The Growth of the American Republic

Franklin Delano Roosevelt *by Elizabeth Shoumatoff*

The Growth of the American Republic

VOLUME TWO

SAMUEL ELIOT MORISON

HENRY STEELE COMMAGER

AND

WILLIAM E. LEUCHTENBURG

SEVENTH EDITION

New York   Oxford

OXFORD UNIVERSITY PRESS

1980

Copyright © 1930, 1937, 1942, 1950, 1962, 1969, 1980
by Oxford University Press, Inc.

Library of Congress Cataloging in Publication Data
Morison, Samuel Eliot, 1887–1976.
The growth of the American Republic.
Includes bibliographies and index.
1. United States—History. I. Commager, Henry Steele, 1902– joint author.
II. Leuchtenburg, William Edward, 1922– joint author. III. Title.
E178.M85 1980 973 79-52432
ISBN 0-19-502595-4 (two-vol. set) ISBN 0-19-502593-8 (v. 1)
ISBN 0-19-502594-6 (v. 2)

9 8 7 6 5 4 3 2

Printed in the United States of America

Preface

The publication of the seventh edition of *The Growth of the American Republic* marks the fiftieth anniversary of this history. It first appeared in 1930 as a single volume, beginning the story in 1763 and terminating it in 1917. Over the next three decades, the two senior authors brought out four more editions, covering a much longer span, from the first arrival of Indians on this continent to the most recent events, an enterprise which required publication in two volumes and a division of editorial responsibility. In the fifth edition, which appeared in 1962, Morison was responsible for the period up to the Civil War, and for the chapters on World War II in Vol. II; Commager for the period since 1860, except for the chapters on World War II.

With the appearance of the sixth edition in 1969, Leuchtenburg joined the two senior authors for the first time. In that edition, Leuchtenburg had the main responsibility for a substantial revision, and for writing new chapters on the Kennedy and Johnson years, but Morison and Commager also made revisions, especially on those chapters which they contributed to the previous edition.

This seventh edition is the first to appear without the direct involvement of Samuel Eliot Morison, though his significant contribution to the sixth edition has been retained. His death on 15 May 1976 evoked widespread expressions of sorrow together with a sense of fulfillment for a life so rich in achievement. In his eighty-eight years Admiral Morison had written more than fifty books, taught with distinction at Harvard for four decades, served his country in two world wars, and, an accomplished mariner, had retraced the voyages of Columbus and Magellan. Born in the nineteenth century, with intimate associations with the world of eighteenth-century Boston, he embraced in his own life much of the history of the American republic about which he wrote with such felicity.

For this seventh edition, the final chapter of the second volume of this work was revised, and new material was added to embrace the period from the fall of 1968 until nearly the end of the next decade, including such momentous events of the Carter presidency as the recognition of the People's Republic of China.

We write for young men and women of all ages, for whom economy in truth-telling is neither necessary nor appropriate. We believe that history embraces the whole of a people's activity: economic and social, literary and spiritual, as well as political and military. We have endeavored therefore to give such stress to these different aspects that our story will be that of a growing and changing civilization in an expanding United States of America.

This new edition, marking a half-century of continuous publication, is dedicated to the rising generation. May they continue to further the Growth of the American Republic!

HENRY STEELE COMMAGER

WILLIAM E. LEUCHTENBURG

Contents

Maps

Illustrations

James J. Hill (1838–1916).

Alexander Graham Bell (1847–1922).

Thomas A. Edison (1847–1931).

The Wright Brothers' First Flight, 1903.

Following page 202

Sixth Avenue Elevated at Third Street by John Sloan.

New York's Lower East Side.

Broadway (*c.* 1910).

Pennsylvania Station, New York.

Following page 330

William Jennings Bryan at the Democratic Convention, 1896.

Eugene V. Debs (1855–1926).

Terence V. Powderly (1849–1924).

Samuel Gompers (1850–1924).

Woodrow Wilson and William Howard Taft.

Robert M. La Follette (1855–1925).

Theodore Roosevelt at Asheville, North Carolina, 1904.

Booker T. Washington (1858–1915).

Jane Addams (1860–1935).

W. E. B. Du Bois (1868–1963).

Following page 426

Big Four at Versailles (Lloyd George, Orlando, Clemenceau, Wilson).

KKK Parade in Long Branch, New Jersey, on 4 July 1924.

Charles Lindbergh (*c.* 1927).

Oliver Wendell Holmes (1841–1935) by Charles Hopkinson.

William James (1842–1910) by Ellen Emmet (Rand).

Ernest Hemingway (1899–1961).

F. Scott Fitzgerald (1896–1940).

Dean Acheson.

John Foster Dulles.

Dean Rusk and Robert McNamara.

President Lyndon B. Johnson and President-elect Richard Nixon.

Albert Einstein and J. Robert Oppenheimer

The Warren Court, 1967–68.

Robert F. and John F. Kennedy.

Following page 778

Atomic Bomb Cloud, Nagasaki, August 1945.

Little Rock, Arkansas, September 1957.

The 1963 March on Washington.

Evacuation of Refugees, Phu Chuong, South Vietnam. Photograph by Philip J. Griffiths.

Student Demonstration, University of California, Berkeley, December 1967.

Men at Work on Buckminster Fuller's Geodesic Dome, Expo 67, Montreal.

Menand I, 1963, by David Smith.

Apollo 8 Earth View, December 1968.

Samuel Eliot Morison
1887–1976

For the whole earth is the sepulchre of famous men, and their
story lives on, woven into the stuff of other men's lives.

PERICLES,   The Funeral Speech

The Growth of the American Republic

The Passing of the Frontier

1. THE LAST WEST

The roaring vitality, the cascading energy of the American people in the postwar years, is nowhere better illustrated than in the history of the West. The generation after the Civil War witnessed the most extensive movement of population in our history; a doubling of the settled area; the rapid development of this population from primitive society to contemporary standards of civilization; the final disappearance of the wild Indian; the rise and fall of the mineral empire and of the cattle kingdom; the emergence of new types of agriculture and of economic life articulated to the geography and climate of the High Plains and the Rocky Mountains; and the organization of a dozen new states with a taste for social and political experiment.

The most notable of these achievements was the conquest of the Great Plains — that region extending roughly from longitude 98 to the Rocky Mountains, and from Texas to the Canadian border. This vast area, comprising roughly one-fifth of the United States, had long interposed a formidable barrier to settlement. In the decade of the 'forties the westward frontier had reached the edge of the Plains. Then, instead of moving progressively westward as it had always heretofore done, the frontier leaped 1500 miles to the Pacific coast. For 30 years the intervening territory was practically uninhabited except by Indians and Mormons; not until the decade of the 'seventies did permanent settlers begin to close in on the Plains and Mountain regions; then the process went on with unprecedented rapidity until by 1890 it was almost complete and the frontier had disappeared.

The Plains region had long been known as 'the Great American Desert'; it was not, of course, a desert, but the designation had some justification. For over 200 years the American pioneer had moved westward from one woodland frontier to another, and in all that time it had never been necessary for him to make any radical readjustment to forest and prairie and stream. But when the pioneer came to the edge of the Great Plains he found an environment fundamentally different from that to which he was accustomed. Here was an immense grassland, sparsely wooded, with few navigable streams, and with a rainfall seldom sufficient for farming as practiced in the East. When the pioneer farmer tried to apply here the experience he had gained and the tools he had developed in the wooded East, he failed. 'The attempt,' as Walter P. Webb has said, 'of a migrating people to cross this line of the 96th or 98th meridian resulted in social chaos and economic ruin which continued until, through invention and much experiment, new weapons were adopted, new implements invented, new methods devised for getting water, making fences, and farming, until new institutions were evolved or old ones modified to meet the needs of a country that was level, devoid of timber, and deficient in rainfall; until a plainscraft took the place of woodcraft.'

Not until the 1870's did the industrial revolution, science, and invention come to the aid of the farmer and enable him successfully to invade the High Plains. Before he could establish himself permanently on the Plains four things were necessary: the elimination of the Indian; new methods of farming to cope with inadequate rainfall; a substitute for traditional wooden fencing; and transportation to take the crops to market. The army and the destruction of the buffalo took care of the Indian; barbed wire solved the fencing problem; the windmill, dry farming, and irrigation went far to overcome the effect of insufficient rainfall and intermittent droughts; and the railroad furnished transportation.

In the course of this long and arduous struggle with the Plains environment, the miner, the cattleman, and the farmer evolved institutions that differed markedly from those which had obtained in the woodlands of the East. The Plains environment necessitated a modification not only of the tools and methods of farming, but of social attitudes, economic concepts, political and legal institutions as well. 'The physical conditions which exist in that land,' Major John Wesley Powell said, '. . . are such that the industries of the West are necessarily unlike those of the East and their institutions must be adapted to their industrial wants. It is thus that a new phase of Aryan civilization is being developed in the western half of America.'

2. THE INDIAN BARRIER

The first step in the conquest of the last West was the solution of the Indian question. The Indians of the Great Plains and the Rocky Mountain regions, perhaps 225,000 in number, presented a formidable obstacle to white settlement. The strongest and most warlike of the tribes that the whites encountered were the Sioux, Blackfeet, Crow, Cheyenne, and Arapahoe in the north; the Comanche, Kiowa, Ute, Southern Cheyenne, Apache, and Southern Arapahoe in the south. Mounted on swift horses, admirably armed for Plains warfare, and living on the millions of buffalo that roamed the open range, these tribes for generations had maintained a stubborn and successful resistance to white penetration of their hunting grounds.

The first serious invasion came with the great migrations of the 1840's. The fate of the California Indians after the gold rush was prophetic of what was to happen elsewhere in the West. There were approximately 100,000 Indians in California in 1850; ten years later the number had been reduced to 35,000, and the Commissioner of Indian Affairs could write that 'despoiled by irresistible forces of the land of their fathers; with no country on earth to which they can migrate; in the midst of a people with whom they cannot assimilate; they have no recognized claims upon the government and are compelled to become vagabonds — to steal or to starve.' The advance of the miners into the mountains, the building of the transcontinental railroads, and the invasion of the grasslands by cattlemen, threatened the other Indian tribes of the West with the same fate. Most serious was the wanton destruction of the buffalo, indispensable not only for food but for hides, bowstrings, lariats, fuel, and a score of other purposes. Scarcely less ruinous were two other developments: the perfection of the Colt repeating revolver, fearfully efficient in Plains warfare, and the spread of smallpox, cholera, and venereal diseases among the Indians.

The story of Indian relations in the period from 1860 to 1887, the year of the passage of the Dawes Act, is a melancholy tale of intermittent and barbarous warfare, broken pacts and broken promises, greed and selfishness, corruption and maladministration, of alternating aggression and vacillation on the part of the whites, of courageous defense, despair, blind savagery, and inevitable defeat for the Indians. President Hayes observed in his annual message of 1877, 'Many, if not most, of our Indian wars have had their origin in broken promises and acts of injustice on our part.'

Until 1861 the Indians of the Plains had been relatively peaceful, but in that year the invasion of their hunting grounds by thousands of frantic and ruthless miners, and the advance of white settlers along the upper Mississippi and Missouri frontier, together with dissatisfaction at their treatment by the government and the breakdown of the reservation system, resulted in numerous minor conflicts. In 1862 the Sioux of the Dakota region went on the warpath, devastated the Minnesota frontier, and massacred and imprisoned almost a thousand white men, women, and children. Retribution was swift and terrible and fell indiscriminately upon the innocent and the guilty. For the next 25 years Indian warfare was constant, each new influx of settlers driving the redskins to acts of desperation which brought on renewed outrage and punishment. In 1864 the Cheyenne, banished from their hunting grounds to the wastes of southeastern Colorado, attacked Ben Halliday's stages and harried the mining settlements to the north; they were persuaded to abandon their depredations and concentrate at Indian posts, and at one of these posts Colonel Chivington ordered a savage slaughter of the Indian men, women, and children which sent a thrill of horror through the nation. General Nelson Miles called the Sand Creek Massacre the 'foulest and most unjustifiable crime in the annals of America,' but Denver hailed Chivington, a former Methodist minister, who exhibited his collection of a hundred scalps at a local theater. Two years later a small force under Colonel Fetterman was in turn massacred by the embittered Sioux. All through the following decade the Sioux fought desperately for their hunting grounds. The climax came in 1875 when prospectors discovered gold in the Sioux reservation in the Black Hills. That summer General Sheridan was able to hold back the importunate gold-seekers, but the next spring they broke through and flooded over the area. Under Sitting Bull and Crazy Horse the Sioux struck back. In June 1876 they ambushed the impetuous 'glory-hunter,' General George Custer, on the Little Big Horn, and annihilated his whole command of 264 men; for two generations, millions of children got their notions of the Indians from the Currier and Ives lithograph of the gory massacre. Punishment was quick; the Sioux were scattered and Crazy Horse captured and murdered by his guard.

In the mountains, as on the plains, the Indians were driven from their ancient homes. In Montana the Crow and the Blackfeet were ejected from their reservations; in Colorado the vast holdings of the Utes were confiscated and opened to settlement; in the Southwest ten years of warfare ended in the capture of the intractable Apache chief, Geronimo, and the practical destruction of the Apache tribe. The discovery of gold on the Salmon river in western Idaho precipitated an invasion of the country of the peaceful Nez Percés. The Indians refused to surrender the lands once guaranteed to them, and fifteen years of intermittent warfare culminated in the decision to drive the recalcitrant tribe entirely out of their hunting grounds. Chief Joseph struck back, but in vain, and in 1877 there began a retreat eastward over 1500 miles of mountain and plain that remains the most memorable feat in the annals of Indian warfare. In the end the feeble remnant of the Nez Percés tribe was captured and exiled to Oklahoma, and Chief Joseph spoke for all his race:

> I am tired of fighting. Our chiefs are killed. Looking-Glass is dead. Too-hul-hut-sote is dead. The old men are all dead. It is the young men now who say 'yes' or 'no.' He who lead the young men is dead. It is cold and we have no blankets. The little children are freezing to death. My people, some of them, have run away to the hills and have no blankets, no food. No one knows where they are, perhaps freezing to death. I want to have time to look for my children and see how many of them I can find. Maybe I can find them among the dead. Hear me, my chiefs. My heart is sick and sad. I am tired.

In the Southwest, after forces led by Kit Carson had inflicted hundreds of casualties, slaughtered their flocks, and laid waste their lands, the Navajo were herded onto a bleak reservation.

Authority over Indian affairs was divided between the Departments of War and of the Interior, and both departments pursued a vacillating and uncertain policy, the one failing to live up to treaty obligations, the other failing to protect the Indians on their reservations from the aggressions of white settlers. By fraud and chicanery large areas of

Indian lands were alienated by 'treaty' or by 'sale' to railroads and other speculators. One railroad acquired 800,000 acres of Cherokee lands in southern Kansas by methods that the governor of the state denounced as 'a cheat and a fraud in every particular,' but nothing was done to cancel the arrangement, and the railroad resold the lands to settlers at 100 per cent profit.

If most frontiersmen believed that the only good Indian was a dead Indian, Easterners, removed by a century from the Indian menace, had a different attitude. Here churchmen and reformers united to urge a policy of humanitarianism toward Indian wards. Statesmen like Carl Schurz, religious leaders like Bishop Whipple, literary figures like Helen Hunt Jackson, whose *A Century of Dishonor* stirred the nation's conscience, were loud in their criticism of the government's treatment of the Indian, and their attitude effected important changes in Indian policy.

In 1865, in the breathing space permitted by the conclusion of the Civil War, Congress had created a Committee on the Condition of the Indian Tribes which recommended dealing with the Indians as individuals and concentrating them in reservations. This substitution of a 'peace' policy for the more belligerent one of the 1860's was dictated partly by humanitarian considerations, and partly by the more cogent argument of economy — for it was obviously cheaper to herd the Indians into government reservations and feed them than it was to fight them. But as one Indian commissioner wrote bluntly, 'That these reservations will cause any considerable annoyance to the whites we do not believe. They consist, for the most part, of ground unfitted for cultivation.'

In 1887 Congress brought a long period of Indian relations to a climax with the passage of the Dawes Severalty Act, which set Indian policy for the next half-century. The Dawes Act was the first serious attempt to teach the Indian the practices of agriculture and social life and merge him in the body politic of the nation. It provided for the dissolution of the tribes as legal entities and the division of the tribal lands among the individual members. To protect the Indian in his property the right of disposal was withheld for 25 years; upon the expiration of this probationary period, the Indian was to become the unrestricted owner and to be admitted to full citizenship in the United States. In October 1901 the Five Civilized Nations of Oklahoma, already assimilated to American social and political institutions, were admitted to citizenship and in 1924 Congress granted full citizenship to all Indians.

The Dawes Act was hailed at the time as an Indian Emancipation Act; it might better have been compared to Appomattox. Under the operation of this misguided act, Indian holdings decreased in the next half-century from 138 to 48 million acres, half of these arid or semi-arid, with no compensating advantages. Whites deprived Indians of their lands by various kinds of deceit and even by murder, in one case the bombing of two sleeping children. Indian timber land was seized by speculators, and in 1917 the Indian commissioner explained blandly that 'as the Indian tribes were being liquidated anyway it was only sensible to liquidate their forest holdings as well.' Tribal funds amounting to more than $100 million were diverted from their proper use to meet the costs of the Indian Bureau — including the costs of despoiling the Indians of their lands. And during the Harding administration, which marked the nadir of Indian welfare, the egregious Secretary of the Interior Albert Fall tried to take their oil lands away from the Navajo Indians as well.

Thus the proud savages who once ruled the American continent were settled on some 200 government reservations, eking out an existence on government doles, cut off from the free life of an earlier day, losing the power to fend for themselves, disintegrating economically and physically, tragic remainders of the race which had helped the white man to adjust himself to the American scene, descendants of the Hiawathas and Pocahontases who for so long fired the imagination of the American people.

3. THE MINING FRONTIER

The vast territory between the Missouri and the Pacific, first explored by the traders of the American and the Rocky Mountain fur companies, had been crossed and recrossed by emigrants along the great trails, but it was the miners who first revealed to the nation the possibilities of this country. The first frontier of the last West was the miners' frontier. In 1849 the lure of gold had drawn to California a turbulent, heterogeneous throng of miners who later formed the nucleus of a large permanent population and who developed the varied agricultural resources of the state. This process was to be repeated time and again in the decade of the 'sixties: in Colorado, Nevada, Arizona, Idaho, Montana, and Wyoming. In each case precious metals were the magnet that attracted the first settlers and advertised the resources of the territory; then, as the big pay dirt was exhausted, the mining population receded, and its place was taken by ranchers and farmers who established, with the aid of the railroads and the government, the permanent foundation of the territory.

In 1859 the discovery of gold in the foothills of the Rockies, near Pike's Peak, drew thousands of eager prospectors from the border settlements and from California, bent on repeating here the fabulous story of California gold. Within a few months the roads from Council Bluffs and Independence to western Kansas were crowded with wagons bearing the slogan 'Pike's Peak or Bust' scrawled on their canvas. Soon brash little mining camps dotted the hills all along Cherry Creek, a branch of the South Fork of the Platte. Denver City, Golden, Boulder, and Colorado City arose almost overnight, the Territory of Jefferson — changed later to Colorado — was organized, and the census of 1860 recorded a population of some 35,000. The mining boom soon spent itself, and the development of Colorado was somewhat retarded by the Civil War and Indian uprisings as well as by inadequate transportation and a failure to appreciate the agricultural and grazing resources of the country. During the ensuing decade population barely held its own; not until the silver strikes of the 1870's, the advent of the railroads, the influx of farmers, and the readjustment of the region to a new economic basis were the foundations for a sounder development laid. Colorado's silver output soared from 600,000 a year in 1870 to more than $3 million in 1874, and in 1877 silver smelters at Leadville also began to turn out large quantities of lead. By 1880 Leadville, already the second city of Colorado, had 13 schools, 5 churches, and 28 miles of streets; its annual silver production soon outdistanced that of any foreign country save Mexico.

In the same year that gold was discovered in Colorado came the announcement of a rich strike of silver on the eastern slopes of the Sierra Nevada, near Lake Tahoe. Here was located the Comstock Lode, one of the richest veins in the world. Within a year the roaring towns of Virginia City, Aurora, and Gold Hill sprang up in the desert waste, the Territory of Nevada was carved out of Utah, and 10,000 men were digging frantically in the bowels of the earth for the precious silver stuff.

Nevada furnishes the most extreme example of a mining community;

nowhere else in history do we find a society so completely and con-
tinuously dependent upon minerals. And the history of this mining
commonwealth for the first decade of its existence is largely that of the
Comstock Lode. Within 20 years the lode yielded no less than $306
million. Very little of these enormous riches, however, remained in Nevada, most of it going to California mining companies or to speculators
in the East. The Comstock Lode is notable not only as the foundation of
the mineral wealth of Nevada, but as the location of one of the greatest
engineering enterprises of the nineteenth century — the Sutro Tunnel.
This tunnel, built by Adolph Sutro over a period of eight years and
penetrating into the heart of the mountain to the depth of three miles,
was a technical marvel; unhappily, it was finished just as the mines were
failing.

The application of engineering skill, machinery, and capital to the
Comstock illustrates a process that was universal in the history of the
mining kingdom. Panning and placer mining as practiced in the diggings of early California and Colorado were wasteful, and the change
from placer mining to quartz mining required the purchase of expensive
machinery, the hiring of engineering skill, and the organization of mining as a big business. So outside capital came in and took over the
mining industry; the miners became day laborers working for wages,
and the profits went to stockholders scattered throughout the United
States and Europe. Mining actually added nothing to the wealth of the
state. It did not create permanent industries or cities, nor provide foundations for healthy growth. This was the history of Comstock, and it was
to a greater or less extent the history of most of the mines of the West in
the following decade.

The story of Idaho and Montana runs parallel to that of Colorado and
Nevada. Gold was discovered in 1860 on the Nez Percés reservation in
the extreme eastern part of Washington Territory. Within a year a wave
of prospectors from Washington and Nevada was rolling into the region.
Lewiston and, farther to the south, Boise City, sprang into existence;
and in 1865 the Territory of Idaho was carved out of Washington and
Montana. 'The Idaho miners,' wrote the historian of the West, H. H.
Bancroft, 'were like quicksilver, a mass of them dropped off in any
locality, broke up into individual globules, and ran off after any atom of
gold in the vicinity. They stayed nowhere longer than the gold attracted
them.' But mining furnished a most insubstantial foundation for the

development of Idaho, and the census of 1870 showed a population of only 15,000 for the Territory.

Gold was discovered east of the Continental Divide along the headwaters of the Missouri, and in the Bitter Root valley in the eastern part of Washington Territory, and soon Alder Gulch (later Virginia City), Last Chance Gulch (Helena), and Bannack City enjoyed a flush rivaling that of the Colorado and Nevada camps. Although Montana produced over $100 million in precious metals in the first decade, the mining kingdom was short-lived, and the census of 1870 recorded a population of only slightly over 20,000. Like other mining camps, those of Montana soon died out or were transformed into respectable towns, with schools, churches, and other institutions of civilization. For a brief time the activities of the notorious Henry Plummer and his gang of highway robbers and cutthroats threatened the prosperity of the Montana camps, and it required a vigilante organization such as that which had arisen in California fifteen years earlier to restore law and order. Virginia City, which may well serve as typical of the mining towns of the West, was thus described by N. P. Langford in his *Vigilante Days and Ways*:

> This human hive, numbering at least ten thousand people, was the product of ninety days. Into it were crowded all the elements of a rough and active civilization. . . . Gold was abundant, and every possible device was employed by the gamblers, the traders, the vile men and women that had come in with the miners to the locality, to obtain it. Nearly every third cabin in the town was a saloon where vile whiskey was peddled out for fifty cents a drink in gold dust. Many of these places were filled with gambling tables and gamblers, and the miner who was bold enough to enter one of them with his day's earnings in his pocket, seldom left until thoroughly fleeced. Hurdy-gurdy dance-houses were numerous, and there were plenty of camp beauties to patronize them. . . . Not a day or night passed which did not yield its full fruition of fights, quarrels, wounds, or murders. The crack of the revolver was often heard above the merry notes of the violin. Street fights were frequent, and as no one knew when or where they would occur, everyone was on his guard against a random shot.
>
> Sunday was always a gala day. . . . Thousands of people crowded the thoroughfares, ready to rush in any direction of promised excitement. Horse-racing was among the most favored amusements. Prize rings were formed, and brawny men engaged at fisticuffs until their sight was lost, and their bodies pummelled to a jelly, while hundreds of onlookers cheered the victor. . . . Pistols

flashed, bowie-knives flourished, and braggart oaths filled the air, as often as men's passions triumphed over their reason. This was indeed the reign of unbridled license, and men who at first regarded it with disgust and terror, by constant exposure soon learned to become part of it, and forgot that they had ever been aught else.[1]

But it would be a mistake to picture the mining camps as mere nests of lawlessness. They had, to be sure, few of the institutions taken for granted in the East — churches, schools, newspapers, theaters — but they hastened to establish these institutions as quickly as they could. Nor did the 'Argonauts' — as the first miners were known — conform to the standards of society or of law which obtained elsewhere; instead they very sensibly formulated their own social standards and developed their own laws. The evolution of common law institutions in the miners' camps is one of the most illuminating chapters in the history of American law. Each miners' camp was an administrative and a judicial district. It had its own executive officers, judges, recorders, it voted laws and regulations suited to its own peculiar needs, and it enforced these laws through public opinion and police officers.

> The Argonauts [said Senator Stewart, himself once a miner] found no laws governing the possession and occupation of mines but the common laws of right. . . . They were forced to make laws for themselves. The reason and justice of the laws they formed challenge the admiration of all who investigate them. Each mining district . . . formed its own rules and adopted its own customs. The similarity of these rules and customs throughout the entire mining-region was so great as to attain the beneficial results of well-digested general laws. These regulations were thoroughly democratic in character. . . .

The legal codes and practices of these mining communities were eventually recognized in the American courts and many of them were incorporated into U.S. statutes and the constitutions and laws of the western states.

The early development of Wyoming and Arizona followed the same general lines of the other mining communities. The mines along the Sweetwater river at South Pass City, Pacific City, and Miners' Delight were soon played out, and after 1865 the future of Wyoming Territory was almost wholly dependent upon cattle and sheep. In the Southwest, silver had been mined by the Spaniards in the Santa Cruz valley of the

1. N. P. Langford, *Vigilante Days and Ways* (1912 ed.), pp. 222–4.

New Mexican Territory and by Americans in the Gadsden Purchase for many years, but the brisk development of mining which began along the Bill Williams fork of the Colorado river was a by-product of the Civil War. Though a few mushroom mining towns sprang up in the Arizona and New Mexico deserts, the majority of the prospectors had poor luck and soon limped back to more promising territory to the north.

Not gold and silver but copper proved the chief resource of Montana, and of Arizona, too. In the 1870's Marcus Daly, once an impoverished Irish immigrant, bought an option on a small silver mine in Butte, the Anaconda, which proved fabulously rich in copper. In the next half-century he and his associates took over two billion dollars' worth of copper out of this 'richest hill in the world.' To control this and other copper mines, Daly, William Clark, and other 'copper kings' bought legislatures and senatorships, corrupted the public life of the state for a generation, and engaged in open warfare with each other. In the end Clark got a senatorship, $100 million, and a mansion on New York's Fifth Avenue with 121 rooms and 31 baths. After the turn of the century, copper mining shifted to Arizona where the Phelps-Dodge interests dominated the economy of the state, and where the single Copper Queen mine at Bisbee yielded more money than all the gold and silver mines of the Territory.

The last domestic gold rush came in the Black Hills region of western Dakota Territory, on the reservations of the Sioux. In 1874 the news of the discovery of gold here precipitated a frantic and lawless invasion. Deadwood had its brief day of glory; here 'Calamity Jane' enjoyed her merited notoriety; here 'Wild Bill' Hickok handed in his checks; here a stock company played Gilbert and Sullivan's *Mikado* for a record run of 130 nights. Within a short time heavily capitalized companies, like the Homestead, took over the mining, and the days of glamour were gone.

The history of the last gold rush is as gaudy as that of California or Colorado, but belongs as much to Canadian as to American history. The discovery of gold along the waters of the Klondike, which flows from Yukon into Alaska, came in 1896; the next year ships from San Francisco were unloading avid fortune-hunters all along the frozen coast. By 1898 there were 30,000 fortune-hunters in the Yukon, washing the icy waters of the Klondike and tributary streams. The gold strike in the Klondike had unanticipated repercussions. By depressing the price of gold and raising that of silver, it took Bryan's issue away from him for the cam-

paign of 1900. It gave rise to a boundary controversy between Canada
and the United States, which President Roosevelt agreed to arbitrate
only on condition that all the issues were settled his way. It furnished
material for a dozen red-blooded novels which gave Jack London an
international reputation; inspired Robert Service to write and a million
hams to recite 'The Shooting of Dan McGrew'; and provided the background for Charlie Chaplin's wonderful movie *The Gold Rush*. More
important, it marked the beginnings of modern Alaska.

Ephemeral as it was, the mining frontier played an important part in
the development of the West and of the nation. The miners familiarized
the American people with the country between the Missouri and the
Pacific, and advertised its magnificent resources. They forced a solution
of the Indian problem, dramatized the need for railroads, and laid the
foundations for the later permanent farming population. Out of the
necessities of their situation they developed codes of law admirably
suited to their needs, and contributed much of value to the legal and
political institutions of the West. They produced, in the 30 years from
1860 to 1890, a total of $1,241,827,032 of gold and $901,160,660 of silver,
enabled the government to resume specie payments, precipitated 'the
money question' which was for well-nigh twenty years the main political
issue before the American people, and then solved it. They added immeasurably to American folklore, enriched the American idiom, and in
the stories of Bret Harte and Mark Twain inspired lasting contributions
to American literature.

4. THE CATTLE KINGDOM

One of the most dramatic shifts in the screen-picture of the West was
the replacement of millions of buffalo that had roamed the Great Plains
by cattle, and of the Indian by the cowboy and the cattle king. The
territory between the Missouri and the Rockies, from the Red river of
the South to Saskatchewan — an area comprising approximately one-
fourth of the United States — was the cattle kingdom, the last and most
picturesque American frontier. Here millions of cattle — Texas longhorns,
full-blooded Herefords, Wyoming and Montana steers — fatted on the
long luscious grasses of the public lands. The cowboys and their liege
lords, the cattle barons who ruled this vast domain, developed therein a
unique culture, folklore, and society.

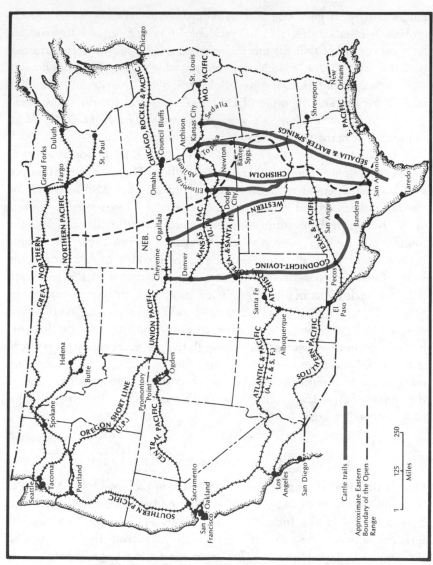

RAILROADS AND CATTLE TRAILS, 1850-1900

The development of the cattle industry on a large scale was due to a peculiar combination of factors: the opening up of the public domain after the Civil War, the elimination of the Indian danger and the annihilation of the buffalo, the extension of the railroads into the High Plains, the decline in the number of cattle raised in the Middle West and the East, the increased consumption of meat here and abroad, the invention of the refrigerator car, and the growth of great packing centers and of world markets.

Since the days when the American Southwest belonged to Spain, the sturdy Texas longhorn, descendant of Spanish *toros* from the plains of Andalusia, had grazed on the limitless prairie grasses north of the Rio Grande. It was not until 1846 that the first herd, valued only for their hides, was driven northward to Ohio, though long before that many had found their way to California. In 1856 a drove of Texas cattle reached Chicago, but not until the middle 'sixties did the 'long drive' to the region of rich grasses and good prices cease to be an experiment. In 1867 the Kansas Pacific began to reach out in the Plains, and in the same year J. G. McCoy established the first of the cow towns, Abilene, Kansas, from which live cattle were shipped to slaughter houses in Chicago. The refrigerator car, in common use by 1875, delivered the western dressed beef to the great eastern centers of population.

On the first of the organized long drives, 35,000 longhorns pounded up clouds of dust all along the famous Chisholm Trail, across the Red and Arkansas rivers and into the land of the Five Nations, to Abilene, Kansas. Two years later no less than 350,000 longhorned kine made their way along the Chisholm and Goodnight trails to fatten on the long northern grasses and find a market at one of the several roaring cattle towns on the Kansas and Pacific Railroad: Abilene, Dodge City, or Newton. Later the 'long drive' extended north to the Union Pacific and even to the Northern Pacific.

> In after years [writes the historian of the cattle kingdom] the drive of the Texas men became little short of an American saga. To all who saw that long line of Texas cattle come up over a rise in the prairie, nostrils wide for the smell of water, dust-caked and gaunt, so ready to break from the nervous control of the riders strung out along the flanks of the herd, there came a feeling that in this spectacle there was something elemental, something resistless, something perfectly in keeping with the unconquerable land about them.[2]

2. E. S. Osgood, *The Day of the Cattleman*, p. 26.

Altogether some 6 million cattle were driven up from Texas to winter on the High Plains of Colorado, Wyoming, and even Montana, between 1866 and 1888. It was this new industry of fattening cattle on the Great Plains that produced the last phase of the Wild West and the highest and most picturesque development of the ancient art of cattle droving. The experience of cattlemen along the Oregon and California trails in the decade of the 'forties had long proved the practicability of wintering cattle in the northern ranges. Now Easterners and Englishmen of a sporting or speculating turn put their money into cattle, establishing their headquarters anywhere from the Rio Grande to the Canadian border, and in the absence of law managed their affairs through some *de facto* commonwealth such as the Wyoming Stock Growers' Association. Texas borderers who learned their horsemanship and 'cowpunching' from the Mexican *vaqueros* were the first and the best *bucaroos* or cowboys. Every spring they rounded up the herds in designated areas, all the way from Texas to Wyoming and the Dakotas, identified their owners' cattle by the brands, and branded the calves, dividing up pro rata the strays or 'mavericks.' The breeding cattle were then set free for another year while the likely three- and four-year-olds were conducted on the 'long drive' to the nearest cow town on a railway. Each 'outfit' of cowboys attended its owner's herd on the drive, protecting it from wolves and cattle rustlers, sending scouts ahead to locate water and the best grazing. The long drive seems romantic in retrospect, but to the cowboys it was hard and often hazardous work. Andy Adams, later one of the cattle barons of Texas, describes a dry drive along the Old Western Trail:

> Good cloudy weather would have saved us, but in its stead was a sultry morning without a breath of air, which bespoke another day of sizzling heat. We had not been on the trail over two hours before the heat became almost unbearable to man and beast. Had it not been for the condition of the herd, all might yet have gone well; but over three days had elapsed without water for the cattle, and they became feverish and ungovernable. The lead cattle turned back several times, wandering aimlessly in any direction, and it was with considerable difficulty that the herd could be held on the trail. Our horses were fresh, however, and after about two hours' work, we once more got the herd strung out in trailing fashion; but before a mile had been covered, the leaders again turned, and the cattle congregated into a mass of unmanageable animals, milling and lowing in their fever and thirst. . . . No sooner was the milling

stopped than they would surge hither and yon, sometimes half a mile, as ungovernable as the waves of an ocean. After wasting several hours in this manner, they finally turned back over the trail, and the utmost efforts of every man in the outfit failed to check them. We threw our ropes in their faces, and when this failed, we resorted to shooting; but in defiance of the fusillade and the smoke they walked sullenly through the line of horsemen across their front. Six-shooters were discharged so close to the leaders' faces as to singe their hair, yet, under a noonday sun, they disregarded this and every other device to turn them, and passed wholly out of our control. In a number of instances wild steers deliberately walked against our horses, and then for the first time a fact dawned upon us that chilled the marrow in our bones—*the herd was going blind.*

The bones of men and animals that lie bleaching along the trails abundantly testify that this was not the first instance in which the plain had baffled the determination of man.[3]

In Wyoming, a country admirably suited by nature for large-scale ranching, but almost entirely unsuited for farming, the great cattle companies ruled supreme. The cattlemen seized most of the public and much of the Indian lands, controlled the politics and wrote the laws of the Territory. For almost 20 years the powerful Wyoming Stock Growers' Association was the *de facto* government of the Territory; it formulated laws and regulations governing land and water rights, the round-up, the disposition of estrays, breeding, and similar matters, and enforced them on members and non-members alike; it agitated ceaselessly for the revision of the land laws of the West, and for the recognition of the prior rights of cattlemen; it attempted, by fraud, intimidation, and violence, to keep Wyoming the exclusive preserve of the ranchers.

This proved impossible. The most dangerous threat to the cattle kingdom, in Wyoming as elsewhere through the West, was not, at first, the farmer but the lowly sheepherder. Before the Civil War, Vermont had been the leading sheep-raising state of the Union; during the war sheep moved west to Ohio. Then came competition from Australia and the Argentine, which Ohio farmers, who had to pay $50 an acre for their lands and had to buy winter forage, could not meet; and the sheep kingdom shifted to the Far West and the Southwest. After the Civil War the sheep moved in from these grazing grounds, and from Oregon and the East as well, onto the rich grasses of Colorado, Wyoming, and Montana. Sheep, like cattle, could graze free on Uncle Sam's inexhaustible

3. Andy Adams, *The Log of a Cowboy*, Houghton Mifflin Co., pp. 63–4.

lands; labor costs were negligible; and the wool clip, protected by high tariffs, was increasingly valuable. The cattlemen, who resented the invasion of their lands by the sheepherders and were convinced that sheep ruined the grass by close cropping, waged open war on their rivals. The Tonto Basin War in northern Arizona, like Kentucky feuds, dragged on for years and ended only when ranchers and sheepherders had wiped each other out. But in the end the sheepmen triumped over the cattlemen, even in Wyoming. In the decade after the great blizzard the number of cattle in that state declined from 900,000 to about 300,000, while the number of sheep increased to some 3 million. Montana, too, counted 675,000 cattle but over 3 million sheep. By that time sheep could safely graze. Oddly enough, though the sheepherder is an older and more beloved figure than the rancher, and one with many Biblical associations, sheep raising never caught the American imagination or acquired a folklore or a literature.

It is clear that a system of laws based upon conditions in the well-watered and well-wooded East, and designed to encourage family farming, was not suitable for the needs of the semi-arid West, nor for the purposes of ranching or sheep raising. As early as 1878 Major Powell had recommended to Congress a thorough revision of the laws governing Western lands, based on realities — on a recognition of the paramount importance of water rather than mere acreage and on the abandonment of the rectangular survey. These recommendations were ignored, and the land-office continued its misguided effort to confine the cattle industry as well as farming within the framework of sections and quarter-sections. It was perhaps inevitable that cattlemen and sheepmen should flout these laws and make their own. By hook or by crook the cattle companies seized control of the grasslands. They leased millions of acres from Indians, strung barbed wire fences around other millions of acres — or across roads and around the approaches to streams and water holes, denying water to farmers who were entitled to it. In 1886 Secretary Lamar reported that 'substantially the entire grazing country west of the 100th meridian' was fenced in by cattlemen. President Cleveland moved with characteristic energy to destroy these illegal enclosures, and in the end government officials and the inexorable advance of the farmer forced the cattlemen to accommodate themselves to the law.

The cattle boom reached its height about 1885. By that time the range had become too heavily pastured to support the long drive and was beginning to be crisscrossed by railroads and the barbed wire fences of homesteads. By that time, too, the range had ceased to be a frontier industry and had become a corporate enterprise, organized, capitalized, and directed in the East or in Britain. The hazards of ranching were increasing enormously. The rapid fencing-in of the open range, the appearance of cattle diseases and the passage of state quarantine laws, the conflict between the cattlemen and sheepherders, between northern and southern cattlemen, and between cattlemen and settlers, the decline of prices because of overproduction, the destruction of the range on account of overgrazing, and the determination of the Federal Government to enforce its land laws in the West — all these presaged the decline of the cow kingdom. Then came the two terrible winters of 1885–86 and 1886–87 which almost annihilated the herds on the open ranges. Cattle owners began to stake out homestead claims in the names of their 'outfit' and to fence off their lands. Almost in a moment the cattle range replaced the open ranges. The cowboy, now a cattleman or ranch employee, was penned in behind wire and no longer knew the joys and dangers of the long drive.

5. THE DISAPPEARANCE OF THE FRONTIER

The picturesque mining and cattle kingdoms and the old, romantic 'Wild West' fell before the pressure of farmers, swarming by the hundreds of thousands out onto the High Plains and into the mountain valleys. During the Civil War, dangers and uncertainties, especially in the border states, induced many to try their luck in the new regions, while the liberal provisions of the Homestead and later land acts, the low cost of railroad lands, and the high rewards of farming proved an irresistible magnet for thousands of others. During the war years the population of nine Western states and Territories increased by over 300,000, while the agricultural states of Illinois, Wisconsin, Minnesota, Iowa, Kansas, and Nebraska received 843,000 immigrants from Europe and the East. In the year 1864 no less than 75,000 persons passed westward bound through Omaha alone. From Council Bluffs, Iowa, eastern terminus of the Union Pacific, the Reverend Jonathan Blanchard wrote in 1864:

> When you approach this town, the ravines and gorges are white
> with covered wagons at rest. Below the town, toward the river side,

long wings of white canvas stretch away on either side, into the soft
green willows; at the ferry from a quarter to a half mile of teams
all the time await their turn to cross. Myriads of horses and mules
drag on the moving mass of humanity toward the setting sun; while
the oxen and cows equal them in number.

All this seems incredibly remote from the Wilderness and marching
through Georgia. It was one of the great pulses of American life that
went on beating amid the din of arms.

The close of the war brought a sharp acceleration of this movement. It
was in part the absorbing power of the West which enabled a million
soldiers to resume civilian life without serious economic derangements.
Southerners by the tens of thousands, despairing of recouping their fortunes in the war-stricken South, migrated westward although excluded
temporarily from the privileges of the Homestead Act. Immigrants,
mostly from northern Europe, found their way to the prairies of Iowa
and Minnesota and eastern Dakota by the hundreds of thousands.

The twenty years following 1870 witnessed the greatest expansion of
the West, the taking up of most of the good public and railroad lands,
and the disappearance of the frontier. The railroads, crossing the continent along half a dozen lines, and immigration, which reached a total of
8 million in these 20 years, were the most influential factors in the
process. Not only did the railroads provide transportation and ensure
markets, but they were the active colonizing agents of the time. Whole
Territories, such as the Dakotas, came into existence largely by virtue of
the railways, while scores of towns and cities, such as Cheyenne, Council
Bluffs, Kansas City, Spokane, and Seattle, were created by and completely dependent upon them.

But it was not enough to provide land and transportation for eager
immigrants to the West. Some method had to be found to overcome the
natural handicaps to agriculture in the semi-arid Plains. The first and
most urgent problem was to provide fencing. Even in the East, where
timber was available, the cost of fencing was an important item: in 1870
the Department of Agriculture estimated that the total cost of fencing in
the entire country was not far from $2 billion and that the annual
upkeep consumed almost $200 million. In the Plains, where lumber had
to be imported, the cost of timber-fencing a quarter-section of land was
prohibitive. Yet if cattle were to be controlled, manure saved, crops
protected from the ravages of cattle, and water holes preserved, fencing
was absolutely necessary. Plains farmers experimented for years with

various substitutes such as earth embankments and almost impenetrable osage orange hedges. In 1874, J. F. Glidden of DeKalb, Illinois, put barbed wire on the market and the fencing problem was solved! By 1883 Glidden's company was turning out 600 miles of barbed wire daily, and the expense of fencing had been reduced to a mere fraction of its former cost. The importance of barbed wire to the development of the Great Plains was comparable to that of the cotton gin in the development of the South.

Fencing made farming on the High Plains possible, but not necessarily profitable. There was still the question of water. 'The Great Plains,' wrote an observer from the Department of Agriculture, 'can be characterized as a region of periodical famine. . . . Year after year the water supply may be ample, the forage plants cover the ground with rank growth, the herds multiply, the settlers extend their fields, when, almost imperceptibly, the climate becomes less humid, the rain clouds forming day after day disappear upon the horizon, and weeks lengthen into months without a drop of moisture. The grasses wither, the herds wander wearily over the plains in search of water holes, the crops wilt and languish, yielding not even the seed for another year.'

Scientific farming and invention modified, though they did not overcome, the menace of drought. For a time irrigation promised to solve the problem. The Pueblo Indians were familiar with irrigation, and the Mormons had reclaimed millions of acres of arid land by this ancient method. In 1894 Congress passed the Carey Act, turning over to the western states millions of acres of public lands to be reclaimed through irrigation. The act was ineffective, and through the Reclamation Act of 1902 the Federal Government took charge of irrigation. By the turn of the century some 5 million acres had been reclaimed: 20 years later this acreage under irrigation had been multiplied fourfold. Yet irrigation was not an unqualified success, and its effects were limited to a comparatively small area of the mountainous West and to California.

Far more effective than irrigation was the use of deep-drilled wells and of the windmill, and the practice of dry farming. By drilling from 100 to 500 feet below the surface it was possible to tap ground water. Such water was brought to the surface not in the romantic 'old oaken bucket' lowered and raised by hand, but in slender metal cylinders lowered and raised by never failing windmills. Windmills were introduced to the Plains in the middle 'seventies; within a short time they became a familiar feature on the landscape, and assured the farmer a steady though sometimes meager supply of water. Dry farming — the scientific conservation of moisture in the soil through the creation of a dust blanket to prevent evaporation — made it possible to grow cereal crops successfully over large parts of the Plains area, though in the more arid sections it failed to bring satisfactory results.

As a result of all these factors — transportation, immigration, the growth of domestic and foreign markets, new methods of fencing and of soil cultivation — the settlement of the last West went on with unprecedented rapidity. In the 20-year period from 1870 to 1890 the population of California doubled, Texas trebled, Kansas increased fourfold, Nebraska eightfold, Washington fourteenfold, and Dakota Territory fortyfold. Altogether, the population of the trans-Mississippi West rose from 6,877,000 in 1870 to 16,775,000 in 1890. In his annual report for 1890, the Superintendent of the Census announced:

> Up to and including 1880 the country had a frontier of settlement, but at present the unsettled area has been so broken into by isolated bodies of settlement that there can be hardly said to be a frontier line.

The 'disappearance of the frontier' was shortly hailed by a great American historian, Frederick Jackson Turner, as the close of a movement that began in 1607, and the beginning of a new era in American history.

The decade of the 'nineties did constitute a watershed in American history, but the 'passing of the frontier' was not a significant feature of that watershed. If the frontier represented an opportunity to stake out a farm in the West, that opportunity did not disappear in the 1890's. Over a million new farms were settled in the last decade of the century, and more land was patented for homestead and grazing purposes in the generation after 1890 than in the previous generation. The great wheat fields of western Canada continued to offer opportunities to American farmers. The westward movement of population, too, continued unabated. Thus, while in the years 1890 to 1930 population increased in the flourishing Middle Atlantic and North Central States by about 90 per cent, in the Mountain and Pacific States it increased threefold, and the greatest era in the history of the westward movement of population was still to come.[4]

4. In the years from 1940 to 1960 the Mountain and Pacific coast states increased their population by not far from 14 million.

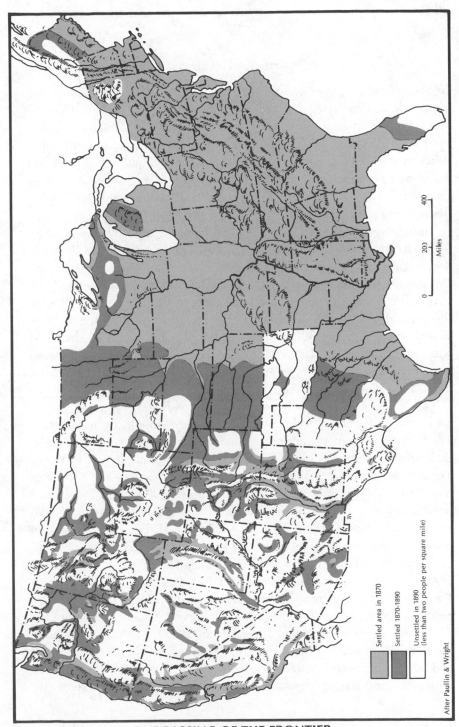

Settled area in 1870

Settled 1870–1890

Unsettled in 1890
(less than two people per square mile)

0   200   400

Miles

After Paullin & Wright

THE PASSING OF THE FRONTIER

25

6. POLITICAL ORGANIZATION

In 1860 something over one-third of the area of the United States was divided into Territories and under the control of the Federal Government. From Minnesota to Oregon, from Texas to the Canadian border, there were no states. Within 30 years all this territory, comprising something over a million square miles, was organized politically, and the major part of it included in states. Statehood was an important step in the assimilation of the West. Federal political control and the frontier disappeared simultaneously.

The admission of Nevada in 1864 had been dictated by the desire to obtain its three electoral votes for Lincoln. The inhabitants of Colorado had rejected the proffer of statehood in the same year, but in 1876 Colorado was admitted as the Centennial State. Nebraska entered the Union in 1867 over President Johnson's veto, in time to cast her vote for the impeachment of that unfortunate chief magistrate. With the creation of Wyoming Territory in 1868 the territorial subdivisions of the West had been rounded out, but few of these Territories, most of them based upon mineral wealth, showed any prospects of being prepared for statehood in the immediate future.

The building of the transcontinental railroads, however, put an entirely different face upon the situation, for they brought to the Western Territories a permanent farmer population and a solid economic foundation for statehood. This became apparent first in the northernmost tier of Territories. In 1870 the population of the Dakota, Idaho, and Washington Territories was only 75,000; by 1890, after the Northern Pacific had been completed and the Great Northern almost finished, their population had increased to one million. The influence of the railroads, both in bringing a permanent population and in providing markets, was central in the creation of most of the other Western states.

Agitation for statehood, especially in the Dakotas and Washington Territory, was continuous, but action was held up for a full decade by political differences in Congress. The decisive influence of Colorado's vote in the disputed presidential election of 1876 brought the statehood question into party politics. Favorable action upon the demand of the Dakotas for admission in 1881 was held up by Eastern fear of Western radicalism, and Eastern resentment over the repudiation of certain railway bonds by Yankton county. By playing politics with the fortunes and the futures of the Western Territories, both parties forfeited the confidence of these embryo states and made them the more willing to follow the banner of Populism in the early 1890's.

The so-called blockade, however, came to an end abruptly in 1888, with the election of Harrison and the prospect of complete Republican control of the government. Both parties and both Houses then made frenzied efforts to get credit for the admission of the Western states. The result of this eager rivalry was the Omnibus Bill of 1889 which, in its final form, provided for the admission of North and South Dakota, Montana, and Washington. No provision had been made in the Omnibus Bill for Wyoming and Idaho, but in both of these Territories constitutional conventions met without specific authority, and a few months later both were admitted by a debate-weary and vote-hungry Republican Congress.

With the admission of these six states there existed for the first time a solid band of states from the Atlantic to the Pacific. The same year that the Omnibus Bill passed, the government purchased a large part of the lands of the Five Civilized Tribes and threw Oklahoma open to settlement under the provisions of the homestead laws. When the gun was fired on 22 April 1889 there ensued a scene without parallel in the history of the West. Let Edna Ferber's Yancey Cravat describe it:

> Well, eleven o'clock and they were crowding and cursing and fighting for places near the line. They shouted and sang and yelled and argued, and the sound they made wasn't human at all, but like thousands of wild animals penned up. The sun blazed down. It was cruel. The dust hung over everything in a thick cloud, blinding you and choking you. The black dust of the prairie was over everything. We were a horde of fiends with our red eyes and our cracked lips and our blackened faces. Eleven-thirty. It was a picture straight out of hell. The roar grew louder. People fought for an inch of gain on the Border. . . . Eleven-forty-five. Along the Border were the soldiers, their guns in one hand, their watches in the other. Those last five minutes seemed years long; and funny, they'd quieted till there wasn't a sound. Listening. The last minute was an eternity. Twelve o'clock. There went up a roar that drowned the crack of the soldiers' musketry as they fired in the air as the signal of noon and the start of the Run. You could see the puffs of smoke from their guns, but you couldn't hear a sound. The thousands surged over the Line. It was like water going over a broken dam. The rush

had started and it was devil take the hindmost. We swept across the prairie in a cloud of black and red dust that covered our faces and hands in a minute, so that we looked like black demons from hell.[5]

The towns of Guthrie and Oklahoma City sprang up overnight. By November, Oklahoma had 60,000 settlers and the following year it was organized into a Territory. Within a decade the population had reached almost 800,000, and the question of statehood became urgent. The problem of the disposition of the Indians of Indian Territory complicated matters considerably, and it was not until 1907, when the population was larger than that of any other Territory on admission, that Oklahoma and Indian Territory were admitted as one state.

When in 1890 the Mormon government in Utah accepted the inevitable and promised to abandon polygamy, it removed the last objection to its admission to statehood. Under the able administration of the Mormon Church the Latter-day Saints had prospered amazingly, and when Utah was finally admitted to statehood, in 1896, it was with a flourishing population of some 250,000. The Territories of Arizona and New Mexico, both containing a large admixture of Mexicans and Indians, had rejected joint admission as a single state in 1907, and it was five years before they were admitted individually.

Thus was completed a process inaugurated by the Northwest Ordinance of 1787. Since that time the United States had grown from 13 to 48 states, embracing the whole continental domain; Alaska and Hawaii were admitted just half a century later. Texas came in as an independent republic; Maine and West Virginia were separated from other states; Vermont and Kentucky were admitted without previous Territorial organization. But all the others, after passing through the Territorial stage, were admitted as states in a Union of equals, in accordance with the policies laid down by the enlightened ordinance. The greatest experiment in colonial policy and administration of modern times had been brought to a conclusion successful beyond the wildest dreams of those who inaugurated it.

The constitutions of the new states differed little from those of the older states; for Americans, on the whole, have hesitated to exploit the opportunity for political experiment and differentiation offered by the federal system. What differences there were took a democratic form.

5. Edna Ferber, *Cimarron*, Doubleday, Doran, pp. 23–5.

The constitutions of Wyoming [6] and Utah provided for woman suffrage from the beginning, and Colorado and other Western states incorporated this provision in their constitutions shortly after. Some of the states provided for the initiative, the referendum, and the Australian ballot, and Arizona went so far as to legalize the recall of judges — a feature which persuaded President Taft to veto her admission to the Union on the ground that it was 'destructive of free government.' All of the new constitutions contained lengthy authorizations for the regulation of railroads and other corporations, and most of them reflected the more liberal attitude of the 'nineties toward labor and social reform. There were provisions for the eight-hour day, the limitation of the hours of labor for women and children, arbitration of labor disputes, and employer liability, and prohibitions against the use of the blacklist. In form, too, these new constitutions differed from those of the Eastern states; they were remarkably long and detailed, strengthened the executive at the expense of the legislative power, and encouraged the growth of the 'fourth branch' of the government by providing for numerous boards and commissions. On the whole they resembled codes of law rather than statements of basic principles of government, and constituted documents in 'the case of the American People *versus* Themselves.'

Yet it would be an error to suppose that the governments of the new states were more liberal, during these years, than those of the old. The contrary was more commonly true, for it was easier for vested interests to capture control of thinly populated and politically immature Western states. For years the Southern Pacific dominated the politics of California — it was 'The Octopus' of Frank Norris's famous novel; the Anaconda Copper Company ruled Montana as a feudal fief; the Wyoming Stock Growers' Association gave the law to that territory; and the copper companies and land speculators controlled by the 'Anglos' imposed their rule on the native peoples of New Mexico. Railroads bought and sold state legislatures; mining companies kept labor in its place; timber and cattle overlords despoiled the public domain; and later on oil companies were strong enough to control not only the states but Congress when their own interests were at stake. And once the Populist

6. The Wyoming proviso was attacked on the floor of the House as a violation of the guaranty clause of the Constitution, for, as one Congressman from Georgia observed, 'female suffrage and the right of females to hold office are antagonistic to republican institutions.'

impulse had spent itself, nowhere were the authorities more ready to put down radicalism than in the Far West. If it is not quite true that the Western farmer held no grievances that dollar wheat would not cure, it is true of the West in general that it was far more interested in economic panaceas than in political freedom, and that it was scarcely interested in intellectual freedom at all.

Transportation and Its Control

1. THE RAILWAY KEY

For almost fifty years after the Civil War the railroad dominated American industry and politics. There were 35,000 miles of steam railway in the United States in 1865, practically all east of the Mississippi. During the next eight years the country doubled its rail network. From 1874 to 1887, some 87,000 additional miles of track were laid, and in 1900, with just under 200,000 miles in operation, the United States had a greater railway mileage than all Europe. Railway expansion touched American life at countless points. It closely interacted with western migration and settlement, with the iron and steel industry, and with agriculture; it greased the way for big business and high finance, helped to pollute politics, and gave birth to new problems of constitutional law and of government policy and governmental mechanisms. By widening the market for manufactured goods, it helped trigger a revolution in the American economy.

Immediately after the war came mechanical improvements such as the gradual replacement of the old type of engine (which looked like a wash boiler hitched to a big funnel and a cow-catcher) by coal-burning expansion-cylinder locomotives, the Pullman sleeping car (1864), the safety coupler, and the Westinghouse air brake. This last, invented in 1869, did more than any other invention to transform the original string of boxes on tracks into the modern train and to make possible safe operation at high speeds. But it was the old wood-burning, spark-belching 'bullgine,' gay with paint and sporting a name instead of a number, tugging unvestibuled coaches with swaying kerosene lamps and quid-bespattered wood stoves, which first wheezed across the Great Divide and linked the Atlantic to the Pacific.

On 1 July 1862 President Lincoln signed the first Pacific Railway Act. This law provided for the construction of a transcontinental railroad by two corporations — the Union Pacific which would build westward from Council Bluffs, Iowa, and the Central Pacific, which was to build eastward from Sacramento, California. It pledged liberal aid in the form of alternate sections of public lands to the depth of ten miles (and later twenty) on either side of the road, and loans ranging from $16,000 to $48,000 for every mile of track completed. Active construction of the Union Pacific, directed by General Grenville Dodge as chief engineer, began in 1865. The road was pushed rapidly westward from Omaha through Nebraska and Wyoming Territories, near the line of the old Oregon and Mormon Trails, and across the Wasatch range of the Rockies into the Great Salt Basin. In the meantime the Central Pacific, chartered in 1858 and directed by Collis P. Huntington and Leland Stanford, built eastward over the difficult grades of the Sierras and across the arid valleys of Nevada to meet the Union Pacific.

The obstacles to be overcome seemed almost insuperable: engineering problems, labor and financial difficulties, the constant struggle with mountain blizzard and desert heat, and — in the mountains — with the Indians as well. As General Dodge recalled:

> All the supplies for this work had to be hauled from the end of the track, and the wagon transportation was enormous. At one time we were using at least ten thousand animals, and most of the time from eight to ten thousand laborers. The bridge gangs always worked from five to twenty miles ahead of the track, and it was seldom that the track waited for a bridge. To supply one mile of track with material and supplies required about forty cars, as on the plains everything — rails, ties, bridging, fastenings, all railway supplies, fuel for locomotives and trains, and supplies for men and animals on the entire work — had to be transported from the Missouri River. Therefore as we moved westward, every hundred miles added vastly to our transportation. Yet the work was so systematically planned and executed that I do not remember an instance in all the construction of the line of the work being delayed a single week for want of material.[1]

1. Grenville Dodge, *How We Built the Union Pacific*.

That the obstacles were overcome must be attributed not only to the indomitable energy and perseverance of men like Dodge and Huntington but also to the courage and devotion of the thousands of laborers — the ex-soldiers, Irish immigrants, and Chinese coolies — upon whose brawny shoulders the heaviest part of the task rested.

> When I think [wrote Robert Louis Stevenson] of how the railroad has been pushed through this unwatered wilderness and haunt of savage tribes . . . ; how at each stage of construction, roaring, impromptu cities full of gold and lust and death sprang up and then died away again, and are now but wayside stations in the desert; how in these uncouth places pigtailed Chinese pirates worked side by side with border ruffians and broken men from Europe, talking together in a mixed dialect mostly oaths, . . . how the plumed hereditary lord of all America heard in this last fastness the scream of the 'bad medicine wagon' charioting his foes; and then when I go on to remember that all this epical turmoil was conducted by gentlemen in frocked coats, and to nothing more extraordinary than a fortune and a subsequent visit to Paris, it seems to me . . . as if this railway were the one typical achievement of the age in which we live. . . . If it be romance, if it be contrast, if it be heroism that we require, what was Troy town to this.[2]

Both the Union and the Central Pacific roads were pushed forward in record time, 20,000 laborers laying as much as eight miles of track in a day in the last stages of the race. The prime motive for this feverish haste was the greed of each group of promoters to obtain the lion's share of federal bounties and land grants. When, amidst universal rejoicing, the two sets of rails were joined with a golden spike at Promontory Point, Utah, 10 May 1869, the Union Pacific was regarded as the winner, but the Central Pacific promoters had made enough to enable them to buy the state government of California.

Meantime there was a wild scramble among other groups of promoters for charters and favors, and within a few years Congress chartered and endowed with enormous land grants three other lines: (1) the Northern Pacific — from Lake Superior across Minnesota, through the Bad Lands of Dakota up the valley of the Yellowstone, to the headwaters of the Missouri, across the Continental Divide at Bozeman, and by an intricate route through the Rockies to the Columbia river and Portland; (2) the Southern Pacific — from New Orleans across Texas to

2. *Across the Plains*, pp. 50–52.

the Rio Grande, across the Llano Estacado to El Paso, and through the territory of the Gadsden Purchase to Los Angeles, up the San Joaquin valley to San Francisco; (3) the Sante Fe — following closely the old Santa Fe Trail, from Atchison, Kan., up the Arkansas river to Trinidad, Colo., across the Raton spur of the Rockies to Santa Fe and Albuquerque, through the country of the Apache and the Navajo, parallel to the Grand Canyon of the Colorado — which thrusts its impassable barrier for 300 miles athwart the southern railway routes — and across the Mojave desert to San Bernardino and San Diego. The Southern Pacific link was completed in 1881; the Northern Pacific and Santa Fe both reached the Pacific in 1883. Thus within 20 years of the Pacific railway legislation there were four transcontinentals; a fifth, the Great Northern, was pushed through in the next decade by the dynamic James J. Hill.

2. THE RAILROADS AND THE WEST

At the end of the Civil War the Plains west of eastern Kansas and Nebraska, the High Plains, and the Rocky Mountain regions were practically unpeopled, save for mining towns in Colorado and Nevada and the Mormon settlements in Utah. Mail coaches of the Overland Stage Line required at least five days to transport passengers and mails from the Missouri river to Denver, where flour was sold for 20 cents a pound and potatoes for $15 a bushel. Prewar pioneers had been confined to subsistence farming until the railway connected them with markets; but the transcontinental railways pushed out into the Plains far in advance of settlers, advertised for immigrants in the Eastern states and Europe, transported them at wholesale rates to the prairie railhead, and sold them land at from $1 to $10 an acre. Thus James J. Hill settled his great domain in the Far Northwest, his agents scouring Europe for settlers and meeting new arrivals at the piers in New York City; Henry Villard of the Northern Pacific employed almost a thousand agents in England and continental Europe, and their advertising literature painted the climate and the soil of the Northwest in such roseate colors that the Union Pacific lands were popularly known as Jay Cooke's banana belt. The immigration department of the Santa Fe Railroad attracted to Kansas, in 1874, 10,000 German Mennonites whose ancestors had colonized the Ukraine, and these in turn brought with them not only piety and industry but the Red Turkey wheat which made Kansas prairies bloom like a garden. Thousands of section-hands entered a free homestead right, saved their wages to buy farm equipment and a team of horses, built a sodhouse or cabin, and became permanent settlers. The termini and eastern junction points of these lines — like Omaha, opposite the old Council Bluffs of the Indians; Kansas City, hard by the old jumping-off place for the Oregon Trail; Duluth, the 'Zenith City of the Unsalted Seas'; Oakland on San Francisco bay; Portland, Oregon; Seattle and Tacoma, Washington — places non-existent or mere villages before the Civil War — became in thirty years metropolitan cities.

Railroading was the biggest business of a big era, and the railway builders were of the mettle that makes leaders and conquerors. The new Northwest was the domain of James J. Hill, the 'Empire Builder,' and the Great Northern Railway his path of empire. St. Paul was a small town on the edge of the frontier when he migrated thither from eastern Canada just before the Civil War, and Minneapolis a mere village at the Falls of St. Anthony on the Mississippi. Such importance as they had was due to their position at the end of a trail from the Red river of the North, which connected Winnipeg with the outside world. Long trains of two-wheeled ox-carts transported the peltry and supplies in 40 or 50 days' time. In the winter of 1870 Donald Smith, resident governor of the Hudson's Bay Company, started south from Winnipeg, and James J. Hill north from St. Paul, both in dog-sleds. They met on the prairie and made camp in a snowstorm; and from that meeting sprang the Canadian Pacific and the Great Northern railways. In the panic of 1873 a little Minnesota railway with an ambitious name, the St. Paul and Pacific, went bankrupt. Hill watched it as a prairie wolf watches a weakening buffalo, and in 1878, in association with two Canadian railway men, wrested it from the Dutch bondholders by a mere flotation of new securities.

The day of land grants and federal subsidies was past, and Hill saw that the Great Northern Railway, as he renamed his purchase, could reach the Pacific only by developing the country as it progressed. So this empire builder undertook to enhance the prosperity of what came to be known as the 'Hill country'; he introduced scientific farming, distributed blooded bulls free to farmers, supported churches and schools, and assisted in countless ways the development of the communities of the Northwest. 'It was,' observes one commentator, 'largely due to his unceasing interest in all that pertained to getting the most out of the soil that the "Hill country" developed more evenly and with fewer tragedies than any other large-scale land enterprise of these years.'

In constructing his railroad Hill showed equal forethought and shrewdness. Construction costs were low, the financial management skillful and conservative, and the Great Northern was the one transcontinental line that weathered every financial crisis. Hill first made connection with Winnipeg by the Red river valley; then, anticipating a diversion of Winnipeg traffic by the Canadian Pacific, he struck almost due west across the Dakota plains, sending out branches in order to people the region and carry wheat to market. In the summer of 1887 he made a record stride, 643 miles of grading, bridging, and plate-laying from Minot, North Dakota, to the Great Falls of the Missouri, at the rate of over three miles per working day. Two years later, the Rockies yielded their last secret, the Marias pass, to a young engineer named John F. Stevens. In 1893 the trains of the Great Northern reached tidewater at Tacoma, Washington. Ten years more, and Hill had acquired partial control of the Northern Pacific Railroad, had purchased joint control of a railway connecting its eastern termini with Chicago, and was running his own fleets of steamships from Duluth to Buffalo, and from Seattle to Japan and China.

The Great Northern, the Northern Pacific, and the Union Pacific (which sent a taproot northwesterly) were responsible for the opening of the great 'Inland Empire' between the Cascades and the Rockies, and for an astounding development of the entire Northwest. This once isolated Oregon country, with its rich and varied natural resources, magnificent scenery, and thriving seaports, became as distinct a section of the Union as New England. The three states of this region — Washington, Oregon, and Idaho — increased their population from 282,000 in 1880 to 763,000 in 1890, and 2,140,000 in 1910. California, which contained only half a million people when the golden spike was driven in 1869, kept pace with them: it stood twenty-fourth in population in 1870, and twelfth in 1910; fifty-five years later it moved past New York into first place. The population of Kansas, Nebraska, and the Dakotas, starting at the same level in 1870, grew sixfold in two decades; Utah and Colorado, where there was a great mining boom in the 1870's, rose from 125,000 to 624,000 in the same period; Oklahoma and the Indian Territory, where not a white man was enrolled in 1880, had over a million and a half palefaces in 1910; and Texas, with the aid of a network of railways and the discovery of oil wells that were seemingly inexhaustible, foreshadowed its future growth by doubling its population between 1880 and 1910.

King Cotton's crown passed to King Wheat, whose dominions increased. Railway penetration of the Far Northwest, improved farm machinery, new strains of rust-resistant wheat, techniques of dry farming, the trans-shipment to lake or ocean steamers by grain elevator companies, and a new milling process which ground Northern spring wheat into superfine flour — all these combined to move the center of wheat production north and west from Illinois and Iowa into Minnesota, the Dakotas, Montana, Oregon, and the prairie provinces of Canada.

While Villard and Dodge, Huntington and Hill, were connecting the Atlantic and the Pacific, another enterprise, no less heroic, was linking the two shores of the Atlantic. As early as the 1840's Samuel F. B. Morse, inventor of the telegraph, and the famous oceanographer Matthew Maury had proposed laying a telegraphic cable under the Atlantic Ocean. But it was Cyrus Field of New York, member of one of America's most distinguished families, who took up the notion and carried it through. In 1856 he enlisted the financier Peter Cooper, British scientists and investors, and the British and American governments in a bold plan to string a giant cable from westernmost Ireland to Trinity Bay, Newfoundland. He quickly connected Trinity Bay with New York, and by summer 1857 two men-of-war were playing out a giant cable off the Irish coast. It broke in mid-ocean — the first of a long series of cruel disappointments. In 1858 a cable was finally laid over 2000 miles of ocean bed, but even as two continents indulged in an orgy of rhetoric and rejoicing, the cable ceased to transmit messages. The Civil War put a stop to further experiments, but after the war the indomitable Field once more took up the project, enlisting this time the scientific genius of Lord Kelvin and the engineering talent of the railroad-builder Isambard Brunel. With the fabulous *Great Eastern* — the world's largest ship — playing out a vastly improved cable, a firm connection between the continents was finally established in 1866. It cost $5 a word to send a message across the ocean, and the public was duly impressed when the Emperor Maximilian of Mexico cabled a message to the Empress Carlotta at a cost of $4780, but soon the price was reduced and the messages improved.

3. FEDERAL AND LOCAL AID

When railroads began to supplant rivers and canals as highways of commerce, connect isolated rural regions with markets, and open up new land to settlement, they were looked upon as an unmixed blessing, and their promoters were regarded as public benefactors. Since every route decided upon by surveyors and railway promoters brought prosperity to some communities and threatened ruin to others, towns, counties, and states outdid one another in bidding for the iron tracks. The Federal Government, too, having definitely abandoned strict construction theories that had embarrassed an earlier generation, regarded the roads as military and postal necessities and aided them with a liberality which at the time seemed commendable but which a later generation came to regard as excessive.

This policy of government aid to internal improvements had its beginnings in grants of land to canal, turnpike, and railroad companies in the decades before the Civil War. In the 1850's no less than 28 million acres of public lands were granted to states to subsidize railroad construction; the Illinois Central alone got some 2.6 million acres in the states through which it passed. With the enactment of the Pacific Railway Acts of 1862 and 1864 the Federal Government inaugurated the practice of making land grants directly to railway corporations.

Besides charters and rights of way across the territories, federal aid was extended to the roads in a number of ways, the most important of which were land grants, loans, subsidies, and tariff remission on rails. The land grants were the most lavish and the most valuable. The Union Pacific received some 20 million acres of public lands; the Sante Fe got 17 million acres from the Federal Government and additional millions from the state of Texas; the Central Pacific and the Southern Pacific each got 24 million acres; while the Northern Pacific obtained the enormous total of 44 million acres, an area equal to the entire state of Missouri. Altogether the Federal Government gave the railroads 155,504,994 acres, of which over 40 million were forfeited because the roads failed to fulfill the conditions of the grants, leaving a net total of 131,350,534 acres from this source.

But this was by no means the whole of the land subsidy to the Western roads. The states — notably Texas and Minnesota — gave the railroads an additional 48,883,372 acres. Other millions of acres were obtained by purchase or chicanery under the easy terms of the Desert Land Act of 1877, the Timber and Stone Act of 1878, and the Forest Lien Act of 1897, which enabled the railroads to exchange barren land for well-timbered land elsewhere on the public domain. Railroads acquired vast acreages at absurdly low prices from Indian tribes, or from states disposing of their swamp lands or their land-grant college scrip.

As most of this land was worth nothing to the roads until it produced crops to be hauled to market, and because they urgently needed money, the railway companies generally disposed of it as rapidly as possible, and at a price of between $4 and $5 an acre. Some of the land, however, covered extensive deposits of coal or oil, or other minerals, and much of it was heavily timbered. So while disposing rapidly of their agricultural and grazing lands, the roads consistently followed the policy of reserving mineral lands, timber lands, and potential town sites for speculative purposes, and in this policy they were encouraged by amiable interpretations of the law by successive land commissioners. Some of these holdings — the Williston Oil Basin, for example, still controlled by the Northern Pacific — proved fabulously rich. The lands granted the Illinois Central brought in a sum equal to the entire construction cost of that railroad. It cost some $70 million to build the Northern Pacific, but in 1917 that road reported gross receipts from land sales of over $136 million, with a substantial part of its most valuable lands still unsold. The lands granted to both the Union Pacific and the Central Pacific yielded enough to have covered all legitimate costs of building these roads.

The Federal Government gave direct financial aid only to the Union Pacific and the Central Pacific railways and their subsidiaries in the form of a loan for every mile of track. These loans, aggregating $64 million, were repaid in 1899 with interest of about $100 million, but the controversy involving their repayment troubled American politics for a decade.

The Federal Government received substantial benefits in return for its largess. Land-grant railroads were required to carry government mail at a reduced price, and also to transport military personnel and supplies at less than normal charges, an arrangement of considerable importance during the First World War. Spokesmen for the railroads estimated the accumulated value of these benefits at more than the total worth of the land grants, but those who have ventured into the labyrinths of this accounting have never been known to emerge.

Aid from states, counties, and municipalities, often competing with one another, was equally lavish and more reckless. The states often granted tax exemption, protection from competition, and liberal charters; some lent the roads their credit, others subscribed outright to the stock of railway companies. Many states made extensive land grants, sometimes under pressure; the La Crosse Railroad managed to get a grant of one million acres from the state government by a judicious distribution of $900,000 in railroad stock to the governor, the legislature, and state judges. Counties and municipalities subscribed liberally to railroad stock and often donated money outright. Counties and towns in Kentucky incurred a debt of over $13 million for railroad construction; 86 counties in Illinois subsidized railroads to the extent of over $16 million. Many railroads 'reorganized' or went bankrupt before they could build the promised roads, but cities and counties were held to their commitments.

Yet it would be unfair to conclude on a note of exploitation and chicanery. Two other observations are called for. First, short of government construction and operation — something unimaginable to Americans of that generation — this was probably the only way to get the Western railroads built at all. Second, the policy of governmental subsidy to transportation is as old as the Republic and as recent as the last session of Congress. The Populists and Progressives were shocked at the spectacle of private profit from government subsidies, but a generation that has seen Congress vote hundreds of millions to subsidize the merchant marine, spend billions on highways used by trucks, and vote additional billions to build airports and subsidize airlines, does not find it so difficult to understand the methods — however incompetent and corrupt — whereby our forebears built the transcontinentals.

4. ABUSES AND STATE REGULATION

This rapid extension of the railroads was not followed by the expected wave of prosperity, except for the insiders who built the roads. On the contrary, within a few years the farmers of the West began to feel the effects of the postwar deflation, followed by the panic of 1873, and many laid the blame on the railroads. The advantages for which Westerners had paid so handsomely seemed to bring only hard times. How far the railroads were responsible for the hard times of the early 1870's through stimulating production ahead of market needs is a matter of dispute; but there is no question of the reality of grave abuses connected with railway expansion.

To the farmer the most grievous of the abuses were the high freight rates charged by the Western roads, rates so exorbitant that the farmers at times burned their corn for fuel rather than ship it to market. The railway masters argued that they were barely able to maintain dividend payments, and it is true that in periods of depression, such as those following upon the panics of 1873 and 1893, a good many roads were in receivership. Furthermore, on competitive routes vigorous competition drove rates below cost. Yet it is equally true that profits, either in the form of dividends, stock splits, or other devices, were often exorbitant, and that both the extortionate freight rates and the financial troubles of the roads were traceable to such things as over-high construction costs, fraudulent purchase of other properties at inflated prices, manipulation of stock, and incompetent management.

The total construction cost of the Central Pacific, for example, from Sacramento to Ogden, Utah, ran something over $90 million, and upon this investment the directors of the road expected to pay dividends; but a congressional committee estimated that 'a road similar to that of the Central Pacific could probably be built for $22,000,000.' The same committee figured the cost of the five transcontinental lines at $634 million, and that these same roads could be duplicated for $228 million. Construction costs were so high partly because of the pressure under which many of the roads were built in order to get land grants, but chiefly because costs were artificially increased by dummy construction companies in order to provide profits for the directors. In the East, Jay Gould and Jim Fisk systematically milked the Erie Railroad, which did not finally recover until the 1940's. This technique of using dummy construction corporations is illustrated by the short-lived Southern Pennsylvania Railroad, a little road started by Vanderbilt in order to force the Pennsylvania Railroad to buy it. A contractor offered to construct it for $6.5 million, but instead Vanderbilt organized a corporation consisting of his clerks, which received $15 million to build the road; the syndicate who furnished them with this money was paid with $40 million in railroad shares. The Pennsylvania, which eventually had to buy this property, not unnaturally expected to earn dividends on the cost of acquiring all this! No wonder Poor's Railroad Manual for 1885 estimated that approximately one-third of all railroad capitalization in the country that year represented water.

Complaint was loud and persistent against other abuses too. Railroad 'pools' did away with competition in large areas by fixing prices and dividing up profits in accordance with agreed-on schedules. Railroads discriminated in rates and in services with secret rebates to powerful shippers which put the small shippers at a hopeless disadvantage. The Standard Oil Company was granted a rebate on each barrel of oil shipped to Cleveland, and an additional drawback on each barrel shipped by a competitor. The long-and-short-haul evil consisted in slashing freight rates at competitive points and making up the losses at non-competitive points. Goods traveling from Boston to Denver direct paid $1.70 a hundredweight, but if they traveled from Boston to San Francisco and then back to Denver, they went for $1.50. Farmers bridled, too, at railroad domination of warehouses and other facilities. The railroads controlled all the great grain elevators in Chicago and through them fixed the price they would pay for wheat from the hinterland; they also owned the Union stockyards which enabled them pretty well to determine the price of beef in the Mid-West. Protests were voiced as well against the corrupt activities of railroads in politics. The Union Pacific agent in Nebraska's state capital admitted that he ordinarily gave out over 400 passes a year to those who might influence legislation.

The power of the Western railways over their exclusive territory was nearly absolute, for until the age of the automobile the West had no alternate means of transportation. Railways could make an industry or ruin a community by a few cents more or less in rates. The money at their disposal, often created by financial manipulation, enabled them to influence both public opinion and legislatures. Railway builders and promoters insisted that railroading was a business wholly private in its nature, no more a fit subject for government regulation than a retail store. 'There is no foundation in good reason,' said Leland Stanford to his stockholders in 1878, 'for the attempts made by the General Government and by the States to especially control your affairs. It is a question of might, and it is to your interest to have it determined where the power resides.'

Leland Stanford, Collis P. Huntington, and their associates who built

Union Pacific Engine No. 119 crosses the high trestle near Promontory, Utah, where the first transcontinental rail line was completed 10 May 1869.

Race for Claims on the Cherokee Strip, Oklahoma, 1889

Sioux Camp, 1891

A sod house in the Dakota Territory, 1885

the Central Pacific and controlled the Southern Pacific, had the might, and in the exercise of that might they were indifferent to all save considerations of gain for themselves and their roads. By distributing free passes to state representatives, by paying campaign expenses, and by downright bribery, they prevented just taxation of their properties and evaded most regulation. By discriminating in freight charges between localities, articles, and individuals, they terrorized merchants, farmers, and communities 'until matters reached such a pass, that no man dared engage in any business in which transportation largely entered without first . . . obtaining the permission of a railroad manager.'[3] The same methods were imitated by the railroad magnates in the rest of the country. For years President Milton Smith of the Louisville and Nashville Railway openly defied legislatures and court orders in four states. The New York Central and the Erie Railroads corrupted not only the Albany legislature but the state courts as well.[4] In New Hampshire, as in California, a 'railroad lobby,' ensconced in an office near the state capitol, acted as a chamber of initiative and revision; and, as the novelist Winston Churchill tells us in his *Coniston* and *Mr. Crewe's Career*, few could succeed in politics unless by grace of the Boston and Maine.

These abuses were tolerated by the American people with a remarkable patience, so imbued were they with laissez-faire doctrine, so proud of progress, improvement, and development, and so averse to increasing the power of government. But the deflation of the postwar years and the panic of 1873 brought an inevitable reaction, centered in the Mid-Western states of Illinois, Iowa, Wisconsin, Minnesota, Missouri, and Nebraska, but also expressed in Eastern states such as Massachusetts and in Western states such as California. It took several forms: denial of further state aid, as in the constitutions of California, Kansas, and Mis-

3. Report of the U.S. Pacific Railway Commission (1887), Vol. I, p. 141.
4. 'War is the natural state of an American railway towards all other authorities and its own fellows, just as war was the natural state of cities towards one another in the ancient world. And as an army in the field must be commanded by one general, so must this latest militant product of an eminently peaceful civilization. The president of a great railroad needs gifts for strategical combinations scarcely inferior to those, if not of a great general, yet of a great war minister — a Chatham or a Carnot. If his line extends into a new country he must be quick to seize the best routes. . . . He must know the Governors and watch the legislatures of the States or Territories through which his line runs; and must have adroit agents at the State capitals well supplied with the sinews of war. . . .' James Bryce, *The American Commonwealth*, Vol. II, pp. 651–2.

souri; recovery of land grants; prohibition of specific abuses such as rebates and passes; and positive regulation of rates and services. The Eastern state governments inclined to supervision by special railway commissions, and that of Massachusetts, under the leadership of the gifted Charles Francis Adams, Jr., attracted widespread attention and became the conservative model for numerous states.

The Mid-Western states were more direct in their methods. The Illinois Constitution of 1870 directed the legislature to 'pass laws to correct abuses and to prevent unjust discrimination and extortion in the rates of freight and passenger tariffs on the different railroads of the state.' Pursuant to this charter the legislature of Illinois outlawed discrimination, established a maximum rate, and created a Railway and Warehouse Commission to regulate roads, grain elevators, and warehouses. These laws, though bitterly denounced as socialistic throughout the East, served as models for similar legislation in other states. At the demand of the farmers, and of businessmen who had suffered from railroad discrimination, the example of Illinois was followed in 1874 by Iowa and Minnesota, and by Wisconsin with its drastic Potter law. Within a few years the railroads of the Middle West found their independence severely circumscribed by a mass of highly restrictive regulatory legislation.

The validity of this legislation was upheld in the 'Granger' cases. The first and most important of these was *Munn* v. *Illinois* (1876) involving the constitutionality of a statute regulating the charges of grain elevators. The warehouse owners contended that the act by depriving them of property without due process of law violated the Fourteenth Amendment. In one of the most far-reaching decisions in American law, Chief Justice Morrison R. Waite upheld the Illinois statute. Basing his opinion upon the historical right of the state, in the exercise of its police power to regulate ferries, common carriers, inns, etc., he announced:

> When private property is affected with a public interest it ceases to be *juris privati* only. . . . . Property does become clothed with a public interest when used in a manner to make it of public consequence, and affect the community at large. When, therefore, one devotes his property to a use in which the public has an interest, he, in effect, grants to the public an interest in that use, and must submit to be controlled by the public for the common good, to the extent of the interest he has created.

The warehouse owners not only challenged the right of the state to regulate their business but contended further that rate-fixing by a legis-

lative committee did not constitute 'due process of law.' This contention
the Court disposed of in cavalier fashion:

> It is insisted, however, that the owner of property is entitled to a
> reasonable compensation for its use . . . and that what is reason-
> able is a judicial and not a legislative question. . . . The controlling
> fact [however] is the power to regulate at all. If that exists, the
> right to establish the maximum charge, as one of the means of
> regulation, is implied. . . . We know that this is a power which
> may be abused; but that is no argument against its existence. For
> protection against abuses by legislatures, the people must resort to
> the polls, not to the courts.

On the same day that the Court sustained the validity of the Illinois
statute, it handed down decisions in the important cases of *Peik* v.
Chicago & Northwestern R.R., *Chicago, Burlington & Quincy R.R.* v.
Iowa, and *Winona & St. Peter R.R.* v. *Blake*. These cases involved the
validity of Granger laws establishing maximum freight and passenger
rates. The statutes had been attacked not only as violations of the Fourteenth Amendment but also as violations of the exclusive control over
interstate commerce by the Congress. The Court, however, sustained the
validity of these laws against both charges. The railroad, said the Court,

> is employed in state as well as interstate commerce, and until Con-
> gress acts, the State must be permitted to adopt such rules and
> regulations as may be necessary for the promotion of the general
> welfare of the people within its own jurisdiction, even though in so
> doing those without may be indirectly affected.

Thus the Court announced three major principles of constitutional
law: first, the right of government to regulate all business affected with a
public interest; second, the right of the legislature to determine what is
fair and reasonable; third, the right of the state, in areas of concurrent
authority, to act where Congress has failed to act. These decisions,
which inaugurated the modern era of regulation of public utilities,
aroused a storm of protest from financial circles in the East. Within
a decade the composition of the Supreme Court became more conservative, and two of the three Granger principles were duly modified. Thus,
in 1886, in the Wabash case, the Court retreated from the third principle
by holding invalid an Illinois statute prohibiting the 'long-and-short-
haul' evil, on the ground that it infringed upon the exclusive power of
Congress over interstate commerce. In the same year, in *Stone* v.
Farmers' Loan Co., the Court intimated that the reasonableness of the

rate established by a commission might be a matter for judicial rather than legislative determination. Three years later, in *Chicago, Milwaukee and St. Paul Railroad Co.* v. *Minnesota,* this obiter dictum became the basis for a decision declaring rate regulation by a legislative commission invalid. These decisions dealt a heavy blow to state regulation of roads and rates, and placed the burden squarely upon the Federal Government. Congress responded with the Interstate Commerce Act of 1887.

5. THE ADVENT OF FEDERAL REGULATION

The Interstate Commerce Act of 4 February 1887 represented a compromise between the Massachusetts or supervisory type of regulation and the Granger or coercive type of regulation. It specifically prohibited pooling, rebates, discrimination of any character, and higher rates for a short haul than for a long haul. It provided that all charges should be 'reasonable and just' but failed to define either of these ambiguous terms. Perhaps most important, it established the first permanent administrative board [5] of the Federal Government, the Interstate Commerce Commission, to supervise the administration of the law. Enforcement was left to the courts, but a large part of the burden of proof and prosecution was placed upon the commission. Although the bill was popularly regarded as a victory for the public, it had the support of the railroads, and railway stocks rose in the market upon its passage.

Administrative regulations were still so foreign to the American conception of government that the federal courts insisted upon their right to review orders of the Interstate Commerce Commission, and took the teeth out of the act by a series of decisions. In the Maximum Freight Rate case (1897), the Supreme Court held that the commission did not have the power to fix rates, and in the Alabama Midlands case of the same year it practically nullified the long-and-short-haul prohibition. It was found almost impossible to require agents of the railroads to testify about railroad malpractices, and witnesses would introduce into the court new testimony which had been withheld from the commission, thus requiring an entirely new adjudication. Reversals of the commission's rulings were frequent; by 1905 fifteen of the sixteen cases appealed to the Supreme Court had been decided adversely to the com-

5. Unless the Civil Service Commission, established in 1883 but spectacularly ineffective, should be regarded as the first.

mission. Furthermore, it was found almost impossible for shippers to collect refunds from recalcitrant roads; down to 1897 shippers had succeeded in getting refunds in only five out of 225 cases. Indeed, the roads evaded the provisions of the act so successfully that Justice Harlan declared the commission to be a 'useless body for all practical purposes,' and the commission itself, in its annual report for 1898, confessed its failure. Nevertheless the principle of federal regulation of railroads had been established, and the machinery for such regulation created. It remained for a later administration to apply the principle and make the machinery effective.

6. THE DECLINE OF STEAMBOATING

I saw the boat go round the bend,
Good-by, my lover, good-by!
All loaded down with gentlemen,
Good-by, my lover, good-by!

The generation that flung the iron tracks across the prairies and mountains of Western America witnessed the passing of one of the most characteristic and colorful phases of American life — steamboating. From the eventful day that Henry Shreve launched the *George Washington* on the Ohio (1817) until the Civil War, steamboats were the major means of inland transportation. For fifty years the waters of the Mississippi and her tributaries floated hundreds of steamboats great and small, their main decks laden with cotton and cattle, grain and furs, and 'fellows who have seen alligators and neither fear whiskey nor gunpowder'; their upper decks, which to the simple dwellers of the valley, appeared 'fairy structures of Oriental gorgeousness and splendor,' bore planters, merchants, dandies, and fine ladies. Swift passenger steamers raced each other recklessly on the lazy Father of Waters or the riotous Missouri, lashing the waters into foam with their churning paddles. While the North and East followed the fortunes and compared the records of Yankee clippers, the people of the interior bet their shirts on the *Robert E. Lee* and the *Natchez* in their historic race from New Orleans to St. Louis, won by the *Lee* in the record time of three days, eighteen hours, and fourteen minutes.

In the decade of the 'fifties river traffic reached its zenith. The value of the river trade at New Orleans was over $289 million in 1860. In those piping times before the war hundreds of new steamboats were launched on the inland waters, and on the outbreak of the conflict over 2000 of them plied the Ohio-Mississippi system alone. Before the coming of the railroads the steamboat almost succeeded in tying the upper part of the great valley to the Cotton Kingdom. At one time 80 per cent of the pork and grain from Cincinnati floated down the Ohio, and Southern Congressmen so far waived their strict-construction principles as to vote over $3 million for river improvements. The greater part of the produce that came down-river was reshipped by sea to Atlantic ports and to Europe.

In the 1850's the Eastern trunk lines provided a short cut, an improvement on this roundabout route which struck at the fancy profits of river steamboating. The Civil War accelerated the movement tremendously. Southern shipping was destroyed, and some of the Southern ports as well, and control of the cotton trade passed to the North. The steamboat fought gallantly for life, readjusting itself to new circumstances, compromising with new conditions. As Mark Twain tells it:

> Boat used to land — captain on hurricane roof — mighty stiff and straight — iron ramrod for a spine — kid gloves, plug hat, hair parted behind — man on shore takes off hat and says:
> 'Got twenty-eight tons of wheat, Cap'n — be great favor if you can take them.'
> Captain says:
> 'I'll take two of them' — and don't even condescend to look at him.
> But nowadays the captain takes off his old slouch and smiles all the way around to the back of his ears, and gets off a bow which he hasn't got any ramrod to interfere with, and says:
> 'Glad to see you, Smith, glad to see you — you're looking well — haven't seen you looking so well for years — what you got for us.'
> 'Nuthin,' says Smith; and keeps his hat on, and just turns his back and goes on talking with somebody else.

But the river captains were not always so unsuccessful. Although passenger traffic almost disappeared from the inland waters, the opening up of the wheat, timber, and iron-ore regions of the Northwest brought an absolute, though not a relative, gain in freight traffic. In 1879 no fewer than 3372 boats and 1320 barges passed Winona, Minnesota, loaded down with lumber and grain, and 1880 witnessed the high-water mark of freight transportation for the lower Mississippi, with over a million bales of cotton unloaded at the levee at New Orleans. After that river shipping declined precipitously. In 1880 two-thirds of the cotton at New Orleans came by river, by 1910 only one-tenth.[6] With the decline of the steamboat passed another phase of American frontier life as unique and as rich as the cattle kingdom.

6. However, Great Lakes tonnage rose from 500,000 in 1869 to 2.6 million in 1920. In 1885 traffic through the newly built Sault Ste. Marie canals amounted to 3.3 million tons; by 1920 it had increased to almost 80 million tons, surpassing the tonnage of both the Suez and the Panama canals.

The Economic Revolution

1. HAMILTON WINS

It was the dream of Jefferson that his country — 'with room enough for our descendants to the hundredth and thousandth generation' — was to be a great agrarian democracy. 'While we have land to labor,' he wrote, 'let us never wish to see our citizens occupied at a work bench, or twirling a distaff,' for 'those who labor in the earth are the chosen people of God.' Within two generations of Jefferson's death the value of American manufactured products was almost treble that of the agricultural, and the spokesmen of big business were appealing to his laissez-faire principles. For a hundred years America progressed economically in the direction that Alexander Hamilton wished: that of a diversified, self-sufficing nation, ruled by the people who controlled the nation's prosperity. When the census of 1920 recorded over 9 million industrial wage-earners producing commodities to the value of some $62 billion, and over 50 per cent of the population crowded into towns and cities, surely Hamilton was able to collect some bets from Jefferson in the Elysian Fields!

By 1910 the United States, hitherto a debtor nation of extractive and predominantly agricultural industry, had become the leading industrial and manufacturing power in the world. This economic revolution was a consequence of the creation of a national market, made possible by the spread of the railway network which linked farms to commercial centers and spurred the growth of cities. As population tripled between 1860 and 1920, and incomes rose at an even more rapid pace, mass demand encouraged the expansion of industry. In 1870 industries were still servicing a rural economy; most were small enterprises manufacturing for a local market. They processed the farmer's products and made goods for him. By the early 1900's many firms were operating on a national scale and not a few were turning out producers' goods for other industries rather than for the consumer. If in the quarter-century before 1900 the main stimulus for economic growth was the mass demand of a national market, in the next quarter-century the most important stimulus would be the application of electric power and the introduction of the internal combustion engine.

By 1903 the great corporation had established itself as the basic unit of American industry. The main industries were dominated by a few huge enterprises which maintained extensive national organizations for buying and marketing. In 1880 the corporation had been a phenomenon almost wholly confined to the railroads. In the next two decades nearly every industry saw the rise of the modern corporation with centralized, bureaucratized control of most phases of production and distribution; especially characteristic was the creation of a national sales department to cope with a national market.

This revolution enhanced national wealth, raised standards of living, and produced cycles of prosperity and depression with attendant periodical unemployment. It depressed agriculture and speeded up urbanization, encouraged immigration, and stimulated the more rapid growth of population. It led to mechanization and standardization of social life, modified social institutions such as that of the family and the church, and changed the intellectual outlook of the people. It helped plunge the United States into world affairs, shifted the balance of international payments, and made the United States a creditor nation. It led to a concentration of wealth and placed the control of the natural resources and the machinery of production and distribution in the hands of a small group of men, so creating, in a nation brought up on Jeffersonian principles, a whole series of antagonisms and difficulties which the teachings of the Fathers did little to illuminate.

2. THE AGE OF INVENTION

The United States Patent Office was created in 1790 largely through the efforts of one of the greatest American inventors, John Stevens of Hoboken, New Jersey. So numerous were the patents granted to ingenious Americans in the following years that in 1833, it was said, the head of the Patent Bureau decided to resign because he felt that everything of importance had been invented! Yet the 36,000 patents granted before 1860 were but a feeble indication of the flood of inventions that was to inundate the Patent Office in the years following the Civil War. In the period from 1860 to 1890 no less than 440,000 patents were issued. The average number of inventions patented in any one year since 1900 equals or exceeds the total number patented in the entire history of the country before 1860.

While the beginnings of many important inventions can be traced to the late eighteenth and early nineteenth centuries, their application on a large scale to the processes of industry and agriculture came after the Civil War. Thus James Watt in Glasgow and Oliver Evans in Philadelphia developed the steam engine before the close of the eighteenth century, but it was not until the construction of the railroad system and the introduction of the De Laval steam turbine in 1882 that steam reached its peak in America. And even at this time, the age of electricity was portended. A hundred years earlier Franklin, Galvani, and Oersted had experimented with electricity; Michael Faraday in England and Joseph Henry of the Smithsonian Institution had developed the principle of the dynamo as early as 1831, but it was not until after 1880 that the genius of Thomas A. Edison, William Stanley, Charles Brush, and a host of others revolutionized American life with the dynamo. Thus Charles Goodyear discovered the secret of the vulcanization of rubber in 1839, but not until the arrival of the automobile did it assume an important place in the economy. Elias Howe invented the sewing machine in 1846, but it did not have general use until popularized by Isaac Singer after 1860, and was first applied to the making of shoes by Gordon McKay in 1862. Eli Whitney of cotton-gin fame adapted for firearms the revolutionary principles of standardization and interchangeability of parts as early as 1798, but the general application of this principle to manufacturing, which has given precedence to American mass production, did not come until after the achievements of Kelly, Holley, and Bessemer ushered in the age of steel. Dr. N. A. Otto of Germany invented the internal combustion engine in 1876, but it did not mean much to the average American until Henry Ford in 1908 placed a motorcar on the market that was not a rich man's toy but a poor man's instrument.

Inventions radically changed transportation. Between 1870 and 1880 Stephen Field and Thomas A. Edison in America and the Siemens firm in Berlin were perfecting the first electric railway, and inside of ten years there were 769 miles in operation in the United States. Within a short time the streetcar, the elevated and subway train, all based upon the dynamo, accelerated that concentration of population in cities which is one of the characteristics of modern America. The steam railway dispersed population all over the land, and the electric railway and motorcar then pulled it, for working-day purposes at least, into a few hundred civic centers and concentrated one-twelfth of the population of the country in a single metropolitan conglomeration, New York.

George Selden of Rochester, New York, had experimented with gasoline cars as early as 1879, but it was not until the turn of the century that the industry of Henry Ford and the genius of Charles Duryea bore fruit in the modern automobile. By 1920 Ford was making more than 6000 cars a day in his Detroit factories, and the automobile industry ranked first in the country in the value of its finished products. 'Darius Green and his flyin' machine' was a favorite comic recitation in the gay 'nineties; 'God never intended man to fly' was a serious conviction in 1900. Yet around 1908 the vision of Samuel P. Langley and the perseverance of the Wright brothers and Glenn Curtiss lifted the airplane out of the experimental stage into the practical.

Other forms of communication — the telegraph, the cable, the telephone, and wireless telegraphy — helped to revolutionize modern life. In 1844 Samuel Morse, a Yankee painter with a talent for mechanics, had flashed over the wires from Washington to Baltimore the first telegraphic message: 'What hath God wrought!' In 1856 the Western Union Company was organized and soon the whole country was crisscrossed with a network of wires. In 1858 the duplex telegraph was invented, and on the modern multiplex telegraph over 100,000 words can be transmitted within an hour. In 1896 an Italian, Guglielmo Marconi, discovered the secret of wireless telegraphy.

In the centennial year of 1876, Emperor Dom Pedro of Brazil, attending the Philadelphia Exposition, sauntered up to the booth of young Alexander Graham Bell; he picked up the cone-shaped instrument on display there, and as he placed it to his ear Bell spoke through the transmitter. 'My God, it talks!' exclaimed His Majesty; and from that moment the telephone became the central feature of the Exposition. Within half a century 16 million telephones had profoundly affected the life of the nation. The tempo of business was enormously quickened, too, by the invention in 1867 of the typewriter by an erratic printer, Christopher Sholes of Milwaukee; of the cash register in 1897 by James Ritty; of the adding machine by Burroughs in 1888; of the dictaphone — an outgrowth of the phonograph — by Edison; and hundreds of other office and business accessories. The linotype composing machine invented by Ottmar Mergenthaler and first used by Whitelaw Reid in 1886 in printing the New York *Tribune,* Hoe's rotary press, the web press, and folding machinery, have made it possible to print as many as 240,000 eight-page newspapers in an hour; and the electrotype has worked a comparable change in the printing of magazines and books. This revolution — plus the benevolent policy of the postal authorities in allowing cheap postal rates — made it possible for new magazines to reach a mass market heretofore unsuspected.

Just as science and invention revolutionized transportation, communication, business, and the conditions of urban living, so they wrought profound changes in agriculture. In 1868 a Scotch immigrant, James Oliver, perfected the chilled plow; in the 1870's John Appleby patented a twine binder; in 1881 Benjamin Holt turned out the first combined harvester and thresher, designed for the bonanza farms of the Far West; in 1888 A. N. Hadley invented a combined corn cutter and shocker; and after the opening of the twentieth century, gasoline power was widely applied to farm machinery.

Meantime a host of inventions affected the daily life of the American people, especially those who flocked to the towns. The 'Wizard of Menlo,' Thomas Edison, gave the world the incandescent lamp in 1880, and within a few years millions of homes were supplied with better, safer, and cheaper light than had ever been known before. It was Edison, too, who perfected the talking machine — which was in time to become a music-playing machine — and in conjunction with George Eastman developed the motion picture. And D. W. Davis's invention of the refrigerator car in the late 1860's changed the diet of the American people.

Machinery, science, and invention have enabled man to increase his productivity a hundredfold. In 1830 it was estimated that the production of a bushel of wheat required something over three hours of human labor; by the turn of the century the application of machine labor — machine seeders and harrows, steam reapers and threshers — had reduced the time to less than ten minutes. Under primitive conditions of weaving it required 5605 hours of labor to produce 500 yards of cotton sheeting; by 1900 cotton manufacturers were able to turn out the same amount with only 52 hours of human labor. One hundred and fifty years ago Adam Smith celebrated the efficiency of machine production with his famous illustration of the pin. Without machinery, he observed, a workingman would need a full day to make a single pin, but machinery then enabled a workingman to manufacture 5000 pins in a single day. A century later the great economist might have pointed his moral even more effectively, for then a single workingman could supervise the manufacture on automatic machines of 15 million pins each day.

3. THE NEW SOUTH

Although the Northeast continued to be the center of the economic revolution, its impact was felt in every region, even the South. In that region urban recovery was slower than agricultural, but once under way went faster and farther. Norfolk was long stagnant; Galveston lost population; Columbia and Charleston were too shattered to rebuild properly for years, and Charleston exported less in 1880 than she had in 1860. New Orleans took a generation to recover from the combined impact of the decline of Mississippi steamboating, Union occupation, the mismanagement of the Reconstruction governments, and yellow fever; and the stricken city of Memphis suffered so severely from the war and the ravages of yellowjack that she temporarily disappeared as a city. But new cities like Birmingham, Chattanooga, and Durham sprang into existence, and Atlanta rose from her ashes and by 1880 boasted a population four times as large as at the outbreak of the war. 'Chicago in her busiest days,' wrote a visitor, 'could scarcely show such a sight as clamors for observation here.'

Here was the 'New South' — the South of cities, factories, and blast furnaces. When, all through the 1880's, Henry Grady proclaimed the New South, what inspired enthusiasm was not so much his celebration of the Union, or his tribute to Lincoln, or even his insistence that the

South would take care of the Negro, but his glorification of the new industrial order — cities, factories, immigrants, tariffs, and all. 'Think of it,' he said in a rapturous outburst —

> In cotton a monopoly. In iron and coal establishing swift mastery. In granite and marble developing equal advantages and resources. In yellow pine and hard woods the world's treasury. Surely the basis of the South's wealth and power is laid by the hand of Almighty God!

But two things were necessary before the South could achieve wealth and power: capital and transportation. Capital presented the most difficult problem. The South itself had no surplus, and the fiscal policies of the Reconstruction governments, Radical and Redeemer alike, were not calculated to inspire confidence in Northern or foreign investors. But gradually the South attracted, or accumulated, money. The Freedmen's Bureau and the army spent large sums; the government appropriated millions for internal improvements; Northerners bought up farms and plantations, and Northern capital went into railroads, timberlands, coal and iron industries. Gradually, too, the South re-entered the world market with her exports, and lifted herself by her financial bootstraps. By the 'eighties money was pouring into the South from the North and from abroad. Much of this went to rebuilding, modernizing, and expanding the railroads. Some of these roads — notably the Louisville and Nashville — had weathered the war in good shape, and others were speedily repaired. The Louisville and Nashville was controlled by Northern capital, and of the twenty directors of the South's largest railroad system, the Terminal, seventeen were New Yorkers. During the 'seventies the South added 5000 miles to her railroad network, and in the 'eighties no less than 23,000 miles.

For two generations Southerners had sent their cotton to the mills of Old and New England where the manufacturing establishments, labor, capital, and facilities for world marketing were well organized. The 'fifties had seen the beginnings of a textile industry in Georgia and South Carolina, and some of the new mills — those of William Gregg at Graniteville, South Carolina, for example — flourished all through the war. Not until the 'seventies, however, did the South seriously challenge the monopoly of New England mills. Proximity to raw materials and to water power, cheap labor, freedom from legal restraints, low taxes, and eager community support all gave Southern mills an initial advantage.

By the end of Reconstruction over 100 Southern mills had almost half a million spindles; twenty years later some 400 mills boasted over 4 million spindles. Yet this was only a beginning. By 1920 the textile industry had moved south, and North Carolina, South Carolina, and Georgia ranked second, third, and fourth among the textile states of the nation.[1]

The rapid growth of the textile industry in the South necessitated grave readjustments. It introduced to Southern economy a labor problem of an explosive nature; to Southern society a social problem that long defied solution; to Southern politics new pressures that acted as a solvent on the old political solidarity. Because Southerners had no experience with the industrial revolution, they blundered as badly as had the English at the beginning of the nineteenth century and took even longer to recover from their mistakes.

The pattern of the Southern textile industry differed in important ways from that of New England. Small mills sprouted on the outskirts of scores of little Carolina and Georgia towns, financed by local capital, managed by local enterprise, supported by local pride, and worked by white labor recruited from the neighborhood. The mill-workers, mostly from the poor-white class, welcomed the opportunity to exchange their drab and impoverished existence for the questionable attractions of the mill village. The great majority of mill-workers were women, and children between the ages of ten and fifteen; these worked an average of seventy hours a week for a wage of about three dollars. No laws limited the hours of labor of women, and such child labor laws as were enacted were universally unenforced.

Though such cities as Gastonia and Winston-Salem in North Carolina became major textile centers, the industry was less concentrated and much less specialized in the South than in New England. The establishment of local mills introduced a new element into many an old Southern town — the 'mill village,' inhabited by laborers recruited from nearby farms, its very existence often ignored by respectable people. A Northern visitor has described the appearance of a typical Georgia mill village in the 'eighties:

> Flung as if by chance beside a red clay road that winds between
> snake fences, a settlement appears. Rows of loosely built, weather-
> stained frame houses, all of the same ugly pattern and buttressed by

1. In 1957 each of these states had more spindles than all the New England states combined.

clumsy chimneys are set close to the highway. No porch, no door-step even, admits to these barrack-like quarters; only an unhewn log or a convenient stone. To the occupants suspicion, fear, and robbery are unknown, for board shutters stretched swagging back leave the paneless windows great gaping squares. A shackling bed, tricked out in a gaudy patchwork, a few defunct 'split-bottom' chairs, a rickety table, and a jumble of battered crockery keep company with the collapsed bellows and fat pine knots by the hearth. The bare floors are begrimed with the tread of animals, and the muddy outline of splayed toes of all shapes and sizes be-token inmates unused to shoes and stockings. Yard there is none, nor plant, nor paling, nor outhouse, in the whole community.[2]

The mill village gathered around the factory as a medieval village clus-tered about a feudal castle, and the mill manager ruled his community as a feudal lord ruled his manor. The company ordinarily owned the entire village — houses, stores, streets, the school, the church; needless to add, it effectively owned the workers, the shopkeepers, the teachers, and the preacher as well. Labor organizers could be denied access to the village, trouble-makers could be evicted, and teachers or preachers who indulged in criticism of the system could be sent packing. By the open-ing of the twentieth century the New South had gone a long way toward substituting industrial autocracy for the old agrarian feudalism.

It was not until the late 'seventies and 'eighties that the pattern of the Southern economy took on a more varied appearance. The South had manufactured most of the nation's tobacco even before the war, and after Appomattox the tobacco industry made a swift comeback. As with the textile industry, it enjoyed the advantages of the proximity of raw material, low transportation costs, and cheap labor; unlike the textile industry, it was concentrated in large cities such as Richmond and Louisville, and used Negro labor. Two circumstances account in large part for the great prosperity it enjoyed: the invention, in 1880, of a cigarette-making machine by James Bonsack of Virginia, and the organ-izing genius of James Buchanan Duke. Starting as a boy peddling his father's tobacco to North Carolina farmers, young Duke rose to be the Rockefeller of the tobacco industry, made his native town of Durham, North Carolina, the tobacco capital of the world, and in 1890 welded together the gigantic American Tobacco Company, whose operations — conducted in New York City — stretched from the tobacco fields of the American South to Europe, Egypt, India, and China. The 'eighties saw,

2. Clare de Graffenried, in *The Century Magazine*, February 1891.

too, the beginnings of a flourishing coal and iron industry centered on Birmingham, Alabama, which quickly became the Pittsburgh of the South, and a lumber industry which moved south from the timber stands of New York and Michigan to exploit and devastate the pine forests of Louisiana and Mississippi. And after the opening of the new century the plains of Texas and Oklahoma, once the domain of Indians and cattle-men, became part of the domain of oil.

The industrialization of the South carried with it changes in the politi-cal outlook of that section. The leaders of the New South were no less sensitive to the demands of industry than the leaders of the Old South had been to the demands of slavery. The 'Bourbons' who ruled the South from Reconstruction to the turn of the century were, for the most part, wholeheartedly committed to a program of industrialization, and it was not long before the South, as well as the North, could boast its 'railroad Senators' and its 'coal and iron Senators.' William Mahone, for example, who was active in Virginia politics for almost twenty years after the war, was a railroad builder and industrialist who used parties and politics for his business purposes. The three men who controlled Georgia politics in the postwar years, General Alfred Colquitt, General John Gordon, and Governor Joseph E. Brown, were all deeply involved in railroad promo-tion, manufacturing, real estate, and other forms of speculation. Louisi-ana politics were dominated by the Lottery Ring, which hired distin-guished Confederate veterans like General Beauregard and General Jubal Early as fronts, while it debauched legislatures and corrupted the press to make fabulous profits. Through Milton Smith and General Basil Duke the Louisville and Nashville Railroad manipulated Kentucky poli-tics for over twenty years; when in 1900 a reformer, Governor William Goebel, threatened that control, he was assassinated.

It was this combination of developments — the emergence of the small farmer and of the free Negro, the rise of industry, and the growth of cities — that persuaded contemporaries that there was indeed a 'New South.' Thus in 1881 Bishop Atticus Haygood asked, rhetorically,

> Does History record an example in any race or age where a people of strong character went so far in fifteen years as the Southern people have gone since 1865 in the modification of opinions, in the change of sentiments that had been, through generations, firmly fixed in all their thinking and feeling? The change of opinions and sentiments of the Southern people since 1865 is one of the most wonderful facts of history.

Yet we must not be deceived by the glib phrase, as so many Southerners were. Industrialization is common to the entire post-Civil War United States, and there was no more a 'New' South than there was a 'New' North or a 'New' West. Indeed the Middle West and the Pacific coast both advanced more rapidly along the path of industry than did the seaboard South, and the South of 1900 accounted for a smaller proportion of the total manufacturing product of the country than did the South of 1860. Far more than other sections, the South escaped those two concomitants of industry — urbanization and immigration. The South was still, in 1900 as in 1860, predominantly rural, and the population of the Southern states remained almost entirely native-born. Notwithstanding the experience of the Civil War, the South remained almost wholly a staple-crop — and even a one-crop — section; if King Cotton had been deposed he was still a lively pretender.

The Old South was, in short, mankind before the Fall, but it was Southern mankind, not Yankee — a special moral and historical experience which Providence had vouchsafed to Southerners and which set them apart. As, with the passing years, the contrast between the dream of the Old South and the reality of the New — between the myth of plantation and slavery and the reality of tenant-farming and the mill villages — became ever more visible, Southerners grew more defiantly insistent upon it. Perhaps most remarkable is that in the end the South imposed this myth not only on itself, but on the North as well.

4. IRON AND STEEL

'The consumption of iron,' wrote the great ironmaster, Abram S. Hewitt, 'is the social barometer by which to estimate the relative height of civilization among nations.' If this is true, the progress of civilization in the United States from the Civil War to World War I was indeed remarkable. The works of man in the United States of 1860 were constructed of wood and stone, with a little brick and iron; by 1920 this had become a nation of iron, steel, and concrete. The United States of 1860 produced less than one million tons of pig iron; 60 years later production had mounted to almost 36 million tons and the United States was easily foremost in the manufacture of iron and steel products among the nations of the world. This transformation resulted from the exploitation of new resources of iron, the discovery of new processes for converting it into steel, the contribution by the government of indirect subsidies in the form of a prohibitive tariff, and the rise of a group of ironmasters with a genius for organization and production.

Iron ore had been mined in the Appalachians from early colonial days; in the early nineteenth century the industry was concentrated in eastern Pennsylvania and northern New Jersey. By the middle of the century the Trenton Iron Works, controlled by the philanthropist Peter Cooper, was producing 35,000 tons of iron annually, but even then the industry was moving westward to the Pittsburgh region. In the late 1840's enormous iron-ore deposits were discovered in the northern Michigan peninsula, and the year of the rush to the California gold diggings witnessed a rush to the iron-ore fields around Marquette scarcely less spectacular and no less significant for the American economy. Transporting the ore by rail was expensive; a water route was essential. The driving energy of young Charles Harvey built a canal connecting Lakes Huron and Superior, which was opened to Great Lakes shipping in 1855. Soon a series of new iron-ore discoveries more than justified the enterprise. In the 1870's the Menominee range in the upper Michigan peninsula was opened, and ten years later the vast Gogebic range lying just below the western end of Superior. That greatest of lakes proved to be rimmed by iron. In the mid-1880's Charlemagne Tower of Philadelphia opened up the rich Vermilion iron range on the north side of the lake, pushed a railroad through from Duluth, and within a few years was shipping one million tons annually through the Soo Canal.

To the west and north lay even richer iron-ore fields. As early as 1844 lumbermen had stumbled on the Missabe (or Mesabi) iron range west of the lake, but it was not until almost fifty years later that the fortitude and faith of the seven Merritt brothers, and the organizational genius of Rockefeller, made the ore commercially available and guaranteed the supremacy of the American steel industry for another half-century. For within a short time this region proved to be the greatest ore producer in the world. The ore of the Mesabi region had, in addition, two inestimable advantages: it lay on the surface of the ground and was therefore easy and cheap to mine, and it was remarkably free of those chemical impurities that made conversion into steel difficult.

The ore fields of the Lake Superior region are hundreds of miles distant from coal deposits, but cheap lake and railway transportation brought the two together. Ore and coal met in smelters of Chicago where the first American steel rails were rolled in 1865, and in Cleveland, Toledo, Ashtabula, and Milwaukee. Much of the ore was carried to Pittsburgh, center of the great Appalachian coal fields and strategically located with reference to water and rail transportation. In the 'eighties the iron and coal beds of the southern Appalachians were first exploited, and soon Birmingham, Ala., became a southern rival to Pittsburgh and Chicago; in the twentieth century Colorado with apparently inexhaustible resources of minerals came to be the Western center of the steel industry.

The Bessemer and open-hearth processes and the application of chemistry and electricity to the making of steel were as fundamental as the new ore beds. The Bessemer process, which consists in blowing air through the molten iron to drive out the impurities, was anticipated in America by William Kelly of Kentucky, a prophet without honor in his own country; but it was not until Henry Bessemer had demonstrated the utility of his process in England that American iron manufacturers adopted it. The Bessemer process gave to U.S. steel producers one incalculable advantage: it was effective only where the phosphorus content of the iron ore was less than one-half of 1 per cent; comparatively little of the English iron ore was free from phosphorus, but practically all the ore of the Lake Superior region was. By 1875 Andrew Carnegie had recognized the advantages of the Bessemer process and adopted it in his great J. Edgar Thomson steel works. Shortly after the Civil War, Abram Hewitt had introduced to this country the Siemens-Martin open-hearth method of smelting, and despite the increased time and expense it involved, the superiority of the steel it produced was soon apparent. In 1880 ten times as much steel was manufactured by the Bessemer as by the open-hearth process, but by 1910 the latter method accounted for 20,780,000 tons of steel and the Bessemer for only 10,328,-000 tons. The Bessemer and open-hearth processes not only made steel of superior quality and in enormous quantities but reduced the price from $300 to $35 a ton.

The application of chemistry to steel making introduced further economies and solved many technical problems. 'Nine-tenths of all the uncertainties were dispelled under the burning sun of chemical knowledge,' affirmed Andrew Carnegie. The introduction of electric furnaces has made it possible to produce hard manganese steel for automobiles and machines and 'high-speed' steel for tools. Carnegie could boast with truth:

Two pounds of iron stone mined upon Lake Superior and transported nine hundred miles to Pittsburgh; one pound and one-half
of coal mined and manufactured into coke, and transported to
Pittsburgh; one-half pound of lime, mined and transported to Pittsburgh; a small amount of manganese ore mined in Virginia and
brought to Pittsburgh — and these four pounds of materials manufactured into one pound of steel, for which the consumer pays one
cent.

Well might the great ironmaster congratulate himself on this combination of engineering and technical skill, science and business enterprise.
By 1890 the United States had passed Great Britain in the production of
pig iron; by 1900 American furnaces turned out as much steel as those of
Great Britain and Germany combined; and this supremacy in iron and
steel manufacture, once attained, was never surrendered. Yet it would
be naïve to suppose that this supremacy was due entirely to the combination of raw materials, science, and business enterprise. An important
element in the growth of the iron and steel industry was the tariff. From
the beginning the ironmasters of Pennsylvania had insisted upon protection for their infant industry, and long after that industry had outgrown
its swaddling clothes it continued to enjoy the blessings of government
paternalism. It was this tariff which enabled American manufacturers to
compete successfully with their English and German competitors and to
pile up fabulous profits. Abram Hewitt, himself one of the greatest of
the ironmasters, put the matter succinctly: 'Steel rails . . . were subject
to a duty of $28 a ton. The price of foreign rails had advanced to a point
where it would have paid (the manufacturer) to make rails without any
duty, but of the duty of $28 a ton he added $27 to his price and
transferred from the great mass of the people $50 million in a few years
to the pockets of a few owners who thus indemnified themselves in a
very short time, nearly twice over, for the total outlay which they had
made in the establishment of their business.' Even Carnegie himself,
when his company showed a profit of $40 million in a single year, felt
that the time had come to abandon protection.

Andrew Carnegie was the greatest leader in the American iron and
steel industry and the archetype of the industrial age. A poor immigrant
boy from Scotland, he followed and helped to perpetuate the American
tradition of rising from poverty to riches, and his success he ascribed
entirely to the democracy which obtained in this country. By dint of
unflagging industry and unrivaled business acumen and resourcefulness,
and especially through his extraordinary ability to choose as his associ-

ates such men as Charles Schwab, Henry Frick, and Henry Phipps and to command the devotion of his workmen, Carnegie built up the greatest steel business in the world, and retired in 1901 to chant the glories of 'Triumphant Democracy' and to give away his enormous fortune of $450 million. This was made possible by the sale of his holdings to a rival organization, directed by the Chicago lawyer Elbert Gary and the New York banker J. Pierpont Morgan. The result was the United States Steel Corporation, a combination of most of the important steel manufacturers in the country, capitalized at the colossal sum of $1400 million — a sum greater than the total estimated national wealth of the United States in 1800. Seven hundred million of this capitalization was 'water,' but by 1924 the company had earned aggregate net profits of $2,108,-848,640.

5. TRUSTS AND MONOPOLIES

The organization of the United States Steel Corporation in 1901 came as the climax to an economic movement which had been underway for a generation: the concentration of industry and transportation in large units — a concentration taking such forms as pools, trusts, corporations, and holding companies. By expanding output for a national market, firms had developed excess capacity, and overproduction threatened to drive prices below costs. To halt this process, corporations welded numerous kinds of combinations.

Combination had a great many advantages. It tended to eliminate competition, removing many of the hazards of unregulated competitive production and facilitating great economies in manufacture, transportation, marketing, administration, and finance. Through combination, capital reserves could be built up as a means to stabilize or expand industry. Where combination was along horizontal lines — the combination, for example, of all manufacturers of typewriters — it was easy to control production and price. Where combination was along vertical lines — the control, by one corporation, of all the elements of raw materials, transportation, manufacture, marketing, and finance of a single product, like the Ford car — it gave a degree of independence and of power that no isolated industry could expect to enjoy. In the steel and oil industries, combination was both horizontal and vertical and created industrial sovereignties as powerful as states.

The development of an industrial monopoly did not require that all the plants under one control be concentrated at a particular place, but only that legal control be concentrated in the hands of a particular group. The primary legal instrument of this process was incorporation. Business corporations were not new in our history, but the widespread use of the corporate device came in the years after the Civil War. Incorporation gives permanence of life and continuity of control, elasticity and easy expansion of capital, limited liability for losses in case of disaster, the concentration of administrative authority and the diffusion of responsibility, and the 'privileges and immunities' of a 'person' in law and in interstate activities.

The concentration of industry developed swiftly in the years after the Civil War. In 1860, 2116 manufacturers of agricultural machinery turned out products which averaged $9845 in value; 40 years later the number of companies had been reduced by two-thirds to 715 but the average output had increased fifteenfold. In 1860, 542 iron and steel companies turned out goods with an average value of a little less than $100,000; by 1900 the number of companies had increased very slightly but the average product had multiplied more than twelvefold.

Large firms expanded at the expense of smaller ones. In 1904, 98 per cent of all the manufacturing establishments in the country had an annual output of less than $1 million, while but 1 per cent boasted an annual output of more than that sum. The former, however, turned out 62 per cent of the manufactured products of the country, while the latter turned out no less than 38 per cent, and of these no less than 33 manufactured products to the value of over $100 million each. But in almost no industry did one firm squeeze out all of its competitors and establish an absolute monopoly. Instead, in many industries, a few great firms created powerful oligopolies.

The trust movement grew out of the period of fierce competition following hard upon the Civil War. Competing railways cut freight rates between important points, in the hope of obtaining the lion's share of business, until dividends ceased and railway securities became a drug on the market. The downward trend of prices from 1865 to 1895, especially marked after 1873, put a premium on labor-saving machinery, on new processes of manufacture, and on greater units of mass production. Pooling — 'gentlemen's agreements' between rival producers or railroad directors to maintain prices and divide business, or even to pro-rate profits — was characteristic of the period after 1872. But on the whole it was found so difficult to maintain these rudimentary monopolies that a 'gentlemen's agreement' came to be defined as one that was certain to be violated.

In the 1880's pools were superseded by trusts — a form of combination in which affiliated companies handed over their securities to be administered by a board of trustees. The trust device was 'invented' by a Standard Oil lawyer, Samuel Dodd, in 1882; first adopted by the great oil combination it quickly became the pattern followed by combinations of every kind in the business world. The term itself shortly outgrew its purely technical meaning, and came to be used as a description of all large-scale combinations. According to the economist Eliot Jones, 'a trust may be said to exist when a person, corporation, or combination owns or controls enough of the plants producing a certain article to be able for all practical purposes to fix its price.' How much is 'enough' is something that not even the courts have been able to determine, and in some ways Mr. Dooley's definition of a trust is more accurate: 'A trust,' he said, 'is somethin' for an honest, ploddin', uncombined manufacturer to sell out to.'

The Standard Oil Company was not only the first trust and — as Allan Nevins observes — 'the largest and richest industrial organization in the world'; it was also in its relations to the industry it dominated, to its rivals, and to the public, the most characteristic, and it provides us with the classic example of the advantages and dangers, the costs and rewards of this form of organization. It was built on the exploitation of a great natural resource; it prospered by the astute application of technology and of scientific management; it combined control of almost every economic activity that affected its welfare — raw material, transportation, wholesale and retail trade, and finances; it was deeply involved in overseas operations; it influenced, perhaps corrupted, the political processes; it inspired, and frustrated, anti-trust legislation and litigation; it piled up unparalleled fortunes for its astute founders and beneficiaries, most of which were poured back into the channels of philanthropy.

Oil had provided light from almost the beginning of history; the America of the 1850's was lighted by candles, and by lamps that used whale oil, coal oil, and the petroleum that was just coming onto the market in small quantities: all of these were expensive. The Seneca Indians of northwestern Pennsylvania had long been familiar with the green viscous fluid that shimmered on the surface of the streams and pools of the Allegheny valley, and as 'Seneca oil' it was sold by traveling medicine men to gullible purchasers at a dollar a bottle as a cure-all for most of the ailments to which the flesh is heir. In 1854 a group of New Yorkers and New Englanders who had organized the Pennsylvania Rock and Coal Company to exploit this surface oil sent a sample of it to Professor Benjamin Silliman of Yale College; his *Report on the Rock Oil or Petroleum from Venango County, Pennsylvania* which predicted the industrial possibilities of the petroleum was a kind of scientific charter for the oil industry. Four years later Edwin Drake, prospecting along Oil Creek, near Titusville, Pennsylvania, sunk a shaft some 70 feet into the ground and struck oil. The word echoed through the East like the cry of 'Gold' in 'forty-eight. Within two years tens of thousands of frantic prospectors were sinking wells along the hillsides and in the gullies of the forsaken countryside that now came to be known as the 'Regions.' The life of the 'Regions' was like that of a mining camp in Nevada or Montana. When a prospector struck oil at Pithole Creek, a town of almost 15,000 grew up overnight, with 50 hotels, theaters, and concert halls, dance halls and brothels, newspapers and churches; five years more and the place was deserted. As prospectors denuded the hills of trees they erected a forest of derricks; the open wells sometimes caught fire, and a pall of smoke hung over the valley at most times; railroads pushed their way into what had been an unprofitable wilderness, and enterprising oil men ran miniature pipelines to the swollen Allegheny, where the barrels were filled and floated down to Pittsburgh.

In nearby Cleveland a young commission-merchant, John D. Rockefeller — he was not yet twenty-five — watched the birth of the oil industry with shrewd understanding, and in 1863 sold out his commission business and acquired an oil refinery. Two years later his was the largest refinery in Cleveland, and in 1870 he and his partners incorporated as the Standard Oil Company of Ohio. Two years later he organized the South Improvement Company to do battle with, or absorb, his competitors in Pittsburgh and Philadelphia. With ample financial backing he weathered the panic of 1873; he bought up weaker competitors or forced them to their knees; he entered into arrangements with shippers that put him in an invulnerable position; he went into the pipeline business and soon had a virtual monopoly on the pipelines of the East. Within a decade he was master of the oil business of the nation.

What accounts for this spectacular achievement? Rockefeller's own explanation of it might apply to almost any one of the major industrial monopolies of the day:

> I ascribe the success of the Standard to its consistent policy to make the volume of its business large through the merits and cheapness of its products. It has spared no expense in finding, securing, and utilizing the best and cheapest methods of manufacture. It has sought for the best superintendents and workmen and paid the best wages. It has not hesitated to sacrifice old machinery and old plants for new and better ones. It has placed its manufactories at the points where they could supply markets at the least expense. It has not only sought markets for its principal products, but for all possible by-products. . . . It has not hesitated to invest millions of dollars in methods of cheapening the gathering and distribution of oil by pipe lines, special cars, tank steamers and tank wagons. It has erected tank stations at every important railroad station to cheapen the storage and delivery of its products. It has spared no expense in forcing its products into the markets of the world among people civilized and uncivilized. It has had faith in American oil, and has brought together millions of money for the purpose of making it what it is, and holding its markets against the competition of Russia and all the many countries which are . . . competitors against American oil.[3]

What Rockefeller failed to mention in this testimony was what made Standard Oil feared and hated by his contemporaries. By playing competing railways one against another, he obtained rebates from their published freight rates, and even forced them to pay to the Standard rebates from competitors' freight payments. If competing oil companies managed to stagger along under such handicaps, they were 'frozen out' by cutting prices in their selling territory until the Standard had all the business. The situation was so notorious that the Hepburn Committee of New York reported in 1880 that the Standard Oil

> owns and controls the pipe lines of the producing regions that connect with the railroads. It controls both ends of these roads. It ships 95 per cent of all the oil. . . . It dictates terms and rebates to the railroads. It has bought out and frozen out refiners all over the country. By means of the superior facilities for transportation which it thus possessed, it could overbid in the producing regions and undersell in the markets of the world. Thus it has . . . absorbed and monopolized this great traffic.

3. *Report of the U. S. Industrial Commission*, I, 796–7 (1899).

The Pennsylvania legislature annulled the charter of the South Improvement Company almost as soon as it had been granted; and in 1892 the Supreme Court of Ohio dissolved the trust on the ground that it had violated its charter, only to have it reorganize under the more lenient laws of New Jersey a few years later.

The Standard Oil trust was soon followed by a number of similar business combinations. The movement for consolidation gathered momentum in the 1880's and early 1890's, and reached its climax in the years of prosperity around the Spanish War. Altogether in this period something over 5000 industrial establishments were consolidated into about 300 trusts or corporations, and of these no less than 198 were formed in the period from 1898 to 1902. The combined capitalization of the consolidations formed in the single year of 1899 was no less than $2,243,995,000 — a sum greater than the total national debt at the time. The most important of the industrial combinations, besides the Standard Oil Company and the United States Steel Corporation, were the Amalgamated Copper Co., the American Sugar Refining Co., the American Tobacco Co., the United States Rubber Co., the United States Leather Co., the International Harvester Co., and the Pullman Palace Car Co., no one of which had a capitalization under $50 million.

In no field was the tendency toward combination and concentration more significant than in transportation. By the turn of the century the major part of the railroad mileage and the railroad business of the country was in the hands of six groups: the Morgan and the Morgan-Belmont alliance controlling 24,035 miles, the Harriman group with 20,245 miles, the Vanderbilt combination with 19,517 miles, the Pennsylvania group with 18,220 miles, the Gould group with 16,074 widely scattered miles, and the Hill network with 10,373 miles of track flung across the Northwest. Of the total railway mileage in the country only some 40,000 was still in the hands of independents. So, too, with other forms of transportation and communication: the expressing business of the country was apportioned out between three companies which by their united influence prevented the United States mails from taking parcels until 1912; the Western Union, until the rise of the Postal Telegraph, had a virtual monopoly on the telegraph business; and the American Telephone and Telegraph Company, capitalized in 1900 at one-quarter of a billion dollars, was already on its way to becoming the greatest of modern combinations.

The role of New York City bankers in putting together many of these great railroad and industrial combinations led many Americans to fear that the greatest and most elusive of all trusts was in the making — the 'money trust.' The House of Morgan, which played a leading role in substituting combination for competition, was exhibit A in this argument. In 1864 Junius Spencer Morgan, long a leader in marketing American securities in England, placed his son John Pierpont in charge of the American branch of the firm. Within a few years young Morgan had tied up with the old banking house of Drexel in Philadelphia, and soon was challenging the supremacy of Jay Cooke and Company. The failure of Cooke in the panic of 1873 put the House of Morgan in a position of immense power. In the 1880's Morgan formed a close association with the New York Central Railroad, and all through that decade and the next the House of Morgan organized and reorganized railroads, extending its influence through the South and even into the Far West where, after the turn of the century, it formed an alliance with the Hill group. Meantime Morgan interests had spread into many other fields, until in the new century there was scarcely an important business which it did not touch except those controlled or influenced by the rival Rockefeller interests. In 1901 the House of Morgan put through the gigantic deal that created the United States Steel Corporation. Morgan brought together the warring manufacturers of agricultural instruments, and emerged with the International Harvester Company. He organized American shipping in the ill-fated Mercantile Merchant Marine combine, and helped finance the American Telephone and Telegraph, the General Electric, and a dozen other giants. He had spent — wasted, his critics said — millions on the attempt to consolidate the whole of New England transportation into a single system. He and his associates controlled a dozen large banks in New York and other leading cities — the Hanover, the Chase, the First National, the Bankers' Trust, and others; more important, from the fiscal point of view, they had tied up with three of the greatest insurance companies — the New York Life, the Mutual Life, and the Equitable.

These developments spelled the doom of local industry and of the self-sufficient community. The social implications can best be read in such novels as Sherwood Anderson's *Poor White:*

> In the days before the coming of industry, before the time of the mad awakening, the towns of the Middle West were sleepy places

Lines	Miles	Lines	Miles
I.—VANDERBILT GROUP		**V.—GOULD GROUP**	
New York Central lines	10,016	Missouri Pacific	5,326
Delaware, Lackawanna, and Western	951	Texas and Pacific	1,599
Chicago and Northwestern	8,550	St. Louis and Southwestern	1,265
	19,517	International and Great Northern	825
		Denver and Rio Grande	1,675
		Missouri, Kansas and Texas	2,423
II.—MORGAN GROUP		Rio Grande Western	603
Southern Railway	6,807	Wabash	2,358
Mobile and Ohio	879		16,074
Queen and Crescent	1,115		
Central of Georgia	1,835		
Georgia Southern and Florida	285	**VI.—HILL GROUP**	
Macon and Birmingham	97	Great Northern	5,185
Philadelphia and Reading	1,891	Northern Pacific	5,188
Lehigh Valley	1,404		10,373
Erie	2,271		
Central of New Jersey	677		
Atlantic Coast Line	1,812	**VII.—BELMONT GROUP**	
	19,073	Louisville and Nashville	3,235
		Nashville, Chattanooga and St. Louis	1,195
			4,430
III.—HARRIMAN GROUP			
Illinois Central	5,000	**VIII.—BELMONT-MORGAN**	
Union Pacific	3,029	Georgia Railroad	307
Oregon Railroad and Navigation Co.	1,137	Atlanta and West Point	87
Oregon Short Line	1,498	Western of Alabama	128
Chicago and Alton	918		532
Southern Pacific	7,723		
Kansas City Southern	833		
Chicago Terminal Transfer	107	**IX.—INDEPENDENT SYSTEMS**	
	20,245	Seaboard Air Line	2,591
		Plant System	2,170
		Chicago, Milwaukee and St. Paul	6,592
IV.—PENNSYLVANIA GROUP		Rock Island	3,819
Pennsylvania system	10,031	Chicago, Burlington and Quincy	8,070
Buffalo, Rochester and Pittsburgh	650	Atchison, Topeka and Santa Fe	7,808
Western New York and Pennsylvania	633	St. Louis and San Francisco (K. C. M.	
Chesapeake and Ohio	1,476	& B.)	3,000
Norfolk and Western	1,671	Chicago & Great Western	1,023
Baltimore and Ohio system	3,156	Colorado Southern	1,142
Long Island	603	Pere Marquette	1,762
	18,220		37,977

SUMMARY

Groups	Mileage	Groups	Mileage
Vanderbilt	19,517	Belmont	4,430
Morgan	19,073	Belmont-Morgan	532
Harriman	20,245		108,464
Pennsylvania	18,220	Independent	37,977
Gould	16,074		
Hill	10,373		

From the *Final Report* of Industrial Commission of 1900, p. 308.

devoted to the practice of the old trades, to agriculture and merchandising. In the morning the men of the towns went forth to work
in the fields or to the practice of the trade of carpentry, horse-
shoeing, wagon-making, harness repairing, and the making of shoes
and clothing. They read books and believed in a God born in the
brains of men who came out of a civilization much like their own.
On the farms and in the houses in the towns the men and women
worked together toward the same ends in life. They lived in small
frame houses set on the plains like boxes, but very substantially
built. The carpenter who built a farmer's house differentiated it
from the barn by putting what he called scroll work up under the
eaves and by building at the front a porch with carved posts. After
one of the poor little houses had been lived in for a long time,
after the children had been born and men had died, after men and
women had suffered and had moments of joy together in the tiny
rooms under the low roofs, a subtle change took place. The houses
became almost beautiful in their old humanness. Each of the houses
began vaguely to shadow forth the personality of the people who
lived within its walls. . . . A sense of quiet growth awoke in sleeping minds. It was the time for art and beauty to awake in the land.

Instead the giant, Industry, awoke. Boys, who in the schools had
read of Lincoln, walking for miles through the forest to borrow his
first book . . . began to read in the newspapers and magazines of
men who by developing their faculty for getting and keeping money
had become suddenly and overwhelmingly rich. Hired writers
called these men great, and there was no maturity of mind in the
people with which to combat the force of the statement, often repeated. . . .

Out through the coal and iron regions of Pennsylvania into Ohio
and Indiana, and on westward into the States bordering on the
Mississippi River, industry crept. . . .

A vast energy seemed to come out of the breast of the earth and
infect the people. Thousands of the most energetic men of the
Middle States wore themselves out in forming companies, and when
the companies failed, immediately formed others. In the fast-
growing towns, men who were engaged in organizing companies
representing a capital of millions lived in houses thrown hurriedly
together by carpenters who, before the time of the great awakening,
were engaged in building barns. It was a time of hideous architecture, a time when thought and learning paused. Without music,
without poetry, without beauty in their lives or impulses, a whole
people, full of the native energy and strength of lives lived in a
new land, rushed pell-mell into a new age.[4]

4. *Poor White*, p. 131 ff. Reprinted by permission of the author and Viking Press.

6. TRUST REGULATION

In the 1880's the American public began to demand effective regulation of the trusts; but the problem of regulation was seriously complicated by the federal form of government. Corporations are chartered by the states, not the nation. The constitutions of many states contained general prohibitions of monopolies or conspiracies in restraint of trade (it was Ohio that broke up the first great trust) but most state prohibitions were singularly ineffective, especially after the federal courts began to interpret broadly the congressional authority over interstate commerce and to limit severely the kind of regulation permitted the states under the Fourteenth Amendment.

A corporation chartered by one state has the right to do business in every other state. Hence it was easy for corporations to escape the restrictions or limitations of strict state laws by incorporating in states such as New Jersey, West Virginia, or Delaware where the laws as to issuing stock, accountability of directors, and the right to hold stock in other corporations were very lax. In its ordinary operations the average corporation came into contact only with state and municipal governments. Lighting and water companies and street railways depended for their very existence on municipalities. Hence the corrupt alliance that was cemented after the Civil War between politics and business. Plain bribery was often practiced with municipal councils, which gave away for nothing franchises worth millions, while their cities remained unpaved, ill-lit, and inadequately policed.

Opposition to trusts and monopolies, however, was not aroused so much by corruption and dishonest practices, which were looked upon with a leniency characteristic of the American people, as by the fear that the natural resources of the country were being ruthlessly exploited and rapidly exhausted by a group of men who used them to aggrandize their own fortunes. Equally effective was the hostility of labor to powerful corporations, the opposition of the small businessman who in many instances was faced with the choice of surrender or ruin, and the widespread disapproval of the growth of great fortunes and the concentration of wealth.

All who recall the conditions of the country in 1890 [said Mr. Justice Harlan in the Standard Oil case] will remember that there

was everywhere among the people generally a deep feeling of
unrest. The nation had been rid of human slavery . . . but the
conviction was universal that the country was in real danger from
another kind of slavery, namely the slavery that would result
from the aggregation of capital in the hands of a few . . . controlling, for their own advantage exclusively, the entire business of
the country, including the production and sale of the necessities of
life.

As a result of widespread agitation, Congress enacted the Sherman
Anti-Trust Act in 1890. This famous law, the joint product of Senators
Sherman of Ohio, Edmunds of Vermont, Hoar of Massachusetts, and
George of Mississippi, passed Congress by an almost unanimous vote
and received the signature of President Harrison on 2 July 1890. Its cen-
tral provisions are to be found in the first two articles:

> 1. Every contract, combination in the form of trust or otherwise,
> or conspiracy, in restraint of trade or commerce among the several
> States, or with foreign nations is hereby declared to be illegal. . . .
> 2. Every person who shall monopolize, or attempt to monopo-
> lize . . . any part of the trade or commerce among the several
> States, or with foreign nations, shall be deemed guilty of a mis-
> demeanor. . . .

It is difficult to determine the precise purpose of this law. At the time
it was alleged that the act sought to give to the federal courts common
law jurisdiction over the crime of monopoly and conspiracy in restraint
of trade; if so the law should have been interpreted in accordance with
common law precedents to the effect that only *unreasonable* restraints of
trade, or monopolies contrary to public interest, were illegal. But there
were no such qualifications in the provisions of the act itself. Nor were
there any definitions of the terms 'trust,' 'conspiracy,' and 'monopoly,'
while the phrase 'in the form of trust or otherwise' left much to the
imagination. In all probability the provisions of the act were purposely
couched in indefinite terms, leaving to the courts the task of interpreting
and applying them. By thus placing responsibility upon the courts the
legislators evaded the problem, and put off its solution indefinitely, for
judicial regulation proved singularly ineffective. As a weapon against
trusts, the Sherman law was a broken reed.

The first important case involving the interpretation and application
of the anti-trust law was that instituted by the government against the

whiskey trust. This suit, *United States* v. *Greenhut,* was summarily dismissed by the Court on the ground that no restraint in trade had been proven. Discouraged by this rebuff, the Federal Government abandoned the prosecution of the whiskey trust and allowed an indictment against the cash register trust to lapse. The attempt to dissolve the powerful sugar trust met with an even more serious reverse. In this case, *United States* v. *E. C. Knight and Company,* the Court in 1895 held that the mere control of 98 per cent of the sugar refining of the country did not in itself constitute an act in restraint of trade:

> Doubtless [said Chief Justice Fuller] the power to control the manufacture of a given thing involves in a certain sense the control of its disposition, but this is a secondary and not a primary sense; and although the exercise of that power may result in bringing the operation of commerce into play, it does not control it, and affects it only incidentally and indirectly. Commerce succeeds to manufacture, and is not a part of it.

In a vigorous dissenting opinion, Justice Harlan warned:

> Interstate traffic . . . may pass under the absolute control of overshadowing combinations having financial resources without limit and audacity in the accomplishment of their objects that recognize none of the restraints of moral obligations controlling the action of individuals; combinations governed entirely by the law of greed and selfishness — so powerful that no single State is able to overthrow them and give the required protection to the whole country, and so all-pervading that they threaten the integrity of our institutions.

But the government was not similarly concerned, and Attorney-General Richard Olney wrote complacently, 'You will observe that the government has been defeated in the Supreme Court on the trust question. I always supposed it would be, and have taken the responsibility of not prosecuting under a law I believed to be no good.'

In case after case the courts emasculated or nullified the act, leading Theodore Roosevelt to declare, later, that the 'courts . . . had for a quarter of a century been . . . the agents of reaction and by conflicting decisions which, however, in their sum total were hostile to the interests of the people, had left both the Nation and the States well-nigh impotent to deal with the great business combinations.' Yet responsibility for the failure of the anti-trust law should not be charged exclusively to the judiciary. The legislature failed to amend the act; the executive failed to enforce it. Altogether only seven suits under the Sherman Act were instituted by Harrison, eight by Cleveland, and three by McKinley; these suits were equally ineffective in reversing or even slowing down the movement toward consolidation. Only when the law was applied to labor unions — happily embraced in the ambiguous term 'or otherwise' — was it somewhat effective; here the government won a series of victories. But more business combinations were formed during the Mc-Kinley administration than in any years of our history until the 1920's.

The persistent and uniform failure of the anti-trust laws and of the machinery of enforcement — failures which persisted into the Roosevelt and Taft administrations — inevitably gave rise to the suspicion that the whole trust-busting movement was something of a sham. Americans were, in fact, caught on the horns of a dilemma. On the one hand their traditions and habits, drawn from a rural background, exalted individualism and idealized the independent yeoman, the self-reliant artisan and shopkeeper; they were firmly convinced that if you made a better mousetrap the world would really beat a path to your door! On the other hand all those forces of technology and science, which Americans so deeply admired, advertised the incomparable advantages of large-scale organization and the elimination of wasteful competition. Had the American people really wished to strike down trusts and liquidate monopolies, they could have done so easily enough by taxing them out of existence. Had they believed wholeheartedly in bigness and efficiency, they could have stimulated these by permitting consolidation to proceed without legal interference. But wanting the best of both worlds — the pastoral world of the eighteenth century and the technological world of the twentieth, they contented themselves with ceremonial gestures. They satisfied their moral scruples by donning the armor of anti-trust legislation and undertaking, from time to time, ritualistic skirmishes against the trusts; they satisfied their passion for efficiency and profits by permitting and even encouraging whatever combinations could be regarded as 'reasonable,' and by supporting them with lavish land-grants, protective tariffs, friendly incorporation laws, and easygoing tax policies. As Thurman Arnold observes:

> In order to reconcile the ideal with the practical necessity, it became necessary to develop a procedure which constantly attacked bigness

on rational, legal and economic grounds, and at the same time never really interfered with combinations. Such pressures gave rise to the anti-trust laws which appeared to be a complete prohibition of large combinations. The same pressures made the enforcement of the anti-trust laws a pure ritual. The effect of this statement of the ideal and its lack of actual enforcement, was to convince reformers either that large combinations did not actually exist, or else that if they did exist, they were about to be done away with just as soon as right-thinking men were elected to office. Trust busting therefore became one of the great moral issues of the day, while at the same time great combinations thrived and escaped regulation.[5]

It is perhaps the crowning irony of this situation that when Mr. Arnold himself was put in charge of the anti-trust division of the Department of Justice, he displayed quite exceptional zeal in the ritualistic enforcement of the Sherman Act!

7. BIG BUSINESS AND ITS PHILOSOPHY

The age was memorable not for statesmen, as in the early years of the Republic, or for reformers and men of letters, as in the middle years, or for soldiers as during the Civil War, but for titans of industry and masters of capital. Schoolboys today who have difficulty in remembering the names of any Presidents between Grant and Theodore Roosevelt identify readily enough the names of John D. Rockefeller, Andrew Carnegie, of John Pierpont Morgan. Few novelists of these years blunted their pens on the portrayal of the political scene, but the most distinguished novels of the age portray the world of business and industry, from Mark Twain's *The Gilded Age* and William Dean Howells's *The Rise of Silas Lapham* to Theodore Dreiser's *The Titan* and Henry James's *The Ivory Tower*. At no other period of our history has the businessman exercised a comparable power. During this half-century the great captains of industry and finance could say, with Frederick Townsend Martin, 'We are rich. We own America. We got it, God knows how, but we intend to keep it.'

Everything seemed arranged to enhance their sense of power and gratify their sense of magnificence. Nature and man conspired to pros-

5. Thurman Arnold, *Folklore of Capitalism*, p. 208.

per and to exalt them. A boundless continent lay open and ready for
their exploitation; willing legislators gave them first chance, and amiable
judges confirmed them in what they had won or seized. Gold and silver,
copper and oil, forest and stream, all the bounties of nature which in the
Old World had belonged, as a matter of course, to the crown — that is,
to the commonwealth — were allowed to fall into the hands of strong
men and powerful corporations. Clever lawyers worked out new devices
for legal aggrandizement of wealth — pools, trusts, holding companies,
and similar mechanisms; legislators made these devices available in their
states, and co-operative courts held that the principle of interstate
comity applied to corporations as to individuals. No income tax impeded
the swift accumulation of private fortunes; no labor laws or workmen's
compensation acts interfered with their profits; no government officials
told them how to run their business; no public opinion penetrated the
walls of their conceit.

Political power and social prestige naturally gravitated to the rich. As
a matter of course they exerted a decisive influence on politics and
parties. They controlled newspapers and magazines; subsidized candidates; bought legislation and even judicial decisions. The greatest of
them, such as John D. Rockefeller or J. P. Morgan, treated state governors as servants, and Presidents as equals, in the exercise of power. And
as wealth came to dominate the political scene, so it came in time to
dominate the social scene. The new rich moved into the great cities,
hired architects to build French châteaux or English country houses on
New York's Fifth Avenue or Cleveland's Euclid Avenue or San Francisco's Nob Hill, and undertook to indulge themselves in luxuries which
Thorstein Veblen was to designate as 'conspicuous waste.' They filled
their houses with paintings and tapestries from the Old World to delight
the eye and gratify their pride; staffed their palaces with innumerable servants and gave parties which they thought were like those of
Versailles; and patronized museums and the opera. They built Gothic
churches, and listened gladly to the gospel as expounded by a Bishop
Lawrence who assured them that 'godliness is in league with riches';
they built schools like Groton to train up an elite that should govern
America as Eton and Winchester governed England. Thus strengthened
they crashed the gates of society. 'I remember very well,' wrote Frederick Martin, 'the first great march of the suddenly rich upon the capitals
of the nation. Very distinctly it comes back to me with what a shock the

fact came home to the sons and daughters of what was pleased to call itself the aristocracy of America, that here marched an army better provisioned, better armed with wealth, than any other army that had ever assaulted the citadels of Society.'

Business even formulated a philosophy which drew impartially on history, law, economics, religion, and biology in order to justify its acquisitiveness and its power: we give this philosophical potpourri the name Social Darwinism. At its most full blown it was made up of four not wholly harmonious ingredients. First, the principle drawn from Jeffersonian agrarianism and Manchester liberalism, that that government was best which governed least, and that government should keep its hands off business. 'All experience,' wrote the most vigorous of the Social Darwinists, Professor William Graham Sumner of Yale, 'is against state regulation and in favor of liberty. The freer the civil institutions are, the more weak and mischievous state regulation is.' Second, the principle of the peculiar sanctity of property — including, of course, corporate charters and franchises — in our constitutional and economic system. This principle was, presumably, written into the Fourteenth Amendment's prohibition of the deprivation of life, liberty, and property without due process of law, and was applied with uncompromising rigor by jurists like Justice Stephen J. Field, and lawyers like Joseph Choate, long leader of the American bar. Third, the quasi-religious principle that the acquisition of wealth was a mark of divine favor, and that the rich therefore had a moral responsibility both to get richer and to direct the affairs of society. Judge Elbert Gary, who had refused to talk to representatives of steel workers who worked twelve hours a day seven days a week in his mills, put it simply: 'Moral principles,' he said, 'are the base of all business success.' Distinguished churchmen, too, endorsed this view; Bishop Lawrence, for example, assured his parishioners that 'in the long run it is only to the man of morality that wealth comes.'

Fourth, perhaps most persuasive of all, was the pseudo-scientific principle of 'the survival of the fittest,' derived from Darwinian biology and applied to the affairs of mankind by the great English philosopher Herbert Spencer and by his many American disciples. 'If we do not like the survival of the fittest,' wrote Professor Sumner, 'we have only one possible alternative, and that is the survival of the unfittest. The former is the law of civilization; the latter is the law of anti-civilization.' John D. Rockefeller stated his own case even more simply. 'The American beauty rose,' he said, 'can be produced in the splendor and fragrance which bring cheer to its beholder only by sacrificing the early buds which grow up about it. This is not an evil tendency in business. It is merely the working out of a law of Nature and of God.' All this added up not so much to an apology for business as to the inescapable conclusion that America itself was a business civilization — and should be kept that way.

IV

Labor

1. GENERAL CONSIDERATIONS

American labor failed to achieve a satisfactory adjustment to industrial capitalism during the years following the Civil War largely because it was unable to act as a unit or to agree upon the nature of the
problem, the instruments of action, or the proper objectives. Throughout
the nineteenth century and well into the twentieth, labor debated
whether to accept or reject capitalism, whether to welcome or sabotage
inventions, whether to trust laissez-faire or seek government patronage,
whether to organize on a broadly industrial or on a narrow craft basis,
whether to embrace unskilled as well as skilled, Negro as well as white
workers, within its organizations.

During most of the nineteenth century the benefits of the application
of science and invention to industry redounded to the advantage of
society as a whole, but more especially to capital rather than to labor.
Machinery made enormous savings in manufacturing and a vast increase
in productivity, but only a small proportion of these savings was passed
on to labor in the form of wages, and the decrease in the hours of
workers did not keep pace with the gains in productivity. Furthermore
the workingman suffered from the fatigue and nervous strain of modern
machine labor.

The mechanization of industry devalued the experience of the skilled
worker by eroding the creative instinct of craftsmanship. Workingmen

were more and more reduced to performing a hundred times a day some monotonous operation. Upton Sinclair described it:

> Each one of the hundreds of parts of a mowing machine was made separately, and sometimes handled by hundreds of men. Where Jurgis worked there was a machine which cut and stamped a certain piece of steel about two square inches in size; the pieces came tumbling out upon a tray, and all that human hands had to do was to pile them in regular rows, and change the trays at intervals. This was done by a single boy, who stood with eyes and thoughts centered upon it, and fingers flying so fast that the sounds of the bits of steel striking upon each other was like the music of an express train as one hears it in a sleeping car at night. . . . Thirty thousand of these pieces he handled every day, nine or ten millions every year — how many in a lifetime it rested with the gods to say. Near by him sat men bending over whirling grind-stones, putting the finishing touches to the steel knives of the reaper; picking them out of a basket with the right hand, pressing first one side and then the other against the stone, and finally dropping them with the left hand into another basket. One of these men told Jurgis that he had sharpened three thousand pieces of steel a day for thirteen years.[1]

As machinery came to represent a large part of capital investment, it was thought necessary to accommodate the worker to machinery rather than machinery to the worker. Thus if efficiency required that machines be run twenty-four hours a day and seven days a week, workers were expected to adjust themselves to that requirement regardless of the social desirability of such a schedule. Furthermore machinery constituted a fixed capital charge which could not well be reduced; when economies were necessary there was a temptation to effect them at the expense of labor. Finally the introduction of increasingly efficient machinery resulted in throwing large groups of laborers out of work. While most of these were eventually absorbed in other industries, and while in the long run mechanization more than balanced losses in factory jobs by the growth of clerical and service positions, the process worked severe hardship on the individual employee and was accompanied by a staggering social waste. At the same time the increasing efficiency of machinery sometimes resulted in the production of more commodities than the public could or cared to buy, thus creating unemployment and lowering of wages and standards of labor. Industrial

1. Upton Sinclair, *The Jungle*.

unemployment, a product of the machine age, grew proportionately with the development of the machine economy until governments intervened to control it.

The rise of the giant corporation as employer had consequences for labor almost as serious as those which flowed from the mechanization of industry. Such corporations subjected the laborer to a new set of circumstances, impersonal and complex as those introduced by the machine. The fiction that a corporation was a person had a certain legal usefulness, but every laborer knew that the distinguishing characteristic of a corporation was precisely its impersonality. A person was responsible for his acts to his own conscience; a corporation was responsible to its stockholders. As individuals, the directors of a corporation might be willing to make concessions to labor, even at personal sacrifice; but as directors they could not indulge themselves in this pleasure, for their first duty was to maintain the solvency of their business and dividend payments.

The change from individual employer to impersonal corporation sharply lessened the worker's bargaining power. It was one thing for an iron-puddler in the mid-nineteenth century to strike a bargain about wages and hours with the owner of a small ironworks; it was a very different thing for a 'roller' in the twentieth century to strike a bargain with the United States Steel Corporation. Theodore Roosevelt put the matter with characteristic clarity:

> The old familiar relations between employer and employee were passing. A few generations before, the boss had known every man in his shop; he called his men Bill, Tom, Dick, John; he inquired after their wives and babies; he swapped jokes and stories and perhaps a bit of tobacco with them. In the small establishment there had been a friendly human relationship between employer and employee.
>
> There was no such relation between the great railway magnates, who controlled the anthracite industry, and the one hundred and fifty thousand men who worked in their mines, or the half million women and children who were dependent upon these miners for their daily bread. Very few of these mine workers had ever seen, for instance, the president of the Reading Railroad. . . . Another change . . . was a crass inequality in bargaining relation between the employer and the individual employee standing alone. The great coal-mining and coal-carrying companies, which employed their tens of thousands, could easily dispense with the services of

any particular miner. The miner, on the other hand, could not dispense with the companies. He needed a job; his wife and children would starve if he did not get one. What the miner had to sell — his labor — was a perishable commodity; the labor of today — if not sold — was lost forever. Moreover, his labor was not like most commodities — a mere thing; it was part of a living, breathing human being. The workman saw that the labor problem was not only an economic but also a moral, a human problem.[2]

When in response to this situation laborers organized, giant corporations representing the combined wealth and strength of scores of companies and thousands of stockholders could afford to fight a strike for months, import strike-breakers, hire Pinkerton detectives, carry their battle through the courts with highly paid lawyers, buy the press and influence politicians, and, if necessary, close down their plants and starve the workers into submission.

At the same time the giant corporation sometimes exercised an industrial dominion menacing not only to labor but to American society. Corporations were able to acquire mining or manufacturing properties and, not infrequently, whole towns and counties; they became, to all intents and purposes, sovereignties within states. Many textile companies in the South came to own the villages in which mills are located — the streets, houses, stores, schools, churches, and utilities — and to control, inevitably, the local administration and police; the inhabitants of such mill villages, most of them operatives in the mills, could remain and work only on sufferance of the mill owners. Similar conditions, in even more aggravated form, were to be found in Colorado, Kentucky, and Pennsylvania mining communities and in many of the lumber camps of the South and the West. In 1914 a United States congressman testified that he had to have a pass to enter one of the towns of Colorado situated on the property of the Colorado Fuel and Iron Company. Thus there developed in certain major industries a species of industrial feudalism in which the laborer occupied a position in many respects less secure than that of the medieval serf.

Unionists viewed with alarm the tidal wave of immigration which spilled almost 18 million persons on American shores in the single generation from 1880 to 1910. When the unions attempted to organize these 'new' immigrants, as the United Mine Workers did, they succeeded. But in part because of the racial and religious antagonisms that embittered

2. *Theodore Roosevelt: An Autobiography*, Scribners, pp. 470–71.

relations between native- and foreign-born workers and between various immigrant groups, partly because much of organized labor was by this time committed to the craft principle, most unions made no serious effort to enlist the immigrants. Almost inevitably labor experienced its most serious difficulties in those industries where the proportion of foreign-born workers was highest — the meat-packing, iron and steel, and mining industries. Although some of the most important labor leaders were foreign-born, many unions became staunch champions of immigration restriction.

The solution of the labor problem was conditioned by the tradition that America was a land of equal opportunity for all, that in America there were not and never would be any classes, and that here any laboring man could rise by his own efforts. The average American looked with suspicion upon any tendency to consider the problems of labor distinct from those of capital or to develop class consciousness among workingmen, and regarded with deep distrust the entry of labor into politics. Throughout the nineteenth century there was a widespread hostility toward labor unions and the closed shop, and even so open-minded a man as President Eliot of Harvard could assert that the closed shop was un-American. The strike, which as late as the 1840's was regarded as a conspiracy against the public interest, continued to be in bad repute, and in 1886 the New York banker, Henry Clews, identified the strike with treason. 'Strikes may have been justifiable in other nations,' he said, 'but they are not justifiable in our country. The Almighty has made this country for the oppressed of other nations, and therefore this is the land of refuge . . . and the hand of the laboring man should not be raised against it.'

The late nineteenth century had a double standard of social morality for labor and capital. Combination of capital was regarded as in accordance with natural laws; combination of labor as a conspiracy. It was the duty of government to protect corporation interests, but government aid to labor was socialism. That business should go into politics was common sense, but that labor should go into politics was contrary to the American tradition. Property had a natural right to a fair return on its value, but the return which labor might enjoy was to be regulated strictly by the law of supply and demand. Appeals to protect or enhance property interests were reasonable, but appeals to protect or enhance labor interests were demagogic. Brokers who organized business combines were respectable public servants, but labor organizers were agitators. The use of Pinkerton detectives to protect business property was preserving law and order, but the use of force to protect the job was violence, and for labor to call in the militia or federal troops to protect its property in jobs was quite unthinkable. To curtail production in the face of an oversupply of consumers' goods was sound business practice, but to strike for shorter hours in the face of an oversupply of labor was unsound.

2. THE RISE OF ORGANIZED LABOR

In the years after the Civil War two rival approaches — reform unionism and trade unionism — vied for the allegiance of the American workingman. The reform unionists rejected the factory system, with its division of labor and its sharp differentiation of interests of employer and employee, and sought to restore a society which valued the independent artisan. Determined not to become machine tenders assigned to a small part of the process of production, they strove to preserve their status as craftsmen. To safeguard equality of opportunity, they fought those forces of monopoly, especially in finance, which they believed aimed to shackle the worker. They viewed themselves as members of a 'producer class' which embraced master as well as journeyman, farmer as well as artisan. Yet as early as 1850, when the National Typographical Union was founded, some workers had abandoned the hope of escaping the factory system, or of becoming entrepreneurs, and accepted their role as wage-earners. Hence, instead of looking for ways to be self-employed, they organized trade unions to bargain with employers, whose interests, they recognized, differed from their own. At the outset, the reform unionists had the larger following, but as the factory system colonized the city and the countryside, the trade union analysis came to seem more appropriate.

In 1866, under the guidance of William Sylvis of the iron molders, labor leaders set up the first national labor federation in America — the National Labor Union. Although it welcomed trade unions, the National Labor Union reflected the reform unionist outlook, for it included various middle-class reform organizations, including women's suffrage leagues. Moreover, it was hostile to the strike weapon and experimented with co-operatives as an alternative to the wage system. The National

Labor Union also plunged into politics; in 1872, it sponsored the country's first national labor party, the Labor Reform Party, with the millionaire Supreme Court justice David B. Davis as its standard-bearer. But when both its presidential and vice-presidential candidates turned down the nominations, the Labor Reform Party was made to look ridiculous; that same year, the National Labor Union collapsed.

The fiasco of the Labor Reform Party proved to be only the first in a series of episodes which persuaded trade unionists that they should shun labor party ventures. In 1876, when Eastern labor reformers joined with Midwestern soft money men to create the National Independent Party, more popularly known as the Greenback Party, they chose as their presidential candidate, Peter Cooper, who suffered the handicap of being 85 years old, and who attracted almost no working-class votes. In 1880, the Greenback-Labor Party nominee, General James Baird Weaver, found little support in the factory towns of the industrial Northeast. In 1884, reform unionists sank to nominating the notorious Ben Butler on an Anti-Monopoly Party ticket, although Butler may well have been in the race as an agent of the Republicans. Trade unionists concluded from these disasters that the attempts of reform unionists to find political solutions for the workers' problems were doomed to failure.

By far the most important organization of reform unionism was the Noble Order of the Knights of Labor, founded in 1869 by a Philadelphia tailor, Uriah S. Stephens, a Mason with a smattering of Greek who was able to contribute his knowledge of ritual to the secret order. Native American in leadership and largely in personnel, it attempted to unite the workers of America into one big union, under centralized control. Membership was open to men and women, white and black, skilled and unskilled, laborers and capitalists, merchants and farmers. Only liquor dealers, professional gamblers, lawyers, and bankers were excluded! The professed object of the order was 'To secure to the toilers a proper share of the wealth that they create; more of the leisure that rightfully belongs to them; more societary advantages; more of the benefits, privileges, and emoluments of the world; in a word, all those rights and privileges necessary to make them capable of enjoying, appreciating, defending, and perpetuating the blessings of good government.' The Order hoped to secure these laudable but somewhat vague ends by co-operation, arbitration of industrial disputes, an eight-hour day, the abolition of child labor, and many other such reforms.

The growth of the Knights of Labor was nothing short of phenomenal. When a Pennsylvania machinist named Terence V. Powderly became Grand Master in 1878, the membership was under 50,000. A vain man, Powderly acted 'like Queen Victoria at a national Democratic convention.' Norman Ware has observed: 'English novelists take men of Powderly's look for their poets, gondola scullers, philosophers and heroes crossed in love but no one ever drew such a looking man as the leader of a million of the horny-fisted sons of toil.' Opposed to the tactics of combative unionism, Powderly said: 'Strikes are a failure. Ask any old veteran in the labor movement and he will say the same. I shudder at the thought of a strike, and I have good reason.' Powderly placed much of his emphasis on co-operatives, and even more on the land question, because 'we must free the land and give men the chance to become their own employers.' Yet under Powderly's leadership the Order made spectacular gains, especially after it shed its secrecy and thus overcame the hostility of the Catholic Church, and, ironically, after it won a great railroad strike on the Gould lines in the Southwest in 1885. Capital then, for the first time, met labor on equal terms, when the New York financier, Jay Gould, conferred with the Knights' executive board and conceded their demands. The prestige of this victory was so great that the Order reached a membership of over 700,000 the following year, a gain of more than half a million members in 14 months.

Parallel with the rise of the Knights of Labor grew a few unions affiliated with the 'Black' International, an anarchistic organization introduced into the United States in the early 'eighties by the German Johann Most. Local units of the Knights of Labor, trade unions, and socialist unions struck for the eight-hour day in 1886, in an era of comparative prosperity. A general strike called for 1 May 1886 was climaxed by a tragedy only indirectly connected in origin with the eight-hour movement, the Haymarket bomb explosion in Chicago. A long drawn-out lockout and strike in the McCormick Harvester Company culminated, on 3 May, in a riot in which the police killed and wounded half a dozen labor demonstrators. On the following day when the police broke up a mass meeting held to protest this massacre, someone threw a bomb into their midst; seven persons were killed and over sixty injured. Though the actual perpetrator of the outrage could not be found, Judge Joseph E. Gray of the Cook County Criminal Court held that those who incited the deed were equally guilty with those who committed the actual murder. Under this ruling the jury found eight anarchists guilty of murder, and sentenced one to imprisonment and seven to death. Of these seven, one committed suicide, four were executed, and the other two had their sentences commuted to life imprisonment. Six years later Governor John Peter Altgeld came to office. Alleging that 'the record of this case shows that the judge conducted the trial with malicious ferocity,' he pardoned the three anarchists who were still serving prison sentences. Although there was no possible doubt of the innocence of these men, Altgeld was denounced from coast to coast as an aider and abetter of anarchy.

The Knights of Labor was in no way responsible for the Haymarket affair and Powderly had even attempted to disassociate the Order from the eight-hour movement, but the popular revulsion against radical organization of any kind embraced it uncritically, and its influence began to wane. Indiscriminate strikes, all failures, the mismanagement of Powderly, and the difficulty of holding skilled and unskilled labor in the same union made serious inroads in their ranks. By the end of the decade membership in the Order had dwindled to about 100,000 and, after a brief and half-hearted flirtation with the Populists, the Knights practically disappeared.

As the Knights of Labor declined in membership and prestige, its place in the van of the labor movement was usurped by a new organization, the American Federation of Labor. This body, which was to dominate the American labor scene for the next half-century, rejected the idea of one big union in favor of the principle of unions of skilled workers on craft lines. The two organizations differed in other respects as well: the A. F. of L. was opportunistic and practical where the K. of L. had been idealistic and vague in its aims; the new organization abjured third parties and relied on the traditional weapons of the strike and the boycott, whilst the old Order had, on occasion, embraced farmer-labor parties and theoretically discouraged strikes. The Federation from the beginning accepted capitalism and chose to work within the framework of the established economic order, whilst the Knights looked forward to a co-operative republic of workers.

The A. F. of L., distinctively American as it was, issued from the brain of a foreign-born worker in the polyglot section of New York. In the late 'sixties a bullet-headed young man named Samuel Gompers, a London-born Jew of Flemish ancestry, was working in a highly unsanitary cigar-making shop in the Lower East Side, and speaking at the meetings of a cigar-makers' union. Cigar making was then a sociable handicraft. The men talked or read aloud while they worked, and both shop and union included German and Hungarian immigrants who could discuss socialism or Darwinism with equal facility. Gompers, as he rose in the councils of his fellow workers, learned to concentrate on the economic struggle and to fight shy of intellectuals who would ride union labor to some private Utopia. He determined to divorce unionism from independent political action, which dissipated its energy, and from radicalism, which served only to arouse the fear of the public and the fury of the police. In the hard times of the 'seventies he experienced cold and hunger, the futility of charity, and the cowardice of politicians. At all times he had reason to bewail the lack of discipline in the labor movement. By 1881 he and other local labor leaders had thought their way through to a national federation of craft unions, economic in purpose, evolutionary in method, and contending for the immediate objects of shorter hours and better wages. Five years later the A. F. of L. was born, and as the Knights of Labor declined the Federation became the fighting spearhead of the American labor movement.

There is a rough analogy between the A. F. of L. and the American system of federalism, although, in fact, the Federation modeled its structure on the British Trades Union Congress. Each national union in the Federation has complete power to contract with or strike against employers within its own jurisdiction. The Federation decides matters of jurisdiction, prevents — or tries to prevent — the establishment of rival unions in the same trade, and relies on salaried organizers and a labor press to keep the ranks of the workers solid. Opportunistic rather than idealistic, animated by the philosophy of the job, the Federation is a purely economic organization of wage-earners for the business of collective bargaining. 'At no time in my life,' said Gompers, 'have I worked out definitely articulated economic theory,' and Gompers's co-worker, Adolph Strasser, was even more emphatic. 'We have no ultimate ends,' he testified. 'We are going on from day to day. We are fighting only for immediate objects — objects that can be realized in a few years.'

By the turn of the century the A. F. of L. boasted a membership of over half a million; by 1914 it would reach 2 million. This rapid growth of the Federation was in great part due to the leadership of Gompers who for 40 years guided its destiny, impressed it with his personality, permeated it with his ideas, inspired it with his stubborn courage, held it steadily to the course of aggressive self-interest, and steered it clear of the shoals of politics upon which so many earlier labor movements had grounded. The A. F. of L. opposed creating a separate labor party nor would it divide its ranks by giving allegiance to either of the two major parties. Instead, it used its power to persuade legislators to adopt specific demands and judged them accordingly. Without respect to party labels, it hewed to a simple line: 'Reward your friends and punish your enemies.'

Although the American Federation of Labor was for 40 years the acknowledged spokesman of American labor, at no time did its membership embrace a majority of the working class. In 1901, only one out of every 14 nonagricultural workers belonged to any union, about half the proportion in Britain. The A. F. of L. never made any effort to organize the great mass of unskilled workers. As late as 1920, for example, when the Federation was strongest, only 23 per cent of the workers in manufacturing plants, 25 per cent in the building trades, and 37 per cent in transportation were organized, and nothing at all had been done for miners and smelters, lumberjacks and migratory farm workers, women in domestic service or in textile mills or tobacco factories, immigrants and Negroes in packing houses.

The Knights, with their philosophy of industrial unionism, had made uncertain gestures toward these people, but with the decline of the Knights there was no one to champion them. The void was only partially filled by ragged.unions that sprang up spontaneously in the mining camps of the West and eventually coalesced into the Industrial Workers of the World. This militant organization, which acted as a catalytic agent in American labor, was born out of the labor warfare in the Coeur d'Alene mines of Idaho in the early 'nineties. To meet assaults upon them, the miners organized the Western Federation of Miners, which in turn conducted a long series of strikes through the West. Theirs was from the beginning a fighting existence. Themselves prone to violence, they were met by violence from mine operators, vigilante committees, and government officials. Thus when the Western Federation of Miners went out on strike at the Cripple Creek mines in Colorado in 1903 and 1904, the governor declared martial law and rushed in state troops without even pausing to investigate; the military commander arrested workers without preferring charges against them, destroyed miners' camps, cooped the miners up in bull pens, deported several hundred of them from the state, seized supplies of food sent in for their relief, shut down offending newspapers, and forced operators who had managed to keep their mines open to discharge union workers.

Out of all this, in 1905, came the Industrial Workers of the World (the I.W.W., or 'Wobblies,' as they came to be known). It was the first labor organization formally committed to the principle of class warfare. This principle was set forth in the preamble of its constitution:

> The working class and the employing class have nothing in common. There can be no peace so long as hunger and want are found among millions of working people, and the few, who make up the employing class have all the good things of life.
>
> Between these two classes a struggle must go on until all the toilers come together on the political as well as on the industrial field, and take and hold that which they produce by their labor, through an economic organization of the working class, without affiliation with any political party.

In its fifteen years of existence the I.W.W. tried to organize the migratory farm workers of the Great Plains, lumbermen of the Far Northwest, copper miners in Arizona, and dock hands along the Pacific waterfront. In 1912 it ventured east to take charge of the textile strike in Lawrence, Massachusetts, where the mill-owners had countered a new state law reducing hours to 54 hours a week by slashing wages, which then stood at $8.56 a week. The I.W.W. won this strike, but lost a parallel strike in the textile town of Paterson, New Jersey. Before its demise in 1918 it had conducted almost 150 strikes, winning an astonishingly large number of them. When its activities threatened to interfere with the war in 1917 and 1918, it was destroyed.

3. INDUSTRIAL CONFLICT

As labor shifted its objectives from social reform to wages and the job, it resorted with increasing frequency to the weapons of industrial warfare — the strike and the boycott — and business retaliated with the lockout, the blacklist, the injunction, and the employment of company police or the National Guard. The result was an uninterrupted industrial conflict that frequently broke out into violence and assumed the ominous character of warfare. In 1900 the Industrial Commission concluded that strikes and lockouts were far more prevalent in the United States than in other industrial countries — possibly a tribute to the independent spirit of the American workingman as well as to the growing pains of big business and big labor; the experience of the next 30 years furnished no ground for modifying the sobering estimate.

The great majority of strikes that occurred after the 1870's involved either hours or wages or both. As late as 1900, 70 per cent of the industrial workers in the country worked ten hours or more each day, and ten years later only 8 per cent were on an eight-hour day. In many industries the hours were shockingly long: the steel industry had a twelve-hour day and a seven-day week, a schedule maintained for many steel workers until 1923. Hours in the textile industry ranged from 60 to 84 a week, even for the women and little children who constituted a large part of the working force. The wage situation was not much better. From 1880 to 1910 the unskilled laborer commonly earned less than $10 a week and the skilled worker rarely more than $20, while the earnings of women ranged from a low of $3.93 a week in Richmond to a high of $6.91 in San Francisco. During the whole of this 30-year period the average annual family income of industrial workers was never more than $650, or of farm laborers more than $400, figures considerably below that fixed as necessary for a decent standard of living. When we recall that unemployment averaged 10 per cent during the entire period and was often higher,[3] that even those employed rarely enjoyed continuous work through the year, and that with the growth of cities the vegetable garden, fruit trees, chicken-coop, and family cow that had supplemented earlier family incomes disappeared, we can understand better the deep discontent of labor and the resort to conflict and even to violence.

The first great industrial conflict in our history came in 1877 when the four Eastern trunk railroads jauntily announced a wage-cut of 10 per cent, the second since the panic of 1873. Without adequate organization the railway employees struck, and with the support of a huge army of hungry and desperate unemployed, the strike flared up into something that seemed to respectable folk like rebellion. During one week in July

3. In the prosperous year of 1898, for example, 14 per cent of the workers in manufacturing and transportation were unemployed. In the same year the average miner in the bituminous coal mines worked 211 days a year, and in the anthracite mines 152 days a year.

traffic was entirely suspended on the trunk lines and demoralized elsewhere in the country, and every large industrial center from the Atlantic
to the Pacific was in turmoil. In Baltimore, Pittsburgh, Martinsburg,
Chicago, Buffalo, San Francisco, and elsewhere, there were pitched battles between militia and the mob, and order was restored only by federal
troops. Pittsburgh was terrorized for three days; fatalities ran into the
scores, and a wall of three miles of flame destroyed every railroad car,
including 160 locomotives, and every railroad building, and almost lev-
elled the city. American complacency received a shock which was only
partially alleviated by the notion, so precious to Americans then and
since, that foreign agitators alone were responsible for the disorder.
Only the most far-sighted realized that the country had reached a stage
of industrial evolution which meant that the 'Great Strike' of 1877 would
be only the first of a long series of battles between labor and capital.

Not until 1892 was the nation again to witness so menacing an outbreak. In that year occurred the terrible strike in the Homestead works
of the Carnegie Steel Company which culminated in a pitched battle
between infuriated strikers and an army of Pinkerton detectives hired by
the president of the Carnegie Company, Henry C. Frick. The strikers
won the sanguinary battle, but the attempted assassination of Frick
alienated public opinion and state militia broke the backbone of the
strike.

Two years later the country was distracted by a strike against the
Pullman Palace Car Company in the model town of Pullman, Illinois.
The strike resulted originally from the arbitrary refusal of Mr. Pullman
to discuss grievances with representatives of his employees, but it came
eventually to involve far larger issues. The cause of the Pullman workers
was taken up by the American Railway Union, a powerful body of
railway workers under the leadership of the magnetic Eugene V. Debs.
When this union voted a boycott against all Pullman cars, the cause of
the Pullman Company was as promptly championed by the newly organized General Managers' Association of Railroads. The result was a
paralysis of transportation throughout the North. Disorder was widespread and the situation explosive. The railroads succeeded in enlisting
the sympathies of President Cleveland and Attorney-General Olney, a
former railroad attorney who had not forgotten his earlier obligations to
the railroads nor failed to consider the railroads' future obligations to
him. On 1 July, Olney appointed as special counsel for the United States

a prominent railway attorney, at whose suggestion the federal circuit court at Chicago served on the officers of the American Railway Union a 'blanket injunction' against obstructing the railways and holding up the mails. Hooligans promptly ditched a mail train and took possession of strategic points in the switching yards. Cleveland declared that he would use every dollar in the Treasury and every soldier in the army if necessary to deliver a single postcard in Chicago. On 4 July he ordered a regiment of regulars to the city. The effect was like that of sending British regulars to Boston in 1768.

Cleveland's antagonist in this conflict was not so much Debs and the Railway Union as Governor John P. Altgeld. This honest and fearless statesman had already been marked for destruction by big business because he had helped Jane Addams to obtain factory regulations in Illinois and because he had pardoned the Haymarket prisoners. During the Pullman strike Altgeld was ready and able to protect law and order with state militia. He sent troops to every point in the state where the authorities called for them, and had an ample force ready to use in Chicago, where, as yet, there was no disorder with which police and militia could not cope. The government appointed Edwin Walker, a career railroad lawyer, as special counsel. Walker called for a federal injunction and federal troops not to preserve order but to break the strike, and the most serious disorder came after the federal injunction had been issued. Altgeld's eloquent protest against this gratuitous interference by the Federal Government and his demand for the withdrawal of federal troops was cavalierly disregarded. Debs defied the injunction, a prosecution for conspiracy failed, but he was given six months' imprisonment for contempt of court. By early August the strike was smashed.

The Supreme Court of the United States, to which Debs appealed his sentence, upheld the government, declaring that even in the absence of statutory law it had a dormant power to brush away obstacles to interstate commerce — an implied power that would have made Hamilton and Marshall gasp. Yet the whole affair was not without a certain educational value to all concerned. Debs, in his prison cell, studied socialism and in time became the organizer and leader of the Socialist party in America; the workers learned the real meaning of the Sherman Anti-Trust Act; business awoke to the potentialities of the injunction in labor disputes; and the country at large was taught a new interpretation of the sovereign powers of the Federal Government. Only George Pullman emerged innocent of new ideas.

Scarcely less spectacular than the Pullman strike was the outbreak in the anthracite coal fields of Pennsylvania in 1902. Then, as later, the coal industry was chaotic, and the miners depressed and insecure. In the 'nineties organization had made some progress among the bituminous miners, but in the anthracite fields the racial antipathies and the bitter hostility of the railway-controlled operators delayed unionization. In 1898, however, the youthful John Mitchell became president of the United Mine Workers union which then numbered some 40,000 members. Within two years he whipped it into shape, extended its membership to the anthracite fields, and wrested favorable terms from the powerful coal companies of eastern Pennsylvania. Two years later the operators abrogated this agreement, and the miners struck for recognition of their union, a nine-hour day, and an increase in wages. The operators were obdurate, and for four tense months the strike dragged on while the strikers maintained an unbroken front and won the support of public opinion. It was in the course of this struggle that President George F. Baer of the Philadelphia and Reading Railroad announced that 'the rights and interests of the laboring man will be protected and cared for, not by the labor agitators, but by the Christian men to whom God in His infinite wisdom, has given control of the property interests of the country.' In October, with both a congressional election and a coal-less winter looming up, Roosevelt brought pressure on miners and operators to arbitrate. The miners were willing, but not Mr. Baer, who rebuked the President for 'negotiating with the fomenters of anarchy.' Outraged by this attitude Roosevelt then threatened to take over the mines and run them with militia unless the stubborn operators came to terms with the miners. This threat, and the force of public opinion, persuaded the mine-owners to arbitrate, and the strike ended in a signal victory for the miners, enhancement of the prestige of John Mitchell and of President Roosevelt, and a triumph for the cause of arbitration.

Labor unrest in the coal fields was chronic. The murderous activities of the Molly Maguires in the eastern Pennsylvania coal fields in the early 'seventies had given the American people their first premonition of class warfare and had helped create a stereotype of the 'alien agitator' that did service for half a century or more. In 1903–04 came a terrible outbreak in the Rockefeller-owned coal fields of Colorado which was crushed by the military. Ten years later the United Mine Workers tried to unionize the Colorado Fuel and Iron Company; the company resisted, armed guards were called in and broke up the miners' camps, and the conflict ended in the 'Ludlow massacre' — a battle between miners and soldiers that plunged Colorado into something like civil war, aroused nation-wide sympathy for the striking miners, and led, eventually, to far-reaching reforms.

4. LABOR LEGISLATION AND THE COURTS

Until the 1930's American social legislation lagged almost a generation behind that of the more progressive European states like Denmark and Germany and behind such Commonwealth nations as Australia and New Zealand. Yet probably more has been accomplished by labor through legislation than through strikes or other violent methods. This included the establishment of an eight-hour day in some industries, limitation of the hours and regulation of the conditions of women's labor, factory inspection, safety and sanitation regulation, arbitration of railroad disputes, workmen's compensation, and restriction of immigration and protection of native labor against foreign competition.

Except for federal employees, the Federal Government was thought to have no jurisdiction over many of these matters, and it was not until the New Deal that ways were found to achieve indirectly what could not be achieved directly. But as early as 1868 Congress established an eight-hour day on public works, and in 1892 enacted an eight-hour day for all government employees. The Adamson Law of 1916 extended this boon to all railway employees. In many other ways, too, the Federal Government responded to the demands of organized labor or of reformers. A Bureau of Labor, created in 1884, was elevated to cabinet rank in 1913 and assigned to a stalwart of the labor movement, William B. Wilson. An act of 1885 prohibited the importation of contract labor, and thereafter a whole series of laws regulated, restricted, or excluded immigration. In 1898 Congress passed the Erdman Act providing for the arbitration of labor disputes on interstate carriers, and in 1908 an Employers' Liability Act whose provisions were likewise confined to railway employees. The La Follette Seaman's Act of 1915 elevated seamen for the first time to the full status of free men. Twice Congress attempted to prohibit child labor through statutory enactment — in 1916 under the guise of a regulation of commerce, and again in

1919 through the medium of taxation, but both laws were nullified by the Court.

Before the 1930's, labor and social legislation lay for the most part in the domain of the individual states, where there was progress in certain lines, particularly in states such as Massachusetts, New York, Oregon, and Washington. The first labor law to be adequately enforced was the Massachusetts Ten-Hour Act of 1874 for women and children in factories. It was not so hard to get such laws passed as it was to provide proper administrative machinery for their enforcement; and until judges began to lose their laissez-faire prepossessions, there was constant danger of judicial nullification. The Massachusetts law was sustained, but similar statutes in Illinois and New York were voided by the courts.

In 1882 New York enacted a law prohibiting the manufacture of cigars in tenement houses which Gompers persuaded young Theodore Roosevelt to sponsor and Grover Cleveland to sign. It was intended as an entering wedge to break up the 'sweating' system, a rapidly growing menace. The highest state court in New York, however, threw it out on the ground that it interfered with the profitable use of real estate without any compensating public advantage. 'It cannot be perceived how the cigarmaker is to be improved in his health or his morals by forcing him from his home and its hallowed associations and beneficent influences to ply his trade elsewhere,' declared the court. Roosevelt, who had personally inspected these one-room 'homes' where whole families and their lodgers ate, slept, and rolled cigars, then began to revise his conception of justice and of the role of the courts in American economy.

> It was this case [he recorded in his autobiography] which first waked me to a dim and partial understanding of the fact that the courts were not necessarily the best judges of what should be done to better social industrial conditions. The judges who rendered this decision were well-meaning men. They knew nothing whatever of tenement-house conditions; they knew nothing whatever of the needs, or of the life and labor, of three-fourths of their fellow-citizens in great cities. They knew legalism, but not life. . . . This decision completely blocked tenement-house reform legislation in New York for a score of years, and hampers it to this day. It was one of the most serious setbacks which the cause of industrial and social progress and reform ever received.[4]

4. *Theodore Roosevelt: An Autobiography*, Scribners, p. 81.

By what theory did the courts declare such labor and welfare laws unconstitutional? It is forbidden in most state constitutions and in the Fourteenth Amendment to the Federal Constitution to deprive persons of liberty or property without due process of law. As no reform can be effected without depriving someone of something that he may deem to be a liberty or a property right, American courts (following English precedents) early elaborated the doctrine of a superior 'police power' — the reserved right of the state to protect the people's health, safety, morals, and welfare. The police power was held to justify even confiscatory legislation such as the prohibition of lotteries or of the sale of alcoholic liquors. But when labor and factory laws began to appear on the statute books, judges began to have second thoughts about the scope of this police power. Corporations engaging the best lawyers found it easy to convince courts that such laws were not a proper exercise of the police power but rather a violation of the 'due process' clause of the Fourteenth Amendment.

For half a century after Reconstruction such judges as Field and Brewer, Peckham and Sutherland, and their disciples in the state courts, turned the judicial bench into a dike against which the surging tides of welfare legislation beat in vain. They interpreted the Constitution as a prohibition rather than an instrument, and read into it limitations on the scope of governmental authority which were in fact merely the conclusions of natural law syllogisms. Insisting that they were without discretion and that their functions were purely mechanical, they struck down hundreds of state police laws on the theory that they deprived somebody of property or of liberty of contract without due process of law. When outraged legislators pointed to the laws themselves, judges answered that laws that deprived corporations of a fair return or workers of the right to work when and where they pleased were arbitrary and therefore denied 'due process.' Two assumptions pervaded these decisions. First, they assumed that the provisions of the Constitution were axiomatic, inflexible, and indisputable and that the judges were the only persons competent to apply them to particular cases. Second, they held that whenever social or economic facts conflicted with the theoretical assumptions of natural law, the facts must give way to the assumptions. Behind all this was the judicial fear that labor and welfare laws constituted 'an assault upon capitalism' or 'the first step towards socialism,' and the judges wrote their fears into legal doctrine. In 1913 Justice Holmes could observe that 'When twenty years ago a vague terror went over the earth and the word socialism began to be heard, I thought and still think that fear was translated into doctrines that had no proper place in the Constitution or the common law.'

The record bore this out. A Pennsylvania act forbidding payment of workers by orders on company stores was voided as an 'infringement on natural inherent rights and an insulting attempt to put the laborer under a legislative tutelage,' and a West Virginia court, confronted by a similar law, held that 'the evil was in the hands of the employee since he is not compelled to buy from the employer' — this in the face of the fact that the company owned the town, the houses, and the stores. A New York statute fixing the hours of labor for municipal contracts was struck down because it 'created a class of statutory laborers.' An Illinois court invalidated an act limiting the hours of labor for women in sweatshops on the ground that women had the same liberty of contract as men, a decision which inspired the Chicago *Evening Post* to protest that 'when Dora Windeguth, her employer at her elbow, says that she cannot earn enough in ten hours to live, our whole chivalry rises to her defense; let her work twelve hours then. We have always contended that nobody need starve in America!' [5] And a few years later the New York Court of Appeals declared void a law prohibiting night work for women. 'When it is sought,' said Judge Gray on behalf of the court, 'under the guise of a labor law, arbitrarily, as here, to prevent an adult female citizen from working any time of day that suits her, I think it is time to call a halt.'

In 1905 the Supreme Court of the United States in the case of *Lochner* v. *New York* took a similar view of a New York statute prescribing the hours of labor in bakeries. If, said the Court in effect, long hours of bakers could be shown to affect the quality of bread, something might be said for the regulation under the police power; but bakers were sufficiently intelligent to make their own labor contracts in their own interest, and 'we think the limit of the police power has been reached

5. The *Post* continued: 'It is interesting to reflect that while Dora's feudal forebears fought for the right to work, it has been left for Dora's generation to fight for the right to work overtime. But there is still a chance — if we all stick together — to save this state from the fate of Massachusetts . . . and other commonwealths, which, given the choice between healthy womanhood and cheap paper boxes, are now going without paper boxes.'

and passed in this case.' In a vigorous dissenting opinion Justice Holmes observed: 'This case is decided upon an economic theory which a large part of the country does not entertain. . . . The Fourteenth Amendment does not enact Mr. Herbert Spencer's *Social Statics*.'

Many of these illiberal decisions have since been reversed, and all of the states today have laws carefully regulating conditions and hours of labor for women and children, and in all dangerous occupations. As early as 1898 the Supreme Court, in the case of *Holden* v. *Hardy*, accepted a Utah law limiting to eight the hours of labor in mines, and this precedent has been commonly followed, though judges have differed on the question of what constituted a hazardous or fatiguing occupation. An Oregon law of 1903 limiting to ten the hours of employment for women was upheld by the Supreme Court in 1908 in the notable case of *Muller* v. *Oregon* — notable especially because the mass of scientific, sociological, economic, and physiological data introduced by the counsel for Oregon, Louis D. Brandeis, was admitted as evidence. Thus the principle was established that the courts could take cognizance of the special circumstances that justified the exercise of the police power. This did not necessarily mean that the courts would accept expediency as a legal argument, but rather that they would acquiesce in legislative findings of reasonableness.

Legislative enactments of minimum wages were for many years less successful. Organized labor itself long opposed such legislation as tending to level the general wage scale down rather than up, but in time labor withdrew its opposition to minimum wages for women and children. Following Australian and British precedents, Massachusetts in 1912 enacted the first minimum wage law for women and children, and within a few years fourteen states had followed suit. In 1916 the learning and logic with which Louis Brandeis and Felix Frankfurter had argued in the state court persuaded the Supreme Court to accept the Oregon minimum wage act,[6] and thereafter all seemed clear sailing. Seven years later, however, in one of the most remarkable reversals in our judicial history, the Court, in the *Adkins* case, found a District of Columbia minimum wage law unconstitutional, and on this rock of judicial intransigence the program of minimum wage legislation was temporarily wrecked.

6. *Stettler* v. *O'Hara* 243 U.S. 629 (1916). On this case the Court divided four to four, thus sustaining the act.

Another series of laws was designed to safeguard the health and lives of workers. In no other industrial nation were the hazards of industry so great or the accident and death rate so high as in the United States. In 1907, for example, there were 4534 fatal accidents and 87,644 non-fatal injuries among railroad workers alone, and in 1917 fatal accidents in manufacturing establishments amounted to 11,338 and non-fatal to the astonishing total of 1,363,080. The most elementary task here was to require the installation of safety devices and to provide for sanitary and fire inspection. It proved easier to pass laws and draw up regulations than to enforce them. Not until inspection was taken out of the hands of spoilsmen and entrusted to civil servants was there any perceptible improvement. The next task was to secure compensation for the injured or incapacitated victims of industry. Before this could be done it was necessary to get rid of the monstrous common law doctrines which made it almost impossible for the injured workingman or his family to collect compensation for injuries or death: if the worker had willingly assumed the risks of his job, if his accident resulted from his own negligence or that of a fellow worker, the company was not responsible! Most European and Commonwealth nations had workmen's compensation legislation by the turn of the century; alone of major industrial nations the United States lagged behind. Congress provided workmen's compensation for interstate railroad workers but when the states — Maryland leading the way — enacted similar laws the courts declared them void. Not until 1917 when the Supreme Court sustained New York's new compensation act were the states able to go ahead with full-dress programs. Within a few years most states outside the South had legislated workmen's compensation.

Veterans of industry were as much the responsibility of society as casualties, but few industries or businesses made the least provision for workers who had outlived their usefulness: they were supposed to fend for themselves or live on the charity of their children. The palpable injustice and inefficiency of this had led Britain and all the advanced European countries to provide unemployment and old-age pension programs even before the turn of the century. Here, too, the United States lagged behind. Although a few companies experimented with pension plans and Wisconsin adopted a pathbreaking unemployment insurance plan, not until the New Deal did the nation begin to take appropriate action.

V

Immigration

1. A NATION OF NATIONS

Immigration is the oldest and most persistent theme in American history, and though its character changed in the twentieth century, the process has remained essentially the same. For 300 years immigrants to America shared common experiences: the English, Dutch, and French of the seventeenth century, the German, Scotch, Irish, and Scandinavian of the eighteenth and nineteenth, the Italian, Slav, Hungarian, and Greek of the twentieth, all had to uproot themselves from Old World homes, break away from familiar folkways, and adjust themselves to a new environment and new institutions in a New World. With the early settlers the process of adjustment was largely physical. Of their experience we can say with Robert Frost

> The land was ours before we were the land's.
> She was our land more than a hundred years
> Before we were her people. . . .

For those who came after the pattern of American life had been in some measure fixed, the adjustment was more largely social and economic; but the cultural and psychological implications of the process of uprooting and transplanting were substantially the same for all. And through these years, from the founding of the Republic to 1917, the United States welcomed all comers, and invited each of them to membership in its political and social community. If the United States was not precisely a melting pot, as the earlier metaphor asserted, it was a loom on which the domestic warp and the imported weft were woven into a pattern in which all the threads, except perhaps the black, blended harmoniously into each other.

The transfer of peoples from the Old World to the New was the most extensive and successful experiment of its kind in modern history, carried out on a larger stage and over a longer period and with fewer convulsive reactions than any comparable enterprise.[1] The disruptive agricultural revolution in Europe, persistent poverty for the peasants, recurrent hard times for workers, war and the constant threat of military service for young men, political oppression, religious persecution, a class system which closed the door of opportunity to the vast mass of the poor and denied education to their children — these were, for 200 years, the main motivations for the emigration of 40 million Europeans to the United States. As for the magnetic attraction of America, that is even more easily explained: open land, work for all who were willing to work, a higher standard of living for ordinary folk than was known in Europe, religious freedom, political democracy, social equality, a second chance for the young — these were the lodestars that drew millions from the Old World to the New.

Ballads and songs, the accounts of travelers printed in the local newspapers, the tales of those who revisited their old homes and boasted of their new-found wealth, a million 'America-letters' — all told the same story:

> They give you land for nothing in jolly Oleana,
> And grain comes leaping from the ground in floods of golden manna,
> And ale as strong and sweet as the best you've ever tasted,
> It's running in the foamy creek, where most of it is wasted . . .[2]

Men and women foregathered in the mill towns of Scotland or the fishing villages of Norway, or along the sanguinary banks of the Dan-

1. It should be noted that this was part of a much larger emigration from the Old World to Canada, Australia, South Africa, the Argentine, Brazil, and many other parts of the globe. And while it is true that in the past century and a half more emigrants went to the United States than to any other country, Argentina and, for long periods, Canada actually received larger numbers of immigrants in proportion to their population. See Frank Thistlethwaite, 'Migration from Europe Overseas in 19th and 20th Centuries,' Reports of the 11th International Conference of Historical Sciences, Vol. V, for a fascinating analysis.
2. 'Oleana,' translated by Theodore Blegen, *Norwegian Emigrant Songs and Ballads*, U. of Minnesota Press.

ube, to sing some new ballad about America or listen to the latest
America-letter: in America you eat meat every day; in America everybody is equal; in America you do not pull your forelock to the priest or
take your hat off to the mayor — he takes his hat off to you; in America
women do not work in the fields; in America all the children go to
school; in America no one makes you serve in the army. When Andrew
Carnegie was a little boy in Dumfermline, Scotland, he used to hear his
father and mother sing

> To the West, to the West, to the land of the free,
> Where the mighty Missouri rolls down to the sea;
> Where a man is a man if he's willing to toil,
> And the humblest may gather the fruits of the soil;
> Where children are blessings, and he who hath most
> Has aid for his fortune and riches to boast.
> Where the young may exult and the aged may rest,
> Away, far away, to the land of the West.

It was this song that induced the elder Carnegie to migrate to America,
where his son amassed a fortune.

In the three-quarters of a century after Appomattox some 33 million
emigrants sought American shores, swarming out onto the rich prairie
lands of the West, transforming the cities into enormous cosmopolitan
beehives, performing the back-breaking labor that made possible the
economic expansion of the nation, creating new problems of social
assimilation and adaptation, and bringing to the United States the richest and most varied cultural heritage vouchsafed any modern nation
— though one all too often dissipated. This migration from the Old
World to the New represents the greatest folk movement in history,
ancient or modern. After a century and a half of colonization and unprecedented natural increase the population of the English colonies in
America was but slightly over 2 millions; every decade from 1850 to
1930 witnessed an immigration large enough to replace this entire
population.

In attempting to interpret the significance of this immigration it may
be well to dispose of some misconceptions at the outset. Neither immigration nor racial heterogeneity is a recent development; immigration
was as large, proportionately, in the later colonial period as in the latter
part of the nineteenth century, and the population of the colonies on the
eve of the Revolution, though predominantly English and African, rep-

resented six or seven nationalities and three or four languages. Nor was there ever any ground for fearing that the 'native stock' would succumb to the alien invasion, or that the foreign infiltration would upset the equilibrium of the American population. Despite the fecundity of many of the immigrant groups, and the very general intermarriage of native- and foreign-born, the number of Americans of foreign or mixed parentage constituted only one-fifth of the population in 1920, and declined steadily thereafter. And though the number of foreign-born in the country more than doubled in the 50 years after 1880, so, too, did the population, and the foreign-born made up a smaller percentage of the population in 1930 than in 1880. Recent immigrant stock has not shown itself less intelligent politically than the earlier stock or less faithful to democracy. At one time the foreign-born element in the population was held largely responsible for crime and disease, and the perpetual object of charity, but this belief has not been substantiated. That the foreign-born figures more largely than the native-born in the statistics of crime and charity was an index of opportunity rather than of character. The material standard of living in America generally kept ahead of that in Europe, and after half a century of large-scale immigration remained higher than in all but a very few countries, such as Denmark and Sweden. The infiltration of new blood into an industry generally makes the people already there ambitious to move on and up; yesterday's pick-hand becomes today's riveter and tomorrow's construction boss or company vice-president. Standards of living for a long time remained lower among the Anglo-Saxon mill hands in the South, where there was no push from below, than among the Finnish and Polish and Lithuanian textile workers in New England; and Polish tobacco farmers in the Connecticut valley boasted cars, radios, and modern plumbing at a time when 'Nordic' farmers in Georgia could not afford electric light.

2. THE 'OLD' IMMIGRATION AND THE 'NEW'

In the decade from 1850 to 1860 about 2.5 million immigrants came to this country; in the 40 years from 1860 to 1900 about another 14 million; in the first 30 years of the twentieth century over 18 million. Of these 35 million immigrants the largest number were from the United Kingdom — some 8.5 million in all — of whom over 4.5 million came from Ireland. Germany accounted for approximately 6 million, Canada for al-

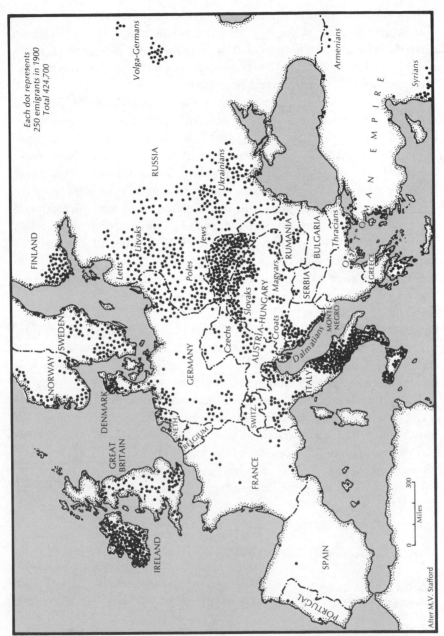

Each dot represents
250 emigrants in 1900
Total 424,700

Volga-Germans

Armenians

Syrians

RUSSIA

Ukrainians

FINLAND

Letts
Litvaks
Poles
Jews

OTTOMAN EMPIRE

RUMANIA

BULGARIA

Thracians

SWEDEN

NORWAY

DENMARK

GERMANY

Czechs

Slovaks

AUSTRIA-HUNGARY

Magyars

SERBIA

GREECE

Croats

MONTE-
NEGRO

Dalmatians

ITALY

GREAT
BRITAIN

NETH.

BELGIUM

SWITZ.

FRANCE

IRELAND

SPAIN

PORTUGAL

300

Miles

0

After M.V. Stafford

EMIGRATION FROM EUROPE TO THE UNITED STATES IN 1900

most 3 million, and the three Scandinavian countries for 2.25 million. The largest number of immigrants from northern and western Europe arrived in the generation immediately after the Civil War — there was a notable decline in immigration from Germany and the United Kingdom after 1890 and from Scandinavia after 1910.

The ingredients that made up the American population in 1870 did not differ markedly from those which had made up the population a hundred years earlier. But in the 1870's there began to appear new types among the thousands who swarmed in at Castle Garden, New York: Austrians and Hungarians from the valley of the Danube, Bohemians from the river Moldau, Poles from the Vistula, and Serbs from the river Save, blue-eyed Italians from the banks of the Arno and olive-skinned Italians from the plains of Campania or the mountains of Sicily, Russian Jews from the Volga and the Dnieper and the steppes of Ukraine. Almost 75,000 of the many peoples of the old Dual Monarchy came over in the 'seventies, over 50,000 Italians and as many Russians. By the 'eighties this trickle from southern and eastern Europe had become a stream, by the 'nineties a torrent, and in the early years of the new century a veritable flood. Altogether, in the 50 years between 1880 and 1930, Italy sent over 4.5 million emigrants, Austria, Hungary, and the succession states over 4 million, Russia and Poland perhaps another 4 million — a total from these countries alone of 13 million.[3]

The proportion of the foreign-born in America in 1910 remained roughly what it had been a half-century earlier, but the sources of immigration had changed drastically. In 1860 southern and eastern Europe made up only 1 per cent of the foreign-born population; in 1910, 38 per cent. While the 'old' immigration was predominantly Protestant, the 'new' arrivals were for the most part Catholic, Greek Orthodox, or Jewish. The United States, in short, had become a much more cosmopolitan country.

3. Change in source of immigration from Europe, 1860–1930.

Period	Total Admitted	Northern and Western Europe		Southern and Eastern Europe	
1861–70	2,314,824	2,031,624	87.8%	33,628	1.4%
1871–80	2,812,191	2,070,373	73.6	201,889	7.2
1881–90	5,246,613	3,778,633	72.0	958,413	18.3
1891–1900	3,687,564	1,643,492	44.6	1,915,486	51.9
1901–10	8,795,386	1,910,035	21.7	6,225,981	70.8
1911–20	5,735,811	997,438	17.4	3,379,126	58.9
1921–30	4,107,209	1,284,023	31.3	1,193,830	29.0

Immigrants from northern Europe tended to go west and take land. Large numbers of Germans, it is true, congregated in the cities of the Middle West, giving a distinctive flavor to such places as Cincinnati, St. Louis, and Milwaukee which lingers on into the twentieth century. Among the Norwegians and Swedes the tendency to go out to the land was marked; the great agricultural states of Minnesota, Illinois, North and South Dakota, Nebraska, and Iowa still have substantial Scandinavian population, and the single state of Minnesota displays no less than 400 Swedish place names, while the influence of these industrious and intelligent farmers was felt south to Texas and west to California. Some of the Irish went west — in 1860 there were 50,000 of them in Wisconsin, and large numbers in Iowa, but most remained in the cities of the Eastern seaboard, where their group loyalty and talent for politics in a democratic medium made them the first and most enduring of racial blocs in American politics. Their control of the local government of New York was long proverbial, and their conquest of New England was so complete that in 1915 the Irish mayor of Boston could boast that his people had first 'made Massachusetts a fit place to live in,' and get away with it.

Like the Irish, the later immigrants — Italians, Russians, Austrians, Poles, Jews, and others from southern and eastern Europe — chose the cities. Most of them were far too poor to buy a farm or invest in the machinery and stock necessary for modern agriculture, and peoples whose language, customs, and religion were very different from those of the older stock naturally tended to live together in colonies rather than isolate themselves on farms or in small towns. For many of them, too, as for many Irish and Danes and Norwegians, migration to America was their urban movement — inspired by the same notions that took native Americans from the farms to the cities. In 1900 two-thirds and in 1930 three-fourths of the foreign-born were living in towns and cities. The proportion of foreign-born in such large cities as New York, Chicago, Cleveland, and Detroit was impressive, but the concentration in the smaller industrial cities, such as Passaic and Paterson, New Jersey, or Lawrence and Fall River, Massachusetts, was even more extraordinary. In 1930 it was not New York City but the industrial town of Hamtramck, Michigan, that had the largest percentage of foreign-born in its population. But New York City, with the largest Jewish population of any city in the world, with almost 500,000 Italians and Russians, 250,000 Poles and Germans, and large numbers of every European and some

Asiatic nationalities, presented the most varied racial picture. The
Danish-born journalist Jacob Riis thus describes the city in 1890 when
the new immigration was just beginning on a large scale:

A map of the city, colored to designate nationalities, would
show more stripes than on the skin of a zebra, and more colors
than any rainbow. The city on such a map would fall into two great
halves, green for the Irish prevailing in the West Side tenement districts, and blue for the Germans on the East Side. But intermin-
gled with these ground colors would be an odd variety of tints that
would give the whole the appearance of an extraordinary crazy-
quilt. From down in the Sixth Ward . . . the red of the Italian
would be seen forcing its way northward along the line of Mulberry
Street to the quarter of the French purple on Bleeker Street and
South Fifth Avenue, to lose itself, after a lapse of miles in the 'Little Italy' of Harlem. . . . Dashes of red would be seen strung
through the District, northward to the city line. On the West Side
the red would be seen overrunning the Old Africa of Thompson
Street, pushing the black of the Negro rapidly uptown. . . . Hardly
less aggressive than the Italian, the Russian and the Polish Jew
. . . is filling the tenements of the old Seventh Ward to the river
front, and disputing with the Italian every foot of available space
in the back alleys of Mulberry Street. . . . Between the dull gray
of the Jew, and the Italian red, would be seen squeezed in on the
map a sharp streak of yellow marking the narrow boundaries of
Chinatown. Dovetailed in with the German population the poor
but thrifty Bohemian might be picked out by the sombre hue of
his life as of his philosophy. . . . Down near the Battery the West
Side emerald would be soiled by a dirty stain, spreading rapidly;
like a splash of ink on a sheet of blotting paper, headquarters of
the Arab tribe. Dots and dashes of color here and there would
show where the Finnish sailors worship their God, the Greek pedlars
the ancient name of their race, and the Swiss the goddess of
thrift.[4]

The same character could be observed in Boston, Chicago, San Francisco, and the other big cities of the country. Problems of housing,
sanitation and health, and education inevitably arose. American cities
came to have their 'ghettos,' their 'little Italy' or their 'Chinatown,' and
'slum' became a familiar word in the American vocabulary. By the
decade of the 'eighties tenement conditions in American cities were as
sordid as in the industrial centers of the Old World: breeding places for

4. Jacob Riis, *How the Other Half Lives*, pp. 25-7.

vice, crime, and epidemics. In 1890 two-thirds of the population of New York City was crowded into tenements.

Desperately poor, without industrial or mechanical skills, and unable to strike out for themselves in a new country, the immigrants from southern and eastern Europe became, for the most part, unskilled laborers in mine, in factory, or on the railroad. The Italians, Magyars, Slovaks, Jews, Czechs, Croats, Poles, and others who came over in the 'nineties, took what work was available, in the steel mills of Pennsylvania or the mines of West Virginia, in the lumber camps or the iron mines of Michigan, in the stockyards of Chicago or the sweatshops of New York. Jews congregated in the garment trade, Finns in mining, Portuguese in the textile towns. In 1907 of 23,337 laborers at the Carnegie steel works, 15,858 were foreign-born; two years later a survey of the workers in the bituminous mines of Pennsylvania discovered 76 per cent to be of foreign birth, and of these 92 per cent from southern and eastern Europe.

Two other groups of immigrants came into the United States in increasing numbers after the turn of the century: Canadians and Mexicans. It was easy for Canadians to drift into the United States, and after the Civil War many of them, attracted by the opportunities for work in the textile or lumber mills, or in the woods, found their way to northern New England, the Great Lakes states, and the Far Northwest. Canadian immigration first took on major proportions after 1910; in the next 20 years 1.5 million Canadians, one-third of them French and about two-thirds of them English-speaking, crossed over the border, cementing the strong ties already binding the two neighboring democracies. Especially in the prairie lands of the West there was a good deal of movement the other way as well; between 1890 and the coming of the War perhaps a million American farmers moved into Canada, and the tier of states on either side of the border from Minnesota to Montana and from Manitoba to Alberta came to constitute something of a social as well as an economic unit.

Immigration from Canada raised few difficulties, except for some of the French, but immigration from Mexico was a more serious matter. The census of 1930 revealed that not far from 750,000 Mexicans were domiciled in the United States, the majority of them in the border states of Texas, New Mexico, Arizona, and California. For the most part poor and illiterate, casual laborers who worked under shocking conditions in

the cotton, rice, and beet-sugar fields of Colorado and the Southwest,
they presented an urgent problem of labor and race relations. Immigration exclusion laws did not apply to the countries of the Western Hemisphere, and in so far as Mexican immigration was regulated at all, it was
under the general provisions giving immigration officials the power to
exclude those who 'might become public charges.' A strict application of
this provision cut the Mexican-born population to a mere 372,000 by
1940.

The United States has held inconsistent attitudes toward the assimilation of the immigrant. The predominant expectation has been that the
newcomer, no matter what his place of origin, would conform to Anglo-
Saxon patterns of behavior and cherish those institutions transported to
the New World from the British Isles. Competing with this view was the
conviction that in this hemisphere a new type of man was being fused
out of a variety of ethnic elements. In 1845 Emerson observed:

> As in the old burning of the Temple at Corinth, by the melting
> and intermixture of silver and gold and other metals a new com-
> pound more precious than any, called Corinthian brass, was
> formed; so in this continent, — asylum of all nations, — the en-
> ergy of Irish, Germans, Swedes, Poles, and Cossacks, and all the
> European tribes, — of the Africans, and of the Polynesians, —
> will construct a new race, a new religion, a new state, a new lit-
> erature, which will be as vigorous as the new Europe which
> came out of the smelting-pot of the Dark Ages, or which earlier
> emerged from the Pelasgic and Etruscan barbarism.

Still a third conception came from the experience of the settlement-
house workers: respect for the cultural heritage of the new arrivals.
Those who saw at first hand the tragic alienation of first from second
generation Americans feared that attempts to 'Americanize' the immigrants would lead to ethnic self-hatred and would deprive the country of
a variety of distinct cultural contributions. Many of the immigrants were
themselves uncertain which attitude to adopt. The consequence has
been a complex set of relationships in which immigrants have been less
likely to marry outside their group than to alter their ideas of participation in civic affairs.

Most newcomers were quick to abandon their Old World loyalties and
profess those of the New. In other countries — Brazil, Chile, India,
South Africa, Poland, Tunisia, for example — European aliens have

been able to preserve their languages and their customs, but not in America. Here everything conspired to root out old attachments and supplant them with new: the vastness of the country which broke up compact settlements; the economy which rewarded speedy acquisition of the American language; the political system which encouraged naturalization and voting; the habit of voluntary association which welcomed most newcomers into political parties, labor unions, granges, and a hundred other organizations; and perhaps most effective of all, the public schools. What the public school meant is movingly recalled by the Russian Jew, Mary Antin:

> Education was free. That subject my father had written about repeatedly, as comprising his chief hope for us children, the essence of American opportunity, the treasure that no thief could touch, nor even misfortune or poverty. It was the one thing that he was able to promise us when he sent for us; surer, safer than bread or shelter. On our second day I was thrilled with the realization of what this freedom of education meant. A little girl from across the alley came and offered to conduct us to school. My father was out, but we five between us had a few words of English by this time. We knew the word school. We understood. This child, who had never seen us till yesterday, who could not pronounce our names, who was not much better dressed than we were; was able to offer us the freedom of the schools of Boston! No application made, no questions asked, no examinations, rulings, exclusions; no machinations, no fees. The doors stood open for every one of us. The smallest child could show us the way.[5]

Books by immigrants like Mary Antin emphasize the immigrant contribution to American society.

> We came not empty-handed here
> But brought a rich inheritance [6]

wrote one of the immigrant poets, and no student of American culture can fail to appreciate the validity of the boast. The immigrant contribution of muscle and brawn is obvious; the contribution to politics and public affairs, industry and labor, science and education, arts and letters, is scarcely less apparent, though to be sure, in these fields it has been an individual rather than a group contribution. To remember the achievements of Carl Schurz and John Peter Altgeld in politics, Jacob Riis and

5. Mary Antin, *The Promised Land,* Houghton Mifflin Co.
6. The Danish poet, Adam Dan.

Nathan Straus in social reform, Joseph Pulitzer, James Gordon Bennett, and E. L. Godkin in journalism, Andrew Carnegie, James J. Hill, and Henry Villard in business, Samuel Gompers and William B. Wilson in unions, Alexander Graham Bell, John Ericson, and Nikola Tesla in the field of invention, Louis Agassiz, Albert Michelson, and Polykarp Kusch in science, Francis Lieber and Herman Von Holst in scholarship, Karl Bitter and Augustus St. Gaudens in sculpture, and Theodore Thomas and Jascha Heifetz in music,[7] is to realize the extent to which the foreign-born have enriched American life.

3. PUTTING UP THE BARS

Although the regulation of immigration is a function of the Federal Government, it was not effectively exercised for well-nigh a hundred years. From the first, regulation of immigration was left largely to the states, and shortly after independence the states undertook to exclude 'undesirables.' South Carolina, for example, passed an Act for Preventing the Transportation of Malefactors in 1788. For the next half-century New York, Massachusetts, and Pennsylvania, to whose ports most of the arrivals came, attempted, through the exercise of the police power, to

7. The foreign-born have, from the beginning, exercised almost a monopoly over musical activities in the United States; only in the last generation is this changing. A partial list of conductors of the leading symphony orchestras in the country illustrates the situation in the 1930's:

Boston	Serge Koussevitsky
Buffalo	Lajos Shuk
Chicago	Frederick Stock
Cincinnati	Eugene Goossens
Cleveland	Artur Rodzinski
Detroit	Ossip Gabrilowitch
Kansas City	Karl Kreuger
Los Angeles	Arnold Schonberg
Minneapolis	Eugene Ormandy
New York	Arturo Toscanini
	John Barbirolli
Omaha	Rudolph Ganz
Philadelphia	Leopold Stokowski
Portland	William van Hoogstraten
Rochester	José Iturbi
St. Louis	Vladimir Golschmann
San Francisco	Pierre Monteux
Syracuse	André Polah
Washington	Hans Kindler

exclude criminals, paupers, and diseased immigrants. The constitutionality of such legislation was sustained, but when New York State, faced with the heavy burden of receiving and protecting the throngs of immigrants who poured in during the 'thirties and 'forties, assessed a small head tax on each immigrant, the Supreme Court declared the tax unconstitutional as an interference with the congressional control of commerce.[8] It was obviously unjust for one or two states to carry the entire burden of welfare work which unrestricted immigration entailed, but the Federal Government steadfastly refused to assume any part of that burden.

Not until 1882 did Congress finally undertake to regulate immigration, and it acted then only because its hand was forced by a situation which was rapidly getting beyond control: the threat of an inundation of the Pacific coast by Chinese coolies. The discovery of gold in 1849 and the consequent demand for cheap labor first brought the Chinese to California, and the great Taiping rebellion of 1850 accelerated the movement. By 1852 there were about 25,000 Orientals on the Pacific coast, and thereafter they came at the rate of 4000 a year, their numbers augmented in the 'sixties by the demand for laborers on the Central Pacific Railroad. By the end of the 'seventies there were almost 150,000 Chinese in California alone, and their low standards of living, long hours of labor, and tractability were said to constitute a serious menace to native labor. At the same time they aroused racial prejudice by their adherence to the Chinese ways of life and religion, their exotic appearance, customs, and language, and their obvious intention to return to China with their savings.[9] As a result an anti-Chinese movement developed in the 'seventies under the leadership of an Irish agitator, Denis Kearney. Taken up by the California Workingmen's party, it culminated in discriminatory legislation and a demand for the prohibition of further Oriental immigration. In response to this demand Congress, in 1882,

8. *The Passenger cases,* 7 Howard 283 (1849).
9. Wrote Robert Louis Stevenson: 'Of all stupid ill-feelings, the sentiment of my fellow-Caucasians towards our companions in the Chinese car was the most stupid and the worst. They seemed never to have looked at them, listened to them, or thought of them, but hated them *a priori.* The Mongols were their enemies in that cruel and treacherous battlefield of money. They could work better and cheaper in half a hundred industries, and hence there was no calumny too idle for the Caucasians to repeat, and even to believe. They declared them hideous vermin and affected a kind of choking in the throat when they beheld them.' *Across the Plains,* 1879.

passed an act excluding Chinese laborers for a period of ten years — a prohibition that was extended in 1890 and again in 1902 until it became permanent. As a result of this policy of exclusion the Chinese population of the country declined from 107,000 to 75,000 in 1930.

Japanese immigration did not become a serious problem until some years later. There were less than 25,000 Japanese in the country at the beginning of the twentieth century, but when the following decade witnessed an extraordinary upturn in immigration from the Nipponese Empire, the Pacific coast became alarmed and demanded that the policy of exclusion be extended to embrace the Japanese as well as the Chinese. Anti-Japanese agitation crystallized into discriminatory legislation, and in order to avoid an international crisis, President Roosevelt, in 1907, reached a 'gentlemen's agreement' with the Japanese government whereby it pledged itself to continue 'the existing policy of discouraging emigration of its subjects of the laboring classes to continental United States.' Despite this agreement a small stream of Japanese continued to trickle into the Pacific coast, and between 1911 and 1913 California and other Western states enacted a series of laws designed to prevent Japanese from owning or even leasing real estate. Once again a diplomatic rupture threatened, which required the personal intervention of the Secretary of State. Ten years later when Congress was assigning mathematical quotas for immigration — an arrangement which would have admitted 246 Japanese a year — it went out of its way specifically to exclude Japan from the operation of the system and to ban Japanese immigration completely. The State Department expostulated in vain against this deliberate affront to a wartime ally. 'Our friends in the Senate have in a few minutes spoiled the work of years,' said Secretary of State Charles Evans Hughes, 'and done lasting injury to our common country.' By its long record of racial prejudice, segregation in schools, prohibition of land-holding, and discrimination in immigration, the United States managed to stockpile for itself a formidable arsenal of ill-will and bitterness among the Japanese people.

Once embarked upon a policy of regulation, Congress faced a number of alternatives among which to choose. Should it adopt a policy of selection, of regulation, or of exclusion? If selection, upon what basis should it be made? If restriction, how far should the government go in denying entry to prospective immigrants? The first general immigration law, that of 1882, was based upon the theory of selection; it imposed a head tax of 50 cents on each immigrant admitted, and excluded convicts, idiots, and persons likely to become public charges. From this time on a long series of federal acts elaborated the policy of selection, increased the head tax, and prohibited contract labor, considerably extended the classes excluded, and provided for more efficient enforcement of the laws. The new statutes excluded the sick and diseased, paupers, polygamists, prostitutes, anarchists, alcoholics, and — by the Act of 1917 — persons with constitutional inferiority complexes!

While this policy of selection afforded protection against some unwelcome additions to the population, it made no dent on the total number who clamored to come in. Beginning early in the century there arose an insistent demand for some plan designed to reduce the total number who would be admitted and to select those thought to be best. Agitation for exclusion came from three disparate groups. First, and most powerful, was organized labor which had long looked upon unrestricted immigration — especially the immigration of unskilled workers — as a major threat. Second were social reformers like E. A. Ross of Wisconsin who had come to the conclusion that there could be no solution of the problems of slums, public health, and the exploitation of the poor as long as illiterate immigrants poured into the great cities. Third were the traditionalists who had been taken in by the doctrines of Nordic supremacy and who deplored the

> Accents of menace alien to our air,
> Voices that once the Tower of Babel knew.[10]

The criterion of selection was to be literacy, and an historic battle was waged over this issue. A bill incorporating a literacy test passed one of the two Houses of Congress no less than 32 times, and on four occasions it was approved by both Houses and went to the President, only to be vetoed each time. Cleveland, in 1897, characterized the measure as 'a radical departure from our national policy.' Taft, in 1913, declared that the literacy test violated a principle which he believed should be maintained. Wilson in 1915 and again in 1917 denounced it as a test of opportunity rather than of character or fitness. On this last occasion, however, the bill was passed over the presidential veto and became a law. By its term no alien over 16 years of age who could not read

10. Thomas Bailey Aldrich, 'Unguarded Gates.' 'A Poem,' wrote Aldrich, 'in which I mildly protest against America becoming the cesspool of Europe.'

English or some other language was to be admitted to the United States. When we note that in the first decade of the century less than 3 per cent of the 'old' immigrants were illiterate, but over half of those from Sicily and southern Italy, we can see that the literacy test provided an easy and certain method of discrimination on racial and national lines.

The Immigration Act of 1917, in method selective, in purpose restrictive, marks the transition from the earlier to the modern policy of immigration regulation — regulation which became increasingly restrictive. During the First World War immigration from Europe fell off sharply, but a renewal of the influx after the cessation of arms led Congress to abandon the policy of selection for one of absolute restriction. By the Immigration Act of 1921, the number of aliens admitted from any European, Australasian, Near Eastern, or African country [11] was to be limited to 3 per cent of the total number of persons of that nationality residing in the United States in 1910. This so-called quota system, specifically designed to reduce the number of immigrants from southern and eastern Europe, drastically restricted the total number that could be admitted in any one year to 357,802. Even this act was criticized because it admitted too many immigrants and it failed to discriminate sufficiently in favor of northern and western Europeans. Consequently a new and more drastic law was passed in 1924 which reduced the annual quota from 3 to 2 per cent, and which, by taking the census of 1890 as a basis, more effectively favored English, Irish, German, and Scandinavian, and discriminated against Italian, Austrian, Russian, and other southern and eastern European immigration. Finally by the National Origins Act of 1929 the total number of immigrants who might be admitted in one year was reduced to 150,000 to be distributed among the various European countries in proportion to the 'national origins' of the American people in 1920. Immigration from other American countries was left undisturbed, except by a Department of Labor ruling that no immigrants should be admitted who might become public charges.

The enactment of the first quota law of 1921 ended an era. In a hundred years the tide of immigration had risen to a flood, engulfing the whole country and depositing millions of people from every land and the cultural accretions of centuries. Then suddenly it ebbed. The Statue

11. The Act of 1917 created a Barred Zone, including India, Siam, Indo-China, and other parts of Asia, from which no immigrants were to be admitted.

of Liberty still stood guard over New York harbor, its beacon light held proudly aloft, the inscription on its base not yet erased:

> Give me your tired, your poor,
> Your huddled masses yearning to breathe free,
> The wretched refuse of your teeming shore,
> Send these, the homeless, tempest-tost to me:
> I lift my lamp beside the golden door.

But it was a symbol of things strange, and but faintly remembered.

VI

Agriculture and the Farm Problem

1. THE AGRICULTURAL REVOLUTION

While manufacturing was advancing with giant strides in the half-century following the Civil War, agriculture still remained the basic industry, the one which engaged the labor of the largest number of people. But agriculture itself was undergoing a revolution. Its main features were the expansion of its domain, the application of machinery and science to farming, the use of modern transportation to convey the products to world-wide markets, and the assumption by the Federal Government of responsibility for the welfare of the farmers. This revolution meant a shift from husbandry to machine-cultivation, and from subsistence to commercial farming; made agriculture an intimate though subordinate part of the industrial system; exposed the farmer to the vicissitudes of the industrial economy and the world market; and brought a vast increase in productivity which did not always bring comparable returns.

In the years from 1860 to 1910 the number of farms in the United States and the acreage of improved farm land trebled. The production of wheat rose from 173 to 635 million bushels, of corn from 838 to 2886 million bushels, and of cotton from 3,841,000 to 11,609,000 bales. More land was brought under cultivation in the 30 years after 1860 than in all the previous history of the nation. While the value of farms and farm products increased, they did not keep pace with returns from manufacturing and business, and there were serious decreases in parts of New England and the South. In 1900 the farmers' share in the national wealth was less than half that of 1860. Farm population grew absolutely, but the proportion of people living on farms declined; while the agricultural domain expanded, the relative political and social position of the farmer contracted.

In the half-century after the Civil War farming had been subjected to a series of shocks. The first was the impact of the war and reconstruction on the South, involving the partial destruction of the plantation system, the redistribution of land, and the rise of the crop-lien and the sharecrop systems. The second came from opening up the High Plains and the West, and the over-rapid extension of farming westward, with a consequent depression of farming in the Middle West and the East. American crops moved westward with the American people. In 1860 Illinois, Indiana, and Wisconsin were the leading wheat-producing states; 50 years later the cereal empire had passed to North Dakota, Kansas, and Minnesota. In 1860 the heart of the corn belt was the Ohio valley; in 1910 it was the Mississippi valley from the Wabash to the Platte. In 1860 Ohio led the nation in the production of wool; by 1900 Wyoming and New Mexico were the leading woolen states. In 1860 Mississippi was the leading cotton state of the South; by the turn of the century the Cotton Kingdom's capital was somewhere on the plains of Texas. All this meant drastic readjustment in the older states and the transition to truck or dairy farming or — as in much of New England — to mere subsistence farming.

A third shock was the rapid growth of world markets, and of world competition, as the productivity of the American farm outstripped the nation's capacity to consume. American wheat competed with the wheat of the Argentine, Australia, and Russia; beef and wool with the products of Australia, New Zealand, and the Argentinian pampas; cotton with Egypt and India. Fourth, and scarcely less disturbing to the agricultural equilibrium, was the impact of new machinery, new crops, and new techniques of farming.

Except in isolated regions like the Southern highlands or the rich Pennsylvania and Maryland country, the average farm ceased to be a self-sufficient unit, where a man and his family raised most of what they ate, wore, and used, and provided their own amusement in neighborhood groups. It became, like the West Indian sugar plantations, a cog in an industrial system, devoted to the raising of a staple crop, mechanized, and tied up with banking, railroading, and manufacturing.

One thing, however, did not greatly change until after the First World War. American agriculture continued to be, as it had always been, extensive rather than intensive, robbing the land of its fertility and leaving desolation behind. Because land was abundant, fertile, and cheap, the American farmer of the early Republic had found it easier and more profitable to take up new land than to conserve the resources of the old. Just as speculators recklessly exploited mineral resources, so the farmer used up the soil and the lumberman cut down the forest, leaving nature to do the replacing unaided. Almost everything conspired to encourage the farmer in his gutting of the soil: not only machinery and world markets, but constant change in farm ownership, untrained Negro labor in the South, an increase in absentee ownership and in tenancy which destroyed the sense of responsibility toward the land, and a laissez-faire policy of government, both state and federal, toward the land and its resources. Not until the sharp rise in farm land values in the early years of the new century dramatized the passing of cheap good land did the government realize the need for conservation, or the farmer the necessity for scientific farming. Then it was almost too late. When economists came to count the cost of our exploitative agriculture, they found that 100 million acres of land — an area equal to Illinois, Ohio, North Carolina, and Maryland — had been irreparably destroyed by erosion; that another 200 million acres were badly eroded; that over large areas the grass lands of the Great Plains had been turned into dust, and that the forest resources of the Eastern half of the country were rapidly disappearing. It remained to be seen whether science and technology could repair the material devastation, whether the drastic remedies of the economists could cure the malaise, and whether the expedient of government support could rehabilitate the farmer class.

2. THE USE AND ABUSE OF THE HOMESTEAD ACT

Under the terms of the Homestead Act any citizen, except one who had served in the Confederate army, could obtain 160 acres on the public domain by living on it or cultivating it for five years. Not content with this, and recognizing, somewhat grudgingly, that the neat little rectangular farm of the East was not really suitable to the West, Congress had passed a complex series of land laws: the Timber Culture Act of 1873, the Desert Land Act of 1877, the Timber and Stone Act of 1878, the Carey Irrigation Act of 1894, and the Enlarged Homestead Act of 1909. These statutes enlarged the areas that could be patented, facilitated entry and final acquisition, and provided government aid to enterprises like reclamation.

All of this should have meant that the immense public domain — perhaps 1 billion acres in 1860 — should have gone into the hands of the independent yeoman. Nothing of the kind happened. Between one-sixth and one-tenth of the public domain went to Homesteaders, and all the rest was not given away but sold — or held off the market by speculators, or by the government itself. By the end of the century Homesteaders had patented about 80 million acres, but the railroads had received — from federal and state governments — 180 million acres, the states had been given 140 million acres, and another 200 million acres — much of it Indian lands — had been put up for sale to the highest bidders.

The Homestead policy had been frustrated by a combination of confusion, incompetence, chicanery, and fraud. It was never suited to the needs of the landless workingman or immigrant; after all, how was he to move himself and his family to the West, build a house and barn, buy farm equipment and cattle, and keep going for a year until the money for his crops came in? Nor was the 160-acre farm suitable for the kind of farming profitable on the plains of the West or in the mountains. Perhaps more important was the fact that government policy was inconsistent; for all their professed concern for the independent yeoman, Congress and the states showed themselves a good deal more interested in satisfying the demands of business and speculator groups. In land policy as in trust policy, the Federal Government contented itself with ceremonial gestures. Just as Congress could have broken up trusts at any time by the simple device of taxation, so Congress could have made sure that the public domain went to genuine farmers, either by refraining from lavish land grants to corporations or by the calculated use of taxation.

Instead, as the Commissioner of Lands stated in 1901, 'immense tracts of the most valuable lands, which every consideration of public interest demanded should be preserved for public use, have become the property of a few individuals and corporations.' The railroads were the most favored beneficiaries, but they were by no means the only ones who enjoyed privileged treatment. Lumber companies, ranchers' associations, emigration and colonization companies, individual speculators like Ezra Cornell of New York or Amos Lawrence of Boston got princely domains. Over 40 per cent of public lands in Kansas, for example, were withdrawn from the operation of the Homestead law and sold to railroads or speculators.

An illuminating example of what happened when enthusiasm for Homesteaders gave way to concern for business is afforded by the history of the disposition of public lands in the South after the War. In 1866 Congress had set aside some 47 million acres of public lands in five Southern states for 80-acre homesteads. Ten years later the pressure of Northern lumber interests forced a repeal of these arrangements, and the land was thrown open to purchase by speculators. One congressman hastened to acquire 111,000 acres in Louisiana; a Michigan firm got 700,000 acres of pine lands. In Louisiana alone Northern businessmen picked up over a million acres, and in Mississippi another 900,000 acres of timber. English firms, too, hurried to be in on the kill. One English company bought 2 million acres of timberland in Florida, another purchased 1.3 million acres in the Yazoo Delta country, and a London firm called the North American Land and Timber Company got 1.5 million acres in Louisiana for 45 cents an acre. In 1906 a government expert could conclude that the exploitation of the South by these and other companies was 'probably the most rapid and reckless destruction of forests known to history.'

Cleveland instituted some far-reaching reforms in the disposal of public lands, and these were carried further under Harrison. An act of 1889 put an end to all cash sale of public lands, and the next year the government limited land acquisitions to 320 acres; in 1891 came the first act setting aside forest reservations on public lands. But these modifications of the land system were both too little and too late.

3. MACHINERY

The application of machinery to agriculture lagged fully a century behind the application of machinery to industry. Henry Adams could truthfully observe of the America of 1800 that

The Saxon farmer of the eighth century enjoyed most of the comforts known to Saxon farmers of the eighteenth. . . . The plough was rude and clumsy; the sickle as old as Tubal Cain, and even the cradle not in general use; the flax was unchanged since the Aryan exodus; in Virginia, grain was still commonly trodden out by horses.[1]

Mechanization of agriculture did not really begin until the 'thirties and 'forties, when Obed Hussey and Cyrus McCormick were experimenting with a reaper, A. D. Church and George Westinghouse with a thresher, and John Lane and John Deere with a chilled plow. Agricultural machinery, moreover, remained relatively unimportant, except in parts of the upper Middle West, before 1860. The Civil War, robbing the farms of their laborers and increasing the price of grain, induced farmers generally to adopt machines such as the reaper, which enabled a woman or even a boy to perform the work of several men. Over 100,000 reapers were in use by 1861 and during four years of war the number increased by a quarter of a million. After the war came countless new inventions — there were over 12,000 patents on plows alone before 1900 — and the pressure of competition eventually made the use of agricultural machinery almost universal in the North. Soon almost every operation from preparing the ground to harvesting the product was transformed by machinery. The Oliver chilled plow, finally perfected in 1877, meant an enormous saving in time and money; within a few years the wonderfully efficient rotary plowed and harrowed the soil and drilled the grain in a single operation. In 1878 the Deering Company marketed George Appleby's twine binder which greatly increased the amount of grain a farmer could harvest, and at the same time the steam threshing machine was perfected to a point where it was both efficient and safe. Within twenty years the bonanza farms of California were using 'combines' which reaped, threshed, cleaned, and bagged the grain in a single operation. During these same years the mowing machine, the corn planter, corn binder, husker and sheller, the manure spreader, the four-plow cultivator, the potato planter, the mechanical hay drier, the poultry incubator, the cream separator, and innumerable other machines entirely transformed the ancient practices of agriculture. At the same time the steady reduction in the price of windmills, the invention of a vane

1. Henry Adams, *History of the United States*, Vol. I, p. 16.

that turned the wheel to the wind, and the mass production of barbed wire, speeded up the conquest of the Plains.

With the hand cradle of 1830 a man could harvest 20 bushels of grain in 61 hours; by 1900 he could perform the same work in less than three hours. It took 21 hours to harvest a ton of timothy hay in 1850; half a century later, four hours. This vast saving in labor made it possible for a proportionately smaller number of farmers to feed an ever-increasing number of city-dwellers and have a surplus left over for export.

In the twentieth century came the application of steam, gasoline, and electricity to the farm. The huge 'combines,' formerly drawn by 20 or 30 horses, were propelled by gasoline tractors, and by 1930 almost 1 million tractors were in use on the farms of the United States. This substitution of power for horses has released not less than 30 million acres formerly devoted to pasture and forage. Electric power came to be used in all up-to-date dairies. The motor truck altered marketing conditions, and the motor car — especially after Henry Ford reduced its price to below $400 — the telephone, and the radio enlarged the social radius of the farm and led farmers to forget their rich heritage of folklore and song in favor of canned entertainment.

The value of farm implements and machines in the whole country increased from about $246 million in 1860 to $750 million in 1900, and then, swiftly, to $3595 million in 1920. This increase was distinctly sectional in character. Mechanization was not profitable in much of New England, with its rolling topography and little specialties, or in the South where cotton and tobacco farming did not take readily to the use of machinery. But the Middle West and the Far West absorbed reapers, mowers, tractors, harvesters, and threshers as fast as they could be turned out of the factories. In 1910 the value of machinery on Northern farms was $800 million, and by 1920 this had increased to over $2300 million, while the corresponding figures for the South were $293 million and $771 million. In 1920 the average value of farm implements and machinery on each South Dakota farm was $1500; on each farm in the Cotton Belt $215.

Farming as a way of life gave way to farming as a business. A stout heart and willing hands were no longer the essential equipment of farming, or a cabin roof and the sky the only 'overhead.' Increase in land values, heavy costs of machinery, and the substitution of chemical fertilizer for manure required capital and commonly involved the farmer in heavy indebtedness. The small diversified farm of the 1860's, with fields of wheat, corn, oats, and barley, orchard and vegetable garden, pasture mowing and woodlot, gave way to the large farm specializing in staple crops which could be produced with one kind of machinery and sold for cash. Another result was an ominous increase in farm mortgages and in tenancy: by 1930 almost every second farmer was a tenant, and one-fifth of the total value of American farms was mortgaged.

4. SCIENTIFIC AGRICULTURE

Interest in scientific agriculture, which had been considerable in the second half of the eighteenth century, waned in the South after the invention of the cotton gin in 1793 made it more profitable to take up virgin land in the newer South than to reclaim farms in Virginia and the Carolinas. In New England, however, where agricultural societies founded in the eighteenth century are still flourishing, Elkanah Watson inaugurated the agricultural fair, and the first agricultural school in the United States opened in 1822. The *American Farmer,* the first agricultural journal in the United States, was established in Baltimore in 1819. By 1840, when the prevalence of 'old-field' land worn out by successive cropping with tobacco had become an eye-sore in tidewater Virginia and Maryland, Edmund Ruffin of Virginia began to devote himself to disseminating knowledge of scientific agriculture; and much of the abandoned land was regenerated by the use of marl. Lord Playfair's translation of Baron von Liebig's great treatise, *Chemistry in Its Application to Agriculture and Physiology* (1840), was read with avidity by the more progressive farmers. By 1860 there were 50 farm papers in the country, many of them in the South; and if the Civil War had not broken out, the teachings of Ruffin and De Bow would undoubtedly have borne fruit in a more diversified and economical agriculture in the South.

Yet the average farmer had little patience with scientific agriculture, and some of them doubtless read with approval the dictum of one book on farming that was published in 1860: 'Scientific agriculture stands today with phrenology and biology and magnetism. No farmer ever yet received any benefit from any analysis of the soil and it is doubtful if any one ever will.' As long as there was an abundance of cheap land and a shortage of labor — a condition which obtained until some time after the Civil War — it was more economical for farmers to abandon worn-out soil and move on to virgin land than to cultivate intensively and invest in expensive fertilizers. The passing of these conditions led to scientific agriculture, conservation, and reclamation.

Scientific agriculture in the United States has depended largely upon government aid. A number of states subsidized agriculture in one way or another even before the Civil War. The Constitution gives Congress no explicit jurisdiction over agriculture, but as early as 1839 Congress made its first appropriation, $1000, for agricultural research. One of the most useful results of the loose-constructionist thinking in the Republican party was the creation by Congress in 1862 of a Department of Agriculture, under the direction of a commissioner with the happy name of Isaac Newton. In 1889 this department was raised to executive grade with a secretary of cabinet rank.

The activities and influence of the Department of Agriculture grew steadily until by 1930 it included some 40 subdivisions and bureaus, and operated with an appropriation of almost $100 million.[2] Its Bureau of Plant Industry introduced over 30,000 foreign plants including alfalfa from Liberia, short-kernel rice from Japan, seedless grapes from Italy, and grass from the Sudan to cover the High Plains; its Bureau of Entomology had field laboratories in every state to fight plant diseases; its Bureau of Animal Husbandry fought and conquered hog cholera, sheep scab, and Texas fever in cattle. It was the first government department to undertake extensive research and was, for a time, the leading research institution in the country. Nor was all of its research confined to the laboratory. In 1903 the department employed perhaps the most distinguished of agricultural scientists, Seaman Knapp of Iowa, to set up 'demonstration' farms throughout the South, and to fight the boll-weevil plague with techniques that every farmer could understand and use.

The Morrill Land-Grant College Act of 1862 not only had a great impact on education but was the most important piece of agricultural legislation in American history. This far-sighted law, which provided for the appropriation of public land to each state for the establishment of agricultural and industrial colleges, discriminated heavily in favor of the more populous states of the East — where farming was of less importance — and against the agricultural states of the West. New York State got almost a million acres of Western lands, while Kansas, which depended entirely on agriculture, got 90,000 acres. Seventeen of the

2. In 1968 the Federal government spent $5.9 billion on agriculture.

states, including Illinois, Wisconsin, and Minnesota, turned the Morrill land-grant money over to the existing state universities; others, like Iowa, Indiana, and Oregon, chose to set up independent agricultural and mechanical colleges. This made for expensive duplication of facilities, but assured educational experiments and paid dividends when the rush of college students got to be more than any one state institution could handle. At first agricultural colleges were looked upon by the practical farmer with suspicion, but in time farmers learned their value and came to take pride in them. Milburn Wilson, an Iowa farm boy later active in the Department of Agriculture, recalled:

> When I went to Ames (Iowa) to study agriculture in 1902 I was not the first boy in my Iowa neighborhood to go to college, but I was the first boy from that neighborhood to go on to an agricultural college. Ten or fifteen years later it was becoming an accepted thing for all who could afford it. A few farmers began to keep books, count costs, and calculate where profit came and loss occurred. Still more farmers began to feed their stock scientifically, following the advice from Feeders' Hints columns in the farm journals. Alfalfa came in, and farmers became aware of nitrogen needs of the soil. Dairymen began building up new herds of high-producing Holsteins. Hardy and rust-resistant strains of wheat were accepted eagerly by more farmers. Hog men improved their stock, and inoculated against cholera. Finally came the popular demand for county agents — for thoroughly trained men to bring to farmers the advantages of scientific training.[3]

Scarcely second to the Morrill Act in importance is the Hatch Act of 1887. Influenced by the valuable work performed by the experimental station of Wesleyan University in Middletown, Connecticut, Congress provided in this act for the creation of agricultural experiment stations in every state in the Union; since that time Congress has steadily supported and expanded the work of education and experimentation in agriculture.

Scientific farming, the conquest of plant and animal diseases, the surmounting of natural obstacles, and the adaptation of plants to American conditions — each has its roll of pioneers and heroes. Mark Alfred Carleton who experienced on the Kansas plains the devastations of wheat rust and rot and the vagaries of Kansas weather, scoured the wilds of Asia for a wheat strong enough to withstand the rust, the droughts, and the

3. *Agriculture in Modern Life*, Harper Bros., pp. 223–4.

frosts of the Middle West. He returned with the famous Kubanka wheat
and later introduced the Kharkov wheat to the American farmer. Within
a few years these plants demonstrated their superiority to the domestic
variety, and by 1919 over one-third of the American wheat acreage was
of the varieties introduced by Carleton. William Saunders and Angus
Mackay of Canada succeeded in crossing Red Fife with Calcutta wheat,
and produced the hardy Marquis, thus opening up millions of acres of
land in the Canadian Northwest to winter wheat. Niels Ebbesen Hansen
of the South Dakota Agricultural College explored the steppes of
Turkestan and the plateaus of inner Mongolia and brought back a
yellow-flowered alfalfa that would flourish in the American Northwest.
From Algeria and Tunis and the oases of the Sahara came the famous
white Kaffir corn, introduced by Dr. J. H. Watkins, and admirably
adapted to the hot dry climate of the great Southwest. George Hoffer
conquered the insidious rot that destroyed the corn of the Middle West;
Marion Dorset found the remedy for hog cholera; and George Mohler
helped to stamp out the dread hoof and mouth disease that threatened
to wipe out a large part of American livestock. Dr. Stephen M. Babcock
saved the dairy farmers of the nation millions of dollars through the use
of the Babcock milk test which determined the amount of butter fat
contained in milk; he gave the patent to the University of Wisconsin.
Seaman Knapp found in the Orient varieties of rice wonderfully adapted
to the Gulf region, and today Louisiana exports rice to China and Japan.
Luther Burbank, working in his experimental garden at Santa Rosa,
California, succeeded in creating a host of new plants by skillful crossing. David A. Coker, on his South Carolina experimental farm, improved
upland cotton and added immeasurably to the wealth of his section, and
George Washington Carver of the Tuskegee Institute developed hundreds of new uses for the peanut, the sweet potato, and the soy bean.

Scientific agriculture, whose benefits were world-wide, made it possible to raise more and better crops on less land, and even before the turn
of the century the American farmer was plagued by over-production.
But the impulse that had for generations sent American pioneers out
looking for virgin soil persisted. Tantalized by the vision of millions of
acres of land in the West that needed only a little damp to blossom like
a garden, the farmers undertook, or persuaded the government to
sponsor, ambitious projects of irrigation and reclamation. Artificial irrigation had been practiced by the Pueblo Indians even before the
coming of the white man, and later by the Spanish missions of the

Southwest, but it first came into general use with the Mormon settlements in Utah. Major Powell had suggested, in his famous Report of 1878, that much of the arid land of the West could be reclaimed by irrigation and had proposed that the Federal Government establish irrigation colonies comparable to those that already flourished in Utah and Colorado. Out of all this came the Carey Act of 1894 and the Newlands Reclamation Act of 1902. Together these opened up some millions of acres of Western land through state-federal co-operation. By 1910 some 14 million acres of land were under irrigation — a figure which increased by only 5 million in the next 20 years.

5. THE AGRICULTURAL REVOLUTION IN THE SOUTH

The Civil War and Reconstruction shattered the old plantation regime in the South and brought about a widespread redistribution of the land and revolutionary patterns of land-tenure. The planter class had been badly crippled by war and emancipation, and during Reconstruction thousands of planters were forced to the wall. Out of this came the most far-reaching transfer of land-ownership since the Revolution, as yeoman farmers, small merchants and businessmen, Northern soldiers, carpetbaggers, and investors snapped up what looked like bargains in land. On the surface this meant not only a redistribution of land-ownership but the breakup of plantations into small farms and a striking increase in land-ownership. In 1860 there were 33,171 farms in South Carolina, 55,128 in Alabama, and 17,328 in Louisiana; twenty years later there were 93,328 in South Carolina, 135,864 in Alabama, 48,292 in Louisiana. Between 1860 and 1880 the number of farms in nine cotton states increased from approximately 450,000 to some 1,110,000, while the average size of farms declined from 347 to 156 acres, and the number of farms under ten acres jumped almost twentyfold.

But these figures are misleading. The years after the war saw a revolution not in land-ownership but in farm labor. The number of large farms (or plantations) remained about the same, but now they were divided up into small 'holdings' and farmed not by slaves but by sharecroppers and tenants. In Louisiana the percentage of farms over 100 acres actually went up in the two decades after secession from 34 to 70 and a census of Louisiana parishes of 1910 which took account of *ownership* rather than of *tenancy* reported the average farm to be 904 acres. In short, if we look to ownership rather than to cultivation the agricultural revolution — like the famous Cheshire cat — fades away, all but the grin. As C. Vann Woodward concludes, the agricultural revolution was in fact

> the plantation minus such scant efficiency, planning, responsible supervision, and soil conservation as the old system provided . . . minus the ordinary minimum of economic virtues associated with proprietorship . . . minus even an owner who lived on its soil, and spent the profits of another's labor on his own family. The evils of land monopoly, absentee ownership, soil mining, and the one-crop system, once associated with and blamed upon slavery, did not disappear, but were instead, aggravated, intensified, and multiplied.[4]

The explanation was to be found in the operation of the sharecrop and the crop-lien systems. These twin evils emerged as a response to the breakdown of the old labor system and the collapse of credit after the war. The sharecrop system was an arrangement whereby planters could obtain labor without paying wages and landless farmers could get land without paying rent. Instead of an interchange of money for labor and rent, there was a sharing of crops. The planter furnished his tenant with land and frame cabin, and, generally, with seed, fertilizer, a mule, a plow, and other farm implements; in return he received at the end of the year one-half of the crop which the tenant raised. The tenant furnished his labor, and received, in return, the rest of the crop as well as whatever he could raise for himself in his vegetable garden. At the close of the war most of the freedmen and many of the poorer white [5] farmers entered into just such an arrangement with the landowners. This system, which appeared at first to be mutually advantageous, was really injurious to all. The sharecropper was rarely able to escape from the tenant class into the farm-owning class; the planter was seldom able to farm profitably or scientifically with sharecrop labor. The method was, said the U.S. Commissioner of Agriculture, 'the best possible plan to destroy fertility and profit and demoralize labor.' With every year the number of tenant farmers increased, the profits from farming and the fertility of the soil decreased. In 1880, when the first records were made, one-third of the farmers of the Cotton Belt were tenants; forty years later the proportion had increased to two-thirds.

4. *Origins of the New South*, pp. 179–80.
5. Four-fifths of the Negro farmers were tenants or sharecroppers, but probably less than one-half the white farmers.

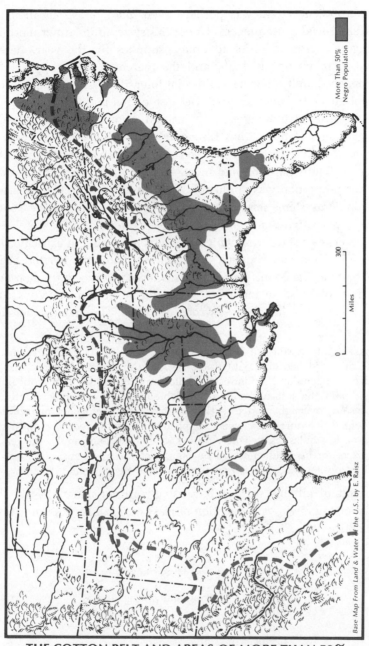

THE COTTON BELT AND AREAS OF MORE THAN 50%
NEGRO POPULATION IN 1910

The crop-lien system was perhaps even more disastrous in its economic and social consequences. Under this system the farmer mortgaged his ungrown crop in order to obtain supplies for the year. Rates of interest were usuriously high, and the merchant who supplied food, clothing, seed, and other necessities customarily charged from 20 to 50 per cent above the normal price. Because cotton and tobacco were sure money crops, creditors generally insisted that most of the land be planted to one of these, thus discouraging diversification of crops and bringing about exhaustion of the soil. As early as 1880 two-thirds of the farmers of South Carolina had mortgaged their ungrown crops, and by 1900 this proportion was applicable to the entire cotton belt. Sharecrop and crop-lien systems served to keep the poorer farmers of the South in a state of perpetual bondage to the large planters, country storekeepers and bankers — a state from which few were ever able to extricate themselves. For when the cropper's share failed to meet the inflated charges against him at the country store, he was forced to renew the lien on his next crop to the same merchant — and often on more onerous conditions. When this happened, wrote Matthew Hammond, the sharecropper

> passed into a state of helpless peonage. . . . With the surrender of this evidence of indebtedness he has also surrendered his freedom of action and his industrial autonomy. From this time until he has paid the last dollar of his indebtedness, he is subject to the constant oversight and direction of the merchant. Every mouthful of food he purchases, every implement that he requires on the farm, his mules, cattle, the clothing for himself and family, the fertilizers for his land, must all be bought of the merchant who holds the crop-lien, and in such amounts as the latter is willing to allow.[6]

The result of all this was an increasing impoverishment of the farm population, a growing stratification of class lines, and a determination to seek political redress.

6. THE 'FARM PROBLEM'

When we've wood and prairie land,
Won by our toil,
We'll reign like kings in fairy land,
Lords of the soil.

6. Matthew B. Hammond, *The Cotton Industry*, p. 149.

So sang Richard Garland and the 'trail-makers of the Middle Border' as
they pushed hopefully westward from the forests of Maine to the
coulees of Wisconsin, the prairies of Iowa, and the sun-baked plains of
Kansas, Nebraska, and the Dakotas. They won their wood and prairie
land, but often won it for others — for absentee landlords, railroads,
banks, and mortgage companies — and they lingered on as slaves, not
lords, of the soil. Within a generation the 'marching song of the Gar-
lands' gave way to a different tune:

> There's a dear old homestead on Nebraska's fertile plain,
>   There I toiled my manhood's strength away:
> All that labor now is lost to me, but it is Shylock's gain,
>   For that dear old home he claims today.

And when young Hamlin Garland wrote his *Main Travelled Roads* he
dedicated it to 'my father and mother, whose half-century of pilgrimage
on the main travelled road of life has brought them only pain and
weariness.'

Why should the pilgrimage of the farmer toward the sunset regions
have ended in weariness and pain? Why did the conquest of a continent
and the creation of a great agricultural domain result not in the realization of Jefferson's dream of a great agrarian democracy, but in a 'farm
problem'? First there was the physical problem of soil exhaustion and
erosion, drought and frost and flood, plant and animal diseases; the
economic problem of over-expansion and over-production, rising costs
and declining returns, exploitation in the domestic market and competition in the world market, mortgages and tenancy; the social problem of
isolation and drabness, inadequate educational, religious, medical, and
recreational facilities, narrowing opportunity and declining prestige.
Finally there was the political problem of wresting remedial legislation
from intransigent state and federal governments, which were much more
responsive to the demands of industry, transportation, and finance than
to the appeals of the farmer.

Of all these problems, the physical difficulties were the most intractable. The reckless mining of the soil, the cultivation of staple crops, the
destruction of the forests, resulted in soil erosion and flood. The use of
untrained Negro labor, the concentration upon cotton and tobacco
which exhaust the soil more rapidly than other crops, and heavy rainfall
made soil erosion peculiarly grave in the South. Almost 100 million acres
of that section — approximately one-sixth of the total — had been hope-

lessly lost or seriously impaired through erosion, and in some sections of the Piedmont as much as half of the arable land had been swept of its topsoil by 1930. Early travelers in the South recorded that the streams were as clear as those of New England, but by the twentieth century the rivers of the South, which every year carried out to the ocean over 50 million tons of soil, were mud-black or clay-red. The abuse of the Southern uplands, says one distinguished geographer, 'is well nigh incredible under the cotton economy, and the necessary breaking of that socio-economic pattern if the country is not ultimately to be left to the foxes and the briars is about as tough a task of regeneration as one can imagine.' Southern farmers have tried to replenish their worn-out soil with fertilizer, but that means an intolerable financial burden on the agricultural overhead. South Carolina, for example, long spent 15 per cent of its total farm income on fertilizer, and the proportion was almost as great in the other seaboard states. Not until the TVA began to produce cheap fertilizer and the New Deal to provide low-cost farm loans was the South able to inaugurate a program of reclamation and restoration.

In the grasslands of the West, too, erosion reached staggering proportions, necessitating irrigation and dry farming, and making the farmer helpless before dust storms and droughts.

> The primeval sod [writes Stuart Chase] has been burned, over-grazed, plowed up and destroyed. Where dry farming for wheat lands has been practised on the Great Plains, the Dust Bowl spreads. Where corn has been planted on the slopes of the tall grass regions, water erosion spreads. The sharp hooves of too many cattle and the close cropping of the grass by too many sheep have torn the cover from the open grazing lands, loosened the ancient sod, and started gullies and dunes of both water and wind erosion. One hundred and sixty-five million acres of grazing lands has been seriously depleted.[7]

Closely connected with erosion, and more serious to the individual farmer, were the recurrent droughts which brought crop failures, bankruptcy, and ruin to the farmers of the High Plains ever since they first ventured out on that forbidding land. Mari Sandoz has graphically described for us the effect of drought in western Nebraska in the early 'nineties:

7. *Rich Land, Poor Land*, McGraw-Hill, p. 41. Denuding the land of topsoil also exposed the farmer to a series of calamitous floods.

The drought exceeded all probability. Corn did not sprout. On the hardland fringe the buffalo grass was started and browned before the first of May. Even lighter soil south of the river produced nothing. The sandhills greened only in stripes where the water-logged sand cropped out. The lake beds whitened and cracked in rhythmical patterns. Grouse were scarce and dark-fleshed. Rabbits grew thin and wild and coyotes emboldened. Covered wagons like gaunt-ribbed, gray animals moved eastward, the occupants often becoming public charges along the way.[8]

Since that time the drought has been an ever-present menace. So hazardous, indeed, was farming in parts of the High Plains that in the 1930's officials of the Department of Agriculture concluded that nature did not design this section for intensive agriculture and seriously proposed the abandonment of farming over large areas.

The ravages of insect pests have been scarcely less serious than erosion and drought. 'Every year,' writes Dr. L. O. Howard of the Bureau of Entomology, 'the damage wrought by insects nullifies the labor of a million men.' Before the attack of the cinch bug and the corn borer, the boll weevil and the alfalfa weevil, the average farmer was all but helpless, and the plagues of grasshoppers have been like the locust plagues of ancient Egypt. What reader of Rölvaag's *Giants in the Earth* can forget how the grasshoppers destroyed not only the wheat but the morale of the farmers of the West:

> And now from out the sky gushed down with cruel force a living, pulsating stream, striking the backs of the helpless folk like pebbles thrown by an unseen hand. . . . This substance had no sooner fallen than it popped up again, crackling and snapping — rose up and disappeared in the twinkling of an eye; it flared and flittered around them like light gone mad; it chirped and buzzed through the air; it snapped and hopped along the ground; the whole place was a weltering turmoil of raging little demons; if one looked for a moment into the wind, one saw nothing but glittering, lightning-like flashes — flashes that came and went, in the heart of a cloud made up of innumerable dark-brown clicking bodies. All the while the roaring sound continued. . . . They whizzed by in the air; they literally covered the ground; they lit on the heads of grain, on the stubble, on everything in sight — popping and glittering, millions on millions of them. The people watched it stricken with fear and awe.[9]

8. *Old Jules,* Little, Brown & Co., p. 179.
9. *Giants in the Earth,* Harper & Bros., pp. 342–3.

More complex, but more readily susceptible to remedial action, was the farmer's economic problem: rising costs and falling prices. So long as farm land increased in value it was possible for individual farmers to sell out at a profit and thus have something to show for a lifetime of toil. But except for this increase in land values — an increase closely related to the general rise in the cost of living — American farming, for most of this period, operated at a loss.

In the generation after the Civil War the agricultural domain expanded too rapidly. This expansion westward brought ruin to the farmers of New England and the seaboard South and placed the Western farmer in a precarious position, because his future rested on unrealistic assumptions about the land, the weather, the market, and the credit system. Even official reports of the Kansas Board of Agriculture told prospective settlers: 'Kansas agriculture means a life of ease, perpetual June weather, and a steady diet of milk and honey.' One Kansas newspaper urged: 'Do not be afraid of going into debt. Spend money for the city's betterment as free as water. Too much cannot be spent this year, if properly applied. Let the bugaboo of high taxes be nursed by old women. Do all you can for Belle Plaine regardless of money, and let the increase of population and wealth take care of the taxes. Double, treble, quadruple our expenditures, and do it in the right manner, and before the year 1886 is passed Belle Plaine will be able to pay them and much more — and Belle Plaine will boom with a double pica, black face B.'

This boom spirit was exacerbated by the eagerness of Eastern banks and loan companies to lend money without discretion. Loan agents were often willing to agree to mortgages far in excess of the assets of the farms. *Rhodes Journal of Banking* estimated that the savings banks of New Hampshire and Vermont had invested 40 per cent of their funds in Western mortgages. So great was the desire of Easterners to speculate that competition existed not among borrowers but among lenders. The manager of one loan company reported: 'During many months of 1886 and 1887 we were unable to get enough mortgages for the people of the East who wished to invest in that kind of security. My desk was piled high every morning with hundreds of letters each enclosing a draft and asking me to send a farm mortgage from Kansas or Nebraska.'

This feverish optimism overlooked the fact that the opening up of the West was paralleled by a no less remarkable expansion of the agricul-

John Pierpont Morgan (1837-1913). Photograph by Edward Steichen

Immigrants. Photograph by Lewis W. Hine

Breaker Boys in a Coal Mine

A Sweat Shop (*c.* 1900)

Child Labor: A Tailor's Porter

Steelworkers' Noontime by Thomas Anschutz

Andrew Carnegie (1835-1919)

John D. Rockefeller, Sr. (1839-1937)

Mark Hanna (1837-1904)

James J. Hill (1838-1916)

Alexander Graham Bell (1847-1922)

Thomas A. Edison (1847-1931)

The Wright Brothers' First Flight, Kitty Hawk, N.C., December 1903

tural domain of Canada, the Argentine, Australia, Russia, and Brazil. So long as farming was primarily for subsistence and the market was largely domestic, this situation was not serious. But when the American farmer grew more than the American market could absorb — a condition with which the cotton planter was long familiar — he had to sell his product in the world market, and the price which he received, at home as abroad, was determined by the world market. Industry, which could regulate its production and which operated behind tariff walls, bought in a world market and sold in a protected market; agriculture, which could not effectively regulate its production and had little to gain from tariffs, bought in a protected market and sold in a world market.

There were two possible means by which the farmers might have overcome these disadvantages. The first was organization, looking to a limitation upon production. Transportation, finance, manufacturing, power, even labor, organized for self-protection, but the farmers were never able to organize successfully or to work out any voluntary limitation upon crops which would be at once effective and profitable. The second alternative was governmental action which would subsidize the farmer. Not until the administration of Franklin D. Roosevelt did the government undertake to aid agriculture as it had long aided industry, through loans, subsidies, and price guarantees.

Furthermore, as agricultural technology expanded, the farmer found himself more and more the victim rather than the beneficiary of the industrial revolution. The expansion of agriculture into the West meant an absolute dependence upon railroads, and freight charges came to consume an increasingly large share of the farmer's income. The *Prairie Farmer* asserted in 1867 that Iowa corn cost eight or ten times as much at Liverpool as the farmer received for it at the local grain elevator; thus corn that sold for 70 cents a bushel in the East might bring the farmer only ten or fifteen cents at the local exchange. In 1880 wheat fetched almost a dollar in the Chicago pit, but it cost 45 cents to ship a bushel of wheat from central Nebraska to Chicago. Almost equally burdensome were certain railroad practices against which the farmer protested in vain. The railroads came to control the warehouse facilities of the West, fixed the price for storage, and controlled grading.

The farmer sold his product in a competitive market, but purchased supplies, equipment, and household goods in a market which was protected against competition. The cost of his transportation was fixed by the railroads, of his manure by a fertilizer trust, of his farm implements by the McCormick Harvester Company, of his fencing by a barbed wire trust. The prices which he paid for daily necessities — for furniture and clothing, for lumber and leather goods — were artificially raised by the operation of protective tariffs.

Above all, the price which he paid for money was prohibitively high. Some states attempted, through usury laws, to fix low interest rates, but such laws were flouted or evaded, and interest rates in the farm belts of the South and West were seldom below 10 per cent and in the 'nineties much higher. Inadequate banking facilities were in part responsible. In 1880 the per capita banking power of the Eastern states was $176, of the Central states $27, and of the Southern states $10. Furthermore, with the rise in the value of money after the Civil War, the farmers' debt appreciated steadily. It took approximately 1200 bushels of wheat, corn, oats, barley, and rye to buy a $1000 mortgage in the years 1867 to 1869; between 1886 and 1888 it took approximately 2300 bushels of the same crops to repay that mortgage.

This was the heart of the matter. During most of the thirty years after the Civil War the farmer of the South and West was the victim not only of rising costs but of falling prices. Wheat which netted the farmer $1.45 a bushel in 1866 brought only 76 cents in 1869, 69 cents in 1889, and 49 cents in 1894, so that while the wheat crop in 1878 and again in 1889 was double what it had been in 1867 the farmers received approximately the same amount on the three crops. Corn which brought 75 cents at Chicago in 1869 fell to 38 cents in 1879 and to 28 cents in 1889. Twenty-three million bushels of rye brought $23 million in 1867 and 28 million bushels brought only $12 million in 1889. Cotton sold at 31 cents a pound in 1866, 9 cents in 1886 and 6 cents in 1893; less than 6 million bales of cotton sold, in 1884, for some $241 million; and approximately 10 million bales sold, in 1894, for $220 million.

Agriculture, which represented not quite half of the national wealth in 1860, accounted for but one-fifth of the national wealth half a century later. The value of manufactured products was 50 per cent higher in 1870 than the value of all farm products; by 1910 it was over twice as large. The farmer received 30 per cent of the national income in 1860, 19 per cent in 1890, 18 per cent in 1910, 13 per cent in 1920 and after the collapse of the early 'thirties, 7 per cent in 1933. Farm mortgages and tenancy increased correspondingly: 27 per cent of the farms operated by their owners were mortgaged in 1890; by 1910 the number had increased to 33 per cent; and by 1930 to 42 per cent. As a large part of these farm mortgages were held by mortgage companies, banks, and insurance companies in the East, the interest payment drained the rural sections for the benefit of the urban areas of the country; to many farmers this annual interest charge came to seem more like a tribute than a just payment for services rendered. Even more alarming were the mounting figures of farm tenancy. In 1880 one-fourth of all American farmers were tenants; by the turn of the century one-third of all farmers were tenants; thirty years later almost half the farmers of the nation were cultivating land which they did not own. In the beginning tenancy was largely confined to the Negroes of the South, but in the early years of the twentieth century it spread rapidly throughout the Middle West, and in the census of 1930 five of the leading Mid-Western farming states — Illinois, Iowa, Kansas, Nebraska, and South Dakota — showed over 40 per cent tenant farmers.

Farming yielded not only decreasing economic returns but also decreasing social returns. Before the coming of the automobile, the telephone, and the radio, the isolation of the farm was fearful. Thousands of families were cut off from companionship and conviviality, church and school. Thousands of mothers died in childbirth, thousands of children died through lack of simple medical care. Hamlin Garland tells us that when he wrote *Main-Travelled Roads,* he determined 'to tell the truth.'

> But I didn't. Even my youthful zeal faltered in the midst of a revelation of the lives led by the women on the farms of the middle border. Before the tragic futility of their suffering, my pen refused to shed its ink. Over the hidden chamber of their maternal agonies I drew the veil.

And when he revisited the Dakota country, he

> revolted from the gracelessness of its human habitations. The lonely box-like farm-houses on the ridges suddenly appeared to me like the dens of wild animals. The lack of color, of charm in the lives of the people anguished me. . . . All the gilding of farm life melted away. The hard and bitter realities came back upon me in a flood. Nature was as beautiful as ever . . . but no splendor of cloud, no grace of sunset could conceal the poverty of these people, on the contrary they brought out, with a more intolerable poignancy, the gracelessness of these homes, and the sordid quality of the mechanical daily routine of these lives.[10]

10. The quotations are from *A Son of the Middle Border,* Macmillan, pp. 356–65, 416.

In 1887, Garland wrote: 'The dress of all the farmers I met seemed unkempt, miserable. George A's house showed rude comfort, but not a trace of beauty. Rag carpets, old gunny sacks on the floor. George and his family were eating their Sunday dinner of bread and milk. He was in his shirt sleeves with bare feet. The table was covered with blue oilcloth with vast pitchers of milk and dishes of pickles. The irritable women dragged their tired and ugly bodies around, unlovely, characterless, finding comfort only in the gospels.' Charles Edward Russell recalled: 'The jolly husbandman was a myth; I think I seldom saw a farmer in those days that did not look worsted in the battle of life.'

It was the women who suffered most from the niggardliness and narrowness of farm life. The confession of Benét's John Vilas might have been that of a whole generation of pioneers:

> I took my wife out of a pretty house,
> I took my wife out of a pleasant place,
> I stripped my wife of comfortable things,
> I drove my wife to wander with the wind.[11]

No wonder it was so often the wives and the mothers who inspired the revolt against the farm, who encouraged their sons and daughters to try their fortunes in the cities.

The cities offered not only business and professional opportunities, but facilities for education and recreation that were not to be found in the average rural community. City life conferred, too, a social prestige that no longer attached to farm life. The farmers, who had once been regarded as 'the chosen people of God,' came to be looked upon as 'hayseeds' and 'hicks,' fit subjects for the comic strip or the vaudeville joke. An ever increasing number of young people, unwilling to accept the drudgery and frustration that their parents had suffered, left the farms for the cities. The same thing was happening in the Old World, and this movement from the farm to the city was a significant part of that immense ferment that brought millions of European peasants to American cities during these years. Between 1870 and 1930 the rural population declined from over 80 to less than 40 per cent of the total, and the decline in the actual farm population was even more precipitous.

It must not be supposed that the farmer made no effort to save him-

11. *John Brown's Body*, p. 143.

self. For almost every problem he had a solution, one that was usually reasonable and intelligent. But those solutions generally required legislative action from state or federal government, and in the generation after the Civil War the farmer was seldom in a position to obtain such action. From Jefferson to Jefferson Davis the politics of the nation had been guided chiefly by those who were responsible to the farmers. But with the shift in population from the farm to the city, the rise of giant railroad and industrial corporations, and the concentration of financial power in the East, this situation changed. The farmers still constituted the largest single economic group in 1870, but they could not bridge the sectional barrier. Although the Southern planter and the Middle Western farmer shared similar problems, they failed to forge an effective alliance. But railroad, banking, and industrial interests, unperturbed by any sectional cleavage, presented a united front to matters that concerned them; and political parties became increasingly subservient to these interests. Farmers everywhere wanted railroad regulation, but the railroad was the most powerful single interest in New Hampshire as in California, in Nebraska as in Georgia, and except for the brief Granger interlude the efforts of farmers to enact railroad rate bills met defeat. The vast majority of farmers wanted cheap money and a more flexible banking system, but they got neither. Nor were the farmers more successful in placing their representatives in state legislatures or in Congress. Lawyers and businessmen constituted the majority of the legislatures even in such states as Georgia and Nebraska, while in the halls of Congress a 'dirt' farmer was something of a curiosity. In the whole period from 1860 to 1928 no candidate of a major party was a genuine farmer.

7. AGRARIAN REVOLT

When the bubble of Civil War prosperity burst in 1868, the collapse of farm prices resulted in the first agrarian revolt. This revolt took various forms: the election of legislatures, governors, and often congressmen sympathetic to the farmers' demands; the passage of laws regulating freight and elevator charges; the organization of co-operative societies and eventually of local and even national political parties.

The first and most important of the societies was the Patrons of Husbandry, commonly known as the Grange. In 1866 President Johnson sent

Oliver H. Kelley, a clerk in the Bureau of Agriculture, on a tour of investigation through the South. Kelley returned deeply impressed with the poverty, isolation, and backwardness of the farmers of that section, and determined to organize a farmers' society which might ameliorate these evils. In 1867 he and a group of government clerks in Washington, D.C., founded the Patrons of Husbandry, and in the following year the first permanent Grange of this society was established in Fredonia, New York. By the end of 1870 there were Granges in nine states and when the panic of 1873 burst, the Grange had penetrated every state but four. Two years later it boasted a membership of over 800,000, organized in some 20,000 local Granges, most of them in the Middle West and the South.

The purpose of the Grange, as set forth in its 1874 declaration, was 'to develop a better and higher manhood and womanhood among ourselves. To enhance the comforts and attractions of our homes, and strengthen our attachments to our pursuits. To foster mutual understanding and co-operation. . . . To buy less and produce more, in order to make our farms self-sustaining. To diversify our crops, and crop no more than we can cultivate. . . . To discountenance the credit system, the mortgage system, the fashion system, and every other system tending to prodigal-ity and bankruptcy.' The major function of the Grange, as conceived by its founders and announced in its declarations, was social, and it was as a social institution that it made its most useful contribution. One secret of its success was the policy of admitting women to membership, and for farmers' wives the Grange, with its monthly meetings and picnics, lectures and entertainments, offered an escape from the loneliness and drudgery of the farm. To the women of the Middle Border the Grange, and later the Alliance, suggested a more generous life, and when the heroine of Garland's *A Spoil of Office* spoke at the farmers' picnic, it was the cultural aspects of the movement that she stressed:

> I see a time [said Ida Wilbur] when the farmer will not need to live in a cabin on a lonely farm. I see the farmers coming together in groups. I see them with time to read, and time to visit with their fellows. I see them enjoying lectures in beautiful halls, erected in every village. I see them gather like the Saxons of old upon the green at evening to sing and dance. I see cities rising near them with schools, and churches, and concert halls and theatres. I see a day when the farmer will no longer be a drudge and his wife a bond slave, but happy men and women who will go singing to their

pleasant tasks upon their fruitful farms. When the boys and girls will not go west nor to the city; when life will be worth living. In that day the moon will be brighter and the stars more glad and pleasure and poetry and love of life come back to the man who tills the soil.[12]

The Grange was formally non-political, but almost from the beginning the movement took on a distinctly political character. In Illinois, Iowa, Wisconsin, Minnesota, Kansas, California, and elsewhere the farmers elected their candidates to legislatures and judgeships, and agitated for farm relief through railway and warehouse regulation. The result was the so-called Granger laws limiting railroad and warehouse charges and outlawing some of the grosser railway abuses.

The Grangers also embarked upon business ventures. In an attempt to eliminate the middleman, they established hundreds of co-operative stores on the Rochdale plan, whereby profits were divided among the shareholders, in proportion to their purchases. They set up co-operative creameries, elevators, and warehouses, organized farmers' insurance companies, and constructed their own factories which turned out excellent reapers, sewing machines, wagons, and similar things for half the price charged by private concerns. Kelley from the first opposed such business activities. 'This purchasing business,' he said, 'commenced with buying jackasses; the prospects are that many will be *sold*.' In the end his sour prophecy was justified. Owing to the relentless opposition by business and banking interests, the individualism of the farmers, overexpansion and mismanagement, most of the co-operative enterprises failed. Yet some good resulted from the foray of the Grangers into business. Prices were reduced, thousands of farmers saved money, and with the establishment of Montgomery Ward and Company in 1872 specifically 'to meet the wants of the Patrons of Husbandry' the mail-order business came into existence. By 1880 Grange membership had fallen to 100,000. Chastened by experience, the Grange confined itself therefore largely to social activities.

The Grange gave way to the more aggressive Farmers' Alliances, and the history of farm revolt during the 'eighties and 'nineties is largely that of the Alliance movement. There were, at the start, several Alliances, but by the late 'eighties consolidation and amalgamation had resulted in the creation of two powerful groups, the Northwestern Alli-

12. A *Spoil of Office*, p. 14.

ance, and the Farmers' Alliance and Industrial Union, commonly known as the Southern Alliance. The first effective organization of the Northwestern Alliance was undertaken by Milton George, editor of the *Western Rural Magazine,* and the platform which he drew up in 1880 proposed to 'unite the farmers of America for their protection against class legislation, and the encroachments of concentrated capital and the tyranny of monopoly.' The Northwestern Alliance was particularly strong in Kansas, Nebraska, Iowa, Minnesota, and the Dakotas, and during the hard times of the late 'eighties it increased its membership by leaps and bounds and became a major power in the politics of the Middle Border. The Southern Alliance dates back to a cattlemen's association in Lampasas County, Texas, in the middle 'seventies. In the late 'eighties, under the guidance of the astute C. W. Macune, this Texas Alliance began to absorb other Southern farmers' organizations such as the Arkansas Wheel and the Louisiana Farmers' Union, and affiliated with the powerful Colored Farmers' National Alliance which claimed more than a million members. By the early 'nineties the Southern Alliance boasted a membership of from one to three million and was the most powerful farmers' organization in the country. It had three times as many members as the Northwestern Alliance, and was much more radical. Despite an obvious community of interest between the Northern and the Southern Alliances, all efforts to achieve an amalgamation of the two organizations foundered on the rocks of sectionalism.

The activities of the Alliances were as diverse as those of the Grange. Social activities embraced not only the customary meetings and picnics, but farmers' institutes, circulating libraries, and the publication of hundreds of farm newspapers and dozens of magazines, so that the Alliance became, in the words of one observer, a farmers' national university. The economic enterprises of the Alliance were more substantial and ambitious than those of the Grange. The Texas Alliance undertook co-operative buying and selling, the North Dakota Alliance underwrote co-operative insurance, the Illinois Alliance organized co-operative marketing. Thousands of farmer's 'exchanges' were established, and it was estimated that in 1890 the various Alliances did a business of over $10 million.

But historically the significance of the Alliance is to be found in its political rather than its social and economic activities. From the first the Alliances entered more vigorously into politics than had the Grange, for the Alliance programs required political action. Those programs embraced demands for strict regulation or even government ownership of railroads and other means of communication, currency inflation, the abolition of national banks, the prohibition of alien land ownership and of trading in futures on the exchange, a more equitable taxation, and various progressive political reforms. An original contribution of the Alliance was the so-called Sub-Treasury scheme, which provided that the government should establish warehouses where the farmers might deposit non-perishable farm produce, receiving in exchange a loan of money up to 80 per cent of the market value of the produce, which might be redeemed when the farmer had sold his produce. This scheme had the triple advantage of enabling the farmer to borrow at a low rate of interest, sell his produce at the most favorable market price, and profit by an expanded and flexible currency. When first advanced, it was regarded as a socialistic aberration, but the Warehouse Act of 1916 and the Commodity Credit Corporation of 1933 adopted a similar proposal as national policy. By 1890, the Alliances, with an ambitious set of legislative demands, were prepared to plunge into national politics to launch the Populist movement, the most far-reaching organization of farm protest in the history of the nation.

Politics

1. MASKS IN A PAGEANT

There is no drearier chapter in American political history than that which records the administrations of Hayes, Garfield, Arthur, Cleveland, and Harrison. Civil War issues were dead, though politicians continued to flay the corpses. National politics became little more than a contest for power between rival parties waged on no higher plane than a struggle for traffic between rival railroads. 'One might search the whole list of Congress, Judiciary, and Executive during the twenty-five years 1870–1895 and find little but damaged reputations,' wrote Henry Adams. 'The period was poor in purpose and barren in results.'

At first glance it would appear that this was an era of Republican supremacy. No Democrat had entered the White House with as much as 50 per cent of the vote since Franklin Pierce in 1852, and none would again until Franklin D. Roosevelt 80 years later. The Republicans came out of the war as the party of the union, the nation's legitimate party, while the Democrats were tarred with secession and even treason. As the Grand Old Party that had stood by the flag, the Republicans claimed the support of all loyal Americans. They 'waved the bloody shirt' to remind voters of the atrocities committed by the Confederacy, and for a generation counselled: 'Vote the way you shot.' The Grand Army of the Republic, the leading veterans organization, mobilized the vote of old soldiers for the Republican party, and for nine of ten campaigns beginning in 1868 the G.O.P. chose a military figure as their presidential nominee;

during that same period, the Democrats did so only once. The party's stronghold was New England and the belt of New England migration across northern New York, the Old Northwest, and sweeping west to Oregon, the region which had been the center of anti-slavery sentiment. Since this sector was rural and Protestant, the party was strongly inclined toward temperance and nativism, especially anti-Catholicism.

As a legacy of the Civil War era, the Republicans won the allegiance of Negro voters. Yet this did not prevent the party from playing a double game in the South. Some leaders wanted to use federal force to protect the freedman's right to vote in the South, either out of solicitude for the Negro or in order to prevail at the polls. But others attempted to create a 'lilywhite' Republican party in the South. This policy was pressed by Northern industrialists, who hoped to find allies in the New South for their tariff policies; by merchants in border cities like Cincinnati who feared that agitating the Negro question would jeopardize North-South trade; and by publicists who had come to share the racial outlook of the old slavocracy. 'The negro will disappear from the field of northern politics,' wrote E. L. Godkin's Nation in April 1877. 'Henceforth the nation, as a nation, will have nothing more to do with him.' Neither strategy succeeded in breaking the Democratic hold on the South, and after the abortive attempt to push through a Force bill in 1890, most Republicans abandoned the Southern Negro. By the end of the century, the South, with Northern acquiescence, had virtually completed black disenfranchisement.

Outside the South, the Republicans commanded the support of the gentry and were accepted by many as the party of culture and respectability. One Republican Senator explained:

> The men who do the work of piety and charity in our churches, the men who administer our school system, the men who own and till their own farms, the men who perform skilled labor in the shops, the soldiers, the men who went to war and stayed all through, the men who paid the debt and kept the currency sound and saved the nation's honor, the men who saved the country in war and have made it worth living in in peace, commonly and as a rule, by the natural law of their being, find their places in the Republican party. While the old slave-owner and slave-driver, the saloon keeper, the ballot-box stuffer, the Ku Klux Klan, the criminal class of the great cities, the men who cannot read or write, commonly and as a rule, by the natural law of their being, find their congenial place in the Democratic party.

Along the elm-lined streets of New England and the Old Northwest, not a few thought of the Democratic party as an almost illegitimate organization. Frederic Howe recalled: 'There was something unthinkable to me about being a Democrat — Democrats, Copperheads and atheists were persons whom one did not know socially. As a boy I did not play with their children.'

Despite these disadvantages, the Democrats showed impressive strength, largely because they were less of a sectional party than the Republicans. In 1880 the Democratic presidential candidate captured every Southern state; thereafter Republicans confronted the formidable obstacle of Democratic monopoly of the 'Solid South.' Powerful not only in the South but in the border states and the Southern belt of migration in the Midwest, the Democrats could capitalize on their following in Northern cities to give the Republicans a close race. In 1880 the Democrats had a plurality of 24,000 in the country's twelve largest cities; by 1892, the margin had reached 145,000. The Democrats could count especially on the vote of most Irish Catholics, while the Republicans recruited the natural enemies of the Irish, especially British immigrants and French Canadians. Burton K. Wheeler remembered that to win Democratic nomination in Butte 'it was best to claim nativity in County Cork and second best to claim birth in some county in Ireland with slightly less prestige in Montana.'

By 1874 the two parties had struck an equilibrium, and for the next two decades each election turned on a very small number of votes. In the five presidential contests from 1872 to 1892, the Republicans failed to capture a majority of the popular vote even once, and in three of these elections the difference between the major party candidates was less than 1 per cent. From 1877 to 1897 the Democrats controlled the presidency and Congress at the same time for but two years; the Republicans achieved this for four years, but in only two of these did they have a working majority. With popular allegiances so closely divided, party leaders sought to put together winning combinations in the Electoral College by concentrating their attention on the 'doubtful states,' especially New York, with its large electoral vote, and Ohio and Indiana, where the belts of Northern and Southern migration were roughly equal. During these years, the Republicans almost always chose their presidential candidate from the Midwest and their vice-presidential nominee from New York; the Democrats generally picked their presidential contender from New York and his running mate from the Midwest.

Since the parties were roughly equal, political leaders were wary about introducing disturbing new issues that might break up their coalitions. In the South, Democrats agitated the race question and clamped a lid on economic issues that might prove divisive. In the North, the Republican party kept alive Civil War memories to distract attention from economic difficulties with which they did not choose to deal or often did not know how to deal, and which might split their party. 'Our strong ground,' Hayes wrote Blaine when he was campaigning for the presidency in 1876, 'is the dread of a solid South and rebel rule. I hope you will make these topics prominent in your speeches. It leads people away from hard times, which is our deadliest foe.' The politics of the period placed a premium not on innovators but on extreme partisans who united their party by reminding their followers of the perfidy of the opposition, and on the reconcilers of faction and of sectional antagonism who blurred issues in order to hold together their heterogeneous coalitions.

During the whole of this period the electorate played a game of blind man's buff, for no consequential issue divided the major parties. Questions of currency and the tariff broke on sectional rather than party lines. In 1876, for example, the Democrats took pains to nominate a hard-money New Yorker for president with a soft-money Indianan for vice-president to balance the ticket. Although America was emerging from her isolation and becoming a part of the community of nations, there was not much appreciation of the responsibilities which this new position involved. The country had recovered from the Civil War, but instead of encouraging sectional friendliness, politicians on both sides exploited sectional ill feeling. The industrial revolution, as it unfolded, made laissez-faire less and less valid; but politicians still prated of individualism. Big business was growing bigger, and thoughtful men recognized the conflict of 'wealth against commonwealth' which Henry D. Lloyd was soon to dramatize; but political leaders showed little awareness of the implications of these developments. The American farmer was threatened on all sides by forces over which he could exercise no effective control; but politicians in Washington lacked the imagination to understand even the existence of a farm problem until it was called to their attention by political revolt. There were issues enough before the American people, but candidates commonly evaded them and fought campaigns on the basis of personality, party, or inherited prejudice.

Behind the colorless titular leaders were the real rulers — men who sat in committee rooms listening to the demands of lobbyists, 'boys' who 'fried the fat' out of reluctant corporations. At the head of their ranks were great bosses like Roscoe Conkling of New York. Then there were the representatives of special interests — Standard Oil senators, sugar-trust senators, iron and steel senators, and railroad senators, men known by their business rather than their political affiliations, like Nelson Aldrich of Rhode Island. Yet there was always a small group of men in politics who preserved integrity and a sense of responsibility, men like Lyman Trumbull of Illinois.

James G. Blaine of Maine, Congressman, Senator, twice Secretary of State, and perpetual aspirant to the presidency, typified this era, as Clay and Webster did an earlier one. A man of indubitable intellectual power and of immense personal magnetism, Blaine was possibly the most popular figure in American politics between Clay and Bryan. Year after year thousands of men marched, shouted, and sang for 'Blaine of Maine' whom devoted followers pictured as the 'Plumed Knight,' paladin of all virtues and defender of the true Republican faith. At one Republican convention, when Blaine was absent on a trip with Andrew Carnegie in Scotland, the convention went wild when the band struck up 'My Heart's in the Highlands, My Heart's Not Here.' A magnificent orator, he could inspire a frenzy of enthusiasm by twisting the British lion's tail or solemnly intoning the platitudes of party loyalty. Yet he made no impression upon American politics except to lower its moral tone. He was assiduous in cementing a corrupt alliance between politics and business. Deliberately and violently he fanned the flames of sectional animosity. His name is connected with no important legislation; his sympathies were enlisted in no forward-looking causes. His vision was narrow and selfish, his ambitions personal and partisan. Nevertheless, he was rewarded with votes, office, power, and almost with the presidency.

Business had no party favorites except insofar as it preferred to invest in successful rather than unsuccessful candidates. Democratic senators such as Hill of New York, Gorman of Maryland, and Brice of Ohio could command the support of business quite as effectively as Republicans like Morton of New York, Cameron of Pennsylvania, or Foraker of Ohio. In a number of states, a single corporation dominated political life; such was the case in Montana under Anaconda Copper. The California rail-road king, Collis Huntington, conceded: 'Things have got to such a state that if a man wants to be a constable he thinks he has first got to come down to Fourth and Townsend streets to get permission.' But even when party leaders were most sympathetic to business, they frequently had institutional interests which were not identical with those of the corporations. And at the beginning of this period, politicians, far from being subservient to business, often preyed on merchants and importers; as a consequence, in cities like New York, businessmen played a prominent role in the campaign for civil service reform to curb the spoilsmen.

2. GLIMMERINGS OF REFORM

In an era of generally issueless politics, one group sought to introduce reforms: the patrician dissenters who advocated a civil service system. Members of the older gentry who were being pushed aside by the newly rising industrialists, they felt themselves plunged into a rude new world which did not accord them the deference they had been led to expect. Henry Adams later wrote of the return of his family to the United States in 1868 after several years abroad: 'Had they been Tyrian traders of the year 1000 B.C., landing from a galley fresh from Gibraltar, they could hardly have been stranger on the shore of a world, so changed from what it had been ten years before.' They looked back to a golden age just beyond their memory. Charles Eliot Norton thought the ideal community 'New England during the first thirty years of the century, before the coming in of Jacksonian Democracy, and the invasion of the Irish, and the establishment of the system of Protection.'

They loathed the industrialization of America and what it was doing not only to American politics but to American culture. 'Between you and me and the barber, I like it not,' wrote Richard Watson Gilder. 'The steam whistle attachment which you can see applied nowadays even to peanut stands in the winter streets; the vulgarizing of everything in life and letters and politics and religion, all this sickens the soul.' They were repelled by the increasing influence of nouveau riche businessmen in the postwar years. Richard Henry Dana wrote his son in 1873: 'Our politics look low and dark. Massachusetts has been represented too largely by mere business men, who have no ideas and no high aims, and go to Congress for business purposes only.'

These genteel reformers sought to emulate the British M.P. and were disappointed that America would not afford them the same recognition their friends in Parliament enjoyed. They were convinced that the hope of democracy lay in the conquest of politics by an educated elite. Like classic British liberals, they favored free trade, hard money, civil service reform, and opposition to both business and labor union monopolies. Their outlook was that of John Stuart Mill tempered by Matthew Arnold and Walter Pater; in his later years, as one writer noted, Godkin sighed because all of America was not like Cambridge, Massachusetts. Their ideas made their way through *The Nation* of Godkin, the *North American Review,* and *Harper's Weekly.* Most were Republicans, but they had bolted their party in 1872 to help launch the Liberal Republican movement and in 1884, as 'Mugwumps,' would leave their party again. In 1876, they found the Republican choice, Rutherford B. Hayes, acceptable, chiefly because they knew him to be honest. Joseph Pulitzer of the Democratic New York *World* cried: 'Hayes has never stolen. Good God, has it come to this?'

A well-educated lawyer, officer in the Union army, elected twice to Congress and for three terms governor of Ohio, Hayes was honest and able, but he was from the beginning seriously handicapped in his efforts to effect constructive measures. Not only the Democrats but even many of his own party followers refused to recognize his election as legitimate; they referred to him as 'His Fraudulency.' The factional disputes which had wrecked the harmony of the second Grant administration and of the Convention of 1876 were not allayed, and from the beginning Hayes incurred the animosity of Blaine, leader of the 'Half Breeds,' and the implacable hostility of Conkling, chieftain of the 'Stalwarts.' The elections of 1876 had preserved Democratic control of the House, and two years later this opposition party captured the Senate as well. At one point Hayes was reduced to the sorry state of having only three supporters in the Senate, and one of these was a relative. In the circumstances it is a tribute to Hayes that his administration was not a total failure.

That it was not a complete failure can be credited to the courage with which Hayes set out to cleanse his party of the corruption which had so seriously damaged it during the Grant administrations and to fulfill his pledges of civil service reform. He named a cabinet of moderates: as Secretary of State, William Evarts of New York who had defended Andrew Johnson at the impeachment trial; the able John Sherman as Secretary of the Treasury; the paladin of the patrician reformers, Carl Schurz, to be Secretary of the Interior. He broke with the principle of vindictive sectional rule by appointing a former Confederate officer, David Key of Tennessee, Postmaster General.

Hayes also attempted, somewhat quixotically, to reform the party system and lessen the control by local politicians of the federal government. He issued an executive order which forbade federal office-holders to manage the party politics of the country. 'Party leaders,' said Hayes to the astonishment of the politicians, 'should have no more influence in appointments than other equally respectable citizens.' Hayes was combatting a system under which the Senate, controlled by local machines, controlled the national party and in turn the federal government. Sherman supported Hayes's efforts at reform, and Schurz introduced new standards of honesty and efficiency into the Department of the Interior and cleaned up the nauseating corruption which disgraced the administration of the Indian Bureau.

But Hayes quickly found that if he was to govern he also had to be a leader of his party. He was soon dispensing patronage to the men who had put him in office like any other politician; especially scandalous was the way he rewarded every member of the notorious Louisiana returning board which had been instrumental in giving him the presidency. John Hay commented acidly: 'Not Pomeroy or Butler or Boss Tweed himself ever attempted to run an administration in the interests of his own crowd as this model reformer has done.' Although he thereafter made genuine efforts toward reform, removing some of Grant's most offensive appointees and cleaning up the New York custom house, he was never able to win the complete confidence of the civil service reformers.

Indecisive as it was, Hayes's struggle with the spoilsmen had considerable effect on American political history. That struggle was precipitated by Hayes's attempt to oust Chester A. Arthur and Alonzo B. Cornell from the New York custom house which was mismanaged and corrupt. Senator Conkling, alarmed at the assault on his political organization, persuaded the Senate to reject the nominations of those whom the President appointed to succeed Arthur and Cornell. Involved in this unseemly squabble was not merely a falling-out between two factions in the Republican party, or 'Senatorial courtesy,' but a larger issue of the American form of government. During the Johnson administration Congress had inaugurated a quasi-parliamentary form of government, and Grant had offered no effective resistance to the continuation of this parliamentary system. By such devices as the profligate use of legislative riders, Congress, since the Civil War, had so largely eaten into the presidential prerogative that the chief executive was by way of becoming a mere figurehead, like the President of the French Republic. The Republican Senate sought, as one writer noted, to turn the presidency 'into an office much like that of the doge of Venice, one of ceremonial dignity without real power.' Against this challenge the President set himself stubbornly, and in the end, with the support of the Democrats, he won out. His appointees were renominated and confirmed, and the normal and constitutional relationship between President and Congress began to be restored.

For the larger task of articulating the government to the new economic forces, Hayes was not prepared. He responded to the 'Great Strike' of 1877 by sending federal troops to put down the strikers. The resumption of specie payments, voted in 1875, caused an appreciation in the value of greenbacks that was hard on debtors, and when Congress tried a different solution of the money problem — the Bland-Allison Silver Act of 1878 — Hayes interposed his veto unsuccessfully. To the problems of railroad malpractices, trusts, and land frauds he gave no attention. He later confessed that 'the money-piling tendency of our country . . . is changing laws, government and morals, and giving all power to the rich, and bringing in pauperism and its attendant crimes and wickedness like a flood,' but when President he did not even hang out danger signals. His administration, for all its political drama, was largely negative.

As the election of 1880 approached, the Stalwarts proposed Grant for a third term, but he was blocked by the Half Breed leader, Blaine. One of the 306 Stalwarts who stuck by Grant to the end had 306 medals struck bearing the legend, 'The Old Guard,' thereby coining a new name for Republican regulars. A 'dark horse' from Ohio, General James A. Garfield, obtained the nomination. He was an educated gentleman with a good military record and long experience in Congress; but his party made a greater virtue of his log-cabin birth and early exploits as a canal bargee. To placate Conkling, who had supported Grant, the convention named his henchman, Chester A. Arthur, to the vice-presidency. The Democrats, to confirm their loyalty, nominated General Winfield Scott Hancock of Pennsylvania. Garfield won with a popular plurality of less than 10,000 in a total of over 9 million votes.

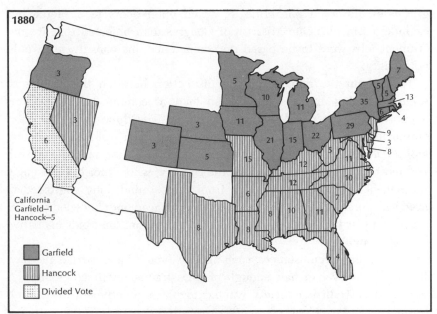

PRESIDENTIAL ELECTION, 1880

Four months after his inauguration, at the climax of another bitter patronage struggle with Conkling, Garfield was shot in the back by a disappointed office-seeker who boasted, 'I am a Stalwart and Arthur is President now.' After a gallant struggle for life, Garfield died on 19 September 1881. The shooting of Garfield, and his assassin's words, indicating he was murdering the President in order to replace him with a factional leader, brought the nation to its senses on the extremism of spoils politics and made the adoption of a civil service reform law all but inevitable.

Yet politicians fought the bill sponsored by 'Gentleman' George Pendleton of Ohio bitterly, some out of desire to preserve their control of patronage, others from a Jacksonian suspicion of the creation of a bureaucratic class. Opponents charged that a permanent civil service would produce an overbearing Prussian bureaucracy or a haughty class of Chinese civil servants. Others objected that a competitive examination was a class device which would discriminate against those too poor to afford a college education. If entrance was to be restricted to college graduates, observed one critic, it would open doors to a Pierce but exclude a Lincoln. One Mississippi Congressman objected that if government jobs were to be based on competence, his constituents would not qualify.

Throughout the debate ran the distinction between the scholar of useless learning and the unschooled man of common sense. Senator Matthew Carpenter of Wisconsin declared: 'The dunce who has been crammed up to a diploma at Yale, and comes fresh from his cramming will be preferred in all civil appointments to the ablest, most successful, and most upright business man of the country, who either did not enjoy the benefit of early education, or from whose mind, long engrossed in practical pursuits, the details and niceties of academic knowledge have faded away as the headlands disappear when the mariner bids his native land goodnight.'

Under other circumstances, such appeals would have carried the day. But the country had had enough of unrestrained factional politics. A rapidly industrializing society wanted to place government on a more businesslike basis. Congress in 1883 wrote the demands of the patrician reformers, the protests of the importers, and the public outcry at Garfield's death into law.

The Pendleton Act created a Civil Service Commission to administer a new set of rules which required appointments to be made as a result of open competitive examinations and prohibited assessments on office-holders for political purposes. By law these new rules were applied only to some 14,000 positions, about 12 per cent of the total, but the President was empowered to extend them to other parts of the service at his discretion. At the turn of the century there were not far from 100,000 in the classified civil service; at the end of Theodore Roosevelt's administration the number had more than doubled, and when Wilson left the White House it had increased to almost half a million. At the same time most states were passing civil service laws of their own. The emoluments were not sufficiently high to attract university graduates and other able men from business and the professions, but morale and efficiency improved greatly. It was fortunate that the merit principle was adopted before the twentieth century when administrative expansion greatly increased the need of honest men and expert service.

To the surprise of many, civil service reform had the ardent support of Garfield's successor, Chester A. Arthur. Long a satellite of the lordly

Conkling, the new President had nothing in his record to justify the hope that he would make more than a mediocre executive and much to arouse fear that he would be a very bad one. Handsome and affable, liked by businessmen and women of the world, he gave Washington its only 'society' administration between those of Buchanan and Theodore Roosevelt. Unexpectedly he developed a genuine independence and became something of a reformer. He severed his connections with the worst of the spoilsmen, vetoed an eighteen million dollar river and harbor bill, and prosecuted, with some vigor, the 'Star Route' frauds in the Post Office Department which had cost the government millions of dollars. Above all, he disappointed his former Stalwart cronies by coming out squarely for the merit system.

In only one other field did the Arthur administration make any contribution to the development of the nation. The War of the Pacific between Peru, Bolivia, and Chile, and the rising interest in an isthmian canal, awakened the American people to a realization of the decrepitude of their navy.[1] Twenty years after the building of the *Monitor* it was inferior to the navy of every principal European country, and to that of Chile. After long discussion Congress authorized on 5 August 1882 'two steam cruising vessels of war . . . to be constructed of steel of domestic manufacture.' The *Chicago* and the *Boston* entered active service in 1887, and a new era in American naval history began.

3. THE ADMINISTRATION OF GROVER CLEVELAND

Arthur's placid administration ended in the most exciting presidential campaign since the Civil War, although the only real issue between the parties was possession of the government. The Republicans, disappointed in Arthur, turned to the magnetic Blaine who had narrowly missed the nomination in 1880. He had served for a few months as Secretary of State under Garfield and Arthur, and had retired to write *Twenty Years of Congress,* a thousand-page celebration of the virtues and triumphs of the Republican party. Now it was his turn for the nomination, and he was not to be denied. But Blaine was more than

1. ' "I don't think I should like America." — "I suppose because we have no ruins and no curiosities," said Virginia, satirically. — "No ruins! no curiosities!" answered the Ghost; "you have your navy and your manners." ' Oscar Wilde, *The Canterville Ghost.*

conscientious Republicans could swallow. The principal charge against him was the prostitution of the speakership to personal gain; in that connection he could not explain the missive to a certain Fisher with the damning postscript, 'Burn this letter.' Even Conkling, when asked to campaign for Blaine, had replied, 'I don't engage in criminal practice.' Under the leadership of Carl Schurz and George William Curtis the reform wing of the party bolted from the convention, promised to support any decent nomination the Democrats might make, and proudly accepted the name 'Mugwump' which was given them in derision.[2] As bolting was the great offense in American political ethics, few of the Mugwumps managed to resume a political career; younger and shrewder politicians like Henry Cabot Lodge and Theodore Roosevelt, who supported Blaine while admitting the worst about him, had their reward.

With the Promised Land at last in sight, the Democrats made an admirable nomination. Grover Cleveland was a self-made man who as reform mayor of Buffalo and governor of New York had distinguished himself for firmness and integrity, to the disgust of Tammany Hall. 'We love him for the enemies he has made,' said General E. S. Bragg of Wisconsin in the nominating speech, and it required only two ballots for the convention to endorse this tribute. Powerful journals such as the *New York Times*, the *Springfield Republican*, *The Nation*, and *Harper's Weekly*, with Nast's telling cartoons, shifted over to Cleveland, as did scores of independents and liberal Republicans of the stripe of Charles Francis Adams and James Russell Lowell.

As the campaign proceeded it became noisy and nasty. Cleveland was charged, among other things, with having an illegitimate child, which he admitted, to the consternation of his supporters. But, as one of them concluded philosophically, 'We should elect Mr. Cleveland to the public office which he is so admirably qualified to fill, and remand Mr. Blaine to the private life which he is so eminently fitted to adorn.' Democratic torchlight processions paraded the streets, shouting,

> Blaine, Blaine, James G. Blaine,
> The continental liar from the State of Maine
> *Burn this letter!*

2. Mugwump, a term applied on this occasion by the New York *Sun,* is the word for 'great captain' in Eliot's Indian Bible.

To which Republican processions retorted:

> Ma! Ma! Where's my pa?
> Gone to the White House,
> *Ha! Ha! Ha!*

The contest was bitterly fought throughout the North; Hendricks, the Democratic vice-presidential nominee, added to the strength of the ticket in the critical state of Indiana, and the Mugwumps played an important role in New Jersey and Connecticut. But New York was the decisive state. Here Blaine had a strong following among the Irish-Americans, which he lost at the eleventh hour through the tactless remark of a clerical supporter. As spokesman for a visiting delegation, a hapless parson named Burchard described the Democracy as the party of 'Rum, Romanism, and Rebellion.' Blaine neglected to rebuke this insult to the faith of his Celtic friends; Cleveland carried New York by a plurality of 1149 in a vote of over a million; and New York's electoral votes gave him the presidency. Yet the crucial point is that the net shift compared to the previous election was the smallest of any in American history.

For a person of such generous bulk, Grover Cleveland was remarkably austere, unbending, and ungenial. He was a man of integrity, courage, and steadfast devotion to duty; but singularly lacking in imagination and never quite at home in the rough and tumble of party politics. Nor did he understand the problems of the farmers of the South and the West or the urban workers. Elected at a period when subservience to the popular will was supposed to be the first political virtue, he remained inflexible in the right as he saw it, and made few departures from his preconceived notions.

Cleveland believed in minimal government intervention. He hated paternalism in all forms: the tariff, land grants to railroads, pensions, social welfare legislation. He reflected his party's suspicion of strong government, a consequence in part of Southern resentment of Reconstruction, in part of the long period out of power which taught the Democrats to act as opposers. They were so much the party of state rights and limited government that Republican Speaker Tom Reed asked: 'Are they but an organized "no"?'

Cleveland's attitude toward government action is exemplified by his veto of the Texas Seed Bill in 1887, with a message that has frequently been quoted in the past generation by opponents of the Welfare State. In reply to requests from sufferers of a severe drought in Texas, Congress had voted the small sum of $10,000 for seed grain. When Cleveland vetoed the measure, he declared:

> I do not believe that the power and duty of the General Government ought to be extended to the relief of individual suffering which is in no manner properly related to the public service or benefit. A prevalent tendency to disregard the limited mission of this power and duty should, I think, be steadfastly resisted, to the end that the lesson should constantly be enforced — though the people support the Government, the Government should not support the people. Federal aid in such cases encourages the expectation of paternal care on the part of the Government and weakens the sturdiness of our national character. The friendliness and charity of our countrymen can always be relied upon to relieve their fellow-citizens in misfortune.

It was character that made Cleveland's administration the most respectable between Lincoln's and Theodore Roosevelt's. He alone of the titular leaders of either party had sufficient courage to defy the groups that were using the government for selfish purposes and to risk his career in defense of what he thought was right. He advanced civil service reform, challenged the predatory interests that were engrossing the public lands of the nation, denounced the evils of protection and dramatized the tariff issue, and called a halt to the raids on the Treasury by war veterans and their lobbyists. If the total achievements of his administration were negative, even that was something of a virtue at a time when too many politicians were saying 'yes' to the wrong things.

Shortly after Cleveland's inauguration the question of patronage arose. Deserving Democrats, deprived of the sweets of office for twenty-five years, demanded as clean a sweep as the law would allow — 88 per cent clean; virtuous Mugwumps insisted on no sweep at all. On one occasion the President broke out, 'The d — d everlasting clatter for office continues to some extent, and makes me feel like resigning, and Hell is to pay generally.' Congress repealed the Tenure of Office Act, which left the President free again to remove incumbents without permission of the Senate; and by the end of his term, Cleveland, despite his intense dislike for the spoils system, had replaced nearly all the postmasters and about half the other officials. Yet Cleveland did more for civil service reform than any President before Theodore Roosevelt. When he entered office some 43,000 places were filled by the merit system; when he left, in 1897, this was the case for 86,932 out of a total of about 200,000. But he pleased neither the Democrats nor the Mugwumps.

Cleveland stirred up the old soldiers by appointing General Lucius Quintus Cincinnatus Lamar, C.S.A., Secretary of the Interior; by proposing to return to their states the captured Confederate battle flags; and above all by his attitude toward pensions. The pension situation, already scandalous, was shortly to become preposterous. The first general Civil War pension bill, passed in 1862, was based upon the sound theory that it was the duty of the government to pension veterans who suffered from disabilities contracted while in military service, and to assist the widows and children of these veterans. Under this law not far from 900,000 claims had been filed by veterans or their dependents prior to the accession of Cleveland to the presidency. Of these some 520,000 had been allowed; the rest had been rejected as invalid. Many of those whose claims were thus rejected had recourse to private pension bills which were presented by greedy pension attorneys and pushed through by Congressmen anxious to make political capital. Charles Francis Adams wrote scathingly, 'We had seen every dead-beat, and malingerer, every bummer, bounty-jumper, and suspected deserter . . . rush to the front as the greedy claimant of public bounty. If there was any man whose army record had been otherwise than creditable . . . we soon heard of him as the claimant of a back pension . . . or as being in the regular receipt of his monthly stipend.' Cleveland actually signed no less than 1453 of these private pension bills — a larger number than any of his predecessors — but it was his vetoes that were remembered.

Soon a second pension theory emerged — that all veterans who suffered from any physical disability, regardless of its origin or its cause, were entitled to pensions. This view had the solid support of the Grand Army of the Republic, of thousands of pension agents, and of business interests anxious to dispose of surplus revenue in order that there might be no downward revision of the tariff. The G.A.R., which by the middle 'eighties boasted a membership of almost half a million, was one of the most powerful pressure groups in the country and had long maintained an intimate alliance with the Republican party. It flooded the country with propaganda, bullied Congressmen, threatened presidents, and intimidated political parties.

We flatter ourselves [said Senator Saulsbury in 1884] that we are great men. We are the Senators of the United States who make laws for the people; but behind us there is another power greater than ourselves, controlling our action if not our judgment. The pension agents who sit around this Capitol issue their circulars and decrees, and petitions come up for pensions, and the Senators of the United States, great and mighty as they may be, bow to the behests of the pension agents and vote the money that they require, and they are afraid not to do it for fear that they would lose political status at home. We all know it, and the country knows it.

In 1887 Congress, at the dictation of the G.A.R. and the pension agents, passed the Dependent Pension Bill granting pensions to all veterans suffering from any disabilities, regardless of how contracted. Cleveland vetoed the bill, and his veto helped defeat him for re-election the following year.

There was a roar of protest, too, from the predatory interests that were despoiling the lands and forests of the West when the President ordered an investigation into the fraudulent practices of cattle ranchers, railroads, timber companies, and squatters on Indian reservations. Lamar and his Land Office Commissioner, William A. Sparks, uncovered frauds that staggered the imagination. Most railroad lands had been granted on terms calling for forfeiture in the event of the non-fulfillment of the contract within a stated time, but during preceding administrations these forfeiture clauses had been blandly ignored. More serious, where railroad grants happened to embrace lands already settled, the railroads had been permitted either to take over the homesteader's land, with all improvements, or to indemnify themselves from valuable forest or mineral lands elsewhere. Lamar put an end to these practices and instituted suits to recover millions of acres of land from the railroads. He proceeded with equal energy against powerful lumber companies like the Sierra Lumber Company and the Montana Improvement Company, subsidiary of the Northern Pacific Railroad, who were ruthlessly despoiling the national forests. He nullified fraudulent leases of Indian lands like that whereby one cattle company leased from the Cherokees 6 million acres for which it paid an annual rental of only $100,000 and which it then subleased for five times that amount. He ordered cattle barons to take down their barbed wire fences enclosing millions of acres of public lands, and instituted reforms long overdue in the administration of the Land Office. Altogether, during his first administration,

Cleveland forced the restoration of some 81 million acres of public lands. At the same time the Interstate Commerce Act of 1887 and the Dawes Act of 1887 furnished points of departure for regulation of the railroads and of Indian affairs.

More dramatic was Cleveland's effort to force action on the tariff problem. In this effort he was moved by two considerations. The high tariff, adopted originally as an emergency Civil War measure, had come to be accepted as a permanent part of national policy. As such it had contributed, in Cleveland's opinion, not only to increases in the prices of protected goods, but to the development of trusts. Furthermore, when government revenues showed a consistent surplus over ordinary expenses of almost $100 million annually all through the decade of the 'eighties, this surplus offered a standing temptation to extravagance of the pork barrel and pension grab variety. The Civil War tariffs had raised the average duties from 18 to 40 per cent, and successive tinkerings in 1867, 1870, 1872, and 1875 had not changed levels in any substantial way, though there had been a gradual upward trend on iron ore and woolens. The clamor for reform became so insistent that the Tariff Commission of 1882, composed though it was of protectionists, recommended a downward revision of not less than 20 per cent. Congress responded the following year with a 'mongrel tariff' that lowered some duties and raised others — a tariff which had the support not only of Republican protectionists like 'Pig Iron' Kelley but also of high tariff Democrats like Randall, another Pennsylvanian.

This was the situation when Cleveland came to office. During the first two years of his administration the Democrats made no sincere effort to redeem their platform pledges of a downward revision of the tariff. In 1887, Cleveland, despite warnings to avoid the explosive subject, startled the nation by devoting his annual message exclusively to the tariff. He denounced the fantastic extremes to which the principle of protection had been pushed, derided the 'infant industry' theory of high tariffs, and emphasized the intimate relation of the tariff to trusts. 'Our progress toward a wise conclusion,' he wrote, 'will not be improved by dwelling upon theories of protection and free trade. It is a condition which confronts us, not a theory.' The New York *Nation* characterized the message 'the most courageous document that has been sent from the White House since the Civil War.' But Blaine denounced it as pure 'free trade,' and the Republicans prepared joyously to make this the issue of the forthcoming campaign. A House bill looking to downward revision of the tariff was deadlocked by Senate Republicans. Yet Cleveland had accomplished his purpose. He had brought the tariff issue sharply to the attention of the country, and he had forced his own party to espouse tariff reform as the paramount issue.

4. THE CLIMAX OF REACTION

The Democrats renominated Cleveland in 1888, and the Republicans picked the innocuous Benjamin Harrison of Indiana, since he came from a critical state and had distinguished ancestry and a war record. In a campaign marked by pronounced ethnic appeals, the Irish vote, which had helped defeat Blaine in 1884, now was turned against Cleveland. A naturalized Anglo-American was inspired to inquire of the British Minister, Sir Lionel Sackville-West, how he should vote in order to serve the mother country. Sir Lionel, with incredible stupidity, advised him by letter to vote for the Democrats. Two weeks before the election, his letter was published, and the mischief was done. Though Cleveland's popular vote exceeded Harrison's by 100,000 the Republicans carried New York State by a few thousand votes, and again New York was decisive.

Benjamin Harrison, grandson of the hero of Tippecanoe, was an Indiana lawyer who made a dignified figurehead in the presidency from 1889 to 1893. Aloof and aristocratic, honest and conscientious, he lacked the insight to comprehend the problems of a new day and the ability to control the spoilsmen of his party. James G. Blaine, who still considered himself the leader of the party, became his Secretary of State; the rest of the cabinet were nonentities. With the autocratic 'Czar' Thomas B. Reed as Speaker of the House, and with a majority in both Houses, the way was clear for constructive legislation. But the Republican party wanted little legislation that was not a raid on the treasury or a hold-up on the consumer, and in this administration statesmanship reached a new low-water mark.

The Republicans returned to office with heavy political debts to pay. The machine politicians had performed yeoman service in rounding up votes, and they expected to be rewarded with the spoils of office. The old soldier vote had proved decisive in critical states, and the veterans counted on more generous pensions. Business and manufacturing interests had contributed liberally to the campaign fund, and they looked forward to an upward revision of the tariff. To all these demands the administration showed itself remarkably complaisant.

Harrison had said, in his acceptance speech, that 'only the interest of the public service should suggest removals from office,' but it was quickly apparent that such interest required a clean sweep of Democratic officeholders. Within a year Postmaster-General Wanamaker had removed over 30,000 postmasters, more than double the number that Cleveland had dismissed in the same period. Cleveland had placed the railroad mail service under civil service rules, but Harrison suspended the operation of the rules until the service could be filled with Republicans, and at the same time refused to extend the rules to the new Census Bureau. Theodore Roosevelt was appointed, as window-dressing, to the Civil Service Commission, but the Civil Service Reform League denounced the President for violation of his campaign pledges.

Harrison, during his campaign, had announced that 'it was no time to be weighing the claims of old soldiers with apothecary's scales,' and he lived up to the implications of that statement. 'God help the Surplus,' said Corporal Tanner who was appointed to the office of Pension Commissioner, and whose liberal interpretations of the existing pension legislation cost the Treasury millions of dollars. In 1890 Congress passed and the President signed a Disability Pension Act which provided pensions to all veterans who had served 90 days and who were unable to perform *manual* labor, or suffered from any disability 'not the result of their own vicious habits.' Even the G.A.R. was satisfied for a time. 'While not just what we asked,' the pension committee of that organization reported, 'it is the most liberal pension measure ever passed by any legislative body in the world, and will place upon the rolls all of the survivors of the war whose conditions of health are not practically perfect.' Yet in course of time the veterans came to demand, and politicians found it expedient to grant, still more. After the turn of the century came a system of Universal Service Pensions, and by a presidential ruling, in 1904, all veterans were granted pensions on the basis of service alone. By 1936 the Civil War pension bill had come to a little less than $8 billion.

That the Harrison administration should fulfill its campaign promises by new tariff legislation was inevitable. The McKinley tariff bill of October 1890 was pushed through as the result of a bargain between Western Republicans who wanted silver legislation and Eastern Republicans who wanted tariff legislation.[3] Its provisions were formulated chiefly by William McKinley of Ohio and Nelson W. Aldrich of Rhode Island, but the important schedules were dictated by such interested groups as the National Association of Wool Manufacturers, the Tin Plate and Iron and Steel Associations, and the Louisiana sugar growers. The bill was a frank recognition of the protective principle: it sought not only to protect established industries, but to foster 'infant industries' and, by prohibitory duties, to create new industries. It embodied three new provisions: it reached out for the farmers' vote with protective rates upon products of agriculture, duties which proved completely ineffective in the forthcoming agricultural depression; it put raw sugar on the free list and compensated the Louisiana and Kansas beet sugar growers with a bounty of two cents a pound — a provision which all but wrecked the Hawaiian sugar industry and brought on a revolution in that island kingdom; it included a reciprocity section which gave the President authority to place duties on sugar, molasses, tea, coffee, and hides if he thought that nations exporting those articles to the United States were imposing unequal and unreasonable duties on American goods. Pension and tariff legislation helped to liquidate the troublesome surplus, and further support to this policy was found in additional legislation of a less important character such as postal subsidies to steamship lines. The total expenditures of the Fifty-first Congress, 2 December 1889 to 3 March 1891, reached the unprecedented sum of almost a billion dollars. 'This is a Billion Dollar country,' was the retort attributed to 'Czar' Reed.

The unpopularity of the McKinley tariff was largely responsible for the political revolution in the congressional elections of 1890. Only 88 Republicans were returned to the new House, as against 235 Democrats and nine Populists; and the Republican majority in the Senate was reduced to eight unstable votes from the Far West. Even rock-ribbed Republican states like Michigan and Massachusetts went Democratic, and McKinley himself failed of re-election. There was more to this verdict, however, than revulsion from the tariff and disgust at Republican chicanery and corruption. It registered a deep-lying unrest that was presently to break forth into a movement that carried Bryan to prominence, Roosevelt to achievement, and Wilson to apotheosis.

3. The year 1890 saw the passage of the McKinley tariff, the Sherman Silver Purchase bill, the Sherman Anti-Trust Act, the Disability Pension Act, and the admission of the last of the 'omnibus' states.

VIII

The Battle of the Standards

1. THE POPULIST REVOLT

In 1890 American politics lost their steady beat and began to dip and flutter in an effort to maintain equilibrium among strange currents of thought that issued from the caverns of discontent.

Almost a generation had passed since the Civil War. The older Republicans had come to revere their 'Grand Old Party' only less than the Union and the flag. It was difficult for the politicians to believe that anything was amiss. The Middle Western men, representative of the party, had grown up with the country. Their experience of life had been utterly different from that of any European statesman. They had seen the frontier of log cabins, stumpy clearings, and razor-back hogs replaced by frame houses and great barns, well-tilled farms, and sleek cattle. Towns with banks, libraries, high schools, mansions, and 'opera houses' had sprung up where once as barefooted boys they had hunted squirrel and wild cat; and the market towns of their youth had become great manufacturing cities. The railroad, the telegraph, the sewing machine, oil and gas lighting, and a hundred new comforts and conveniences had come within reach of all but the poorest and remotest during their lifetime. If discontented workmen and poverty-stricken farmers sometimes intruded into the picture, it must be foreign agitators or the law of supply and demand that were to blame. How could there be anything wrong with a government which had wrought such miraculous changes for the better, or with a Grand Old Party which had saved the nation from disunion?

The Democratic party, too, was conservative and complacent. Its stronghold was in the most conservative areas of the country — the South and the industrial centers; and its strength in these sections rested not on any policies it might embrace but upon race, tradition, and the loyalty of local organizations. There was little reason to believe that either the Bourbon Democrats of the South or Tammany Hall and kindred organizations in the North would be open to new ideas. The Solid South, irrevocably committed to the one principle of maintaining white supremacy, hung like a dead weight on party leadership; the local machines in the North, no less irrevocably committed to the single principle of getting and keeping office, were willing to sell out on any other issue to the highest bidder.

Yet many Americans felt that something was radically wrong and groped for a remedy. Industrial unrest was acute; 1890 witnessed the largest number of strikes in any one year of the nineteenth century. Railroad regulation had proved all but futile, and the anti-trust law was to be effective only against labor organizations. Discontent with the McKinley tariff was widespread, and the prospect of any effective reduction in duties dim. Money was tight, credit inflexible, and banking facilities inadequate. The political machinery was not geared to democracy: the Senate, chosen not by popular vote but by state legislatures, was the stronghold of special interests; the Supreme Court reflected the ideas of the privileged.

Dissatisfaction was most acute on the farms of the South and the West. The Middle Border began, in 1887, to suffer the devastating effects of deflation after a great land boom. After several years of excessive rainfall there came in 1887 a summer so dry that the crops withered all along the border of the Plains. Eight of the next ten years in western Kansas and the Dakotas were too arid, and the region suffered also from chinch bugs, high winds, and killing frosts. In the four years from 1889 to 1893 over 11,000 farm mortgages were foreclosed in Kansas alone and in fifteen counties of that state over three-quarters of the land was owned by mortgage companies. The West was literally in bondage to the East. During these years the people who had entered that new El Dorado trekked eastward again; on their wagons one could read the scrawl, 'In God we trusted, in Kansas we busted.' William Allen White described some of these:

> There came through Emporia yesterday two old-fashioned mover wagons, headed east. . . . These movers were from western Kansas. . . . They had come from that wilderness only after a ten years' hard vicious fight, a fight which had left its scars on their faces, had beat their bodies, had taken the elasticity from their steps and left them crippled to enter the battle anew. For ten years they had been fighting the elements. They had seen it stop raining for months at a time. They had heard the fury of the winter wind as it came whining across the short burned grass and cut the flesh from their children huddling in the corner. These movers have strained their eyes watching through long summer days for the rain that never came. . . . They have tossed through hot nights wild with worry, and have arisen only to find their worst nightmares grazing in reality on the brown stubble in front of their sun-warped doors. They had such high hopes when they went out there; they are so desolate now — no, not now, for now they are in the land of corn and honey. They have come out of the wilderness, back to the land of promise.

Whole sections of the West were left without a single person. Half the people of western Kansas deserted the country between 1888 and 1892. Little wonder that Oliver Goldsmith's 'The Deserted Village' was the favorite work of Populist orators. The misery of the Middle Border was more than matched in the South where cotton growers struggled on from year to year against a falling market, while mortgage indebtedness and tenancy grew at an ominous rate.

In the 1890 elections the angry Southern farmer struck back. The Southern Alliance, spurning third party tactics, launched a campaign to capture control of the Democratic party, and scored a series of stunning victories. It won control of the legislatures in eight states, and elected six governors and more than 50 Congressmen, including Tom Watson of Georgia, apostle of the new Jeffersonianism, who championed the cause of tenant farmers and mill hands, wrote biographies of Jefferson and Napoleon, and earned the dubious title of the 'Sage of Hickory Hill.' In South Carolina, 'Pitchfork Ben' Tillman placed himself at the head of the underprivileged farmers, pushed a series of reforms through the legislature, and created a political machine to do his bidding.

That same year the Alliance helped launch a series of state third parties in the West. These new parties elected five of seven Congressmen and a U.S. Senator in Kansas and won the balance of power in South

Dakota and Minnesota. Kansas called its organization the People's Party, which two years later was to be the name of the national party. A generation which knew its Latin found it an easy transition from People's Party to calling its followers Populists and the movement Populism.

The rank and file of the new party was recruited from the Farmers' Alliances, Greenbackers, Knights of Labor, free-silverites, disciples of Edward Bellamy, and followers of Henry George; the leadership came almost exclusively from the Alliances. David H. Waite, Governor of Colorado, friend of the farmers and the miners and of all the underprivileged of the earth, was known by his admirers as the 'Abraham Lincoln of the Rockies' and by his critics as 'Bloody Bridles Waite' because he had said that it was better 'that blood should flow to the horses' bridles rather than our national liberties should be destroyed.' Minnesota boasted the Sage of Nininger, the inimitable Ignatius Donnelly, discoverer of the lost Atlantis, advocate of the theory that Bacon wrote Shakespeare's plays, author of the prophetic *Caesar's Column*, undismayed champion of lost causes and desperate remedies. A reform meeting in Minnesota without Donnelly, observed one newspaper, would be 'like catfish without waffles in Philadelphia.' Kansas, where, as William Allen White remembered, the farm revolt became 'a religious revival, a crusade, a pentecost of politics in which the tongue of flame sat upon every man and each spake as the spirit gave him utterance' was most prolific of leadership. Here the sad-faced Mary Lease went about advising farmers to 'raise less corn and more Hell.' Here Jerry Simpson, the sockless Socrates of the prairie, espoused the doctrines of Henry George and exposed the iniquities of the railroads. Here Senator William A. Peffer of the hickory-nut head and long flowing beard, whom Roosevelt, with his usual impetuosity denounced as 'a well-meaning, pin-headed, anarchistic crank,' presented with logic and learning *The Farmer's Side, His Troubles and Their Remedy.*

The Populist convention that met in Omaha on Independence Day of 1892 presented a sharp contrast to the conventions of the two major parties. Decorum and apathy had marked these conventions, and the nominations of Cleveland and Harrison had excited neither surprise nor enthusiasm. But a camp-meeting atmosphere characterized the convention of the People's party. The platform, drawn up by the eloquent Ignatius Donnelly, raked both the major parties and painted a melancholy picture of the American scene:

We meet in the midst of a nation brought to the verge of moral, political, and material ruin. Corruption dominates the ballot-box, the legislatures, the Congress, and touches even the ermine of the bench. The people are demoralized; . . . The newspapers are largely subsidized or muzzled; public opinion silenced; business prostrated; our homes covered with mortgages; labor impoverished; and the land concentrating in the hands of the capitalists. The urban workmen are denied the right of organization for self-protection; imported pauperized labor beats down their wages; a hireling standing army, unrecognized by our laws, is established to shoot them down, and they are rapidly degenerating into European conditions. The fruits of the toil of millions are boldly stolen to build up colossal fortunes for a few, unprecedented in the history of mankind; and the possessors of these in turn, despise the republic and endanger liberty. From the same prolific womb of governmental injustice we breed the two great classes — tramps and millionaires.

Specifically, the platform demanded the free and unlimited coinage of silver; a flexible currency system, controlled by the government and not by the banks, with an increase in the circulating medium to $50 per capita; a graduated income tax; the sub-treasury scheme; postal savings banks; public ownership and operation of railroads, telegraph, and telephones; prohibition of alien land ownership and reclamation of railroad lands illegally held; immigration restriction; the eight-hour day for labor; prohibition of the use of labor spies; the direct election of Senators, the Australian ballot, the initiative and referendum. The platform was regarded throughout the East as little short of communism, yet within a generation almost every one of the planks was incorporated into law in whole or in part. The Populist party was a seed-bed of American politics for the next half-century. For their standard-bearer the Populists chose James Baird Weaver of Iowa, a veteran of the reform movement too well known to excite curiosity and too respectable to justify abuse.

Weaver received over a million popular votes, better than 8 per cent of the national total, and 22 electoral votes, all west of the Mississippi. The Populists were the only third party to break into the electoral column between 1860 and 1912. Save for the Republicans, no new party had ever done so nicely in its first bid for national power. The Populists ran reasonably well in the Middle Border, where they elected governors in North Dakota and Kansas, but their new stronghold was the Mountain states, where they captured almost twice as many counties as both major parties combined, and in a single election established themselves as the majority party. However, this new strength threatened to drive the Populists even farther in the direction of an obsession with the one issue of silver.

No party could hope to forge a winning combination if its sectional alliance was limited to the sparsely populated Middle Border and Mountain West. In 1892 the Populists failed completely to crack the South, where Alliance leaders were reluctant to divide the white vote by abandoning the one-party system. In Tillman's South Carolina, the Populists fielded no candidates at all, and Weaver, as a former Union general, was, as Mrs. Lease observed wryly, 'made a regular walking omelet by the Southern chivalry of Georgia.' Most disturbing, the new party made almost no impression on the farmers of the Old Northwest. The Populists took only one county north of the Ohio and east of the Mississippi. Even states west of the Mississippi which had once been centers of agrarian unrest proved disappointing. Weaver, a native son of Iowa, got only 5 per cent of the vote of that state. Donnelly, who ran third as Populist candidate for governor of Minnesota, wrote in his diary: 'Beaten! Whipped! Smashed! . . . Our followers scattered like dew before the rising sun.'

In a three-cornered race, Cleveland swept the Solid South and seven Northern states, and for the third successive time received a popular plurality. Harrison polled a smaller vote than he had in his first campaign, and the labor and tariff policies for which his party was held responsible forfeited the support of the industrial states of the East. Cleveland's triumph was the biggest victory for the Democrats in forty years. But the victory was deceptive, for it encouraged Cleveland and his supporters to adopt policies which would lead to the disruption of their party.

2. THE MONEY QUESTION

Grover Cleveland, a little stouter and more set in his ideas, was inaugurated President on 4 March 1893, and promptly confronted the money question. Business investor classes entertained the orthodox or classical theory of money. This bullion theory held that money was actually only a token of coin, that its value was determined by the bullion which was held as security for its redemption, and that any interference by government with this value was economically unsound. It required therefore that all money in circulation have behind it some substantial metallic value, and that government confine itself to issuing money on security of bullion actually in the treasury vaults, either directly or indirectly through banks. As long as the ratio between gold and silver remained relatively stable, the bullion theory of money accepted a bimetallic standard; when the decline in the value of silver disrupted that long-established ratio, orthodox economists turned to the single gold standard.

This classical view was disputed by those who regarded money as a token of credit rather than of bullion, and maintained that it was the proper business of the government to regulate money in the interests of society at large. Advocates of this theory pointed out that bullion, and especially gold, did not provide a sufficiently large or flexible basis for the money needs of an expanding nation, and that any financial policy which tied money to gold placed the whole monetary system of the nation at the mercy of a fortuitous gold production. They insisted that bullion security for money was unnecessary or necessary only in part; that the vital consideration was the credit of the government, and that 'the promise to pay' of the United States was sufficient to sustain the value of any money issued by that government. These proponents of credit money demanded that currency be expanded whenever essential to provide for the business needs of the country and to hold commodity prices stable. Enthusiastic support for this school of economic thought was found among the farmers of the South and the West and among the debtor groups everywhere — groups who had favored easy money since the days of the Massachusetts land bank scheme and Shays's Rebellion of the eighteenth century.

The roots of the money question are to be found in the financing of the Civil War. At that time, it will be remembered, the Federal Government issued $450 million in greenbacks — money with no security but the promise of the government to pay. These greenbacks were legal tender for all purposes except customs duties and interest on certain government bonds. In part because of this discrimination against them, in part because of lack of confidence that the government would redeem them in coin, they promptly depreciated in value. Yet though the fluctuation in the value of greenbacks was a constant temptation to speculation, they nevertheless proved useful and came in time to command the confidence of a large part of the people. They not only helped to finance the war, but by expanding the currency they served to lower interest rates and to raise commodity prices.

On the conclusion of the war hard money spokesmen presented three demands: resumption of specie payments on all government obligations, retirement from the currency of all legal tender notes, and refunding of the national debt on a gold basis. These demands aroused the bitter opposition of such men as Thaddeus Stevens and Wendell Phillips, but they were in large part complied with. Congress, in 1869, pledged the faith and credit of the United States to the payment of the principal and interest of government bonds in gold; the amount of legal tender notes was contracted; and on 1 January 1879, the government resumed specie payments.

As a result of these policies, so their critics averred, commodity prices fell sharply and the public debt burden was vastly increased. As per capita circulation of money declined from $31 in 1865 to $19 in 1875, money became dear. Since there were fewer dollars to go around in 1875 than there had been a decade earlier, it took more corn, wheat, and cotton to buy a dollar, than it had formerly taken. As for the public debt, it was argued that as the government had borrowed greenback dollars worth anywhere from 50 to 80 cents in gold, it was not morally obliged to pay back dollars worth a dollar in gold. The Specie Resumption Act of 1875, however, ended the greenback question as a practical issue.

After the middle 'seventies the inflationists transferred their zeal from greenbacks to silver, and for the next twenty years 'free silver' was the most exciting political issue before the American people. This shift was brought about by three considerations. In the first place silver satisfied the requirement that there should be some substantial security behind money, for to the conservative economists silver bullion seemed a sounder security than the mere promise of the government to pay. In the second place, dependence upon silver and gold would ensure a reasonable expansion of the currency but guard against any such reckless inflation as might result from the use of mere legal tender notes. In the third place, silver had behind it the silver-mine owners and investors, a powerful group, vitally interested in silver legislation and prepared to finance 'educational' and political campaigns looking to such legislation.

In 1861 the mines of the country had produced approximately $43 million worth of gold but only $2 million worth of silver. The coinage ratio between silver and gold of 15.988 to 1 actually undervalued silver, and in consequence silver was sold for commercial purposes and only gold was carried to the mints for purposes of coinage. During the 'sixties and early 'seventies, however, came the discoveries of immense deposits of silver in the mountains of the West; by 1873 the value of silver mined in the United States had increased to $36 million while the value of gold had declined to the same figure. As a result of this relative and absolute increase in silver production, the price of the metal gradually slumped until by 1873 it reached approximately the legal ratio. The next year, for the first time since 1837, it fell below that ratio, and it became profitable to sell silver to governments for coinage instead of selling it for commercial purposes.

But when the silver-mine owners turned to governments, they found their market gone. Germany in 1871 had adopted a gold standard; the Latin Union consisting of France, Italy, Switzerland, Belgium, and Greece hastened to suspend the free coinage of silver; and all the other European states came tumbling after. Worst of all, from the point of view of the silver interests, the United States had, by the coinage act of 1873, demonetized silver. This demonetization had been effected by the simple device of omitting from the act any specific provision for the coinage of silver dollars. Silverites hotly charged a trick, and the act became known as 'the Crime of '73.' The schoolmaster in *Coin's Financial School* — a book which was to the free silver crusade what *Uncle Tom's Cabin* was to the anti-slavery crusade — wrote:

> It is known as the crime of 1873. A crime, because it has confiscated millions of dollars worth of property. A crime, because it has made tens of thousands of tramps. A crime, because it has made thousands of suicides. A crime, because it has brought tears to strong men's eyes and hunger and pinching want to widows and orphans. A crime because it is destroying the honest yeomanry of the land, the bulwark of the nation. A crime because it has brought this once great republic to the verge of ruin, where it is now in imminent danger of tottering to its fall.

From the middle 'seventies to the middle 'nineties, the money question took the form of a demand for the free and unlimited coinage of silver. In 1878 the silverites pushed through, over a presidential veto, the Bland-Allison Act which provided that the government must purchase each month not less than $2 million nor more than $4 million worth of silver, to be coined into silver dollars at the existing legal ratio with gold. Successive secretaries of the treasury followed the minimum amount, and the addition to the currency was not sufficient to increase in any appreciable way the per capita circulation of money or to halt the steady decline in the price of silver in the world market.

The hard times of the late 'eighties brought a renewal of the silver agitation. Domestic production of the white metal jumped from $36 million in 1873 to $57 million by 1890, and the gain in world production was proportionately great. This increase, of course, depressed the price of silver and raised the price of gold. At the same time per capita circulation of money in the United States barely held its own, and in some sections of the country declined sharply. The relation between the limited coinage of silver and the low price of the metal was not lost upon mine interests. The connection between low commodity prices and high gold prices, between low per capita circulation of money and high interest rates, was not lost upon the farmers.

Yet silver agitation might have come to nought had it not been for the admission of the 'Omnibus' states. When the enabling acts of 1889 and 1890 brought into Congress representatives from six new Western states, the Senate at once became the stronghold of silver sentiment. The result was the enactment of a new and more generous silver bill — the Sherman Silver Purchase Act of 1890. This curious measure, the product of a bargain whereby Western Republicans voted for a tariff bill which they disliked and Eastern Republicans voted for a silver bill which they feared, satisfied no one. It provided that the Treasury Department purchase each month 4.5 million ounces of silver at the market price, paying for such silver with Treasury notes of the United States. It contained further the fateful provision that 'upon demand of the holder of any of the Treasury notes . . . the Secretary of the Treasury shall, under such regulations as he may prescribe, redeem such notes in gold or silver coin, at his discretion, it being the established policy of the United States to maintain the two metals on a parity with each other upon the present ratio.'

The Sherman Act proved a futile and dangerous compromise. It neither raised the price of silver, nor increased the amount of money in circulation, nor halted the steady decline in crop prices. The failure of the Sherman Act to effect these ends was variously explained by two opposing schools of thought. Gold monometallists insisted that the act revealed the hopelessness of the effort to do anything for silver, and that it proved that the price of silver could not be raised artificially by government action. Silverites argued that the act proved the futility of compromise and the necessity for free and unlimited coinage. The act provided, to be sure, for the purchase of practically the entire domestic production of silver. But the world output was almost three times the domestic production, and as long as there were huge quantities of silver seeking a market, the price would be sure to slump. The solution, said the gold forces, was to abandon silver to its fate and return to the gold standard. The solution, said the silverites, was to open our mints to unlimited coinage of silver, and peg the price at the traditional ratio of 16 to 1.

It is impossible now to determine which alternative was the better. In the end the gold standard was victorious, and before the 1930's historians were inclined to regard that victory as providential. Yet logic, at least, would seem to be with the bimetallists. Certainly if the United States stood ready to exchange, with all comers, one ounce of gold for sixteen ounces of silver, no one would sell silver for less than that sum. That is, if the United States could absorb all the silver that would be brought to her mints, she could peg the price, and bimetallism would be an established fact. But that *if* was crucial. The success of the operation depended upon the ability of the United States to pay out gold for silver until speculators were convinced of the futility of trying to break the price, or until the increased demand for silver raised its commercial value.

There was a third solution, one upon the desirability of which both bimetallists and many monometallists were agreed. That was international bimetallism. If the United States could persuade the other great powers of the world to co-operate with it in re-establishing bimetallism, the normal market for silver would be restored, silver would rebound to its traditional price, and the money question would be solved. Hopefully, year after year, delegates journeyed to International Monetary Conferences. Practically every conference concluded that international bimetallism was economically expedient and financially sound. But on the political expediency of bimetallism there was no agreement. Each nation distrusted the sincerity of its neighbors, and no nation was ready to take the plunge.

If bimetallism were to be tried, then, it would have to be tried as a national policy. The mere statement of this fact created an emotional tension unfavorable to the intelligent consideration of the question. 'Gold-bugs' talked of an 'honest dollar,' and, smugly denounced their opponents as wicked and immoral men. 'The eagerness of the advocates of free silver,' wrote the conservative economist, J. Laurence Laughlin, 'is founded on an appeal to dishonesty and cheating on the part of those who would like to repudiate and scale one-half of their obligations.' Silverites retorted by branding the monometallists as 'Shylocks' and 'vampires,' and hurled back at them the charge of dishonesty. 'A dollar approaches honesty,' argued Mr. Bryan, 'as its purchasing power approaches stability. . . . Society has become accustomed to some very nice distinctions. . . . The poor man who takes property by force is called a thief, but the creditor who can by legislation make a debtor pay a dollar twice as large as he borrowed is lauded as the friend of sound currency. The man who wants the people to destroy the Government is an anarchist, but the man who wants the Government to destroy the people is a patriot.'

We can see now that the issue was both deeper and less dangerous than contemporaries realized. It was deeper because it involved a struggle for the ultimate control of government and of economy between the business interests of the East and the agrarian interests of the South and the West — a struggle in which gold and silver were mere symbols. It was less dangerous because, in all probability, none of the calamities so freely prophesied would have followed the adoption of either the gold or the silver standard at any time during these years. When the country finally adopted the gold standard in 1900, the event made not a ripple. When the gold standard was abandoned by Great Britain and by the United States a full generation later, the event led to no untoward results.

3. THE PRESIDENT AND THE PANIC

The Cleveland administration was just two months old when the failure of the National Cordage Company inaugurated the panic of 1893. The long drawn-out agricultural depression which began in 1887 had seriously curtailed the purchasing power of one large group of consumers, and had similarly affected railway income. The collapse of our markets abroad, owing to business distress in Europe and Australia, had serious repercussions on American trade and manufacturing. Over-speculation attendant upon the organization of trusts and combines endangered stability, while industrial disorders like the Homestead strike and the Coeur d'Alene strike reduced profits and cut down purchasing power. Finally the silver policy of the government impaired business confidence at home and abroad, and persuaded many European creditors to dump their American securities on the market and drain the nation of its gold.

By midsummer of 1893 the panic was in full swing. The Reading Railroad failed early in the spring. In July came the failure of the Erie, and shortly thereafter the Northern Pacific, the Union Pacific, and the Santa Fe all went into the hands of receivers. Within two years one-fourth of the railroad capitalization of the country was under control of bankruptcy courts, and 60 per cent of railroad stocks had suspended dividend payments. Banks everywhere felt the strain and called in their loans, often with consequences fatal to business firms and individuals unable to meet their obligations; over 15,000 failures were recorded for the year 1893. In the rural sections banks toppled like card-houses; of the 158 national bank failures in 1893, 153 were in the South and the West. 'Men died like flies under the strain,' wrote Henry Adams, 'and Boston grew suddenly old, haggard, and thin.' Adams was thinking of the Boston financiers; the characterization was equally applicable to the 4 million jobless who, by the summer of 1894, walked the streets of factory towns in a vain search for work.

Convinced that monetary uncertainty was the chief cause of the panic, President Cleveland summoned a special session of Congress to repeal the Sherman law and to enact legislation which should 'put beyond all doubt or mistake the intention and the ability of the Government to fulfill its pecuniary obligations in money universally recognized by all civilized countries.' The result was the liveliest session of Congress in a generation. The administration forces were led by William L. Wilson of West Virginia and the eloquent Bourke Cockran of New York; silver was championed by the veteran 'Silver Dick' Bland and by young William Jennings Bryan of Nebraska.

> On the one hand [said Bryan] stand the corporate interests of the United States, the moneyed interests, aggregated wealth and capital, imperious, arrogant, compassionless. . . . On the other side

stand an unnumbered throng, those who gave to the Democratic party a name and for whom it has assumed to speak. Work-worn and dust-begrimed, they make their mute appeal, and too often find their cry for help beat in vain against the outer walls, while others, less deserving, gain ready access to legislative halls.

Cleveland's discreet manipulation of the patronage provided enough Democratic votes, to help the Republicans repeal their own silver-purchase act at the request of a Democratic President and a bimetallist Secretary of the Treasury! Business and finance breathed more freely, but the farmers cried out betrayal, and Bland warned the President that Eastern and Western Democrats had finally come to 'a parting of the ways.'

Nor did the repeal of the Sherman Act bring about that restoration of prosperity so confidently predicted. The Treasury Department was freed of its obligations to purchase silver but Secretary of the Treasury John Carlisle's troubles had just begun. Distrust of the monetary policy of the government was by no means allayed, and there began a steady raid on the gold reserves of the Treasury. The Sherman Act had provided that silver certificates might be redeemed in gold or silver coin and had announced the policy to maintain the two metals at a parity with each other. Holders of silver certificates, fearful for the future, began to bring them to the Treasury and ask for gold. Cleveland and Carlisle agreed that the government had no legal right to refuse their request. The resultant drain on the gold reserve not only carried that reserve below the established mark of $100 million, but threatened to wipe it out altogether. To the frightened President it seemed that the hour was fast approaching when the government would be unable to meet its legal obligations in gold and would therefore be pushed onto the silver standard. There was, so he thought, but one recourse: to sell government bonds for gold. When the public market for $50 million worth of government bonds proved unresponsive, Carlisle turned in desperation to the New York bankers. A banking syndicate, headed by the House of Morgan, took the issue, and a howl went up that the administration had sold out to Wall Street. Worst of all, this bond sale did not permanently help the Treasury. Purchasers of the bonds simply drew from it the gold with which to pay for their bonds. An 'endless chain' was thus set in operation, and the gold supply of the Treasury was depleted at one end as fast as it was replenished at the other. More bond sales thus became inevitable, and twice again, in November 1894 and February 1895, the same thing happened. Cleveland thought that he was doing the right thing; Morgan and his fellow bankers thought that they were doing the patriotic thing; but the farmers of the country were convinced that a traitor was in the White House and a Judas in the Treasury Department. Finally in 1896, the Treasury floated a $100 million bond issue through popular subscription. With the success of this fourth and last bond issue, the crisis was passed.

The financial difficulties of the government were ascribable not only to the gold drain, but to a sharp decline in revenues. The McKinley tariff had actually reduced income from customs duties, and the depression cut into internal revenues, while the 'billion dollar Congress' had committed the government to a number of new and heavy expenditures. As a result the surplus of 1890 became a deficit of $70 million by 1894. In the face of this situation Cleveland tried to force the Democratic party to redeem its pledge of tariff reduction. But vested interests had been built up under Republican protection, and Democratic Senators from the East were no less averse to tariff reduction than their Republican colleagues. The Wilson tariff as prepared by the House represented an honest effort to reduce duties, but when it emerged from the joint committee of the House and the Senate it was no longer recognizable. Protectionist Democrats like Gorman of Maryland had introduced no less than 634 changes, most of them upward. The new tariff abolished the sugar bounty, but restored the tariff on raw sugar, and fixed rates on refined sugar that were entirely satisfactory to the Sugar Trust — but ruinous to Cuban sugar planters. Cleveland, who had insisted that 'a tariff for any other purpose than public revenue is public robbery,' denounced the bill as smacking of 'party perfidy and party dishonor.' Believing, however, that the Wilson-Gorman tariff was some improvement on the McKinley act, he allowed it to become a law without his signature.

The sponsors of the Wilson bill had anticipated a reduction in customs duties, and they had wisely added a provision for a tax of 2 per cent on incomes above $4000. This income tax upon which the administration had confidently relied for necessary revenue was, however, declared unconstitutional by a five to four decision of the Supreme Court which fifteen years earlier had passed favorably and unanimously upon the war income tax. As some of the opinions, notably that of Mr. Justice Field,[1] were characterized by gross prejudice and as one judge had changed his mind at the eleventh hour, this decision seemed a further proof to the farmers and workingmen that they had no voice in their government.

Even while the Senate was debating the Wilson bill and the House was making futile gestures toward free silver, one proposal was advanced which pointed the way to a statesmanlike solution of some of the most pressing problems created by the money stringency and the depression. This proposal came from 'General' Jacob Coxey, a wealthy quarry owner of Massillon, Ohio, who with his wife and his infant son, Legal Tender Coxey, was shortly to lead an army of unemployed on a march to Washington. Coxey's attack on the depression and the money question was a double-barreled one: non-interest-bearing bonds for public works and appropriations for good roads. One bill provided that any county or town desiring to undertake public improvements might issue non-interest-bearing bonds which should be deposited with the Secretary of the Treasury in exchange for legal tender notes, and which must be retired by taxation within twenty-five years. Public improvements thus financed were to be a form of work relief, employment being guaranteed to any jobless man at not less than $1.50 for an eight-hour day. The Good Roads Bill called for an issue of $500 million of legal tender notes to be used for the construction of a county road system throughout the country at the same rate of pay. These measures were designed to inflate the currency, bring down interest rates, inaugurate much-needed public improvements especially in the rural regions, and provide work for the unemployed. The program was not unlike that later inaugurated by Franklin D. Roosevelt, but at the time it excited only contempt or amusement.

This year, 1894, year of the Wilson tariff and the income tax decision, was the darkest that Americans had known for thirty years. Everything seemed to conspire to convince the people that democracy was a failure. Half a million laborers struck against conditions which they thought intolerable, and most of the strikes were dismal failures. Ragged and

---

1. *Pollock* v. *Farmers' Loan and Trust Co.* 158 U.S. 601 (1895). 'The present assault upon capital,' said Mr. Justice Field, 'is but the beginning. It will be but the stepping-stone to others, larger and more sweeping, till our political contests will become a war of the poor against the rich. . . .'

hungry bands of unemployed swarmed over the countryside, the fires from their hobo camps flickering a message of warning and despair to affrighted townsfolk. Coxey's army, consisting of broken veterans of the armies of industry, inspired by the pathetic delusion that a 'petition on boots' might bring relief, marched on Washington where they were arrested for trespassing on the Capitol grounds — a charge which was never preferred against silk-hatted lobbyists who there presented their petitions for higher tariffs. The corn crop was a failure; wheat fell below 50 cents a bushel, cotton to 6 cents a pound, and bitterness swept over the South and West like a prairie fire. Never did the government seem more unfriendly, or democratic processes more futile. When Pullman workers struck for a living wage, every agency of the government was enlisted to smash the strike. When representatives of the people in the lower House tried to reduce tariff duties, representatives of privilege in the Senate made a farce of the effort. Congress passed an anti-trust law and it was enforced not against the trusts but against labor unions; when the great Sugar Trust was finally called into court, the Attorney-General of the United States sabotaged the prosecution. Congress enacted an income tax and it was voided in the highest court. And the President sold bonds to Wall Street, while silver, the poor man's friend, was disinherited and disgraced!

In countless country schoolhouses and Grange halls toil-worn men and women read from the graphic pages of *Coin's Financial School* the story of the Crime of '73, and auditors applauded with delight when the author refuted all the arguments of the 'gold-bugs.' Tenant farmers cheered lustily as 'Pitchfork Ben' Tillman demonstrated how he would stick his fork into the ribs of Grover Cleveland, and the rebel yell resounded again in the red hills of Georgia as flaming Tom Watson denounced the vampires of Wall Street. On the plains the 'Kansas Pythoness' Mary Lease warned the East that 'the people are at bay, let the bloodhounds of money beware,' and in Nebraska young William Jennings Bryan, the 'Boy Orator of the Platte,' rallied the farmers to a new crusade. There was ferment, too, in the intellectual world. Everywhere men were discussing the revelations of Lloyd's *Wealth against Commonwealth*, the first great broadside against the trusts. Edward Bellamy's Utopian novel, *Looking Backward*, sold by the hundred thousand, and a chain of Nationalist Clubs, inspired by that book, planned hopefully for a new and saner world. Jacob Riis told the sordid story of *How the*

Other Half Lives and respectable people, who had scarcely known the
meaning of the word 'slum,' were shocked into a realization of conditions
in their own backyards. And William Dean Howells, who had described
American society in so many placid novels, wrote a poem called 'Society'
which was published in the sedate pages of *Harper's Magazine*.

> I looked and saw a splendid pageantry
> Of beautiful women and of lordly men,
> Taking their pleasure in a flowery plain,
> Where poppies and the red anemone,
> And many another leaf of cramoisy,
> Flickered about their feet. . . .
> I looked again, and saw that flowery space
> Stirring, as if alive, beneath the tread
> That rested now upon an old man's head,
> And now upon a baby's gasping face,
> Or mother's bosom, or the rounded grace
> Of a girl's throat; and what had seemed the red
> Of flowers was blood, in gouts and gushes shed
> From hearts that broke under that frolic pace,
> And now and then from out the dreadful floor
> An arm or brow was lifted from the rest,
> As if to strike in madness, or implore
> For mercy. . . .

4. BRYAN, BRYAN, BRYAN, BRYAN

The party in power is always blamed for hard times. The crisis of 1894
had more impact on political alignments than any event between the
Civil War and the Great Depression. The 1894 elections ended the 20-
year period of political equilibrium and began an era of Republican
supremacy. In 24 states the Democrats failed to elect a single member of
the House, and for the next 16 years the Republicans would control both
houses of Congress. The G.O.P. did particularly well in winning over
urban voters who had previously been in the Democratic camp. During
the next 36 years, the Democrats would win only three Congressional
elections.

The Democratic party seemed on the verge of disintegration, and it
was apparent that one of two courses was open to it. Either the silver
wing of the party would capture control of the organization and unite all
silver forces under the Democratic banner, or the silverites would secede

to the lusty young Populist party and make that one of the great major parties. It was Cleveland's insistence upon the repeal of the Sherman Act that drove the first wedge into the Democratic party. 'Silver Dick' Bland then warned the President: 'We have come to the parting of the ways. . . . I believe I speak for the great masses of the great Mississippi Valley when I say that we will not submit to the domination of any political party, however much we may love it, that lays the sacrificing hand upon silver.' In 1893–94 silver Democrats everywhere effected a fusion with the Populists, and in many Western states it was difficult to distinguish between the two parties. But the silver leaders were unwilling to abandon the party without a final effort to mold it to their way of thinking. In the closing days of the Fifty-third Congress, March 1895, Bryan and Bland drew up an eloquent 'Appeal of the Silver Democrats' calling upon 'rank and file' Democrats to seize control of the party organization. The tactics thus suggested were promptly put into effect, with results described by Bryan in his 'Cross of Gold' speech a year later:

> Then began the struggle. With a zeal approaching the zeal which inspired the Crusaders . . . our silver Democrats went forth from victory unto victory. . . . In this contest brother has been arrayed against brother, father against son. . . . Old leaders have been cast aside when they have refused to give expression to the sentiments of those whom they would lead, and new leaders have sprung up to give direction to this cause of truth.

While the Democratic party was being torn apart, the Republicans concluded that in 1896 any Republican could be elected — a boast that Mark Hanna made a prophecy. Marcus Alonzo Hanna was a businessman satiated with wealth but avid for power, naturally intelligent though contemptuous of learning, personally upright but tolerant of corruption, shrewd and cynical in his management of men, but capable of deep loyalties and abiding friendships; he was the nearest thing to a national 'boss' that ever emerged in this country. Hanna was genuinely convinced that the business interests should govern the country, and he believed ardently in the mission of the Republican party to promote business activity, whence prosperity would percolate to the farmers and wage-earners below. Since 1890 he had been grooming for the presidency his friend William McKinley, whom he rescued from bankruptcy in the hard times of 1893. One by one McKinley's competitors were eliminated, as 'Uncle Mark' won over the delegations from the Southern and Mid-Western states. When the convention met, McKinley, 'advance agent of prosperity,' was nominated on the first ballot, 18 June 1896. Only one untoward event marred the jollity of the occasion: as the convention committed itself to the gold standard, the venerable Senator Henry Teller of Colorado bade farewell to the party which forty years earlier he had helped to found. And up in the press gallery William Jennings Bryan looked on with palpitating interest as Teller led a grim band of twenty-two silver delegates from the convention hall.

Three weeks later, when the Democratic convention met at Chicago it became apparent that the tactics of Bryan and Bland had been successful. Instead of going over to the Populists, the silver Democrats had captured control of the party organization and were prepared to write a silver platform and name a silver candidate. Trainload after trainload of enthusiastic delegates swarmed into the streets of the Windy City, silver badges gleaming from their lapels, silver banners fluttering in the breeze. 'For the first time,' wrote one Eastern delegate, 'I can understand the scenes of the French Revolution!' It was indeed a revolution; the Democratic party had been taken over by spokesmen for the farmers of the South and the West who had long since decided to repudiate their own President. Champ Clark of Missouri called Cleveland one of the three great traitors of our history, linking him with Benedict Arnold and Aaron Burr, while Altgeld had put it even more bluntly: 'To laud Clevelandism on Jefferson's birthday is to sing a Te deum in honor of Judas Iscariot on Christmas morning.'

'All the silverites need,' said the New York *World* on the eve of the Convention, 'is a Moses. They have the principle, they have the grit, they have the brass bands and the buttons and the flags, they have the howl and the hustle, they have the votes, and they have the leaders, so-called. But they are wandering in the wilderness like a lot of lost sheep, because no one with the courage, the audacity, the magnetism and the wisdom to be a real leader has yet appeared among them.' The lament was premature. In the person of William Jennings Bryan of Nebraska, the silver forces found their leader.

Only 36 years of age, Bryan had already distinguished himself as the most aggressive and eloquent spokesman of silver in the country. Elected to Congress in 1890 he had received the extraordinary tribute of appointment to the powerful Ways and Means Committee; his speeches on the tariff, the income tax, and silver had attracted national attention and made him one of the leaders of his party. Defeated for election to the Senate in the landslide of 1894, he had turned his talents to the task of whipping up silver sentiment and clearing the way for his own nomination. His preconvention campaign was thorough and shrewd; his convention strategy astute; his nomination came as a surprise to the East only because the East did not know what was going on elsewhere in the country.

Bryan's opportunity came in the debate on the platform. The champions of gold had made eloquent appeals, 'Pitchfork Ben' Tillman had failed to do justice to silver, and the great throng of 20,000 sweltering men and women were anxious and impatient. Bryan's was the closing speech, and as he made his way nervously down the aisle, a great shout went up, and Bryan banners appeared miraculously in every part of the great hall. His opening words, clear and mellifluous, stilled the vast throng and set the tone of his speech — dignified but impassioned:

> It would be presumptuous, indeed, to present myself against the distinguished gentlemen to whom you have listened if this were a mere measuring of abilities; but this is not a contest between persons. The humblest citizen in all the land, when clad in the armor of a righteous cause, is stronger than all the hosts of error. I come to speak to you in defense of a cause as holy as the cause of liberty — the cause of humanity.

Bryan reviewed the contest between the silver and the gold forces within the party, and reminded the delegates that they were 'now assembled, not to discuss, not to debate, but to enter up the judgment already rendered by the plain people of this country.' That judgment might run counter to the interests of Big Business, but,

> when you come before us and tell us that we are about to disturb your business interests, we reply that you have disturbed our business interests by your course. We say to you that you have made the definition of a business man too limited in its application. The man who is employed for wages is as much a business man as his employer; the attorney in a country town is as much a business man as the corporation counsel in a great metropolis; the merchant at the crossroads store is as much a business man as the merchant of New York; the farmer who goes forth in the morning and toils all day, who begins in the spring and toils all summer, and who by the application of brain and muscle to the natural resources of the coun-

try creates wealth, is as much a business man as the man who goes
upon the Board of Trade and bets on the price of grain; the miners
who go down a thousand feet into the earth, or climb two thousand
feet upon the cliffs, and bring forth from their hiding places the
precious metals to be poured into the channels of trade, are as much
business men as the few financial magnates who in a back room,
corner the money of the world. We come to speak for this broader
class of business men.

And they came, said Bryan, not as petitioners, but as a victorious army.

We have petitioned, and our petitions have been scorned; we
have entreated and our entreaties have been disregarded; we have
begged, and they have mocked when our calamity came. We beg
no longer; we entreat no more; we petition no more. We defy them.

The convention had found its spokesman at last, and every sentence was
punctuated by a frenzied roar of applause. Like a skillful fencer Bryan
found the weakness in the gold armor and drove home every thrust.
Swiftly he reviewed the minor planks in the platform — the income tax
which was 'not unconstitutional until one of the judges changed his mind,
and we cannot be expected to know when a judge will change his
mind'; the bank-note plank — 'the issue of money is a function of government, and banks ought to go out of the governing business'; the
tariff, which was less important than the money question, for while
'protection has slain its thousands, the gold standard has slain its tens of
thousands.' For the paramount issue was the gold standard. Then followed the peroration which drew the class and sectional lines:

You come to us and tell us that the great cities are in favor of the
gold standard; we reply that the great cities rest upon our broad
and fertile prairies. Burn down your cities and leave our farms, and
your cities will spring up again as if by magic; but destroy our farms
and the grass will grow in the streets of every city in the country.
. . . Having behind us the producing masses of the nation and the
world, supported by the commercial interests, the laboring interests
and the toilers everywhere, we will answer their demand for a gold
standard by saying to them: You shall not press down upon the
brow of labor this crown of thorns, you shall not crucify mankind
upon a cross of gold.

Bryan might have been nominated even without the 'Cross of Gold'
speech, but that speech made his nomination a practical certainty. Yet
five ballots were necessary before Bland's support disintegrated and the

'Boy Orator of the Platte' was selected as the Democratic standard-bearer in the Battle of the Standards.

Not only on the silver issue, but on banks, trusts, the injunction, and other issues, the Democrats had stolen the Populist thunder, although they failed to adopt the full Populist program. When the People's party met in St. Louis the fusionists were in complete control, to the distress of those like Henry Demarest Lloyd who charged that the social emphases of their party were being superseded by the single questionable issue of silver. Under the skillful leadership of men like Weaver and Senator Allen of Nebraska, the Populists chose Bryan as their candidate, but balked at accepting the Democratic vice-presidential nominee, a banker from Maine, and named Tom Watson instead, thereby giving Bryan two different running mates. Within a short time silver Republicans bolted to Bryan; Gold Democrats named a separate ticket but actually threw their support to McKinley. For the first time in 30 years the country divided roughly along class and sectional lines, and the electorate was confronted with a clean-cut issue. And that was not merely the money issue, but the more fundamental one of the control of the government by the business interests of the East or the agrarian interests of the South and the West.

In Bryan the agrarians had an ideal leader:

> Prairie avenger, mountain lion,
> Bryan, Bryan, Bryan, Bryan,
> Gigantic troubadour, speaking like a siege gun,
> Smashing Plymouth Rock with his boulders from the West.[2]

Radical only on economic questions of money, banks, and trusts, strictly orthodox in matters of morality and religion, Bryan was an honest, emotional crusader. More fully than any other candidate since the Civil War he represented the average middle-class American, and as the common denominator of the people of his generation he was able to retain his extraordinary hold upon their affections for so many years. Everything about him illustrated that quality which justified his title, 'the Great Commoner.' Born in a small farming town in southern Illinois, he came from mixed Scotch, Irish, and English stock from both North and South. One of his parents was Baptist, one Methodist; he himself joined the Presbyterian church. For generations his family had participated in the westward movement — from the Virginia tidewater to the Valley, from

2. Vachel Lindsay, 'Bryan, Bryan, Bryan, Bryan,' *Collected Poems*, Macmillan.

the Valley to the banks of the Ohio, from the Ohio to the Mississippi valley; he continued the process by moving out to the last frontier in Nebraska. He attended a small denominational college, studied law, dabbled in politics, and finally found himself in the championship of a great popular cause. Realist enough to appreciate the significance of the economic revolution, and astute enough to appeal to man's emotions as well as interests, he was thoroughly equipped for politics. But it was his qualities of character rather than of mind that won for him such loyalty as no other leader of his generation could command. Irreproachable in private and in professional life, his career was characterized by sincerity, courage, audacity, faith in the wisdom of the plain people and the processes of democracy, religious belief in the identity of morals and politics, and an undismayed conviction that the right must eventually triumph over the wrong.

The campaign was such a one as the country had not witnessed since Jackson and would not see again until 1928. For the farmers, wrote William Allen White,

> It was a fanaticism like the Crusades. Indeed the delusion that was working on the people took the form of religious frenzy. Sacred hymns were torn from their pious tunes to give place to words which deified the cause and made gold — and all its symbols, capital, wealth, plutocracy — diabolical. At night, from ten thousand little white schoolhouse windows, lights twinkled back vain hope to the stars. . . . They sang their barbaric songs in unrhythmic jargon, with something of the same mad faith that inspired the martyr going to the stake. Far into the night the voices rose — women's voices, children's voices, the voices of old men, of youths and of maidens, rose on the ebbing prairie breezes, as the crusaders of the revolution rode home, praising the people's will as though it were God's will and cursing wealth for its iniquity.

Conservatives responded as though the Hun were thundering at the gates. The New York *Tribune* denounced 'the wretched rattle-pated boy, posing in vapid vanity and mouthing resounding rottenness.' None of this seems to have disturbed Bryan. Mark Sullivan wrote: 'Bryan used to repeat what his enemies said, with a smile and manner that was subtly designed as half-way between Christ forgiving his persecutors and John L. Sullivan showing himself a good sport.'

Mark Hanna, who managed the Republican campaign, shook down metropolitan banks, insurance companies, and railroad corporations for colossal contributions. His committee reported campaign expenditures of $3.5 million, but estimates of the amount actually spent by local and national organizations ran as high as $16 million. Employees were ordered to vote for McKinley on pain of dismissal, and their fears were aroused by the prospect of receiving wages in depreciated dollars or by the even more serious danger of wage-slashes and unemployment. The silver-mining interests contributed to the Democratic funds, but the Democrats had not one-tenth of the 'sinews of war' that their opponents commandeered. Bryan bore the brunt of the battle; traveling day and night, speaking ten, twenty times a day to vast throngs, he inaugurated a new kind of campaign which struck terror into the hearts of his opponents.

William Allen White recalled:

> Men now in middle age, grown respectable themselves and staid Republicans, still remember some weird night in a Kansas or Nebraska boyhood when, well toward midnight, they waited in tingling excitement on the fringe of a crowd which packed the station plaza. The train roared in, as a hastily assembled band played Sousa's new march, 'El Capitan,' and from the back platform a man with longish black hair began to speak. Men grown old still sit in crossroads grocery stores, listening to the radio, and tell of the giants who once lived: Blaine, perhaps, and Foraker of Ohio, and Major McKinley and Roosevelt. They had heard them all, but Bryan, then 36 years old, had been the greatest.

In the 1896 election Bryan received more votes than had ever before been cast for a presidential candidate and more than any Democratic nominee would get for another twenty years. But McKinley not only outpolled him by half a million votes but won a sharp victory in the Electoral College. Bryan carried the late Confederacy and most of the Middle Border and the Mountain West; but the electoral votes of the populous East and the Middle West together with the trans-Mississippi states of Iowa, Minnesota, North Dakota, Oregon, and California gave McKinley an emphatic victory. In the silver region, Bryan won by prodigious margins — Montana, 4-1; Colorado, 6-1. In the East, he met disaster; he lost every county in New England, all but one in New York. The Eastern worker was repelled by a Western rural movement which, by spurring inflation, threatened his real wages. As Daniel De Leon said, labor feared it might be crucified 'upon a cross of silver.' McKinley ran

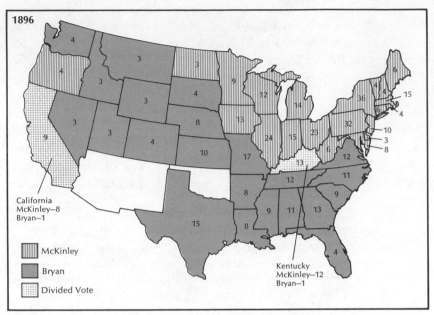

PRESIDENTIAL ELECTION, 1896

so well in the cities that the Democratic plurality of 145,000 in the twelve largest cities in 1892 became a Republican margin of 352,000 in 1896.

Bryan lost chiefly because he failed to carry the old Granger areas. The more settled the Midwestern states became, the less they were dependent on outside forces they could not control. Farmers had nearby city markets for many of their crops; they had established railroad systems; they were not as subject to the whims of the world market; and their operations were generally less speculative than they had been at the outset. They lived in a different world from the Southern tenant farmer or the wheat grower on the Middle Border. Furthermore, this section was increasingly industrialized and urbanized. The election demonstrated that the industrial Northeast had extended its empire to embrace all of the Old Northwest, and the Republicans would hold this region for most of the next generation.

> The great fight is won [wrote Mrs. Henry Cabot Lodge] a fight conducted by trained and experienced and organized forces, with

both hands full of money, with the full power of the press — and of prestige — on one side; on the other, a disorganized mob, at first, out of which burst into sight, hearing, and force — one man, but such a man! Alone, penniless, without backing, without money, with scarce a paper, without speakers, that man fought such a fight that even those in the East can call him a Crusader, an inspired fanatic — a prophet! It has been marvellous. Hampered by such a following, such a platform . . . he almost won. We acknowledge to 7 millions campaign fund, against his 300,000. We had during the last week of the campaign 18,000 speakers on the stump. He alone spoke for his party, but speeches which spoke to the intelligence and hearts of the people, and with a capital P. It is over now, but the vote is 7 millions to 6 millions and a half.[3]

The significance of the campaign, indeed, was not lost upon contemporaries. The election of McKinley constituted a triumph for big business, for a manufacturing and industrial rather than an agrarian order. 'For a hundred years,' Henry Adams observed, 'the American people had hesitated, vacillated, swayed forward and back, between two forces, one simply industrial, the other capitalistic, centralizing, and mechanical. . . . The issue came on the single gold standard, and the majority at last declared itself, once and for all, in favor of a capitalistic system with all its necessary machinery. All one's friends, all one's best citizens, reformers, churches, colleges, educated classes, had joined the banks to force submission to capitalism; a submission long foreseen by the mere law of mass.'

McKinley left no doubt that he regarded the election as a mandate for the policies industry wanted. He named a lumber baron Secretary of War, the president of the First National Bank of Chicago Secretary of the Treasury, a New York banker Secretary of the Interior, a post that had been conceded to the West. He summoned Congress into special session to rush through the mountain-high Dingley Tariff Act. In the 1898 elections the Populists were all but wiped out. 'For the first time in twenty years the silver menace is cleared away from the financial horizon,' wrote The Nation. 'The silver lining no longer adorns the Western sky.' With the silver forces routed, McKinley was able to push through the Gold Standard Act of 1900.

Actually the election of a Democratic administration in 1896 could

3. Quoted in Stephen Gwynn, Letters and Friendships of Sir Cecil Spring Rice, Vol. 1.

have served no useful purpose. The Democrats were not prepared, nor was the country ripe, for measures to bring financial giants under control, and the enormously increased production of gold in Australia and the Klondike soon made the money question, in its traditional form, one of mere historical interest. Yet Bryan's campaign had a significance quite independent of any question as to the soundness of its first principles. It was not only the last protest of the old agrarian order against industrialism, it was also the first attempt to create a new order. Bryan was the bridge between Andrew Jackson and Franklin D. Roosevelt.

IX

Philosophy, Arts, and Letters

1. PHILOSOPHY AND RELIGION

From the year 1859, when Darwin published his *Origin of Species,* we can date a revolution in thought as in science. The leaders of practically every Christian sect except the Unitarian fought hard for the book of Genesis and special creation, and Louis Agassiz of Harvard University attacked evolution of species on scientific grounds. But with the support of scientists like Asa Gray and of popularizers like Edward Youmans and John Fiske, the doctrine of evolution spread rapidly, and by the 'eighties had triumphed in most scientific and intellectual circles, and was making heavy inroads on the popular consciousness.

This doctrine of evolution was chiefly responsible for the abandonment of transcendentalism and the formulation of a new philosophy known as instrumentalism or pragmatism. Rooted in the eighteenth century, transcendentalism was a kind of philosophical romanticism which celebrated many of the things dear to the romanticists: Nature, individualism, spontaneity, the imagination. Transcendentalist philosophy rested upon primal intuitions not susceptible to proof, such as the benevolence of God and of Nature, and preferred the assurances of *a priori* principles to the findings of the laboratory.

Such a philosophy, unscientific and basically anti-intellectual, was clearly irrelevant to the kind of universe unveiled by Charles Darwin and described by the sociologist Herbert Spencer. Truth could no longer be something plucked from the inner consciousness of man, nor yet what

God revealed to man; it must be a hypothesis that would stand laboratory tests. Moral standards, when discovered to be the product of social
evolution and environment, could no longer be absolute and changeless.
Laws, by the same test, were neither eternal nor cosmic; they derived
from the social needs of the day. Fixed ideas were as out of place in
politics and economics as in science and religion.

Between the transcendentalism of Kant and Coleridge and Emerson
and the new doctrine of organic evolution as expounded by Darwin and
Huxley and John Fiske, there could be no logical compromise. The St.
Louis school of philosophy, founded in the 1860's by the German immigrant Henry Brockmeyer and the educator William T. Harris, simply
ignored the new science and devoted itself to the futile task of sowing
the seeds of Hegelian idealism in the unfertile soil of the Middle West.
The Scottish, or 'common sense,' school of philosophy, represented in the
United States by President James McCosh of Princeton, attempted to
effect a compromise between science and theology by arguing that 'evolution proceeded from a universal causation — namely God'; this did
not prove very helpful.

It was clearly necessary to formulate a new philosophy which would
harmonize with science and yet avoid the pitfalls of materialism, explain
an organic world and a dynamic society. This task was undertaken by a
remarkable group of philosophers who came to maturity in the last third
of the nineteenth century: Chauncey Wright, Charles Peirce, William
James, and John Dewey — all from New England. Pragmatism is the
name of the philosophy that they formulated; and although European
philosophers cried out with one voice that its concern with consequences
was just a piece of American sordidness, it may yet be admitted that
pragmatism was one of the really important novelties in the history of
thought through the ages.[1]

It is not easy to define pragmatism; the Italian Papini observed that
pragmatism was less a philosophy than a method of doing without one.
James certainly, and Dewey probably, would have admitted the validity
of this criticism, for they insisted that pragmatism was less an independent system of thought than a method of thinking about philosophical
questions. The philosophy which they elaborated was meant not for the
schoolroom but for the world of affairs. 'Better it is,' wrote Dewey, 'for

1. Parts of it were as old as the fifth century B.C., when Protagoras was exiled from
Athens for proclaiming the universal right of every man to find his own truth.

philosophy to err in active participation in the living struggles and issues of its own age and times than to maintain an immune monastic impecca-bility.' The pragmatists regarded truth not as an absolute, but as a social achievement, and James sometimes summed up his point of view in the phrase 'Damn the absolute!' Truth was something that each society and each thinking individual had to make for himself. 'The truth of an idea,' wrote James, 'is not a stagnant property inherent in it. Truth *happens* to an idea. It becomes true, it is *made* true by events.' The test of truth was to be found in its consequences; the business of the philosopher was to find out what worked to the best possible purposes. 'The ultimate test of what a truth means,' wrote James, 'is the conduct it dictates or inspires.'

The pragmatists conceived of our world as still in the making, for they accepted the fullest implications of organic evolution. To the field of morals and thought, as to social and political institutions, they applied but one test: the test of consequences. The effect of such an attitude on politics, law, economics, social institutions, education, art, and morals was little less than revolutionary, and the revolution, inaugurated in the 'eighties, is still going on. Its influence was not limited to America, but it was far greater in the United States than in other parts of the world, for it accommodated itself readily to the American environment and admir-ably expressed the national style. 'It is beyond doubt,' wrote John Dewey, 'that the progressive and unstable character of American life and civilization has facilitated the birth of a philosophy which regards the world as being in a constant formation, where there is still place for indeterminism, for the new, for a real future.'

What all this meant was a shift from the deductive to the inductive, from the intuitive to the experimental, from form to function, from pattern to process, from the static to the dynamic, from principle to practice.

Progressive teachers abandoned the idea that education was the mere acquiring of a body of information, and tried to make it a function of society. Political scientists talked less about abstractions such as 'sover-eignty' and the 'state' and more about institutions like the 'political party' and the 'spoils system.' Jurisprudents ceased to regard the law as a body of changeless truth and sacred precedent, and accepted the doc-trine that law was a creation of society and that every generation must make its own precedents. Economists reluctantly surrendered axioms which they had long regarded as inviolable, and 'economic laws' went down the drain. Sociologists came to reject the dour doctrine that man is the creature of his environment, and taught instead that man could transform and master his environment. Moralists ceased to speak so pontifically of 'self-evident' truths; liberal clergymen cited the Old Testament less frequently than the New; even historians admitted that historical truth was relative to each generation. That is one reason why textbooks so quickly become out-of-date!

The Protestant churches, whose doctrines were based exclusively on the Bible, suffered most from the new philosophy. Beginning with the Tübingen school in Germany in the 1830's, theological scholars had applied to the Bible critical standards long accepted in other fields of scholarship, testing the Scriptures by the facts of history, philology, geology, archaeology, and other sciences. In the hands of such devout ministers as Theodore Parker this 'higher criticism' was employed to justify an allegorical rather than a literal interpretation of sacred Scriptures. This application of the scientific method to religion paved the way for the rejection of much that seemed incongruous to modern life, and for a liberal religion based upon ethics rather than upon revelation. In the course of time the 'higher criticism' came to be accepted by many Protestant churches, and for them the Bible lacked Divine authority. Much was lost in this process, for when the Bible ceased to be regarded as God's word, it was no longer assiduously read, and one of the priceless heritages of English literature which had imparted beauty, wisdom, and imagination for three centuries was neglected.

The Protestant churches were more afraid of Darwinism than of the 'higher criticism,' and several Southern states actually passed laws forbidding the teaching of evolution in the public schools. For a time leaders of almost all denominations joined in the hue and cry against evolution, and a famous battle raged along the whole intellectual front. Orthodox defenders of the faith quoted with approval Disraeli's famous declaration, 'Is man an ape or an angel? I, my Lords, am on the side of the angels.' Stout champions of science countered with vigorous attacks upon what they denominated religious bigotry: John William Draper's *History of the Conflict Between Religion and Science* (1874) and Andrew D. White's 'Warfare of Science' (1876) [2] ran through innumerable editions, while the professional agnostic, Colonel Robert Ingersoll, lec-

2. Elaborated later (1896) into the two-volume *History of the Warfare Between Science and Theology.*

tured on 'Some Mistakes of Moses' to rapt audiences in all parts of the country. Moderates on both sides, meantime, attempted to effect a reconciliation between religion and evolution. The task was undertaken first by the English scientists, Huxley and Tyndall, who lectured widely in the United States. It was shortly taken up by a group of American scholars of whom the most successful was the philosopher John Fiske. Fiske, a very behemoth of a scholar, who wrote on history, ethnology, and sociology, expounded a reconciliation of science and religion to the students of Harvard College as early as the 'sixties, published his elaborate *Outlines of Cosmic Philosophy* in 1874, and thereafter, by books and lectures throughout the North, spread his message that evolution was simply God's way of doing things. Soon the most popular of American preachers, Henry Ward Beecher, announced his conversion, and shortly thereafter such distinguished clergymen as President McCosh, James Freeman Clarke of Boston, and William Tucker of the Andover Seminary came over to the side of the evolutionists.

While 'higher criticism' and Darwinism caused some churchmen to gird on armor and do battle for their faith, others chose to meet a third challenge of the times, that of the industrial revolution which was making it increasingly difficult for people to lead the life that Christ commanded. They discarded all but the essentials of the gospel and concentrated on making the Church an instrument of social reform. They were troubled by the conviction that industrial society had severed the bonds that had once held simpler village communities together. Class divisions had fractured the nation and atrophied the capacity of people of different social groups to feel toward one another. They were especially concerned that the ministers had become alienated from the poor in the great cities. From his parsonage in Columbus, Ohio, Washington Gladden championed the cause of industrial peace and succeeded in persuading labor and capital to arbitrate their differences. The venerable Edward Everett Hale of Boston — he had written 'The Man Without a Country' — was Theodore Parker's successor in rescuing the dangerous and perishing classes of Boston. The presses teemed with such volumes as George Herron's *The Christian Society*, Shailer Mathews's *Social Teachings of Jesus*, and Washington Gladden's *Applied Christianity;* and millions of copies were sold of Charles Sheldon's *In His Steps*, describing a congregation which followed consistently the teachings of Jesus.

Probably the most influential books came from the pen of the gifted

Walter Rauschenbusch. Upon graduation from seminary, he was sent to the Second German Baptist Church of New York, a small, impoverished congregation on the fringe of Hell's Kitchen. Here, in the depression of the 1890's, he saw good men go 'into disreputable lines of employment and respectable widows consent to live with men who could support them and their children. One could hear human virtue cracking and crumbling all around.' This experience convinced Rauschenbusch that evil was the consequence not of individual frailty but of environment. He wrote that his social view 'came through personal contact with poverty, and when I saw how men toiled all their life long, hard, toilsome lives, and at the end had nothing to show for it; how strong men begged for work and could not get it in hard times; how little children died — oh, the children's funerals! They gripped my heart — that was one of the things I always went away thinking about — why did the children have to die — why a single human incident of that sort is enough to set a great beacon fire burning, and to light up the whole world for you.'

In place of the emphasis of religion on individual salvation to make possible eternal life in another world, Rauschenbusch sought to achieve the Kingdom of God on earth. He interpreted literally the words of the Gospel: 'Thy Kingdom come; Thy will be done on earth. . . .' 'The kingdom of God,' he wrote, 'is not something wholly future, or remote from our present participation in it, but is a real power and an actual reign of God already begun on earth — a kingdom of heaven into which we may now enter.'

When Rauschenbusch went as professor to the Rochester Theological Seminary, it was to train up a generation of preachers imbued with his social gospel and to produce a series of books, the most notable of which was *Christianity and the Social Crisis* (1907).

> Competitive commerce [he wrote] exalts selfishness to the dignity of a moral principle. It pits men against one another in a gladiatorial game in which there is no mercy, and in which ninety per cent of the combatants finally strew the arena. It makes Ishmaels of our best men and teaches them that their hand must be against every man, since every man's hand is against them. It makes men who are the gentlest and kindliest friends and neighbors relentless taskmasters in their shops and stores who will drain the strength of their men and pay their female employees wages on which no girl can live without supplementing them in some way.

Sixth Avenue Elevated at Third Street by John Sloan

Courtesy of the Los Angeles County Museum of Natural History

New York's Lower East Side

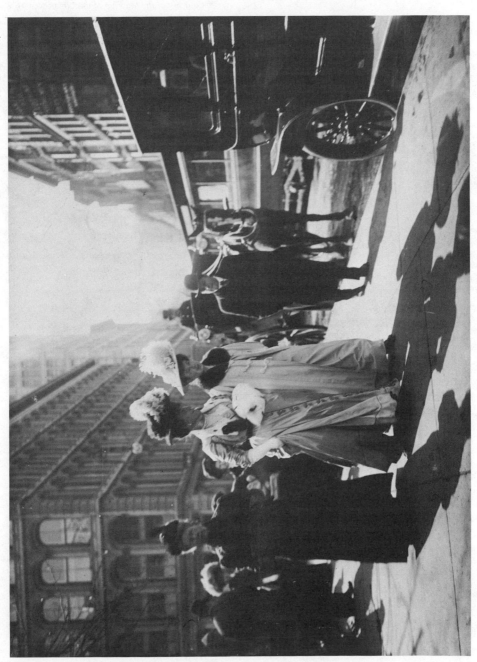

Broadway (c. 1910)

Pennsylvania Station, New York

Meantime, the fundamentalist churches closed their doors — and their minds — to the new currents of thought that were sweeping across the country. In a world that trembled and reeled beneath them they clung with passionate faith to the simple orthodoxies of the past, content with Henry Lyte's great prayer

> Swift to its close ebbs out life's little day;
> Earth's joys grow dim, its glories pass away;
> Change and decay in all around I see;
> O Thou who changest not, abide with me.

While the Protestant churches sought to come to terms with the new forces, the Roman Catholic Church was under no pressure to conform to the new science. It specifically repudiated 'modernism' in the papal encyclical *Pascendi Dominici Gregis* of 1907, although in the encyclical *Rerum Novarum* of 1891 the Church had sharply attacked the evils of unregulated capitalism and encouraged far-ranging social and economic reforms.

Perhaps in the long run the most important development of these years was neither the reconciliation of science and religion, which was never complete or harmonious, nor the formulation of the Social Gospel, but the growth of American Catholicism. In 1890 the Roman Catholic Church counted some 9 million communicants in the United States; thirty years later the number had doubled, and every sixth person and every third church member was Catholic. This growth coincided with and was in large part the product of the flood of immigration which brought 16 million people from the Old World to the New during these years; well over half of these came from the Catholic countries of central and southern Europe. No church that had been in the Americas a century before the Jamestown plantation could be called an immigrant church, but probably the majority of Catholic communicants were first- or second-generation Americans, while the Church hierarchy was long dominated by those who were Irish in background or in origin; thus Cardinal Gibbons of Baltimore and Archbishop Ireland of St. Paul. The unassailable unity of the Catholic Church, its centralized control and discipline, its elaborate organization, its comprehensive control of education from the parochial school through the seminary and the university, all contrasted sharply with the secularism, liberalism, decentralization, and fragmentation of Protestantism.

As in the past the growth of Catholicism gave rise to anti-Catholic movements that were inspired in part by religious considerations, in part by racial and economic. Most prominent of these was the American Protective Association which flourished, chiefly in the Middle West, during the 'nineties. Like the Know-Nothing Movement of the 'fifties and the later Ku Klux Klan of the 1920's, the A.P.A. was wholly lacking in intellectual content and wholly negative in character; unlike them it did comparatively little damage.

2. SOCIAL AND LEGAL THOUGHT

The eighteenth century — the Age of Reason — had believed that government, society, and economy were subject to the same great laws of Nature as the physical universe. Romanticism, with its exaltation of the imaginative, the subjective, and the irrational, dealt a heavy blow to this philosophy. The doctrine of evolution, however, appeared to restore to it something of its former lustre, for it argued progress not as conformity to great natural laws, but as part of the long process of evolution itself — an inevitable consequence of the survival of the 'fittest' in the long struggle for existence. The trouble with this doctrine was that while it guaranteed 'progress,' it did so only as a reward for acquiescence in a process that required several thousand years to work itself out.[3]

Frank Lester Ward, the father of American sociology, formulated a philosophy which, while fully accepting Darwinian evolution in the realm of Nature, resolutely rejected its authority in the realm of human nature. Man, he argued — and he was a distinguished zoologist and paleontologist — is not subject to the same iron laws that govern the animal world, for while environment, or Nature, masters and transforms the animal world, man masters and transforms Nature. What is more, he does this not by a blind struggle for existence, but by co-operation and applied intelligence.

> We are told [wrote Ward] to let things alone, and allow nature to take its course. But is not civilization itself, with all it has accom-

3. Discussing corruption in New York City politics, Henry George said to Youmans, 'What do you propose to do about it?' 'Nothing,' replied Youmans, 'You and I can do nothing at all. It's all a matter of evolution. Perhaps in four or five thousand years evolution may have carried men beyond this stage of things.'

plished, the result of man's *not* letting things alone, and of his *not* letting nature take its course. . . . Every implement or utensil, every mechanical device . . . is a triumph of mind over the physical forces of nature in ceaseless and aimless competition. All human institutions — religion, government, law, marriage, custom — together with innumerable other modes of regulating industrial and commercial life are only so many ways of meeting and checkmating the principle of competition as it manifests itself in society.[4]

In book after book — *Dynamic Sociology, Applied Sociology, Psychic Factors in Civilization* — Ward hammered home this scientific moral: that although for all other creatures environment controlled life, man alone was able to control his environment. It was the fittest who survived, to be sure, but fitness meant the application of organized intelligence, and the institution best qualified to organize man's intelligence was government. Ward called, therefore, for a sociology that would recognize that progress was something to be achieved and that would rely confidently on education and on government as the means whereby it was to be achieved. Though neglected in his own lifetime, he raised up a school of disciples, and his arguments came in time to be accepted as the common sense of the matter. One of the original leaders of pragmatism, Charles Peirce, observed that 'soon a flash and a quick peal will shake economists out of their complacency.'

The same forces that shaped sociology shook the study of economics to its foundations. Economists, like sociologists, had acquiesced passively in a series of iron laws that were said to control the economy. The full-throated attack upon this notion came from a new generation of academic economists, most of them trained in Germany where they were taught that the State should be an agency to produce a more humane social order. In 1885, a group of young Turks, all of whom had studied in Germany — Simon Patten, Herbert Baxter Adams, John Bates Clark, Edwin James, and E. R. A. Seligman — founded the American Economics Association. They boldly asserted: 'We regard the state as an educational and ethical agency whose positive aid is an indispensable condition of human progress. . . . We hold that the doctrine of laissez faire is unsafe in politics and unsound in morals.'

Men such as these wished to place the American university at the service of government. At the University of Wisconsin, they played an

4. *Psychic Factors of Civilization*, p. 262.

important role in aiding the administration of Governor Robert M. La
Follette. John R. Commons drafted bills for civil service, railroad regulation, workmen's compensation, and the regulation of municipal utilities,
and Charles McCarthy, a Wisconsin Ph.D. in history, headed a legislative drafting service responsible for numerous other measures. The professors also helped staff the government agencies which had been created by these laws: Commons served on the Industrial Commission, T. S.
Adams on the Income Tax Commission, B. H. Meyer on the Railroad
Commission; the president of the university, Charles Van Hise, on five
different commissions. Finally, the university, especially the School of
Economics, Politics and History headed by Richard T. Ely, trained students for careers in public administration; it even offered a course in bill
drafting.

Wisconsin is only the most spectacular example of what was happening across the country in these years. A similar relationship existed in
New York between Governor Charles Evans Hughes and Professor
Seligman of Columbia, in New Jersey between Governor Woodrow
Wilson and a group of reformers with close ties to Princeton and Columbia. On the national level, government commissions looked into problems of conservation, rural life, and industrial strife. By the time America entered World War I, it was accepted as a matter of course that
professors like Felix Frankfurter and Leo Wolman, as well as many
university-trained experts, would man the wartime agencies.

No economist did more to change old ways of viewing society than
Thorstein Veblen, a rugged individualist who was too independent to
stay long with any institution. A Norwegian farm-boy who had grown
up in the Middle West, Veblen was all his life something of an outsider,
and able therefore to look at institutions and practices of the American
economy without emotional or intellectual commitments. This he did in
The Theory of the Leisure Class (1899) and *The Theory of Business
Enterprise* (1904) and in a long series of volumes dealing with the more
ostentatious manifestations of the economy and the social system.
Veblen's books constituted an uncompromising attack on orthodox laws
of economics — indeed on the notion that there are any such laws —
and on the clichés with which privileged groups adorned their practices. Veblen himself emphasized the irrational element in the economy;
the role of conspicuous leisure, conspicuous consumption, and conspicuous waste; the conflict between the instinct for craftsmanship and the

instinct for pecuniary gain, the engineer and the price system. Since, he argued, those engaged in industry were subject to the discipline of tools and of the machine, they dealt with facts and were impatient of doctrines; but those who engaged in business were given to 'de jure rather than de facto arguments,' exalted precedent, and valued not production but pecuniary gain. Veblen called for an economy which would serve what he held to be the real interests and desires of men, one which would be controlled by the engineers and technicians rather than by businessmen or financiers.

Evolution and pragmatism profoundly affected the interpretation of politics and history as well. There was a widespread revolt against Newtonian concepts of government — against the tyranny of abstract concepts like sovereignty, the state, the separation of powers, and the illusion that there could be such a thing as 'a government of laws and not of men.' Instead scholars and statesmen turned to the analysis of constitutions and governments as they actually functioned: to the Constitution as a mechanism that often broke down and had to be tinkered with rather than as a sacred Covenant which (as one judge put it) meant precisely the same in his day as it had meant in 1787! They studied actual administration rather than impersonal government; analyzed what presidents and judges did rather than abstractions called The Executive Power or The Judiciary; explored the battlefields of party politics or the misty fogs of public opinion rather than the formal documentary record. Woodrow Wilson, who was a professor of politics at the time, explained the revolution with characteristic clarity:

> Government is not a machine but a living thing. It falls not under the theory of the universe, but under the theory of organic life. It is accountable to Darwin, not to Newton. It is modified by its environment, necessitated by its tasks, shaped to its functions by the sheer pressure of life. . . . Government is not a body of blind forces; it is a body of men. Living political constitutions must be Darwinian in structure and in practice.[5]

History, in many ways closer to literature than to the social sciences, responded somewhat more sedately to the new teachings. In the 'nineties the elder statesmen who had dominated the historical stage for two generations were passing from the scene. The venerable George Bancroft completed the Author's Last Revision of his great history just in

5. *Constitutional Government in the United States,* pp. 56–7.

time to have it go out of date on publication. In 1892 the indomitable Francis Parkman published the last panel of his great historical series on the struggle between the French and English peoples for the control of North America — the most impressive achievement of the age of historical romanticism. With the death of Bancroft in 1891 and of Parkman in 1893 the golden age of American history came to an end and the iron age set in. Three names dominate the new generation. In 1890 Captain Alfred Mahan published the remarkable *Influence of Sea Power upon History;* the next year Henry Adams completed his brilliant nine-volume study of the administrations of Jefferson and Madison and turned from the writing of history to the study of historical forces; in 1893 young Frederick Jackson Turner announced a frontier interpretation of American experience that was to bemuse the imagination of American historians for another half-century. These historians — and others of their generation — shared a rejection of romanticism and of moral considerations, together with an interest in history as a science.

Frederick Jackson Turner and Charles A. Beard both came out of the Middle Border and both were deeply influenced by the Populist revolt and the Progressive movement, but they responded with very different formulas. In a series of epoch-making essays Turner argued that what chiefly differentiated America from the Old World was the frontier, which took a European and transformed him into an American. 'American democracy,' he wrote, 'is fundamentally the outcome of the experience of the American people in dealing with the West.' Turner's habit of looking at American history from the vantage point of the West made for emphasis on environment rather than on heredity, and put a premium on isolation and the concept of uniqueness. Beard's emphasis, too, was environmental; in a prodigious flow of books and articles he read an economic interpretation into much of American history from the making of the Federal Constitution to American participation in two world wars. A crusader as much as an historian, Beard was incessantly active in public affairs, and used scholarship as a weapon in the struggle for Progressivism and reform, and eventually for isolationism.

Of all the social sciences, the study of law responded most decisively to evolution and pragmatism. Under the compelling pressures of the new exegesis Natural Law gave way to historical jurisprudence, and this in turn to sociological jurisprudence. Dean Roscoe Pound of the Harvard Law School characterized it as 'a movement for pragmatism as a philosophy of law; for the adjustment of principles and doctrines to the human conditions they are to govern rather than to assumed first principles; for putting the human factor in the central place and relegating logic to its true position as an instrument.'

This concept of the law as a living, growing organism owes much to the most distinguished American jurist of his generation, Oliver Wendell Holmes, who sat on the Supreme Court of Massachusetts and that of the United States for half a century, from 1882 to 1932. A product of Harvard and of the Union Army, Holmes had early associated with Charles Peirce, William James, John Fiske, and other members of the Metaphysical Club of Cambridge, and he took in pragmatism as naturally as his father, the famous Dr. Holmes of the Harvard Medical School, accepted the new teachings about antisepsis. From the beginning he confessed the pragmatist's distrust of systems and absolutes. 'The life of the law has not been logic,' he wrote in that famous treatise *The Common Law*, which he published in 1881, 'it has been experience. The felt necessities of the time — the prevalent moral and political theories, intuitions of public policy, avowed or unconscious, even the prejudices which judges share with their fellow men — have had a good deal more to do than the syllogism in determining the rules by which men should be governed. The law embodies the story of a nation's development through many centuries and cannot be dealt with as if it contained only the axioms and corollaries of a book of mathematics.'

In the hands of jurists like Justices Holmes, Brandeis, and Cardozo and of scholars like Professors Pound, Ernst Freund, and Felix Frankfurter, sociological jurisprudence was a program as well as a method. It held that the truth of law, like truth in general, was something to be found by experience; that good law was what worked best for society; and that the actual day-by-day workings of the law were more important than abstractions. It brought law squarely into the social sciences and required that it conform to social ends; it emphasized administration and enforcement — the cop on the beat as well as the judge on the bench; it affirmed that the past had not exhausted the creative capacities of jurists and lawmakers; it insisted that law was concerned with the collective good of society and embraced in its scope the whole range of social interests and needs.

If law was an organic growth rather than a body of fixed principles, it could be studied as a science rather than as a 'brooding omniscience in the sky' — the phrase is Holmes's. Creating a science of law was the special function of the law schools, the most notable of which were the Harvard Law School, revitalized by the appointment of C. C. Langdell as Dean in 1870, and the new University of Chicago Law School which called Ernst Freund to its faculty in 1894. Langdell introduced the case method, which speedily supplanted the older lecture and textbook system throughout the United States, though it has not yet been accepted in Europe, while Freund established administrative law as a major division of jurisprudence and, by his studies of the police power, paved the way for the 'legal realism' of our own day.

3. LITERATURE

The three writers who had emerged during the Civil War and Reconstruction years continued to dominate the literary scene: Mark Twain, William Dean Howells, and Henry James. In background, character, temperament, literary interests, and style they seemed to have little in common: Mark Twain, a child of the frontier, product of the rough and tumble mining camps and of life on the Mississippi; Howells, so proper and respectable, editor of the dignified *Atlantic* and the no less dignified *Harper's Monthly;* Henry James, fastidious and elegant, an exile from his own country spiritually as well as physically, preoccupied with problems of social and moral relationships too subtle for Mark Twain and too eccentric for Howells. Yet these three in fact had much in common: a revolt against the pervasive romanticism which plagued so much of the speech and the style of the time; an obsession with the relations between the New World and the Old — all three lived much of their lives abroad; disillusionment with many aspects of American society; and a common concern for moral values.

Mark Twain had published *Tom Sawyer* in 1876; now he entered into the era of his greatest productivity and his highest achievement. In the course of the following twenty years he wrote *The Prince and the Pauper,* an enlarged version of *Life on the Mississippi, A Connecticut Yankee at the Court of King Arthur, Pudd'nhead Wilson, Joan of Arc,* and, of course, the immortal *Adventures of Huckleberry Finn.*

Huckleberry Finn (1884) is, by common consent, the greatest of Mark Twain's books and one of the two or three greatest of American novels. The wonderful device of the raft floating down the Mississippi through the heartland of America enabled Mark Twain to pass in review American society at mid-century. Huck's voyage is the Odyssey of American literature; not even the voyage of Melville's *Pequod* can compare with it. It is not a pleasant society that we see through the eyes of the two innocents, Huck Finn and his friend Jim, escaping, as they think, from slavery; it is a society ravaged by cruelty, violence, and greed, pretentiousness, hypocrisy, and superstition, with only occasional glimmerings of decency and kindness. Mark Twain's disillusionment with 'the damn'd human race' was implicit in *Huckleberry Finn.*

All modern American literature comes from *Huckleberry Finn,* said Ernest Hemingway, and if we emphasize the word *American* there is a good deal of truth in the aphorism. For *Huckleberry Finn* is the first novel so unmistakably American in subject matter, setting, characters, idiom, and style that it could not have been written elsewhere. Though Mark Twain himself was the product of the frontier he was, in a deeper sense, the product of the whole of America of the Gilded Age — the America of business and speculation and politics as well as of mining and river-boating. In his fresh and idiomatic speech, his exuberant style, his wild imagination, his extravagant humor, he was indubitably American, and so too in his philosophy. 'Emerson, Longfellow, Lowell, Holmes, I knew them all, and all the rest of the sages, poets, seers, critics, humorists,' wrote Howells. 'They were like one another and like other literary men. But Mark Twain was sole, incomparable, the Lincoln of our literature.'

For the generation that came after his own *Gilded Age,* Mark Twain was a symbol not only for what he was but for what he failed to be and to do. Though he made his countrymen rock with laughter at the conventions and follies of the Old World, he accepted most of the conventions and follies of American materialism without protest. He settled down to respectable society in Hartford, Connecticut, devoted himself to business and money-making, curbed his Rabelaisian humor, and aspired to be accepted by the 'genteel' literary figures of New England. Yet he was never really content with any of his roles — humorist, novelist, lecturer, businessman — or, for that matter, with life itself. Increasingly he was embittered not so much by particular follies and immoralities as by human nature. 'I have been reading the morning paper,' he wrote to Howells. 'I do it every morning, well knowing that I shall find in it the usual depravities and basenesses and hypocrisies and cruelties that make up civilization and cause me to put in the rest of my day pleading for the damnation of the human race.' This note recurred increasingly as the years took their toll of him in failures and betrayals, in public disillusionments and private tragedies. As Henry Adams found some consolation for his misery in contemplating the cathedrals of Mont St. Michel and Chartres, so Mark Twain took refuge in adoration of the Maid of Orleans or in flight to Italy and Switzerland. To these last years belong his sentimental *Personal Recollections of Joan of Arc*, the savage *Man that Corrupted Hadleyburg*, and the allegorical *Mysterious Stranger* with its comforting conclusion that, after all, nothing was real.

> Strange, indeed, that you should not have suspected that your universe and its contents were only dreams, visions, fiction! [says Satan to the boy Theodor] Strange because they are so frankly and hysterically insane. . . . It is all a dream — a grotesque and foolish dream. Nothing exists but you. And you are but a thought — a vagrant thought, a useless thought, a homeless thought, wandering forlorn among the empty eternities.

For forty years Mark Twain carried on a literary love affair with William Dean Howells. 'You are really my only author,' he wrote to his Boston friend and mentor, 'I am restricted to you. I wouldn't give a damn for the rest.' Howells responded with affection and understanding. He was the first major critic to recognize that Mark Twain was not just a humorist but an authentic genius, just as he was the first to recognize talent in his young friend Henry James.

Howells's relationships with Mark Twain and with James illustrate something of the position he held in American intellectual society. Not the greatest novelist of his generation, nor the most profound critic, nor the most talented editor, nor the most perspicacious biographer, he combined these roles more successfully than any other individual, and for almost half a century functioned as Dean — or Pope — of American letters. He had begun, pleasantly enough, with essays and travel sketches — *Venetian Life*, for example — then had turned to recording 'the more smiling aspects of American life,' and then gone on to describe and interpret that life in almost every aspect. In some forty novels, thirty plays, a dozen books of criticism, and a score of biography and travel, Howells provided the most comprehensive description of middle-class Victorian America to be found in our literature. In these volumes Howells drew genre pictures of New England villages and Ohio towns, of the frontier and of the summer resort, of autumnal Boston and vigorous New York, of suburbia and Bohemia, and of the trans-Atlantic ship and European watering places; he crowded his literary canvas with farmers and workingmen, journalists and clergymen, timorous maidens and elderly spinsters, criminals and reformers, the new poor and the new rich — representative samples of American society north of the Potomac and east of the Mississippi. 'Stroke by stroke,' wrote Henry James, 'and book by book, your work was to become for this exquisite notation of our whole democratic light and shade and give and take, in the highest degree documentary.' Howells was the American Balzac, fascinated by the homely details of social relationships. A *Foregone Conclusion* and *The Kentons* explored the contrast between American and European manners; *The Rise of Silas Lapham* drew a classic portrait of the self-made man; *A Modern Instance* interpreted a Victorian marriage and its breakdown; *A Hazard of New Fortunes* dramatized industrial conflict in New York City, and *Annie Kilburn* work in the New England mill towns; *Dr. Breen's Practice* dealt with the new woman; *The Leatherwood God* returned to the Ohio frontier of the past, and *Through the Eye of a Needle* looked to a utopian future. In all of this, as James wrote, 'he adores the real, the natural, the colloquial, the moderate, the optimistic, the domestic, and the democratic.'

The 'optimistic' note was there, but gradually it died out as Howells came up against 'the riddle of the painful earth.' More and more he was caught up in the conflicts of the day — the Haymarket riot, the Populist revolt, the rights of labor, socialism. In the late 'eighties he moved to New York, and thereafter devoted himself increasingly to commentary on the economic order. 'After fifty years of optimistic content with civilization and its ability to come out all right in the end,' he wrote, 'I now abhor it, and feel that it is coming out all wrong in the end, unless it bases itself anew on a real equality.' Yet while Howells criticized the America of his day more sharply than did Mark Twain, he never suffered the desperate bitterness that ravaged the author of *The Man that Corrupted Hadleyburg*. Thus, Howells wrote *A Traveler from Altruria* to show what men could do to save themselves, while Mark Twain wrote *The Mysterious Stranger* to show that man was not worth saving.

Howells was not only an American Balzac, he was an American Sainte-Beuve as well. 'Yours is the recognized critical Court of Last Resort in the country,' Mark Twain wrote him, and few would have challenged the statement. If realism triumphed over romanticism, much of the credit goes to Howells. He did more than any one else to obtain a hearing for the rebellious younger novelists who were coming to the fore: he found a publisher for Stephen Crane's *Maggie, A Girl of the Streets*, wrote an introduction to Hamlin Garland's *Main-Travelled Roads*, championed Thorstein Veblen and Edward Bellamy, and welcomed a host of European naturalists like Henrik Ibsen, Björnson, Turgenev, Thomas Hardy, and Émile Zola.[6]

Where Mark Twain wrote of rivermen and miners and smalltown boys and slaves, and Howells of the proper middle classes, Henry James took for his theme the sophisticated relationships of an aristocratic — or sometimes merely a very rich — international society. Unlike the Old World, America he found thin and arid, lacking color, drama, intensity, and the marrow of literature. After 1875 James lived mostly abroad, and though a few of his novels — *The Bostonians, Washington Square*, and *The Ivory Tower*, for example — have an American setting, generally he set his stories in the great houses, the hotels, or the boulevards of London, Paris, and Rome. He was fascinated by the trappings and machinery of society — houses, gardens, dinners, teas, travel, manners, and ceremonies — but only because these reflected, or concealed, traditions and values with a deeper moral significance. A long shelf of novels and stories — and James wrote almost as voluminously as Howells — elaborates on two basic themes: the interaction of New World innocence and Old World sophistication, and the interaction of the values of the artist and of fashionable society. The first of these is the theme of the greatest of his books — *The American* (1877), *The Portrait of a Lady* (1881), *The Ambassadors* (1903), *The Wings of the Dove* (1903), *The Golden Bowl* (1904) — all exploring with subtlety and compassion the complex moral relationships of the American and the European, innocence and corruption, renunciation and moral triumph. The second — the theme of the artist and society — permeates much of these books as well as *Roderick Hudson* (1876), *The Aspern Papers*

---

6. One disgruntled romanticist, Thomas Bailey Aldrich, wrote:

> The mighty Zolaistic Movement now
> Engrosses us — a miasmatic breath
> Blown from the slums. We paint life as it is,
> The hideous side of it, with careful pains,
> Making a god of the dull Commonplace . . .

(1888), *The Lesson of the Master* (1892), *The Ivory Tower* (1917), and others. Because James wrote of subjects and characters far removed from the interest of the average American, and in an intricate style, he had few readers in his own lifetime. Like Melville, he has been rediscovered in our time, and is now generally acknowledged to be one of the great masters of the modern novel.

These three novelists grew to literary maturity during the period of the Darwinian controversy, but their writings do not reflect the new philosophy. Few of the younger men of letters, born after the Civil War, enjoyed a comparable immunity. Almost all of these were deeply influenced by Darwin's teachings, some bemused by the notion of evolutionary progress, others fascinated by the principle of the struggle for existence and the survival of the fittest. Thus, among the first, the poet William Vaughn Moody (b. 1869) in the sardonic 'The Menagerie':

> Survival of the fittest, adaptation,
> And all their other evolution terms,
> Seem to omit one small consideration,
> To wit, that tumblebugs and angleworms
> Have souls; there's soul in everything that squirms . . .

So, too, the philosopher-poet George Santayana held that Nature

> hath not made us, like her other children,
> Merely for peopling of her spacious kingdoms,
> Beasts of the wild, or insects of the summer,
> Breeding and dying
> But also that we might, half knowing, worship
> The deathless beauty of her guiding vision . . .

The most philosophical poet of his generation, Edwin Arlington Robinson (b. 1869), accepted evolution and scientific determinism but, like his contemporaries in Victorian England, refused to acquiesce in negation or despair. Fascinated by failure and renunciation, he peopled his Tilbury Town (really his own town of Gardiner, Maine) with a wonderful gallery of misfits and derelicts — Luke Havergal, Richard Cory, Miniver Cheevy, and others — who were unable to cope with life but often triumphed over misfortune and tragedy. Himself a confirmed bachelor, Robinson gave us, in his Arthurian trilogy — *Merlin, Lancelot,* and *Tristram* — the greatest love poetry in our literature, poetry which celebrates not so much the high noon but the twilight of passion, not the failure of men to live up to their own expectations but the enduring of the expectations. Robinson agreed with Mark Twain that man's fate was tragic, but he admonished man to meet the fate with fortitude and wrest from material defeat some spiritual victory. As he wrote in the autobiographical 'Captain Craig':

> It is the flesh
> That ails us, for the spirit knows no qualm,
> No failure, no down-falling; so climb high
> And having set your steps regard not much
> The downward laughter clinging at your feet . . .
>   only know
> As well as you know dawn from lantern light
> That far above you, for you, and within you
> There burns and shines and lives, unwavering
> And always yours, the truth. Take on yourself
> But your sincerity, and you take on
> Good promise for all climbing; fly for the truth
> And hell shall have no storm to crush your flight.

Meantime a host of less philosophical writers were carried away by the literary possibilities of the doctrine of the survival of the fittest. Not a subtle idea, it made few demands upon the mind or the imagination; mostly it took the literary form of celebrating passion, self-indulgence, violence, or malign fate. In Frank Norris's *Vandover and the Brute*, the central character reverts to a kind of animal brutality. The argument was put crudely by Jack London's Wolf Larsen:

> I believe that life is a mess. It is like a yeast, a ferment, a thing that moves or may move for a minute, an hour, a year, or a hundred years, but that in the end it will cease to move. The big eat the little that they may continue to move, the strong eat the weak that they may retain their strength. The lucky eat the most and move the longest, that's all.

So too Frank Norris in the best of his books, *The Octopus*, the story of the struggle of the sheep-ranchers against the Southern Pacific:

> Force only existed — Force that brought men into the world — Force that crowded them out of it to make way for the succeeding generation — Force that made the wheat grow — Force that garnered it from the soil to give way to the succeeding crops.

In Theodore Dreiser's writings, man was less animal than fool, victim of his own vagrant impulses, pitiful vanities, insatiable lusts and greeds. Like London, Dreiser was obsessed with power, but it was the complicated power of control over social and economic machinery: the city provided his background, and his characters pitted their cunning and ruthlessness against their fellow men in the desperate battlefields of business or of love. Frank Cowperwood, the hero — if we can use that word — of *The Titan* and *The Financier* is a far more sophisticated creature than Wolf Larsen, but not therefore more admirable. Through a quarter-century of writing, from *Sister Carrie* (1900) to *An American Tragedy* (1925), Dreiser played variations on the theme of determinism.

Determinism was by its very nature amoral, but few of the writers who subscribed to it could regard the contemporary scene with scientific detachment; not only London and Norris and Dreiser but most of the other poets and novelists of their day found themselves protesting against just those malpractices of business and politics which they had explained away as inevitable. The note of protest was struck by representatives of the old order, in a vocabulary which accorded ill with the modern temper. Thus as early as 1875 the romantic Lanier had asked:

> Yea, what avail the endless tale
> Of gain by cunning and plus by sale?
> Look up the land, look down the land,
> The poor, the poor, the poor, they stand
> Wedged by the pressing of Trade's hand . . .
> Does business mean, Die you — live I?
> Then 'trade is trade' but sings a lie:
> 'Tis only war grown miserly.

And so too William Vaughn Moody in his 'Gloucester Moors' (1900):

> But thou, vast outbound ship of souls,
> What harbour town for thee?
> What shapes, when thy arriving tolls
> Shall crowd the banks to see?
> Shall all the happy shipmates then
> Stand singing brotherly?
> Or shall a haggard ruthless few
> Warp her over and bring her to,
> While the many broken souls of men
> Fester down in the slavers' pen
>   And nothing to say or do?

Writers expressed a many-sided revolt against social evils. Robert Herrick, professor at the new University of Chicago, drew a somber picture of Chicago life against the background of the Haymarket riot in the *Memoirs of an American Citizen* and a savage indictment of the delinquencies of business in *The Common Lot*. Brand Whitlock, soon to be mayor of Toledo, Ohio, portrayed municipal corruption in *The Thirteenth District,* and William Allen White of the *Emporia Gazette* dramatized national corruption in 'The Mercy of Death.' Even the incurably romantic Booth Tarkington, in the best of his novels — *The Magnificent Ambersons* and *Alice Adams* — drew a picture of what happened to a gracious small town, his own Indianapolis, when it grew into an unlovely big city.

The cruel contrast between the high ideal of the independent, self-sufficient farmer and the tragic reality of farm life on the Middle Border brought a literary revolt similar to that against the industrial order. Edward Howe's grim *Story of a Country Town* (1884) fixed the type in our literature, but Hamlin Garland was destined to be the literary spokesman of the Middle Border. In his first and best book of short stories, *Main-Travelled Roads,* he presented farm life in Wisconsin and Iowa in all its unprepossessing actuality, 'with a proper proportion of the sweat, flies, heat, dust and drudgery of it all.' Eventually Garland achieved eminence and prosperity, settled in the East, and in his old age waved the magic wand of romance over the scenes of his boyhood and enveloped them in a nimbus of romance and of beauty. The result was *A Son of the Middle Border,* a classic narrative of life in the West, recounting the heroic saga of the pioneer. But if Garland himself had abandoned the realism of his youth, others had taken it up. Willa Cather in novels which lifted her to a high position in American literature — *My Ántonia* and *O Pioneers!* — painted the Nebraska prairie-land in somber hues, 'its fierce strength, its peculiar savage kind of beauty, its uninterrupted mournfulness'; and in that exquisite and moving portrayal of *A Lost Lady* she presented a memorable example of the spiritual disintegration that was a part of the pioneering process. The Norwegian-American, O. E. Rölvaag, in *Giants in the Earth* (1927) wrote the epic story of the immigrant farmer in the Dakota country. *Giants in the Earth* caught the spirit of the westward movement; but instead of being the proud story of man's conquest of the earth, it is the record of earth's humbling of man.

4. JOURNALISM

The same developments which were changing American life as a whole altered the character of American journalism. First there was the subordination of politics to 'news,' with a consequent development of the highly efficient machinery of reporting and news-gathering, made possible largely by improvements in the telephone, telegraph, cable, and printing machinery. Second, we note the passing of the personal element in journalism and the growth of editorial anonymity. With few exceptions newspapers ceased to be vehicles of opinion and became impersonal business enterprises. Third, there was centralization and standardization through the creation of chains, the elimination of competition, and the use of syndicated editorials and features. Fourth, there was the enlargement and improvement in the appearance of the newspapers, accomplished in large part through machinery such as the Hoe rotary press, the Mergenthaler linotype and rotogravure processes, the organization of news-gathering agencies like the United Press and the Associated Press, and the immense growth of advertising which gave newspaper-owners the money to install expensive machinery and maintain elaborate services. And last, the co-operation of the Federal Government in the form of low postal rates for newspapers and magazines, and rural free delivery.

The late 'seventies and 'eighties marked a dividing line in American journalism. Adolph Ochs bought the Chattanooga *Times* in 1878, and used it as a kind of trial run for the New York *Times*, which he acquired in the mid-'nineties. Joseph Pulitzer took over the moribund St. Louis *Post-Dispatch* that same year, and the New York *World* in 1883; Frank Munsey descended on New York in 1882; William Randolph Hearst acquired the San Francisco *Call* in 1887 and was already launched on a gaudy career in journalism and politics when he entered the New York newspaper arena a few years later.

No one better represented the new journalism than Joseph Pulitzer. A Hungarian-German Jew, trained under Carl Schurz, he first made the St. Louis *Post-Dispatch* a respectable newspaper, then moved on to New York where he acquired the almost defunct *World* from the speculator Jay Gould. By elaborating on the sensationalism of James Gordon Bennett, Pulitzer pushed the circulation of the *World* up to unprecedented figures, passing the million mark during the hectic days of the Spanish-American War. His paper, popular in appeal, played up crime, scandal, and sensational news in screaming headlines and illustrations, while its bold political program recommended it to the poor. Yet the *World* under Pulitzer was never merely a 'yellow' journal. There was a wide gap between the news stories and the editorial page, which was conducted on a high intellectual and moral plane. Pulitzer's ambition was to reach the masses through sensationalism, and then indoctrinate them with his liberalism — an ideal which did not work out very well. In the course of time the *World,* like the *Herald* and the *Sun,* became entirely respectable; after the retirement of Pulitzer and the accession of Frank I. Cobb to the editorship it became the leading Democratic organ in the country, a position which it maintained under the able direction of Walter Lippmann until its lamented demise in 1931.

The success of Pulitzer in tapping substrata of newspaper readers was contagious. Hearst, who had inherited a vast mining fortune, bought the New York *Journal* in 1896. Soon Hearst was outsensationalizing Pulitzer himself, and there ensued one of the fiercest struggles in the history of American journalism, a struggle which sent the circulation of both papers soaring, but degraded the press. Hearst, in the *Journal,* and in the nation-wide chain of papers he subsequently acquired, brought 'yellow' journalism to its most extreme development, but without the editorial compensations offered by the *World.* Lavish use of enormous black leaders, colored paper, blaring full-page editorials, and colored cartoon strips assured the Hearst papers an extraordinary popularity, but sensationalism became a national menace when, in order to boost the circulation of his papers, Hearst exploited the Cuban revolution to whip up popular demand for war with Spain. E. L. Godkin, in one of his last editorials, hotly denounced 'a regime in which a blackguard boy with several millions of dollars at his disposal, has more influence on the use a great nation may make of its credit, of its army and navy, of its name and traditions, than all the statesmen and philosophers and professors in the country.'

Pulitzer and Hearst, for all their faults, were real journalists, and Pulitzer at least contributed greatly to making journalism a respected profession. Not so a third powerful figure, Frank A. Munsey, who in 1882 came down to New York City from Portland, Maine, and began to deal in magazines and newspapers the way Daniel Drew had dealt in stocks. An entrepreneur, who at one time owned more valuable newspaper properties than anyone else in the country, Munsey had no interests outside business, subscribed to no ascertainable policies beyond an uncritical attachment to the status quo, and recognized no responsibility to the public. Shrewd, single-minded, and possessed by a driving ambi-

tion to make money, Munsey bought and sold newspapers and magazines as he bought and sold real estate. Those he did not sell he frequently killed off, for he believed in the survival of the fittest, by which
he meant, of course, the most profitable. At one time or another Munsey
owned the New York *Press, Sun, Mail, Globe, Herald,* and *Telegram,*
the Baltimore *American* and *News,* the Philadelphia *Times,* the Washington *Times,* and the Boston *Journal;* most of these he merged or
killed. 'Frank Munsey,' wrote William Allen White in one of the bitterest
of obituaries, 'contributed to the journalism of his day the talent of a
meat packer, the morals of a money changer, and the manners of an
undertaker. He and his kind have about succeeded in transforming a
once-noble profession into an eight per-cent security.'

Despite this vulgarization of the press, the professional standards and
ethics of journalism were on the whole improving during these transition
decades. This was brought about through voluntary agreements,
through the establishment of schools of journalism — of which those at
Columbia and the University of Missouri were the most influential —
and through the example of such papers as the *New York Times.* When
Ochs bought the *Times* in 1896, it was bankrupt and on the verge of
collapse; by printing only the news 'that's fit to print,' eschewing sensationalism, insisting on standards of integrity in reporting as high as those
for the editorial page, and building up a staff of skillful correspondents
around the world, Ochs made the *Times* at once the American counterpart of *The Times* of London and the Manchester *Guardian,* and an
immensely profitable enterprise. The vigorous growth of such papers as
the St. Louis *Post-Dispatch,* the Baltimore *Sun,* and the Chicago *Daily
News* went far to offset the low standards of the mass circulation press.

The 'eighties saw something of a revolution in magazines as well. The
magazine field had long been dominated by respectable family journals
like *Harper's,* content with a modest circulation and catering to middle-
class readers whose tastes were primarily literary. In 1886 came the
Forum, designed — as its title announced — for the discussion of controversial issues. Three years later Benjamin Flower launched the lively
Arena, which opened its pages to radicals, socialists, reformers, and
heretics of all stamps. Then came a flood of weekly and monthly magazines devoted to agitation rather than to entertainment — Bryan's *Commoner,* for example, and *La Follette's Weekly,* and a revived and revised
Independent. In 1912 Oswald Garrison Villard obtained control of *The*

Nation, and transformed it into a radical weekly of opinion. The *New Republic,* launched two years later under the auspices of Herbert Croly, and with an editorial staff that included Walter Lippmann and Randolph Bourne, was designed 'to start little insurrections,' and assumed at once a commanding position among the magazines of the country.

5. EDUCATION

No nation was ever more fully committed to the ideal of education, free, universal, and comprehensive, than the United States. Yet in 1870 only 6,871,000 pupils were enrolled in the public schools of the country, and of these only 80,000 were in the high schools.[7] Even these figures were misleading, for the average daily attendance was barely four million, while the average number of days of schooling for each pupil was seventy-eight. By 1900, however, enrollment had increased to 15,503,000 and by 1920 to 21,578,000,[8] of whom over two million were in the high schools. In the same half-century the percentage of children between five and seventeen who were in school increased from 57 to 78, while the average daily attendance increased fivefold. In 1870 Americans spent some $63 million on their public schools; by 1920 expenditures had passed the billion mark. In the half-century from 1870 to 1920 the per capita expenditure for public education rose from $1.64 to $9.80; and the sum spent on each pupil rose from $9 to $48.

The qualitative changes were more important than the quantitative. Progressive education, anticipated in the 'seventies, now came into its own. The leaders in the transformation of the school were Lester Ward, who thought education 'the great panacea' for all social ills and the mainspring of progress; William James, whose *Principles of Psychology,* published in 1890, provided inspiration for the new dispensation; G. Stanley Hall, first professional psychologist in America and president of Clark University, who wrote a pioneer work on *Adolescence;* Edward L. Thorndike of Columbia University's new Teachers' College, who carried out psychological and educational experiments which shattered orthodox assumptions about the learning process; and above all John Dewey, who

7. Compare, however, Great Britain, which had a population roughly two-thirds that of the United States; only 1,450,000 children were enrolled in schools, and the number who attended was much smaller.
8. Non-public school enrollment for 1900 was 1,334,000 and for 1920 was 1,700,000.

in time was to be not only the philosopher but the symbol of the whole progressive education movement. Dewey believed that the school was a legatee institution which had to carry on functions previously attended to by other groups in the community. In *The School and Society* (1899) he wished to use the school as a lever for reform to make society more 'worthy, lovely, and harmonious.' In *Democracy and Education* (1916) he argued that in an 'intentionally progressive' society culture could not be divorced from vocation.

The 'revolution' that these men and their disciples carried through involved a shift from emphasis on instruction to emphasis on the processes of learning, from subject matter to the training of the pupil, from teaching by rote to teaching by experience, from education as a preparation for life to education as life itself. It called for actual participation in the learning process by the children themselves — the original principle of the *Kindergarten* — through such activities as woodwork, cooking, printing, and map-making; did away with much of the formality of the classroom; greatly broadened the curriculum, often at the expense of thoroughness and discipline; encouraged children to play an active role in such affairs as student government; and attempted to make each school, in the words of Dewey, 'an embryonic community life, active with types of occupations that reflect the life of the larger society.' Within a short time Dewey and his associates at Teachers' College succeeded in imposing their educational philosophy on a large part of the country.

In higher education, too, there was an immense quantitative expansion: the 52,000 students who attended some five hundred colleges in 1870 — all of them financially and most of them intellectually impoverished — increased to 157,000 by 1890; the census of 1920 showed no less than 600,000 students in institutions of 'higher learning' — more than in all the universities of the Old World. The terms 'college' and 'university' still had the most varied meaning. Yet in 1888 Bryce was able to find ten or twelve institutions in the New World that he thought worthy to be ranked with the older universities of Britain and the European continent.

Soon this number increased, for the habit of building new universities overnight, from the ground up, was contagious. In 1889 John D. Rockefeller made the first of his munificent gifts to create the new University of Chicago, which promptly (1892) took its place among the leading institutions of learning of the New World. In the 1880's, too, the railroad magnate, Leland Stanford, endowed a university at Palo Alto, California, in memory of his son; supported by an initial gift of some $20 million, the Leland Stanford, Jr., University became at once the leading private institution of learning west of the Mississippi — an area heretofore committed almost entirely to public education. A third major creation of private benevolence was Clark University in Worcester, Massachusetts, which, under the guidance of the eminent psychologist G. Stanley Hall, undertook to be a New England version of the Johns Hopkins University. From these new universities came many educational innovations: the quarter system, for example, the summer session, extension divisions, the university press, and above all the creation of new graduate and professional schools.

More prophetic of future educational developments was the rapid growth of state universities after the turn of the century. California, which attracted only 197 students in 1885, enrolled over six thousand in 1915; during the same period student enrollment at the University of Illinois increased from 247 to 5500, at Minnesota from 54 to 4500, and at Ohio State from 64 to 4600. Pressures from state legislatures often required these institutions to be general service stations, and pressures from public opinion tended to lower academic standards. But many of the best state institutions, such as Michigan, Wisconsin, Illinois, and California, were able to hold their own academically with the older private universities.

Some of the educational pioneers of the earlier generation lived on into the new, and new educational statesmen came to the fore. William Rainey Harper, a Hebrew scholar from Yale, gathered about him on Chicago's Midway perhaps the most remarkable group of scholars to be found in America in the 1890's and inaugurated far-reaching experiments that contrasted sharply with the traditional Gothic architecture of the institution. Nicholas Murray Butler, founder and first director of Teachers' College, was elected President of Columbia University in 1901, and for over forty years directed the destinies of that institution, changing it from a small residential college to one of the largest of the world's universities and the leading center for graduate research in the country. Influenced by the example of German universities, these men were interested primarily in graduate and professional training and in the university as a center for research. Woodrow Wilson, who came to the presidency of Princeton just as Butler took over the helm at Columbia, favored the English rather than the German model. He raised standards, toughened the intellectual fiber of the college, and introduced something like the Oxford tutorial system, all with marked success; when he was defeated in his attempt to add on top of this a great graduate school, he resigned to become Governor of New Jersey.

One important feature of the upsurge of these years was the interest in adult education and in the organized popularization of culture. Bishop John Vincent founded Chautauqua in 1874, on the principle that 'mental development is only begun in school and college, and should be continued through all of life.' Though Chautauqua originally emphasized religion, the institution became increasingly secular, and devoted more and more of its energies to the popularization of literature, the arts, music, and drama. With permanent headquarters on the shores of Chautauqua Lake in western New York, Chautauqua was peripatetic, carrying its message of cultural cheer to small towns in America. With the coming of the movies and the radio, and with a growing sophistication in the rural and small town population, the influence of Chautauqua declined, and it withdrew to its lakeside refuge.

An essential instrument of education, and of popular culture, was the library — public, school, and university. The first of the great modern public libraries was founded in Boston in the 'fifties, and soon attracted not only public support but generous private bequests. The Chicago Public Library was developed around the gift of 7000 volumes presented after the great fire of 1871 by Thomas Hughes of England, author of *Tom Brown at Rugby*. The New York Public Library, which quickly became the largest of its kind in the Western world, was formed by the merger of three privately endowed libraries — the Astor, the Lenox, and the Tilden — with the library resources of the city. The Library of Congress was built around the nucleus of Thomas Jefferson's private library; it is not only the largest and the most effective library in the world, but through its Library of Congress classification system simplifies the tasks of scholars everywhere.

The major impulse to the public library movement came not from official sources or from public demand, but from the generosity of Andrew Carnegie. Inspired by a genuine passion for education, persuaded that the public library was the most democratic of all highways to learning, and mindful of his own debt to books and his love of them, the Pittsburgh iron-master devoted some $45 million of his vast fortune to the construction of library buildings throughout the country. His philanthropies were not only munificent but far-sighted, for by requiring a guarantee of adequate support to the libraries he built he laid the foundation for healthy growth of library facilities after his own gifts had served their initial purpose.

If the United States did not 'invent' the public library, it did, in a very real sense, invent library science. Three things were essential here: trained librarians and the development of librarianship as a profession; adequate systems of cataloguing and classification to make the vast and disparate literary records available to students; and a new attitude that invited the public into the library, put books in circulation, and dedicated the library to public service. By 1900 these objectives were achieved, thanks in great part to three remarkable men. Charles Cutter, long librarian of the Boston Athenaeum, devised a *Dictionary Catalogue* which was largely responsible for systemizing and giving uniformity to library cataloguing. Melvil Dewey, librarian at Amherst College and at Columbia University, not only invented the Dewey Decimal system of book classification — a system still used in almost every public library in the country — but launched the American Library Association and the first professional library journal, and set up the first school of library science. And at Newark, New Jersey, John Cotton Dana showed how a public library could be made an effective instrument of the cultural life of the whole community.

If, as most Americans from Jefferson to John Dewey confidently believed, education could be counted on to provide a sound basis for 'a happy and a prosperous people,' Americans at the turn of the century had reason to be cautiously optimistic. The principle of universal free public education from kindergarten through the university had been established; it only remained for the practice to catch up with the principle. That would take another half century or so.

6. ART AND ARCHITECTURE

The advance in American architecture might be measured by comparing the buildings of the Centennial Exposition of 1876 with those of the Columbian Exposition at Chicago in 1893. The first had been a helter-skelter of frame and iron buildings without either design or harmony —

doubtless the ugliest collection of buildings ever deliberately brought together at one place in the United States. The Chicago Exposition, by contrast, was elaborately designed, with the planning assigned to the gifted Richard Morris Hunt. Hunt promptly enlisted the assistance of the most distinguished artists and architects in the country: Daniel Burnham of Chicago, Stanford White of the ubiquitous firm of McKim, Mead, and White, and the brilliant young Louis Sullivan among the architects; Augustus Saint-Gaudens, Daniel Chester French, and Frederick MacMonnies among the sculptors; Gari Melchers, Edwin Blashfield, and Mary Cassatt as painters; while the famous Frederick Law Olmsted was put in charge of landscaping the exhibition — a task which he carried out with dazzling success. Saint-Gaudens's outburst at one of the planning sessions, 'Look here, old fellow, do you realize that this is the greatest meeting of artists since the fifteenth century?' was not wholly rhetorical.

Together these artists created along the shores of Lake Michigan the best designed and most beautiful exposition of modern times. Yet the design was conventional and the beauty mostly derivative, for the overall plan was classical. As Richard Watson Gilder exclaimed:

> Say not, 'Greece is no more,'
> Through the clear morn
> On light wings borne
> Her white-winged soul sinks on the New
>   World's breast
> Ah, happy West —
> Greece flowers anew, and all her temples soar!

The individual buildings were almost uniformly good, but they were good archaeologically rather than functionally. Hunt's Administration Building was a brilliant copy of St. Paul's Cathedral in London; Charles Atwood's Art Building had been unequalled — so Burnham said — since the Parthenon. Almost everything reminded the visitor of something he had read about or heard about, and most of the buildings had all the virtues of the originals except originality. The whole exposition proclaimed that there had been little advance in architecture since Rome. The most promising artist of the Fair, Louis Sullivan, whose exquisitely decorated Transportation Building did reveal originality, said of the Exposition that it was a 'fraudulent and surreptitious use of historical documents.' That was a palpable exaggeration. There was nothing surreptitious about the adoption of Roman classicism and little that was fraudulent. The fact is that Americans had not yet developed an indigenous architectural style.

Under the influence of the World's Fair, and under pressure from the now dominant firm of McKim, Mead, and White, the classical style spread over the whole United States. As Burnham said to the young Frank Lloyd Wright: 'The American people have seen the Classics on a grand scale for the first time. I can see all America constructed along the lines of the Fair, in noble, dignified classic style.' He was a good prophet. Washington adopted the classical as the official style; soon most public buildings, railroad stations, libraries, banks, and college dormitories were being constructed in this style. In 1894 McKim and Burnham established the American Academy at Rome where architects and artists could learn at the source; in 1897 the citizens of Nashville voted to build a replica of the Parthenon in their city; within a few years state legislatures were crowning their capitols with domes; and in time even the homespun Lincoln was to find himself in a memorial more fitting for a Caesar than for a rail-splitter from Illinois.

More clearly than any other architect of his time, Louis Sullivan saw the connection between architecture and society. 'What people are within,' he wrote, 'the buildings express without; and inversely what the buildings are objectively is a sure index to what the people are subjectively.' This interpretation of the functional character of architecture was not meant to flatter Americans of the 'nineties; Sullivan added that 'the unhappy, irrational, heedless, pessimistic, unlovely, distracted and decadent structures which make up the bulk of our contemporaneous architecture point with infallible accuracy to qualities in the heart and soul of the American people.' The most gifted architect of his generation — he built the great Auditorium Building in Chicago, and the Carson, Pirie, and Scott store with its daring use of glass and metal and its rich ornamentation — Sullivan failed in the end to sustain this early promise. It remained for his student and disciple, Frank Lloyd Wright, to vindicate his philosophy and realize his vision.

Born in 1869 and trained in the architectural office of Adler and Sullivan, Wright had helped Sullivan on the Transportation Building of the World's Fair, and taken to heart Sullivan's guiding principle that function determines form and form follows function. He conceived a building not as something superimposed upon the landscape, but as part of an organic whole embracing the structure and its furnishings, the grounds and gardens about it, the people who use it or live in it, and even the community of which it is a part. He began to apply these ideas in the 'nineties as soon as he set up on his own, in such early prairie-style buildings as the Isabel Roberts House at River Forest, Illinois, the Coonley House at Riverdale, and the Robie House on Chicago's Wood-lawn Avenue, as well as in the first Taliesin House at Spring Green, Wisconsin, where he worked and taught. In 1906 he built the Unity Temple in Oak Park, Illinois, the first of those remarkable churches which did so much to revolutionize ecclesiastical architecture in the United States. At the same time he was putting up office buildings and factories, among them the dazzling Larkin Building in Buffalo. All this was but preparation for those masterpieces of the later years — houses like Falling Waters near Pittsburgh where the rocks and waterfalls were incorporated into the house itself; the Imperial Hotel in Tokyo built to withstand earthquakes — but not bombing; office buildings like the futuristic Johnson wax works in Racine, Wisconsin; desert residences like his own Taliesin West in Arizona. Not only as a master architect — indubitably the greatest produced in the New World — but as a highly articulate social philosopher, Wright waged a lifelong war against all that was meretricious, derivative, and imitative, against exploitation of the land for profit, and the megalomania of the skyscraper. His artistic life spanned two generations; he tied together the world of Louis Sullivan and the world of Mies van der Rohe; he did more than any other person to change the character of American architecture.

Three major figures dominated American painting during the transition years: Winslow Homer, Albert Ryder, and Thomas Eakins. Fed up with his genre paintings, good as they were, Homer went abroad in the early 'eighties, and returned to take up a solitary residence on the Maine coast and devote himself to painting the sea and the wilderness. In one great canvas after another — 'The Life Line,' 'Fog Warning,' 'Lost on the Banks,' 'The Undertow,' 'Eight Bells,' and 'Gulf Stream' — he portrayed the struggle of man against the elements. By the 'nineties Homer was the acknowledged dean of American painting, but without a school or disciples.

Albert Ryder, like Herman Melville, lived obscurely in New York, and achieved wide recognition only after his death. Like Melville, too, he lived in 'a dark, moon-ridden world, stirring with strange beauty that indicated unexplored realities, deeper than the superficial levels of being.' [9] His imagination was lyrical and mystical, and he transferred to his varnish-covered canvases the mysterious world of his imagination — clouds flitting across the moon, ships forever lost scudding before the wind, dim figures out of the mythological past — thus his 'Death on a Pale Horse,' 'The Flying Dutchman,' 'Jonah,' 'Siegfried and the Rhine Maidens,' which make us fancy for a moment, in Justice Holmes's phrase, 'that we heard a clang from behind phenomena.'

In these years, too, the Philadelphia artist Thomas Eakins reached maturity. A kind of Thorstein Veblen among artists, Eakins had no use for the salon or the academy; he was fascinated by the spectacle of men and women at their normal activities; by the body, not as an aesthetic object, but at work and at play. (As Mumford says, 'He made art face the rough and brutal and ugly facts of our civilization, determined that its values should grow out of these things, and should not look for its themes to the historic symbols of Europe.') He thought no subject without interest or dignity. Thus he gave us young men swimming, oarsmen rowing, professors lecturing, surgeons operating, singers on the concert stage, scientists in their laboratories. When he painted President Hayes it was at his desk, working, and in his shirt sleeves; as presidents were not supposed to have shirt sleeves, the painting was rejected. 'I never knew but one artist, and that's Tom Eakins, who could resist the temptation to see what they think ought to be rather than what is,' said Walt Whitman, whose portrait is one of Eakins's masterpieces.

In the first decade of the new century, a group of Eakins's disciples launched the 'Realistic' movement. Robert Henri, George Luks, Everett Shinn, William Glackens, and John Sloan had all studied at the Philadelphia Academy under Eakins's disciple, Thomas Anschutz, and had absorbed Eakins's philosophy and something of his technique as well. Most of them had worked as pictorial reporters on the old Philadelphia Press, where they had come to know the seamy side of life in the great city, and most had studied in Paris where they had come under the influence of Daumier and Toulouse-Lautrec. During the 'nineties they drifted to New York where they formed a loose-knit brotherhood of independents and were joined by other young rebels and independents like George Bellows and Maurice Prendergast. The leader of the group

9. The phrase is from Mumford's *The Brown Decades*; it is suggestive that Mumford is also the biographer of Melville.

was the gifted Robert Henri, who conducted a famous school that was as much philosophical as artistic.

> When we packed our paint boxes and journeyed to the new Henri School [wrote one of his pupils] it was equivalent to throwing our gauntlets in the face of the old order. Life seemed somehow to flow richer and freer in Bowery bars and flop houses than at Sherry's or the Waldorf, and the mother who wrapped her baby in a tattered shawl seemed a more poignant embodiment of maternity than her more fortunate sisters. . . . In the Henri School we learned that art was only another medium for interpreting life, and we were taught that all the arts are kindred and relevant to painting.

The philosophy of the group was that of Walt Whitman — unpretentious, robust, and equalitarian:

> See in my poems immigrants continually coming and landing . . .
> See in my poems cities, solid, vast, inflamed, with
> paved streets, with iron and stone edifices,
> ceaseless vehicles, and commerce . . .
> Hear the loud echoes of my songs, there, read the
> hints come at last.

Affectionately and sensitively they painted the color of the great city — McSorley's Bar, boys swimming off East River piers, children dancing in the teeming streets of the Five Corners; Bowery bums lounging under the 'El'; Yeats dining at Petipas; girls drying their hair on the roofs of tawdry tenements; a prize-fight at Sharkey's; the Staten Island ferry.

In 1908 these Manhattan realists gave their first exhibition at the Macbeth Galleries in New York, and were promptly dubbed the 'Ash-Can School.' When two years later they presented an exhibition of Independent Artists, two thousand visitors tried to crash the gates on opening day. These exhibits mark the beginnings of modern art in America as truly as the much-touted Armory Show of 1913.

Meantime another group of painters — they cannot be denominated a school — took up impressionism, that new technique, vision, and philosophy of painting which artists like Monet were revealing to an enraptured world. Inness had anticipated something of impressionism in his later years, and so, too, the remarkable John La Farge, who was equally talented in oils, water colors, murals, and stained glass and who had returned from Paris in the 'sixties determined that his paintings 'indicate very carefully in every part the exact time of day and circumstance of light.' In 1874 Mary Cassatt — whose brother was president of the Pennsylvania Railroad — settled permanently in Paris, where she studied with Degas, exhibited with the Impressionists, bought their paintings, and saw to it that they were to be found in American collections; and herself experimented both with impressionism and with techniques of Japanese art with notable success. Others who revealed the influence of the Impressionists were the enormously successful Childe Hassam, who painted the New England countryside in shimmering light and New York City in its gayer and more colorful moods; the frail Theodore Robinson, who had studied at Giverncy with Monet and whose early death deprived his country of its most promising Impressionist; and John Twachtman, who preferred the melting snows, the frozen waterfall, the purple light on snow to the warmer landscapes that attracted his fellow Impressionists.

Professionally the most successful of all American painters belonged to no school — unless it was the school of Velasquez — and to no country. John Singer Sargent was born in Florence, Italy; studied in Dresden, Venice, and Paris; kept studios in London and Boston; traveled incessantly in the Old World and the New; painted hundreds of portraits, acres of murals, and preferred to do water-colors. The most dazzling technician of his generation, he became society's idol — and victim. The rich and the great flocked to his studios: the President, millionaires, and the leaders of society; to be painted by Sargent became as essential to social success as to be presented at Court.

In sculpture as in architecture American artists had first struck roots in the classical soil of Greece or Italy, and then moved to modern France. Heretofore sculpture, like architecture, had been mostly derivative. The statues and decorations of Hiram Powers, Thomas Crawford, and Horatio Greenough had been faithful copies of Canova or Thorwaldsen, and so, for the most part, had the designs of that odd combination of lawyer, poet, dramatist, and sculptor, William Wetmore Story. The first American sculptor to give evidence of originality was John Quincy Adams Ward, whose statues of Henry Ward Beecher and President Garfield were completely divorced from neo-classical insipidity. But modern American sculpture begins with the work of Augustus Saint-Gaudens, who for a generation towered over all of his artistic contemporaries. Born in Ireland of Irish and French parentage, he nevertheless recorded the American genius with rare sympathy and understanding. His Lincoln, in Lincoln Park, Chicago, with its intuitive comprehension of the combination of rugged shrewdness and spirituality, is so convincing that 'no one, having seen it, will conceive him otherwise thereafter.' The Farragut Monument (1881), its base executed by Stanford White, and the Shaw Memorial (1897) in Boston established him as indubitably the foremost monumental sculptor of his day. The loveliest of Saint-Gaudens's statues is the figure he made for the tomb of Mrs. Henry Adams. 'From Prometheus to Christ, from Michael Angelo to Shelley,' wrote Henry Adams, 'art had wrought on this eternal figure almost as though it had nothing else to say.'

Less powerful and less original than Saint-Gaudens, American-trained and in the American grain, Daniel Chester French made his reputation with the colossal figure of The Republic at the Columbian Exposition and brought it to a climax with the enormous bronze Lincoln for the Lincoln Memorial in Washington. Frederick MacMonnies, a student of Saint-Gaudens and of Falguière in Paris, did the great foundation The Ship of State for the World's Fair, and soared at once to spectacular popularity; his playful but unmistakably shameless Bacchante which was considered too improper for the Boston Public Library found more appropriate refuge in the court of the New York Public Library. Equally impressive were contributions from George Gray Barnard, a disciple of Rodin who is best known for his collection of medieval art appropriately housed in The Cloisters overlooking the Hudson River; Karl Bitter, director of sculpture of three major Expositions; and Lorado Taft, whose towering statue of Blackhawk overlooking the Rock River in Illinois is one of our most impressive historical monuments. And already younger and more original sculptors such as Paul Manship and Jo Davidson were on the way.

Imperialism and World Power

1. THE UNITED STATES IN WORLD AFFAIRS

Writing in 1889 Henry Cabot Lodge, later to win distinction as one of
the most chauvinistic of American politicians, observed that 'our relations with foreign nations today fill but a slight place in American politics, and excite generally only a languid interest.' This generalization
applied with equal force to the whole generation which had come to
maturity since Reconstruction. From the settlement of the Alabama
Claims and the successful weathering of the *Virginius* crisis to the erup-
tion of Hawaii and Venezuela into American politics in the 1890's, the
relations of the United States with the outside world were singularly
placid. To be sure, businessmen stepped up investments overseas; interest in Latin America quickened; and the government began to refurbish
the navy. But most Americans, proverbially parochial in their outlook,
were busy with their internal affairs — repairing the devastations of the
war, settling the continent, constructing their transportation and industrial system, absorbing new racial groups, and enjoying the game of
politics.

The change came in the 'nineties, and it synchronized with the passing
of the frontier, the shift from the 'old' to the 'new' immigration, the rise
of the city, and the coming of age of our industrial system. As fast as the
population of the United States grew, the productivity of its economy
increased still more rapidly. Almost every year before 1876 the United
States suffered an unfavorable balance of trade; almost every year

thereafter the balance was decidedly in its favor. In 1865 the foreign trade of the United States had been $404 million; by 1890 it had reached $1635 million, but the increase in the export of manufactured goods was proportionately far greater than the rise in the export of agricultural products.

The emergence of the United States as a world power was not an isolated phenomenon, for the closing years of the nineteenth century witnessed everywhere an international struggle for new markets and sources of supply. Great Britain, after a long and stated indifference, was fired once more with enthusiasm for expansion; France found compensation for defeat by Germany in consolidating her African empire; Germany, having proved herself the strongest Continental power, demanded her share of colonial pickings; Japan startled the world with her smashing victory over China in 1895. Europe, having almost completed the partitioning of Africa, began, in rivalry with Japan, to break pieces from the weak Chinese Empire. But in the Western Hemisphere the Monroe Doctrine stood as an insuperable barrier against fresh acquisition of American territory by European powers, although it did not prevent the exploitation of Latin America by European or North American capital.

After the Civil War the two traditional policies in American foreign relations — the Monroe Doctrine and expansion in the Pacific area — persisted. American interest in the Pacific and the Far East dated back to the old China trade and became vital with the acquisition of Oregon and California. As early as 1844 Caleb Cushing negotiated a treaty with China granting trade and tariff concessions similar to those enjoyed by Great Britain. Nine years later Commodore Perry steamed past the forts at Yedo Bay and opened Japan to the commerce of the Western world. 'It is self-evident,' wrote Perry, who anticipated much of our subsequent Pacific policy, 'that the course of coming events will ere long make it necessary for the United States to extend its jurisdiction beyond the limits of the western continent,' and he recommended a naval base in the Far East.

America's interest in the Pacific came increasingly to center on the Hawaiian islands, 2300 miles southwest of California. Hawaii, or the Sandwich Islands, had been discovered by Captain Cook in 1778, and early served as a convenient port of call in the China trade and recruiting station for Yankee whalers. By 1840 Honolulu, with whalemen and merchant sailors rolling through its streets, shops filled with Lowell shirtings, New England rum, and Yankee notions, orthodox missionaries living in frame houses brought around the Horn, and a neo-classic meeting house built of coral blocks, was a Yankee outpost. As early as 1842 Webster assured the islanders that the United States could not permit Hawaii to become the possession of any other foreign power; but it just missed becoming a British protectorate in 1843. A few years later, Secretary Marcy negotiated with King Kamehameha III a treaty of annexation which failed of ratification because by its terms Hawaii was to be made a state of the Union. Seward, too, moved toward annexation, but despite the approval of President Johnson and later of Grant, nothing was done. In 1875, however, the United States concluded with the Hawaiian monarch a reciprocity treaty which granted exclusive trading privileges to both nations and guaranteed the independence of the islands against any third party; twelve years later the Senate approved a treaty which renewed these privileges and ceded Pearl Harbor on the island of Oahu to the United States.

These treaties greatly stimulated the sugar industry, which the sons of thrifty missionaries had established in Hawaii. American capital poured in, sugar production increased fivefold within a decade, and by 1890, 99 per cent of the Hawaiian exports, then valued at $20 million, went to the United States. The islands had, in fact, become an American commerical appendage. In 1881 Secretary Blaine declared Hawaii to be part of the 'American system' and announced somewhat cryptically that if Hawaiian independence were endangered, the United States 'would then unhesitatingly meet the altered situation by seeking an avowedly American solution for the grave issues presented.' Native Hawaiians became increasingly disturbed by the growing determination of the American government to establish a protectorate, the ambitions of American settlers, and the overdependence of the islands on the American economy. Then came the McKinley tariff of 1890, which by providing a bounty of 2 cents a pound to domestic sugar dealt a catastrophic blow to the Hawaiian economy; sugar fell overnight from $100 to $60 a ton, and property values collapsed. American planters and industrialists who had opposed annexation out of fear that it would hamper their importation of Asiatic labor, now concluded that only annexation could restore to Hawaiian sugar interests their American market on equal terms.

They were even more alarmed when, in 1891, Queen Liliuokalani

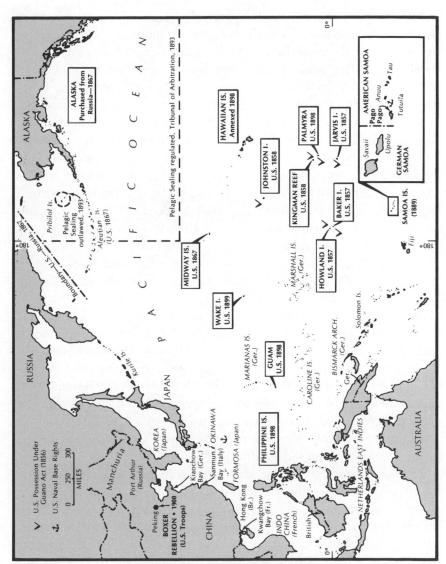

UNITED STATES IN THE PACIFIC

237

came to the throne and inaugurated a policy looking to the elimination
of American influence and the restoration of autocracy. This threat to
the position of the powerful American element excited a prompt counteroffensive. After marines had been landed from the U.S.S. *Boston,*
with the connivance of the American minister John L. Stevens, a Committee of Safety consisting largely of missionaries' sons deposed the
hapless Queen on 17 January 1893. A provisional government under
Chief Justice Sanford B. Dole was set up, which promptly opened negotiations for annexation to the United States. 'I think we should accept
the issue like a great Nation,' wrote Minister Stevens, 'and not act the
part of pigmies nor cowards'; [1] he did his part by hoisting the American
flag over the government house at Honolulu. President Harrison, in full
sympathy with this 'white man's burden' attitude, precipitately accepted
a treaty of annexation on 14 February; but before the Senate got
around to it, Grover Cleveland became President and hearkened to
the appeal of 'Queen Lil.' 'I mistake the Americans,' he said, 'if they
favor the odious doctrine that there is no such thing as international
morality; that there is one law for a strong nation and another for
a weak one.' He withdrew the treaty from the Senate and sent out a
special commissioner to investigate the situation. When the commissioner reported that the Hawaiian revolution was the work of American interests, aided by Minister Stevens, he denounced the affair and
endeavored to persuade the provisional government to step down. The
gesture was ineffective and, under the presidency of an American, the
provisional government became permanent, and Cleveland was forced
to recognize the Republic of Hawaii.

Between 1893 and 1898 two developments in the Far East sharpened
the demand to annex the Hawaiian islands. The first was the rise of
Japan to world power, and the fear of a Japanese inundation of the
islands. The second was the prospective annexation of the Philippines,
which gave Hawaii a new significance as a naval base. Toward annexation McKinley had no such scruples as had animated his predecessor,
but there was still sufficient opposition in the Senate to necessitate action

1. Compare Tennyson's birthday tribute to Queen Victoria:

> We sailed wherever ship could sail;
> We founded many a mighty state;
> Pray God our greatness may not fail
> Through craven fear of being great.

by a Joint Resolution instead of through the normal method of a treaty — as in the case of Texas half a century earlier. Annexation was finally consummated by the Joint Resolution of 7 July 1898. An organic act of 1900 conferred American citizenship on all subjects of the short-lived republic and the full status of a Territory of the United States, eligible for statehood, on the islands.

Our official relations with Samoa were equally confused. The Samoan, or Navigators', Islands were to the South Pacific what the Hawaiian were to the North Pacific, and from the 1830's on they had offered refuge to whalers and a virgin field for missionary activities. Not until the late 'sixties did American commercial interests with the islands become important enough to attract official attention; and in 1878 a treaty granted the United States trading privileges and the right to build a coaling station at Pago Pago in the island of Tutuila. Shortly thereafter Great Britain and Germany secured comparable concessions in the islands, and there followed ten years of ridiculous rivalry for supremacy among the three powers, each supporting a rival claimant to the native kingship. The danger of involving the United States in serious international complications was averted by the establishment in 1890 of a tripartite protectorate guaranteeing the independence and neutrality of the islands and confirming American rights to Pago Pago. Unimportant as this episode was, it constituted nevertheless, in the words of Secretary of State Gresham, 'the first departure from our traditional and well established policy of avoiding entangling alliances with foreign powers in relation to objects remote from this hemisphere.' After another embarrassing native civil war, and intensified bad feeling between the United States and Germany, the tripartite agreement was abrogated in 1900, and the islands divided between Germany and the United States, Great Britain obtaining compensation elsewhere.

In the years between Polk and Lincoln, the Monroe Doctrine had lapsed into something approaching desuetude; Seward's vigorous action against the French in Mexico proved that it was still a basic factor in American foreign policy. Other objectives of our foreign policy were to maintain the leadership of the United States in all American questions, promote the commercial interests of the country, and keep peace, all of which involved diplomatic controversies with powers who still had colonies and capital in America.

United States policy toward Latin America headed in new directions under the vigorous leadership of James G. Blaine, who emphasized a Pan-Americanism primarily economic in character. Although the high priest of protection, Blaine realized that protective tariffs impaired commercial relations between the United States and Latin America, because those countries, still regions of extractive industries, sold to us an excess of raw materials such as coffee, sugar, and cocoa, but purchased their manufactured articles in the cheaper markets of Europe. Since 87 per cent of Latin American exports to the United States entered duty free, Blaine threatened to clamp a tariff on them unless the Latin American countries lowered their duties on United States products. To promote a Pan-American customs union, a series of uniform tariffs which would give reciprocal preference to American products or goods in all American countries, he called a Pan-American Conference in 1881. President Garfield's death was followed by a change in the State Department, and President Arthur revoked the invitations. Eight years later President Harrison placed Blaine once more in a position to advance his cherished project. In October 1889 the first International American Conference, representing eighteen countries, convened at Washington to consider Blaine's proposals for a Pan-American customs union and the arbitration of international disputes. To the Latin Americans both seemed like the invitation of the spider to the fly, and were politely rejected. But the Conference resulted in the creation of a Commercial Union of American States, renamed the Pan American Union in 1910, which served as a clearinghouse for the dissemination of scientific, technical, and economic information and set a precedent for future inter-hemispheric meetings.

His ardor for Pan-Americanism somewhat dampened, Blaine endeavored to secure the same thing by taking advantage of provisions in the McKinley tariff of 1890 to negotiate reciprocity agreements with ten nations. These agreements were abrogated by the Wilson tariff of 1894, but the Dingley tariff of 1897 made provision for a new series of reciprocity arrangements which were effected not only with the Latin American states but with European countries. On the eve of his assassination President McKinley announced his conversion to reciprocity as a universal policy:

> The period of exclusiveness is past. The expansion of our trade and commerce is the pressing problem. Commercial wars are unprofitable. A policy of good will and trade relations will prevent reprisals. Reciprocity treaties are in harmony with the spirit of the times; measures of retaliation are not. If perchance some of our

tariffs are no longer needed for revenue or to encourage and protect our industries at home, why should they not be employed to
extend and promote our markets abroad?

In spite of this persuasive argument from a high source, the Republican
Senate, sensitive to the interests of American manufacturers, stubbornly
refused to ratify any of the reciprocity treaties that were negotiated.

Although the Pan-American Conference did not accept arbitration as
a formal policy, the principle itself was often invoked. President Hayes
had arbitrated the Argentine-Paraguay boundary dispute; Cleveland
arbitrated a similar quarrel between the Argentine and Brazil; and Secretary Blaine intervened in no less than four boundary disputes. The
principle of arbitration won a victory, too, in another quarter: the fur-
sealing controversy in the Bering Sea. Anxious to prevent the ruthless
extermination of the seal in Alaskan waters, and convinced that Canadian practices violated both property rights and morals, Blaine sought to
extend American jurisdiction over the whole of the Bering Sea, and
ordered the seizure of Canadian fishing vessels operating in these waters. He was right in principle but wrong in law, and the controversy
took an ugly turn. But in 1891 the United States and Great Britain had
the good sense to resort to arbitration. The tribunal decided all points of
law adversely to the United States, but implicitly admitted the wisdom
of Blaine's efforts to save the seal by drawing up regulations looking to
that end.

Far more dangerous than this sealing controversy was the dispute
over the Venezuela boundary which afforded an opportunity both to
expand the Monroe Doctrine and to apply the principle of arbitration.
British Guiana and Venezuela had long quarreled over their boundary
line, but the whole question suddenly took on new importance with the
discovery of gold in the hinterlands of both countries. Both Britain and
Venezuela advanced ambitious claims, but Venezuela's was especially
extravagant; Lord Salisbury refused to submit the question to arbitration because, not unreasonably, he feared arbiters would split the difference, and sent troops to the disputed area. Secretary of State Olney
promptly dispatched a note which gave a definition of the Monroe Doctrine that alarmed Latin America, insulted Canada, and challenged England:

> Today the United States is practically sovereign on this continent,
> and its fiat is law upon the subjects to which it confines its inter-

position. . . . Distance and three thousand miles of intervening
ocean make any permanent political union between a European
and an American state unnatural and inexpedient.

Lord Salisbury allowed four months to go by before acknowledging this
astonishing note — and rejecting it. On 17 December 1895 President
Cleveland informed Congress of Salisbury's refusal, asked Congress to
set up a commission to determine the proper boundary line, and added
that any attempt by Britain to assert jurisdiction beyond that line should
be resisted by every means in the nation's power. Panic ensued in Wall
Street, dismay in England, and an outburst of jingoism in the United
States.

No facts of the controversy could justify these extreme claims and
provocative language. Why did Olney and Cleveland use it? They had
become disturbed by British encroachments in Latin America, including
support of a Brazilian rebellion, the occupation of Trinidad, a blockade
of Nicaragua, and the seizure of Belize (British Honduras). Congressmen put Cleveland on the defensive by insisting that after having refused to take a strong line on Hawaii and Samoa he could not permit an
Old World monarchy to discipline a New World republic. Seventeen
years later Olney explained his language on the ground that 'in English
eyes the United States was then so completely a negligible quantity that
it was believed only words the equivalent of blows would be really
effective.'

In fact, only the felt necessity for friendship with the United States
induced the Salisbury government to let this challenge lie. The British
navy's numerical strength over the American was at least five to one, but
Britain, as Bayard wrote, 'has just now her hands very full in other
quarters of the globe. The United States is the last nation on earth with
whom the British people or their rulers desire to quarrel. . . . The other
European nations are watching each other like pugilists in the ring.' And
so they were. The first Boer War was already in the making, and England was beginning to find 'splendid isolation' a bit precarious. On 2
January 1896 came Jameson's raid in the Transvaal, and the next day the
whole world was reading that masterpiece of diplomatic blundering,
Kaiser Wilhelm's congratulatory telegram to the Boer leader Kruger.

The South African crisis reinforced Britain's determination to avoid
war. On 25 January, Joseph Chamberlain declared that war between the
two English-speaking nations would be an absurdity as well as a crime,

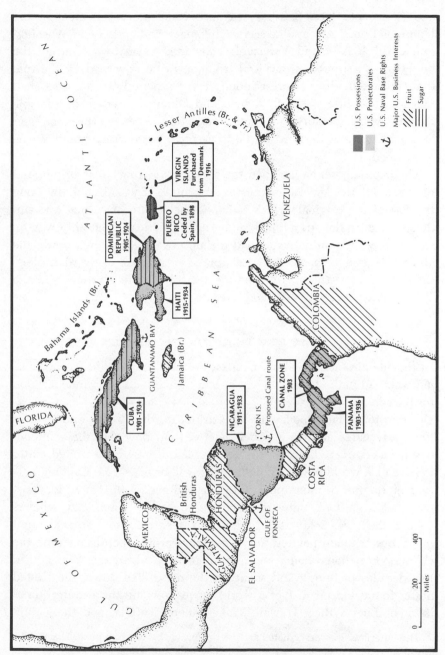

Legend:
- U.S. Possessions
- U.S. Protectorates
- ⚓ U.S. Naval Base Rights
- Major U.S. Business Interests
  - Fruit
  - Sugar

ATLANTIC OCEAN

Lesser Antilles (Br. & Fr.)

VENEZUELA

VIRGIN ISLANDS Purchased from Denmark 1916

PUERTO RICO Ceded by Spain, 1898

DOMINICAN REPUBLIC 1905-1924

HAITI 1915-1934

Bahama Islands (Br.)

CARIBBEAN SEA

COLOMBIA

GUANTANAMO BAY

Jamaica (Br.)

FLORIDA

CUBA 1901-1934

GULF OF MEXICO

British Honduras

MEXICO

GUATEMALA

HONDURAS

EL SALVADOR

GULF OF FONSECA

NICARAGUA 1911-1933

CORN IS.

Proposed Canal route

CANAL ZONE 1903

PANAMA 1903-1936

COSTA RICA

0   200   400
Miles

UNITED STATES IN THE CARIBBEAN

243

and two weeks later Salisbury made a conciliatory statement in the House of Lords. After some secret diplomacy at London and Washington, Great Britain and Venezuela concluded a treaty submitting the boundary question to an arbitral tribunal, to be governed by the rule that 'adverse holding or prescription during a period of fifty years shall make a good title.' Thus Cleveland and Olney secured their principle that the whole territory in dispute should be subject to arbitration, and Salisbury his, that the British title to *de facto* possessions should not be questioned.

The tribunal, which included the Chief Justices of Great Britain and the United States, gave a unanimous decision in 1899, substantially along the line of the original British claim. So the Monroe Doctrine was vindicated, arbitration triumphed, and Anglo-American friendship was restored. But such outbursts of bad feeling always leave their mark; the abusive language in the American press so affected Rudyard Kipling, then living in Vermont, that for the rest of his life references to the United States were sarcastic and bitter.[2]

2. MANIFEST DESTINY IN THE 'NINETIES

In the 'nineties, the spirit of 'manifest destiny,' long dormant, was once more abroad in the land. The phrase had once served as a rationalization for the conquest of Texas and California; it was now to serve as a rationalization for a 'large policy' in the Caribbean, the Pacific, and the Far East. Advocates of such a policy asserted that now that the continent had been conquered, it was the ineluctable destiny of the United States to become a world power. 'Whether they will or no,' wrote Captain A. T. Mahan, the naval philosopher of the new imperialism, 'Americans must now begin to look outward.' Politicians, businessmen, and scholars echoed the idea. Scholars furnished the scientific and historical argument; businessmen pointed to the potential profits; politicians rang the changes on national honor and glory and party advantage. When, after two decades of tumult and shouting, the noise died down, the United States found herself in fact a world power, owning the extraterritorial lands of Puerto Rico, Hawaii, Wake, Guam, Tutuila, and the Philip-

2. His bitterness was exacerbated by the readiness of American publishers to take advantage of international copyright; see 'The Ballad of Three Captains.'

pines, exercising protectorates over Cuba, Panama, and Nicaragua, and asserting interest and influence in the Far East.

This policy, which within half a century carried the United States to world leadership, was merely one manifestation of an international trend toward imperialism. Britain, France, and Germany were busy carving up Africa, and Russia and Japan joined them in scrambling for special concessions in China. Everywhere, too, historians, journalists, poets, novelists, and clergymen provided a convenient rationalization of what came to be called, quite simply, the 'white man's burden.'

Nowhere was such rationalization more full-blown than in the United States. Captain A. T. Mahan, whose influence was world-wide, demonstrated in his brilliant series on the history of seapower that not the meek, but those who possessed big navies, inherited the earth. Professor John W. Burgess of Columbia University claimed that Teutonic nations were 'peculiarly endowed with the capacity for establishing national states, and are especially called to that work; and therefore that they are entrusted, in the general economy of history, with the mission of conducting the political civilization of the modern world.' The Reverend Josiah Strong, author of the enormously popular tract, *Our Country,* asked rhetorically, 'Does it not look as if God were not only preparing in our Anglo-Saxon civilization the die with which to stamp the peoples of the earth, but as if he were massing behind that die the mighty power with which to press it?'

The Washington *Post* stated on the eve of the Spanish War:

> A new consciousness seems to have come upon us — the consciousness of strength — and with it a new appetite, the yearning to show our strength . . . ambition, interest, land hunger, pride, the mere joy of fighting, whatever it may be, we are animated by a new sensation. We are face to face with a strange destiny. The taste of Empire is in the mouth of the people even as the taste of blood in the jungle. It means an Imperial policy, the Republic, renascent, taking her place with the armed nations.

Republicans, Democrats, and even Populists joined in the hue and cry for more land, more trade, and more power. Henry Cabot Lodge asserted:

> From the Rio Grande to the Arctic Ocean there should be but one flag and one country. . . . In the interests of our commerce . . .

we should build the Nicaragua canal, and for the protection of that canal and for the sake of our commercial supremacy in the Pacific, we should control the Hawaiian islands, and maintain our influence in Samoa. England has studded the West Indies with strong places which are a standing menace to our Atlantic seaboard. We should have among those islands at least one strong naval station, and when the Nicaragua canal is built, the island of Cuba . . . will become a necessity.

Other Republicans like Theodore Roosevelt and Albert J. Beveridge were equally emphatic, but neither Democrats nor Populists would permit the Republicans to monopolize so popular an issue. Although Democrats, as befitted a party of state rights and limited government, tended to oppose a 'large' policy; some like Senator Morgan of Alabama supported expansionism; Populists like Allen of Nebraska were no less enthusiastic.

If the United States was to be a world power, she would have to be able to act like one in a crisis. In the 'eighties Americans had awakened with something of a shock to the discovery that their navy was, in the words of the *Army and Navy Journal,* 'a heterogeneous collection of naval trash.' Cleveland's energetic Secretary of the Navy, William C. Whitney, pushed through an ambitious program reorganizing the Navy Department, and starting construction on some thirty armored ships — a program which was sweetened for the American businessman by his very sensible requirement that the armor be of American manufacture. All through the 'nineties Captain Mahan made clear, in a flood of books and articles, that the command of the seas was the price of survival, and his friends, Theodore Roosevelt and Henry Cabot Lodge, spread his gospel where it would do most good — in legislative chambers and executive departments. In 1880 the U.S. Navy had ranked twelfth among the navies of the world; by 1900, with 17 battleships and 6 armored cruisers, it was third.

3. CUBA LIBRE

The Cuban revolution of 1895 brought this latent imperialism and chauvinism to a head. From the days of Jefferson, Cuba had been an object of peculiar interest to the United States, and regarded as properly within the American sphere of influence. As long as Spain owned the island, most Americans were inclined to let matters rest, but the possibility of ultimate acquisition was never out of the minds of American statesmen. 'In looking forward to the probable course of events,' wrote John Quincy Adams, 'it is scarcely possible to resist the conviction that the annexation of Cuba to our Federal Republic will be indispensable to the continuance and integrity of the Union itself.' Polk had tried to purchase the island, and the effort was renewed under the Pierce administration, but without results other than the aggravation of sectional hostilities in the United States. On the very eve of the Civil War a Senate Committee announced that 'the ultimate acquisition of Cuba may be considered a fixed purpose of the United States.' Yet curiously enough, when the opportunity came, during the Ten Years' War of 1868–78, the United States was coy. That Ten Years' War was characterized by all the disorder, cruelty, and affronts to American interests and honor that later marked the course of the revolution of 1895. Yet in the first instance the United States carefully avoided any commitment to the cause of the rebels, and in the second it entered the war on their side.

How did it happen that the inhumanities of the 'sixties had not shocked American sensibilities as did those of the 'nineties? How did it happen that the murder of the crew of the *Virginius* in 1873 did not create a demand for war while the explosion of the *Maine* in 1898 was followed by a wave of war hysteria? How did it happen, finally, that the destiny which necessitated American control of the Caribbean in the 'nineties, was not manifest in the 'sixties? The explanation of this change in the temper of the people and in the policy of the government is fourfold.

In the first place, Americans of the 'nineties had come to share with the British, Germans, and French a willingness to take up 'the white man's burden,' and to this had added their own special sense of 'manifest destiny.'

In the second place, the technique of journalism had become enormously elaborated and its methods increasingly sensational. Newspaper editors found that circulation responded to atrocity stories, and it became immensely profitable to exploit them. The New York *World* and the New York *Journal,* then engaged in a titanic struggle for circulation, were the worst offenders in the business of pandering to the popular taste for sensation, but they were by no means alone. Most of the metropolitan papers throughout the country bought news service from the New York papers, and most of them subscribed to the Associated Press, which served up daily concoctions of atrocities for the delectation of the public. For three years, from 1895 to 1898, this campaign of propaganda went on until at last the American people were brought to the point where they demanded intervention on behalf of 'humanity.'

In the third place, the economic stake of the United States in Cuba had increased enormously during these thirty years. Even more important than the $50 million invested in Cuban sugar and mining industries was our trade with Cuba, which by 1893 had passed the $100 million mark, and all the varied business and shipping interests dependent upon that trade. The United States was particularly disturbed by the destruction of the Cuban sugar industry which resulted from the insurrection. As the American Minister to Spain told one of his diplomatic colleagues: 'The sugar industry of Cuba is as vital to our people as are the wheat and cotton of India and Egypt to Great Britain.'

In the fourth place, the United States had developed a new set of world interests which made it seem necessary that the entire Caribbean area be under American control. American interests in the Pacific and the Far East enhanced the importance of an isthmian canal, and the prospect of having to defend an isthmian canal made the islands that guarded the route strategically important. A big navy was needed to protect our far-flung island possessions; new island possessions were essential in order to provide harbors and coaling stations for our navy.

It is in the light of these changing attitudes and interests that we must interpret the events leading up to the War of 1898. That war was fought to liberate Cuba, but it did not begin until the Cubans had already struggled three years for their own liberation. The fundamental cause of the Cuban revolution which broke out in 1895 was Spanish political oppression and economic exploitation; the immediate cause was the prostration of the sugar and tobacco industries which resulted from the operation of tariffs, both in the United States and in Spain. The price of sugar which had been 8 cents per pound in 1884 fell to 2 cents in 1895. The consequent misery in Cuba furnished the impetus for revolution.

From the beginning the United States was inextricably involved in the Cuban revolution. The United States made little effort to enforce neutrality: a Cuban 'junta' in New York spread propaganda and sold bonds, and scores of filibustering expeditions sailed out from American ports. Americans with property interests in Cuba clamored for intervention to safeguard those interests; Cubans with suspiciously fresh citizenship papers claimed the protection of the United States government. When, within a fortnight of the outbreak of war, a Spanish gunboat fired upon an American vessel, the *Alliance,* an outburst of jingoism revealed the temper of the country. 'It is time,' said Senator Cullom, 'that some one woke up and realized the necessity of annexing some property,' a point of view echoed by others prominent in public life. Thereafter one incident after another aggravated the already tense relations between the United States and Spain and excited American sympathies for the insurrectionists, and if there happened to be a dearth of such incidents, they were brazenly fabricated by the yellow press.

In the face of a mounting demand for intervention, President Cleveland remained imperturbable. He issued a proclamation of neutrality, recognizing the existence of a state of rebellion but not the belligerency of the rebels, and he did his best to enforce neutrality laws and protect American interests. Beyond that he would not go, and when Congress, in April 1896, passed a concurrent resolution recognizing the belligerency of the Cubans, Cleveland ignored it, and in the summer of 1896 he confessed that 'there seemed to be an epidemic of insanity in the country just at this time.' Yet by the end of that year even Cleveland's patience had been strained well-nigh to the breaking point by Madrid's refusal to conciliate the rebels. In his annual message to Congress he warned Spain that if the war went on and degenerated into a hopeless struggle the United States would have to intervene.

McKinley had been elected on a platform calling for Cuban independence, yet at first he too moved with circumspection. 'You may be sure,' he confided to Carl Schurz, 'that there will be no jingo nonsense under my administration,' and shortly after his inauguration he pledged his opposition 'to all acquisitions of territory not on the mainland — Cuba, Hawaii, San Domingo, or any other.' In September 1897 McKinley tendered the good offices of the United States to restore peace to Cuba, but even though a new and more liberal government had come to power in Spain the American overture was rejected. Nevertheless the Spanish government did inaugurate some long overdue reforms. General Weyler, who had earned the unenviable title of 'Butcher Weyler' was recalled; the policy of herding Cubans into concentration camps, where many of them died of disease and mistreatment, was disavowed; all political rights enjoyed by peninsular Spaniards were extended to the Cubans; and a program looking to eventual home rule for Cuba was inaugurated.

Home rule no longer satisfied the Cubans, who were increasingly confident that the United States would intervene. They would accept nothing but independence, the one demand Madrid felt it could not grant. Reforms which might have headed off the revolution had they been offered in 1895 had come too late, and the war of extermination continued. Yet the sincere desire of the Spanish government for peace did much to moderate the attitude of the American government if not of the American people. In his annual message of December 1897 McKinley repudiated the idea of intervention and urged that Spain 'be given a reasonable chance to realize her expectations and to prove the asserted efficacy of the new order of things to which she stands irrevocably committed.' But it was not to the interest of the Cuban junta to permit a policy of neutrality, and on 9 February 1898 the New York *Journal* printed a private letter to Washington from the Spanish Minister, Enrique de Lôme, which had been stolen from the Havana post office. 'McKinley's message,' wrote the tactless Minister, 'I regard as bad. . . . It once more shows what McKinley is, weak and a bidder for the admiration of the crowd, besides being a would-be-politician who tries to leave a door open behind himself while keeping on good terms with the jingoes of his party.' De Lôme resigned at once, but the relations of the United States and Spain were exacerbated.

At this juncture the nation was horrified by the news that in the night of 15 February 1898 the battleship *Maine* had blown up in Havana harbor with the loss of 260 lives. 'Public opinion,' Captain Sigsbee wired, 'should be suspended until further report,' but when a naval court of inquiry reported that the cause of the disaster was an external explosion by a submarine mine, 'Remember the Maine!' went from lip to lip. Without a dissenting vote Congress rushed through a bill appropriating $50 million for national defense. McKinley continued to exercise restraint, but war fever was mounting. Redfield Proctor, a fair-minded Vermonter who had opposed war, gave the Senate on 17 March a vivid description of the horrors of the concentration camps he had seen in Cuba. Still Spain procrastinated. On 25 March McKinley sent to Madrid what turned out to be his ultimatum, suggesting an immediate armistice, the final revocation of the concentration policy, American mediation between Spain and Cuba, and, ambiguously, the independence of Cuba. Spain's formal reply was unsatisfactory, but the Sagasta government, anxious to avoid war, moved toward peace with a celerity unusual at Madrid. Orders were given revoking the concentration policy and a desperate effort was made to persuade the Pope to request a suspension of hostilities — a request to which the Spanish government could agree without loss of face. The American Minister at Madrid, Stewart L. Woodford, cabled to know whether such a solution would be satisfactory to McKinley. 'I believe,' he said, 'that this means peace, which the sober judgment of our people will approve long before next November and which must be approved at the bar of final history. I believe that you will approve this last conscientious effort for peace.' But McKinley's reply was non-committal. On 9 April the Spanish government accepted every demand but Cuban independence, and Woodford thought, perhaps too optimistically, even that might be worked out. Hostilities were suspended, and Woodford cabled that if nothing were done to humiliate Spain further the Cuban question could be settled in accordance with American wishes. Any President with a backbone would have seized this opportunity for an honorable solution.

But by now McKinley's course was set. He had lost faith in Spain's ability to resolve a conflict which was both unhumane and injurious to American interests. Nor did he have the courage to withstand public sentiment. If Mark Hanna, much of big business, and the Republican Old Guard wanted peace, Congress, the press, and much of the country were clamoring for war. Theodore Roosevelt wrote in a private letter, 'the blood of the murdered men of the *Maine* calls not for indemnity but for the full measure of atonement, which can only come by driving the Spaniard from the New World.' By going to war, McKinley would silence such critics within his own party, and deny the Democrats the opportunity to campaign for Free Silver and Free Cuba.

On 11 April the President sent Congress the war message which he had already prepared. At the very conclusion of that message he added a casual reference to the fact that Madrid had capitulated on almost every point at issue.

> This fact, with every other pertinent consideration, will, I am sure, have your just and careful attention in the solemn deliberations upon which you are about to enter. If this measure attains a successful result, then our aspirations as a Christian, peace-loving people will be realized. If it fails, it will be only another justification for our contemplated action.

That action, of course, was war.

4. EXIT SPAIN

Lightheartedly the United States entered upon a war that brought quick returns in glory, but new and heavy responsibilities and problems that were to persist and grow all through the next century. It was emphatically a popular war. Although imperialistic in result, it was not so in motive, as far as the vast majority of its supporters were concerned. To the Joint Resolution of 20 April 1898, authorizing the use of the armed forces of the nation to liberate Cuba, had been added the self-denying Teller Amendment, declaring that 'The United States hereby dis-claims any disposition or intention to exercise sovereignty, jurisdiction or control over the said Island, except for the pacification thereof, and asserts its determination, when that is accomplished, to leave the government and control of the Island to its people.'

With what generous ardor the young men rushed to the colors to free Cuba, while the bands crashed out the chords of Sousa's 'Stars and Stripes Forever!' And what a comfortable feeling of unity the country obtained at last, when Democrats vied in patriotism with Republicans, when William J. Bryan had himself appointed Colonel and donned a uniform alongside the irrepressible T. R.; when the South proved as ardent as the North for the fight, and Joe Wheeler, the gallant cavalry leader of the Confederacy, became a high commander of the United States Army in Cuba! To most Americans, the war arrayed hip-hip-hurrah democracy against all that was tyrannical, treacherous, and fetid in the Old World. How they enjoyed the discomfiture of the Continental powers, and how they appreciated the hearty good will of England! Every ship of the smart little navy, from the powerful *Oregon*, steaming at full speed round the Horn to be in time for the big fight, to the absurd 'dynamite cruiser' *Vesuvius*, was known by picture and reputation to every American boy. And what heroes the war correspondents created — Hobson who sank the *Merrimack*, Lieutenant Rowan who delivered the 'message to Garcia,' Commodore Dewey ('You may fire when ready, Gridley'), Captain Philip of the *Texas* ('Don't cheer, boys, the poor fellows are dying'), and Teddy Roosevelt with his horseless Rough Riders! [3]

3. Roosevelt's volume celebrating the deeds of the Rough Riders was the inspiration for one of Mr. Dooley's choice comments:

'I haven't time f'r to tell ye the wurruk Tiddy did in ar-hmin' an' equippin' him-

This was no war of waiting and endurance, of fruitless loss and hope deferred, of long casualty lists and 'vacant chairs.' On the first day of May, one week after the declaration, Dewey steams into Manila Bay with the Pacific squadron and without losing a man reduces the Spanish fleet to old junk. The Fifth Army Corps safely lands in Cuba and wins three battles in quick succession. Admiral Cervera's fleet issues from Santiago Bay and in a few hours' running fight is completely smashed, with the loss of a single American sailor. Ten weeks' fighting and the United States has wrested an empire from Spain.

Prince Bismarck is said to have remarked, just before his death, that there was a special providence for drunkards, fools, and the United States of America. On paper Spain was a formidable power. If the United States had more battleships, Spain had more armored cruisers and torpedo craft. While Spain had almost 200,000 troops in Cuba before the war, the American regular army included less than 28,000 officers and men, scattered in small detachments from the Yukon to Key West. So weak were the harbor defenses of the Atlantic coast, and so apprehensive were the people of bombardment, that the North Atlantic fleet was divided: the one-half blockading Havana and the other, reassuringly called 'the Flying Squadron,' stationed at Hampton Roads. Against any other nation such strategy might have been disastrous. But the Spanish navy was inconceivably neglected, ill-armed, and untrained; while the United States Navy — a new creation of the last fifteen years — was smart, disciplined, and efficient. John D. Long, Secretary of the Navy, was honest and intelligent; and when the energetic assistant secretary, Roosevelt, left to lead the Rough Riders, his place on the board of naval strategy was taken by Captain Mahan.

In a military sense the United States was entirely unprepared. An elderly jobbing politician headed the War Department. There were enough Krag rifles for the Regulars, but the 200,000 volunteers, whom the President insisted on calling to the colors, received Springfields and black powder. There was no khaki cloth in the country, and thousands of troops fought a summer campaign in Cuba clothed in the heavy blue

self, how he fed himself, how he steadied himself in battles an' encouraged himself with a few well-chosen worruds whin th' sky was darkest. Ye'll have to take a squint into the book ye'erself to l'arn thim things.'

'I won't do it,' said Mr. Hennessy. 'I think Tiddy Rosenfelt is all r-right an' if he wants to blow his horn lave him do it.'

'True f'r ye,' said Mr. Dooley . . . 'But if I was him I'd call th' book "Alone in Cubia."'

uniform of winter garrison duty. The Commissary Department was disorganized, and soldiers complained that they were fed on 'embalmed beef.' Volunteers neglected even such principles of camp sanitation as were laid down in Deuteronomy, and for every one of the 286 men killed or mortally wounded in battle, 14 died of disease. Transporting 18,000 men to Cuba caused more confusion than conveying 2 million men to France twenty years later. The Regulars were encamped at Tampa, Florida, but there was no adequate railroad connection between Tampa and Port Tampa, nine miles distant, and no adequate pier or transport facilities at the latter place. General Miles recorded his impression of conditions at Tampa:

> Several of the volunteer regiments came here without arms, and some without blankets, tents, or camp equipage. The 32nd Michigan, which is among the best, came without arms. General Guy V. Henry reports that five regiments under his command are not fit to go into the field. There are over 300 cars loaded with war material along the roads about Tampa. . . . To illustrate the confusion, fifteen cars loaded with uniforms were side-tracked twenty-five miles away from Tampa, and remained there for weeks while the troops were suffering for clothing. Five thousand rifles, which were discovered yesterday, were needed by several regiments. Also, the different parts of the siege train and ammunition for the same, which will be required immediately on landing, are scattered through hundreds of cars on the side-tracks of the railroads.

Yet the little expeditionary force which finally got under way was allowed to land on the beach at Daiquiri without opposition (20–25 June), and the Captain-General of Cuba, with six weeks' warning, and with almost 200,000 men on the island and 13,000 in the city of Santiago, was able to concentrate only 1700 on the battlefields of Las Guasimas, El Caney, and San Juan, against 15,000 Americans. These 1700 Spaniards, well armed and entrenched, gave an excellent account of themselves and helped to promote Theodore Roosevelt from a colonelcy to the presidency.

It was the navy, however, that clinched the conquest of Cuba. Late in April the Spanish Admiral, Cervera, with four armored cruisers and three destroyers, had steamed out of the Cape Verde Islands to destinations unknown. There was panic all along the Atlantic coast, and timid people hurried their valuables to points of safety well in the interior. But Cervera was not bound on offensive operations. On 19 May he sneaked into the narrow land-locked harbor of Santiago Bay and was promptly bottled up by the American navy under Admiral Sampson and Commodore Schley. With the army closing in on Santiago, Cervera had no alternatives but surrender or escape, and he was ordered to do the latter. On 3 July the Spanish battle-fleet sailed forth from Santiago Bay to death and destruction:

> Haste to do now what must be done anon
> Or some mad hope of selling triumph dear
> Drove the ships forth: soon was *Teresa* gone
> *Furór, Plutón, Vizcaya, Oquendo,* and *Colón*.[4]

Not since 1863 had there been such a Fourth of July in America as that Monday in 1898 when the news came through. Santiago surrendered on the 16th and except for a military promenade in Puerto Rico, which Mr. Dooley described as 'Gin'ral Miles' Gran' Picnic and Moonlight Excursion,' the war was over.

The most important event of the war had occurred not in the Caribbean but in the Far East. Two months before the actual declaration of war Theodore Roosevelt, then Assistant Secretary of the Navy, had cabled to Commodore Dewey in command of the Asiatic Squadron: 'Secret and confidential. Order squadron to Hong Kong. Keep full of coal. In the event of declaration of war Spain, your duty will be to see that the Spanish squadron does not leave the Asiatic coast, and then offensive operations in Philippine Islands.' As soon as war was declared, Dewey set out under full steam for the Philippines, and on the night of 30 April he slipped through the narrow channel of Boca Grande and into the spacious waters of Manila Bay, where a Spanish fleet was anchored. Gridley fired when ready; they all fired; and when the smoke and mist cleared away it was apparent that the Spanish fleet had been utterly destroyed. Dewey moved on the shore batteries, which promptly displayed a white flag, and the battle of Manila Bay was over. Not until 13 August — one day after the signing of the peace protocol — did an American expeditionary force, with the support of Aguinaldo's Filipino army, take the city of Manila.

The collapse of her military and naval power forced Spain to sue for peace. McKinley dictated terms on 30 July — immediate evacuation and relinquishment of Cuba, cession of Puerto Rico and an island in the Ladrones, and American occupation of the city, harbor, and bay of

4. 'Spain in America' in *Poems* by George Santayana, Scribner, p. 118.

Manila pending the final disposition of the Philippine Islands. Spain signed a preliminary peace to that effect on 12 August, sadly protesting, 'This demand strips us of the very last memory of a glorious past and expels us . . . from the Western Hemisphere, which became peopled and civilized through the proud deeds of our ancestors.' But John Hay wrote to his friend Theodore Roosevelt in a very different vein: 'It has been a splendid little war; begun with the highest motives, carried on with magnificent intelligence and spirit, favored by that fortune which loves the brave.'

5. THE FRUITS OF VICTORY

In the formal peace negotiations which began at Paris on 1 October 1898, the United States was represented by a commission consisting of Whitelaw Reid, editor of the powerful New York *Tribune*, Secretary of State Day, and three Senators. Four of these commissioners had already committed themselves to a 'large policy' of imperialism and expansion; the fifth, Senator Gray, came around eventually to the majority point of view. To the American demand for the independence of Cuba and the cession of Puerto Rico and Guam, the Spanish representatives interposed no objections, and they even agreed to assume the Cuban debt of some $400 million. The question of the disposition of the Philippines, however, offered serious difficulties. If they had been contented under Spanish rule, there would have been no question of annexing them. An insurrection had just been partially suppressed when the Spanish War broke out, but Dewey had encouraged Emilio Aguinaldo, leader of the *insurrectos,* to return from exile after the battle of Manila Bay; and upon the fall of the city of Manila the Filipino leader had organized the 'Visayan Republic' in the province of Luzon and made a bid for foreign recognition. The obvious thing to do was to turn the Philippines over to the Filipinos, as Cuba to the Cubans. But Dewey cabled that the 'republic' was only a faction, unable to keep order within its nominal sphere. Yet the fact remained that Aguinaldo represented government in the islands, that if the United States expected to retain the Philippines it would first have to conquer them.

McKinley was in a quandary. In his message of December 1897 he had laid down with respect to Cuba the rule that 'forcible annexation . . . can not be thought of. That, by our code of morality, would be criminal aggression.' Did the same rule hold good for the Philippines? The question was to be answered not by logic, but by a combination of interest and emotion. Already the newspapers were clamoring 'Keep the Philippines.' Already navalists were emphasizing the military importance of the islands and suggesting the danger to American interests should Germany or Japan annex them. Senator Beveridge was speaking hopefully of 'China's illimitable markets' and Whitelaw Reid wrote that the Philippines would 'convert the Pacific ocean into an American lake.' Popular feeling was being aroused by the cry, 'Don't haul down the flag,' and when McKinley returned from a trip through the Middle West he found 'a very general feeling that the United States is in a situation where it cannot let go.' The President's instructions to the Peace Commission presented all of these considerations:

> The presence and success of our arms at Manila imposes upon us obligations which we cannot disregard. The march of events rules and overrules human action . . . We cannot be unmindful that, without any desire or design on our part, the war has brought us new duties and responsibilities which we must meet and discharge as becomes a great nation . . . Incidental to our tenure in the Philippines is the commercial opportunity to which American statesmanship cannot be indifferent.

Yet there were still several alternatives. The United States might simply guarantee and protect the independence of the Philippines as it was to do in Cuba. It might take only the island of Luzon, leaving the rest of the archipelago to the Filipinos. It might take the Philippines in trust, as it were, with a promise of independence — the principle of the Bacon bill that was defeated only by the casting vote of the Vice-President in the Senate. Or it might annex all the Philippines.

McKinley hesitated long and prayerfully, but finally concluded to fulfill manifest destiny by taking them all. 'One night late it came to me this way,' he told his Methodist brethren, '(1) That we could not give them back to Spain — that would be cowardly and dishonorable; (2) that we could not turn them over to France or Germany, our commercial rivals in the Orient — that would be bad business and discreditable; (3) that we could not leave them to themselves — they were unfit for self-government — and they would soon have anarchy and misrule over there worse than Spain's was; and (4) that there was nothing left for us to do but take them all, and to educate the Filipinos, and uplift and Christianize them.' Quite aside from the fact that the Filipinos had been 'Christianized' for some centuries, it is an interesting question whether, in the light of the constitutional separation of Church and State, a President can constitutionally commit the United States to the task of 'Christianizing' another people. So Spain was required to part with the islands for $20 million, and on 10 December 1898 the Treaty of Paris was signed and the United States became, officially, a world power.

But the prospect of the annexation of an alien people without their consent aroused the fierce indignation of many Americans who thought it a monstrous perversion of the ideals which had inspired our crusade for Cuba. Old-fashioned Senators like Hoar of Massachusetts girded on their armor to fight for the principles of the Declaration of Independence, and for two months the fate of the treaty hung in suspense. Lodge led the fight for ratification, and he was particularly concerned with the disgrace involved in repudiating what the President, through his envoys, had concluded in Paris. 'I confess,' he wrote, 'I cannot think calmly of the rejection of that Treaty by a little more than one-third of the Senate. It would be a repudiation of the President and humiliation of the whole country in the eyes of the world, and would show we are unfit as a nation to enter into great questions of foreign policy.' The administration invoked patronage and party regularity to save the treaty, and in its efforts, it received unexpected aid from William Jennings Bryan. Although unalterably opposed to imperialism, Bryan thought that a question of such magnitude as this should be decided on its own merits, and not as part of the general question of peace, and that it should be submitted to the verdict of the people at large. On 6 February 1899 the necessary two-thirds majority for ratification was obtained, but Lodge called it 'the hardest fight I have ever known.'

McKinley, in 1897, had rejected a proposal to buy Cuba because he did not care to buy an insurrection; the United States now found that it had purchased, for $20 million, a first-class Filipino insurrection. For the Filipinos, who had been good Catholics for over three centuries, did not wish to be 'uplifted and Christianized' by the Americans; but when, on 4 February 1899, Aguinaldo's troops disregarded the command of an American sentry to halt, the United States army undertook to 'civilize them with a Krag.' Before the Philippine insurrection was stamped out it had cost the United States almost as many lives as the Spanish War, in hellish fighting between white soldiers and men of color. Colonel Frederick Funston boasted he would 'rawhide these bullet-headed Asians until they yell for mercy' so they would not 'get in the way of the bandwagon of Anglo-Saxon progress and decency.' The United States found itself doing in the Philippines precisely what it had condemned Spain for doing in Cuba. Soon stories of concentration camps and 'water-cures' began to trickle back to the United States, and public opinion became inflamed. The result was a vigorous anti-imperialism crusade which commanded the support of men from all parties and all walks of life. It was not inappropriate that the nineteenth century should be ushered out with a passionate appeal to the Declaration of Independence, and the twentieth century ushered in with a victory for the forces of imperialism.

To the banner of anti-imperialism rallied people of the most diverse views. Party lines were disregarded: Republicans like Senators Hoar and Edmunds, Secretary Sherman, and Speaker Reed joined hands with Democrats like Cleveland and Bryan, Ben Tillman and John G. Carlisle. Samuel Gompers spoke for labor, and Andrew Carnegie paid the bills. The press was represented by E. L. Godkin of *The Nation* and Bowles of the *Springfield Republican*. President Eliot of Harvard spoke for the intellectuals of New England and President David Starr Jordan of Leland Stanford combatted jingoism on the Pacific coast. Philosophers like William James, clergymen like Henry Van Dyke, social workers like Jane Addams, all worked together for a common cause. Effective aid came from the men of letters. Mark Twain, deeply embittered by our conquest of the Philippines, suggested that Old Glory should now have 'the white stripes painted black and the stars replaced by the skull and cross bones.'

The most powerful indictment of imperialism came from the young poet, William Vaughn Moody. In 'An Ode in Time of Hesitation,' he appealed from the chauvinistic spirit of the 'nineties to the idealism of the 'sixties:

> Lies! lies! It cannot be! The wars we wage
> Are noble, and our battles still are won
> By justice for us, ere we lift the gage.
> We have not sold our loftiest heritage.
> The proud republic hath not stooped to cheat
> And scramble in the market-place of war . . .

Ah no!
We have not fallen so.

We are our fathers' sons: let those who lead us know! . . .
Tempt not our weakness, our cupidity!
For save we let the island men go free,
Those baffled and dislaureled ghosts
Will curse us from the lamentable coasts
Where walk the frustrate dead . . .
O ye who lead,
Take heed!
Blindness we may forgive, but baseness we will smite.[5]

The argument against the annexation of the Philippines rested not only on an old-fashioned repugnance to government without the consent of the governed and a humanitarian revulsion against the manner in which the war was conducted, but on political, constitutional, and economic grounds as well. Opponents recognized that the possession of colonies in the Pacific would require for their protection a larger military and naval establishment and would involve us in the whole complex of Far Eastern politics. They pointed out that the conquest, defense, and administration of the Philippines would cost us far more than the islands would ever bring in return. They warned that the flouting of the principles of democracy in the Philippines would impair the vitality and integrity of democracy at home. Some of those who opposed the creation of an American empire did so out of dislike of incorporating other races and cultures in white American society. Tillman cried: 'Coming . . . as a Senator from . . . South Carolina, with 750,000 colored population and only 500,000 whites, I realize what you are doing, while you don't; and I would save this country from the injection in it of another race question.' Finally they argued that the Constitution did not permit the acquisition of extraterritorial possessions and the government of alien peoples without their consent. This last argument was eventually rejected by the Supreme Court, but in a series of decisions so contradictory that no one has ever been able to unravel their logic.

In 1900 the Democrats, determined to make imperialism the 'paramount' issue of the campaign, once again named Bryan, who also got the nominations of the Silver Republicans and one wing of the Populists. The Democrats held their convention on the Fourth of July to empha-

5. William Vaughn Moody, *Selected Poems,* Houghton Mifflin, 1931.

size that the Republicans, by acquiring the Philippines, had perverted the American tradition. Their platform warned: 'The Filipinos cannot . . . be citizens without endangering our civilization; they cannot be subjects without imperiling our form of government. . . . To impose upon any people a government of force is to substitute the methods of imperialism for those of a republic.' But Bryan had played such an ambiguous role in the treaty debate that he obscured the imperialism issue. Moreover, during the campaign he insisted that silver was still the nation's chief concern; as Tom Reed remarked, 'Bryan would rather be wrong than President.'

The Republicans held all the trump cards and played them well. The end of the economic crisis that had begun in 1893 appeared to justify the claim that McKinley was the 'advance agent of prosperity.' McKinley left the campaigning to his running mate, Colonel Theodore Roosevelt, who stormed through the West crying 'Don't lower the flag,' and even referred to Bryan as 'my opponent.' By sweeping all of the agricultural West, including the Middle Border, McKinley improved on his performance in 1896; Byran won only the South and four silver states. Never again would the imperialism issue figure largely in a presidential contest; henceforth, for good or evil, we were a world power with an overseas empire.

6. THE OPEN DOOR

Many Americans feared that the annexations of the year 1898 were only a beginning; that the United States was destined to become a great colonial power. Imperialism in the Roman sense did not, however, appeal to the American people; even the word signified a reproach. The political control of islands densely populated with inhabitants of foreign tongue and alien race was a very different matter from the traditional expansion into sparsely inhabited regions readily capable of full fellowship in the Union. But if the United States had no more than a passing desire to acquire an overseas empire, the country had an avid interest in developing and protecting foreign markets not only in Latin America but in Asia, where the partition of China jeopardized the American position.

The Japanese victory in the War of 1894–95 had revealed to the world the weakness of China: to forestall the Japanese, the European powers hurried to obtain for themselves special concessions and spheres of influence in China. 'The various powers,' said the Dowager Empress of China, 'cast upon us looks of tiger-like voracity, hustling each other in their endeavors to be the first to seize upon our inner-most territories.' Japan had already acquired Formosa (Taiwan) and established her ascendancy in the 'Hermit Kingdom' of Korea; in 1897 and 1898 Russia took Port Arthur and the Liaotung Peninsula, which gave her access to the interior of Manchuria; Germany seized Kiaochow in Shantung, France consoled herself with a lease to Kwangchow bay, adjoining Indo-China; Italy got Sanmun bay, south of the Yangtze river; and England added to her holdings the port of Wei-hai-wei. Along with these leases went valuable railway concessions, which promised to give to the European powers all but complete control over the internal trade of China.

Since the Cushing mission of 1844 the United States had demanded for itself the same commercial and extraterritorial privileges that were granted to other powers, and in this policy it had been entirely successful. Now with the acquisition of the Philippines, American interest in the Chinese trade vastly increased, and so, too, strategic concern over who controlled the western Pacific. The carving up of China into foreign concessions, protectorates, and spheres of influence appeared to threaten American trade, especially in Manchuria, and to nullify part of the value of the Philippines. Businessmen, especially cotton exporters and financiers seeking concessions in China, pressed Secretary John Hay to act. He received similar advice from two men who sought not to advance American interests but to preserve China from foreign encroachment: an 'old China hand,' the Englishman Alfred E. Hippisley, and W. W. Rockhill, unofficial State Department adviser on Chinese affairs. Together they drafted a proposal urging all the major powers to accept the principle of trade equality in China, and to refrain from violations of Chinese territorial integrity. Hay accepted these proposals and incorporated some of them into his own 'open door' policy for China. In a circular note of 6 September 1899 addressed to the major European powers, Hay, while recognizing the existence of the 'spheres of influence,' requested from each power a declaration that each, in its respective sphere, would maintain the Chinese customs tariff, and levy equal harbor dues and railway rates on the ships and merchandise of all nations. The powers made ambiguous replies, with Britain most favorable, Russia least, but Hay promptly announced the agreement of all the powers as 'final and definitive.'

The 'open door' policy, as originally announced, aimed solely at safe-guarding American commercial interests in China, but within less than a year it was given a new and far-reaching interpretation. The brazen exploitation of China by the great powers had created a deep antipathy to foreigners, and in June 1900 a secret organization called the Boxers tried to expel the 'foreign devils.' Within a short time the Boxers had massacred some 300 foreigners, mostly missionaries and their families; others were driven into Peking, where they took refuge in the British legation. An expeditionary force to rescue the beleaguered Europeans was hurriedly organized; the United States contributed some 5000 soldiers. Concerned that the situation might deteriorate into a general war, Hay bent all his energies to localizing the conflict. On 3 July, in a circular note to all the powers, he tried to limit the objectives of the joint intervention:

> The policy of the government of the United States is to seek a solution which may bring about permanent safety and peace to China, preserve Chinese territorial and administrative entity, protect all rights guaranteed to friendly powers by treaty and international law, and safeguard for the world the principle of equal and impartial trade with all parts of the Chinese Empire.

These were not the objectives entertained in the chancelleries of Berlin, St. Petersburg, and Tokyo, but these powers, fearful of each other and of war, found it easy to concur. The danger of war subsided, and the Chinese government permitted the joint expedition to save the legations. Punishment, however, was exacted from the guilty Boxers, and China saddled with an outrageous indemnity of $333 million. Of this some $24 million went to the United States; half of it was eventually returned to the Chinese government which established therewith a fund for sending Chinese students to American colleges.

Now the United States was committed to maintain not only an 'open door' to China but the political integrity of that decrepit empire. Yet what did the commitment mean? Only by alliance with some European power like England could the United States have enforced this policy, and at no time did the exigencies of American politics permit an open alliance. American public opinion rejoiced in the spectacle

of the United States teaching a moral lesson to the wicked imperi-
alists of the Old World, but as Secretary Hay himself said, 'the talk of
the papers about our pre-eminent moral position giving us the authority
to dictate to the world, is mere flap-doodle.' And when, in 1901, Japan
made cautious inquiries about the American reaction to Russian encroachments in Manchuria, Hay assured them that the United States
was not prepared 'to attempt singly, or in concert with other Powers, to
enforce these views in the east by any demonstration which could
present a character of hostility to any other Power.' In short the United
States wanted an 'open door' but would not fight for it.

Yet we cannot dismiss the 'open door' policy quite this easily. It faithfully expressed America's sentimental interest in China; may have delayed for a time the attack on China from Japan; probably enhanced
American prestige in China and other parts of the globe; and may have
earned the United States English backing for its Caribbean policy. And,
like the Monroe Doctrine, it came in time to take on symbolical meaning: that America would have no part in imperialistic designs on China
and would discourage such designs in others. It helped build up popular
support for resistance against Japan's aggression in China, and this in
turn exacerbated Japanese resentment toward the United States.

7. THE SUPREME COURT AND THE INSULAR CASES

The annexation of extra-continental territory, already thickly populated
by alien peoples, created new problems in American government. The
petty islands and guano rocks that had already been annexed had never
raised, as Puerto Rico and the Philippines did, the embarrassing question of whether the Constitution followed the flag, or the difficult matter
of the nature and extent of congressional control. The Treaty of Paris
had provided that 'The civil rights and political status of the native
inhabitants hereby ceded to the United States shall be determined by
Congress' but this provision threw little light on the subject. Opinions of
the Supreme Court in the 'Insular Cases,' a muddle of split decisions, left
the status of the new possessions very unclear, but eventually, as in the
British Empire, a theory was evolved from practice. Insular possessions
are of two categories: incorporated and unincorporated; and the question of what constitutes incorporation is one to be determined on the
basis of fact and intention as revealed in congressional legislation. Thus

at the turn of the century Alaska was held to be incorporated, but Puerto Rico was unincorporated, and this despite the fact that after 1917 the inhabitants of the island became citizens of the United States. Unincorporated territories are not foreign, however, and their exports are not controlled by American customs duties unless by special act of Congress. But Congress may, nevertheless, impose such duties as it sees fit. This meant, according to a dissenting opinion by Chief Justice Fuller, that

> if an organized and settled province of another sovereignty is acquired by the United States, Congress has the power to keep it like a disembodied shade, in an intermediate state of ambiguous existence for an indefinite period: and more than that, after it has been called from that limbo, commerce with it is absolutely subject to the will of Congress, irrespective of constitutional provisions.

Thus the country was able to eat its cake and have it; to indulge in territorial expansion and yet maintain the tariff wall against such insular products as sugar and tobacco which might compete with the home-grown products.

The question of the civil and political rights of the inhabitants of these new possessions proved even more perplexing. Organic acts of Congress became the constitutions of the Philippines, Hawaii, and Puerto Rico, but to what extent was Congress bound, in enacting these laws, and the courts, in interpreting them, by the provisions of the Constitution and the Bill of Rights? How far, in short, did the Constitution follow the flag? To this question the Court returned an ingenious answer. It distinguished between 'fundamental' rights and 'formal' or 'procedural' rights. Fundamental rights are extended to all who come under the sovereignty of the United States, but mere procedural rights, such as trial by jury or indictment by grand jury, extend to the inhabitants of unincorporated territories only if Congress so chooses. Hence, the President and Congress, though limited in power within the United States, possess powers that are practically absolute over American dependencies — powers limited only by the moral sanction of principles of natural justice. Like eighteenth-century London, the government at Washington was reluctant to admit the existence of an empire. No colonial office was established or colonial secretary appointed, and the administration of what we must call our 'non-colonies' was characterized by diversity and opportunism.

XI

The Progressive Movement

1. THE PROMISE OF AMERICAN LIFE

At the turn of the century, Americans could look back over three generations of material progress unparalleled in history. The nation had advanced, in Jefferson's prophetic words, to 'destinies beyond the reach of
mortal eye.' The continent was subdued, the frontier was gone, and
already Americans were reaching out for new worlds to conquer. From a
small struggling republic, menaced on all sides, the nation had advanced
to the rank of a world power. The political foundations upon which the
nation had been established had endured the vicissitudes of foreign and
civil war, of prosperity and depression. No standing army menaced
personal liberty; no permanent bureaucracy endangered political liberty; and the institution of slavery, which had threatened to destroy not
only the Union but democracy, had been itself destroyed. Population
had increased from 5 to 76 million, and 28 million Europeans of all races
had been absorbed without warping social institutions. In the half-
century from 1850 to 1900 national wealth had increased from $7 to $88
billion, and the standard of living for the common man compared favorably with that to be found anywhere else in the world. In agriculture
and in industry the American people had advanced with giant strides.
Nor were the achievements of Americans merely material. The ideal of
free public education had been substantially realized; the ideal of a free
press maintained; the ideal of religious freedom cherished. In literature,
art, and science, Americans had made contributions of enduring value.

When, in 1888, James Bryce finished his magisterial survey of the *American Commonwealth,* he concluded that life was better for the common man in America than elsewhere on the globe.

Yet thoughtful Americans did not look with complacency upon their institutions. For, as Woodrow Wilson would point out in his Inaugural Address:

> The evil has come with the good, and much fine gold has been corroded. With riches has come inexcusable waste. . . . We have been proud of our industrial achievements, but we have not hitherto stopped thoughtfully enough to count the cost, the cost of lives snuffed out, of energies overtaxed and broken, the fearful physical and spiritual cost to the men and women and children upon whom the dead weight and burden of it all has fallen pitilessly the years through. . . . With the great Government went many deep secret things which we too long delayed to look into and scrutinize with candid, fearless eyes. The great Government we loved has too often been made use of for private and selfish purposes, and those who used it had forgotten the people.

The continent had been conquered, but the conquest had been attended by reckless exploitation of soil, forest, and water. The greatest of manufacturing nations, the United States permitted the exploitation of women and children and neglected the aged, the incompetent, and the infirm. Unemployment and child labor both persisted; machinery was marvelously efficient, but no other industrial nation confessed to so many industrial accidents. Wealth was gravitating rapidly into the hands of a small portion of the population, and the power of wealth threatened the political integrity of the Republic. In a land of plenty there was never enough food, clothing, and shelter for the underprivileged; and cyclical depressions plunged millions into actual want. In the great cities the slums grew apace, and from the slums spread disease, crime, and vice. Science taught how to control many of the illnesses that plagued mankind, but poverty interposed between science and health, and tuberculosis, hookworm, malaria, and other diseases of want and ignorance took an annual toll that ran into the millions. Man's inhumanity to man was illustrated in the penal code, in prison conditions, in the treatment of the aged, the poor, the incapacitated, the defective, and the insane, and in the attitude toward the criminal and the prostitute. The Civil War had ended slavery but the degradation and exploitation of the Negro was a blot on American civilization. The educational system was an object of pride, but its benefits were unevenly distributed, and the census of 1900 discovered over 6 million illiterates. Everyone gave lip service to the principles of democracy, but political corruption poisoned the body politic from head to foot. On all sides thoughtful men feared that the nation which Lincoln had called 'the last best hope of earth' would prove instead the world's illusion.

Against the crowding evils of the time there arose a full-throated protest which distinguished American politics and thought from approximately 1890 to World War I. It demanded the centralization of power in the hands of a strong government and the extension of regulation or control over industry, finance, transportation, agriculture, labor, and even morals. It found expression in a new concern for the poor and the underprivileged, for women and children, for the immigrant, the Indian, and the Negro. It called for new standards of honesty in politics and in business. It formulated a new social and political philosophy, which rejected laissez-faire and justified public control of social and economic institutions on the principles of liberal democracy.

This progressive revolt of the 'nineties and the early years of the new century did not essentially differ from the reform movement of the 'forties and 'fifties. The new progressivism, like the old, had a distinctly moral flavor, and its leaders — Bryan, La Follette, Roosevelt, Wilson — were moral crusaders. Its roots went deep into American experience, but it profited from the teachings and the practices of the more enlightened European nations. It was basic in its criticism, but opportunistic in its program, accepting in practice Justice Holmes's dictum that 'legislation may begin where an evil begins.' The progressive movement laid the philosophic and some of the legislative foundations for the New Deal of the 1930's.

2. CHALLENGES TO AMERICAN DEMOCRACY

The problems which faced reformers on the threshold of the new century were many and complex. For the sake of convenience we may note six problems which embraced, in one form or another, practically all of the particular evils which the progressives hoped to eliminate. The first of these was the confusion of ethics which resulted from an attempt to apply the moral code of an individualistic, agrarian society to a highly industrialized and integrated social order. The second was the rise of big business and the consequent exploitation of natural resources and labor by trusts and monopolies. The third was the grossly unequal distribution of wealth and the sharpening of social distinctions. The fourth was the rise of the city with its demand for a new type of social engineering. The fifth was the breakdown of political honesty and the application of antiquated administrative institutions to the new problems of government. And sixth was the denial to Negroes of their elementary rights and the persistence of gross discrimination against them and other minority groups.

The ethical confusion which overtook American society in the industrial age resulted from the growing complexity and interdependence of the social organism and the diffusion of personal responsibility through the use of the corporate device. In a simple agrarian society, personal and social morals were much the same, and the harm that a bad man could do was pretty well limited to crimes against individuals. Such crimes — mainly violations of the Ten Commandments — were easy to recognize and comparatively easy to control. But in a highly complex industrial society personal crimes and social sins were very different, and the old moral standards were no longer applicable. As society grew more interdependent, it grew more vulnerable. Society could be hurt in a thousand new ways, many of them not recognized in the old moral codes or in the law codes. 'The growth of credit institutions,' wrote the sociologist E. A. Ross, whose *Sin and Society* attracted the attention of such men as Theodore Roosevelt and Justice Holmes, 'the spread of fiduciary relations, the enmeshing of industry in law, the interlacing of government and business, the multiplication of boards and inspectors — all invited to sin. What gateways they open to greed! What fresh parasites they let in on us! How idle in our new situation to intone the old litanies!'

The men who were guilty of the new sins against society were for the most part upright and well-intentioned gentlemen, often quite unaware of the consequences of their actions. 'Unlike the old-time villain,' Ross observed, 'the latter-day malefactor does not wear a slouch hat and a comforter, breathe forth curses and an odor of gin, go about his nefarious work with clenched teeth and an evil scowl. . . . The modern high-powered dealer of woe wears immaculate linen, carries a silk hat and a lighted cigar, sins with calm countenance and a serene soul, leagues or months from the evil he causes. Upon his gentlemanly presence the eventual blood and tears do not obtrude themselves.' These men were caught in the meshes of a business system which had not yet developed a moral code of its own and to which the old codes were irrelevant. The manufacture and sale of impure foods, dangerous drugs, infected milk, poisonous toys, might produce disease or death, but none of those involved in the process — retailers, wholesalers, manufacturers, advertisers, corporation directors, or stockholders — realized that they were guilty of murder. Misleading advertisements, the use of the shoddy in manufacture, improper inspection, and short-weight packages, all might cheat purchasers, but none of those involved knew they were guilty of theft. Failure to observe fire regulations, to install safety appliances in factories and in mines and on railroads, to inspect unseaworthy boats, might take a fearful toll in lives, but none of those involved thought they were guilty of manslaughter. Improper inspection of banks, insurance companies, and trust companies, false statements in a company prospectus, speculation in stocks, in gold, or in grain, might bring poverty and misery to thousands, but none of those involved recognized they were guilty of larceny. Business competition might force the employment of children of eight or nine years of age in mines and in mills or dictate the use of woman labor in sweatshops, but none of those involved realized that they were guilty of maintaining slavery. The purchase of votes, the corruption of election officials, the bribing of legislators, the lobbying of special bills, the flagrant disregard of laws, might threaten the very foundations of democracy, but few of those involved recognized that they were guilty of treason to representative government.

The impersonality of 'social sin,' the diffusion of responsibility, presented perhaps the gravest problem which the reformers had to face. It was necessary for them to formulate a new social ethics and to educate the people to that new code, and much of the work of the 'muckrakers' was directed toward this end. They also had to devise new administrative machinery for discovering the consequences of industrial malpractices and new legal machinery for fixing responsibility, and the effort to do this can be read in the struggle over trust, labor, factory, pure food, housing, and similar legislation.

We have already traced the second problem — the rise of big business, the growth of trusts and monopolies, and the efforts to bring combinations of capital and industry under government control. Many reformers were concerned with the problems that flowed from the new industrial order — child labor, factory inspection, unemployment, the exploitation of immigrant workers, the use of natural resources for private or corporate aggrandizement. Roosevelt's reputation as a progressive rests upon his gestures toward 'trust-busting,' railroad regulation, conservation, and similar efforts to grapple with the industrial revolution. Wilson's 'New Freedom' was directed toward similar ends. Robert M. La Follette attacked the railroads and the lumber interests that controlled Wisconsin, and throughout his long career labored for social democracy through the regulation of industrial and financial monopolies. Bryan, after abandoning the money issue and imperialism, concentrated his energies upon the task of regulating business, industry, and finance. A host of lesser leaders in the progressive movement — Hughes of New York, Pingree of Michigan, Tom Johnson of Ohio, Altgeld of Illinois, Johnson of California, to name only a few — comprehended with equal realism the economic basis of the reform movement and fought the campaign for democracy by a series of flank attacks on the citadels of industrial and financial privilege. Political reformers learned that to cleanse politics it was necessary to regulate the business interests that controlled politics; social reformers found that to eliminate child labor or the sweatshop or the slums it was essential to control the industrial and corporate interests that profited by these evils; humanitarian reformers discovered that the improvement of race relations, of penal conditions, and even of morals depended upon the improvement of general economic circumstances. Henry Demarest Lloyd concluded his analysis of *Wealth Against Commonwealth* with the prophetic observation: 'The word of the day is that we are about to civilize industry.'

No less serious than the issues raised by the industrial revolution, and intimately connected with them, was the third problem — the distribution of wealth. Benjamin Franklin had found 'a general happy mediocrity.'

> There are few great proprietors of the soil [he wrote] and few tenants; most people cultivate their own lands, or follow some handicraft or merchandise; very few are rich enough to live idly upon their rents or incomes or to pay the high prices given in Europe for Paintings, Statues, Architecture, and other works of Art, that are more curious than useful.

The first half of the nineteenth century saw the rise of a few large fortunes, most of them either in land or in shipping, and the wealthy men of the time, like John Jacob Astor or James Lenox, were designated 'landlords' or 'merchant princes' rather than 'captains of industry' or 'titans of finance.' Moses Yale Beach of the New York *Sun* who published in the 1850's a pamphlet on 'Wealthy Men of New York' discovered only nineteen who could be called millionaires, and the richest, John Jacob Astor, boasted a fortune of only $6 million.

The industrial revolution changed all this. Men discovered a hundred new ways of making money, and many of the new fortunes were gained through speculation, and carried with them no sense of responsibility. In 1888 Bryce warned Americans that they were developing greater extremes of wealth and poverty than were to be found even in England. An estimate made in 1890 indicated that one-eighth of the people of the country owned seven-eighths of the property. Subsequent surveys suggested that this estimate was perhaps too moderate. In 1896 Charles B. Spahr concluded that 1 per cent of the population owned over half the total national wealth, and that 12 per cent owned almost nine-tenths. This disparity between the rich and the poor did not decrease during the next twenty years, and when O. Henry contrasted New York's Four Million with her 'Four Hundred' the proportions were felt to be too embarrassingly close to the truth for the purposes of humor.

The great fortunes of the day came not from land but from the exploitation of natural resources, manufacturing, banking, and speculation. When in 1892 the New York *Tribune* compiled figures on the millionaires of the country, it discovered that almost 1000 had earned their fortunes in 'merchandising and investment,' over 600 in manufactures, over 300 in banking and brokerage, over 200 in transportation. Some hint of the concentration of natural resources in the hands of the few could be found in the fact that the *Tribune* counted 178 millionaires in the lumber industry, 113 in coal and lead mining, 73 in gold and silver mining, and 72 in oil. Sixty-five lawyers had become millionaires, but only 26 farmers had made the grade, and most of them were absentee landlords.

The fourth problem which challenged the ingenuity of the progressives was the rise of the city. By 1890 nine of every ten people in Rhode Island clustered in town, and Massachusetts had a larger proportion of people in towns of 10,000 than any nation in Europe. One district of New York's Eleventh Ward, with a density of 986 per acre, was probably the most crowded spot on earth; even the notorious Koombarwara district of Bombay had but 760 persons per acre. In the twenty years from 1880 to 1900 the population of New York City increased from a little less than two to almost three and a half millions; Chicago grew from half a million to a million and a half, and became the second city in the nation; such cities as Detroit, Cleveland, Buffalo, Milwaukee, Indianapolis, Columbus, Toledo, Omaha, and Atlanta more than doubled. In 1880 there were 19 cities with a population of 100,000 or more; by 1900 the number had increased to 36, and by 1910 to 50. Those who came to the great cities, either from the farms or from foreign lands, had torn up their roots, and the process of transplantation was often painful.

The rapid and unregulated growth of cities created perplexing problems. How should the teeming thousands who thronged into the towns be housed? What provision could be made to guard against the diseases and epidemics that resulted from impure water, inadequate sewage disposal, filth, congestion, and poverty? What measures should be adopted to control crime and vice; what measures to prevent the recurrence of fires such as that which devastated Chicago in 1871 and Boston in 1872? Could the cities build enough schools for their children and find room between the crowded streets for playgrounds? All of these tasks of housing, sanitation, fire protection, policing, traffic regulation, education, devolved upon the city governments. Under their impact the administrative machinery of many cities broke down, and many governmental functions had to be assumed by private agencies. Yet private agencies, no matter how well intentioned or well financed, could not permanently carry on the administrative work of the great cities. In no field was the progressive movement more vigorous than in municipal reform, where it borrowed liberally from European and especially English and German experience, and the cities were the experimental laboratories in which many of the new progressive ideas were tested.

But whether working within the framework of municipal, state, or federal government, the reformers frequently confronted the fifth major problem — the prevalence of political corruption. Observers like James Bryce, critics like E. L. Godkin, feared that inertia and corruption would, in the long run, destroy democracy, and the exposures of the 'muckrakers' proved that their fears were not wholly unfounded. Corruption, although not unique to America, flourished more shamelessly in the United States than in other democratic nations. This resulted in part from America's tradition of lawlessness, in part from the unstable character of its social life, a consequence of the continuous social disintegrations involved in the westward movements, the migration from the country to the city, and the exodus from the Old World to the New World; in part from the absence in America of a 'patriciate' — a class with the habits, the leisure, and the skill for public service; and in part from the American emphasis on results rather than methods.

There were, too, more practical explanations. First, the administrative organization, inherited from a simpler day, broke down from sheer weight of the duties placed upon it. Second, the deep-rooted belief, inherited from the Jacksonian period, that any honest man could fill any office, and the fear of a permanent bureaucracy, kept the expert out of politics and made municipal and state administration a paradise for the incompetent and a happy hunting ground for privilege. Third, the legitimate financial rewards of politics were so meager that able men preferred business or the professions, and incompetents brought the prestige of office so low that 'gentlemen' did not go into politics.

Too often, the fight against corruption yielded disappointing results. After the reformers had won a victory over the local 'ring' or the state 'boss,' the public often lost interest in the house-cleaning that followed, and permitted corrupt groups to regain lost ground. The exposure of the 'Shame of the Cities' or of dishonesty in state politics loomed large in the newspapers and magazines of the time, but was actually of little importance. Far more significant was the effort of progressives to devise new political techniques and administrative agencies to ensure a more effective operation of democracy.

Sixth was the race question. In the generation after the restoration of self-government to the white South, the position of the freed man had steadily worsened. The vast majority of Southern Negroes were every year more deeply sunk in the tenancy-mortgage morass. The flickering promise of better educational facilities that Reconstruction had held out was not fulfilled; as late as 1900 only some 8000 Negro boys and girls were in the high schools of the entire South. Political and civil rights presumably guaranteed by the Fourteenth and Fifteenth Amendments were eroded by judicial interpretation or flouted by public opinion, and in 1896 *Plessy* v. *Ferguson* stamped judicial approval on the 'separate but equal' theory which gave segregation a spurious respectability. There had been little separation of the races in public facilities in the 70's and 80's, but after *Plessy* v. *Ferguson* 'Jim Crow' became almost universal, and segregation took on the character of a cosmic law. With the decline of the old planter class and the rise to power of the classes represented by men like Tillman of South Carolina and Vardaman of Mississippi, racial violence became the order of the day: in the fifteen years after 1885 almost 2500 Negroes were lynched. Nor were conditions much better in the North. Negroes who found their way to Northern cities were herded into ghettos, segregated in most public places, fobbed off with inferior schooling, cold-shouldered by labor unions, and consigned to the most menial and ill-paid jobs.

3. THE ERA OF MUCKRAKERS

In 1906 President Roosevelt applied to those engaged in uncovering corruption in American society the epithet 'muckrakers':

> In Bunyan's *Pilgrim's Progress,* you may recall the description of the Man with the Muck-rake, the man who could look no way but downward with the muck-rake in his hands; who was offered the celestial crown for his muck-rake, but would neither look up nor regard the crown he was offered, but continued to rake the filth of the floor.

Like many other epithets — Puritan, Quaker, Democrat — the term became in time almost a title of nobility. For the muckrakers did the work that no one else was prepared to do. They exposed the particular iniquities that afflicted American life, stirred public opinion to the point where it was willing to support men like Roosevelt and Wilson in their reform programs, and planted the seeds of progressivism which the politicians were to harvest.

The term 'muckraker' is reserved for the journalists and novelists of the Roosevelt era, but the literature of protest began some two decades earlier and was the work of philosophers, and social scientists, too, men like Lester Ward and Thorstein Veblen as well as Henry George and Edward Bellamy.[1] Henry George's *Progress and Poverty,* published in 1879, is one of the great books of the nineteenth century, but like most great books its influence was provocative rather than didactic. George, one of the few original economic thinkers that this country has produced, set himself to resolve the paradox of progress and poverty through a 'formula so broad as to admit of no exceptions.' The formula

1. Ward and Veblen are discussed in Chapter IX.

which he found was the Single Tax — a tax which would wipe out
unearned increment on land, ensure equal access to the land and its
resources, and thus destroy monopoly, eliminate speculation, and restore
economic equality in all classes of society. George's diagnosis of the
causes of poverty and inequality was more profound than his single-tax
cure, and a whole generation of progressives confessed their indebtedness to this 'Bayard of the Poor' — men like Hamlin Garland, Tom Johnson, Clarence Darrow, and Brand Whitlock in the United States, Sidney
Webb, H. G. Wells, and Bernard Shaw in England, Tolstoy in Russia,
and Sun Yat-sen in China. Nor was George's influence confined to the
intellectuals. Over two million copies of his book were sold in America
alone, and on the dusty plains of Kansas, in the slums of Liverpool and
of Moscow, on the banks of the Ganges and of the Yangtze, poor men
painfully spelled out the message of *Progress and Poverty* to grasp a
new vision of human society.

Discontent often found literary form in utopian romances, of which
the most famous was Edward Bellamy's *Looking Backward, 2000–1887*.
Bellamy's utopia was a co-operative industrial society, where not only
profit but even money was eliminated. The book enjoyed an enormous
popularity, and hundreds of Nationalist Clubs, dedicated to the nationalization of industries and natural resources, were established throughout the country. 'In those days,' wrote William Dean Howells, 'the
solution of the riddle of the painful earth through the dreams of Edward
Bellamy, through the dreams of all the generous visionaries of the past,
seemed not impossibly far off.' Howells added his own fantasy to the
dream, *A Traveler from Altruria*, a novel in which Mr. Homos contrasted
the inequities of American life with the ideal society of Altruria.

Despite the fact that the literature of exposure had developed well
before the turn of the century, historians often date the start of muckraking with Lincoln Steffens's 'Tweed Days in St. Louis,' in the October
1902 issue of *McClure's*, for it was not until then that such writing
captivated the nation. By January 1903, *McClure's* was publishing an
installment in Ida Tarbell's series on Standard Oil, Ray Stannard Baker's
indictment of labor violence, and Steffens's 'The Shame of Minneapolis.'
'Shame' suggests that muckraking was a kind of secular Great Awakening, for, with imagery borrowed from Protestant evangelism, the journalists sought to arouse the country to a consciousness of guilt. Muckraking
was primarily a magazine phenomenon, made possible by the develop-

ment of the inexpensive periodical with mass circulation willing to deal with controversial questions. But it could not have succeeded without a public eager to hear the worst about American institutions. The January issue of *McClure's* was sold out, and people clamored for more. By the end of 1903, newsstands were covered with magazines featuring muck-raking articles, and the demand had not begun to be sated.

'Time was,' Mr. Dooley remarked to his friend Hennessy, when the magazines 'was very ca'ming to the mind.' But no more:

> Now whin I pick me fav-rite magazine off th' flure, what do I find? Ivrything has gone wrong. . . . All th' pomes by th' lady authoresses that used to begin: 'Oh, moon, how fair!' now begin: 'Oh, Ogden Armour, how awful!' Read th' horrible disclosures about th' way Jawn C. Higgins got th' right to build a bay-window on his barber-shop at iliven forty-two Kosciusko Avnoo, South Bennington, Arkansaw. . . . Graft ivrywhere. 'Graft in th' Insurance Companies,' 'Graft in Congress,' 'Graft be an Old Grafter,' 'Graft in Its Relations to th' Higher Life,' be Dock Eliot. . . .
>
> An' so it goes, Hinnissy . . . till I don't thrust anny man anny more. I niver did much, but now if I hear th' stealthy step iv me dearest frind at th' dure I lock th' cash dhrawer. I used to be nervous about burglars, but now I'm afraid iv a night call fr'm th' prisidint iv th' First National Bank.

Exposure of corporate malpractices was a characteristic form of muck-raking. As early as 1894 Henry Demarest Lloyd of Chicago had fixed the type and the method of the later muckraking literature with his *Wealth Against Commonwealth*, a vigorous assault on the malpractices of the Standard Oil Company. Ten years later Ida Tarbell stumbled on the same theme when she was free-lancing for *McClure's Magazine:* the result was the classic *History of the Standard Oil Company*, which analyzed with a wealth of statistical data the methods whereby Standard Oil had crushed competitors, seized natural resources, and purchased legislative favors. Within a few years appeared a whole cluster of books of this type: Charles Edward Russell's *Greatest Trust in the World*, an attack on the beef trust; Thomas Lawson's *Frenzied Finance*, the exposé of Amalgamated Copper by a Wall Street insider; Burton J. Hendrick's *Story of Life Insurance*, which did much to create public demand for regulation of that business; and Gustavus Myers's *History of the Great American Fortunes*, which surveyed American fortunes from the colonial era to the twentieth century and concluded that many of them were based on fraud or favor. Works like Myers's and Russell's series, 'Where Did You Get It, Gentlemen?', by taking much of the respectability away from accumulated wealth aided the movement to redistribute income.

The muckrakers also leveled their guns at political corruption and the alliance between corporations and politics. In a notable series on municipal misrule which appeared in *McClure's* and was later gathered into the classic *Shame of the Cities*, Lincoln Steffens, greatest of the muckrakers, exposed 'Philadelphia: Corrupt and Contented'; 'Pittsburgh, a City Ashamed'; and 'The Shamelessness of St. Louis.' In Minncapolis, Steffens achieved one of the great coups in the history of reporting. He obtained the ledger in which graft collectors had entered their accounts and the names of the persons to whom money was paid, and photographed its pages. In *McClure's*, he told how, under a mayor who had been elected twice by the Republicans, twice by the Democrats, the chief of detectives, an ex-gambler, had invited criminals to Minneapolis, fired 107 honest policemen, and freed prisoners to collect revenues for the gang. Steffens's writings helped Joseph Folk win the governorship of Missouri and Robert La Follette to gain re-election as governor of Wisconsin.

Steffens worked out a law of municipal government: privilege controlled politics. In Colorado, Judge Ben Lindsey found the same rule applicable to state politics, and in *The Beast* told with compelling fervor the story of corporation control of the Centennial State. Nor were national politics immune from the muckraker's rake; in 'The Treason of the Senate' written for the *Cosmopolitan* the novelist David Graham Phillips called the roll of Senators he found loyal to their business masters but traitors to their constituents: Depew of New York, Aldrich of Rhode Island, Gorman of Maryland, Lodge of Massachusetts, Elkins of West Virginia, and others of the same stamp.

At no other time in our history has literature been more vitally concerned with social problems. Book for book the novelists matched the journalists, and for every volume of sociological analysis there was a companion volume of fiction. Theodore Dreiser's *The Financier* and *The Titan* made it easier to understand *Frenzied Finance*, as his leading character, Frank Cowperwood, was a fictional portrait of the Chicago speculator Charles Yerkes. Frank Norris's *The Octopus* complemented Bryan's attacks on the railroad monopolies, and Norris's picture of wheat speculation in *The Pit* explained much of the agrarian protest. Russell's exposure of the meat trust was not nearly as effective as Upton Sinclair's account of life in the stockyards, *The Jungle* — a book which contributed directly to the enactment of meat inspection legislation. David Graham Phillips's best novel, *Susan Lenox: Her Fall and Rise*, found more readers than George Kibbe Turner's exposure of the white slave traffic, *Daughters of the Poor*. And the story of corruption in politics was never better told than in Winston Churchill's *Coniston* and *Mr. Crewe's Career*, unless it was in Brand Whitlock's *The Thirteenth District*. One critic has characterized this literature of protest as the 'minority report of the novelists.' As we note its sweep and depth and trace its influence, we must conclude that it represented rather a majority report.

4. HUMANITARIAN REFORM

'The world is too full of amateurs who can play the golden rule as an aria with variations,' wrote H. D. Lloyd in 1894. 'The only field for new effects is in epigrams of practice.' Into this field the reformers entered with buoyant enthusiasm. Men and women banded together in innumerable charitable and rescue and humane societies. They introduced the methods of big business into the organization of philanthropy, and the study of social pathology became a science, with its own professional standards, technique, and vocabulary. Private philanthropy poured millions of dollars into the channels of reform; the churches adjusted themselves to the demands of 'socialized Christianity' and the state supplemented the work of private agencies through legislative regulations and appropriations.

Inspired by the example of Toynbee Hall in London, social workers established settlement houses in the slums of the great cities. In 1886, only two years after Toynbee Hall was founded, Stanton Coit created the first settlement house in this country in New York City, and by the turn of the century almost a hundred such settlement houses had been founded, including Lillian Wald's Henry Street Settlement in New York, Robert Woods's South End House in Boston, and, best known of all, Hull House, established by Jane Addams in Chicago in 1887. Designed originally to end the estrangement between social classes, they became in time elaborate social service agencies and foci for social reforms. Hull House, with its day nursery, boys' club, gymnasium, music and drama and art schools, handicrafts shop, and many other activities, quickly became a laboratory for social work. But, as Jane Addams wrote:

> We early found ourselves spending many hours in efforts to secure support for deserted women, insurance for bewildered widows, damages for injured operators, furniture from the clutches of the installment store. The Settlement is valuable as an information and interpretation bureau. It constantly acts between the various institutions of the city and the people for whose benefit these were erected. The hospitals, county agencies, and State asylums are often but vague rumors to the people who need them most. Another function of the Settlement to its neighborhood resembles that of the big brother whose mere presence on the playground protects the little one from bullies.

The social settlements made their influence felt not only in the slums but in the legislative chambers. Social workers, regarded by politicians and businessmen as misguided zealots, came to be recognized as the most effective reformers of their generation. Not content with charity, Miss Addams — and her associates like Dr. Alice Hamilton — spearheaded drives for effective regulation of the labor of women and children, the establishment of the first juvenile court, protection for immigrant girls, improved sanitary inspection, and better schools. The proposal for a Children's Bureau originated with Lillian Wald, and the first two heads of the bureau, Julia Lathrop and Grace Abbott, had been trained at Hull House. They also helped launch ambitious surveys of cities like Pittsburgh modeled on Charles Booth's study of London. Hull House attracted the attention of university sociologists and economists, of jurists interested in the reform of the law, of professional students of education, and even of politicians. Presidents listened to what Miss Addams had to say, and legislatures did her bidding. Hull House became in time a world institution, and Jane Addams more nearly a world figure than any other woman of her day.

Settlement workers early engaged in a 'battle with the slums.' It had proved impossible to build dwellings fast enough to house the teeming thousands who poured in from the Old World and from the countryside to such cities as New York, Boston, and Chicago. Furthermore, land values and construction costs were so high that poor immigrants could not afford individual houses, even had they been available. Out of this situation came the tenement house of malodorous fame — a huge, compact structure of five or six stories, with scores and often hundreds of rooms and apartments. The rooms were small, dingy, airless, and sunless; the halls long and dark; the sanitation shockingly primitive; and many of the tenements were fire traps. As early as 1866 a report of the New York City Council described the 'filth, overcrowding, lack of privacy and domesticity, lack of ventilation and lighting, absence of supervision, and sanitary regulation' prevalent in the tenements, and in the following decades conditions became worse. By 1890 over a million New Yorkers were packed into 32,000 tenements; some of these were decent apartment houses, but many were 'crazy old buildings, rear yards, dark, damp basements, leaking garrets, shops, outhouses, and stables converted into dwellings though scarcely fit to shelter brutes.'

Doctors had long warned that these tenements were breeding places of disease and vice, and statistics revealed a death rate in New York and Boston 50 per cent higher than that of London. But it was not until 1890, when a Danish immigrant, Jacob Riis, published *How the Other Half Lives,* that public opinion was thoroughly aroused to the menace of the slums. Riis told of one of these tenements which housed over 700 and confessed a death rate of 75 per 1000. One typical block in New York's Lower East Side contained '2,781 persons on two acres of land, nearly every bit of which was covered with buildings. There were 466 babies in the block, but not a bathtub, except one that hung in an air-shaft. Of the 1588 rooms, 441 were dark, with no ventilation to the outer air; 635 rooms gave upon "twilight air-shafts." In five years 32 cases of tuberculosis had been reported from that block, and in that time 660 different families in the block had applied for charity.' The names of some of these tenement blocks — Blind Man's Alley, Murderers' Alley, Poverty Gap, Misery Row, and Penitentiary Row — were as eloquent of their character as pages of description.

Riis sketched vividly the lives of the poor in the slums of New York's East Side:

> Cherry Street. Be a little careful, please! The hall is dark and you might stumble over the children pitching pennies back there. Not that it would hurt them; kicks and cuffs are their daily diet. They have little else. Here where the hall turns and dives into utter darkness is a step, and another, another. A flight of stairs. You can *feel* your way, if you cannot see it. Close? Yes! What would you have? All the fresh air that ever enters these stairs comes from the hall-door that is forever slamming, and from the windows of dark bedrooms that in turn receive from the stairs their sole supply of

the elements God meant to be free, but man deals out with such niggardly hand.

Theodore Roosevelt, after reading *How the Other Half Lives*, stopped by at Mulberry Street and left his card, saying: 'I have your book and I have come to help.'

The country responded to such accounts with an outburst of humanitarian activity of a sort that had not been seen since before the Civil War. The American people suddenly discovered the poverty in their midst, for in the United States each generation has to discover all over again, with innocent surprise, that we have poor among us. Others came to feel that if they did not reform the city, it would menace their own safety. 'The city has become a serious menace to our civilization,' warned Josiah Strong. 'Not only does the proportion of the poor increase with the growth of the city, but their condition becomes more wretched. Dives and Lazarus are brought face to face.'

Even when doing humane errands at considerable personal sacrifice, some reformers were awed by an apocalyptic vision of an uprising of the ignorant poor. Riis wrote of 'the sea of a mighty population, held in galling fetters, heav[ing] uneasily in the tenements.' He reminded his readers that for three days in 1863 during the draft riots, slum-dwellers had taken over the city. Riis cautioned: 'Once already our city . . . has felt the swell of its resistless flood. If it rise once more, no human power may avail to check it. The gap between the classes in which it surges, unseen, unsuspected by the thoughtless, is widening day by day.' Many of the reformers responded to such warnings by seeking to impose upon the immigrants in the slums the middle-class way of life; their interest in tenement house legislation represented less humanitarianism than an effort at social control.

The revelations of writers like Riis led to a battle with anti-social property owners who profited from rents derived from tenements. For as financial investments, tenements stood high. Of the tenement described above, for example, Riis remarked 'the rent-roll was all right. It amounted to $113,964 a year.' Despite opposition from vested interests, public opinion rallied to the reformers. A tenement house commission, appointed by Governor Theodore Roosevelt, recommended a series of changes, and most of these were incorporated in the model tenement house law of 1901 which did away with the old lightless and airless 'dumbbell' tenements and ensured more decent housing for the poor.

State after state followed the example of New York, and by 1910 most of the great cities had inaugurated housing reform. Yet though the worst conditions were eliminated, the slums remained.

This same period witnessed the climax of the movement for the organization of charity. The misery which accompanied the panic of 1873 had led to the establishment of a National Conference of Charities and Correction in the following year. Soon almost every large city in the country had a Charity Organization Society similar to that founded in New York in 1882, designed to introduce efficiency into the haphazard administration of charity by scores of private agencies. These charity societies maintained shelters for homeless men, undertook the care of dependent children, 'rescued' delinquent girls, provided legal aid to the poor, fought loan sharks, and attempted in scores of ways to alleviate the burden of poverty. Boards of Charity were created in almost every state, and cities supplemented the contributions of private philanthropy. Professional social work started with Mary Richmond of Baltimore, who trained young women prepared to make social service a career. In 1909 the Russell Sage Foundation established a Charity Organization Department to serve as a clearing house for this work and inaugurated a series of far-reaching investigations into the causes of poverty, crime, and disease.

Social workers paid particular attention to children, the innocent victims of urban growth and industrialism. High ground rents forced children out into the streets or into littered alleyways to play, tenements deprived them of air and light, and industry exploited them as a cheap source of labor. Two of Jacob Riis's most effective tracts were *Children of the Poor* and *Children of the Tenements,* while John Spargo, echoing *The Bitter Cry of the Children,* told of little girls toiling 16 hours a day in factories and nine-year-old 'breaker boys' working ten hours a day picking slate out of moving coal. And Jane Addams, who had created the first summer camp for poor children, wrote in *The Spirit of Youth and the City Streets* the best argument yet made for playgrounds and parks. By 1915 over 400 cities had opened community playgrounds. Baby clinics and day nurseries were established for the benefit of mothers who had to work; free milk was distributed at milk depots; settlement houses and Visiting Nurses' Associations gave medical care to children; and eventually medical and dental examination became a routine at most public schools.

The problem of juvenile delinquency was especially vexatious. At common law, children above seven were held capable of crime, and those above fourteen had the same responsibility as an adult; as late as 1894 these common law principles were incorporated into the penal code of New York. Children were tried by the same laws as were applied to adults and, when convicted, were jailed with adult offenders, and thus schooled in a career of crime. In 1899 Miss Addams persuaded Illinois to establish special courts for children, and soon the institution spread throughout the country. Most notable of those who labored for a more humane attitude toward the juvenile delinquent was Judge Ben Lindsey of the Denver Juvenile Court, whose judicial practices and writings eventually commanded international attention.

The 'emancipation' of women had proved a mixed blessing; for many, emancipation from the drudgery of the home merely meant a change to the worse drudgery of the sweatshop. The shift from the country home to the city apartment and the declining size of the family circumscribed the domestic activities of women, but when they turned their energies and talents into industry or business or the professions, they found discrimination everywhere. Scarcely less serious were the legal and political discriminations against women. In few states did married women enjoy the same property rights as men; marriage and divorce laws worked to their disadvantage; and they were denied participation in politics where they might improve their status. Furthermore, the strict social and moral codes of the time imposed a double standard of morality. But during these years the women's rights movement achieved equality in the schools and in some of the professions, improvement in the legal status of married women, reform of marriage and divorce laws, regulation of hours and conditions of woman labor, prenatal care and maternity aid, women's clubs, and, in 1920, the Nineteenth Amendment granting woman suffrage.

Society's misfits as well as society's wards excited the concern of humanitarians, and particular attention was given to prison and penal reform. Everywhere efforts were made to improve prison conditions, mitigate the penalties of the law, and humanize the administration of justice. Since the 1840's the United States had been peculiarly 'the home of penitentiary science.' Under the leadership of Frederick Wines, the Cincinnati Prison Conference of 1870 inaugurated a new era in penal and prison reform, and within a generation many of the recommendations of that conference had been incorporated into law. Altgeld had written a slashing attack on *Our Penal Machinery and Its Victims* as early as 1884; as Governor of Illinois he did much to reform that machinery and rescue its victims. It was reading Altgeld's book that started Clarence Darrow on his life-long career as champion of the underdog. The fundamental idea that 'the supreme aim of prison discipline is the reformation of criminals,' was everywhere acknowledged in principle, though rarely in practice. Reformatories were established for juvenile delinquents; first offenders were separated from hardened criminals; the indeterminate sentence and the parole system were widely adopted; state prison farms were established; convict labor and the lease system were outlawed in some states at least; some of the most barbarous features of the penal codes were repealed; and several states abolished capital punishment. The relation of feeble-mindedness to vice and crime was argued by studies such as Dugdale's *The Jukes* and McCulloch's *The Tribe of Ishmael,* and eugenicists began to urge sterilization of the feeble-minded to protect society.

Most importunate of all the crusades of this generation was that against Demon Rum, a movement which in the United States dates back to the early days of the Republic. By 1851 the temperance forces had established prohibition in Maine and had won minor victories in other states, but between 1860 and 1880 the liquor business increased almost sevenfold, and by the end of the century New York, Chicago, St. Louis, and other large cities with heavy Irish and German populations contained one saloon for every 200 inhabitants. Old stock, Protestant middle-class Americans, especially in rural areas and small towns, waxed indignant at the mores of urban immigrants, who flouted such values as self-control, discipline, and sobriety. The churches denounced drinking as a sin; women attacked the saloon as a menace to the American home; reformers exposed the unholy alliance of the liquor business with crime and the connection between intemperance and poverty; businessmen discovered that drinking affected the efficiency of the workingman and increased the dangers of industrial accidents; while Southern whites insisted on denying liquor to the Negro. For many of the progressives, prohibition was as crucial a reform as social welfare legislation. As Andrew Sinclair has written they looked forward to 'a world free from alcohol and, by that magic panacea, free also from want and crime and sin, a sort of millennial Kansas afloat on a nirvana of pure water.'

Prohibition, as distinct from temperance, was furthered by three well-organized agencies: the Women's Christian Temperance Union, founded in 1874 and long dominated by Frances Willard; the Anti-Saloon League, founded in Oberlin, Ohio, in 1895 and financed by churches and businessmen; and the Methodist Church, most active of all religious denominations. By the turn of the century these organizations, working through the schools, the press, the church, and politics, had succeeded in drying up five states, all of them predominantly rural. A sixth state, South Carolina, had embarked upon the experiment of a state dispensary system not dissimilar from that subsequently adopted in Sweden, but the experiment did not prove a success. In the first fifteen years of the new century the cause of prohibition advanced with rapid strides, and by the time the United States entered World War I over two-thirds of the states were dry, and almost three-fourths of the population lived under 'local option' dry laws. The large cities, however, continued to be wet and from them supplies of liquor flowed unimpeded into thirsty dry areas. One prohibitionist insisted: 'Our nation can only be saved by turning the pure stream of country sentiment and township morals to flush out the cesspools of cities and to save civilization from pollution.'

The demand for national prohibition arose out of the ease with which liquor could be imported from wet into dry territory and the inadequacy of local enforcement machinery. State legislation restricting the importation of liquor had been held unconstitutional as early as 1888, and subsequent efforts by Congress to delegate to the states control over the interstate liquor traffic proved ineffective. 'The Interstate Commerce Clause,' said the U.S. Attorney-General, 'has been made a weapon of offense by which the liquor producing States have compelled prohibition States to receive intoxicating liquors willy-nilly, and thus have made the enforcement of local prohibition substantially impossible.' To remedy this intolerable situation Congress passed, in 1913, the Webb-Kenyon Act penalizing the shipment of liquor into any state where the sale of such liquor was illegal. During World War I, Congress, allegedly for reasons of national economy and efficiency, prohibited the wartime manufacture or sale of all intoxicants. While this law was still in force Congress wrote prohibition into the Constitution in the form of the Eighteenth Amendment. With a unanimity and promptness unique in our constitutional history up to that time, forty-six of the states ratified the amendment.

The achievements of the humanitarians were impressive, yet much that they did was only palliative. There was a growing impatience among the reformers themselves, a changing attitude illustrated in the career of the most distinguished of the social workers, Josephine Shaw Lowell. Founder of the New York Charity Organization Society, active in work for dependent children, for delinquent girls, and for the insane, she decided finally to withdraw from much of this work. Explaining her decision to resign from the State Board of Charities, she wrote:

> If the working people had all they ought to have, we should not have the paupers and the criminals. It is better to save them before they go under than to spend your life fishing them out when they're half drowned and taking care of them afterwards.

As a result of this more realistic attitude toward social reform, progressives turned from organized charity and humanitarianism to political and legislative action.

5. PROGRESSIVISM IN POLITICS

In its political manifestations the progressive movement sought broader democracy and greater efficiency in administration. Most of the progressives had a boundless faith in the efficacy of democracy, and for all the ailments that assailed American institutions their panacea was more democracy. The abandonment of traditional doctrines of laissez-faire in favor of the principle of governmental regulation revealed not so much a disillusionment with liberty as a new confidence in government. Yet the progressives were acutely aware of the need for more adequate administrative machinery. The effort to achieve democracy took the form of agitation for woman suffrage, the Australian ballot, direct primaries, direct election of Senators, the initiative, referendum and recall, municipal home rule, and governmental regulation of railroads, utilities, labor, banking, and finance. The attempt to improve administrative efficiency took the form of agitation for civil service reform, the short ballot, regulation of campaign expenditures, executive leadership, tax reform, and the commission and city manager plan for municipal government.

The progressives achieved their most notable results in state and municipal politics. Some of the older state constitutions were thoroughly revised; others were liberalized by amendments, over 900 of which were adopted in the first two decades of the new century. South Dakota in

1898, Utah in 1900, and Oregon in 1902 adopted the initiative and referendum, and by the time of the First World War over 20 states had provided in some form or other for these devices. In 1908 Oregon committed itself to the recall, and within six years its example was followed by ten states, all but one west of the Mississippi. At first confined to executive officers, the recall was extended by Arizona to judges, and by Colorado, to judicial decisions. The campaign for direct primaries was even more successful. Governor La Follette, who had been twice defeated for the governorship by a boss-ridden convention, persuaded Wisconsin to adopt this reform in 1903; Oregon followed in 1905, and within a decade two-thirds of the states had enacted direct primary and presidential preference laws. Yet the direct primary proved a distinct disappointment, for professional politicians quickly found ways to control the primaries, and by 1912 one advocate of the plan confessed that 'some bosses are wondering why they feared the law, and some reformers why they favored it.' No such dissatisfaction followed the adoption of the Australian or secret ballot which soon became universal. More popular than any of these was the demand for the direct election of Senators. As early as 1899 Nevada formulated a method for circumventing the constitutional requirement of election by state legislatures, and by 1912 some thirty states had provided for the expression of popular opinion in the choice of Senators. The Seventeenth Amendment, ratified in 1913, was therefore rather a recognition of an accomplished fact than an innovation.

From New York to California reform governors gave their support not only to these measures but to enlarging the scope of government control over business. Charles Evans Hughes, elected Governor of New York after exposing spectacular corruption in the great insurance companies, obtained the establishment of a public utilities commission. In Wisconsin Robert La Follette broke the power of the bosses, regulated railroads and public utilities, reorganized the system of taxation, established an industrial commission, made the state university an effective instrument of the regeneration of the state, and reconstructed the administration along more democratic lines. Hazen Pingree in Michigan, Albert Cummins in Iowa, and Hiram Johnson in California shattered the domination of the railways over state politics and brought the roads under strict governmental supervision. In the South, Charles B. Aycock made North Carolina into the most progressive of Southern common-

wealths, Charles A. Culberson brought Texas into the main current of
the reform movement, and 'Alfalfa Bill' Murray, who had played a
leading role in the Constitutional Convention of 1907, made Oklahoma
for a brief time an experimental laboratory of Bryan democracy.

The progressives also scored gains in municipal politics. The framework of American municipal governments had been designed for smaller
and simpler communities; few cities were prepared to undertake the
new tasks of traffic, lighting, sanitation, fire prevention, policing, education, and other costly and complex functions which the great cities demanded. Nor were the cities always able to adapt their administrations
to these new duties.

> The ills from which our cities suffer [wrote Brand Whitlock, re-
> form mayor of Toledo] are not the ills incident to democracy; they
> are ills incident to a lack of democracy. The American city is not
> fundamentally democratic, because it is governed from without.
> . . . Cities are ruled by legislatures from the State capital; they are
> governed, that is, by men from the country who know nothing of
> city problems or city life, and have indeed no real conception of
> just what cities need. In league with them . . . are the public
> utility corporations and political machines. The first requisite,
> therefore, for municipal reform, is home rule.[2]

Men like Whitlock in Toledo and Tom Johnson in Cleveland fought,
with limited success, for home rule, but far more spectacular was the
revolt against boss rule and corruption. Tom Johnson, a wealthy manufacturer who had come under the influence of Henry George, rescued
Cleveland from the grip of the utilities and the domination of Mark
Hanna and made it, for a time, the best governed city in the country. He
left as his disciples two young men who later figured prominently in
national politics: Frederic Howe and Newton D. Baker. In Toledo,
'Golden Rule' Jones guided the city in accordance with his interpretation
of the Golden Rule, and after his death Brand Whitlock carried on the
work of reform — including municipal ownership of public utilities — in
the same spirit and with even more acute understanding. Emil Seidel,
Socialist mayor of Milwaukee, gave that city efficient and honest government. In Jersey City, Mark Fagan fought the corrupt alliance of
bosses and utility interests, and in San Francisco, Fremont Older exposed the skulduggery of a political ring controlled by the president of

2. *The Letters of Brand Whitlock,* edited by Allan Nevins, p. 114.

the Union Pacific. Even New York, under mayors like Seth Low and John Purroy Mitchel, lapsed into respectability, only to repent and reinstate the Tammany Tiger.

The reformers also tried to find permanent solutions to the vexatious problems of city government. The merit system was extended into municipal administration, and bureaus of municipal research inaugurated the study of the science of local government. Various schemes to divorce city government from politics were proposed, and two eventually found wide favor: the city manager and the city commission. Both were first adopted as a result of emergencies. The commission plan grew out of the Galveston flood of 1900; adopted with modifications by Houston and Des Moines, it was soon widely copied throughout the country. The council-manager plan was Dayton's solution for a similar crisis — the Dayton flood of 1913. Both forms made rapid progress in the early years of the century, especially in cities of medium size. By 1940, some 332 cities had adopted the commission form, and 315 cities the council-manager.

Much of this progressive zeal was naïve, some of it was misguided. Fundamentally moralists, the reformers assumed that most of the failings of government could be ascribed to Bad Men — bosses, spoilsmen, vested interests, 'malefactors of great wealth' — and assumed, too, that if only Men of Good Will would devote themselves to public service, all would be well. Progressivism had a touching faith, too, in mechanical contrivances like the initiative and referendum, or the direct primary, or the short ballot; Wilson once said that the 'short ballot was the key to the whole problem of the restoration of popular government in this country.' Yet progressives like Jane Addams, Lincoln Steffens, Louis Brandeis, and Robert La Follette were as hard-headed as any of their successors. If their faith failed to move mountains, it did remove many of the obstacles in the way of effective popular government. Insofar as politics was more honest, society more enlightened, in 1914 than in 1890, much of the credit goes to the embattled and indefatigable progressives.

6. THE STRUGGLE FOR NEGRO RIGHTS: WASHINGTON AND DU BOIS

The most conspicuous failure of the progressive movement was in race relations. After the arduous struggle for abolition, the convulsions of war, and the confusions of Reconstruction, Northern liberals wearied of the Negro issue. Southerners who were 'liberal' on the race question —

like the novelist George Washington Cable — found it healthier to go north. Worse yet, in the decade of the 'nineties and the early years of the new century, Southern progressives themselves often exploited the race issue in their appeal to tenant farmers and mill workers; men like Josephus Daniels of North Carolina, who on most matters went along with Bryan and La Follette, readily sacrificed the Negro to their political ambitions. Daniels stated, 'We abhor a northern policy of catering to Negroes politically just as we abhor a northern policy of social equality.'

Left to fend for himself, the Negro developed two conflicting approaches: one represented by Booker T. Washington of Tuskegee Institute in Alabama, the other by the Massachusetts-born W. E. B. Du Bois of Atlanta University. The issues these two towering figures raised, the controversies they agitated, the programs they sponsored, have dominated Negro thought and thought about the Negro to this day. Born in slavery, raised in abject poverty, catching an education as best he could at the new Hampton Institute in Virginia, Booker T. Washington came to be in truth the Washington of his people, the most distinguished leader of his race after Frederick Douglass, and one of the most influential men in the country between Reconstruction and the First World War. When *Up From Slavery* appeared in 1901, William Dean Howells called Washington 'a public man second to no other American in importance.' Persuaded that the Negro must win economic independence before he could expect to command social or political equality, Washington opened the Tuskegee Normal and Industrial School for Negroes in 1881, with the object of teaching students habits of work, thrift, and good citizenship.

> About eighty-five per cent of the colored people in the Gulf States [he wrote] depended upon agriculture for their living. Since this was true we wanted to be careful not to educate our students out of sympathy with agricultural life, so that they would be attracted from the country to the cities and yield to the temptation of trying to live by their wits. We wanted to give them such an education as would fit a large proportion of them to return to the plantation districts and show the people there how to put new energy and new ideas into farming as well as into the intellectual and moral and religious life of the people.

Over a period of almost forty years Washington counseled progress by evolution rather than by agitation or violence, temporary acquiescence in policies of segregation, and co-operation with the ruling white class.

'In all things that are purely social,' he said, in a widely noted speech at the Atlanta Cotton Exposition of 1895, 'we can be as separate as the fingers, yet one as the hand in all things essential to mutual progress.' 'The wisest among my race,' he insisted, 'understand that the agitation of questions of social equality is the extremest folly.' To win his immediate objective of economic progress, Washington told Negroes to shun politics and scolded them not to forget that they were to work with their hands. This philosophy of accommodation won the enthusiastic support of the white community, relieved to hear a Negro leader consign his brethren to an inferior status. In time Washington came to command the confidence of Presidents; he influenced newspaper editors throughout the country; and he became the confidant of Northern white philanthropists who poured money into Tuskegee and other projects that had Washington's blessing.

At the same time that Washington was playing the public role of 'Uncle Tom,' he was acting in a very different fashion behind the scenes. He surreptitiously lobbied against discriminatory legislation and financed litigation against disfranchisement laws. While loudly deploring office-holding by Negroes, he advised Roosevelt and Taft on patronage; at his suggestion, Negroes were named to such posts as collector of internal revenue in New York and assistant attorney general, appointments that were not to be matched or surpassed by a Negro until after World War II.

Yet for all his dedication Washington fought a losing battle, in part because his program was irrelevant to the urban Negro. He trained Negroes for jobs on the land and in handicrafts at a time when America was rapidly industrializing. He told the black man to stay in the rural South, but as early as 1879 Negroes had begun to move to the cities in large numbers. By 1910 Washington and New York each had more than 90,000 Negroes. In the city the Negro met discrimination from most unions, an ever-tightening cord of residential segregation, and a pattern of legitimized violence. The new century began with the lynching of more than 100 Negroes in its first year, and in 1909 a Memphis newspaper reported that no white man had been hanged in Shelby County since 1890, but noted, 'Since then we have had a hanging of negroes pretty much regularly every year.'

At the beginning of the century the young W. E. B. Du Bois, trained at Harvard and Berlin, challenged the Washingtonian program of compromise and concession.

> So far as Mr. Washington apologizes for injustice, North or South, does not rightly value the privilege and duty of voting, belittles the emasculating effects of caste distinctions, and opposes the higher training and ambition of our brighter minds — so far as he, the South, or the Nation does this — we must unceasingly and firmly oppose him. By every civilized and peaceful method we must strive for the rights which the world accords to men.

Negroes, said Du Bois, could never win economic security without the vote, or achieve self-respect if they acquiesced in a position of inferiority, or attain true equality if they preferred vocational to intellectual training. Du Bois argued in *Souls of Black Folk* that the Negro would be raised by the 'Talented Tenth' who had a liberal arts education. In 1905 Du Bois and his followers met at Niagara Falls, Canada, to inaugurate what came to be called the Niagara Movement. The Niagara platform, as elaborated at subsequent meetings, asserted:

> We want the laws enforced against rich as well as poor; against Capitalist as well as Laborer; against white as well as black. We are not more lawless than the white race, we are more often arrested, convicted, and mobbed. . . . We want the Constitution of the country enforced. We want Congress to take charge of Congressional elections. . . . We want the Fourteenth Amendment carried out to the letter. . . .

The Niagara Movement made slow progress against the opposition of Washington and the hostility of white America, but white reformers who had previously backed Washington now decided that more militant action was needed. Moved by an ugly race riot in Lincoln's town of Springfield, Illinois, in August 1908, William English Walling wrote in the *Independent:* 'Either the spirit of the abolitionists, of Lincoln and of Lovejoy, must be revived and we must come to treat the Negro on a plane of absolute political and social equality or Vardaman and Tillman will soon have transferred the Race War to the North. . . . Yet who realizes the seriousness of the situation and what large and powerful body of citizens is ready to come to their aid?' Stirred by Walling's challenge, a group of Northern whites sent out a call for a National Negro Conference in 1909; the call was written by the publisher of the New York *Evening Post,* Oswald Garrison Villard, the grandson of William Lloyd Garrison. To the conference came many of the Niagara Movement participants as well as such luminaries as Jane Addams, William Dean Howells, and John Dewey.

The conferees laid plans for a permanent organization which led to the creation of the National Association for the Advancement of Colored People with Moorfield Storey of Boston as president, Walling chairman of the executive committee, and Du Bois director of publicity and research. Although Du Bois was the only black official, the strength of the Association lay in its 'Talented Tenth' of college-educated Negro members. With Du Bois as editor, the NAACP organ, the *Crisis,* reached a circulation of 100,000 a month by 1918. Under the leadership of Arthur B. Spingarn, white and Negro lawyers carried out a strategy of litigation which resulted in important legal victories. In 1915, the Supreme Court invalidated the grandfather clauses in the Oklahoma and Maryland Constitutions, and in 1917 the Court ruled unconstitutional a Louisville ordinance imposing residential segregation. To assist urban Negroes, the National Urban League was established in 1911, sparked by George Edmund Haynes, who as a Negro graduate student at Columbia had surveyed conditions in New York City.

The creation of the NAACP marked the victory of the Du Bois approach over the Washington approach. Yet the passing years showed how deeply indebted the Negro was to both of these great leaders. The struggle of the 1950's vindicated both Du Bois's argument that the vote was essential to economic progress and Washington's contention that economic pressure could be the most persuasive of arguments.

Unlike Walling and Storey, most white progressives were either indifferent to race or shared in the prejudices of their day. Theodore Roosevelt's administration was marred by an ugly episode of discrimination against Negro soldiers, and in 1912, Roosevelt, who had outraged the South by inviting Booker T. Washington to dine at the White House, insisted that the Progressive party be a lily white organization in the South. Woodrow Wilson's administration, largely Southern, appointed whites to posts previously granted to Negroes and deliberately imposed racial segregation on the national government. Not until the 1940's would civil rights for the Negro take a prominent place on the agenda of American liberalism.

XII

The Reign of Roosevelt

1. THEODORE ROOSEVELT

On 6 September 1901, six months after his second inauguration, President McKinley was shot by an anarchist. Eight days later he died, and Theodore Roosevelt became President of the United States. Not yet forty-three, Roosevelt was the youngest by several years in the line of Presidents; yet few have been better equipped to administer the office. Building on a broad paternal inheritance of wealth, culture, and public service, he had already achieved prominence as a naturalist, a man of letters, a soldier, and a statesman. He had served his political apprenticeship as a member of the New York State Assembly and, later, as Civil Service Commissioner under Harrison and Cleveland; in both capacities, he had identified himself with the reform element of his party. In between he had found time to write the four-volume *Winning of the West,* and to win a bit of it himself as a Dakota ranchman. In 1895 he had returned to New York City and accepted the thankless post of Police Commissioner. His achievements up to this point were more sensational than permanent, but this work served to throw him into intimate contact with the social reformers and to give him a lasting sympathy with the underprivileged. Two years later McKinley was persuaded to offer him the position of Assistant Secretary of the Navy, but this office proved too confining for his ebullient energies and with the outbreak of the Spanish War he organized the famous Rough Riders and fought his way to fame and glory at San Juan Hill. Elected Governor of

New York in 1898 on his return from war, he had struck at corruption in that state with such vigor that in self-defense Boss Platt and the machine politicians had boomed him for the vice-presidency. His accession to the presidency, regarded with dismay by the conservatives of his party,[1] inaugurated a new era in American politics.

No American of his time was more national in his interests or universal in his friendships than was Roosevelt. University men and the well-to-do in the Eastern states regarded him as one of themselves. He had identified himself with the West by ranching in the Bad Lands of Dakota, leading the Rough Riders, and writing Western history. A dude mocked as 'Four Eyes' as he rode horseback wearing spectacles, a patrician New Yorker who would call out to wranglers in a high-pitched voice, 'Hasten forward quickly there,' a man who neither smoked nor drank and whose favorite swear word was 'By Godfrey,' he nonetheless won the lifelong devotion of the cowboys. The South remembered that his Bulloch uncles had been warriors in the Lost Cause. People everywhere knew him as a red-blooded, democratic American whose every action showed dynamic vitality. Henry Adams said: 'Roosevelt more than any other man living, showed the singular primitive quality that belongs to ultimate matter — the quality that medieval theology ascribed to God — he was pure act.'

Like Bryan and Wilson, Roosevelt was a moralist in politics. It was almost impossible for Roosevelt to think of a political question except in moral terms. Pancho Villa, he remarked, was a 'murderer and a bigamist.' 'Theodore,' Tom Reed said to him, 'if there is one thing more than another for which I admire you, it is your original discovery of the ten commandments.' His morality was positive, but not subtle; he was never in doubt as to the right or wrong of any question, and he regarded those who differed with him as either scoundrels or fools. His habit of injecting moral considerations into political and economic matters served to dramatize the need for reform, but tended to confuse the problems with which he coped. Roosevelt's capacity for action, and for insisting that each of his acts had moral force, led John Morley to call him 'an interesting combination of St. Vitus and St. Paul.'

1. H. H. Kohlsaat tells of riding in the McKinley funeral train with Mark Hanna. 'He was in an intensely bitter state of mind. He damned Roosevelt and said, "I told William McKinley it was a mistake to nominate that wild man at Philadelphia. I asked him if he realized what would happen if he should die. Now look, that damned cowboy is President of the United States." ' *McKinley to Harding*, p. 101.

Roosevelt was a man of fixed convictions and implacable prejudices, but political realism and a talent for opportunism saved him from becoming doctrinaire. He was an ardent nationalist, but his nationalism was often a matter of flags and martial airs. He was a faithful Republican, looked upon Democrats with deep suspicion and, until he himself bolted his party in 1912, upon bolters with positive loathing. He was a thorough democrat, but his democracy was a matter of intellectual conviction rather than of instinct. He took a just pride in his versatility and in the catholicity of his taste: he could lasso a bucking steer, turn out an historical essay, hunt lions, run a political convention, play tennis, lead a regiment, and hypnotize an audience with equal facility; he could hold his own in the company of cowboys, ward politicians, Methodist clergymen, newspaper reporters, foreign diplomats, and Henry Adams. He read widely, and his judgments on literature and science were as dogmatic as his judgments on politics and morals. He had a talent for friendship and commanded a loyalty as near to hero-worship as that which was given to Bryan, and more personal. Wonderfully energetic, bubbling over with good spirits, fascinating in private intercourse, and magnetic in public, he communicated to the American people something of his own wholesome enthusiasm for morality, his own zest for 'the strenuous life.' In time the legend grew that Roosevelt was the 'typical American.' Actually he was less typical, in background, in character, in mind, than Bryan or La Follette or Wilson, but he was more exciting than any of them.

Roosevelt believed that as President he had two important functions: to serve as moral leader of the American people, and to enforce the national interest against special interests. The country, he thought, faced two great dangers: the mob, which could be whipped up by demagogues to overthrow our institutions, and the plutocracy, which lacked the necessary virtues for leadership, and, by its excessive greed, incited the mob. He sought to strengthen the government as a mediating force, for he had, as he once said, a horror of extremes. He aimed to carry out a program that would be neither populistic nor representative of the men he called 'malefactors of great wealth.' Such a program appealed especially to those groups whose values differed from those of the bankers and businessmen: patricians, and the newly rising class of bureaucrats with a sense of mission.

Roosevelt's interest in reform was always qualified by his distaste for most progressives. His own program was general rather than specific, moral rather than realistic. He advocated 'trust-busting,' but his moral sense led him to distinguish between 'good' trusts and 'bad' trusts, and actually the trusts were more powerfully entrenched when he left than when he entered office. He denounced 'malefactors of great wealth' but was critical of the 'muckrakers' who exposed their malefactions, and took no positive steps to curb individual fortunes or to secure a more equitable distribution of wealth through taxation. He demanded a 'square deal' for labor, but no one in the country was more vitriolic in his denunciation of men like Altgeld, Debs, and Bryan, who tried to inaugurate the 'square deal.' He avoided dangerous issues such as tariff and banking reform; and even on those issues to which he committed himself, he was usually ready to compromise on 'half a loaf' rather than risk a break with the Old Guard of his party. His chief service to the progressive cause was to dramatize the movement and make it respectable. Yet Roosevelt's dramatics often distracted attention from the big tent to the side shows. After the seven years of tumult and shouting had passed, many reformers came to feel that they had been fighting a sham battle and that the citadels of privilege were yet to be invested.

2. THE TRUSTS

'It shall be my aim,' said the new President immediately upon his accession to office, 'to continue absolutely unbroken the policy of President McKinley for the peace, prosperity and honor of our beloved country.' But aside from reciprocity, in which Roosevelt had no interest, McKinley had formulated no policy except that of standing pat, and it was inconceivable that Roosevelt should emulate him in this. Indeed, Roosevelt's conception of the presidency was utterly different from McKinley's. McKinley had been willing to follow the leadership of Congress, but Roosevelt believed in executive leadership and gave an exhibition of it that recalled Andrew Jackson and anticipated his own cousin Franklin. According to his conception of the presidency, 'it was not only his right but his duty to do anything that the needs of the Nation demanded, unless such action was forbidden by the Constitution or by the laws,' and he soon indicated his conviction that the needs of the nation were multifarious. McKinley had been content to let well enough alone in business and politics, but Roosevelt, acutely discontented with existing practices in both, demanded reform. In his first message to Congress he gave the country a sample of his political program: the regulation of trusts, railroads, and banks, the creation of a Department of Commerce, new immigration legislation, more conservation, irrigation and reclamation, improvement of the merchant marine, a larger army and navy, construction of an isthmian canal, civil service reform, more generous support to the Smithsonian Institution and the Library of Congress, reform in the consular service and the Indian service, and fifteen or twenty additional items.

Roosevelt came to power at a time of a swelling demand for a more effective enforcement of the anti-trust laws and for additional legislation empowering the Federal Government to regulate all corporations engaged in interstate business. A governmental investigation of 1900 revealed 185 manufacturing combinations, with a total capitalization of over $3 billion. Seventy-three of these trusts had a capitalization in excess of $10 million. Four years later John Moody discovered a total of 318 manufacturing combinations with a total capitalization of over $7 billion — altogether some two-fifths of the manufacturing capital in the country. As 184 of these trusts had been organized since 1898, it was clear that anti-trust laws were not taken seriously. This process of consolidation was even more marked in the realm of transportation, the control and exploitation of natural resources, and especially of finance. Gradually in the course of the first decade of the century, horizontal consolidations and vertical combinations came under the control of great banking houses located for the most part in New York City. The Houses of Morgan, Rockefeller, Vanderbilt, and Baker came to exercise an influence over the economic life of the nation comparable to that of the Houses of Bardi and of Fugger in the Renaissance. Moody struck a popular note when he concluded that 'viewed as a whole, we find the dominating influences in the trusts to be made up of an intricate network of large and small capitalists, many allied to one another by ties of more or less importance but all being appendaged to or parts of the greater groups which are themselves dependent on and allied with the two mammoth, or Rockefeller and Morgan groups. These two mammoth groups jointly . . . constitute the heart of the business and commercial life of the nation.' [2]

In many cases the merger of competing or complementary industries

2. John Moody, *The Truth about the Trusts,* p. 493.

marked a technical advance. But trust methods, however suitable for industries such as meat packing and oil refining, were also extended to others where they were less suitable; and the economies of mass production were not often shared with workers or consumers. The United States Steel Corporation combined the already swollen corporations of Gates, Rockefeller, Carnegie, and others in a trust capitalized at $1400 million, of which nearly one-half was water and nearly one-tenth was issued to promoters for their services. Prices were maintained, although 10 to 12 per cent was being earned on the real capitalization, and the wages of steel workers were kept down by importing cheap labor from southern Europe. The great insurance companies of New York, instead of reducing premiums for their policyholders, paid salaries of $100,000 or more to executives who were often mere figureheads, used their profits recklessly to form industrial consolidations, and corruptly to influence legislation. E. H. Harriman purchased the bankrupt Union Pacific Railway in 1893 with reserve funds of the Illinois Central system and made it one of the best railways in the country; but other lines which he absorbed were sucked dry and cast aside after the stockholders had been ruined. J. Pierpont Morgan, successful in reorganizing railroads and savings banks, came a cropper when at the end of his career he tried to unite all the transportation lines of New England under one management; his effort to consolidate the major transatlantic steamship companies into the International Mercantile Marine was equally disastrous to the stockholders.

Roosevelt proceeded with caution and circumspection. He had not come into power as an opposition leader, but was President 'by act of God.' To most Republican leaders the election of 1900 appeared a mandate to let business alone, and Roosevelt knew that no one of the four Vice-Presidents who had previously succeeded to the presidency had obtained the party nomination at the next election. He knew too, however, that the country was ready for action. He tried to distinguish between the use and the abuse of corporations, and he had the common sense to see that the problem was complicated. 'In dealing with the big corporations we call trusts,' he said in 1902, 'we must resolutely purpose to proceed by evolution and not by revolution. . . . Our aim is not to do away with corporations; on the contrary these big aggregations are an inevitable development of modern industrialism. . . . We can do nothing of good in the way of regulating and supervising these corporations until we fix clearly in our minds that we are not attacking the corporations, but endeavoring to do away with any evil in them. We are not hostile to them; we are merely determined that they shall be so handled as to subserve the public good.'[3] To this end the President recommended the creation of a Department of Commerce and a thorough investigation of the business of corporations. Both recommendations were accepted by Congress. In 1903 a Department of Commerce and Labor was established with cabinet rank, and a Bureau of Corporations was authorized to investigate the operations and conduct of interstate corporations. At first the new bureau was innocuous, but eventually it investigated the oil, packing, tobacco, steel, and other industries and furnished material for prosecution under the anti-trust laws.

More dramatic was Roosevelt's decision to re-invigorate the Sherman law. 'As far as the Anti-Trust Laws go,' he announced, 'they will be enforced . . . and when suit is undertaken it will not be compromised except upon the basis that the Government wins.' In 1902 he shocked Wall Street by instructing Attorney-General Philander C. Knox to enter suit against the Northern Securities Company, a consolidation of the Hill-Morgan and the Harriman railways which embraced the Northern Pacific, the Great Northern, and the Chicago, Burlington and Quincy systems. Morgan and Hanna hurried to Washington to dissuade the President, but their intervention was futile.[4] Nor was their distinguished counsel more successful in the Supreme Court. By a five to four vote the Court sustained the government and overruled its previous decision in the E. C. Knight case,[5] thereby stopping a process of consolidation that

3. Roosevelt's practice of arguing both sides of this question inspired one of Mr. Dooley's happiest comments: ' "Th' thrusts" says he [Roosevelt], "are heejous monsthers built up by th' inlighted intherprise ov th' men that have done so much to advance progress in our beloved counthry," he says. "On wan hand I wud stamp them undher fut; on th' other hand, not so fast. What I want more thin th' bustin' iv th' thrusts is to see me fellow counthrymen happy an' continted. I wudden't have thim hate th' thrusts. Th' haggard face, th' droppin' eye, th' pallid complexion that marks th' inimy iv thrusts is not to me taste. Lave us be merry about it an' jovial an' affectionate. Lave us laugh an' sing th' octopus out iv ixistence." '
4. On the conclusion of this interview, according to Roosevelt's biographer, J. B. Bishop, the President said to Mr. Knox, 'That is a most illuminating illustration of the Wall Street point of view. Mr. Morgan could not help regarding me as a big rival operator, who either intended to ruin all his interests, or else could be induced to come to an agreement to ruin none.' *Theodore Roosevelt and His Time*, Vol. I, p. 184.
5. *Northern Securities Co.* v. *U.S.* 193 U.S. 197 (1904).

Harriman proposed to continue until every important railway in the country came under his control. Roosevelt asserted: 'It was necessary to reverse the Knight case in the interests of the people against monopoly and privilege just as it had been necessary to reverse the Dred Scott case in the interest of the people against slavery.' This decision aroused consternation in financial circles,[6] proved to the nation that industrial magnates were not immune from the law, and enormously enhanced the popularity of the President.

In part as a consequence of the Northern Securities suit, the President grew steadily in popularity. Merely by being himself — greeting professors and pugilists with equal warmth, teaching his boys to ride and shoot, leading major-generals on a point-to-point ride, exercising with his 'tennis cabinet,' praising the good, the true, and the beautiful and denouncing the base, the false, and the ugly — Roosevelt became an institution. Even the journals most opposed to his policies were forced to advertise him in their columns. When the campaign of 1904 came around, the Republicans nominated Roosevelt by acclamation; the Democrats discarded Bryan and put up a conservative New York judge, Alton B. Parker. Roosevelt polled a stunning 56.4 per cent of the vote, the greatest proportion any Republican had ever received, and on 4 March 1905 became 'President in his own right.'

Encouraged by this mandate, Roosevelt turned with new enthusiasm to the enforcement of his trust policies. In the first two years of his second term, big business was further discredited by the muckrakers' attacks on Standard Oil, the beef trust, and the railroads, by the shocking disclosures of the New York insurance investigations of 1905, by the discovery that the sugar trust had swindled the government out of $4 million in customs duties by false weights, and by the panic of 1907. In that year Roosevelt sent Congress a pungent message in which he attributed the panic to 'the speculative folly and flagrant dishonesty of a few men of great wealth,' described the current malpractices of business and industry, and concluded that 'our laws have failed in enforcing the performance of duty by the man of property toward the man who works for him, by the corporation toward the investor, the wage-earner, and

6. 'It seems hard,' wrote J. J. Hill, 'that we should be compelled to fight for our lives against the political adventurers who have never done anything but pose and draw a salary. . . .'

the general public.' Yet legislation giving the Federal Government plenary power to regulate all corporations engaged in interstate business was not forthcoming. Consequently Roosevelt could do little else than demand continued prosecutions under the Sherman law. Altogether there were forty-five such prosecutions, and in notable instances they were successful, but they simply punished the grosser mischief after it had been committed and did not always do that. The beef trust was dissolved, but managed somehow to reintegrate; the fertilizer trust was broken up but miraculously reappeared some years later in different form; the American Tobacco Company was dismembered, but the constituent parts continued to maintain a community of interest.

Unscrambling the eggs, indeed, proved to be a delicate and often impossible operation. As early as 1905, Roosevelt had reached an informal gentleman's agreement with the House of Morgan, although the President never accepted the view that a Morgan corporation like U.S. Steel was co-equal with the Federal government. However, he did leave the impression that he would avoid court action against Morgan companies in return for their co-operation. Roosevelt came to conclude that the mere size and power of a combination did not necessarily render it illegal; there were 'good trusts' such as the International Harvester Company, another Morgan firm, which traded fairly and passed on their economies to consumers; and there were 'bad trusts' controlled by 'malefactors of great wealth.' The Supreme Court raised this moral distinction to the dignity of a legal one when, in the Standard Oil case of 1911, it accepted the common-law doctrine that only those acts or agreements of a monopolistic nature 'unreasonably' affecting interstate commerce were to be construed as in restraint of trade under the anti-trust law. Justice Harlan, in a vigorous dissenting opinion, denounced this 'rule of reason' as 'judicial legislation' and a 'perversion of the plain words of an Act in order to defeat the will of Congress.' But the 'rule of reason' became the guiding rule of decision, notably in the case against the United States Steel Corporation in 1920. Subsequent prosecutions have been based not on size or power, or community of interest — which came in time to be encouraged rather than discouraged — but on unfair, dangerous, or illegal use of power.

3. THE EXTENSION OF GOVERNMENT REGULATION

'The great development of industrialism,' said Roosevelt early in 1905, 'means that there must be an increase in the supervision exercised by the Government over business enterprise.' Early in his first administration Roosevelt had extended the scope of supervision into the realm of labor relations. 'I found the eight hour law a mere farce,' he wrote. 'This I remedied by executive action.' Other aspects of the labor problem likewise felt the impact of 'executive action.' On demand of the President, Congress enacted a workmen's compensation law for all government employees, factory inspection and child labor laws for the District of Columbia, and safety appliance legislation for interstate carriers. But the most notable example of 'executive action' was Roosevelt's high-handed intervention in the anthracite coal strike of 1902, an act which revealed a resourcefulness that no former executive had possessed.[7] Yet despite his enthusiasm for the 'square deal' in labor, and for 'social and industrial justice,' Roosevelt failed to support Senator Beveridge in his struggle for national legislation against child labor.

The railways provided the clearest example of the extension of government supervision; indeed they furnished the fireworks for the second Roosevelt administration as the trusts had for the first. Abandoned by Congress, ignored by Presidents Harrison, Cleveland, and McKinley, and emasculated by court decisions, the Interstate Commerce Act of 1887 had proved all but useless. Yet the necessity for regulation was as urgent in the first decade of the new century as it had been in the 1880's. Concentration of control was growing: by 1904 six major railway systems, representing a combination of almost 800 independent roads and a capitalization of over $9 billion, controlled approximately three-fourths of the mileage in the country.[8] After the Spanish War, freight charges had increased sharply without any corresponding increase in wages or improvement in service, while rebates, discrimination, and favoritism, forbidden by the Act of 1887, continued unabated. And the railroads still enjoyed a practical monopoly on transportation. Only river and lake

7. See above, Chapter IV.
8. The Vanderbilt, Morgan-Belmont, Harriman, Pennsylvania, Gould, and Hill systems.

steamboats furnished any competition; the day of motor and air competition was still far ahead.

The railroads themselves were anxious to make the prohibition of rebates effective, and in 1903 they supported the Elkins Act, described as 'a truce of the principals to abolish piracy.' This act made the published freight rates the lawful standard, substituted civil for criminal penalties, and provided that shippers were equally liable with the railroads for obtaining rebates. Under the provisions of this act the Attorney General instituted prosecutions against the Chicago & Alton and the Burlington for granting rebates and against a group of Chicago packing houses for accepting them. Soon the government went after bigger game. In 1907 Judge Kenesaw Mountain Landis assessed a fine of $29,240,000 against the Standard Oil Company for accepting rebates, but the sentence was set aside by a higher court.

In 1904 Roosevelt pronounced railway regulation the 'paramount issue.' The House promptly passed an act authorizing the Interstate Commerce Commission to fix railway rates, but the Senate refused to concur and substituted instead a bill providing for an investigation of the entire subject. When testimony before the investigating committee revealed the continuation of malpractices, the country rallied behind the President. Roosevelt charged Congress to confer on the Interstate Commerce Commission the power to revise rates and regulations.

Congress responded with the Hepburn Act of 1906, a compromise between the House demand for radical reform and the Senate desire for innocuous regulation. This act made rate regulation for the first time possible and extended it to include storage, refrigeration, and terminal facilities, sleeping car, express, and pipeline companies; regulation was further extended in 1910 to include telephone and telegraph companies. It authorized the Interstate Commerce Commission to determine and prescribe maximum rates and order conformity therewith after thirty days. The railroads could appeal, but the burden of proof was now on the carrier, not the commission. Free passes were prohibited for other than railroad employees, and the railways were required to disgorge most of the steamship lines and coal mines which they had bought up to stifle competition — a requirement which they managed to evade. The Hepburn Act represented a substantial advance in railway regulation; within two years the commission heard almost twice as many complaints as in the previous nineteen years, and by 1911 it had reduced almost 200,000 rates by as much as 50 per cent. Yet as Senator La Follette contended, it did not get to the heart of the matter, for it failed to give the commission power to evaluate railroad properties and the cost of service by which alone it could determine reasonable rates. Not until 1913 was provision made for any valuation of the railroads, and another decade was to elapse before that valuation came to be used for purposes of rate-making. By that time the problem had taken on an entirely new character.

Another gesture toward federal centralization was the extension of governmental supervision over foods and drugs designed for export, but not of meat or food consumed in the United States. Yet investigations of Dr. Harvey Wiley, chief chemist of the Department of Agriculture, and others revealed an almost universal use of adulterants and preservatives in canned and prepared foods. One chemist found that an average menu for breakfast, dinner, and supper might contain forty different doses of chemicals and dyes! At about the same time, the *Ladies' Home Journal* inaugurated a campaign against poisonous patent medicines and misleading advertising, and Samuel Hopkins Adams contributed to *Collier's Weekly* a series of articles on 'The Great American Fraud.' In 1905 Roosevelt asked Congress to act, and, with the support of the American Medical Association and despite the frantic efforts of the Liquor Dealers' Association and the patent-medicine interests, Congress enacted in 1906 a Pure Food and Drugs Act which was strengthened in 1911 by an amendment forbidding misleading labeling of medicines.

The main spur for a pure food and drugs bill came from a book which, ironically, was written for a very different purpose. In March 1906 Upton Sinclair published *The Jungle*, a novel which made a frankly Socialist appeal and boasted an introduction from Jack London, who assured readers that the book was 'straight proletarian.' A story of the tribulations of a Lithuanian immigrant and his conversion to socialism, *The Jungle* was a startling success; for a year, it was the best-selling book not only in the United States but in the British empire. But not, in Sinclair's view, for the right reasons. Instead of rising to indignation about the exploitation of the workers, the American public focused on a dozen pages vividly describing the processing of diseased cattle. When men who worked in the tank rooms fell into open vats, Sinclair wrote, 'sometimes they would be overlooked for days, till but the bones of them had gone out to the world as Durham's Pure Leaf Lard.' As Mr. Dooley said, it was 'a sweetly sintimintal little volume to be r-read durin' Lent.' The public outcry against poisoned meat swept all before it; it not only rescued the pure food and drugs bill from defeat but led to the adoption of federal meat inspection. Though this legislation still left much to be desired, it did give American consumers better protection than the laws of any other country then afforded.

4. CONSERVATION

Unquestionably the most important achievement of the Roosevelt administrations came in the conservation of natural resources. Roosevelt's love of nature and knowledge of the West gave him a sentimental yet highly intelligent interest in the preservation of soil, water, and forest. Even more important, he understood the need to rely on technicians to develop resource policy. It was high time to put some brake on the greedy and wasteful destruction of natural resources that was encouraged by existing laws. Of the original 800 million acres of virgin forest, less than 200 million remained when Roosevelt came to the presidency; four-fifths of the timber in this country was in private hands, and 10 per cent of this was owned by the Southern Pacific, the Northern Pacific, and the Weyerhaeuser Timber Company. The mineral resources of the country, too, had long been exploited as if inexhaustible. The conservationists sought both to halt the waste of such resources and to develop scientific recommendations for their use.

As early as 1873 the American Association for the Advancement of Science had called attention to the reckless exhaustion of our forest resources, but the majority of Americans continued to hug the comfortable delusion that our resources were infinite. Not until 1891 did Congress pass a Forest Reserve Act authorizing the President to set aside timber lands. Under this authority Harrison withdrew some 13 million, Cleveland 25 million, and McKinley 7 million acres of forest from public entry. Despite this promising beginning, the process of exploitation was going on more rapidly than that of conservation when Roosevelt assumed office.

Taking advantage of the law of 1891 Roosevelt set aside almost 150 million acres of unsold government timber land as national forest reserve, and on the suggestion of Senator La Follette withdrew from public entry some 85 millions more in Alaska and the Northwest, pending a study of their mineral and water power resources by the United States geological survey. The discovery of a gigantic system of fraud by which railroads, lumber companies, and ranchers were looting and devastating the public reserve enabled the President to obtain authority to transfer the national forests to the Department of Agriculture, whose forest bureau, under the far-sighted Gifford Pinchot, administered them on scientific principles.

Realizing the necessity for arousing public opinion to the imperative need for conservation, Roosevelt secured wide publicity for the work of the Forest Service, and enlisted the co-operation of local and state groups throughout the country. In 1907 he appointed an Inland Waterways Commission to canvass the whole question of the relation of rivers and soil and forest, of water power development, and of water transportation. That same year, in response to the recommendations of this Commission, the President invited all the state governors, cabinet members, justices of the Supreme Court, and notables from the fields of politics, science, and education to a White House conference. This conference, one of the most distinguished gatherings in American history, focused the attention of the nation upon conservation and gave to the movement an impetus and a prestige that enabled it to survive later setbacks. The conference issued a declaration of principles stressing not only the conservation of forests but of waters and minerals, and the problems of soil erosion and irrigation as well. It recommended the retention by the government of all lands containing coal, oil, phosphate, natural gas, and power sites, the separation of title to surface and sub-surface, the regulation of timber-cutting on private lands, the improvement of navigable streams and the conservation of watersheds. As a result of its recommendations a number of states established conservation commissions, and in 1909 a National Conservation Association, with President Eliot of Harvard as chairman, was organized as a center for propaganda and education. Another outgrowth of the conference was a National Commission, headed by the indefatigable Gifford Pinchot, which undertook an inventory of the natural resources of the nation. Roosevelt realized that the problems of conservation were international in character, and through a North American Conservation Commission he succeeded in securing the co-operation of the other American states in the great work which he had at heart.

By sponsoring an ambitious irrigation program, Roosevelt helped bring new life to barren regions of the West. The Carey Act of 1894, giving the states the right to appropriate public lands for irrigation, had proved inadequate, and in 1902 Roosevelt secured the enactment of the Newlands Reclamation Act which provided that irrigation should be financed out of the proceeds of public land sales under the supervision of the Federal Government. A new Reclamation Service, of which Frederick Newell was the guiding spirit, was established. Under the terms of this act the government constructed, over the next generation, Roosevelt dam in Arizona, Arrowrock in Idaho, Hoover dam on the Colorado river, Grand Coulee on the Columbia river, and a dozen others. At the same time Roosevelt put an end to the acquisition of water-power sites by private utility interests, withdrew over 2000 such sites from entry, and granted others only on fifty-year leases. In addition Roosevelt created five new national parks together with four game preserves and over fifty wild bird refuges. Alone of our Presidents up to this time, Theodore Roosevelt grasped the problem of conservation as a whole. Unfortunately, until the accession of Franklin D. Roosevelt to the presidency, none of his successors had the boldness or the breadth of vision to carry on the work he so hopefully inaugurated.

5. THE BIG STICK

'There is an old adage that says, "speak softly and carry a big stick." ' This familiar quotation, from one of the President's earlier speeches, provided cartoonists with a vivid image to depict Roosevelt's aggressive foreign policy. Yet, paradoxically, it was Roosevelt who gave the Hague Tribunal its first case (the Pious Fund dispute with Mexico), who instructed his delegation at the second Hague Conference to work for the restriction of naval armaments, who was responsible for the return of the Boxer indemnity, who smoothed over a dangerous controversy with Japan, participated in the Algeciras Conference, and won the Nobel peace prize for successful mediation between Russia and Japan.

Roosevelt inherited from McKinley a Secretary of State, John Hay, whose experience as ambassador in London made him eager to meet halfway the new British policy of friendship. And that friendship persisted; there was in effect, during the entire progressive era, an Anglo-American understanding. Downing Street readily conceded to Washington a free hand in the New World; and in return the State Department refrained from any act or expression that would unfavorably affect British interests, and supported British diplomacy in the Far East. The entente, if we may so call it, was consummated by the appointment of the author of *The American Commonwealth*, James Bryce, to the Washington embassy in 1907.

A first fruit of this understanding was the Panama Canal. The voyage of the U.S.S. *Oregon* round the Horn in 1898 touched the popular imagination; and new island possessions in the Caribbean and the Pacific made the construction and operation of an interoceanic canal appear vital to American interests. The Clayton-Bulwer Treaty of 1850 stood in the way of its realization, but not the government of Lord Salisbury. John Hay negotiated with Sir Julian Pauncefote in 1899 a treaty which the Senate, much to his chagrin, rejected because it prohibited fortifying the canal and suggested instead an international guarantee. With the informal aid of Senator Lodge, chairman of the Committee on Foreign Relations, a new Hay-Pauncefote Treaty was signed on 18 November 1901, and promptly ratified. This abrogated the earlier agreement, permitted the United States to construct a canal and control it, and provided that the canal would be open to all nations on equal terms.

The project for an isthmian canal was no new thing; it had been talked of since the sixteenth century and had entered into United States foreign policy since Polk's administration. In 1876 French interests purchased from Colombia the right to build a canal across Panama, and by 1889 DeLesseps, engineer of the Suez canal, had spent over $260 million in a vain effort to cut a canal through the mountains and jungles of Panama. DeLesseps's company was forced into bankruptcy, but a new organization, the Panama Canal Company, was formed for the sole purpose of selling the dubious assets of the old to the United States.

With the quickening of interest in the canal project Congress became a battleground of rival groups: the new Panama Company, which wished to sell its concession on the Isthmus, and an American syndicate which had purchased a concession from the Republic of Nicaragua. McKinley appointed a commission to investigate the merits of the rival routes and that commission, finding that the Panama Company wanted $109 million for its concession, reported in favor of the Nicaragua canal route which had the added advantage of sea-level rather than lock construction. The Panama Company countered by reducing its price to a mere $40 million and by engaging the services of a prominent New York lobbyist, William Nelson Cromwell, who tactfully contributed $60,000 to the Republican campaign fund and enlisted the powerful support of Senator Hanna. Heaven itself came to the aid of the Panama Company; in May 1902, while Congress was considering the rival routes, Mont Pelé in Martinique erupted with a loss of 30,000 lives. Mont Monotombo in Nicaragua followed suit, and when the Nicaraguan government denied that an active volcano existed in that republic, the Panama lobbyists triumphantly presented each Senator with a Nicaraguan postage stamp featuring a volcano in full action. Under these genial auspices Congress on 28 June 1902 passed the Spooner Act. This law authorized the President to acquire the French concession for $40 million if the Colombian Republic would cede a strip of land across the Isthmus of Panama, 'within a reasonable time' and upon reasonable terms; if not, the President was to open negotiations with Nicaragua. On 22 January 1903 Secretary Hay induced the Colombian chargé at Washington to sign a treaty granting the United States a hundred-year lease of a ten-mile wide canal zone, for the lump sum of $10 million and an annual rental of $250,000.

The Colombian government procrastinated about ratifying the treaty — as other governments have been known to do — in spite of a truculent warning from Hay that something dreadful would happen in case of amendment or rejection. We need not take too seriously the constitutional scruples of the Colombian government, since after the dreadful thing did happen the President of the Republic offered to summon a congress with 'new and friendly members' and rush the treaty through. Nor need we give much weight to Roosevelt's argument that 'foolish and homicidal corruptionists' placed him in a dilemma, the other horn of which was the inferior Nicaragua route. The real obstacle to ratification was the $40 million coming to the Panama Canal Company, whose financial affairs were now in the expert hands of the banking house of J. P. Morgan. That company had no right to sell its concession without the permission of Colombia, and there is some ground to believe that the charter of the company would have expired within a year, leaving it without anything to sell! There is no good evidence that Colombia attempted to 'hold up' the United States for a higher price than the treaty provided, although its chargé at Washington had not obtained the conditions required by his instructions.

Colombia's recalcitrance outraged Roosevelt. 'I do not think the Bogotá lot of obstructionists should be allowed permanently to bar one of the future highways of civilization,' he exclaimed to Hay. Neither did Mr. Cromwell nor the Panama junta, dominated by the colorful Philippe Bunau-Varilla, a former agent for the French canal company; and in July 1903 at New York an informal meeting of Panama businessmen, agents of the Panama Company, and United States army officers agreed on a way out: the secession of Panama from the Republic of Colombia. Without making any promise or receiving any of the plotters, Roosevelt and Hay let their intentions become so notorious that Bunau-Varilla advised the revolutionary junta at Panama to proceed in perfect assurance of American assistance.[9] On 19 October three United States war vessels were ordered to the probable scene of hostilities, and on 2 November their commanders were instructed to occupy the Panama railway if a revolution broke out, and to prevent Colombia from landing troops within fifty miles of the Isthmus. The acting Secretary of State cabled the United States consul at Panama, 3 November 1903, 'Uprising on Isthmus reported. Keep Department promptly and fully informed.' The consul replied that afternoon, 'No uprising yet. Reported will be in the night'; and a few hours later, 'Uprising occurred tonight 6; no bloodshed. Government will be organized tonight.'

The description was brief but accurate. The revolution had come off according to schedule. The Governor of Panama consented to being arrested, the Colombian Admiral on station was bribed to steam away, and United States warships prevented troops from being landed by the Colombia government to restore authority. Three hundred section hands from the Panama Railroad and the fire brigade of the city of Panama formed the nucleus of a revolutionary army commanded by General Huertas, former commander in chief of Colombian troops. On 4 November a Declaration of Independence was read in the Plaza, and General Huertas addressed his soldiers. 'The world,' he said, 'is astounded at

9. 'Of course,' Roosevelt wrote some months later, 'I have no idea what Bunau-Varilla advised the revolutionists, or what was said in any telegrams to them as to Hay or myself; but . . . he is a very able fellow, and it was his business to find out what he thought our Government would do. I have no doubt that he was able to make a very accurate guess and to advise his people accordingly. In fact he would have been a very dull man had he not been able to make such a guess.' J. B. Bishop, *Theodore Roosevelt and His Time*, Vol. I, p. 295.

our heroism. President Roosevelt has made good.' Two days later Secretary Hay recognized the Republic of Panama, which by cable appointed Mr. Bunau-Varilla its plenipotentiary at Washington. With him, twelve days later, Hay concluded a treaty by which the Canal Zone was leased in perpetuity to the United States.

As Roosevelt afterwards declared in a speech, 'I took Panama.' Considering the circumstances, one would wish that he had not defended himself by citing a treaty of 1846 with Colombia in which she granted the United States the right of transit and in return was guaranteed her 'right of sovereignty and property over the said territory.' It would also have been better taste on Mr. Roosevelt's part to have refrained from hurling opprobrious epithets at fellow citizens who questioned the righteousness of his action. After all, the only issue at stake was the money to be paid to the speculators who controlled the Panama Canal Company and the construction of the canal might well have waited six months or a year. Colombia was hit by the big stick, but all Latin America trembled. Subsequently, in 1921, the United States paid $25 million to quiet Colombia; it would have been better to have paid this sum eighteen years earlier.

Open to commercial traffic in August 1914, and formally completed six years later, the Panama Canal was a triumph of American engineering and organization. No less remarkable was the sanitary work of Colonel Gorgas, which gave one of the world's greatest pestholes a lower death rate than any American city, while Colonel George Goethals converted the spot described by Froude as 'a hideous dung-heap of moral and physical abomination' into a community of healthy workers.

Elsewhere in the Caribbean area Roosevelt wielded the big stick with redoubtable energy. In 1902 a crisis arose over the question of international intervention for the collection of the Venezuelan debt. Great Britain, Germany, and Italy established a blockade to force the recalcitrant dictator, General Castro, to come to terms. Castro appealed to Roosevelt to arbitrate the claims, but inasmuch as American rights were involved, Roosevelt very properly refused. Yet he deprecated the use of force for the collection of debts, and looked askance at the potential threat to the Monroe Doctrine. A crisis was avoided, however, when Germany, breaking away from the lead of Great Britain, agreed to submit her claims to arbitration. The Hague Tribunal settled the dispute satisfactorily, scaling down the demands from some $40 million to $8 million,[10] and accepting the doctrine of the Argentinian jurist Luis Drago which denied the propriety of coercion for the collection of claims.

For the first time the United States had a President the rulers of Europe looked upon as one of themselves. Roosevelt, like Edward VII, could inject his personality into world politics. In the Russo-Japanese War, the President, at the suggestion of the Japanese and the German Emperors, negotiated directly with premiers and crowned heads. He brought the two belligerents together and broke the deadlock, from which the Treaty of Portsmouth emerged; but not everyone will admit the wisdom of that treaty. Roosevelt preserved for the time being the integrity of China, but the Treaty of Portsmouth merely substituted Japan for Russia in Manchuria and embittered the Japanese people toward the United States. Yet Roosevelt's action had been dictated by friendship for Japan, and the President later declared that he had served notice on France and Germany that the United States would support Japan if either power went to the aid of Russia.[11] It is difficult to find any difference between this sort of thing and the system of secret treaties and balance-of-power diplomacy that Roosevelt, like other Americans, professed to abhor. He played the game of world politics with native audacity and amateur skill, sounding out every step in advance; but if something had gone wrong the American people would have found themselves morally committed by their President to a fighting membership in the Anglo-Japanese alliance. Yet it is inconceivable that the American people would have accepted any such commitments, and if the door held open by John Hay swung to shortly after his death it was, according to Tyler Dennett, because Roosevelt's policy 'could not be continued except at the expense of the Constitution of the United States.'

By the conclusion of the Treaty of Portsmouth, Roosevelt established for his country a right that she did not at that time want — to be consulted in world politics. Again, in the Moroccan crisis of 1905-6, he quietly intervened to preserve peace with justice. French policy of hegemony in Morocco threatened a war with Germany that might easily have become a world conflagration. At the suggestion of the German

10. The United States claims were reduced from some $4 million to $81,000.
11. It is difficult to know whether Roosevelt really made such a threat, or whether his memory played tricks on him.

Emperor Roosevelt urged France to consent to a conference on the North African question, and the American representative, Henry White, was in large part responsible for the Algeciras Convention which, whatever its inadequacies, did keep peace for some years. The Senate ratified the Convention, but with the qualifying amendment that ratification did not involve any departure 'from the traditional American foreign policy which forbids participation by the United States in the settlement of political questions which are entirely European in their scope.' It is interesting to note, by contrast, that President Taft carefully refrained from any participation in the second Moroccan crisis of 1911.

6. THE AMERICAN COLONIAL SYSTEM

Cuba was not a colony, but until 1902 the island was ruled by the United States Army, with General Leonard Wood as military governor. The outstanding feature of this military regime was the remarkable clean-up of Havana under the direction of Major William C. Gorgas which cut the average annual death rate in half. In 1900 came one of the worst yellow-fever epidemics in years. A commission of four army surgeons under Dr. Walter Reed was appointed to investigate the cause. Working on the theory advanced by a Cuban physician, Dr. Carlos Finlay, they proved that the pest was transmitted by the stegomyia mosquito; and two of them, Dr. James Caroll and Dr. Jesse W. Lazear, proved it with their lives. Major Gorgas then declared war on the mosquito; and in 1901 there was not a single case of yellow fever in Havana. One of the greatest scourges of the tropics was at last under control.

By the Teller Amendment the United States had disclaimed any intention of exercising sovereignty over Cuba, and had promised to leave the government in the hands of the Cuban people. Few persons in Europe expected the United States to live up to this altruistic promise, and many Americans regarded it with skepticism. But on the conclusion of the war General Wood provided for the meeting of a constitutional convention to draw up a form of government. The convention met in November 1900 and drafted a constitution modeled upon that of the United States, but without any provision for future relations with that country. The American government was unwilling to acquiesce in this situation, and discreet pressure was applied to induce the Cubans to add a series of provisions known collectively as the Platt Amendment. The chief provisions of the Platt Amendment were those giving the United States an ultimate veto over the diplomatic and fiscal relations of Cuba with foreign powers, recognizing the right of the United States to intervene to preserve Cuban independence and to protect life and property, and committing Cuba to sell or lease a naval base on the island.

Under terms of the Platt Amendment the United States leased and built the naval base at Guantánamo, which she retained even after the Amendment itself was abrogated. The right of intervention was first exercised in 1906, upon the request of the President of Cuba, Estrada Palma. Roosevelt sent his Secretary of War, William Howard Taft, to take charge of the island. When peace and stability were restored, the United States withdrew, leaving the affairs of Cuba in sound condition. At the same time Roosevelt somewhat gratuitously warned the islanders that 'if elections become a farce and if the insurrectionary habit becomes confirmed . . . it is absolutely out of the question that the Island remain independent; and the United States, which has assumed the sponsorship before the civilized world for Cuba's career as a nation, would again have to intervene, and see that the government was managed in such an orderly fashion as to secure the safety of life and property.'

Even more important as a precedent was Roosevelt's intervention in Santo Domingo, and the enunciation of what came to be called the 'Roosevelt corollary' to the Monroe Doctrine. The financial affairs of the Dominican Republic were in a desperate state, and in 1904 the Dominican Minister appealed to Roosevelt 'to establish some kind of protectorate' over the island and save it from its European creditors. Roosevelt had no desire to get involved in the affairs of the Republic — 'about the same desire,' he said, 'as a gorged boa constrictor might have to swallow a porcupine wrong-end-to' — but he agreed that something had to be done to avoid anarchy and European intervention. He set forth his solution in an open letter to Elihu Root: 'If a nation shows that it knows how to act with decency in industrial and political matters, if it keeps order and pays its obligations, then it need fear no interference from the United States. Brutal wrongdoing, or an impotence which results in a general loosening of the ties of civilizing society may finally require intervention by some civilized nation; and in the Western Hemisphere the United States cannot ignore this duty.' In February 1905 he signed a protocol with the Dominican Republic placing an American receiver in charge of Dominican customs, and arranging that 55 per cent of the customs receipts should be applied to the discharge of debts and 45 per cent to current expenses. The Senate refused to ratify the protocol, but Roosevelt went ahead anyway, and in 1907 the Senate came around. In a little more than two years Santo Domingo was transformed from a bankrupt island to a prosperous and peaceful country, with revenues more than sufficient to discharge its debts and pay its expenses, and Roosevelt congratulated himself that he had 'put the affairs of the island on a better basis than they had been for a century.' But a dangerous precedent had been established, and within a decade the United States found herself deeply involved in the domestic as well as the foreign affairs of other Caribbean and Central American nations. So burdensome did this responsibility become, that a quarter-century later the Department of State officially repudiated the 'Roosevelt corollary.' But in the 1960's the United States was still meddling in Dominican affairs.

The Philippine Islands presented peculiar difficulties, especially since from the beginning it was felt that our tenure of these islands was temporary. The Bacon Resolution, promising immediate independence upon the establishment of a stable government, had been defeated by the casting vote of Vice-President Hobart, but the McEnery Resolution had been adopted in its stead. This Resolution announced that 'it is not intended . . . permanently to annex said islands as an integral part of the territory of the United States; but it is the intention of the United States to establish on said islands a government suitable to the wants and conditions of the inhabitants . . . to prepare them for local self-government. . . .' There was, to be sure, a certain ambiguity about this declaration of intention, but the Filipinos were early given to understand that their aspirations for independence would have support of the United States.

The Filipino Insurrection dragged on until 1902, but as early as 1900 military government gave way to a civil Philippine Commission, under William Howard Taft, first Governor-General of the islands. The Commission, entrusted with executive, legislative, and judicial powers, was authorized to reconstruct the government of the islands from the bottom up. Enlarged by the addition of three Filipinos, the Commission was instructed to 'bear in mind that the government which they are establishing is designed . . . for the happiness, peace and prosperity of the people of the Philippine Islands, and the measures adopted should be made to conform to their customs, their habits, and even their prejudices' so far as was consistent with the principles of good government. The Organic Act of 1 July 1902, which regularized this arrangement, recognized the islands as unincorporated territory of the United States and the inhabitants as 'citizens of the Philippine Islands' entitled to the protection of the United States, and provided for the ultimate creation of a legislature.

The United States gave the Philippines as enlightened an administration as is possible in an imperial system which, however well-intentioned, is inevitably paternalistic and self-interested. The insular population in 1900 was about seven million, of whom only 85 per cent were Christian Filipinos, a fairly homogeneous group and intelligent. Their ideas of justice and administration were Oriental, but caste distinctions were lacking; their thirst for education was keen, and Tammany Hall could teach them little in the way of politics. Under American rule they made a remarkable advance in education, well-being, and self-government. Through Taft's diplomacy at Rome, the United States acquired title to vast areas of agricultural land from the religious orders, and sold them on easy terms in small holdings to the peasants. 'Uncle Sam' provided the islands with honest, intelligent, and sympathetic, if somewhat expensive, administrators such as Taft and W. Cameron Forbes; with schools, sanitation, good roads, a well-trained native constabulary, a representative assembly, and baseball. The number of pupils attending school rose from 5000 in 1898 to over a million in 1920, and all but three hundred of the teachers at that date were native. The infant death rate in Manila declined from 80 to 20 per thousand between 1904 and 1920; and smallpox and cholera were practically stamped out. Although the islanders defrayed the entire cost of civil administration, their per capita taxation in 1920 was only $2.50, and their per capita debt, $1.81. But American economic policy left the islands at the mercy of the U.S. market, and as late as 1946 an act of Congress required the Filipinos to grant special privileges to American businessmen. From the outset the islands were an American hostage to Japan, and the Filipinos sensed that someday their country might have the unhappy fate of serving as a battleground for imperial powers. For good or evil, American mores penetrated to parts of the interior where the Spaniards had never ventured. Remote forest glades where savage tribes once met in deadly combat were transformed into baseball diamonds and the jungle resounded to cries of 'Strike him out!'

7. CHANGING THE GUARD

Roosevelt's growing radicalism had alienated conservatives and moderates even of his own party, and his willingness to compromise had forfeited the confidence of many reformers. His vigorous assertion of executive leadership had antagonized Congress and powerful party leaders; and his sense of what constituted fair play brought down upon him at one time or another the wrath of labor and of capital, of Negroes and of Southern whites. Yet no President since Jackson was so popular with the 'plain people.' Only fifty years old in 1908, Roosevelt could have been renominated if he had only said the word. But he had declared in 1904 that 'under no circumstances' would he be a candidate to succeed himself; and in deference to the third-term tradition he contented himself with persuading the Republicans to name William Howard Taft as his successor. After Parker's calamitous defeat in 1904 with less than 38 per cent of the vote, Bryan was able to gain the nomination a third time from a Democratic convention subservient to his every wish. The differences between the two parties were insignificant, and except for charges and counter-charges of financial irregularities, the campaign was apathetic. Bryan carried only the Solid South, Kansas, Nebraska, Colorado, and Nevada, but his popular vote was a million more than that of Parker in 1904, and 43 per cent of the total. Still, save for Parker's race, this was the poorest showing by a Democratic candidate since the party split in 1860. The Republicans captured not only the presidency but both houses of Congress.

To Taft, then, on 4 March 1909, Roosevelt handed over a government that had grown rapidly in prestige and power during the last seven years, and a government that was by way of becoming once more a servant of the people. The entire civil service had been stimulated by Roosevelt's vitality no less than by the knowledge that efficiency would be rewarded. The whole temper of public life had changed for the better, and popular interest in public affairs had never been so keen since the Civil War. If his record of legislative achievement was disappointing, he had helped forge a re-examination of American life. Yet in one respect Roosevelt had failed as a leader. He inspired loyalty to himself, rather than to his ideals and policies. With the conceit of a strong man he had forced and fascinated men of other beliefs to his and the public's service, while neglecting to build up a progressive staff within the Republican party. Still, it would never be quite the same party again, and the Old Guard drew a sigh of relief when Roosevelt took ship to Africa.

XIII

The Taft Administration

1. INEPTITUDE AND INSURGENCY

Strong-willed Presidents have generally managed to nominate their successors, and Roosevelt bequeathed his office to William Howard Taft, a man he loved as a brother and believed the ideal person to carry out his policies. Many progressives welcomed the change, for except in the realm of conservation the last year of Roosevelt's administration was without achievement; as soon as the Republican leaders in Congress had learned that Roosevelt would retire in 1909, they ignored alike his recommendations and his threats. 'Big Bill' Taft, it was hoped, would apply the emollient of his humor and good nature to the wheels of legislation.

If Roosevelt appeared to be less conservative than he really was, Taft seemed more so. He wished to clinch the Roosevelt policies, but in his own fashion; and he was unprepared to go forward with a program of his own. Roosevelt was primarily a man of action, Taft of inaction. As a constitutional lawyer he did not share Roosevelt's view that the President could do anything not forbidden by law; rather, the executive could do only those things for which he had specific authority under the Constitution. Roosevelt had given the presidency an organic connection with Congress; under Taft the relationship became formal, almost diplomatic, and the initiative passed to House and Senate leaders who thought reform had gone far enough, if not too far. In this they were wrong, but Taft was not prepared to disabuse them of their error. Cautious and vacillating, Taft was by instinct conservative, by training 'regular.' In theory he agreed with much of the insurgent program; actually he was unwilling to antagonize the Old Guard. 'Uncle Joe' Cannon of Illinois was its representative in the House, Nelson W. Aldrich of Rhode Island in the Senate, and so certain were these men of their power that they openly professed contempt for democracy.

Roosevelt went to Africa in March 1909, as much to avoid embarrassing the new President by his presence as for the pleasure of big game hunting. The new President and the old parted with warm expressions of trust and affection. But Roosevelt returned fifteen months later to find the Republican party divided, the progressive program halted, and reformers alienated; and in fifteen months more the two old friends were exchanging bitter reproaches before the public. That this happened was in large part President Taft's fault; the manner in which it happened was Roosevelt's.

When Roosevelt sailed for Africa, he left his successor with many critical problems, especially the tariff and the trusts, unsolved. In August 1908, he explained, 'Well I'm through now. I've done my work. People are going to discuss economic questions more and more: the tariff, currency, banks. They are hard questions, and I am not deeply interested in them; my problems are moral problems, and my teaching has been plain morality.' John Hay noted in his diary: 'Knox says that the question of what is to become of Roosevelt after 1908 is easily answered. He should be made a bishop.'

The Republican platform of 1908 contained a pledge to revise the tariff: an issue that Roosevelt had gingerly avoided. Revision was popularly understood as reduction, and Taft had specifically committed himself to this interpretation. A student of William Graham Sumner's at Yale, Taft had never thereafter favored high protection. 'Mr. Taft is a very excellent man,' wrote Senator Foraker in 1909, 'but there never was a minute since I first knew him when the tariff was not too high to suit him.' For downward revision there was, by 1909, pressing demand, especially in the Midwest, a region which exported many of its commodities. The tariff was blamed for the rising cost of living and was thought to be 'the mother of trusts.' In his inaugural address the new President asked that 'a tariff bill be drawn in good faith in accordance with the promises made before the election,' and he summoned Congress into special session to take action.

When Congress assembled, Sereno Payne of New York was ready with a tariff bill which placed iron ore, flax, and hides on the free list and reduced duties on steel, lumber, and numerous other items. The bill promptly passed the House and went to the Senate, where representatives of interested industries fell upon it. When it emerged from the Senate as the Payne-Aldrich tariff it was seen that of the 847 changes, some 600 were upward and that the free list was a joke.[1] Accused of violating the party's promise to revise the tariff, Aldrich retorted: 'Where did we ever make the statement that we would revise the tariff *downward?*' Senator Heyburn was still more brazen; even if the Republicans had pledged downward revision, the people, he reasoned, had been wise enough not to believe them. The Progressive Republicans were outraged, and La Follette, rapidly emerging as the leader of American progressivism, organized the Midwestern Senators to fight the proposed measure item by item. There followed one of the most stirring debates in American history. La Follette attacked the woolens schedule, Beveridge the tobacco, Cummins the steel, Bristow the sugar, Dolliver the cotton, and if in the end they failed, they did at least enlighten the country on the connection between tariffs and trusts, and laid the dynamite for the political explosion of 1910. The President was perturbed. The insurgents urged him to veto the bill as a violation of party pledges, but after painful vacillation he decided to sign it.

To heal this deep sectional wound in the party would require deft diplomacy on Taft's part. But the President promptly made a bad situation worse by deciding to go on tour of the Middle West in the summer of 1909, to 'get out and see the people and jolly them.' He began his trip by paying tribute to Aldrich in the East; in Winona, Minnesota, in the heart of progressive discontent, he enraged insurgents by calling the Payne-Aldrich measure 'the best tariff bill that the Republican party has ever passed, and therefore the best tariff bill that has been passed at all'; and he capped off the tour by having himself photographed with his arms around Speaker Cannon.

1. 'Th' Republican party,' explained Mr. Dooley to Mr. Hennessy, 'has been thrue to its promises. Look at th' free list if ye don't believe it. Practically ivrything nicessary to existence comes in free. Here it is. Curling stones, teeth, sea moss, newspapers, nux vomica, Pulu, canary bird seed, divvy-divvy, spunk, hog bristles, marshmallows, silk worm eggs, stilts, skeletons, an' leeches. Th' new tariff bill puts these familyar commodyties within th' reach iv all.' Mr. Dooley on The Tariff in *Mr. Dooley Says*, p. 148.

The progressive Republicans, already uneasy about Taft's conservative inclinations, came to suspect him of playing traitor to Roosevelt's policies when they looked into his conservation record. James R. Garfield, Roosevelt's lieutenant in conservation, had been supplanted in the Interior Department by R. A. Ballinger, who was presently charged by Chief Forester Gifford Pinchot with letting a Morgan-Guggenheim syndicate obtain reserved coal lands in Alaska. The President dismissed Pinchot, an act interpreted as a dramatic reversal of Roosevelt's conservation program. Actually Taft was not unfriendly to conservation. He was the first President to withdraw oil lands from public sale. He asked for and obtained from Congress the authority to reserve the coal lands which Roosevelt had set aside without specific authority, and made the Bureau of Mines guardian of the nation's mineral resources. Pinchot was replaced by the head of the Yale School of Forestry, and his policy was continued by the purchase, in 1911, of great timbered tracts in the Appalachians.

The progressives directed their indignation not only against the President but against the Old Guard upon whom he depended. In the Senate, La Follette, Beveridge, and Dolliver excoriated Aldrich to such effect that he decided not to stand for re-election. In the House, insurgency took the form of a revolt against Speaker Cannon, 'a hard, narrow old Boeotian,' who controlled a well-oiled legislation mill which rejected progressive grist. On 18 March 1910 George Norris offered a resolution depriving the Speaker of membership on the powerful Committee on Rules and making that committee elective, and Democrats joined with progressive Republicans to pass the resolution.

If the progressive cause gained, legislative efficiency lost. Authority was needed to enforce party discipline in a body so unwieldy and fluctuating as the House of Representatives. Some of the progressives denied any right of national party leaders to regularize the flow of legislation. Victor Murdock later described his attitude as 'merely reflecting Jonathan Edwards' philosophy that nothing should come between God and man, in maintaining that nothing should come between the people and their representatives.' Cannon bridled at such notions: 'The Speaker does believe and always had believed that this is a government through parties, and that parties can act only through majorities.' Although at the time the defeat of Cannon struck a blow for progressivism, modern-day liberals believe that the Speaker's concept of party government is more appropriate to liberal democracy than that of the insurgents who spoke for the autonomy of the Congressman.

The fights over Payne-Aldrich, Ballinger-Pinchot, and Cannonism caused an irrevocable split between Taft and the progressive Republicans, and in the 1910 campaign the President attempted to drive the insurgents out of office. In many Midwestern states, the breach was made formal: 'Taft Republican' clubs fought 'Progressive Republican' clubs. Taft, who had come to office as a Roosevelt progressive, took personal charge of the campaign against the insurgents; he called a meeting of Iowa regulars, sent the Vice-President to campaign against La Follette in Wisconsin, and worked with the Southern Pacific crowd against Hiram Johnson in California. But the progressives handed him and the Old Guard a stunning set of defeats. Iowa Republicans booed and voted down a resolution to endorse Taft; Johnson, who said his Republicanism came not from Washington but from Iowa and Wisconsin, overwhelmed the Taft Republicans; and La Follette won an impressive triumph. This factionalism in the primaries proved devastating for the Republicans in November. Maine elected a Democrat to the U.S. Senate for the first time since 1857, and as Maine went so went the nation. The Democrats captured the governorships of Massachusetts, Connecticut, and New York; sent Dr. Woodrow Wilson, lately president of Princeton University, to the State House in New Jersey; and won control of the House for the first time since 1894.

The ineptitude of Taft's administration and the growing revolt against him must not blind us to his achievements. During his term much valuable legislation was enacted. The Mann-Elkins Act of 1910 strengthened the Interstate Commerce Commission by empowering it to suspend any rate increases until and unless the reasonableness thereof was ascertained, and created a new Commerce Court to hear appeals from the commission. The Department of Commerce and Labor, established at Roosevelt's instance in 1903, was wisely divided; and Congress set up a Children's Bureau in the new Department of Labor. A postal savings bank and a parcel post — conveniences long overdue — were provided. A Commission of Economy and Efficiency to examine the national administration was created, and a measure requiring publicity for campaign expenditures adopted. The merit system was expanded by the addition of second- and third-class postmasters to the civil service list. Alaska, peevish and discontented since the collapse of the Klondike gold bubble, at last obtained full territorial government in 1912. New Mexico and Arizona, last of the continental Territories except Alaska, became the forty-seventh and forty-eighth states of the Union. Here again Taft unnecessarily antagonized the progressives by refusing to certify the admission of Arizona until it expunged from its constitution a provision for the popular recall of judges; once admitted as a state, Arizona promptly restored the device. Approximately twice as many prosecutions for violation of the Sherman Act were instituted during Taft's four years in office as during Roosevelt's seven.

Significant of the rapidly expanding envelope of law were two amendments to the Constitution. As James Bryce pointed out, the difficulties of this process were such that the Constitution had not been amended since 1802, excepting 'in the course of a revolutionary movement which had dislocated the Union itself.' The Sixteenth, or income-tax, Amendment and the Seventeenth Amendment, which transferred the election of United States Senators from state legislatures to the people, were adopted by Congress in 1909 and 1912 respectively and ratified by the requisite number of states in 1913.

From direct election of Senators much had been expected. It would make that body more democratic; it would put an end to indirect corruption; it would open more widely the door to talent, even to impoverished talent. Few of these expectations were realized. The Senate may have become more representative, but the cost of elections has gone up, and it is not certain that the general level of ability has.

2. CANADIAN RECIPROCITY AND DOLLAR DIPLOMACY

Even developments in foreign affairs served to lessen Taft's popularity and tear his party asunder, despite the fact that the unlucky President's foreign policy was often more sensible and more restrained than Roosevelt's had been. With a lawyer in the White House and in the Department of State, American diplomacy returned to its traditional channels. By an exchange of notes in 1908, Japan and the United States had agreed to support the independence and integrity of China, and the 'open door.' Japan, nevertheless, with the full approval of the Triple Entente, began to consolidate her position in Manchuria. Secretary Knox attempted to meet this situation by proposing, in 1909, that the United States and European powers lend China sufficient money to buy back all the railroads controlled by foreign interests. This, said Knox, 'was perhaps the most effective way to preserve the undisturbed enjoyment by China of all political rights in Manchuria and to promote the development of those Provinces under a practical application of the policy of the open door.' But he had not felt out the Powers, as Roosevelt would have done, and his plan was rejected somewhat contemptuously by Russia and Japan. Failing in this effort to assist China out of her difficulties, Taft insisted that American bankers be allowed to participate in a four-power consortium to finance railway construction in the Yangtze valley, 'in order that the United States might have equal rights and an equal voice in all questions pertaining to the disposition of the public revenues concerned.' But this plan, innocent enough in purpose, was repudiated by Wilson within two weeks of his accession to office.

It was fear of Japan, too, which provoked the so-called Lodge corollary to the Monroe Doctrine. In 1911 an American company proposed to sell Magdalena Bay in Lower California to a Japanese fishing syndicate. On hearing of the proposal, Senator Lodge, suspicious that the syndicate might be a cover for the government itself, introduced and the Senate passed a resolution announcing that the purchase or control by any non-American government of any part of the American continents which had a potential naval or military value would constitute an unfriendly act. Though Taft declared that he was not bound by the resolution, it further aggravated Latin American public opinion, already exasperated by Roosevelt's Panama and Caribbean policy. The doctrine was strictly a one-way affair; designed to prevent foreign establishments in the Western hemisphere, it did not limit the expansion of American economic power to other continents.

A comparison of the Roosevelt and Taft policies in Central America recalls the old adage that some persons can make off with a horse, while others cannot look over the stable wall. Secretary Knox signed treaties with Nicaragua and Honduras similar to Roosevelt's treaty with Santo Domingo, underwriting American loans by guaranteeing the bankers against revolution and defalcation. But the Knox treaties were rejected by the Senate, and Taft's policy both in Central America and the Far East was denounced as 'dollar diplomacy.' In 1911 Taft, a warm friend to international peace, concluded treaties with both England and France for the arbitration of all disputes, including those involving 'national honor.' The German-American press and the professional Irish-Americans broke out into shrieks of dissent. A presidential election was approaching, and the Senate rejected the treaties.

Again it was Taft's misfortune, not his fault, that tariff reciprocity with Canada failed. In November 1910 three United States commissioners concluded with two members of the Dominion Parliament a reciprocity agreement to be adopted by identical legislative acts. The agreement provided free trade in primary food products, which would naturally flow from Canada southward, and a large reduction on manufactures, which would obviously go the other way: It was a sincere effort by President Taft to cement friendly relations but bad politics. The insurgent Republicans, representing for the most part Western agrarian states, were able to argue that reciprocity was a good bargain only for the trusts, which would gain a new market and free raw materials at the farmer's expense; yet many Eastern industrialists opposed it too. Democratic votes pushed the bill through Congress. In the debate, Champ Clark, the new Democratic Speaker, said, 'I am for it because I hope to see the day when the American flag will float over every square foot of the British North American possessions clear to the North Pole.' Mr. Clark awoke the next day to find himself notorious. His words may have been a joke, as he feebly explained; more likely they were spoken for effect, and certainly they expressed no current American sentiment. But they aroused the fighting spirit of Canadian loyalty, were repeated in Parliament, and awoke to loud entreaty Rudyard Kipling's lyre. Sir Wilfred Laurier, the Canadian Prime Minister, was forced to appeal to his country. Canadian manufacturers, who feared to lose the protected home market they had so carefully built up, financed the conservative opposition, and in September 1911 the treaty and Sir Wilfred went down to defeat.

Taft's foreign policy also widened a division between the President and his predecessor that had far-reaching political repercussions. Roosevelt disliked Taft's Latin American policy, and he fiercely denounced the President's proposal for blanket arbitration treaties as 'maudlin folly' and the product of 'sloppy thinking.' He expressed such views publicly in *The Outlook* and in a seven-page letter to the *New York Times*. Stung by Roosevelt's attack, Taft commented privately: 'The truth is that he believes in war and wishes to be a Napoleon and to die on the battlefield.'

3. ROOSEVELT AND THE PROGRESSIVE PARTY

Theodore Roosevelt, after enjoying good hunting in Africa and a triumphal progress through Europe, returned to New York in June 1910. Greeted with hysterical enthusiasm that somewhat dismayed him, he insisted on settling down at Sagamore Hill to pursue his many non-political interests. *The Outlook* made him associate editor and afforded him an organ. But the role of sage was not congenial to 'Teddy,' and the people would not be denied the delight of seeing and hearing their hero. Before the summer was over, he was making public addresses in the West which showed unmistakably that shooting lions and dining with crowned heads had not dulled his fighting edge for reform. His ideas, clarified and systematized as the 'New Nationalism,' included not only the old Roosevelt policies of honesty in government, regulation of big business, and conservation of natural resources, but a relatively new insistence on social justice. This principle involved some vigorous and wholly justified criticism of recent Supreme Court decisions, which had nullified social legislation in the states. He urged the country to rely not on the courts but on a Chief Executive who would be 'the steward of the public welfare,' and he boldly asserted the rights of the community over 'lawbreakers of great wealth.' At Osawatomie on 31 August 1910, T.R. stated: 'The man who wrongly holds that every human right is secondary to his profit must now give way to the advocate of human welfare, who rightly maintains that every man holds his property subject to the general right of the community to regulate its use to whatever degree the public welfare may require it.'

Conservative Republicans shuddered at the 'New Nationalism' and feared a split in the party. Taft was worried. 'I have had a hard time,' he confessed to his old friend. 'I have been conscientiously trying to carry out your policies, but my method of doing so has not worked smoothly.' Roosevelt visited the President at the temporary summer capital, and continued a friendly correspondence for several months. Yet the two men were being pulled apart. Insurgents and displaced progressives like Pinchot were continually telling Roosevelt that the President had surrendered to the Old Guard, and entreating him to be a candidate in 1912. Taft, on the other hand, was surrounded by friends and relatives whose advice resembled that of George III's mother: 'George, be a King!'

After the Democratic victories of 1910 and the revolt on reciprocity, it seemed unlikely that Taft could succeed himself. In December 1910 Senator La Follette, spokesman for the insurgents, drafted a declaration of principles for a Progressive Republican League, and the next month the league was formally organized to liberalize the Republican party. On obtaining what he thought was Roosevelt's assurance that he would not enter the contest, La Follette became a candidate for the Republican presidential nomination. His strength, however, was confined largely to the Mississippi valley, and his radicalism frightened many who agreed in theory with the principles that he advocated. In the midst of a speech on the 'money trust,' on 2 February 1912, La Follette collapsed. He recovered by the following day, but insurgents who had used him as a stalking horse for Roosevelt promptly deserted and went over to the old leader.

Roosevelt had declared in 1904 that 'under no circumstances' would he again be a candidate for the presidency. Taft was his friend and his own choice; to oppose him would be to impeach his own judgment. But Roosevelt, who despised Taft's foreign policy and was uneasy about his domestic program, was infuriated when on 26 October 1911 the Taft administration filed an anti-trust suit against U.S. Steel which, by implication, impeached Roosevelt's judgment in sanctioning a special dispensation when he was President. Even before La Follette's candidacy fell flat, Roosevelt was planning how best to get into the race. At his own suggestion the Republican governors of seven states addressed to him, on 10 February 1912, an open letter urging that he announce his candidacy. A few days later President Taft publicly denounced persons who had supported the 'New Nationalism' as destructive radicals, 'political emotionalists,' and 'neurotics.' These words touched Roosevelt on the raw, since a rumor that he was losing his reason was being circulated. They were exactly the sort of challenge to dissolve his lingering doubts and arouse a violent spirit of combat. 'My hat is in the ring,' he announced on 21 February.

That same day he delivered an address before the Ohio Constitutional Convention which opened his campaign. He spoke of big business as 'inevitable and desirable,' but he also insisted that the rich man 'holds his wealth subject to the general right of the community to regulate its

William Jennings Bryan at the Democratic Convention, 1896

Eugene V. Debs (1855-1926)

Terence V. Powderly (1849-1924)

Samuel Gompers (1850-1924)

Woodrow Wilson and William Howard Taft

Robert M. La Follette (1855-1925)

Theodore Roosevelt at Asheville, North Carolina, 1904

Booker T. Washington (1858-1915)

Jane Addams (1860-1935)

W. E. B. Du Bois (1868-1963)

business use as the public welfare requires,' and urged that the police power of the state be broadened to embrace all necessary forms of regulation. Further, he advocated not only the initiative and the referendum, but the recall of decisions by state courts. 'It is both absurd and degrading,' he said, 'to make a fetish of a judge or of any one else.' His radicalism alienated thousands of Republican voters, cost him the support of friends like Lodge, Knox, Root, and Stimson, and made his nomination by the Republicans extremely improbable.

La Follette stayed in the fight, and the contest for the Republican nomination became unseemly and bitter. In the Ohio primary campaign, Taft and Roosevelt called one another Jacobin, apostate, demagogue, and fathead. Wherever the law permitted, Roosevelt entered the presidential preference primaries. Thirteen states chose their delegates to party conventions through popular primaries, and in these states Roosevelt obtained 278, Taft 46, and La Follette 36 delegates. Roosevelt had the overwhelming support of the rank and file of the Republican party, but the bosses were with Taft. Where delegates were chosen by conventions, the President was almost uniformly successful, and the Southern districts, the Republican rotten boroughs, returned a solid block of Taft delegates who represented little more than the federal officeholders in that region. The credentials of some 200 delegates were in dispute, but the conservatives retained control of the convention machinery. Roosevelt, who charged that his legitimate majority was being stolen, told his enraptured followers, 'We stand at Armageddon and we battle for the Lord.' When the party organization awarded practically all the contested seats to Taft men, Roosevelt instructed his delegates to take no further part in the proceedings; and Taft was renominated easily.

Roosevelt and his followers at once took steps to found a new party. On 5 August 1912 the first Progressive party convention met at Chicago amid scenes of febrile enthusiasm that recalled Populism and the early days of the Republican party. The delegates paraded around the convention hall singing 'Onward Christian Soldiers' and

> Follow! Follow!
> We will follow Roosevelt,
> Anywhere! Everywhere,
> We will follow on.

The new party welcomed social workers like Jane Addams, municipal reformers like Harold Ickes of Chicago, and social scientists such as

Charles Merriam, as well as disgruntled politicians and moneyed men like Frank Munsey and George Perkins, known as Secretary of State for the House of Morgan. Since Perkins, like Roosevelt, favored recognizing the inevitability of the growth of trusts, and then regulating them, while many of the delegates were anti-trusters, the party equivocated on its trust plank. But the rest of the platform, which reflected the social justice aspirations of leaders like Jane Addams, was so radical that Gene Debs declared that the red flag of socialism had been replaced by the red bandannas of the Progressives. The convention nominated Roosevelt by acclamation, and picked Governor Hiram Johnson of California to be his running mate. A phrase of the beloved leader, 'I am feeling like a bull moose,' gave the new party an appropriate symbol, beside the Republican elephant and the Democratic donkey.

In the perspective of history the formation of the Progressive party appears to have been a mistake from every point of view save that of the Democrats. Roosevelt's secession with his following lost many good men their political careers and ended all chance of liberalizing the Republican party; for although the Progressives eventually returned to the fold, it was with their tails between their legs. The true progressive strategy of the moment was to remain within the party, let the Old Guard lead it to defeat, and wait for 1916. Roosevelt's mistake was so contrary to his long-settled principles of party regularity, that one naturally asks whether an appetite for power was not his moving force. Like the elder Pitt, Roosevelt believed that he, and he alone, could save the country; unlike Pitt, he did not win the opportunity to justify his faith.

4. WOODROW WILSON AND THE ELECTION OF 1912

The year after Taft entered Yale, and the year before Roosevelt entered Harvard, Woodrow Wilson, son and grandson of Scots Presbyterian ministers, came up to Princeton. At the Hasty Pudding Club of Harvard, Roosevelt would become so excited in debate as to lose the power of articulation. Wilson was remembered at Whig Hall, Princeton, for having lost an interclub debating contest rather than defend protection against free trade. Before graduating from Harvard, Roosevelt wrote his first book, *The Naval History of the War of 1812*, which sounded the note of preparedness for war upon which his life closed. In his last year at Princeton, Wilson published an article exposing the irresponsibility of congressional government, which he later did so much to remedy. Roosevelt entered public life in 1881; Wilson, after a brief and unprofitable practice of law, took his doctorate at Johns Hopkins, and began a quiet career of teaching and scholarship. In 1890, the year after Roosevelt was appointed to the Civil Service Commission, Wilson became a professor of political science at Princeton; and in 1902, the year after Roosevelt became President of the United States, Wilson was chosen president of Princeton University.

While Roosevelt fought political privilege in the nation, Wilson contended with social privilege at Princeton. Originally an austere Presbyterian college, Princeton had become a haven of the well-to-do, where young bloods monopolized the amenities of university life. Wilson attempted somewhat arbitrarily to transform the aristocratic undergraduate clubs into more democratic dormitory groups. Dean Andrew F. West, a classical scholar, spoiled the symmetry of the scheme, and Wilson met his first defeat. Soon arose an even more important dispute over the organization and control of the graduate school which Wilson insisted must be integrated with the college. The whole country was interested when Wilson refused a bequest of half a million dollars which carried qualifying provisions that he deemed fatal to the proper functioning of the graduate school. The issue, to Wilson, was more than academic; it went to the very heart of the problem of democracy. 'The American college,' he said, 'must become saturated in the same sympathies as the common people. The colleges of this country must be reconstructed from the top to the bottom. The American people will tolerate nothing that savours of exclusiveness. . . . The people are tired of pretense, and I ask you . . . to heed what is going on.' But Princeton refused to heed what was going on; and when a new bequest of several million dollars was placed at the disposal of Wilson's enemies, he stepped out of the academic picture.

As a scholar, publicist, and leader in education Wilson enjoyed a national reputation; but active politics was considered a closed sphere to professors. George Harvey, the arch-conservative editor of *Harper's Weekly*, in search of a Democratic candidate for the presidency, mentioned Woodrow Wilson in 1906. Harvey was attracted by Wilson's conservatism; an anti-Bryan Democrat, Wilson had denounced 'the crude and ignorant minds of the members of the Farmers Alliance.' He deplored the 'passion for regulative legislation,' and as late as January

1909 described himself as 'a fierce partizan of the Open Shop.' Harvey's suggestion was greeted skeptically, but the professor took it to heart. In 1910 the Democrats of New Jersey — an amorphous state, half bedroom to New York and half to Philadelphia, under the control of corporations attracted by the laxity of its laws — wished to achieve respectability with a new sort of candidate. They had long been out of power and their none too savory reputation might be sweetened by a scholar. At George Harvey's suggestion the bosses nominated Wilson, and the people elected him governor. Within a year Wilson had repudiated the bosses, broken the power of the sinister 'Jim' Smith, won the enthusiastic allegiance of reformers like George Record and Joseph Tumulty, and written more progressive legislation into the statute books than had been enacted in the previous half-century. He split with Harvey, but a silent politician from Texas, Colonel Edward M. House, took him up; and Wilson became a leading candidate for the presidential nomination in 1912. At the Democratic convention in Baltimore, Champ Clark of Missouri had a majority of the delegates, but he was never able to muster the necessary two-thirds, and on the forty-sixth ballot Wilson was nominated.

The presidential election, then, became a three-cornered contest between Taft, Roosevelt, and Wilson; but really between the last two. Roosevelt ran on a more advanced program of social reform, while Wilson during the campaign opposed both a national child labor law and minimum-wage legislation. Roosevelt believed that big business was inevitable and that it should be regulated. Wilson subscribed rather to the doctrine of Louis Brandeis, that bigness was a curse and government had a responsibility to break it down and to encourage competition. The solution, as Brandeis saw it, was regulated competition instead of regulated monopoly. While Roosevelt's 'New Nationalism' borrowed from European experience with a directive state, Wilson's 'New Freedom' derived from classic British liberalism. 'The history of liberty,' Wilson asserted, 'is the history of the limitation of governmental power.' Their personalities and styles of campaigning differed even more than their programs. Henry Stoddard observed: 'In my study of the two men Wilson stands out, clear cut and rigid, in the sharp definite lines of a steel engraving; when I turn to Roosevelt he is revealed in strong human tints, the warm flesh tones of a Rembrandt or a Franz Hals.' Roosevelt, with biblical imagery and voice like a shrilling fife, stirred men to wrath, to combat, and to antique virtue; Wilson, serene and confident, lifted men out of themselves by phrases that sang in their hearts, to a vision of a better world.

Wilson polled less than 42 per cent of the vote; save for Arizona, no state outside the South gave him a majority. But he won an overwhelming victory in the electoral college. Roosevelt, with 27 per cent, carried six states. Taft, with 23 per cent, carried only Utah and Vermont. Nine hundred thousand voted for the Socialist nominee, Eugene Debs. The Democrats swept Congress, carrying the House by 290 to 145 and the Senate by 51 to 45, and they were victorious in twenty-one of the state gubernatorial contests.

Progressives thought of 1856 and were confident of triumph in 1916. The Grand Old Party, as they saw it, had gone the way of the Whig party — killed by a great moral issue that it would not face. Another bland Buchanan was in the White House. But the Old Guard neither died nor surrendered. The Progressives were little more than a candidate and his following, certainly not an organic party. And Woodrow Wilson, instead of playing the part of Buchanan, welded his party into a fit instrument of his great purpose 'to square every process of our national life again with the standards we so proudly set up at the beginning and have always carried at our hearts.'

XIV

The New Freedom

1. THE INAUGURAL

Few men have ever come to high office in the United States so unprepared politically as was Woodrow Wilson, but no man ever showed a firmer grasp of the problems of statesmanship with which he had to cope, or a shrewder understanding of the game of politics which he was to play. Before he became President he had held only one elective office. Possibly his most remarkable characteristic was his capacity for growth, his ability to immerse himself in new problems, to master them and to re-interpret them in the light of the past and of his own convictions. By birth and training a conservative and a Hamiltonian, he became the greatest leader of the plain people since Lincoln and a democrat who accommodated the ideals of Jeffersonian democracy to the conditions of a new day.

Few even of the new President's friends expected more than a respectable presidency. Wilson lacked the common touch, and loved humanity in the abstract rather than people in particular. Unlike T.R., he could not descend into the market-place or emulate the prize-ring; throughout his eight years of office he was always aloof and often alone; no one ever called him W.W. or Tommy! His humor and warm affections appeared only to a few intimate friends. The obstinacy that had been his undoing in the academic world was not likely to be a useful virtue in the presidency, if Cleveland's career was a fair test; and it was clear that Wilson would not sacrifice a principle either for friendship or for political expediency. 'Wilson is clean, strong, high-minded and cold-blooded,' wrote F. K. Lane, the warm-hearted man who became his Secretary of the Interior; but he was also the kind of person to take refuge from facts in generalities. In an era of fierce contention, and without Lincoln's ability to express himself in simple, homely language, he was certain to be misunderstood.

Woodrow Wilson came to power at a propitious time. The progressive movement was nearing its culmination, and new men in the Democratic party were eager to transform it from a diffuse alliance of rural Southerners and machine bosses into a modern national organization. It was one of those moments in history when the situation called for a particular kind of man, and the man was there. Wilson, who had minimized the importance of the presidency in his *Congressional Government in the United States,* had come to think of the Chief Executive as 'the only national voice in affairs.' A month before his inauguration he wrote that the President 'must be prime minister, and he is the spokesman of the Nation in everything.' And more perhaps than anyone who had ever held the office Wilson understood the force of words as a political weapon. In 1909 he had cried: 'I wish there were some great orator who could go about and make men drunk with this spirit of self-sacrifice . . . whose tongue might every day carry abroad the golden accents of that creative age in which we were born a nation.'

The Democratic party for which he was now the spokesman had undergone little change since Andrew Jackson's time. The elements in it that counted were the emotional and somewhat radical Western wing represented by Bryan; Irish-Americans of the industrial states, who wanted the power and office denied them during the Republican dynasties; a large segment of labor and the Solid South, including almost every white man in the late Confederacy, and many in the new Southwest — Oklahoma, New Mexico, and Arizona. Tradition, habit, and common suspicion of Big Business and Wall Street held these sections together, and the issues of liquor and religion that almost split the party in 1924 and again in 1928 had not yet arisen; the small farmers of the South and West had much in common while the rural tories of the South could sympathize with rebels against the Northern industrial bosses.

In only one election since Reconstruction had the Democratic party polled less than 42 per cent of the popular vote cast for a President, and in five of the ten presidential elections it received a plurality. But the party wanted leadership. Cleveland's victories had proved barren, Bryan had thrice failed, and the majority leaders in Congress were elderly and timid. For the task of leadership Wilson proved himself peculiarly equipped. He had inherited a Calvinistic philosophy which placed the halo of moral necessity on expediency, and he had developed an intellectual arrogance which inclined him to rely largely upon his own judgment, while from a prolonged professional study of the science of government he had learned the necessity of executive leadership in the modern state.

Wilson's inaugural address, striking a note of high idealism and couched in words reminiscent of Jefferson's first inaugural, aroused hope and enthusiasm.

> No one can mistake the purpose for which the Nation now seeks to use the Democratic Party. It seeks to use it to interpret a change in its plans and point of view. Some old things with which we had grown familiar, and which had begun to creep into the very habit of our thought and of our lives, have altered their aspect as we have latterly looked critically upon them, with fresh, awakened eyes. . . . Some new things . . . have come to assume the aspect of things long believed in and familiar, stuff of our own convictions. We have been refreshed by a new insight into our own life.

By the light of this new vision Wilson examined the processes by which America had achieved her greatness and revealed the ruthlessness, waste, and corruption, and reckoned anew the cost, not by the balance sheet of business but in the ledger of social well-being.

> We have been proud of our industrial achievements, but we have not hitherto stopped thoughtfully enough to count the human cost of lives snuffed out, of energies over-taxed and broken, the fearful physical and spiritual cost to the men and women and children upon whom the dead weight and burden of it all has fallen pitilessly the years through. The groans and agony of it all had not yet reached our ears, the solemn, moving undertone of our life, coming up out of the mines and factories and out of every home where the struggle had its intimate and familiar seat. . . . The great Government we loved has too often been made use of for private and selfish purposes, and those who used it had forgotten the people.

The inaugural itemized with some degree of particularity the things that ought to be altered. These included the tariff, 'which makes the Government a facile instrument in the hands of private interests'; an antiquated and inadequate banking and currency system; a burdensome and wasteful industrial system, which 'exploits without renewing or conserving the natural resources of the country'; an inefficient and neglected agricultural system; 'water-courses undeveloped, waste places unreclaimed, forests untended, unregarded waste heaps at every mine.' Government was not negative —

> it must be put at the service of humanity, in safeguarding the health of the Nation, the health of its men and its women and its children, as well as their rights in the struggle for existence. . . . There can be no equality of opportunity . . . if men and women and children be not shielded in their lives, their very vitality, from the consequences of great industrial and social processes, which they can not alter, control, or singly cope with. . . . Sanitary laws, pure food laws and laws determining conditions of labor which individuals are powerless to determine for themselves are intimate parts of the very business of justice and legal efficiency. The Nation has been deeply stirred by a solemn passion, stirred by the knowledge of wrong, of ideals lost, of government too often debauched and made an instrument of evil. The feelings with which we face this new age of right and opportunity sweep across our heartstrings like some air out of God's own presence, where justice and mercy are reconciled and the judge and the brother are one.

No administration of modern times has been inaugurated with more passionate eloquence. Yet Wilson himself was neither a fighting progressive like La Follette, nor a spokesman for agrarian and labor discontent like Bryan. He was rather a nineteenth-century liberal, suspicious of special interests whether they were of Wall Street or of the Grange or the labor union, and distrustful of the new breed of intellectuals who were calling for government to intervene directly in the economy. 'I don't want a smug lot of experts to sit down behind closed doors in Washington and play Providence to me,' he said. Wilson's beliefs, noted Walter Lippmann, were 'a fusion of Jeffersonian democracy with a kind of British Cobdenism. This meant in practical life a conviction that the world needs not so much to be administered as to be released from control.'

Wilson spoke for 'the man on the make,' the risk-taking entrepreneur who asked only a fair chance to make his fortune. He inquired: 'Are you not eager for the time when the genius and initiative of all the people shall be called into the service of business? when newcomers with new ideas, new entries with new enthusiasms, independent men, shall be welcomed? when your sons shall be able to look forward to becoming, not employees, but heads of some small, it may be, but hopeful business?' The new President offered a three-point program designed to foster the interests of the small capitalist: a lowered tariff to deny the trusts an unfair advantage; a changed banking structure to make credit more available to the small businessman; and new trust legislation to prevent big business from squeezing out the small competitor.

Wilson, who had entered politics as an admirer of J. P. Morgan, had become increasingly critical of financial interests which he believed were crushing the independent businessman. By the end of 1911, Harvey was writing Colonel House: 'Everybody south of Canal Street was in a frenzy against Wilson.' Even before he took office, Wilson attempted to build up public support by a blunt attack on Wall Street. If any tycoon dared to frustrate his program, he warned, 'I promise him, not for myself but for my countrymen, a gibbet as high as Haman — not a literal gibbet, because that is not painful after it has been used, but a figurative gibbet, upon which the soul quivers as long as there are persons belonging to the family who can feel ashamed.' Yet however radical his rhetoric, Wilson proposed to do little to disturb vested interests, and his program ignored many of the realities of life in industrial America.[1]

2. THE UNDERWOOD TARIFF

On 8 April 1913, hardly more than a month after he was inaugurated, Wilson made the dramatic move of coming before Congress in person to

1. Lippmann commented: ' "Have you found trusts that thought as much of their men as they did of their machinery?" he [Wilson] asks, forgetting that few people have ever found competitive textile mills or clothing factories that did. . . . The pretty record of competition throughout the Nineteenth Century is forgotten. . . . You would think that competitive commercialism was really a generous, chivalrous, high-minded stage of human culture. . . . The New Freedom means the effort of small business men and farmers to use the government against the larger collective organization of industry. . . . That is the push and force of this New Freedom, a freedom for the little profiteer, but no freedom for the nation from the narrowness, the poor incentives, the limited vision of small competitors.'

deliver his message on tariff reform. Not since John Adams had a President appeared before Congress. One Democratic Senator protested: 'I am sorry to see revived the old Federalistic custom of speeches from the throne. . . . I regret all this cheap and tawdry imitation of English royalty.' But Wilson was determined to seize the initiative in law-making by narrowing the distance between 'the two ends of Pennsylvania Avenue.' A slight thing in itself, this act caught the popular imagination.

On the very day he took office, Wilson had summoned Congress to special session, as in 1909, to revise the tariff. It was a dangerous issue; in the preceding twenty years only one tariff revision had not resulted in defeat at the polls, and the fate of the Wilson-Gorman tariff was as familiar to Democrats as that of the Payne-Aldrich to Republicans. But Wilson did not hesitate, would not compromise. 'The tariff duties must be altered,' he said. 'We must abolish everything that bears even the semblance of privilege, or of any kind of artificial advantage, and put our business men and producers under the stimulation of a constant necessity to be efficient, economical and enterprising.' Hearings on the new tariff bill had begun as early as January 1913, and House leaders such as Underwood of Alabama, Kitchin of North Carolina, and Hull of Tennessee were ready with a bill. After a brief debate, the Underwood tariff, as it came to be known, passed the House by a strict party vote, 281 to 139. The real struggle, as everyone anticipated, came in the Senate.

On 8 May the Underwood tariff went to the Senate, which prepared to exercise its ancient prerogative of rewriting the House measure. To assist in this task, representatives of vested interests descended upon Washington. Senator Thomas of Colorado described the scene:

> By telegram, by letter, by resolutions of commercial and industrial associations and unions, by interviews, by threat, by entreaty, by the importunities of men and the clamor of creditors, by newspaper criticism and contention, by pamphlet and circular, by the sinister pressure of a lobby of limitless resources, by all the arts and power of wealth and organization, the Senate has been and will be besieged, until it capitulates or the Underwood bill shall have been enacted.

In a public statement of 26 May Wilson lashed out at the sinister activities of the lobbyists. 'It is of serious interest to the country,' he said, 'that the people at large should have no lobby, and be voiceless in these matters, while great bodies of astute men seek to create an artificial opinion and to overcome the interests of the public for their private profit.' His appeal was effective, and consideration of the tariff bill went forward in a more wholesome atmosphere. Through the hot months of a Washington summer the President held Congress to its appointed task. He himself set an example of ceaseless vigilance, scrutinizing every section of the measure with meticulous care and appearing with embarrassing frequency at the Senate committee rooms to participate in conferences. Through such adroit personal leadership, Wilson secured passage of the measure with almost unanimous Democratic support. In September the bill passed the Senate, and on 3 October 1913 it received the signature of the President.

The Underwood tariff was far from a free-trade measure, but it did reverse a tariff policy which had been almost unchallenged for fifty years. A London editor called it 'the heaviest blow that has been aimed at the Protective system since the British legislation of Sir Robert Peel.' The act lowered average duties from some 37 per cent to some 27 per cent, but more important were reductions in specific schedules and additions to the free list. Duties were decreased on 958 articles, raised on 86, and maintained on 307. Reductions embraced important commodities such as cotton and woolen goods, iron and steel, while wool, sugar, iron ore, steel rails, agricultural implements, hides, boots, cement, coal, wood and wood pulp, as well as many agricultural products were to enter duty free. To meet the anticipated reduction in customs revenues, Representative Cordell Hull of Tennessee added a provision for a graduated tax on incomes of $4000 and over, ranging from 1 to 6 per cent.

3. BANKING AND CURRENCY REFORM

While Congress was still wrestling with the Underwood tariff, Wilson presented a proposal to reorganize the banking system. The need for a thorough overhauling of our banking and currency system was almost universally recognized. The 'bankers' panic' of 1907 reflected no basic unsoundness in the economic system, but a ruinous shortage of currency and inelasticity of credit; only by hasty importations of gold from abroad and by resort to extra-legal forms of currency was business able to weather the crisis. Recognizing that the whole question of banking and currency required further study, Congress created a National Monetary Commission, whose final report listed no less than seventeen serious defects in the American banking system, among them the concentration of financial power in New York.

The extent of that concentration of money and credit was not fully realized until the investigations of the Pujo Committee of 1912 were made public. Those investigations revealed that the firm members or directors of two sets of New York banks, controlled by the Morgan and Rockefeller interests, held:

> One hundred and eighteen directorships in 34 banks and trust companies having total resources of $2,679,000,000 and total deposits of $1,983,000,000.
>
> Thirty directorships in ten insurance companies having total assets of $2,293,000,000.
>
> One hundred and five directorships in 32 transportation systems having a total capitalization of $11,784,000,000 and a total mileage (excluding express companies and steamship lines) of 150,000.
>
> Sixty-three directorships in 24 producing and trading corporations having a total capitalization of $3,339,000,000.
>
> Twenty-five directorships in 12 public utility corporations having a total capitalization of $2,150,000,000.
>
> In all, 341 directorships of 112 corporations having aggregate resources of capitalization of $22,245,000,000.

If all agreed to the necessity of reform, they disagreed vigorously about what form it should take. Conservatives, even within the President's own party, wanted a central bank such as the old Bank of the United States without its branches, with control of credit in the hands of the bankers. Bryan's followers, on the other hand, insisted that the power to issue notes should be a government not a private function, that control of the new banking system should be exclusively governmental, and that the system should be decentralized. On 23 June Wilson appeared before Congress to outline his own program.

> We must have a currency, not rigid as now, but readily, elastically responsive to sound credit. . . . And the control of this system of banking and of issue which our new laws are to set up must be public, not private, must be vested in the Government itself, so that the banks may be the instruments, not the masters of business and of individual enterprise and initiative.

Carter Glass was ready with a bill which carried out these general principles, and for six months Congress wrangled over this administration measure while metropolitan bankers and Western farmers criticized it with equal severity. Wilson had little to fear from the opposition of the bankers, but he could not afford to forfeit the support of Bryan and his followers. In the end the provisions of the new law recognized both of Bryan's demands: that there should be no active banker representation on the banking board and that all Federal Reserve currency should be governmental obligations. So disciplined had the party become under Wilson's leadership that not a single Democratic Senator voted against the bill.

The Federal Reserve Act of 23 December 1913 created a new national banking system upon regional lines. The country was divided into twelve districts,[2] each with a Federal Reserve Bank owned by the member banks, which were required to subscribe 6 per cent of their capital. These regional banks acted as agents for their members. All national banks were required and state banks permitted to join; within a decade one-third of the banks, representing 70 per cent of the banking resources of the country, were members of the Federal Reserve system. A Federal Reserve Board, consisting of the Secretary and the Comptroller of the Treasury and six others appointed by the President, was to supervise the business of the regional banks. The law authorized a new type of currency: Federal Reserve notes secured by short-term commercial paper and backed by a 40 per cent gold reserve. The new system was designed to introduce greater elasticity into the credit of the country, a sounder distribution of banking facilities, and more effective safeguards against speculation. In time the bankers themselves admitted that the Federal Reserve system had added immeasurably to the financial stability of the country.

The Federal Reserve Act aimed to provide easier credit for farmers, but the law did little to bring down farm interest rates or ease farm credit. These objects were partially achieved, however, by the Federal Farm Loan Act of May 1916 which purposed to 'reduce the cost of handling farm loans, place upon the market mortgages which would be a safe investment for private funds, attract into agricultural operations a fair share of the capital of the nation, and lead to a reduction of interest.' Specifically the act created a Federal Farm Loan Board and 12 regional

2. District banks were established at Boston, New York, Philadelphia, Cleveland, Richmond, Atlanta, Chicago, St. Louis, Minneapolis, Kansas City, Dallas, and San Francisco.

Farm Loan banks similar in general character to the Federal Reserve banks. These Farm Loan banks were authorized to extend loans on farm lands, buildings, and improvements up to 70 per cent of their value to co-operative farm loan associations. Loans were to run from 5 to 40 years, interest rates not to exceed 6 per cent, and profits were to be distributed to the members of the subscribing farm loan associations. By 1930 over 4000 such farm loan associations had been established and the Farm Loan banks held over a billion dollars of farm mortgages. A further step toward the creation of better credit facilities for farmers was taken in the Warehouse Act of 1916, which authorized licensed warehouses to issue against farm products warehouse receipts which might be used as negotiable paper. Thus were the Populists vindicated a quarter-century after their sub-treasury scheme had been rejected with contempt.

4. THE REGULATION OF BUSINESS

With the enactment of the Underwood tariff and the Federal Reserve Act the Democrats had gone far toward translating their platform promises into law, but the most emphatic of the party pledges was as yet unfulfilled. 'A private monopoly,' said the platform, 'is indefensible and intolerable. We therefore . . . demand the enactment of such additional legislation as may be necessary to make it impossible for a private monopoly to exist in the United States.' Since reliance upon the Sherman law had proved clearly futile, Wilson, in his acceptance speech, had called for 'new laws' to meet 'conditions that menace our civilization.'

As soon as the tariff and banking reform bills were disposed of, Wilson appeared before Congress to ask for legislation on trusts and monopolies. His address of 20 January 1914 included five specific legislative recommendations: the prohibition of interlocking directorates of corporations, banks, railroads, and public utilities; the grant of authority to the Interstate Commerce Commission to regulate the financial operations of railways; the explicit definition of the meaning of the anti-trust laws; the creation of a federal interstate trade commission to supervise and guide business; and the penalization of individuals, not business, for violations of the anti-trust laws. Congress responded with two bills: the Clayton bill, which prohibited numerous forms of unfair trade practices, and a measure to set up a commission with limited authority. When the

Clayton bill was denounced as inadequate, Wilson embraced a proposal from Brandeis to establish a strong regulatory commission, although this was an idea that the New Nationalists had advanced and Wilson opposed in 1912. The Federal Trade Commission Act replaced Roosevelt's Bureau of Corporations with a new non-partisan commission of five, appointed by the President for seven-year terms. The law declared unfair methods of competition unlawful and authorized the commission to investigate alleged violations of the anti-trust laws; to issue 'cease and desist' orders against any corporation found guilty of unfair methods of competition; and, if this failed, to bring the accused firm into court.

Once Wilson accepted the FTC approach, he lost interest in the Clayton bill, which emerged as a weak law. Senator Jim Reed complained: 'It was a raging lion with a mouth full of teeth. It has degenerated to a tabby cat with soft gums, a plaintive mew, and an anaemic appearance. It is a sort of legislative apology to the trusts, delivered hat in hand, and accompanied by assurances that no discourtesy is intended.' The Clayton Act prohibited discriminations in price which might tend to lessen competition or create monopoly and 'tying' agreements limiting the right of purchasers to deal in the products of competing manufacturers. It forbade corporations to acquire stock in competing concerns, and outlawed interlocking directorates in corporations with a capital of more than one million dollars and banks with a capital of more than five million dollars. In accordance with the President's recommendation, officers of corporations were made personally responsible for violations of the law.

Wilson, who opposed grants of special privilege to any group, set himself stiffly against a demand to exempt unions and farm organizations from anti-trust prosecutions. Faced by a party revolt, he agreed only to a provision that such organizations were not, per se, in restraint of trade. Unions were exempted from the terms of the act as long as they sought legitimate objectives, and the use of the injunction in labor disputes 'unless necessary to prevent irreparable injury to property . . . for which there is no adequate remedy at law' was explicitly forbidden. Gompers hailed these provisions as 'labor's charter of freedom,' yet the act did not outlaw the notorious 'yellow-dog' contracts or, unlike the British Act of 1906, relieve unions from corporate responsibility for damage caused by their members; and subsequent developments were to reveal its inadequacy.

'With this legislation,' said Wilson optimistically, 'there is clear and sufficient law to check and destroy the noxious growth [of monopoly] in its infancy.' But the courts reserved to themselves the right to determine what constituted 'unfair methods of competition' just as they reserved the right to interpret the phrase 'irreparable injury to property,' and in the war and postwar years judicial rulings became increasingly conservative. The effort to enforce the provision making directors responsible for corporation malpractices broke down when the government failed to prove its case against the directors of the New Haven Railroad. During the war the Clayton Act was tacitly suspended, and in the postwar period of Republican ascendancy it was seldom invoked, while the Federal Trade Commission, by encouraging the formulation of codes of trade practices, entered into something suspiciously like an alliance with the trusts. When, twenty years after the enactment of the Wilsonian anti-trust legislation, Franklin D. Roosevelt came into office, the trusts were as numerous and monopolies as powerful as ever, and the whole problem had to be studied afresh. Perhaps all this merely demonstrates the validity of Thurman Arnold's theory that the function of anti-trust agitation and legislation is purely ceremonial — that it provides us the satisfaction of declaiming against the 'evil' part of a 'necessary evil' while retaining what is necessary about it. Yet if the legislation did not break up trusts or curb monopolies, it may well have imposed on them a pattern of good behavior.

In pushing through his three-point program, Wilson had demonstrated that he was a great leader: of his party, of Congress, of the nation. He had held the 63rd Congress in Washington for over a year and a half, the longest session in history, and he had kept relentless pressure on its members. The *New York Times* commented: 'President Cleveland said he had a Congress on his hands, but this Congress has a President on its back, driving it pitilessly. . . . Never were Congressmen driven so, not even in the days of the "big stick." ' Above all, Wilson had proven what many reasonable men had long doubted — that the Democratic party could govern.

Yet by the autumn of 1914 Wilson was content to call a halt to further reforms. As spokesman for the Democratic party's Jeffersonian equal rights tradition, Wilson rejected three types of legislation: social welfare reforms that sought to hurdle constitutional barriers; proposals aimed at benefiting special interests, including workers; and measures which reflected the New Nationalist approach of reconciling business and government. He blocked a bill to provide long-term rural credits, refused to support a woman's suffrage amendment, and in March 1915 almost vetoed the La Follette Seamen's bill. When A. Mitchell Palmer led a fight for a federal law to abolish child labor, Wilson opposed it. Until alarmed by the storm of liberal disapproval, he permitted members of his cabinet to practice racial discrimination. For all his rhetoric against big business, his appointments to government agencies were so conservative that one Senator said of his selections for the Federal Reserve Board that they looked as though they had been chosen by the head of the National City Bank.

Wilson might have continued his cautious drift to the right had it not been for the collapse of the Progressive party, which carried the threat that Roosevelt's ardent following might move back into the Republican fold. Having won less than 42 per cent of the vote in 1912, Wilson was doomed to defeat in 1916 if a reunited Republican party polled its full strength. To attract voters of a progressive inclination, Wilson decided to turn to the left. Moreover, just as his views in New Jersey had shifted, Wilson's convictions were no doubt changing as the result of his White House experience. He began the transformation with the appointment on 28 January 1916 of the distinguished reformer, Louis D. Brandeis, to the Supreme Court, a selection that was confirmed despite an appalling outburst of anti-Semitism. In rapid succession he reversed himself to support social welfare measures, including a law excluding the products of child labor from interstate commerce and a Workmen's Compensation Act for federal employees. He gave his blessing to special interest legislation for farmers and workers, including the Rural Credits Act, which provided long-term farm loans, and the Adamson Act, imposing an eight-hour day on all interstate railways. The New Nationalist program of business-government co-operation won a partial victory with the creation of a tariff commission and the exemption of exporters from the anti-trust laws. If Wilson had not accepted the idea that the national government would play a directing role in the economy, or the conception of a managerial class ruling in the national interest, he could nonetheless boast that the Democrats had 'come very near to carrying out the platform of the Progressive Party' as well as their own.

In four years Wilson had reasserted presidential leadership, converted a state-rights party to enlightened nationalism, convinced the average citizen that the government was at last his servant, and made clear that progressivism transcended party lines.

5. NEIGHBORS AND DEPENDENCIES

Wilson had not mentioned foreign affairs in his inaugural address nor had he discussed them in his campaign; yet his first administration was concerned largely, his second almost exclusively, with problems of international relations. When he assumed office the United States was at peace with the world, but faced with many vexatious controversies which demanded early attention. Japanese aggressions in Manchuria threatened the open door policy, and Japan was assuming a menacing attitude toward the anti-alien land laws of the Pacific coast states; Colombia was still sore over the Panama episode, and England was aggrieved at our discrimination in favor of American coastwise shipping through the Panama Canal; American marines controlled Nicaragua, and conditions elsewhere in the Caribbean were unsettled, while Mexico was in the throes of a revolution which affected American interests. To the solution of these difficulties the new President brought neither experience nor detailed information, but a body of broad principles which not only required the maintenance of peace but American leadership in that effort. And to those principles, most of which he might justly claim to be his own, Secretary Bryan subscribed with enthusiasm. For while Wilson was for the most part his own Secretary of State, Bryan's contribution to Latin-American policy was not negligible; his interpretation of the problem of neutrality, when that arose, however, differed from that of his chief.

In principle and to a lesser extent in practice, Wilson reversed much of the foreign policy of his predecessors. The first hint of that reversal was the statement of 19 March 1913 withdrawing support from the proposed bankers' loan to China as incompatible with Chinese sovereignty. This was widely interpreted as a formal repudiation of 'dollar diplomacy.' Shortly thereafter came recognition of the new Chinese Republic. At the same time Secretary Bryan launched that program of conciliation treaties which he had been advocating ever since 1905 and in whose success he had a touching faith. Altogether Bryan concluded thirty agreements submitting all disputes — including those involving questions of 'national honor' — to arbitration, and providing a 'cooling-off' period of one year before resort to arms; of the major powers only Germany refused to sign such an agreement.

Bryan had campaigned in 1900 on a platform promising independence to the Philippines, and in 1912 the party had once again pledged itself to that policy. In 1914 a Bryan follower, Representative Jones of Virginia, introduced a bill largely drafted by young Felix Frankfurter granting immediate self-government to the Filipinos and promising complete independence in the near future. Under pressure from the War Department, which was alive to the strategic importance of the Philippines, and from Catholics who feared confiscation of church property in the islands, Wilson maneuvered for a less drastic measure, which would not stipulate a specific time-limit on American control. The Jones Act, passed in 1916, formally pledged the United States to withdraw from the Philippines 'as soon as a stable government can be established therein,' and inaugurated far-reaching political and administrative reforms. It abolished the Philippine Commission, provided for a legislature of two houses, both elected by popular vote, and gave the legislature authority to reorganize the government. At the same time Governor-General Harrison filled the civil service with native Filipinos and encouraged the Philippine government to establish state-controlled railroads, banks, mines, and manufacturing industries. Under these auspices the Filipinos made such progress that President Wilson, in his last annual message, reminded Congress that the time had now come to fulfill the promise of the Jones Act. But the incoming Republican administration had no sympathy with such a program. A new commission, dominated by General Leonard Wood, reported that the islands were not ready for independence, and Wood, who stayed on as Governor-General, reversed practically all of Harrison's enlightened policies. In 1927 Wood died, but not before he had destroyed in large part the reputation he had made in Cuba; his successor, Henry L. Stimson, returned to the policy of conciliation which had been so successful. Not until 1934 did Congress finally pass a bill providing for Philippine independence; not until 1946 did the bill take effect.

As so often before, and since, Latin America provided the crucial test of the new policy, and furnished the arena for its triumph and its defeat. Nothing better illustrates the high-mindedness of the new administration than Wilson's reaction to two Panama Canal problems that he had inherited from his predecessors. The first was the long-standing dispute with Colombia, which still bitterly resented the part that President Roosevelt had played in detaching Panama and setting her up as an independent state in 1903. In 1914 Bryan negotiated a treaty with Colombia which expressed 'sincere regret' for whatever injury the United States might have inflicted, paid an indemnity of $25 million, and granted Colombia free use of the Panama Canal. That a powerful nation should apologize to a weak one was something new in international relations. To Roosevelt it was nothing less than an outrage, and his friend Senator Henry Cabot Lodge led a successful fight against ratification of the obnoxious treaty, thus delaying for seven years the restoration of good relations with Colombia and getting in some good practice for his more ambitious battle against the Versailles treaty a few years later.

The second dispute grew out of the special exemption which Congress had granted American coastwise shipping from paying tolls on the canal. The British protested this as a violation of earlier treaty agreements. Convinced that the British were right, and anxious to have British support in Mexico, Wilson persuaded Congress to repeal the exemption.

Within two weeks of his inauguration Wilson announced that one of the chief objects of his administration would be to cultivate the friendship of Latin America. A few months later, in a speech at Mobile, Alabama, he announced that his administration would be concerned more with 'human rights, national integrity and opportunity' than with 'material interests,' and promised that 'the United States will never again seek one additional foot of territory by conquest.' Yet despite these entirely sincere protestations of altruism, Wilson and Bryan continued without modification many of the Caribbean policies of Roosevelt and Taft. Marines remained in Nicaragua, a new and exacting bankers' loan received the approval of the State Department, and in 1914 Bryan negotiated a treaty leasing the Gulf of Fonseca, the Great Corn and Little Corn Islands, and granting the United States the right to intervene to maintain orderly government and protect property, which so seriously infringed on Nicaraguan sovereignty that it was denounced by the Central American Court of Justice. In Santo Domingo Bryan authorized 'an enlargement of the sphere of American influence beyond what we have before exercised'; and as minister to that hapless republic he sent an ex-pugilist named James Sullivan who introduced the worst Tammany methods into Dominican politics, exploited his office for personal profit, deliberately misled the State Department about the true condition of affairs, and in the end helped precipitate a revolution. In 1916 Wilson ordered a military occupation of the Dominican Republic, which lasted for eight years. Anarchy in Haiti, too, led to American intervention. In 1915 the United States Marine Corps occupied the island after fighting which cost the lives of over 2000 Haitians. Under the terms of the treaty which the Wilson administration dictated to the helpless Haitians, American control was continued until 1930 when public opinion in the United States forced its discontinuance.

Elsewhere in the Caribbean, relations were less troubled. During the First World War Cuba experienced an unprecedented prosperity, but that prosperity was accompanied by extravagance and corruption. At the close of the war the Cuban sugar market collapsed, and Cuban politics reflected the economic and financial disorder. President Wilson sent a personal representative, General Enoch Crowder, to help the Cubans out of their troubles. Crowder, for all his abilities, was only partially successful, and when prosperity returned he was discredited by the Cuban nationalists who resented his extra-legal status and feared the economic implications of his advisory activities — fears not unjustified by the rapid growth of American investments and banking influence in the island. Crowder's anomalous position was soon regularized by his appointment as ambassador to Cuba, and thereafter Cuban-American relations returned, for a time, to a less troubled basis. Under the long regime of the tyrant, Gerardo Machado (1925–33), unrest was chronic, but even when that unrest broke out into revolution, the United States avoided any official intervention. By the 1920's the rising tide of Cuban nationalism made intervention in Cuban affairs a highly dangerous business. Not until 1934 was President Roosevelt able to negotiate a treaty abrogating the Platt Amendment — except for the provision permitting the maintenance of a naval base.

Puerto Rico, like Cuba, was governed for a time by the United States military, but in 1900 the Foraker Act had established civil government of the old crown colony type: an elective assembly, with an executive council appointed by the President acting as an upper house. This, too, was contrary to the Wilsonian philosophy, and in 1917 Congress passed an act granting American citizenship to the inhabitants of the island, and a semi-responsible government. Not until 1947 were the islanders permitted to elect their own Governor, but in 1952 the island achieved

Commonwealth status, whatever that term might mean in American constitutional law. Intervention in Nicaragua, Santo Domingo, and Haiti, then, were balanced, in a sense, by a more enlightened policy toward Cuba and Puerto Rico.

Mexico presented the real test of Wilson's Latin American policy, and one of the achievements of his administration was the maintenance of peace with that distraught republic. In 1911 Porforio Díaz, dictator of Mexico for thirty-five years, resigned as a result of a revolutionary movement that he could no longer suppress. Díaz had given his country order at the expense of every sort of liberty. The national domain of 135 million acres was cut up into latifundia, or used to augment the already swollen estates of less than a thousand great landowners. At the same time Díaz pursued a policy resembling the enclosures of eighteenth-century England, expropriating and allotting in severalty the communal lands of the Indian villages. The new owners exacted forced labor from the landless peons by keeping them in perpetual debt for food and supplies. Education remained in the hands of the Catholic Church. The government was autocratic, the ruling class concentrated and powerful, the condition of the common people desperate. Foreign, especially English and American, mining and business interests, to which Díaz gave generous concessions and protection, enthusiastically supported his rule.

The revolution of 1910–11 was conducted by a small doctrinaire middle class under Francisco I. Madero, but supported by the peons in the hope of recovering their communal lands. Installed as constitutional President in 1911, Madero neither kept order nor satisfied the aspirations of the landless. A counter-revolution of the landowners, supported by foreign investors, displaced him by assassination in February 1913, and installed Victoriano Huerta as President. Although unable to exert his authority over the greater part of the country, which was fast falling into anarchy, Huerta was promptly recognized by Great Britain and most of the Powers. Strong pressure was exerted on President Wilson by the American ambassador and by American business interests to do the same. How powerful those business interests were is indicated by reports of a congressional committee which calculated American investments in Mexico at $1.5 billion and estimated that Americans owned 78 per cent of the mines, 72 per cent of the smelters, 58 per cent of the oil, 68 per cent of the rubber plantations, and some two-thirds of the railroads of Mexico.

But President Wilson refused to be moved by the importunities of business. In his statement of 11 March he anticipated his refusal to recognize Huerta:

> We hold that just government rests always upon the consent of the governed, and that there can be no freedom without order based upon law and upon public conscience and approval. . . . We can have no sympathy with those who seek to seize the power of government to advance their own personal interests or ambition.

Such a policy, importing moral considerations into the realm of international law, was a departure from the traditional practices of the United States as well as of other nations. The easier course would have been to accord the Huerta government *de facto* recognition, and leave to the Mexicans the solution of their problems of constitutional law and democracy. The other policy was fraught with peril, for it placed upon the United States the responsibility of deciding which government was moral, and there was no assurance that the decision would be disinterested. Furthermore in the event that Huerta failed to back down, Wilson faced the awkward alternatives of some kind of intervention, which would be an invitation to imperialism, or of a serious loss of prestige.

Wilson, after persuading the British to withdraw support for Huerta, moved toward a showdown with him. On 3 February 1914 he revoked the arms embargo and permitted American arms to go to the leader of the Constitutional forces, Venustiano Carranza. The landed aristocracy and the Catholic Church rallied to Huerta, and the situation seemed as unsolvable as ever. What could Wilson do short of outright intervention — an intervention that would have turned both the Huerta and the Carranza forces against the invader? At this juncture the zeal of a Mexican colonel made history. When the paymaster and crew of an American warship landed, without permission, at Tampico they were arrested. The Mexican commander instantly apologized and returned the men, but Admiral Mayo demanded not only an apology but a salute to the American flag, and President Wilson, eagerly looking for an excuse to intervene, backed him up. Inasmuch as the United States refused to recognize the Huerta government, the situation presented obvious and embarrassing legal difficulties. Huerta, hoping that American aggression might consolidate Mexican sentiment behind him, refused to budge further — though he did sardonically promise to exchange salute for salute! On 21 April a force of American marines landed at Vera Cruz which they took with slight loss to themselves but at the cost of several hundred Mexican casualties. However, war with Mexico did not begin, partly because Wilson realized that his legal case was ridiculous and his moral case far from strong, but chiefly because he wished above all to help the people of Mexico find themselves. He tried to distinguish between the Mexican people and the Mexican government — just as he later distinguished between the German people and the German government — and insisted that 'if armed conflict should unhappily come . . . we should be fighting only General Huerta and those who adhere to him.'

At this acute juncture, Wilson was rescued by a proposal from Argentina, Brazil, and Chile for a joint mediation. The President gladly took this way out of the impasse, especially as he was confident that he could control the proceedings, and a conference with these 'A.B.C.' powers met at Niagara Falls in May 1914 to compose the differences between the warring Mexican factions. The conference — the first of its kind in the history of the Americas — averted war and proposed a new constitutional government for Mexico. Huerta stood out stiffly against the terms of the mediation; unable, however, to obtain arms or credit from the United States or from an otherwise-occupied Europe, he was forced out of office. Late in July he fled the country, and on 20 August, Venustiano Carranza, leader of the Constitutional party, entered Mexico City and took over the presidency.

But there was to be no peace for stricken Mexico. No sooner had Carranza won Mexico City than his ablest lieutenant, Francisco Villa, raised the standard of revolt. With incomparable ineptitude the Wilson administration now decided to back Villa, mistakenly supposing him more tractable than the stubborn and independent Carranza. Carranza, however, took the field, and shattered the Villa forces, and the United States had no alternative but to accord him recognition.

During the five years that followed there were occasional outbreaks of peace in Mexico. Fundamentally the trouble was that the underlying force of the revolution — the land hunger of the peasants — was unable to find a leader with the honesty to adopt fundamental reforms and the ability to carry them through. All other approaches having failed, President Wilson adopted a policy of 'watchful waiting,' while endeavoring, without much success, to create a Pan-American machinery for dealing with the situation. The State Department advised all Americans to withdraw from the country, and some 40,000 did so. Many who remained to protect their property suffered at the hands of the revolutionists and bandits. Estimates of American losses vary, but it is probable that between 1910 and 1922 over 400 American civilians lost their lives in Mexico or along the Mexican border, and that property losses totaled not far from $200 million. Not all the losses were on one side: the Mexicans, too, suffered loss of life and property from American intervention.

Defeated by Carranza and abandoned by the United States, Villa took to banditry. In 1916 he launched repeated raids across the border on American towns. Wilson mobilized the regular army along the Rio Grande border and in March sent an expeditionary force under General John Pershing after Villa. Pershing's force, 6000 strong, pursued Villa deep into the interior but failed to capture him. The practice it afforded the army was hardly worth the cost, for this violation of Mexican soil outraged Carranza and aroused the suspicion of most of the peoples of South America.

When American troops and Mexican regulars clashed at Carrizal, war seemed unavoidable. War, and even annexation, would have been popular with vociferous groups in the United States, but once again Wilson refused to take advantage of Mexican weakness. Instead he sent a commission to Mexico to try to patch things up. The commission was not very successful, but it gained time, and time was decisive. In March 1917, Wilson formally recognized the Carranza government. Carranza had proved himself more determined even than Wilson. As for Wilson, although he had, as his biographer Arthur Link observes, 'embittered Mexican-American relations, for many years to come,' he had also,

> almost alone, stood off Europe during the days of the Huerista tyranny, withstood the powerful forces in the United States that sought the undoing of the Revolution, and refused to go to war at a time when it might have insured his re-election.

XV

The Road to War

1. THE UNITED STATES AND THE WORLD WAR:
FACTORS AND CONDITIONS

Since the early years of the twentieth century Europe had been preparing for war, and hoping to avoid it. Peace was maintained only by a precarious balance between two sets of alliances: the Triple Alliance or Central Powers (Germany, Austria-Hungary, Italy) and the Triple Entente (France, Russia, and Great Britain). General war had threatened on several occasions: the Moroccan question in 1905, when Germany backed down; the Agadir crisis of 1911; and two or three times during the Balkan War of 1912–13. That local war had lessened the prestige of the Central Powers which backed the wrong horse, and increased both the power and the bumptiousness of Serbia and Rumania, the Balkan kingdoms that obtained the lion's share of the loot. And as soon as the war was over, Serbia went fishing in the troubled waters of the Dual Monarchy.

On 28 June 1914 the shot was fired that closed an era of progress, liberalism, and democracy and inaugurated the age of warfare, destruction, revolutionary upheavals, and dictatorships, which is not yet ended. Archduke Franz Ferdinand, heir to the throne of Austria-Hungary, was assassinated at Sarajevo in the province of Bosnia. The murderer belonged to a Serbian revolutionary group active in breaking up the Dual Monarchy, but that was not generally known until after the war. Austria determined once and for all to put an end to the Slavic threat and, supported by Germany, presented stringent demands with which Serbia could not comply save at the cost of her independence. On 28 July Austria declared war on her. Russia, as the leader of the Slavic world, could not stand by while Serbia, whom she had secretly encouraged, was crushed; she mobilized her army. Germany, fearing to be caught between two enemies, declared war first (1 August) on Russia and then (3 August) on France, which was bound to come to Russia's aid in any case. In order to crush France before unwieldy Russia fairly got going, Germany struck at her through Belgium, whose neutrality she and the other powers were bound by treaty to respect. Great Britain then (4 August) declared war on Germany. The First World War was on.[1]

President Wilson at once tendered American good offices, which were politely but firmly rejected, and proclaimed the neutrality of the United States. 'The occasion is not of our making,' he said in his message to Congress of 4 September 1914. 'But it is here. It affects us directly and palpably almost as if we were participants in the circumstances which gave rise to it. . . . We shall pay the bill, though we did not deliberately incur it.' The statement was exact and the warning prophetic. From the very beginning the United States was vitally affected by the war. The most powerful of nations that remained neutral, we were likewise the most vulnerable. Our population included representatives of every racial group whose homelands were involved in the war, and their emotions were naturally aroused. Our commercial and financial relations extended to every European nation and were particularly bound up with England and Germany. Our cultural relations were very close with England and France. And no European war in which England was involved could fail to raise problems of neutral rights, which, as the experience of Jefferson's time recalled, might easily become points of national honor.

Yet in 1914 the suspicion hardly dawned on the average American that his country might be drawn into the war, and there was an almost universal determination to stay out. A century had passed since the

---

1. Turkey joined the Central Powers about a month later. Italy disregarded her alliance with the Central Powers, and after a highly profitable neutrality and much astute bargaining, threw in her lot with the Entente Allies in 1915. Japan also joined the Allies before the United States came in, but confined her efforts to the Far East. Rumania and Portugal joined the Allies; Bulgaria, the Central Powers. Greece tried to remain neutral, but the Allies occupied Salonica as a base, and finally she joined their side.

Treaty of Ghent and the fall of Napoleon, a hundred years for the sentiment of isolation from the 'broils of Europe' to deepen. And although the United States, in view of her wars with the Indians and with Mexico and Spain, could hardly be called a pacific nation, she had early taken the lead in the peace movement and from the beginning of her history had subscribed to the principle of the arbitration of international controversies.[2]

America had a long tradition of neutrality and neutral rights, and one of the most important of these rights was freedom of the seas. From the Franco-American treaty of 1778, the United States had made it a consistent policy to enlarge the right of neutrals and decrease the power of belligerents to disturb the peaceful part of the world. She went to war with England in 1812 to protect her rights as a neutral. She adhered to most of the Declaration of Paris of 1856, which adopted the principle that free (neutral) ships make free goods; took part in the Hague Conventions of 1899 and 1907, and helped draft the Declaration of London of 1909, which drew up a code of naval warfare based on the Declaration of Paris. American determination to preserve and enforce neutrality traversed class, sectional, and party lines, and found eloquent expression from the President, who pleaded with the country to 'be neutral in fact as well as in name . . . impartial in thought as well as in action.'

There is no easy answer to the question of why we fought, and those who look for simple explanations will be disappointed or misled. It is possible to discover the causes of wars such as that of 1812 or the one with Mexico, but after a century and a half, no two scholars are agreed upon the precise causes of the American Revolution; and the schoolboys of North Dakota and South Carolina grow up with very different notions of responsibility for the Civil War. The immediate provocations of these wars, to be sure, can be fixed; the underlying causes are still in dispute. So, too, with our entry into the First World War: the provocation is easy to discover, but the fundamental causes are lost in a maze of controversy, and most of the available literature on the subject is tinged by

2. The Jay Treaty, the Rush-Bagot agreement, the Treaty of Guadelupe-Hidalgo, the Geneva arbitration, the arbitration of the fur-sealing, the Canadian and the Venezuela boundary controversies, the provisions of various Pan-American conferences declaring arbitration to be a principle of 'American international law,' the Root and Bryan treaties, all testified to the persistence and the sincerity of American faith in this method of settling disputes.

emotion. We must guard against reading back into the period 1914–17 our present-day judgments and preconceptions. And if our generation is disillusioned about 'making the world safe for democracy' we must not assume that the phrase was insincere or the ideal naïve.

Let us then retrace the path to war. It is necessary that we keep in mind several considerations of a general character as well as a particular train of facts and circumstances. For while it is true that American entry into the war was precipitated by the German submarine warfare, and that without this we probably should not have fought, it is important to know why Germany resorted to submarine warfare, and why the United States reacted to it as she did.

From the outbreak of World War I American public opinion predominantly favored the Allies. It matters little how much of this opinion was due to Allied propaganda, since propaganda can be effective only on receptive minds. The majority of Americans were English-speaking, and regarded some part of the British Empire as their mother country, with whom war would have seemed immoral. For one thing, it would have involved us in war with our sister democracy, Canada. Ties of language and literature, law and custom, as well as those of a more personal character, bound America to the British Empire in a hundred ways. With France our relations were more sentimental than intimate, but the tradition of Franco-American friendship went back to the Revolution: Lafayette's gallantry was one thing that schoolchildren did not forget when they grew up.

With Germany and her allies, on the other hand, American relations were amicable but not cordial. To be sure, the presence of millions of Germans in America made for understanding and even sympathy with the German people; but many even of these were critical of their fatherland's policies, and few, as Ambassador von Bernstorff lamented, were inclined to place the interest of Germany before that of the United States. And since the Spanish war, there had grown up in America a feeling that the German government was militaristic, hostile to democracy, and unfriendly to the United States. To many Americans there was something ridiculous in the posturings and saber-rattlings of William II, when they were not odious. Suspicion of Germany was intensified by her cynical violation of Belgian neutrality, and by the widespread conviction, supported by seemingly irrefutable documentary evidence, that she alone was responsible for the war. American opinion was further exacerbated by Germany's persistence in her U-boat policy, which most Americans regarded as a flagrant violation of international law and of morality.

France was the most popular of the countries at war. Germany had declared war upon her, apparently without the slightest provocation, caught her unprepared, and taken an unfair advantage by striking through Belgium; and the French armies aroused admiration by their desperate stand along the Marne. American novelists such as Edith Wharton and correspondents such as Frank Simonds glorified France. A group of wealthy young Americans formed the *Lafayette Escadrille* in the French flying corps; thousands of other youngsters enlisted in the British and Canadian armies and air forces — among them William Faulkner — and their letters and articles all stimulated the feeling that the least America could do was not to let our historic ally be crushed by insisting on too strict a neutrality.

While the American friends of France worked for her, the British issued first-class propaganda for themselves. They had an initial advantage in speaking the same language as the Americans and having much the same modes of thought. The Allies, moreover, controlled the most important avenues of communication, had ready access to American newspapers and journals, and could command the services of many intellectuals and leaders of American society. Yet that propaganda probably did not hasten by a day the decision to fight. It did break down resistance in some quarters and silence it in others, and encourage Americans to rationalize their war on broad humanitarian grounds. No one now believes the more preposterous atrocity stories, to the authenticity of which even Lord Bryce lent his name; but the hatred that they engendered served to give the war the moral character of a wolf hunt.

This basic friendliness for the Allies and suspicion of Germany made our entry into the war on the side of Germany unthinkable, our entry on the side of the Allies not inconceivable. Wilson himself illustrated this attitude. Of mixed Scots and English ancestry, steeped in English literature and history, and an admirer of British political institutions, he found it easier to grasp the British than the German point of view, and his sympathies were from the first enlisted on the side of the Allies. He tried to be neutral, but he was willing to endure almost any provocation rather than risk war with England; and Bryan was right in protesting that the President was quicker to hold Germany than England to 'strict

accountability' for violations of neutral rights. And when Russia —
temporarily—went republican, just as we were about to enter the war,
Wilson was quick to identify the cause of the Allies with that of democracy and of civilization itself.

The United States also developed an economic stake in the war. Even
before 1914 a large part of American trade had been with the Allied
nations. On the outbreak of the war the Allies began to apply trade-
restriction measures — commonly called the blockade — to the Central
Powers; and they were very shrewd in developing these restrictions progressively. Cotton, for instance, was added to the list of contraband only
after the *Lusitania* was sunk; and when a Southern Senator complained,
Senator Lodge remarked that he was more moved by the spectacle of
American women and children drowning in the ocean than by that of
American cotton sitting on a wharf. Trade with Germany became negligible; trade with Great Britain and France mounted impressively. This
increase in our foreign trade, in full swing by the middle of 1915, rescued the United States from a commercial depression that had lasted a
year. Cotton, wheat, and beef, as well as manufactures, found a highly
profitable market; and when the Allies seized American cargoes destined
directly or indirectly for Germany, it was possible to claim and eventually to collect damages. Within a year after the outbreak of war the
whole fabric of our economic life was so closely interwoven with the
economy of the Allies that any rupture would have been ruinous. It was
the realization of this, in addition to sympathy for the Allies, that persuaded Wilson and his cabinet to reject an embargo on munitions of
war.

Countenanced by international law, the munitions trade was theoretically open alike to all belligerents. In fact, Allied sea power prevented
the Central Powers from procuring American munitions; the Allies got
all they wanted; and our munitions exports increased in value from
some $40 million in 1914 to $1290 million in 1916, and our total trade to
the Allied countries from $825 million to $3214 million. Germany never
officially denied the legality of this trade, but she protested bitterly that
its one-sided nature violated the spirit of neutrality. To the suggestion
that the United States place an embargo upon munitions exports, the
American government replied that it could not change the rules of neutrality to the advantage of one belligerent while the war was in progress.
As a technical defense this was sound; but both belligerents were chang-

ing the rules of war, and it was within the rights of Congress to stiffen our neutrality requirements as, for instance, the Dutch did, by treating armed merchantmen as warships and interning them. But neither Congress nor most of the nation wished to do so.

Without credit the belligerents could not buy American goods. At the beginning of the war the United States was a debtor nation: this situation was promptly reversed as foreign investors dumped their securities on the American market. Soon the Allies found it advisable to finance their purchases in the United States through loans floated in Wall Street, a scheme Bryan opposed. 'Money,' he said, 'is the worst of all contrabands because it commands everything else.' For this and other reasons the State Department on 15 August 1914, informed American bankers that 'in the judgment of this Government, loans by American bankers to any foreign nation which is at war are inconsistent with the true spirit of neutrality.' Yet within a month this position was modified to authorize 'credit loans,' and bank credits were promptly extended to belligerent governments. By the late summer of 1915 Bryan was out of the cabinet, and his successor Secretary Robert Lansing, as well as Secretary McAdoo, warned the President that the country was 'face to face with what appears to be a critical economic situation.' 'Popular sympathy,' wrote Lansing, 'has become crystallized in favor of one or another of the belligerents to such an extent that the purchase of bonds would in no way increase the bitterness of partisanship or cause a possibly serious situation.' Before this united pressure, Wilson gave way, and on 14 September 1915 the State Department withdrew altogether its opposition to loans. By the time the United States entered the war, over $2 billion had been lent by the American public to the Allied governments, as opposed to only $27 million to the Central Powers.

That the American economic stake in an Allied victory may have inclined some people toward war is possible. But the financial community as a whole preferred American neutrality, which afforded Wall Street all the profits of war without the corresponding sacrifices and taxation. Furthermore, most of the loans were secured by pledged collateral which would be unaffected by the outcome of the war. And there is not a shred of evidence to support the allegations that Wilson himself was at any time influenced by the financial stake in his relations with Germany, or that the decision to fight in April 1917 would have been retarded or reversed had financial relations been otherwise. It was neither trade, nor munitions, nor loans, nor propaganda that persuaded the administration of the necessity of war; it was the German submarine policy.

2. THE STRUGGLE FOR NEUTRAL RIGHTS

From the beginning the United States waged a losing struggle to preserve her rights as a neutral. There were two fundamental difficulties: lack of international law to deal with unforeseen circumstances, and the immense stakes and savage fighting which made the belligerents ready to flout law or morality if that was necessary for their survival. Laws purporting to protect the rights of neutrals had been formulated with reference to the last naval war, the Russo-Japanese conflict of 1905; but at that time the big naval powers were neutral, and the technique of offense developed so fast in World War I that there was no generally recognized law to deal with it. The Declaration of London of 1909 represented a hopeful effort to codify and modernize the laws of neutrality, but that declaration had been rejected by Great Britain as too favorable to neutral rights, and had no legal standing. With reference, therefore, to many controversial matters international law was vague; with reference to new problems presented by the submarine, it was silent. And as Lloyd George subsequently remarked: 'Nations fighting for their lives cannot always pause to observe punctilios. Their every action is an act of war, and their attitude to neutrals is governed, not by the conventions of peace, but by the exigencies of a deadly strife.'

America's first and most prolonged dispute came with Great Britain. Promptly upon the outbreak of the war, Britain blockaded Germany. This was no mere policing of German ports but a new type of blockade. It extended considerably both the contraband list and the 'continuous voyage' doctrine which justified confiscating cargoes of enemy destination in neutral ships, even when billed for neutral ports; and declared that the North Sea and the English Channel were 'military areas.' The Allies' command of the sea enabled them to enforce these Orders in Council, even when their diplomacy was hard put to justify them on legal grounds. American direct trade with the Central Powers was entirely, and her indirect trade largely, cut off. In addition the Allies employed such devices as the rationing of trade to neutrals and the blacklisting of firms suspected of trading with the Central Powers.

Against these palpable violations of American neutral rights, the United States protested in vain. England's determination to enforce her own interpretation of neutral rights was inflexible. The United States faced three possible courses of action: war, an embargo partial or complete, or temporary acquiescence accompanied by formal protest. But from the start our means of defense and retaliation were circumscribed by pro-Allied sentiment; and by 1916 they were still further restrained by the economic tie-up with the Allied cause. At any time after the middle of 1915 a real threat of an American embargo on munitions would probably have brought the Allies to heel. But Wilson and the State Department had no intention of taking a stand for neutral rights which, if persisted in, might land us in war on the side of autocracy, as had happened in 1812. So they chose the course of protest and persuasion in order to keep the record clear while avoiding the catastrophe of war. As a consequence, until the beginning of 1917, the British and French continued to violate neutral rights, while the State Department filed protests and the Germans fumed. At any time after the middle of 1915 a real threat of an embargo on munitions of war would probably have brought the Allies to heel. Their own factories were unable to supply the enormous demand of their armies for high explosives; the cutting off of supplies from America would have lost them the war. Jefferson's embargo had not accomplished anything, but Madison's non-intercourse, it will be remembered, forced the repeal of the Orders in Council; and the situation of 1915–17 was analogous to that of 1811–12, not to that of 1807–9.

Faced with economic strangulation, Germany struck back with the only weapons at her disposal: mines and submarines. As early as August 1914 she began to plant mines in the North Sea and the Irish Sea, and on 4 February 1915 she announced that all the waters around the British Isles constituted a war zone in which Allied vessels would be destroyed and warned neutral ships to keep out in order to preclude accidental attacks, which seemed highly likely. Thus was inaugurated the submarine warfare which eventually forced the United States into war. That the sinking of unarmed neutral ships was a clear violation of existing international law, Germany did not deny; but she justified her policy on the ground that it was necessitated by the equally lawless British blockade.

Wilson and most Americans distinguished between British and German violations of neutral rights. As Mr. Asquith said, 'Let the neutrals complain about our blockade and other measures taken as much as they may, the fact remains that no neutral national has ever lost his life as the result of it.' (To be sure, if the United States had insisted on full freedom of the seas, American lives might well have been lost to British mines in the North Sea.) But the U-boat warfare took a toll of 209 American lives on the high seas — twenty-eight of them on American ships.[3] Damages for property losses entailed by Allied violations of American rights could be settled after the war; damages for American lives that had been lost in the U-boat campaign could never be adequately paid.

Alarmed at the threat of submarine warfare, Wilson informed the German government on 10 February 1915 that 'the United States would be constrained to hold the Imperial German Government to a strict accountability' for 'property endangered or lives lost.' Thereby the Wilson administration took the stand that must inevitably lead to war, unless either the United States or Germany backed down.

The trouble with requiring submarines to follow the time-honored procedure of visit and search was that U-boats were extremely vulnerable; and a merchantman armed with a single 6-inch rifle could sink any that appeared above the surface. The Dutch government early in the war adopted a principle for which there was ample precedent in earlier naval wars: armed merchantmen were warships and were forbidden to trade with the Netherlands. If the United States had adopted and enforced a similar law, the Allies would have had to stop arming their merchantmen, and the German submarines in that event could have afforded to observe the proprieties and humanities when making captures at sea. Our government might also have warned American citizens against traveling on belligerent merchant ships. But we must remember that they had the right to do that and to expect that if the ship they traveled in was sunk they would first be placed in safety. And the American public, with its strong tradition of defending neutral rights, would have treated any failure to hold the U-boats to 'strict accountability' as pusillanimous and the Democratic party would have lost the election of 1916. As it was, Wilson was accused of

3. Borchard and Lage give the number as 195. Other neutrals suffered far more. During the war over 3000 Norwegian sailors lost their lives through submarine and mine, and over 50 per cent of the Norwegian merchant marine was destroyed.

insincerity, cowardice, and pro-Germanism by the Republican press and also by the growing proportion of the American people who sincerely believed that the Allies must win, or the Prussian heel would be upon our necks.

Soon came a test of the meaning of 'strict accountability.' On 28 March 1915 an American citizen went down with the British ship *Falaba;* on 29 April an American merchant vessel, the *Cushing,* was attacked by a German airplane; and on 1 May the American tanker *Gullflight* was torpedoed. Germany offered to make reparations for an 'unfortunate accident' but refused to abandon submarine warfare.

Matters were brought to a head when on 7 May the crack Cunard liner *Lusitania* was torpedoed off the coast of Ireland with a loss of over 1100 lives, including 128 American citizens. Germany justified the sinking as one of the hazards of war: the *Lusitania* was a 'semiwarship' carrying munitions and troops, passengers had been duly warned, and if Americans were unprepared to take the risks of war they could have sailed on American vessels instead. Yet the sinking violated international law as it then stood, and it was a piece of criminal folly as well. Nothing except the invasion of Belgium did so much to inflame American sentiment against Germany. Public leaders like Theodore Roosevelt clamored for war, and the press took up the cry.

But the country was not yet mentally prepared for war, and Wilson in 1915, like Jefferson in 1807, refused to be stampeded into any irrevocable act. On 13 May he demanded that the German government disavow the sinking of the *Lusitania,* 'make reparation so far as reparation is possible for injuries that are without measure, and take immediate steps to prevent the recurrence of anything so obviously subversive of the principles of warfare.' Germany, persuaded that Wilson was playing to the gallery, tried to drag out the issue by a series of technical objections. Impatient of procrastination, Wilson sent, on 9 June, a second peremptory note; this brushed aside German extenuations and technicalities and insisted upon a formal disavowal of the outrage.

Bryan, who felt that this protest was dangerously close to an ultimatum, resigned from the cabinet rather than sign the note. His own solution for the difficulty was to renounce responsibility for the lives of Americans who chose passage on belligerent ships. 'Germany,' he said, 'has a right to prevent contraband from going to the Allies, and a ship carrying contraband should not rely upon passengers to protect her from attack — it would be like putting women and children in front of an army.' This plausible argument, not without precedent in our own history, commanded the support of many of the most influential congressional leaders — Senators Stone and Gore, Congressmen Clark, Lindbergh, Kitchin, and McLemore, among them. It was embodied, early in 1916, in the Gore-McLemore Resolutions refusing passports to American citizens who purposed to travel on the armed ships of belligerents. Wilson moved promptly to defeat the resolutions. 'Once accept a single abatement of right,' he wrote to Senator Stone, 'and many other humiliations would certainly follow, and the whole fine fabric of international law might crumble under our hands piece by piece.' As a result of executive pressure, the resolutions were defeated, and the 'whole fine fabric of international law' was saved — for the moment.

On 19 August 1915, before the *Lusitania* controversy had been settled, the English liner *Arabic* was torpedoed with the loss of two American lives. A diplomatic rupture seemed inescapable, but Bernstorff, fully alive to the seriousness of the situation, hastened to disavow the action and to promise that in the future 'liners will not be sunk by our submarines without warning and without safety of the lives of non-combatants.' A month later his disavowal was confirmed by the German government, and the crisis passed. In Berlin, Chancellor Bethmann-Hollweg recognized that if the submarine brought America into the war his country faced defeat; hence he sought to persuade U-boat enthusiasts in Germany that undersea warfare must be restrained.

For six months American relations with Germany were undisturbed by any new U-boat sinkings, but this peaceful interlude was rudely shattered when in February 1916 the German government announced a renewal of submarine warfare on armed merchant vessels. On 24 March the unarmed channel steamer *Sussex* was torpedoed without warning. Outraged at this violation of the pledge which had been given after the *Arabic* affair, Wilson warned Germany that unless she immediately abandoned her submarine warfare against freight and passenger vessels the United States would be forced to break off diplomatic relations. Faced with this threat, the German government capitulated, promising, on 4 May, that henceforth no more merchant vessels would be sunk without warning, provided the United States held England also to 'strict accountability.' The State Department continued to protest England's violations, and German submarines spared merchant vessels until February 1917; during the intervening nine months American relations with Germany were less disturbed than at any time since the *Lusitania* tragedy. Indeed, in the summer and fall of 1916 the United States had sharper differences with England than with Germany. Angered by British controls over commerce, including mail censorship and blacklisting, Wilson contemplated strong retaliatory measures.

3. PREPAREDNESS AND THE ELECTION OF 1916

Despite this apparent settlement of the U-boat controversy, President Wilson became more and more persuaded that the only way in which the United States could avoid war was to end the war. Proffers of good offices and of mediation had been repeatedly rejected, but all through 1916 Wilson labored to bring about a peace on the basis of mutual compromises and concessions. The task was hopeless from the first, for none of the belligerents wanted such a peace; none of the politicians dared face their peoples without some compensation for their terrible sacrifices. In all Europe there was no statesman with vision to foresee and courage to proclaim the disastrous consequences of a Pyrrhic victory.[4] Wilson alone appreciated the ultimate cost of a dictated peace to victors and vanquished alike; he alone had the courage to call for a 'peace without victory.'

So eager was Wilson to achieve peace that he went to the somewhat inconsistent extreme of suggesting he might fight for it. In February 1916 Lord Grey, after a series of conferences with the ubiquitous Colonel House, was able to assure his government that 'President Wilson was ready . . . to propose that a Conference should be summoned to put an end to the war. Should the Allies accept this proposal, and should Germany refuse it, the United States would probably enter the war against

4. 3 January 1917. 'The Allies' reply to the peace overture of Germany is published today; about as weak a document as could be imagined. Neither the German proposal nor the Allies' response rises to any level of statesmanship. The chancelleries of Europe, so far as character is concerned are bankrupt, and the conceptions of the men in them are no higher than those of the fish-wives down at the Fish Market; they plot and wrangle all the time.' Allan Nevins, ed., *The Letters and Journal of Brand Whitlock*, ii, 341. Cf. the situation in our own Civil War, Vol. I.

Germany. . . . If such a Conference met, it would secure peace on terms not unfavorable to the Allies; and if it failed to secure peace, the United States, would probably leave the Conference as a belligerent on the side of the Allies, if Germany was unreasonable.' But Grey did not take these overtures seriously; the British did not want to negotiate at a time when Germany held the upper hand, and like the French and Germans they wanted the spoils of an eventual victory.

Profoundly discouraged, Wilson turned early in 1916 toward a program of military preparedness. This policy resulted in part from conviction, in part from political expediency. A presidential campaign was in the offing, and the Democrats could not afford to permit their Republican opponents to capitalize on the popular issue of national defense. As early as November 1915 Wilson had set forth a program of preparedness, justifying his conversion by a reference to Ezekiel xxxiii: 'But if the watchman see the sword come, and blow not the trumpet, and the people be not warned; if the sword come, and take any person from among them, he is taken away in his iniquity; but his blood will I require at the watchman's hand.' In the following months Wilson blew the trumpet, and the people were warned. A series of monster preparedness parades in Eastern cities indicated support from the business and industrial sections of the country, but the South and the Middle West were lukewarm. Nevertheless, during the summer of 1916, the administration urged through Congress a series of measures strengthening the military and naval forces of the nation. The National Defense Act of 3 June enlarged the regular army to some 220,000, integrated the national guard into the National Defense system, and provided for an officers' reserve corps; the Naval Appropriation Bill of 29 August authorized the construction of a large number of new battleships and cruisers. To lessen the dependency of American traders on belligerent or Scandinavian merchantmen to carry their exports, the United States Shipping Board Act of 7 September 1916 appropriated $50 million for the purchase or construction of merchant ships. To co-ordinate industries and resources, Congress created a Council for National Defense and an advisory board drawn from the ranks of industry and labor.

Having thus made appropriate gestures toward the more militant elements, the President embarked upon a campaign for re-election under the slogan, 'He kept us out of war.' As a statement of fact it was accurate; those Americans who read into it a promise of future policy failed to consider the possibility of a change in the circumstances on which the promise was conditioned.

If the Republicans could lure the Progressive bolters back into the party, they were sure to win, for the combined GOP and Bull Moose ballots in 1912 totaled a clear majority of the vote. Progressives hoped that the Republican convention would effect a merger by nominating Roosevelt, but the GOP turned instead to Charles Evans Hughes, Justice of the Supreme Court. With Warren Harding as their keynoter, the Republicans were no more interested in social reform than they had been in 1912, but by now many Progressives shared the chauvinistic outlook of the Republicans on foreign affairs. For his part, Roosevelt, his attention focused on the single issue of war, hoped that the Progressives would not 'go off into a mass of resolutions . . . about social and industrial justice.' He dismissed the last Progressive convention with the advice that the delegates follow him back to the Grand Old Party. Some did; others, more concerned than he with domestic reform, went over to the Democrats.

All the well-known portents — the September election in Maine, the trend in New York, the betting odds of 10 to 7 — indicated a Republican victory. But Hughes proved a disappointing candidate; Wilson's progressive reforms were not forgotten; and hundreds of thousands of Socialists, more loyal to peace than to party, gave their votes to the candidate who had kept us out of war. Most of the social workers, including Jane Addams, and many of the free-lance intellectuals and radicals like Lincoln Steffens, Herbert Croly, and John Dewey supported Wilson. When the early returns showed that Hughes had carried New York, New Jersey, and Indiana, his election was taken for granted. But the Far West had not yet been heard from; and the electoral vote of that section had grown with its population. Hughes, who had made several errors during an electioneering tour of California, lost that state by less than 4000 votes, and its electoral vote was just enough to give Wilson a majority in the electoral college. The margin was uncomfortably narrow, but Wilson's popular plurality of 600,000 was a better indication of the relative strength of the two candidates, and the increase of almost 3 million in his popular vote since 1912 was a measure of the extent to which he had won the confidence of the American people. Never before had a Democrat come to power without substantial backing in the Northeast. By forging a new alliance of the South and West, Wilson had overcome the massed strength of the reunited Republican party. But the future of this coalition rested on a precarious supposition: that the President could continue to keep the country out of war.

4. WAR

As soon as his re-election was assured, Wilson determined to renew his appeal to the belligerents for a negotiated peace. Such an appeal seemed well-timed. The Battle of the Somme cost a million casualties; the Russian offensive in Galicia a million and a half more. Unfortunately, Wilson postponed his overture a week too long. Germany, having beaten Rumania to her knees in a quick summer campaign, issued an invitation to the Allies to open direct negotiations (12 December 1916). Six days later President Wilson addressed to every belligerent government a note asking for a statement of 'the precise objects which would, if attained, satisfy them and their people that the war had been fought out.' Coming at that time, this appeared to echo the German invitation, which queered the Wilson overture in the sight of the Allies. Lloyd George announced that Britain's terms would be 'complete restitution, full reparation, and effectual guarantees' for the future; Germany's terms, announced confidentially to Washington, included a slice of France, economic control of Belgium, parts of Russian Poland, and plenty of indemnities. Clearly there could be no getting together on either basis; and although Wilson had at his hand one weapon — embargo — that could have forced the Allies to a conference, he had as yet no means to compel Germany.

Faced with this intransigence on the part of the belligerents, and convinced that the time had come when the United States must co-operate in securing and maintaining world peace, Wilson, in a memorable speech on 22 January 1917, formulated the conditions upon which such co-operation might be extended. Those conditions, anticipating in a general way the subsequent 'Fourteen Points,' included government by the consent of the governed, freedom of the seas, limitation of military and naval armaments, and a League to enforce peace. Fundamental to all of these principles was the requirement that the settlement must be a 'peace without victory.' Victory, said the President prophetically,

> would mean peace forced upon the loser, a victor's terms imposed upon the vanquished. It would be accepted in humiliation, under duress, at an intolerable sacrifice, and would leave a sting, a re-

sentment, a bitter memory upon which terms of peace would rest, not permanently, but only as upon quicksand. Only a peace between equals can last.

This appeal fell upon deaf ears, and even in the United States critics branded the phrase 'peace without victory' as pusillanimous. There was no hope that the Allies, bound hand and foot by secret treaties, or that Germany, now that Rumania was crushed and Russia reeling, would agree to a reasonable settlement; and though Wilson proposed, the Allies disposed. Yet it was not pressure from the Allies, or even from American interests favorable to the Allies, which within two months swept the United States into war. Actually the die was cast, even before Wilson made his 'peace without victory' speech. Late in August 1916 the war-lords Hindenburg and Ludendorff had been elevated to the supreme military command in Germany. Determined to break the blockade and to destroy British morale, they insisted upon unrestricted U-boat warfare. At a conference on 9 January 1917, Chancellor Bethmann-Hollweg once more warned against the peril of American intervention, but the submarine faction won out.

The Germans decided to embark upon unrestricted submarine warfare with a full comprehension of the effect upon relations with the United States. 'I know full well,' wrote Bethmann-Hollweg to Bernstorff, 'that by taking this step we run the danger of bringing about a break and possible war with the United States. We have determined to take this risk.' And on an official Admiralty memorandum suggesting that war with the United States might be avoided if submarines 'overlooked' American boats, the Kaiser penciled, 'Now, once and for all, an *end* to negotiations with America. If Wilson wants war, let him make it, and let him then have it.' The German high command believed that American participation in the war would not materially increase their contributions of money, munitions, and supplies, and they discounted American naval and military assistance. With over 120 submarines ready for service they calculated to a nicety the destruction of British and neutral merchant tonnage and promised victory in six months. In that time, the United States, it was thought, could do nothing important.

On 31 January 1917 Bernstorff informed the American government that beginning the next day German submarines would sink on sight all merchant vessels, armed or unarmed, within a military zone around the British Isles and in the Mediterranean. The two countries promptly severed diplomatic relations, and though Wilson still hoped that Germany would not commit the supreme folly of aggressive acts against the United States, the nation prepared for war. Wilson himself took the first step in this direction by calling upon Congress for authority to arm American merchant vessels. A Senate filibuster, led by La Follette and what Wilson described as 'a little group of willful men,' prevented congressional action until the adjournment of 4 March, when the President discovered a piracy statute of 1819 that authorized him to act. But events moved so rapidly that armed neutrality was soon forgotten. Late in February the British secret service handed over to the United States State Department a copy of the incredibly stupid 'Zimmermann note' in which the German government proposed that, if the United States declared war, Mexico conclude an offensive alliance with Germany and Japan; Mexico to have Texas, New Mexico, and Arizona for her share of the loot. This note, released to the newspapers on 1 March, immensely strengthened the popular demand for war. On 17 March came news that a revolution in Russia had overthrown the Tsar and established a provisional republican government; the last taint of autocracy in the Allied cause disappeared. When, also during March, German submarines torpedoed five American merchant vessels, Wilson decided that Germany was warring upon the United States and that the time had come to proclaim the existence of this war.

In the 'twenties and 'thirties that decision was denounced as a mistake, for in the end the war brought the United States nothing but debts and disappointments. Yet what was the alternative? We must not let ourselves be deceived by wishful thinking into the theory that a fair and lasting peace would have been negotiated in 1917 if the United States had stayed neutral. Those who indulge in that hypothesis are invited to examine the terms of the Treaty of Brest-Litovsk that Germany imposed upon Russia early in 1918. The Russian revolution would soon take that great country out of the war; the submarine campaign would shortly have starved England; France, unable to budge the German armies from the Hindenburg line, had shot her bolt. The resulting peace settlement would have left Imperial Germany bestride the narrow world like a colossus. In January 1916 Wilson had warned his countrymen that considerations of national honor might require participation in the war:

> I know that you are depending upon me to keep this Nation out of the war. So far I have done so and I pledge you my word that, God helping me, I will — if it is possible. But you have laid

> another duty upon me. You have bidden me see to it that nothing stains or impairs the honor of the United States, and that is a matter not within my control; that depends upon what others do, not upon what the Government of the United States does. Therefore there may at any moment come a time when I cannot preserve both the honor and the peace of the United States. Do not exact of me an impossible and contradictory thing.

The preservation of both honor and peace, in March 1917, seemed to Wilson an 'impossible and contradictory thing.' Whatever others might think of the desirability of war in order to protect investments, enhance munitions profits, or preserve gains in trade, Wilson himself did not respond to these considerations, and it was Wilson who made the decision to fight. To him the logic of that decision was crystal clear. 'The United States entered the war,' he said,

> not because our national interests were directly threatened or because any special treaty obligations to which we were parties had been violated, but only because we saw the supremacy, and even the validity, of right everywhere put in jeopardy and free government likely to be everywhere imperilled by the intolerable aggression of a power which respected neither right nor obligation. . . .
> We entered the war as the disinterested champions of right.

That Wilson's faith in a peace without victory was betrayed, that his vision of a new and better world order was dissipated, was not his fault, but the fault of the European and American peoples who proved themselves incapable of living up to his ideal. Wilson's error was in failing to take a sufficiently realistic view of human nature, and it was an error that a later generation found difficult to condone.

Despite his keen intelligence and sensitiveness, Wilson did not sufficiently appreciate the strength of the traditions of diplomacy or of New World isolation. He did not contemplate the betrayal of his peace program by the Allies or realize that his own power and influence would be drained from him by repudiation at home, nor, needless to say, was he aware of those qualities in his own character that would contribute so much to that rejection.

So on 2 April 1917, President Wilson appeared before Congress and read his message asking for a declaration of war:

> It is a fearful thing to lead this great peaceful people into war, into the most terrible and disastrous of all wars, civilization itself seeming to be in the balance. But the right is more precious than

peace, and we shall fight for the things which we have always carried nearest our hearts, — for democracy, for the right of those who submit to authority to have a voice in their own Government, for the rights and liberties of small nations, for a universal dominion of right by such a concert of free peoples as shall bring peace and safety to all nations and make the world itself at last free. To such a task we can dedicate our lives and our fortunes, everything that we are and everything that we have, with the pride of those who know that the day has come when America is privileged to spend her blood and her might for the principles that gave her birth and happiness and the peace which she has treasured. God helping her, she can do no other.

In the small hours of Good Friday morning, 6 April 1917, Congress passed a joint resolution declaring war on the German Empire.

XVI

War and Peace

1. INDUSTRIAL AND FINANCIAL MOBILIZATION

'It is not an army that we must shape and train for war,' said President Wilson, 'it is a nation.' The real history of American participation in the First World War is not so much the story of Belleau Wood and St. Mihiel and Château-Thierry as of mobilizing industrial resources at home. The task was not only gigantic, but urgent. In April 1917 German submarine warfare was succeeding beyond the expectations of the Germans themselves, and the Allies were almost at the end of their tether.

The United States not only had to raise an army but provide clothing, arms, ammunition and explosives, light and heavy artillery, gas and gas masks, airplanes and balloons, and a hundred other things equally essential. It was necessary to build a 'bridge' across the Atlantic, set up dockage facilities and arrange railroad, motor, and horse transportation in France, string thousands of miles of telephone wires, create a vast medical and nursing corps, and construct hundreds of hospitals in the United States and overseas. No task of similar magnitude had ever been attempted before by this nation.

Spurred by necessity Congress conferred upon the President extensive powers to commandeer essential industries and mines, requisition supplies, control distribution, fix prices, and take over and operate the entire system of transportation and communication. The President in turn delegated these powers to a series of boards, organized under the supervision of the Council for National Defense. These boards mobilized

377

America's industrial, agricultural, and even intellectual resources for war purposes, and gave the country an experience in government planning that went far beyond anything the prewar reformers had contemplated.

To mobilize the nation's industrial resources, the Council set up a War Industries Board in the summer of 1917, but not until the economy verged on collapse did the WIB get the sweeping powers it needed. On 4 March 1918 Wilson called in the Wall Street broker, Bernard Baruch, and made him virtual economic dictator of the country. Under Baruch, the board regulated all existing industries that produced war materials, developed new industries, facilities, and sources of supply, enforced efficiency and eliminated waste, fixed prices, determined priorities of production and delivery, and managed all war purchase for the United States and the Allies. The production of some 30,000 articles came under the minute supervision of the War Industries Board. Baby carriages were standardized; traveling salesmen were limited to two trunks; and the length of uppers on shoes was cut down. It was such a regimentation of the economy as had never before been known, and it later served as a model for the New Deal mobilization of 1932.[1]

The United States Shipping Board Act of 1916 had already called into existence an organization prepared to cope with the task of providing ships to replace the vessels which the submarines were destroying at the rate of over half a million tons monthly. On 16 April 1917 Congress authorized the creation of a subsidiary of the Shipping Board, the Emergency Fleet Corporation, to build ships. This operation moved at a snail's pace; the first vessel from the enormous shipyard at Hog Island in the Delaware river was not delivered until a month after the armistice. But by seizing interned German ships, commandeering or buying neutral vessels, taking over all private shipping, and by a modest amount of new construction, the Shipping Board succeeded in increasing the available tonnage from one million to ten million tons and overcoming the submarine danger.[2]

The administration also had to reorganize transport within the United

---

1. The two men chiefly instrumental in working out the details of this mobilization of industrial and agricultural resources were Hugh S. Johnson and George Peek, who later applied to the NRA and AAA the technique they learned under Baruch.
2. 'Appalling prices,' wrote Secretary McAdoo, 'were paid for everything that had to do with a ship. Engines and other equipment were purchased at such a staggering cost that I fancied more than once that the machinery we were buying must be made of silver instead of iron and steel.' *Crowded Years.*

States, for under the impact of war orders and troop movements the American railroad system broke down. In December 1917 the government took it over, and proceeded to operate the railroads as a unified system, guaranteeing adequate compensation to the owners. Secretary of the Treasury William G. McAdoo resigned to become Director-General of the railroads. By consolidating terminal facilities, standardizing equipment, shutting down little-used lines, spending more than $500 million on sorely needed improvements, discouraging passenger traffic, and co-ordinating freight traffic, he succeeded in bringing the railroads to a peak of effectiveness heretofore unknown. Because the rental paid was too high, and the freight rates too low, this experiment in federal operation of the railroads cost the government $714 million. During the war the government also took over other agencies of transportation and communication — terminals, express companies, sleeping-car companies, elevators, warehouses, and telephone, telegraph, and cable lines.

The Food Administration more than any other government agency brought the war home to the American people. Herbert Hoover, who had carried through Belgian relief and whose prestige was second only to the President's, was put in charge of the work. His job was to increase production and decrease the consumption of food in America so that the Allies might have enough. In accomplishing this task he displayed extraordinary ingenuity. By law he was empowered to fix prices of staples, license food distributors, co-ordinate purchases, supervise exports, prohibit hoarding or profiteering, and stimulate production. His administration fixed the price of wheat at $2.20 a bushel, established a grain corporation to buy and sell it, organized the supply and purchase of meat, and bought the entire Cuban and American sugar crop and resold it. Meantime a systematic campaign persuaded the American people to cut down food consumption. 'Wheatless Mondays,' 'Meatless Tuesdays,' and 'Porkless Thursdays' became an accepted part of the national regimen, and Americans experimented with such unattractive comestibles as sugarless candy, vegetable lamb chops, and shark steak. As a result of 'Hooverizing' the United States was able to export in 1918 approximately three times the normal amounts of breadstuffs, meats, and sugar.

The war spawned a great many other agencies. A fuel administration, under the direction of Harry A. Garfield, president of Williams College, introduced daylight saving and 'Fuelless Mondays,' banned electric displays, and closed down non-essential plants in an effort to conserve coal. A war trade board licensed exports and imports and black-listed firms suspected of trading with the enemy. A war finance corporation supervised the flotation of all security issues of $100,000 or over and in addition was empowered to underwrite loans to industries engaged in the production of war materials.

The war produced unprecedented changes in the government's relationship to labor unions. The War and Navy departments broke new ground by setting up such agencies as a Cantonment Adjustment Commission which fixed wage and hour policies for construction workers in army camps, and a Board of Control for Labor Standards which regulated manufacturers of uniforms. Wilson appointed a War Labor Policies Board which, under the direction of Felix Frankfurter, standardized wages and hours and for the first time gave the government a national labor policy. As a consequence, a newly created United States Employment Service placed nearly four million workers in vital war jobs. But the most important new agency was the War Labor Board, headed by former President Taft and the brilliant labor lawyer, Frank P. Walsh. While many of the prewar progressives had frowned on unions as monopolies which denied equality of opportunity and threatened middle-class interests, the WLB threw the power of government behind the right of workers to organize and bargain collectively. When the Smith & Wesson Arms plant in Springfield, Massachusetts, rejected a WLB decision, the board boldly commandeered the plant. The various labor boards also made progress in imposing the eight-hour day on many industries and in protecting women and children from exploitation. When the Supreme Court overturned the Child Labor Act of 1916, Congress quickly enacted a new law using the taxing power to discourage the employment of child labor. As a result of all of these actions and of the insatiable manpower demand, the A. F. of L. gained more than a million members; hours of labor declined sharply; and real wages rose 20 per cent.

The government had to find money not only for our own but for Allied expenses. As early as July 1917 the British Chancellor of the Exchequer, Lord Northcliffe, informed Colonel House that 'our resources available for payments in America are exhausted. Unless the United States government can meet in full our expenses in America . . . the whole financial fabric of the alliance will collapse.' During and immediately after the war the United States Government lent some $10 billion to the Allies and associated governments, practically all of which was spent in this country. American expenditures to October 1919 came to $26 billion. The total direct cost of the war for the United States therefore amounted to about $36 billion; indirect costs in the form of interest on the national debt, pensions, soldiers' bonuses, and so forth brought the total to well over $42 billion by 1936.

The country financed approximately one-third of the war cost by taxation, two-thirds by loans. To avoid a repetition of the unhappy experience of Cleveland's negotiations with Wall Street, Congress insisted that bonds be sold through popular subscription. The five loans which were floated between May 1917 and May 1919 — four Liberty loans and one Victory loan — were all handsomely oversubscribed. Congress stepped up income, inheritance, corporation, and excess profit taxes, and levied new taxes on transportation, spirits, gasoline, amusements and entertainments of all kinds. The war demonstrated the potential of the steeply graduated income tax as an instrument for distributing the costs of government more equitably. In the Revenue Act of 1918 Congress not only raised the excess profits tax to 65 per cent but increased the surtax so that the total levy on the wealthy reached 77 per cent. Although the war created new millionaires and resulted in swollen profits in some instances, it also showed that in a time of crisis the government can impose its will on the rich in a way that is rarely possible in peacetime.

Notwithstanding the many achievements, the war mobilization fell short of its goal. Despite the enormous upsurge of industrial production the American army depended heavily on English and French arms and supplies. Before the end of the war American factories had produced only 64 tanks, the Liberty aviation engine was just getting into production, field artillery was almost exclusively supplied with French 75 mm. field guns, and more American troops went to Europe in British transports than in American vessels.

2. MOBILIZING PUBLIC OPINION

When Congress declared war, a very large part of the public was indifferent to the issues, and an important minority disaffected. Millions of Americans — anti-war Socialists, German, Irish, and other ethnic groups, pacifists, Wobblies, many progressives — opposed American intervention. When Socialist candidates ran in municipal elections in 1917, they polled a startling 22 per cent in New York City, 34 per cent in Chicago, 44 per cent in Dayton. In Oklahoma, a leading Socialist state, an uprising of tenant farmers, including Indians and Negroes, burned bridges and cut pipelines in protest against participation in the war. When this 'Green Corn Rebellion' was put down by militia, thousands fled to the Winding Stairs mountains to evade arrest. Anti-war progressives charged that the poor people of the country had been dragooned into war by greedy profiteers. 'We are going into the war,' George Norris had asserted, 'upon the command of Gold.' Furthermore, among the many who did not oppose the conflict, the boy on the farm and the man in the street who were to do the fighting, the girl in the factory who was to make supplies, and the woman in the kitchen who was to do the saving had very little idea what the war was about. By an act of 14 April 1917 Congress established the Committee on Public Information. Its chairman, George Creel, combined, as Mark Sullivan observed, 'incredibly efflorescent imagination, fertile ingenuity, and prodigious energy.' He undertook to mobilize the mind of America as Baruch was mobilizing industry and Baker the manpower. Creel enlisted artists, advertisers, poets, historians, photographers, educators, and actors in the campaign, and they inundated the country with a flood of propaganda pamphlets, posters, magazines, and newspapers. Altogether the indefatigable Creel distributed over 100 million pieces of 'literature,' while 75,000 'four-minute men' let loose a barrage of oratory at movie houses and public gatherings which all but paralyzed the intelligence of the country. Motion pictures displayed to horrified audiences the barbarities of the 'Hun'; pamphlets written by learned professors proved to the more skeptical that the Germans had always been a depraved people; and thousands of canned editorials taught the average man what to think about the war. In this campaign none was neglected: school children learned to lisp the vocabulary of hatred; women's clubs were titillated by atrocity stories; and foreigners were taught to be ashamed that they had not been born in America. Nor were the delights of education confined to the United States; no people was safe from Creel's zeal, no country too remote for his concern. Three hundred Chinese newspapers supplied the palpitating Celestials with 'the truth about the war'; pictures of the American President and the American flag hung on walls of cottages of Russian peasants and Peruvian *mestizos*.

The Administration directed its propaganda too toward international opinion. Charges by Bolshevik and Socialist leaders that the war was being fought for imperialistic aims encouraged Wilson to enunciate a declaration of principles. He hoped not only to inspirit the Allies but to break down the will to fight in the Central Powers. From the first Wilson had tried to distinguish between the German people and their government, and had held out to minority races of the Dual Monarchy the hope of independence from the Hapsburgs. In his war message of 2 April he had announced that 'we have no quarrel with the German people. We have no feeling toward them but one of sympathy and friendship,' and throughout the war he reiterated his policy of 'war on the German government, peace with the German people.' The struggle was, he said, 'a war for freedom and justice and self-government amongst all the nations of the world, a war to make the world safe for the peoples who live upon it and have made it their own, the German people themselves included.' Wilson sought two ends: to establish a moral basis for peace upon which all belligerents — including the Allies — must agree, and to sow dissatisfaction among the peoples of Germany and Austria-Hungary.

To achieve these goals Wilson announced, on 8 January 1918, the Fourteen Points upon which it would be possible to formulate terms of peace. They included the principle of 'open covenants openly arrived at,' freedom of the seas, the reorganization of much of Europe on the basis of self-determination, and the creation of a 'general association of nations.' Wilson's statement, assiduously circulated throughout Germany, eventually helped to drive a wedge between the people and the government, and when Ludendorff's army met defeat on the Western front, Germany hastened to comply with Wilson's insistence upon a popular government, and opened negotiations for an armistice upon the basis of the Fourteen Points.

3. CIVIL LIBERTIES IN WARTIME

In 1917–19 the people of the United States abandoned themselves to a hysteria of fear of German conspiracies and of Communist subversion, and the government indulged in greater excesses than at any previous crisis of our history. The Espionage Act of 15 June 1917 fixed a maximum penalty of a $10,000 fine and 20 years' imprisonment for anyone who interfered with the draft or encouraged disloyalty, and empowered the Postmaster General to deny the mails to any materials he thought seditious. The Sedition Act of May 1918 extended these penalties to anyone who should obstruct the sale of United States bonds, incite insubordination, discourage recruiting, 'wilfully utter, print, write or publish any disloyal, profane, scurrilous or abusive language about the form of government of the United States, or the Constitution, or the flag, or the uniform of the Army or Navy, or bring the form of government . . . or the constitution . . . into contempt . . . or advocate any curtailment of production of anything necessary to the prosecution of the war.' In addition a Trading-with-the-Enemy Act of October 1917 gave the President authority to censor all international communications, and the Postmaster General power over the foreign-language press in the United States.

Under these harsh laws the government instituted widespread censorship of the press; banned two Socialist newspapers from the mails; held up circulation of a tax-journal, *The Public*, because it advised that more of the costs of the war should be borne by taxation; and banned Thorstein Veblen's *Imperial Germany and the Industrial Revolution* — while Creel's committee was using it for propaganda purposes! A hapless film-producer was sentenced to ten years in jail for producing a film on the American Revolution called *The Spirit of Seventy-six*, because it was thought that it might excite anti-British sentiments; a Vermont minister was sentenced to fifteen years' imprisonment for citing Jesus as an authority on pacifism; South Dakota farmers went to jail for petitioning for a referendum on the war and on the payment of war costs through taxation; the son of a Chief Justice of New Hampshire was convicted for sending out private letters upholding the German interpretation of U-boat warfare; and a New Hampshire judge, trying a radical who said that 'this was a Morgan war and not a war of the people,' observed that 'out West they are hanging people for saying such things' and vindicated New Hampshire justice by jailing the man for only three years. A drive against conscientious objectors, who were theoretically excluded from the draft, netted 4000 men, of whom more than 400 were hurried to military prisons.

Altogether, the government carried out 1500 prosecutions under the Espionage and Sedition laws. Among those convicted, the two most

distinguished were Eugene V. Debs and Victor Berger. Debs had been
four times a candidate for the presidency of the United States; in 1912
he had polled almost 900,000 votes and in 1920 he was to poll almost a
million. He was sentenced to 20 years in jail for a speech which was held
to have a tendency to bring about resistance to the draft, though there
was no evidence to prove that it did. Berger, editor of the Milwaukee
Leader and Congressman from Milwaukee, also received a 20-year sentence for editorials in his newspaper branding the war as a capitalist
conspiracy. Twice re-elected by his constituents he was twice refused his
seat. C. T. Schenck, General Secretary of the Socialist party, was convicted on the same charge; Justice Holmes's opinion sustaining the conviction is memorable because it announced for the first time the 'clear
and present danger' test which was to stand as a safeguard for freedom
of speech until whittled away in the 'fifties by the counter-doctrine of
the 'balance of interests.' 'The question in every case,' wrote Holmes,

> is whether the words are used in such circumstances and are of
> such a nature as to create a clear and present danger that they will
> bring about the substantive evils that Congress has a right to pre-
> vent. It is a question of proximity and degree.

Holmes's standard was not adhered to in a more controversial case
where a miserable garment-worker, Jacob Abrams, was sentenced to
twenty years' imprisonment for distributing a pamphlet calling on the
workers of the world to rise against the American military expedition to
Siberia — an expedition conceived in folly, conducted in vain, and abandoned in disorder. The opinion of the Court in 1919 evoked from
Justice Holmes the most moving of his many eloquent dissents:

> When men have realized that time has upset many fighting faiths,
> they may come to believe even more than they believe the very
> foundations of their own conduct that the ultimate good desired is
> better reached by free trade in ideas — that the best test of truth
> is the power of the thought to get itself accepted in the competi-
> tion of the market, and that truth is the only ground upon which
> their wishes can be safely carried out. That at any rate is the theory
> of our Constitution. It is an experiment, as all life is an experiment.
> Every year if not every day we have to wager our salvation upon
> some prophecy based upon imperfect knowledge. While that ex-
> periment is part of our system I think that we should be eternally
> vigilant against attempts to check the expression of opinions that

we loathe and believe to be fraught with death, unless they so
imminently threaten immediate interference with the lawful and
pressing purposes of the law that an immediate check is required
to save the country.

No less disturbing than this official crusade against sedition was the
unofficial witch-hunting that engaged the energy of sundry old ladies of
both sexes and of members of filiopietistic organizations. The war
offered a great opportunity to bring patriotism to the aid of personal
grudges and neighborhood feuds. The independent-minded sort of citizen who was known to his conforming neighbors as a 'Tory' in the Revolution, a 'Jacobin' in 1798, and a 'Copperhead' in the Civil War became
a 'pro-German traitor' in 1917 and a 'Bolshevik' in 1918, and was lucky if
he did not have garbled scraps of his conversation sent in to the Department of Justice or flashes from his shaving mirror reported as signals to
German submarines. German-Americans, the vast majority of them loyal
to the United States, were subjected to all sorts of indignities. Schools
dropped German from their curricula, and even some universities abolished their German departments; German books were withdrawn from
public library circulation and German publications driven under cover.
The Governor of Iowa decreed that 'conversation in public places, on
trains, or over the telephone' should be in the English language. Frederick Stock, distinguished conductor of the Chicago Symphony Orchestra, was deprived of his baton; the patriotic mayor of Jersey City refused to allow Fritz Kreisler to appear on the concert stage; and some
universities revoked degrees they had conferred on distinguished Germans, thus giving academic sanction to the doctrine of retroactive guilt.

'The only way to keep men from agitating against grievances,' said
President Wilson in 1919, 'is to remove the grievances. An unwillingness
even to discuss these matters produces only dissatisfaction and gives
comfort to the extreme elements in our country which endeavor to stir
up disturbances in order to provoke Governments to embark upon a
course of retaliation and repression. The seed of revolution is repression.'
It would be difficult to improve on this as a short description of what
actually happened. Yet it was Wilson who signed the Espionage and
Sedition Acts and supported Attorney General A. Mitchell Palmer's request for an even more extreme Sedition Act in 1919; who refused to
release men like Eugene Debs or Victor Berger from the savage sentences pronounced on them in wartime; and who would sit by while

Palmer carried through his high-handed raids and deportations in 1919 and 1920. This high-minded scholar who read and admired those great libertarians, John Stuart Mill and Walter Bagehot, sanctioned, and at times even encouraged, an unprecedented program of repression.

4. NAVAL AND MILITARY OPERATIONS

'Force to the utmost, force without stint or limit' had been Wilson's promise, yet neither the Germans nor the Allies expected much military and naval contribution from the United States. In one sense this estimate was correct; it was fully a year after the declaration of war before American soldiers were available in sufficient numbers to affect the military situation on the Western front, and the Germans confidently expected to win the war in less than a year. When American military aid did come, it was decisive. But even before American soldiers turned the tide at Château-Thierry, the navy had co-operated to destroy the effectiveness of German submarine warfare.

General Joffre early assured American officials that half a million soldiers was the largest number the Allies expected the United States to send to France, but the government organized its military machine upon a far more ambitious basis. Within eighteen months the United States created an effective army of 4 million men, transported over 2 million to France, and placed 1.3 million on the firing line. This was a result of the organizing genius of Newton D. Baker, who, despite pacifist inclinations, proved himself one of the ablest of all secretaries of war.

Even before the actual declaration of war, General Hugh L. Scott, Chief of Staff, had convinced Mr. Baker of the need to raise an army by conscription rather than by the volunteer system, and in turn won over Wilson. Although our experience with the Civil War draft had not been happy, European experience in the First World War proved conscription to be a necessity. The Selective Service Act of 18 May 1917 required all men between the ages of twenty-one and thirty to register for service. Some Congressmen, recalling the New York draft riots of 1863, prophesied that conscription would be attended by 'rioting all over the United States,' and that 'we will never get a conscript on the firing line in France,' but these predictions proved erroneous. When the registration offices closed at sundown on 5 June, 9,586,508 men had registered and there had not been the slightest disorder or opposition. Subsequent registrations of all men between the ages of eighteen and forty-five brought the total registration up to 24,234,021. Of these, 2,810,296 were inducted into the army. The regular army, national guard, navy, and marine corps continued to be recruited by voluntary enlistment. Including these and 'minor branches of service,' the total number of men in the armed forces of the United States at the end of the First World War was nearly five million.

The first American contingent, the 1st Infantry Division, arrived in France in June 1917, and on Independence Day paraded through the streets of Paris. This and subsequent contingents in 1917 served chiefly to bolster Allied morale, and for this purpose the Americans were distributed among French and English troops along the quieter sectors of the front. By the end of 1917 some 200,000 American soldiers were in France, but only a few Engineer Regiments of the 1st Division had seen active service at the front, in the Cambrai offensive.

The United States Navy got into the thick of the action much sooner, but only after a bad start. Although Secretary Daniels and his Assistant-Secretary, Franklin D. Roosevelt, had done a great deal to build up the morale and efficiency of the fleet, the new construction provided for in the summer of 1916 was still mostly in the blueprint stage and the 'bridge' of merchant ships to France was as yet largely a bridgehead, at Hog Island on the Delaware. Admiral William S. Benson, the Chief of Naval Operations, had no war plan ready when war was declared, and the one he promulgated on 11 April looked to little more than a defensive patrol by battleships and cruisers on the American side of the Atlantic, and a considerable Pacific Fleet to watch Japan — which was an ally! Fortunately, the President had been prevailed upon by Ambassador Page to send the gifted and energetic Rear Admiral William S. Sims to London a few days ahead of the declaration of war; and Sims's pungent dispatches described a situation so appalling that the navy almost completely altered its plans.

Admiral Jellicoe, First Lord of the Admiralty, told Sims that sinkings of Allied merchant vessels averaged almost 570,000 tons per month in February and March, and bade fair to reach 900,000 tons in April 1917.[3]

3. Compare figures for World War II: only in six months of 1942 and in March 1943, did sinkings by submarines in the Atlantic and Arctic pass 500,000 tons, the highest being 637,000 tons in November 1942. Morison, *Battle of the Atlantic*, p. 412.

England had only a three weeks' supply of grain on hand, the German U-boats were increasing in numbers and efficiency, and if something was not done promptly to stop these losses and repair the life line, the Allies would have to throw in the sponge before the end of the year. Sims found, to his surprise, that the Allies had not yet adopted the convoy system of operating merchant ships in groups so that they could be protected from submarine attack by an escort of cruisers and destroyers. Sims threw his influence on the side of convoys, and they were promptly adopted. The predicted frictions and collisions proved to be few and unimportant, and the convoy system, more than any single factor (and this was as true of World War II as of World War I), enabled American troops and supplies to cross the Atlantic safely.[4]

Sims also persuaded the navy to send as many destroyers as it could spare to Queenstown, Ireland, to be operated for escort-of-convoy and anti-submarine patrol under the British. The first six of them arrived on 4 May and went right to work; by 5 July there were 34 American destroyers at Queenstown together with several ancient 400-ton torpedo boats of the Asiatic Fleet, which Lieutenant Commander Harold R. Stark had brought halfway around the world. Never before had American warships operated under British or indeed any foreign command. The British commander, Vice Admiral Sir Lewis Bayly, was an austere, crusty old sea-dog, but the experiment was a success. The American destroyer officers (including in their junior ranks such men as Halsey, Kirk, Carpender, Hewitt, and Lee, who emerged as distinguished admirals in World War II) came to have a feeling amounting almost to veneration for 'Uncle Lewis.'

These destroyers experimented successfully with listening gear that detected submarines' propellers, and with depth charges ('ashcans') which could destroy a submerged U-boat if properly placed; both were primitive in comparison with the sonar and depth weapons of World War II, but effective against the small submarines of World War I. It was not until 17 November that American destroyers made their first kill of a U-boat, but in the meantime the new convoy tactics and aggressive

4. The comparatively small U-boats of 1917–18 had so short a cruising range that it was necessary to convoy vessels for only a few hundred miles west of Europe. It is true that the German navy, as a stunt, sent six submarines into U.S. coastal waters in 1918, but they sank only 24 ships of 2000 tons and over and their operations were little more than a nuisance raid which failed even to disrupt coastal shipping.

patrolling had reduced Allied monthly shipping losses from 881,000 tons (April) to 289,000 tons (November), and these losses were more than replaced by new construction; submarine operations now became very hazardous and the United States could send troops and supplies abroad with confidence that they would arrive. Not one loaded transport was lost. In several other ways, too, the U.S. Navy contributed to put the squeeze on Admiral Tirpitz's underwater fleet. A fleet of 120 SC's (subchasers), commanded entirely by naval reservists fresh out of college, proved their value against the Austrian navy in the Adriatic. Naval aviators, flying the old Curtiss float planes that few would dare to fly now, began operating in Europe, and by the end of the war the United States had some 500 planes and three 'blimps' on 27 different European bases reporting U-boats, and before the end of the war they joined the army air force in bombing raids on Germany. Finally, it was the U.S. Navy that initiated, planned, and executed the colossal mine barrage across the North Sea which, beginning in June 1918, practically closed that exit to enemy submarines. Previous to the laying of this barrage, an American battle fleet under Rear Admiral Hugh L. Rodman, with a complement of destroyers, was sent to augment the British Grand Fleet at Scapa Flow in the Orkney Islands. These combined fleets contained the German high-seas navy in port and reduced its efficiency and morale to a point that contributed strongly to the German surrender in November 1918.

Without the work by the U.S. Navy, the Allies might have been defeated before American ground forces could have arrived. Nevertheless, it was the American Expeditionary Force which, in conjunction with the British, French, and (to a limited extent) Italian armies, secured Allied victory.

Late in 1917 the military situation turned radically against the Allies. In October the Italian army cracked at Caporetto and the Austrians poured onto the plains of Friuli; the Italians dug in along the Piave, but the Allies had to hurry troops from the Western front to stem the Austrian tide. A month later came the Bolshevik revolution in Russia; the new Soviet government sued for peace, and the inauguration of negotiations at Brest-Litovsk, 22 December 1917, released hundreds of thousands of German soldiers for the Western front. By the spring of 1918 the Germans had a clear numerical superiority in the West, and the German high command prepared with confidence for a drive on Paris that would end the war.

A Macedonian cry went up for American troops, and there began a 'race for France.' Could the United States speed up her troop shipments sufficiently to restore the numerical balance between the Allies and the Central Powers? 'Would she appear in time to snatch the victor's laurels from our brows?' asked Hindenburg. 'That, and that only was the decisive question! I believed I could answer it in the negative.' Troop shipments were given right of way over supplies, new transports were pressed into service, and soldiers were rushed from American training camps to France. In March 80,000 troops were shipped abroad, in April 118,000, in May 245,000. Altogether, during the critical months from March to October 1918, 1,750,000 American soldiers landed in France. 'America,' wrote the German Commander-in-Chief von Ludendorff, 'thus became the decisive power in the war.'

The great German offensive began on 21 March 1918 with a terrific assault on the British line from Arras to La Fère. Within a week the Germans had severely crippled the British Fifth Army, captured 90,000 prisoners, and rolled the British line back 25 miles. On 9 April came the second offensive; once again the British were hurled back on a broad front from Ypres to Armentières. In late May and early June the Germans launched their third offensive, this time against the French armies along the sector between Noyon and Rheims. Within a week the Germans smashed supposedly impregnable defenses, captured 40,000 prisoners and 650 guns and, standing on the right bank of the Marne, threatened Paris. At this crisis of the war the Allies placed General Foch in supreme command of all their forces, and the premiers of Great Britain, France, and Italy warned the United States that 'as there is no possibility of the British and French increasing the numbers of their divisions . . . there is great danger of the war being lost unless the numerical inferiority of the Allies can be remedied as rapidly as possible by the advent of American troops.'

Pershing, Baker, and Wilson wanted the American army in France to form a separate and independent unit, but temporarily Pershing waived this claim and placed all his forces at the disposal of Foch, who dispersed them among the Allied armies where they were most needed. On 28 May the 1st Division helped to repulse the German drive on Montdidier and in a counter-attack captured the heights of Cantigny. A few days later a marine brigade of the 2nd Division was rushed to the front to stop the German onslaught at Château-Thierry; for 96 hours the marines, assisted by the French colonials, fought off the Germans, hurling them back to the right bank of the Marne. On 5 June the 2nd Division took the offensive at Belleau Wood, and after three weeks of fighting cleared the woods of Germans and penetrated their lines to a depth of over three miles. The actual military importance of these engagements was not great, but their morale importance was incalculable.

On 15 July came the fourth and last phase of the great German offensive, known as the Second Battle of the Marne. The Germans launched their heaviest attack at the Château-Thierry salient; had they broken through, Paris could not have been saved. American troops, 275,000 strong, supported the French in stemming a tide which at first seemed irresistible. In three days the German offensive was exhausted, and on 18 July, without giving the enemy an opportunity to consolidate his position, Foch called upon the 1st and 2nd American and the First French Morocco Divisions to form the spearhead of a counter-attack, which was brilliantly executed. The German Chancellor Hertling later confessed that 'at the beginning of July 1918, I was convinced . . . that before the first of September our adversaries would send us peace proposals. . . . That was on the 15th. On the 18th even the most optimistic among us knew that all was lost. The history of the world was played out in three days.'

With the passing of the crisis on the Marne, Pershing revived his cherished plan for an independent American army. The Allied command of necessity acquiesced, and on 10 August the American army began its official existence. It was assigned the task of straightening out the St. Mihiel salient, south of Verdun. St. Mihiel, which had been in the possession of the Germans since September 1914, was strategically important because it commanded the Mézières-Sedan-Metz railway and the great Briey iron basin. The Germans were preparing to withdraw when, early in the morning of 12 September, blanketed by a heavy fog, the American army of over half a million men went into battle. 'The rapidity with which our divisions advanced overwhelmed the enemy,' wrote Pershing, 'and all objectives were reached by the afternoon of September 13.' In two days the American army wiped out the St. Mihiel salient, captured 16,000 prisoners and over 400 guns and established their line in a position to threaten Metz, all with only 7000 casualties.

General Foch now assigned the American army a crucial role in a gigantic Allied offensive all along the line from Ypres to Verdun. The time was propitious for such a drive. The last Austrian offensive against

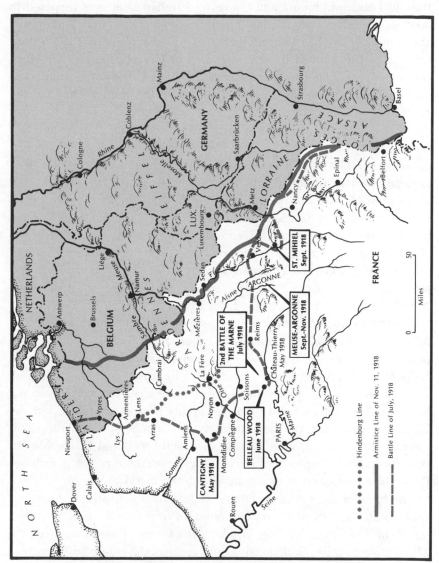

THE AMERICAN ARMY IN FRANCE—1918

Italy had ended in failure and the revived Italian army was prepared to take the offensive; Bulgaria had cracked in September, and Turkey was about to follow; while the uninterrupted Allied success on the Western front since July proved the disintegration of German morale. American contingents were fighting alongside the Belgians in the north and played an important part in the British offensive on the Somme, but for the main attack the American First Army was assigned the sector between the Meuse and the Argonne Woods, with Sedan and the Sedan-Metz railway as the ultimate objective. The Meuse-Argonne battle, launched on 26 September, was the greatest in which American troops had been engaged so far. Stretched out over a period of 40 days, it engaged 1,200,000 soldiers, 840 airplanes, and 324 tanks, and cost 117,000 American casualties. Despite stout resistance from the badly depleted German troops, the movement scored a complete success. The Allies broke the Hindenburg line, and American forces and their French allies captured over 25,000 prisoners, 874 cannon, and 3000 machine guns, and inflicted more than 100,000 casualties on the enemy. Similar success attended the Allied offensive along the whole front from Flanders to Rheims.

As early as August Ludendorff recognized that the end was near. The Allies had now regained numerical superiority. Foch was planning a new offensive in the spring of 1919, and Pershing was asking for an army twice the size of that already under his command. On 2 October Ludendorff informed the German government that the army could not hold out 48 hours. In this he was, as events proved, mistaken, but the German government was panic-stricken. In the hope of conciliating Wilson [5] a parliamentary system was hastily established and Prince Max of Baden was called upon to form a liberal government. On 3 October Prince Max addressed to President Wilson the first overture for peace — on the basis of the Fourteen Points. Wilson handled these negotiations with a skill that belied his reputation as an impractical idealist. After a month of diplomatic fencing, in which the Germans were worsted, the Allied governments instructed Foch to negotiate for an armistice. Mutiny in the German navy and revolution in Munich, the Rhine cities, and Berlin rendered the Germans impotent to offer further resistance; but in the vain hope that a complete change in the form of government might win milder terms of peace, the Kaiser was forced to abdicate, and

5. Austria-Hungary had inaugurated peace overtures as early as 14 September, but without success.

on 9 November he fled across the border to Holland. Two days later an armistice was officially proclaimed, and the greatest and most costly war that the world had yet known came to an end.

5. THE RUSSIAN REVOLUTION AND THE SIBERIAN MISADVENTURE

Of all our political decisions in this era intervention in Russia proved the most ill-considered, of all diplomatic adventures the most maladroit, of all military escapades the most misguided.

The collapse of Russia in November 1917 and the separate treaty of Brest-Litovsk the following March administered a double shock to American, and Allied, opinion. First, not only was Russia out as a military ally, but her defeat released scores of veteran German divisions for service in the spring offensives on the Western front. Second, the Bolshevik revolution, by its nature world-wide in scope and in thrust, threatened the very bases of Western institutions.

What, then, should be the American policy toward the Bolsheviks, fighting to stay afloat in the turbulent seas of war, revolution, invasion, famine, and civil strife? There appeared to be two alternatives. The policy of bolstering the moderate Alexander Kerensky had failed, but some thought it might still be possible to encourage the Bolsheviks to continue to fight the Germans. This meant recognition of Bolshevism and taking the chance that it might spread throughout Europe and beyond. In fact, it is questionable that anything could have kept the war-weary Russians in the war. The other policy was to support the White Russians or any other forces hostile to the Bolsheviks, including the Japanese who promised to continue the war against Germany.

From the beginning the French and British, speaking through the Supreme Allied Command, favored the second course. Alone of major statesmen, President Wilson counseled patience with the Russian people and set himself against intervention. In the early months of 1918 some of the American representatives in Russia — notably the old-time Progressive, Raymond Robins — tried to work out some arrangement with Lenin and Trotsky whereby the Russians would keep on fighting in return for American military and economic aid. But by this time neither side could deliver: the United States could not get aid through to Russia, and if the Bolsheviks took up arms again, the Germans would sweep into Moscow and Petrograd. Robins was recalled, and Ambassador David Francis and the influential Edgar Sisson, who held a somewhat ambiguous position as director of American propaganda, won the ear of the President. Sisson's contribution was to 'prove' with documents palpably forged that Lenin and Trotsky were 'German agents.' [6]

Wilson himself was torn by indecision. 'I have been sweating blood over the question of what is right and feasible to do in Russia,' he wrote. 'It goes to pieces like quicksilver under my touch.' All of his instincts counseled him to sympathize with the Russian masses in their hour of agony, and his training taught him to mistrust anything that smacked of imperialistic ventures in Europe or Asia. But he feared that Germany would gain too great a military advantage from the Bolshevik defection, and he found the pressure from the British and French for intervention almost impossible to resist. As he explained to his Secretary of War, he felt obliged to do it, because the British and French were pressing it on his attention so hard, and he had refused so many of their requests that they were beginning to feel that he was not a good associate, much less a good ally.

Out of all this came a series of compromises and improvisations by which the United States managed to get the maximum of trials and tribulations with the minimum of advantages. In July Wilson agreed to send a token force to the Arctic front which the British were trying to establish at Murmansk and Archangel, on condition that they were to be used only 'to guard military stores and make it safe for Russian forces to come together in organized bodies in the north,' and not for offensive operations. But the British naval commander ignored these reservations. In September some 5000 bewildered American infantrymen from Michigan and Wisconsin, who had been headed for France, found themselves fighting in the frozen forests of Arctic Russia, for purposes never clear, and against an enemy who had never officially been recognized as such.

In far-eastern Siberia, a situation of unusual complexity had devel-

6. These documents played a decisive role in the conviction of Jacob Abrams and his associates for printing leaflets calling on American workers to refuse to have any part in the invasion of Russia — conduct which earned them 20-year sentences. If we were not technically at war with Russia, such advice could not be a violation of the Espionage Act, which penalized activities designed to hinder the conduct of the war. The Court got around this by assuming, on the basis of the Sisson documents, that the Russian Revolution was all a German plot! See Zechariah Chafee, *Free Speech in the United States,* chap. III.

oped. More than 45,000 Czech prisoners, who had been released after the collapse of Russia, had seized the Trans-Siberian railroad and were fighting their way across thousands of miles of Russia and Siberia to Vladivostok, where they expected to embark for the Western front in France. When this plan proved impracticable, they 'captured' Vladivostok — with the aid of the Japanese who had moved in to keep an eye on things — and then prepared to take the offensive against alleged armies of German and Austrian prisoners in eastern Siberia.

Here, quite fortuitously, was a justification for Allied intervention: they could come to the aid of the heroic Czechs and enable them to return to the Western front! Besides, it was a good idea to be on hand and see to it that the Japanese did not dig in too deeply in Russian Siberia or in Manchuria. Once again France and Britain brought pressure on Wilson; once again he yielded to pressure — but in his own way. There was to be no 'intervention' in Russia's internal affairs and no fighting the Bolsheviks; the American expeditionary force was to be limited to helping the Czechs, blocking enemy advances, and 'steadying' efforts at self-government; to these laudable purposes the United States and Japan would each contribute not more than 7000 troops. We were riding the tiger, and we ended up inside.

The situation speedily got out of hand; as George Kennan says, 'the American forces had scarcely arrived in Russia when history invalidated at a single stroke almost every reason Washington had conceived for their being there.' The Czechs had won their freedom and no longer needed help; as there were no Germans or Austrians to fight, they were fighting the Bolsheviks instead. The Japanese sent in not 7000 men, as agreed, but 72,000. The American General Graves found himself, in 1919, fighting the wrong war, at the wrong time, in the wrong place, and against the wrong enemy. Yet Wilson at least helped to avert a large-scale, overtly Bolshevik intervention which would have been even more costly.

The Archangel and Siberian adventures attracted very little attention at a time when the war had entered its final stages. But their long-term consequences were formidable. Americans forgot the intervention, but the Bolsheviks did not. To them it meant that the United States had joined the capitalist countries of the Old World in an attempt to destroy them at a time when they were struggling for their life. 'The Siberian situation,' wrote Secretary Baker, 'will always illustrate the eccentricities of a remote and irrational emanation from the central madness of a warring world.'

6. THE PEACE CONFERENCE, THE TREATY, AND THE LEAGUE

Wilson had been successful in carrying the war to a victorious conclusion; he was to discover that it was easier to win a war than to make a peace. Like Lincoln, he failed to guard against the forces of vindictiveness, hatred, and greed that are inevitably loosed by war. The only statesman representing a major power who combined intelligence, magnanimity, and vision, he nevertheless bore some of the responsibility for inspiring emotions of vindictiveness and greed in others and for creating a situation in which they would have free play. He had acquiesced in the suppression of freedom of expression in the United States; he had supported George Creel's campaign to inoculate Americans with the germs of hatred for the Central Powers; and he had encouraged utopian expectations about the outcome of the war.

Even before the armistice Wilson determined to shatter precedent by taking personal charge of the peace negotiations. On 24 October 1918 he had appealed to the American electorate for a vote of confidence: 'If you have approved of my leadership and wish me to continue to be your unembarrassed spokesman in affairs at home and abroad, I earnestly beg that you will express yourselves unmistakably to that effect by returning a Democratic majority to both the Senate and House of Representatives.' Two weeks later Americans went to the polls and chose a majority of Republicans for both houses of Congress. By winning control of the Senate by two votes, the Republicans were able to place Henry Cabot Lodge in the chairmanship of the critically important Senate Foreign Relations Committee.

Wilson's critics charged him with hurting his cause by fecklessly ending a political truce. In fact, well before the election the Republicans had not only behaved in a partisan fashion, as was inevitable in an election year, but party leaders like Roosevelt and Lodge had made clear that they opposed Wilson's plans for a postwar association of nations. Roosevelt, who had long had an intense hatred of Wilson, was a bitter partisan who believed that casualty lists were being suppressed in order to hide the fact that two-thirds of the American war dead were Republicans. The former President insisted that the United States had

gone to war strictly to seek vengeance for insults to American honor, and
he demanded that the peace be dictated by 'hammering guns' instead of
'clicking . . . typewriters.' Lodge, who regarded himself as a Scholar in
Politics, resented the renown Wilson had won in the same field. (In fact,
Senator Depew's remark is to the point: Lodge had a mind like the New
England landscape — 'naturally barren, but highly cultivated.')

The party out of power normally gains seats in a midterm election, and
the Republicans did not win by an unusual margin in 1918. Moreover,
the Democratic setback resulted less from resentment at Wilson's appeal
than from Western grievances over price regulation. Since wheat and
wool were regulated, while the price of cotton was not, the Republicans
were able to exploit the suspicion that the Southern-controlled Democratic party was playing sectional favorites in administering the war. Yet
in his Gladstonian appeal for a vote of confidence, Wilson left himself
open to the Republican claim that the President, after drawing the line
on foreign policy, had been rejected. When on 13 December he sailed
for France, ex-President Roosevelt warned 'our allies, our enemies and
Mr. Wilson himself' that 'Mr. Wilson has no authority whatever to speak
for the American people at this time. His leadership has just been emphatically repudiated by them.'

As members of the American peace delegation Wilson took with him
Secretary of State Lansing, General Tasker H. Bliss, Colonel House, and
Henry White, a career diplomat. It was not a strong delegation. Prudence would have counseled the appointment of more prominent Republicans than White, leaders of international repute and experience
such as William H. Taft and Elihu Root. Along with the American delegation went hundreds of experts to assist in the historical, ethnographical,
and economic work of the peace commission. The Paris Conference,
whatever its defects, had the benefit of more expert advice than any
political arrangement ever concluded.

In the preliminary armistice negotiations with the Allies, Wilson had
been made painfully aware of the conflict in war aims between the
United States and the Allied powers. While he had clung tenaciously to
his Fourteen Points, he had been forced to admit qualifications with
respect to the important items of 'freedom of the seas' and reparations.
Aware of the existence of secret treaties which in part nullified the
Fourteen Points, he persuaded himself to ignore their significance. These
secret treaties, which had been revealed by the Soviet government in

Russia to discredit imperialist diplomacy, had been concluded between the major Allies and powers like Japan, Italy, and Rumania, in order to induce them to join the Allied side. This did not indicate any peculiar obliquity on the part of the Allies — for Italy and Rumania would certainly have joined the Central Powers otherwise — but the treaties were contrary in spirit and letter to the principle of self-determination, and Wilson should have tried to obtain formal abrogation or modification of them before sending American troops to Europe.

In the Peace Conference which held its first formal session 18 January 1919, all the Allied and associated powers were represented, but the 'Big Four' — England, France, Italy, and the United States — made the important decisions. Like the conference at Brest-Litovsk, this one gave the defeated powers no part in the negotiations; they were merely called in when the treaty was ready and ordered to sign on the dotted line. Nor was Russia officially represented, since the Allies hoped that the Soviet government would shortly collapse. Moreover, the jingo atmosphere of Paris and the personalities of the leaders made a just peace exceedingly difficult to attain. David Lloyd George, the British prime minister who represented his country, was an able leader, but a self-seeker and demagogue. He had won a general election since the armistice on the slogans 'Hang the Kaiser' and 'Make Germany Pay.' Georges Clemenceau, the 'tiger' of French politics, was an able and disillusioned old man who regarded Wilson liberalism with complete skepticism and assailed it with mordant wit: 'Mr. Wilson bores me with his Fourteen Points; why, God Almighty has only ten!' Clemenceau cared only for France, and France wanted but one thing, security; the English and Americans were never able to convince the 'logical' French that the worst way to security was the way that had always made for insecurity in the past — a humiliating peace that placed intolerable burdens on the vanquished. Orlando, the prime minister who represented Italy, was the exponent of *sacro egoismo*, the prisoner of his own propaganda; he must bring home the Austrian bacon to Rome. All four leaders were responsible to the public opinion of democratic states; even the most enlightened and generous statesmen had to reduce the standards of their own thoughts to the level of popular feeling. Many Europeans regarded Wilson as little short of a new Saviour come to bring peace on earth. In Poland university men greeted one another with the word 'Wilson.' But too many had been outraged, impoverished, and wounded by a war which they regarded as entirely Germany's fault; they were in no mood to support the sort of peace that Wilson wanted.

Wilson, who had denounced 'punitive damages, the dismemberment of empires, the establishment of exclusive economic leagues,' stood steadfast for his Fourteen Points. Once, exasperated by the intransigence of his three associates, he was on the point of giving up and going home. But it is easy to see why he stayed. His departure would have been a confession of failure and would have laid him open to the charge of caring more for Germany than for the Allies — an accusation that leading Republicans were already making. And, above all, the menace of Bolshevism hung over Paris like a dark cloud. At one point Hungary went Bolshevik, and rumors that both Germany and Italy were slipping terrified the entire bourgeois-capitalist world. Any peace seemed better than prolonging the uncertainty, and if America deserted the Allies would not Bolshevism reap the profit? So Wilson stayed. In the end he was forced to agree to many compromises, but he imposed upon his colleagues something of his own ideas of a 'just' peace and wrung from them some concessions. Perhaps no one could have done more.

The Treaty of Versailles to which the Germans affixed their signature on 28 June, after a peace conference of over six months' duration, was not as drastic as France wanted, nor harsh enough to keep Germany down. It required Germany to admit her war guilt, stripped her of all colonies and commercial rights in Africa and the Far East, of Alsace-Lorraine, Posen, and parts of Schleswig and Silesia, rectified the Belgian boundary line, confiscated the coal mines of the Saar basin, imposed military and naval disarmament upon her, saddled her with an immediate indemnity of $5 billion and a future reparation bill of indeterminate amount, and placed practically the whole of her economic system under temporary Allied control. Other treaties drawn up simultaneously or shortly after recognized Czechoslovakia, greatly enlarged the territories of Italy, Rumania, and Serbia at the expense of the old Dual Monarchy, and from the historic Polish territories that had been parts of three empires, created a new Poland with a corridor to the sea.

Wilson successfully resisted some of the more extreme demands of the Allies. He prevented France from annexing the Saar basin, substituting instead a temporary control under League mandate — eventually the

Saar went back to Germany. He denied Fiume to Italy, an action which caused Orlando to withdraw from the conference in a huff. He persuaded Japan to promise an early evacuation of Shantung province, a promise which was fulfilled. He refused to permit the Allies to charge Germany with the whole cost of the war — a sum which Lloyd George estimated at approximately $120 billion — pointing out that this was 'clearly inconsistent with what we deliberately led the enemy to expect.' He resisted Clemenceau's desire to detach the entire Rhineland from Germany, the Polish demand for East Prussia, and the ambition of many to intervene actively in Russia. And finally he wrote into the treaty the covenant of the League of Nations. This, he felt, was the heart of the treaty, the part that justified the whole. 'The settlements,' he said, 'may be temporary, but the processes must be permanent.'

Wilson insisted that the League should be an integral part of the treaty, and on 25 January the Peace Conference sustained him and assigned to a special committee, of which he was chairman, the task of drawing up the League covenant. For this task he and his advisers were abundantly prepared. Since 1915 the idea of a League to Enforce Peace had been agitated in the United States and in Great Britain. The American society of that name, a British committee, and various individuals like Colonel House had plans, and all these contributed something to the final draft of the league covenant, drawn up by Sir Cecil Hurst and David Hunter Miller. The Peace Conference adopted this draft on 14 February 1919.

The League of Nations was 'to promote international co-operation and to achieve international peace and security.' Membership was open to all nations and self-governing dominions; every member nation should be represented and have an equal vote in the Assembly, which was a deliberative body, while the United States, Great Britain, France, Italy, and Japan should be permanent and four other nations temporary members of the Council, which was more largely an executive body. A secretariat, attached to the League at Geneva, and an independent Permanent Court of International Justice, established at The Hague, completed the machinery for world organization. The members of the League pledged themselves to 'respect and preserve as against external aggression the territorial integrity and existing political independence of all Members of the League' (Art. X); to bring to the attention of the League any circumstance threatening international peace; to give publicity to treaties and to armaments; to submit to inquiry and arbitration all disputes threatening international peace, breaches of treaties, and questions of international law, and refrain from war until three months after the award by the arbiters; to refrain from war with the nations complying with the award of the League; and to employ on the recommendation of the League Council, military, naval, financial, and economic sanctions against nations resorting to war in disregard of their covenants under the League. The Council was further authorized to make plans for the reduction of armaments; give publicity to treaties; exercise mandates over the former colonies of Germany and Turkey; and set up an International Labor Bureau which should have jurisdiction over conditions of labor, traffic in women and children, drugs, arms, and munitions, and the control of health. The covenant specifically recognized 'the validity of . . . regional understandings like the Monroe Doctrine.'

The President called Congress into special session to consider the treaty and the League of Nations, but when he returned to the United States, early in June, he found the Senate in an ugly mood. Opposition to the League had been growing from the time of the armistice, and prospects for ratification seemed unfavorable. The opposition was compounded of diverse elements: personal hostility to Wilson, partisanship, and senatorial pique; indignation of German-Americans who felt that their country had been betrayed, Italian-Americans angry over Fiume, Irish-Americans stirred up against England, then engaged in trying to suppress the Sinn Fein revolution; conservative disapproval of what was alleged to be leniency toward Germany, liberal disapproval of severity toward Germany; and a general feeling that Wilson and America had been tricked, and that the country should avoid future European entanglements. In the Senate three groups could be discerned. At one extreme stood the 'irreconcilables' — Borah, Johnson, Knox, Moses, McCormick, La Follette, and others who were adamant against any departure from the traditional policy of isolation and determined to undo the whole of Wilson's handiwork; at the other extreme were the President's faithful followers who were ready to ratify the treaty as it stood. In between a large number believed in the wisdom of reservations to protect American interests. At all times, during the prolonged debate over the treaty, more than three-fourths of the members of the Senate were ready to accept membership in the League in some form or other.

Both opposition to the League and support of it broke on party lines. Of the 47 Democrats in the Senate, only four were outright opponents of the treaty, a remarkable record of party solidarity. The great weakness of the Democrats was that they had almost no imposing figures who could lock horns with men like Lodge and Borah; their floor leader died during the debate, and the active leadership fell to Senator Gilbert Hitchcock of Nebraska, a man of modest talents in whom Wilson never fully confided. Yet with Democratic votes Wilson could easily overcome the irreconcilables like Borah. His crucial problem was how to cope with the pivotal group of Republican reservationists. He might be able to assuage the anxieties of mild reservationists like Senator Frank Kellogg. But the more powerful faction of strong reservationists led by Lodge were not only jealous of American sovereignty but wanted to deny the Democrats the opportunity to go to the country in 1920 as the party which had led the nation not only through a victorious war but to a successful peace. Lodge insisted on altering the treaty proposal so that it no longer bore Wilson's stamp; if this failed, he preferred to see it die.

Wilson, unwilling to accept any but the mildest 'interpretations,' showed himself almost as stubborn as the irreconcilables, although he did make some effort to conciliate his critics. Failing to make headway against the senatorial clique, he resorted to a policy which he had often before employed with spectacular success — a direct appeal to the people. On 4 September he set out on a speaking tour which carried him through the Middle West and Far West. He spoke with superb eloquence and passionate conviction. In Omaha, he warned: 'I tell you, my fellow citizens, I can predict with absolute certainty that within another generation, there will be another world war if the nations of the world do not concert the method by which to prevent it.' But against the rising tide of isolationism and illiberalism he made little headway, and much of the effect of his speeches was spoiled by the counter-arguments of the irreconcilables who stalked him relentlessly from city to city. On 25 September he spoke at Pueblo, Colorado; that night as his train sped eastward to Wichita he suffered a physical collapse. And with his collapse went all the hopes of ratification.

On 19 November 1919, the Treaty of Versailles went down to defeat in the Senate, both with and without reservations. Yet a large majority of Senators favored ratification with some kind of reservations, as did a large majority of the American people. Senator Lodge would not budge; would Wilson? Colonel House urged him to accept reservations in order to save the treaty, but his letters went unread; Bryan pleaded with him, and so did the Democratic leader, Senator Hitchcock, but in vain; the British sent over Sir Edward Grey to urge compromise, but the President would not see him. The treaty was brought up for reconsideration again in February 1920, but another full-dress debate did nothing but exacerbate tempers. The final vote came on 19 March. Twenty-three Democrats joined the twelve Republican irreconcilables to defeat ratification with reservations by a vote of 49 to 35; a change of seven Democratic votes would have approved the treaty and put the United States in the League of Nations.

'If the President desires to make a campaign issue on the treaty,' said Senator Lodge, 'the Republicans are willing to meet that issue.' The President did so desire. Calling for a 'solemn referendum' on the League of Nations, Wilson and his followers made that the issue of the presidential campaign of 1920, and went down to defeat. On 25 August 1921, almost three years after the armistice, Congress by joint resolution officially declared the war with Germany at an end.

Responsibility for the defeat of the League lies first on the Republican irreconcilables who were animated by blind partisanship, personal vindictiveness, or misguided parochialism; next on President Wilson, shattered in body but not in will, uncompromising and implacable, insulated in his own sense of virtue; and third on the handful of Democrats also lacking in courage to break with their chief and vote their convictions. Thus was sacrificed the fairest prospect for world order which had yet been opened to mankind. Thus was the world condemned to seek solutions once more along those paths which had always, in the past, led to slaughter and ruin.

Like a British prime minister with a balky Parliament, Wilson waited for the next general election to vindicate his policies and give him a more malleable legislature. The 1920 election, Wilson declared, should be 'a solemn referendum' on American membership in the League of Nations. But the League question was obfuscated in the campaign, and it never again figured as a vital issue in a national election. As early as 1922 the United States began to send 'unofficial observers' to League conferences, and by 1925 it was officially represented at a League meeting. Yet after 1920 no party dared advocate membership in the League of Nations, and the United States never took a direct part in the League's peace-keeping machinery.

7. LIQUIDATING THE WAR

No sooner had the war ended than the country moved precipitately to erase all evidence of the war experience, most especially the experiment in an enhanced role for government. 'When the war closed,' said Herbert Hoover, 'the most vital of all issues both in our own country and throughout the world was whether governments should continue their wartime ownership and operation of many instrumentalities of production and distribution.' Wilson called for a rapid liquidation of governmental activities, and legislation returning the railroads to private operation and promoting a privately owned merchant marine was passed during his administration. The twelve-year reign of the Republicans, beginning with Warren Harding's election in 1920, was marked by an insistence on private ownership and operation even of such things as airmail and hydroelectric power. 'We want,' said Harding, 'a period in America with less government in business and more business in government,' and the sentiment was echoed, in varying forms, by his successors.

The most immediate problem concerned the railroads which had been taken over and operated by the Federal Government during the war. That act had been an emergency measure, but it was felt that the roads should not be relinquished to private operation without some positive guarantees that the advantages of unified operation, achieved under government control, should be retained. The Esch-Cummins Transportation Act of 28 February 1920 differed from previous railroad regulation in that it sought to encourage rather than discourage consolidation. Dealing with the railroad system of the nation as a unit, it provided that the Interstate Commerce Commission should evaluate all railroad property and fix a 'fair return' to the stockholders and fair rates on freight and passenger traffic. A so-called recapture clause stipulated that net earnings over 6 per cent should be divided equally between the carrier and the government, the latter to use such earnings as a revolving fund for the benefit of weaker roads. The clause proved unworkable and was repealed. Furthermore, the law gave the commission complete jurisdiction over the financial operations of the railways in order to protect the investing public and its stockholders and set up a Railway Labor Board to mediate disputes about wages, hours, or working conditions. This act, together with subsequent Supreme Court decisions, effectually deprived the states of control over a large part of even intrastate commerce, and thus wrote finis to a question which had agitated the courts since the Granger cases. With the railroad system considered as a unit, it became almost impossible to distinguish between interstate and intrastate commerce.

Plenary government regulation ended the necessity for artificial competition, and the railways were encouraged to combine with a view to economical operation. To further this end, the Interstate Commerce Commission, under the guidance of Professor W. Z. Ripley, worked out a plan for the consolidation of all railroads into 19 major systems. The revolutionary character of the Esch-Cummins Act is perhaps best indicated by the fact that this Ripley plan called for the consolidation of the Northern Pacific, Great Northern, and Chicago, Burlington and Quincy railroads into one system — which had been prohibited by the Northern Securities decision of 1904 — and for the combination of the Central and Southern Pacific railroads — which had been attempted in 1911 but forbidden by the Supreme Court in 1922. Three years later a federal coordinator of railroads, Joseph B. Eastman, undertook to work out a scheme to combine all the railroads in the country in regional systems. Yet consolidation came slowly, and almost forty years later the major Eastern roads were still finding difficulty in gaining I.C.C. approval for consolidations.

The other features of the Transportation Act did not work well. The Railway Labor Board failed to prevent the railway shopmen's strike of 1922, and it was replaced, in 1926, by boards of adjustment, mediation, and arbitration with which the Federal Government had only the most tenuous connection, and the attempt to fix a 'fair rate' of return ran afoul of the old difficulty of evaluation. The effort of the Interstate Commerce Commission to estimate values upon reproduction costs of 1914 — which was thought to be near 'actual original costs' — encountered bitter opposition from the carriers who much preferred an estimate based upon costs in the 1920's. This difference of opinion — involving billions of dollars — was threshed out in the Supreme Court, and in the O'Fallon decision of 1929 the Court sustained the contention of the roads.

Meantime the whole railroad problem was changing fundamentally. For almost sixty years state and federal governments had fought to regulate railroad rates and curb railroad malpractices, and during most of that time the railroads had fought back. Now the railroads were faced with new and more formidable threats. A network of highways, built at public expense, covered the country; buses and private cars competed for passenger traffic; trucks took away freight; pipelines carried oil. Airplanes threatened to make railway travel an anachronism. Within a quarter-century the railroads were to throw in the sponge, invite federal intervention, and solicit federal aid. Unhappily, instead of managing the railroads in the public interest, the government chose to subsidize highways which scarred the countryside and spewed traffic into crowded cities, while the railroads, which in other lands were the basis of an efficient transportation system, faced extinction.

Congress took another step toward liquidating the wartime structure with the passage of the Jones Merchant Marine Act of 5 June 1920. The law permitted the Shipping Board to sell the government-owned merchant fleet to private companies, and Albert D. Lasker, the chairman of the Shipping Board who had characterized government ownership as 'poison ivy in the garden of industry,' hastened to dispose of the government ships on liberal terms. Yet the Act of 1920 failed to revive the languishing merchant marine, and in 1928 Congress passed the Jones-White bill, increasing mail subsidies, appropriating $250 million for construction loans, and authorizing the sale of the remaining government-owned vessels. This law permitted private companies to obtain first-class ships at about one-tenth original cost and underwrote the construction of 68 new vessels. The drastic decline of international trade which set in with the depression made it impossible to know whether our merchant marine might have prospered under these liberal arrangements, and the United States was further from having a self-sufficient merchant marine in 1940 than in 1920.

The government deliberately encouraged aviation by subsidizing private operation. The first airmail lines had been operated by the government, but from the beginning the ultimate objective of private operation was kept in view; in 1925 Congress authorized contracts for the transfer of airmail to private air lines, and during the following years the shift was effected. Encouraged by airmail subsidies of approximately $8 mil-

lion annually and by municipal and federal construction of airports for
the use of commercial companies, the airplane industry prospered.
Charles Lindbergh's solo flight across the Atlantic in the *Spirit of St.
Louis,* in May 1927, had caught the public imagination as nothing had
since the opening of the Panama canal, and the American public became
increasingly air-minded.

A far more vexatious problem created by the war was that of veterans'
benefits. In the years after the First World War, agitation to reward the
veteran took two forms; disability compensation and adjusted compensation for war service. To the first there could be no reasonable objection, and the government adopted a liberal policy toward disabled soldiers and their dependents, providing not only outright pensions and
hospitalization, but vocational rehabilitation. By 1936 almost 500,000
World War veterans and dependents were receiving such aid.

Of a different character was the demand for adjusted compensation,
commonly called a bonus. Many soldiers who had served for $30 a
month while their civilian friends were earning $10 or $12 a day in
industry felt that the government owed them additional compensation.
On the conclusion of the war seventeen states provided bonuses ranging
from $10 to $30 for each month of service; but the veterans wanted
something more liberal than this and looked to the Federal Government
for satisfaction. In 1922 representatives of the American Legion pushed
through Congress a bill calling for a bonus of $50 for each month of
service, but were unable to override the presidential veto. Two years
later Congress passed over Coolidge's veto an Adjusted Compensation
Act, which gave every World War veteran an endowment and insurance
policy. Some 3.5 million veterans thus received policies whose average
value was about $1000. But even this did not end the vexatious question
of the bonus, which would help drive Herbert Hoover out of office and
would trouble the administration of Franklin Roosevelt.

Yet another legacy of the war roiled the waters of international affairs.
In addition to the more than $7 billion the United States Government
lent to the Allies in the war, $3.25 billion more in loans and credits were
extended to our late associates and to some of the succession states after
the armistice. America's efforts to collect these debts involved it in a
series of abortive enterprises in which financiers like Charles G. Dawes
and Owen D. Young attempted to develop a viable relation between the

debts and German reparations. The insistence by the United States that the debts be repaid proved to the Europeans that 'Uncle Shylock' was heartless, and by June 1933 only Finland was meeting its obligations in full. The whole business addled American politics and poisoned relations with Europe for more than a decade.

8. THE UGLY AFTERMATH

The hatred generated by war does not subside when an armistice is proclaimed but lingers on to envenom the next generation. This was especially true of America's participation in World War I which terminated so abruptly it left a residue of pent-up violence that found expression in a number of ugly forms.

Between 1917 and 1925, some 600,000 Negroes moved north, a development which jeopardized the pattern of racial segregation in America. Negro soldiers returned from the war more independent and less willing to accept second-class citizenship. Southern whites responded by using violence and intimidation to compel the Negro to acquiesce in the rituals of the white supremacy. In the first year after the war, seventy Negroes were lynched, some still wearing their Army uniforms. In Washington, D.C., on a sultry Sunday in the summer of 1919, gangs of whites, many of them restless unemployed ex-servicemen, set upon isolated Negroes and beat them; two Negroes were mauled right in front of the White House. The next day, Negroes struck back, firing shots into crowds of whites, attacking a streetcar, emptying their guns at random at whites in the street. One Negro explained: 'We have been through war and gave everything, even our lives, and now we are going to stop being beat up.'

That same year the government itself contributed to the postwar acrimony by playing an active role in the Red Scare, in which Wilson's Attorney General, A. Mitchell Palmer, tried to make political capital by persecuting alien radicals. Using private spies and *agents provocateurs*, Palmer conducted a series of lawless raids on private houses and labor headquarters, rounded up several thousand aliens, and subjected them to drumhead trials. In the end some five hundred aliens were deported — many of them quite illegally; the vast majority of those arrested were found to be harmless.

Socialism as well as Communism and pacifism came under the ban,

and in 1920 the Empire State distinguished itself by expelling five Socialist members from the state legislature. It was not alleged that the party
was illegal or that the Socialist members were guilty of any crime, but
merely that socialism was 'absolutely inimical to the best interests of the
State of New York and of the United States.' This palpable violation of
elementary constitutional rights inspired vigorous protests from liberals
and conservatives alike. The distinguished Charles Evans Hughes, later
to be elevated to the chief justiceship, hastened to expose the illogic of
the Albany legislature, but his call for sanity fell on deaf ears. Even the
Supreme Court shortly revealed a spirit scarcely more enlightened than
that of legislative bodies. In two notable cases it denied citizenship to
a woman and to an elderly professor in a theological school who proclaimed their pacifism. 'I would suggest,' wrote Justice Holmes in one of
the last of his many dissenting opinions — subsequently accepted by the
Court — 'that the Quakers have done their share to make the country
what it is, that many citizens agree with the applicant's belief, and that I
had not supposed hitherto that we regretted our inability to expel them
because they believed more than some of us do in the teachings of the
Sermon on the Mount.'

Hostility to radicals, antipathy to foreigners, and a jealous protection
of the status quo were revealed in the most sensational murder trial
since that of the Haymarket anarchists — the Sacco-Vanzetti case
(1920–27). The principals, again, were foreigners and philosophical
anarchists — Nicola Sacco and Bartolomeo Vanzetti — accused of murdering a paymaster at South Braintree, Massachusetts. When they were
convicted and sentenced to death there was a widespread belief that the
jury had been moved more by their radical views and their evasion of
military service than by the evidence. For seven years men and women
of all shades of opinion and in almost every country labored to obtain a
retrial, and Governor Fuller of Massachusetts so far heeded this opinion
as to appoint an investigating committee consisting of the presidents of
Harvard and Massachusetts Institute of Technology and a judge of pro-
bate. Although this committee found the trial judge guilty of 'grave
breach of official decorum,' it reported that justice had been done. When
Sacco and Vanzetti were electrocuted on 23 August 1927, a cry of horror
at the injustice of it went around the world. Edna St. Vincent Millay
wrote:

As men have loved their lovers in times past
And sung their wit, their virtue and their grace,
So have we loved sweet Justice to the last,
That now lies here in an unseemly place.
The child will quit the cradle and grow wise
And stare on beauty till his senses drown;
Yet shall be seen no more by mortal eyes
Such beauty as here walked and here went down.
Like birds that hear the winter crying plain
Her courtiers leave to seek the clement south;
Many have praised her, we alone remain
To break a fist against the lying mouth
Of any man who says this was not so;
Though she be dead now, as indeed we know.[7]

Citizens of Massachusetts who loved justice remembered John Adams
and the Boston Massacre case and Judge Sewall's retraction in the case
of the Salem witches and hung their heads in shame.

7. Edna St. Vincent Millay, *Wine from These Grapes*, p. 43 (Harper & Brothers).

XVII

'Normalcy' and Reaction

1. RETURN TO 'NORMALCY'

The decade after the First World War, like the decade after the Civil War, featured conservatism in politics and in social philosophy. In both eras the Republican party enjoyed almost undisputed control of national affairs. It avowed the philosophy of laissez faire, but in practice made government an instrument of large corporations. Both decades saw a rapid change in manufacturing and business techniques and a florid but badly distributed industrial prosperity accompanied by agricultural distress and succeeded by acute and prolonged depression. Both were characterized by a decline in liberalism and an ardent nationalism. And both moved into the future with their eyes fixed on the past; as the post-Civil War decade looked back toward ante-bellum days, the 1920's sought to preserve the rural values of nineteenth-century America from the rude intrusion of the great city.

The point of view of the dominant group in the 1920's was best expressed by the titular leaders of the party in power. President Harding called for a 'return to normalcy,' President Coolidge announced that 'the business of the United States is business,' and President Hoover insisted that the 'American system' was a product of 'rugged individualism.' There was a bold assertion that the nation was in greater danger from 'mistaken government activity' than from 'lack of legislation,' and an acknowledgment that the government should assist and encourage business — by high tariffs, the search for markets and raw materials, a

413

suspension of embarrassing regulatory legislation, a reduction of taxation, and outright subsidies to merchant marine and aviation.

As the country approached its first postwar national election in 1920,
no national leader in either party could make an effective challenge to
the forces of reaction. Woodrow Wilson was grievously ill, Theodore
Roosevelt had died in 1919. One commentator observed: 'No voice
carries more than a hundred yards.' Unlike every other previous war in
which we had engaged, World War I produced no military hero who
aimed for a political career. The only man to come out of the war with
a brilliant reputation was Herbert Hoover, but for a time no one knew
what party he was in (Democrats like Franklin D. Roosevelt thought
well of him), and he had no organization behind him.

After years of playing second fiddle to strong leaders like Theodore
Roosevelt within their own party and to a strong-minded Democratic
President, the Republican Old Guard was determined to nominate a
pliable candidate, one who would not attempt to dictate to the Senate.
They had such a man in the undistinguished Senator from Ohio, Warren
Harding, who announced that the country needed a return to 'not heroism but healing, not nostrums but normalcy . . . not experiment but
equipoise, not submergence in internationality but sustainment in triumphant nationality.' Harding's manager, the unsavory Harry Daugherty, predicted that the Republican convention would deadlock and the
winner would be chosen by a gathering of tired men sitting in a smoke-
filled room 'about eleven minutes after two o'clock on Friday morning.'

For a time events followed Daugherty's scenario. The convention deadlocked, and in a smoke-filled suite in the Blackstone Hotel at
about 1 a.m. party leaders summoned Harding. But it was not until late
the next day that the convention, less as a result of a conspiracy in a
smoke-filled room than because Harding expressed perfectly the conservatism of the delegates, gave Warren Harding the Republican
nomination. No one was more astonished than Harding, who had been
walking around the convention with a two-day growth of beard, certain
of defeat. When he learned of his victory, Harding said, 'I feel like a
man who goes in with a pair of eights and comes out with aces full.' For
the party's vice-presidential nominee, the delegates nominated Calvin
Coolidge. Fame had recently thrust herself upon Governor Coolidge
when, in the course of a Boston police strike, he declared that there was
'no right to strike against the public safety by anybody, anywhere, any-

time.' This resounding declaration caught the imagination of a public jittery about the 'Red menace.'

The Democrats met in San Francisco, the first time that a convention had been held west of the Rockies. Badly divided, they took forty-four ballots to choose Governor James Cox of Ohio as their nominee with Franklin D. Roosevelt of New York, who had been Wilson's Assistant Secretary of the Navy, as his running mate. Wilson's followers attempted to make the election a 'great and solemn referendum' as their leader wished by pushing for a strong plank on the League. Homer Cummings ticked off the nations which had not joined the League: 'Revolutionary Mexico, Bolshevist Russia, unspeakable Turkey, and — the United States of America.' But the Wilsonian internationalists were forced to compromise with reservationists at the convention, and Cox's statements during the campaign added to the ambiguity of the Democratic position. For their part the Republicans drafted an indecipherable plank, and Harding's masterly obfuscation of the issue was his supreme intellectual achievement. One Republican observed with pardonable pride: 'One half of the speeches were for the League of Nations if you read them hastily, but if you read them with care every word of them could have been read critically against the League of Nations. The other half were violent speeches against the League of Nations if you read them carelessly, but if you read them critically every one of them could be interpreted as in favor of the League of Nations.'

The Republicans exploited the national mood of weariness with the tensions and discord of the Wilson years — the war, the draft, the meatless days and Spartan life of the war economy, the League fight, the Red Scare. Since much of this dissatisfaction found a personal target in Wilson, many of the Republicans directed their fire not against Cox but against the President. At the Republican convention, Lodge cried: 'Mr. Wilson and his dynasty, his heirs and assigns, or anybody that is his, anybody who with bent knee has served his purposes, must be driven from all control, from all influence upon the Government of the United States.' The Democrats, who were hurt by the difficulties of operating a war economy which splintered their coalition into warring interest groups, also bungled the transition from war to peace, which resulted in severe economic dislocations. The middle class was angered by the postwar inflation, labor by the cut in take-home pay after the war and the suppression of strikes. The administration, which had lost the support of many conservatives who disliked Wilson's progressive measures, was now blamed by liberals for the Palmer raids, the compromises at Versailles, and the increasingly conservative orientation of the government.

In the 1920 election the Republicans won a crushing victory which restored them as the majority party, a position they would hold for the next twelve years. With the electorate swollen by millions of new women voters, Harding won over 61 per cent of the vote, the largest proportion ever achieved in a presidential contest up to that time. He received 16 million votes to Cox's 9 million, and took 404 electoral votes to Cox's 127 by capturing the entire North and West and breaking the Solid South by carrying Tennessee. Eugene V. Debs, intellectually the most respectable of the three candidates, received a little less than a million votes, although he was serving a term in the federal penitentiary at Atlanta. The Democrats did badly in the urban Northeast; Harding swept every borough in New York City, and Cox won but one county in all New England. He suffered from northern disapproval of the conduct of the war, and the animosity of ethnic groups toward Wilson's foreign policy. Cox ran even more poorly in the West, where he lost every county on the Pacific Coast. The West continued to resent wartime controls on wheat, and it was dismayed by Wilson's failure to keep the country out of war. Although the League issue had been muddled, isolationists claimed Harding's landslide victory as a triumph for their views. The Tulsa *World* concluded: 'The voice of America . . . intones the death of internationalism.' Even more emphatically, the election marked an end to an era of political intensity and discouraged the forces of reform.

Warren Gamaliel Harding of Marion, Ohio, was a small-town politician and newspaper editor whose appearance and career recalled that of his old neighbor William McKinley. Like McKinley, Harding seemed to represent virtues dear to the American heart: simplicity, friendliness, generosity. He was a thoroughly commonplace person, without intellectual or social pretensions, disposed to let well enough alone, and sure that in the United States everything was well enough. Like McKinley, too, he was politically regular, convinced that the Republican party was the only one fit to rule and that the Old Guard had accumulated most of the wisdom of the United States. His political advancement, as McKinley's, had been promoted by local bosses and friends who expected gratitude, and Harding was not inclined to disappoint them. But unlike

McKinley, Harding was morally weak, unable to resist the influence of stronger and more unscrupulous wills or to deny the importunities of his friends.

Save for the Washington arms conference and the creation of the Bureau of the Budget, Harding's administration was barren of accomplishment and tarnished by scandal. When Harding moved into the White House, he took with him his Ohio friends, and for three years the 'Ohio gang' made the most of the opportunity. One of them, Harry Daugherty, was awarded the position of Attorney-General. If Harding found room in his cabinet for Charles Evans Hughes as Secretary of State and Herbert Hoover as Secretary of Commerce, he dismayed conservationists by naming Albert B. Fall to the Department of the Interior. Fall, with the acquiescence of Secretary of the Navy Denby, entered into a corrupt alliance with the Doheny and Sinclair interests to give them control of immensely valuable naval oil reserves. The Elk Hill reserve in California was leased to Doheny's company; the Teapot Dome reserve in Wyoming to Sinclair's. In return the government obtained some oil storage tanks in Pearl Harbor, Hawaii, and Fall got at least $100,000 from Doheny and $300,000 from Sinclair. Investigations conducted by Senator Thomas Walsh of Montana forced the resignations of Denby and Fall; civil prosecutions in the federal courts brought the cancellation of the oil leases; criminal prosecutions sent Fall and Sinclair to prison and threw a lurid light upon the activities of other oil men connected with the Sinclair and Doheny interests.

Other scandals, too, besmirched the Harding administration. Colonel Charles R. Forbes, director of the Veterans' Bureau, was charged with the corrupt sale of government property, liquor, and narcotics, and misconduct in office, and was sentenced to a term in the federal penitentiary. Colonel Thomas W. Miller, the alien-property custodian, who sold valuable German chemical patents for a song, was dismissed from office and convicted of a criminal conspiracy to defraud the government. Daugherty, who regarded his office as an opportunity to reward his friends and smite the 'Reds,' was dismissed for misconduct involving the illegal sale of liquor permits and pardons; a Senate committee found him guilty of these and other malpractices, but on a criminal trial he escaped conviction.

Harding seems to have been personally innocent of participation in or profit from this orgy of corruption, but he could not have been entirely unaware of it or of the consequences when the inevitable exposures came. Demoralized by these betrayals, his health broke; a trip to Alaska failed to restore him, and on 2 August 1923 he died. Eight years later, at the belated dedication of the Harding Memorial at Marion, Ohio, President Hoover said, 'Warren Harding had a dim realization that he had been betrayed by a few men whom he trusted, by men whom he had believed were his devoted friends. It was later proved in the courts of the land that these men had betrayed not alone the friendship and trust of their staunch and loyal friend, but they had betrayed their country. That was the tragedy of the life of Warren Harding.'

When Vice-President Coolidge succeeded Harding, Republicans breathed a sigh of relief. For Calvin Coolidge, whatever his limitations, represented probity and economy; if he displayed little zeal in tracking down the malefactors who had wrecked the Harding administration, he did not permit a continuation of their malpractices. A person of respectable mediocrity, Coolidge had little to his credit in the way of constructive legislation or political ideas and equally little to his discredit. So completely negative a man never before lived in the White House; it is characteristic that Coolidge is best remembered for his vetoes and his silence. 'Mr. Coolidge's genius for inactivity is developed to a very high point,' observed Walter Lippmann. 'It is far from being an indolent inactivity. It is a grim, determined, alert inactivity which keeps Mr. Coolidge occupied constantly.'

Yet this dour, abstemious, and unimaginative figure became one of the most popular of all American Presidents. For his frugality, unpretentiousness, and taciturnity gave vicarious satisfaction to a generation that was extravagant, pretentious, and voluble. To people who had pulled up their roots and were anxiously engaged in 'keeping up with the Joneses,' there was something vaguely comforting about the fact that Coolidge had been born in a village named Plymouth, that his first name was Calvin, that he had attended an old-fashioned New England college, that he had been content with a modest law practice and half of a two-family house in a small Massachusetts city, and that the oath of office which inducted him into the presidency had been administered in a Vermont farmhouse by his aged father, and by the light of a kerosene lamp. Actually Coolidge was democratic by habit rather than by intellectual conviction; his frugality indicated no distrust of wealth; his taciturnity no philosophic serenity; his simplicity no depth. Coolidge lacked such

Yankee traits as idealism, a desire to make the world better, and a fighting devotion to a cause. He believed in the *status quo* and regarded the
entire progressive movement since Theodore Roosevelt's day with cynical distrust. Consequently, although 'Silent Cal' had a moral integrity
wanting in his predecessor, his administration, more fully even than
Harding's, represented a return to 'normalcy.'

2. PROGRESSIVES AT BAY

The progressive movement, which had reached its zenith under Woodrow Wilson, suffered a serious setback in the 1920's. Even before the war
some of the progressives, content with such modest reforms as the short
ballot, had dropped by the way. The war, although it brought such
achievements as government labor boards and progressive taxation,
deeply divided the reformers. The aftermath was even more costly, for
progressives disagreed with one another about the League, and some of
them played an active role in the Red Scare. In the early 1920's a progressive element took part in the attempt to build a farmer-labor party,
but the effort failed, chiefly because both farmers and workers were on
the defensive throughout the decade.

During most of the 1920's, the farmer was in distress, and the government did little of value to help him out. High war prices had persuaded
the farmer to expand, with an increase in borrowings and mortgage
indebtedness, but farm prosperity did not last long enough to enable
farmers to liquidate their debts. Even more important was the collapse
of the foreign market. For a brief period, farmers took effective steps to
meet their difficulties. During the Wilson administration the Farmers'
Non-Partisan League, organized in North Dakota, spread into fifteen
states of the West. In 1916 the League captured control of the government of North Dakota and in the ensuing years enacted a far-reaching
program: state-owned warehouses and elevators, a state bank, exemption of farm improvements from taxation, creation of a hail-insurance
fund, a Home Building Association to encourage home ownership, and
the establishment of an industrial commission to organize state-owned
and state-financed industries. After the war, the more conservative
American Farm Bureau Federation came to dominate farm politics. In
the Harding regime a bipartisan 'farm bloc' pushed agrarian legislation
through Congress. But by the Coolidge era the Non-Partisan League

had disintegrated, and the farm bloc had lost much of its power.

When farm leaders came up with schemes to enlist government support for agriculture as the tariff engaged its support for industry, they ran into a stone wall in the Coolidge administration. Out of the medley of plans, two emerged: the equalization fee and the export debenture. The first, which became the controversial McNary-Haugen bill, proposed a government corporation which would buy selected farm products at a 'parity' price and sell the surpluses at a lower price in the world market; the costs would be paid by an 'equalization fee' on processing and by the taxpayer. ('Parity' would insure the farmer that the prices he received for his crops bore the same relationship to the prices of the goods he bought as had prevailed in the good years before World War I). Passed in 1927 this plan was vetoed by President Coolidge. The export debenture plan provided a 'bounty' on six agricultural commodities, to be paid in 'export debentures' that could be used for paying tariff duties, but Hoover killed this bill by the threat of a veto.

Union labor fared little better than the organized farmer. Labor's time of troubles came right after the war when the return of millions of veterans to their jobs, the threat of cheap labor and cheap products from abroad, and the cancellation of wartime contracts with its resulting drastic readjustments in industry all led to industrial unrest. More than 3000 strikes involving over 4 million workers erupted in 1919, and almost as many the following year. Business, and some elements in the government, made a concerted effort to establish the 'open shop' and to break the power of the unions, once and for all. During the 'twenties the position of organized labor deteriorated steadily; membership in unions declined from 5.1 million in 1920 to 3.6 million in 1929.

A series of spectacular strikes in steel, coal, railways, and textiles marked the beginning and the end of this decade of 'normalcy.' The most dramatic of the 1919 strikes came in the steel industry. One-third of all steel workers still labored twelve hours a day, seven days a week, and most of the rest worked a ten-hour day. The giant corporation that dominated the steel industry set itself with adamantine stubbornness against unionization; and when the steel workers demanded an eight-hour day, Judge Gary of the U.S. Steel Corporation refused even to discuss the matter with them. An impartial commission of the Federal Council of Churches reported that the grievances of labor were acute: 'the average week of 68.7 hours . . . and the underpayment of unskilled labor, are all inhumane. The "boss system" is bad, the plant organization is military, and the control autocratic.' The strike was attended with the customary violence on both sides, and in Pennsylvania the Constitution was, in effect, suspended. The Steel Corporation managed to persuade public opinion that the strike was the entering wedge of communism, and it collapsed.

The coal industry had long been sick, in the United States as in England. Coal miners worked without adequate safeguards in dangerous underground pits, and the record of accidents and deaths was appalling; the work was seasonal and many miners could count on only two or three days' work a week; miners who lived in company-owned towns could call neither their homes nor their souls their own. When in 1919 the coal miners of West Virginia went out on strike, President Wilson pronounced the walkout a violation of wartime regulations, and the governor of West Virginia used state militia to smash it. Three years later another and more widespread coal strike exploded in the 'massacre' of imported strikebreakers at Herrin, Illinois. President Harding set up a commission to study the coal situation; its report sustained most of the complaints of the miners, but no one in the government paid any attention to it. So shattered was the United Mine Workers by this series of strikes, and by hard times in the mines, that between 1920 and 1932 it declined from half a million to 150,000 members.

Railroad workers had won a signal victory in the Adamson Act of 1916, but by 1920 their wages lagged behind those of comparable labor groups, and that year the newly created Railway Labor Board authorized a substantial increase in wages. Two years later, however, a new board appointed by President Harding took a fresh look at the situation, and voted a slash in wages instead. The railway shopmen, 400,000 strong, went out on strike. The President set up a mediation board whose terms were accepted by the shopmen but rejected by the railway operators, or the bankers who controlled them, and the strike continued. At this juncture Attorney-General Daugherty invoked the law, not against the operators but against the strikers; he obtained a sweeping injunction which outlawed any word or gesture that encouraged or aided the strike in any way. The injunction was probably unconstitutional, but the strike ended before this could be determined.

The textile industry, like coal mining, had chronic difficulties. Originally centered in New England, it was now shifting to the South where

422 GROWTH OF THE AMERICAN REPUBLIC

there was less nonsense about limitations on hours of work or on child labor. Successful strikes in New England and in Paterson, New Jersey, persuaded the United Textile Workers that the time had come to invade the South. They were mistaken, for Southern textile companies owned not only their mills but the mill villages, and usually the local sheriffs and politicians as well. A strike in 1927, in Elizabethton, Tennessee, where girls worked 56 hours a week for 18 cents an hour, was broken by a combination of local vigilantes, company militia, and state troops. In 1929 the union tried to organize the textile workers of North Carolina and Virginia, but once again the familiar combination of vigilantes and police smashed both strike and strikers.

In almost every instance of industrial conflict the government threw its support to the side of management, and the courts also caught the contagion of reaction. The Supreme Court held two child-labor laws unconstitutional, one of them on grounds so untenable that they were wholly repudiated a generation later. It struck down a minimum wage law for women, sustained yellow-dog contracts, voided a Kansas statute authorizing an impartial court to set wages in business affecting the public health and safety, assessed triple damages against an unincorporated union, and threw out an Arizona anti-injunction law. Not until 1932 when the Democrats controlled both houses of Congress did the Norris-LaGuardia law erect effective safeguards against the misuse of the injunction in labor disputes and against the yellow-dog contract.

Both labor unions and farm organizations looked increasingly toward the national government to redress their grievances, but both of the major parties turned their backs. In 1924 the Republicans nominated Coolidge for a full term at a convention dominated by eastern business elements headed by the Massachusetts textile manufacturer, William Butler. The leading candidate for the Democratic nomination, Wilson's son-in-law William McAdoo, had been besmirched by the oil scandals. The oil-leasing policy had been inaugurated under a law passed in Wilson's administration; Doheny, a loyal Democrat, for years had paid an annual retainer of $50,000 to McAdoo's law firm. Not only did this make it difficult for the Democrats to make the most of the Republican scandals but the party became a national laughing stock when it took 103 ballots to choose a presidential nominee. After the convention deadlocked between McAdoo and Governor 'Al' Smith of New York, the

Democrats repeated the mistake of 1904 when they tried to compete with the Republicans by nominating an ultraconservative. John W. Davis, Solicitor-General under Wilson and Ambassador to Great Britain, was a leading Wall Street attorney. 'I have a fine list of clients,' Davis declared. 'What lawyer wouldn't want them? I have J. P. Morgan and Company, the Erie Railroad, the Guaranty Trust Company, the Standard Oil Company, and other foremost American concerns on my list. I am proud of them.' The choice of Charles W. Bryan, brother to the 'Great Commoner,' as Davis's running mate did little to remove from the ticket the taint of Wall Street. 'How true was Grant's exclamation,' observed Hiram Johnson, 'that the Democratic Party could be relied upon at the right time to do the wrong thing!'

Despairing of both major parties, leaders from the ranks of labor and farming joined with the Socialists and old Bull Moosers to run a third ticket with 'Fighting Bob' La Follette as their presidential candidate. For their vice-presidential nominee the Progressives chose Senator Burton K. Wheeler, Montana Democrat, who declared: 'When the Democratic party goes to Wall Street for its candidate I must refuse to go with it.' The Progressive platform stressed the ancient issue of anti-monopoly but also advocated public ownership of water power, downward revision of the tariff and railway rates, farm relief, abolition of the injunction in labor disputes, a federal child labor amendment, the election of all federal judges, legislation permitting Congress to override a judicial veto, the abolition of conscription, and a popular referendum on declarations of war.

At a time of boom prosperity most of the nation was satisfied enough with Republican policies to give Coolidge a lopsided victory with more than 54 per cent of the vote to Davis's less than 29 per cent, the least ever registered by a Democratic presidential candidate. Davis, with 136 electoral votes to Coolidge's 382, won only 12 states, all in the South. La Follette ran ahead of Davis in much of the West, and with nearly 5 million votes (better than 16 per cent) he made a respectable showing. But his failure to win any state but his own Wisconsin shattered the movement for a farmer-labor party, and his death the following year deprived the Progressives of their commander. Many of the reformers simply waited out the rest of the decade.

3. THE NEW ERA

Businessmen interpreted Coolidge's victory as a ratification of the policies of the 'New Era' in which a benevolent capitalism would develop the American economy in the national interest. In the Coolidge years the nation reaped the benefits from the application of electricity to manufacturing and the adoption of the scientific management theories of Frederick Winslow Taylor. In 1914, electricity operated only 30 per cent of American factory machinery; by 1929, it sparked 70 per cent. The war nurtured an American chemical industry, and the electrochemical revolution drastically altered factory procedures and improved output in industries like petroleum and steel. As a consequence of all these changes, the productivity of the worker increased at a startling rate and the real income of each person gainfully employed rose from $1308 in 1921 to $1716 in 1929.

These spectacular achievements added to the stature of the businessman and encouraged Republican administrations to heed his demands, such as tax reduction. Instead of liquidating the public debt of $24 billion left by the war, Secretary of the Treasury Andrew Mellon, an aluminum magnate who held this post under all three Republican presidents, sought to reduce taxes, especially the steep war levies. For a few years, an alliance of Democrats and Republican progressives balked him, but after the 1924 landslide Democratic conservatives outdid the Coolidge administration in calling for reductions on taxes for the well-to-do and on conservatives. A series of revenue acts wiped out excess profit levies, drastically reduced surtaxes, granted rebates on 'earned income' and refunds to corporations of over $3.5 billion. This policy encouraged speculation and transferred much of the burden of taxation from the rich to the middle and poorer classes. Thus under Mellon's benign direction, taxes on incomes of a million dollars fell from $600,000 to $200,000. Yet notwithstanding these reductions, the national debt was lowered by 1930 to $16 billion. No wonder the business community asserted with one voice that Andrew W. Mellon was 'the greatest Secretary of the Treasury since Hamilton.'

This policy of tax reduction, however, was not maintained with respect to the most pervasive of all taxes — the tariff. The Underwood tariff had never really been tried under normal conditions, for the war itself afforded protection to American manufactures and fostered the establishment of new industries. On the conclusion of the war these 'infant' industries — chemicals, dyes, toys, hardware, rayon, and so forth — clamored for protection. Fearful that the United States would be inundated with the produce of depressed European labor, a Republican Congress, in March 1921, pushed through an emergency tariff bill which Wilson promptly vetoed. 'If there ever was a time when America had anything to fear from foreign competition,' he observed in his veto message, 'that time has passed. If we wish to have Europe settle her debts, governmental or commercial, we must be prepared to buy from her.' But this elementary logic failed to sink in.

Within a month of his accession to the presidency, Harding announced that 'the urgency for an instant tariff cannot be too much emphasized.' Congress responded with the emergency tariff of 27 May 1921, historically important because its prohibitive agricultural schedules, while affording no actual relief to farmers with surplus crops to sell, did commit them to the principle of protection. More important was the Fordney-McCumber tariff of 19 September 1922, which established rates higher than ever before in our history. Duties on sugar, textiles, pig iron, rails, and chinaware were restored to the old Payne-Aldrich level, while increases on toys, hardware, chemicals, dyes, and lace ranged from 60 to 400 per cent. The law also authorized the President, on recommendation of the tariff commission, to raise or lower duties as much as 50 per cent, but Harding and Coolidge used this discretionary authority only thirty-seven times. Thirty-two of these changes, including such things as butter, cheese, pig iron, and chemicals were upward; on five articles duties were reduced. These five were mill feed, bobwhite quail, paint-brush handles, cresylic acid, and phenol, but there was no Mr. Dooley to see the joke. The Fordney-McCumber act provoked a tariff war which cut seriously into our foreign trade, persuaded many manufacturers to establish branch plants abroad, and inspired among the large manufacturers and bankers their first serious misgivings about the wisdom of protection.

Continued prosperity, however, confirmed the Republicans in their devotion to high tariffs, and the shift in Democratic strength from the rural South to the industrial North tempered that party's traditional hostility to protection. In the campaign of 1928 the Republicans reaffirmed their faith in the economic blessings of high tariffs, and the Democrats hedged on the issue. There was no urgent need for further tariff revision, but no sooner was Hoover inaugurated than he summoned Congress in special session to consider farm relief and 'limited changes in the tariff.' The new Hawley-Smoot tariff bill represented increases all along the line, but particularly in minerals, chemicals, dyestuffs, and textiles. Objections from the American Bankers Association and from industries with foreign markets were brushed aside and a vigorous protest from 1028 economists had no effect on President Hoover, who signed the bill on 17 June 1930. The reaction was immediate: within two years twenty-five countries established retaliatory tariffs, and American foreign trade took a further slump.

Yet the Republican administrations could not be impervious to considerations of foreign markets, raw materials, and investments. During the First World War the position of the United States had changed from a debtor to a creditor nation. American private investments abroad, estimated at less than $3 billion before the war, increased to $14 billion by 1932. These investments were distributed over all parts of the globe and in every variety of business: government bonds, railroads, utilities, manufactures, mines, oil, fruit, sugar, rubber, and so forth. Part of this investment reflected the determination of American industry to control its own sources of raw material, and in this policy the government co-operated, just as governments had co-operated in the mercantilism of the seventeenth and eighteenth centuries. It encouraged foreign trade associations, discovered new trade opportunities abroad, and helped American oil interests obtain concessions in Latin America and in the Middle East.

Characteristically, the neo-mercantilists of the 1920's fostered large-scale combinations. Herbert Hoover, as Secretary of Commerce, inaugurated a policy of 'alliance with the great trade associations.' His sense of engineering efficiency was outraged at the spectacle of competition with its inevitable waste, and in his first report as Secretary of Commerce he proposed modifications of the Sherman Act to permit business organizations to combine for purposes of information, standardization, arbitration of industrial disputes, elimination of unfair practices, transportation, and research. He placed his department at the disposal of business as a clearing house for exchange of information; and under his auspices, trade associations not only pooled information, advertising, insurance, traffic, and purchases, but drew up codes of fair practice.

Big Four at Versailles (left to right: Lloyd George, Orlando, Clemenceau, Wilson)

KKK Parade in Long Branch, New Jersey, on 4 July 1924

Charles Lindbergh (*c.* 1927)

Oliver Wendell Holmes (1841-1935) by Charles Hopkinson

William James (1842-1910) by Ellen Emmet (Rand)

Ernest Hemingway (1899-1961)   F. Scott Fitzgerald (1896-1940)

Sinclair Lewis (1885-1951)   Eugene O'Neill (1888-1953)

Ezra Pound (1885–1972)
Photograph by Boris de Rachewiltz

T. S. Eliot (1888-1965)

John Dewey (1859-1952)

Robert Frost (1875-1963)

William Faulkner (1897-1962)

Over two hundred such codes were in existence at the end of the Hoover administration. 'We are passing,' said Hoover perspicaciously, 'from a period of extreme individualistic action into a period of associational activities.'

In part as a result of this official encouragement, the concentration of control in American industry and banking grew apace. The decade from 1919 to 1929 saw 1268 combinations in manufacturing and mining, involving the merging of some 4000 and the disappearance of some 6000 firms. The same process took place in utilities, finance, transportation, and trade. In the eight years after the war 3744 public utility companies disappeared through merger. In 1920 there were 30,139 banks; fifteen years later the number had been reduced by failures and mergers to 16,053. In 1920 the twenty largest banking institutions in the country held about 14 per cent of all loans and investments; ten years later the proportion had increased to 27 per cent. One great corporation came to dominate the telephone, and one the telegraph systems. In retail trade, chain stores ate heavily into the business of the independent shopkeeper. The inevitable result of this process was the domination of American industry, transportation, and finance by giant corporations. In 1933, some 594 corporations, each capitalized at $50 million or more, owned 53 per cent of all corporate wealth in the country; the other 387,970 owned the remaining 47 per cent.

In few fields had concentration gone further than in the realm of hydroelectric power. In the years after World War I the electric light and power industry grew with extraordinary rapidity; between 1917 and 1932 production increased more than threefold and capitalization more than fourfold, to over $12 billion. Largely through the holding-company device, control over power production was concentrated in the hands of six giant financial groups — General Electric, Insull, Morgan, Mellon, Doherty, and Byllesby.

Senators Walsh of Montana, La Follette of Wisconsin, and the indomitable Norris of Nebraska led the most important contest in this sphere, that for government operation of the water-power dams at Muscle Shoals on the Tennessee river. These had been constructed to furnish power for nitrate plants during World War I, at the conclusion of which conservatives wanted to turn them over to private companies. President Coolidge recommended that the property be sold to the highest bidder and vetoed a bill providing for government operation of the dams. But the high cost of privately produced electricity and the depression kept the power issue alive; and in 1931 Congress once more passed the Norris bill, calling for the construction of a second dam on the Tennessee river and for government manufacture and sale of fertilizer and power. President Hoover issued a veto message:

> I am firmly opposed to the Government entering into any business the major purpose of which is competition with our citizens. . . . This bill raises one of the important issues of Federal Government ownership and operation of power and manufacturing business not as a minor by-product but as a major purpose. . . . I hesitate to contemplate the future of our institutions, of our country, if the preoccupation of its officials is to be no longer the promotion of justice and equal opportunity but is to be devoted to barter in the markets. That is not liberalism, it is degeneration.

Even this *ex cathedra* statement as to the nature and purposes of government, however, did not settle the matter. Two years later, with the creation of the Tennessee Valley Authority, the Roosevelt administration entered jauntily upon the course of 'degeneration.'

4. THE QUEST FOR PEACE

Although all three Republican administrations followed a generally isolationist course, American traditions dictated effective co-operation for disarmament and the outlawry of war. In the first year of office President Harding, pursuant to a resolution sponsored by Senator Borah, called a conference of the nine powers with interests in the Pacific area to consider a limitation on armaments. On 12 November 1921 delegates from the United States, Great Britain, France, Italy, Belgium, Holland, Portugal, China, and Japan heard Secretary Hughes propose an itemized plan for scrapping warships and limiting naval armaments to prevent a naval 'race.' The United States, Great Britain, Japan, France, and Italy agreed upon a program calling for the maintenance of a battleship and carrier ratio of 5-5-3 for the first three countries and 1.7 for the others, the scrapping of designated ships, and a ten-year naval holiday in the construction of capital ships.

At the time, this Washington Treaty of 1922 and the London Naval Treaty of 1930, which extended its provisions to other classes of ships, were regarded as outstanding victories for peace. Yet no well-meaning reform of the twentieth century, except prohibition, proved so disappointing as naval limitation. The United States sacrificed an opportunity to become the world's greatest naval power, which in the troublous years ahead could have made her an effective keeper of the world's peace. The U.S. Navy scrapped 15 new capital ships on which over $300 million had already been spent, and no other nation had a comparable building program with which to match this sacrifice. Britain retained the prestige of parity at the expense of weakening the naval power that in a few years' time would be essential to her existence. And, in order to induce Japan to consent to the 5-5-3 ratio, the United States and Great Britain had to agree not to strengthen any of their fortifications and naval bases in the Pacific between Singapore and Hawaii. This action virtually doubled the value of Japanese tonnage quotas for naval operations in the Orient and rendered the defense of Guam, Singapore, and the Philippines virtually impossible. Moreover, in spite of these concessions, Japan was insulted rather than appeased; their militarists used the slogan '5-5-3' to discredit the liberal government which had accepted limitation, and to get into power. When that had been accomplished, at the end of 1934 Japan denounced the naval-limitation treaties and started a frenzied building program which, by the time war broke out in the Pacific, rendered the Japanese navy more powerful in every type of ship than the United States and British Pacific and Asiatic fleets combined. And American and British budgets, now geared to meager naval appropriations, followed suit slowly and reluctantly.

The Washington conference was designed not only to achieve disarmament but to avoid conflict in the Far East where Americans had to deal with three major elements. First there was the great and ancient empire of China, nominally a republic on the Western model since 1912 but actually torn by civil wars between generals that left little power to the national government. Second there was the ancient but streamlined empire of Japan, nominally a constitutional monarchy but actually at the mercy of the Emperor's army leaders whenever they chose to assert their authority. Japan by 1920 had acquired an economic position in the Orient similar to that of Britain in the Occident a century earlier; by techniques learned in the West, combined with native energy, the Japanese had built up an industrial empire in textiles, steel, and consumer goods that was capturing the former European-dominated markets all around the Pacific. Underneath this modern industrial skill, however, Japan was a country of primitive ideas, where the military were venerated, *Bushido* (the code of the warrior) was the highest morality, and *Hakko Ichiu* — 'bringing the eight corners of the world under one roof,' the probably mythical slogan of a possibly mythical Emperor in 600 B.C. — lay in the back of the popular mind. Unless Westernized liberal elements kept control of the Japanese government, Japan, like Germany in 1914, would not be content with industrial expansion but would go in for foreign conquest. And third, there was the colossus of Russia. Her new leaders had not forgotten the humiliating defeat that Japan had inflicted upon their nation in 1905; they burned with resentment against the Allied powers who had invaded her territories in her hour of mortal peril; they were conscious of a great historical past and determined to have a greater future.

The Anglo-Japanese alliance gave Japan a welcome excuse to participate in World War I, from which she profited greatly. First she seized the German islands in the North Pacific and the German concessions in Shantung. Then she took advantage of the involvement of the European powers and the isolation of the United States to consolidate her position in Manchuria and to browbeat China into submission to her will.

Early in 1915 the Japanese government presented to China, in the form of an ultimatum, Twenty-one Demands that would give her a practical protectorate over China more complete than any the United States had ever exercised over Cuba. They were a clear violation of the Root-Takahira agreement of 1908 to maintain the independence and territorial integrity of China and the 'open door' for commerce. Bryan protested, but he acted from a position of weakness rather than of strength. For it was just at this time that California, contemptuously rejecting President Wilson's plea for moderation, went ahead with its program of forbidding Japanese to own land in the state. Such discriminatory legislation clearly violated the most-favored nation agreement with Japan, and outraged the Japanese, who found it difficult to distinguish between an affront from the United States and one from one of its sovereign states. Therefore, when Bryan informed the Japanese government that the United States would not recognize any impairment of American rights, or of the territorial integrity or political sovereignty of China, the Japanese abandoned a few of their extreme demands, forced China to accept the others, and continued a stealthy but sure advance toward domination of the Far East. Secret agreements with the European powers secured support for the Japanese claim to Shantung, the German islands in the Pacific, and special concessions in China. In 1917 Viscount Ishii came to the United States on a special mission to quiet American apprehension of Japanese policies and obtain definite recognition of Japan's 'paramount' interest in China. From the point of view of the Japanese, the Lansing-Ishii Agreement of 2 November 1917 accomplished just that, but the American interpretation of the agreement was very different. It reaffirmed the 'open door,' pledged both nations to respect the independence and territorial integrity of China, and disclaimed any desire for 'special rights or privileges.' At the same time, however, it specifically recognized that 'territorial propinquity creates special relations, and that Japan has special interests in China, particularly in that part to which her possessions are contiguous.' At the Paris Peace Conference Japan succeeded in legalizing her claims to Shantung and the former German islands in the Pacific.

This was the situation which confronted President Harding in 1921. The 'open' door had been partly shut, the territorial integrity and political sovereignty of China had been impaired, and Japan had entrenched herself firmly in Shantung, Manchuria, Mongolia, and eastern Siberia. Most of the agreements, declarations, and understandings by which the United States had sought to impose her own policy upon Japan had proved to be scraps of paper, and short of war — which nobody wanted — there was no way by which she could enforce them.

From this embarrassing situation the United States tried to extricate herself by the Washington Conference. The American government aimed to convert bilateral into multilateral understandings, thus freeing the United States from sole responsibility for a policy which she could not in any event enforce and making that responsibility a common one. By the Four Power Treaty (13 December 1921) the United States, Great Britain, France, and Japan engaged mutually to 'respect their rights in relation to their insular possessions in the region of the Pacific Ocean' and pledged themselves to confer about any controversy that might arise over these rights. By the Nine Power Treaty (6 February 1922) the same powers, plus Italy, Belgium, the Netherlands, Portugal, and China, agreed to respect China's sovereignty, independence, and territorial and administrative integrity, maintain the principle of the 'open door,' and refrain from creating 'spheres of influence,' seeking privileges or concessions, or abridging therein the rights and privileges of citizens of friendly states. The Four Power Treaty buried the Anglo-Japanese alliance, and the Nine Power pact gave treaty form to the open door. But these agreements had one serious weakness: they set up no machinery for enforcement.

Lack of enforcement machinery was also the glaring weakness of the Pact of Paris, sometimes known as the Kellogg Peace Pact. When in 1927 the French foreign minister, Aristide Briand, offered a bilateral treaty to the United States for the outlawry of war, Secretary of State Frank B. Kellogg countered with the suggestion of a multilateral treaty of the same character. The result of these negotiations, the Pact of Paris of 27 August 1928, provided that the contracting powers 'condemn recourse to war for the solution of international controversies, and renounce it as an instrument of national policy,' and that 'the settlement or solution of all disputes or conflicts of whatever nature or of whatever origin they may be . . . shall never be sought except by pacific means.' Adhered to eventually by 62 nations, it was ratified by the United States Senate on 15 January 1929 by a vote of 81 to 1. The most thoroughgoing commitment to peace that great powers ever made, the Pact of Paris may fairly be called an attempt to keep peace by incantation.

Little more than three years after the Pact of Paris was negotiated, Japanese militarists riddled its pretensions. World War II in the Far East really began on 18 September 1931 when General Hayashi, seizing the excuse of a bomb explosion on the South Manchuria Railway, moved his army into Manchuria and overran that great Chinese province. The Japanese government, which had not authorized this 'Manchuria Incident,' was forced to acquiesce under threat of assassination, and in 1932 Japan declared Manchuria the independent kingdom of Manchukuo, under a puppet monarch.

This, of course, violated the Nine Power Treaty, the Kellogg Pact, and the Covenant of the League of Nations, by each of which Japan was bound; all but the last of these concerned the United States. Secretary of State Henry L. Stimson met the Japanese aggression by enunciating the Stimson doctrine of refusing to recognize forceful acquisitions of territory. He also talked about joining with Britain and the League in a threat of economic sanctions against Japan. But President Hoover was alarmed equally by the prospect that we might get into war with Japan or that we might get involved in too close an association with the League. When the British minister, Sir John Simon, asked for assurance of American co-operation with League of Nations sanctions, Hoover refused, and Japan went right ahead with her aggressions. Hoover's conduct in this episode is a classic example of the futility of relying on purely moral suasion when dealing with international banditry.

5. THE METAMORPHOSIS OF THE MONROE DOCTRINE

Modification of the Monroe Doctrine had been inaugurated, in theory at least, by Wilson's administration. The Mobile address had held out the promise of a new Latin-American policy, and the A.B.C. Conference at Niagara Falls recognized the right of South American states to co-operate in the formulation of policies affecting the Western Hemisphere. Yet Wilson himself, as we have seen, was not constant to his ideal; the occupation of Vera Cruz and intervention in Nicaragua and Hispaniola caused his sincerity to be seriously questioned south of the Rio Grande. To his successors he left a heritage not only of fine principles but of tough problems, such as the protection of oil and mineral investments in Mexico and the Caribbean occupations. His successors subscribed to his principles but liquidated his problems.

Mexico was the center of trouble for six years. Article 27 of the Constitution of 1917 had vested in the Mexican nation ownership of all mineral and oil resources, and limited future concessions to Mexican nationals. American investments in mining and oil amounted to about $300 million; if Article 27 should be interpreted as retroactive, all that would be confiscated. President Obregon, who succeeded Carranza, would not at once commit himself in regard to the interpretation of this article. Consequently President Wilson refused to recognize his government, and the Harding administration declined to do so unless Mexico gave formal guarantees that American interests would not suffer. Obregon, resenting this demand as an affront to Mexican sovereignty, refused. There followed a war of hard words for two years, during which American troops were deployed along the Rio Grande, and war seemed imminent. At this juncture a timely decision of the Mexican Supreme Court, holding that Article 27 was not retroactive, averted a crisis, and negotiations in the summer of 1923 resulted in the resumption of friendly relations.

The new President, Plutarco Calles, favored nevertheless a retroactive interpretation of the troublesome Article 27, and at the same time promoted agrarian legislation that threatened American land investments and ecclesiastical legislation that affronted Roman Catholics. Secretary Kellogg, who had succeeded Hughes in the State Department, declared:

> The government of Mexico is now on trial before the world. . . . We have been patient and realize, of course, that it takes time to bring about a stable government, but we cannot countenance violation of her obligations and failure to protect American citizens.

Despite this threat, the Calles government remained firm. Kellogg, unable to enlist popular support for an aggressive defense of American oil interests, early in 1927 dragged the red herring of Communism across the controversy and, further to complicate the issue, accused the Mexican government of opposing American policy in Nicaragua. Nevertheless, on 25 January 1927 the Senate voted unanimously to arbitrate the Mexican controversy.

Sobered by this rebuke, President Coolidge appointed as ambassador to Mexico his Amherst classmate, Dwight W. Morrow, a member of the House of Morgan who had publicly avowed his opposition to 'dollar diplomacy.' Through a remarkable combination of character, intelligence, shrewdness, and charm, Morrow succeeded in repairing most of the damage that his predecessors in Mexico City and his superiors in Washington had done. In response to new Supreme Court rulings the Mexican Congress modified some of its oil and mineral legislation in line with American objections, while Morrow obtained an adjustment of land questions, claims, and the Church question. Throughout the decade of the 1930's this new understanding so auspiciously inaugurated by Morrow remained undisturbed, while in the United States a widespread admiration for Mexican culture (especially the paintings of Rivera and Orozco) and a growing appreciation of the social ideals of the Mexican revolution made a good base for the future. And, in contrast to World War I, when Mexico was a center of German propaganda, the Southern Republic loyally supported the United States in World War II.

Elsewhere in the Caribbean the United States declined to pick up the 'big stick' that Theodore Roosevelt, Taft, and Wilson had successively brandished. Impatience of public opinion with 'dollar diplomacy' was back of it, but the Caribbean countries co-operated by an awakened sense of order, and American investments in them increased to a point where their direct influence on the local governments rendered the old cry 'Send the Marines!' unnecessary. Americans owned about one-third of the wealth of Cuba, while investments in Central America amounted to almost $300 million. In 1924 the Dominican flag displaced the American in that distracted republic. In 1925 United States marines were withdrawn from Nicaragua; they returned that same year to put down a revolution and supervise elections, but the acrimonious criticism which greeted this brief revival of intervention led to a more circumspect policy and eventually to a final withdrawal in 1933. Indeed, it was upon the foundation of the Latin American policy of Herbert Hoover that Franklin Roosevelt built his Good Neighbor Policy.

6. NINETEENTH-CENTURY AMERICA'S LAST STAND

In the years after World War I the older America of the Protestant, old-stock culture felt deeply threatened by the burgeoning city and erected barriers against change. The census of 1920 revealed that for the first time most Americans lived in urban areas, a frightening statistic for those on the farms and in small towns whose way of life had prevailed for three centuries. They attributed to the metropolis all that was perverse in American society: the revolution in morals associated with the flapper and Sigmund Freud, the corner saloon, the control of government by urban immigrants, and the modernist skepticism of the literal interpretation of the Bible.

Religious fundamentalism, which gained new strength from the conviction that modernism was an import from Germany, America's enemy in World War I, took an aggressive form after the war. Under the leadership of William Jennings Bryan, now turned crusader for religious orthodoxy, several southern states enacted laws forbidding the teaching of evolution in state-supported schools. In 1922 Bryan moved into Kentucky and kicked up a storm; an anti-evolution measure failed by only a single vote. That same year, a Kentucky father removed his children from school because the teacher declared the earth was round; hauled into court, he convinced the judge that the world was flat, and the teacher was dismissed. In 1923 the Oklahoma legislature passed a measure forbidding schools to use any textbook containing the 'Darwin theory of creation.'

In 1925 the whole country became caught up in the fundamentalist controversy when a high-school biology teacher, John T. Scopes, was tried for violating a Tennessee statute forbidding the teaching of evolution. To Dayton, Tennessee, swarmed armies of reporters to watch William Jennings Bryan, who joined the prosecution, match wits with Clarence Darrow, the iconoclastic attorney. Into the town came colporteurs, itinerant hymn singers, and chimpanzee-swinging circus men who hoped to be called to testify at the 'monkey trial.' The roads leading into Dayton were placarded with signs: 'Where Will You Spend Eternity?' and 'Sweethearts, Come to Jesus,' and each night revivalists held meetings by lantern light. Through it all Bryan marched serenely, walking the streets of Dayton in shirtsleeves and a pith helmet, the idol of the town. But on the witness stand Bryan was subjected to a savage examination by Darrow, who revealed the ignorance of the Commoner and spotlighted the inconsistencies of his argument. Bryan said at Dayton: 'Thank God I am going to spend the latter years of my life in a locality where there is a belief in God, and in the Son of God, and in a civilization to be based on salvation through blood.' Within a few days after his ordeal, Bryan was dead, and with him died much of the older America. The judge found Scopes guilty; the anti-evolution laws remained on the statute books; but the fundamentalist crusade, although it now had a martyr, no longer had the same force.

The impulse to use coercion to preserve the values of the older America took a much uglier form in the creation of the Ku Klux Klan. Founded in 1915 by Colonel William Joseph Simmons, a Methodist circuit rider who had been a member of numerous fraternal orders and who appears to have derived his title from his rank in the Woodmen of the World, the KKK got off to a very slow start. In 1920, it probably had fewer than 2000 members, but that year applicants clamored to join the order.

An organization of white, native-born Protestants, the Klan was aggressively anti-Negro, but its chief ethnic target was not the Negro but the Catholic. The Klan fought Catholic influence with a humorless fanaticism. Some members of the KKK believed President Harding had died from hypnotic telepathic thought waves directed at him by the Jesuits, and one zealot even thought the sinking of the *Titanic* was an expression of God's wrath at immigrants and Catholics. The chief organ of the KKK in Illinois advertised '12 red hot anti-Catholic postcards, all different.' The Klan was also anti-Semitic and anti-foreign-born. The Catholics, it argued, dominated the nation's politics; the Jews, the country's economy.

Although the Klan was founded in Georgia, it had its greatest strength not in the Deep South but in the Midwest, where the dominant figure was the Grand Dragon of the Realm of Indiana, David Stephenson; it was also powerful in the Southwest and the Far West. It appealed especially to those who felt themselves losing out to the increasingly powerful city. In its war against 'metropolitan morality' the Klan blamed the city for the waning of church influence over young people, the defiance of parental control, and the jettisoning of the old moral code. It opposed all the forces turning cities into 'modern Sodom and Gomorrahs.' To compel adherence to its moral code, the KKK employed social ostracism against individuals judged guilty of moral infractions, but it also sometimes resorted to violence — church burnings, lynchings, mutilations, and whippings.

The Klan had a reciprocal relationship to the evils it attacked. It denounced city vices, but was drawn to them. It appealed for law and order, and resorted to violence; demanded civic virtue, but once in office engaged in wholesale corruption. It insisted on sexual purity, but throughout its history became implicated in sexual scandals. There was something close to pathological about the attitude of some Klansmen toward sex and violence, and it is fitting that an act of sexual sadism should have brought about the downfall of the Klan in its Indiana stronghold.

Wherever it had strength, the Klan reached out for political power. In some states the KKK was so potent that elections were held in Klaverns before the regular primaries. Five U.S. Senators and at least four governors were Klansmen. The Klan infiltrated both major parties. In 1924, it captured the Republican primaries in Colorado, elected a governor, one house of the legislature, several judges and sheriffs, and the Denver chief of police. In Alabama, it ended the career of the veteran Senator Oscar Underwood, whom it denounced as the 'Jew, jug, and Jesuit candidate,' and replaced him with Hugo Black, who accepted a gold-engraved life membership in the KKK. In the 1924 presidential campaign it silenced the Republicans and fractured the Democrats, who voted not to mention the Klan by name, 543 $\frac{3}{20}$ to 542 $\frac{3}{20}$. No longer did the KKK hide in the shadows. On 8 August 1925, in a brazen assertion of their strength, more than 50,000 Klansmen marched for 3 hours and 30 minutes down Pennsylvania Avenue in the nation's capital.

But the Klan declined even more rapidly than it rose to power. It was fought by the various ethnic groups it attacked; by liberals and old-stock conservatives; by corruptionists and bootleggers; and by courageous southern governors and mayors. In Indiana in 1925, after a sordid episode, Stephenson was convicted of second-degree murder and sentenced to life imprisonment. When the governor refused to come to his aid, Stephenson made public the corruption and violence in the order. Within a year, the Klan was headed downhill, and by the end of the decade only small pockets of power remained.

Many who abhorred the Klan shared the order's conviction that the older Americans of Anglo-Saxon stock owned the United States and its fear that republican institutions were being undermined by the tidal wave of European immigrants. During the 'twenties Congress enacted three sweeping laws which drastically limited immigration. The Act of 1921 restricted the total number of aliens who would be admitted from outside the Western Hemisphere to 357,000; the more drastic Act of 1924 set up a quota system that discriminated sharply in favor of the 'old' and against the 'new' immigration; the Act of 1929 reduced the total who might come in to 150,000 a year. As a result of this legislation, of Department of Labor rulings excluding any who might become a public charge, and, above all, of the Great Depression, immigration from the Old World fell to about 35,000 during the 1930's, while during that decade almost 100,000 more aliens returned to their homes than came to America.

At the very outset of the decade rural America had scored an emphatic victory when the Eighteenth Amendment, forbidding the 'manufacture, sale or transportation of intoxicating liquors,' went into effect in January 1920. Prohibition permitted the Protestant countryside to coerce the Newer Americans in the city to accept its abstemious way of life. One 'dry' asserted: 'Our nation can only be saved by turning the pure stream of country sentiment and township morals to flush out the cesspools of cities and so save civilization from pollution.' Many of the drys believed that the Eighteenth Amendment was a landmark in the development of civilization. Dr. Louis Henry Smith, president of Washington and Lee University, called prohibition 'the longest and most effective step forward in the uplift of the human race ever taken by any civilized nation.'

In the cities opposition to prohibition, once strongest among foreign-born workingmen, spread through every class of society, and the thirst for liquor was sublimated into a philosophy of 'personal liberty.' The satirical essayist H. L. Mencken claimed that prohibition had caused suffering comparable only to that of the Black Death and the Thirty Years War, and Dr. Samuel Harden Church, president of the Carnegie Institute of Technology, told a Senate committee that rum was 'one of the greatest blessings that God has given to men out of the teeming bosom of Mother Earth.' Drinking not only continued, but even became fashionable; the corner saloon gave way to the speakeasy, and home-brewing became a national pastime. States with large urban populations sabotaged prohibition laws just as Northern states had once nullified the fugitive slave acts. Agents of the Prohibition Bureau entered into corrupt alliances with bootleggers like Chicago's vicious Al Capone, and there was a breakdown not only of law but of respect for the law.

Both political parties tried to avoid the troublesome issue, but without success. The Republicans, in office during most of the life of national prohibition, and strongest in rural, Protestant communities, were inclined to stand behind what Hoover called 'an experiment noble in motive and far-reaching in purpose.' The Democrats were in a quandary. Their strength came in almost equal proportions from southern and western rural constituencies which were immovably dry and northern industrial constituencies which were incurably wet. In the Northeast Democratic leaders reflected the rage of foreign-born and second-generation Americans at the moralistic attitudes of the drys. 'The government which stands against the founder of Christianity cannot survive,' declared Senator David I. Walsh of Massachusetts. If Christ came back to earth and performed the Cana miracle again, 'he would be jailed and possibly crucified again.' But Democratic leaders like William Jennings Bryan and Cordell Hull found their Methodist and Baptist followers no less intensely in favor of prohibition. This division almost split the party in 1924 and deeply affected the outcome of the 1928 election.

In 1928 the Democrats, who had been impaled on the urban-rural split four years earlier, decided to ride with the forces of urbanism by nominating Alfred E. Smith, the able governor of New York and *beau ideal* of the newer Americans from the slums of the great cities. A product of the 'Sidewalks of New York,' he was a Tammany brave, wringing wet, and the first lifetime city-dweller to receive the presidential designation of a major party. The *New Republic* observed: 'For the first time, a representative of the unpedigreed, foreign-born, city-bred, many-tongued recent arrivals on the American scene has knocked on the door and aspired seriously to the presiding seat in the national Council Chamber.' The 1928 election would be perceived as a test of how widely this group had won acceptance, and as a challenge to the continued pre-eminence of other groups. 'Here is no trivial conflict,' wrote Walter Lippmann. 'Here are the new people, clamoring . . . and the older people defending their household gods. The rise of Al Smith has made the conflict plain, and his career has come to involve a major aspect of the destiny of American civilization.'

Since the Democrats were as solicitous as the Republicans of business interests in 1928, they erased any real difference on economic issues be-tween the candidates, permitting much of the campaign to revolve around a single fact: that for the first time in American history a major party had nominated a Roman Catholic for President. The minister of the First Methodist Church of Lynn, Massachusetts, called Smith 'the greatest menace that has faced America since the Civil War,' and the pastor of Oklahoma City's largest Baptist Church warned: 'If you vote for Al Smith you're voting against Christ and you'll all be damned.' Smith's detractors not only whispered that if he were elected all Prot-estant children would be declared bastards, but distributed photographs of Governor Smith at the dedication of the Holland Tunnel in 1927 and charged that he was planning to extend the tunnel to the basement of the Vatican.

When bigots were not warning that Smith's election would make the White House an outpost of the Vatican, they were depicting the election of a wet like Smith as a religious affront to rural Protestants. An edi-torial in the *Christian Endeavor World* entitled 'City against Country' proclaimed:

> 'The wet city is trying to impose its will on the dry country. The wet north on the dry South!'
> 'What is to be done about it?'
> 'In the cities the Christian vote must be got out on election day.'

If the Christian vote did not go to the polls, 'we shall see our towns and villages rumridden in the near future and a whole generation of our chil-dren destroyed.'

Finally, the religious assault on Smith was closely linked to an attack on the foreign-born in the northern cities. 'Elect Al Smith to the presi-dency,' declared one southern churchman, 'and it means that the floodgates of immigration will be opened, and that ours will be turned into a civilization like that of continental Europe. Elect Al Smith and you will turn this country over to the domination of a foreign religious sect, which I could name, and Church and State will once again be united.'

The objection to Smith expressed not simply anti-Catholicism but a pervasive anti-urbanism that embraced antagonism to his religion, his views on liquor, his tie to Tammany Hall, his identification with the new immigrants, and his association with the city itself—in short with all that seemed threatening in the metropolis. A leading Republican dry declared:

> The stability and continuation of our democratic form of government depends on keeping in the political saddle what we used to call the frontier and what today we call Main Street; the virile, clean-minded, middle class mentality. . . . America stands at the crossroads. Can her democracy survive if she puts in the White House what Bryce calls 'her failures in government'—the big cities? Here is the question of the hour!

Smith's opponent, Herbert Clark Hoover, had not only made a brilliant record as an administrator but could summon up the image of a pristine, rural America. He wrote of boyhood memories of gathering walnuts in the fall, carrying grain to the mill, fishing for catfish and sunnies, and finding 'gems of agate and fossil coral' on the Burlington track. His family, he recalled, had woven its own carpets, made its own soap, preserved 'meat and fruit and vegetables, got its sweetness from sorghum and honey.' He was taught, he said, by a 'sweet-faced lady who with infinite patience and kindness drilled into us those foundations of all we know today.'

Hoover won by the decisive vote of 21 million to Smith's 15 million, over 58 per cent of the popular vote to Smith's less than 41 per cent. While Cox had taken eleven states and Davis twelve, Smith captured only 8. For the first time since Reconstruction, the Republicans cut deeply into the Solid South, winning Virginia, Texas, Tennessee, North Carolina, and Florida. Smith, who received a much higher proportion of the popular vote than Davis or Cox had, ran well in the large cities inhabited by newer Americans and captured the industrial states of Rhode Island and Massachusetts. In Irish wards in Charlestown and South Boston, he won as much as 90 per cent of the vote; he did almost as well in Boston's Italian North End and in a French-Canadian ward in

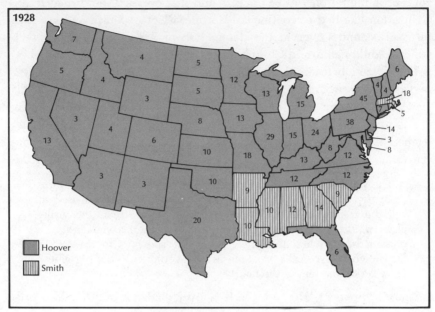

PRESIDENTIAL ELECTION, 1928

Holyoke. Yet for all Smith's gains, he had suffered an overwhelming de-feat. Hoover won because he ran as a candidate of the majority party at a time of boom prosperity, but Smith's background had also proved costly. 'America is not yet dominated by its great cities,' concluded a Minnesota newspaper after the election. 'Control of its destinies still re-mains in the smaller communities and rural regions, with their tradi-tional conservatism and solid virtues. . . . Main Street is still the prin-cipal thoroughfare of the nation.'

7. COLLAPSE

Herbert Hoover entered the White House with the brightest of reputa-tions. His successful administration of relief organizations in Belgium, Russia, and the Mississippi valley had earned the sobriquet of great hu-manitarian; his vigorous administration of the Commerce Department won him the confidence of business, if not of Wall Street. Innocent of any previous elective office, Hoover seemed to be a new type of political leader, a socially minded efficiency expert, able and ready to chart a new Utopia. The people who had come to regard wealth as the infallible hallmark of success did not resent the fact that he had become a millionaire; a society which had come to view the mechanics of life as of primary importance took pride in the fact that he was a world-famous mining engineer. Hoover, in short, carried into the White House with him all of the shining promises of the New Era.

President Hoover came to office committed to the ideal of abolishing poverty. 'We in America are nearer to the final triumph over poverty,' he said during the campaign, 'than ever before in the history of any land. . . . We have not reached the goal, but, given a chance to go forward with the policies of the last eight years, we shall soon with the help of God be in sight of the day when poverty will be banished from this nation.' Swept into the presidency by an overwhelming majority, Hoover prepared to go forward with the policies of the previous eight years which he had, in large measure, inspired. His election was the signal for a boom on the Stock Exchange, and most businessmen and investors prepared to reap still higher profits and to enjoy a still higher standard of living.

For a time their confidence seemed justified. The average value of common stocks soared from 117 in December 1928 to 225 the following September, and a few stocks such as U.S. Steel and General Electric rose to dizzy heights. Inspired by these dazzling gains, stockbrokers increased their bank borrowings from $3.5 billion in 1927 to $8.5 billion two years later and bought more extravagantly than ever before. The public appeared willing and able to absorb limitless quantities of stock: in the single month of January 1929 no less than a billion dollars' worth of new securities were floated. Factory employment, freight car loadings, construction contracts, bank loans, almost all the indices of business, showed a marked upward swing.

Even as Hoover announced in his inaugural address that 'in no nation are the fruits of accomplishment more secure,' shrewd investors were cashing in on their paper profits and pulling out of the market; but the Federal Reserve Board, though alarmed at the speculative mania, did little to reverse the policy of easy credit which it had inaugurated in 1927. There were, indeed, many reasons for concern. The world economic situation was discouraging. War debts were uncollectable, foreign trade had declined precipitously, and the interest on billions of dollars of private investments was in default. Prosperity, even during the height of the boom, was spotty. Agriculture was depressed; industries such as coal and textiles had not shared in the general well-being; technical improvements worked hardships on many older industries and created temporary unemployment. In 1921 joblessness was estimated at over 4 million, and at no time did it fall below 1.5 million. Much of the new wealth had gone to the privileged few, and 5 per cent of the population enjoyed one-third of the income. Business plowed a disproportionate amount of the gains in productivity into new plants or passed them on as dividends rather than wages. So long as industry turned out mountains of goods but denied workers the purchasing power to buy them, a breakdown was inevitable. Meantime public and private debts had mounted to staggering sums; by 1930 the total debt burden was estimated at between $100 billion and $150 billion — approximately one-third the national wealth. Debts, installment buying, and speculation had strained credit to the breaking point, and because few understood the dangers involved in the process, credit was gravely abused. Too many Americans were living on the future. When confidence in the future disappeared, the system collapsed.

The crash came in October 1929. On the twenty-first of that month the prices of stocks began to sag; on the twenty-fourth over 12 million shares changed hands; on 29 October came a catastrophic crash. In less than a month stocks suffered an average decline of 40 per cent. At the outset Hoover, and most of the nation, assumed that the Wall Street crash, although devastating, was only the latest of those familiar financial panics that America had experienced before. In fact, it triggered a depression which would be a watershed in American life. 'The stock market crash,' wrote the literary critic Edmund Wilson, 'was to count for us almost like a rending of the earth in preparation for the Day of Judgment.' Before the Great Depression ended, some thirteen years later, it would alter the whole landscape of American society, terminate the long reign of the Republicans as the majority party, cut short the political career of Herbert Hoover, and bury in its ruins the bright prospects of the New Era.

XVIII

American Society in Transition

1. THE NEW SOCIETY

In the interwar decades American society underwent far-reaching changes, many of which were foreshadowed in the years before the United States entered World War I. As early as 1908 the photographer Alfred Stieglitz had hung Matisse canvases in his Fifth Avenue gallery, and that same year the expatriate Ezra Pound reached Gibraltar. In 1909 Sigmund Freud came to Worcester, Massachusetts, to lecture at Clark University, and by 1916 some 500 psychoanalysts were practicing in New York. At Mabel Dodge's salon in Greenwich Village, writers, artists, and revolutionaries discussed the ideas of Henri Bergson and Georges Sorel, of Nietzsche and Shaw and those insurgent thinkers who stressed spontaneity, instinct, emotion, and movement, and assaulted nineteenth-century conceptions of morality and decorum. In 1913, the same year that the Provincetown Players began to perform, a dance craze swept the country, a symbol of the growing sense of sexual liberation; disturbed by the intimacy of movement, Columbia University stipulated that six inches must separate the dancers. By 1915, the year T. S. Eliot's 'The Love Song of J. Alfred Prufrock' appeared in Harriet Monroe's *Poetry*, H. L. Mencken had identified the new American woman as 'the Flapper.' In intellectual circles at least, there was a quickening awareness of taking part in an insurrection against the old order, and a vivid anticipation of the coming of great events.

445

The prewar rebels, for all their earthshaking manifestos, lived in an exuberant age of confidence and optimism, an era that World War I shattered beyond repair. The war created a divide which separated the world of Booth Tarkington from that of Nelson Algren, the universe of Billy Sunday from that of Reinhold Niebuhr. Too many had known the young men who, in Ezra Pound's words, 'walked eye-deep in hell/believing in old men's lies,' or, as E. E. Cummings wrote, had heard 'death's enormous voice,' which left 'all the silence / filled with vivid noiseless boys.' The war blighted the immense sense of promise of the 1912 period and left a sense of outrage at the killing and maiming. 'I got hurt in the war,' Hemingway's mutilated hero, Jake Barnes, says. 'Oh, that dirty war.'

Hemingway caught much of the spirit of the postwar years in his story of the Oklahoma boy who returned from the war 'much too late' and who 'did not want any consequences ever again.' Although some of the old progressives remained faithful to the earlier ideals, many rejected public involvement for a preoccupation with self. Like the 'Hamlet' of Archibald MacLeish, they would 'Cry I! I! I! forever.' This private vision inspired the literature of the 1920's but impoverished the politics. The socialist Norman Thomas protested: 'The old reformer has become the Tired Radical, and his sons and daughters drink at the fountain of the *American Mercury*. They have no illusions but one. And that is that they can live like Babbitt and think like Mencken.'

George Babbitt, the protagonist of Sinclair Lewis's novel, personified the materialistic aspirations of this period in which Americans turned with unashamed enthusiasm to the business of getting rich and enjoying themselves, to the distress of critics of American manners. Santayana wrote:

> No space for noonday rest or midnight watches,
> No purest joy of breathing under heaven!
> Wretched themselves, they heap, to make them happy,
> Many possessions.[1]

During the piping years of the 'twenties, population grew by 17 millions in a decade — the greatest absolute increase in history until then — and the growth in national wealth was equally spectacular; those who en-

1. *Poems*, Charles Scribner's Sons, p. 73.

joyed this new prosperity congratulated themselves that it was universal and permanent, and that the millennium had arrived. But the wealth of the nation was unevenly distributed: 25 million families — or over 87 per cent of the population — had incomes of less than $2500, while only about a million families — or less than 3 per cent — had incomes of over $5000.

While the rich grew richer, there was less they could do with their money to distinguish them from those who were not rich. Technology provided a standardized product, advertising looked to a mass market, and social habits put a premium on formal equality. The gap that separated white from black remained painfully deep, but the lines that distinguished different classes of whites were increasingly blurred.

The war had made this generation conscious of impermanence and impatient for the gratification of wants. Even President Hoover's Committee on Social Trends took note of this 'new attitude toward hardship as a thing to be avoided by living in the here and now, utilizing installment credit,' and other devices, to telescope the future into the present.' Business co-operated with these desires by building obsolescence into its products and providing credit that was easy if not always liberal, and the public responded by buying what it wanted on the installment plan. No longer inclined to regard thrift as a virtue, they speculated avidly on the stock market or in Florida real estate.

These changes contributed to significant alterations in the national character, for as Joseph Gusfield has noted, 'In an easygoing, affluent society, the credit mechanism has made the Ant a fool and the Grasshopper a hero.' The nation was swiftly moving toward a society in which styles of consumption would determine status. The New Middle Class — from the white collar clerk to the Madison Avenue executive — was captivated by the wealth of new consumer products, and his wife eyed them even more avidly. In Montgomery Ward catalogues, toasters and irons made their first appearance in 1912, vacuum cleaners in 1917, the electric range in 1930, the refrigerator in 1932.

These new products first found their way in an urban market, for rural America still lacked electricity, but in this period America was becoming a predominantly urban nation. In 1890 the population was 65 per cent rural; in 1930 it was 56 per cent urban. Many cities, especially in Florida and California, grew tenfold during these years, while increases in the larger cities of the older parts of the country were spectacular.[2] The whole nation became urbanized — in its psychology as well as in its economy. Big towns copied the cities, and little towns copied the big towns, while few villages were so small or isolated as to be without moving pictures and supermarkets and parking problems. Nearly half the population of the country lived within easy access of cities of 100,000 inhabitants or more; these cities became the shopping, entertainment, educational, and cultural centers of the nation. The city promised excitement and adventure. In a Floyd Dell novel, the protagonist has a recurring image of a map at the depot 'with a picture of iron roads from all over the Middle West centering in a dark blotch in the corner. . . . "Chicago!" he said to himself.' On the other hand, rural America was now often perceived as mean and narrow. In 1923 Veblen's *Absentee Ownership and Business Enterprise* denounced the rural town as 'the perfect flower of self-help and cupidity standardized on the American plan.'

To this process of urbanization the automobile especially contributed. At the close of World War I there were some 9 million motor cars in use; a decade later the number had soared to 26 million. Originally a luxury, the automobile quickly became a necessity; when hard times hit a family, the car was the last thing to go, and with the return of prosperity it was not a house but a car that the workingman bought. For many Americans the automobile was a symbol of freedom, a badge of equality, useful for transportation but essential for social intercourse and self-respect. It gave the national propensity for mobility and the restless mania for speed new and easy outlets. The automobile broke down isolation and provincialism, promoted standardization, accelerated the growth of cities at the expense of villages and then of suburbs at the expense of cities, created a hundred new industries and millions of new jobs, and required the destruction of large parts of the country to make way for roads and by-passes. It precipitated new problems of morals

2. Thus, in thousands:

	1890	1930		1890	1930
Atlanta, Ga.	65	270	Minneapolis, Minn.	164	464
Detroit, Mich.	205	1568	Pittsburgh, Pa.	238	669
Grand Rapids, Mich.	60	170	Rochester, N.Y.	130	320
Hartford, Conn.	60	150	Syracuse, N.Y.	88	209
Indianapolis, Ind.	105	305	Toledo, Ohio	81	290
Kansas City, Mo.	130	400	Washington, D.C.	189	487

and of crime, and took an annual toll of life and limb as high as that exacted by the First World War.

The radio, like the automobile, began as a plaything and became a necessity and a promoter of social change. The first broadcasting station opened at Pittsburgh in 1920; within a decade there were almost 13 million radios in American homes, and by 1940 there were close to 900 broadcasting stations and 52 million receiving sets. From the beginning radio was privately owned and controlled, not — as in Britain and on the Continent — in public hands. Most of the wave-lengths were controlled by a few great networks — the Columbia, the National, and the Mutual leading the field.[3] Government regulation was tardy, feeble, and fragmentary. Not until 1927 did Congress establish a Federal Radio Commission to license stations, assign wave-lengths, and supervise policies. In 1934 this commission was abolished and general supervision over radio assigned to the Federal Communications Commission. This body is authorized to require that all radio and television broadcasts conform to the 'public interest, convenience and necessity,' a requirement that has always been interpreted so loosely as to be almost meaningless.

In the 1930's judicious and conscientious commentators like Raymond Gram Swing and Elmer Davis, as well as demagogues like Father Coughlin, came to wield an influence comparable to that exercised by Horace Greeley in his time. The radio — soon to be dramatically augmented by television — brought world affairs into the living room, and by making it possible for every American to hear the 'fireside chats' of Roosevelt, the bitter harangues of Hitler, and the somber eloquence of Churchill, did a great deal to break down provincialism. Because the radio competed with the newspaper, publishers began to acquire radio, and later television, stations; in many cities a single company came to control all the media of news.

Second only to the radio as diversion, but well behind it as education, were the 'movies.' Invented by the resourceful Thomas Edison at the turn of the century, the motion picture grew steadily in popularity. David Griffith's *The Birth of a Nation*, shown to rapt audiences in 1915, introduced the spectacle film which another producer, Cecil B. de Mille, shortly made his peculiar property. Stars of the silent screen supplanted

3. Eventually these gave way to the big three: National Broadcasting Company, Columbia Broadcasting System, and American Broadcasting Corporation, which exercised a virtual monopoly of radio and television.

luminaries of the 'legitimate' stage in the democratic heavens: Mary Pickford, 'America's sweetheart'; Charles Chaplin, greatest of comedians; Douglas Fairbanks, handsome and acrobatic; Bill Hart, always in cowboy costume; Pearl White, whose endless series of escapades left her audience palpitating each week for the next installment. Sound, introduced in 1927, greatly expanded film potentialities (as television later did radio), and allied movies to the theater. Many former stars disappeared, and talking cinema increasingly recruited artists and adapted dramas from the more sophisticated boards. Film versions of *David Copperfield, Wuthering Heights, Anna Karenina, Little Women,* and other books introduced millions to classics they would never have read; Greta Garbo, Charles Laughton, W. C. Fields, Katherine Hepburn, and Humphrey Bogart gave performances worthy of the best stage tradition. The development of the cartoon movie by Walt Disney, creator of Mickey Mouse and Donald Duck, delighted adults as well as children, and opened up a new dimension of the art. By 1937 the motion-picture industry was fourteenth in volume of business and eleventh in assets among the industries of the nation, and some 75 million persons visited the movies every week.

Every other form of entertainment revealed the same quality of commercialization. Sport, even 'amateur' competition, became big business. Professional baseball teams played to capacity crowds, and so too did boxers and wrestlers. Intercollegiate football attracted millions of spectators, and high-school basketball tournaments became events of statewide importance. Few Americans saw any connection between the exaltation of competitive sports and the low standards of public education. Daylight-saving time and the five-day week gave a new popularity to tennis and golf, while such old-fashioned games as croquet, which required well-kept lawns and family groups, all but disappeared. Card games, once looked upon as a form of gambling, became fashionable, and adeptness at bridge came to be as important an ingredient in social success as membership in a country club.

The 'emancipation' of women came closer to achievement in the years after the First World War. Women had been in process of winning the suffrage ever since Wyoming Territory granted them the vote back in 1869. With the introduction of co-education at Oberlin in the 1830's and the admission of women to the Universities of Iowa, Michigan, and Cornell after the Civil War, women had won something like equality in education. They had long enjoyed the privilege of working, side by side with children of both sexes, in textile mills, and the invention of the typewriter and the telephone opened up to them new worlds of office work. Gradually, too, they had made their way into the professions of medicine, law, and the ministry, and had pretty much taken over elementary and high-school teaching. All of these things came to a head in the years of the First World War, when manpower shortages put a premium on woman power. Woman suffrage was written into the Constitution in 1920; millions of women crowded into jobs in factory and office; and increasing numbers of them took part in public life. A generation that observed Jane Addams and Eleanor Roosevelt could not seriously believe women less competent than men in public affairs. The greatest changes came in the social and psychological realms. Labor-saving devices emancipated millions of women from the stove and the wash-tub, and knowledge of birth control from the demands of large families, while education and prosperity opened up new careers. As women won freedom from the kitchen and the nursery, and won economic independence as well, they had some success in replacing the old double standard of morality with a single standard. Soon sociologists were muttering darkly about an American matriarchy, while comic strips, the radio, and James Thurber's cartoons presented the American male as dithering and childish and the American woman as firmly in command.

Marriage came to seem less permanent than had long been supposed; even the remarkable upswing in the Catholic population did not seriously retard the mounting divorce rate. In 1890 out of every one hundred marriages, six ended in divorce; forty years later eighteen of every one hundred marriages were thus terminated, and that year some 200,000 couples were legally separated. In many other respects family life came to seem less stable. Those who continued to live in the town where they were born became objects of curiosity, and for the inhabitants of the large cities, moving came to be an almost annual junket, while the shift from roomy Victorian houses to city flats made it difficult for large families — the grandparents and the maiden aunts — to live together.[4] With the passing of the family homestead, many of the old

4. The expatriate poet, Ezra Pound, made a virtue of this:

> O, how hideous it is,
> To see three generations of one house gathered together!

bonds and disciplines that had moulded generations of young men and women slipped away, and the cities furnished no immediate substitute. For millions of Americans the Depression was to reveal that

> Home is the place where when you have to go there,
> They have to take you in.[5]

For millions it was that, and nothing more.

2. LITERARY INTERPRETATIONS

In the 'lyric years' before the war almost everything was 'new': the new poetry, the new criticism, the new art, the 'New Freedom,' the 'New Nationalism,' the new history. A new generation was getting ready to break new paths, launch new ventures, think new thoughts, and discover new worlds. Harriet Monroe founded *Poetry* in Chicago; Herbert Croly established the *New Republic;* Max Eastman and Art Young started the socialistic *Masses,* and soon the staid *Dial* moved from Chicago to New York and found a new youthfulness. Walter Lippmann published his *Preface to Politics,* followed by *Drift and Mastery;* Jocl Spingarn, who had written the *New Criticism,* helped start the NAACP; the Armory Show of 1913 exploded traditional art; the Provincetown Players welcomed young Eugene O'Neill; William C. Handy composed the 'Memphis Blues' and jazz was born, and Serge Diaghileff brought the Russian Ballet to America. It was an American Renaissance and, wrote Ezra Pound extravagantly from London, 'it would make the Italian Renaissance look like a tempest in a teapot.'

'The fiddles are tuning up all over America,' wrote John Butler Yeats. So they were, but it was in Chicago that Harriet Monroe whipped them together into a kind of orchestra. This indomitable woman of fifty decided that poetry had been too long neglected and that it ought to have a subsidy and a magazine, and in 1912 she launched *Poetry: A Magazine of Verse,* and a parlor revolution in poetry was under way. Within six years almost all the poets who would dominate the literary scene for the next fifty years made their bow, and most of them in the pages of this little magazine: the 'prairie' poets, Carl Sandburg and Vachel Lindsay; the imagists, Amy Lowell and Conrad Aiken; the lyricists, Sara Teasdale, Edna St. Vincent Millay, and Elinor Wylie; Freudians like

5. Robert Frost, 'Death of the Hired Man.'

Edgar Lee Masters; and Robinson Jeffers, who went his own way. Over in England three Americans who were to achieve fame in their lifetime — Ezra Pound, T. S. Eliot, and Robert Frost — were publishing their first books. Not since New England's golden day had there been anything like it.

When Carl Sandburg published 'Chicago' in *Poetry*:

> Hog Butcher for the World,
> Tool Maker, Stacker of Wheat,
> Player with Railroads and the Nation's Freight Handler;
> Stormy, husky, brawling,
> City of the Big Shoulders

a jaundiced critic wrote that 'the typographical arrangement for this jargon creates a suspicion that it is intended to be taken as some form of poetry.' So it was. A disciple of Whitman, Sandburg thought nothing too undignified for poetry; in this he was like the members of the 'Ash-Can' school, who thought nothing too undignified to paint. Born of Swedish parents, Sandburg was as authentically American as Lincoln, whose biography he later wrote in six huge volumes; like Lincoln he was instinctively equalitarian; his most important collection of poetry is called *The People, Yes*.

Another son of Illinois, Vachel Lindsay, poet and minstrel, wandered from town to town preaching the 'Gospel of Beauty,' and 'trading his rhymes for bread.' In 1913 he brought out *General Booth Enters Heaven* with its moving tribute to Governor Altgeld, the 'Eagle Forgotten,' and thereafter the famous 'Congo' and 'The Chinese Nightingale.' His poems, made to be chanted rather than read, led Lindsay to a career on the lecture circuit which laid a heavy toll on his energy. When in December 1931 he took his life, he was paid handsome tributes; Sherwood Anderson commented: 'We do very well by our poets here, when they are dead.'

Imagism was an altogether more sophisticated affair, intellectually closer to abstract painting and modern music than to the kind of poetry being written by Vachel Lindsay. A revolt against the verbose pretentiousness of late nineteenth-century rhymesters, it valued the intense, concrete image. Ezra Pound, who led the movement, explained that there was to be no Tennysonianness of speech; nothing — nothing that you couldn't in some circumstance, in the stress of some emotion, actually say.' When Pound wearied of it, Amy Lowell — sister to Harvard's

President Lowell — assumed leadership of the group and aggressively promoted *vers libre*. The 'Amygists,' as Pound called them, not only encouraged free verse, but like Pound sought to write 'hard and clear' poetry and sometimes succeeded.

The Idaho-born Ezra Pound and the Missouri-born T. S. Eliot were both in London when Miss Monroe launched *Poetry;* Pound became its London editor, and Eliot contributed to it his first important poem, 'The Love Song of J. Alfred Prufrock.' Impetuous and scholarly, adventurous and reactionary, Pound spent a lifetime trying to work out new techniques of verse, immersing himself in new intellectual interests, and living in new countries. He championed Eliot, James Joyce, and a score of other writers; edited little magazines; and poured out a steady stream of translations, criticisms, and original verse — notably the endless series of *Cantos* composed with brilliant and calculated obscurity. Where Pound dissipated his talents, Eliot grew in stature and in influence until he became one of the commanding figures of his age. Like Henry James he lived by preference in London, and eventually became a British citizen; like James, too, he became increasingly the champion of traditionalism. Equally distinguished as a poet, a dramatist, and a critic, Eliot did as much to change the nature and character of modern poetry as had Wordsworth and Whitman in earlier generations, and his *The Waste Land* (1922), subtle and profound, became the *vade mecum* of a whole generation. Yet some rebelled against the imagery of disintegration and sterility. 'After this perfection of death,' concluded Hart Crane, 'nothing is possible but a motion of some kind.' But it was Crane himself who chose death.

The American traditionalists looked to Henry James rather than to Eliot for inspiration, notably the three intrepid women who bridged the gap between the realism of Howells and the social protest of a Dos Passos or a Steinbeck: Edith Wharton, Ellen Glasgow, and Willa Cather. Mrs. Wharton wrote of New York in the age of gaslight and horses, and of the Hudson Valley when the dominant architecture was Hudson River bracketed. In a series of novels that began with *The House of Mirth* (1905) and concluded with *Hudson River Bracketed* (1929), she presented complex social problems against a background of fashionable New York where Civil War profiteers and the new rich were crashing the gates of society, shattering old standards of elegance and taste, and calling in question old moralities. She was fascinated by the impact of the clash of cultures, and though she began as a rebel against the traditional social standards, she ended as something of an apologist for them. Even when, as in *Ethan Frome* and *Summer,* she turned from the New York scene to rural New England, it was the moral implications of the violation of custom and code that interested her. Like James, too, Mrs. Wharton was a master of the short story and of the ghost story; like him she lived much abroad; like him she was, for all the documentation of her novels, primarily a moralist.

Ellen Glasgow was a penetrating literary historian of the South. She began, at the turn of the century, as a simple chronicler of the Old South, describing its lingering pretensions with ironic detachment; she moved on to trace in elaborate detail the rise of the plain people of the New South and the clash of cultures and values that accompanied this rise. By the 'twenties the threat to those values which she herself cherished came not so much from the sentimentality of the Old South, but from the absence of tradition in the New. Beginning with *Barren Ground* (1925), Miss Glasgow expressed a mounting distaste for the emptiness of the new day and a grudging appreciation of the older virtues; with *The Sheltered Life* (1932) the appreciation was ardent; and with *Vein of Iron* (1935) there was an open appeal for the re-creation of the older values. As Miss Glasgow herself tells us:

> Although in the beginning I had intended to deal ironically with both the southern Lady and the Victorian tradition, I discovered as I went on, that my irony grew fainter, while it yielded at last to sympathetic compassion.

Willa Cather, too, recorded and celebrated the virtues of the past — the recent past of Nebraska, the historic past of Spanish New Mexico and of French Quebec; like Ellen Glasgow, she valued the past for its moral qualities rather than for its romance or antiquity. All her novels and stories — those of the Arcadian Virginia of her childhood, the golden Nebraska of her youth, the shimmering Southwest of Bishop Latour, the Quebec of the Ursulines — were animated by this single theme: the superiority of the moral values of the past over the material interests of the present. Willa Cather shared with Miss Glasgow a passion for the land — as she said of Alexandra Bergson in *O Pioneers!* 'it fortified her to reflect upon the great operations of nature.' She was fascinated, too, by the great Rock of Acoma — the 'utmost expression of human need,' she called it, 'the highest comparison of loyalty in love and friendship,' and so too by the rocks of Quebec on which the French had built their city. 'When an adventurer carries his gods with him into a remote and savage country,' she wrote, 'the colony he founds will have grace, tradition, riches of the mind and spirit. Its history will shine with bright incidents, slight perhaps, but precious, as in life.' This was what she found in the American West — that West which had been settled

> by dreamers, great hearted adventurers who were unpractical to the point of magnificence; a courteous brotherhood strong in attack but weak in defence, who could conquer but could not hold. . . .

All this now was gone; industry, business, and speculation had destroyed it: that was the moral of the most nearly perfect of her books, *A Lost Lady,* and of *The Professor's House.*

All three of these writers counted themselves disciples of Henry James, who in this period came into his own. The rediscovery of James was both a sign of growing maturity in American readers — the new generation could take both Ezra Pound and T. S. Eliot in its stride — and, more deeply, a sign of nostalgia for the traditions which James championed, and for the subtlety and depth of his insights into human nature.

The most popular serious poet of this generation was both classicist and modernist, traditionalist and innovator. Robert Frost made his first appearance just as the fiddles were tuning up, but he belonged to no school, took part in no movement, fits into no pattern. For half a century he went his own way, growing steadily in stature and in fame, developing a philosophy deceptively homespun and a style deceptively simple, as was so much about Frost. Born in San Francisco, he was unmistakably a New Englander; raised in cities, he was a countryman to the marrow; authentically American, he did not gain recognition until he expatriated himself to England, where he published his first two volumes of poetry: *A Boy's Will* (1913), and *North of Boston* (1914), with 'Mending Wall,' 'Death of the Hired Man,' 'Home Burial' — poems not surpassed in our literature for beauty and insight. In 1916 came *Mountain Interval,* with 'The Road Not Taken,' 'Birches,' and others — colloquial, philosophical, lyrical; all through the 'twenties and 'thirties, Frost turned out book after book: *New Hampshire, West Running Brook, A Further Range,* until by the end of this period he was the grand old man of American letters, and with yet another quarter-century of honors ahead of him.

If the second decade of the new century had been one of experimentation and affirmation, the decade of the 'twenties was one of disillusionment and revolt. The most vociferous critic of his generation, Henry L. Mencken of Baltimore, made it his special business to expose bourgeois complacency and his 'Americana' column in the *American Mercury* recorded with melancholy faithfulness the fatuousness and vulgarity of contemporary American life. Through the *American Mercury*, and through the well-named *Prejudices*, Mencken imposed his style on young writers and his iconoclastic views on a large part of the nation. Those views were almost all malicious, for Mencken was catholic in his dislikes: he disapproved of the rich and the poor, the ignorant and the intelligent, the mob and the elite, fundamentalism and advanced thought, devotion to the past and confidence in the future. 'From Boy Scouts, and from home cooking, from Odd Fellows' funerals, from Socialists, and from Christians — Good Lord, deliver us': this was typical of his prayers. He was a kind of domestic Ezra Pound who seceded from the United States not by going abroad, but by staying home and finding everyone out of step. While his influence was for the most part negative, Mencken made some positive contributions: a magazine that attracted the brightest writers of the day; a free-swinging and irreverent style that went far to liberate writing from pedantic pretentiousness; and three learned volumes on *The American Language*.

The 'revolt from the village' found its bards in Edgar Lee Masters and Sherwood Anderson. In *The Spoon River Anthology* (1915) Masters recorded, in the spirit of the Greek Anthology, the drab existence of some two hundred victims of life in a little Illinois town — a kind of prairie Tilbury Town — where dreamers were always defeated and idealists ended as cynics. Sherwood Anderson's grotesques revealed the unhinging experience of alienation and loneliness. *Winesburg, Ohio*, which caused something of a sensation when it was published in 1919, was a declaration of war against the small town, the factory, industry, the ties of marriage and of family; and almost all other conventions.

It was Sinclair Lewis, however, whose *Main Street* (1920) and *Babbitt* (1922) made the revolt against the small town and against business a popular preoccupation. Lewis satirized the ideals of the smug middle-class society to which he had been born, and in which he moved so uneasily. He rebelled against the dullness and provincialism of Gopher Prairie and Zenith City rather than against the moral anarchy of the industrial order which they represented. Like Mark Twain, he was very much a part of the world he repudiated, and he had a grudging affection for the characters he ridiculed.

Meantime, inspired by Sigmund Freud of Vienna, whose books and teachings were becoming increasingly known, usually second hand, the revolt against Puritanism and rationalism flared all along the literary front. Freudianism took the form of exploration of the irrational and the unconscious, fascination with the primitive and with violence, obsession with sex, and a search for new forms and a new vocabulary. It influenced such varied writers as Sara Teasdale, Edna Millay, Elinor Wylie, and Robinson Jeffers among the poets; Fitzgerald, Hemingway, and Faulkner among the novelists; and Eugene O'Neill among the playwrights.

Not since Emily Dickinson had America produced women poets to rank with the three who now appeared on the literary scene. Sara Teasdale's was the earliest, and the thinnest, talent, but in *Rivers to the Sea* and *Love Songs,* she made permanent contributions to our literature. Edna St. Vincent Millay, the poetess of her special generation, was not only the gay spirit who boasted that she burned her candle at both ends because it gave a lovely light, but the idealist who protested movingly against the injustice to Sacco and Vanzetti. Elinor Wylie was more purely a lyrical poet, and a kind of American Shelley, the most finished master of the sonnet in the whole of our literature; her 'Angels and Earthly Creatures' is one of the masterpieces of American poetry.

American poetry ranged widely in the interwar period. Wallace Stevens wrote sensual, elegant poems distinguished by the vivid hues of their imagery: 'pungent oranges and bright, green wings,' 'porcelain chocolate and pied umbrellas,' and 'a dove with an eye of grenadine.' In *The Bridge* Hart Crane attempted to create an ambitious synthesis of American experience; and although he failed, his brilliant employment of symbol and myth made his failure a greater achievement than lesser men's successes. William Carlos Williams wrote poetry spare in form, conversational in idiom, like 'The Red Wheelbarrow,' and Marianne Moore peopled 'imaginary gardens with real toads.'

The 'Harlem Renaissance' produced in quick succession Countee Cullen's *Color* in 1925, Langston Hughes's *The Weary Blues* in 1926, and James Weldon Johnson's *God's Trombones* in 1927. (Cullen's moving poem, 'Heritage,' reflected a fascination with the Negro's African origins which prompted Marcus Garvey to lead an abortive back-to-Africa movement in the 1920's.) 'I can never put on paper the thrill of the underground ride to Harlem,' Hughes wrote. 'I went up the steps and out into the bright September sunlight. Harlem! I stood there, dropped my bags, took a deep breath and felt happy again.' The exuberant 'Negro Renaissance' resulted not only in poems but novels, plays, and social analyses by writers such as Claude McKay, Jean Toomer, Alain Locke, and E. Franklin Frazier. White novelists also 'discovered' Harlem. Yet the Harlem Renaissance often burdened the black writer with unrealistic expectations, and the white world's celebration of 'exotic' Harlem gave a distorted image of the 'laughing, swaying' black and glossed over the grim reality of slum life.

Robinson Jeffers's poetry expressed, in uncompromising form, a revolt against society and civilization, and a fascination with Nature and violence and death. Man is born to pain — so says Jeffers in 'The Double-Axe' — as are all living things, but man alone adds depravity to the pain; man alone is inhuman.

> Lord God, exterminate
> The race of man. For only man in all the world, except a few kinds
> of insect, is essentially cruel.
> Therefore slay also these if you will . . . the driver ant,
> And the slave-maker ant, and the slick wasp
> That paralyzes living meat for her brood; but first
> The human race.

The most significant and most widely read writers. of this period were those who confessed that theirs was a 'lost generation.' 'Lost, and forever writing the history of their loss, they had become specialists in anguish,' writes Alfred Kazin. Theirs was the generation of 'the hollow men, the stuffed men,' and their spiritual home was 'the waste land.' Some, like Robinson Jeffers, rejected all human values; others, like Hemingway, took refuge in physical violence — in the bull fight or the prize ring or hunting big game in Africa, or in war. All of them might have said, with Eugene O'Neill, that 'the writer must dig at the roots of the sickness of today as he feels it — the death of the old God and the failure of science and materialism to give any satisfactory new one for the surviving religious instinct to find a new meaning in life.'

F. Scott Fitzgerald became the chronicler of the peculiar disillusionment that afflicted the very rich in the postwar years that he taught us to
call the Jazz Age. *This Side of Paradise,* published in 1920, became a
Baedeker of the new generation 'grown up to find all Gods dead, all
wars fought, all faiths in man shaken.' Fitzgerald depicted the world of
glitter and of wealth, of Princeton and the St. Regis roof, the Riviera and
the Ritz Bar in Paris, West Egg and Hollywood. He is the historian, too,
of ambition that cannot be gratified, of wealth that in the end makes no
difference, of pleasures that bring ennui and passion that cannot achieve
lasting love. 'My millionaires,' he wrote, 'were as beautiful and damned
as Thomas Hardy's peasants.' Still, his characters do not experience the
nightmare that broods over the novels of a Kafka or a Camus; for all
their wealth and sophistication, in the vacuity of their lives and the aim-
lessness of their loves, they differ little from the denizens of Gopher
Prairie or Zenith City. In *The Great Gatsby* (1925), one of the notable
novels of the generation, Fitzgerald offered a melancholy commentary
on the Jazz Age; his account of Jay Gatsby, who put his life at 'the service of a vast, vulgar and meretricious beauty,' is a curious counterpart
of Willa Cather's *A Lost Lady.* In the 1930's Fitzgerald wrote one of
his finest novels, *Tender Is the Night,* but the depression decade was
no longer interested in Fitzgerald's sad young men.

The year after the appearance of *The Great Gatsby,* the 28-year-old
Ernest Hemingway published his first novel, *The Sun Also Rises;* it carried a quotation from Gertrude Stein, 'You are all a lost generation.'
Hemingway was, like Fitzgerald, an historian of that generation, but
his characters were more hopelessly and desperately lost than were the
playboys and girls who disport themselves across Fitzgerald's tinseled
stages. He wrote about those who wanted to be counted out; all of his
characters, except possibly the idealist Robert Jordan in *For Whom the
Bell Tolls,* were engaged in a massive repudiation of their society. All of
them might have repeated the prayer of the old waiter in 'A Clean Well-
Lighted Place' — 'Hail nothing full of nothing, nothing is with thee.'
Like Robinson Jeffers, and Faulkner too, Hemingway was obsessed with
violence, pain, and death, themes that run through *The Sun Also Rises,*
which shifts frenetically from Paris to the bull rings of Spain; *A Farewell
to Arms* which is set against the background of the Italian retreat after
Caporetto; *For Whom the Bell Tolls,* which caught something of the
passion and despair of the Spanish Civil War; *The Green Hills of Africa;*
the last of his books, *The Old Man and the Sea;* and collections of short

stories like *Men Without Women* and *Winner Take Nothing*. In such works, Hemingway sought to work out his preoccupation with senseless, violent injury, especially the wound he had received in the war, and to develop a code whereby a man may live with honor in the face of violence and annihilation.

Hemingway was to become a legend even during his own lifetime. 'For the young men born between 1918 and 1924,' wrote one of them, 'there was a special charm about Hemingway. By the time most of us were old enough to read him, he had become a legendary figure, a kind of twentieth century Lord Byron.' He lived the flamboyant life which was the stuff of his novels and stories — he drove an ambulance in war-torn Italy, was a correspondent in the Spanish Civil War, and hunted big game in Africa. Yet he remained a man apart, independent and uninvolved.

Hemingway's great influence, however, came not from his manner of living but from his literary style. He had gone to school to Mark Twain, he had practiced journalism, he had come under the influence of Gertrude Stein and Ezra Pound; but his style was his own achievement. 'I was always embarrassed,' says one of his characters,

> by the words sacred, glorious, and sacrifice, and the expression in vain. . . . There were many words that you could not stand to hear and finally only the names of places had dignity. Certain numbers were the same way and certain dates and these with the names of the places were all you could say and have them mean anything. Abstract words such as glory, honor, courage, or hallow were obscene beside the concrete names of villages . . . the names of rivers, the numbers of regiments and the dates.[6]

He hammered out a style that was direct, pithy, nervous, idiomatic, simple, and honest. Though no others quite mastered it, almost all the writers of his generation imitated it.

A third major literary figure of the 'twenties, Eugene O'Neill, has the distinction of being the first, and perhaps the only, American dramatist to achieve the kind of fame accorded Ibsen, Chekhov, and Shaw. Born of a theatrical family and trained at the famous Harvard Workshop and in the Provincetown Theater, O'Neill combined a high order of technical competence with imagination, passion, and a sense of the theater. Very much a child of his age, he reflected almost all the intellectual currents

6. *A Farewell to Arms*, p. 196 (Scribners).

of the day, responding — as he put it — to the 'discordant, broken, faith-less rhythms of our time.' He indulged himself in naturalism in his early plays of the sea and the waterfront: *Anna Christie, The Hairy Ape, The Moon of the Caribbees;* participated in the revolt from the village — particularly the New England village — in *Beyond the Horizon* and *Desire Under the Elms;* shot his arrows at Babbitry in *Marco's Millions* and *The Great God Brown;* confessed a brief nostalgia for a homespun past which he had never known in the charming *Ah, Wilderness!;* exper-imented with expressionism in *Lazarus Laughed;* immersed himself in Freudianism in *Strange Interlude* and in *Mourning Becomes Electra* where he boldly invited comparison with the Agamemnon trilogy of Aeschylus. When he died he left a searing autobiographical drama, *Long Day's Journey into Night,* which, like *The Iceman Cometh,* re-turned to the naturalism of his early plays and confessed once again his deep debt to August Strindberg. A note of desperation resounds in this the best of O'Neill's plays, which recapitulate his painful childhood memory of his intimidating father, his drug-addicted mother, and his al-coholic elder brother; and in his final autobiographical *cri du cœur* there is a sense of hopelessness and of doom.

The fourth major figure to emerge during these postwar years, Wil-liam Faulkner came in time to share with Hemingway dominion of the American literary scene and, like Hemingway, to win the Nobel Prize in literature. All of his books are laid in the South, and most of them in that Yoknapatawpha County which he created — the most famous and most commonly misspelled locale in literature since Swift's Brobdingnag. Like Ellen Glasgow, Faulkner wrote of the transformation of the Old South into the New, of the disintegration of the values of the Old and the failure of the New to create substitutes, but in their philosophy and their style the two writers are as far apart as Trollope and Virginia Woolf. Faulkner was much more than a regionalist. He wrote of such eternal problems as the conflict of freedom and necessity and Man's quest to liberate himself from the burden of history.

Faulkner is the greatest of American literary experimenters — a writer of dazzling virtuosity who can reproduce the folk speech of the poor white and the rhetoric of the Old Testament, the crude, and often per-verse, humor of a Mark Twain and the complex symbolism of a T. S. Eliot. He had learned something from Proust, something from James Joyce, but his use of the stream of consciousness technique, the flash-back, interior monologues, tortured syntax, and jumbled time sequences is all his own.

Over the years, beginning with *The Sound and the Fury* (1929), and including such masterpieces as *Light in August, As I Lay Dying,* and *The Hamlet,* Faulkner traced the pathology of the South, Old and New — the collapse of standards, the ineffectiveness of the old families — like his own Falkners — and the irredeemable vulgarity and corruption of the new — like the Snopeses and the Sutpens. He gives us a region wracked by guilt, permeated by an all but universal debasement. For thirty years he attempted, by literary catharsis, to

> Minister to a mind diseased,
> Pluck from the memory a rooted sorrow,
> Raze out the written trouble of the brain
> Cleanse the stuff'd bosom of that perilous stuff
> That weights upon the heart.

But in vain.

A host of lesser writers, successors to Garland and Norris and Dreiser, addressed themselves to the crises that bedeviled the postwar years. Four made a powerful impression on their own generation: John Dos Passos, James T. Farrell, Thomas Wolfe, and John Steinbeck. Dos Passos's great, sprawling *U.S.A.* trilogy, a profoundly pessimistic work, portrays a society that is rootless and disintegrated, hurrying to wealth and pleasure without faith or purpose. Farrell was perhaps Dreiser's most faithful disciple; his *Studs Lonigan* series — another massive and formless social document — depicts the Chicago of the 'twenties with unrelenting bitterness.

Thomas Wolfe, the promise of whose *Look Homeward, Angel* (1929) was never wholly fulfilled in his later and more popular books, belongs only marginally to this group. Gargantuan, tempestuous, capable of both bathos and beauty inextricably intermixed, Wolfe was something of a genius and something of a charlatan. But he provided a sense of the clamorous life of Boston and New York during these exciting years, and through them of the whole of America. Coming up from North Carolina to Harvard and New York City, he experienced at first hand the tragedy of the depression and

> The staggering impact of this black picture of man's inhumanity to his fellow men, the unending repercussions of the scenes of suffering, violence, oppression, hunger, cold, and the filth and poverty

going on unheeded in a world in which the rich were still rotten with their wealth, left a scar upon my life.

Forever a young man — he died at 38 — Wolfe was like Rousseau in his volatile passions, his public confessions, his torrential eloquence, and his hatred of injustice.

John Steinbeck's greatest work, too, came out of the depression. His early books — *Tortilla Flat, In Dubious Battle,* and the enchanting *Red Pony* — revealed a high technical skill and a deep understanding of the Mexican Americans and the migratory workers of California. His *Grapes of Wrath* (1939), a moving saga of the trek of the Joad clan from their dust-blown Oklahoma farm to the promised land of California, was the one great story to come out of the depression that caught the tragedy of the Dust Bowl, the gallantry as well as the meanness of the rural pro-letariat.

There had been something artificial about the studied cultivation of despair with which so many of the writers reacted to the materialism of the 'twenties. When, after 1935, the shadows of totalitarianism spread and a long night threatened to blot out the values of Western civiliza-tion, many of the leading poets and novelists rallied to the defense of the things they had long taken for granted. Thus Sinclair Lewis sounded an alarm bell to a lethargic democracy in *It Can't Happen Here* — which sought to show that it could. Ernest Hemingway turned briefly to cele-brate the life and death struggle of the Spanish Loyalists in their fight against Franco; Thomas Wolfe recorded the destruction of the older Germany in *The Web and the Rock;* and Dos Passos, who had long wandered aimlessly about the *U.S.A.* found at last *The Ground We Stand On* — democracy and freedom; and Steinbeck celebrated Nor-wegian resistance to Nazi tyranny in *The Moon Is Down.* The poets, too, returned to the tradition of Whittier. Carl Sandburg reaffirmed his faith in *The People, Yes;* in a series of eloquent poems — 'Public Speech,' 'The Land of the Free' — MacLeish called on the people to summon up cour-age for a fight for survival; and in his solemn 'Nightmare at Noon' Stephen Vincent Benét reminded his people that

> There are certain words,
> Our own and others', we're used to, words we've used,
> Heard, had to recite, forgotten,
> Rubbed shiny in the pocket, left home for keepsakes,
> Inherited, stuck away in the back-drawer. . . .

Liberty, equality, fraternity.
To none will we sell, refuse or deny, right or justice.
We hold these truths to be self-evident.

I'm merely saying — what if these words pass?
What if they pass and are gone and are no more.[7]

3. PAINTING AND MUSIC

A new chapter in American art began when the Armory Show opened its
doors in February 1913. In the next month or so over a hundred thousand people crowded into the vast hall to gaze with incredulity or indignation at paintings by Impressionists and post-Impressionists, Fauvists
and Cubists and Modernists of all kinds. Here for the first time Americans could see the paintings of Cezanne and Matisse, Toulouse-Lautrec
and Redon, Van Gogh and Picasso as well as that forever baffling 'Nude
Descending the Staircase' by Marcel Duchamp. The new sculptors were
there too — figures by Epstein and Maillol and the baffling Brancusi as
well as by the newly Americanized Gaston Lachaise. This new art
deeply shocked the conservatives; Royal Cortissoz, dean of art critics,
called it 'not a movement, or a principle, but unadulterated cheek.' However the ever-versatile Theodore Roosevelt, emerging as an art critic,
welcomed a departure from the conventional.

Yet the triumph of the Modernists still lay well ahead, and preoccupation with the social scene became the most pronounced feature of American painting. In 1936 the artist George Biddle, reviewing an exhibition
of contemporary American and French painting, found that while
among the French pictures there was not one that was concerned with
social problems, among the American works 'seventy-four dealt with the
American scene or with a social criticism of American life; six with
strikes or with strikebreakers; six with dust, sand, erosion, drought, and
floods. There were no nudes, no portraits, and two still lifes. Out of the
hundred not one could be said to enjoy, reflect, participate in our inherited democratic-capitalist culture.' [8] Biddle himself was preoccupied
with the social scene. So, too, with those abler artists, Charles Burchfield
and Edward Hopper. Burchfield spread before us a panorama of

---

7. *Selected Works of Stephen Vincent Benét*, Vol. I, p. 466 (Farrar & Rinehart,
Inc.).
8. *An American Artist's Story*, p. 292.

ugliness — the ugliness of the small town in Ohio or Indiana, of the factory in that Buffalo where he chose to live, of rain-swept nights on dreary streets. He set himself, writes Sam Hunter, 'the task of exploring in humble visual metaphors the failures behind the American success story, the corruption of the landscape that followed in the wake of industrial progress and which most Americans had managed to ignore.' [9] So too with Edward Hopper, painter of the poignant isolation of people in the great cities. Social criticism is to be found in the political cartoons of William Gropper, in Henry Varnum Poor's murals of labor; in Reginald Marsh's gaudy pictures of Coney Island, the Bowery, and other gathering places of those who have nowhere to go; and in Ben Shahn's Daumier-like commentaries.

The regionalists were closely identified with the social critics, but not always in revolt against what they portrayed. Thomas Hart Benton was as authentically American as his ancestor the statesman; like Mark Twain, he transcribed the social history of the Mississippi, of the South and the West. John Steuart Curry celebrated the plains of Kansas and the cottonfields of Dixie; Waldo Peirce was at his best in depicting the coast of Maine; Edward Bruce divided his allegiance between New York and California; Grant Wood bathed the rolling hills and the gimcrack houses of Iowa in rich color and sentiment, though in such paintings as 'American Gothic' and 'Daughters of the Revolution' he showed that he too could indulge in social criticism.

Meantime the Modernists were rebelling against mere representational art. During a brief transition period, craftsmen like Jonas Lie, Bernard Karfiol, and John Marin still clung to representational art but moved into new experiments in the use of color or — as with Charles Sheeler — in geometric designs. They were succeeded by the Modernists like Max Weber, Marsden Hartley, Charles Demuth, Stuart Davis, and the brilliant Georgia O'Keefe. And, after them, the pure abstractionists like Mark Tobey and Jackson Pollock were just around the corner.

American music was not as advanced as American art. With the notable exceptions of folk music and Negro spirituals, America had always imported her music and her musicians, and the most determined efforts to cultivate here a 'native' music had failed. Edward MacDowell's sonatas and concertos were applauded on two continents, but most of the music of this generation now seems second-rate and derivative. More

9. *Modern American Painting and Sculpture*, p. 111.

vitality appeared in the new generation of composers that came to maturity after World War I — John Powell, Virgil Thomson, John Alden
Carpenter, Roy Harris, Aaron Copland, Jerome Kern, and George
Gershwin. Powell, Harris, and Gershwin exploited the resources of folk
music and Negro spirituals, while Carpenter and Copland, influenced by
such modernists as Stravinsky and Schönberg, explored the symphonic possibilities of jazz and translated into music the nervous and
explosive character of our mechanical civilization. Harris's *American
Overture,* Schelling's *Victory Ball,* Rodgers and Hammerstein's *Oklahoma,* Kern's *Show Boat,* and Gershwin's *Rhapsody in Blue* and *Porgy
and Bess* are nominated for permanence.

America's musical genius was best revealed not in the classical forms,
but in folk melodies and their modern equivalents, ragtime, jazz, blues,
and swing. The wealth of Negro folk music was first exploited by
Stephen Foster in the nineteenth century, and the Jubilee singers of Fisk
University was the first American choir to be well received in Europe.
The Negro carried jazz north from New Orleans up the river to Chicago,
and by 1915, the year W. C. Handy wrote 'St. Louis Blues,' jazz had
reached New York's Harlem. In the ensuing years for the first time in
America composers and performers became popular heroes. Benny
Goodman and Duke Ellington and Louis Armstrong won a loyal follow-
ing among millions of Americans ranging from 'bobby-soxers' to musical
sophisticates. No less important is the wealth of folk music only now
being discovered and exploited. Lumberjacks, miners, cowboys, sailors,
Appalachian mountaineers, canal boys, all had their own body of songs.

What we have lacked in music of our own has been partly made up
for in appreciation of the music of others. In World War I music became
a normal part of the curriculum of every school. The radio enabled the
whole nation to enjoy symphonies and operas, and sales of phonograph
records reached almost astronomical heights. Few cities were so be-
nighted as to lack a symphony orchestra — no less than eighty-four new
ones were established in the depression decade — and if the nation
could support few opera companies, that was rather a comment on the
decline of the leisure-class tradition than an indictment of musical taste.
The totalitarian terror recruited to our shores some of the most distinguished of contemporary European composers — Stravinsky, Hindemith, Bartók, Schönberg, to mention only a few. Musical conservatories
like the Juilliard, Eastman, and Curtis flourished, and great foundations

like the Guggenheim stood ready to give such patronage to budding genius as Mozart and Schubert never knew.

4. SCIENCE

It is possible that American civilization during these years will be judged neither by material achievements nor by arts and letters, but by contributions to science. While the Nobel Prize in literature went to Americans only three times before 1945 (Sinclair Lewis, Eugene O'Neill, Pearl Buck), eight Americans received the prize in physics, seven in medicine, and three in chemistry.

Tocqueville had observed, back in the 1830's, that 'in America the purely practical part of science is admirably understood, and careful attention is paid to the theoretical portion which is immediately requisite to application . . . but hardly any one in the United States devotes himself to the essentially theoretical and abstract portion of human knowledge.' That was still true, a century later, yet by then not only universities but industry were liberally underwriting research in pure science. What is more, the United States greatly benefited from the migration of European scientists, and other intellectuals, which set in with the advent of Hitler to power in 1933. Einstein was merely the most famous of hundreds of physicists, chemists, and medical men who found in America refuge from oppression and an opportunity to pursue their researches in the most favorable circumstances. The most striking advances came in astronomy and physics. Working with the giant telescope of Mt. Wilson Observatory, which enabled them to plot thousands of new galaxies, astronomers postulated an expanding universe. Physicists, meantime, invented the cyclotron to break down the composition of the atom and held out the hope that we might obtain from some elements — uranium, for example — fabulous new sources of energy that would end dependence on fuel.

Yet, able as they were to chart a new universe of infinite vastness or to penetrate to the secret of the atom, this generation of scientists held out no assurance of ultimate understanding of the laws that governed the universe or even that there were any laws. Under the impact of the new science ancient certainties faded, and with them the illusion that the cosmos was governed by laws that man could comprehend. According to Percy W. Bridgman:

The physicist finds himself in a world from which the bottom has dropped clean out; as he penetrates deeper and deeper it eludes him and fades away by the highly unsportsmanlike device of just becoming meaningless. No refinement of measurement will avail to carry him beyond the portals of this shadowy domain which he cannot even mention without logical inconsistency. A bound is thus forever set to the curiosity of the physicist. What is more, the mere existence of this bound means that he must give up his most cherished convictions and faith. The world is not a world of reason, understandable by the intellect of man, but as we penetrate ever deeper, the very law of cause and effect, which we had thought to be a formula to which we could force God Himself to subscribe, ceases to have any meaning. The world is not intrinsically reasonable or understandable; it acquires these properties in ever-increasing degree as we ascend from the realm of the very little to the realm of everyday things; here we may eventually hope for an understanding sufficiently good for all practical purposes.[10]

Throughout this generation doctors and chemists and bacteriologists, working in the laboratories of universities, the Federal Government, or the great foundations, waged war against diseases that had baffled medical science for centuries. The results were spectacular. In the first third of the century, infant mortality declined in the United States by two-thirds and life expectancy increased from 49 years to 59 years. The death rate for tuberculosis dropped from 180 to 49 per 100,000, for typhoid from 36 to 2, for diphtheria from 43 to 2, for measles from 12 to 1, while pneumonia fatalities decreased from 158 to 50 and were still going down rapidly; sulfa drugs and, later, penicillin almost ended them. Yellow fever and smallpox were practically wiped out, and the war on malaria, pellagra, hookworm, and similar diseases was brilliantly successful. A new study of the role of the glandular system led to the discovery of specifics against endocrine disorders. Within a few years insulin had cut the death rate of diabetes from over 700 to 12 per 1000 cases. Pernicious anemia, long regarded as fatal, yielded readily to the use of liver and liver extracts and, later, to vitamins. Adrenalin proved helpful in cardiac disorders and gave relief to sufferers from asthma. Tannic acid worked cures on apparently fatal burns. In anesthesia, too, the perfection of avertin and cyclopropane made possible new miracles of surgery. Chemistry opened the way to an appreciation of the role of vitamins in maintaining health and building up resistance to dis-

10. 'The New Version of Science,' *Harper's Magazine*, March 1929.

eases; numerous ailments like pellagra and rickets yielded to vitamin treatment, and the discovery led to dietary reforms, as well as to considerable proprietary quackery.

The most sensational medical development was the successful fight against coccus infections. In 1935 the German Dr. Domagk announced that prontosil was effective in arresting streptococcal infection. At the Pasteur Institute in Paris, prontosil was broken down and sulfanilamide isolated as the effective ingredient. English and American doctors promptly experimented with sulfanilamide and its numerous derivatives and found that it could be used with spectacular success against a host of coccal infections—streptococcus, meningitis, gonorrhoea, gangrene, pyelitis, and, above all, pneumonia.

These immense advances in medical science put better health within the reach of all, yet the general health of the American people was not a matter for complacency. Infant mortality was still higher than in such countries as Norway and Sweden, and the draft statistics of the early 'forties revealed that an astonishingly high proportion of American men suffered from poor eyesight, bad teeth, and other ailments caused by poverty or neglect, and that the incidence of venereal disease was shockingly high, especially in the rural counties of the South. The clear correlation between health and income suggested the desirability of government support to public health comparable with that given to public education, a goal that America did not even begin to take seriously until the 1960's and has yet to achieve.

XIX

The Great Depression and
the New Deal

1. THE GREAT DEPRESSION

The stock market crash of 1929 soon confronted the United States with its greatest crisis since the Civil War. Once under way the spiral of the depression swept out in an ever-widening curve. Millions of investors lost their savings; thousands were forced into bankruptcy; over 5000 banks closed their doors in the first three years of the depression. Debts mounted, purchases declined, factories cut down production, workers were dismissed, wages and salaries slashed. Real estate sagged in value and tax collections dropped alarmingly, forcing governments to cut essential services. Construction work, except for government operations, practically ceased. Foreign trade declined in three years from $9 billion to $3 billion. One writer observed: 'We seem to have stepped Alice-like through an economic looking-glass into a world where everything shrivels. Bond prices, stock prices, commodity prices, employment — they all dwindle.'

The depression struck a devastating blow at the farmer, already hard hit, and when he was unable to meet his obligations, his mortgage was foreclosed, sometimes on land that had been held in his family for generations. Between 1920 and 1932 total farm income declined from $15.5 billion to $5.5 billion. In these years corn fell from 61 cents to 32 cents; cotton from 16 cents a pound to 6 cents; wheat from $1.82 a bushel to 38

471

cents. 'Wheat on the Liverpool market,' noted one observer, 'fetched the lowest price since the reign of Charles II.'

As the depression wore on, unemployment mounted to staggering levels, and suffering became intense. Of New England's 280,000 textile millhands, 120,000 had no work a year after the crash. New Bedford was bankrupt; Lowell and Lawrence seemed like ghost towns. By 1933 the number of jobless was variously estimated at from 12 to more than 15 million, as factory payrolls fell to less than half the level of 1929. In a country of some 120 million people, probably more than 40 million were either unemployed or members of a family in which the main breadwinner was out of work. Those who did have jobs often worked for a pittance. Women in Tennessee textile mills got $2.29 for a fifty-hour week which was better than the $1.10 a week paid young girls for sweatshop labor in progressive Connecticut. Grown men worked for 5 cents an hour in sawmills. Negroes learned the cruel truth of the saying that they were the 'last to be hired, first to be fired.' Yet this desperate deprivation came at a time when orchards were heavy with fruit, granaries bulging with grain, factories burdened with inventories of clothing. Pennsylvania coal miners froze in the midst of mountains of coal, while their children lived on weeds and dandelions.

Perhaps as many as two million were wandering the country by the summer of 1932; of these, the Children's Bureau estimated that 200,000 were young boys and girls. In 1932 the Southern Pacific ejected 683,000 trespassers, mostly young men from 16 to 25. By the end of the year, the railroads, fearing the raiding of sealed cars and hoping to cut down on the rising number of boys maimed or killed in leaping for cars, surrendered to the 'Vagabond Army' and added empty freight cars to accommodate the migrants. In cold weather riding the rods was a grim business. One investigator wrote: 'Last winter in one Western city thirty-five young men and boys were removed from box cars, seriously ill, some in an advanced stage of pneumonia.' If they entered a town, they risked a jail term for having no visible means of support. *Fortune* reported: 'Atlanta, a natural way station of the hobo route in the South, gives thirty-day sentences in the city stockade or the chain gang — both of which are filled with degenerates — to anyone caught on a freight train within Fulton County. . . . Yet 6,000 wandering boys were listed there through September, 1932.'

The magisterial historian of these tragic years has described the second winter of the depression:

> The cold was bitter in unheated tenements, in the flophouses smelling of sweat and Lysol, in the parks, the empty freight cars, along the windy water-fronts. With no money left for rent, unemployed men and their entire families began to build shacks where they could find unoccupied land. Along the railroad embankment, beside the garbage incinerator, in the city dumps, there appeared towns of tar-paper and tin, old packaging-boxes and old car-bodies. . . . Symbols of the New Era, these communities quickly received their sardonic name: they were called Hoovervilles. And, indeed, it was in many cases only the fortunate who could find Hoovervilles. The unfortunate spent their nights huddled together in doorways, in empty packing cases, in box-cars. At the bread lines and soup kitchens, hours of waiting would produce a bowl of mush, often without milk or sugar, and a tin cup of coffee. The vapours from the huge steam cookers mingling with the stench of wet clothes and steaming bodies made the air foul. But waiting in the soup kitchen was better than scavenging in the dump. Citizens of Chicago could be seen digging into heaps of refuse with sticks and hands as soon as the garbage trucks pulled out. On June 30, 1931, the Pennsylvania Department of Labor reported that nearly one-quarter of the labor force of the state was out of work. 'Have you ever heard a hungry child cry?' asked Lillian Wald of Henry Street.[1]

The depression seriously impaired confidence in business leadership. Nowhere else in the world had the titans of finance and the moguls of industry enjoyed such prestige, or had their titles of leadership been so uncritically accepted as in the United States. But by 1932 businessmen who in the 1920's had taken credit for prosperity now found themselves saddled with the blame for hard times. One economist wrote: 'It is easier to believe that the earth is flat than to believe that private initiative alone will save us.' Marriner Eccles, the head of a Utah economic empire, wrote that his friends, his family, and the community all expected him 'to find the way out of the pit,' but he felt that after 17 years in the world of finance and production he 'knew less than nothing about its economic and social effects.' He recalled: 'Night after night following that head-splitting awakening I would return home exhausted by the

1. Arthur Schlesinger, Jr., *The Crisis of the Old Order*, p. 177.

pretensions of knowledge I was forced to wear in a daytime masquerade.'

Yet business leaders became discredited not merely because they were judged responsible for the depression and proved unable to restore prosperity but because so many revealed themselves derelict in duty and guilty of grave malpractices and even of outright corruption. The public learned with astonishment that the dignified House of Morgan kept a 'preferred list' of influential public men to whom it sold securities below the market price, and that in the depression years of 1930 and 1931 not a single partner of that banking firm had paid any income tax; that Charles E. Mitchell of the great National City Bank of New York made $2.5 million of stockholders' money available to bank officers for speculation, without interest or security; that great banking houses palmed off on gullible investors South American bonds that they knew to be almost worthless; and that a powerful banker like former Vice-President Charles E. Dawes used his position and influence to obtain favors for his bank. 'The belief that those in control of the corporate life of America were motivated by ideals of honorable conduct was completely shattered,' observed the millionaire Joseph P. Kennedy. Not for another quarter of a century did the business community recover something of its former prestige.

The crisis in confidence produced by the depression was far graver than even this disaffection with business leadership suggested. Throughout the Western world, men brooded over whether the great society of the West which had grown in strength since the days of Charlemagne had not begun to disintegrate. In Marc Connelly's play, *Green Pastures*, produced in 1930, the angel Gabriel told de Lawd: 'Everything nailed down is comin' loose.' The British historian Arnold Toynbee commented: 'The year 1931 was distinguished from previous years — in the "post-war" and in the "pre-war" age alike — by one outstanding feature. In 1931, men and women all over the world were seriously contemplating and frankly discussing the possibility that the Western system of Society might break down and cease to work.' If in Europe men wondered whether the Western world had not reached the stage of the Roman empire after Theodosius, most Americans were of a more optimistic frame of mind. Yet even in the United States the cold fear that the world Americans had known might be at an end could not easily be overcome. 'With the present breakdown, we have come to the end of something,'

Edmund Wilson wrote in 1931. The depression might 'be nothing less than one of the turning-points in our history.' The following year Colorado's Senator Edward Costigan told a reporter: 'Sometimes, of course, in history the door is finally closed.'

2. THE HOOVER RESPONSE

The Hoover administration discounted the seriousness of the depression, for to those who had guided the destinies of the nation throughout the unprecedented prosperity of the 1920's, it seemed inconceivable that the economic structure should collapse. The panic, they were convinced, was a stock market panic, induced by speculation and precipitated by fear; all that was necessary for a return of prosperity was a restoration of confidence. To this end the administration directed its energies. In conference after conference with the industrial leaders of the country, President Hoover urged the maintenance of employment and wages; in speech after speech he exhorted the nation to keep a stiff upper lip. But he did more than this. Assuming responsibilities no president had ever taken on before, he stepped up federal public works and encouraged construction by state and local governments; announced a tax cut; and, through the Federal Reserve System, pursued an easy credit policy. To support crop prices, the Federal Farm Board purchased vast quantities of wheat and cotton.

Yet these measures were largely nullified by other policies. Committed to budget-balancing, Hoover took away with one hand what he gave with the other. When he asked governors to accelerate public works, he instructed them to be 'energetic but prudent.' The increase in federal spending for public works was so modest that it was more than offset by the drastic cut in state and local spending. Although he insisted that the source of America's troubles lay overseas, he agreed to the Hawley-Smoot tariff which raised new barriers to international trade. Above all, he persisted in relying on voluntary agreements even when this faith proved misplaced.

Nothing demonstrates so well the inadequacy of voluntarism as the sad experience of Hoover's Federal Farm Board. Despite the loans the Board granted to co-operatives, cotton prices skidded from 17½ cents in October 1929 to less than 12 cents in the summer of 1930. In June 1930 the Board intervened in the market to buy crops, but in a single season prices fell to 8 cents. The program failed because the Board was attempting to support crop prices without restricting production, and it was swamped by surpluses. In the summer of 1931, faced by glut of millions of bales of cotton, the chairman of the Board wired cotton state governors 'to induce immediate plowing under of every third row of cotton now growing.' But Hoover continued to hold out against controls. By June 1932 cotton prices had slumped to 4.6 cents. The Board had financed the removal of 3½ million bales from the market only to see ten million bales added to the surfeit. Since Hoover would not sanction acreage control, the Farm Board abandoned the hope of maintaining prices and contented itself with liquidating losses running into hundreds of thousands of dollars. After the collapse of these voluntary price stabilization operations, Hoover had nothing more to offer. The farmer faced ruin, and because of his importance to the economy of agrarian states, he threatened to pull the nation's banks down with him.

Despite mounting evidence of the breakdown of his program for recovery, Hoover spurned appeals for more vigorous federal action. He shared the common belief that federal spending would prolong the depression by discouraging business investment and inviting inflation. A man touted as a Great Engineer, he brought to government none of the engineer's insistence on testing theories by their results. One who prided himself on his willingness to consult experts, he ignored advice which ran counter to his preconceptions. For all of his enterprise in Washington at the outset of the depression, not once in the first two years of the crisis did he call on Congress to take a significant step. In March 1931, Congressman Fiorello La Guardia reflected: 'Every day as I lie here in bed I try to think of what the last Congress accomplished to meet the depression. With the exception of additional appropriations for public improvements, nothing constructive was done.'

'As a nation,' said President Hoover just a year after the crash, 'we *must* prevent hunger and cold to those of our people who are in honest difficulties.' But the administration was unwilling to grant direct relief; that burden was one for local governments and private charity to shoulder. In vain did progressives like La Follette, Costigan, and Cutting plead for a large-scale program of public works, financed directly by federal funds. In vain did they present statistics proving the breakdown of private charity and the inability of municipal and state authorities to carry the burden any longer. Every proposal for generous relief was met by the stubborn opposition of Bourbon Democrats and Republican Tories whose devotion to the fictions of states' rights and the shibboleth of a balanced budget blinded them to realities. When the House threatened to pass a bill appropriating some $2 billion for public works, the President warned: 'This is not unemployment relief. It is the most gigantic pork-barrel ever perpetrated by the American Congress.'

In 1931 European financial squalls struck the United States in full force. In June Hoover braved the displeasure of isolationists by proposing a one-year moratorium on reparations and war debt payments, a constructive move but one which failed to save the day. The European panic caused a fresh financial crisis in America. In August 158 banks failed, in September, 305, in October, 522. When the Federal Reserve Board raised the rediscount rate sharply, it halted the flow of gold but did untold damage. As credit tightened, production fell off, stocks plummeted, and a typhoon of bank failures swept areas that had been hardly touched before: New England, the Carolinas, the Pacific Northwest.

Hoover responded first by encouraging bankers to set up their own credit organization, and then by asking Congress for an eight-point program intended chiefly to shore up the great financial institutions. In December 1931 he called on Congress to establish a Reconstruction Finance Corporation, which was the old War Finance Corporation in new guise. The RFC, chartered by Congress in 1932, was authorized to lend money to banks, railroads, and other institutions threatened by destruction. Congress also approved most of the remainder of Hoover's requests in 1932, including the creation of such institutions as the Federal Home Loan Banks to discount mortgages.

Yet Hoover's new program proved no more successful than his original efforts, and for the same reasons: he acted on too small a scale and his faith in voluntarism was misplaced. The RFC made so little use of its power that it frustrated the intent of Congress. The Federal Home Loan Banking System neither averted collapse of the mortgage market nor helped the distressed homeowner. The credit organization fell apart when the bankers refused to co-operate. As Hoover himself later wrote: 'After a few weeks of enterprising courage, the bankers' National Credit Association became ultra-conservative, then fearful, and finally died. It had not exerted anything like its full possible strength. Its members — and the business world — threw up their hands and asked for government action.'

This same misplaced faith in voluntarism marked Hoover's approach to relief for the unemployed. Despite widespread hardship, Hoover claimed that federal relief was not needed, and that the traditional sources — private charity and local government — would meet the needs of the unfortunate. But neither private agencies nor municipal governments could hope to meet distress in a city like Cleveland where 50 per cent of the work force were jobless, or in Akron or East St. Louis when unemployment reached 60 per cent, or Toledo where it mounted to 80 per cent. At the start of the depression Allen T. Burns, director of the Association of Community Chests, opposed federal aid, but in December 1931 he told a Senate committee that when he looked at the situation in even the best cities, he was 'just appalled, absolutely dumbfounded as to how they are going to get through.' Confronted by the harsh arithmetic of relief needs four times greater than the community chests could collect, Burns announced that he now supported federal action. Nor was local government action any more satisfactory. Even when cities vastly increased their spending for relief, the sums did not begin to be enough. Chicago paid $100,000 a day for relief in a city where workers were losing $2 million a day in wages.

By the spring of 1932 the country confronted a relief crisis. New York City, where the average family stipend for relief was $2.39 a week, had 25,000 emergency cases on its waiting list. Houston, Texas, announced: 'Applications are not taken from unemployed Mexican or colored families. They are being asked to shift for themselves.' In May 1932, the vice chairman of the Mayor's Unemployment Commission of Detroit saw 'no possibility of preventing widespread hunger and slow starvation . . . through its own unaided resources.' In Chicago, families were separated, and husbands and wives sent to different shelters. On 25 June 1932, Philadelphia ran out of funds — private, municipal, state — and suspended aid to some 52,000 families. But Hoover, doggedly, stubbornly, continued to insist that he had the situation well in hand.

3. THE ELECTION OF 1932

The failure of Hoover to liquidate the depression placed the Republicans in an extremely vulnerable position; every indication pointed to a Democratic victory in 1932. This prospect dampened Republican zeal;

Hoover's renomination was neither contested nor greeted with enthusiasm. But in the Democratic camp competition for the nomination was sharp. Alfred E. Smith's large popular vote in the previous election justified him in believing that he might now overcome the handicaps that had then thwarted him and lead his party to victory. Others regarded the anti-Catholic prejudice as insuperable and called for new leadership. By far the most prominent of the several aspirants was Franklin Delano Roosevelt.

A distant connection of the famous T. R., and married to the former President's niece, Franklin D. Roosevelt was born to wealth and position, educated at Groton School, Harvard, and the Columbia Law School. As a child, Roosevelt had learned a patrician's conviction of *noblesse oblige*. At Groton this sense had been reinforced by Rector Endicott Peabody who preached the duty of service to the less fortunate, a faith modeled on that of the Cambridge professor, Charles Kingsley. Like all the Roosevelts except the Oyster Bay branch, he was born a Democrat. At the age of 29 he was elected state senator from the 'silk-stocking' Dutchess County district where he had inherited a country estate, and promptly caught the public's eye by opposing the election of Boss Murphy's candidate to the United States Senate. After supporting Wilson in 1912, he was appointed Assistant Secretary of the Navy. Contact with Wilson served to deepen Roosevelt's liberal convictions, companionship with Bryan and Daniels broadened his democratic sympathies, while acquaintance with party leaders taught him the political ropes. In 1920 he was nominated as Cox's running mate; the following year his promising political career was apparently ended by a severe case of infantile paralysis. During the next seven years, he stubbornly fought his way back to health.

Roosevelt returned to politics in 1928 rugged in health, although permanently crippled, rejuvenated in spirit, better known in the party than before, and one of the best-informed men in the country on a wide range of subjects. That year, the voters of New York elected Roosevelt governor when they rejected Smith for President. Two years later Governor Roosevelt was re-elected by a majority of 700,000 and thus became the leading contender for the next presidential nomination. Smith, embittered, broke with his former friend whom he denounced as a demagogue. Roosevelt also faced the formidable opposition of Speaker John

Nance Garner. But after a closely fought contest, Roosevelt mustered the necessary two-thirds vote, and Garner was chosen as the vice-presidential nominee.

Partly to prove his physical vigor, partly to capitalize on his personal magnetism, Roosevelt chose to embark upon an old-fashioned stump-speaking tour which took him into almost every state of the Union. Running safely ahead, FDR straddled a number of important questions and was silent on others. He also made some statements, especially on the need for government economy, that were to seem hilarious in retrospect. At Forbes Field in Pittsburgh, he scolded Hoover as a spendthrift and expressed his horror that by June 1933 the federal deficit might reach 1.6 billion dollars, 'a deficit so great that it makes us catch our breath.' Yet Roosevelt also made clear that he favored unemployment relief, farm legislation, and 'bold and persistent experimentation' to give a 'new deal' to the 'forgotten man.' Furthermore, he showed a willingness to turn to the universities for counsel, since his 'Brain Trust' of speech writers and advisers included three Columbia University professors: Raymond Moley, Rexford Guy Tugwell, and Adolf A. Berle, Jr.

President Hoover, laboring under the dead weight of hard times, made matters worse when in June 1932 a 'bonus army' marched on Washington to demand immediate payment of the bonuses voted to veterans of World War I. Camping on the flats within sight of the Capitol building, this 'petition on boots' seemed to Hoover an offense against the dignity of the government and with singular ineptitude he called on the National Guard to break up the camp and drive out the veterans. Swords in hand, cavalrymen rode down the marchers and their wives and children, burning their hovels and scattering their pitiful possessions. The smouldering ruins of Anacostia flats created deep indignation and confirmed the impression that the President was hostile to the dispossessed. 'Never before in this country,' commented one writer, 'has the government fallen to so low a place in popular estimation, or been so universally an object of cynical contempt. Never before has the chief magistrate given his name so liberally to latrines and offal dumps, or had his face banished from the screen to avoid the hoots and jeers of children.'

Hoover could only recite his efforts to cope with the depression, prophesy that a Democratic tariff would mean that 'the grass will grow in the streets of a hundred cities, a thousand towns,' and reaffirm his

COMPOSITION OF CONGRESS, 1928-1969

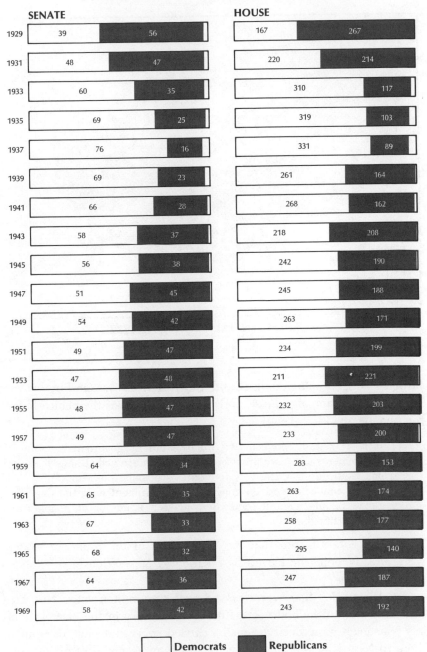

	SENATE	HOUSE
1929	39 / 56	167 / 267
1931	48 / 47	220 / 214
1933	60 / 35	310 / 117
1935	69 / 25	319 / 103
1937	76 / 16	331 / 89
1939	69 / 23	261 / 164
1941	66 / 28	268 / 162
1943	58 / 37	218 / 208
1945	56 / 38	242 / 190
1947	51 / 45	245 / 188
1949	54 / 42	263 / 171
1951	49 / 47	234 / 199
1953	47 / 48	211 / 221
1955	48 / 47	232 / 203
1957	49 / 47	233 / 200
1959	64 / 34	283 / 153
1961	65 / 35	263 / 174
1963	67 / 33	258 / 177
1965	68 / 32	295 / 140
1967	64 / 36	247 / 187
1969	58 / 42	243 / 192

☐ Democrats   ■ Republicans

Other parties and independents shown by white at end of bar.

481

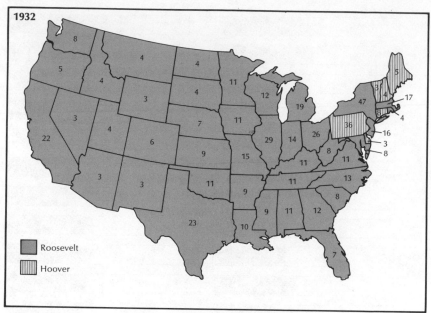

PRESIDENTIAL ELECTION, 1932

faith in rugged individualism and the American system. In his last speech of the campaign he set forth his conception of the choice before the people:

> It is a contest between two philosophies of government. . . . Our opponents . . . are proposing changes and so-called new deals which would destroy the very foundations of our American system. . . . You cannot extend the mastery of government over the daily life of a people without somewhere making it master of people's souls and thoughts.

Too many voters feared that the foundations of the American system were already being destroyed by attrition to take seriously this impassioned warning.

On election day Roosevelt received almost 23 million votes, Hoover a little less than 16 million votes. Roosevelt's victory in the electoral college was even more decisive, for he carried every state but six, four of them in New England. Hoover, with less than 40 per cent of the vote, sustained the worst defeat ever inflicted on a Republican presidential nominee in a two-party race. The Democrats also won their greatest majority in the House since 1890 and their largest margin in the Senate since before the Civil War. The Great Depression had ended the reign of the Republicans as the nation's majority party and fastened on the GOP the unwelcome reputation of the party of hard times.

Franklin Roosevelt would not take office for another four months since the Twentieth Amendment, the 'lame duck' proposal advanced by Senator George Norris, had not yet been ratified. The harsh interregnum was a time of exaggerated worry over the peril of incipient revolution, as Iowa farm rebels recalled the insurrection of Daniel Shays, but it was even more a time of torpor. Harold Clurman recalled the drab anxiety of New York City that winter: 'It seemed as if the very color of the city had changed. From an elegant bright gray by day and a sparkling gold by night, the afternoons had grown haggard, the nights mournful.' The morale of the country had been shattered, and many seemed almost palsied by fear. Charles M. Schwab of Bethlehem Steel was quoted as saying: 'I'm afraid, every man is afraid.' One periodical thought the clue to the period lay in Shakespeare's words:

> I find the people strangely fantasied;
> Possess'd with rumours, full of idle dreams;
> Not knowing what they fear, but full of fear.

The premonitions of disaster seemed well-founded when, on the eve of Roosevelt's inauguration, banks closed their doors in every section of the country and on the morning of inauguration day the Stock Exchange closed down. As the financial system collapsed, all eyes looked toward Washington. It seemed to many that it mattered less what the incoming President did than that he act boldly. 'A fool who will do something and stick to it and pound out a policy in this crisis, a fool who can lead is better than a wise man who can fumble,' wrote William Allen White. On the eve of the inauguration, *Editor and Publisher* asserted:

> What this country needs, if we are to shake off the torpor of fear and hopelessness, is a series of blinding head-lines proclaiming action, resolute leadership, a firm grip at the controls. . . .
> Blinding head-lines . . . let them come! The people and the press await with bated breath.

4. WALL STREET AND WASHINGTON

When Roosevelt took the oath of office on 4 March 1933, he made no effort to minimize the danger. He said in his inaugural address:

> Values have shrunken to fantastic levels; taxes have risen; our ability to pay has failed; government of all kinds is faced by serious curtailment of income; the means of exchange are frozen in the currents of trade; the withered leaves of industrial enterprise lie on every side; farmers find no markets for their produce; the savings of many years in thousands of families are gone. More important, a host of unemployed citizens face the grim problem of existence and an equally great number toil with little return. Only a foolish optimist can deny the dark realities of the moment.

There followed an excoriation of the 'unscrupulous money changers' who 'stand indicted in the court of public opinion,' and of the 'false leadership' which had attempted to solve problems through exhortation. 'They have no vision,' said Roosevelt, who like Bryan and Wilson knew the value of biblical phrases, 'and where there is no vision the people perish.'

Roosevelt had no intention of emulating his predecessor in relying upon exhortation. 'This nation,' he said, 'asks for action, and action now!' He warned Congress and the country that the emergency called for emergency measures.

> It is to be hoped that the normal balance of executive and legislative authority may be wholly adequate to meet the unprecedented task before us. But it may be that an unprecedented demand and need for undelayed action may call for temporary departure from that normal balance of public procedure. I am prepared under my constitutional duty to recommend the measures that a stricken nation in the midst of a stricken world may require.

If Congress failed to support these recommendations,

> I shall not evade the clear course of duty that will then confront me. I shall ask the Congress for the one remaining instrument to meet the crisis — broad Executive power to wage a war against the emergency as great as the power that would be given me if we were in fact invaded by a foreign foe. . . . The people of the United States have asked for discipline and direction under leadership. They have made me the present instrument of their wishes.

The speech, with its criticism of the old order and its promise of executive leadership toward a new, typified the outlook of Franklin D. Roosevelt, who combined qualities that perhaps no President since Jefferson possessed in such happy proportion. He had political acumen, the ability to work through established political machinery and to champion reform without antagonizing party bosses. He had personal charm equally effective in social intercourse, public appearances, or over the radio. A cultivated gentleman, he did not distrust scholarship in politics and was able to command the services of an enthusiastic and loyal group of experts to furnish ideas, formulate legislation, and implement policies. He combined audacity and courage; tenacious of ultimate ends, he was almost recklessly opportunist as to means. He knew how to dramatize himself and his policies and how to create a favorable climate of opinion in which to work, and he inspired loyalty to his ideas as well as to his person.

The legislation of the first Roosevelt administration did not constitute a revolution; the popular name, New Deal, is more correct. Its philosophy was deeply rooted in the American tradition. New Deal legislation was an attempt to catch up the political lag of the postwar years and to articulate government to the facts of a depressed economy. Three bodies of precedents illuminated the course of the New Deal: the federal regulation of business and railroads dating back to the 1880's; the social legislation of progressive states such as Massachusetts, New York, Wisconsin, and Oregon; and the experiments in social welfare carried on by some of the more progressive nations of Northern Europe and the British Commonwealth; while the organization of American industry and business, which had long accepted such practices as price-fixing agreements, codes, and cartels, provided antecedents for some of the economic regulations.

Roosevelt moved swiftly to deal with the financial crisis. His first task was to rehabilitate the nation's banks. In the Treasury, lights burned all through the night as Hoover and Roosevelt lieutenants worked together in a spirit of wartime unity to cope with the banking disaster. On the day after his inauguration, the President issued two edicts: one summoned Congress into special session; the other halted transactions in gold and proclaimed a national bank holiday. When Congress convened on 9 March, it took only seven hours to pass Roosevelt's banking bill which validated presidential powers over banks and facilitated the re-opening of liquid banks under proper regulation. Three days later, in the first of his radio 'fireside chats,' the President told his listeners it was safer to 'keep your money in a reopened bank than under the mattress'; when the bank holiday ended the next morning in Federal Reserve cities, deposits exceeded withdrawals. The crisis had been ended. Although the powers of government had been greatly enhanced, the nation's financial institutions remained in private hands.

Roosevelt had issued the bank holiday edict under authority of the Trading-with-the-Enemy Act of 1917, and the New Dealers frequently resorted to metaphors of wartime unity to rally support for their program during the 'Hundred Days.' From 9 March until Congress adjourned on 16 June, Roosevelt sent fifteen different proposals to Congress and saw all fifteen adopted. In quick succession, he followed up his banking message with proposals for government economy and to amend the Volstead Act to legalize light wine and beer.[2] Within two weeks after FDR took office, the country seemed to have regained a large share of its sense of purpose, a recapture of morale, said Walter Lippmann, comparable only to the news of the second battle of the Marne. From Britain, James Louis Garvin commented in *The Observer:* 'America has found a man. In him at a later stage, the world must find a leader. Undaunted by the magnitude of his stupendous task and cool in the face of its urgency, Mr. Roosevelt has made a splendid beginning.'

Yet the weight of Roosevelt's early actions was deflationary, and he recognized that he must experiment with ways to raise prices, especially in order to alleviate the debt burden. In a bold series of actions, he took the United States off the gold standard.[3] The President also moved slowly toward some kind of managed currency, but cheap money advocates from the South and West compelled him to act more swiftly by foisting on him discretionary powers to undertake various kinds of inflation. That fall, Roosevelt tried to raise prices through buying gold, and

2. Before the year was out, the Twenty-first Amendment repealing the Eighteenth (Prohibition) Amendment had been ratified.

3. A Joint Resolution of 5 June, designed to avoid the difficulties which had attended Civil War legal tender, canceled the gold clauses in all government and private obligations and made all debts payable in legal tender. When the resolution was challenged in the courts, the Supreme Court in a 5–4 decision sustained congressional power over legal tender and held that though the cancellation of gold clauses in government contracts was both illegal and immoral the plaintiff had suffered no damage and had no grounds for suit.

he later bowed to the demand of Mountain State senators to undertake silver purchases.

Currency manipulation did not effect any appreciable increase in commodity prices, and in January 1934 the President, 'to make possible the payment of public and private debts at more nearly the price level at which they had been incurred,' obtained authority to devaluate the dollar, impound all gold in the Treasury and the Federal Reserve Banks, and create out of the accruing profit a stabilization fund of $2 billion. He fixed the value of the dollar at 59.06, and the nation returned to this modified gold standard. Friends of the administration credited improvement of commodity prices to this dollar devaluation; critics averred that improvement would have come in any event, and that devaluation worked unwarranted hardship upon security holders. Perhaps the only indisputable effect was to attract much of the world's gold to the United States, where it was buried in the vaults of Fort Knox, in Kentucky. None could deny, however, that the goal of controlled inflation had been carried through with utmost caution or that the dangers of printing-press money had been skillfully avoided.

Roosevelt also dealt with the debt burden more directly. In the five years from 1927 to 1932 not less than 10 per cent of the country's farm property had been foreclosed at auction; in certain sections these foreclosures had become so numerous that farmers banded together to intimidate prospective purchasers, close courts, and terrorize judges. In late April, 1933, a mob dragged an Iowa judge off his bench and came close to lynching him. The following month Congress authorized the creation of a new Farm Credit Administration which made possible the refunding of farm loans at drastically lower rates of interest, provided more than $100 million for new mortgages in a few months, and set up machinery for equitable adjustment of farm debts. Within eighteen months, the FCA had refinanced a fifth of all farm mortgages in the United States. Congress also came to the aid of the distressed home owner, in the cities as well as in the country. In June 1933 it established a Home Owners' Loan Corporation to refinance small mortgages on privately owned homes; within a year this corporation had approved over 300,000 loans amounting to almost a billion dollars.

Roosevelt, who had a patrician's distrust of Wall Street and a Wilsonian's memory of the machinations of the 'money trust,' was determined to discipline the financiers. The congressional investigation of banking and securities practices under the skillful direction of Ferdinand Pecora, which revealed conditions characterized as 'scandalous,' and the banking collapse of 1932–33 dramatized the need and furnished the opportunity for reform. A group of Senators led by Robert M. La Follette Jr. of Wisconsin and Bronson Cutting of New Mexico tried to persuade the President to seize the opportunity to nationalize the entire banking system, but the proposal was either too radical or too novel to win the President's backing. Instead he gave his approval to the Glass-Steagall Banking Act of 16 June 1933. This measure provided for the separation of commercial and investment banking, severe restrictions on the use of bank credit for speculative purposes, and the expansion of the Federal Reserve System to embrace banks heretofore excluded. To prevent a recurrence of the epidemic of bank failures of the 1920's the act set up a Federal Deposit Insurance Corporation to insure bank deposits up to a fixed sum. Roosevelt accepted this proposal with reservations, and the American Bankers Association denounced it as 'unsound, unscientific, unjust and dangerous,' but it turned out to be one of the most constructive devices of the whole New Deal era. Bank failures, which had averaged a thousand a year in the previous decade, became almost non-existent. During the 'Second Hundred Days' of the summer of 1935, Congress put the final stone in the new structure of government regulation of banking with the passage of the Banking Act of 1935 which expanded the powers of the reorganized and newly named Board of Governors of the Federal Reserve System.

On 29 March the President asked Congress to add 'to the ancient rule of caveat emptor, the further doctrine "let the seller also beware." ' Modeled closely upon the British Companies Act and Directors' Liability Act, the Securities Act of 27 May 1933 provided that all new securities offered or advertised for interstate sale should be registered with a government agency, subsequently the Securities and Exchange Commission; that every offering should contain full information to enable the prospective purchaser to judge the value of the issue and the condition of the corporation; and that the directors and officers of the corporation were to be criminally liable for any deliberate omission of significant information or any wilful misstatement of fact.

The following year came legislation to curb malpractices on the Stock Exchange. The financial community was outraged at this interference but had nothing to propose in its stead. An act of 6 June 1934 created a

Securities and Exchange Commission, licensed stock exchanges and required the registration of all securities in which they dealt, prohibited pools, options, and other devices for manipulating the market, and empowered the Federal Reserve Board to determine the extension of credit for marginal and speculative loans. Joseph P. Kennedy of Boston, financier and speculator, was appointed chairman of the commission because, as Roosevelt said, he knew the tricks of the trade. Much of this legislation reflected the influence of the followers of Justice Louis Brandeis — Professor Felix Frankfurter of the Harvard Law School, Benjamin Cohen, Thomas Corcoran. In the Second Hundred Days, the Brandeisians scored their greatest triumph when Congress passed legislation to level the public utility holding companies and to place these companies, too, under the SEC.

Although the New Deal left the system of private control of credit and investment intact, it markedly altered the relationship between government and the world of finance. As early as 1934 one writer noted: 'Financial news no longer originates in Wall Street. The sources of such news have been moved to Washington. . . . The pace of the ticker is determined now in Washington, not in company board-rooms, or in brokerage offices.' The new securities and banking legislation, the expansion of the Reconstruction Finance Corporation under the Houston banker Jesse Jones, the enhanced powers of the Federal Reserve System under Marriner Eccles, and the accelerated rate of government spending gave Washington a significantly new position as senior partner in the management of the nation's finances.

5. FARM RELIEF

In consultation with national farm leaders, Roosevelt's Secretary of Agriculture, Henry A. Wallace, prepared a farm relief plan of unexpected boldness. On 12 May 1933 Congress passed the Agricultural Adjustment Act, in order to re-establish 'parity' between agriculture and industry by raising the level of commodity prices and easing the credit and mortgage load. Its most important provisions authorized the Secretary of Agriculture to make agreements with staple farmers whereby, in return for government subsidies, they undertook to reduce production of certain staple commodities. They would either rent the government land taken out of cultivation or restrict allotments in return for benefit payments. The costs of these payments were to be met from taxes on the processing of the products involved. The Secretary could also negotiate marketing agreements for commodities like citrus fruits and dairy products.

It was expected that this plan would not only bring cash payments but would raise crop prices and in this expectation farmers hastened to avail themselves of its benefits. Almost three-fourths of the cotton growers agreed to reduce their acreage by approximately one-third in return for cash payments of from $7 to $20 an acre or an option on the purchase of cotton held by the government up to the extent of their reduction the previous year. Altogether, in 1933, slightly over 10 million acres of land were taken out of production, thus reducing the cotton crop by at least 4 million bales. For this reduction planters received from the government some $200 million in benefit payments. In addition the price of cotton rose from 5.5 to 9.5 cents a pound. The total cash income of the cotton farmers for 1933 was thus more than double the income of the previous year. Subsequent arrangements, in 1934 and 1935, buttressed by the coercive Bankhead Cotton Control Act of April 1934, which empowered the AAA to impose marketing quotas, held the cotton crop down to about 10 million bales, continued generous benefit payments to planters, and maintained the price at 10 cents a pound or better.

The wheat program proved equally successful. Contracts with over 550,000 wheat farmers removed some 8 million acres from production, brought the co-operating wheat growers over $100 million in benefit payments, and contributed to an increase in the price of wheat and in the total income of wheat growers of approximately 100 per cent. The drought of 1934 and adverse crop conditions in 1935 necessitated a modification of the crop reduction program, and by the end of this period the government had disposed of surplus stocks held over from the Federal Farm Board operations, and the nation was importing wheat. The effort to reduce corn acreage and remove hogs from the market was attended with even greater success. In 1933 over a million corn and hog producers signed contracts with the AAA to reduce acreage by approximately 25 per cent; at the same time the government purchased and slaughtered for relief or other purposes some 6 million pigs and hogs. The result was the smallest corn crop since 1881, benefit payments totaling over $300 million, and higher prices for corn and pork. Corn growers, like cotton raisers, also had the opportunity to secure Commodity Credit Corporation loans which permitted them to store crops until prices rose. The reduction of the tobacco crop was spectacularly successful — from the farmers' point of view. Over 95 per cent of Southern farmers entered into agreements to cut tobacco production by almost one-third. Southern tobacco growers, who had received $56 million for their 1930 and $43 million for their 1933 crop, got $120 million for their 1934 crop. Comparable results were attained in other less important farm commodities. In part because of the AAA program of crop reduction, in part because of drought and government payments, and in part because of the devaluation of the dollar, farm income increased from $5,562,000,000 in 1932 to $8,688,000,000 in 1935.

On 6 January 1936 in a 6-3 decision the Supreme Court invalidated the AAA's processing tax as an improper exercise of the taxing power and an invasion of the reserved rights of states. 'This is coercion by economic pressure,' said Justice Owen Roberts, who conjured up the terrifying consequences that would flow from the taxation of one part of the community for the benefit of another.

> The expressions of the framers of the Constitution, the decisions of this court interpreting that instrument, and the writings of great commentators will be searched in vain for any suggestion that there exists . . . in the Constitution the authority whereby every provision and every fair implication from that instrument may be subverted, the independence of the individual states obliterated, and the United States converted into a central government exercising uncontrolled police power in every state of the Union, superseding all local control or regulation of the affairs or concerns of the states.

But Justice Harlan Fiske Stone, in his powerful dissenting opinion, protesting that this objection 'hardly rises to the dignity of argument' pointed out that 'the present levy is held invalid, not for any want of power in Congress to lay such a tax . . . but because the use to which its proceeds are put is disapproved' and observed, with some asperity, that 'courts are not the only agency of government that must be assumed to have capacity to govern.'

The Court's decision in the Butler case compelled the administration to piece together a stopgap measure: the Soil Conservation and Domestic Allotment Act of 1936. This law subsidized farmers for increasing acreage of soil-conserving crops and reducing acreage of soil-depleting crops, which, conveniently, were the surplus staples; it financed this program directly, rather than through the illegal processing tax. Although this law speeded the development of soil conservation, it proved unsatisfactory as a price-raising device since the government had no way to compel compliance. In 1938 Congress adopted a second AAA which embraced a number of earlier programs in addition to such new approaches as the 'ever normal granary,' crop insurance, and the extension of the coercive principle of the Bankhead Act to other commodities.

The administration also took steps to cope with the long-range problems of agriculture. In 1935 the President set up a Resettlement Administration which, under the guidance of Rexford Tugwell, embarked upon a program of rehabilitation. It removed from cultivation some 10 million acres of marginal land; gave financial aid to 635,000 farm families, and adjusted farm mortgages to save debtors over $25 million; built model farmhouses, suburban 'greenbelt' developments, and camps for migratory workers; and, through the development of health, education, and recreation services, attempted to make rural life more attractive.

An even more ambitious plan to rehabilitate agriculture was embodied in a presidential proposal of 1937 to rid the country of the curse of tenant farming. In the five years between 1930 and 1935 the number of tenant farmers had increased by 200,000; in the latter year two-fifths of the farmers of the country — and in eight Southern states over one-half — were tenants. Efforts to organize the tenant farmers of the South had resulted in disorder and in violent reprisals, but had dramatized to the country a situation which called for prompt remedial measures. Representatives from some Southern states looked askance at federal interference in this new 'peculiar' institution, but it was everywhere admitted that only the national government could institute the necessary reforms. In July 1937 Congress passed a bill providing that the Federal Government subsidize the purchase of farms for tenants on easy terms. The Farm Security Administration, which succeeded the Resettlement Administration, lent tenants almost $260 million to purchase farms and over $800 million in rehabilitation loans; helped organize co-operatives, including medical co-ops; and built camps for migratory workers, like the Joads of Steinbeck's *The Grapes of Wrath*. But as the spokesmen for the poorer farmers, the FSA incurred the opposition of the powerful Farm Bureau Federation, and FSA funds were never large enough to meet the need. World War II did more than the New Deal to bail out the tenant farmer. By 1950 only one state — Mississippi — reported more than half

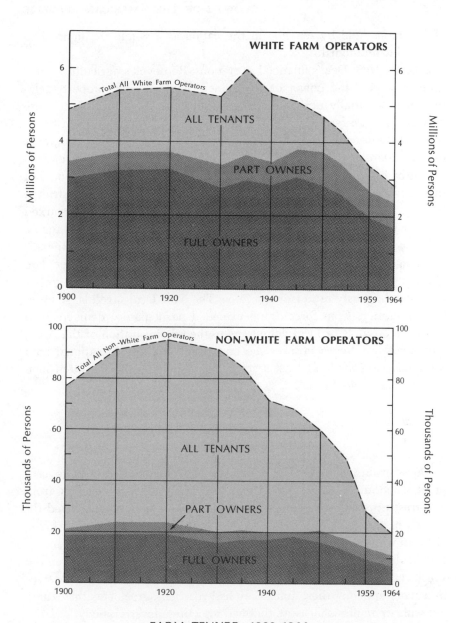

FARM TENURE, 1900-1964

493

of her farms held by tenants; in the nation as a whole the figure had dropped to one-fourth.

Like the New Deal's financial operations, Roosevelt's agricultural program expanded the power of government while leaving property relationships essentially undisturbed. AAA subsidies gave disproportionate benefits to large farmers, and the crop reduction campaign even drove some of the tenants and sharecroppers off the land. Furthermore, as a humanitarian movement, the New Deal remained perpetually embarrassed by its scarcity economics, even though the plow-up of cotton and the slaughter of the little pigs were only emergency measures restricted to 1933. Yet, for all its weaknesses, the New Deal's farm program marked a great improvement on the single-interest government of the 1920's. While net farm income in 1939 still fell well under that of 1929, the administration rescued the farmer from his desperate plight of the late Hoover period. Between 1932 and 1936 gross farm income rose 50 per cent and the parity ratio from 55 to 90. The New Deal saved large numbers of farmers from foreclosure; extended participatory democracy to involve thousands of local volunteers in the administration of the AAA; gave Southern Negro farmers the opportunity to vote in national crop referenda; and made at least a start toward helping the forgotten men of American agriculture.

6. INDUSTRY UNDER THE NEW DEAL

The New Deal's program for industrial recovery had multiple origins. Business groups like the U.S. Chamber of Commerce wanted government sanction for trade associations to draft agreements exempt from anti-trust prosecution. Planners such as Tugwell sought centralized direction of the economy. Labor leaders like John L. Lewis and Sidney Hillman wanted guarantees for workers. Progressive senators led by La Follette had been pressing for massive public works spending. When the President told advocates of these different proposals to lock themselves in a room and stay there until they had reached agreement, they came out with an omnibus measure that had something for everybody.

The National Industrial Recovery Act of 16 June 1933, like so many of the New Deal measures, had the dual purpose of recovery and reform. It was designed to spread employment, reduce hours and raise wages, and provide money for a system of public works. It proposed, at the same time, to eliminate child labor, throw new safeguards about the rights of unions, and reduce the waste of competition without encouraging monopolies. To attain these laudable ends the law provided for the organization of industries through codes drawn up by businessmen in conjunction with government administrators, subject to approval by the President. Monopolies or monopolistic practices were prohibited, but at the same time the operation of the anti-trust laws was suspended for the duration of the statute. Pending the formulation of codes for major industries, the President requested business to adhere to a blanket code, promulgated 27 July as a model for industrial code-makers. It prohibited child labor, limited hours of work to 36 for industrial and 40 for clerical workers, established a minimum wage of 40 cents an hour, and included the mandatory protection to labor provided for in Section 7a of the act. The Recovery Act also set up a Public Works Administration with an appropriation of $3.3 billion, and the President designated his Secretary of the Interior, Harold Ickes, to head the PWA.

In the hot summer months of 1933 thousands of representatives of American industry descended on Washington to discuss, argue, and frame codes. This titanic task exhausted even the cascading energy of the national administrator, General Hugh Johnson. The NRA administrators were familiar only with the general principles of the new program, businessmen and their legal advisers were familiar with all the details; the inevitable result was that big business generally imposed its own codes upon both government and small business. Yet out of the welter of conference and debate there emerged a pattern of industrial organization that met many of the requirements laid down by the act. To rally support, Johnson hit on the Blue Eagle as a symbol of compliance with the wage and hour provisions of the codes, and for a short time the Blue Eagle was almost as popular as the flag. Within a year some 500 codes had been adopted and some 200 more were in process of formulation, and it was estimated that over 23 million workers were under codes. Under Johnson's aegis, industry reabsorbed unemployed workers, and went far toward abolishing child labor and the sweatshop.

But the NRA overextended itself in trying to regulate small enterprises, and it could not muster enough power to discipline the big corporations. Shortly after the creation of the NRA, President Roosevelt appealed to business to defer price increases until recovery was under way. But for the most part industry disregarded Roosevelt's appeal. Even more ominous was the growth of monopoly and the continuance of unfair practices under the NRA codes. In July 1934 an investigation found that code authorities were controlled by the larger firms and fostered monopoly. Reforms were promptly inaugurated, but were ineffective, and during 1934 and 1935 the NRA was assailed with increasing bitterness from all sides: by large businessmen who resented government control of their labor relations; by small businessmen dismayed at the growth of monopoly; by liberals who lamented the suspension of the anti-trust laws and feared the long-range consequences of a 'planned economy' dominated by business; by consumers outraged at price increases; by labor disappointed in the practical results of the codes.

The NRA was breaking down of its own weight when in May 1935 the Supreme Court destroyed it by undermining its legal foundations in a unanimous decision, the Schechter case. The Recovery Act, said the Court, involved an illegal delegation of legislative power to the Executive. Furthermore, it constituted an improper exercise of the commerce power and an invasion by the Federal Government of the realm reserved to the states, for 'if the commerce clause were construed to reach all enterprises and transactions which could be said to have an indirect effect upon interstate commerce, the federal authority would embrace practically all the activities of the people and the authority of the state over its domestic concerns would exist only by sufferance.' Thus came to an end a law which President Roosevelt had described with palpable exaggeration as 'the most important and far-reaching ever enacted by the American Congress.' Never again would big business play so large a role in the New Deal, but neither would the planners like Tugwell ever have so promising, but illusory, an opportunity to impose centralized planning on the economy.

The framers of the Recovery Act hoped, too, that the $3.3 billion appropriation for public works would be an important lever for industrial recovery. But Roosevelt, committed to budget-balancing, was skeptical of the value of public works and repeatedly raided the grant for other projects. Ickes operated the PWA so cautiously that it did little to stimulate the economy. Worried about the possibility of another Teapot Dome, Ickes insisted on reviewing every word of every PWA contract. The industrious, sardonic Ickes won himself the reputation of 'Honest Harold,' but neither he nor the President realized the economic potentialities of public works spending.

7. LABOR UNDER THE NEW DEAL

Roosevelt came to office with his policy toward labor unresolved, but the appointment of Frances Perkins, distinguished social reformer, to the post of Secretary of Labor augured well for the workingman. He took another important step when he approved the National Industrial Recovery Act which attempted to raise wages, reduce hours, eliminate child and sweatshop labor, and safeguard the right of organization and collective bargaining. This latter policy was embodied in Section 7a which provided:

> Employees shall have the right to organize and bargain collectively, through representatives of their own choosing, and shall be free from the interference, restraint, or coercion of employers of labor, or their agents, in the designation of such representatives or in self-organization or in other concerted activities . . . and that no employee and no one seeking employment shall be required as a condition of employment to join any company union or to refrain from joining . . . a labor organization of his own choosing.

Under the impetus of the NRA, organized labor more than recovered all the losses which it had suffered in the preceding decade. Using the magic name of FDR, John L. Lewis launched an organizing drive in the coal fields in the summer of 1933 which gained the United Mine Workers 300,000 members in two months, and by the tens of thousands workers signed union cards in industries that had long been resistant to organization — rubber, automobiles, textiles.

But in 1934 employer resistance stiffened. By manipulating the device of the company union, industrialists complied with the letter of the Recovery Act while keeping union organizers out of their factories. At the same time the craft union leaders of the A.F. of L., hostile or indifferent to the unskilled recruits flocking to the Federation, treated their new members with such disdain that many tore up their union cards. Many workers turned to radicals for leadership, and in 1934 an epidemic of strikes under radical sponsorship hit such cities as San Francisco, Milwaukee, Toledo, and Minneapolis. But most failed, and the general strike in San Francisco was smashed by the militia and by self-constituted vigilantes. The Roosevelt administration was dismayed by these strikes, which impeded its recovery effort. As it fumbled for a labor policy it antagonized employers, who resented any kind of intervention, and industrial unionists, who protested that the government labor boards were powerless to cope with employer defiance. By 1935 membership in the rubber union had slumped from 70,000 to 3000, in the auto workers from 100,000 to 10,000.

In the Second Hundred Days, Congress, led by Senator Robert Wagner of New York, gave labor an emphatic victory with the passage of the National Labor Relations Act of 5 July 1935, better known as the Wagner Act. This measure, which won the last-minute endorsement of President Roosevelt, not only embraced some of the provisions of the recently invalidated Recovery Act but also significantly expanded the government's powers. The act set up an independent National Labor Relations Board authorized to conduct plant elections and issue 'cease and desist' orders against unfair practices. These 'unfair practices' included interference with or coercion of employees in collective bargaining, domination of a labor union through financial contributions, discrimination against union members in employment or tenure, and refusal to bargain collectively with employees. By stipulating that a majority of workers should have exclusive bargaining rights, the law all but destroyed the divisive tactic of the company union.

Under the umbrella of government protection, organized labor carried out a dramatic campaign to organize industrial workers. In 1935 Lewis led a secession from the A.F. of L. of unions impatient with the resistance of the Federation's leadership to organizing factory workers. The C.I.O., which was first known as the Committee for Industrial Organization and later as the Congress of Industrial Organizations, frequently employed the novel technique of the 'sit-down,' seizing possession of the machinery and property of employers and refusing to yield until demands had been granted. When on 11 February 1937 General Motors agreed to a settlement after a forty-four-day sit-down, the C.I.O. gained immense prestige. Before the year was out such giants as U.S. Steel, Chrysler, and General Electric had also surrendered. The C.I.O. insurrection also awakened the A.F. of L., which emerged even more powerful than its upstart rival. As one historian has noted: 'John L. Lewis and his CIO were to the AFL what Luther's Ninety-five Theses and the Reformation were to the Catholic Church.'

The New Deal had helped make possible one of the most important developments of twentieth-century America: the unionization of the mass production industries. For the most part this transfer of power was carried out peacefully, although in June 1937 the nation was shocked by the outbreak of open warfare at the Republic Steel Company in South Chicago. The benevolent neutrality of the administration (including Roosevelt's refusal to countenance force to oust the sit-down strikers), the sympathy of local leaders like Governor Frank Murphy of Michigan, and the aid of congressional liberals such as Wagner and La Follette, who headed a Senate committee that exposed employer violence, had all proved immensely beneficial to the unions. For a few more years anti-union holdouts like Republic would still bar the door to unionism, but by World War II even Henry Ford had recognized the worker's right, long granted in other industrial nations, to unionize and to bargain collectively.

8. CONSERVATION AND THE TVA

No part of the New Deal was more imaginative than that which looked at the conservation of natural resources; none, certainly, was closer to the heart of the President. A country gentleman, he was passionately interested in the preservation of soil, forests, water, and wild life; his ideal for the American people was really a 'balanced civilization' in which all workers had a stake in the land and all farmers enjoyed the advantages of urban life. The contrast between President Hoover's veto of the Muscle Shoals Bill in 1931 and Roosevelt's sponsorship of the TVA in 1933 is the measure of the change in social philosophy that occurred in two years.

The initial step in Roosevelt's conservation policy was the creation (31 March 1933) of the Civilian Conservation Corps, designed to give emergency work relief to young men from 17 to 25. In the eight years of its existence the CCC enlisted almost 3 million young men, who, under the direction of army officers and foresters, added over 17 million acres of new forest land, checked forest fires, fought plant and animal diseases, stocked hatcheries with over a billion fish, built 6 million check dams to halt soil erosion, and by mosquito control helped stamp out malaria. And — as President Roosevelt said — 'no one will ever be able to estimate in dollars and cents the value to the men themselves and to the nation in morale, in occupational training, in health, and in adaptability to later competitive life.'

Of all New Deal projects the most dramatic was the Tennessee Valley Authority. Not content with government operation of Tennessee river dams for nitrate production, Roosevelt insisted on expanding the program to a vast experiment in regional reconstruction. The law of 18 May 1933 created the Tennessee Valley Authority, with power to acquire, construct, and operate dams in the Tennessee valley, manufacture nitrate and fertilizer, generate and sell electric power, inaugurate flood control, withdraw marginal lands from cultivation, develop the river for navigation, and in general 'advance the economic and social well-being of the people living in the said river basin.'

The Tennessee valley embraces an area of some 40,000 square miles in seven states; a natural geographical unit, it presented a tempting challenge to long-range planning. It was a region rich in natural resources which were rapidly being exhausted, and in water power which was going to waste. Once the Promised Land, it had been cruelly ravaged and neglected; its soil was depleted, its once beautiful forests heedlessly cut or destroyed by fire; its people living in primitive economy, scratching a precarious living from the soil. Could all this be changed? Could the intelligence of science and the resources of government combine to restore the natural richness of the region and to rehabilitate its people? Certainly the experiment of government operation of power plants, regulation of agriculture, preservation of water resources, and co-operation with industry might be expected to throw some light on the problem of a planned economy.

To direct the destinies of the new agency Roosevelt appointed Arthur Morgan, president of Antioch College and an engineer with a long record of idealism and with a predilection for a planned society. To balance him on the three-man commission were Harcourt Morgan, president of the University of Tennessee and a practical agriculturalist, and the brilliant young David Lilienthal, chairman, at 36, of the Wisconsin Public Service Commission. The directors, interpreting the act broadly, undertook to make the project a laboratory for social experiment and an instrument for the regeneration of local government. They acquired or constructed in the course of time some 25 dams for flood control, nitrate production, and the generation of electric power; to these they eventually added a series of steam generator plants. The government built some 5000 miles of transmission lines and sold surplus power to nearby communities at rates low enough to ensure widespread consumption.

In 1932 only two farms out of one hundred in the valley were electrified; five years later the proportion was one out of seven, and by 1960 electrification was well-nigh complete.

As an agency to foster 'an orderly and proper physical, economic, and social development' of the valley, the TVA withdrew marginal lands from cultivation, resettled marginal farmers, promoted public health and recreational facilities, and encouraged local industry. All this was done in close co-operation with the people of the valley, for the TVA was from the beginning dedicated to the principle of decentralized administration. Too often, decentralized administration meant that decisions were made by the wealthy white farmers and the TVA bowed to the local pattern of racial segregation. But the TVA also left a substantial record of achievement. Within a few years millions of abandoned acres were returned to cultivation, forests grew in burnt-over land, industry returned to the valley, vacationers crowded its artificial lakes, and the river, navigable now over its entire length from Knoxville to the Ohio river, was one of the busiest streams in the country. The TVA itself became a model which attracted the attention and emulation of the whole world.

The Tennessee Valley Authority was the most notable of several such experiments in regional rehabilitation. Almost as important was the ambitious program for the Columbia river basin. In 1933 the government began construction of the Grand Coulee Dam, some 90 miles west of Spokane, and in 1937 of the Bonneville Dam on the lower Columbia, to develop some 2.5 million kilowatts of electric power and to make possible the irrigation and reclamation of over a million acres of farm land.

Government competition with private power companies and the use of the 'yardstick' to determine fair rates inspired acrimonious criticism and challenge. Wendell Willkie, president of the Commonwealth and Southern, a great holding company, was the most prominent and effective of critics. TVA was attacked on economic grounds as a threat to the $12 billion invested in private utilities, on social grounds as tending to undermine private enterprise, and on legal grounds as an exercise of unauthorized power. The first two issues were fought in the arena of public opinion and politics, and in both arenas the government policy was endorsed. The third came before the Supreme Court for adjudication in the Ashwander case. On 17 February 1936 the Court, with only McReynolds dissenting, sustained the government.

The Roosevelt administration initiated a host of new enterprises in conservation and electric power. It not only disciplined the utility-holding companies and strengthened the Federal Power Commission but set up the Rural Electrification Administration which radically changed life on the farm. At the outset of the New Deal, only one out of nine American farms had electricity; by the end of the Roosevelt era, eight out of nine enjoyed electric power. The alarming spread of the 'dust bowl' on the high plains inspired the planting of a 100-mile-wide shelter belt of trees, stretching from Texas to Canada. The program to stop soil erosion enlisted one-fourth the farmers of the country and embraced almost 300 million acres. The New Deal found a home for the brilliant head of the Soil Conservation Service, Hugh H. Bennett; for the thoughtful planner, Morris Llewellyn Cooke, who turned out landmark reports on the nation's resources; for John Collier, who, as Indian Commissioner, sought to save the Indian's lands at the same time that he preserved his culture; and Pare Lorentz, who produced such film epics as *The River* and *The Plough That Broke the Plains*. Not even in Uncle Teddy's day had the conservation movement enjoyed such brilliant leadership.

9. THE WELFARE STATE

The most urgent problem facing the administration was that of relief for the millions of unemployed victims of the depression. Roosevelt had promised during his campaign that no one should starve, but millions were perilously near starvation, and the resources of state and local governments and of private charities were well-nigh exhausted. The emergency was clearly one that called for the energetic intervention of the Federal Government. Outright relief had the advantages of economy and efficiency; work relief, on the other hand, promised to maintain morale, repair and improve the economic plant, and facilitate the transfer of workers to private industry. Relief, however, no matter how generously contributed or how intelligently directed, offered no solution to the problem of unemployment nor guarantee of security. In a message to Congress in mid-March 1933, Roosevelt proposed three types of relief: the enrollment of workers by the Federal Government for public employment, grants to the states for relief work, and a broad program of public works. Congress adopted all three. The first step in emergency relief was the creation of the Civilian Conservation Corps. In May, Congress adopted the second proposal by setting up the Federal Emergency Relief Administration to make grants to state and local governments to get public projects under way; where necessary the FERA made direct grants to the needy. Under the experienced social-work administrator, Harry Hopkins, the FERA in the next two years disbursed $4 billion for relief, three-fourths from federal and one-fourth from local funds. By 1934 more than twenty million people — one out of every six Americans — were receiving public assistance.

When Roosevelt realized that not even FERA would get the country through the first New Deal winter of 1933–34, he named Hopkins to head a temporary Civil Works Administration, and the resourceful Hopkins quickly put four million jobless on federal projects. Frank Walker, the head of the President's National Emergency Council, reported on the operation of the CWA in his native state of Montana: 'I saw old friends of mine — men I had been to be school with — digging ditches and laying sewer pipe. They were wearing their regular business suits as they worked because they couldn't afford overalls and rubber boots.' One of them pulled out some silver coins and said: 'Do you know, Frank, this is the first money I've had in my pockets in a year and a half? Up to now, I've had nothing but tickets that you exchange for groceries.' Another told him: 'I hate to think what would have happened if this work hadn't come along. The last of my savings had run out. I'd sold or hocked everything I could. And my kids were hungry. I stood in front of the window of the bake-shop down the street and I wondered just how long it would be before I got desperate enough to pick up a rock and heave it through that window and grab some bread to take home.'

The third major program of relief was provided by the Public Works Administration. If the PWA under Ickes did not provide much stimulus to the economy, it did put men to work on construction projects which helped change the face of the land. The PWA engaged in such diverse enterprises as the construction of schools, flood control, the rebuilding of aircraft carriers and submarines, and the construction of army posts. PWA burrowed Chicago's new subway, built the Skyline Drive in Virginia, and constructed the carrier *Yorktown*. It gave Kansas City a municipal auditorium, Denver a new water-supply system, and the state of Washington a set of university buildings. In the six years of its existence it helped build two-thirds of all new school buildings in the nation and one-third of the new hospitals.

In January 1935 President Roosevelt proposed that a distinction be made between employables and unemployables, that new and more satisfactory provision be made for the former, and that the burden of supporting the latter be transferred to state and local authorities. In accordance with these suggestions, Congress created a Works Progress Administration, and appropriated nearly $5 billion to be expended for relief, loans and grants on non-federal projects, reforestation, flood-control, housing and slum clearance, public health, rural electrification, and education. The responsibility for carrying through this immense enterprise was assigned to the dynamic Harry Hopkins, whose influence with the President was growing apace. Inevitably it was attended with confusion and waste: administrative costs were high, construction was often shoddy. Nor did the government provide for all who were in need. Yet what is most impressive is the scope of the projects. By 1943 when the WPA terminated its activities, it had given work to over 8 million unemployed, and spent $11 billion on a bewildering variety of projects. These included 600,000 miles of highways, 125,000 public buildings, 8000 parks, 850 airport landing fields, and thousands of hospitals, municipal power plants, and school buildings.

To make use of the special skills of people with creative talent, Hopkins set up a Federal Arts Project under the WPA. The Federal Theatre produced the classic works of Euripides, Molière, and Ibsen; offered the plays of contemporaries like Elmer Rice and Eugene O'Neill; sponsored vaudeville troupes, marionettes, and circuses; and offered such innovations as the 'Living Newspaper,' a series of kaleidoscopic scenes which dramatized contemporary issues. The Federal Writers' Project gave jobs to established writers like Conrad Aiken, unknown men such as John Cheever and Richard Wright, and, mercifully, jobless historians. It turned out a thousand publications, including the immensely useful series of state guides. The Federal Music Project employed 15,000 jobless musicians; encouraged composers like William Schuman; and put together three orchestras — the Buffalo Philharmonic, the Oklahoma Symphony, and the Utah State Symphony — which became the established orchestras in their communities. 'Nowhere in Europe is there anything to compare with it,' said the Austrian composer Erich Wolfgang Korngold. The Federal Arts Project supported such painters as Stuart Davis, Jackson Pollock, and Charles Alston, and sponsored the influential *Index of American Design*.

Another progeny of the relief act of 1935, the National Youth Administration, sought to rescue young people from home relief rolls and either help them stay in school or retrain them in new job skills. Under the direction of Aubrey Williams, the NYA found part-time jobs for more than 600,000 college and 1.5 million high-school students, and 2.5 million who were out of school.

The New Deal's housing program joined together a number of separate aims: to provide public works projects to employ the jobless; to revive the construction business; and to wipe out noisome slums. The National Housing Act of 1934 set up the Federal Housing Administration which insured mortgages to encourage the repair and building of private homes. Of benefit chiefly to the middle class, the FHA had by 1945 financed more than one-third of all privately constructed homes, and proved a boon to builders and savings and loan associations. On a much more modest scale the PWA constructed low-rent public housing, but Ickes moved so slowly that, as Charles Abrams wrote, 'a great opportunity to rebuild many of America's decayed urban centers was lost.' Roosevelt, too, was much more interested in bootless schemes to return city-dwellers to the land than in massive urban housing projects. But in his inaugural address in 1937 he called attention to 'one-third of a nation ill-housed,' and that year he committed himself for the first time to the public housing measure Senator Wagner had been sponsoring. As a consequence, Congress created the U.S. Housing Authority to assist local communities in slum clearance and the construction of low-cost housing. The USHA eventually built 165,000 family units. If the New Deal failed to take full advantage of the opportunity that housing offered, both as a humanitarian enterprise and as a lever for recovery, it did establish a new principle: federal responsibility for clearing slums and housing the poor.

As early as 1934 the President had called for a broad program of old-age and unemployment insurance. 'There is no reason,' he said to Secretary Perkins, 'why every child from the day he is born, shouldn't be a member of the social security . . . cradle to grave — they ought to be in a social insurance system.' Pressure for an old-age pension scheme was also exerted by advocates of the Townsend Plan, concocted by Dr. Francis Townsend of California who advocated monthly payments of $200 to all persons over 60 years of age, on the sole proviso that they retire from work and spend the money; the plan was championed by

Townsend Clubs claiming close to a million members. The proponents of some kind of national welfare program overwhelmed the opposition of Republican conservatives like Senator Daniel Hastings of Delaware who said: 'I fear it may end the progress of a great country and bring its people to the level of the average European.'

On 14 August 1935 Congress enacted the Social Security law, an omnibus measure which provided for pensions to needy aged, old-age insurance, unemployment insurance, benefit payments to the blind, dependent mothers and children, and crippled children, and extensive appropriations for public health work. Pensions of not more than $15 a month were to be extended to indigent persons over 65 on the understanding that co-operating states would contribute a like amount. The national system of old-age insurance gave benefits to participants in accordance with a complicated system of graduated premiums paid by both employer and employee. To persuade the states to establish systems of unemployment insurance, the act required payments by employers of a percentage of their payroll for insurance purposes, but provided that 90 per cent of the federal levy would be returned to states whose insurance plans conformed to standards approved by a Social Security Board. In addition the act appropriated to the states $25 million for aid to dependent children and called for annual appropriations of $25 million for maternal and child health service, crippled children, the blind, state and local public health service, and vocational rehabilitation. In the course of the next two years every state set up old-age pensions and unemployment insurance systems that met the requirements fixed by the Social Security Board.

The United States still had a long way to go to provide adequately for the impoverished and the handicapped, but the New Deal had taken giant strides in that direction. One writer noted: 'During the ten years between 1929 and 1939 more progress was made in public welfare and relief than in the three hundred years after this country was first settled.' The New Deal not only engaged in an unprecedented range of activities — vast relief programs, slum clearance, aid to tenant farmers, opposition to the sweatshop and child labor, minimum labor standards, a social security system — but had established the principle of federal responsibility for society's victims. 'Government has a final responsibility for the well-being of its citizenship,' Roosevelt declared. 'If private co-operative endeavor fails to provide work for willing hands and relief for the unfortunate, those suffering hardship from no fault of their own have a right to call upon the Government for aid; and a government worthy of its name must make fitting response.'

XX

The End of the New Deal

1. THE ROOSEVELT COALITION

The Great Depression made a deeper impact on American politics than any event since the Civil War. By identifying the Republican party with the collapse, the voters in 1932 had given the Democrats an opportunity to establish themselves as the majority party for the next generation, and Roosevelt made the most of it. By 1936 he had forged a new party coalition which would prevail not only in his lifetime but for many years thereafter. From 1930 to 1968 the Republicans would win control of the House in only two elections.

The Roosevelt coalition was centered in the great cities. In 1932 FDR had taken every metropolis in the Midwest, West, and South; the Democratic vote in Los Angeles jumped from 29 per cent in 1928 to 60 per cent. In 1936 he improved on this performance, capturing all but two of the 106 cities of 100,000 population or more. The cities showed their power when the 1936 Democratic convention abolished the century-old two-thirds rule. The New Deal found its greatest appeal among urban elements, especially labor and ethnic groups. John L. Lewis, who had endorsed Hoover in 1932, opened his union treasury to Roosevelt in 1936; the Mine Workers contributed nearly half a million dollars. Labor's Non-Partisan League rallied union workers for the Democrats; in 1936, the President swept every ward in Pittsburgh. To the Democratic standard too came a variety of ethnic elements, grateful not only for New Deal measures but for being granted recognition by a party

508

whose national chairman, James A. Farley, was an Irish-Catholic, and whose leader named the first Italo-American ever appointed to a federal judgeship.

In 1932 the Negro had still given his allegiance to the party of Lincoln; despite Hoover's 'lily-white' policies, a black ward like Cincinnati's Ward 16 gave Roosevelt less than 29 per cent of its ballots. In the early years of the New Deal, Negro leaders were distressed by NRA wage differentials, which worked against the Negro; discrimination in agencies like the CCC; the AAA crop-reduction programs which drove black farmers from the land; and a pattern of segregation which excluded Negroes from the TVA's model town of Norris. Yet never before had the Federal Government shown such concern for the Negro. He received a lion's share of relief jobs; got one-third of the federal housing units; and won appointments to important national posts. Roosevelt's 'black cabinet' included such able leaders as Mary McLeod Bethune and Robert Weaver. If the President refused to antagonize Southern committee chairmen by pressing civil rights legislation, Eleanor Roosevelt intervened repeatedly on behalf of the Negro. When a Negro minister opened one session of the 1936 Democratic convention and a Negro congressman seconded Roosevelt's nomination, 'Cotton Ed' Smith stormed out of the convention. 'I cannot and will not be a party to the recognition of the 14th and 15th Amendments,' the South Carolina senator explained. By 1934 Negro voters had been switching to the Democrats in large numbers, and in 1936 they rolled up big majorities for FDR, as Cincinnati's Ward 16 now gave Roosevelt better than 65 per cent.

In the 1930's, class gradually replaced section as the most important determinant of voting. Roosevelt, conscious of his lower-income following and angered by the attacks of business leaders, exploited class antagonisms in the 1936 campaign. At Madison Square Garden on the eve of the election, the President charged:

> For twelve years this Nation was affiliated with hear-nothing, see-nothing, do-nothing Government.
> They had begun to consider the Government of the United States as a mere appendage to their own affairs. We know now that Government by organized money is just as dangerous as Government by organized mob.
> Never before in all our history have these forces been so united against one candidate as they stand today. They are unanimous in their hate for me — and I welcome their hatred.

I should like to have it said of my first Administration that in it the forces of selfishness and of lust for power met their match. I should like to have it said of my second Administration that in it these forces met their master.

Although many of the Republican leaders fit Roosevelt's description, they found a presidential candidate in 1936 who was a decent man with a respectable record of reform. Governor Alfred M. Landon of Kansas had been a Bull Mooser in 1912, had fought the Klan in the 1920's, and had been a fairly progressive governor. Republicans offered him as a 'liberal Coolidge,' who combined a belief in tightfisted administration with liberal social policies. But Landon was embarrassed by the Hoover wing of the party which took the campaign away from him. Some of the Republican campaign literature heaped contempt on reliefers, and Landon's running mate, the Chicago publisher Frank Knox, invited disbelief when he claimed: 'The New Deal candidate has been leading us toward Moscow.' Landon also had the support of Democratic defectors like Al Smith and of the American Liberty League; but Smith was accused of trading his brown derby for a silk hat, and the Liberty League's charges were so extreme that the Republicans asked them not to issue any more statements. Nor, in contrast to the eloquent Roosevelt, was Landon a good speaker. H.L. Mencken wrote that Landon 'is an honest fellow, and would make an excellent President, but he simply lacks the power to inflame the boobs.'

An ill-assorted group of Roosevelt's opponents fielded a third party in 1936. No critic of the President's had been more formidable than Louisiana's Senator Huey Pierce Long, but the flamboyant 'Kingfish,' advocate of a share-the-wealth scheme, had been assassinated in September 1935. Long's putative successor, Gerald L.K. Smith, hatemonger extraordinary, joined with Dr. Townsend and Father Coughlin, the rabble-rousing radio priest of Royal Oak, Michigan, to back North Dakota's Representative William Lemke for the presidency on a Union party ticket. Had the effervescent Huey Long lived he might have welded these dissident groups into the semblance of a party. But without him the coalition crumbled, and all three of its leaders were discredited.

On 2 November Roosevelt's campaign manager, Postmaster General Jim Farley, wrote the President: 'I am still definitely of the opinion that you will carry every state but two — Maine and Vermont.' Farley hit it right on the button. With 523 votes to Landon's 8, Roosevelt won the

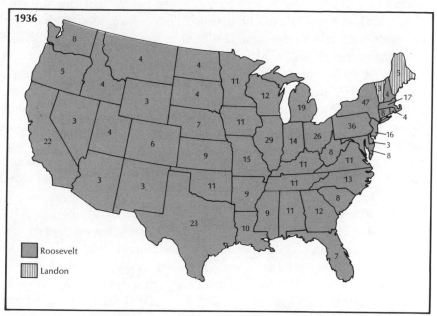

PRESIDENTIAL ELECTION, 1936

greatest electoral margin of any presidential candidate since Monroe. 'I knew I should have gone to Maine and Vermont,' the President said glee-fully, but Jim wouldn't let me.' Never before had a major party suffered so overwhelming a defeat as the Republicans had sustained. So great was the Democratic margin in the Senate that a number of Democrats had to sit on the Republican side of the aisle. 'It was not an election the country has just undergone,' said William Allen White, 'but a political Johnstown flood.' Buoyed by this impressive vote of confidence, Roose-velt faced his second term in office with high hopes.

2. COURT REFORM AND CONSTITUTIONAL REVOLUTION

Outnumbered in Congress, humiliated at the polls, the Republicans lifted their eyes to the Supreme Court. The G.O.P. 'retired into the judi-ciary as a stronghold, and from that battery all the works of republican-ism were to be beaten down and erased.' So Jefferson had said of the Federalists over a century earlier, and his successor in the White House had reason to echo the bitter charge. Never before had the Supreme Court worked such havoc with a legislative program as it did in 1935 and 1936 with that of the New Deal, nor in so short a time invalidated so many acts of Congress. It overthrew the NRA in part on the novel ground of improper delegation of power. It struck down the AAA through what a dissenting justice called a 'tortured construction of the Constitution.' It rejected the railroad retirement plan on the curious theory that there was no legitimate connection between interstate commerce and the welfare of those who conducted it, while the Bituminous Coal Act went into the judicial wastebasket because the Court, in the Carter case, insisted that coal mining was a purely local business. It invalidated congressional legislation to protect farm mortgages on the ground of conflict with the esoteric 'due process' clause of the Fifth Amendment and nullified the Municipal Bankruptcy Act on the assumption that such legislation invaded the domain of the states — even though the Act required state consent, which many states had already given. The Federal Government had long been denied the power to enact minimum-wage legislation; when in the Tipaldo case it denied this power to the states as well, it created a no-man's-land where neither federal nor state power might be applied. In the realm of administration the Court rejected the precedent of the Myers decision and denied to the President power to remove a recalcitrant member of the Federal Trade Commission. Even in the two instances where the Court sustained the New Deal — the gold clause and the TVA cases — it did so on narrow grounds and with ill-grace.

The 1935–36 decisions were so sweeping in character that they appeared to foreclose amendment of the objectionable legislation and to foredoom further legislation along liberal lines. The Court, in fact, had taken upon itself the responsibility of nullifying the electoral verdicts of 1932 and 1934 and of negating in advance any consequences of a comparable verdict in 1936. Furthermore, the Court's reasoning in recent cases suggested that within a few months it would obliterate such New Deal landmarks as the Wagner Act and the Social Security law.

What to do? The question was not a new one; it had confronted Jefferson, Jackson, Lincoln, and Theodore Roosevelt, and had commanded the attention of a long line of political thinkers from Taylor of Caroline to Borah of Idaho. Yet the most anxious study of the problem had not yielded a solution. Impeachment had failed, with the acquittal of Justice Chase in 1805; withdrawal of jurisdiction had been tried during Reconstruction and proved dangerous; proposals to require more than a mere majority of votes for the nullification of legislative acts or to permit Congress, by a two-thirds vote, to override such nullifications were of dubious constitutionality; the process of constitutional amendment was slow and uncertain. In the past the judiciary had been brought to acquiescence in majority will only by the process of new appointments. But Roosevelt was the first president in more than a century to serve a full term without having the opportunity to appoint at least one new justice, although six of the judges were over seventy years of age.

If the trouble lay not in Constitution but in the Court, that could be remedied by appointing new members. So at least Roosevelt thought, and this was the crucial part of the proposal for the reform of the federal judiciary which he submitted to a startled Congress on 5 February 1937.

In the proposed bill the President would obtain the 'addition of younger blood' by the appointment of one new judge, up to a maximum of six, for every justice of the Supreme Court who, having passed the age of seventy and served for ten years, failed to retire. Roosevelt argued that such a measure would speed judicial procedures.

The proposal was simplicity itself, and on this score, at least, had much to commend it. It fixed upon seventy as the logical retirement age, and if the examples of Holmes and Brandeis made this age seem premature, the rules in effect in the civil service, the army and navy, universities, hospitals, and similar institutions, suggested that it was not unreasonable. The presidential proposal did not compel retirement at seventy, but merely provided an additional judge for every incumbent over seventy; if the incumbent wished to avoid an enlarged court he had the alternative of leaving the bench at full pay. The bill raised no constitutional question, for the power of Congress to control membership was clear. Nor was its method without precedent; the number of judges had been changed six times in the past.

Nevertheless, the proposal was greeted with cries of alarm and dismay. It was denounced as a plan to 'pack' the Supreme Court; as an attack on the independence of the judiciary; as the end of constitutional government in the United States. Many resented Roosevelt's tactic of arguing that he wanted to improve court procedures by lightening the burden of aged justices as disrespectful to the Court and a ruse to disguise his insistence on having a more malleable judiciary. Conservatives rejoiced that they could now identify opposition to presidential policies with the defense of the Constitution. Liberals like Senators Wheeler, Borah, and Johnson, who had long held something of a monopoly on criticism of the highest court, now ranged themselves on the side of judicial supremacy.

Throughout the spring and summer of 1937 as the debate went on, the tide of public opinion was rising against the presidential proposal. Yet in the end it was the strategic retreat of the Court that brought about the defeat of the plan. For even as the bill was under consideration, and before there had been any change in its membership, the Court found ways of making the constitutional sun shine on legislation which had heretofore been under a judicial cloud. Nine months after the Court had struck down the New York minimum-wage law, it sustained a similar act of the state of Washington. On the same day it approved a revised farm-mortgage act and a new Railway Labor Act. A few weeks later came five decisions, all upholding various provisions of the National Labor Relations Act which a committee of sixty distinguished lawyers had advised their clients to disregard as incontestably unconstitutional. The Court, which had circumscribed the government's powers over labor relations in the Carter case only a year before, now said, in Chief Justice Hughes's words:

> The fact remains that the stoppage of those operations by industrial strife would have a most serious effect upon interstate commerce. It is idle to say that the effect would be indirect or remote. It is obvious that it would be immediate and might be catastrophic. We are asked to shut our eyes to the plainest facts of our national life and to deal with the question of direct and indirect effects in an intellectual vacuum. . . . When industries organize themselves on a national scale, making relation to interstate commerce the dominant factor in their activities, how can it be maintained that their industrial labor relations constitute a forbidden field into which Congress may not enter when it is necessary to protect interstate commerce from the paralyzing consequences of industrial war?

A month later, and the controversial Social Security legislation was vouchsafed judicial blessing with a sweeping endorsement of the power of government to act for the national welfare. In all but one of these decisions, the conservative 'Four Horsemen' — McReynolds, Sutherland, Butler, and Van Devanter — took an adamant stand, but they now constituted a minority, because Justice Roberts had joined the liberal triumvirate of Brandeis, Cardozo, and Stone, together with Chief Justice Hughes, whom many credited with frustrating the President by marshalling the Court in support of new interpretations.

At the same time that the Court gave Roosevelt approval for New Deal laws, it spiked the 'court packing' scheme, for many saw no point in altering the judiciary now that the reform legislation had been validated. As one commentator quipped: 'A switch in time saved nine.' The Senate Judiciary Committee voted 10-8 to reject the measure, and although the fight continued into the month of July, the opponents prevailed. The President, at the height of his power, had suffered a stinging rebuke.

Roosevelt claimed that though he had lost the battle, he had won the war. Even while the Court debate was under way, Justice Van Devanter announced his retirement, and his example was shortly followed by Sutherland and Butler as well as the revered Brandeis, one of the intellectual godfathers of the New Deal. Within a few years, the Court was entirely remade. To fill vacancies created by retirement and death President Roosevelt appointed Hugo Black of Alabama, distinguished for his fight against the power trust; Stanley Reed of Kentucky, former solicitor-general; Felix Frankfurter of the Harvard Law School, teacher of a generation of social-minded lawyers and jurists; William Douglas of the Yale Law School and the Securities and Exchange Commission; Attorney-General Robert Jackson of New York; and Frank Murphy, former governor of Michigan and Governor-General of the Philippine Islands; while the talents and tolerance of Mr. Justice Stone were recognized by his elevation to the chief justiceship.

This new court hastened to retreat from the untenable constitutional positions seized by its predecessor. Since 1937 the Court has not invalidated a single congressional statute in the realm of regulation of business, and very few laws, national or state, in any realm. It repudiated the unrealistic limitation on the commerce power written into the Constitution by *Hammer v. Dagenhart,* and in a series of decisions nullified the curious divorce of commerce from manufacturing affirmed in the Schechter and Guffey coal cases. Another series of decisions, in 1939, swept away any lingering doubts about the power of the Federal Government to regulate agricultural production through marketing agreements. The limitation imposed upon congressional spending by the Butler decision was withdrawn; uncertainties about federal control over navigable rivers and water power, conjured up in the TVA decision, were abandoned; and the right of the Federal Government to regulate even potentially navigable streams and to exercise jurisdiction over the development of hydroelectric power re-established.

Nor were all the new decisions in the direction of the enlargement of federal powers. The Court took a sympathetic attitude toward the exercise of state police power, while in the complex and controversial domain of taxation, it acquiesced in the search for new sources of revenue through discriminatory taxation of out-of-state corporations. And, finally, *Swift v. Tyson,* which for a century had permitted the federal courts to disregard decisions of the state courts on matters of state law, was formally pronounced mistaken.

The 'Roosevelt Court,' as it was called, continued even more assiduously than the Court had before 1937 to throw new safeguards around civil liberties, although even in the 1920's important gains had been made in protecting the rights of minorities. In *De Jonge v. Oregon,* the Court voided a criminal-syndicalism law which made mere attendance at a Communist meeting a crime. 'The greater the importance of safeguarding the community from incitements to the overthrow of our institutions by force and violence,' said Chief Justice Hughes, 'the more imperative is the need to preserve inviolate the constitutional right of free speech, free press, and free assembly in order to maintain the opportunity for free political discussion, to the end that government may be responsive to the will of the people and that changes, if desired, may be obtained by peaceful means.' In *Herndon v. Lowry,* the Court ruled that the mere possession of Communist literature could not be held to be an 'incitement to riot.' *Thornhill v. Alabama* interpreted picketing as a form of expression and extended to it the constitutional guarantees of free speech, and *Hague v. C.I.O.* vindicated the right of liberal groups to hold public meetings in boss Frank Hague's bailiwick, Jersey City. Two notable decisions went far to assure Negroes a fair trial in the South: *Powell v. Alabama* — the notorious Scottsboro case — held that failure to include Negroes on the panel from which jurors were drawn constituted in effect a denial of due process; while in *Chambers v. Florida* a unanimous court, speaking through the new Associate Justice from

Alabama, Mr. Hugo Black, reversed the conviction of a Negro obtained through the use of the 'third degree.'

Equally significant was the judicial insistence upon a broad reading of the guarantee of a free press. American devotion to freedom of the press was deep-rooted, and not until the First World War was there any serious challenge to the principle that there should be no previous restraint upon any publication. When, in 1925, Minnesota provided punishment without jury trial for any 'malicious, scandalous and defamatory' newspaper article, making truth a defense only if the motives were good and the ends justifiable, the Supreme Court in *Near v. Minnesota* voided the law. A more dangerous, because more subtle, attack upon the freedom of the press came when Huey Long's pliant legislature in Louisiana imposed a discriminatory tax upon newspapers with a circulation of over 20,000 — a tax neatly designed to embarrass the few papers still opposed to the Long regime. Refusing to be diverted by the vexatious question of the taxing power of the state, the Court in *Grosjean v. American Press Co.* nullified the act squarely on the ground of its conflict with the guarantees of the First Amendment.

In striking down state legislation impairing personal liberties, the Court forged a new constitutional weapon: the doctrine whereby the federal Bill of Rights was interpreted as a limitation upon state as well as upon national action. It had long been assumed that the Bill of Rights limited only the national Congress. Beginning, however, in the 1920's, especially with *Gitlow v. New York* in 1925, the Court intimated that the rights of 'life, liberty and property,' guaranteed against state impairment by the Fourteenth Amendment, might be presumed to embrace those rights set forth in the federal Bill of Rights. This dictum, at first only cautiously advanced, was within a decade incorporated into constitutional law. Since, historically, most limitations upon personal liberties had come from the states, this new principle of law gave support to the hope that the Fourteenth Amendment might at last be interpreted to mean what its framers had originally intended.

In its decisions on property rights even more than on civil liberties, the Court had wrought a Constitutional revolution that appeared to justify Roosevelt's claims that he had won the war; yet in another sense he lost the war. The Supreme Court fight, together with such other developments in 1937 as the recession and resentment at the sit-down strikes, cost the President much of his middle-class following and dealt a heavy blow at the Roosevelt coalition. By the time Congress ended its session in late August in 'spasms of bitterness,' the *New York Times* noted that the session had been the 'stormiest and least productive in recent years.' The Court struggle helped weld together a bipartisan coalition of anti-New Deal senators who soon held a pivotal position. If Roosevelt's Court proposal secured the legitimization of the vast expansion of the power of government, it also played an important role in the untimely end of the New Deal.

3. THE RECESSION OF 1937

Middle-class enthusiasm for Roosevelt owed much to the fact that the President appeared to be leading the country out of the depression, for in the spring of 1937 the nation had finally achieved 1929 levels of production, but in August the economy suddenly slumped. From September 1937 to June 1938, in a decline of unparalleled severity, national income fell 13 per cent, industrial output 33 per cent, payrolls 35 per cent, and profits 78 per cent. Middle-class support for Roosevelt, already shaken by the Supreme Court and sit-down episodes, was now even more seriously tried, for no longer did the President seem a magic-maker who had a formula for ending the depression.

Yet, ironically, the recession had been produced by Roosevelt's acquiescence in the most cherished of middle-class prescriptions for recovery: balancing the budget. Denounced as a wild spender, the President had, in fact, from the very beginning favored government retrenchment. As Tugwell later reflected: 'Roosevelt felt just as much convicted of sin when the budget was unbalanced as Hoover had been.' But to provide relief for the jobless the President had been compelled to accept an unbalanced budget as an unpleasant necessity. All through the New Deal years expenses exceeded income, and the national debt mounted. By 1936 there was a deficit of $4 billion; the gap closed a bit in 1937 and 1938, then widened once more to $4 billion by 1940. The national debt soared from $22 billion when Roosevelt first took office to almost $36 billion at the beginning of his second term, and by 1940 to an unprecedented $42 billion. All this staggered a generation brought up on Micawber's simple prescription for happiness, yet five years later that same generation accepted a debt of $258 billion without visible perturbation.

Early in 1937, as the economy continued to show steady improvement, Roosevelt concluded that he could safely return to more conservative fiscal policies, and he even entertained himself with the mirage of a balanced budget. The Federal Reserve Board contracted credit, and government spending was radically slashed. Since it had been the deficit spending that had been largely responsible for the gains of Roosevelt's first term, his abrupt reversal produced a convulsive reaction.

Through the winter of 1937-38, Roosevelt's advisers belabored him with conflicting advice. Secretary of the Treasury Henry Morgenthau, Jr. urged him to commit himself to orthodox finance to win business 'confidence.' But men like Harry Hopkins and Federal Reserve Chairman Marriner Eccles argued that when private investment fell off, the government should step up spending. 'In other words,' Eccles insisted, 'the Government must be looked upon as a compensatory agency in the economy to do just the opposite to what private business and individuals do.' In addition, these New Dealers believed that the government should curb monopoly, because they felt that the inflexible 'administered' price practices of the monopolies was prolonging the depression.

Some of these ideas reflected the influence of the British economist, John Maynard Keynes, but Keynes made rather little impact on Roosevelt; he served chiefly to reinforce views which the New Dealers already held. During the recession, Keynes urged Roosevelt to step up investment in durable goods like housing, public utilities, and railroads if he wanted to regain the lost momentum toward recovery. While he admired much of the New Deal, he thought the President's handling of housing had been 'really wicked.' Housing, he argued, offered the best prospect for revival. 'I should advise putting most of your eggs in this basket, caring about this more than anything, and making absolutely sure they are being hatched without delay,' he wrote. If Roosevelt did not intend to nationalize the railroads and utilities, then he should forget past grievances and extend them a helping hand, for 'what is the object of chasing the utilities round the lot every other week?' 'To an Englishman,' Keynes commented, 'you Americans, like the Irish, are so terribly historically-minded.' Roosevelt, who thought Keynes's prescriptions for deliberately unbalancing the budget flew in the face of common sense, turned Keynes's letter over to Morgenthau, the Cambridge economist's chief critic within the administration, and the Secretary framed a purposefully noncommittal response.

Yet by the early spring of 1938, Roosevelt had concluded that he must take hold of the reins, for the recession was taking too great a toll of the unemployed. On 2 April 1938, at his Southern home in Warm Springs, Georgia, the President announced he had decided to spend. Two weeks later, he asked Congress to approve a large-scale 'lend-spend' program, and Congress responded by voting nearly a billion for public works and almost three billions more for other federal activities. Roosevelt gave his liberal advisers something else to cheer about when he asked Congress for a full-dress investigation of the concentration of economic power, which led to the creation of the Temporary National Economic Committee, and when he appointed Thurman Arnold of Yale Law School to be Assistant Attorney-General in charge of the Antitrust Division. That same year Congress established the second AAA and passed a Fair Labor Standards Act which ended child labor and put a floor under wages and a ceiling on hours for workers in industries engaged in interstate commerce.

In the remainder of Roosevelt's second term, the economy painfully climbed up toward its earlier levels, but the New Dealers could not escape the fact that whatever they had done had not been sufficient to avert the recession, and that in 1939 there were still ten million unemployed. Nor had the New Deal substantially changed the pattern of income. In May 1940, Ickes noted in his diary: 'This is our weakness. The New Deal has done a great deal during the last seven years, but we have not been able to force from those who own and control the preponderant part of our wealth the social and economic security that the people are entitled to.' Never before had any administration been so responsive to the nation's social needs or built so many useful economic institutions, but it would require the coming of World War II to restore the country's prosperity.

4. POLITICAL AND ADMINISTRATIVE REFORM

The number of civil servants in the employ of the Federal Government had increased from some 370,000 before World War I to over half a million during the Hoover administration. Under the New Deal, with the establishment of new boards and bureaus and the enlargement of old ones, the number rose from 583,000 in 1932 to 920,000 in 1939. Both the increase in governmental activity and in the number of civil servants had every appearance of permanence.[1]

Yet the government which had thus come to play so crucial a part in the life of the nation had developed in an opportunistic and haphazard fashion. Every student of government knew that the administrative machinery was inefficient and extravagant, while to the layman bureaucracy was synonymous with red tape. Scientific management, which had been applied to the business of large corporations, had never been tried out in this largest and most important of all businesses. Every President since Theodore Roosevelt had been aware of the problem and anxious for reform, but none had been able to achieve more than piecemeal improvement.

By orthodox standards Roosevelt was a poor administrator. He did not work through channels, or a chain of command, but through any persons or methods that caught his fancy; his intellectual processes were not orderly but intuitive, and he liked to match his 'hunches' against the logic of his advisers. He allowed a thicket of overlapping and even conflicting bureaus and agencies to grow up almost in the White House grounds; he found it difficult to fire anyone, and those who had outlived their usefulness were often kicked upstairs to make further trouble. He liked to play his assistants off against each other; he had a pawky sense of humor; he was by turns confiding and secretive, generous and vindictive, clear cut and deliberately fuzzy. Yet in a larger sense he was wonderfully effective: he got things done. He made Washington so exciting that first-rate men left good jobs and came to work for him, and he inspired them with such loyalty that they worked far beyond the ordinary call of duty. Superficially less efficient than President Hoover, Roosevelt was in fact far more effective, and his presidency dramatized once again the vital principle that politics is neither a business nor a science, but an art.

Roosevelt was convinced that a thorough overhauling of the executive branch of the government was imperative, and in 1936 he appointed a Committee on Administrative Management to formulate plans for reform. Early the next year he laid their recommendations before Congress: a reorganization of the civil service and an extension of the merit

1. As indeed it was; by 1940 the total had passed 1 million and by 1950 it passed 2 million.

system; the addition of two new departments of cabinet rank; the establishment of budget and efficiency agencies, and of a planning agency through which the President might co-ordinate executive functions; an increase in the White House staff; and the creation of an independent auditing system for the executive departments.

The proposals were innocuous enough, but Congress, alarmed by the presidential 'attack' on the Supreme Court, jealous of any enlargement of executive authority, and sensitive to the bogey of dictatorship, rejected them. The President, however, persisted, and in 1939 — after the Supreme Court issue had been settled and the congressional elections were safely out of the way — had the satisfaction of obtaining congressional approval for most of this program.

One important aspect of the problem remained — that concerned with the extension of the merit system and the divorce of administration from politics. To prevent exploitation of government employees or relief workers, Senator Hatch of New Mexico introduced and Congress passed two bills forbidding federal employees or state employees paid from federal funds to engage in 'pernicious political activities.' More specifically these bills made it unlawful for any officeholder to coerce or intimidate any voter, or 'to use his official authority or influence for the purpose of interfering with an election or affecting the result thereof.' Just what these esoteric words meant was not entirely clear, nor was their meaning clarified in the following decade.

5. THE END OF THE NEW DEAL

After the passage of the Fair Labor Standards Act in 1938, Congress did not adopt any other reform legislation for the rest of the decade. The impetus of the New Deal came to an end not only because it failed to bring recovery, but because the forces opposed to further change were too powerful. The informal conservative bipartisan coalition forged during the Court fight showed its strength in the special session of Congress in the fall of 1937 when the President could not gain approval of a single measure. In 1938 Democratic insurrectionists joined with Republicans to bury Roosevelt's plan for executive reorganization. That same spring the House set up a Committee on Un-American Activities which, under the chairmanship of the Texas Democrat Martin Dies, became a forum for right-wing forays against the Roosevelt administration. 'Stalin

Wall Street, 29 October 1929

Franklin D. Roosevelt and Herbert Clark Hoover, 4 March 1933

A Breadline, New York

Secretary of Labor Frances Perkins
(1882-1965)

Senator Robert Wagner (1877-1953) and
Senator Robert M. La Follette, Jr. (1895-1953)

Father Charles Coughlin

Senator Huey Long (1893-1935)

Secretary of the Interior Harold Ickes

John L. Lewis

Senator George Norris at TVA's Norris Dam

The Supreme Court, 1937

American Tragedy, 1937 ("Republic Steel Massacre") by Philip Evergood

Pearl Harbor, 7 December 1941

baited his hook with a "progressive" worm,' Dies said, 'and New Deal suckers swallowed bait, hook, line, and sinker.'

This series of setbacks exasperated New Dealers who recalled that many of the Democrats who were now attacking Roosevelt had come in on the President's coattails only a short time before. Since the last time the nation had spoken it had given Roosevelt a landslide triumph, liberal Democrats were convinced that he had the country with him. They persuaded the President to attempt to 'purge' a number of legislators in the Democratic primaries, in particular Senators Walter George of Georgia, 'Cotton Ed' Smith of South Carolina, and Millard Tydings of Maryland. The President succeeded in eliminating a Tammany congressman, but George, Smith, and Tydings all won handily, leaving the party's conservatives more cocksure than ever. That fall, the Republicans picked up 81 seats in the House, 8 in the Senate, and 13 governorships; all but given up for dead two years before, they introduced to the national spotlight that year such new faces as Thomas Dewey, Robert Taft, and Harold Stassen.

Without enough votes to carry his program through Congress before the election, the President now faced a greatly bolstered conservative alliance. Resigned to the inevitable, Roosevelt in his annual message to Congress in January 1939 for the first time advanced no new measures. 'We have now passed the period of internal conflict in the launching of our program of social reforms,' he told Congress. 'Our full energies may now be released to invigorate the processes of recovery in order to preserve our reforms.' As an innovating force, the New Deal was at an end, and the President henceforth directed most of his attentions to the critical problems of foreign policy.

6. THE NEW DEAL: AN EVALUATION

What, then, is the significance of the New Deal in our history, and what are its permanent contributions? First, there is the physical rehabilitation of the country. For generations Americans had been laying waste their natural resources without restoring them. The New Deal attack on this problem was thoroughgoing; it involved an ambitious program of soil conservation, building dams and planting trees to prevent floods, reclaiming the grass lands of the Great Plains and millions of acres of sub-marginal lands, developing water-power resources, and inaugurating vast regional reconstruction enterprises like the TVA and the Columbia river projects. All this changed the face of the country and restored to productive use much of the national domain.

Second, the establishment of the principle that government has responsibility for the health, welfare, and security of all its citizens. The New Deal embraced social security, public health, and housing, and entered the domain of agriculture and labor, and of the arts and sciences. Verbal and ceremonial opposition persisted for the next generation, but in fact the new principle was accepted by the Republican as well as the Democratic party after 1940.

Third, three major developments in the realm of politics and government. One of these was the strengthening of the executive branch and the reassertion of presidential leadership characteristic of every period of progressivism in our history: Roosevelt made clear — as had his forceful predecessors from Jackson through Wilson — that the presidential power was pretty much what the President made it. It was ratified judicially by the reapplication of a 'broad construction' to the Constitution where federal authority was involved.

Although the New Deal did more to strengthen than weaken the capitalist economy, the expansion of governmental regulation and functions meant a steady socialization of the economic life of the nation — a socialization going forward under the auspices of private enterprise as well. The immediate impulse to socialization came from practical considerations of the inability of private enterprise to undertake necessary large-scale social and economic programs; its manifestations were chiefly in the economic realm such as government development of hydroelectric power, operation of merchant marine, and partnership in banking. Equally significant was the growing government participation in business activities that came with the depression and the defense program of the late 'thirties. During the early years of the depression the Federal Government had to come to the rescue of banks, railroads, utilities and industries, and inevitably financial aid involved supervision and effective partnership. As the attempt to manage the whole economy was abandoned, regulation of particular departments of the economy became stricter. The Wheeler-Rayburn Public Utilities Act of 1935 gave the government effective control and veto-power over holding companies; and the Eccles Banking Act of the same year transferred to the Federal Reserve Board substantial control over all market transactions in government bonds. War brought a vast expansion of governmental activity — the financing and operation of defense industries, construction of low-cost housing, and so forth. States, too, expanded not only their regulatory activities but their participation in economic life, setting up systems of state insurance and employment agencies, while cities took on such diverse activities as transportation, the sale of gas and electricity, the distribution of milk, and radio broadcasting.

Even more significant than the extension of democracy in the domestic realm was the maintenance of a democratic system of government and society in a world swept by confused alarms of struggle and flight. 'The only sure bulwark of continuing liberty,' Roosevelt had observed, 'is a government strong enough to protect the interests of the people, and a people strong enough and well enough informed to maintain its sovereign control over its government.' The proof that in the United States it was possible for such a government to exist and such a people to flourish was of fateful significance, and it helped restore the United States to its traditional position as 'the hope of the human race.' For in the 'thirties it became doubtful whether liberty or democracy could survive in the modern world, and at the end of that decade totalitarian states felt strong enough to challenge the democracies in a war for survival. It was of utmost importance to the peoples of the world that the American democracy had withstood the buffetings of depression and the vicissitudes of world affairs and emerged strong and courageous; that the American people were refreshed in their faith in the democratic order, prepared to defend it wherever it was threatened.

XXI

Gathering Storm

1. THE CHALLENGE OF THE DICTATORS

If there was one principle upon which the vast majority of the American people agreed in 1937, it was that what was happening in Europe was no concern of theirs; and that if Europe were so wicked or stupid as to get into another war, America would resolutely stay out of it. Even the President reflected this feeling by failing to mention foreign relations in his second inaugural address, which, owing to the ratification of the Twentieth Amendment to the Constitution, was delivered on 20 January 1937 instead of the traditional 4 March. Yet within two years, developments in Europe and Asia made a mockery of this negative attitude.

A system known as collective security was supposed to maintain the territorial and other settlements made after World War I, but to make minor adjustments necessary to serve justice and prevent any new war. It worked well enough until challenged by demagogues and dictators whose main object was unrestrained power. In pursuance of their several ambitions they set up totalitarian regimes in which the rule of law and traditional liberties such as freedom of speech, assembly, elections, and the press were suppressed, and the citizen became powerless under a monster state. Russia, Communist since 1918, fitted this category, but Russia in the 1930's did not threaten the peace of the world. Stalin was too deeply concerned with his country's problems to brandish the spear, and in 1934 he had joined the League of Nations and used his influence to check Hitler. Benito Mussolini also had set himself up as *duce* of Italy in 1922, but waited until the rise of Hitler before taking a first step to 'restore the Roman Empire' by attacking helpless Ethiopia.[1]

Mussolini would have been powerless to upset the peace of Europe but for the rise of Adolf Hitler. The hold of that uneducated paranoiac over the German people, with their long tradition of culture and decency (to which they have since returned), is a phenomenon which even the Germans themselves have been unable to explain. In part, no doubt, it was due to the poverty and disorganization of Germany after her defeat in World War I; but other nations, notably Austria and Poland, had suffered even more than Germany and made little trouble. Hitler rose on a tide of resentment over the Treaty of Versailles; but the victor powers had redressed most of the severities imposed by that treaty and (with the aid of American loans) had relieved Germany from the burden of war reparations before Hitler reached power. There was much talk of *Lebensraum*, room for expansion; but the Netherlands and Scandinavia suffered similar pressures without trying to wreck the European world. Possibly the conclusion that Franklin D. Roosevelt reached is the right one. Hitler, a frustrated fanatic, based his National Socialist (Nazi) party on the residuary hatred, barbarism, and cruelty inherent in modern society. He hated the Jews, he hated democracy, he hated the Christian religion in which he was reared, he hated all foreigners, and in general anything that was good, true, or beautiful. For brutality, sadistic cruelty, and villainy he may be compared only with Genghis Khan in ancient days, or to Stalin in ours. As Winston Churchill wrote, Hitler 'called from the depths of defeat the dark and savage furies latent in the most numerous, most serviceable, ruthless, contradictory, and ill-starred race in Europe.'[2]

Hitler's objective was to reunite all Germans at home and abroad as a 'master race' which would rule Europe and dictate to the world. He was willing only to tolerate rulers whose objectives in other areas were similar to his. When Marshal von Hindenburg, President of the German Republic, allowed Hitler to take office as Chancellor on 30 January 1933, it was as if President Roosevelt, seeing his end approaching, had abdicated

1. The other dictators — Franco in Spain, Salazar in Portugal, Perón in Argentina, Trujillo in the Dominican Republic, Castañeda in Guatemala — were relatively powerless outside their own countries, although the three Latin Americans nourished a 'fifth column' of Nazis who were potentially dangerous to the New World.
2. *The Second World War*, pp. 170–71.

in favor of Huey Long or Gerald Smith. And when Hindenburg died (2 August 1934) Hitler made himself chief of state, using his party title of *Fuehrer*. He promptly abolished the republican constitution, made Germany a military dictatorship in which he was the source of all authority, and surcharged the German flag with the party swastika.

Hitler had a devilish ability to play off rivals against each other and to profit by their weakness and folly. The only nations capable of stopping him in his early aggressions were Great Britain and France; and in both countries, decimated as they had been by the First World War (France lost some million and a half men, and the British Empire a million), sound leadership was wanting; lassitude, timidity, and class hatred were paramount, especially in France. The Western powers acquiesced in one aggression after another, in the vain hope of 'appeasing' Hitler, until the time came when they had to dig in and fight. Nor can our country escape censure. If American influence had been exerted in time, directly or through the League of Nations, it might have galvanized flabby British politicians like MacDonald, Baldwin, and Chamberlain, timid French politicians like Daladier and Georges Bonnet, into action; and there were still elements in Germany, especially in the army, who wanted only encouragement from abroad to liquidate Hitler.

2. THE PACIFIST MOOD

Never since Jefferson's time had America been in so pacifist a mood. Yet at a time when the Fascist powers were planning to pounce on the democratic states and when the system of collective security was breaking down, it was not clear that isolation would bring peace. Edna St. Vincent Millay wrote:

> Longing to wed with Peace, what did we do? —
> Sketched her a fortress on a paper pad;
> Under her casement twanged a love-sick string;
> Left wide the gate that let her foemen through.[3]

As early as 1933, writers like Leland Stowe were cautioning: 'Nazi Means War.' Supporters of the League of Nations warned that fascism constituted the greatest threat the Western world had ever faced, and

3. *Make Bright the Arrows*, Harper & Brothers, 1942, copyright 1939, 1940 by the author.

they counselled the democracies to join together to contain Hitler. Such admonitions fell on deaf ears. They sounded too much like the slogans of World War I, an event now recalled with bitter resentment. Ostensibly fought to preserve democracy, the war had left Europe a continent where democracy appeared to have only the barest chance to survive. In 1925, Prime Minister Stanley Baldwin had asked: 'Who in Europe does not know that one more war in the West and the civilization of the ages will fall with as great a shock as that of Rome?' The war had taken millions of lives, wiping out much of the younger generation in many European countries and maiming thousands more. In America, fifteen years later, the grim reminders of that conflict still lay in veterans' hospitals.

Many thought the greatest danger of war came not from Hitler but from war-mongering internationalists who would attempt to embroil the United States. Historians argued that the idealistic statements of Wilson in 1917 had cloaked the greed of profiteers and that the nation had been manipulated by adroit Allied propaganda. It was but a short step to the conclusion that idealism and false propaganda were one and the same and that the real peril lay in the possibility that people would once again permit themselves to be manipulated by the pronouncements of some new idealist.

Leaders who had urged America's entry into World War I felt a sense of guilt and humiliation, and they promised that this time they would prove worthy of their positions of leadership. The Chicago Federation of Churches made public atonement: 'In humble penitence for past mistakes and sincere repentance for our want of faith and devotion to the ideals of the Kingdom of God . . . we declare ourselves as unalterably opposed to war.' In 1932, celebrating twenty-five years as rabbi of New York's Free Synagogue, Stephen Wise apologized to the country for his support of the First World War and promised 'without reservation or equivocation' never to repeat the error. 'I would as little support a war to crush Hitlerism as a war for the strengthening of Jewish claims on Palestine,' Rabbi Wise announced. At the Northern Baptist annual meeting in 1933, the preacher of the Convention Sermon confessed that he had personally 'helped to kill men,' and swore, 'before enough witnesses so that it may be remembered: "I will never do it again." ' Robert Osgood has commented: ' "Never-again" vows were as much the order of the day in the 1930's as temperance pledges had been in the days before Prohibition.'

Disillusionment with World War I not only fortified isolationists but nourished a pacifist movement that won millions of adherents. Textbooks played down martial heroes, and military history was all but eliminated. Children were encouraged to abandon war games and were denied war toys. On May Day each year, hundreds of thousands of college and high school students walked out of their classes to 'strike' for peace; at Vassar and Mt. Holyoke, the college presidents took part. New York University, the University of Minnesota, and other institutions abolished military training.

Opponents of war charged that munitions makers had precipitated World War I and were intriguing to touch off a new arms race that would lead to a second world war. 'The thumbprints of our munitions makers are smudged all over the budgets of the United States army and navy,' protested one writer. He claimed that the arms makers had trapped the government into buying armaments far beyond our actual needs. 'Since the United States is protected on both coasts by oceans too wide for any known hostile airplane to cross under war conditions, 1,800 planes seems a fantastic number for this country to possess.' As conservative a senator as Arthur Vandenberg of Michigan damned the arms traffic as 'unutterable' treason and urged the confiscation of virtually all individual income in excess of $10,000 in the event of war.

America's pacifist mood received official sanction in 1934 from a Senate investigation into the bankers and munitions makers during World War I. The committee, headed by Senator Gerald Nye of Wisconsin, concluded that America had intervened not to defend its own interests, nor for the altruistic purpose of saving the world for democracy, but as a consequence of the intrigues of financiers and armament interests. If Europeans had to fight, Nye scolded, 'let them pay for their own wars. If the Morgans and other bankers must get into another war, let them do it by enlisting in the Foreign Legion.' Although the Nye committee failed to prove anyone's responsibility for the war, it did reveal scandalously high profits, and the public concluded that Wall Street wanted the war for financial reasons. Historians like Charles A. Beard, journalists like Colonel McCormick of the Chicago *Tribune* and William Randolph Hearst, converted a substantial part of public opinion to the naïve view that America had been stampeded into war in order to make money for 'merchants of death,' and that our intervention in any future European war would be a crime.

3. WATCHFULLY WAITING

On the very day Roosevelt took the oath of office, the Japanese marched into the provincial capital of Jehol in China, and on the following day the last free elections in Germany consolidated the power of Adolf Hitler. Throughout the Hundred Days, news of the TVA and NRA jostled for attention side by side with accounts in the nation's press of Nazis beating Jews in the streets of Germany. Roosevelt, who came to office with extensive knowledge of foreign affairs, recognized the perils of the breakdown of the world order, but isolationist and pacifist opinion left him little room to maneuver, and the crisis of the Great Depression persuaded him he must concentrate his energies on domestic affairs. 'I shall spare no effort to restore world trade by international economic readjustments,' he said in his inaugural address, 'but the emergency at home cannot wait on that accomplishment.'

In his first months in office Roosevelt encouraged the world to believe that he held out high hopes for the international economic conference scheduled for London in June. But by the time the delegates convened, he had come to fear that France and the other gold bloc countries were seeking to commit him to a policy that would destroy his efforts at price-raising at home. He not only killed a currency stabilization agreement but sent the conference a harsh message scolding the delegates for succumbing to the 'old fetishes of so-called international bankers.' Some like Keynes thought that the President was 'magnificently right,' but Roosevelt's 'bombshell message' undoubtedly reinforced the isolationists and persuaded Europe it could not count on the United States.

Despite this initial setback, Roosevelt's Secretary of State, Cordell Hull, unsympathetic to the philosophy of national autarchy, persisted in exploring the possibilities of the recapture of foreign markets through reciprocity agreements, a solution President McKinley had proposed in 1901. Under the terms of the Trade Agreements Act of June 1934, Secretary Hull negotiated unconditional most-favored-nation reciprocity treaties with Cuba, Canada, France, Russia, and some twenty other countries. Within a year trade with Cuba had doubled, and trade with Canada, Sweden, France, and South American and Central American countries had improved materially. Hull hoped that the new commercial policy would operate not only for economic improvement at home and abroad but that it would break down nationalist barriers and advance international understanding and peace. In fact, the agreements failed to have important economic consequences but did serve to win political good will. Even more illusory as a panacea for improved trade was the recognition of the Soviet Union in 1933, an event which twenty years later would be denounced as a treasonable act by liberal marplots. The truth of the matter is that recognition was widely applauded by businessmen avid for Russian markets, and Roosevelt's decision simply brought American practice in line with that of most of the rest of the world.

Roosevelt had the greatest leeway in foreign affairs when he sought to liquidate American commitments. 'In the field of world policy,' he said in his inaugural address, 'I would dedicate this Nation to the policy of the good neighbor.' The 'Good Neighbor policy' soon became the descriptive term for Roosevelt's willingness to disavow America's intention to intervene in the internal affairs of Latin American nations. In 1934 the United States agreed to abrogate the Platt Amendment, thereby giving up its right to intervene at will in Cuba, and that same year it pulled the last Marines out of Haiti, recognized a revolutionary government in El Salvador, and established the Export-Import Bank which extended credit to Latin American republics. Before the decade was over, the Administration had ended financial controls in the Dominican Republic and resisted pressures to prevent Mexico from expropriating American oil. On the other side of the world, the Philippines won a promise of independence in 1946 when Congress approved the Tydings-McDuffie Act of 1934.

But such actions defined the limits of Roosevelt's power, for when he sought to use his influence in European affairs Congress would have none of it. In 1933 isolationists like Hiram Johnson warned the President away from a proposal to co-operate in League sanctions against an aggressor, and in 1935 the Senate killed a measure to permit the United States to join the World Court. After this unexpected defeat, Roosevelt wrote Elihu Root, 'Today, quite frankly, the wind everywhere blows against us.' That same year Congress passed the first of a series of neutrality measures which prohibited private loans or credits to belligerent nations, embargoed shipments of arms or munitions to belligerents, and required they 'pay cash and carry' for any other articles. That is, belligerents who wanted to buy nonmilitary goods had to pay for them on delivery and haul them away in their own vessels or those of some country other than the United States. As Italy marched into Ethopia in 1935 and Germany reclaimed the Rhineland the following year, Roosevelt found himself powerless to do anything effective. 'I am "watchfully waiting,"' he wrote one of his envoys, 'even though the phrase carries us back to the difficult days from 1914 to 1917.'

By August 1936, when he spoke at Chautauqua, the President appeared to have capitulated to the pacifist mood. In case of an overseas conflict Roosevelt foresaw that some Americans would seek to 'break down or evade our neutrality' to hunt for 'fools' gold.' 'We shun political commitments which might entangle us in foreign wars; we avoid connection with the political activities of the League of Nations,' the President asserted. He added:

> I have seen war. I have seen war on land and sea. I have seen blood running from the wounded. I have seen men coughing out their gassed lungs. I have seen the dead in the mud. I have seen cities destroyed. I have seen two hundred limping, exhausted men come out of line — the survivors of a regiment of one thousand that went forward forty-eight hours before. I have seen children starving. I have seen the agony of mothers and wives. I hate war.

When in July 1936 anti-republican forces plunged Spain into a 'civil war' that Hitler and Mussolini soon made a testing ground for World War II, Roosevelt outdid the isolationists in his plea that Congress impose an arms embargo. Most of the nation approved, secure in the belief that the United States, by this series of steps, was avoiding the mistakes that had led to its unhappy involvement in the First World War. Claude Bowers, Roosevelt's ambassador to Spain, was unconvinced. 'My own impression,' he wrote in July 1937, 'is that with every surrender beginning long ago with China, followed by Abyssinia and then Spain, the fascist powers, with vanity inflamed, will turn without delay to some other country — such as Czechoslovakia — and that with every surrender the prospects of a European war grow darker.'

4. 'FOR WHOM THE BELL TOLLS'

When President Roosevelt signed the Neutrality Act of 1937, he seemed to be endorsing all the assumptions of the isolationists. In fact, he was a

troubled man. 'One cannot help feeling that the whole European panorama is fundamentally blacker than at any time in your life time or
mine,' the President had written Ambassador Jesse Straus the year before. People were saying that Europe had muddled through one crisis
after another for the past three years and would continue to do so,
Roosevelt noted. 'I hope that point of view is right but it goes against
one's common sense. The armaments race means bankruptcy or war —
there is no possible out from that statement.' The spread of fascism constituted a threat not only to America's safety and well-being but to the
whole heritage of Western civilization. In his novel *For Whom the Bell
Tolls,* Ernest Hemingway, recalling the solemn words of John Donne,
wrote that the bell in Spain tolled not just for that unhappy country; '*it
tolls for thee.*'

By 1937 Roosevelt's alarm at the actions of Hitler and Mussolini in
Europe was matched by concern over the ambitions of the Japanese in
the Far East. That year, Japan engaged in hostilities in China which
raised so critical a challenge to the post-Versailles order that the President decided to reappraise his foreign policy. In his first term, Roosevelt
had pursued an even more isolationist line in the Far East than Hoover
had. By the end of that term, Japan had denounced the Washington
naval treaty, walked out of the London Naval Conference, and signed
an Anti-Comintern Pact with Nazi Germany. But neither the President
nor advisers like Ambassador to Japan Joseph Grew favored strong measures against Tokyo. 'Then if moral ostracism is ineffective how can we
implement the Kellogg Pact?' Grew asked. 'Certainly not by force of
arms, which would be contrary to the very principle for which the Kellogg Pact stands,' he responded.

But Roosevelt recognized that Japan's war in China in 1937 represented a new situation. The Japanese militarists, from 1937 on, made a
concerted effort to drive American and European missionary, educational, medical, and cultural activities out of China permanently. American churches, hospitals, schools, and colleges were bombed despite flag
markings on their roofs; American missionaries and their families were
killed; there were so many 'accidents' of this sort that cynical Chinese
reported the most dangerous spot in an air raid to be an American
mission. Japan conducted its war in China with a barbarity, as in the
bombing of Shanghai and the sack of Nanking, that appalled American
opinion. Moreover, the militant faction in Tokyo had been growing in-

creasingly closer to the leaders in Berlin and Rome. The rest of the world, Roosevelt knew, would soon be confronted by a crisis in which it would either have to resist the aggression of the three powers or submit to it. He was still committed to peace, but he looked for some way to build a concert of powers to curb the expansion of Germany, Italy, and Japan.

In October 1937 Roosevelt sought to warn the country of the peril it faced and ask the world to take steps to avert the impending war. In an address in Chicago, the isolationist capital, the President warned that, if aggression triumphed elsewhere in the world, 'let no one imagine that America will escape, that America may expect mercy, that this Western Hemisphere will not be attacked.' Roosevelt noted that 'the epidemic of world lawlessness' was spreading, and he added: 'When an epidemic of physical disease starts to spread, the community approves and joins in a quarantine of the patients in order to protect the health of the community against the spread of the disease.' The President's 'quarantine' speech was interpreted as a new departure in Roosevelt's foreign policy — the abandonment of isolation for collective security, and advance notice to Tokyo of sanctions against Japan. In fact, Roosevelt had not yet committed himself to any project to contain the Axis powers, and while public response to the quarantine speech was generally favorable, the nation resolutely opposed any commitment of American forces abroad. On 12 December 1937 a small river gunboat of the American navy's Yangtze river patrol, U.S.S. *Panay*, was bombed and sunk by Japanese naval planes. When the Japanese government apologized and offered to pay indemnity to the victims, a sigh of relief passed over the length and breadth of America. In a Gallup poll conducted during the second week of January 1938, 70 per cent of the American voters who were interviewed and had an opinion on the subject, favored complete withdrawal from China —Asiatic Fleet, marines, missionaries, medical teams, and all.

By 1938 the Fascist powers were on the march. Hitler called Austrian Chancellor Kurt von Schuschnigg to his retreat in Berchtesgaden to bully him into submission. 'Perhaps I shall be suddenly overnight in Vienna, like a spring storm,' he warned. 'Do you want to turn Austria into another Spain?' On 11 March 1938 Schuschnigg resigned. Immediately afterwards, Nazis swarmed into Vienna's Kärnsterstrasse; they ripped badges off Austrian officials, broke the shop windows of Jewish merchants, ran up the swastika over the Chancellery. The next morning,

German tanks and troops poured over the border and, to the pealing of church bells and deafening cheers from Nazi followers, Adolf Hitler entered Austria at Braunau, his birthplace. In Vienna the following night, the Gestapo arrested no fewer than 76,000 Viennese. Yet when at Munich in September 1938 Britain and France succumbed to Hitler's demand that Czechoslovakia be dismembered and the Sudetenland incorporated in the Reich, Americans had an overwhelming feeling of relief. The New York *Herald Tribune* declared that 'only heartfelt applause' should greet Chamberlain's 'scrupulous integrity' and 'self-sacrificing devotion.' However, the Munich crisis served also to heighten isolationist sentiment in the United States, for it seemed to prove that the European democracies were concerned only with self-interest. The New York *Post* commented: 'If this transcendental sellout does not force the Administration at Washington to return to our policy of isolation — then Heaven help us all!' Two months later, the Nazis carried out an appalling pogrom which drove numbers of German and Austrian Jews to America, but the United States, in one of its most shameful acts, refused to lower immigration barriers in any substantial way. Many who were denied visas later died in Hitler's gas chambers.

Much of Hitler's appeal to the rest of the world rested on his invocation of the Wilsonian doctrine of self-determination. Many in the West accepted Hitler's professed aim to incorporate all German peoples in one Reich as not unreasonable. In September 1938, the Fuehrer had said that once the Sudeten problem was settled, there would be 'no further territorial problem in Europe.' He added: 'We want no Czechs.' But less than six months later, on the Ides of March, Hitler gobbled up most of Czechoslovakia. On the night of 15 March 1939 the Gestapo roved the streets of Prague making mass arrests; no Jewish shops opened the next day. On the tower of Hradschin Castle, the palace of the Kings of Bohemia, the Nazis hoisted a gold-bordered swastika, the Fuehrer's standard.

Germany had made a mockery of the Munich settlement. It was now clear that Hitler's aims were not limited, as Chamberlain remarked, by 'racial affinity or just claims too long resisted.' The Fuehrer had, in a single stroke, destroyed any pretext that his ambitions were restricted to the desire to reunite Germans; had exposed appeasement as a failure; and had rendered general war all but inevitable.

At an off-the-record conference with the American Society of Newspaper Editors in April 1939, the President unburdened himself of his thoughts on the state of foreign affairs. He confided that his informants had told him that there was now an even chance of war in Europe. 'That is something to think about, whether it be in Washington, D.C., or Watertown, New York, a fifty-fifty chance there will be a war in Europe.' They also advised him that it was even money on which side would win. 'I don't like it,' Roosevelt said. If the totalitarian countries triumphed, the President went on, the United States would face serious economic problems just as this country would have 'if Napoleon Bonaparte had won out that time that he organized the fleet to invade England.'

'Today they have somewhere around 1500 planes which can leave their countries tonight, be in the Cape Verde Islands tomorrow morning and be in Brazil tomorrow afternoon,' Roosevelt pointed out. 'We have eighty planes that could get there in time to meet them.' They could bring 'economic slavery to South America, and by flying from Brazil to Yucatan and Tampico, dominate Mexico.' The President pointed the moral: 'I think I am a lot safer on the Hudson River than I would be if I were in Kansas. They [in Kansas] are awfully close to Mexico.' Roosevelt concluded: 'Now, we all hope it is not going to happen and that we are not going to get into this game, except this: we know where the sympathies of the American people will lie. We are not going to send armies to Europe. But there are lots of things, short of war, that we can do to help maintain the independence of nations who, as a matter of decent American principle, ought to be allowed to live their own lives.'

Roosevelt did all that he could, 'short of war.' He asked Congress for larger appropriations to rebuild the army, which in 1933 ranked seventeenth in the world, and got approval for a Naval Expansion Act. He solidified friendship with Canada by promising in August 1938 at Kingston, Ontario, 'that the people of the United States will not stand idly by if domination of Canadian soil is threatened by any other Empire.' On 14 April 1939 he sent a personal message to Hitler and Mussolini asking them to promise not to attack some twenty small countries in Europe. Hitler made an insulting reply and then bullied some of the countries (which he was about to swallow) into assuring Roosevelt that they had no cause to fear good neighbor Germany. Mussolini sneered to his underlings that the message was 'a result of infantile paralysis.' To strengthen his hand, the President asked Congress to repeal the Neutrality Act. But on 11 July 1939 the Senate Foreign Relations Committee voted, 12-11, to postpone such action, in part out of the conviction that there would be no war. Less than two months later, on 1 September 1939 Germany attacked Poland and brought the 'Long Armistice' to an end.

5. AND THE WAR CAME

Three weeks after the outbreak of war, the President asked Congress, called into special session, to repeal the arms embargo and return to our 'traditional neutrality.' The one previous experiment with an embargo, Roosevelt warned, had been a 'major cause' of the War of 1812, during which the enemy had burned 'part of this Capitol in which we are now assembled.' The President said of the Neutrality law: 'I regret that the Congress passed that Act. I regret equally that I signed that Act.'

Roosevelt preferred no neutrality legislation at all, but isolationist sentiment was still too strong. 'If you try that you'll be damn lucky to get five votes in my committee,' Senator Pittman told him. The President was forced to compromise on a bill continuing the principle of cash-and-carry, and even this brought forth violent denunciations from isolationists. But after six weeks of heated debate, Congress repealed the arms embargo and applied the cash-and-carry requirement to munitions as well as raw materials. Events in Europe had moved America another step toward war. Yet the anti-war forces were still strong enough to include a provision in the new law forbidding American ships to sail to belligerent ports and, if the President stipulated, to combat zones. The Neutrality Act of 1939 abandoned the doctrine of freedom of the seas that had been maintained since the days of the Napoleonic wars and the incursions of the Barbary pirates.

Although the United States had taken a step toward war, the nation still did not feel that its own security was at stake in Europe — and, so long as it did not, further commitments were stoutly opposed. Not even Russia's attack on Finland in November shook this determination. The war in the West settled down to a long siege; some Americans even complained about the lack of excitement in the 'bore' war. When Henry Ford was asked in December 1939 how long he thought the war would last, he answered: 'That's no war.' 'Figure it out for yourself,' he said. 'Millions of men under arms. Great, unbreakable fortifications strung

along the borders. Fierce propaganda. And what else? Practically nothing. Something is holding it up. I think it is the culminating power of all
the past Christmases.' Since the war seemed so unreal, there was little to
shake the conviction that Hitler would be defeated in a war of attrition,
and the United States, without danger to itself, could be the quartermas-
ter for the Allied forces.

Early in April 1940, the 'phony war' came to a dramatic end. Without
warning Germany moved into Denmark, a nation with whom Hitler had
just recently concluded a non-aggression pact, and then into Norway.
Denmark fell within hours, Norway in less than two months. One month
after the invasion of Scandinavia came the blow in the West. Here the
French army trusted to a series of modern forts, but the Maginot line
ended at the frontier of Belgium, whose king was so scrupulously neutral and so eager to keep out of war that he neglected even rudimentary
defense. On 10 May the German army invaded his country and neutral
Holland, while the *Luftwaffe,* the German air force, rained death on
those countries and on northeastern France. In five days the Netherlands
was conquered, Rotterdam laid in ruins by a cruel air assault. Three
days later Antwerp fell. Already the German Panzer (armored) divisions, slipping around the end of the Maginot line, had crashed through
the Ardennes Forest, enveloped a French army, and smashed ahead toward the Channel ports. On 21 May — only eleven days after the attack
on Holland — the Germans reached the English Channel, cutting off the
British expeditionary force which had been rushed to the aid of Belgium
and France. A week later Belgium surrendered, and the British were left
to their fate. Their evacuation has well been called 'the miracle of Dunkirk.' Every available warship, yacht, power boat, fisherman, barge, and
tug, to the number of 848, was pressed into service; and with a suicide
division holding the front and the Royal Air Force screening, 338,000
men were transported to England. But they did not bring their weapons,
and evacuations do not win wars.

The German army now swung south, and in two weeks cut the French
army to pieces. On 10 June 1940 Mussolini, with his jackal instinct to be
in at the kill, entered the war. Five days later Paris fell, and Premier
Reynaud, in desperation, appealed to Roosevelt for 'clouds of planes.'
But Roosevelt could give only sympathy, and a hastily formed French
government under the aged Marshal Pétain sued for peace. Hitler exacted a savage price. He occupied half of France, leaving the southern

part to be ruled, from Vichy, by Pétain and Premier Laval, who were forced to collaborate with the victors, even to recruit workers for German war industry and to deliver French Jews to torture and death. In one month Hitler's mechanized armies had done what the forces of William II had been unable to accomplish in four years.

Now England stood alone. 'We have just one more battle to win,' said Hitler's propaganda minister Goebbels to cheering thousands; but Hitler, having foolishly counted on England's not fighting, was not prepared with landing craft and equipment to launch a massive amphibious operation. While these instruments were being built and assembled in northern France, Hitler's air force leader Marshal Goering tried to 'soften up' England by massive bombing attacks. All that summer and fall the German bombs rained on Britain. In September 1940 this air assault rose to a furious crescendo. Cities like London, Coventry, and Birmingham suffered massive destruction; civilian casualties ran into the tens of thousands. England at that juncture was saved by her scientists, such as Watson-Watt and Tizard, who developed radar and persuaded the government to set up a chain of radar warning posts about southern and eastern England; and by the gallantry of her Spitfire and Hurricane fighter pilots, who exacted an insupportable toll of the invaders. By October the German air force had to acknowledge that it had failed.

In this hour of mortal peril England found her soul, under the inspiration of a great leader. The reins of government, on 11 May 1940, had passed from the faltering hands of Chamberlain into the iron grip of Winston Churchill, who announced, when he took office, that he had naught to offer his countrymen but 'blood, sweat, and tears.' Undismayed by disaster, he confronted life with antique courage and infused that courage into freedom-loving peoples everywhere. At the threat of invasion, he thus hurled defiance at the German legions:

> We shall not flag or fail, we shall go on to the end, we shall fight in France, we shall fight on the seas and oceans . . . we shall fight on the landing grounds, we shall fight in the fields and in the streets, we shall fight in the hills; we shall never surrender. And even if . . . this island . . . were subjugated and starving, then our Empire beyond the seas, armed and guarded by the British Fleet, would carry on the struggle, until, in God's good time, the new world, with all its power and might, steps forth to the rescue and liberation of the old.

The news from across the Atlantic stunned America. In Boston, crowds on Washington Street bunched in front of placards where news dispatches were being posted; in New York, they spilled into Times Square to watch bulletins circling the Times Building. The Nazi *Blitzkrieg* had shattered America's illusions about the outcome of the European war and its own impregnability. France had capitulated, Britain might soon go under. Walter Lippmann wrote: 'Our duty is to begin acting at once on the basic assumption that the Allies may lose the war this summer, and that before the snow flies again we may stand alone and isolated, the last great Democracy on earth.'

For the moment even Roosevelt's severest critics rallied to him as the nation's leader in a time of crisis. Some were now willing to concede that Roosevelt had been foresighted in warning of the dangers abroad. (The President told a group of businessmen: 'I was a sort of — who was the fellow? John the Baptist — "voice crying in the wilderness" all last Summer.') Under the spur of presidential prodding, Congress voted immense sums for defense. Within a year after the invasion of the Low Countries, Congress appropriated $37 billion for rearmament and aid to the Allies — a sum larger than the total cost to the United States of World War I. To take advantage of the support by elements in both parties for his foreign policy, Roosevelt replaced the colorless Secretaries of War and of the Navy in his cabinet with two prominent Republicans — the 72-year-old Henry Stimson, who had been Secretary of War under Taft and Secretary of State under Hoover, and Frank Knox, the G.O.P. vice-presidential candidate in 1936.

At Charlottesville, Virginia, on 10 June the President pledged to 'extend to the opponents of force the material resources of this nation,' but Congress was less willing to approve aid to Britain than to agree to strengthening American defenses. Only 30 per cent of the country still thought the Allies would triumph, and the President's military and naval advisers warned that, with America's own stocks below the safety point, stepped-up aid to Britain would be highly precarious. If the United States extended such aid, and Britain surrendered, leaving the United States, stripped of its arms, to face an Axis invasion, Roosevelt would be hard put to justify his decision. Nonetheless, Roosevelt released navy planes to be sold to the Allies and made available supplies of arms and ammunition. He went even further, at great political risk, by con-cluding a swap with Britain which was, as Winston Churchill later observed, 'a decidedly unneutral act,' which by 'all the standards of history' would have 'justified the German Government in declaring war' on the United States. In early September the President announced an arrangement whereby the United States transferred to Britain 50 World War I destroyers and received in return 99-year leases on a series of naval and air bases in the British West Indies.[4] Roosevelt called the deal 'the most important action in the reinforcement of our national defense that has been taken since the Louisiana Purchase.'

Nor was Anglo-American co-operation a one-way affair. A British scientific mission, headed by Sir Henry Tizard, reached Washington in August 1940 with blueprints of radar and the latest secret weapons (rockets, underwater detectors, etc.) which they were authorized to place at the disposition of our armed forces; and the National Defense Research Committee, organized that summer and including such distinguished scientists as Vannevar Bush and James B. Conant, reciprocated.

By the time the destroyer-bases deal was announced, Congress was in the closing stages of a bitter debate over a proposal to conscript men for military service in time of peace. Mail to Congressmen ran 90 per cent against the bill; in the halls of Congress, twelve mothers in black conducted a Death Watch, while on Capitol Hill angry women hanged internationalist Senator Claude Pepper in effigy. But as the Nazis poised to strike across the English Channel, polls revealed a rapid shift of opinion in favor of selective service. In mid-September, Congress voted to conscript men between the ages of twenty-one and thirty-five. A month later, Secretary Stimson, blindfolded, plucked from a fishbowl the first of the numbers which would determine the order men would be called into uniform.

Roosevelt's foreign policy precipitated one of the greatest debates in American history. Critics charged that the President was dragging the United States inexorably into an 'imperialistic' war with which we had no legitimate concern; supporters insisted that only by helping Britain and France to defeat Hitler could we save democracy from destruction and ourselves from ultimate attack. The issue was fought out in the halls of Congress, in the press, over the radio, on public platforms, and in private houses. Party lines were shattered, labor organizations split, busi-

4. The Argentia (Newfoundland) and Bermuda bases were free gifts. The U.S. Navy also transferred ten Coast Guard cutters to Britain.

ness relations were strained, old friendships broken. William Allen White's Committee to Defend America by Aiding the Allies organized branches in a thousand towns, sent out hundreds of speakers and millions of letters and pamphlets to arouse the nation to its danger. The opposition organization, the America First Committee, top-billing Charles Lindbergh, paraded, picketed, protested, and preached an amalgam of isolationism and pacifism. Most Americans wanted both to halt Hitler and to stay out of war, but in pursuing the first aim it was not clear that they could fulfill the second.

6. THE ELECTION OF 1940

In the midst of this debate came the presidential election. The German *Blitzkrieg* made it inadvisable for the Republicans to chose an isolationist for their presidential candidate, and the three leading contenders — Senator Robert Taft of Ohio, Senator Arthur Vandenberg of Michigan, and District Attorney Thomas Dewey of New York — were isolationists in varying degree. This gave an opportunity to a group of amateur politicians who had been building up a political maverick, Wendell Willkie, a Wall Street lawyer who had voted for Roosevelt in 1932 and, as a lifelong Democrat, had once even served on a committee of Tammany Hall. He had become the utility interests' most articulate critic of the New Deal. He was no isolationist, but a frank proponent of aid to the Allies. His sincerity and charm appealed to an electorate wearied with political clap-trap, and this former Hoosier inspired a devotion such as no other Republican has enjoyed between 'Teddy' and 'Ike.' When the Republican convention met at Philadelphia in June, seasoned politicians found that they could not hold back the rising tide of Willkie sentiment, although as late as April he had not had a single delegate. On the sixth ballot he was nominated.

Events in Europe also assured Franklin Roosevelt the Democratic nomination for a third term. Tommy Corcoran quipped: 'The Democratic convention was held in Copenhagen.' Although Jim Farley insisted that his name be placed in nomination, thereby denying Roosevelt the unanimous 'draft' he wanted, the President was chosen by an overwhelming margin on the first ballot. Roosevelt, who had long since parted company with Jack Garner, brought pressure on the delegates to accept the much more liberal Henry Wallace, a former Republican, as

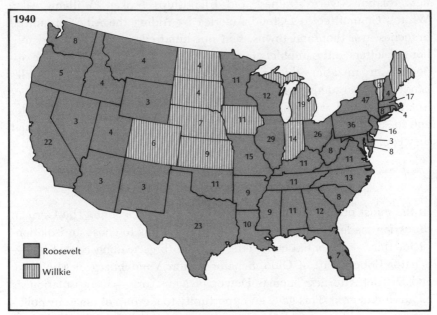

PRESIDENTIAL ELECTION, 1940

his running mate. The President had demonstrated convincingly to people who thought he had lost control in the purge of 1938 that he still dominated the Democratic party.

Willkie looked forward to a personal battle with FDR, but the President refused to recognize him; instead, he played his role as commander in chief to the hilt. One Republican Congressman complained: 'Franklin Roosevelt is not running against Wendell Willkie. He's running against Adolf Hitler.' In such a contest, Willkie was at a decided disadvantage, especially because he shared Roosevelt's outlook on foreign policy. In his acceptance speech, Willkie warned: 'We must face a brutal but terrible fact. Our way of life is in competition with Hitler's way of life.' To be sure, before the campaign was over, both candidates had succumbed to the temptation to make extravagant appeals to the voters. Willkie said that if Roosevelt were elected 'you may expect war in April 1941,' and the President asserted, 'I have said this before, but I shall say it again and again and again. Your boys are not going to be sent into any foreign wars.' But the isolationists knew that neither candidate was their man, and the conviction that the nation had never had a fair choice between war and peace in 1940 was to poison American politics for many years to come.

In the November election Roosevelt received 449 electoral votes, Willkie only 82, but FDR's share of the popular vote had fallen to less than 55 per cent. He continued to run very well in lower income districts. In an analysis of the election, Samuel Lubell wrote: 'The New Deal appears to have accomplished what the Socialists, the I.W.W. and the Communists never could approach. It has drawn a class line across the face of American politics.'

7. YEAR OF DECISION

The President naturally interpreted re-election as an endorsement of his foreign as well as his domestic policies. When Congress met early in January 1941 he appealed to it for support of nations who were fighting in defense of what he called the Four Freedoms — freedom of speech, freedom of religion, freedom from want, freedom from fear. Four days later he submitted a program which was the result of an urgent message the President received a month after his election to an unprecedented third term. The Prime Minister wrote that Britain was in 'mortal danger' and that it was fast reaching the point when it would not be able to pay cash for the vast quantities of American arms it needed. For some months, Roosevelt had been mulling over the idea of leasing supplies to Britain, and Churchill's letter brought this notion to a head. On 16 December the President unveiled a new proposal: to lend arms directly on the understanding that they would be returned, or replacements for them provided, when the war ended. 'What I am trying to do,' he explained, 'is to eliminate the dollar sign.'

The lend-lease plan aroused fierce opposition. 'Lending war equipment is a good deal like lending chewing gum,' Senator Taft grumbled. 'You don't want it back.' Robert Maynard Hutchins, president of the University of Chicago, declared that American democracy had so many shortcomings that it was unqualified to lead the world against totalitarianism. Not until British millionaires stripped themselves of castles, steeds, dogs and jewels should the 'one-gallused, overall-class' American farmer or laborer be asked to pay, insisted Senator Reynolds of North Carolina. Montana's Senator Wheeler called lend-lease the 'New Deal's 'triple A' foreign policy — to plow under every fourth American boy.' (Roosevelt told newspapermen two days later: 'That really is the rottenest thing that has been said in public life in my generation.')

By mid-January 1941, aid to Britain even at the risk of war was favored by 70 per cent of those polled; and when the rolls were called in March, Congress voted passage of the Lend-Lease Act by sizable margins. The law authorized the President to 'sell, transfer, exchange, lease, lend,' any defense articles 'to the government of any country whose defense the President deems vital to the defense of the United States.' It also made available to such nations the facilities of American shipyards. By the end of the month Congress had voted the staggering sum of $7 billion, and this would be only the first installment in a mammoth program to arm the Allies that would total more than $50 billion.

Events now moved speedily. During the lend-lease debate, Jesse Jones had blurted: 'We're in the war; at least we are nearly in it; we're preparing for it.' A few weeks after the passage of lend-lease, the United States seized all Axis shipping in American ports. In April 1941 it took Greenland under protection and announced that the Navy would patrol the sea lanes in defense zones. In May came the transfer of 50 oil tankers to Britain, and, after the sinking of an American freighter by a U-boat, the proclamation of an 'unlimited national emergency.' In June the United States froze all Axis assets in this country and closed all Axis consulates. And on 24 June the President announced that lend-lease would be extended to a new ally — Russia. For on 22 June, Hitler, in one of the astounding about-faces common to dictators, broke his 1939 pact and set out to conquer that vast country. It was one of those colossal mistakes in strategy which undid the earlier mistakes of England and France. Now they had an ally capable of pinning down the bulk of the Germany army on an Eastern front. And the Communist party in America, which had been sneering at the 'imperialist war,' now demanded our participation in a 'crusade.'

Roosevelt, like Wilson a generation earlier, moved to obtain a statement of war aims from the Allies. On 14 August 1941 he and Winston Churchill met afloat in Argentia Bay, Newfoundland, and there drew up the Atlantic Charter, containing certain 'common principles' on which they based 'their hopes for a better future for the world.' These included the already proclaimed Four Freedoms, a renunciation of territorial aggrandizement, a promise of the restoration of self-government to those deprived of it, and a pledge of equal access to trade and raw materials.

The Atlantic also appeared likely to be the place where the United States would be drawn into World War II. On 4 September a German submarine attacked the United States destroyer *Greer* in the waters off Iceland, where American troops had been stationed some weeks earlier. The President denounced this 'piracy' and ordered the navy to 'shoot on sight' these 'rattlesnakes of the Atlantic.' Roosevelt stated indignantly: 'I tell you the blunt fact that the German submarine fired first upon this American destroyer without warning, and with deliberate design to sink her.' The President was being less than frank. The *Greer* had not only informed a British plane of the presence of the German U-boat but had pursued the sub and broadcast its position for three and a half hours. During this period, the British plane had dropped four depth charges. Only then had the U-boat fired at the *Greer*. The *Greer* had, in turn, dropped eight depth charges and kept up its pursuit of the sub.

Two days after the shoot-on-sight speech, the Atlantic Fleet was ordered to protect all vessels on the run between North America and Iceland, even convoys which numbered no American ships. Since the Fleet had also been instructed to destroy any Nazi ship it sighted, the order of 13 September brought the United States Navy into all-out, even though undeclared, war in the Atlantic.

On 9 October, the President asked Congress to repeal the 'crippling provisions' of the Neutrality Act of 1939. Isolationists in Congress organized themselves for a protracted struggle to defeat the President, but they failed to reckon on the impact of events in the North Atlantic. On 17 October, news arrived that the destroyer *Kearny* had been torpedoed southwest of Iceland; eleven sailors were lost. Three days later, the destroyer *Reuben James* was sent to the bottom of the sea off western Iceland; it was the first armed American vessel to be sunk by Germany. Ninety-six officers and men lost their lives. Within two weeks both houses of Congress had voted to repeal restrictive sections of the neutrality law; henceforth, the President could arm merchantmen and send ships directly into combat areas. Little wonder that the nation's attention in the autumn of 1941 was focused on these reverberations of the war in Europe. But when war came to America, it would come not as the result of developments in the Atlantic but as a consequence of less-noticed but even more momentous events across the Pacific, where the sands of peace were swiftly running out.

XXII

World War II: The Defensive Phase

1. PEARL HARBOR — 7 DECEMBER 1941

For over a year, tension had been mounting in the Far East. The Japanese war lords, meeting unexpected resistance in China, now planned to swing south and conquer the Philippines, Malaya, Burma, Indo-China, and Indonesia. In order to realize this 'Greater East Asia Co-Prosperity Sphere,' Japan had to risk fighting Great Britain, France, the Netherlands, and the United States, which controlled the coveted territories. The Japanese government was of two minds about risking open war with the West. It still had considerable respect for the United States, but after the German victories of May-June 1940, it became more difficult for moderate elements in Japan to restrain the militarists. Now that France and Holland were conquered, Indo-China and the Netherlands East Indies were ripe for the picking; Malaya, Burma, and even India looked easy, when and if Hitler invaded Britain. In the summer of 1940 Japan wrested permission to build airfields in Indo-China from the helpless Vichy government of France. The United States struck back with a small loan to China and a partial embargo on exports to Japan. In July 1940 Congress gave the President power to restrict the export of any war materials required for American defense or to license export to friendly nations, and passed the Two-Ocean Navy Act. Very cautiously, Roosevelt began imposing embargoes on strategic materials, including scrap iron; and a Gallup poll indicated 96 per cent popular approval.

In July 1941 events began moving toward a crisis. On the 25th, Japan announced that she had assumed a protectorate of the whole of French Indo-China. Next day, President Roosevelt took three momentous steps. He received the armed forces of the Philippine Commonwealth into the Army of the United States, appointed General Douglas MacArthur to command all army forces in the Far East, and issued an executive order freezing Japanese financial assets in the United States. Great Britain and the Netherlands followed suit, cutting off Japan's source of credit and imports of rubber, scrap iron, and fuel oil. The Japanese war lords decided to make war on these three countries within four months unless the flow of oil and other strategic supplies was restored. For Japan was 'eating her own tail' in the matter of oil; the armies must have fuel or evacuate China and Indo-China, and the military could not contemplate any such retreat.

The subsequent negotiations were a sparring for time by two governments that considered war all but inevitable. The Japanese wanted time to organize their military and naval push to the south; the United States wanted time to prepare the defense of the Philippines and strengthen the navy. Through the summer and fall of 1941 Secretary Hull made it clear that Japan could have all the goods and credits she wanted from America, if she would begin a military evacuation of China and Indo-China. Prince Konoye, the Japanese premier, on 14 October asked General Tojo, the war minister, to begin at least a token withdrawal. Tojo refused. He was confident that Japan could beat America, Britain, and any other country that stood in her way; and a few days later Tojo became prime minister. On 20 November he presented Japan's ultimatum. He promised to occupy no more Asiatic territory if the United States would stop reinforcing the Philippines; he would evacuate southern Indo-China only if the United States would cut off aid to Chiang Kai-shek and 'unfreeze' Japanese assets in the United States, leaving Japan free to complete her subjugation of China. Tojo did not expect the United States to accept such terms, suitable only for a defeated nation, and his plans for further aggression were already hardened. On 26 November 1941 the Japanese striking force of six big carriers with 353 battle-ready planes, two battleships, two heavy cruisers, and eleven destroyers sortied from its rendezvous in the Kurile Islands for the fatal destination of Pearl Harbor.

No inkling even of the existence of that force leaked out. A few days earlier, however, Japanese troop-laden transports with escorting warships were reported steaming south off Formosa, and on 27 November Washington sent a 'war warning' message to Pearl Harbor and Manila, indicating an attack against either the Philippines, Thailand, or the Malay Peninsula. Nobody suspected that Pearl Harbor would be attacked, but General Short was warned against sabotage.

Oahu was in a relaxed Sunday morning mood at 7:55 a.m. 7 December, when the bombs began to drop. Despite the war warning of 27 November, Admiral Kimmel had not interrupted his training schedules or canceled week-end leave and liberty; General Short had his army planes parked wing-to-wing, fearing only danger from sabotage. A midget submarine launched from an advance Japanese force was sighted off Pearl Harbor at 3:42 a.m. 7 December and sunk at 6:45, but the word did not reach naval headquarters for over an hour. An army search radar on northern Oahu picked up scouting planes from the Japanese carriers at 6:45, and the first wave of attack planes at 7:02; but the watch officer laughed off the report. General Marshall and Admiral Stark, in Washington, hearing that the Japanese ambassador was about to present a note breaking off diplomatic relations to Secretary Hull, at an hour corresponding to 7:30 a.m. at Pearl Harbor, sent out an alert to the effect that something, they knew not what, was about to happen; the alert, sent by commercial wire, was delivered after the attack.

At the end of this sad and bloody day, the 'day that shall live in infamy' as President Roosevelt called it, 2403 American sailors, soldiers, marines, and civilians had been killed, and 1178 more wounded; 149 planes had been destroyed on the ground or in the water; battleship *Arizona* was shattered and sunk beyond repair; *Oklahoma* shattered and capsized; *Tennessee, West Virginia,* and *California* were resting on the bottom; *Nevada* run aground to prevent sinking; two naval auxiliaries destroyed; three destroyers and a few other vessels badly damaged. All at a cost of fewer than 30 planes and about the same number of men to the Japanese striking force, which returned undetected to its home waters.

Nor was this all. Although General MacArthur's Far Eastern command was notified of the attack on Pearl Harbor at 3:00 a.m. 8 December (corresponding to 8:00 a.m. 7 December at Oahu), a Japanese bomber attack from Formosa caught the army air force grounded on fields near Manila at noon and all but wiped it out — a major disaster.

At 8:30 a.m. Guam was bombed from nearby Saipan, and before dawn Japanese troops landed on the Malay Peninsula.

To millions of Americans, sitting down to Sunday dinner, or with radios tuned in to some musical program, this news of disaster after disaster came as something fantastic and incredible. As the awful details poured in, hour after hour, incredulity turned to anger and an implacable determination to avenge these 'unprovoked and dastardly' attacks. Next day Congress declared a state of war with Japan; on 11 December Germany and Italy, faithful to their tripartite pact with Japan, declared war on the United States.

The American people were not content merely to avenge Pearl Harbor; they wished to know why it happened. Investigations followed, culminating in an exhaustive one by Congress after the war was over, with testimony and reports filling forty volumes. In these investigations, and in discussion in Congress and in the press, every effort was made by Roosevelt's critics to prove that the administration was responsible; that it withheld vital news of Japanese ship movements from the commanders at Pearl Harbor, either from sheer stupidity or from a vicious design to get the country into full-fledged war, since Hitler seemed determined not to resent our unneutral aid to Great Britain. Yet more than a quarter of a century later, no substantial evidence has been found to support this far-fetched hypothesis.

Naval and army intelligence had broken the Japanese secret code, and were 'reading the mail' that passed between Tokyo and Japanese representatives abroad; but the Japanese war lords never let their consuls or their ambassadors at Washington in on the secret. The United States government knew that reports were being sent from the Japanese consulate at Honolulu about American ship movements; but similar reports were being filed by Japanese consuls from every important world port, and nobody noticed that those from Honolulu also gave the exact position of every ship in Pearl Harbor. Washington knew that mighty Japanese forces were moving south — that was the reason for the 27 November war warning — but none of the 'top brass' thought that Tokyo was capable of launching another attack eastward. Nor, putting themselves in the place of Japan, could they imagine that any nation in its senses would dare bring the United States, angry and unified, into war; for the isolationists in Congress would probably have prevented a declaration of

war on Japan had she attacked only British or Dutch possessions. Peacetime relaxation in Hawaii was matched by Sunday somnolence in Washington. General Marshall, chief of the army general staff, did not omit
his Sunday morning horseback ride on 7 December, although he had
been warned that something was about to break. Two ranking officers of
the war plans division of the Navy Department, when they heard the
terrible news, decided to go down to the department and get secret war
plans out of the safe. They found that the combination had a time-lock
which would not be released until Monday morning!

In attacking Pearl Harbor, Japan conferred a moral and strategic favor on the nation which was the chief object of her rage. Senator Arthur
Vandenberg of Michigan, who had been one of the leading isolationists
before December 1941, remarked five years later that Pearl Harbor
'drove most of us to the irresistible conclusion that world peace is indi-
visible. We learned that the oceans are no longer moats around our ram-
parts. We learned that mass destruction is a progressive science which
defies both time and space and reduces human flesh and blood to cruel
impotence.'

2. HOW THE WAR WAS DIRECTED

Owing to ample warning of impending hostilities on two oceans, and the
administration's foresight, the United States was relatively better prepared for a world-wide war in 1941 than she had been for a limited one
in 1917. In that year the United States had entered the war with no
plans, nor any agreement with associated nations how to operate. But
early in 1941, warned by the German blitz on neutral nations of Europe,
the United States service chiefs decided that, if and when America entered the war, her primary military effort would be exerted in the European theater.

This concept was arrived at, because the Rome-Berlin Axis by knocking out France had control of the entire western coast of Europe, thus
threatening with her U-boats sea communication between the Old
World and the New. Furthermore Germany, with a greater war potential than Japan, might uncork some devastating secret weapon if given
the time — as indeed she did, but too late to win. Since Japan was
fighting only China, there was still hope of keeping her from further
aggressions. This decision, which dictated the major strategy of World

War II, became the more pressing after Hitler attacked Russia; for if Germany obtained control over Soviet manpower and resources, the geopolitical 'heartland' would be under Hitler's control, from Finisterre to Vladivostok and from the North Cape to the bulge of Africa.

The informal alliance thus formed continued throughout the war. Meeting together, the American Joint Chiefs of Staff (as the heads of army, navy, and army air force shortly became) and the British Chiefs of Staff were called the Combined Chiefs of Staff. They, under President Roosevelt and Prime Minister Churchill, initiated strategy, drafted plans, allocated forces, and directed the war. Russia was represented by Marshal Stalin, and China by Chiang Kai-shek, at the Teheran and Cairo C.C.S. conferences, respectively; but each of these two allies fought his own war, not without aid from the others, but with little regard to their wishes or strategy.

America was fortunate in having very able war direction. The vital members of the Joint Chiefs of Staff throughout the war were General H. H. ('Hap') Arnold, head of the air force, which until after the war was part of the army; the army chief of staff General George C. Marshall, a Virginian who combined in his character the patient wisdom of a Washington with the strategic savvy of a Lee; Admiral Ernest J. King, chief of naval operations and commander in chief of the fleet, a hard-bitten, experienced naval officer who took a world-wide view of strategy and seldom, if ever, made a mistake. These three in concert with President Roosevelt formed a winning team. There had been nothing like that in American history since the Lincoln-Grant-Sherman combination of 1864–65.

The cabinet was equally strong. Secretary of State Cordell Hull was becoming rather infirm, but he had an energetic under secretary, Sumner Welles, and several able assistant secretaries, such as Dean Acheson and Adolf Berle, Jr.; Henry M. Stimson, the elderly Secretary of War, was still full of brains and energy, and profited by his cabinet experience under two earlier presidents. Frank Knox, Secretary of the Navy, also had a capable under secretary, James Forrestal, who handled all matters of procurement for the navy, as assistant secretary Robert Patterson did for the army. Forrestal succeeded Knox after the latter's death in 1944, and later became the first Secretary of Defense.

Roosevelt was a great war President, in a class with Lincoln; and, like Lincoln's, his greatness came more from a capacity to lead and inspire than from skill in administration. He was an opportunist, with a flair for the attainable, rather than, as in the case of Wilson, for the ideal; but, no less than Wilson, he looked ahead to a world of peace and justice. His warm understanding of other nations enabled him to deal successfully with Latin America, neutrals, and representatives of the overrun democracies; at his death, when victory was in sight, he was almost universally mourned. He respected his military advisers, and his considered judgment was almost always sound. He sometimes worked in devious ways, as through his much detested but shrewd confidential assistant, Harry Hopkins; but the wisdom of the serpent was necessary to deal with clashing personalities and opposing interests. It was F.D.R. who glimpsed the dangers of Axis and Japanese militarism before any other American leader and who, with tact and patience, persuaded a reluctant Congress to prepare for war. It was he, too, who led America into war, not as an Associated Power as in World War I, but as a full-fledged member of the 'United Nations,' a grand alliance that would ultimately embrace 46 nations resolved to fight to the finish.

3. PROCUREMENT AND PRODUCTION

Although much had been accomplished in military preparedness when Pearl Harbor broke, yet even more remained to be done. Congress promptly repealed its prohibition against sending draftees outside the Western Hemisphere and extended their period of service to six months after the war's end — no 'three months men' in this war. All men between 18 and 45 were made liable to military service. Standards of physical fitness and intelligence were exacting, and many failed to qualify; rejections ran to over 40 per cent in Georgia and the Carolinas. Including voluntary enlistments, over 15 million people served in the armed forces during the war; 10 million in the army, 4 million in the navy and coast guard, 600,000 in the marine corps. About 216,000 women served as nurses, and in the auxiliary 'Waves' and 'Wacs' or as lady marines.

Although not confined to labor battalions, as he largely had been in World War I, the Negro was generally segregated in barracks and mess halls, and often was confined to menial tasks and subjected to various kinds of discrimination. Seven thousand Negroes were commissioned as officers. The all-Negro 99th Fighter Squadron won distinction in Europe and a combat team of the 93rd Infantry Division at Bougainville.

The problem of training was prodigious. The average 'G.I.' (General Issue), the nickname for infantrymen in this war, was a more or less unwilling draftee, who had been brought up in a pacifist atmosphere. He could be trained *to* fight, but it was well said of General Patton that he alone could make them *want* to fight. And more was required of the G.I. than of the 'doughboy' of World War I, or the 'boys in blue' — or gray — of 1861. In those days all that a man needed to become a soldier was close-order drill and the manual of arms; modern warfare required him to be something of an athlete, a mechanic, and a scientist as well as a fighting man. A sailor had to be taught almost everything except to sail — basic navigation, ship handling, and gunnery; but modern warships are as complicated as the modern industrial state, and new devices like sonar, radar, and loran were constantly being added. There were any number of specialized forces, such as the army rangers for raiding, and the navy's UDT's or 'frogmen,' who swam up to enemy-held beaches, made soundings, and blew obstacles. Air forces had become highly specialized. There were fighter planes, high-level bombers, torpedo- and dive-bombers, and several other types for which pilots and crewmen had to be trained. To fight a global war it was necessary to build naval bases, army bases, and airfields all over the world. Specially packaged units called Lions, Cubs, Oaks, and Acorns were organized with men and matériel ready to rush in and build a base or airfield as soon as a site was secured.

The work of the service forces was no less important. In this war the average soldier required at least double the World War I equipment. An infantry division of 10,000 fighting men required 6000 more to keep it fed, supplied, paid, doctored, amused, transported, and its equipment repaired. Remarkable progress was made by the medical corps. Infection and disease had always been the bane of armies, and in every American war before 1917 had accounted for many more deaths than did actual battle. Thanks to abundant food, proper clothing, and hospitals competently staffed, the health of the armed forces in World War II compared favorably with that of the civilian population in the same age groups. The development of sulfa drugs and penicillin, given by injections, the use of plasma for transfusions, control of mosquitoes and other insects, new techniques for the treatment of the terrible burns incident to bursting shells and Japanese kamikaze tactics, and prompt evacuation of the wounded reduced the death rate from wounds to less than half that of

World War I, and enabled about two-thirds of all wounded to return to duty. The increasing role of the artillery shell and the bomb in warfare is shown by the fact that, whilst 94 per cent of wounds in the Civil War were caused by rifle bullets, 72 per cent of those in the two world wars and the Korean War were inflicted by shell fragments.

The United States Navy entered the war well prepared except for anti-aircraft and antisubmarine defense, both pressing needs. Fortunately, in conjunction with the marines, it had undertaken training for amphibious warfare. As early as 1933 the navy realized that in Asia certainly, and Europe probably, delivering troops to a fighting area would be no simple matter of transporting them by sea and landing them on a wharf; men, supplies, and heavy equipment would have to be landed under fire on enemy-held beaches. Consequently the navy began building a new line of vessels specially designed for amphibious warfare: the 460-foot LSD (Landing Ship, Dock), which spawned loaded landing craft from a miniature lake in its bowels; the 330-foot LST (Landing Ship, Tank), a two-decker floating garage, which became the workhorse of the fleet; the 180-foot LCI (Landing Craft, Infantry) for bringing soldiers directly to a beach; and a variety of small landing craft that could be carried on the davits of a big transport. After 1940, with money available for high wages in the shipyards, it became possible to build a destroyer in five months instead of a year, and a big carrier in 15 months instead of 35.

The United States Merchant Marine Cadet Corps, established in 1938, was expanded to provide officers; the National Maritime Union, with the slogan 'Keep 'em Sailing,' co-operated in keeping merchant seamen on their jobs despite losses to U-boats. In November 1941, when Congress repealed the Neutrality Act forbidding merchantmen to arm in self-defense, the navy began installing guns with bluejacket crews on freighters. The Maritime Commission, created by Congress in 1936 and headed by Rear Admiral Emory S. Land, received new powers in July 1941 and drew up blueprints for an emergency freighter that could be built quickly and inexpensively. The first of these Liberty ships — appropriately named *Patrick Henry* — was launched in September, and 139 more came out that year. The bigger and faster Victory ship followed.

Although the United States became an 'arsenal of democracy' while fighting the war, there were ominous lags and shortages. Donald Nelson, the merchandising expert who became director of procurement in 1940, said, 'We almost lost the war before we ever got into it.' Many leading industrialists, distrusting 'that man in the White House,' could not believe that the country would ever go to war, and hung back from incurring the expense of conversion. By Pearl Harbor only 15 per cent of industrial production was going to military needs.

The genius of ship construction, Henry J. Kaiser, trimmed the time for turning out merchant ships from 105 days to 46, then 29, then 14. In mid-November 1942, Kaiser's Richmond, California, yard launched 'Hull 440,' the *Robert E. Peary*, in 4 days, 15½ hours. It went down the ways fitted out with life belts, coat hangers, electric clocks, and ink wells. By the middle of 1942, Kaiser, still a landlubber who spoke of the 'front-end' of a ship, was building one-third of the government's vessels, and his pace-setting records fixed the standard the Maritime Commission demanded of other firms. As a consequence, merchant shipping construction, which amounted to only one million tons in 1941, surpassed 19 million just two years later.

In January 1942 the President set up the War Production Board to direct the mobilization. Nelson, the WPB administrator, did not have the personal force to impose priorities, and not until 1943 was an effective system of allocation developed. As a consequence of Nelson's failings, the President named 'czars' to handle the critical problems of oil and rubber, and in October 1942 appointed Supreme Court Justice James F. Byrnes to head an Office of Economic Stabilization. In May 1943 he gave Byrnes, who proved an able administrator, still greater authority as director of the Office of War Mobilization. Reporters referred to Byrnes, who operated out of the White House, as 'Assistant President.'

To curb inflation, the government not only stepped up taxes and sold nearly $100 billion in war bonds but controlled prices directly through the Office of Price Administration which Roosevelt had set up in August 1941 under Leon Henderson, an ebullient New Deal economist. After experimenting with selective controls of prices and rents, Henderson imposed a general price freeze in April 1942. The OPA also rationed scarce commodities like meat, gasoline, and tires. But the agency ran into trouble from businessmen who resented controls, from the farm bloc which insisted on 110 per cent of parity, and from union labor which protested that even the War Labor Board's formula of a 15 per cent wage increase did not meet the rising cost of living. In 1943, to counter a strike by John L. Lewis's Mine Workers, the government took over the coal mines; at the same time, it rolled back food prices. By the middle of 1943, prices had reached a plateau, and for the rest of the war, the OPA, under the advertising executive Chester Bowles, held the increase in the cost of living to less than 1.5 per cent, one of the remarkable achievements of the war.

When the Allies launched their cross-Channel invasion in 1944, the armies 'lurched forward,' wrote Allan Nevins, 'like a vast armed workshop; a congeries of factories on wheels with a bristling screen of troops and a cover of airplanes.' The mobilization built a magnesium industry, gave an enormous impetus to aluminum production, enlarged electricity output to nearly half again as much as in 1937, increased machine tool production sevenfold, and turned out more iron and steel than the whole world had produced a short time before. In 1939 America's airplane industry employed less than 47,000 persons and produced fewer than 6000 planes; in the peak year of 1944, the industry employed 2,102,000 workers and rolled out more than 96,000 planes. Medium tank production advanced at so rapid a pace that it had to be cut back. By the beginning of 1944, the output of American factories was twice that of all the Axis nations.

Mighty as America's effort was, it did not add up to total war. There was no firm control over manpower, no conscription of women, little direction of talent to useful activities. A few edibles were rationed, but most Americans ate more heartily than before. Gasoline and tires were rationed, but hundreds of thousands of cars managed to stay on the road for purposes remotely connected with the war. Personal and corporation taxes were increased, but there was no limit on profits, or to what workers could earn, if they chose to work overtime; and as prices of most essentials were kept down, the standard of living rose. The country was never invaded, except by U-boats penetrating the three-mile limit, and a large measure of the 'blood, sweat and tears' that Churchill promised his countrymen were spared his country's ally.

Yet even for Americans it was a grim, austere war. In contrast to the utopian statements of the Creel Committee in World War I, the Office of War Information, under the sensible newspaperman, Elmer Davis, presented the war not as a utopian struggle, but, in the President's words, simply as 'the survival war.' For the American fighting forces there were no brass bands or bugles, no 'Over There' or marching songs, no flaunting colors; not even a ship's bell to mark the watches. It was typical that when the Japanese surrendered on board *Missouri* on 2 September 1945 'The Star Spangled Banner' had to be played from a disk over the intercom system, and Admiral Halsey had no better beverage than coffee to offer his guests.

4. SOCIAL CONSEQUENCES OF THE WAR

World War II had a profound impact on American society, because it wrought changes, for good or evil, that had not been possible even in the turbulent thirties. Of the many changes, none had more immediate importance than the termination of the Great Depression. The demands of the armed services and the war industries brought to an end more than a decade of unemployment. Indeed, there quickly developed a shortage of workers which gave women opportunities not only in the traditional white collar fields but in aircraft plants and shipyards. Women accounted for one-third of all workers on the B-29's. The war brought unparalleled prosperity to millions of Americans. The farmers' net cash income more than quadrupled between 1940 and 1945, and the weekly earnings of industrial workers rose 70 per cent.

Wartime full employment, together with progressive tax legislation, resulted in a redistribution of income that had not been achieved in the halcyon days of the New Deal. Although tax laws hit millions of Americans for the first time, through the new device of 'withholding,' the top 5 per cent of income receivers were soaked more than at any time in our history. Their share of disposable income dropped from 26 per cent in 1940 to 16 per cent in 1944, as the federal income levy reached a maximum of 94 per cent of total net income. With a corporation income tax as high as 50 per cent and an excess profits tax stepped up to 95 per cent, few corporations enjoyed 'swollen profits.' Net corporation income in 1945 was less than in 1941.

World War II reshuffled more Americans than had any internal migration over the same time span in the nation's history. During the war years, the West showed a net gain of 1,200,000 people, three-fourths of them from the South. Within a few months after Pearl Harbor, the Pacific Coast states were building one-fourth the nation's war planes, one-third of its ships. Southern California, which ranked second only to Akron as a rubber manufacturing center, even boasted a steel plant. A nation in which 27 million people moved during the war counted the social costs of this upheaval: a critical housing shortage, lack of civic facilities in jerry-built war plant towns, and a spectacular rise in juvenile delinquency occasioned by the uprooting of families.

During the war, 25,000 Negroes moved from the Deep South to New York, 60,000 to Detroit, 100,000 to Chicago, 250,000 to the West Coast, and wherever they went they encountered discrimination. When they gave their blood to the Red Cross, it was segregated from that of whites. When war plants cried for more help, Negro applicants were rejected. When they got jobs, as in the Mobile shipyards, white workers organized 'hate strikes' against them.

But Negroes fought with increased militance for their rights. By 1944 NAACP membership had risen to 500,000, five times the total at the time of Pearl Harbor, and much of this gain came in the Deep South. Dismayed by the reluctance of employers to hire Negro labor even in boom times, A. Philip Randolph, president of the Brotherhood of Sleeping Car Porters, issued a call for 50,000 Negroes to march on Washington in protest. Randolph cancelled the call only after Roosevelt had issued Executive Order 8802 on 25 June 1941. The President's edict forbade discrimination in work under defense contracts and established a Fair Employment Practices Committee. In part as a result of the FEPC's activities, but more because of the critical labor shortage, the Negro's share of jobs in war industries increased from 3 to 8 per cent of the whole, while the number of black employees in the Federal Government jumped from 40,000 to over 300,000.

Despite such brutal episodes as a race riot in Detroit in which 25 Negroes and nine whites were killed, World War II resulted in marked advances for black Americans and for relations between the races. Georgia repealed the poll tax; the Supreme Court outlawed the white primary in Texas; and governors appealed for anti-discrimination statutes. In Chicago, the American Council on Race Relations was created; in Atlanta in 1944, Negro and white leaders sat down together to organize the Southern Regional Council. The doctrine of white supremacy met a formidable intellectual challenge. Gunnar Myrdal's two-volume *An American Dilemma* offered an imposing scholarly analysis, and Lillian Smith's novel, *Strange Fruit*, found a wide audience; perhaps most influential of all was Ruth Benedict's pamphlet, *Races of Mankind,* even though the USO and the YMCA forbade its distribution to American soldiers.

Although America's performance on civil liberties was generally much better than in World War I, in large part because there was far less internal opposition to this war, one dreadful blot stained this record: the relocation and internment of Japanese-Americans. The Roosevelt administration attempted to quiet demands for the evacuation of the 112,000 Japanese or Americans of Japanese descent (*Nisei*) from the West Coast, but it was overwhelmed by the outcry against them. The Hearst columnist Henry McLemore demanded: 'Herd 'em up, pack 'em off and give 'em the inside room in the badlands. Let 'em be pinched, hurt, hungry and dead up against it. . . . Let us have no patience with the enemy or anyone whose veins carry his blood.' The army commander on the West Coast, Lt. General John DeWitt, was a man of marked racial bias who reasoned: 'The fact that no sabotage has taken place to date is a disturbing and confirming indication that such action will be taken.' Even men long regarded as friends of civil liberties beat the drums for evacuation: Senator Hiram Johnson, California's Attorney-General Earl Warren, Walter Lippmann.

On 19 February 1942, Roosevelt, bowing to the anti-Japanese hysteria, hastily approved an edict surrendering control to the Army. DeWitt ordered the removal of every 'Japanese' (more than two-thirds were American citizens) from the western parts of Washington, Oregon, and California and the southern quarter of Arizona. Thousands of American citizens were driven from their homes and herded into assembly centers. After a stay in the assembly centers, the prisoners were dumped into relocation centers in the western deserts and the Arkansas swamplands.

The expulsion and internment of thousand of Americans of Japanese origins were based wholly on racial grounds. No such action was taken against German or Italian aliens, let alone Americans of German or Italian descent. Much of the justification for the removal rested on fears of sabotage. Yet in Hawaii, where people of Japanese birth were much more concentrated than on the West Coast (and where they were not interned), not one act of sabotage was committed. Nonetheless, the Supreme Court sanctioned the government's action in the Korematsu case, although Justice Murphy commented that the evacuation of Japanese-Americans bore 'a melancholy resemblance' to the Nazis' treatment of the Jews. When the Army reversed its policy and recruited *Nisei,* they proved to be the toughest of all fighters in the Italian campaign. But when Japanese-Americans returned to the West Coast after the war, they still encountered gross discrimination and personal indignities.

5. AT BAY IN THE ATLANTIC

Hitler, in one of his more flagrant and (for us) fortunate misjudgments, did not expect to fight England before 1944. He concentrated German naval efforts on building up a high-seas fleet to challenge the 'mistress of the seas' at that distant date when he expected to have all Europe in his grasp. In September 1939 he had fewer than fifty U-boats ready to fight, half of them too small for oceanic work. But this submarine fleet, under command of the young and daring Rear Admiral Karl Doenitz, served notice on the first day that no holds would be barred and no treaties respected. A U-boat torpedoed and sank the unescorted, unarmed, and lighted British passenger ship *Athenia,* with the loss of 112 lives, many of them women and some of them Americans. German propaganda then compounded the felony by claiming that the British sunk her themselves, to get America into the war.

The Royal Navy, though ill-prepared for defense, got on top of the submarine problem very quickly. Merchantmen on the most vital trade routes were organized into convoys, and Canadian corvettes helped to escort them. A separate Coastal Command of the Royal Air Force was specially trained to hunt U-boats. Echo-ranging sound gear ('sonar') was installed on escort vessels to detect submarines.[1] During the first ten months of the war, the Germans destroyed more British, French, and neutral ships by surface raids, mines, and aircraft than by submarines, and the total loss was staggering—616 vessels, amounting to 2.2 million tons.

By June 1940 the fall of France enabled the Germans to construct bombproof submarine pens in the harbors of Brest, Lorient, Saint-Nazaire, and La Pallice, which doubled the range of their U-boats. Admiral Doenitz worked out the technique of night attack on convoys by 'wolf-packs' of eight to twenty U-boats which would dog a convoy for

---

1. The 10-mm or microwave radar for submarine-hunting aircraft, which Doenitz declared to be the most important gadget for defeating U-boats, was also a British invention, adopted in early 1943. All these methods and inventions were freely given to the United States.

days, submerging in daylight. During the first eleven months of 1941 almost a thousand Allied or neutral merchantmen, totaling over 3.6 million tons, had been lost by enemy action, half of it by U-boats, and very few of those noxious craft were forfeited.

Since the basic strategic decision was to beat Hitler first, the Atlantic sea lanes had to be kept open for supplies and to build up a United States army in England for eventual invasion of the Continent. American destroyers now helped to escort convoys all the way across. Sinkings in the North Atlantic fell off promptly; soon we knew why. Admiral Doenitz was moving wolf-packs over to the American east coast, where he rightly anticipated rich pickings from non-convoyed tankers and merchantmen. The navy, pressed to build more carriers and cruisers, had neglected small vessels suitable for coastal convoying, hoping to improvise them if the need arose; but the Germans were not so accommodating as to wait.

The U-boat offensive opened on 12 January 1942 off Cape Cod, and a severe one it was. Most United States destroyers were tied to North Atlantic escort duty; only five subchasers were in commission; there were fewer than a hundred planes to patrol coastal waters between Newfoundland and New Orleans; no merchantmen had yet been armed. Under these conditions, frightful destruction was wrought by the submarines in shipping lanes between the Canadian border and Jacksonville. During January-April 1942, almost 200 ships were sunk in North American, Gulf, and Caribbean waters, or around Bermuda. Doenitz then shifted his wolf-packs to the Straits of Florida, the Gulf of Mexico, and the Caribbean; and in those waters 182 ships totaling over 751,000 tons were sunk in May and June 1942. Vessels were torpedoed 30 miles off New York City, within sight of Virginia Beach, off the Passes to the Mississippi, off the Panama Canal entrance. Since tourist resorts from Atlantic City to Miami Beach were not even required to turn off neon signs and waterfront lights until 18 April 1942, or to black out completely for another month, hapless freighters and tankers passing them were silhouetted to the benefit of the U-boats. Over half the victims in southern waters were tankers, the sinking of which not only roasted the water-borne survivors in burning oil, but threatened the success of military operations in Europe and the Pacific. Puerto Rico suffered from inability to move crops or import necessary food; sugar and coffee had to be rationed in the United States; 'good neighbors' in Latin America began to doubt big neighbor's ability to win. New construction of merchantmen in Allied and neutral countries amounted to less than 600,000 tons in June 1942 when the total loss almost touched 800,000 tons; and in half a year the British and American navies had sunk less than one month's production of new U-boats. If this ratio continued, a 'torpedo curtain' would soon be dropped between the United States and Europe.

Fortunately Admiral Ernest J. King, who as 'Cinclant' had directed the 'short of war' phase, had become 'Cominch,' commander in chief of the United States fleet, on 20 December 1941. At once he took energetic measures to combat the submarine menace. To supply small escort vessels, the slogan 'sixty vessels in sixty days' was nailed to the mast in April 1942, and 67 vessels actually came through by 4 May, when a second 60–60 program was already under way. Scientists were mobilized to find more efficient means of tracking and sinking U-boats; inshore and offshore patrols were organized into a 'Hooligan Navy' of converted yachts, and an interlocking convoy system was worked out. In the second half of 1942 coastal convoys lost only 0.5 per cent of their ships; the transatlantic convoys lost only 1.4 per cent in a whole year. By April 1943 there were every day at sea in the American half of the North Atlantic an average of 31 convoys with 145 escorts and 673 merchant ships, as well as 120 ships traveling alone and unescorted, and the heavily escorted troop convoys.

6. RETREAT IN THE PACIFIC

In the Far East in the days after Pearl Harbor, the news was calamitous. Thailand surrendered to the Japanese, who promptly landed troops at various points on the Malay Peninsula and began a relentless march on the British base at Singapore. On 10 December the Rising Sun flag was hoisted on Guam, which had been bravely but pitifully defended by a few hundred Americans and Chamorros. Other Japanese task forces occupied the British Gilbert Islands, captured Hong Kong and the Borneo oilfields. Japanese bombers based in Indo-China eliminated British naval strength in the Pacific. On Wake Island, lonely outpost in the Central Pacific, Commander W. S. Cunningham and a small marine defense force beat off a Japanese attack on 11 December, only to be overwhelmed by another on the 23rd, before the navy came to their rescue. In the Philippines, after the blitz of 8 December, American air forces were reduced to about 17 bombers and 40 fighters. General MacArthur evacuated Manila on 27 December, withdrew his army to the Bataan Peninsula, and set up headquarters on the island fortress of Corregidor.

The defense of Bataan and Corregidor, valiant and inspiring though it was, had no other effect than to deny the use of Manila Bay to the enemy for a time. The campaign was a melancholy confirmation of Mahan's theory of sea power. The Japanese, controlling all sea approaches and the air too, enveloped both peninsula and Rock in a tight blockade, and landed fresh troops behind the American lines almost at will. Over half the fighting men were disabled by wounds or by disease, and all were at the point of starvation by early April. On the 9th the 'battling bastards of Bataan,' about 12,500 Americans and over 60,000 Filipinos, had to surrender unconditionally. Only a couple of thousand escaped to Corregidor before the ranks of the prisoners were thinned by the infamous 65-mile 'death march' from Bataan to Japanese prison camps. In the hope of restoring confidence to the Australians, who now expected a Japanese invasion themselves, President Roosevelt ordered General MacArthur to leave the Philippines and set up headquarters in the sub-continent. He left by motor torpedo boat on 11 March 1942, promising to return; as he did. On 6 May, after the Japanese had captured the main defenses of Corregidor, General Jonathan M. Wainwright was forced to surrender the Rock together with its 11,000 defenders, and a Philipppine army of over 50,000 on the Visayas and Mindanao. There had been no such capitulation in American history since that of Appomattox. Many troops in the southern islands refused to surrender and continued guerrilla resistance to the Japanese with supplies sent from Australia by submarine.

In the meantime the Japanese had won all their objectives in Southeast Asia. Rabaul in New Britain fell in January 1942. The Malay barrier (Sumatra, Java, Bali, Timor, and smaller islands), which barred the enemy from the Indian Ocean and Australia, was desperately defended by soldiers, sailors, and aviators of the United States, Great Britain, the Netherlands, and Australia, but they had a hopeless task. The Japanese would seize a strategic point in Borneo or Celebes, operate or build an airfield there, soften up the next objective by air bombing, occupy it with an amphibious force and go on to the next. Admiral Hart's Asiatic Fleet, with British and Dutch allies, fought a series of valiant engagements in January and February 1942 — Balikpapan, Bali, Badung Strait,

Java Sea — always heavily outnumbered, always defeated. The great naval base of Singapore, on which England had lavished millions of pounds, fell on 15 February. On Java and in the surrounding waters the soldiers, sailors, and aviators of the three united nations fought and fought until they could fight no more. On 9 May 1942 Java surrendered. Rangoon, capital and chief seaport of Burma, had been occupied by the Japanese the day before. The Japanese now ruled East Asia, west to British India and south to the waters adjacent to Australia and Fiji. India, as threatened by nationalists within as by enemies without, and Australia trembled that their turn might come next.

Never in modern history has there been so quick and valuable a series of conquests; even Hitler's were inferior. The prestige of the white races fell so low that even victory over Japan could not win it back; and the areas that the Japanese conquered, though no longer Japanese, are now also independent of Europe.

XXIII

First Offensives, West and East

1. 'VICTORY DISEASE'

On Christmas Eve 1941 Admiral King warned, 'The way to victory is long; the going will be hard.' And hard it was. Admiral Chester W. Nimitz, who at the same time received the command of the Pacific Fleet, was forced to bide his time until new naval construction and more trained troops gave him adequate reinforcements. No British fleet remained in the Pacific. The Combined Chiefs of Staff, having entrusted the conduct of the Pacific war to America, the Joint Chiefs of Staff perforce adopted a strategy of active defense. A glance at the map of the Pacific will show why. Distances were immense, and the only hope of eventually defeating Japan was to hold fast to what we still had, and prepare for future offensives. Islands still in American possession such as the Hawaiian and Samoan groups had to be defended; the sea-air lanes to New Zealand and to Australia had to be protected; and that meant tying up a large part of the fleet to escort transports and supply ships.

Nothing much could be done for five months except to make hit-and-run raids with carrier planes. Of these the most spectacular was the air assault on Tokyo 18 April 1942. That was delivered by Colonel James H. Doolittle's B-25's from carrier *Hornet*, a base that President Roosevelt humorously called 'Shangri-La,' after the mystery city in James Hilton's *Lost Horizon*. The planes did little damage, and most of the crews had to bail out over China; but the news that Tokyo had actually been bombed lifted American morale and encouraged the Japanese high com-

567

mand to retrieve face by an imprudent offensive. America learned more from adversity than Japan did from victory.

Instead of sitting pretty in their new conquests until attacked and organizing their resources to make their country invincible, the Japanese succumbed to what one of their admirals after the war ruefully called 'victory disease.' They decided to wrest more Pacific territory — Papua, Fijis, New Caledonia, Solomons, western Aleutians, Midway Island — from the Allies and set up an impregnable 'ribbon defense.' Admiral Yamamoto, greatest Japanese sea lord since Togo, wished to provoke a major battle with our Pacific Fleet. A good prophet, he pointed out that the United States Navy must be annihilated, if ever, in 1942, before American productive capacity replaced the Pearl Harbor losses. He expected that after another defeat, the 'soft' American people would force their government to quit and leave Japan in possession of her most valuable conquests. Then she could proceed at her leisure to overwhelm the rest of China and so become the most powerful empire in the world, capable of defying even Germany, if Hitler conquered all Europe.

The Japanese navy in 1942 by any standards was a great navy. It included the two most powerful battleships in the world, displacing 68,000 tons, with 18-inch guns; the American *Iowa* class (none completed before 1943) were of 45,000 tons with 16-inch guns. She had a fleet of fast and powerful 8-inch gunned cruisers, the fastest and most modern destroyers, twice as many big carriers as the American navy, and carrier planes superior in the fighter and torpedo-bomber types. Japanese torpedoes were faster, more powerful, and more sure-firing than those made in the United States, and employment of them was at once more lavish and more intelligent. Japanese naval gunnery was excellent; their warships were intensely trained for night fighting, as the Americans were not. They lacked only radar, which American ships began to install in 1942. The army was well trained and well equipped, and its air force excellent. Flushed with triumph after triumph in the Southwest Pacific, the Japanese army and navy were confident of victory.

Why, then, did Japan fail? Because, owing to a combination of stupid strategy on her part and good strategy and good luck on ours, the numerically inferior Pacific Fleet defeated her in the battles of the Coral Sea, Midway, and Guadalcanal, and the army and Marine Corps learned to deal with the Japanese army. After 1942 it was too late, as Yamamoto predicted. The American armed forces had learned many salutary lessons, had acquired unprecedented strength, and had become an irresistible force in the air, on the surface, and under water.

2. BATTLES OF CORAL SEA AND MIDWAY: MAY–JUNE 1942

The Battle of the Coral Sea (7–8 May 1942) frustrated the first forward lunge in the new Japanese offensive to capture Port Moresby, a strategic base in Papua, New Guinea. This was the first naval battle in which no ship of either side sighted one of the other; the fighting was done by carrier plane against carrier plane, or carrier plane against ship. Admiral Nimitz, commanding the Pacific Fleet, sent carriers *Lexington* and *Yorktown* and a support group of cruisers into the Coral Sea, under the command of Rear Admiral Frank Jack Fletcher. The resulting engagement was almost a comedy of errors. Each side in this new sort of naval warfare made mistakes, but the Japanese made more; and although their losses were inferior to ours, they dared not press on to occupy Port Moresby. For Australia, Coral Sea was the decisive battle, saving her from possible invasion.

In the next and more vital Japanese offensive, Yamamoto went all-out. Personally assuming command, he deployed almost every capital ship of the Japanese navy. His first objective was to capture Midway, a tiny atoll at the tip end of the Hawaiian chain, 1134 miles northwest of Pearl Harbor, where the United States had an advanced naval and air base. Yamamoto wanted Midway as a staging point for air raids to render Pearl Harbor untenable by the Pacific Fleet. Minor objectives were Attu and Kiska, two barren islands in the western Aleutians which he wanted as the northern anchor of his defense line. Yamamoto's dearest object, however, was to force Nimitz to give battle with his numerically inferior Pacific Fleet. He had his wish, but this time the battle did not go to the strong.

Nimitz guessed what Yamamoto was up to, but had only a small fleet to stop him. First, he reinforced Midway with planes to the saturation point. Next, he sent out Rear Admiral Raymond A. Spruance to command carriers *Enterprise* and *Hornet* with their attendant cruisers and destroyers; Rear Admiral Fletcher in carrier *Yorktown* hastened to join. On 4 June 1942, the Japanese four-carrier force, advancing undetected under a foul-weather front, was near enough Midway to batter the air base. A brave group of 26 obsolete marine fighter planes and army B-17s, together with anti-aircraft guns on the island, disposed of about one-third of the enemy attackers. The rest bombed Midway severely but not lethally.

Admiral Nagumo, the Japanese carrier-force commander, had a painful surprise on the morning of 4 June, when he learned from a reconnaissance plane that American flattops were approaching. Nagumo then made the fatal decision of the battle. He ordered his reserve attack group, then arming for a second strike on Midway, to be rearmed with the different sort of bombs used against ships, and turned his prows northeastward to close with the American carriers. Spruance and Fletcher already had several flights of torpedo-and dive-bombers flying toward the Japanese; and, owing to Nagumo's mistake, they had the good fortune to catch three of his four carriers in the vulnerable situation of rearming and refueling planes. But the carrier-plane battle opened ill for the Americans. Nagumo's combat air patrol of fast fighter planes shot down 35 of the 41 slow torpedo-bombers that came in first. Minutes later, the American dive-bombers hit three carriers and left them exploding and burning. The fourth Japanese carrier, *Hiryu*, unseen by the American fliers, got off two plane strikes, which found and disabled *Yorktown*. Fletcher's flagship, however, was promptly avenged, for an attack group from her deck and from *Enterprise* jumped *Hiryu* that afternoon and put her down. A lucky shot by a Japanese submarine later sank *Yorktown* as she was under tow.

Yamamoto, having lost his four best carriers, ordered his vast fleet to retire. He had sustained the first defeat to the Japanese navy in modern times. The carriers and their air groups were wiped out, and the Stars and Stripes still flew over Midway; Kiska and Attu — poor consolation prizes — had been taken by a Japanese task group. Ambitious plans for capturing New Caledonia, the Fijis, and Samoa had to be scrapped; and the Japanese high command was forced into an unaccustomed defensive position.

This glorious Battle of Midway on 4 June 1942, called the most decisive battle since Jutland, marked a clean-cut ending to the defensive phase in the Pacific war. For two months there was an ominous pause, each contestant licking his wounds. There then broke out a bloody and desperate six months' campaign over two focal points — Buna-Gona in New Guinea, and Guadalcanal.

3. OPERATION 'TORCH' — THE RECONQUEST OF NORTH AFRICA

While Winston Churchill was conferring with President Roosevelt at the White House in June 1942, news came of the German capture of Tobruk in North Africa. Publicly, Churchill described the situation as 'a bit disconcerting'; privately, he confessed that he was the most miserable Englishman in America since the surrender of Burgoyne. For the fall of Tobruk opened a German road into Egypt and beyond. If Alexandria and the Suez Canal fell, nothing short of a miracle could keep the Axis out of India, on whose eastern frontier the Japanese were already poised.

At their White House meeting neither Roosevelt nor Churchill nor their military advisers could agree on the time or place for the first combined military operation against the Axis. The Americans wanted a cross-Channel operation in France to come first; a beachhead to be secured in 1942 and the big invasion in 1943. The British opposed any such attempt before the Allies had overwhelming air and ground forces and plenty of amphibious equipment, lest it be thrown back with heavy loss. Roosevelt, who had received Molotov at the White House just before Churchill arrived, was deeply impressed with the effort being made by Russia and the need for a second front in Europe to prevent Russia's being overrun. Something had to be done in 1942 — Churchill and Roosevelt could not stand the obloquy of fighting another 'phony war.' They decided, overriding most of their military advisers, on an occupation of French North Africa (25 July 1942) — Operation 'Torch.'

Oran and Algiers on the Mediterranean, and Casablanca on the Atlantic coast of Morocco, were selected as the three strategic harbors to be seized by amphibious forces. General Dwight D. Eisenhower was appointed commander in chief, with Admiral Sir Andrew Cunningham as over-all commander of naval forces.

With less than four months in which to plan, equip, and launch this operation, it was very risky. The United States and Great Britain had to train thousands of troops for amphibious warfare, divert hundreds of ships to new duties, and, as General Eisenhower wrote, occupy 'the rim of a continent where no major military campaign had been conducted for centuries.'

On 23 October General Sir Bernard Montgomery launched the second

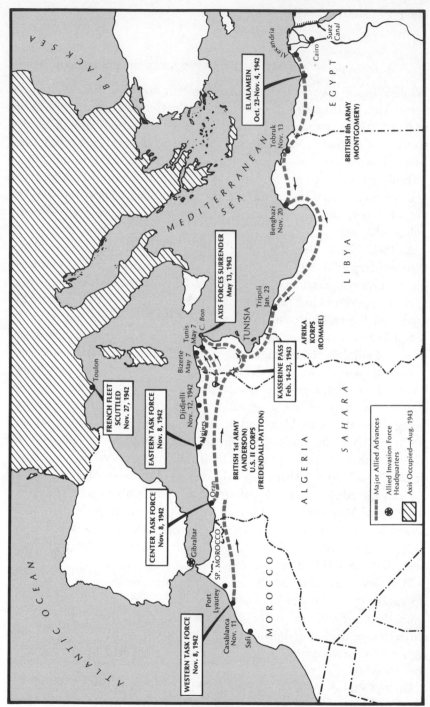

BLACK SEA

ATLANTIC OCEAN

MEDITERRANEAN SEA

EL ALAMEIN
Oct. 23–Nov. 4, 1942

Alexandria

Suez Canal

Cairo

E G Y P T

**BRITISH 8th ARMY
(MONTGOMERY)**

Tobruk
Nov. 13

L I B Y A

Benghazi
Nov. 20

AXIS FORCES SURRENDER
May 13, 1943

Tripoli
Jan. 23

**AFRIKA
KORPS
(ROMMEL)**

TUNISIA

C. Bon

Tunis
May 7

Bizerte
May 7

KASSERINE PASS
Feb. 14–23, 1943

**FRENCH FLEET
SCUTTLED**
Nov. 27, 1942

Toulon

Djidjelli
Nov. 12, 1942

EASTERN TASK FORCE
Nov. 8, 1942

Algiers

BRITISH 1st ARMY
(ANDERSON)
U.S. II CORPS
(FREDENDALL–PATTON)

S A H A R A

A L G E R I A

CENTER TASK FORCE
Nov. 8, 1942

Oran

Gibraltar

SP. MOROCCO

Port
Lyautey

M O R O C C O

WESTERN TASK FORCE
Nov. 8, 1942

Casablanca
Nov. 11

Safi

Major Allied Advances

Allied Invasion Force
Headquarters

Axis Occupied—Aug. 1943

THE WAR IN NORTH AFRICA
1942–1943

battle of El Alamein against Rommel, and on the same day Rear Admiral H. Kent Hewitt, commanding the Western Naval Task Force, sailed from Hampton Roads. Never before had an amphibious operation been projected across an ocean, but the complex operation went like clockwork. By midnight 7–8 November all three task forces (the two for Oran and Algiers under British command) had reached their destinations, unscathed and unreported. Admiral Hewitt had to fight a naval battle with the French fleet off Casablanca, and sink most of it, in order to get General Patton's troops ashore safely, but there was little resistance from the French army. Admiral Darlan, second to Marshal Pétain in the Vichy government, was so impressed by the strength of the Anglo-American landings that Eisenhower was able to persuade him to issue a cease-fire order to all French forces in North Africa on 11 November. Defended as a military expedient, this 'Darlan deal' was denounced by liberals as capitulation to a Nazi collaborator. Darlan was assassinated on Christmas eve, but not until October 1944 did the United States recognize Charles de Gaulle as the leader of the French nation.

Although caught flat-footed by the invasion, the Germans reacted promptly, flying 20,000 men across the Sicilian straits within a few days and establishing fighter and bomber bases on Tunisian airfields. General Eisenhower moved, too, but the difficulties he faced from mountain and desert, narrow twisting roads, the rainy season which grounded his aircraft, and, not least, from half-trained troops, prevented his reaching Bizerte and Tunis in 1942.

Early in January 1943 Roosevelt and Churchill and the Combined Chiefs of Staff met at Casablanca to plan future operations. For the first time Allied prospects seemed favorable; this was, as Churchill said, 'the end of the beginning.' The Russians had turned the tide at the decisive battle of Stalingrad; Auchinleck and Montgomery had saved Egypt; air and naval forces were fast being built up in Morocco and Algeria; Mussolini could no longer call the Mediterranean *mare nostrum*.

Allied chiefs at Casablanca granted antisubmarine warfare top priority, decided to invade Sicily as soon as Tunisia was secured, gave America the green light to start Admiral Nimitz and General MacArthur on an offensive against the Japanese, and promised 'to draw as much weight as possible off the Russian armies by engaging the enemy as heavily as possible at the best selected point.' And they made the momentous announcement that the war would end only with 'unconditional surrender' of all enemies, European and Asiatic. That formula, borrowed from General Grant's declaration before Fort Donelson, was the second major strategic decision of the war. It was prompted by the failure of the armistice of 11 November 1918 to eliminate the German menace, propaganda about the Darlan deal suggesting that Roosevelt and Churchill were contemplating a similar deal with Mussolini and Hitler, and a desire to reassure Russia that we would not let her down. The formula was subsequently criticized as helping Hitler to persuade his people to fight to the bitter end, but it is not clear that it actually had much effect.

While Roosevelt and Churchill were discussing grand strategy, the Germans seized the initiative. Swift counterattacks and the arrival of Rommel's Afrika Korps gave them ground superiority, which Rommel exploited in brilliant fashion. On 14 February 1943 he hurled his armor through the Kasserine Pass, turned northward toward Tebessa, and threatened to cut the Allied armies in two. The untried American forces were badly beaten for a time. But General Patton, the opportune arrival of two armored divisions from Oran, the employment of powerful new tanks, and clearing skies that permitted the North African Air Force to deliver punishing blows turned the tide.

This was Rommel's last offensive. Montgomery had caught up with him, and the two antagonists squared off for a last round. Hammered front and rear, pounded by the most devastating aerial attack of the North African campaign, Rommel acknowledged defeat and retreated northward into Tunisia. The Allied armies, now half a million strong, closed in for the kill. As Montgomery broke the German lines in the south and raced for Tunis, Omar Bradley, commanding II Corps, United States Army, smashed into Bizerte. Each city fell on 7 May 1943. Cornered on Cape Bon, the German army, still 275,000 strong, surrendered on 13 May. It was the greatest victory that British and American arms had yet won.

Now that North Africa was cleared of the enemy, the Mediterranean became open to Allied merchant ships throughout its entire length, though still subject to air attack from Italy and southern France, which the Germans occupied as soon as they heard of the Darlan deal. The now spliced lifeline of the British Empire to India through Suez made it possible to reinforce Russia via the Persian Gulf. And the way was open at last for a blow at what Churchill mistakenly called 'the soft underbelly' of Europe.

4. THE GUADALCANAL AND PAPUA CAMPAIGNS

After the Coral Sea and Midway victories, Allied forces in the Pacific were based mainly at four points. Operating from Dutch Harbor in Alaska, a small American force watched the Japanese in the western Aleutians. At Pearl Harbor the main Pacific Fleet was based, and on the Hawaiian islands several army divisions were being trained for jungle warfare. At Nouméa in New Caledonia and at Espiritu Santo was based the South Pacific force, at first under Admiral Ghormley, later relieved by the dashing Admiral Halsey. In Brisbane, Australia, General MacArthur headed the Southwest Pacific command of American, Australian, and New Zealand troops, together with a small United States and Australian naval force.

In July 1942 the Japanese still held Tulagi on Florida Island in the Solomons, Rabaul on New Britain, and New Ireland. These were anchors to a formidable island barrier to an Allied advance toward Japan. The islands are so close to one another that the surrounding waters could be controlled by land-based planes. The Joint Chiefs of Staff decided that this barrier must be breached. And the campaign to do this was sparked by the news that the Japanese had taken Buna and Gona on the north coast of Papua, and were building an airfield on Guadalcanal, whence they would be able to batter our advance base at Espiritu Santo. Since massive forces were being assembled for the invasion of North Africa, the South Pacific command got only what was left; the campaign was well nicknamed Operation 'Shoestring.' Presently nineteen transports, escorted by cruisers and destroyers, with an airsupport force of three carriers, were converging on the mountainous, jungle-clad Solomon Islands. On 7 August 1942, the 1st Marine Division under General Alexander A. Vandegrift landed at Tulagi and Guadalcanal, surprised the enemy, and seized the harbor of the one island and the airfield on the other.

There then began the prolonged and bloody struggle for Guadalcanal; an island worthless in itself, like the battlefield of Gettysburg in 1863, but even more violently contested. The Japanese could not afford to let us establish a base there, and we could not afford to let it go. Seven major naval battles were fought,[1] until Iron Bottom Bay, as our sailors

1. (1) Battle of Savo Island, 9 Aug. 1942, won by Admiral Mikawa against a cruiser force commanded by Rear Adm. Crutchley, R.N., with a loss of three U.S.

named Savo Island Sound, was strewn with the hulls of ships and the bodies of sailors. Every few nights the Japanese ran fast reinforcement echelons, the 'Tokyo Expresses,' down the central channel, the Solomons' 'Slot'; every few days American reinforcements came in, and daily air battles became routine. On shore, the marines, reinforced by army divisions, fought stubbornly and, in the end, successfully. On 9 February 1943, six months after the landings, the Japanese evacuated Guadalcanal.

In this campaign American soldiers — marines under General Vandegrift, army under General A. M. Patch — took the measure of the supposedly invincible Japanese foot-soldiers, who had overrun half of Eastern Asia, and found that they could be beaten. And the navy learned, the hard way, how to fight night battles and shoot down enemy planes. After this deadly island had been secured, the navy won every battle with the Japanese fleet.

In the meantime the western prong of this Japanese offensive had been stopped on the north coast of Papua, New Guinea, in the villages of Buna, Gona, and Sanananda. This was done by General MacArthur's command, executed by American and Australian troops under Generals Eichelberger and Sir Edmund Herring. The fighting, in malaria-infested mangrove swamps against a trapped and never-surrendering enemy, was the most horrible of the entire war. With the aid of air power the com-

---

and one Australian heavy cruisers; (2) Battle of the Eastern Solomons, 24 Aug., in which carriers *Saratoga* and *Enterprise* under Vice Adm. F. J. Fletcher beat off a Japanese carrier force under Vice Adm. Kondo and sank one; (3) Battle of Cape Esperance, 11–12 Oct., in which a cruiser force under Rear Adm. Norman Scott defeated a reinforcement group under Rear Adm. Goto, sinking four destroyers and losing one; (4) Battle of the Santa Cruz Islands, 26–27 Oct., in which a carrier force under Rear Adm. Thomas C. Kinkaid beat off Kondo again, but lost *Hornet;* (5) the two-night naval Battle of Guadalcanal, 12–15 Nov., in which Rear Admirals D. J. Callaghan, Norman Scott, and Willis A. Lee sank two Japanese battleships, a cruiser, two destroyers, and 11 transports, but paid for it with the lives of Callaghan and Scott, two cruisers, and seven destroyers; (6) Battle of Tassafaronga, 30 Nov., in which we lost a cruiser but frustrated an attempt at reinforcement; (7) Battle of Rennell Island, 29–30 Jan. 1943, in which we lost cruiser *Chicago* to air attack. The final score was 24 warships lost to each side. There was almost continuous fighting by ground troops on the island itself, scores of air battles, and frequent night bombardments by Japanese warships. The principal ground actions were the battle of the Tenaru River (21 Aug.), of the Bloody Ridge (12–14 Sept.), of the Metanikan River (23–27 Sept. and 7–9 Oct.), the battle for Henderson Field (19–26 Oct.), of Point Cruz (19–22 Nov.), of Mt. Austen (17–24 Dec.), and Bonegi Ridge (1 Feb.).

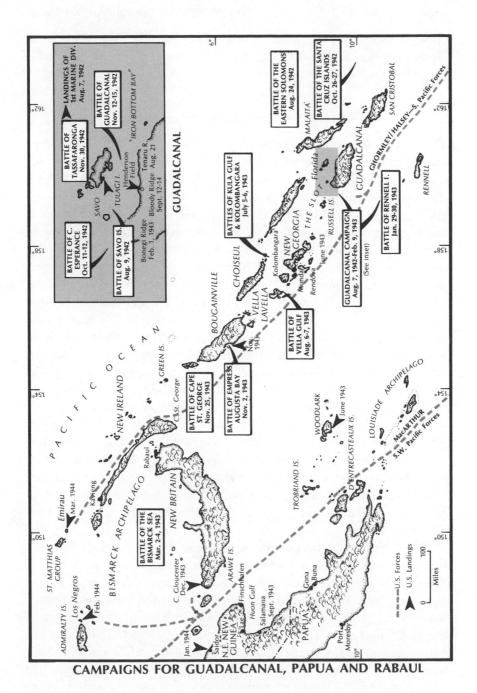

CAMPAIGNS FOR GUADALCANAL, PAPUA AND RABAUL

577

bined armies won through, and by the end of January 1943 Papua up to Huon Gulf was in Allied hands. The defensive period in the war with Japan had finally come to an end.

5. THE TIDE TURNS AGAINST THE U-BOAT

The crucial period in the Battle of the Atlantic came in the first half of 1943. At the turn of the year Hitler appointed as head of the German navy his submarine expert, Admiral Doenitz, and concentrated on producing more and better U-boats. The number operating in the Atlantic more than doubled, and their effectiveness was increased by sending big supply subs — 'milch cows' — into waters around the neutral Azores, enabling U-boats to replenish without returning to France. But the number of allied ships and planes capable of dealing with them more than quadrupled. The North African campaign required so many troop and supply convoys to Casablanca and Algiers that the United States Navy took charge of them, while the British and Canadian navies escorted the North Atlantic merchant convoys. A fresh German blitz in March 1943, accounted for 108 merchant ships aggregating over 625,000 tons. Echelons of wolf-packs, preceded by U-boats whose sole duty was to shadow convoys, attacked by day as well as night. These sinkings, occurring at the worst season in the North Atlantic when the temperature of the water hovers around 30° F, were accompanied by heavy loss of life. And although the United States Navy, which escorted transatlantic troop transports, lost none of those going to and from Great Britain or the Mediterranean, it lost three army transports en route to Greenland and Iceland; one of these, the *Dorchester,* on 3 February 1943, with heavy loss, including four army chaplains. But by April the Allies were definitely ahead.

The increased number of convoys and escorts, improved devices and training, and the work of scientists and technicians were getting results. The British put on a great surface and air drive in the Bay of Biscay against U-boats that were approaching or departing from their French bases. This, in conjunction with successes elsewhere, brought the total bag of U-boats up to 41 in May. At the same time the United States began using new escort carriers in convoys between Norfolk and the Mediterranean. These went out after every submarine detected within 300 miles of the convoy route and sank a considerable number, even some of the big 'milch cows.' The latter were already driven from their pastures when Portugal permitted the Allies to use air bases in the Azores; that closed the last stretch in the North Atlantic which long-range bomber planes had been unable to reach. And merchant ship new construction was now well ahead of losses.

Germany built 198 U-boats between 1 May 1943 and the end of the year, and lost 186. Transatlantic convoys were now so well defended that tonnage losses during these eight months totaled only 592,000 tons, less than in the single months of June and November 1942. Admiral Doenitz, feeling that he must make a tonnage score, no matter where, now began sending his best long-legged U-boats into the Indian Ocean, where as yet there were no convoys. But he kept enough in home waters occasionally to send wolf-packs full cry after transatlantic traffic; the Battle of the Atlantic did not end until Germany surrendered.

6. THE INVASION OF SICILY AND ITALY

If the North African campaign could have been concluded early in 1943, it might have been possible to invade the continent of Europe that year; but operation 'Torch' flickered too long to permit that, and 'Overlord,' the invasion of Normandy, had to be postponed to 1944. Something had to be done during the rest of 1943, and the obvious thing was to hit the Axis on its backside, which might make 'Overlord' less difficult.

The plan selected was to overrun Sicily, cross the Strait of Messina to Calabria, and work up the Italian peninsula. This offered complete control of the Mediterranean, as well as an objective dear to Churchill's heart, knocking Italy out of the war. D-day for the attack on Sicily was 10 July, General Eisenhower ran the show; under him Admiral of the Fleet Sir A. B. Cunningham, General Sir Harold Alexander, and Air Chief Marshal Tedder were the top naval, ground-force, and air commanders. This invasion of Sicily was the biggest amphibious assault of the war, not excepting 'Overlord.' About 250,000 British and American troops landed simultaneously, eight divisions abreast, and in black darkness. The 350,000 Italian and German defenders of Sicily were surprised and thrown off balance. The American Seventh Army (General Patton) was landed on the southwestern shore of Sicily; the British Eighth Army (General Montgomery), which included a Canadian division, landed on the American right flank and up to a short distance from Syracuse.

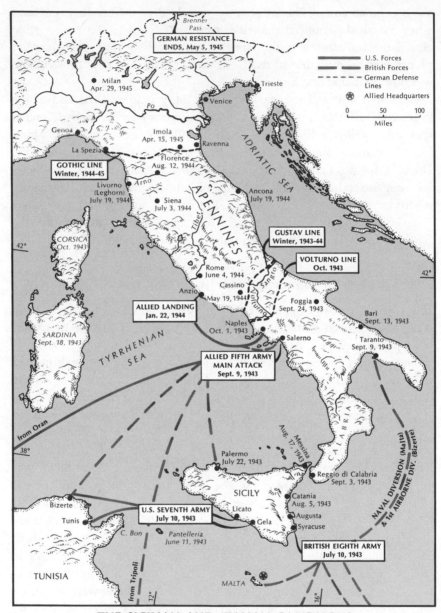

Brenner Pass

GERMAN RESISTANCE ENDS, May 5, 1945

U.S. Forces
British Forces
German Defense Lines
Allied Headquarters

0   50   100
Miles

Milan
Apr. 29, 1945

Trieste

Po

Venice

Genoa

Imola
Apr. 15, 1945

Ravenna

La Spezia

ADRIATIC SEA

Florence
Aug. 12, 1944

GOTHIC LINE Winter, 1944-45

Livorno
(Leghorn)
July 19, 1944

Arno

Siena
July 3, 1944

Ancona
July 19, 1944

APENNINES

Tiber

CORSICA
Oct. 1943

42°

42°

GUSTAV LINE Winter, 1943-44

VOLTURNO LINE Oct. 1943

Rome
June 4, 1944

Cassino

Sangro

Foggia
Sept. 24, 1943

Bari
Sept. 13, 1943

Anzio
May 19, 1944

ALLIED LANDING Jan. 22, 1944

Volturno

SARDINIA
Sept. 18, 1943

Naples
Oct. 1, 1943

Salerno

Taranto
Sept. 9, 1943

TYRRHENIAN SEA

ALLIED FIFTH ARMY MAIN ATTACK Sept. 9, 1943

CALABRIA

NAVAL DIVERSION (Malta) & 1st AIRBORNE DIV. (Bizerte)

from Oran

38°

Aug. 17, 1943

Messina

Reggio di Calabria
Sept. 3, 1943

Palermo
July 22, 1943

SICILY

Catania
Aug. 5, 1943

Bizerte

U.S. SEVENTH ARMY July 10, 1943

Licato

Gela

Augusta

Syracuse

Tunis

C. Bon

Pantelleria
June 11, 1943

BRITISH EIGHTH ARMY July 10, 1943

TUNISIA

from Tripoli

12°

MALTA

16°

THE SICILIAN AND ITALIAN CAMPAIGNS

After a sharp battle at the Gela beachhead with a German armored division, the Seventh Army swept across Sicily, marching at a rate that matched Stonewall Jackson's 'foot cavalry' in the Civil War. On 22 July General Patton made his triumphal entry into Palermo and set up headquarters in the ancient palace of the Norman kings. By 17 August the great island was in Allied hands. Unfortunately some 40,000 German troops escaped across the Strait of Messina with most of their weapons and equipment.

Italy, though not mortally wounded, was heartily sick of the war into which Mussolini had dragged her. On 25 July, six days after Allied air forces had delivered a 560-plane bombing raid on Rome, King Victor Emmanuel III summoned up enough courage to force Mussolini to resign. Marshal Badoglio, who told the king that the war was *perduto, perdutissimo* (absolutely and completely lost), now headed the government and began to probe for peace. Owing to the Italian love of bargaining and the Allies' 'unconditional surrender' slogan, which made bargaining difficult, negotiations dragged along until 3 September. This gave the Germans, who suspected what was cooking, plenty of time to rush reinforcements into Italy and to seize key points such as Genoa, Leghorn, and Rome.

General Eisenhower had already been ordered to plan an invasion of Italy at the earliest possible date. Salerno, south of the Sorrento Peninsula, was chosen for the main landing in Italy, as the point farthest north where Allied fighter planes could protect amphibious forces from German air attack. In early September 1943 the American Fifth Army, commanded by General Mark W. Clark, with two British and two American infantry divisions in the assault, took off from a dozen ports between Oran and Alexandria. En route to the objective the familiar voice of General 'Ike' was heard broadcasting news of the Italian surrender, so all hands expected a walk-over. They had a bitter surprise. Some very tough and unco-operative Germans were at the beach. D-day for Salerno, 9 September, was very costly. The German air force tried a new weapon, the radio-guided bomb, which put several ships out of business, and a Panzer division laid on a series of vicious tank attacks. But by 16 September the beachheads were secured, and the Germans started an orderly retirement northward. The Fifth Army on 1 October entered Naples, which the Germans had done their best to destroy. Commodore William A. Sullivan, with a mixed Anglo-American salvage team, did a remarkable job in clearing the bay and the waterfront, so that by the end of the year more tonnage was being discharged in Naples than in time of peace.

Here, at the Volturno line north of Naples, the Italian campaign should have been halted. But Churchill and General Sir Alan Brooke, chief of the Imperial General Staff, justified continuing on the ground that the battle of Italy pinned down and used up German divisions which might resist the Normandy landing in 1944. Actually the Italian campaign failed to draw German reserves from France, and by June 1944 the Allies were deploying in Italy double the number of the Germans in that area. Marshal Kesselring, fighting a series of delaying operations along prepared mountain entrenchments, exploited natural advantages to the full. From Naples to Rome is but a hundred miles; yet the Allies, with numerical superiority on land and in the air, and with control of adjacent waters, took eight months to cover that ground. Fighting in the Apennines, wrote the war correspondent Ernie Pyle, consisted of 'almost inconceivable misery,' in mud and frost. GIs 'lived like men of prehistoric times, and a club would have become them more than a machine gun.'

Rome was the objective of the winter campaign of 1943–44, but some of the most mountainous terrain in Europe barred the way. Churchill persuaded the C.C.S. to try to break the stalemate by an amphibious landing in the rear of the Germans at Anzio, 37 miles south of Rome. Although the Anzio landing (22 January 1944) by one British division and the United States 3rd Infantry Division was a complete surprise, Kesselring reacted swiftly; his air force sank a number of British and American transports and warships, and the troops had to dig into an open plain, where they were subjected to constant air and infantry counterattack. Anzio beachhead, which should have been a spearhead, became instead a beleaguered fort.

To the south, the Eighth Army (General Montgomery) launched a series of savage attacks against Monte Cassino, anchor of the German 'Gustav line.' For three months the Allies wore themselves out in futile attempts to take the place by storm. Finally, the Eighth Army, which by this time included American, British, Polish, Indian, and French divisions, enveloped and captured Monte Cassino (19 May); a Canadian force advanced up the Adriatic coast; Mark Clark's Fifth Army burst through the iron ring around Anzio on 25 May, and advanced north against stubborn rear-guard resistance. By the morning of 4 June 1944, as Kesselring's forces were retiring toward a new defense line, columns of Allied troops were rushing along all roads that led to Rome. By midnight the Fifth Army was there. American troops in Italy, who often felt they were the forgotten men of the war, for one brief day held the attention of the Allied nations. Then, on 6 June, came the news that the Allies had landed on the coast of Normandy, and the soldiers in Italy, their brief share of the limelight quickly ended, plodded northward to meet the Germans at the Gothic line another 150 miles to the north.

7. FORWARD IN THE PACIFIC

For five months after Guadalcanal was secured in early February 1943, there was a lull in the Pacific war, in large part because of lack of aircraft carriers. By mid-1943, when the new *Essex* class carriers began to join the fleet, it was ready to go.

Japan was the final objective, but before invasion of her tightly defended home islands, positions had to be taken within air-bombing distance. But how to get there? The short northern route, via the Aleutians, was ruled out by bad flying weather.[2] In the Central Pacific, hundreds of atolls and thousands of islands — the Gilberts, Marshalls, Carolines, Marianas, and Bonins — plastered with airfields and bristling with defenses, sprawled across the ocean like a maze of gigantic spider webs. South of the equator, Japan held the Bismarck Archipelago, the Solomons north of Guadalcanal, and all New Guinea except its slippery tail. General MacArthur wished to advance by what he called the New Guinea-Mindanao axis; but Rabaul, planted like a baleful spider at the center of a web across that axis, would have to be eliminated first. And as long as Japan held the island complex on MacArthur's north flank, she could throw air and naval forces against his communications at will. So it was decided that Admiral Nimitz must take a broom to the Gilberts, the Marshalls, and the Carolines, while MacArthur and Halsey cleaned

2. The western Aleutians, however, were first reconquered for their nuisance value. Following the naval victory by Rear Adm. Charles A. McMorris off the Komandorski Islands on 24 March 1943, the 7th Infantry Division was landed on Attu and after a very tough fight cleared out the enemy, which then evacuated Kiska. These islands and Adak were then developed as air bases.

out the Bismarcks. All could then join forces for a final push into the Philippines and on to the coast of China.

Accordingly the plans for mid-1943 to mid-1944 began with preliminary operations to sweep up enemy spiders' webs. The central Solomons were the first objective. After three sharp naval actions up the Solomons' Slot in July and a number of motor torpedo boat actions (in one of which John Fitzgerald Kennedy distinguished himself), the United States Navy won control of surrounding waters, and Munda field with adjacent positions was captured by XIV Corps, General Oscar W. Griswold, on 5 August 1943, after a tough jungle campaign. In New Guinea and on Cape Gloucester, New Britain, a series of shore-to-shore amphibious operations secured the main passage from the Coral Sea through the Bismarcks barrier into the Western Pacific.

Japan could now be approached in a series of bold leaps instead of a multitude of short hops. Independently, General MacArthur and Rear Admiral Theodore S. Wilkinson thought up 'leap-frogging,' or, as Wilkinson called it in baseball phraseology, 'hitting 'em where they ain't.' The essence of this strategy was to by-pass the principal Japanese strongpoints like Truk and Rabaul, sealing them off with sea and air power, leaving their garrisons to 'wither on the vine,' while the allies constructed a new air and naval base in some less strongly defended spot several hundred miles nearer Japan. After the war was over General Tojo told General MacArthur that leap-frogging, the success of United States submarines against the Japanese merchant marine, and the projection of fire power by aircraft carriers deep into enemy territory were the three main factors that defeated Japan.

In November 1943 began the first important Pacific offensive, the campaign to break the Bismarck barrier by neutralizing Rabaul. Admiral Wilkinson, commanding the III Amphibious Force, selected a slice of undefended coast on Bougainville, within fighter-plane distance of Rabaul, landed troops there on 1 November, and established a defensive perimeter inside which the Seabees began building fighter and bomber strips. The Japanese fleet based on Truk and Rabaul promptly came out to challenge, only to be decisively beaten (Battle of Empress Augusta Bay, 2 November 1943) by Admiral A. Stanton Merrill's cruiser and destroyer force. On the 5th and 11th, carrier-based planes pounded Rabaul, and day by day 'Airsols' bombers of three nations based on Bougainville continued the work of wearing away the enemy air forces.

By 25 March 1944, Rabaul was ringed. The Bismarck barrier to MacArthur's advance was decisively breached, and almost 100,000 Japanese troops were neutralized at Rabaul.

8. GILBERTS, MARSHALLS, NEW GUINEA, MARIANAS

The Gilberts and Marshalls campaigns were the first full-scale amphibious operations in the Pacific. Some 200 sail of ships, the Fifth Fleet carrying 108,000 soldiers, sailors, marines, and aviators under the command of Raymond Spruance, Kelly Turner, and Major General H. M. ('Howling Mad') Smith converged on two coral atolls of the Gilbert group. Makin, where the enemy had no great strength, was taken methodically by a regiment of the 27th Infantry Division, but Tarawa, a small, strongly defended position behind a long coral-reef apron, was a very tough nut. The lives of almost a thousand marines and sailors were required to dispose of 4000 no-surrender Japanese on an islet not three miles long. But Tarawa taught invaluable lessons for future landings and provided another airfield. The Gilberts became bases from which aircraft helped to neutralize the seven Japanese air bases in the Marshalls. These islands were sealed off by fast carrier forces under Rear Admiral Marc Mitscher which roved about the group, ships pounding and aircraft bombing. Consequently, not one Japanese plane was available in the Marshalls on D-day, 31 January 1944. Massive amphibious forces under Admirals Harry Hill and Turner, with close air and gunfire support, covered landings at both ends of the great atoll of Kwajalein. On 17 February 1944 another force moved into Eniwetok, westernmost of the Marshalls. The Japanese troops, as usual, resisted to the last man; but the Marshalls cost many fewer casualties than tiny Tarawa. The Japanese navy dared not challenge because its air arm had been sliced off to defend Rabaul; and on 20 February 1944 both ships and aircraft were chased out of the important naval base on Truk, with heavy loss, by a round-the-clock carrier air raid.

Mobile surface forces and mobile naval air power needed mobile logistics, and got them. Outstanding in the pattern for Pacific victory was the mobile supply base — Service Squadron 10, a logistic counterpart to the fast carrier forces. While the flattops carried the naval air arm to within striking distance of the enemy, 'Servron 10,' composed of tankers, ammunition ships, refrigerator ships, repair ships, fleet tugs, escort car-

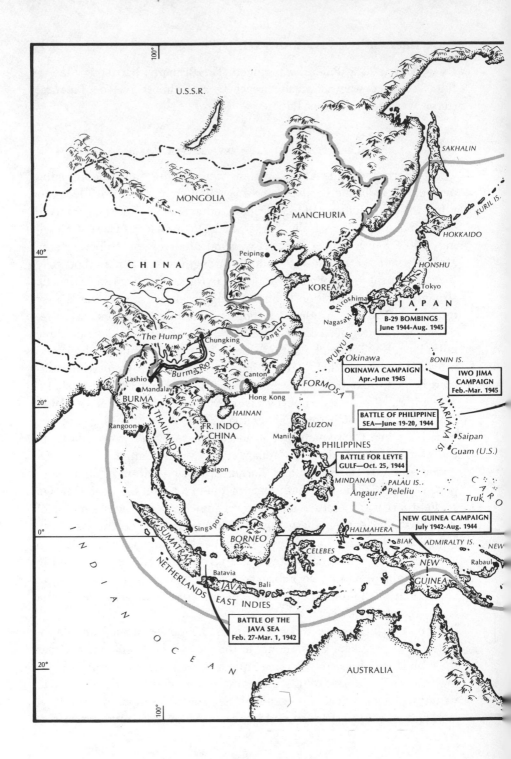

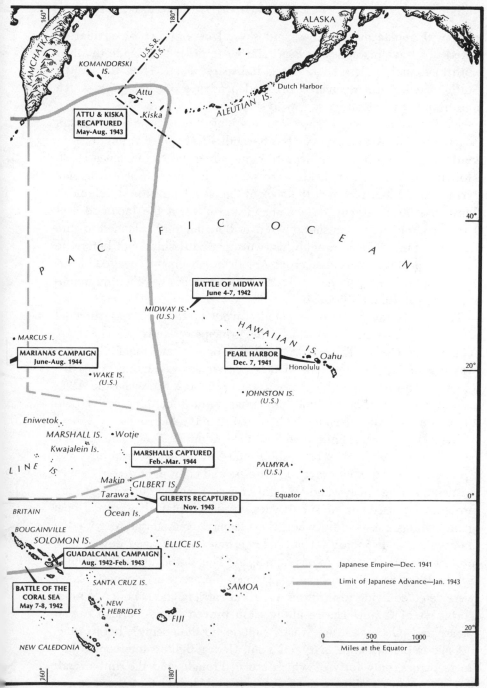

KAMCHATKA

KOMANDORSKI IS.

U.S.S.R.
U.S.

ALASKA

Attu • Dutch Harbor

ATTU & KISKA RECAPTURED May-Aug. 1943

.Kiska

ALEUTIAN IS.

P A C I F I C   O C E A N

40°

P A C I F I C

BATTLE OF MIDWAY June 4-7, 1942

MIDWAY IS.•
(U.S.)

• MARCUS I.

MARIANAS CAMPAIGN June-Aug. 1944

H A W A I I A N   I S.

PEARL HARBOR Dec. 7, 1941

Oahu

Honolulu

•WAKE IS.
(U.S.)

20°

• JOHNSTON IS.
(U.S.)

Eniwetok •.

MARSHALL IS.   •Wotje

Kwajalein Is.

MARSHALLS CAPTURED Feb.-Mar. 1944

PALMYRA •
(U.S.)

L I N E   I S.

Makin•
Tarawa•

GILBERT IS.

GILBERTS RECAPTURED Nov. 1943

Equator

0°

BRITAIN

Ocean Is.

BOUGAINVILLE

SOLOMON IS.

ELLICE IS.

GUADALCANAL CAMPAIGN Aug. 1942-Feb. 1943

BATTLE OF THE CORAL SEA May 7-8, 1942

SANTA CRUZ IS.

SAMOA

NEW HEBRIDES

FIJI

NEW CALEDONIA

Japanese Empire—Dec. 1941

Limit of Japanese Advance—Jan. 1943

20°

0   500   1000

Miles at the Equator

160°   180°

160°   180°

THE PACIFIC THEATER OF WAR—1941–1945

587

riers with replacement planes, and several other types of auxiliaries, acted as a traveling annex to Pearl Harbor in order to provide the fleet with food, fuel, bullets, spare parts, and spare planes. Thus, the United States Pacific Fleet recovered that independence of land bases which had been lost when sail gave way to steam.

While Spruance and Turner were crashing through the Gilberts and Marshalls, 'MacArthur's navy,' the Seventh Fleet under Admirals Kinkaid and Dan Barbey, were leap-frogging along the New Guinea coast. Hollandia and Aitape airfields were secured by the end of April. Biak Island, poised like a fly over the neck of the New Guinea bird, fell on 17 May 1944. Admiral Toyoda, commander in chief of the Japanese fleet (Yamamoto having been shot down over Bougainville), planned to stop the Americans right there with his two super-battleships; but before he got around to it, a more dangerous American movement engaged his attention, and by 15 September MacArthur's air forces were within bombing distance of the Philippines.

The new offensive that engaged Toyoda's attention was directed against the Marianas, of which the principal islands were Saipan, Tinian, and Guam. This group, with the Bonins and the Philippines, was part of Japan's inner line of defense. Saipan was within flying distance of southern Japan by the new B-29 bombers. So, when the Allies moved into Saipan on 15 June, Japan had to do something better than the last-ditch local resistance she had offered in the Marshalls.

Deploying into the Philippine Sea, Vice Admiral Ozawa commanded nine carriers, with five battleships and seven heavy cruisers. The Spruance-Mitscher fleet (seven *Essex*-class and eight light carriers, seven battleships, three heavy and six light cruisers) moved out to meet him, preceded by a screen of submarines. Spruance played his usual cool game, taking risks boldly when they seemed commensurate with the damage he might inflict, yet never forgetting that his main duty was to protect the amphibious forces at Saipan. The Battle of the Philippine Sea broke at 10 a.m., 19 June 1944, when hundreds of Japanese planes were detected flying toward the American carriers, then about 100 miles northwest of Guam. The resulting clash proved that American carrier planes and pilots were now vastly superior to the enemy's, both in tactics and in performance. Sixty miles out, Hellcat fighters intercepted Japanese planes, only forty of which broke through; and the anti-aircraft fire of Spruance's ships was so accurate and deadly that these scored only two hits, on tough battleships that suffered little damage. As a result of this 'great turkey shoot,' the Japanese lost over 345 planes at the cost of only 17 American aircraft. The enemy lost three carriers, two of them to United States submarines; Ozawa's air groups were wiped out, and he had no time to train new ones before the next great battle, in October.

Now the conquest of the Marianas could proceed without outside interference. On 6 July, the Japanese general and his staff committed suicide, and the rest of his army jumped off cliffs or holed up in caves. Turner's amphibious forces then captured Tinian and Guam, which were much less strongly held than Saipan. By 1 August 1944 these three big islands of the Marianas were in American possession. Airfield and harbor development went on briskly, Admiral Nimitz moved his headquarters to the hills above Agaña, and by fall, Marianas-based B-29's were bombing southern Japan.

The more sagacious Japanese now knew they were beaten; but they dared not admit it, and nerved their people to another year of bitter resistance in the vain hope that America might tire of the war when victory was within grasp.

XXIV

Victory in Europe
and in the Pacific

1. THE AIR ASSAULT ON GERMANY

While waiting for an appropriate moment to launch the cross-Channel invasion of Hitler's 'Fortress Europe,' the R.A.F., in conjunction with the United States Army Air Force, was doing its best to render invasion unnecessary by bombing Germany into submission. On 30 May 1942 came the first 1000-bomber raid against Cologne. In 1943 the Americans began taking an increasing share. Largely British, but assisted by B-17's of the Eighth Army Air Force, was the most destructive air bombing of the European war — the series of attacks on Hamburg in July-August 1943, which, by using incendiary bombs, wiped out over half the city, killed 42,600, and injured 37,000 people. 'Those who sowed the wind are reaping the whirlwind,' said Winston Churchill.

They certainly were, and worse was to come; but this strategic air offensive never succeeded as an alternative to land invasion. The bombing of German cities, almost nightly by the R.A.F. and every clear day by the A.A.F., did not seriously diminish Germany's well-dispersed war production and conspicuously failed to break civilian morale. It was also frightfully expensive. In six days of October 1943, culminating in a raid on the ball-bearing plants at Schweinfurt, deep in the heart of Germany, the Eighth lost 148 bombers and their crews, mostly as a result of battles in the air. This was its worst week.

During 1944 the strategic bombing effort was far better directed. On New Year's day America's most famous aviator, General Carl Spaatz, was appointed commander of the United States Strategic Air Force in Europe. Air power, besides obstructing the movement of German armies, was now applied with increasing precision and violence to the key centers of German war production. One reason for the heavy casualties of October 1943 was the lack of fighter planes long-legged enough to escort the bombers; by the spring of 1944 we had the P-38 Lightning, P-47 Thunderbolt, and P-51 Mustang, which could fly to Berlin and back, fighting a good part of the way. In the 'Big Week' of 19-25 February 1944, 3300 heavy bombers of the England-based Eighth, and over 500 of the Italy-based Fifteenth Air Force, escorted by about the same number of fighter planes, attacked twelve targets important for the German aircraft industry, as far south as Ratisbon and Augsburg. Our losses were 226 bombers, 28 fighters, and about 2600 men; but some 600 German planes were shot down in the air. German aircraft production recuperated to be sure; but these February bombing missions, organized by Major Generals Frederick A. Anderson and William Kepner USA, did deny many hundreds of aircraft to the enemy when he needed them most. By 14 April, when the almost two-year-old Combined Bomber Offensive ended and control of the U.S. Strategic Air Forces in Europe passed to General Eisenhower, the Allied air forces had established a thirty-to-one superiority over the German air force, and during the next seven weeks, before the Normandy invasion, they co-operated to make that operation a success. On D-day, 'Ike' told his troops, 'If you see fighting aircraft over you, they will be ours,' and so they were.

The air war in Europe cost the lives of some 158,000 British, Canadian, and American aviators. In this new dimension of warfare, many mistakes were made; but the Germans made even more. Without victory in the air there could have been no victory anywhere.

2. OPERATION 'OVERLORD,' JUNE–JULY 1944

In planning for the continental invasion, Roosevelt and Churchill decided to appoint General Eisenhower, who in the conduct of North African and Mediterranean operations had revealed military and diplomatic talents of high order, to command all invasion forces of both nations. In January 1944 'Ike' flew to London where he received his directive from the Combined Chiefs of Staff: 'You will enter the continent of Europe and, in conjunction with the other United Nations, undertake operations aimed at the heart of Germany and the destruction of her armed forces.'

Never before in modern times had an invading army crossed the English Channel against opposition, and Hitler's coastal defenses were formidable: underwater obstacles and mines, artillery emplacements, pill boxes, wire entanglements, tank traps, land mines, and other hazards designed to stop the invaders on the beaches. Behind these defenses were stationed 58 divisions. Yet the Allies had reason for confidence. They could select their point of attack. For six weeks Allied air forces had been smashing roads and bridges in northern France, reducing the transportation system to chaos. The Allied force of soldiers, sailors, aviators, and service amounted to 2.8 million men, all based in England. Thirty-nine divisions and 11,000 planes were available for the initial landings, and the Allied supporting fleet was overwhelmingly superior to anything the Germans could deploy; the U-boats had been so neutralized by the Allied navies that not one of the thousands of vessels engaged in the invasion was torpedoed. Hitler's army commanders, fooled by an elaborate deception to the effect that a major army group under General Patton was about to cross the Strait of Dover to the Pas de Calais, concentrated their strongest forces on the wrong stretch of coast.

The Allied command selected as target a 40-mile strip of beach along the Normandy coast between the Orne river and the Cotentin peninsula. The eastern sector was assigned to the British, the western to the Americans. By the end of May southern England was one vast military camp, crowded with soldiers awaiting the final word to go and piled high with supplies and equipment awaiting transport to the far shore of the Channel. This 'mighty host,' wrote Eisenhower, 'was as tense as a . . . great human spring, coiled for the moment when its energy should be released.' Shortly after midnight 5 June three paratroop divisions were flown across the Channel to drop behind the beaches. During the night the invasion fleet of 600 warships and 4000 supporting craft, freighted with 176,000 men from a dozen different ports, the British commanded by Admiral Sir Philip Vian and General Sir Miles Dempsey, the Americans by Admiral Alan Kirk and General Omar Bradley, moved over to the Norman coast. The transports and large landing craft anchored off the invasion beaches at 3:00 a.m.; battleships, cruisers, and destroyers closed the beaches and began hurling shells ashore at 5:30. Before naval bombardment ended, landing craft, lowered from transports over ten miles from shore, began their approach. It was D-day, 6 June.

The first assault troops, who touched down at 6:30, achieved tactical surprise. On the American right — designated Utah Beach — VII Corps (Generals J. L. Collins and Theodore Roosevelt, Jr.) got ashore against light opposition, surmounted barriers of marsh and swamp, and linked up with elements of the 82nd Airborne Division. But 1st and 29th Divisions (General C. R. Huebner), landing on four-mile Omaha Beach, found the going tough. Heavy overcast prevented the air force from bombing that beach, and naval bombardment did not destroy German artillery emplacements. For a time the issue was in doubt. Soldiers were wounded in a maze of mined underwater obstacles, then drowned by the rising tide; those who got through had to cross a 50-yard-wide beach, exposed to cunningly contrived cross-fire from concrete pill boxes. Men huddled for protection under a low sea wall until company officers rallied them to root the defenders out of their prepared positions. Plain guts and training saved the day at Omaha, not forgetting the naval gunfire support that rained shells on the Germans as soon as shore fire control parties were able to indicate targets.

The numerically superior British assault force under General Dempsey had a somewhat less difficult landing on beaches Gold, Juno, and Sword, but it bore the brunt of the next week's fighting. Caen was the hinge of the Allied beachhead, and the Germans counterattacked strongly at that point. In both sectors paratroops played an essential part by confusing the Germans and harassing their communications. All in all, the D-day assault on that ever memorable 6th of June was a brilliant success.

Once the initial landings had been effected, the Allies rushed over men, armor, and supplies to build up the invading army faster than the Germans could reinforce theirs. By 12 June the Allies controlled a continuous beachhead some 70 miles in length and from five to fifteen miles in depth. On the left the British were battling for Caen; in the center the 101st Airborne had entered Carentan; and on the right VII Corps was pushing swiftly across the Cotentin peninsula and sweeping north toward Cherbourg. In a single week the Allies landed 326,000 men, 50,000 vehicles, and over 100,000 tons of supplies.

'The history of war,' said Marshal Stalin, in one of his rare compli-

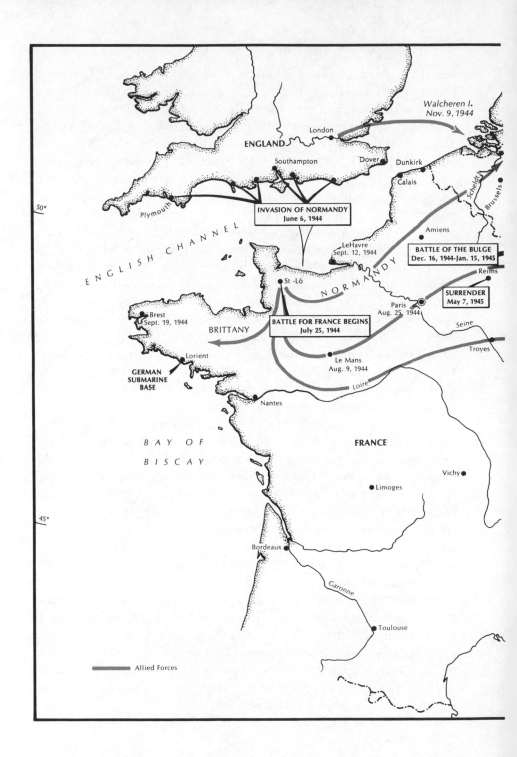

Walcheren I.
Nov. 9, 1944

London

ENGLAND

Southampton

Dover

Dunkirk

Calais

Brussels

Amiens

Reims

Plymouth

50°

**INVASION OF NORMANDY
June 6, 1944**

LeHavre
Sept. 12, 1944

E N G L I S H   C H A N N E L

St -Lô

N O R M A N D Y

**BATTLE OF THE BULGE
Dec. 16, 1944-Jan. 15, 1945**

**SURRENDER
May 7, 1945**

Brest
Sept. 19, 1944

BRITTANY

**BATTLE FOR FRANCE BEGINS
July 25, 1944**

Paris
Aug. 25, 1944

Seine

Lorient

Le Mans
Aug. 9, 1944

Troyes

**GERMAN
SUBMARINE
BASE**

Loire

Nantes

B A Y   O F

B I S C A Y

FRANCE

Vichy

45°

Limoges

Bordeaux

Garonne

Allied Forces

Toulouse

594

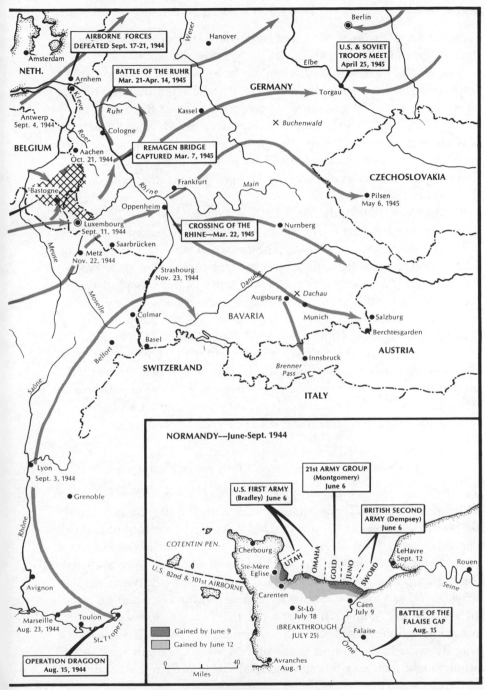

THE CONQUEST OF GERMANY
1944-1945

595

ments to his allies, 'does not know any undertaking so broad in conception, so grandiose in scale, and so masterly in execution.'

Two artificial harbors off the landing beaches created out of sunken ships with connecting pontoon units facilitated a rapid build-up of supplies; but a northwest gale blew up on 19 June and in three days badly damaged the 'mulberrys,' as these harbors were called. Now the capture of Cherbourg became highly urgent. The Germans there, bombarded from land, air, and sea, surrendered on 26 June, but they wrecked the harbor first, and for weeks more stuff came in over the beaches than through Cherbourg.

The Battle of Normandy lasted until 24 July. By that time the British, after very tough fighting, had captured Caen; the Americans had taken Saint-Lô, gateway to the South. The enemy, unable to bring up reinforcements, his communications wrecked and planes grounded, was bewildered. Rommel thought the situation hopeless and was preparing to try to negotiate with Eisenhower for a separate peace when he was arrested and killed, on Hitler's orders. Other high-ranking officers attempted to assassinate Hitler at his headquarters on 20 July, to take over the German government and to surrender; but the Fuehrer survived, they and hundreds of others were tortured to death, and the war went on. Hitler now trusted to his 'secret weapons' such as the new U-boat to win. His new V-1 'buzz bombs,' launched from Belgium and northern France, were spreading death and destruction on London.

3. NORMANDY TO THE RHINE, JULY-SEPTEMBER 1944

The battle for France began on 25 July 1944, when General Patton's Third Army hit the German lines west of Saint-Lô. By the end of July the Americans stood at the threshold of Brittany. In the face of this fast and furious attack the German withdrawal turned into something like a rout. And after the breakthrough came the breakout. One wing of Patton's army turned west and within a week overran Brittany; another wing turned east and within two weeks reached the Loire and Le Mans. In a desperate gamble Hitler ordered the German Seventh Army to break through the funnel of the American army at Avranches. Most of it was destroyed in the ensuing Battle of the Falaise Gap; only remnants of armor fought their way through and sped east to prepare for the defense of Germany.

On 15 August, as the Germans were being ground to bits in the Falaise gap, the Allies launched their long-awaited invasion of southern France. General Eisenhower insisted on this Operation 'Dragoon' for two reasons: to deploy General Patch's American Seventh Army and General de Lattre de Tassigny's First French Army on his southern flank for the final invasion of Germany; and to capture the major port of Marseilles for logistic supply. 'Dragoon,' commanded by Admiral Hewitt, was a push-over. Toulon and Marseilles were soon taken by the French, while the Seventh Army rolled up the Rhine valley, captured Lyons, and raced to close the German escape corridor at the Belfort gap. By mid-September Patch had linked up with Patton.

'Liberate Paris by Christmas and none of us can ask for more,' said Churchill to Eisenhower. General Hodges's First Army raced for the Seine; Patton's Third boiled out onto the open country north of the Loire and swept eastward through Orléans to Troyes. Paris rose against her hated masters, and with the aid of General Leclerc's 2nd Armored Division, was liberated on 25 August, four months ahead of Churchill's request. General Charles de Gaulle entered the city in triumph and assumed the presidency of a French provisional government.

Only lack of gasoline could stop Patton. His spearheads reached the Marne on 28 August, pushed through Château-Thierry, overran Rheims and Verdun. To the north, Montgomery's British and Canadians drove along the coast into Belgium. They captured Brussels and entered Antwerp 4 September; but that great port was no use while the Germans blocked the lower Scheldt. By 11 September the American First Army had liberated Luxembourg and near Aachen crossed the border into Germany. Within six weeks all France had been cleared of the enemy, and from there to Switzerland Allied armies stood poised for the advance into Germany. The Germans had lost almost half a million men; but Hitler's amazing hold over them had not relaxed, and they were ready for a last counterblow that cost the Allies dear.

On other fronts, the German position was becoming equally bad. The Russian offensive that began in July 1943 had recovered most of the invaded territory, and in the spring of 1944 the Red armies reached the Dnieper in the north and the Carpathians in the south. Stalin, having promised to launch a new offensive when the Allies entered Normandy, on 23 June did so along an 800-mile front. In five weeks the Russians swept across the Ukraine and Poland and up to the gates of Warsaw where, despicably, they paused instead of helping Polish patriots to liberate their capital; they hoped to reduce Poland to a satellite state, and they did. Rumania threw in the sponge when another Red Army crossed her borders, and so deprived the Germans of their last source of crude oil. By October the Russians had linked up with Tito forces in Yugoslavia. In Italy the Germans were driven back to their last line of defense, the 'Gothic Line' guarding the Po valley — a formidable barrier, which held up further advance in 1944.

Although the Allies still held the initiative in France, they were unable to exploit it. They had run into a serious problem of logistics; the speed of their advance had outrun supply and a stubborn defense still denied them the water approach to Antwerp.

This situation presented Eisenhower with one of his most difficult strategic decisions. Montgomery wanted to push ahead through Holland into the heart of Germany; he was confident that with proper support he could plunge through to Berlin. Patton was no less confident of his ability to smash into Germany from the south. Logistics permitted a modest advance on a broad front, or a deep stab on a single front, but not both. Because Eisenhower deemed it essential to clear the way to Antwerp, capture Calais and Dunkirk, and overrun the V-1 and V-2 bomb emplacements, which were raining guided missiles on London, priority in the scarce gasoline supply was given to Montgomery, who wasted it. But the root of Allied trouble at this moment of supreme opportunity was lack of foresight. The top planners, not having anticipated the collapse of German resistance in France in August, had made no preparation for exploiting it instantly. Thus, by mid-September, when airborne forces dropped on Arnhem were defeated, and the ground offensive halted, the sad prospect of another winter's campaign in Europe loomed.

4. LEYTE, OCTOBER 1944

By 1 August 1944, when the three largest Marianas and the entire northern coast of New Guinea were in American hands, the question of the next move became acute. Several previous plans for victory had envisioned an Allied base somewhere on the coast of China as a springboard for invading Japan, as Great Britain had been a springboard for invading Germany. But the Japanese army, in a fresh offensive starting in April 1944, captured most of the airdromes from which General Chen-

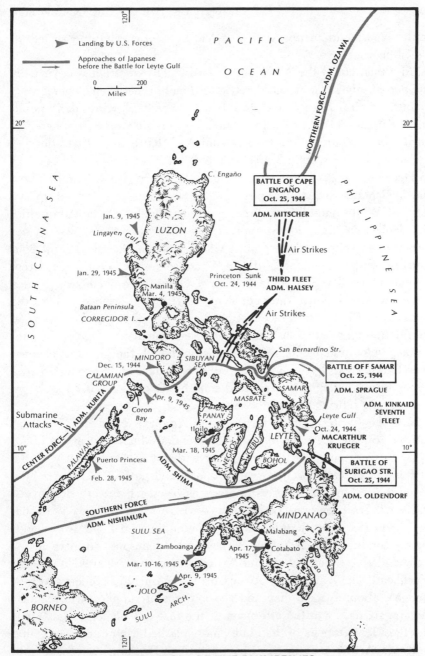

LIBERATION OF THE PHILIPPINES

nault's Fourteenth Army Air Force had been operating and sealed off the China coast.

How then could the Allies get at Japan? The question was virtually decided in July 1944, in a conference at Honolulu between General Mac-Arthur, Admiral Nimitz, and President Roosevelt. The President, pointing to Saipan on the map, said, 'Douglas, where do we go from here?' — 'Leyte, Mr. President; and then Luzon!' And that is how it was done.

The Joint Chiefs of Staff first set the date for the invasion of Leyte as 20 December 1944. At the suggestion of the aggressive Admiral Halsey, and to General MacArthur's pleasure, the timetable was stepped up two months. While amphibious forces were marshaling at the Admiralties and Hollandia, and slowly approaching their target, the fast carrier forces, four groups under Admiral Mitscher — nine fleet and eight light carriers, with attendant battleships, cruisers, and destroyers — rendezvoused in the Philippine Sea on 7 October, and embarked on a three-day 'knock-down, drag-out fight,' as Halsey described it, over the Ryukyus and Formosa. They destroyed over 500 planes at the cost of 89 aircraft and 64 aviators lost and two cruisers damaged. None of the supposedly vulnerable carriers was touched, although the Japanese claimed over the radio to have sunk them all — to which Halsey retorted in a dispatch to Nimitz, 'Ships reported sunk by Tokyo have been salvaged and are now retiring toward the enemy.'

Now the Central Pacific forces under Admirals Nimitz and Halsey, and the Southwest Pacific forces under General MacArthur and Admiral Kinkaid, were combined in one massive thrust in Leyte. Early in the morning of 20 October 1944, 73 transports and 50 LST's, covered by a dozen battleships and cruisers and a flock of escort carriers, destroyers, and small craft, entered Leyte Gulf — where Magellan, 423 years before, had discovered the Philippines. The landings on Leyte were handsomely conducted by Admirals Barbey and Wilkinson, and Sixth Army, commanded by General Walter Krueger, promptly secured a 20-mile beachhead. The X and XXIV Army Corps (Generals F. C. Sibert and J. R. Hodge), about 132,400 men and 200,000 tons of supplies, were landed the first six days. On the afternoon of the first day General MacArthur and President Osmeña of the Philippines splashed ashore from a landing craft. MacArthur announced: 'I have returned. By the grace of Almighty God our forces stand again on Philippine soil. . . . Rally to me. . . . Let no heart be faint.'

At Tokyo the war lords decided that now was the time to commit the entire Japanese fleet, defeat American forces afloat, and isolate MacArthur, so that he would be virtually back at Bataan. From that decision there resulted, on 25 October, the battle for Leyte Gulf, greatest sea fight of this or of any other war.

Admiral Toyoda put in execution a plan based on ruse and surprise, factors dear to Japanese strategists; but his plan required a division of the Japanese fleet into three forces, which proved to be fatal. Admiral Nishimura's Southern Force of battleships and cruisers was to come through Surigao Strait, break into Leyte Gulf at daybreak 25 October, and there rendezvous with Kurita's more powerful Center Force, which was to thread San Bernardino Strait and come around Samar from the north. Either separately was strong enough to make mincemeat of Admiral Kinkaid's amphibious forces in Leyte Gulf and cut off General Krueger's troops from their seaborne lifeline. Way was to be cleared for Kurita by Admiral Ozawa's Northern Force built around four carriers, whose mission was to entice Halsey's Task Force 38, the American carrier force, up north.

That part of the plan worked only too well, but the rest of it worked not at all. Admiral Kinkaid deployed almost every battleship, cruiser, and destroyer that had supported the Leyte landings, and placed them under the command of Rear Admiral Jesse Oldendorf, to catch Nishimura as he came through Surigao Strait in the early hours of 25 October. First a flock of motor torpedo boats fired their 'fish,' missed, but sent word ahead. Then, two destroyer torpedo attacks nicked Nishimura of one battleship and three destroyers. What was left of his 'T' was crossed by Oldendorf's battleships and cruisers. Their high-calibre fire sank the other enemy battleship and killed Admiral Nishimura; and what was left of the Southern Force fled, most of it to be harried and sunk after dawn by carrier planes. This emphatic night victory was the battlewagons' revenge for Pearl Harbor — five of the six there engaged had been sunk or grounded on 7 December 1941.

Scarcely was the Surigao Strait battle over when the most critical of the three actions began. Kurita's massive Center Force, built around his biggest battleships and heavy cruisers, had been damaged and delayed en route, first by two American submarines in Palawan Passage, then by carrier planes in the Sibuyan Sea, on 24 October. Halsey overestimated the damage that his bombers had done; and, after his search planes had found Admiral Ozawa's Northern Force of carriers coming down from Japan (with the express mission of luring him north), Halsey could think of just one thing — to sink those carriers. So, without leaving even a destroyer to watch San Bernardino Strait, Halsey tore up north to dispose of the enemy flattops.

Thus, Kurita, to his great astonishment, was able to leave the strait unopposed and approach the northern entrance to Leyte Gulf undetected. Off the island of Samar, at 6:45 a.m., 25 October, he ran smack into a force of six escort carriers under Rear Admiral Clifton Sprague. One of three groups of 'baby flattops' that were providing air cover for the amphibious forces in Leyte Gulf, it had expectation of fighting battleships, heavy cruisers, and destroyers. The ensuing battle off Samar was the most gallant naval action in our history, and the most bloody — 1130 Americans killed, 913 wounded. As soon as the Japanese big guns opened at a range of 14 miles, Sprague turned into the wind to launch planes, called for help from two other escort carrier groups, and sent his destroyers and DE's to make desperate gunfire and torpedo attacks. After a running fight of an hour and a half, two American destroyers and a DE were sunk; but the American bombs and torpedoes had sunk three Japanese heavy cruisers and, by repeated air attacks relentlessly pressed home, so badly mauled and scattered the other enemy ships that Admiral Kurita broke off action and retired. Thus, because the enemy commander lacked gumption and Sprague had plenty; and, still more, because the Japanese had no air support, a fleet more than ten times as powerful as the Americans in gunfire power was defeated.

Up north, Admiral Mark Mitscher's carriers were slicing off bombers and fighter planes against Ozawa's carriers which had decoyed him and Halsey up north. In this battle off Cape Engaño, all four Japanese carriers (including the last survivor of those which had struck Pearl Harbor) were sunk, with a trifling loss of planes and pilots on our side.

This three-part battle for Leyte Gulf on 25 October 1944 left the United States Navy in complete command of Philippine waters; never again could the Japanese navy offer a real threat. But two months' fighting ashore were required against the hard-fighting, no-surrender Japanese infantry before Leyte and Samar were in MacArthur's hands.

5. POLITICAL INTERLUDE

As the Allied armed forces fought ahead, another presidential election came up — the first in wartime since 1864 although in no war had the United States ever suspended elections. In World War II America's energies were devoted not only to winning the struggle against the Axis but to political and ideological battles for control at home. In some respects, the war was a boon to the New Dealers. TVA, Grand Coulee, and the other public power projects proved indispensable, private utility spokesmen who had claimed there would never be a marke : for so much power had to eat their words. Under the approving eye of the War Labor Board, union membership jumped to nearly 15 million by 1945.

The war resulted, too, in a revolutionary change in fiscal policy. By the middle of 1943, the United States was spending almost $190,000 a second to prosecute the war. Total Federal spending in the war years rose above $320 billion — twice the total of Federal expenditure in all the previous history of the republic. The national debt reached $280 billion, nearly six times the sum at the time of Pearl Harbor. When in 1936 the government outlay totaled eight billion dollars, critics had cried that the New Deal was inviting national bankruptcy. When the government spent $98 billion in 1945, few were concerned, for the country was enjoying boom prosperity. The war amply demonstrated the Keynesian hypothesis: with mounting deficits, unemployment disappeared.

Inevitably, the war enhanced the powers of the President and accelerated the aggrandizement of Federal bureaus. When Sewell Avery, the anti-union head of Montgomery Ward, resisted a government edict, Roosevelt ordered the Commerce Department to seize Ward's Chicago plant, even though the firm's operations were only remotely connected with the war. (Attorney General Francis Biddle boldly told a Federal court: 'No business or property is immune to a Presidential order. Particularly in time of war the Court should not substitute its judgment for that of the Executive.') Three olive drab army trucks rolled up to the doors, and a 44-man unit of battle-helmeted military police took over the plant. Told he could not return to his office, Avery flushed angrily and treated Biddle to the choicest invective he could think of: 'You New Dealer!' When the sixty-nine-year-old, white-haired Avery refused to budge, he was picked up and carried out by two helmeted soldiers,

Avery sitting, as though still reclining in his leather chair — his face grim but composed, his hands held together stoically, a white handkerchief neatly arranged in his breast pocket. A widely distributed photograph of this incident incensed conservatives. 'If the President has the power to take over Montgomery Ward,' said Senator Eastland, 'he has the power to take over a grocery store or butcher shop in any hamlet in the U.S.'

Yet if such episodes as the Avery affair demonstrated the strength of the New Dealers in wartime, it is also true that the war enhanced the power of the conservatives. The President frankly confessed that 'Dr. New Deal' had given way to 'Dr. Win-the-War.' Roosevelt and aides like Hopkins became preoccupied with the grand design of military strategy and diplomatic alliances. As the New Deal lost its momentum, political power shifted perceptibly to what Samuel Lubell has called the 'border state Democrats': men like Jimmie Byrnes and Fred Vinson who could mediate conflicts between the White House and Capitol Hill. Respected by Congress as tough legislative tacticians who were unlikely to advance 'visionary' ideas, the 'border state Democrats' headed the crucial war agencies and fixed the boundaries of what Roosevelt could hope to achieve in domestic affairs. When the 'visionary' Henry Wallace, who in 1942 proclaimed 'the century of the common man,' brawled with the business-minded Jesse Jones, Roosevelt was compelled to resolve the conflict by awarding victory to the Jones faction.

In the 1942 elections, the Republican Congressional candidates received more votes than Democrats for the first time since 1928. In New York, Thomas Dewey became that state's first Republican governor since 1920; in California, Attorney General Earl Warren was chosen governor. Although the meaning of the election was murky, for many Americans could not vote that year, conservatives interpreted it as a mandate for reaction. Ever since 1937 the coalition of conservative Southern Democrats and Republicans had been gaining power, and in World War II this alliance was cemented. The next session of Congress set out to dismantle the New Deal and drive liberals out of war agencies, and it had considerable success in both aims.

In 1944 organization Democrats insisted that Roosevelt drop Vice-President Wallace as his running mate and choose instead Missouri's Senator Harry S. Truman whose management of a Defense Investigating Committee (the 'Truman committee') had won him a national reputation for courage and fair-dealing. Another 'border state Democrat,' Truman satisfied the demand for a candidate who would be acceptable both to the New Dealers and the party bosses; the New York *Times* called him 'the new Missouri Compromise.' With no need this time for a 'draft,' Roosevelt won his party's presidential nomination for a fourth term on the first roll call. By 1944 millions of Americans could not recall when there had been anyone in the White House but FDR. The Chicago *Daily News* commented: 'If he was good enough for my pappy and my grandpappy, he is good enough for me.'

While the Democrats were using the vice-presidential nomination as a contest for party control, the Republican party was carrying on a similar struggle between its internationalist and isolationist wings for the GOP Presidential nomination in 1944. Leader of the internationalist wing was Wendell Willkie who in 1943 published an account of a trip around the world that had taken him to wartime Russia and China. The most influential book published during the war, *One World* both reflected and helped to create a remarkable shift of opinion away from traditional isolationism. By early 1943 the polls revealed that 76 per cent of respondents thought the United States should 'take an active part in world affairs' rather than 'stay out of world affairs as much as we can.' Yet much of isolationism had not died but submerged; it mushroomed in new forms such as support for General MacArthur and an 'Asia-first' strategy. Willkie learned the latent strength of the isolationists when Wisconsin voters failed to give him a single delegate; shut out in the Wisconsin primary, Willkie withdrew from the race, his political career at an end. With Willkie out, the contest for the Republican nomination in 1944 proved a runaway for New York's competent but colorless Governor Thomas E. Dewey.

Dewey, wanting the personal charm that made Willkie and F.D.R. so formidable, was a poor campaigner, and the issue was never in doubt. Although the President had less than 53 per cent of the vote, his following in the big cities swung large states with big blocks of electoral votes. Roosevelt carried 36 states with 432 electoral votes; Dewey, 12 states with 99 electoral votes; Roosevelt's popular plurality was about 3.5 million; the Democrats won 242 seats in the House, as against 190 for Republicans. Isolationists like Gerald Nye and Hamilton Fish went down to defeat, and internationalists like J. William Fulbright and Wayne Morse arrived in the Senate to strengthen the forces favoring world organization. The election marked the end of isolationism as a potent political factor. But, in a sense, it 'went underground,' to emerge nastily as Mc-Carthyism.

6. VICTORY IN EUROPE, SEPTEMBER 1944–MAY 1945

After the failure of the Arnhem air drop, the war temporarily lost its momentum and settled down to what General Eisenhower called 'the dirtiest kind of infantry slugging.' The Germans now held their strongest defensive positions since the beginning of the invasion. Rundstedt and Kesselring, ablest of their generals, were now commanders in the West and in Italy. And the winter of 1944–45 was one of the worst in memory: floods, cold, and snow combined to help the defense.

In the confused fighting that stretched from October to mid-December 1944 we can distinguish a series of battles, each as bitter as any of those that had been fought since Tunisia, and as costly. The first, taking them in geographical order, was the battle for the Scheldt estuary. The bloody task of clearing the enemy out of the islands, whose possession by the Germans prevented Allied use of Antwerp, was assigned to the Canadian First Army. Walcheren's reduction cost the Allies more casualties than the conquest of Sicily. Mine-sweeping and harbor clearance took so long that not until the end of November could Allied ships unload at Antwerp, and so shorten the logistics line.

The second major battle was for Aachen, near the junction of Belgium, Holland, and Germany. General Courtney H. Hodges's American First Army launched the attack on 2 October, fighting through five miles of Siegfried line fortifications. Before the end of the month, the ancient capital of Charlemagne capitulated. It was the first German city to fall to the Allies.

General Omar Bradley now brought the Ninth Army north to cooperate with the First in a campaign to capture the Roer river dams — third of the major battles. An assault by seventeen divisions through the Hürtgen Forest failed to do it. The country was not unlike that Wilderness in which Grant and Lee had tangled eighty years earlier. Three divisions alone, the 4th, 9th, and 28th, suffered almost 13,000 casualties. The Americans reached the Roer river on 3 December, but there they were stalled until early February.

To the south, General Patton's Third Army jumped off early in November to capture Metz, northern Lorraine, and the industrial Saar basin. Only once before in modern times — in 1871 — had the fortress city of Metz fallen to an invader. Patton proved that if need be, he could be methodical, instead of dashing. First he enveloped Metz, reducing one by one the forts that encircled it. Then came a week of street fighting. The city fell on 22 November, and the Third Army, fighting its way through the heaviest fortifications of the Siegfried line, plunged into the Saar. This campaign cost the Americans 29,000 battle casualties but netted them 37,000 prisoners.

In conjunction with Patton's advance, General Devers's Sixth Army Group launched an attack into Alsace; Strasbourg fell on 23 November. The French then turned north along the Rhine, the Americans south. These operations, obscured by the more dramatic fighting to the north, cost the Allies 33,000 more casualties.

By mid-December the Allied armies were poised all along the border from Holland to Switzerland, ready to plunge into Germany. Then came a dramatic change of fortune: a German counteroffensive. Rundstedt's name was given to this desperate thrust through the Ardennes Forest, but the idea was Hitler's. His objective was to split the Allied army groups, drive through to the coast, and recapture Antwerp. Eisenhower had taken the calculated risk of spreading thin his forces in the rugged Ardennes, through which Rundstedt had crashed with his main force in May 1940. Now the Germans prepared to repeat that successful campaign. Because bad weather prevented Allied air reconnaissance, they achieved surprise and success along a 50-mile front on 16 December. The Germans concentrated on the center of the Allied line, and as they thrust toward the Meuse, which they almost reached on 26 December, maps of the Western front showed a marked 'bulge' to indicate the advance of the Germans. But they were checked at Bastogne, a name long to be remembered. This little Belgian town, headquarters of General Troy Middleton's VIII Corps, was a center of a network of roads essential to the Germans. Middleton decided to hold it at all costs. Late in the night of 17 December the 101st Airborne Division, then in a rest center 100 miles behind the lines, was ordered to Bastogne; the men piled into trucks and jeeps and pulled into Bastogne on the 18th, just before the German tide flooded around the town. This reinforcement beefed up the strength of the defenders to some 18,000 men.

There followed one of the fiercest land battles of the war. The Americans seized outlying villages and set up a perimeter defense. For six days the enemy hurled armor and planes at them, persistently probing for a weak spot, and found not one. Foul weather prevented aerial rein-forcement of the defenders. On 22 December the American situation ap-peared hopeless, and the Germans presented a formal demand for sur-render, to which General 'Tony' McAuliffe of the 101st Airborne gave the simple answer 'Nuts!' Next day the weather cleared, and planes be-gan dropping supplies; by Christmas Eve, with bomber and fighter sup-port, the situation looked more hopeful. In the meantime, Patton's Third Army had made a great left wheel and started pell-mell north to the res-cue of the besieged garrison. On 26 December his 4th Armored Division broke through the German encirclement and Bastogne was saved. The Battle of the Bulge was not over, but by 15 January 1945 the original lines of mid-December had been restored. Rundstedt had held up the Allied advance by a full month, but at a cost of 120,000 men, 1600 planes, and a good part of his armor. Never thereafter were the Ger-mans able to put up an effective defense.

At the end of January, Eisenhower regrouped his armies and resumed advance toward the Rhine. In the meantime the Russians had sprung their winter offensive, which surpassed the campaign in the West in numbers involved and territory recaptured. The Russian army jumped off on a thousand-mile front early in January, crossed the Vistula, and swept toward Germany. While one group of armies in the center took Warsaw and raced across Poland to the Oder, others stabbed into Ger-many from the north and south, moved into Hungary and Czecho-slovakia, and threatened Vienna. This gigantic pincer movement inflicted over a million German casualties.

In the final Allied campaign in the West we can distinguish three stages: the advance to the Rhine, from late January to 21 March; the crossing of the Rhine and the Battle of the Ruhr, 21 March to 14 April; and the annihilation of all enemy opposition, 14 April to the surrender on 7 May.

First came a series of systematic mopping-up operations designed to clear the Germans out of all territory west of the Rhine. The Canadian First Army launched an attack in the north and reached the Rhine at Kleve. The American First and the Ninth fought through the Hürtgen Forest, crossed the Roer, and plunged on toward Cologne. Patton's Third Army, wheeling to the right again after the Ardennes battle, fought its way through the Siegfried line into Trier, and further south the French First Army cleared out the Colmar pocket. By the first week of March the Allied armies occupied the left bank of the Rhine from Holland to Switzerland, except in the triangle formed by the Eifel and the Palatinate.

That triangle did not remain long in German hands. Early in March, Patton broke loose again and drove forward in a great sweeping advance. Within five days he reached the Rhine, then wheeled south and raced through the Palatinate, mopping up over 60,000 prisoners at a cost of less than 800 men killed. 'No defeat suffered in the war, except possibly Tunisia,' wrote Eisenhower, 'was more devastating in the completeness of the destruction inflicted' on enemy forces. The 7th of March 1945 was one of the dramatic days of the war. On that day a detachment of the 9th Armored Division of the First Army captured the bridge over the Rhine at Remagen, just as the Germans were about to blow it. And on 22 March Patton began crossing the Rhine at Oppenheim, beating 'Monty' to the historic river.

The next move after vaulting the Rhine barrier was to encircle the Ruhr. Moving at breakneck speed — the 3rd Armored Division covered 90 miles in a single day — Hodges's First Army swung north, Simpson's Ninth turned south, and a giant pincer closed on the Ruhr, trapping some 400,000 Germans. Encircled, pounded on all sides, hammered day and night by swarms of bombers, the German armies caught in the pocket disintegrated. By 18 April the bag of prisoners reached a total of 325,000, and organized resistance ceased in the Ruhr. It was, said General Marshall, the largest envelopment operation in the history of American warfare; and it should be noted that this was Marshall's idea, violently opposed by Alan Brooke and 'Monty,' who wanted all Allied ground forces to be concentrated in one knifelike thrust across northern Europe, a concept which would have caused an impossible congestion and left the Ruhr in enemy hands.

Montgomery now drove toward Bremen and Hamburg, Patton raced for Kassel, and Patch sped through Bavaria toward Czechoslovakia.

As the Allied armies drove deep into Germany, Austria, and Poland, they came upon one torture camp after another — Buchenwald, Dachau, Belsen, Auschwitz, Linz, Lublin — and what they reported sickened the whole Western world. These atrocity camps had been established in 1937 for Jews, gypsies, and anti-Nazi Germans and Austrians;

with the coming of the war the Nazis used them for prisoners of all nationalities, civilians and soldiers, men, women, and children, and for Jews rounded up in Italy, France, Holland, and Hungary. All were killed in the hope of exterminating the entire race. In these camps, hordes of prisoners had been scientifically murdered; other multitudes had died of disease, starvation, and maltreatment. Much of this wholesale murder was done in the name of 'science,' and with the criminal collusion of German physicians. Nothing in their experience had prepared Americans for these revelations of human depravity. The total number of civilians done to death by Hitler's orders exceeded 6 million. And the pathetic story of one of the least of these, the diary of the little Jewish girl Anne Frank, has probably done more to convince the world of the hatred inherent in the Nazi doctrine than the solemn postwar trials.

As German resistance crumbled and victory appeared certain, the Western world was plunged into mourning by the news that a great leader had died. President Roosevelt, returning from the Yalta conference of the Combined Chiefs of Staff in February a sick man, went to his winter home in Warm Springs, Georgia, to prepare for the inauguration of the United Nations at San Francisco, which he hoped would usher in a new era of peace and justice. On 12 April, as he was drafting a Jefferson Day address, he suffered a cerebral hemorrhage which brought instant death. The last words he wrote were an epitome of his career: 'The only limit to our realization of tomorrow will be our doubts of today. Let us move forward with strong and active faith.'

The end was now in sight for Hitler's Germany. The Western Allies were rolling unopposed to the Elbe; the Russians were thrusting at Berlin. Advance detachments of the two armies met at Torgau on 25 April, severing Germany. On the last day of April, Hitler died a coward's death, killing first his mistress and then himself in a bombproof bunker under Berlin. German resistance was also collapsing in northern Italy. On 4 May General Mark Clark's Fifth Army, which had fought all the way up the boot of Italy, met, at the Brenner Pass, General Patch's Seventh, coming down through Austria, and next day German resistance in Italy ceased. Italian partisans had already captured Mussolini, complete with mistress, and killed them on 28 April. Thus ended, in ruin, horror, and despair, the Axis that pretended to rule the world and the Reich which Hitler had boasted would last a thousand years.

Admiral Doenitz, Hitler's designated heir and second Fuehrer, tried desperately to arrange a surrender to the Western Allies instead of Russia. Loyalty to our Eastern ally caused General Eisenhower sternly to decline these advances. And on 7 May General Jodl signed an unconditional surrender at Allied headquarters in Rheims.[1] Bradley, awakened by a telephone call from Eisenhower with the news, roused Patton, then opened his mapboard and smoothed out the tabs of the 43 divisions under his command.

'With a china-marking pencil, I wrote in the new date: D day plus 335.'

'I walked to the window and ripped open the blackout blinds. Outside the sun was climbing into the sky. The war in Europe had ended.'

7. VICTORY OVER JAPAN, 1945

Well before the landings at Leyte on 20 October 1944 the Joint Chiefs of Staff decided that as soon as the Third Fleet, with its carriers, could be relieved from supporting MacArthur in the Philippines, it should be used to secure island bases for a final assault on Japan. Tokyo, Saipan, and Formosa make an isosceles triangle with legs 1500 miles long. The eastern leg, Saipan-Tokyo, was already being used by the B-29 Superforts to bomb the Japanese homeland, but a halfway house was wanted through which fighter support could stage or where these Superforts could call if damaged. Iwo Jima, a desolate little island of coal-black lava, fitted the bill. After a two weeks' preliminary bombardment, a three-day intensive naval and carrier-plane bombardment drove the Japanese from the landing beaches, and Kelly Turner's seasoned Fifth Fleet team, with Major General Harry Schmidt commanding the marines, went in on 19 February 1945. Mount Suribachi, scene of the famous flag-raising, was captured on 23 February; after that it was a steady, bloody advance of the marines against the holed-up enemy, with constant naval fire support. Even before organized resistance ceased on 14 March, the B-29's began using the Iwo airfields; and it is estimated that by this means thousands of American lives were saved. But Iwo, which cost the navy and marine corps some 6800 deaths and 21,000 other casualties, was remembered with a special kind of horror, for the island seemed too small for all the killing it absorbed.

1. V-E Day is celebrated on 8 May because the surrender became effective at 2301 that day, Central European time.

In the meantime another angle of the triangle, whose apex was Tokyo, had been shifted to Okinawa in the Ryukyus, several hundred miles nearer Japan than is Formosa and less stoutly defended. Sixty-mile long Okinawa, where Commodore Perry had called in 1853, was an integral part of Japan. It was expected that when we attacked the Japanese would 'throw the book at us,' and they did. They had few warships left and American command of the sea prevented reinforcement of the island garrison; but they had plenty of planes and self-sacrificing pilots to employ the deadly kamikaze tactics. The Kamikaze ('Divine Wind') Corps was organized as a desperate expedient after the use of proximity-fused anti-aircraft shells by the United States Navy had made it almost impossible for a conventional bomber to hit a ship. The kamikaze pilots were trained to crash a ship, which meant certain death for a large part of its crew and probable loss of the vessel. These tactics had already been tried in the Philippines campaign, with devastating success, and no defense against them had yet been found, except to station radar picket destroyers around the fleet, to take the rap and pass the word.

The Spruance-Turner team was in charge of the amphibious assault on Okinawa, with General Simon B. Buckner (who lost his life there) commanding Tenth Army. And, as the war in Europe was drawing to a close, the British contributed a task force built around four carriers with steel decks — useful insurance against kamikaze-kindled fires — which neutralized the Japanese airfields between Okinawa and Formosa.

American amphibious technique was now so perfected that when the four divisions went ashore on Okinawa on Easter Sunday, 1 April, the Japanese abandoned beaches and airfields and retired to prepared positions on the southern end of the island. Here they put up a desperate resistance, exacting a heavy toll of American lives, before the island was finally conquered late in June. In the meantime the navy, which had to cover the operation and furnish fire support, took a terrific beating from the kamikaze planes. Twenty-seven ships, fifteen of them destroyer types, were sunk, and sixty-one others were so badly damaged as to be out of the war; casualties were heavy even on the ships that survived. Seven carriers were badly damaged by kamikazes — *Franklin*, *Wasp*, and *Bunker Hill* between them lost 2211 men killed and 798 wounded — but not one was sunk. The total cost to the United States of the invasion of Okinawa was over 12,500 killed and over 62,500 wounded; but the island as a base proved indispensable not only in the closing weeks of World War II but in the cold war that followed and the war in Vietnam.

With Germany defeated, the Allies could give their undivided attention to knocking out Japan. A new British offensive, by land and sea, captured Mandalay and Rangoon in the spring of 1945 and soon pushed the Japanese out of Burma. While in great secrecy scientists were preparing the atomic bombs at Los Alamos, the navy and the army air force redoubled the fury of their attacks on the Japanese home islands. There were bombings by carrier planes, naval bombardments, and B-29 bombing raids directed by General LeMay of the Air Strategic Command. Large parts of Tokyo and other industrial cities were destroyed by incendiary bombs.

During the assaults on the outlying Japanese islands, General Eichelberger's Eighth Army and Admiral Kinkaid's Seventh Fleet — both under General MacArthur — were completing the liberation of the Philippines. They captured the ruins of Manila, where the Japanese made a house-to-house defense, on 4 March 1945. There the Philippine Commonwealth, soon to become the Philippine Republic, was promptly reestablished. Before Japan surrendered, the rest of the archipelago was liberated.

Destruction of merchant shipping by the submarines of the Pacific Fleet was one of the three main factors that brought victory over Japan. The 50 American submarines (at a maximum) operating daily in the Pacific in 1944 were almost twice as effective as over 100 German U-boats operating daily in the Atlantic in 1942–43. Japan had 6 million tons of merchant shipping at the start of the war and added another 4 million tons by conquest and new construction; but at the end she had left only 1.8 million tons, mostly small wooden vessels in the Inland Sea, and was completely cut off from her early conquests. United States forces alone sank 2117 Japanese merchant vessels of almost 8 million tons during the war, and 60 per cent of this was done by submarines, of which 50 were lost in action. The Japanese submarines did sink several big American warships, but inflicted slight damage on the merchant marine and lost 128 of their number, U.S.S. *England* sinking six in thirteen days of May 1944. Admiral Charles A. Lockwood, commanding all submarines of the United States Pacific Fleet, was one of our outstanding naval leaders in the war.

The Combined Chiefs of Staff, meeting at Quebec in September 1944, figured that it would take eighteen months after the surrender of Germany to defeat Japan. Actually, the war in the Pacific ended with a terrific bang only three months after V-E Day. President Truman and Winston Churchill, meeting with the C.C.S. at Potsdam, presented Japan with an ultimatum on 26 July 1945. The surrender must be complete, and must include an Allied occupation of Japan and the return of all Japanese conquests since 1895 to their former owners. But the Japanese people were assured that the occupation would end as soon as 'a peacefully inclined and responsible government' was established and that they would neither 'be enslaved as a race or destroyed as a nation.' The alternative was 'prompt and utter destruction.' If the government of Suzuki, the Japanese premier, had made up its mind promptly to accept the Potsdam declaration as a basis for peace, there would have been no atomic bomb explosion over Japan. But Suzuki was more afraid of Japanese militarists than of American power.

The fearful consequences resulted from long experiment and development in atomic fission. In 1939 Albert Einstein, Enrico Fermi, Leo Szilard and other physicists who had sought refuge in the United States from tyranny in their native countries warned President Roosevelt of the danger of Germany's obtaining a lead in uranium fission. In the summer of 1940 Fermi, assisted by members of Columbia's football team, began to build an atomic pile. Using a mighty cyclotron, or 'atom smasher,' Dr. Ernest Lawrence of the University of California solved the problem of turning out fissionable material in sufficient quantities. The President assigned responsibility for further developments to the Office of Scientific Research and Development, set up in May 1941 under the direction of Vannevar Bush and James B. Conant.[2] (One unanticipated consequence of this war research was a marriage of the university to the military operations of the national government which in the postwar years would raise a serious threat to the independence of the American university.) By December Fermi and others, working in the squash court at the University of Chicago's Stagg Field, achieved the first self-sustaining nuclear chain reaction, halfway mark to the atomic bomb. Army engi-

2. The Office of Scientific Research and Development supervised such developments in military technology as the proximity fuse and short-range rockets, notably the 'bazooka.' The government also fostered the achievement of the 'miracle drug,' penicillin, soon to be followed by streptomycin. DDT also proved effective during the war.

neers under General Leslie Groves then took over, under the code name 'Manhattan District,' and built small cities at Oak Ridge, Tenn., and Hanford, Wash., to make plutonium. As research progressed, a special laboratory was erected at Los Alamos, New Mexico, for which J. Robert Oppenheimer was responsible.

On 16 July 1945, scientists and military men gathered before dawn on the New Mexico desert, their eyes covered with dark glasses, their faces with anti-sunburn cream, some of the young scientists unnerved by the tension, Oppenheimer holding onto a post to steady himself. With the word, 'Now!' the bomb was detonated. A blinding flash illuminated the desert, and an enormous fireball, changing colors from deep purple to orange to 'unearthly green' erupted skyward. Following the fireball, a great column rose from the ground, eventually taking the mushroom shape that was to symbolize the new age; pushing through the clouds, it reached a height of 41,000 feet. Then came a wave of intense heat and a thunderous roar; the ground trembled as though shaken by an earthquake. Oppenheimer was reminded of the passage from the *Bhagavad-Gita:* 'I am become Death, the shatterer of worlds.' Another scientist commented: 'This was the nearest to doomsday one can possibly imagine. I am sure that at the end of the world — in the last millisecond of the earth's existence — the last man will see something very similar to what we have seen.'

President Truman conveyed the news at Potsdam to Winston Churchill, who remarked 'This is the Second Coming, in wrath.' That, indeed, it was for Japan; eventually, perhaps, for the entire world.

We had it, but whether or not to use it was another question. President Truman's committee of high officials and top atomic scientists recommended that atomic bombs be exploded over Japan at once, and without warning. On 25 July the President issued the necessary order to prepare to drop the bombs at the first favorable moment after 3 August, if Japan had not accepted surrender. He hoped that the enemy would reconsider his scornful answer to the Potsdam declaration; but, as he did not, the fateful order stood.

'Enola Gay,' as the chosen B-29 was called, was commanded by Colonel Paul W. Tibbets. At 9:15 a.m., 6 August, the bomb was toggled out at 31,600 feet, at a speed of 328 m.p.h., over Hiroshima. This city had been given the tragic target assignment as the second most important military center in Japan. The bomb wiped out the Second Japanese Army to a man, razed four square miles of the city, and killed 60,175 people including the soldiers. That morning the dreadfully-burned survivors moved through the city, eerily silent, holding their arms out before them to prevent the burned surfaces from touching, hoping in vain that someone could ease their pain. Of the 1780 nurses in the city, 1654 had been killed instantly or were too badly hurt to work; most of the doctors were dead or wounded. That afternoon people who seemed to have escaped unharmed died, the first signs of the effects of radiation. At about noon 9 August, a few hours after Russia declared war on Japan, the second atomic bomb was exploded over Nagasaki, killing 36,000 more.

Should the United States have used this most terrible of weapons? Having revealed its dreadful potentialities over Hiroshima, should we have used it a second time over Nagasaki? That is a question men will ask for a hundred years, if the atomic weapon allows mankind another hundred years. On the one hand it can be said that had we not brought Japan to her knees by this awful display of power, the war might have dragged on for another year, with incomparably greater loss of lives, both Japanese and American; for Japan still had more than 5000 planes with kamikaze trained pilots, and a million ground troops prepared to contest every beachhead and every city. The explosion over Hiroshima caused fewer civilian casualties than the repeated B-29 bombings of Tokyo, and those big bombers would have had to wipe out one city after another if the war had not ended in August. On the other hand it is asserted that destruction of her merchant marine and the blockade had brought Japan to the verge of defeat, that she could have been strangled without invasion. Long-range considerations are likewise surrounded by uncertainty. It can be said that had we not used atomic weapons, others would have done so, for neither their mechanisms nor their potential were secrets. But it can be argued, too, that had we shown restraint, others might have shown comparable restraint and that in any event, no matter what the future held, the responsibility — or guilt — of the use of this most dreadful of all weapons would not be ours. Honorable and humane men made the fateful decision to drop the two atomic bombs; honorable and humane men may, in time, conclude that it was the most mistaken decision in the history of warfare.

Even after the two atomic bombs had been dropped, and the Potsdam declaration had been clarified to assure the Japanese that they could keep their emperor, the surrender was a very near thing. Hirohito had to override his two chief military advisers, Admiral Toyoda and General Umezu, and take the repsonsiblity of accepting the Potsdam terms. That he did at 10:50 p.m., 14 August. Even thereafter, a military *coup d'état* to sequester the emperor, kill his cabinet, and continue the war was narrowly averted. Yet the gloom of the postwar years owed not a little to the awareness that a liberal, democratic government had not scrupled to unleash a weapon which might mean the end of mankind.

After preliminary arrangements had been made at Manila with General MacArthur's and Admiral Nimitz's staffs, an advance party was flown into Atsugi airfield near Tokyo on 28 August. Scores of ships of the United States Pacific Fleet, and of the British Far Eastern Fleet, then entered Tokyo Bay. On 2 September 1945 General MacArthur, General Umezu, the Japanese foreign minister, and representatives of Great Britain, China, Russia, Australia, Canada, New Zealand, the Netherlands, and France signed the surrender documents on the deck of battleship *Missouri,* a few miles from the spot where Commodore Perry's treaty had been signed 82 years before.

At 9:25 a.m., as the formalities closed, a flight of hundreds of aircraft swept over *Missouri* and her sister ships. General MacArthur then addressed a broadcast to the people of the United States:

> A new era is upon us. . . . Men since the beginning of time have sought peace . . . military alliances, balances of power, leagues of nations, all in turn failed, leaving the only path to be by the way of the crucible of war. . . . The utter destructiveness of war now blots out this alternative. We have had our last chance. If we do not devise some greater and more equitable system, Armageddon will be at our door.

In this stern and solemn setting, Japan acknowledged her total defeat in a war forced upon her by a clique of ambitious and reckless militarists.

XXV

A Fair Deal

1. RECONVERSION

When, on 12 April 1945, Franklin D. Roosevelt died and the Vice-President took the oath of office as President, there were some who affected to ask, 'Who is Harry S. Truman?' just as a century earlier some had asked, 'Who is James K. Polk?' At both times the questions were rhetorical. Truman came to the presidency with longer experience in politics than Theodore Roosevelt, Woodrow Wilson, or Herbert Hoover. Twelve years in Missouri politics had trained him to appreciate the realities of party organization, and two terms in the United States Senate had quickened his mind and enlarged his views. He seemed — as he looked — the very epitome of the average small-town American: pithy and idiomatic in speech, easy-going, friendly and self-confident, hating all pretense and injustice. Like Lincoln and Wilson, once in office he revealed an astonishing capacity for growth. In matters of domestic politics and personalities he often spoke, and acted, impulsively; intensely loyal to his friends, he was inclined to overlook even their more flagrant shortcomings. Too often he surrounded himself with men unsympathetic to the cause he espoused. But these failings appeared venial when contrasted with his virtues: boldness, decisiveness, and courage. Truman's domestic record, which seemed modest by comparison with that of his predecessor, came to seem more respectable when compared with that of his successor, and no other President in our history — not even FDR — did so much to shape our foreign policy as did this unassuming man from Missouri.

Truman not only had to lead the country in the final months of the war but guide it through the difficult transition from war to peace. Fortunately, reconversion presented fewer and less onerous problems than had been anticipated. Twelve million service men and women were absorbed into civilian life with no greater difficulty than half that number in 1919. Industry changed over easily enough from a war to a peace basis. The postwar depression many had feared never materialized. But if there was no political reaction comparable to that which had been dramatized by the change from Wilson to Harding, the nation experienced something even more unpleasant: the cold war and the security hysteria.

Unlike the aftermath of World War I, the Truman years saw a continuation and expansion of wartime prosperity. Veterans had little difficulty finding work, and unemployment remained low; reconversion to civilian economy was swift; the dammed-up demand for consumer goods seemed insatiable. In the five years after the war, national production increased from $213 billion to $284 billion, national income from $181 billion to $241 billion, and consumer income from $151 billion to $208 billion. More important, the maintenance of full employment, high wages, and high farm prices accelerated the redistribution of national income. In 1935 over one-half the workers of the country earned less than $1000; by 1950 only one-tenth of the workers were in this unhappy category. In 1935 only one out of six American families enjoyed an income of over $2000 a year, and only 6 per cent over $3000; by 1950 three fourths of all families earned over $2000, and half over $3000, a year. A sharp increase in the cost of living, to be sure, qualified these statistics, but even so it was clear that the war and postwar prosperity, together with the new tax policies, had achieved a greater approach to economic equality than Americans had known since the Civil War.

Even the farmers, the group most sensitive to the economic cycle, continued to enjoy unprecedented prosperity. Sustained by an insatiable demand for foodstuffs abroad, by higher standards of living at home, and by government subsidies, farm income actually increased by $5 billion between 1945 and 1948: total farm income in 1948 was over $30 billion as compared with $11 billion in 1941 and $5.5 billion in 1933. As a consequence, farm mortgages fell by $2 billion between 1940 and 1950, and farm tenancy to the lowest point in the twentieth century.

What was the explanation of this phenomenon, which appeared to justify the claims of private enterprise and to confound the Communists, who had confidently expected an economic collapse in the United States? It was, in part, that five years of war had created a vast demand for consumer and durable goods; in part, the market for American surpluses assured by the program of relief and reconstruction abroad; in part, the explosive increase in private investment; in part, the continuation of heavy government spending after the war. At the depth of the depression the Federal Government had spent about $9 billion; five years after the war the Federal budget ran over $40 billion, most of which was pumped into the domestic economy.

The government underwrote the expansion in a number of other ways, not least in speeding demobilization, which got under way with the surrender of Germany and proceeded swiftly — perhaps too swiftly — after victory in the Pacific. Within a year the armed services had been reduced from 12 million to 3 million, and by 1950 to well below one million. The shock of the transition from the armed services to civilian life was cushioned by elaborate laws providing mustering-out pay, unemployment pay for one year, job reinstatement and seniority rights, civil-service preferment, insurance, loans for home building and the purchase of farms or businesses, generous subsidies for education or apprentice training, and elaborate provision for health and medical care. Eventually some 12 million veterans took advantage of the education subsidies of the 'G.I. Bill of Rights,' and the college population of the country increased by over a million.

Yet if reconversion went more smoothly than had been expected, Truman nonetheless faced one grievous problem: inflation. Manufacturers and farmers, who had bridled at wartime controls, wanted to exploit a sellers' market, and consumers, their pockets bulging, demanded goods that had been denied them during the war. The President was expected both to get rid of controls and prevent inflation, and he could anticipate political reprisals if he failed to achieve this impossible assignment. While Roosevelt in the depression years had been able to distribute benefits to interest groups as a part of his recovery program, Truman had to discipline interest groups at the very time when peace encouraged them to expect new gains.

When Truman sided with John Snyder, a conservative Missouri banker whom he had named director of the Office of War Mobilization and Reconversion, against Chester Bowles, the OPA administrator who

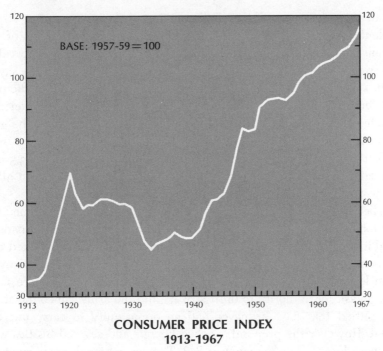

CONSUMER PRICE INDEX
1913-1967

represented the consumer, he antagonized New Deal liberals who wanted to keep a tight lid on prices. Roosevelt's followers had been impressed when on 6 September 1945 Truman outlined a twenty-one point program of far-reaching reforms, but they were dismayed by Truman's support of Snyder and his appointment of other conservatives to his cabinet and the Supreme Court. Before long, Roosevelt stalwarts like Harold Ickes had fled the government in protest.

Yet when Truman did take a firmer stand against inflation, he added to his difficulties with the liberal wing of his party, because he ran into a head-on conflict with union labor. After the war, fear of rising costs of living, the prospect of a return to the 40-hour week with consequent loss of overtime pay, and the belief that labor had not shared as fully in the general prosperity as had capital, brought a demand for substantial wage increases. Clearly, too, this was the ideal time to strike: business was eager to get back to normal production, and ready enough to pass higher costs on to the consumer; the public was eager to buy. Within a month after victory over Japan half a million workers were out on strike, while the year 1946 saw 4.6 million workers on strike, with a loss of 116 million man-days of work. If Truman did not find some way to call a halt, wages and prices threatened to chase one another up to the sky.

On 1 April 1946 John L. Lewis led 400,000 coal miners out of the pits, and for forty days the strike cut off the nation's supply of fuel and threatened European recovery. On 21 May, after a brief truce, the government took over the mines. When Lewis refused to order his men back to work, a Federal court slapped the union with a fine of $3.5 million, later reduced to $700,000. Yet, eventually, Lewis won almost all of his demands, but at the cost of mounting anti-union sentiment.

When in the midst of this crisis railway union leaders threatened the first total strike on the roads since 1894, Truman seized the railroads to head it off. But in defiance of the President the rail workers walked out, marooning 90,000 passengers and stopping 25,000 freight cars, many of them loaded with perishables. On 25 May, Truman went before Congress to ask for authority to draft strikers into the army. Since the strike was settled that day, he never had an opportunity to carry out this threat. However the proposal shocked liberals and severed his ties with union leaders. 'Labor,' announced R. J. Thomas, national secretary of the CIO Political Action Committee, 'is through with Truman.' Yet when Congress enacted a milder labor measure, Truman irked conservatives by vetoing it. The politics of inflation was costing the President support at both ends of the political spectrum.

Five weeks after Truman's threat to draft the rail strikers, he confronted a showdown on price control, for on 1 July 1946 the authority of the OPA would expire. When just before the deadline Congress passed a bill which eviscerated the OPA, Truman vetoed it, although this left the nation temporarily with no controls. In two weeks prices jumped 25 per cent, more than in the previous three years. When Congress enacted a new measure, stockmen held back their cattle, and meat all but disappeared. Truman's popularity fell from a peak of 87 per cent to 32 per cent, and Republicans jeered at 'Horsemeat Harry.' Unfairly blamed for the meat shortage, Truman on 14 October announced he had no alternative but to take off controls on meat. When meat returned to the butcher's counter, housewives were incensed to find that it commanded sharply increased prices.

At the height of national annoyance over the price control controversy, the country went to the polls in the 1946 elections. Exasperated by high prices, inexplicable shortages,[1] and administrative incompetence, voters gave the Republicans a majority of Congress for the first time since 1930. They sent to the Senate for the first time that year such conservatives as John Bricker of Ohio and the little known Joseph McCarthy, who toppled the La Follette dynasty in Wisconsin, and to the House thirty-three-year-old Richard Nixon. The election was interpreted as a brutal repudiation of Truman's leadership. Democratic Senator William Fulbright of Arkansas advised the President to name a Republican Secretary of State and resign from office, a proposal supported by such Democratic newspapers as the Chicago *Sun* and the Atlanta *Constitution*. Mr. Truman rejected this gratuitous advice, but four days after the election he removed most of the remaining controls.

2. THE EIGHTIETH CONGRESS

The 1946 elections gave the Republicans an opportunity to demonstrate that they were a party of moderation, but the Eightieth Congress misinterpreted the vote, which reflected a momentary impatience over reconversion, as a mandate for reaction. They not only rejected Truman's proposals to raise the minimum wage and extend social security coverage but turned down modest proposals by Republican Senator Robert Taft of Ohio for Federal action in education and housing. Bricker complained: 'I hear the Socialists have gotten to Taft.' While turning in a creditable performance on foreign policy, the 80th Congress squandered the political advantage of the 1946 elections by antagonizing farmers by failing to provide adequate crop-storage facilities, Westerners by slashing funds for power and reclamation projects, and various ethnic groups by enacting an anti-Semitic, anti-Catholic displaced persons law. When the lifting of controls resulted in a price rise from 1946 to 1947 greater than in all of World War II, people on fixed incomes were caught in the inflationary squeeze.

If Senator Taft differed with the Bricker wing of his party on some welfare measures, he shared their determination to curb organized labor. The Taft-Hartley Act of 1947, which he co-sponsored, outlawed the closed shop and the secondary boycott; made unions liable for breach of

1. Wrote the commentator David Cohn, 'A housewife who cannot get hamburger is more dangerous than Medea wronged.'

contract or damages resulting from jurisdictional disputes; required a
60-day cooling-off period for strikes; authorized an 80-day injunction
against strikes that might affect national health or safety; forbade political contributions from unions, featherbedding, and excessive dues;
required union leaders to take a non-Communist oath; and set up a conciliation service outside the Labor Department, which was suspected of
being too friendly to labor. Truman vetoed this bill on the ground that it
would

> reverse the basic direction of our national labor policy, inject the
> government into private economic affairs on an unprecedented scale,
> and conflict with important principles of our democratic society. Its
> provisions would cause more strikes, not fewer. It would contribute
> neither to industrial peace nor to economic stability and progress.
> . . . It contains seeds of discord which would plague this nation
> for years to come.

Congress, however, re-enacted the bill by thumping majorities. Whether
the Taft-Hartley bill 'plagued the nation' or not, it certainly plagued the
Republican party. It drove organized labor back into Truman's arms, and
in 1948 union members returned to private life many Republican supporters of the act, including Representative Fred Hartley, Jr.

The Republicans muffed an even more promising opportunity to
capitalize on Democratic vulnerability when they failed to enact civil
rights legislation and chose instead to coalesce with Southern Democrats
to block reforms. It was President Truman who seized the initiative, in
part because he understood that at a time when the United States was
competing with Soviet Russia for the allegiance of the uncommitted nations events in Mississippi and Alabama were watched closely in Accra
and Nairobi. In his famous Peoria speech Abraham Lincoln had charged
that slavery

> deprives our republican example of its just influence in the world;
> enables the enemies of free institutions with plausibility to taunt us
> as hypocrites; causes the real friends of freedom to doubt our sin-
> cerity; and forces so many good men among ourselves into an open
> war with the very fundamental principles of civil liberty.

The denial of civil and political rights to Negroes and other minority
groups during World War II and after had much the same effect. As
Secretary of State Dean Acheson observed:

The existence of discrimination against minority groups in this country has an adverse effect upon our relations with other countries. . . . Frequently we find it next to impossible to formulate a satisfactory answer to our critics in other countries; the gap between the things we stand for in principle and the facts of a particular situation may be too wide to be bridged.

In response to protest against a number of racial murders in the South in 1946, the President that December appointed a President's Committee on Civil Rights which on 29 October 1947, after ten months of study, issued its historic report, 'To Secure These Rights.' On 2 February 1948 Truman asked Congress to implement this report by approving a ten-point program which embraced a permanent Civil Rights Commission, a Federal Fair Employment Practices Act, and legislation to protect the right to vote, do away with poll taxes, and prevent lynching.

Spurned by the Republican 80th Congress and denounced by Southern senators in his own party, Truman refused to back down. He increased the pace of desegregation of the armed forces and issued an executive order which stipulated that there was to be no discrimination in Federal employment. No President in at least seventy-five years had done so much for the cause of civil rights. Yet by his actions Truman infuriated Southern whites who feared that their social system was collapsing at a time when the Supreme Court was ruling restrictive covenants unenforceable and when Jackie Robinson was breaking the color line in baseball. The President appeared to have ensured his defeat in the 1948 election.

Only in the area of governmental reorganization did the 80th Congress make important contributions, and here too Truman played an important role. The Presidential Succession Act of 1947 provided that the Speaker of the House and the President of the Senate should be next in line of presidential succession after the Vice-President. That same year Congress wreaked posthumous vengeance on FDR by adopting a proposed Twenty-second Amendment limiting Presidents to two terms; the amendment was ratified in 1951, an indication of growing concern over presidential power. In 1947 Congress also voted to establish a commission to study the whole problem of governmental administration. Truman appointed Herbert Hoover chairman of the commission, which made a series of reports recommending the reduction of Federal departments and agencies from 65 to 23 and the creation of a Department of

Health and Welfare. Congress authorized the President to submit plans for reorganization which would go into effect unless it disapproved, an unusual arrangement under which Truman submitted no less than 36 reorganization plans, all of which went through except the one calling for a Department of Health and Welfare; that was blocked temporarily by Southern votes.

To end bickering, jealousy, and competition between the army, navy, and air force, an act of 1947 created a single National Defense Establishment under a Secretary of Defense; two years later this was reorganized as the Department of Defense. The National Security Act also set up a National Security Council, a Central Intelligence Agency, and a National Security Resources Board, and gave legal status to the Joint Chiefs of Staff. The passage of the act owed much to the leadership of President Truman and the skill of Secretary of the Navy James V. Forrestal, who become the first Secretary of Defense, an office with cabinet rank.

The Truman years marked a transition from the informal personal presidency of the Roosevelt era to the institutionalized White House of the Eisenhower years. By 1947 the President was filing three separate messages to Congress: State of the Union, Budget, and Economic Report, the latter as a consequence of the Employment Act of 1946 which created a three-man Council of Economic Advisers to aid the President. Although Congress insisted on leaving the main responsibility for economic decision-making in private hands, this law indicated that Congress recognized a degree of government responsibility for the health of the economy, and in subsequent years the reports of the Council helped educate the country in the new economics. That same year the Atomic Energy Act, drafted by Senator Brien MacMahon, created yet another agency, the Atomic Energy Commission. This proliferation of institutions enabled the President to cope with a wider range of problems than had faced any of his predecessors.

3. THE 1948 ELECTION

The Democratic convention in July 1948 opened in gloom. The setbacks in 1946 and subsequent rifts in the party convinced almost everyone that Truman could not win; delegates wore campaign buttons reading, 'We're just Mild about Harry.' But when a last-minute attempt to persuade General Eisenhower to take the nomination failed, Truman was nominated by default. The administration sought to unite the party on a moderate civil rights plank, but Hubert Humphrey, the young mayor of Minneapolis, fought for a stronger commitment. 'I say the time has come to walk out of the shadow of states' rights and into the sunlight of human rights,' Humphrey cried. When the convention adopted Humphrey's substitute plank, Mississippi and Alabama delegates, waving the battle flag of the Confederacy, marched out of the hall. Within a week the 'Dixiecrats' had organized a States Rights party with Governor J. Strom Thurmond of South Carolina as their presidential nominee.

At the same time that the Dixiecrats were cutting off one flank of the Democratic party, opponents of Truman's foreign policy were severing another. In September 1946 the President had dropped Henry Wallace from his cabinet because he had become too vocal a critic of the administration's Cold War tactics. In July 1948 his followers organized the Progressive party with Wallace as their candidate. Although the platform of the new party included such demands as the nationalization of basic industries, it centered its fire at such fixtures of Truman's foreign policy as the Marshall plan. The party's uncritical attitude toward Soviet Russia deprived it of much of its potential support, but observers reckoned that Wallace would cut heavily into Truman's vote in the North and West.

All but guaranteed victory, the Republicans felt confident enough to nominate a former loser, Thomas E. Dewey, with the liberal governor of California, Earl Warren, as his running mate. Dewey ran a deliberately cautious campaign, during which he made such startling observations as 'We need a rudder to our ship of state and . . . a firm hand at the tiller,' 'Our streams should abound with fish,' and 'Our future lies before us.' Dewey sought the presidency, one writer noted, with the 'humorless calculation of a Certified Public Accountant in pursuit of the Holy Grail.'

Truman, on the other hand, made full use of the powers of his office to wage a vigorous campaign to remould the Roosevelt coalition. Throughout the election year he fired a series of messages to Congress calling for specific reforms, and that summer he called Congress back into a special session on 26 July, the day turnips are planted in Missouri. When the 'turnip Congress' did nothing, Truman was well on his way to making the issue of the campaign not Dewey's record but the performance of the 'do-nothing, good-for-nothing' 80th Congress. On a 22,000-mile 'give-em hell, Harry' whistle-stop tour, the President met an enthusiastic response. Still, almost every political expert, and pollsters like George Gallup and Elmo Roper, predicted defeat for Truman. The heavy Dewey margin, Roper noted, bore 'an almost morbid resemblance to the Roosevelt-Landon figures.'

To the astonishment not only of the prognosticators but of the nation, Truman scored the biggest political upset of the century.[2] *Le Figaro*, stealing a line from Henri IV, advised, 'Brave Gallup, Go Hang Yourself.' Thurmond captured four Southern states, and Wallace, while winning no electoral votes, deprived Truman of New York, Michigan, and Maryland. But the President ran well among workers, Negroes, and farmers, many of whom resented the failings of the 80th Congress. Dewey had 'snatched defeat out of the jaws of victory,' while Truman, running as the candidate of the majority party in an election with a surprisingly low turnout, got enough of the party faithful to the polls to prevail.

Truman benefited too from the strong array of Democratic candidates running for Congress and governorships. The party recaptured control of both houses of Congress, winning a majority of 12 in the upper chamber and 93 in the House. To the Senate came Humphrey of Minnesota, Paul Douglas, a University of Chicago economics professor, from Illinois, Estes Kefauver of Tennessee, and, by the tiny margin of 87 votes, 'Landslide Lyndon' Johnson of Texas. The Democrats won 21 out of 33 gubernatorial contests, and among the Democratic victors were prominent liberals like Chester Bowles in Connecticut and Adlai Stevenson in Illinois. The Roosevelt coalition, which had seemed shattered two years before, had taken a new lease on life.

4. FAIR DEAL LEGISLATION

The 81st Congress, which met for the first time in January 1949, enacted more liberal legislation than any Congress since 1938. It increased social

2. The vote was:	Popular	Per Cent	Electoral College
Truman	24,179,345	49.6	303
Dewey	21,991,291	45.1	189
Thurmond	1,176,125	2.4	39
Wallace	1,157,326	2.4	0

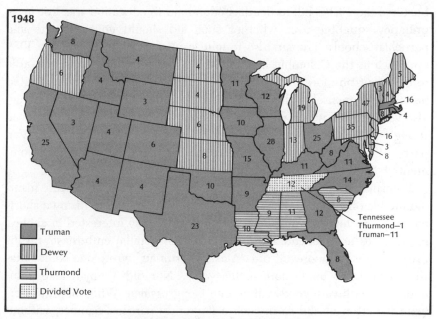

PRESIDENTIAL ELECTION, 1948

security benefits and extended coverage to ten million more people; raised the minimum wage from 40 to 75 cents an hour; expanded public power, rural electrification, soil conservation, and flood control projects; approved a more generous, but still inadequate, Displaced Persons Act; set up a National Science Foundation; and granted the President powers to cope with inflation. By adroitly exploiting middle-class dissatisfaction with the housing shortage, Truman put through a law which authorized new public housing for the slum-dweller. The National Housing Act of 1949 provided for the construction of 810,000 subsidized low-income housing units over the next six years, as well as grants for slum clearance and rural housing.

However, most of this legislation represented only extensions of New Deal measures; and when Truman tried to break new grounds for his 'Fair Deal,' he had little success. Congress bowed to the American Medical Association's campaign against Truman's proposal for national health insurance, rejected a new approach to farm subsidies, and filibustered the FEPC bill to death. Federal aid to education was lost in an unhappy squabble over whether such aid should go to private and parochial schools. Truman also fought losing battles to extend the TVA approach to the Columbia and the Missouri river valleys, and was able to carry out no more than a delaying action to preserve for the United States the immensely valuable oil reserves under the 'tidelands.' Truman also vetoed a bill which would have raised the price of natural gas, even though the measure was supported by powerful elements in his own party. When Senator Douglas heard of Truman's nervy veto, he commented: 'God bless the President of the United States.'

Truman's troubles with Congress resulted largely from the insurmountable obstacles he faced, but owed something too to his own shortcomings as a legislative leader. Although genuinely interested in achieving change, he never could arouse the kind of popular enthusiasm for his proposals that a Roosevelt did. 'Alas for Truman,' wrote one commentator, 'there is no bugle note in his voice.' Nor did Truman take pains enough to cultivate good will among Congressmen. When he did intervene too often he did so in such a flagrantly partisan manner, without proper sensitivity to the institutional interests of Congress, that he hurt his cause. But much more significant was the powerful opposition he faced, especially the rural-based, bipartisan conservative coalition entrenched in the committee structure in Congress. In addition the obsession with Communist subversion distracted attention from reforms, and the Korean War not only contributed to the Democratic setback in the 1950 elections, which strengthened the conservative coalition, but compelled the President to reimpose the unpopular economic controls.

The economic requirements of the Korean War mobilization led to one final rebuff for President Truman. When steel workers gave notice of an intention to strike in the midst of the war, the Wage Stabilization Board recommended an increase of 18 cents an hour without corresponding rises in steel prices. The operators refused this solution; the union called a walkout; and Truman on 8 April 1952 seized the mills. One of the mills — Youngstown Sheet and Tube Company — challenged the constitutionality of the President's act; and after a district court granted an injunction against the President, the Supreme Court struck down the presidential order on the ground that it constituted executive lawmaking. The Court's decision, and the President's helplessness in the face of the 54-day strike in wartime that ensued, further impaired Truman's prestige. In his final months in office Truman, his program frustrated, was reduced to fighting a rearguard action against those who wished to repeal the New Deal and detonate an explosion of ill feeling that would rival and in some respects surpass the Red Scare of 1919.

5. LOYALTY AND SECURITY

Although the Cold War with Russia and the hot war in Korea provided most of the fuel for McCarthyism, anxiety over subversion preceded World War II. Even before the war there was suspicion that Communists had infiltrated into government service, labor unions, and schools, and that they were hiding behind the guarantees of the Bill of Rights to destroy freedom. As early as 1938 the House established a committee on un-American activities. This committee, which at no point in its long and shabby career defined the term 'un-American,' embarked upon a relentless search for subversive activities — chiefly communistic and radical. Although it distracted congressional attention from more important matters, spent millions of dollars, produced voluminous reports, and made the headlines of newspapers with great regularity, it found nothing that was not already known to the Department of Justice.

However, when a raid in 1945 on the magazine *Amerasia* turned up quantities of classified State Department documents, another House committee began a study of disloyalty and subversion which resulted in Truman's issuing Executive Order 9835 on 21 March 1947. While this order to investigate the loyalty of civil servants set up intelligent standards and procedural safeguards and provided for non-judicial review, it, too, embraced the doctrines of guilt by intention and by association. Under its terms activities that might be evidence of disloyalty included 'membership in, affiliation with, or sympathetic association with . . . any organization, movement, group or combination of persons, designated by the Attorney-General as having adopted a policy of approving the commission of acts of force or violence to deny other persons their rights under the Constitution.' [3] On the whole the enforcement of the order was characterized by moderation. Of the 3 million persons passed on, only a few thousand were actually investigated. Of these, 212 were dis-

3. A supplementary executive order of 28 April 1951 authorized the firing of Federal employees even if there was only 'reasonable doubt' as to their loyalty.

missed, but none, apparently, had committed offenses serious enough to warrant prosecution. Potentially the most ominous feature of the executive order was the one authorizing the Attorney-General to prepare lists of subversive organizations and giving these lists a quasi-legal character. 'If there is any fixed star in our constitutional constellation,' Justice Jackson had said, 'it is that no official, high or petty, can prescribe what shall be orthodox in politics, nationalism, religion or other matters of opinion, or force citizens to confess by word or act their faith therein.' The executive order discouraged independence and originality in government employees, put a premium on conformity, and dissuaded many valuable citizens from entering government service.

Even the executive order did not free the Truman administration from charges of being 'soft on communism,' and on 20 July 1948 it precipitately took steps to indict the eleven top Communists on the charge of violating the Smith Act of 1940, which made it a crime to conspire to 'advocate and teach' the violent overthrow of government. The defendants challenged the constitutionality of the law, but in the Dennis case the Supreme Court accepted Judge Learned Hand's modification of the 'clear and present danger' test: 'in each case courts must ask whether the gravity of the evil, discounted by its improbability, justifies such invasion of free speech as is necessary to avoid the danger' — and concluded that the Smith Act was constitutional and that the Communists were in fact guilty of conspiracy to advocate the overthrow of government.

Wallace's defection from the Democratic party neutralized the Communist issue in the 1948 campaign, but the outcome of the election left the Republicans feeling embittered: to be beaten by Roosevelt was disappointing but familiar; to be rejected in favor of Truman seemed intolerable. And then two prodigious events upset the global balance of power shortly after the election: the final defeat and retreat of Chiang Kai-shek, and the Soviet detonation of the atomic bomb. On top of this came the Korean War.[4] How did it happen? How did we 'lose' China, and the atomic monopoly all at once, and then come close to losing the Korean War as well? To the average American it was unthinkable that Communism could win on its own and incredible that Soviet scientists were as clever as American or British. The answer must lie elsewhere — in subversion and treachery, perhaps by intellectuals and 'one-worlders'

4. The Korean War is discussed in the next chapter.

in the State Department who were secret sympathizers with Russia, or atomic scientists who had sold themselves to the Communists or been seduced by them into treason.

To support this fantastic interpretation came the Hiss case. In August 1948 Whittaker Chambers, onetime editor of *Time* magazine, accused Alger Hiss of having been a Communist. Hiss had been a State Department official before becoming president of the Carnegie Endowment for International Peace. Since the unprepossessing Chambers produced nothing convincing to back up his charge, and since the House Un-American Activities Committee had an unfortunate record of permitting itself to be used as a forum for false allegations, President Truman seemed right to dismiss the affair as a 'red herring' designed to distract attention from the failures of the 80th Congress. But in December 1948 Chambers produced microfilms of classified State Department documents — out of a pumpkin! — and asserted that Hiss had not only been a party member but a spy. When Hiss denied all of Chambers's charges, a New York grand jury indicted him for perjury; since the statute of limitations had expired, Hiss could not be indicted for espionage, but everyone understood that it was treason that was really at issue. After two trials Hiss was found guilty and sentenced to five years in jail.

It was highly improbable that Hiss had ever influenced policy, but in 1945 he had been with Roosevelt in a minor capacity at the Yalta conference where, irresponsible critics charged, American interests had been 'sold out' to the Russians. Moreover, Hiss was tailor-made for the role of a villain: a graduate of the Harvard Law School, a New Dealer, a friend of Secretary Acheson, who said he would not turn his back on him, an international 'do-gooder'; even his name suggested perfidy! Clearly he was 'fit for treason, stratagems, and spoils.' And if Hiss, why not scores of others?

While the country was shaken by the furor over Hiss, the government made two other disquieting announcements — China had fallen to the Reds, and Russia had exploded an atomic bomb, three years ahead of schedule. Two weeks after Hiss's conviction came news from England that Klaus Fuchs, an atomic physicist who had worked at the Los Alamos laboratory, had been found guilty of systematically feeding atomic information to the Russians. Here was the explanation of Russian success with the atomic bomb!

This series of events provided the background for that phenomenon known as McCarthyism. Senator McCarthy himself was a finished demagogue of a type more familiar to Europe than to America: brutal, unscrupulous, cunning, and adroit, he hoped to achieve power by exploiting the Communist issue; his methods were wild charges, fake evidence, innuendoes and lies, appeals to ignorance, prejudice, hatred, and fear. On 9 February 1950 he alleged that he had the names of 205 — or was it 57? — 'card-carrying Communists' in the State Department. He never actually produced any of these names, but he did charge that Professor Owen Lattimore of the Johns Hopkins University, one of the leading experts on Far Eastern affairs, was 'Russia's top espionage agent' in the United States. Lattimore denied under oath that he was a Communist, or a 'follower of the communist line'; when some years later Attorney-General Herbert Brownell, who was still playing McCarthy's game, indicted Lattimore for perjury, the case was contemptuously thrown out of court.

In July 1950 a Senate committee under Senator Tydings of Maryland reported that McCarthy's charges were 'a fraud and a hoax perpetrated on the Senate of the United States and on the American people. They represent perhaps the most nefarious campaign of half-truth and untruth in the history of the Republic.' Nothing daunted, McCarthy moved on to larger game. 'It was Moscow,' he cried, 'which decreed that the United States should execute its loyal friend, the Republic of China. The executioners were that well-defined group headed by Acheson and George Marshall.'

Out of the sense of panic aroused by McCarthy, and by the course of events, came the McCarran-Nixon Internal Security Act of 1950. This law required all Communist-front organizations to register with the Attorney-General, excluded Communists from employment in defense plants, made it illegal to *conspire* to perform any act that would 'substantially contribute' to the establishment of a dictatorship in the United States, debarred from the United States anyone ever affiliated with a totalitarian organization, or with organizations looking to the revolutionary overthrow of government,[5] authorized deportation for aliens involved in suspect organizations, barred passports to Communists, pro-

5. The McCarran-Walter Immigration and Nationality Act of 1952, also passed over Truman's veto, featured provisions harsh on immigrants and aliens; however, it also mitigated some of the discriminatory aspects of regulations on Asiatic immigration and citizenship.

vided for the internment of subversives in the event of war, and set up a Subversive Activities Control Board. Truman vetoed the bill, alleging that it was 'worse than the Sedition Acts of 1798,' but Congress passed it over his veto by acclamation. Given the threat of Communism, said the Illinois Democrat Scott Lucas, Senate majority leader, 'there is nothing too drastic.'

The subversion issue highlighted the 1950 elections in which the Republicans picked up five seats in the Senate and twenty-eight in the House. McCarthy, who received more invitations from Republican senators to speak in their states than all other senators combined, received credit for the defeat of Governor Bowles in Connecticut and of Senator Tydings in Maryland, where a fraudulent composite photograph was used to unseat McCarthy's critic. In California, Richard Nixon won a Senate seat by exploiting McCarthyite issues. The 1950 elections not only sealed the fate of the Fair Deal but encouraged the Republicans to anticipate that the same tactics would win them the White House in the 1952 presidential race.

6. THE 1952 ELECTION

By the spring of 1952 Americans were ready to listen to the Republicans' contention that it was 'time for a change' from twenty years of Democratic administration. Prices were too high; there was a 'mess in Washington'; the Russians had the atom bomb; the State Department had 'lost' China; the war in Korea was at a stalemate, and nothing in their experience had prepared Americans for a war which they could not hope to 'win.' It was not surprising that many people came to believe that they were the victims not of circumstances, or even of Communist aggression, but of subversion and incompetence in high places.

The right wing of the Republican party, rallying behind Senator Taft, contended that the Republicans had failed to capture the presidency in the three previous elections because they had offered no real alternative to the policies of liberal Democrats, and they called now for a return to 'rugged individualism' and isolationism. Republican moderates, convinced that the nomination of a member of the Old Guard would be disastrous, looked to General Eisenhower, Supreme Commander of NATO on leave from the presidency of Columbia University, to provide more progressive and more internationally minded leadership.

At the Republican Convention which met in Chicago the Taft forces gave the impression that they were acting like the Taft forces back in 1912: deals, intrigues, steam-rollers, and smoke-filled rooms! Eisenhower, by contrast, appeared remote and aloof, above partisanship and above the battle, although the General's political lieutenants were in fact adept manipulators. Governor Dewey marshaled the Eisenhower cohorts; wavering delegates fell in line under a conviction that only 'Ike' could win; and the General was uproariously named on the first ballot. Senator Nixon, who had distinguished himself only by his zeal in exploiting the issue of 'subversion,' was nominated for Vice-President.

The Democrats, who followed the Republicans to Chicago, faced the necessity of choosing a candidate not too closely identified with the Truman administration, which was blemished by scandals involving such agencies as the RFC. Senator Kefauver of Tennessee had won a large following by his investigation of organized crime, the first political event to attract an avid television audience, but the convention turned instead to Adlai Stevenson of Illinois, a man of wit, charm, intelligence, and eloquence. Born to Democratic politics (his grandfather had been Vice-President in Cleveland's second term), he had served in the Agriculture, Navy, and State departments, as delegate to the United Nations, and as reform governor of Illinois. Stevenson was nominated on the third ballot, with Senator John Sparkman of Alabama as his running-mate.

In his acceptance speech Stevenson stated:

> The ordeal of the Twentieth Century — the bloodiest, most turbulent era of the Christian age — is far from over. Sacrifice, patience, understanding, and implacable purpose may be our lot for years to come.
>
> Let's face it. Let's talk sense to the American people. Let's tell them the truth, that there are no gains without pains, that we are now on the eve of great decisions, not easy decisions, like resistance when you're attacked, but a long, patient, costly struggle which alone can assure triumph over the great enemies of man — war, poverty, and tyranny — and the assaults upon human dignity which are the most grievous consequences of each.

Eisenhower at first showed himself unwilling to repudiate policies of the Truman administration which he had helped to shape, but after a momentous meeting with Senator Taft, he began to give aid and comfort to the right wing of his party. He accepted the support of demagogues like McCarthy and Senator Jenner of Indiana, denounced the Truman administration for harboring subversives, charged Acheson with responsibility for the Communist attack on Korea, and poured scorn on the 'eggheads' who had rallied to the support of Stevenson. It was to no avail that Stevenson reminded the country that 'Korea, corruption, and communists in government are really not controversial issues between the two candidates at all. No one is running on a pro-corruption ticket or in favor of treachery.'

With ample funds at their command, the Republicans exploited to the full the possibilities of television which, for the first time, played an important part in a presidential campaign. Thus when Nixon was revealed to have been subsidized by a secret fund subscribed by California millionaires, he converted the liability into an asset by a dramatic television appearance, which critics denounced as 'soap opera' but to which the public responded favorably. However, the greatest advantage the Republicans enjoyed was neither control of the mass media, the smoke screen of 'subversion,' nor the corruption issue, but Eisenhower himself. 'The crowd is with him,' wrote one correspondent. 'Idolatry shows in their solemn, up-turned faces.' Moreover, at a time when casualties were mounting in Korea, with no end to the war in sight, Eisenhower struck a popular chord when he promised he would go to Korea to bring the war to an early end.

The election returns provided an accurate index of the General's popularity. Eisenhower won with more than 55 per cent of the popular vote and captured 39 states with 442 electoral votes, while Stevenson carried only 9 states with 89 votes in an election marked by a sharply increased turnout. Eisenhower even won four states of the not so solid South: Virginia, Tennessee, Texas, and Florida. The personal nature of Eisenhower's triumph was apparent when contrasted to the congressional vote. In spite of all the advantages they enjoyed, the Republican party barely carried the House by a majority of 8, and managed no better than a tie in the Senate. Clearly the election was less a triumph for the Republicans than a vote of confidence in Eisenhower; and if the support of the people is the secret of presidential power, the new President should have been one of the strongest of American executives.

XXVI

The Cold War

1. THE NEW WORLD

The problems of the postwar years were so many and so complex that neither the American people nor their government seemed able to understand or to master them. It was not merely that large areas of the globe were ravaged by famine, disease, and anarchy, though this in itself placed a heavy responsibility upon the United States. Nor was it merely that Russia and the Western powers had reached a dangerous state of disagreement, though this threatened to prolong world unrest indefinitely. It was rather that profound and revolutionary changes were under way throughout the globe. The western European states which for centuries had directed world affairs were declining in authority, and power gravitated to the United States and the Soviet Union. Empires dissolved almost overnight as the peoples of Asia and Africa claimed the right to govern themselves. Science and technology were binding nations ever closer together in time and space, making them at once more interdependent and more vulnerable than ever before.

In a century and a half — a short time in history — the United States had vaulted from insignificance to pre-eminence, and from isolation to leadership. Rejecting responsibility, she had been unable to escape it. Inclined to parochialism, she had been thrust into the center of internationalism. The only great nation to emerge from the war materially unscathed, she elected to assume responsibility for relief and reconstruction, and to put her technological skills and wealth at the disposal of less

638

fortunate peoples. The only democratic power able to resist the advance of Communism, she committed herself to that perilous task throughout the world.

Because America felt compelled to sustain the peoples of the Old World, to occupy parts of Germany, Austria, and Korea, defend Greece, re-arm Turkey, establish air and naval bases across the world, become an Atlantic power, a Pacific power, and a Hemispheric power all at once, she stretched not only her physical but her intellectual resources thin. Because the wealth of the United States was essential to recovery almost everywhere, many Americans assumed that all that was needed was American money. Because so many ancient nations appeared unable to exist without U.S. support, Americans were tempted to forget the force of tradition and assume that they could rearrange other countries' politics as simply as they rearranged their own. Because U.S. military might was the most formidable the world had ever seen, many Americans thought it was absolute and proposed to use it wherever democracy or liberty was challenged by hostile forces.

But as the United States advanced in strength, so too did Russia. As America poured financial aid into western Europe, the Soviet Union revolutionized the economies of eastern Europe. As the United States built up a system of alliances, the USSR created its own blocs. And as the United States made atom bombs, so too did the Russians. With the emergence of nuclear bombs as absolute weapons, it became clear that notwithstanding her might the United States was as vulnerable as any of her rivals. At the moment in history when Americans attained their greatest power, they were confronted with implacable limits on power.

Thus Americans needed to make multiple adjustment. They had to adjust themselves first to the notion and the practice of world responsibility. Americans who had barely acquainted themselves with the geography of their own country had to learn overnight about Burma and Indo-China, Pakistan and India, Eritrea and Ethiopia. They had to learn about foreign trade and currency controls, the intricacies of Continental politics, the strategic importance of Palestine and Transjordan. They had to learn to work with new international organizations and to acquire a new vocabulary and grammar of international politics. World responsibility meant, too, a new political orientation at home: a bipartisan foreign policy, a vastly enlarged State Department, a closer correlation between foreign and domestic policy and between civilian and military economy than ever before, the elaboration of far-reaching security controls, and the creation of an alert, intelligent, and prudent public opinion. The cost of national defense meant a terrific tax burden. Americans were called upon to display a degree of political maturity such as they had displayed only once before — in the Revolutionary generation, 1765–1800. It was asking a good deal to expect Americans to learn all this at once. Yet, to an impressive degree, the American nation did fulfill the obligations that had been thrust upon it, although not without making some painful errors.

2. ORGANIZATION FOR PEACE

We seek peace — enduring peace. More than an end to war, we want an end to the beginnings of all wars — yes, an end to this brutal, inhuman and thoroughly impractical method of settling the differences between governments. . . . We are faced with the pre-eminent fact that, if civilization is to survive, we must cultivate the science of human relationships — the ability of all peoples, of all kinds, to live together and work together in the same world, at peace. . . . Today, as we move against the terrible scourge of war — as we go forward toward the greatest contribution that any generation of human beings can make in this world, — the contribution of lasting peace — I ask you to keep up your faith.

These were the last words that Franklin Roosevelt wrote, and they were eloquent of that profound concern for peace, and for the creation of machinery to keep it, that possessed him throughout the war years. Roosevelt's interest in peace went back to his service in the Wilson administration during World War I. That he had been deeply impressed by Wilson's idealism is clear; that he was determined not to repeat Wilson's mistakes is equally clear; 'the tragedy of Wilson,' wrote Robert Sherwood, 'was always somewhere within the rim of his consciousness.'

The Atlantic Charter had called for 'the establishment of a wider and permanent system of general security,' and thereafter the construction of a peaceful postwar order was second in Roosevelt's thoughts only to the war, and never wholly separated from it. The great coalition that was to guarantee peace took embryonic form in the wartime United Nations of 1 January 1942, and thereafter every major conference of the Allied leaders gave increasing attention to this problem. All through 1944

Allied leaders were busily engaged in drafting proposals for a post-war international organization, and in August of that year their representatives met at Dumbarton Oaks, in Washington, and drew up the blueprint which was adopted, with some changes, as the Charter of the United Nations. On Roosevelt's return from the Yalta Conference of February 1945 in the Crimea — the last and most important of the Roosevelt-Churchill-Stalin meetings — he gave Congress a report which, in the light of the subsequent breakdown of world peace, takes on an almost tragic character. 'I come from the Crimea Conference,' he said,

> with a firm belief that we have made a good start on the road to a world of peace. . . . This time we are not making the mistake of waiting until the end of the war to set up the machinery of peace. . . . The Conference in the Crimea was a turning point — I hope in our history and therefore in the history of the world. There will soon be presented to the Senate of the United States and to the American people a great decision that will determine the fate of the United States — and of the world — for generations to come. There can be no middle ground here. We shall have to take the responsibility for world collaboration, or we shall have to bear the responsibility for another world conflict.

The wartime alliance between Russia and the Western powers had been a marriage of convenience, not of love. Yet it was no less effective for that: witness the $11 billion of Lend-Lease that went to the USSR. During the whole of the wartime alliance the leaders of the West hoped that after the war Russia, freed from the fear of Germany and Japan, protected by friendly border states, and strengthened by American help, might abandon her hostility and associate herself with the work of creating a new international order. These expectations, it must be admitted, animated Roosevelt rather than Churchill, who was more cynical, or more realistic. Roosevelt saw clearly the importance of Russian co-operation to assure peace after the defeat of the Axis; he did not see so clearly the forces in the Soviet world militating against such co-operation.

Relations between Russia and the West were strained even during the war. Sharp differences over such matters as the sharing of military secrets, the policy toward the Polish Army in Exile and the Polish underground and toward the contending forces in Yugoslavia, the timing of the second front, and the treatment of Italy foreshadowed the even deeper divisions that emerged after the war. Roosevelt hoped that these frictions would yield to the emollient of wartime comradeship, and that particular misunderstandings could be cleared up by personal consultations, and to this end he went to Teheran and to the Crimea.

The Yalta Conference appeared to have achieved the end to which Roosevelt so ardently looked. Later Yalta came to be regarded as a defeat for the West, but it was not so regarded at the time, nor is there convincing evidence that it was so in fact. The Yalta agreements involved mutual concessions from Russia and the Western powers; on paper the concessions from the West seemed more far-reaching than those from the USSR, but in reality Roosevelt and Churchill conceded nothing substantial that Russia could not have taken anyway, while the Soviet Union yielded on important points to the Western point of view. Of primary importance was Russia's agreement to enter the war against Japan 'within two or three months' of the defeat of Germany. In return she was promised the Kurile Islands, the southern half of Sakhalin, and privileges in Manchuria and at Port Arthur and Dairen: in all probability she could have taken all these as easily without as with Anglo-American permission. Nor should it be forgotten that when this agreement was made, the Allied armies had not yet crossed the Rhine, nor had the atom bomb been exploded at Alamagordo, and Roosevelt's military advisers anticipated that the war with Japan would go on for at least another year. As for the other postwar arrangements, Stalin acquiesced in the American formula for the admission of Latin American states to the United Nations and for their voting in the Security Council, withdrew his preposterous demand for 16 votes in the General Assembly, agreed to permit France a zone of occupation in Germany, accepted the reparation figure as tentative only, and — presumably — left open to further negotiation the reorganization of the Polish government. Roosevelt and Churchill conceded the Curzon line as Russia's western boundary, accepted a tentative reparations figure far beyond what they thought proper, promised the USSR three votes in the General Assembly, and left open for future negotiation such thorny questions as Soviet rights in the Dardanelles and in Iran, the future of the Baltic countries, and the disposition of Italian colonies.

Roosevelt and his adviser Harry Hopkins thought that the Yalta agreements ushered in a new era of peace and hope. 'We really believed in our hearts,' said Hopkins, that this was the dawn of the new day we had all been praying for and talking about for so many years. We were absolutely certain that we had won the first great victory for peace — and by we I mean *all* of us, the whole civilized human race. The Russians had proved that they could be reasonable and farseeing and there wasn't any doubt in the minds of the President or any of us that we could live with them peacefully for as far into the future as any of us could imagine.[1]

Actually it is doubtful whether the course of history was changed in any important particulars by the Yalta Conference.

Roosevelt died on 12 April, but invitations had already gone out for a United Nations Conference to meet at San Francisco to draft a charter for the new international organization, and late in that month delegates from 50 nations gathered at that city whose very choice suggested the new importance of the Pacific area. Secretary of State Stettinius headed the American delegation, Anthony Eden the British, and — in the end — Molotov the Russian. Determined to avoid Wilson's mistake in ignoring both the Republicans and the Congress, Roosevelt had appointed two Republicans — Senator Vandenberg and Representative Eaton — and two Democrats — Senator Connally and Congressman Bloom — to the American delegation.

The conference lasted for two months and was marked by many sharp disagreements over such matters as the Polish delegation, the admission of Argentina, separate votes for the Ukraine and White Russia, and the veto power; it ended on a note of surface harmony with all 50 nations signing the Charter. The United States was already committed to the Charter in principle by the Fulbright-Connally Resolutions of 1943, and the Senate ratified the document on 28 July 1945 with only two votes in opposition.

The United Nations Charter resembled the Covenant of the League of Nations in some respects, differed from it in others. Like the League, it created an Assembly, whose functions were largely deliberative, and a Council whose functions were executive; like the League, it provided for a system of mandates, an International Court of Justice, a Secretariat, and other affiliated organizations; and like the League, too, it recognized the validity of regional agreements. However, unlike the League, it was not tied to the peace treaties, but existed independently of any that

1. Robert Sherwood, *Roosevelt and Hopkins*, p. 870.

might be made; it permitted any one of the five great powers (the United States, Britain, Russia, France, and China) to exercise a veto on any but procedural questions — a power which Soviet Russia grossly abused; and it authorized the use of force against aggressor nations.

The Charter provided for a General Assembly in which each nation had one vote, and whose functions were limited almost entirely to discussion, investigation, and advice, and a Security Council to consist of five permanent [2] and six elected members, which alone had power to act in international disputes. The Assembly could call to the attention of the Council any situation likely to endanger peace, recommend measures for the settlement of disputes, and promote international co-operation in economic, social, and cultural fields. The Council was authorized to hear complaints from member nations, investigate disputes that might lead to war, and take such measures 'by air, sea or land forces' as might be necessary to preserve peace. All members agreed to make available to the Council such armed forces and facilities as were agreed on and called for. Article 52 of the Charter permitted the creation of regional agreements and agencies, and it was in accordance with this permissive article that the Rio de Janeiro and the North Atlantic treaties were subsequently negotiated.

The Charter created a number of other agencies: an International Court of Justice with powers comparable to those formerly exercised by the World Court; an Economic and Social Council to promote social and cultural welfare and human rights; a trusteeship system to replace the unsatisfactory mandate system of the old League; a permanent Secretariat. Under the Economic and Social Council there was a proliferation of special agencies — UNESCO, a Food and Agricultural Organization, an International Labor Organization, a World Health Organization, and eventually many others of a technical character.

Launched with high hopes, the United Nations soon ran into the dangerous waters of the East-West conflict. Yet in the first few years of its existence it had some substantial accomplishments to its credit. It succeeded in settling — after a fashion — three major disputes: that between Russia and Iran, the series of problems connected with the

2. Great Britain, France, Russia, the United States, and China. The kind of problem presented, after 1950, by the existence of Nationalist and Communist governments each claiming to represent China was neither anticipated nor provided for in the Charter.

emergence of Israel as a nation, and the complex and inflammable Indonesia issue. Its principal achievements were not, however, in the settlement of explosive disputes, but in serving — in Senator Vandenberg's phrase — as a 'town meeting of the world' and as a vehicle for reforms. In a quiet way such agencies as the International Health and the International Labor Organizations performed important services for the whole world.

Yet it could not be denied that the United Nations disappointed those who had hoped that it would succeed where the League had failed. The ostensible difficulty was the veto; designed for use only in emergencies, and then to avoid a rupture between the great powers, it was invoked by Russia some fifty times in the first four years, often for purposes that were trivial. But the real difficulty of the United Nations was not mechanical but substantial: the division of the world into hostile camps led by the United States and the Soviet Union. For within an ominously brief period after the end of World War II, the two great powers had come to a total impasse over policy toward their wartime enemy, Germany.

3. DIVIDED GERMANY

It was the irrepressible Winston Churchill who said, 'We shall not make the same mistakes after this war that we made after the last; we shall make a lot of new ones.' As it turned out, we made plenty of them and many of the old ones as well, although we achieved some unexpected successes too. Twenty years after victory no permanent settlement had been achieved for Germany. Disagreements among the victors, restrained during the war itself, broke out virulently after the war and grew increasingly acrimonious with the passing years.

The victors faced formidable tasks. They had to cleanse Germany of the Nazi contamination and do all they could to ensure against a revival of Hitlerism. They had to provide the mechanism for demobilization, dispose of the millions of prisoners of war, set up military government during the interregnum between surrender and peace, and get temporary civil government under way. They had to start the economy functioning once more, supply food and clothing, heat and shelter, medicine and protection for the defeated populations, and re-create such social institutions as church, schools, and the press.

What was to be the Allied policy toward Germany? World War I afforded no precedent; when Germany quit in November 1918 a German government was functioning and the country's economy was intact. The Allies — already by mid-1945 as much rivals as allies — had to tailor their policies to fit new and unpredictable circumstances. For a time the United States seriously considered the Morgenthau plan of reducing Germany to a pastoral economy. Tentatively endorsed at the Quebec Conference, over the protest of the British, it was soon abandoned.

The Moscow Conference of 1943 set up a European Advisory Commission, which worked out the basic principles for the treatment of Germany after the war: the destruction of German militarism and military potential; the dissolution of the Nazi party and the punishment of war criminals; creation of zones of control; and the payment of reparations 'to the greatest extent possible.' The Yalta Conference reaffirmed these principles, added the provision that France might share in the occupation, named, as a basis for discussion only, the sum of $20 billion for reparations, and tentatively conceded the territory east of the Curzon line to Russia and the right of Poland to compensation from German territory.

At the Potsdam Conference, held in July 1945, Truman, Stalin, and Clement Attlee — who had replaced Churchill as spokesman for the British government — spelled out the details of these agreements and added certain others. That conference created a Council of Foreign Ministers, which was to draw up peace treaties with Italy and the Axis satellites; regularized an Allied Control Council for the military administration of Germany; gave Poland administrative control over all German territory east of the Oder and Neisse rivers; decided that notwithstanding the division into occupation zones, Germany should be treated as an economic unit; and provided that each occupying power should take reparations from its own zone but that, in addition, the U.S.S.R. might receive reparations in the form of industrial equipment from the West in exchange for food and other products from the East. Eastern Germany was assigned to Russia; northwestern Germany to Britain; southwestern Germany, including Bavaria, Württemberg, and Hesse, to the United States; while France received two smaller areas — Baden and the Saar. Austria, too, was carved up into four occupation zones, while both Berlin and Vienna were parceled out to the victors.

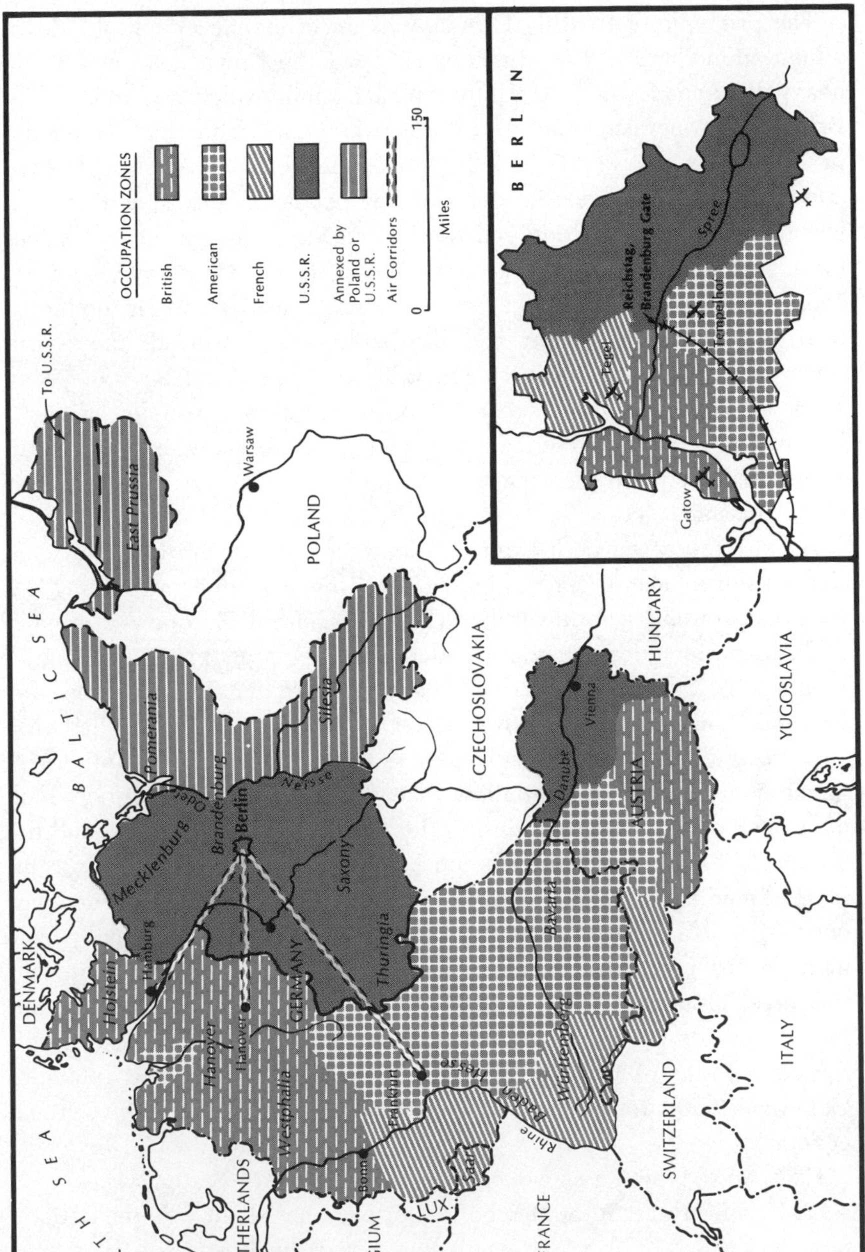
OCCUPATION ZONES
British
American
French
U.S.S.R.
Annexed by Poland or U.S.S.R.
Air Corridors
0
150
Miles
To U.S.S.R.
East Prussia
Warsaw
POLAND
BALTIC SEA
Pomerania
Silesia
Oder
Neisse
Brandenburg
Berlin
Mecklenburg
Hamburg
Holstein
DENMARK
Hanover
Westphalia
GERMANY
Saxony
Thuringia
CZECHOSLOVAKIA
NORTH SEA
NETHERLANDS
BELGIUM
LUX.
Saar
Bonn
Frankfurt
Hesse
Rhine
Baden
Württemberg
Bavaria
Danube
AUSTRIA
Vienna
HUNGARY
YUGOSLAVIA
ITALY
SWITZERLAND
FRANCE
BERLIN
Reichstag, Brandenburg Gate
Spree
Tempelhof
Tegel
Gatow

ZONES OF OCCUPATION, GERMANY AND AUSTRIA

The principle of treating Germany as an economic unit broke down almost immediately. The Russians stripped their own zone and made heavy demands for factories, power plants, rolling stock, and tools in the British and American zones. But the Potsdam declaration had included a precautionary clause to the effect that the conquerors 'should leave enough resources to enable the German people to subsist without external assistance.' If Britain and the United States permitted their zones to be gutted, German economy would collapse and Germany would become a permanent burden on their taxpayers. Furthermore, if the industrial potential of the Ruhr and the Saar were destroyed, the consequences for European recovery generally would be disastrous. On 3 May 1946, almost exactly one year after the German surrender, General Lucius Clay, deputy American commander in Germany, announced an open break between the victors when he halted delivery of reparations to the Russians.

Behind these sharp differences of opinion on reparations lay even sharper differences of general policy. The Russians aimed at nothing less than the communization of the whole of Central Europe — Germany and Austria included. They proceeded as if the purely provisional agreements at Yalta and Potsdam were permanent. When Truman called for free elections in Hungary, Rumania, and Bulgaria, Stalin replied that 'any freely elected government in these countries will be an anti-Soviet government, and we cannot allow that.' The Soviet Union not only took over the Baltic states seized during the war, part of East Prussia, and the whole of Poland east of the Curzon line, but undertook a vigorous campaign to win eastern Germany for Communism. Poland regarded her occupation of Germany west of the Oder-Neisse line as equally permanent and proceeded to oust some 10 million Germans living in that rich area. This mass expulsion worked grave hardship on its victims, but in the long run proved highly beneficial to them and to the West; it permitted millions of Germans to live under freedom rather than under Communist dictatorship, and it greatly strengthened the West German economy.

Exasperated by Russian truculence, Secretary of State Byrnes, in a speech at Stuttgart in September 1946, enunciated the administration's new "get tough" policy. Although he offered the Russians a forty-year security treaty, Byrnes plainly implied that he no longer contemplated agreement with the Russians over Germany. The United States, which had started out determined to reduce Germany's industrial potential, would henceforth seek to spur the country's economic revival. To that end, he invited Britain to fuse her zone with the American zone, a fusion that was achieved on 1 January 1947. Furthermore, he suggested uniting Germany politically, for the aim of occupation was not 'a prolonged alien dictatorship' but the creation of a political democracy. So within less than two years after the defeat of Hitler's Reich, Germany was being divided into two nations, each owing its allegiance to one of the great powers, and Russia and the Western Allies were bidding against each other for control of the German people.

Meantime the Big Three went ahead with the trial of major war criminals, and the Western powers with their denazification program and with re-establishing a German government. That Associate Justice Robert Jackson was appointed to represent the United States in establishing an International Military Tribunal and to serve as chief counsel for the prosecution indicated the importance Roosevelt and Truman attached to the trials of Nazi leaders. Jackson's report designated three major types of crime: violations of international law, crimes against humanity and against established criminal law, and aggressive warfare in violation of the Kellogg Pact and other international commitments. Jackson proposed the trial not only of major war criminals but of criminal organizations such as the Gestapo, the SS, and the Nazi party as well, but left to military tribunals and to the German courts the punishment of lesser criminals.

The London Agreement of August 1945 accepted these proposals and established an international judicial tribunal with representatives from the four occupying powers. The International Military Tribunal then presented indictments against 24 major criminals and six criminal organizations. The trials, lasting ten months, published the whole ghastly record of Nazi aggression, atrocities, mass murders, looting, and destruction. Nineteen war criminals were found guilty, and twelve, including such notorious figures from the Nazi high command as Goering, Keitel, Jodl, Ribbentrop, and Seyss-Inquart, sentenced to death. In addition there were numerous trials of lesser war criminals by the military authorities and by denazified German courts. The Americans conducted a series of 12 trials, each centered on an occupational group — doctors and lawyers, military leaders, SS and police, industrialists, and government ministers. All the members of these groups were tried individually for specific crimes: 35 were acquitted, 24 given death sentences, and 128 condemned to varying terms of imprisonment.

The war trials came in for heavy criticism in Britain and the United States. It was alleged that by making aggressive warfare a crime the tribunal was guilty of *ex post facto* legislation, that trials by judges from the victor nations did not deserve the term 'judicial,' and that trials by military tribunals were equally flawed with impropriety. The trials, Churchill warned, created the dangerous precedent that 'the leaders of a nation defeated in war shall be put to death by the victors.' To this it was replied, unpersuasively, that the legal justification for the trials lay in the Kellogg-Briand Pact which had outlawed war, and the trials therefore were not *ex post facto*. However, the tribunals which tried the accused observed the highest standards of due process. And, as Jackson pointed out, 'Either the victors must judge the vanquished or we must leave the defeated to judge themselves,' and there was ample reason for doubting the wisdom of the latter course.

While these trials were proceeding to their somber conclusion, the work of sterilizing German society of its Nazi infection went ahead. The Potsdam declaration had looked not only to outlawing the Nazi party and all of its affiliates but to eliminating Nazis from the civil service, schools, industries, and all important private organizations, and replacing them with persons capable of developing genuine democratic institutions. This was easier said than done. The Nazi regime had so extended itself into every field of activity that almost the only Germans free of Nazi taint were those in exile, concentration camps, or cemeteries. Confronted with this situation, the military administration was forced to compromise, and the denazification that had begun with a bang petered out with a whimper. Notorious Nazis were ousted from places of authority and, in some instances, punished, but most of the small fry went free or were subjected to mild penalties. Under the Germans, denazification became something of a joke. Of the 836,000 Nazis tried, less than 0.1 per cent were classified as major offenders, and as of May 1948 only 1677 were serving jail sentences. But by then the world was less interested in punishing the perpetrators of World War II than in avoiding the outbreak of World War III, a prospect to which the atomic bomb gave a special horror.

President Truman and General MacArthur on Wake Island, October 1950

Dwight D. Eisenhower and Robert A. Taft at Republican Convention, 1952

Eleanor Roosevelt and Adlai Stevenson

Dean Acheson

John Foster Dulles

Dean Rusk and Robert McNamara

President Lyndon B. Johnson and President-elect Richard Nixon

Photograph by Alfred Eisenstaedt (Life Magazine)

Albert Einstein and J. Robert Oppenheimer

The Warren Court, 1967-68

Robert F. and John F. Kennedy

4. THE CONTROL OF ATOMIC ENERGY

On the day the United Nations Conference convened at San Francisco, Secretary Stimson presented to President Truman a memorandum on the atomic bomb, which pointed out:

> The world, in its present state of moral advancement, compared with its technical development, would be eventually at the mercy of such a weapon. . . . Modern civilization might be completely destroyed. To approach any world peace organization of any pattern now likely to be considered without an appreciation by the leaders of our country of the power of this new weapon would seem to be unrealistic. No system of control heretofore considered would be adequate to control this menace. . . . Our leadership in the war and in the development of this weapon has placed a certain moral responsibility upon us which we cannot shirk without very serious responsibility for any disaster to civilization which it would further.[3]

The explosions at Hiroshima and Nagasaki and the 1946 experiments in the Bikini Lagoon [4] justified the validity of this warning. How to prevent the use of atomic energy for destructive ends and encourage its use for constructive purposes was the most urgent problem that confronted the statesmen of the world at mid-twentieth century.

It was a problem of peculiar difficulty as well as of peculiar urgency. In the first place, there were no 'secrets' about the atom bomb; physicists everywhere in the world knew how to make the bomb, and it was certain that within a few years any country that cared to spend the money and effort could have bigger and more devastating bombs than those that had already been exploded. Within a few years Russia, Britain, and France all had 'the bomb.' In the second place, given existing international machinery, there was no effective means of controlling either the manufacture of atom bombs or nuclear experiments; any method that would be effective required some surrender of national sovereignty. In the third place, there was no defense against an atomic attack except the desperate measure of counterattack.

3. Henry Stimson, *On Active Service*, p. 638.
4. There were two tests. One bomb, dropped from the air, sank five ships and heavily damanged the superstructure of many more. The second, exploded under water, sank two battleships and an aircraft carrier and did major damage to many other vessels; it also created radioactivity in the water that lasted for several months.

American policy on atomic energy, first outlined by Secretary Stimson, was clearly formulated by two committees headed by Dean Acheson and David Lilienthal. This Acheson-Lilienthal Plan, published in March 1946, called for the creation of an International Atomic Development Authority, which should have exclusive control over such raw materials as uranium and thorium and over every stage of the production of atomic energy throughout the world, and should act as custodian of atomic weapons and stockpiles of fissionable materials.

At its first session the General Assembly of the United Nations had created an Atomic Energy Commission to consist of representatives from all eleven members of the Security Council plus Canada. President Truman appointed Bernard Baruch as American representative on this commission, and in a notable address in June 1946 Baruch presented a proposal that incorporated the main features of the Acheson-Lilienthal Plan plus provision for rigid international inspection and for the elimination of the veto in cases involving illegal manufacture of atomic bombs. Under the Baruch Plan, the proposed International Atomic Development Authority would control the whole field of atomic energy through ownership, licenses, operation, inspection, research, and management, and concern itself not only with the prevention of the manufacture of atomic weapons but with the production of atomic energy for peaceful benefits. If this program were adopted, the United States stood ready to destroy its stock of atom bombs, stop further manufacture of bombs, and share its scientific knowledge with the rest of the world. Since at this time the United States had a monopoly on the atomic bomb, Americans viewed this proposal as not only enlightened but magnanimous.

The United Nations Atomic Energy Commission endorsed the American plan by a vote of 10–0; the USSR and Poland abstained. Russia rejected it for two reasons: inspection would be an intolerable invasion of national sovereignty, and the suspension of the veto would destroy the unanimity principle that was the very basis of the Security Council. The Russians objected that the plan would give the United States the advantage of knowing how to make an atomic bomb while restricting experimentation by other countries. Furthermore, the United States would almost certainly control the international atomic agency. Gromyko proposed an alternative plan: the immediate destruction of all atom bombs and the prohibition of the manufacture of atomic weapons. Such a plan was unacceptable to the United States or to her Western associates. It required the surrender by the United States of its advantage, and, in the absence of inspection, gave no corresponding assurance that Russia would not proceed secretly to make atomic weapons.

Russian intransigence on the veto and on inspection condemned the work of the United Nations Atomic Energy Commission to futility, and in July 1949 the commission suspended its deliberations. Meantime the United States pushed steadily ahead with her own atomic program. The atom bomb had originally been made by civilian scientists, but under the jurisdiction of the military. With the end of the war there was strong pressure for civilian control of the whole field of atomic energy. The plan worked out by Congress, after lengthy debate, placed the atomic-energy program under the jurisdiction of a five-man civilian Atomic Energy Commission but provided for close military liaison and elaborate security measures; the AEC was to have a monopoly on all fissionable materials, processes, facilities, patents, and technical information. Lilienthal, whose administrative abilities had been tested by his work as head of the TVA, was appointed first chairman of the new commission.

When the Russians detonated an atomic device in September 1949, and the United States, a few months later, announced plans for a hydrogen bomb, a thousandfold as powerful as the atomic bomb, the quest for effective international control assumed a new urgency. Speaking with deep solemnity, the venerable philosopher-scientist Albert Einstein, who had originally called President Roosevelt's attention to the potentialities of nuclear fission, warned the world,

> The armament race between the U.S.A. and the U.S.S.R., originally supposed to be a preventive measure, assumes hysterical character. On both sides, the means to mass destruction are perfected with feverish haste, behind respective walls of secrecy. The H-bomb appears on the public horizon as a probably attainable goal. . . . If successful, radio-active poisoning of the atmosphere and hence annihilation of any life on earth has been brought within the range of technical possibilities. The ghost-like character of this development lies in its apparently compulsory trend. Every step appears as the unavoidable consequence of the preceding one. In the end, there beckons more and more clearly general annihilation.

5. RELIEF AND RECONSTRUCTION

The organization to bring relief to the stricken millions of the Old World, which eventually got caught up in the politics of the Cold War, began as a wholly humanitarian venture. For five years the Nazis and the Communists had systematically looted and destroyed wherever they went. Tens of millions of workers had been drawn into non-productive war industries; perhaps 20 million men and women had been killed in battle, or in the rubble of cities, or in concentration camps. Food production had fallen to half the prewar level. Towns and cities were destroyed, factories smashed, power plants wrecked, mines flooded, ports clogged, shipping sunk, railroads torn up, and rolling stock in ruins; money was almost worthless. Ten to twelve million bewildered refugees wandered aimlessly on the roads or clung to the camps that had been hastily established for them. Herbert Hoover, sent abroad to survey the food situation, reported, 'It is now 11:59 o'clock on the clock of starvation.' Most continental Europeans were living on less than 1500 calories a day: the American average was 3500. Starvation, disease, and anarchy threatened to take more lives and to leave worse scars than war itself. Over large parts of Asia, too, the situation was desperate, and with crop failures in 1946, it grew worse: it was estimated that almost 400 million people of Asia were close to starvation.

The burden of relief fell most heavily upon the United States, which alone of major nations had a transportation system and shipping intact, and surplus food. As early as June 1943 the United States proposed to her allies the creation of an international relief organization, and out of this proposal came the United Nations Relief and Rehabilitation Administration (UNRRA), of November 1943, to which 48 nations eventually adhered. Under the vigorous leadership first of Herbert Lehman and then of Fiorello La Guardia, UNRRA distributed not only food and clothing but seed, fertilizer, livestock, machinery, and medicine. Altogether, in four years of troubled existence, UNRRA spent some $4 billion for relief purposes; of this sum the United States gave $2.75 billion. In addition the U.S. Army fed large areas of occupied Europe, Lend-Lease continued to pour foodstuffs and other supplies into Allied countries, and private gifts and CARE supplemented governmental contributions on a generous scale. Yet if the United States did much for relief, she did less than her resources permitted; there was no postwar rationing, cereals continued to be fed to livestock rather than exported to the starving abroad, and Lend-Lease was abruptly terminated in August 1945, one week after the capitulation of Japan.

UNRRA devoted much of its attention to the millions of refugees who came to be known as Displaced Persons. At the close of the war there were perhaps ten million of these hapless victims of modern war; many of them had been pressed into Nazi military service and were mingled with other prisoners of war; others were labor slaves, or inmates of prison camps. By the end of 1946 the military had repatriated most of these refugees, but there remained a hard core of perhaps a million non-repatriables: Jews who wanted to go to Palestine, or Balts, Poles, Yugoslavs, and Russians who had fought communism and were unable or unwilling to return to their own countries. Many of these were eventually resettled in Palestine, New Zealand, Brazil, Colombia, Australia, and other countries who were ready to welcome the labor and skills that they possessed. The United States lagged badly behind in this program of resettlement of Displaced Persons, admitting only some 6000 by the end of 1947. In 1948 Congress passed legislation to admit an additional 200,000, on terms far from generous; in 1950 this legislation was liberalized and another 200,000 refugees admitted.

The reconstruction of the war-shattered economy of western Europe called for boldness and imagination. Europe needed everything but was able to buy nothing; the United States had — or was capable of producing — almost everything, but could sell nothing to a bankrupt Europe. If the European economy collapsed, the American economy would take a tailspin. Some method must be found, therefore, not only to get the European economy functioning on an emergency basis, but to make it permanently self-supporting, so that European countries could resume their traditional role in international trade. Moreover, if the United States stood idly by while western Europe plunged into economic chaos, she would be faced, in a few years, with a Soviet-dominated continent.

The United States moved on many fronts to ease restrictions on trade, stabilize currencies, and encourage investments. The Reciprocal Trade Agreements, inaugurated in 1934, had been renewed in 1945, and in 1947 some 40 nations, meeting at Geneva, agreed on sweeping reductions in tariffs. Under the terms of this agreement the United States cut duties on thousands of items; the general effect was to reduce duties to the 1913 level. At the same time the United States took the lead in establishing an International Trade Organization to promote the expansion of world trade. In response to these moves American imports increased from a prewar average of less than $3 billion to a total of over $7 billion in 1948. Yet this still left a gap of almost $8 billion between what the rest of the world bought and what it sold to the United States: if trade were to continue, this gap would have to be closed.

As early as 1943 the Treasury Department began laying plans to stabilize national currencies and make available credit for international trade and investment, and in the summer of 1944 a United Nations Monetary and Financial Conference met at Bretton Woods, New Hampshire, to crystallize these plans. This conference set up and Congress ratified two new agencies: an International Monetary Fund and an International Bank for Reconstruction. The first, designed to maintain stable exchange rates and discourage restrictions on the transfer of funds from nation to nation, had a capital of $8.8 billion, to which the United States contributed one–fourth. The World Bank, as it came to be called, was authorized to borrow and lend money and to underwrite private loans for production purposes. But by 1950, the bank had made loans of only $700 million and had been unable to attract private capital to any large-scale investment in European recovery.

Roosevelt and Truman both deplored the war-debt business that had plagued America's relations with her Allies after World War I, so Lend-Lease was settled on the simple principle of wiping all wartime debts and credits off the books and requiring repayment only of postwar grants, and that on easy terms. Settlements were speedily concluded with Britain, France, China, and other wartime associates; for a long time Russia refused to discuss the matter. These settlements removed what would have been a heavy impediment to European reconstruction. Nonetheless, the abrupt termination of Lend-Lease precipitated a serious economic crisis in Britain.

The British had not only disposed of most of their foreign investments but had incurred heavy debts abroad; they had lost one-third of their shipping as well as a substantial part of their foreign markets; and their industry was partially destroyed and almost wholly run down. They could neither recapture their export market nor pay for imports with accumulated capital. At the same time they were unable to escape expensive external commitments: occupation costs in Germany and Austria, military expenses in Palestine, Greece, and the Far East, assistance to their colonies, contributions to the World Bank, and so forth. To ward off a catastrophe the British asked for a loan of $5 billion from the United States. After protracted negotiations a sum of $3.75 billion was agreed upon, plus an additional credit for the $650 million outstanding on Lend-Lease; the loan was to run for 50 years and carry interest at 2 per cent. It had been hoped the loan would carry Britain through the next five years but, notwithstanding the maintenance of wartime austerity and heroic efforts to regain foreign markets, the money ran out in two years. By 1947 Britain again faced economic disaster.

6. THE TRUMAN DOCTRINE AND THE MARSHALL PLAN

Britain's tribulations came at a time when the West was becoming growingly disturbed by the defiant actions of the Soviet Union in Europe and in Asia. By January 1946 Truman was writing his Secretary of State: 'Unless Russia is faced with an iron fist and strong language another war is in the making. Only one language do they understand — "how many divisions have you?" . . . I'm tired of babying the Soviets.' Two months later he accompanied Sir Winston Churchill to Fulton, Missouri, where the former Prime Minister declared: 'From Stettin in the Baltic to Trieste in the Adriatic, an iron curtain has descended across the Continent.' To curb the Kremlin's 'expansive tendencies,' Churchill proposed an Anglo-American alliance. East-West relations were further exacerbated by wrangling at a series of conferences of the Council of Foreign Ministers, chiefly representatives of the Big Three, which took until the end of 1946 to hammer out peace treaties with Italy, Finland, Hungary, Rumania, and Bulgaria.

The first showdown between Russia and the West took place in the Mediterranean and the Near East. The importance of the Mediterranean lifeline had been proved by the war, and the prospect of Soviet dominance in this area raised basic questions of strategy. If Russia could take over Iran with its rich oil resources, bring Turkey and Greece into her orbit, retain her strong ties with Yugoslavia, and get a foothold in North Africa, she would turn the flank of the West. Italy would be unable to resist communism; the Near and Middle East would fall to Russia; the whole Moslem world would be threatened; and India would be open to attack from north, east, and west.

The British, who kept a tenuous foothold in Greece and Palestine, announced on 24 February 1947 that they could no longer carry this burden and proposed to pull out. Rarely in history had there been so dramatic a moment when one nation turned over the responsibilities of empire to another. In desperation Greece and Turkey turned for financial and military assistance to the United States, which had just succeeded in turning back a Soviet threat to Iran. On 12 March, President Truman sent a message to Congress embodying not only a request for appropriations for Greece and Turkey, but what came to be known as the Truman Doctrine. 'One of the primary objectives of the foreign policy of the United States,' he said,

> is the creation of conditions in which we and other nations will be able to work out a way of life free from coercion. We shall not realize our objectives unless we are willing to help free peoples to maintain their free institutions, and their national integrity against aggressive movements that seek to impose on them totalitarian regimes. . . . I believe that it must be the policy of the United States to support free peoples who are resisting attempted subjugation by armed minorities or by outside pressures.

While this doctrine affected immediately only Greece and Turkey, it was potentially world-wide in its application.

Congress voted the money — eventually close to $700 million — and American power moved into the vacuum created by Britain in the Near East. After prolonged fighting the Greek guerrillas were beaten, Greek government and economy were reformed, Turkish defenses were strengthened, and the situation in the Mediterranean was stabilized.

In July 1947 *Foreign Affairs* published an article under the enigmatic signature of 'X' which took a hard-headed view of Russian-American relations. 'X,' shortly revealed to be one of the State Department's veteran Russian experts, George Kennan, warned that, at least for some time to come, there could 'never be on Moscow's side any sincere assumption of a community of aims between the Soviet Union and powers which are regarded as capitalist.' In enunciating what came to be known as the 'containment' policy, Kennan argued that it must be made clear to the USSR that expansion beyond a given perimeter would be met with force. Kennan stressed:

> The United States has it in its power to increase enormously the strains under which the Soviet policy must operate, to force upon the Kremlin a far greater degree of moderation and circumspection than it has had to observe in recent years, and in this way to promote tendencies which must eventually find their outlet in either the breakup or the gradual mellowing of Soviet policy.[5]

5. *Foreign Affairs*, July 1947.

Kennan, who thought the Truman Doctrine too negative an application of the containment doctrine, made an important contribution to a more imaginative development in American foreign policy: the Marshall Plan. As early as 1946 he had admonished our government to

> put forward for other nations a more positive and constructive picture of the sort of world we would like to see. . . . It is not enough to urge people to develop political processes similar to our own. Many foreign peoples are tired and frightened by experiences of the past and are less interested in abstract freedom than in security. They are seeking guidance rather than responsibilities. We should be better able to give them this. And unless we do the Russians certainly will.[6]

The next year Secretary Marshall set up a policy-planning staff headed by Kennan; this staff recommended short-term aid to stop further deterioration of the European economy, and a long-range program looking to European economic integration. Early in May 1947 Dean Acheson announced that national self-interest required that western European nations become self-supporting, and to this end the United States must be prepared to contribute. Speaking at a Harvard Commencement in June, Secretary Marshall summed up all of these recommendations by advising Europe to work out a joint plan for reconstruction. 'Our policy,' he said, 'is directed against hunger, poverty, desperation and chaos. Its purpose should be the revival of a working economy in the world so as to permit the emergence of political and social conditions in which free institutions can exist.' Any government willing to assist in the task of recovery, he added, would find full co-operation on the part of the United States.

Marshall's speech came at a time when not only Britain but much of western Europe neared economic breakdown. By 1947 the world owed the United States $11.5 billion for goods it had acquired but could not pay for, and emergency measures to close this 'dollar gap,' such as the loan to Britain, gave only temporary relief. In March 1947, as UNRRA came to an end at the same time that Europe was buffeted by a vicious winter, the people of western Europe faced starvation; bread rations in Italy and France fell to half a pound a day. So critical was the coal

6. Quoted in W. C. Mallalieu, 'Origin of the Marshall Plan,' 73 *Political Science Quarterly* 481.

shortage in England that, for hours every day, London shut off electric power. The financial editor of Reuter's wrote: 'The biggest crash since the fall of Constantinople — the collapse of the heart of an Empire — impends.' The political consequences of the impending disaster would be as serious as the economic cost. Europe, wrote Winston Churchill, was 'a rubble heap, a charnel house, a breeding ground of pestilence and hate.'

The invitation from Marshall found an instantaneous response in Europe. The Prime Ministers of Britain and France promptly issued an invitation to 22 nations, including Russia, to meet at Paris the following month to draw a blueprint for European recovery. Though Molotov came to Paris to discuss preliminaries, the Kremlin decided it was unwise to take part in a project that would extend American influence in Europe. Molotov withdrew, and all the Soviet satellites followed; poor Czechoslovakia, which had already accepted an invitation to the Paris conference, sent regrets.

In the end representatives of 16 nations met at Paris and, under the leadership of the Oxford philosopher Sir Oliver Franks, drafted an elaborate plan for European recovery. This plan fixed new production targets, promised financial and monetary stability, advised the abandonment of trade barriers, called for the restoration of the industrial economy of western Germany, and fixed the bill at approximately $22 billion over a period of four years; it was assumed that most of this would come from the United States.

In December 1947 President Truman submitted this plan to Congress together with his own recommendations for an appropriation of $17 billion over a four-year period. Opposition to the proposal, led by Senator Taft, came chiefly from those who felt that the American economy could not stand so heavy a burden and those who regarded any further aid to the Old World as 'Operation Rathole.' Liberals of both parties as well as powerful business, farm, and labor organizations rallied to the bill, whose leading senatorial champion was Arthur Vandenberg, architect of the bipartisan foreign policy. What finally turned the tide was not so much economic arguments as the Communist coup in Czechoslovakia in March 1948, together with new Russian demands on Finland and the fear of Communist success in the forthcoming Italian elections. A program to halt the advance of Communism appealed to many who were immune to an appeal on economic or humanitarian grounds, and the

Foreign Assistance Act — providing an immediate grant of $5.3 billion for European recovery plus $463 million for China and $275 million for Greece and Turkey — passed both houses of Congress by thumping majorities and became law on 3 April 1948. Thus once more, in the great words of Churchill, 'the new world with all its power and might, stepped forth to the rescue and liberation of the old.'

The Marshall Plan mounted the most effective counterattack on poverty, despair, and disintegration in modern history. Altogether Congress voted some $12 billion to carry it out. Critics had predicted that the enterprise would bankrupt the United States; instead the country enjoyed unparalleled prosperity. At the same time, Europe, which had a sound economic basis in industrial resources and skilled labor, prospered. When the Economic Cooperation Administration — set up to administer Marshall-aid money — reported in 1951, it could point to an over-all increase of production in Marshall-aid countries of 37 per cent, a growth in agricultural production of 25 per cent, while steel output almost doubled. More important was the dramatic change in morale. As the economy rebounded, so did the confidence of the peoples of western Europe, not only in their ability to fend for themselves but in their democratic institutions.

7. THE COLD WAR

If the Marshall Plan succeeded in reviving western Europe, it also served to deepen divisions between the United States and Russia. On 16 April 1947, in a speech at Columbia, South Carolina, Bernard Baruch declared: 'Let us not be deceived — today we are in the midst of a cold war.' Increasingly, American institutions — the government, the corporation, the university, the foundation — were called into the service of the Cold War. Economic aid, too, came chiefly to be a stratagem in the Cold War. At the outset, Congress stipulated that not one penny of Marshall Plan aid was to be used for military purposes. In less than three years the United States was informing Europe that every cent of aid would be allotted so as to contribute to Western defenses.[7]

7. When the United States set up 'Point Four' (named after the fourth point of Truman's inaugural address of 1949), the program began as a modest venture in providing technological aid to underdeveloped nations, but by 1951 had been brought under the Mutual Security Act as another weapon in the Cold War arsenal.

This new military posture resulted in large part from concern over Soviet aggressiveness in Germany. The Russians had been disturbed when the French fused their zone with the British and the American zones to create a 'Trizonia' with the richest industrial resources in Germany and a population of 50 million which outstripped the Soviet zone's 17 million. In the spring of 1948 the Western powers alarmed the Kremlin by inviting the Germans to elect delegates to a convention to create a new government for West Germany. (Subsequently, in May 1949, the German Federal Republic was established at Bonn.) In June 1948 the Allies carried out a drastic currency reform which triggered a remarkable economic revival that would result in prosperity for western Germany such as no other Continental power enjoyed.

On June 24 the Russians retaliated by clamping a tight blockade around Berlin. Through some inexplicable oversight the Western powers had not guaranteed access to their zones of Berlin, and as a result the Russians were able to cut all land communication by the simple device of erecting road blocks and stopping railroad trains. Confronted with the alternatives of mass starvation for the 2 million Germans of the western zones of Berlin or an ignominious evacuation of that city, the American commander, General Lucius Clay, rejected both. 'We have lost Czechoslovakia,' he said,

> Norway is threatened. We retreat from Berlin. When Berlin falls, western Germany will be next. If we mean to hold Europe against Communism we must not budge. . . . If we withdraw, our position in Europe is threatened. If America does not understand this now . . . then it never will, and communism will run rampant. I believe the future of democracy requires us to stay.

The American and British governments rejected the temptation to ram an armored train through the Russian blockade, for this might have precipitated general war. Instead they embarked upon an 'airlift' operation to supply the beleaguered capital not only with food but with coal and other necessities. To the consternation of the Russians the airlift was a spectacular success: by the spring of 1949 American and British planes were flying in up to 10,000 tons of supplies daily; altogether they dropped 2.5 million tons of provisions into the city. On 12 May 1949, outwitted by the West, Russia ended the blockade.

The Berlin crisis and the Czech coup prompted negotiations for a military alliance that would weld western Europe into a unified military force. The Brussels Pact of 1948, joining Britain, France, and the Benelux nations in a defensive alliance, provided the springboard. That June the Senate adopted Arthur Vandenberg's resolution pledging American support to collective security arrangements between the free nations of the West, and Truman immediately took steps to implement this resolution. The North Atlantic Treaty of 4 April 1949 brought together the United States and Canada and ten nations of western Europe in an alliance against aggression; eventually it embraced several Mediterranean nations as well. The treaty pledged that an armed attack against any one member would be considered an attack upon them all.

Never before had the United States gone so far in a practical surrender of part of its sovereign power, or so clearly recognized that its frontier henceforth lay overseas along the lines that divided noncommunist nations from the Soviet Union. The overwhelming public support for the pact was measured by the alacrity with which the Senate ratified it, by a vote of 82 to 13. The administration then proposed a military assistance program, giving the North Atlantic Treaty Organization (NATO) authority to spend over a billion dollars on arms and other military needs, and giving further aid to Greece and Turkey — soon to join the organization — and Iran.

The next year saw NATO make a real beginning in armed power. The first American shipments of arms reached Europe in April; Great Britain and France both undertook to re-arm; and General Eisenhower was persuaded to leave the presidency of Columbia University to become Supreme Commander of NATO forces. Within a few years West Germany was admitted to NATO and her armed forces integrated into the NATO army. Not surprisingly, Russia looked upon the creation of NATO as an open declaration of hostility, and upon the re-arming of Germany and her admission to the new international organization as an act of defiance.

8. THE KOREAN WAR

While Americans were preoccupied with the problems of Europe, the Far East burst into flames. When Truman took over, he continued the Roosevelt policy of regarding China as the mainstay of American interests in Asia and of supporting the Nationalists against the Communists.

At the end of the war U.S. forces enabled the Nationalists to secure control of Shanghai, Nanking, and the region south of the Yangtse. But the Chiang Kai-shek regime, torn by dissension, corroded by corruption, and without strong popular support, proved wholly unable to stem the tide of Chinese Communism. Even during the war the Chinese had been as zealous to fight among themselves as to fight the Japanese; after the war, as the Japanese moved out, Russian and Chinese Communist armies moved in. Efforts by the United States to reform and strengthen the Nationalist regime and to force some settlement of the Chinese civil war proved abortive. Early in 1946 General Marshall arranged a truce between the Nationalists and the Communists, but it was speedily violated by both and, exasperated with both factions, Marshall withdrew most of the American troops from China and washed his hands of the whole muddle. Yet notwithstanding this official shift in policy, the United States continued to pour military and financial aid into Nationalist China. This aid, which came to some $2 billion by 1950, disappointed the Nationalists who expected further assistance. Although the United States continued Lend-Lease shipments to China after it had halted such aid to other countries, Truman would not make a massive commitment to the Nationalists because he and his advisers did not believe that Chiang could be salvaged. By the end of 1949 the Communists had swept the whole of the mainland, and Chiang, with the remnant of his forces, had fled to the island of Formosa (Taiwan).

The 'fall' of China had a number of momentous consequences. By allying the 500 million Chinese with the Russians, it shifted the balance of power in the Cold War in Asia. It led to a fierce attack on the Truman administration from Republican 'Asia-firsters' and publicists like the Luce empire which strengthened McCarthyism, helped bring the twenty year reign of the Democrats to an end, and served to lock American policy in Asia in the matrix of an inflexible anti-Communism. The Administration's policy was vulnerable to criticism, for Roosevelt had led the country to believe that Nationalist China was a major power and some diplomats had misconceived the nature of the Communist threat. Yet, as John King Fairbank pointed out, 'The illusion that the United States could have shaped China's destiny assumes that we Americans can really call the tune if we want to, even among 475 million people in the inaccessible rice paddies of a subcontinent 10,000 miles away.' When the Administration, shocked by indignities to American consular officials and sensitive to criticism of its Asia policy, refused to recognize Red China and blocked attempts to admit Mao Tse-tung's government to the United Nations, it enraged the Chinese Communists, widened the gulf between the United States and Russia, and strained relations with allies like Britain that recognized Mao. Finally, the 'loss' of China resulted in a dramatic reversal of American policy toward Japan.

At the end of World War II, the United States had but one aim in Japan: to make certain that the Japanese would never again constitute a military threat in Asia. To this end the American occupation authorities sought both to democratize Japan and to reduce that country to a second-rate power by returning its economy to the level of 1930–34. Within a few months after the surrender, General MacArthur in cooperation with liberal elements in Japan revolutionized the country's society and government. He demobilized 4 million soldiers, destroyed Japanese military potential, purged the civil service, abolished the secret police and 'patriotic' societies, broke up cartels and the family trusts, democratized the landowning system, ended press censorship, prohibited racial and religious discrimination, abolished Shintoism as a state religion, and required the Emperor, who was not deposed, to repudiate his own divinity. Meantime an International Tribunal tried the leading war criminals and sentenced Prime Minister Tojo and a dozen of the leading generals to death for their part in war crimes and atrocities. High ranking officers of the army and navy were tried by local tribunals for offenses against the laws of war; 4200 of them were convicted and no less than 720 of them were executed.

At the same time MacArthur inaugurated far-reaching reforms. A new Diet, elected under a law permitting woman suffrage, drafted a democratic constitution that provided for popular sovereignty and parliamentary government, reduced the Emperor to a figurehead, and included a bill of rights. The United States took special pride in one provision of the constitution, written in part by Americans, which stipulated that 'the Japanese people forever renounce war as a sovereign right of the nation.'

With the fall of China, American policymakers did a complete about face. The United States now came to value Japan as a military counterweight against Red China. As a consequence, it took steps to help the Japanese win industrial supremacy in Asia, partly in order to restore Japan's war potential. No longer did the Americans press Tokyo for a permanent renunciation of war; and when in 1951 the United States signed a treaty which put a formal end to the war and the occupation, it put through another treaty that same day which permitted the United States to maintain troops and air bases on the Japanese islands. Long before then the State Department's Policy Planning staff was boasting that Japan, with its industrial might, was a better prize than China.

The United States little reckoned that the focus of its attention would shortly become neither Japan nor China but the ancient nation of Korea. Military occupation was as unsuccessful in Korea as it was successful in Japan. Long part of China, then briefly independent, the 'Hermit Kingdom' had been annexed to Japan in 1910; the Cairo Conference had promised Koreans freedom 'in due course.' Russia's last-minute declaration of war against Japan enabled her to move troops into the Korean peninsula, and Korea was divided along the 38th parallel into zones of occupation: the United States in the more populous south, and Russia in the north. All efforts to unify either administration or economy proved vain; as the Russians proceeded to communize their area, the American authorities threw their support to the conservative elements of South Korea, represented by the aged and stubborn Syngman Rhee, a kind of Korean Chiang Kai-shek. Late in 1946 the administration was turned over to the Koreans, and in 1948 a popular election adopted a republican constitution. Syngman Rhee was elected President for what proved to be a 12-year term, and the American military occupation came to an end.

The triumph of the Communists in the north and in China made Korea's strategic position highly vulnerable, while economically the nation continued to be a heavy drain on the American taxpayer. Since the United States, under a tight military budget, did not have enough men even to defend airstrips in Alaska, Korea seemed a luxury America could not afford, especially at a time when the United States was trying to build up her strength in Europe. On 12 January 1950 when Secretary Acheson outlined a 'defensive perimeter' vital to national security, he included neither Korea nor Formosa. Yet two months later he warned: 'The Chinese people should understand that . . . they can only bring grave trouble on themselves and their friends, if they are led by their new rulers into aggressive or subversive adventures beyond their borders.'

On 25 June 1950, just five months after Acheson's 'perimeter' speech,

North Korean troops launched a full-scale attack upon the South, and within three days they had captured the capital at Seoul and threatened to overrun the entire country.

Once again, as at the time of the threat to Berlin, Truman reacted decisively. The President reflected: 'I recalled some earlier instances: Manchuria, Ethiopia, Austria. I remembered how each time that the democracies failed to act it had encouraged the aggressors to go ahead. . . . If this was allowed to go unchallenged, it would mean a third world war.' On 27 June he announced that he was sending American air and naval forces to the aid of the South Koreans. That same day the United Nations Security Council — with Russia momentarily absent on a boycott — called on member nations to repel aggression in Korea. Truman ordered American troops to the battlefront, and within a few days a dozen other members of the United Nations responded to the appeal and in time sent small contingents to the front. When the Security Council asked Truman to create a unified command, he appointed General MacArthur commander in chief of the United Nations forces, and before long the UN banner waved over a motley world army — the first of its kind in history. But since the United States sent more than five times as many troops as the rest of the world combined, most Americans regarded the conflict as a U.S. war.

For nearly six weeks North Korean armies advanced down the peninsula driving the smaller South Korean and American forces before them. Fighting desperately, the outnumbered defenders retreated over jagged mountains, across tangled ravines, and through malodorous rice paddies to the southernmost tip of Korea. There they held firm while reinforcements poured into the port of Pusan from Japan and the United States, and MacArthur built up naval and air support. In mid-September, MacArthur carried out a brilliant, and daring, amphibious landing at Inchon, the first engagement in a well-conceived counteroffensive that smashed the North Korean lines and drove the stricken armies in full retreat to the north. On 26 September Seoul was once more in South Korean hands, and the United Nations armies were pounding on the North Korean border.

The United States had gone to war when North Koreans crossed the 38th parallel; would China go to war when South Koreans — and Americans — crossed it going the other direction? From the beginning, Truman had insisted that the intervention in Korea would be limited; he had no intention of getting bogged down in a land war in Asia, or in a direct conflict with Russia or China. To this end, he had dispatched the Seventh Fleet to serve as a barrier between Formosa and the Chinese mainland. Exponents of containment like George Kennan now argued that the UN had achieved its objective of expelling the North Koreans; the UN should consolidate its lines along the 38th parallel and negotiate a settlement. But MacArthur, buoyed by his success at Inchon, was convinced that the only way to end the war, and unite Korea, was to conquer the North. For a brief interval, both Acheson, under pressure from the Asia-firsters, and the UN were persuaded by MacArthur's argument. In the teeth of a Chinese warning that they might enter the war, the UN General Assembly authorized MacArthur to cross the parallel.

So concerned was President Truman with the threat of Chinese intervention that in mid-October he flew to Wake Island for a conference with MacArthur. The General assured him that the Chinese would not attack, and if they did 'there would be the greatest slaughter.' On this advice, Truman approved an advance to within a few miles from the Chinese border on the Yalu river. MacArthur predicted that enemy resistance would be ended by Christmas, and for a time it seemed he might be right. On 20 October the North Korean capital of Pyongyang fell to UN forces. By the end of the month MacArthur was approaching the Manchurian border, while the battleship *Missouri* bombarded Chongjin, only 50 miles from Siberia. Yet even as Truman and MacArthur spoke, masses of Red Chinese soldiers were streaming across the Yalu into Korea.

On the night of 25 November Mao's 'volunteers' unleashed a ferocious assault on the UN forces. Three days later MacArthur issued a chilling communiqué: 'We face an entirely new war.' An army of more than a quarter-million Chinese, provided with the best arms and equipment and supported by ample air power, drove MacArthur's armies out of all the territory they had won in North Korea, pushed them out of Seoul, and sent them reeling back across the 38th parallel.

That winter saw some of the cruelest warfare in American history. The shocking cold and blinding storms, the rugged terrain of jagged mountains, treacherous swamps and unbridged streams, the ferocity of the enemy giving no quarter, the power of Russian-made tanks and planes, the desperate nature of many of the battles, the inhuman treatment of prisoners — all this added a new dimension to terror.

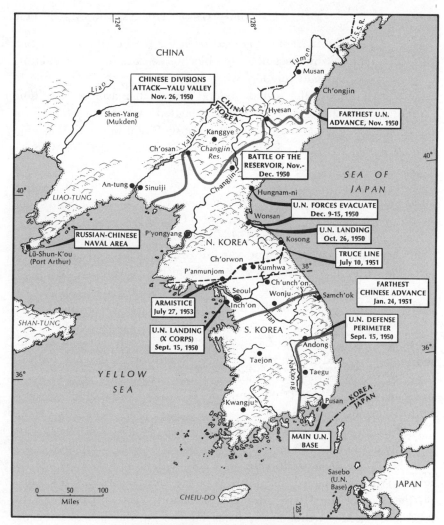

CHINA

CHINESE DIVISIONS
ATTACK—YALU VALLEY
Nov. 26, 1950

Musan

Ch'ongjin

Shen-Yang
(Mukden)

Hyesan

FARTHEST U.N.
ADVANCE, Nov. 1950

Kanggye

Ch'osan

Changjin
Res.

BATTLE OF THE
RESERVOIR, Nov.-
Dec. 1950

SEA OF
JAPAN

An-tung   Sinuiji

Changjin

LIAO-TUNG

Hungnam-ni

U.N. FORCES EVACUATE
Dec. 9-15, 1950

Wonsan

RUSSIAN-CHINESE
NAVAL AREA

P'yongyang

N. KOREA

Kosong

U.N. LANDING
Oct. 26, 1950

Lü-Shun-K'ou
(Port Arthur)

Ch'orwon

TRUCE LINE
July 10, 1951

P'anmunjom

Kumhwa

38°

FARTHEST
CHINESE ADVANCE
Jan. 24, 1951

Ch'unch'on

Seoul

Wonju

Samch'ok

SHAN-TUNG

ARMISTICE
July 27, 1953

Inch'on

Han

S. KOREA

U.N. DEFENSE
PERIMETER
Sept. 15, 1950

U.N. LANDING
(X CORPS)
Sept. 15, 1950

Andong

36°

Taejon

Taegu

YELLOW

SEA

Kwangju

Pusan

KOREA

JAPAN

MAIN U.N.
BASE

Sasebo
(U.N.
Base)

JAPAN

0   50   100
Miles

CHEJU-DO

THE KOREAN WAR, 1950-1953

MacArthur, who in September had been the hero of the Inchon success, found himself by December an object of censure for miscalculating Chinese intentions and for deploying his troops ineptly. Never one to take reproof lightly, the proud general turned increasingly to issuing public and private statements which intimated that the real blame for the discouraging situation in Korea lay not with him but with Washington's decision to fight a limited war. He proposed bombing China's 'privileged sanctuary' in Manchuria, pursuing MIGs across the Yalu into China, a blockade of the Chinese coast, air attacks on the densely populated industrial cities of the Chinese mainland, and an invasion of China by the well-trained but untested armies of Chiang Kai-shek.

Truman firmly rejected MacArthur's policy of extending the war and announced that 'our goal is not war but peace.' Chastened by its costly flirtation with a liberation policy, the Administration returned to the old policy of containment. It did not want MacArthur to lead the United States into the 'gigantic booby trap' of an all-out war with Red China. Moreover, the military situation in Korea in early 1951 offered new hope for peace. UN forces under General Matthew Ridgway blunted the Chinese offensive, and in March recaptured Seoul for the second and last time and recrossed the 38th parallel. With the Republic of Korea cleared of Communist soldiers, Truman and the UN believed the time had come to press for negotiations.

MacArthur would have none of it. Although he had been warned repeatedly not to make statements which conflicted with UN policy, on 24 March 1951 he defiantly threatened China with an attack, a declaration which Truman believed killed any hope for an early truce. On 5 April, on the floor of the House, Republican minority leader Joseph Martin read a letter MacArthur had written him on 19 March criticizing the President and insisting, 'There is no substitute for victory.' It was the boldest challenge to civilian authority since McClellan had tried to take direction of the war out of Lincoln's hands; and it was equally intolerable, and even more dangerous for what was at stake this time was not merely American peace but world peace. After consulting with Secretary Marshall and General Bradley, Truman dramatically dismissed General MacArthur from command.

The General came home to receive tumultuous ovations, address both houses of Congress, and defend his position at elaborate hearings conducted by the Congress and in speeches throughout the country. In all of these he made clear that he was indifferent to the fate of Europe, thought the United States could get along without European allies, and felt that the future destiny of America lay in the Pacific and Asiatic theaters.

Nor did MacArthur speak for himself alone. Ever since Seward's 'large' policy in the Pacific and McKinley's 'open door' policy in China, the Republican party had been deeply committed to intervention in Pacific affairs; the isolationism upon which it embarked in 1919 did not embrace Asia, and indeed the very consciousness of isolationism toward Europe tended to exaggerate the vigor of interventionism in the Far East. MacArthur's position was endorsed by the two most powerful figures in the Republican party: Herbert Hoover and Robert A. Taft. Even as the General was trying to impose his program upon the President, Hoover urged that the United States withdraw its forces from Europe and become a 'Western Hemisphere Gibraltar.' Hoover saw MacArthur as 'a reincarnation of St. Paul into a great General of the Army who came out of the East,' and when MacArthur addressed Congress, Republican Congressman Dewey Short, who had studied at Harvard, Oxford, and Heidelberg, cried out that he had seen 'a great hunk of God in the flesh' and had heard 'the voice of God.' But popular enthusiasm for MacArthur died down out after it was revealed that all three Chiefs of Staff backed Truman against the General. If MacArthur's counsel had been followed, the President's military advisers declared, the United States would have won the enmity of all of Asia, wrecked the coalition of free nations, and diverted its strength in a costly struggle with China while Russia would have been unscathed. MacArthur's approach, General Omar Bradley observed, 'would involve us in the wrong war, at the wrong place, at the wrong time, and with the wrong enemy.'

By the spring of 1951 the Korean conflict had been deadlocked; and when in June 1951 the Soviet delegate to the United Nations suggested an armistice with mutual withdrawal behind the 38th parallel, Washington welcomed the proposal. Early the next month leaders of the opposing forces began discussions looking to an armistice; these dragged on interminably over two issues: the exact boundary line between North and South, and the fate of prisoners. The first was settled by accepting the current status quo, which meant the United Nations forces would be a bit north of the famous parallel; the second proved more vexatious.

The United Nations held some 132,000 prisoners; the Chinese admitted to only 11,502, of which 3198 were Americans; either the Chinese lists were incomplete, or they had killed most of their prisoners. The Communists insisted on mutual repatriation of all prisoners, but most of the North Koreans and Chinese did not want to be repatriated. The armistice negotiators were at an impasse when the timely 'escape' of some 20,000 North Koreans from their prisons, the election of Eisenhower to the presidency, and the death of Stalin brought about a change of atmosphere. In a more conciliatory mood the Communists accepted a plan of voluntary repatriation, and on 27 June 1953 a truce put an end to the three-year war.

The war had cost the United States some 30,000 dead and over 100,000 wounded and missing. South Korean casualties approached a million, and North Korean and Chinese were estimated at a million and a half. Korea lay in ruins, North and South alike; it was to be another decade before South Korea would achieve some kind of recovery and a stable government, while the chains that bound North Korea to China were tightened. In return for all this South Korea was saved from communism, and the prestige of the United Nations was enhanced. Above all, the limited war which arrayed American against Chinese soldiers had not escalated into World War III.

XXVII

The Eisenhower Administration

1. PRESIDENT EISENHOWER

President Eisenhower, who was sixty-two years old when he took office, personified the American success story. Born in Denison, Texas, in 1890 into a humble family of Pennsylvania-Dutch descent, Dwight Eisenhower grew up in Abilene, Kansas, long one of the famous 'cow-towns' of the West, still very much part of the frontier. Appointed to West Point at the age of twenty-one, Eisenhower spent the whole of his adult life in government service. From 1915 to 1941 he rose methodically through the grades of the army, serving for four years on General MacArthur's staff in the Philippines, and in Washington. The outbreak of World War II found him Chief of the War Plans Division of the General Staff; his outstanding performance brought him to the attention of General Marshall, who recommended him to the President for the command of the Allied forces invading North Africa. Eisenhower's success in this enterprise led to his appointment as Supreme Commander of the Allied Forces in Europe, a post which he filled with distinction. After the war General Eisenhower remained Chief of Staff until 1948, when he became, briefly, president of Columbia University and, from 1950 to June 1952, Supreme Commander of NATO. In these positions he displayed transparent honesty, integrity, prudence, a talent for mediating among men of diverse views, and the ability to inspire loyalty among subordinates and confidence among associates.

Eisenhower belonged to the McKinley-Taft rather than the Roosevelt-

Wilson tradition of the presidency. He thought of the President as neither party leader nor Chief Legislator but as a combination chief of
staff, mediator, and father of his people. He repudiated the 'left-wing
theory that the Executive has unlimited powers' and adopted the Whig
view that the prerogatives of his office should be used as little as possible. His general outlook, noted Walter Johnson, was: 'What will we refrain from doing now?' Convinced that Roosevelt and Truman had
usurped congressional authority, Eisenhower limited himself, for the
most part, to suggesting policies and leaving congressmen free to 'vote
their own consciences.' Unlike his Democratic predecessors and successors in the White House, he disliked politics and politicians, and tried to
keep aloof from the contest for patronage and the Billingsgate of campaigns. Thoroughly American as 'Ike' was, he nevertheless conceived his
role to be somewhat like that of a constitutional monarch: he was to be
a symbol above the battle. He hoped to smooth over party differences,
to offend nobody in Congress, to preside over a scene of harmony and
peace, to use his immense popularity to bring about a new 'Era of Good
Feelings.'

Eisenhower's long military experience predisposed him toward a 'staff'
system, which he had used so successfully in Europe. He preferred to
work through subordinates who would shelter him from demands on his
time and protect him from personal involvement in the hurly-burly of
politics. Members of his cabinet who enjoyed his confidence exercised
more power than had been customary in the history of the American
presidency. Impatient of detail and of administrative routine, Eisenhower was not disposed to probe deeply into any subject; and he liked
to have every problem, even the most complex, summarized for him on a
single sheet of paper. Because he insulated himself from public affairs,
he was often taken by surprise on learning things that almost everyone
knew — book burning by the Department of State underlings in American overseas libraries, for example, or sit-ins by Negro students in the
South.

As his special assistant Eisenhower chose one of his original backers,
Governor Sherman Adams of New Hampshire. This dour Yankee, who
became a kind of unofficial alter-ego of the President's, wielded a power
out of all proportion to his official position. Under the Eisenhower staff
system he controlled access to the President: 'The Governor' decided
who could see the President and selected letters and papers to be sub-

mitted to his consideration. He was to Eisenhower what Colonel House had been to Wilson and Harry Hopkins to Roosevelt, and had far more power than either. 'I need him,' Eisenhower said when Adams's position was threatened through his indiscretions. Increasingly, as the President took refuge on his Gettysburg farm from routine work and social demands, the burden of running the presidential office fell on the hardworking Adams. On the whole he performed his thankless task well.

Eisenhower's conception of his office unsuited him for the exacting and importunate role of the President in time of crisis, but it seemed appropriate for the mood of many Americans in the 1950's, a mood the President himself helped to set. In the 1952 campaign some, like Walter Lippmann, backed Eisenhower because they hoped he would lead the nation in new ventures, while others did so because they wished him to repeal the past. Yet many, perhaps most, who voted for him did so because they anticipated that the General would give the country a respite from the stress of politics. By 1952 the American people had experienced a generation of unrelieved crisis: a disastrous depression, a world war, a cold war, an enervating limited war. Kept in a constant state of tension by two activist Presidents, they had reached a point of weariness with the intrusion of public issues into their lives. They expected Eisenhower not to solve problems but to serve as a good-luck amulet to charm them away.

The country demanded too much of the new President; and, since he was asked to do contradictory things, he was bound to disappoint some of his followers. Men like Lippmann who anticipated that Eisenhower would lead the country in new directions were quickly disillusioned. For a time he showed some tendency to placate both those who desired a sharply conservative turn in domestic affairs and those who favored a more aggressive foreign policy. But in the end Eisenhower would satisfy only that large segment of his supporters who hoped he would bring a new spirit of quiescence and moderation.

2. DYNAMIC CONSERVATISM

Eisenhower's election marked the return of the Republican party to power after twenty years; many Republicans looked forward to a complete reversal of Democratic policies which (their platform asserted) led toward socialism and the wrecking of the free enterprise system. They knew what they wanted: New Deal and Fair Deal to be discredited and scrapped; no more welfare-state 'creeping socialism'; an end to unbalanced budgets and sky-rocketing debt; a reversal to centralization and the invasion of states' rights; and, in foreign policy, no more 'giveaways.' Yet, once in power, the Republicans found they could do no more than modify practices which had been woven into the fabric of American life through the inescapable needs of the age. For better or worse, both government and people were irretrievably committed to many elements of the welfare state, such as Federal responsibility for full employment, social security, control of natural resources, and regulation of business. There could be no major reversal.

In the 1952 campaign Eisenhower had indicated sympathy with the Taft conservatives; and when he took office he aimed to achieve a 'revolution' in the national government, 'trying to make it smaller rather than bigger and finding things it can stop doing instead of seeking new things to do.' But the new President also carried the hopes of those Republicans who wanted to demonstrate that the party was responsible and enlightened. Eisenhower's two favorite phrases were 'middle of the road' and 'dynamic conservatism.' His administration turned out to be more conservative than dynamic, but in the end it was apparent that the President had not moved far from the middle of the road.

Eisenhower, who admired men of business and preferred them for his associates, named to his first cabinet six prominent businessmen, several of whom were multimillionaires. Secretary of Defense Charles E. Wilson, who had been head of the General Motors Corporation, achieved a kind of immortality by his statement that 'what was good for our country was good for General Motors, and vice versa.' Arthur Summerfield, also of General Motors, distinguished himself as Postmaster General by trying to put the department on a 'businesslike footing,' regardless of the impact on postal service, and by his crusades against books that he considered too 'obscene' for the mails. Secretary of the Interior Douglas MacKay of Oregon, yet a third product of General Motors, had a long record of hostility to conservation and public power. Secretary of Commerce Sinclair Weeks, a Massachusetts manufacturer, began his administration by firing the head of the Bureau of Standards, Dr. Allen Astin, because he was oblivious to 'the business point of view'; but in the face of nation-wide protests Weeks reversed himself and restored Dr. Astin to his job. Secretary of the Treasury George Humphrey, president of

Mark Hanna's old firm, regarded a balanced budget as the supreme test of economic statesmanship. The new Secretary of Agriculture, Ezra Taft Benson, a devout elder of the Mormon Church, had strong convictions about the dangers of Federal centralization and the welfare state. Attorney-General Herbert Brownell, a prominent New York lawyer, represented the Dewey wing of the party as did the leader of the cabinet, John Foster Dulles, the new Secretary of State. Dulles employed his talents chiefly in foreign affairs, but as a Wall Street lawyer he too weighted the cabinet on the conservative side. In this atmosphere it is little wonder that Secretary of Labor Martin Durkin, a Stevenson Democrat and union official, felt thoroughly out of place and resigned before the year was out; his post was filled by James P. Mitchell of New Jersey, a former personnel manager.

Eisenhower frequently appointed men to the independent regulatory commissions who did not believe in government regulation at all. Thus John C. Doerfer, new chairman of the Federal Communications Commission, opposed regulation of radio or television by the government; in the end he had to be dropped because of his intimacy with network officials. The Federal Power Commission was stacked with opponents of public power, and William B. Conole, who had fought against increases in the price of natural gas, and whose dissenting opinions in cases before the Federal Power Commission had been sustained by the Supreme Court, was dismissed because the President thought him too deeply committed 'to the consumer point of view.' The policies of the Civil Aeronautics Board, favoring the major airlines at the expense of the smaller ones, practically put the 'non-scheduled' independent airlines out of business.

Nowhere did the conservatism of the Eisenhower administration express itself more emphatically than in the attitude toward natural resources. The disposition of off-shore oil was a case in point. President Truman had twice vetoed bills giving the states control of the underseas oil deposits lying off their shores. In 1947 and 1950 the Supreme Court, while recognizing the special claims of Texas, held that these oil resources belonged to the entire nation. In 1952 Truman assigned underseas oil to the navy as a reserve for use in time of war. But within a few months of Eisenhower's accession he signed a Submerged Lands Act, put through by Republicans and Southern Democrats, which nullified all earlier arrangements and assigned Federal rights to the off-shore oil to the seaboard states — three miles in the Atlantic and Pacific Oceans and ten and one-half miles in the Gulf of Mexico.

In the realm of atomic energy also, private interests gained. The Atomic Energy Act of 1954 provided for government financing of atomic research but farmed out the operation of the new atomic energy plants to private corporations: General Electric at Hanford, Washington, Union Carbide at Oak Ridge, Tennessee. 'In turning a twelve billion dollar investment over to private industry,' wrote Walter Adams and Horace Gray, 'the statute was a milestone in government abdication from the public domain.'

Almost all Republicans agreed upon the paramount importance of private enterprise in the production of hydroelectric power. Not only would Federal control of hydroelectric power paralyze local enterprise, Eisenhower declared, but it would 'pose a threat deadly to our liberties.' And the President, promoting the issue to a celestial plane, added, 'there are spiritual as well as physical values to protect.' The Eisenhower administration cut the budget of the various Federal power administrations, abandoned projects already approved by Congress, and jettisoned a Democratic plan for a federally built and controlled dam at Hell's Canyon on the Snake river in Idaho in favor of a series of small dams to be built and operated by the Idaho Power Company.

Early in his administration, Eisenhower cited the TVA as an example of that 'creeping socialism' against which he so insistently warned his countrymen, and Clarence Manion, whom he had appointed chairman of the Commission on Inter-governmental Relations, went so far as to advocate selling TVA to private industry. Between 1952 and 1960 appropriations for the TVA fell from $185 million to $12 million. It was the administration's reluctance to expand this great enterprise that led in 1954–55 to the Dixon-Yates imbroglio. When Congress denied the Authority money to build a new generating plant to serve the needs of the Memphis area, the Atomic Energy Commission signed a contract for the plant with two private utilities, represented by Edgar Dixon and Eugene Yates. The terms of the contract were more than generous. Dixon and Yates were required to contribute only $5.5 million of a total investment of $107 million; the AEC guaranteed a 9 per cent return and exempted them from all taxes. However, a congressional investigation revealed that the contract had been written by a consultant to the Bureau of the Budget who, by an odd coincidence, was also vice-president of the corporation which would finance the operation; and the Atomic Energy Commission was compelled to void the contract. When Dixon-Yates sued to recoup its losses, the Administration was placed in the awkward position of claiming that the contract, in which it had taken such pride, had been illegal and 'contrary to the public interest' from the very beginning.

Devotion to private enterprise, and suspicion of public, persisted throughout the Eisenhower administration. Shortly after assuming office the President ended all price and rent controls and did away with the Reconstruction Finance Corporation. He vetoed a school construction bill which he thought interfered unduly with local autonomy, acquiesced in a sharp reduction in Federal aid to public housing, and opposed medical insurance amendments to social security bills.

The rising cost of farm subsidies typified the problem that bedeviled the Eisenhower administration. It was an axiom of Republican orthodoxy that an unbalanced budget was the road to ruin, and to this Eisenhower himself subscribed with almost religious fervor. But he soon discovered that it was one thing to preach the virtues of economy and another to practice them. As a result of expanding costs and of economic recession with the consequent reduction of tax revenue, the administration achieved a balanced budget in only three of its eight years. In 1959 the government ran the biggest peacetime deficit, and in Eisenhower's eight years the total of deficit over surplus came to some $20 billion.

Eisenhower sought both to slash Federal spending and to limit the intervention of the government in the economy, but he was finding it difficult to achieve either goal, as the intractable farm question soon demonstrated. Disturbed by the cost of government subsidies, Eisenhower embraced Secretary Benson's recommendation for flexible instead of rigid price supports for leading agricultural commodities, and Congress reluctantly approved. But Benson's program proved a costly failure. Farm income fell drastically, surpluses mounted. In 1954 Senator Hubert Humphrey revived Henry Wallace's idea of paying farmers to take their land out of production. This 'soil bank' scheme was at first rejected by Eisenhower, but in 1956 he came around to it, and even persuaded Congress to adopt it. Although the Republican platform of 1952 had charged the Democrats with using 'tax money to make farmers dependent upon government,' federal expenditures for agriculture multiplied during Eisenhower's two terms. By 1958 the government was spending six times as much as in 1952.

The Eisenhower administration stayed in the 'middle of the road' not only by maintaining a significant, if restrained, role for government in the economy but by balancing conservative policies in fields like natural resources with more liberal responses in other areas. Under the President's prodding — at times merely with his tacit approval — Congress extended reciprocal trade agreements; enlarged social security to embrace some ten million additional persons in agriculture, government employment, and domestic work; raised the minimum wage to a dollar an hour; pushed through two civil-rights bills designed to extend federal guarantees of the political rights of Negroes; established a new Department of Health, Education and Welfare; created an Air Force Academy and a National Aeronautics and Space Administration; authorized a far-reaching reorganization of the Department of Defense; amended the Atomic Energy Act of 1954 to permit more effective co-operation in atomic research and the exchange of scientific information with allied nations; admitted Hawaii and Alaska to statehood; provided some $887 million for student loans and the support of science and language teaching under the National Defense Education Act; carried through some modest tax reductions; provided for the admission of an additional 214,000 refugees outside the normal immigration quotas; and authorized the construction of the Great Lakes-St. Lawrence seaway, which Hoover, Roosevelt, and Truman had all urged in vain and which Canada and the United States completed within the decade. In short Eisenhower, partly by intent, partly by inadvertence, pursued a course of moderation in domestic affairs that much of the country seemed to approve.

3. LIQUIDATION OF MC CARTHYISM

For one of the long-needed accomplishments in Washington, the Senate rather than the President deserves credit: the liquidation of Senator McCarthy as an effective force. Yet in truth both performed ingloriously. Only a rare senator like Herbert Lehman dared to stand up to McCarthy, and the administration at times seemed bent on diverting the Wisconsin senator by outdoing him. Shortly after taking office Eisenhower extended the security system to all agencies of the government, replaced the earlier criterion of 'loyalty' with a broader and vaguer criterion of 'security risk,' and authorized the discharge of any person whose employment was not 'clearly consistent with the interests of national security.' Between May 1953 and October 1954 no fewer than 6926 'security risks' were 'separated' from their government jobs. Very few of these were even charged with subversion, and not one had committed any crime or breach of duty for which he was brought to trial in a court of law. Secretary Dulles appointed a McCarthyite as the State Department's security officer and sacrificed valued officials to appease the Senator. In December 1953 the Atomic Energy Commission, on orders from Eisenhower, withdrew security clearance from the 'father of the atomic bomb,' J. Robert Oppenheimer.

All this display of zeal, however, failed to assuage McCarthy, who, not impressed with the administration's house-cleaning, now trained his guns on the administration itself. McCarthy objected to Eisenhower's new Ambassador to Russia, Charles Bohlen, because he had been at Yalta; he charged that the Army Signal Corps at Fort Monmouth was riddled with subversion; he sent to Europe two bumbling assistants to track down and destroy 'subversive' literature (such as the works of Emerson and Thoreau) in libraries of the American Information Service — a usurpation of State Department authority in which Dulles readily acquiesced in the hope of appeasing McCarthy. Early in 1954, McCarthy seized on the case of an obscure army dentist, a major who had been given a routine promotion and an honorable discharge from the Army notwithstanding a suspicion of Communist sympathies. In the course of an investigation of this trivial episode of the 'pink dentist' McCarthy browbeat the major's superior, General Zwicker, and then turned on Robert Stevens, Secretary of the Army, who allowed himself to be bullied into signing a 'memorandum of agreement' with the Senator.

But on 11 March 1954 the army struck back with the charge that McCarthy had demanded preferential treatment in the army for one of his aides who had been drafted. The Senator counterattacked with forty-six charges against the army, and the war was on. The month-long hearings to determine the facts were televised on national networks, and the whole country watched with a kind of horrified fascination the spectacle of McCarthy bullying high officials and army officers. After it became clear that opinion was turning against McCarthy, the administration's backbone stiffened. When the Senator arrogantly asserted that government employees were 'duty bound' to give him information 'even though some bureaucrat may have stamped it secret,' Eisenhower was moved to denounce usurpation by an individual who undertook 'to set himself above the laws of our land or to override orders of the President of the United States.' No sooner was the investigation concluded than Republican Senator Ralph Flanders of Vermont moved that the Senate formally censure McCarthy for improper conduct. A Senate committee headed by Watkins of Utah, another Republican, recommended censure, and on 2 December 1954 the Senate formally 'condemned' McCarthy by a vote of 67 to 22, with Republicans casting all the opposition votes. Thereafter McCarthy's influence declined rapidly. On 2 May 1957 he died, his force largely spent, his name an 'improper noun' for a guiltily-remembered episode in American history.

Yet if McCarthy was gone, McCarthyism left as a heritage a large body of laws and administrative practices based on the notion that there were litmus tests for such things as loyalty, security, and Americanism, and that it was the business of governments to apply these tests to all those who served in any public capacity. 'Un-American activities' committees functioned without ever defining either 'American' or 'Un-American'; 'loyalty' tests and oaths lacked any clear notion of what loyalty meant; elaborate 'security' screenings sought to assure security by aimless inquiries into the private activities, beliefs, and intellectual interests of civil servants. A person's conduct, which since the Middle Ages had been considered the only proper test of loyalty or security, was now ignored in favor of inquests into a person's intentions, ideas, associations, and other tests so vague as to guarantee confusion and error.

What was new in the 'fifties was not American impatience with nonconformity — Tocqueville had observed that as far back as the 1830's — but the notion that it was the government's business to set up standards of conformity and force citizens to live up to them.[1] The elaborate apparatus improvised in the 'forties now hardened as a permanent engine of the American security system. To the Smith Act of 1940 and

1. Thus Senator McCarthy charged the distinguished lawyer and judge, Dorothy Kenyon, with being 'affiliated with' 28 Communist-front organizations. A congressional committee exonerated her from this charge, but nevertheless undertook to criticize her for being 'less than judicious' in her choice of associates and organizations. The notion that a congressional committee may supersede individual judgment in the choice of friends, clubs, churches, or organizations is certainly an innovation not only in constitutional law but in American history.

the Internal Security Act of 1950 was added the Communist Control Act of 1954 outlawing the Communist party. Self-appointed guardians of 'true' Americanism — patriotic, filiopietistic, and ultra-conservative organizations of all stripes — joined to preserve the true marrow of Americanism. Just as in pre-Civil War days Southern hostility to abolition gradually became hostility to all liberal nineteenth-century ideas, so now hostility to 'subversion' became also a bitter opposition to the United Nations and UNESCO, to those who championed the rights of Negroes, favored recognition of Communist China, supported Federal aid to schools and medical care for the aged, or even — as Arthur Schlesinger said — those who believed in the income tax, the fluoridation of water, and the twentieth century.

Many aspects of these security programs raised important constitutional questions, and increasingly in the 'fifties the federal courts found themselves preoccupied with civil liberties cases. The Supreme Court tended to divide sharply in interpreting such cases, with Justice Frankfurter speaking for one group — usually the majority — and Justice Black or Chief Justice Warren for the other. The philosophical difference between the two groups was subtle but important.[2] The Frankfurter wing tended to support the right of the legislature to qualify or suspend some of the guarantees of the First Amendment where it felt that the security of the commonwealth was at stake. The Black group believed that because security was ultimately best served by the exercise of freedom, legislatures should not be permitted to plead the necessity of security as a justification for overriding constitutional guarantees.

In the Dennis case of 1951 the Court had found the balance of interest to be on the side of security — as interpreted by the Congress — rather than of freedom. After 1954 there was a shift toward a more restrictive view of governmental power and a stronger emphasis on the guarantees of the First Amendment. The next four or five years saw a series of decisions that substantially enlarged the area of freedom. In 1955 the federal

2. It would be naïve to characterize these two groups as 'liberal' and 'conservative.' No judges were in favor of license or (the Birch Society to the contrary) were dupes of Communism; no judges were against the guarantees of the Bill of Rights. The real issue, as men like Frankfurter and Douglas saw it, was whether the Court or the legislature should determine, in the last analysis, whether the balance of interest was to be found in the preservation of particular freedoms or in the security of society. This particular issue may have been factitious, but not the issue whether it should be decided by the legislatures or by the courts.

courts rejected — and rebuked — the blundering attempt of Attorney General Brownell to indict the scholar Owen Lattimore for perjury because he had denied Communist affiliations. The next year, in *Cole v. Young*, the Court drastically curtailed the scope of the executive security program by restricting it to 'sensitive' positions only, and also in 1956, in *Pennsylvania v. Nelson*, it invalidated a state security program on the ground that the Federal government had already pre-empted the field. *Yates v. United States* (1957) curtailed the scope of the Dennis opinion by holding that even advocacy of forcible overthrow of government was not illegal if it confined itself to mere advocacy and made no effort to inspire action. The same year *Watkins v. United States* curbed the authority of the Un-American Activities Committee to punish uncooperative witnesses at will, and in two notable cases — *Kent v. Dulles* and *Dayton v. Dulles* — the Court denied the State Department the right to deny passports on arbitrary grounds. In *Sweezy v. New Hampshire* the Court rejected the claims of a state attorney general that he had a right to spy on state university professors in quest of subversive doctrines; in *NAACP v. Alabama* (1958) the Court nullified an Alabama ordinance requiring full disclosure of membership and activities of that organization, as an unconstitutional interference with freedom of association. That same year, too, the courts invalidated a California law requiring clergymen to take loyalty oaths as the price of tax exemption for their churches.

With the sharpening of the Cold War after 1958 there was a perceptible shift to the side of security. Thus in the Barenblatt, the Uphaus, and the Wilkinson cases the Court sustained the activities of legislative investigating committees even when these were palpably bent on exposure rather than on acquiring information, or when the relevance of the information they accumulated was negligible. It upheld the constitutionality of a requirement that subversive organizations register with the Department of Justice (*Communist Party v. Subversive Activities Board*) and applied the penal provisions of the membership clause in that act, thus all but officially endorsing the doctrine of guilt by association (*Scales v. United States*). In two decisions (*Konigsberg v. State Bar of California* and *In re Anastaplo*) it sustained the right of a state to exclude from the bar candidates otherwise qualified if they refused to answer questions about their associations and affiliations. Perhaps the most far-reaching — and potentially the most dangerous — opinion was one that attracted very little attention: *Perez v. Brownell*. This decision sustained an act of Congress depriving a native-born American of citizenship because he voted in an election of a foreign country. As Congress has control of foreign affairs, said Mr. Justice Frankfurter, it may punish actions which embarrass the conduct of foreign affairs.

4. THE CIVIL RIGHTS REVOLUTION

If the Supreme Court failed to speak with a clear voice on civil liberties, it acted emphatically on behalf of Negroes who, as the centenary of the Civil War approached, were still second-class citizens throughout the South. Negro children were fobbed off with schools that were not only segregated but physically and academically inferior, and Negro youths were denied entrance to the state universities they helped to support by taxation. When Negroes traveled they were forced to use segregated waiting rooms and sections of buses and denied access to Pullman cars. They were not permitted to sit with white people in theaters, movies, restaurants, or at lunch counters; even in many churches. Their right to vote was flouted by various devices, and without fellow Negroes on juries it was impossible for many to obtain a fair trial. Half a century after Booker T. Washington's famous Atlanta speech calling for economic partnership between white and black, Negroes were mostly tenant farmers or unskilled laborers. In the North urban Negroes met various kinds of discrimination and were confined to slum dwellings in black ghettos.

Between 1940 and 1960 Negroes in the North increased from 2.8 to 7.2 million, while in the South they barely held their own. New York in 1960 boasted the largest black population of any state in the Union. In the 1960's Washington, D.C., was more than 60 per cent nonwhite; by 1962 Philadelphia's public schools had more Negro than white pupils; and by early 1967 white pupils in New York City's public school system were a minority classified with 'others.' This meant that economically and politically Negroes were a power to be reckoned with, for it was not practical to deny social rights to those who had achieved economic independence or political rights to those who might hold the balance of power.

The conscience of the American people had been deeply disturbed by what the great Swedish sociologist, Gunnar Myrdal, called the American

Dilemma — the dilemma of commitment to both equality and to white superiority — and by the spectacle of the ravages of racism in Nazi Germany. Furthermore, at a time when the colonial peoples of Africa and Asia were bursting their bonds and emerging into the sunshine of liberty, and when the United States was trying to win them to the side of the democracies, it was embarrassing to maintain at home a policy that made a dark skin a badge of inferiority.

The new attitude toward the Negro received judicial sanction in a number of Supreme Court decisions which chipped away at the stone wall of separation and prejudice erected by the states of the South. One series of Court decisions looked to the practical implementation of due process and fair trial by requiring Negro representation on juries; another required political parties to act as public, not private bodies; a third announced the beginning of the end of discrimination in public facilities such as housing and interstate transportation.

The climax of the judicial assault on white supremacy, and one of the historic decisions of the Supreme Court, came in the 1954 school segregation case, *Brown v. Board of Education of Topeka*. In 1896 the Supreme Court had held — over the protest of Justice Harlan — that the Fourteenth Amendment did not require that Negroes and whites share all public facilities and that it was not illegal for such facilities to be 'separate' as long as they were 'equal.' The principle of this ruling, though subject to serious qualification, had survived. In the Brown case a unanimous Court, speaking through Chief Justice Earl Warren, an Eisenhower appointee, reversed this decision and held that 'separate educational facilities are inherently unequal.' It followed this ruling with another in May 1955 which required that Southern states proceed with desegregation 'with all deliberate speed' and assigned to the lower courts responsibility for applying this principle in the school districts of the South.

Deliberateness became more apparent than speed. In the border states, except Virginia, desegregation encountered only sporadic resistance, but in the Deep South, the segregationists stood firm, hoping that district judges would find some legal means to frustrate the Court's decision or delay its implementation. When, in decision after decision, the courts ordered school boards to proceed with integration, the beleaguered defenders of segregation resorted to less formal and more drastic measures. Organizing themselves into White Citizens' Councils, they whipped up opposition sentiment to fever pitch, brought pressure on state officials and on congressmen, and, in the words of Senator Byrd of Virginia, confronted the Federal authorities — and the Negroes — with 'massive resistance.' In March 1956 one hundred Southern congressmen sought to legitimize these acts of defiance by a 'Declaration' of constitutional principles. 'We commend the motives of those states,' it said, 'which have declared the intention to resist forced integration by any lawful means. . . .' Southern legislatures hastily threw up a barricade of legislation and regulation designed to impede integration; within a few months five Southern states adopted forty-two segregation measures. Georgia made it a felony for any school official to spend tax money for public schools in which the races were mixed; Mississippi made it a crime for any organization to institute desegregation proceedings in the state courts; North Carolina withheld school funds from any school district which integrated its public schools. Some states sanctioned segregation on the ground not of 'race' but of 'public health, morals, and good order'; some segregated pupils according to 'scholastic ability'; some put the burden of initiating action for desegregation on the individuals in each school district, thus assuring endless litigation; some made a gesture of purely token integration. Virginia went to the extreme of closing public schools altogether and enrolling white children in segregated 'private' schools. Where these methods failed, or where Negroes attempted to nullify them, there was resort to force. In February 1956, when Autherine Lucy became the first Negro to register at the University of Alabama, a howling mob of students drove her from the campus. That September a mob attempting to prevent twelve Negro students from attending classes at the high school in Clinton, Tennessee, had to be restrained by the National Guard.

Out of patience with resistance in the Deep South, where not a single child attended a desegregated school at the beginning of Eisenhower's second term, a Federal court ordered a start of desegregation in the schools of Little Rock, Arkansas, a city known for racial progress, in the fall of 1957. But Governor Orval Faubus responded by creating an atmosphere of violence and then calling out the National Guard, not to protect the Negro children in their right to attend the public schools but to deny them that right. When these troops were withdrawn on order of the Federal district judge, a mob prevented Negro students from entering Central High School. President Eisenhower, who had not lifted a finger to enforce the Brown decision and would not even indicate that he approved the Court's ruling, now confronted an act of defiance that could not be permitted to go unchallenged.

On 24 September the President dispatched Federal troops to Little Rock to preserve order and protect Negro children. 'Mob rule,' he said, 'can not be allowed to override the decisions of our courts.' The people of Arkansas, however, rallied to this new nullification by re-electing Faubus to the governorship, and he continued his tactics of obstruction. In June 1958 the Little Rock school board obtained from a Federal district judge a delay of two and one-half years for integration. When the Circuit Court of Appeals overturned this decision, the school board appealed to the Supreme Court. On 12 September the Court unanimously refused to permit further procrastination. 'The constitutional rights [of the children] are not to be sacrificed or yielded to the violence and disorder which have followed the actions of the Governor and Legislature. . . . Law and order are not to be preserved by depriving the Negro children of their constitutional rights.'

This decision seemed to represent the limits of the Court's power to enforce its desegregation order. Further action would have to come from the President or Congress. But the President spurned suggestions that he use his immense prestige to educate the country on civil rights. Even after the Little Rock episode, Eisenhower observed: 'I have never said what I thought about the Supreme Court decision — I have never told a soul.' Congress proved somewhat more responsive. In 1957, under the leadership of Lyndon Johnson of Texas, the Senate Majority Leader, it enacted the first civil rights law in 82 years. Although weakened by amendments, it provided a degree of Federal protection for Negroes who wanted to vote and set up a Civil Rights Commission. A second statute in 1960 authorized the appointment of Federal referees to safeguard the right to vote and declared that a threat of violence to obstruct a Court order was a Federal offense. However, Congress did nothing effective to speed enforcement of the Court's decisions. Six years after the Court had called for desegregation with 'all deliberate speed,' not a single school was integrated in South Carolina, Georgia, Alabama, Mississippi, or Louisiana.

The real spark for the civil rights revolution came not from the President or Congress, not even from the Supreme Court, but from the Negroes themselves. The pathbreaking Court decisions would not have

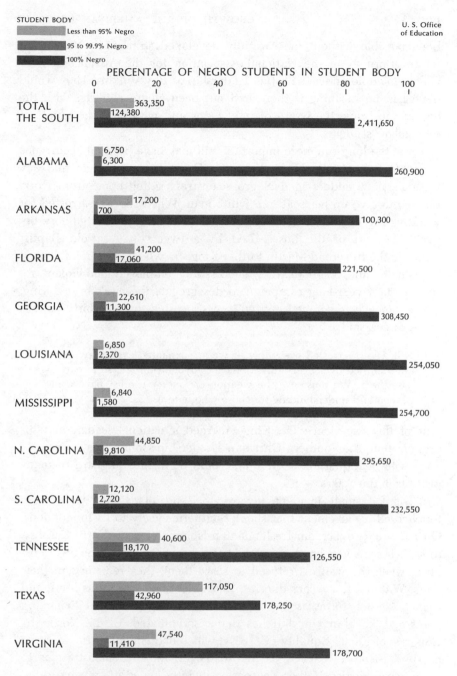

U. S. Office
of Education

PERCENTAGE OF NEGRO STUDENTS IN STUDENT BODY

0   20   40   60   80   100

TOTAL
THE SOUTH
363,350
124,380
2,411,650

ALABAMA
6,750
6,300
260,900

ARKANSAS
17,200
700
100,300

FLORIDA
41,200
17,060
221,500

GEORGIA
22,610
11,300
308,450

LOUISIANA
6,850
2,370
254,050

MISSISSIPPI
6,840
1,580
254,700

N. CAROLINA
44,850
9,810
295,650

S. CAROLINA
12,120
2,720
232,550

TENNESSEE
40,600
18,170
126,550

TEXAS
117,050
42,960
178,250

VIRGINIA
47,540
11,410
178,700

NEGRO ENROLLMENT IN SOUTHERN SCHOOLS, FALL 1966

689

been possible without the carefully developed strategy of Negro and white attorneys in the National Association for the Advancement of Colored People under the astute leadership of Roy Wilkins. They would have had no meaning if there had not been Negro children with the courage to brave the wrath of ugly mobs and withstand the taunts of their fellow students.

Yet in the long run more important still may have been an occurrence on a Montgomery, Alabama, bus on 1 December 1955. Late that day Rosa Parks, a middle-aged Negro seamstress riding home from work, refused to give up her seat to a white man. When she was arrested for violating the city's Jim Crow statutes, the Negroes of Montgomery began a boycott of the buses. Led by a twenty-five-year-old Baptist minister, the Reverend Martin Luther King, Jr., who had been influenced by Gandhi and Thoreau, they successfully employed non-violent resistance in a year-long campaign to desegregate the city's buses. King, whose home was bombed and who was arrested, one of thirty jailings in his career, said:

> If we are arrested every day, if we are exploited every day, if we are trampled over every day, don't let anyone pull you so low as to hate them. We must use the weapon of love. We must have compassion and understanding for those who hate us. . . .

Out of this experience Dr. King emerged a national leader, and his organization, the Southern Christian Leadership Conference, formed in 1957 with headquarters in Atlanta, would be in the vanguard of many protests in the 1960's.

A similar small incident toward the end of Eisenhower's reign touched off a movement that shook Southern society to its foundations. On 1 February 1960, four freshmen at a Negro college in North Carolina took their seats at a lunch counter in Woolworth's in downtown Greensboro; when the waitress refused to serve them, they remained in their seats. Within a few weeks the sit-in movement had swept the South and soon took such forms as 'wade-ins' in motel and municipal swimming pools and 'kneel-ins' in churches that discriminated. In the North the Congress of Racial Equality (CORE), which had employed the tactic of passive resistance as early as the 1940's, organized demonstrations to break racial barriers. Other Negroes and whites joined in 'freedom rides' to end segregated facilities in interstate transportation. The demonstrations, together with the pressure of economic boycott by Negroes, scored spectacular successes and within a brief period Northern hotels and restaurants ended their subtle forms of discrimination, Southern department stores and lunch counters were desegregated, and WHITE and COLORED signs were pulled down from waiting rooms in hundreds of Southern rail, air, and bus terminals.

5. THE POLITICS OF THE CENTER

In the 1950's neither party established its predominance. The Republicans had possession of the executive branch, but in 1954 their slim margin in Congress vanished, and for the next six years Eisenhower had to work with a Congress controlled by the Democrats. The Eisenhower era, noted one political scientist, 'was one of almost unprecedented ambiguity in regard to partisan responsibility for the conduct of the government.' Eisenhower himself was perceived to be a man 'above party.' A former Republican Speaker, Joseph Martin, said of him: 'Republican was a word that was not on the tip of his tongue.' After Taft's death in July 1953 Republican conservatives were much more undisciplined, and Eisenhower found that he had to depend on the support of the Democratic leadership to enact administration bills. As a result both conservatives and liberals had to settle for a government of the center which was in keeping with the quiescent spirit of the 'fifties.

According to public opinion polls no President — not even F.D.R. — had been more generally liked than 'Ike,' and it was taken for granted that he would win a second term. In the latter part of 1955 he made a remarkable recovery from a heart attack (thanks largely to his physician, Dr. Paul Dudley White), and by January 1956 was back at his desk in the White House. Next month he set speculation at rest by announcing that he would stand for re-election that fall. A second serious operation in June 1956, for ileitis, did not alter his plans.

The Republican convention, in August renominated President Eisenhower by acclamation and, after only token opposition, named Nixon as his running mate. The Democrats once again turned to Adlai Stevenson and chose Senator Kefauver, a Southern liberal whose pose of homespun simplicity masked sharp intelligence and bold independence, as their vice-presidential nominee.

Neither candidate generated as much excitement as he had four years earlier, and both appealed to the country as men of moderation. Only toward the end of the campaign did Governor Stevenson inject some interest into it, with two controversial proposals: that the selective service system be discontinued and the army rely henceforth on a small corps of highly trained professionals, and that the United States suspend hydrogen bomb tests as a practical step toward disarmament and as a moral gesture. Both recommendations were sensible enough, and Eisenhower — who dismissed the hydrogen bomb proposal as 'a theatrical gesture' — actually adopted it within two years, but each had the disadvantage of raising a military question which asked the country to choose between Stevenson's competence and that of a successful general.

Eisenhower likewise profited from developments in foreign affairs, because he was regarded as a man of peace, yet at the same time as a general who would be needed if war loomed. He had impressive credentials as an evangel of peace. He had ended the 'police action' in Korea; avoided war over Vietnam; ridden out the threat of a conflict with China. But he benefited too from turmoil abroad. The very week of the election the long-festering Suez crisis came to a head when Israel, France, and Britain sent armed forces against Nasser's Egypt. Eisenhower took to the air to recall the West to its moral principles and could claim that he had won a cease-fire agreement — though the Russians had something to do with it too. That same week the Hungarians revolted against their Communist overlords and Russian tanks poured into the hapless country to suppress the revolt. Stevenson charged that both events revealed the bankruptcy of Eisenhower's foreign policy, but to most Americans this was no time to 'change horses.'

The election resulted in a triumph for Eisenhower — but not for his party. The President polled 35,590,000 votes (57.4 per cent) and swept 41 states with a total electoral vote of 457; Stevenson received 26,-023,000 votes (42 per cent), winning 7 states with 73 electoral votes, all in Southern or border states. It was the most one-sided victory since Roosevelt had defeated Landon in 1936. The President broke into the once-solid South, winning Florida, Virginia, Tennessee, Texas, and Louisiana, a state which had been Democratic since 1876. He carried most of the large cities of the North — traditionally the strongholds of the Democracy — and made heavy inroads on both the labor and the Negro vote. Yet, astonishingly, despite Eisenhower's overwhelming victory, the Democrats held control of both houses of Congress. While the President was winning with a 9.6 million margin, Democratic candidates for the House were outpolling their Republican opponents by 1.6 million votes. Not since Zachary Taylor had a President been elected without carrying at least one house of Congress for his party. Once again the politics of equilibrium had been reaffirmed.

In Eisenhower's second term a hornet's nest of troubles swarmed around him, from difficulties at home like the Little Rock crisis to reversals abroad on almost every continent. Late in 1957 a severe recession brought an abrupt and unanticipated end to the 'Eisenhower prosperity,' and unemployment soared to the highest rate since 1941. With the country reeling from the shock of lay-offs in the auto and steel industries, it learned that Eisenhower's 'crusade' for decency in government had also turned out unhappily. 'Not one appointee of this Administration has been involved in scandal or corruption,' the President had boasted. But in his second term a series of scandals rocked the administration. The worst blow of all fell in September 1958 when Sherman Adams had to resign as confidential assistant to the President after a congressional committee had exposed his indiscreet relations with an industrial promoter.

As a consequence of these developments, American voters in 1958 handed the Republicans their third consecutive congressional defeat, an event unprecedented in the history of a party that controlled the executive branch. The Democrats swelled their margin in the Senate from a one-seat advantage to almost 2-1, and they gained the largest proportion in the House that any party had won since Roosevelt's landslide in 1936. Reactionary senators like Bricker of Ohio failed to win re-election while others like Jenner of Indiana and Malone of Nevada withdrew voluntarily to private life. The Republicans breasted this current of discontent only in New York, where Nelson Rockefeller, regarded as a liberal and an internationalist, won an impressive victory. The main consequence of the election was to diffuse authority even further by attenuating the ranks of the President's party without transferring the responsibility for policy-making to his opponents.

In the last two years of Eisenhower's tenure a conflict between the President and the liberal wing of the Democratic party in Congress created a virtual deadlock in Washington. Eisenhower, who had insisted during the 1958 campaign that the country faced a choice between 'left-wing government or sensible government,' seemed bewildered by the rejection of his appeal. Convinced that the Democrats were leading the country down the road to socialism, he set himself obdurately against proposals for Federal action in areas like education and housing; liberal Democrats knew that they could enact such legislation only if they were able to muster a two-thirds vote to override the President's veto, an unlikely circumstance. On the other hand Eisenhower could not impose his will on Congress since he confronted the largest opposition majority in the twentieth century. In such a situation an unusual share of the responsibility for leadership fell to such Southern moderates as Majority Leader Lyndon B. Johnson and Speaker Sam Rayburn, both veteran Texas Democrats. Priding themselves on their mastery of politics as the art of the possible, they pursued a course of compromise with the administration. In vain, liberal Democrats protested that the Johnson-Rayburn strategy of slicing appropriations to escape vetoes blurred the party's identity and surrendered crucial legislation to the President's 'reckless frugality spree.' Despite the large Democratic majorities, accomplishments were meager.

Hence the Eisenhower administration ended as it began, somewhat to the right of 'the middle of the road.' The President had fulfilled the expectation that he would promote domestic tranquility. The querulous partisanship of the late Truman years had been mitigated, the acerbity of the national temper had been sweetened. Whereas Truman had provoked political controversy, Eisenhower made politics seem needlessly divisive. His style of leadership muffled issues instead of meeting them; even his prolix prose and his involuted manner of speaking served to blur issues rather than define them. His place in history will probably rest less on what he did than on what he did not do. He gave the nation a chance to consolidate past gains, take stock of itself, and renew its spirits for future struggles.

Yet Eisenhower's achievements came at a price. By the very nature of his role as a moderator of differences, he could not risk dividing the country by raising new questions. Moreover, he had a limited interest in such matters and, at times, limited strength. Never did he risk his great popularity to help the nation solve problems too long postponed. One writer observed: 'When he leaves office in January 1961, the foreign policies and the domestic policies of the past generation will be about where he found them in 1953. No national problem, whether it be education, housing, urban revitalization, agriculture, or inflation, will have been advanced importantly toward solution nor its dimensions significantly altered.' Critics like the Harvard economist John Kenneth Galbraith charged that America's preoccupation with the output of consumer goods was starving the public sector, and Adlai Stevenson protested that the United States had become a society characterized by the 'contrast of public squalor and private opulence.' A country with a half-trillion dollar economy permitted crowded classrooms and hospital wards, antiquated transportation systems and festering slums. If America was more tranquil, the uneasy peace in the South had been bought at the expense of the Negro. None could doubt that Eisenhower had made an important contribution toward unifying the nation, but not a few asked whether the price that had been paid was too high.

XXVIII

World Power in the Nuclear Age

1. THE NEW LOOK AND THE OLD VIEW

The administrations of Roosevelt and Truman had been the most troubled in American history since Lincoln's, and the election of Eisenhower, if not a mandate for 'normalcy,' was clearly a vote for peace and security. The campaign attempted to fasten responsibility for the advance of Communism on the Democrats; and there was a lively expectation that with the return of the Republicans history would reverse itself. But alas for expectations, Americans continued to live in a world of turmoil. The eight years of the Eisenhower administration, in foreign affairs, were to be filled with danger and frustration. Yet if there was no dramatic reversal of the lava flow of history, there was, at least, a kind of peace. In the circumstances that was something of a triumph.

Turn where you would, there was crisis: crisis in Vietnam, in the Straits of Formosa, in Jordan and Suez, in Hungary, in Berlin, in the Congo, in Kashmir, in Guatemala, in Cuba. Inevitably the United States became involved in every one — such was the price of power. And all the time, filling the horizon and darkening the skies, was the huge black cloud resulting from the implacable growth of Soviet and Chinese power, and the relentless threat of atomic annihilation. A people who for generations had come to expect peace and security and who, in every major struggle had imposed their will on the seeming chaos of history, now had to learn to live with fear and uncertainty. No wonder there was a mounting sense of exasperation and a quest for quick solutions. With the best of intentions the postwar administrations were able to provide neither certitude nor peace nor help for pain.

The new Secretary of State, John Foster Dulles, brought an internationalist outlook to the conduct of foreign affairs. Grandson of one Secretary of State and nephew of another, he had been secretary to the Hague Peace Conference of 1907 and an adviser to the United States delegation at Versailles in 1919. 'Dulles', noted one biographer, 'was trained for diplomacy as Nijinsky was for the ballet.' One of the architects of the United Nations and of the peace treaty with Japan, Dulles, like Eisenhower, had been so closely identified with the programs of the outgoing administration that it seemed probable that there would be substantial continuity in policy. Yet Eisenhower had won election on a platform which attacked 'the negative, futile and immoral policy of containment' and Dulles denounced the Truman-Acheson approach as 'treadmill policies which, at best, might perhaps keep us in the same place until we drop exhausted.'

Dulles advanced as alternatives to containment a series of policies which would permit the United States to seize the initiative in world affairs. A prominent Protestant layman with a moralistic view of America's responsibilities, he objected that containment abandoned 'countless human beings to a despotism and Godless terrorism' and proposed the 'liberation' of the captive peoples of eastern Europe. The satellites were to be liberated not by force but 'by intelligent care' and by the intensity of our moral indignation. Those who minimized the power of moral pressure and propaganda, he claimed, 'just do not know what they are talking about.' The mere announcement by the United States 'that it wants and expects liberation to occur would change, in an electrifying way, the mood of the captive peoples.' 'Never before,' noted one writer, 'had the illusion of American omnipotence demanded so much of American diplomacy.'

At the same time that Dulles would roll back the Iron Curtain and 'unleash' Chiang to assault the Chinese mainland, he would cut military spending. He shared the fear of men like Senator Taft that America's security was threatened less from abroad than by the heavy burden of taxation to support foreign commitments, a millstone that discouraged incentive. Under what Admiral Arthur Radford, chairman of the Joint Chiefs of Staff, called the 'New Look' policy, the United States would cut back on expensive ground forces and place more reliance on nuclear bombs, which the air force would deliver. The New Look responded to America's pride in air power and its revulsion at trench warfare. (Elmer Davis once observed that it was generally understood in Washington that only ground troops have mothers.) Although it reduced military spending, the administration insisted it was providing greater security by getting 'more bang for a buck.'

On 12 January 1954 Dulles announced that henceforth the United States would rely less on local defenses and more on 'the deterrent of massive retaliatory power . . . a great capacity to retaliate instantly, by means and at times of our own choosing.' Dulles's speech, wrote a historian sympathetic to the administration, marked 'the zenith of the cold war.' The doctrine of 'massive retaliation' reflected the irritation of much of the country with limited war, as a result of the Korean experience. The United States, declared Secretary Humphrey, had 'no business getting into little wars.' If the country had to intervene, he said, 'let's intervene decisively with all we have got or stay out.' But the trouble with the massive retaliation doctrine is that it escalated every dispute into an occasion for a war of annihilation, and, if carried to its logical conclusion, left the country with no alternative save surrender or a nuclear holocaust. Moreover, since the threat of nuclear retaliation had not proved effective even when the United States held an atomic monopoly, it seemed even less likely to work now that Russia had its own nuclear arsenal.

In a sense the Republicans were the prisoners of their campaign propaganda. Since they publicized the dogma of 'betrayal' at Yalta and in China, they were committed to the support of Chiang Kai-shek. Because the doctrine of 'containment' was associated with the Truman administration, they felt it incumbent on them to replace it by the principle of 'liberation' — which they were unable to implement. Because they had persuaded themselves that Soviet advances in atomic science resulted not from Russian scientific skill but from the betrayal of atomic secrets by American Communists, they were unprepared for the Russian invention of the hydrogen bomb and for Soviet leadership in satellites and missiles. Because they had told themselves that the State Department was riddled with subversives, they played into the hands of extremists like Senator McCarthy, who demoralized the Department and the Foreign Service, and deprived themselves of experienced diplomats and experts just when most needed.

Too often the new administration wanted clear military supremacy — but a balanced budget; as a consequence, it frequently pursued contradictory aims or adopted tactics certain to frustrate the achievement of its goals. It desired closer ties with our European associates, but by indulging in such rhetoric as threatening the French with an 'agonizing reappraisal' impaired relations. It hoped to win over the uncommitted nations, but by identifying the American version of private enterprise with freedom, it antagonized important elements in those countries. It recognized that the real struggle was for the minds of men, but put disproportionate emphasis — and money — on military rather than on economic or cultural programs. It championed the United Nations but worked through regional or bilateral agreements which tended to weaken that organization. It advocated change but yearned for stability; encouraged revolution but expected revolution to be respectable; and in fact misjudged such revolutions as occurred, notably in Cuba. Like its predecessors it supported such friends as Chiang Kai-shek, Syngman Rhee, Batista, and Trujillo, even though such support forfeited the confidence of liberal elements elsewhere on the globe who questioned the sincerity of America's commitment to reform.

The Truman administration had succeeded in strengthening the non-Communist countries and preventing further extension of Communism by force. In Iran, Turkey, Greece, Berlin, and Korea, the Reds had discovered that no such easy victories lay open to them as had been achieved by Hitler as a result of Western apathy. But Communism was both more flexible and more ingenious than Nazism. Balked in attempts at military expansion, the Communists turned instead to exploiting the grievances of Asians and Africans emerging from the long night of colonialism into the uncertain day of national independence. In the struggle for the support of these peoples, the Communists played upon the hostility of ex-colonials toward the West and the resentment of colored peoples against the whites.

Would Western policy prove sufficiently resourceful to meet these challenges? The logical response was that of the Marshall Plan and the Point Four program — to support the economies of new nations so that they would themselves be strong enough to defeat aggression and stamp out subversion. This called for a heavy concentration on economic aid, for a strong information program which would make clear how the free world differed from the Communist world, and above all for patience and understanding. But to the new administration, that approach seemed negative and sterile. Instead Dulles fell back on phrases like 'massive retaliation,' which gave the appearance of great deeds without actually committing the country to action.

In the end the Eisenhower foreign policies differed little from those of Truman, for the new administration discovered that it had far less room for maneuver in the conduct of world affairs than it imagined. There was a 'New Look,' to be sure, but the view remained dismally the same: the might of Russia, the immensity of China, the ambitions of France, the nationalist revolts of the non-European peoples against imperialism and colonialism, the hostility of the Arabs to Israel, of Pakistan to India, the pull of neutralism, the population explosion, the technological revolution, the threat of atomic fission. These stubborn facts fixed the latitude and longitude of foreign policy.

Yet if Eisenhower's foreign policies marked no significant new departure in substance, they had a distinctive style and method. The President shared Dulles's faith in 'personal' diplomacy; not only was everything to be talked out in front of microphones and television lights but the participants should be principals, not subordinates. Eisenhower inaugurated this 'new' diplomacy successfully by flying to Korea to arrange an armistice, and thereafter he preferred, when possible, to negotiate 'at the summit'; while Dulles, flitting from continent to continent, turned out to be the most traveled Secretary of State in American history.[1]

2. THE FAR EAST AND THE SUMMIT CONFERENCE

Elected on a platform which charged the Democrats with waging war in Korea 'without the will to victory' and with 'ignominious bartering with our enemies,' Eisenhower quickly scored one of the most important achievements of his administration by bartering with the enemy to secure a peace without victory in Korea. In obtaining a cease-fire in that stricken country, the President fixed the pattern for the remainder of his

1. During the seven years of his secretaryship he flew 480,000 miles outside the bounds of the United States.

years in office: war-like rhetoric would yield to deeds of peace. Korea, divided absurdly at the waist, faced an uncertain and gloomy future. It was threatened hourly by the 'People's Republic' on its northern boundary and by Communist China and Russia on its flanks; lacking a sound economic basis, it subsisted largely on the vast sums which the United States poured in as economic and military aid. It was governed by the patriot leader Syngman Rhee, who grew more and more dictatorial with the passing years and was eventually ousted by a popular rebellion. But the United States was committed to support this unhappy republic by a mutual defense treaty, by far-reaching political and military considerations, and by deep moral obligations. Still, if the outcome was less than satisfactory, Eisenhower had fulfilled his pledge to go to Korea, and the fighting had stopped.

In 1954 the revolution against colonialism which was sweeping Asia and Africa presented another test of the doctrines of the administration. For almost seven years Communist guerillas known as the Viet-Minh had been waging war against the French in the jungles of Indo-China. By the summer of 1953 they had overrun much of the northern half of Vietnam, largest of the three states comprising French Indo-China, and threatened the neighboring state of Laos. Fearful that the Communist wave might engulf the whole of southeastern Asia, and eager to take the pressure off the French so that they could fulfill their obligations toward the European Defense Community, Truman sent a military mission to Saigon and stepped up aid to the French in Vietnam. By 1954 America was paying almost four-fifths of the cost of the war.

When the French position became critical in the spring of 1954, Dulles insisted that Indochina could not be permitted to fall; Admiral Radford proposed an air strike to save the beleaguered jungle fortress of Dienbienphu; and Vice President Nixon favored, if necessary, 'putting our boys in.' But the British as well as elements in America, including all the other members of the Joint Chiefs of Staff and such Democratic Congressional leaders as Lyndon Johnson, opposed action which might lead to another Korea. Eisenhower believed that the United States had a vital stake in Vietnam. 'You have a row of dominoes set up,' he explained. 'You knock over the first one, and what will happen to the last one is that it will go over very quickly.' But despite his attraction to this 'domino theory,' he was persuaded by the arguments of men like the Army Chief of Staff, General Matthew B. Ridgway, and the Chief of Plans, General James M. Gavin, to veto the plan to intervene. When the United States permitted Dienbienphu to fall on 7 May, the doctrine of massive retaliation died an early death. The French decided to give up the unequal struggle and settle for a compromise line, as the United States had done in Korea. As a consequence of a conference at Geneva of the great powers, which for the first time included Red China, the kingdoms of Cambodia and Laos emerged as nominally independent new nations, while Vietnam was divided provisionally in two along the 17th parallel until free elections could be held.

To counter Communist influence in this region, Secretary Dulles took steps to create an Asiatic defense community that would parallel NATO. In November 1954, Pakistan, Thailand, and the Philippines joined with the United States, Britain, France, Australia, and New Zealand to set up a Southeast Asia Treaty Organization (SEATO). The treaty provided that in the event of a threat of armed aggression the members would 'meet in order to agree on the measures which should be taken for common defense.' SEATO differed from NATO in four important respects. Neither we nor any of our allies in the Southeast Asia organization had significant armed forces for waging a general war in the treaty area; there was no permanent command structure and no standing military organization, such as NATO maintained in Paris; important states such as India and Indonesia refused to join; and the signatories had no obligation save to consult, although in the 1960's it would be falsely argued that the United States was compelled by its SEATO commitment to intervene militarily in Vietnam.

At the same time that Dulles was negotiating the SEATO pact a comparable situation developed in Formosa, whither Chiang Kai-shek and the Chinese Nationalists had betaken themselves when driven by the Reds from the mainland in 1949. Whereas Dr. Rhee had at least the formal credentials of a popular election, Chiang ruled as if by divine right. The United States, already bound to him by a wartime alliance, by participation in a common front against Chinese Communism, and now by the exigencies of American politics, committed itself to the theory that Chiang, representing the true and rightful government of all China, would eventually recross the Formosa Strait and reconquer the mainland. With the passing of years, this became an increasingly unrealistic policy, but the Eisenhower administration — and its successors, to date — refused to recognize the existence of Red China and opposed her admission to the United Nations. A powerful element in Eisenhower's own party, headed by Taft's successor as Republican leader in the Senate, William Knowland, called the 'Senator from Formosa,' identified the party leadership with the Nationalist cause.

Chiang multiplied the dangers of the Formosan problem by occupying not only the nearby Pescadores Islands but a group of smaller islands — Quemoy, Matsu, and the Tachens — close to the Chinese mainland. On his accession to the presidency, Eisenhower had announced that he was lifting the 'blockade' of Taiwan by the U.S. Seventh Fleet, thus 'unleashing' Chiang Kai-shek for an attack upon the mainland, an enterprise that existed largely in the minds of men like Senator Knowland, for Chiang lacked the strength to carry it out. The Chinese premier, Chou En-lai, responded that Taiwan was part of China proper and the Nationalist regime there must be liquidated. When, in the summer of 1954, the Communists began a heavy bombardment of the off-shore islands, the United States negotiated a 'mutual defense' treaty with Chiang, and the President told the Congress that 'in the interest of peace the United States must remove any doubt regarding our readiness to fight.' Congress responded with a somewhat ambiguous resolution declaring that 'an attack against territories . . . in the region of Formosa and the Pescadores would be dangerous to the peace and safety' of the United States, and authorizing the President to use the armed force of the nation 'as he deems necessary' to defend this region. This was one of the few times in history that Congress formally gave the Executive power to involve the nation in war at his discretion. But Eisenhower once again pulled back from a war of liberation, and Chiang gave up the Tachens to the Communists.

The danger passed, but the problem remained. Were Quemoy and Matsu part of those 'territories' to whose defense the United States now stood committed? When, in August 1958, the Communists opened another and heavier bombardment of the islands, Secretary Dulles promptly declared that an attack on them would be a prelude to an invasion of Formosa and that the United States stood ready to repel it; the Seventh Fleet escorted troops which Chiang rushed to garrison the beleaguered islands. Public opinion at home and abroad reacted sharply to the threat of war over these islands, which were almost as close to the Chinese mainland as Staten Island is to Manhattan. Were they really worth an atomic war — or even a 'conventional' war? On 30 September,

Dulles executed a stunning reversal. He stated that Chiang had been 'rather foolish' and declared that the United States had 'no commitment to help Chiang back to the mainland'; Eisenhower, who had recklessly committed himself to the ambitions of the Nationalists, now said that Chiang's build-up of troops on the offshore islands was 'a thorn in the side of peace.' On 23 October, Dulles 'released' Chiang by compelling him to renounce publicly the use of force to regain control of the mainland of China. So ended another experiment in 'liberation.'

In a magazine interview Dulles offered an explanation of his approach to foreign affairs which gave birth to a new term: "brinkmanship." He stated:

> You have to take chances for peace, just as you must take chances in war. Some say that we were brought to the verge of war. Of course we were brought to the verge of war. The ability to get to the verge of war without getting into the war is the necessary art. If you cannot master it, you inevitably get into wars. If you try to run away from it, if you are scared to go to the brink, you are lost. We've had to look it square in the face — on the question of enlarging the Korean War, on the question of getting into the Indo-China war, on the question of Formosa. We walked to the brink and we looked it in the face.

Critics not only disputed the accuracy of Dulles's account of these incidents but asked whether, in a world of nuclear terror, such an attitude was not irresponsibly provocative.

By 1955 a series of events combined to bring about a mild thaw in the Cold War: the death of Stalin, truce in Korea, a cease-fire in the Formosa Strait, a compromise peace in Vietnam. Eisenhower himself had become a symbol of peace. In a dramatic gesture before the United Nations Assembly in December 1953 he had proposed that the major scientific nations of the world jointly contribute to a United Nations pool of atomic power to be used exclusively for peaceful purposes. On four crucial occasions — Korea, Taiwan, Indo-China, and in negotiations with China over prisoners [2] — he had thrown the weight of his influence

2. Discussing the Chinese detention of thirteen American fliers, on 2 December 1954, the President said: 'In many ways the easy course for a President . . . is to adopt a truculent, publicly bold, almost insulting attitude. A President experiences exactly the same resentments, the same anger, the same kind of sense of frustration . . . when things like this occur to other Americans, and his impulse is to lash out.

to the side of peace. The European defense community was now a reality. A wave of prosperity surged through Western Europe, giving West Germany, France, and Italy self-confidence and greatly diminishing fear of Communist subversion or aggression. Russia, having detonated a hydrogen bomb, showed signs of a more reasonable relationship with the West. While the official repudiation of Stalin awaited the advent to power of the bold Nikita Khrushchev, the new government was already proving itself less intransigent. Meantime Russia badly needed a period of internal calm in which to settle the question of succession, and a period of peace in which to reconsider relations with China — a junior partner now threatening to take over the firm. As if to dramatize the new spirit, the Soviet Union in May 1955 ended its long and harsh occupation of Austria and gave that little nation its freedom. Thus the stage was set for the 'summit' conference at Geneva in mid-summer 1955.

As early as May 1953 Winston Churchill had proposed a conference of the heads of major states, but neither Russia nor the United States was then ready for it. The British Foreign Minister, Harold Macmillan, reopened the issue in a more favorable climate of opinion; and President Eisenhower, Sir Anthony Eden, Bulganin, and Edgar Faure agreed to represent their respective countries. On 18 July 1955, Eisenhower opened the-conference on a note of hope and of good will:

> The American people want to be friends with the Soviet peoples. There are no natural differences between our peoples or our nations. There are no territorial or commercial rivalries. Historically our two countries have always been at peace. . . . It is time that all curtains whether of guns or laws or regulations should begin to come down.

Specifically, Eisenhower proposed a new approach to the problem of German unification, free communication between the East and the West, the peaceful use of atomic power, with some practical contribu-

[But] when one accepts the responsibilities of public office, he can no longer give expression freely to such things; he has got to think of results. That would be the easy way. . . .
The hard way is to have the courage to be patient, tirelessly to seek out every single avenue open to us in the hope of finally leading the other side to a little better understanding of the honesty of our intentions.' *Public Papers of President Eisenhower,* 1955, pp. 1075–6.

tions to disarmament. It was the disarmament plan that caught the popular imagination, for it called upon Russia and the United States to:

> give each other a complete blueprint of our military establishments, from beginning to end, from one end of our countries to the other; lay out the establishments and provide the blueprints to each other. Next to provide within our countries facilities for aerial photography to the other country, ample facilities for aerial reconnaissance where you can make all the pictures you choose and take them to your own country to study, you to provide exactly the same facilities for us, and we to make these examinations, and by this step to convince the world that we are providing as between ourselves against the possibility of great surprise attack, thus lessening danger and relaxing tension.

'What I propose,' he added, 'would be but a beginning.'

Bulganin, in turn, advocated prohibiting the manufacture of atomic weapons and limiting the armies of the United States and the USSR to 1.5 million men. But Moscow would not even consider Eisenhower's generous offer. The Russians' suggestion of prohibiting atomic weapons meant nothing once they would not admit inspection, and in modern conditions of warfare a limitation of the size of the ground force was completely anachronistic. So nothing came of the Geneva conference.

3. CRISIS IN THE MIDDLE EAST

The 'spirit of Geneva' which had inspired such high hopes in the West — and possibly even in the East — quickly evaporated under the hot sun of power politics. Within a few months events in Central Europe and in the Middle East again strained East-West relationships to the breaking point.

At the celebration of the Twentieth Communist Party Congress, in February 1956, Nikita Khrushchev, the new leader of the USSR, startled the world by a savage attack on his predecessor, Stalin. Josef Stalin, he asserted, had been a monstrous tyrant. That kind of savage leadership, Khrushchev implied, was a thing of the past. Seven months later the festering discontent of the Poles broke out into the open; and under the leadership of Wladyslaw Gomulka, the Poles demanded freedom from Soviet bayonets and autonomy within the Communist system. When Khrushchev accepted these demands for a new kind of partnership, it looked like the dawn of a new and better day.

But alas for all such hopes. When that same autumn the long-suffering Hungarians revolted against Communist misrule, Khrushchev's response would have done credit to Stalin whom he had just denounced. Two hundred thousand soldiers and thousands of tanks poured into the hapless country; and while the United Nations passed frantic resolutions of protest, and the West looked on in despair, this heroic revolt of the Hungarians was ruthlessly stamped out. Tens of thousands of Hungarian patriots were killed, and almost 200,000 fled across the border into Austria, and eventually into other Western countries. The events in Hungary revealed the hollowness of 'massive retaliation' and 'liberation.' Eisenhower refrained from intervening in the Soviet sphere of eastern Europe, but the repression of the Hungarian revolt snuffed out whatever remained of the 'spirit of Geneva.'

The crisis in the Middle East, which erupted the very same week the Hungarian revolt was put down, had been long in the making. That vast area, stretching from the Mediterranean to the Caspian Sea, and from the Hellespont to the Gulf of Oman, and embracing some twelve countries,[3] seethed with unrest. Long the pawn of European politics, its peoples governed by distant rulers, and its rich oil resources exploited for the benefit of distant economies, it was now quickened into new life — and revolt — by the currents of anticolonialism, nationalism, and religion that were racing through all the non-European world. World War II accelerated the pace of change. In Iran, Dr. Mossadegh nationalized oil; and although he was later ousted (with the help of the West) the oil remained nationalized. Syria and Lebanon asserted their independence, and in 1946 the last French troops left these two Arab nations. In 1948 the British gave up their mandate in Palestine; the Israelis struck for freedom and, when invaded by the combined forces of Egypt, Lebanon, Jordan, and Syria, broke the invaders and secured their independence. Egypt was then swept by revolt; in 1952 the fat King Farouk was driven into exile, and two years later Colonel Gamal Abdel Nasser took over the government. Arab nationalism surged through the whole Moslem world, from Morocco halfway across the globe to Pakistan and Indonesia.

Secretary Dulles precipitated the Middle East crisis in 1953-54 by attempting to create a regional defense against Soviet penetration which would parallel NATO in the Atlantic and SEATO in the Pacific areas.

3. Turkey, Lebanon, Syria, Iraq, Iran, Jordan, Israel, Egypt, and Saudi Arabia; also Kuwait, Yemen, and the Sudan.

The result was the Baghdad Pact of 1954 to which Turkey, Iraq, Iran, and Pakistan adhered, but not the United States! The Pact did not in fact intimidate the Soviets; it did, however, antagonize Nasser, who saw it as a deliberate attempt to undermine his own leadership and to split the Moslem world in two.

Under pressure to vindicate his newly won position, Nasser was now following the well-worn precedent of distracting his people from their difficulties at home by creating quarrels abroad. First he negotiated for the withdrawal of all British troops from the Suez Canal zone by 1956. Second came the formation of a close military alliance with Syria, Jordan, and Saudi Arabia. Third was a deal with Czechoslovakia for arms — presumably to use against the Israelis. Fourth he launched a war of nerves — and of attrition — against Israel by denying Israeli ships passage through the Suez Canal, by subversion, and by ceaseless threats of destruction. Finally he made a constructive gesture — a project for a vast dam and irrigation system at Aswan on the upper Nile; it was to be the largest dam in the world. Since Egypt could not finance this herself, Nasser entered on the dangerous game of inviting the United States and the USSR to bid against each other for the privilege of financing the enterprise. Dulles first offered to help Egypt build the dam, then abruptly withdrew the offer.

On 26 July 1956, one week after Dulles's about-face, Nasser precipitated a serious world crisis by seizing the Suez Canal in clear violation of treaty agreements. Faced with the prospect of being cut off from essential Middle East oil supplies, the British and French determined to use force to recover control of the Canal. This provided Israel with an opportunity to launch her own offensive against Egypt; Nasser having denied Israel access to the Canal on the grounds that the two countries were at war, the Israeli legal and moral position seemed strong. On 29 October, as Russian tanks were rumbling into the streets of Budapest, Israeli troops invaded the Sinai peninsula, scattered a much larger Egyptian army, and within a few days were across the peninsula and on the banks of the Canal. Britain and France joined hastily in the war with aerial attacks on the Egyptian air force; Nasser responded by sinking enough ships in the Canal to close it to traffic for an indefinite time.

Here were the makings of another major war, for India and the Soviet bloc threatened to pile in unless there was an immediate cease-fire. A possibly fatal rift between East and West was avoided when the United Nations, too, denounced the war as aggression and the United States supported the U.N. position. 'We believe these actions [of Britain and France] to have been taken in error,' said Eisenhower. 'We do not accept the use of force as a proper instrument for the settlement of international disputes.' Confronted by the prospect of a long and wearing war in Egypt, by the threat of retaliation from Russia, by disapproval from the United States and India, and by the condemnation of the United Nations, England and France bowed to the inevitable and brought their hostilities to a close.

Israel, however, balked at withdrawing her troops from their advanced positions until she had obtained assurances of equitable treatment. Eisenhower assured the Israelis that if they drew back, the United States would support their efforts to end Egyptian hostility and the exclusion of Israeli ships from the Canal. This commitment became binding when Israel complied with the President's request; but nothing came of it. The Suez affair drove a wedge between the United States and her allies, dramatized the growing power of the Soviet Union, enhanced the prestige — but not the strength — of Israel, and played into the hands of Nasser, who now presented himself as the very symbol of Arab nationalism in its struggle against Western imperialism. The peaceful settlement was a victory for Eisenhower; but a few more such victories and the Western alliance would be in ruins.

The Suez dispute had created a situation favorable to the extension of Communist influence throughout the Middle East and compelled the United States to assume responsibilities that had previously been shouldered by Britain and France. Eisenhower now turned his attention to that threat and, in a message of 5 January 1957, warned that if the nations of the Middle East should

> lose their independence, if they were dominated by alien forces hostile to freedom, that would be both a tragedy for the area and for many other free nations whose economic life would be subject to near strangulation. Western Europe would be endangered just as though there had been no Marshall Plan, no NATO. The free nations of Asia and Africa, too, would be placed in serious jeopardy. . . . All this would have the most adverse, if not disastrous, effect upon our own nation's economic life and political prospects.

To avoid such a catastrophe, the President asked for authority to extend economic assistance to Middle Eastern countries and to use the armed forces to protect any nation 'threatened by aggression from any country controlled by international communism.' On 9 March Congress authorized some $200 million for economic and military aid to implement this 'Eisenhower Doctrine.' The response from the West generally was enthusiastic, but not so from many of the Middle East countries, India or Russia. Nasser's and Soviet influence grew all through that stormy region. The Eisenhower Doctrine could not prevent the capture of the government of Syria by a clique favorable to Nasser, the forced retirement of the pro-Western king of Saudi Arabia, or the assassination of King Faisal of Iraq and the establishment there of a pro-Nasser government.

When in the spring of 1958 Syria and Egypt undertook to subvert the pro-Western government of Lebanon, President Chamoun appealed to the United Nations for help. As usual the United Nations machinery worked slowly. The revolt in Iraq added a new urgency, and Chamoun turned to the United States for aid. There was some doubt about the applicability of the Eisenhower Doctrine, but Eisenhower immediately ordered the Sixth Fleet to steam into the eastern Mediterranean and dispatched 9000 — eventually 14,000 — marines to Lebanon. (Britain also sent troops to Jordan.) When the nearby Arab states agreed to refrain from armed intervention in Lebanon, and Chamoun consented to retire, peace returned to that troubled country, and in October Eisenhower withdrew the marines. Russia hurriedly announced that she would help finance Egypt's Aswan dam, and henceforth the United States would have to cope with the fact that the Soviet Union was in the Middle East to stay.

4. THE GOOD NEIGHBOR POLICY TESTED AND RECONSTRUCTED

Preoccupied with affairs in Europe and Asia, the United States failed to take note of what was happening in the Western hemisphere. The abrupt cessation of wartime purchases dealt a heavy blow to Latin American economies; the population explosion was pressing implacably on existing resources; the gap between rich and poor was growing wider; Latin American friendship was taken for granted. Down to 1951 all the Latin American republics together had received about the same amount of foreign aid as Greece; and in the next ten years Latin America received only $3.4 billion out of a total of some $80 billion in aid: that was less than Japan, Taiwan, or Korea got.

Events in Guatemala shocked the United States out of its complacency. For years that little Central American state had groaned under the dictatorship of General Jorge Castañeda; in 1954 he was overthrown and after a period of confusion the government came under the control of Jacobo Arbenz, who was sympathetic to Communism. He and his followers carried through a wholesale confiscation of land, dominated the labor unions, ran the government-owned newspapers, and obtained arms from Poland. Alive to the proximity of Guatemala to the Panama Canal, Dulles moved to check Communist infiltration; mindful of the prohibition against intervention in the internal affairs of any American state, he worked through the existing machinery of the Organization of American States. The tenth Inter-American Conference condemned 'any dominion or control of the political institutions of any American state by the international Communist movement.' Fortified by this resolution, Dulles then shipped arms in to the Guatemalan rebels gathering along the Honduras border, and on 18 June 1954 these forces invaded Guatemala, overthrew the Arbenz government, and set up a new regime under a liberal constitution but led by ultra-conservatives. What Secretary Dulles cheered as a triumph for constitutionalism and hemispheric solidarity, most Latin Americans condemned as old-fashioned intervention. That same year Eisenhower presented the Legion of Merit to the dictators of Venezuela and Peru. When in 1958 Vice-President Nixon visited South America on a good will tour he met alarming manifestations of ill will; he was showered with anti-American pamphlets in Uruguay, stoned in Peru, mobbed in Venezuela.

Now, with exemplary dispatch, the United States applied itself to mending its Latin American fences. It stepped up foreign aid; helped establish an Inter-American Development Bank with a capital of one billion dollars; encouraged the creation of a free-trade area in the major Latin American states; and at the Bogotá conference authorized a grant of $500 million to advance social and economic welfare throughout Latin America. To dramatize this aid, President Eisenhower himself made a visit to South America in 1960. 'We are not saints,' he said at Santiago. 'We know we make mistakes, but our heart is in the right place.'

Cuba provided a hard test of the new departure. That long-suffering island had been ruled for years by a ruthless military dictator, Fulgencio Batista. Although evidence of his cruelty was overwhelming, the United States continued to recognize him as the legitimate governor until 1958. Two years earlier a student leader, Fidel Castro, had launched an invasion from Mexico; taking refuge in the remote mountains of the Sierra Maestra, he gathered support from long-oppressed peasants and the middle class. On 1 January 1959 he succeeded in ousting Batista. A 'fellow traveler' from the first, and influenced by his Argentine Communist economic adviser, 'Che' Guevara, Castro apparently planned to turn the 'Pearl of the Antilles' into the first Communist country in the New World. This was not evident for some time. Castro, who had been hailed as a liberator by the American press, made a triumphant tour of the eastern states in 1959, and in Washington was promised economic aid and help in building Cuban schools and social services. But when Castro returned to Cuba, he dispensed with elections, threw thousands of Cubans who opposed his ruthlessness into jail, and expropriated sugar plantations, major industries, utilities, and banks, with scarcely a pretense at compensation.

When the United States protested, Castro adopted a policy of overt hostility and moved ever closer to the USSR, which was delighted to establish a Communist beachhead only a few hours steaming from the United States. The Russian Deputy Premier Mikoyan visited Cuba in 1960, extended a credit of $100 million, arranged to buy five million tons of Cuban sugar over a five-year period, and provided technical — and eventually military — assistance. For the first time the Soviet Union had a foothold in the Western hemisphere.

5. THE THREAT OF NUCLEAR WARFARE

Throughout all the vicissitudes of the 'fifties one overwhelming menace loomed over mankind: the danger that the two great powers, the United States and the USSR, would plunge the world into nuclear war and shatter the great globe itself. Driven by mutual fears and animosities, these two powers piled up the most formidable armories in the history of mankind, and, like figures of classical Greek tragedy, called on the innermost secrets of nature, long imprisoned in stone and water, to serve them for purposes of mutual destruction. How to avoid a nuclear holocaust—that was the question that haunted the minds of statesmen and dictators throughout these years.

Almost everyone agreed on the imperative necessity of controlling the arms race, but when it came to ways and means 'their weak noddles,' as Benjamin Franklin had said almost two centuries earlier, 'are perfectly distracted.'

Every year the two great powers devoted more and more of their resources to building nuclear weapons — and defenses against nuclear
weapons. The 'fifties saw the development not only of bigger and more
devastating hydrogen bombs but of Polaris-equipped nuclear submarines, rockets, guided missiles, and antimissile missiles, and a revelation
of the staggering potentialities of outer space for military purposes. In
this contest the Russians for a time made more rapid progress than the
United States. In October 1957 they put their first satellite — Sputnik I
— in orbit around the globe; a month later Sputnik II, more than six
times heavier and carrying a live dog, orbited the earth; and in 1959 they
fired a rocket past the moon and in orbit about the sun. Within a few
months of Sputnik the United States, too, had launched a whole series of
rockets; in December 1958 America sent a monkey into outer space and
brought him safely home. Earlier that year, on 1 August 1958, a nuclear-
powered United States submarine, *Nautilus* (Commander William R.
Anderson) submerged north of Alaska, steamed for 1800 miles under the
polar ice cap, and emerged on the 5th on the European side of the pole.
Another U.S. nuclear sub, *Triton* (Captain Edward L. Beach), circum-
navigated the globe under water between 16 February and 10 May
1960, breaching only twice in the 84 days — once to land a sick seaman
at Montevideo, and once at Cadiz to honor the memory of Magellan,
whose course she had followed. It soon became clear that neither major
power could hope to win a resounding lead over the other and that if
they were not to exhaust and bankrupt themselves, they would do well
to consider co-operation instead of competition.

Nuclear weapons — unlike all earlier weapons — were dangerous in
peace as in war. To 'keep up' in the nuclear race required continuous
experiments which spread radioactive materials through the atmosphere; these tests might do incalculable damage not only to this but to
future generations. In 1954 when the United States exploded a 20-mega-
ton hydrogen bomb in the Bikini atoll in the Pacific, it spread a lethal
amount of radioactive material over an area of 7000 square miles. Another seven years and the Russians would be exploding 50-megaton
bombs — and boasting bombs of 100 megatons, powerful enough to
destroy the largest metropolitan areas in the world. While members of
the Atomic Energy Commission talked about 'tolerable' levels of radioactivity, geneticists made clear that all radioactivity was harmful and
that the damage from it was cumulative. Nor was it possible to confine
the damage from radioactive fall-out to particular countries; like the

rain, it falls upon the just and the unjust. Of all the problems President Eisenhower faced, none troubled him so deeply as the threat of nuclear war to the future not only of the republic but of mankind.

6. A WORLD IN TURMOIL

In Eisenhower's last years in office he took more direct responsibility for the conduct of foreign affairs, expecially after April 1959 when Dulles, fatally ill, resigned. Dulles's successor, Christian Herter, was much less self-assertive, and, with both Dulles and Adams gone, the President now grasped the reins more firmly. In the next year he made unprecedented trips which rivaled Dulles's peregrinations: a 22,000-mile journey to eleven countries from Spain to India and a good-will tour of Latin America. 'There is no place on this earth to which I would not travel, there is no chore I would not undertake, if I had any faintest hope that by so doing, I would promote the general cause of world peace,' Eisenhower said. On these travels, as at the conference in Geneva, the President's personal commitment to avoid a nuclear war was unmistakable. In India people showered him with flowers until he stood a foot deep in them, and he was hailed with signs: 'WELCOME PRINCE OF PEACE.' Yet he was to find before his term expired that dedication was not enough and that the world was rapidly spinning out of control.

If a nuclear war came, the German problem might well be what would trigger it. The separation into East and West Germany, and the parallel division of the city of Berlin, was originally designed to last only during the Allied occupation, but like other temporary arrangements it gradually took on permanence. That it did so was the product of the failure to write a formal peace treaty; of the fear of a resurgent Germany that was deeply ingrained in the peoples of Central and Eastern Europe she had victimized in the past; of Russian insistence on a thick padding of satellite states along her western border; and of the Communists' belief that they could extend their system by this kind of political osmosis. Under the auspices of Russia the Communists sought to make East Germany not only a willing satrapy in the Russian empire but a kind of show-place of Communism which would win over the hesitant neighbors in the West. To their intense mortification this plan did not work out. East German economy never recovered; and every week thousands of East Germans escaped into West Germany, while few

West Germans went east. West Germany prospered beyond any other European state, and it was West Berlin, a glittering jewel in the drab fabric of East Germany, that was the showpiece. West Germany, which had never acquiesced in the division, refused to recognize an East German government. A rearmed West Germany, its NATO forces possibly equipped by the United States with nuclear weapons, raised a threat which the Communist bloc regarded with grave misgivings.

In 1958 Khrushchev delivered an ultimatum to Berlin and the Germanies: either negotiate a settlement within six months, recognizing the permanent partition of Germany, or Russia would make a separate treaty with East Germany, giving her control of East Berlin and the air lanes into West Berlin. Committed to the defense of West Germany, and of Berlin as an outpost of freedom, and dependent on West Germany's contribution to the European defense system, the United States refused to back down. For the rest of Eisenhower's term, the Berlin controversy smoldered.

Yet at the same time Khrushchev showed an interest in conciliation, and Eisenhower was more than willing to meet him halfway. Confident that person-to-person talks would solve problems that defied conventional diplomacy, Eisenhower invited Khrushchev to the United States to see for himself how well intentioned the American people really were, and to discuss with him the most urgent problems of world politics. In September 1959 the Russian dictator made his first visit to the United States; he toured the country, talked with workingmen, farmers, shopkeepers, and housewives, and wound up his trip with a visit at President Eisenhower's rural retreat, Camp David. The two leaders appeared to get along famously, and the 'spirit of Camp David' supplanted the defunct 'spirit of Geneva' as the Western world prepared for yet another summit meeting to lay the foundations for a permanent settlement of the problems of Berlin, nuclear weapons, and disarmament. Not since the beginning of the Cold War had hopes for a peaceful world run so high.

Once again everything went wrong. On 5 May 1960, only eleven days before the summit conference was to have convened in Paris, Khrushchev announced that the Russians had shot down an American U-2 reconnaissance plane in the heart of Russia. After trapping the administration in a lie, the premier gave further details: they had captured the pilot, Francis Powers, who admitted that he was employed by the U.S. Central Intelligence Agency and engaged in aerial photographic espionage, as the Secretary of State eventually confirmed. Khrushchev chose to use this incident as an excuse to wreck the summit conference, and, in a deliberate insult, withdrew his invitation to the President to visit the Soviet Union. American 'aggressors,' he cried, should be treated as a boy handled an erring cat: 'We would catch such a cat by the tail and bang its head against the wall.' A month later, the Russians broke up the ten-nation disarmament conference in Geneva. Eisenhower's hopes for a *detente* had been shattered.

Within less than two months of the U-2 fiasco, the friendly nation of Japan told Eisenhower it would be unsafe for him to visit their country; relations with Castro's Cuba fell to a new low; and Africa burst into flame. After centuries of subjugation and exploitation the Africans were impatient to throw off their bonds. In the vast area of tropical Africa, one former colony after another won its independence: Nigeria, Ghana, the Ivory Coast, Cameroun, Mali, Sudan, and others. In some states the change-over from European to native governments was carried through with a minimum of unpleasantness and a maximum of co-operation. But in the Congo (as well as in Algeria) prolonged violence attended the transfer of power.

When, in response to urgent demands for independence, the Belgians pulled abruptly out of the Congo, that vast nation — or congeries of tribes — fragmented three ways, and flared into civil war. Confronted by the twin dangers that the war might spread through tropical Africa and be metamorphosed into a race war, and that the Congolese might be used as pawns in a game of power politics played by Russia and the West, the United Nations stepped in. Under the leadership of the far-sighted and intrepid Secretary-General, Dag Hammarskjöld, the UN raised an international military force to maintain the peace. But to extend Soviet influence south of the Equator, Khrushchev disrupted the work of the UN. In the same year that Soviet Russia penetrated the Western hemisphere for the first time, the Communists made their presence felt in the jungles of Africa. Soviet bloc technicians infiltrated the Congolese government, and Red China used Guinea as a base of operations in other African countries. The UN eventually brought the war under control and set the Congo on the road to nationhood, but the attempt to negotiate a settlement cost Hammarskjöld his life and the Congo crisis provided a dreadful example of how Cold War rivalries might envelop the whole world.

The session of the United Nations which opened in September 1960 revealed the tumultuous changes that had taken place in the Eisenhower years. When Eisenhower took office, the West dominated the UN; now the Afro-Asian nations were the largest voting bloc, and African states that did not exist in 1953 — countries like Dahomey, Niger, and Upper Volta — each had parity with the United States in the General Assembly. To Manhattan came a group of prominent leaders none of whom held power in 1953, all of whom were antagonistic to the United States: Khrushchev, Nasser, Castro, as well as spokesmen for the revolution of rising expectations like Sukarno of Indonesia and Nkrumah of Ghana. As Khrushchev banged his shoe on a table to show his boorish displeasure, Castro assaulted the delegates with an interminable harangue, and American Negroes stormed the chambers to protest the murder of the Congolese leader, Patrice Lumumba, it seemed that the winds of violence from every quarter of the globe were racing through the sheltered corridors of the pristine buildings on the East River, once so freighted with hopes for peace.

In foreign policy even more than in domestic affairs it seemed likely that Eisenhower's place in history would rest largely on what he did not do. Above all he did not go to war: he achieved a peace in Korea and resisted the temptation to intervene in Vietnam and Quemoy, in Hungary and Suez. Even the Lebanon episode was quickly ended. Elected on a platform of denouncing containment, he had gone beyond the Truman-Acheson policies to explore the possibility of peaceful coexistence with the Communist world. And he ended his tenure by warning against 'the acquisition of unwarranted influence, whether sought or unsought, by the military-industrial complex.'

Yet it could fairly be asked whether Eisenhower and Dulles had not, by rhetoric and deed, often contributed to the atmosphere of violence and to the recurrent crises which brought the world to the 'brink' of war. Even in his last months in office the President was heading toward a collision with the Russians in Laos and promoting an invasion of Castro's Cuba. And once again Eisenhower's achievements carried a price. He did not solve problems but postponed them, although sometimes this may have been all he could have done. He went out of office with his hopes for peace unfulfilled and with America's world prestige diminished, and he left to his successor a legacy of difficulties — in Berlin, in Cuba, in the Middle East, in Southeast Asia — which might, at any moment, bring on that war of annihilation that he so conscientiously sought to prevent.

XXIX

Society and Culture
in Modern America

1. GROWTH

'The time will come,' wrote Tocqueville in 1835, 'when 130 millions of men will be living in North America, equal in condition, the progeny of one race, owing their origin to the same cause, and preserving the same civilization, the same language, the same religion, the same habits, the same manners, imbued with the same opinions propagated under the same forms. The rest is uncertain, but this is certain.' A century after Tocqueville, demographers anxiously scanning the birth rate predicted that the population of the United States might reach 150 million by the 1960's, and thereafter barely hold its own. For reasons not wholly clear, but connected with the war and the vast upswing of prosperity, the total population reached 150 million by 1950 and passed 200 million at the beginning of 1968. This astonishing increase resulted largely from higher birth and lower death rates. During World War II early marriages and larger families began to make up for the sharp falling off of immigration; and the boom in babies showed no sign of slowing up after the war. It had taken 250 years for the population of the United States to reach 29 million; the single decade of the 'fifties added almost that number. Gratification over the disclosures of the census was tempered by the prospect of a population of 300 million by the year A.D. 2000. In the world-wide 'population explosion,' no European country, except possibly Portugal, increased as did the United States, which in the 1950's had a rate of growth about the same as that of India.

718

With this growth in population came a modest shift in racial and national composition. Europe generally failed to fill the immigration quotas set by earlier restrictive legislation, and of the more than three million immigrants admitted to the United States in the fifteen years after the end of the war, about half came from the countries of the Western hemisphere, especially Puerto Rico — which was part of the United States — and Mexico. There were now more Puerto Ricans in New York City than in San Juan and more Mexicans in Los Angeles than in any Mexican city except the capital. Yet by 1960, 95 per cent of the American population was native-born, and the overwhelming majority of Americans belonged to families who had lived in this country at least two generations.

The population shifted markedly from the Northeast to the South and West. During the 'fifties the population of New England increased only 12 per cent and that of the South Central states only 5 per cent, while some of the plains states barely held their own; but the population of California jumped 50 per cent, and Florida, which in 1920 had not one million inhabitants, went over the five million mark to become one of the ten largest states of the Union. By 1960 the statistical center of population had moved to the edge of the Mississippi river, and in 1964 California moved past New York and became the first state in the Union.

Even more spectacular was the flight from farm and village to the cities and their burgeoning suburbs. Some 70 per cent of the population lived in metropolitan areas by 1960. While several of the major cities actually declined in population, their metropolitan areas spread uncontrollably. The New York metropolitan region, which sprawled across three states, passed the 14 million mark; Los Angeles reached almost 7 million. By 1960 the ten largest metropolitan areas — if we include the Washington-Baltimore complex among them — embraced 50 million people.

The Union expanded too. After the admission of New Mexico and Arizona to statehood in 1912, it was assumed that the Union had crystallized permanently into forty-eight States. But World War II and the Cold War proved the strategic and economic importance of Hawaii and Alaska. As candidates for statehood, Alaska, with almost 600,000 square miles but only 225,000 people had the size; Hawaii with over 600,000 inhabitants but only 6400 square miles, the population. Because neither of them was contiguous with the American mainland, and both vindicated their claims by appeal to strategic considerations, their applications were coupled; both were admitted in 1959.[1] Unless Puerto Rico evolves from its preferred commonwealth status and demands statehood, and unless (as is extremely unlikely) other Caribbean islands demand annexation, it would seem that the United States has reached its maximum territorial limits.

2. THE DECLINE OF THE CITY

The census of 1960 revealed what had long been foreseen — the erosion of the great cities: eight of the ten largest cities had fewer people in 1960 than in 1950. As population fled to the suburbs, newcomers from the cotton fields of Mississippi, the mountains of West Virginia, and the teeming villages of Puerto Rico poured in to fill the void partially. The movement to the suburbs began well before the war, but after 1945 it became something like a mass migration. Driven by the urge for space and privacy, better schools and recreation facilities, by the desire for status, and sometimes by the lure of all-white communities, some 40 or 50 million Americans had by 1960 found refuge in suburbia or, as the fringes came to be called, 'exurbia.'

The well-to-do led the exodus to outlying areas, thus depriving the central cities of much of their tax base; city residential districts deteriorated into ghettos of the poor. American cities lacked a burgher class such as had flourished in the Old World and for centuries had preserved the beauty and civic vigor of Florence, Frankfurt, Bordeaux, and Bruges. There had been something similar in colonial and Federal Charleston, Philadelphia, Boston, and Salem, but most descendants of the old patricians had given up the struggle and moved out. Few cared to preserve the beauties and amenities of the old cities and resist the ravages of industrialism. A few cities, such as New Haven and Pittsburgh, had some success in arresting the erosion that was eating them away, but for the most part the efforts of cities to stop decay were like those of Alice in her race with the Red Queen: they found that they had to run at least twice as fast if they expected to get anywhere.

1. Neither the political fears of those who had opposed nor the hopes of those who had favored their admission were fulfilled. The two new states divided precisely down the middle in the election of 1960. Alaska went Republican by 1200 votes, Hawaii went Democratic by 115 votes!

Many came to question whether the American city was governable. The city was blighted by slums, which were warrens of racial bitterness, wretched housing, and crime. Yet efforts to raze slums through 'urban renewal' often resulted in sterile housing projects which destroyed the old neighborhoods. Strikes of municipal employees crippled essential services for weeks at a time; white policemen and black residents viewed one another with mutual suspicion; and by 1968 the welfare population of New York City passed 900,000, with one person on welfare for every three employed in private industry. City demands for schools, law enforcement, roads, sanitation, and welfare services loomed much larger than in the prewar years. Thus a vicious circle was set up where declining revenues led to poorer schools and lax law enforcement and these, by driving business and the middle classes to the suburbs, brought a still further loss in revenues. Lewis Mumford wrote mordantly: 'Lacking any sense of an intelligent purpose or a desirable goal, the inhabitants of our great American cities are simply "waiting for Godot."'

The automobile not only made it possible to live in the suburbs, or far out in the country, and do business in the city, but also, by creating insoluble traffic problems, ruining public transportation, devouring space for parking lots (two-thirds of central Los Angeles has been given over to streets, freeways, parking lots, and garages) and filling the air with noxious fumes, made it disagreeable to live in the central city. Intended as a vehicle for quick mobility, the automobile no longer served this function in many cities. In 1911 a horse and buggy paced through Los Angeles at 11 m.p.h.; in 1962 an auto moved through the city at rush hour at an average of 5 m.p.h. Yet while commuter railroads received little government aid, federal and local governments poured money into highways which funneled yet more traffic into the city.

As the city declined, the countryside became citified. By 1963 there were fewer than four million farms in the whole country. Although many still thought the family farm was the keystone of democracy, only 8 per cent of America's families lived on the land. The old rural patterns, which had loomed so large in American economy, politics, and literature, almost disappeared. Almost no part of the country was so remote as to be denied the advantages of good roads and electricity. Electricity brought efficiency, convenience, leisure, and recreation to the farmhouse, while the automobile and paved roads ended isolation. For generations farmers had taken pride in sending their children to agricultural colleges; now these schools dropped the word 'agricultural' from their names, and the students turned to everything except tilling the soil. The romantic or sentimental images drawn from Whittier's poems, Currier and Ives prints, and a century of political oratory faded out, as did the counter-images of the city slicker and Wall Street.

3. THE ECONOMY

The economy expanded at a phenomenal rate. By 1955 the United States, with only 6 per cent of the world's population was turning out half the world's goods. From 1945 to 1967 the gross national product increased from $213 billion to $775 billion a year; even when adjusted for inflation, this was an astonishing gain. Other statistics were almost equally impressive: an upsurge in electrical energy in the twenty years after 1940 from 150 to 800 trillion kilowatt hours, a 100 per cent gain in the production of natural gas and petroleum, and a growth of the labor force by 1967 to over 75 million. The economy was sparked by the emergence of new industries like plastics and electronics and by the huge investments of business and government in research. Not content with the vast home market, American corporations bought control of great automobile, drug, and electrical companies overseas.

If growth continued, so did concentration. The giant corporation came to be more and more gigantic; and notwithstanding the most zealous efforts of the anti-trust division of the Department of Justice, mergers and combinations spread into almost every field. The ten years after 1948 saw no fewer than 2191 mergers and combinations of corporations worth over $10 million. Between 1940 and 1960 bank deposits increased fourfold, but the number of banks declined by over one thousand and branch banking came to be almost as common in the United States as in Great Britain. Three great corporations — General Motors, Ford, and Chrysler — dominated the automobile industry, although in the 'fifties a fourth, American Motors, entered the competition. Three networks all but monopolized the air; six tobacco companies fed the insatiable appetite of Americans for cigarettes. Even in the realm of news the process seemed inexorable. In 1910 almost 700 cities and towns in the United States had competing daily newspapers; by 1967 the number had fallen to 64, and 17 states were without any locally competing newspapers. In many cities newspaper publishers held a news monopoly by owning the radio and television station as well.

As the automobile, the bus, the truck, and the airplane took over much of passenger and freight service, railroads, which had long dominated the economy of the nation, fell into desperate straits. Between 1940 and 1960 total railroad mileage actually declined by 17,000, and many parts of the nation which had been well served by railroads in 1890 found themselves isolated in 1960. The railroad companies, which had once fought Federal intervention, now appealed, almost desperately, for aid from Washington; the Federal Government, which had once frowned on combinations as 'conspiracies in restraint of trade,' now encouraged mergers. In the meantime, air service expanded rapidly; every city had an airport and some needed two or three to handle the traffic that filled the skies. Transatlantic air freight even threatened transatlantic shipping, and great monarchs of the sea like the *Queen Mary* that had excited the imaginations of an earlier generation lost out to the anonymous jet plane.

Automation increased apace. Not just a continuation of that speeding-up process introduced by the industrial revolution, it was something new, which tended to supplant the boss as well as the operative — to provide thinking and judgment as well as labor. Computers could store and use information to control, adjust, and correct complex operations. Walter Reuther described the automation of one of the Ford plants:

> I went to work in the automotive industry back in 1927. At that time, it took us about twenty-four hours to take a rough engine block, as it was cast in the foundry, and to machine that block, ready for assembly. . . . We kept making progress. We cut it down to 18 hours, and then 14 hours, then 12, then 9 hours. If you'll go through the Cleveland Ford engine plant, which is fully automated, you will see a Ford V-engine, 8 cylinders — a very complicated piece of mechanism — in which the rough castings are automatically fed into this automated line, and in fourteen and six-tenths minutes later, it is fully machined, without a human hand touching it. . . . There are acres and acres of machines, and here and there you will find a worker standing at a master switchboard, just watching green and yellow lights blinking off and on, which tell the worker what is happening in the machine.[2]

Automation presented labor with the menace of falling employment — and industry with the peril of declining purchasing power among

2. Walter P. Reuther, *Selected Papers*, Henry M. Christman (ed.), pp. 178, 180.

workers;[3] made inevitable the shorter working day, week, and year; gave rise to an urgent demand for the annual wage; and created a massive problem of leisure. At a time when the numbers of young and old were growing at the expense of the numbers in between, it denied employment to the young and retired the old, thus putting on the 20- to 55-year-olds an ever increasing burden of support for the rest of the community.[4] Since the new technology raised skill requirements for jobs, the school 'dropout' was at a disadvantage, and educational opportunities assumed increased urgency.

America had never known an economy of scarcity in the Old World sense of the term, but in the past it had always been able to dispose of its abundance by a steady rise in the standard of living and by exports. Now the capacity of farm and factory to produce far more than could normally be consumed created a new series of problems. Four responses were adopted in whole or in part. One was to build obsolescence into the product itself, thus making reasonably sure that there would be a continuous demand for new models. A second was to create new consumer wants: this task was the special responsibility of the advertisers, who rose to so prominent a position in American life that the term 'Madison Avenue' came to take on some of the connotations that 'Wall Street' had held a generation earlier. A third technique was to dump vast quantities of surplus goods abroad — to give wheat or airplanes, dynamos or books, to 'needy' nations. These were the more conventional solutions. The fourth, ardently advocated by John Kenneth Galbraith in *The Affluent Society*, was to divert an ever larger part of the economy to building schools, hospitals, museums, playgrounds, public housing, and the like. Because this smacked of the welfare state, business did not approve. Yet it was government expenditures in the public area — highways, airports, the military, the exploration of outer space, foreign aid — which helped keep the economy going.

In the postwar years organized labor achieved both prosperity and

---

3. Mr. Reuther tells us that one of the management who conducted him through the new fully automated Cleveland plant, 'with a slightly gleeful tone in his voice said to me, "How are you going to collect union dues from all those machines?" And I replied, "You know, that is not what's bothering me. I'm troubled by the problem of how to sell automobiles to all these machines." ' *Selected Papers*, p. 180.
4. Between 1950 and 1960 the number of persons under 18 increased by 37 per cent and the number over 65 by 35 per cent, while the number between the ages 19 to 64 grew only 7 per cent.

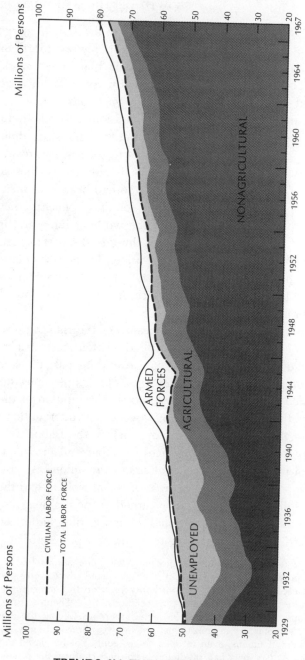

From Economic Report of the President 1968

Millions of Persons

Millions of Persons

CIVILIAN LABOR FORCE

TOTAL LABOR FORCE

UNEMPLOYED

ARMED FORCES

AGRICULTURAL

NONAGRICULTURAL

TRENDS IN THE LABOR FORCE
1929-1967

725

stability. In 1955 when the A.F. of L. and the C.I.O. merged, they boasted a joint membership of 17 million; still only one-fourth of the entire labor force, it was well over one-half of 'blue collar' workers who had always been the core of labor strength. By then organized labor generally had secured the 40-hour week, vacations with pay, welfare benefits, and in some industries old-age pensions as well. In 1946 John L. Lewis set a precedent which workers in other industries quickly took up when he persuaded the coal operators to set aside a 'royalty' of 20 cents on every ton of coal, to be used for health and welfare and pensions of $100 a month. Since only those who had been with their companies for long periods would be eligible for these benefits, the pension system put a premium on stability of the working force and indicated that the day of the casual laborer was a thing of the past. As labor prospered, it became increasingly conservative. European union officials claimed that the only way they could tell the difference between businessmen and labor leaders in America is that the union chieftains dressed better and drove bigger cars.

The old militancy waned in part because of the role the government played in labor relations. Government had written most of labor's goals into law, including the right to organize and to bargain collectively, workmen's compensation, minimum wages, old age pensions, unemployment insurance, limitations on hours, and the prohibition of the injunction. Along with this came increasing government intervention in union affairs, first in the Taft-Hartley Act and then in the Labor Act of 1959, which set up codes of ethical practices for labor and provided Federal supervision of many of the internal affairs of the union.[5] As government took over responsibility for broad areas of social welfare and the protection of the rights of workers, labor turned to new objectives that involved it deeply in the whole national economy: the guaranteed annual wage, a redistribution of work time to fit the new pattern of automation,

5. 'For about a decade beginning in the mid-1930's the unions had enjoyed the best of both possible legal worlds. On the one hand they were permitted to negotiate for closed shops by statutory authority . . . on the other, they continued to enjoy the status of voluntary, nonprofit associations. . . . Then, in 1947, Congress opened the shops to a very considerable degree, thereby obliging the unions better to qualify . . . as voluntary organizations. But in 1959 the community decided that the internal affairs of unions, even in open shops, could not be closed to regulation and supervision. As Gompers had predicted in the last century, the price of governmental protection was governmental control.' Lloyd Ulman, 'Unionism and Collective Bargaining,' in Seymour Harris (ed.), *American Economic History*, p. 471.

profit sharing and management sharing, co-operation with business to preserve vested interests in particular areas, and a livelier concern with global economy and international economic policies. Organized labor was fast becoming one of the great conservative forces in American economy and politics.

4. THE HOMOGENEOUS SOCIETY

Tocqueville had predicted that American society would become 'equal not only in condition, but preserving the same civilization, habits and manners.' But in the 1940's and 1950's a school of sociologists stressed the inequalities of American society and distinguished no less than nine classes, ranging from lower-lower and middle-lower to middle-upper and upper-upper. They found indices of class in such common denominators as family background, education, residence, work, profession, church and club affiliations, and similar stigmata. Other sociologists were impressed with the frenetic quest for status which, they insisted, pervaded the whole of American society, but particularly suburbia. Still others, especially the influential C. Wright Mills, discovered the emergence of a new power elite, made up of closely interrelated leaders in politics, finance, industry, communications, and the military.

Although World War II resulted in a redistribution of income, the postwar years saw a halt, and then a reversal, of this trend. The share of total wealth held by the richest 1 per cent in the United States increased from 20.8 per cent in 1949 to 26 per cent in 1956. At a time of boom prosperity, one careful survey found that nearly half the population, some 77 million Americans, lived at levels 'short of minimum requirements for a modestly comfortable level of living,' and in 1960 between one-fifth and one-fourth of American families were impoverished. As late as 1967 an estimated 32 million Americans, most of them city-dwellers, had an annual income which, by the most commonly accepted definition, placed them beneath the poverty line.

Yet the most impressive social development from the mid-nineteenth to the mid-twentieth century was the growth, rather than the decline, of equalitarianism. Nineteenth-century American society, equalitarian by Old World standards, contained marked class distinctions, and the gulf between rich, white, native-born Protestants and poor immigrants and Negroes was wide and deep. The America described as late as 1900 by an Upton Sinclair or an Edith Wharton, a Theodore Dreiser or a Henry James, was in many respects a stratified and class-conscious society.

In the course of the twentieth century the gap between rich and poor, native and foreign-born, Protestant, Catholic, and Jew, gradually narrowed, and during and after World War II the progress toward equality was spectacular. The leveling of standards of living, the increase in income (for in a time of staggering economic growth each man's share tended to rise, even if not proportionately), the cessation of large-scale immigration, the advent of all but universal high school education and the enormous increase in college and university enrollments, the standardization of consumer products — all of these developments tended to make American society at mid-twentieth century more equalitarian.

Deference to first families declined, as representatives of newer stocks like Governor DiSalle and Governor Rosellini, Secretary Ribicoff and Secretary Goldberg, moved into the seats of power. With 95 per cent of the population native-born, only Puerto Ricans and Mexicans remained in any substantial numbers to remind Americans of their earlier habit of associating class with place of birth. And as Negroes achieved an ever larger measure of economic, political, and educational equality, they also came closer to social equality. Technology, mass production, and advertising brought a leveling up and standardization of innumerable products, from canned foods to reproductions of the Old Masters. Where, in England, a Morris and a Rolls-Royce clearly proclaimed their class affiliations, in the United States Fords and Cadillacs came to look more and more alike. As the ranks of the middle class swelled, millions of Americans went to the same schools, dressed in the same ready-made clothes, shopped in the same supermarkets, ate the same packaged foods, drank the same beverages, listened to the same radio and television programs, read the same mass-produced magazines, drove the same cars, and vacationed on the same beaches. Differences in wealth remained very great, but differences in what money would buy were less significant. While blatant class distinctions persisted even in a democratic society like that of the English in such things as church and chapel, Oxbridge and Redbrick, barrister and solicitor, 'U' and 'non-U,' American society acknowledged no decisive class distinctions other than those fixed by color, although subtle differences remained.

Automation in industry, mechanization on the farm, and labor-saving devices in the home combined to add to the hours of leisure. For thousands of years most men and women, and many children too, had worked from sun-up to sun-down; now, abruptly, the work day was cut to seven hours and the work week to five days or occasionally even less. Work followed a more easy-going schedule: morning and afternoon coffee breaks, chats at the water cooler, the long lunch, paid holidays, and more extended vacations. Industries catering to leisure flourished: radio and television, boating, golf, skiing, camping, touring, and swimming pools. Travel became a national habit, and for many the winter vacation almost as normal as the summer. Because calculated relaxation was more tiring than hard work, 30 million Americans turned hopefully to adult — now renamed 'continuing' — education, immersing themselves in the study of the Hundred Great Books or indulging in amateur music, painting, and ceramics. The import of vintage wines soared; symphonic records sold briskly; and the sale of paperback books neared a million a day.

As fewer and fewer farmers and workers were required to produce the food and goods for an affluent society, the service industries swiftly became central to the economy, a development which also served to obliterate class lines. In 1956 for the first time white collar workers outnumbered blue collar employees. Between 1947 and 1957, the number of factory operatives declined 4 per cent while clerical workers increased 23 per cent and the salaried middle class 61 per cent. In the two decades after the war the percentage of the working force contributed by professional and technical workers almost doubled. The census of 1960 revealed some 35 million workers in service, sales, professional, and managerial jobs — the traditional white collar occupations — and fewer than 32 million working on the farms or in factories, shops, and mines.

The proportion of self-employed dropped sharply, and an increasing number of Americans spent their lives in a world of organizations, a phenomenon which many found alarming. In the world of W. H. Whyte, Jr.'s *The Organization Man*, C. Wright Mills's *White Collar*, Vance Packard's *The Status Seekers*, and Sloan Wilson's *The Man in the Gray Flannel Suit*, a bureaucratized society discouraged the free-wheeling individual and placed a premium on conformity, and in John Hersey's *The Child Buyer* a pupil is marked down as a troublesome deviate because he scores poorly in 'followership.' The 'other-directed man' described by David Riesman, whose aptly titled *The Lonely Crowd* was the prophetic book of this generation, engaged in 'smooth, unruffled manipulation of the self' to satisfy an 'irrational craving for in-discriminate approval.'

The economy of the second half of the century created a new type of employee whose talents lay primarily in adaptability and team work rather than independence and ingenuity; and it discouraged dominant personalities, even at the top. Just as the academic system no longer pro-duced strong presidents like Charles W. Eliot, Nicholas Murray Butler, and William R. Harper, and the military no longer turned out generals like Grant, Sherman, and Lee, so the new economy rarely brought to the fore new Rockefellers, Carnegies, McCormicks, and Morgans. Even in organized labor, where the tradition of personal leadership was strong, warriors like Samuel Gompers and John L. Lewis and idealists like Terence Powderly and Eugene Debs gave way to bureaucrats who ran large and flourishing organizations from comfortable well-staffed offices. Yet if there was social loss in the failure of innovative and strong-willed leaders to emerge, few deplored the passing of the type represented by George Baer, Tom Girdler, or Sewell Avery; if leadership was blander, it was also more enlightened and responsive.

Social critics who had long been disturbed by the inequalities in American life now expressed their anxiety about the trend toward a homogenized society. They drew a dismaying picture of the American suburb which displayed the same 'ranch houses' on single or split levels, with picture windows, television antennae, and a two-car garage; the same well-manicured back gardens with little swimming pools; the same country clubs and shopping centers and supermarkets, all built to a pattern. Almost all the men commuted to nearby cities, society was matriarchal, and the well-protected young gravitated from the local high or country-day school to the state university or the Ivy League college of the East. For many Americans suburbia represented a new way of life — one that contrasted sharply with the older habits of the countryside or the city. Max Lerner observed:

> The suburbanites found new roots for their lives in a new sense of neighborhood which was closer than anything in previous American experience except college dormitories or fraternities or the com-munal settlements of the early nineteenth century. . . . Not only did the doors within houses tend to disappear, but the outside doors ceased to have much function. . . . Newcomers were expected to be 'outgoing' and to 'join the gang'; introversion was frowned

upon, and the society of ex-introverts was like the society of ex-sinners. There was intensive 'joining' in club work and community participation, including greatly increased church membership. . . . Instead of 'conspicuous consumption' the rule became 'inconspicuous consumption' so that no one would embarrass anyone else. There were car pools for shuttling children to school and back; there was an almost communal use of bicycles, books, and baby toys; there was an enforced intimacy so that everyone's life was known to everyone, and no one had to face his problems alone.[6]

American society had more variety than such a portrait suggests. To be sure, in the Eisenhower years, many observers sensed that 'the bland were leading the bland,' and the college generation of the 1950's seemed exceptionally passive. But not even the suburbs were uniform: in New York's Westchester County Negroes in the river streets of Ossining lived different lives from bankers on Scarsdale estates, as the world of Cicero differed from that of Oak Park, and Daly City from Tiburon. No doubt standardization and conformity are tributes that a mobile, equalitarian society is often compelled to pay, but this same movement toward equality opened up new opportunities for many Americans, and the United States still had far more diversity than many of its critics, and some of its admirers, would concede.

5. EDUCATION

America was the first country in modern history where each generation had more education than its forebears — an elementary consideration which goes far to explain that child-centered society which puzzled foreign observers. The familiar process of enlarging both the base and the height of the educational pyramid was greatly accelerated in the years after the Second World War. Prosperity, the G.I. Bill of Rights, leisure, the achievement of equality for women and the beginnings of equality for Negroes, the urgent demands for expertise and professional skills — all of these combined to give a powerful impetus to education, particularly at the secondary and higher levels. In the twenty years after 1940 the educational level of the country rose by two or three years. By 1960 the college occupied about the same position in the educational enterprise as the high school in 1920 and the junior college in 1940. Between

6. Max Lerner, *America as a Civilization*, p. 178.

1920 and 1960, when the population grew about 75 per cent, the high school population increased 500 per cent. The total number of students at institutions of higher education in 1920 was less than 600,000, and that year universities granted some 53,000 degrees. By 1960 the university population was 3.6 million, and of these, 479,000 earned degrees — a sixfold increase in enrollment and a ninefold increase in earned degrees. Substantial numbers of college graduates — in some colleges as high as 85 or 90 per cent — moved on to graduate professional schools.

The new demands on schools and universities raised many perplexing problems, of which the most urgent was money. How were the American people to finance twice as much education for twice the number of students as they had for an earlier generation? Total public school expenditures in 1950 ran around $6 billion — not an impressive sum when compared with the $7 billion spent for liquor, to be sure, but heavy enough to cause widespread complaint. In the next decade the population explosion threatened to overwhelm the nation's schools; the number of children aged 5 to 14 increased 49 per cent. By 1960 public school expenditures had soared to over $15 billion. The average varied greatly from state to state. In 1958 New York spent more than $500 per pupil, Oregon and Delaware over $400, but Mississippi, South Carolina, and Arkansas less than $200; nevertheless Southern states were actually spending a larger proportion of their tax income on schools than were their rich Northern and Western neighbors. Inability, assumed or real, of the poorer states to support public schools adequately led to a widespread demand for federal aid to education, but this was not achieved until the Johnson administration.

These material problems of education reflected deeper and more important intellectual ones. Education had been controversial ever since Plato's day, and it was not to be expected that society would cease to debate its character, content, or purposes when it became 'universal.' What troubled many Americans at mid-century was that somehow education had failed to educate: that a generation of which almost everyone went to high school and unprecedented numbers to the university, was still content with largely pictorial journalism, television programs fit for imbeciles, politics conducted with the technique of the circus, and race relations that reflected the tribal enmities of primitive peoples.

When, in 1957, the Russians launched Sputnik, thereby dramatizing the superiority of their engineers, the United States took a hard look at its educational system. It found that Russia was spending a larger proportion of her income on education than was the United States, and Russian and Western European students who left school at eighteen were better educated than the average American of college age and experience. Not a few blamed the inadequacies of American schools on 'progressive' education, which valued 'adjustment' more than intellectual discipline. Some of the detraction arose from concern that progressive education inspired in the young a disrespectful attitude toward the status quo; some by the simple desire to recapture not only the pastoral pleasures of the 'little red schoolhouse' with its McGuffey Readers and Blue-backed Spellers but its modest budgets as well.

Dissatisfaction centered on the high school. Writers alleged that it taught badly in four years what should be learned well in two or three; that it failed to provide a sound knowledge of mathematics, English grammar, or a foreign language; that it encouraged social and athletic activities at the expense of intellectual; that it favored mediocrity at the expense of excellence and laid waste the talents of its brighter students. The most judicious critic of the high schools, James B. Conant, formerly president of Harvard University, in his *The Child, the Parent, and the State* (1959) supported some of these charges, recommended increased emphasis on mathematics and foreign languages, and endorsed the comprehensive high school. In his *Slums and Suburbs* (1961) he warned against the development of two school systems in America, one for the poor children of the slums and the other for the privileged children of the suburbs — a division which would dangerously sharpen cleavages in American society.

Our thousand or more colleges and universities presented a fantastically varied pattern, from vocational institutions which were inferior to a good high school academy to some of the best universities in the world. Whilst in the nineteenth century Americans eager for post-graduate instruction had to go to Germany or France, and in the twentieth many continued to do so, there was now a reverse movement; thousands of graduates of the universities of Latin America and the Old World flocked to the universities and technological institutes of the United States and Canada.

Higher education confronted as great a pressure of students as the high schools; the three million or so of 1960 promised to grow to five million by 1970, beyond which few cared to peer. As armies of students invaded the great state universities, dormitories and student unions, field houses and university airports mushroomed over the landscape. Private philanthropy and public generosity, together with increased tuition charges, helped meet the mounting costs.

American graduate schools had not turned out enough first-rate scholars to take care of the two million or so students of the 1940's; by the 'sixties the shortage of talent was alarming, and it promised to become desperate. Two developments exacerbated this shortage of talent: the growing complexity of science and the rapid enlargement of the areas of knowledge. The facts of sciences like biology, with new developments such as DNA, were increasing faster than men's ability to absorb them; the areas and disciplines which Americans were expected to master — the Near East, the Far East, Indonesia, the African and Indian languages, Japanese culture, the economics of the Common Market — all of these clamored for attention. At the same time foundations, business, and government competed with universities for such talent as was available. Scholars could take some satisfaction in the reflection that professors now jostled doctors and lawyers in the prestige ratings that the sociologists solemnly compiled.

Originally universities had been cosmopolitan in character, and some European institutions, like Paris, Göttingen, and Edinburgh, had continued this tradition throughout their history; but not until after the Second World War did American universities begin to attract large numbers of students from abroad or to take on formal responsibility for training foreign students. Provisions of the Smith-Mundt and other congressional acts brought tens of thousands of students, chiefly from Germany, to American campuses, and by 1960 there were well over 50,000 foreign students enrolled in American universities — most of them in graduate and professional schools. Individual institutions like Columbia, Michigan, and California numbered their foreign students by the thousands. At the same time the Fulbright Act of 1946, revised and enlarged in 1961, enabled thousands of American students and scholars to study and teach in universities throughout the world.

Great foundations like the Ford, Rockefeller and Guggenheim added to this stream of Americans studying overseas, and the American student became as familiar a sight on the Boul' Mich' or the Via Veneto as the American scholar in the archives of Vienna or the museums of Florence. Another interesting postwar development has been the creation of

American university centers abroad — the Salzburg Center for American Studies in Austria, a branch of the Johns Hopkins in Bologna, outposts of Stanford and Syracuse universities in Florence, Frankfurt, and Japan. All of these activities — the interchange of students and scholars, the transplanting of educational facilities, the beneficent work of the foundations, the activities of UNESCO — went far to re-create that community of Western learning which had flourished from the Middle Ages to the rise of modern nationalism; and in all this the United States played a generous and enlightened role.

6. LITERATURE AND THE ARTS

In the postwar years the new generation lived on the literary capital accumulated by the old. No new novelists emerged to supplant Hemingway or Faulkner; no major poet took up the torch which had been held aloft for so long by writers like Robert Frost; neither Eugene O'Neill nor Thornton Wilder had a truly formidable successor in the theater, although Tennessee Williams, Arthur Miller, William Inge, and Edward Albee showed the wealth of talent Broadway still drew. Most of the major critics were hold-overs from an earlier generation: the cosmopolitan Edmund Wilson, gathering strength with the years, Lionel Trilling, a kind of American Georg Brandes, the learned Richard Blackmur, and the iconoclastic Yvor Winters. In other cultural pursuits the auspices were more hopeful. Painters and sculptors no longer permitted Europe to set the style; architects, after a long period of enthrallment with Frank Lloyd Wright, began to emancipate themselves from the functional and return to the imaginative; and the musical renaissance launched in the 'thirties flourished and gathered strength.

Americans congratulated themselves that their literature had vitality, and even English critics, deprecating their own preoccupation with form and style, accepted this estimate, but many of the postwar novels were primarily documentary. As Saul Bellow wrote, 'The American desire for the real has created a journalistic sort of novel which has a *thing* excitement, a glamor of *process;* it specializes in information, satisfies the readers' demand for knowledge. It seldom has much independent human content and it is more akin to popularized science or history than to the fiction of Balzac or Chekhov.'[7] The Second World War, as clearly as

7. New York *Times Book Review,* 18 Feb. 1962.

the Civil War, involved moral issues, but these somehow failed to command interest or allegiance, and the war itself evoked for the most part a meager and ineffectual literary response. The novels of World War II were longer and stronger than those of World War I, but there was no *The Sun Also Rises,* no *Soldiers' Pay,* no *The Enormous Room,* and very little war poetry that caught the imagination. Only a few war novels compelled attention: Norman Mailer's *The Naked and the Dead,* James Jones's *From Here to Eternity,* both badly flawed works, and Joseph Heller's *Catch-22,* with its outrageous black humor.

Much of the best writing reflected a special vantage point — that of Negro authors like James Baldwin and Ralph Ellison, of Jewish novelists such as Bernard Malamud and Saul Bellow, and most particularly in these years, of Southern self-consciousness. William Faulkner still dominated the literary scene: *Intruder in the Dust, Requiem for a Nun, The Town,* and *The Mansion* continued that study of the pathology of the South which Faulkner had inaugurated in the early 'thirties, and which now became the most elaborate literary analysis of one segment of American society since Henry James. Faulkner's influence was pervasive, but he had few disciples; most of the new Southern writers traced their lineage to Ellen Glasgow or Willa Cather or even to Stark Young rather than to him. In *Delta Wedding, The Ponder Heart,* and a large number of short stories, Eudora Welty showed herself one of the most faithful interpreters of the present-day South; Carson McCullers (*Reflections in a Golden Eye, The Heart Is a Lonely Hunter, The Member of the Wedding*), perhaps the most brilliant of the younger generation of writers, combined psychological insight with an impressive technical competence. The most substantial of the Southern writers was doubtless Robert Penn Warren, a Kentuckian and a member of the remarkable Vanderbilt University group (which included the poet John Crowe Ransom and the critic Allen Tate). In a series of novels outwardly historical but fundamentally philosophical, Warren examined critical episodes of history that dramatized Southern traits of character. *Night Riders* recreated the war between the tobacco farmers and the companies in the early years of the century; *World Enough and Time* explored the passions involved in a famous Kentucky murder case more than a century earlier; *All the King's Men* was a fictional tour de force about the career of Huey Long.

The literature of these years reflected the anxiety of 'the lonely crowd.'

Many novels dealt with the search for identity, notably Bellow's *The Adventures of Augie March* and the writings of J. D. Salinger, who, one critic observed, presented 'madness as the chief temptation of modern life, especially for the intelligent young.' Salinger's *The Catcher in the Rye,* which sold almost two million copies, became the special favorite of adolescents in the 1950's. Writers often sounded the theme of loneliness, isolation, and the inability of men to communicate with one another. In one of Tennessee Williams's plays a character says, 'We're all of us sentenced to solitary confinement inside our own skins for life.' If America's mobile society permitted unparalleled freedom, it also cut people off from tradition and a sense of community, a rootlessness which concerned almost all of these writers. In Truman Capote's *Other Voices: Other Rooms,* one character protests, 'We go screaming round the world, dying in our rented rooms, nightmare hotels, eternal homes of the transient heart.'

The leader of the postwar poets, Robert Lowell, voiced the same absorbed interest in the quest for identity in such works as *Lord Weary's Castle,* but the new generation failed to command the kind of following that their elders had enjoyed. Many of the older poets — Robert Frost, Carl Sandburg, Conrad Aiken, John Crowe Ransom, Marianne Moore (all born before 1890) — carried on into the 'sixties with no apparent diminution of powers, providing an example for the younger poets, most of whom preferred to experiment with new forms. Rarely had poetry had so many practitioners; never had they demanded so much of their readers. Younger poets like Robert Lowell and Theodore Roethke, Richard Eberhart, and Richard Wilbur, combined an astonishing technical competence, an intricate and allusive style, and philosophical maturity. Like so many of the painters and sculptors of the day they had to be content with a critical rather than a popular success.

In 1946 abstract expressionism burst on the American art scene, and New York replaced Paris as the center of advanced painting. Hans Hofmann was the father of this school, characterized by big splashes of paint, but its most important practitioner was Jackson Pollock, the founder of 'action painting.' The abstract expressionists believed that, to paraphrase Archibald MacLeish, a painting must not mean but be. In the 'sixties the United States again was the originator of new approaches which reverberated through the art world. 'Pop' artists satirized America's consumer society by painting canvases with multiple images of soup cans or film goddesses, although often they produced paintings that suggested that they had been swallowed up by the consumer culture they sought to lampoon. Still more subjective was the work of 'op' painters who created illusions of movement in dazzling canvases that clearly had no meaning save in the patterns perceived by the viewer. Most Americans preferred the painting of more traditional artists like Andrew Wyeth, often admired for the wrong reasons, but even Wyeth insisted he was an abstractionist.

With the passing of Frank Lloyd Wright a new group of architects, some trained in Europe but transplanted to America, came to the fore: Eero Saarinen, Miës van der Rohe, Walter Gropius, Gordon Bunshaft, and Wallace K. Harrison. The postwar years saw a reaction against both the functionalism of Wright and the mechanical impersonality of the all-glass skyscrapers and a return to some of Louis Sullivan's ideas of decoration. This resulted in such achievements as the American Embassy at New Delhi erected by Harrison and Abramowitz, Saarinen's American Embassy building in London, Gordon Bunshaft's Lever building and Mies van der Rohe's magnificent bronze and glass Seagram building in New York's midtown area, and Le Corbusier's United Nations Secretariat building alongside the East river in New York. No less original was the new airport architecture, which could be seen at its best in St. Louis, and the combination of functional interiors, decorative exteriors, and landscaping in the complex of the Connecticut General Life Insurance buildings outside Hartford planned by Skidmore, Owings and Merrill and landscaped by the gifted Isamu Noguchi.

The musical renaissance which had set in between the two world wars, with the coming of distinguished European refugees like Paul Hindemith, Arnold Schoenberg, Igor Stravinsky, Bela Bartók, and Darius Milhaud, flourished and gathered strength. Colleges and universities appointed many distinguished composers to university faculties: Randall Thompson and Walter Piston at Harvard, Roger Sessions at Princeton, Douglas Moore at Columbia, Lukas Foss at California, Darius Milhaud at Mills College in California, and Leonard Bernstein at Brandeis University. Although America still could not boast an opera company as good as those in Vienna or Milan, the number of small, local opera companies and small-town symphony orchestras increased tremendously.

From Haydn and Mozart to Dvořak and Brahms, musicians had

drawn on folk music for their compositions, and American composers followed in the same tradition. Aaron Copland wrote 'native' music for Steinbeck's *Red Pony* and for Emily Dickinson's poems, and drew on folk music for his own ballets. Leonard Bernstein, gifted conductor of the New York Philharmonic, composed the music for *On the Town* and *West Side Story* out of familiar materials. Douglas Moore, who provided probably the largest operatic repertory of anyone of his generation, composed in authentic American style *The Ballad of Baby Doe, The Devil and Daniel Webster, Giants in the Earth,* and *The Wings of the Dove.* The Italian-born Gian-Carlo Menotti wrote, for the American stage, *Amahl and the Night Visitors, The Medium,* and *The Saint of Bleecker Street.*

7. THE CHALLENGE OF SCIENCE

In a lecture on 'The Two Cultures,' in 1959, the British novelist C. P. Snow admonished his contemporaries not to think of 'culture' as meaning exclusively art, music, and letters, but to remember that science, too, is a culture, with its own traditions, laws, and empire. America has made significant contributions to this scientific culture, increasingly so to theory and principle rather than to those 'purely practical arts' toward which Tocqueville thought that the American genius would be exclusively directed. 'Today, in almost all fields of natural science,' wrote Robert Oppenheimer, 'our country is pre-eminent in theory as it is in experiment, invention, and practice. . . . Today the young man wishing the best training in theoretical physics, or mathematics, theoretical chemistry or biology, will be likely to come to this country, as three decades ago he would have gone to the schools of Europe.' Science, to be sure, is universal, and scientific findings are the product of co-operative action spread over many countries and long periods of time. Yet no period of American history has seen more far-reaching advances in science than the quarter of a century after the outbreak of World War II. Americans did notable work in atomic physics, the exploration of outer space and of the seas, calculating machines, medicine, and public health.

Doubtless the most spectacular development came in the realm of atomic physics. The peaceful uses of atomic energy either through fission (the atomic bomb) or fusion (the hydrogen bomb) held out the most dazzling prospects to mankind. One pound of uranium could provide the power of 1300 tons of coal, and five pounds of hydrogen could create enough energy to meet all the power requirements of New York City for twenty-four hours. Uranium was scarce, but the supply of hydrogen, processed from water, was limitless. Once fully harnessed, nuclear fusion could take care of the power needs of the entire world for all time. Although some of these expectations proved premature, by 1960 there were atomic power reactors in the United States, Britain, France, and Russia, and atomic energy was being used to speed up the desalination of ocean water, for logging oil wells and detecting gas-bearing and oil-bearing geological strata, for combating agricultural pests and diseases, in many fields of medicine, and in electronics and engineering.

For thousands of years mankind had lived in an economy of scarcity, and even optimistic Americans, with a continent at their disposal, were haunted by the specter of the exhaustion of natural resources. Now science was able to dissipate some of these fears. Vast deposits of oil were discovered in the off-shore and tidal lands of the Gulf States and California, and by the 1960's this oil was being pumped out. Science also found the way to extract oil from the inexhaustible shale mountains of Colorado, although costs are high. Reforestation and check dams slowed up soil erosion; chemical fertilizers restored the fertility of worn-out land; and new sources of food such as the ocean gave some hope that the world-wide 'population explosion' would not mean starvation for mankind. Programs of desalination of sea water through vapor compression, solar distillation, or more complex processes run by atomic power were holding out the bright promise of enough water to make ancient deserts once again blossom as gardens and to meet the needs of cities and industry.

The exploration of outer space realized the dream of Icarus, which had bemused generations of astronomers, physicists, and philosophers. American as well as Russian satellites photographed the moon and relayed messages from space. This penetration of outer space not only aided activities such as satellite communication and long-range weather prediction, but enabled man to penetrate the mysteries of the stellar universe and held out hope that man may in time establish contact with other planets. Thus, at the very moment in history when man peered into the abyss of total self-destruction through atomic weapons, he glimpsed the farthest reaches of the universe.

Spectacular developments took place in the field of electronics. Computers capable of combining thousands of separate items in a single formula, of solving almost instantly mathematical questions beyond the control or even the grasp of the human mind, and of directing the most delicate machines in the most complicated processes — all these promised to extend the mental powers of man as steam and electricity had extended his physical powers in the nineteenth century. Already on the horizon were computing machines that would not only work on material fed into them, but would 'think' for themselves on subjects formulated for them.

The decades in which war, implemented by science and technology, destroyed many million lives, also saw advances in medicine that wiped out long-familiar diseases, reduced infant mortality, extended the life span, and made those added years more useful and comfortable than old age had ever been.

In 1920, 82 out of every 1000 white babies and 131 out of every 1000 Negro babies born in the United States died at birth or in their first year. By 1959 infant mortality had been reduced to 23 out of 1000 white babies and 44 out of 1000 colored. Thus a 1960 baby had about three or four times the chance of survival of a 1920 baby, a sensational gain although the figures on race were deplorable. The improvement in life expectancy was almost equally dramatic. The average child born in 1850 could expect to live only to the age of 40; the child born in 1900 might live to be 47; but the child born in 1960 should — if atomic war can be avoided — live out the Biblical three score and ten.

Medicine is the least national of scientific activities, yet it is eloquent testimony to medical research in the United States that since 1945 the Nobel prize in medicine has gone to fourteen Americans, four of them European-born. Dr. Herman Muller's discovery of DDT made possible a world-wide attack on malaria; the Russian-born Dr. Selman Waksman discovered streptomycin; Doctors Jonas Salk and Albert Sabin developed vaccines that promised to wipe out poliomyelitis; Dr. Max Theiler found a vaccine against the ancient scourge of yellow fever. New techniques of anesthetics and new surgical refinements made possible open-heart surgery, the grafting of arteries and veins, massive blood transfusions, and the transplanting of eye corneas and of other vital organs. The postwar years saw steady advances in vitamin research, the development of cortisone for treating arthritis, and of orinase for diabetes.

The Atomic Energy Commission sponsored research into the effect on cancer of radiation, and for its diagnosis and treatment made available radio-isotopes.

Much of this research was made possible by lavish appropriations from the Federal Government. That government had long interested itself in some fields of science — geology, oceanography, paleontology, and botany, for example — but during the war and the postwar years it entered boldly into almost every area of scientific activity. This new alliance of government and science was dictated in the first instance by the exigencies of national defense; as it became clear that no aspect of science from cancer research to the exploration of outer space was unrelated to national security, government came to be the chief support to all kinds of research. By 1960 the Federal Government was subsidizing research in universities to the tune of over a billion dollars a year. California Tech and Michigan received almost half their income from this source; and, with Federal funds, a single institution like M.I.T. was enabled to spend more money on scientific research than all the universities of the British Isles combined. The cost of atomic research and the probing of outer space was of course far larger. There were two serious dangers: that government subsidies might deflect research into those areas that seemed most important to government officials rather than encourage it in those areas that appealed to the scientists themselves, and that the government's insistence on supervision, regulation, and security would endanger scientific and academic independence.

XXX

John F. Kennedy and the New Frontier

1. THE 1960 ELECTION

In 1960, as the elderly Eisenhower prepared to leave office, both major parties turned to younger men, each of whom had been identified with the unadventurous politics of the 1950's. The Republicans named the forty-seven-year-old Vice-President, Richard Nixon, who easily overcame a challenge from Nelson Rockefeller, a critic of the Eisenhower administration. To balance the ticket with an Easterner and an internationalist, the convention chose as his running mate Henry Cabot Lodge of Massachusetts, member of a distinguished political family and, since his defeat by John F. Kennedy for re-election to the Senate in 1952, chief United States representative at the United Nations. Kennedy, four years younger than Nixon, won the Democratic nomination after thrashing Senator Hubert Humphrey, a forthright liberal, in the West Virginia primary and turning aside a movement for Adlai Stevenson at the Democratic convention. To the dismay of the liberals, Kennedy persuaded Lyndon Johnson, the middle-of-the-road Majority Leader, to take second place on the ticket.

Neither candidate aroused much enthusiasm among those who had been critical of America's failure to develop a strong sense of national purpose under Eisenhower. Nixon, who had played a dubious role in the McCarthy era, seemed manipulative and unimaginative. By failing to take a stand against McCarthy, Kennedy, who had won a Pulitzer Prize for his book *Profiles in Courage*, opened himself to the taunt that he

743

should have shown less profile and more courage. Liberals feared he was too affected by the views of his wealthy financier father, Joseph P. Kennedy, who as ambassador to the Court of St. James's had given comfort to the isolationists. Like Nixon, Kennedy appeared to be too calculating and too detached.

But in his acceptance speech at Los Angeles, Kennedy gave indications that his critics may have misjudged him, for he began to elaborate the theme of his campaign: the need for sacrifice, imagination, and boldness in a 'supreme national effort' to 'get the country moving again.' Kennedy stated:

> We stand today on the edge of a New Frontier — the frontier of the 1960s — a frontier of unknown opportunities and perils — a frontier of unfulfilled hopes and threats.
>
> Woodrow Wilson's New Freedom promised our nation a new political and economic framework. Franklin Roosevelt's New Deal promised security and succor to those in need. But the New Frontier of which I speak is not a set of promises — it is a set of challenges. It sums up, not what I intend to offer the American people, but what I intend to ask of them. It appeals to their pride, not their pocket-book — it holds out the promise of more sacrifice instead of more security.

For all his eloquence, Kennedy ran under formidable handicaps. To be sure he had the advantage of campaigning as the candidate of the majority party; he was charming and handsome; and he had the appeal of a war hero who had shown exemplary courage and devotion to his men as a PT-boat commander in the Solomons. But he was a Roman Catholic, and Al Smith's defeat was well remembered. Furthermore, no one so young had ever been elected President; and he seemed much less experienced than Nixon, who had actually held the reins of government during Eisenhower's illnesses. Nor did Negroes, a mainstay of the Roosevelt coalition, rally to Kennedy, who had not been a leader of the civil rights forces in the Senate.

Kennedy surmounted each of these obstacles. He met the religious issue directly by addressing the Greater Houston Ministerial Association and answering frankly any question the ministers chose to ask. Kennedy declared:

> I believe in an America where the separation of Church and State is absolute — where no Catholic prelate would tell the President

(should he be a Catholic) how to act, and no Protestant minister would tell his parishioners for whom to vote — where no church or church school is granted any public funds or political preference — and where no man is denied public office merely because his religion differs from the President who might appoint him or the people who might elect him.

By his forthrightness he succeeded in muting, if not eliminating, the religious issue.

Polls still showed Nixon running ahead of his rival when he agreed to a series of four nationally televised debates in late September and October. Nixon, who had used television skillfully in 1952, thought he would improve his advantage, but he was outpointed in the crucial first debate in which Kennedy displayed a poise and maturity that erased any impression of callow upstart. Kennedy moved into the lead in the polls, and he maintained a narrow edge for the rest of the campaign. When, on 19 October, Martin Luther King was sentenced on a technicality to four months' hard labor in a Georgia penitentiary, from which many feared he would not emerge alive, Kennedy phoned Dr. King's wife to express concern; and Kennedy's brother, Robert, secured the minister's release. This act appears to have swung large numbers of Negro voters to Kennedy, and the Negro ballots provided the margin of victory in several critical states.

Kennedy won, but in the closest race since 1888. He gained a popular majority of only 118,000 out of a total of some 68 million votes, a mere two-tenths of 1 per cent, but he had a more comfortable majority of 303 to 219 in the electoral college.[1] His Catholicism helped him in the industrial Northeast, hurt him in Protestant rural areas. He ran strongly in the Northeast and in the South, where Lyndon Johnson kept Texas and other states in the Democratic column; Nixon swept most of the West. Although the Democrats held most of their 1958 gains, the Republicans picked up two seats in the Senate, 22 in the House. Yet, by however small a margin, Kennedy and Johnson had ended eight years of Republican rule at a time when the nation was enjoying both peace and prosperity. They had overcome the immense popularity of Eisenhower and the experience of Nixon, despite the handicaps of youth, Catholicism, and a discontented South.

1. Fifteen votes went to Senator Harry F. Byrd of Virginia. They included Mississippi's eight, six from Alabama, and one from a Republican elector in Oklahoma.

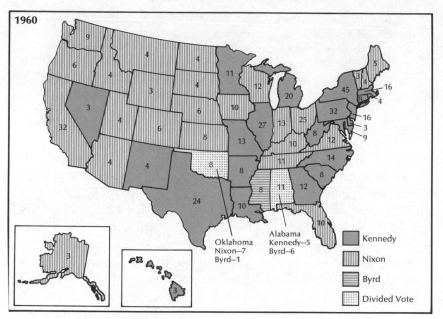

PRESIDENTIAL ELECTION, 1960

Ten weeks later, as blustery winds and snow flurries swept across Washington, one hundred million Americans watched the inauguration ceremonies on television and heard the new President reaffirm their revolutionary inheritance:

> Let the word go forth from this time and place, to friend and foe alike, that the torch has been passed to a new generation of Americans — born in this century, tempered by war, disciplined by a hard and bitter peace, proud of our ancient heritage, and unwilling to witness or permit the slow undoing of those human rights to which this Nation has always been committed.

He called upon his generation

> to bear the burden of a long twilight struggle, year in and year out, 'rejoicing in hope, patient in tribulation' — a struggle against the common enemies of man: tyranny, poverty, disease and war itself.

And he concluded with a characteristic affirmation of confidence and of faith:

> I do not believe that any of us would exchange places with any other people or any other generation. The energy, the faith, the devotion which we bring to this endeavor will light our country and all who serve it — and the glow from that fire can truly light the world.
>
> And so, my fellow Americans: ask not what your country can do for you — ask what you can do for your country.

Kennedy, who so deliberately made himself the spokesman for 'a new generation of Americans,' put together an administration notable for its youth. His cabinet, which included his thirty-five-year-old brother Robert as Attorney-General, was ten years younger than Eisenhower's. The youngest man ever elected to the Presidency, he often appointed to key positions still younger men, who were, as one observer said, the junior officers of World War II now come to power. Although he still suffered the effects of serious illnesses which had plagued him for years, Kennedy, whose favorite catchword was 'vigor,' found an enthusiastic following for touch football, sailing, and even fifty-mile hikes. More important, he contributed to that change in the national mood which saw the 'Silent Generation' of the 1950's give way to the deeply committed young people of the 'sixties.

From the very first day in the brilliant winter sunshine of the inauguration, at which Robert Frost read a poem, Kennedy gave a tone to the White House which not only contrasted sharply to that of the Eisenhower years but which differed from anything Washington had ever seen before. It was not merely that professors now streamed to Washington — they had done so in New Deal days — but that Kennedy and his circle developed a style that reminded some of an eighteenth-century French court, others of the Whig society of early nineteenth-century Britain, and still others only of the 'jet set' of Palm Beach and St. Tropez. Led by a President who quoted Madame de Staël on television, Kennedy's world found a place for both Oleg Cassini gowns and Pablo Casals at the White House, for the glitter of the party for Princess Lee Radziwill and for a Postmaster-General who had published a novel.

In contrast to the Eisenhower era, in which the 'egghead' was an object of contempt, the new administration welcomed the contributions of men of ideas to public affairs. Kennedy, who enjoyed the company of brilliant men, made a point of honoring Nobel prize winners at a White House dinner; with characteristic felicity he greeted them as 'the most extraordinary collection of talent, of human knowledge, that has ever been gathered together at the White House, with the possible exception of when Thomas Jefferson dined alone.' He also sought to encourage the arts. 'I look forward to an America which will not be afraid of grace and beauty,' he said. Kennedy took steps to improve the appearance of Washington by inviting architects like Mies van der Rohe and Marcel Breuer to design Federal buildings. His wife, Jacqueline, a member of the Newport aristocracy who was the youngest mistress of the White House since Frances Cleveland, refurbished the White House to make it a cherished 'national object,' and introduced good music and even, for the first time in the century, good cooking.

As early as the 1960 campaign, in which Jack Kennedy revealed a quick wit and a talent for epigram, there had begun to be talk of 'the Kennedy style.' Yet no one was more impatient than Kennedy with the notion that the success of a Presidency could be measured by style. The real test of his administration, he knew, would be whether he could achieve significant substantive changes. 'I run for the Presidency,' he had declared, 'because I do not want it said that the years when our generation held political power . . . were the years when America began to slip. I don't want historians writing in 1970 to say that the balance of power . . . began to turn against the United States and against the cause of freedom.' He approached this task full of hope, yet soberly, and he was to find that, although he scored successes, the world was even more intractable than he had thought.

2. THE END OF THE POSTWAR WORLD

At the same time that he sought to explore the 'New Frontier' of American society, Kennedy faced the formidable task of shaping a foreign policy which would accommodate to a world in flux. The Cold War had entered its sixteenth year, yet the situation in 1961 differed so dramatically from that of 1945 that commentators wrote of 'the end of the postwar world.' The bipolar alignment of 1945 was breaking apart in both East and West. Within the Communist camp, the Soviet Union confronted the rivalry of Red China. In the West a prosperous Europe no longer recognized the United States as the unchallenged leader of the free world. The emerging nations of three continents, comprising more than half of the world's population, refused to commit themselves to either side in the Cold War and often found the East-West conflict irrelevant to their own needs.

Kennedy comprehended the nature of these changes, and he recognized that the United States had only a narrow range of options. In an article in *Foreign Affairs* in 1957 he had observed: 'Americans have always displayed a faith in self-enforcing moral principles and have hankered for apocalyptic solutions and fixed patterns; they must learn that most current issues in international politics do not encourage such unrealistic hopes.' Weary of Dulles's chiliastic rhetoric, Kennedy doubted that the struggle with Communism was a holy war that must end in total victory for the United States. In November 1961 he declared:

> We must face the fact that the United States is neither omnipotent nor omniscient — that we are only six per cent of the world's population — that we cannot impose our will upon the other ninety-four per cent of mankind — that we cannot right every wrong or reverse every adversity — and that therefore there cannot be an American solution to every world problem.

Yet Kennedy also sought to advance American interests. Indeed he had charged during the campaign that under Eisenhower the United States had lost its 'position of pre-eminence,' and he intended to regain that position at the earliest opportunity. He chose as Secretary of State the president of the Rockefeller Foundation, Dean Rusk, who shared some of Dulles's unfortunate quality of moralistic rigidity, and on occasion the President's own rhetoric suggested that he anticipated a showdown with the Kremlin. In his first State of the Union message, he warned: 'Before my term has ended, we shall have to test anew whether a nation organized and governed such as ours can endure. The outcome is by no means certain. The answers are by no means clear.' For all of his emphasis on restraint, he was destined, in a number of fearful episodes, to carry brinkmanship farther than Dulles had ever dared.

After his election, Kennedy learned the startling news that plans were far advanced for an invasion of Cuba to overthrow Fidel Castro, whose regime served as a center of subversion throughout Latin America. Since the spring of 1960 the Central Intelligence Agency had been secretly training and arming hundreds of anti-Castro exiles in Florida and Guatemala. Kennedy, who had been publicly critical of Eisenhower for not moving more vigorously against the Cuban dictator, gave the bizarre scheme his reluctant approval. 'What do you think about this damned invasion?' an adviser asked. 'I think about it as little as possible,' the President answered.

On 17 April 1961 the invaders landed at the Bahía de Cochinos (Bay of Pigs) on the swampy southern coast of Cuba. In short order Castro's forces pinned down the beachhead and overwhelmed the rebels, who lacked adequate air cover. Even more important, the CIA had failed to work with the anti-Castro underground in Cuba, and the anticipated internal uprising never took place. The United States was denounced for trying to destroy the government of a weaker nation and jeered for botching the attempt. The fiasco badly impaired the prestige of the Kennedy regime and put an end to the euphoria of the young administration. The President shouldered the blame, although not without observing wryly 'that victory has a hundred fathers and defeat is an orphan.'

Six weeks later, in a grim confrontation with Khrushchev in Vienna, Kennedy had a chilling confirmation of the realities of the Cold War. The disaster at the Bay of Pigs apparently persuaded the Soviet premier that the young President would crumple under pressure. But Kennedy refused to be intimidated. At one point when Khrushchev pointed out that the medal he wore was the Lenin Peace Prize, Kennedy said, 'I hope you keep it.' When the Russian leader threatened to make a treaty with East Germany before the end of the year which would extinguish Western rights of access to West Berlin, Kennedy responded, 'It will be a cold winter.'

That summer the threat of nuclear war mounted dangerously. In response to appeals from Kennedy, Congress authorized the calling up of reserves and passed huge military appropriations, and a frenzy of air-raid shelter building swept the country. At border points in Berlin, American tanks eyed Soviet tanks. In August the crisis reached its peak when East Germany sealed the Berlin border and erected an ugly wall of concrete and barbed wire to halt the flow of refugees into West Berlin, a tacit admission of the Communist world's inability to compete with the West. To reassure West Berliners that the United States would not be driven out of the old German capital, Kennedy sent Vice-President Johnson and General Lucius Clay to Berlin and ordered a battle force of American troops down the 100-mile Autobahn from Western Germany through the Communist zones into Berlin. In another move in the war of nerves, the USSR that fall exploded some fifty nuclear devices, including a bomb nearly 3000 times more powerful than the one which had leveled Hiroshima.

By the end of the year the crisis had eased, and in January 1962 the United States pulled back its tanks. Fallout shelter companies went bankrupt, and civil defense units folded. Critics charged that Kennedy, after behaving provocatively in Cuba, had over-reacted in Berlin. Yet just as he had resisted demands for full-scale American intervention in Cuba after the Bay of Pigs debacle, he had shown restraint as well as firmness in Berlin. In particular he had rejected counsel to smash through the Berlin Wall, for he recognized the danger of a nuclear exchange. The President told the country, 'In the thermonuclear age, any misjudgment on either side about the intentions of the other could rain more devastation in several hours than has been wrought in all the wars of human history.'

The Berlin experience reinforced Kennedy's determination to diversify America's military forces. Whereas Dulles had relied inordinately on nuclear power, which at worst offered a choice between a war of annihilation or capitulation, Kennedy favored a more flexible response to counter unorthodox methods of Communist expansion. His Defense Secretary, Robert McNamara, formerly president of the Ford Motor Company, established firm civilian control over the military establishment and developed a more balanced fighting capability. Kennedy won from Congress the biggest military and naval build-up in the country's history, which increased the nuclear arsenal but placed more emphasis on mobile Polaris submarines than on overseas missile sites. The administration stressed the importance of conventional forces that could fight limited conflicts and special forces trained for jungle and guerilla warfare.

Even the exploration of space from Cape Canaveral became implicated in the Cold War. From the moment on 20 February 1962 when Lieutenant Colonel John Herschel Glenn, Jr., radioed gleefully, 'Cape is go and I am go,' at the beginning of the first of three orbits of the earth, through Astronaut Gordon Cooper's landing in May 1963 'right on the money' after twenty-two orbits, the United States, which had once known little but the bitter taste of failure in its space efforts, scored a series of spectacular successes in the 'space race' with the Russians. In May 1961, Kennedy announced plans to land a man on the moon 'before this decade is out,' and Congress responded with huge appropriations for 'Project Apollo.'

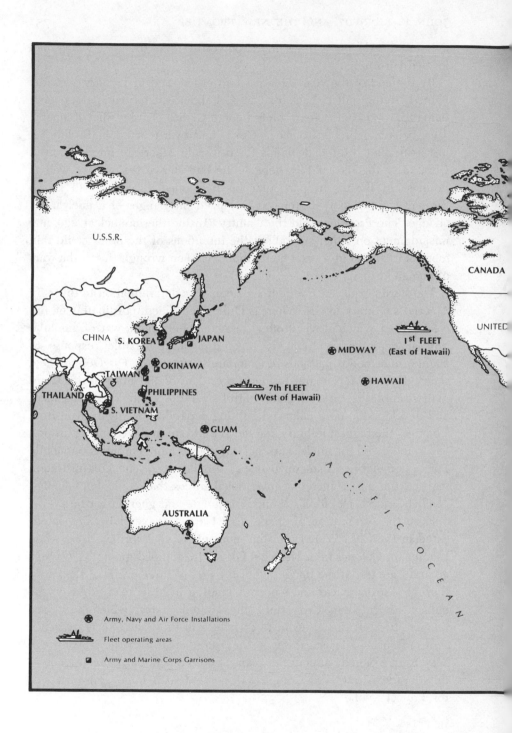

U.S.S.R.

CANADA

UNITED

CHINA   S. KOREA   JAPAN

MIDWAY   1st FLEET
(East of Hawaii)

TAIWAN   OKINAWA

THAILAND   PHILIPPINES

HAWAII

7th FLEET
(West of Hawaii)

S. VIETNAM

GUAM

PACIFIC OCEAN

AUSTRALIA

⊛   Army, Navy and Air Force Installations

   Fleet operating areas

▪   Army and Marine Corps Garrisons

752

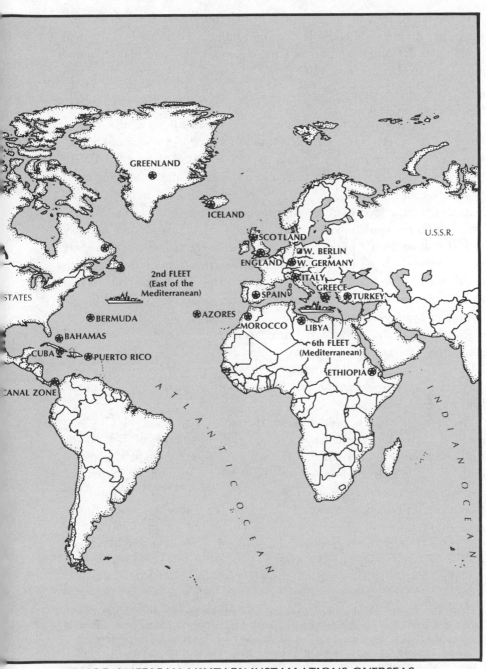

GREENLAND

ICELAND

SCOTLAND

U.S.S.R.

W. BERLIN
ENGLAND   W. GERMANY

2nd FLEET
(East of the
Mediterranean)

ITALY
GREECE

STATES

SPAIN   TURKEY

BERMUDA   AZORES

BAHAMAS

MOROCCO   LIBYA

CUBA   PUERTO RICO

6th FLEET
(Mediterranean)

CANAL ZONE

ETHIOPIA

ATLANTIC OCEAN

INDIAN OCEAN

MAJOR AMERICAN MILITARY INSTALLATIONS OVERSEAS

In the fall of 1962 the United States came to the very brink of nuclear war. That summer, ships displaying the hammer and sickle had steamed boldly past the American base at Guantánamo, Cuba, and had unloaded missiles, patrol boats, and MIG fighters, as well as Russian technicians and instructors. Hard-pressed to take action against this Soviet build-up, the President refused to risk a calamitous war so long as photographic reconnaissance showed no evidence of offensive missiles. On 16 October, however, he received shocking news: an Air Force U-2 had spotted Russian medium-range missiles in place near San Cristobal, and the USSR, despite solemn assurances to the contrary, was rushing launching pads to completion. Missiles from these sites could deliver hydrogen warheads to targets as distant as Minneapolis, Denver, and Lima, Peru.

Kennedy responded with a combination of determination and restraint. He would not permit the USSR to shift the balance of power by establishing a missile base only ninety miles from America's shores. Instead, on 22 October he imposed a quarantine on arms shipments to Cuba and issued orders to intercept Russian vessels headed for the island. Furthermore he warned the Kremlin that a nuclear attack from Cuba on any nation in the Western hemisphere would require a 'full retaliatory response on the Soviet Union' by the United States. Yet he rejected the advice of all his military advisers, many of his civilian aides, and even Senator Fulbright that he order an air strike, for this might lead to general war.

As Soviet vessels headed toward Havana where U.S. ships of war awaited them, the world shuddered at the imminence of Doomsday. Robert Kennedy later recalled, 'I felt we were on the edge of a precipice with no way off.' But the President's firm stand prevailed. At the end of two weeks, Kennedy, confronted by two letters from Khrushchev offering conflicting replies, chose to acknowledge the more acceptable one. Russia agreed to remove all offensive weapons and accept international inspection if the United States promised not to invade Cuba; the President consented, and the crisis ended.[2] After a time the bases were dismantled and the missiles crated and withdrawn. Kennedy had won the war of

2. Robert Kennedy later described a conference with his brother after the gratifying news of Khrushchev's message: 'I went back to the White House and talked to the President for a long time. . . . As I was leaving, he said, making reference to Abraham Lincoln, "This is the night I should go to the theater." I said, "If you go, I want to go with you." ' *Thirteen Days* (W. W. Norton, 1969), p. 110.

nerves. Yet he took pains not to humiliate Khrushchev, for he recognized there were limits to 'eyeball to eyeball' diplomacy.

Kennedy hoped to avoid these perilous showdowns and to encourage instead new areas of co-operation and peaceful development. The missiles crisis, which threatened a disastrous war, had the ironic consequence of improving hopes for peace and permitting the President to direct his attention to more constructive programs, many of which he had initiated earlier. Kennedy believed that the main struggle no longer centered in Europe, save for Berlin, but in the Southern Hemisphere where, since 1945, forty new nations, embracing nearly a billion people, had won their independence. He appointed envoys sympathetic to the aspirations of the emerging nations; expanded Food for Peace shipments of farm surpluses to almost $1.5 billion each year; and shifted the emphasis of foreign aid from military to economic assistance. The newly created Peace Corps, under the President's brother-in-law, R. Sargent Shriver, sent enthusiastic volunteers to offer educational or technical services to underdeveloped regions. Kennedy abandoned the Dulles attitude of condemning neutralism as immoral and gave his support to the attempt of the UN to build a central government in the Congo which would resist both Communist-oriented elements and right-wing secessionists. To save the United Nations from bankruptcy when the USSR and other countries refused to pay the costs of the Congo operation, which after much bloodshed resulted in a defeat for the Communist bloc, Kennedy persuaded Congress to buy 100 million dollars' worth of UN bonds.

In August 1961, four months after the Bay of Pigs miscarriage, Kennedy proposed an ambitious program for Latin America: the Alliance for Progress. At a meeting of the Inter-American Economic Council in Punta del Este, Uruguay, the United States sought a new goal in foreign aid, 'controlled revolution.' Upon agreement to basic reforms of their social structure to end the grievances Castroism might exploit, Latin American nations would be eligible for a ten-year, $20 billion program of aid, half of it provided by the United States. One writer commented: 'It is a monumental commitment which for size and complexity makes the Marshall Plan look puny by comparison.' But the *Alianza,* joined by every American republic save Cuba, got off to a poor start, and engineers of social change found that progress came slowly.

When on the morning before his inauguration Kennedy met with Eisenhower at the White House, the outgoing President pointed to a map of Southeast Asia and said: 'This is one of the problems I'm leaving you that I'm not happy about. We may have to fight.' In Laos it seemed that the conflict of pro-Western, pro-Communist, and neutralist forces would lead to American intervention. But Kennedy, recognizing that the conservative regime backed by Eisenhower lacked popular support, abandoned the idea of an anti-Communist crusade and sought instead 'a neutral and independent Laos, tied to no outside power.' To persuade the Kremlin to accept a neutralization solution he landed 5000 combat troops in Thailand and ordered units of the Seventh Fleet into the area, and to overcome the objections to neutralization of their balky rivals he suspended aid to the pro-Western government. Negotiations in Geneva resulted in the creation of a tripartite regime, with the aim of removing Laos from the Cold War; stability of a sort was achieved eventually.

Elsewhere in Southeast Asia, Kennedy found the going more difficult. The Geneva settlement of 1954, which ended the Indochinese war, had stipulated the calling of free elections to unify Vietnam, but the elections were never held, and the United States backed Ngo Dinh Diem, who rapidly established authoritarian rule in the Republic of South Vietnam. When the Communist dictatorship of Ho Chi Minh in North Vietnam gave aid to the Viet Cong, the Communist guerillas of South Vietnam, Kennedy stepped up his support of Diem and sent military 'advisers' to assist the Saigon regime. In the spring of 1963 the Diem government took harsh repressive measures against the Buddhists; when some of the Buddhists set themselves afire in protest, they aroused the indignant opposition of many Americans to the Diem regime. Kennedy urged Diem to undertake reforms to win the loyalty of landless peasants, and he expressed doubts about the extent of America's commitment to the South Vietnamese. 'In the final analysis,' he said in September 1963, 'it is their war. They are the ones who have to win it or lose it. We can help them, we can give them equipment, we can send our men out there as advisers, but they have to win it, the people of Vietnam.' However at the same time he believed that he could not afford a Dienbienphu, and his advisers assured him that a military victory was within grasp. On 1 November 1963 the situation entered a new, and more turbulent, phase when a military junta deposed Diem and murdered him and his brother; the United States lost no time in recognizing the new government. At that point the American contingent in Vietnam was still small, but Kennedy, by making the fateful error of confusing a political problem with a military one, had planted the grapes of wrath which the next administration would nurture and harvest.

In Europe, President Kennedy sought to re-create the transatlantic community fractured by the independence of France's premier, Charles de Gaulle. The 'Grand Design' aimed to tie the United States into a European Common Market which would also admit the British. To make this possible, Kennedy secured from Congress the Trade Expansion Act of 1962 which empowered the President to lower tariff barriers in return for trade concessions. But when in Jaunary 1963 de Gaulle vetoed the admission of Britain to the Common Market, he ended Kennedy's dream of an 'Atlantic Partnership,' and when he insisted on developing an independent nuclear force, he jeopardized the unity of NATO. No longer could the United States count on getting its way in the Western world.

During his 1960 campaign Kennedy promised 'a supreme effort to break the log jam on disarmament and nuclear tests,' because 'the world was not meant to be a prison in which man awaits his executioner.' For more than two years the Russians balked. On 31 August 1961 they stunned the world by announcing that they were breaking the moratorium on nuclear testing, and the subsequent explosions, which increased the radioactive contamination of the atmosphere by half, made clear that the USSR had been feigning an interest in a test-ban agreement at the same time that it was planning to resume tests. In September 1961, Kennedy made an eloquent plea to the United Nations in which he warned that the world faced a choice between arms control or 'a flaming funeral pyre' and offered a series of constructive suggestions which the Russians turned down. When the Kremlin showed no interest at all in disarmament proposals, even rejecting a proposition they had previously suggested, the President reluctantly ordered the resumption of atmospheric testing in the spring of 1962.

After the missiles crisis Kennedy renewed his efforts toward achieving a test ban and a *détente* with the USSR. In June 1963 in a remarkable address at American University in Washington he stated that the United States should not see 'only a distorted and desperate view of the other side,' and urged: 'Let us reexamine our attitude toward the Soviet Union.' He declared: 'The wave of the future is not the conquest of the world by a single dogmatic creed but the liberation of the diverse energies of free nations and free men.' One commentator observed: 'For the first time in eight years, a President was speaking of American policy without making the cold war the paramount matter of concern. . . . Indeed, he spoke at times of the cold war as if it hardly existed any longer.'

As a consequence of Kennedy's appeal, and perhaps even more of the growing breach between the USSR and Red China, the Russians agreed to enter into negotiations toward a limited test ban in environments where physical inspection would not be required. At Moscow in July 1963 the United States, Great Britain, and the USSR signed a pact banning atmospheric and underwater testing of nuclear devices. It was a small step, but for the first time the powers had reached agreement on controlling The Bomb. The treaty, the President declared, was an important start toward getting 'the genie back in the bottle.' Many doubted whether the pact marked the beginning of a prolonged period of Soviet-American amity, but by the summer of 1963 there was renewed optimism about a thaw in the Cold War. The Kremlin agreed to the installation of a 'hot line' which would connect it with the White House by telephone in the event of a future crisis that might result in nuclear war, and the President approved the sale of 250 million dollars' worth of wheat to Russia. Yet fundamental disagreements persisted, and in Southeast Asia the Vietnamese war was a running sore.

3. THE NEW FRONTIER

The Kennedy circle hoped that the first session of Congress in 1961 would rival Roosevelt's Hundred Days, but the young President quickly found that in domestic legislation as in foreign policy he could score only limited gains. The conservative coalition of Southern Democrats and Northern Republicans which had blocked almost all innovative social reform measures for a generation had no interest in moving America toward new frontiers. Although Kennedy, unlike Eisenhower, was determined to use the powers of his office, his relations to Congress bore a melancholy resemblance to those of his predecessor. Congress turned down his pleas for medical care for the aged (Medicare); for a Department of Urban Affairs and Housing; and for mass transportation legislation. The Federal aid to education bill was blocked once again, because of an inability to resolve the problem created by the demand of Roman Catholic bishops for grants to parochial schools.

Kennedy's critics deplored his failure to take advantage of his popularity to win support for administration measures, and his lack of finesse in dealing with congressmen. They conceded that the conservative coalition posed difficulties, but pointed out that he had top-heavy Democratic majorities in both houses and claimed that a little more skill as a party leader would have shifted the two votes needed to put Medicare through the Senate and won other close contests. Above all they complained that the President was too cautious and too unwilling to risk defeat. Kennedy believed that such censure underrated the obstacles he faced, and he doubted that direct appeals to the nation would find an effective response. He recalled that when in Shakespeare's *Henry IV, Part I,* Owen Glendower boasts, 'I can call spirits from the vasty deep,' Hotspur retorts:

> Why, so can I, or so can any man;
> But will they come when you do call for them?

Moreover Kennedy could point to a number of accomplishments. He pushed through legislation which raised the minimum wage, liberalized social security benefits, set up a program to retrain jobless workers, extended emergency unemployment compensation, appropriated funds for mental health, provided new housing, and funneled public-works money into depressed areas. Kennedy won approval for a Federal Water Pollution Control Act, and Congress established three national seashores, one of them at the President's favorite vacation place, Cape Cod. By a narrow margin he won a tough fight to dislodge conservatives from control of the Rules Committee. Although he did not secure Federal aid to education, he did advance its chances by easing concerns over the religious issue.

Kennedy played an important part, too, in sparking an economic revival, although at the outset he moved too prudently. He came to office at a time when the economy was behaving sluggishly. The rate of growth lagged, and nearly 7 per cent of the working force was unemployed in the fourth recession since World War II. Some of the President's liberal advisers urged him to stimulate the economy through social spending, but at a time of near-crisis in the international balance of payments, Kennedy feared that massive expenditures might accelerate the gold drain and augment the danger of inflation. Instead, he adopted a more modest program which included easier credit, adroit handling of the balance of payments problem, and an investment tax credit. Together with stepped-up military and highway spending, these measures lifted the country out of the recession.

To preserve these gains, Kennedy emphasized the importance of maintaining the price level. The President was delighted when he and Secretary of Labor Arthur Goldberg persuaded steel workers to accept a non-inflationary wage contract. Ten days later he received the unwelcome news from Roger M. Blough, chairman of the board of U.S. Steel, that his company was raising prices six dollars a ton; other steel firms quickly followed Blough's lead. Kennedy, who believed he had been betrayed by the steel corporations, denounced the rise angrily in public and in private employed more colorful language to express his displeasure. To compel the companies to back down, the President mobilized the power of the Federal government: antitrust suits, a tax investigation by the Treasury, an FTC inquiry into collusive price-fixing, a Defense department boycott. Steel capitulated within 72 hours. After Blough surrendered, Kennedy was asked what he had said to the steel magnate. The President responded: 'I told him that his men could keep their horses for the spring plowing.'

Although Kennedy's skillful management helped promote an economic upturn, unemployment remained distressingly high. The President recognized the need for new measures if full employment was to be achieved, and under the tutelage of Walter Heller, chairman of the Council of Economic Advisers, he embraced the ideas of the New Economics. While the New Deal theorists had approved of deficit spending only in periods of depression, the apostles of the New Economics urged the deliberate creation of deficits at a time when indices were climbing. Kennedy set out to win the support of sophisticated businessmen for these heresies; and, when the time seemed ripe, he asked Congress for a multibillion dollar tax cut to encourage consumer spending and business investment and thus stimulate economic growth. The President did not live to see the tax cut adopted, but historians will mark the Kennedy years as a watershed in American thinking about the economy.

In the field of civil rights, too, Kennedy at first moved slowly. He sought to avoid jeopardizing the rest of his program by antagonizing Southern Democrats over civil rights legislation, and consequently relied instead on executive action to advance civil rights. Unlike Eisenhower, he left no doubt that he supported the Brown decision. He appointed a number of Negroes to high places, notably Thurgood Marshall, general counsel of the NAACP, to the United States Circuit Court, Robert Weaver to head the Housing and Home Finance Agency, and Carl Rowan as ambassador to Finland. On 6 March 1961 he set up a Committee on Equal Employment Opportunity under Vice-President Johnson who persuaded large defense contractors to agree to hire members of minority groups. When in two Tennessee counties an economic boycott was imposed on Negroes who had dared to try to register to vote, the President ordered surplus food sent to them.

His brother, Attorney-General Robert Kennedy, played a crucial role in the strategy of executive action. Under Assistant Attorney-General Burke Marshall and his first assistant John Doar, the civil rights division was greatly expanded. 'Bobby' Kennedy took special pains to recruit Negroes for the Department of Justice, and he nominated the first two Negroes ever appointed to a Federal district court in the continental United States. The Department of Justice acted far more vigorously than the Eisenhower administration in bringing suits on denial of voting rights, and it took the initiative in requesting a Federal court to compel the opening of schools in Prince Edward County, Virginia, which had been closed to forestall desegregation. When in the spring of 1961 Alabama mobs mauled 'freedom riders' traveling through the South to challenge Jim Crow bus terminals, and bombed and set afire a 'freedom bus,' the young Attorney-General dispatched hundreds of Federal marshals to Montgomery. Later that year, at the goading of the Department of Justice, the ICC ordered bus companies to desegregate interstate buses and to stop only at restaurants and terminals that took down their 'white' and 'colored' signs.

When James H. Meredith, a Negro Air Force veteran, was denied admission to the University of Mississippi in his native state, a United States Circuit Court issued an injunction on 25 June 1962 to compel his acceptance, and the Supreme Court on 10 September sustained this order. Meredith tried to register later that month, but Governor Ross Barnett, defying court orders, physically interposed himself and used state police to rebuff Meredith. On 30 September President Kennedy sent several hundred Federal marshals to escort Meredith to the campus at Oxford. That night a howling mob engulfed the marshals, and Kennedy dispatched Federal troops and federalized national guardsmen; before the rioting ended, two were killed and seventy wounded. Under Federal bayonets, Meredith was registered.

The actions of the administration made the names of 'the Kennedy brothers' anathema in the Deep South, but civil rights leaders criticized them severely for not acting more forcefully. During the campaign the President had said that discrimination in public housing could be wiped out 'tomorrow' with a stroke of the pen; but pens flooded the White House mail before he decided to act, and then administrative interpretation weakened his order of 20 November 1962. Martin Luther King stated:

> This Administration has outstripped all previous ones in the breadth of its civil rights activity. Yet the movement, instead of breaking out into the open plains of progress, remains constricted and confined. A sweeping revolutionary force is pressed into a narrow tunnel.

In the spring and summer of 1963, one hundred years after the Emancipation Proclamation had been effected, the Negro's cry for equality resounded throughout the land. Dr. King announced: 'We're through with tokenism and gradualism and see-how-far-you've-comeism. We're through with we've-done-more-for-your-people-than-anyone-elseism. We can't wait any longer. Now is the time.' North and South, the Negroes came out on the streets. In one week they carried out sixty separate demonstrations. That spring in Birmingham, where King led massive street protests, civil rights marchers were met with snarling police dogs, electric cattle prods, and high-pressure fire hoses that sent demonstrators sprawling; and the police commissioner, Eugene 'Bull' Connor, crowded the jails with hundreds of young marchers. But the Negroes would not be put down. They sang their freedom anthem:

> Black and white together
> We shall overcome some day.

The combination of passive resistance — 'Refrain from violence of fist, tongue or heart' — and the latent threat of violence won speedy results. In the first two weeks of June 1963 all the leading hotels and motels of Nashville agreed to desegregate; Atlanta announced plans to integrate its swimming pools; and Negroes played golf on the municipal course in Jackson, Mississippi. The University of Georgia graduated two Negroes; Texas A & M enrolled its first Negro students; and the University of Kentucky erased the color line in its athletic program.

By 1963 only one state in the Union, Alabama, had no Negro attending any state-supported school with white students. Its governor, George C. Wallace, promised to stand in the doorway to bar the entrance of any Negro to the University of Alabama. When in June two young Negroes appeared in Tuscaloosa to register, Wallace barred their way. But it was only a charade. After the President ordered the Alabama National Guard into Federal service, the Governor submitted. In 1956 Eisenhower had done nothing to help Autherine Lucy, but seven years later Kennedy had thrown the full weight of Federal power behind the black students.

One week after the tawdry melodrama in the doorway, the President delivered a notable civil rights message calling for far-reaching Federal legislation to curb discrimination and segregation. He said:

> Surely, in 1963, 100 years after Emancipation, it should not be necessary for any American citizen to demonstrate in the streets for the opportunity to stop at a hotel, or to eat at a lunch counter in the very department store in which he is shopping, or to enter a motion picture house, on the same terms as any other customer.

Other American Presidents, notably Harry Truman, had spoken out against discrimination, but Kennedy will go down in history as the first President to identify himself with the elimination of racial segregation.

Yet Kennedy's eloquence failed to move Congress to enact civil rights legislation that year, and his last months in office saw a rising tide of ugly rhetoric and violent deeds. A white racist murdered Medgar Evers, the head of the Mississippi NAACP. A war veteran, Evers received a hero's burial in Arlington National Cemetery, but in Jackson police used clubs, tear gas, and dogs against marchers who sought to pay tribute to their slain leader. A bomb in a Birmingham church killed four little Negro girls while they attended Sunday school. To win passage of Kennedy's comprehensive civil rights bill 200,000 people, 'black and white together,' took part in a 'March on Washington,' but although the House Judiciary Committee reported the measure in late October it was clear that Congress would not pass the bill at that session. When Congress also balked Kennedy's bid for tax-cut legislation, *Time* called the 88th Congress 'the do-nothingest of modern times,' and on 12 November, the *New York Times* wrote: 'Rarely has there been such a pervasive attitude of discouragement around Capitol Hill and such a feeling of helplessness to deal with it. This has been one of the least productive sessions of Congress within the memory of most of the members.'

4. THE DEATH OF A PRESIDENT

Ten days later, on Friday 22 November 1963, the President arrived in Dallas, recently the scene of displays of violence by the radical right. As the motor caravan of open cars moved through the streets of the city, the wife of Texas's governor, John Connally, remarked to Kennedy: 'You can't say that Dallas isn't friendly to you today.' An instant later, at 12:30, the President was struck twice by rifle bullets; his head cradled in his wife's lap, he was sped to a hospital where within minutes he was pronounced dead. Over that frightful weekend, yet another act of violence stunned a grief-stricken nation. Before a national television audience, the President's assassin, Lee Harvey Oswald, who had once expatriated himself to Russia, was murdered in a corridor of the city jail by Jack Ruby, the operator of a sleazy night club. A commission under Chief Justice Warren subsequently concluded that the assassination of the President was the work of Oswald, acting alone. The commission's findings have frequently been challenged by critics who claim that the President was the victim of a conspiracy, but no substantial evidence has been offered to support these charges.

Within a short time after the painful grief over the President's death, writers began to debate the meaning of his life. Some said that a President must be judged by his accomplishments, and that Kennedy's were small. Kennedy himself had been puzzled by why historians ranked Theodore Roosevelt as 'near great' when he had gotten so little through Congress. Many regretted that a man who had held out so much promise of fulfillment would be consigned to the history books as a President of minor stature. They granted that the output of his administration had been meager, but insisted that Kennedy, if he had lived, would have achieved much more. Kennedy, one writer observed, was a Prince Hal who died before Agincourt.

Others, many of whom conceded that his accomplishments were slim, concluded he was a man of greatness less for what he did than for what he was. They recalled his gallantry in the face of an intimate acquaintance with death and misfortune. His brother Robert said afterwards: 'President Kennedy would be forty-seven in May. At least one-half of the days that he spent on this earth were days of intense physical pain.' Many remembered his disarming wit: When asked how he became a wartime hero, he retorted, 'It was involuntary. They sank my boat.' Or his definition of Washington, D.C.: 'a city of southern efficiency and northern charm.' Adlai Stevenson called him 'the contemporary man,' and Kennedy did display many of the qualities of the existential hero. At the time of his death, *Le Figaro* wrote: 'What remains as the loss . . . is a certain feeling of possibilities, of an *élan,* and — why not say it? — of an impression of beauty. These are not political qualities, but surely they are enduring legendary and mythological qualities.' It is the legend that is swiftly building — of the gallant young prince taken before his time, of the romantic protagonist brutally dispossessed from Camelot.

But still others contended there was more to Kennedy's short Presidency than the gossamer of legend, that his brief tenure embraced significant achievements. Arthur Schlesinger, Jr., who served on Kennedy's staff, wrote:

> Yet he had accomplished so much: the new hope for peace on earth, the elimination of nuclear testing in the atmosphere and the abolition of nuclear diplomacy, the new policies toward Latin America and the third world, the reordering of American defense, the emancipation of the American Negro, the revolution in national economic policy, the concern for poverty, the stimulus to the arts, the fight for reason against extremism and mythology. . . . He re-established the republic as the first generation of our leaders saw it — young, brave, civilized, rational, gay, tough, questing, exultant in the excitement and potentiality in history.

Both critic and admirer tended in retrospect to be more sympathetic toward Kennedy's reluctance to divide the nation to achieve his goals. In the summer before his death he read to White House visitors the speech of Blanche of Castile from *King John:*

> The sun's o'ercast with blood; fair day, adieu!
> Which is the side that I must go withal?
> I am with both: each army hath a hand;
> And in their rage, I having hold of both,
> They whirl asunder and dismember me.

No legacy of John F. Kennedy is more important than his championing of reason against the anarchy of Right and Left and his understanding that liberty is possible only in an ordered society. But in the end the whirling forces of violence, pulling the nation asunder, overcame him.

XXXI

War and Political Change

1. THE GREAT SOCIETY

At 2:38 p.m. on 22 November 1963, in the plane bearing the late President's body back to Washington, Lyndon Baines Johnson took the oath of office as President of the United States. A self-made man from the bleak Texas hill country, Johnson lost no time in imprinting the LBJ brand on the White House. At fifty-five he was only a decade older than his predecessor; yet they seemed a generation apart, for Johnson had first come to Washington while Kennedy was a student at Choate, and he had won election to Congress, as an advocate of FDR's 'Court-packing' plan, when Kennedy was a freshman at Harvard. Intimidating, irascible, egocentric, he radiated a desire for power. 'The President,' wrote an English observer, 'comes into a room slowly and warily, as if he means to smell out the allegiance of everyone in it.' Yet at the same time he was sensitive to criticism and obsessively anxious for approval. As Jackie's *truite amandine* gave way to Lady Bird Johnson's recipes for Pedernales River chili and Kennedy's patrician grace to Johnson's country manners, the Eastern 'Establishment' so deplored the change in style that it frequently refused to give the new President his due.

For as Chief Legislator Johnson had infinitely greater experience and talent than Kennedy. A veteran of twenty-three years in Congress, he had served in both houses and had risen to Majority Leader of the Senate, where he had won renown for his skill as a legislative tactician. Even his harshest critics conceded his political adroitness. 'Politics, and

national politics in particular, seems to be Johnson's only possible vocation,' noted Richard Rovere. 'He is as specifically and precisely a national politician as Henry James was a man of letters, as Isaac Stern is a
violinist.' Liberals, recalling his role as a moderate in the 1950's, feared
he had only a lukewarm commitment to the Kennedy reforms; but Johnson, who came out of a Populist background and had been a protégé of
Franklin Roosevelt's, had known hard times and the direct benefits of
government as Kennedy had not, and he was determined to be a national, not a sectional, leader. He believed he could achieve the best results by creating a spirit of 'consensus'; he was fond of quoting Isaiah,
'Come, let us reason together.' Yet he would move this 'consensus' toward particular legislative and partisan ends; as he explained ingenu-
ously, he favored 'uniting our people, by bringing our capital and our
management and our labor and our farmers all under one great Democratic tent.'

Johnson came to power at a time when political scientists were be-
wailing 'the deadlock of democracy,' but in short order he broke up the
log jam of Kennedy legislation and demonstrated not only the continuity
but the strength of America's political institutions. Within a month of his
accession to office, Congress had voted $1.2 billion for college construc-
tion projects. He quickly won congressional approval for a mass transit
bill and legislation to protect wilderness areas. By his stress on consensus
and by symbolic acts (such as dimming lights in the White House to
reduce electric bills), he gave an impression of fiscal responsibility that
not only consolidated business interests behind liberal measures but induced congressmen to approve an $11.5 billion tax cut. The economy
responded immediately; in 1964 gross national product soared $38 bil-
lion over the previous year.

The first resident of a Southern state to enter the White House since
Andrew Johnson a century earlier, the new President urged Congress to
enact the civil rights bill as a memorial to Kennedy. With the co-
operation of the Democratic whip, Senator Hubert Humphrey, and
Republicans like Senator Everett Dirksen, he dislodged the bill
from the House Rules Committee and broke the Southern filibuster
in the Senate. The Civil Rights Act of 1964 prohibited discrimination in
places of public accommodation; authorized the Attorney-General to
bring suits to speed school desegregation; strengthened voting rights statutes; set up an Equal Opportunity Commission to wipe out job discrimi-

nation; and empowered Federal agencies to withhold funds from state-administered programs that discriminated against Negroes.

Johnson not only won congressional approval for proposals that had been stymied under Kennedy but he began to enunciate his own program. In his State of the Union Message on 8 January 1964, the President announced: 'This Administration today, here and now, declares unconditional war on poverty in America.' Starting with the Economic Opportunity Act of 1964, Congress in the next two years approved funds for such anti-poverty projects as VISTA, the domestic peace corps; a Job Corps for school dropouts; Upward Bound, to encourage bright slum children to go to college; a Neighborhood Youth Corps for jobless teenagers; Operation Head Start, to give preschool training to children; and a Community Action Program to permit 'maximum feasible participation' of the poor. In an address at Ann Arbor in the spring of 1964, Johnson emphasized that he wanted to improve the quality of American life in order to achieve a 'Great Society,' which he described as 'a place where the city of man serves not only the needs of the body and the demands of commerce but the desire for beauty and the hunger for community.'

In the 1964 campaign the credo of the Great Society faced a sharp challenge from a new kind of Republican candidate who broke the pattern of recent American politics. If in the past quarter of a century advocates of strong Federal action had failed to win a commanding majority, neither had spokesmen for the Right been able to prevail. No matter how conservative the Republican contingent in Congress, the GOP during these years had always chosen a man of the Center as its presidential candidate. But in 1964, Barry Goldwater, aggressively a spokesman for the Right, won the Republican nomination after a campaign in which he attacked the domestic and foreign policies that had been pursued by both parties for the preceding generation.

The victory of the senator from Arizona at the San Francisco convention reflected the conviction that Johnson could be defeated by an unprecedented coalition of the South and West. Goldwater once remarked: 'Sometimes I think this country would be better off if we could just saw off the Eastern Seaboard and let it float out to sea.' The Right had long argued that outside the Northeast there was a vast silent vote — conservative and isolationist — which had never been drawn to the polls. It took comfort from such episodes as the vote in 1963 of the Wyoming legislature, under the influence of the John Birch Society, to take the United States out of the United Nations, abolish the Federal income tax, and deny the authority of the Supreme Court. By offering 'a choice not an echo,' Goldwater, it was claimed, would pull a huge support which 'Me Too' Republicans like Willkie and Dewey had never been able to attract.

Certainly Goldwater offered voters a clear choice in 1964. He appealed to all those elements discontented with modern America. At a time when the country was deeply troubled by extremists, he told the Republican convention, 'Extremism in the defense of liberty is no vice.' In Cleveland, a scene of racial strife, Goldwater, who had voted against the civil rights bill, exploited white 'backlash' by speaking for the freedom not to associate. In the Tennessee valley, he suggested the sale of the TVA to private interests. To the old folks of St. Petersburg he criticized social security. Such statements permitted Johnson to campaign both as the liberal candidate and as the 'safe' candidate.

Over and over again, Goldwater, who had voted against the test ban treaty, preached a militant foreign policy and raised uneasy feelings about whether he could be trusted with The Bomb. In particular he denounced the Administration's 'no win' policy in Vietnam. But Johnson took much of the sting out of this charge when in August he ordered retaliatory air raids against North Vietnam in response to an attack by North Vietnamese gunboats on American destroyers in the Gulf of Tonkin. (Subsequently a Senate inquiry disclosed that the order for 'retaliation' against the North had been prepared long before the Tonkin Gulf incident, and raised the question whether the whole 'incident' had not been deliberately designed to provoke a military response which could be used as justification for bombing North Vietnam.) The President seized advantage of the occasion to secure from Congress the 'Tonkin resolution' authorizing him 'to take all necessary measures to repel any armed attack against the forces of the United States and to prevent future aggression,' a resolution so ambiguously worded that it could be interpreted as a blank check authorization for escalating the war. Yet at the same time Johnson stressed that 'we still seek no wider war,' and in contrast to Goldwater he appealed to the nation as the peace candidate. When Goldwater advocated enlarging the war by bombing North Vietnam, Johnson stated: 'We are not going to send American boys nine or ten thousand miles away from home to do what Asian boys ought to be doing for themselves.'

Goldwater's appeal received a sharp rebuke. The electorate exploded the theory of the silent vote and gave Lyndon Johnson the biggest popular majority in American history. With 43 million votes (61.1 per cent) to Goldwater's 27 million (38.5 per cent), and an electoral margin of 486-52, Johnson captured 44 states and the District of Columbia which, as a consequence of the Twenty-third Amendment ratified in 1961, voted in the national election. The Republicans surrendered such strongholds as Vermont, which turned to a Democratic presidential nominee for the first time in its history. Negroes, once a mainstay of the GOP, voted better than 90 per cent for Johnson, and the Irish supported the President more strongly than they had Kennedy. The Republicans had the electoral votes only of Goldwater's Arizona and four Deep South states which backed him on the race issue. For the first time the South provided the main electoral base for a Republican presidential candidate. Yet even in the South, Goldwater ran less well than had other Republicans in recent years.

The 1964 elections gave the Democrats their greatest majority in Congress since the 1930's. For the first time since 1938, the bipartisan conservative coalition would not hold the balance of power. When the 89th Congress convened in January 1965, Johnson fired a fusillade of legislative messages, and before Congress recessed in October he had gotten almost everything he had asked. Among the new measures were a number long deferred, including Medicare, to provide medical care for the aged under the social security system, Federal aid for elementary and secondary education, and the creation of a cabinet-level Department of Housing and Urban Development. Congress also expressed the Great Society's concern for 'quality' with the Highway Beautification Act.

Throughout 1965 the United States witnessed a new national rite: the pageant of presidential bill-signing. Johnson signed the Voting Rights Act of 1965 in the President's Room of the Capitol where exactly 104 years before Abraham Lincoln had signed a bill freeing slaves impressed into the Confederate service. He put his name to a Federal aid to elementary education bill at the one-room schoolhouse in Texas he had attended as a child. At the National Institute of Health in Bethesda, Maryland, he signed a measure authorizing a multimillion-dollar program for

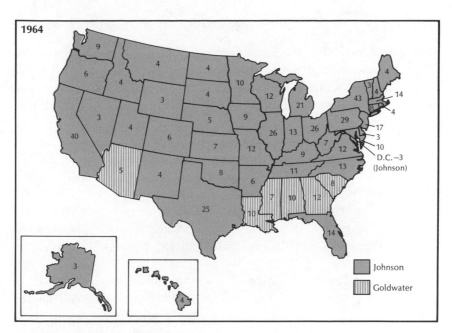

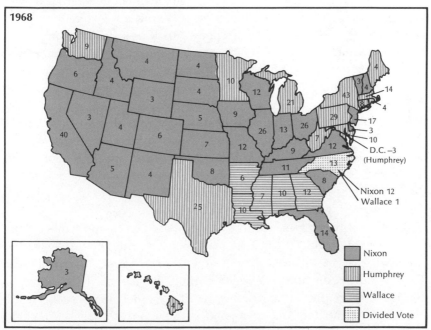

PRESIDENTIAL ELECTIONS, 1964, 1968

medical research. On a bright autumn day in the Rose Garden of the
White House, attended by such luminaries as Agnes de Mille, Ben
Shahn, and Katherine Anne Porter, he affixed his name to a Federal-aid-
to-the-arts bill. And in the shadow of the Statue of Liberty, facing Ellis
Island, the President signed into law the bill which ended racist restrictions on immigration to the United States, although for the first time it
placed a ceiling on immigration from the Western Hemisphere. In 1965
and 1966, the 89th Congress, the most productive since the New Deal,
sent to the President for his approval such innovations as legislation for
rent subsidies, demonstration cities, a teacher corps, regional medical
centers, 'vest pocket' parks, a rescue operation for the economically
depressed region of 'Appalachia,' and 'Medicaid' to provide medical care
for the poor.

The Voting Rights Act of 1965 resulted from a series of demonstrations organized by Martin Luther King early in 1965 to point out the
obstacles to voting by Negroes that persisted despite the provisions of
civil rights statutes. In Dallas County, Alabama, where Negroes of voting age outnumbered whites, there were 28 whites registered for every
one Negro. A series of violent responses to King's demonstrations, including the murder of the Rev. James J. Reeb, a Unitarian minister from
Boston, in Selma, the county seat of Dallas County, led the President to
ask Congress on 17 March for sweeping new legislation. He also gave
Federal support to a massive civil rights march from Selma to Montgomery, the state capital, which it reached on 25 March. That August
the President approved the new law which, in place of the protracted
earlier method of individual lawsuits to secure voting rights, provided
for direct Federal intervention. In districts where 50 per cent or more of
the voting-age population was unregistered, Federal examiners would
enroll voters.

Together with Supreme Court decisions based on the principle of 'one
man, one vote,' which struck at malapportionment (especially in the
landmark case of *Baker v. Carr*), and the ratification in 1964 of the
Twenty-fourth Amendment, which curbed the use of the poll tax to
abridge suffrage, the Voting Rights Act of 1965 took another long stride
toward democratizing American politics. In the next three years Federal
voting examiners registered more than 150,000 Negroes in five Deep
South states. Some states showed spectacular gains; Mississippi, with 6.7
per cent of voting-age Negroes registered in November 1964, had 59.8

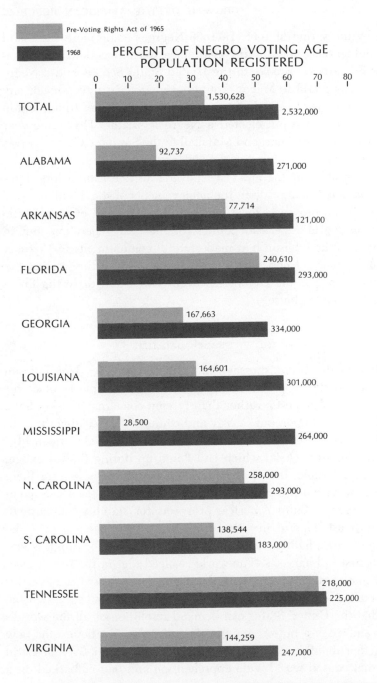

PERCENT OF NEGRO VOTING AGE POPULATION REGISTERED

0   10   20   30   40   50   60   70   80

TOTAL
1,530,628
2,532,000

ALABAMA
92,737
271,000

ARKANSAS
77,714
121,000

FLORIDA
240,610
293,000

GEORGIA
167,663
334,000

LOUISIANA
164,601
301,000

MISSISSIPPI
28,500
264,000

N. CAROLINA
258,000
293,000

S. CAROLINA
138,544
183,000

TENNESSEE
218,000
225,000

VIRGINIA
144,259
247,000

REGISTRATION OF NEGRO VOTERS IN THE SOUTH

per cent by the spring of 1968. In 1966 Negroes made more successful bids for public office than in any year since Reconstruction. Massachusetts sent Edward W. Brooke to the United States Senate, and a Negro won election as sheriff in Macon County, Alabama. In 1967 a major city chose a Negro mayor for the first time when Carl B. Stokes triumphed in Cleveland, and Mississippi elected a Negro legislator. That same year the President elevated Thurgood Marshall to the Supreme Court; he was the first Negro to be appointed to the highest tribunal.

Returned to office by the greatest landslide in American history, Lyndon Johnson could take pride in the achievements of the 'fabulous 89th' which opened up prospects for a new era of reform and of Democratic party domination of American politics for the next generation. But in these same months Johnson had made fateful commitments in Vietnam which would snuff out hopes for reform, undo much of the work of the 89th Congress, topple the Democrats from power, and drive the President from the White House.

2. THE VIETNAM QUAGMIRE

In his State of the Union message in January 1965 President Johnson found the international picture so bright that he was able to place his main emphasis on domestic rather than foreign concerns. 'World affairs will continue to call upon our energy and courage,' he declared. 'But today we can turn increased attention to the character of American life.' To be sure, Southeast Asia, which had flared up during the campaign, remained troublesome, but as the President began his new term there were still only 23,000 American 'advisers' in Vietnam and no U.S. combat force there. In Latin America, prospects for stability and growth seemed the most hopeful in years, for friction with Panama over the Canal Zone in 1964 had been reduced and the Alliance for Progress was reaping its first full harvests. The world rejoiced that in the recent election the United States had emphatically rejected a reckless Cold Warrior and given decisive backing instead to a candidate who had scoffed at the 'illusion that the United States can demand resolution of all the world's problems and mash a button and get the job done.' Yet before the new term was four months old the President had taken initiatives in Latin America that caused world-wide apprehension and had embarked on a course in Southeast Asia that would embroil the United States in the fourth largest war in its history.

In April 1965 civil strife erupted in the Dominican Republic, which had failed to find stability after the assassination of the ruthless dictator Trujillo. From the outset the American embassy as well as the State Department sided with conservative generals against the forces loyal to Juan Bosch, a democratic reformer. Persuaded that Bosch's movement had been taken over by Communists, Johnson, without seeking the prior approval of Latin American republics, landed more than 20,000 marines on the island. 'We don't expect to sit here on our rocking chairs with our hands folded and let the Communists set up any government in the Western Hemisphere,' the President explained. Critics at home and abroad deplored Johnson's misjudgment, for there was scant evidence that Communists controlled the movement, and denounced the President's heavy-handed, unilateral action that revived memories of gunboat diplomacy. The Dominican venture ended in a compromise solution, but it raised disquieting doubts about whether the United States intended to impose a Pax Americana on the world and about Johnson's ability to use power with discrimination.

Two months before the Dominican affair the President had made a much more critical decision about Vietnam, where he sharply altered his earlier position. Determined to maintain continuity with Kennedy's policies, Johnson had only limited options when he took power in November 1963. He inherited from his predecessor the architects of what Arthur Schlesinger, Jr. has called Kennedy's 'great failure in foreign policy': Secretary of State Rusk, Secretary of Defense McNamara, and such advisers as McGeorge Bundy and Walt Rostow. For the remainder of his truncated term, Johnson did little, save for the Tonkin Gulf episode, but follow the contours of Kennedy's policy, and this may well have been all he could have done.

His landslide victory in the 1964 election, however, not only made Johnson President in his own right but gave him the prestige to disentangle the country from Vietnam, if this were his choice. By January 1965 American policy had reached a cul-de-sac, as the fourth military coup in fifteen months revealed the instability of the Saigon government. Johnson's advisers warned him that if he did not step up America's military contribution the anti-Communist forces in South Vietnam would be overwhelmed. Prudence might have suggested a reconsideration of America's commitment if after more than a decade of U.S. aid the army of the Saigon government could not overcome the Viet Cong forces it outnumbered six to one. But Johnson believed too much was at stake to permit withdrawal. Two days after he took office he had told the U.S. ambassador to Saigon, Henry Cabot Lodge, 'I am not going to lose Vietnam. I am not going to be the President who saw Southeast Asia go the way China went.'

On 7 February 1965 when a mortar attack by the Viet Cong on an American camp at Pleiku killed eight Americans and wounded 108 others, Johnson retaliated by ordering carrier-based air strikes against North Vietnam, for he viewed the Viet Cong in the South only as agents of Hanoi. So quickly did the President respond that it seemed clear that the administration had planned such a strike well in advance. Johnson still insisted, 'We seek no wider war,' and he emphasized that the bombing was only a measured reprisal. But by 2 March, American planes were bombing the North with no pretense that they were retaliating for specific acts against American soldiers. Five days later, only one month after the Pleiku assault, two battalions of marines, the first U.S. combat units, landed in Vietnam. McNamara explained that they would have only defensive duties and would not 'tangle with the Viet Cong.' But by 28 June they had moved into battle in the land war on the Asian continent that had so long been dreaded and against which almost every military expert had warned. Nor were American planes confining their operations to limited sorties against the North. On 17 June 1965 twenty-nine B-52 jet bombers flew 2500 miles from Guam to drop explosives on Viet-Cong-held territory in South Vietnam.

Month by month the war reeled farther out of control. Each escalation ordered by Johnson called forth an increased effort by the enemy, and this led in turn to reciprocal action by the United States. Like the generals in World War I who thought 'one more push' on the Western front would terminate the war, the administration believed 'one more step' would bring an early victory; in each case it served only to raise the cost of the war. The Pentagon found it hard to believe that a little more firepower would not overcome these miserable guerillas, clad in black pajamas and supplied with ammunition carried over jungle trails on the backs of old women. As a result the war steadily became Americanized. During some weeks in the spring of 1966, U.S. casualties were greater than those of the South Vietnamese. By the middle of 1968 the total of American forces had passed half a million, and by the end of the year casualties exceeded 30,000 dead and 100,000 wounded.

The bombing, too, found new justifications. In a speech at the Johns Hopkins University on 7 April 1965 the President offered to begin 'unconditional discussions' to end the war in Vietnam and pledged a $1 billion investment in Southeast Asia including North Vietnam. When the Communists replied with a demand that the United States get out of Vietnam altogether, the administration expanded the bombing raids on the grounds that only additions to 'the quotient of pain' in North Vietnam would bring Hanoi to the bargaining table. Instead the bombing strengthened the will to fight in North Vietnam and cost the United States heavily in the loss of aircraft and crews who had to fly into murderous flak. Nor did the bombing stop the infiltration of supplies and of troops from the North, which did not, in fact, reach serious proportions until after the bombing began. On 29 June 1966, bombers, which had previously been restricted, struck close to the heavily populated cities of Hanoi and Haiphong, and by the end of 1968 the United States had dropped more tons of bombs on Vietnam than fell on Germany and Japan in World War II.

In the face of sharpening criticism Johnson and his associates asserted that they must persist in Vietnam, because they were committed to do so by SEATO and other pacts. Secretary Rusk protested that 'those who would place in question the credibility of the pledged word of the United States under our mutual security treaties would subject this nation to mortal danger. If any who would be our adversary should suppose that our treaties are a bluff, or will be abandoned if the going gets tough, the result could be catastrophe for all mankind.' If Vietnam went Communist all Southeast Asia would tumble, the Pacific would become a 'Red Sea,' and America's defense line would fall back to California. Hence the war, Johnson asserted, was 'a contest as far-reaching and as vital as any we have ever waged.'

The Johnson administration insisted that the Vietnamese conflict was not a civil war but a scheme by 'the Sino-Soviet military bloc' and more particularly by Red China to expand into Southeast Asia through its agents, the Communist regime of Ho Chi Minh in Hanoi and the Viet Cong. Rusk warned of the future peril of 'one billion Chinese armed with nuclear weapons' and declared that the United States sought

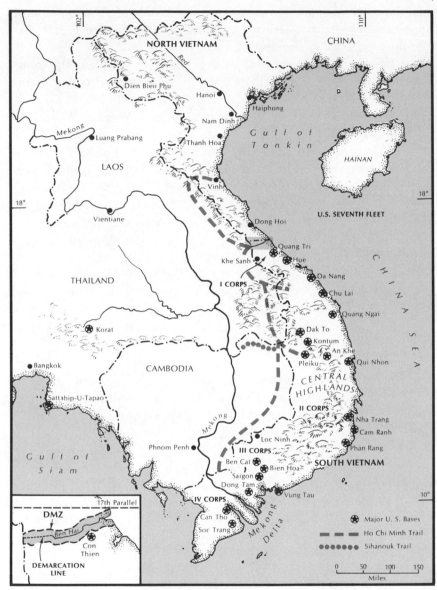

NORTH VIETNAM

CHINA

Red

Dien Bien Phu

Hanoi

Nam Dinh

Haiphong

Luang Prabang

Mekong

Thanh Hoa

Gulf of Tonkin

HAINAN

LAOS

18°   18°

Vinh

U.S. SEVENTH FLEET

Vientiane

Dong Hoi

Quang Tri

Khe Sanh   Hue

I CORPS

Da Nang

THAILAND

Chu Lai

C H I N A   S E A

Quang Ngai

Korat

Dak To

Kontum

An Khe

Pleiku   Qui Nhon

CAMBODIA

CENTRAL HIGHLANDS

Bangkok

II CORPS

Sattahip-U-Tapao

Nha Trang

Cam Ranh

Mekong

Loc Ninh

Phnom Penh

III CORPS

Phan Rang

Gulf of Siam

Ben Cat

Bien Hoa

SOUTH VIETNAM

Saigon

Dong Tam

10°

Vung Tau

IV CORPS

Can Tho

Soc Trang

Mekong Delta

⊛ Major U. S. Bases

- - - Ho Chi Minh Trail

••••• Sihanouk Trail

17th Parallel

DMZ

Ben Hai

Con Thien

DEMARCATION LINE

0   50   100   150
Miles

VIETNAM

Atomic Bomb Cloud , Nagasaki, August 1945

Little Rock, Arkansas, September 1957

The 1963 March on Washington (Martin Luther King, Jr., Whitney M. Young, Roy M. Wilkins, A. Philip Randolph, Walter Reuther)

Evacuation of Refugees, Phu Chuong, South Vietnam. Photograph by Philip J. Griffiths

Student Demonstration, University of California, Berkeley, December 1967

Men at Work on Buckminster Fuller's Geodesic Dome, Expo 67, Montreal

Menand I, 1963, by David Smith

Apollo 8 Earth View (December 1968)

to 'prevent Red China from establishing its hegemony over the East Asian land mass.' The Vietnam war represented the crucial test of the feasibility of 'wars of national liberation'; if this one succeeded, such techniques would be employed throughout the Southern Hemisphere. A victory for the Communists would lead Southeast Asian nations to turn to China as Balkan nations had sought out Nazi Germany after Munich. 'I'm not the village idiot,' Rusk said. 'I know Hitler was an Austrian and Mao is Chinese. . . . But what is common between the two situations is the phenomenon of aggression.' The administration claimed that it was as important to achieve stability in Asia as it had been to build an anti-Communist bulwark in Europe in the Marshall Plan–NATO era. It charged that its opponents were Europe-firsters who did not value the freedom of darker-skinned Asians and who were behaving toward Asia as pre-Pearl Harbor isolationists had acted toward Europe.

Critics of Johnson's policy mounted a formidable assault on the administration's arguments. 'Hawks,' especially strong among conservative Republicans, urged the President to escalate the war more rapidly; and as late as the spring of 1967 polls showed that a preponderance of opinion favored strong measures to end the war quickly. Yet more dangerous to the administration were the objections of the 'doves,' embracing both those who wanted to end the bombing in order to encourage negotiations and those who favored withdrawal, for the 'doves' threatened to disrupt the Johnson coalition. In the Senate the 'dove' faction, which in 1965 consisted of only a few mavericks like Wayne Morse of Oregon and Ernest Gruening of Alaska, came by 1967 to include such respected Democratic leaders as Majority Leader Mike Mansfield and the chairman of the Senate Foreign Relations Committee, J. William Fulbright, as well as such prominent liberal Democrats as Robert Kennedy of New York, Eugene McCarthy of Minnesota, Joseph Clark of Pennsylvania, and George McGovern of South Dakota, along with high-ranking Republicans like George Aiken of Vermont.

The confusing and contradictory statements issued by the administration created a 'credibility gap' between Johnson and the nation which swelled the ranks of his critics. So often were administration statements that the war would not be widened followed by some new escalation that each peace offer came to be viewed as a signal that a new expansion of the fighting could be expected shortly. Richard Goodwin, the draftsman of Johnson's 'Great Society' speech and an early supporter of the

Vietnam policy, wrote subsequently, "The continual downpour of contradiction, misstatements and kaleidoscopically shifting attitudes has been so torrential that it has almost numbed the capacity to separate truth from conjecture and falsehood.' After Johnson declared that the bombing of North Vietnam had been 'aimed at military targets and . . . controlled with the greatest of care,' Harrison Salisbury of the *New York Times* reported on Christmas day, 1966, of his visit to Namdinh in North Vietnam:

> For blocks and blocks I could see nothing but desolation. Residential housing, stores, all the buildings were destroyed, damaged or abandoned. I felt that I was walking through the city of a vanished civilization. . . . Even by the Pentagon's least strict definition there were no very remarkable targets in Namdinh.

So many reports promised victory 'within a year' or declared that the corner had been turned that every claim of progress came to be viewed with skepticism.

The administration's critics viewed the Vietnam conflict as primarily a civil war in which the Viet Cong were an indigenous force; they pointed out that the Viet Cong controlled most of the countryside before there was any substantial infiltration from the North. Furthermore, they denied that the North Vietnamese, with a long history of distrusting the Chinese, were pawns of Peking. They thought it absurd to speak of a monolithic 'Sino-Soviet bloc' at a time when Peking warred with Moscow, Belgrade went its own way, and the Communist world was moving toward diversity. They ridiculed the claim that SEATO obligations made military action mandatory, since Dulles had specifically denied this at the time the treaty was written, and none of the other major signatories of the SEATO treaty — Britain, France, Pakistan — interpreted it to require intervention. They scoffed at the Munich analogy and the domino theory; General David M. Shoup, former commandant of the Marine Corps, thought it 'ludicrous' to believe that if the Communists won in Vietnam, they would 'soon be knocking at the doors of Pearl Harbor.'

Opponents of the administration also regretted the international consequences of the war. Many of America's allies deplored the attempt of the United States to set itself up as judge, jury, and executioner for mankind, and Afro-Asian nations resented the bombing of non-white populations. The war doomed prospects that the administration could 'build bridges' between East and West and distracted the President's attention from areas of the world more vital to American interests. As early as March 1965, James Reston of the *New York Times* observed caustically: 'For lack of an over-all strategy, Saigon has become the major capital of the State Department's world, the Gulf of Tonkin larger than the Atlantic, Vietnam more important than Europe or Latin America.' Critics charged that Johnson and his advisers were unwittingly encouraging a resurgence of isolationism, for the country was becoming increasingly unwilling to assume obligations in other parts of the world.

The 'doves' denied that the United States was advancing the causes either of democracy or a stable peace. The corrupt, repressive regime of Air Marshal Nguyen Cao Ky made a mockery of Washington's claim that it was defending the right of the Vietnamese to govern themselves; the election of 3 September 1967 was riddled with fraud and resulted in the imprisonment of the leading opposition challenger. Even if this dirty war, in which the United States employed napalm, and the South Vietnamese (as well as the Viet Cong) tortured prisoners, could be 'won,' Vietnam would be destroyed in the process, its countryside defoliated and gutted by bomb craters, its society shattered. Critics asked whether the administration was motivated less by a desire to liberate the Vietnamese than by the aim of establishing a beachhead of American power on the mainland. Although Johnson did agree to several bombing pauses, they accused him of spurning opportunities for negotiations and hardening his demands, especially by denying the claims of the National Liberation Front, the political arm of the Viet Cong. Administration opponents argued that the war, far from being a setback to Communism, had given Russia and China an enormous propaganda victory without the loss of a Soviet or Chinese soldier. Finally, the 'doves' insisted that escalation was doomed to failure, for each increase in America's commitment would be matched by the other side, with the consequence at best of a bloody ground war with no end in sight and at worst of nuclear war. Over the whole military venture, critics charged, there brooded an air of fatuity and futility. As Richard Goodwin put it:

> If I were to tell you today there was a guerilla war going on in a small Asian country, and that you could send one-half million men, and spend billions of dollars, and suffer thousands of casualties, and still have no hope of winning, could anyone possibly choose that course?

Such criticism fell on deaf ears. Johnson jeered at 'nervous Nellies,' and Dean Rusk remarked, 'I sometimes wonder at the gullibility of educated men and the stubborn disregard of plain facts by men who are supposed to be helping our young to learn — especially to learn how to think.' As the administration ignored the counsel of opponents of its Vietnam policy, its critics escalated their activities too, from 'teach-ins' on campuses and demonstrations at which draft cards were burned to more violent confrontations with authority. Dr. Benjamin Spock, author of an immensely popular guide book on babies, and the Rev. William Sloane Coffin, Jr., chaplain of Yale University, were convicted of encouraging draft resistance. Johnson's policies, by reversing the apparent mandate of the 1964 election, soured many Americans, especially young people, on a political system which appeared to give them so little effective voice and put enormous strains on the bonds that held American society together. 'Our Saigon expedition,' warned Archibald MacLeish, 'may well turn out to have played the part in our ultimate destiny which the Syracusan expedition played in the destiny of Athens.'

By draining money and energy from critical domestic problems, the war brought to an abrupt halt the most promising reform movement in a generation. By 1966 the government was spending more for Vietnam than for the entire welfare program. The Vietnam conflict divided labor leaders, most of whom supported Johnson's policies, from liberals, most of whom did not, and turned civil rights leaders against the administration. Martin Luther King declared:

> To do too little to relieve the agony of Negro life is as inflammatory as inciting a riot. To put an Asian war of dubious national interest far above domestic needs in the order of priorities and to pit it against reforms that were delayed a century is worse than a blind policy; it is a provocative policy.

The cost of the war, running some $28 billion a year, overheated the economy, as prices and interest rates soared and a new gold crisis loomed. Johnson, who had once put through a tax cut with the most salutary results, now asked for increased levies and sought to curb foreign travel. After the 1966 elections, in which the Democrats lost 47 House seats and three in the Senate, Congress adopted a few items of reform legislation — Federal housing, protection for the consumer — but it slashed funds for Great Society projects, undid the work

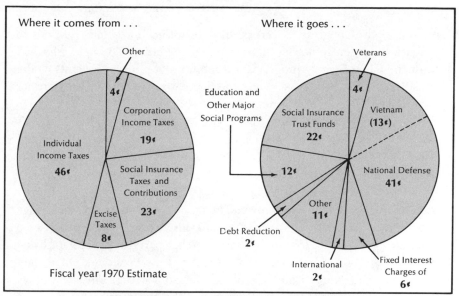

Where it comes from . . .

Other
4¢

Corporation Income Taxes
19¢

Individual Income Taxes
46¢

Social Insurance Taxes and Contributions
23¢

Excise Taxes
8¢

Fiscal year 1970 Estimate

Where it goes . . .

Veterans
4¢

Education and Other Major Social Programs
12¢

Social Insurance Trust Funds
22¢

Vietnam
(13¢)

National Defense
41¢

Other
11¢

Debt Reduction
2¢

International
2¢

Fixed Interest Charges of
6¢

THE FEDERAL GOVERNMENT DOLLAR

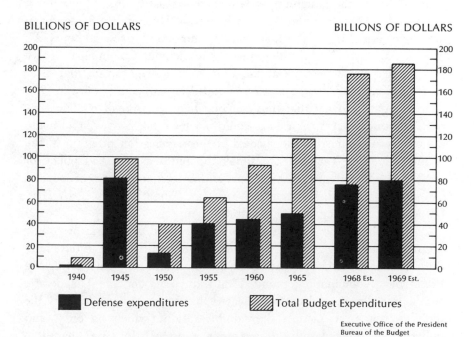

BILLIONS OF DOLLARS   BILLIONS OF DOLLARS

1940 1945 1950 1955 1960 1965 1968 Est. 1969 Est.

■ Defense expenditures   ▨ Total Budget Expenditures

Executive Office of the President
Bureau of the Budget

NATIONAL SPENDING 1940-1969

of the 89th Congress in areas like beautification, and refused to embark on urgently needed departures in the cities. The men who had built the Great Society programs — such first-rate public servants as the President's aide, Bill Moyers, and the Secretary of HEW, John Gardner — now fled the administration.

As early as April 1965 Senator Wayne Morse predicted that Johnson's policy in Vietnam would send him 'out of office the most discredited President in the history of this nation'; but few doubted that Johnson, after his unprecedented victory in 1964, would win another four-year term in 1968. When on 30 November 1967 Senator Eugene J. McCarthy announced he would enter several Democratic primaries to challenge the President over the issue of Vietnam, his decision was viewed as a quixotic gesture, for Johnson's control of his party appeared unshakeable. Yet the tide of events soon overwhelmed the President. On 23 January 1968 four North Korean gunboats seized the U.S. *Pueblo,* a Navy intelligence-gathering ship, as it cruised off the North Korean coast (and held its officers and crew captive for the next eleven months). One week later, on 30 January, as Vietnam began to celebrate the Tet (lunar New Year) holiday, the Communists launched a massive assault on thirty provincial capitals, overran the ancient city of Hue, and in Saigon even held a portion of the American embassy compound for several hours. Although the offensive did not result in the clearcut Communist victory that seemed quite possible at the time, it did demonstrate that after years of effort the United States and South Vietnam could not even safeguard Saigon, showed that the Vietcong had widespread civilian support, without which such attacks could not have taken place, and made a mockery of claims for the success of the pacification program in the countryside. The Tet offensive shook the faith in Johnson's policy of some of the President's most stalwart supporters, and scores of journals of opinion joined the influential *New York Times* and *St. Louis Post-Dispatch* in rebuking the administration.

On 12 March 1968, Senator McCarthy surprised the nation by rolling up 40 per cent of the vote in the New Hampshire primary. Four days later Robert Kennedy, who had previously been committed to supporting the President's renomination, plunged into the race for the Democratic nomination. Private polls now indicated that McCarthy would carry the state of Wisconsin against the administration (which he did), and public polls showed only 26 per cent approved Johnson's handling of the Vietnam situation. On 31 March, in a major address to a national television audience, Johnson declared that he was restricting the areas of North Vietnam to which bombing missions would be sent and invited Hanoi to discuss a settlement, an invitation which was quickly accepted. He concluded his address with a statement that stunned the country: 'I shall not seek and I will not accept the nomination of my party for a second term as your President.' The war in Vietnam, which had claimed so many victims, had now consumed the President's ambitions too.

3. A DIVIDED NATION

In the last years of Johnson's tenure, spasms of violence rocked the nation as bitterness over Vietnam, racial strife, and a series of shocking assassinations raised doubts about the stability of American society. Antiwar leaders, insisting that riots had been 'legitimized' by the savagery in Vietnam, called for a 'new politics.' 'The rage to demolish,' in John Gardner's phrase, threatened the most venerable institutions: the university, party organization, the Electoral College. Reverberations of the war against 'the Establishment' shook the Catholic Church as priests led open revolt against the authority of the hierarchy. Even movements dedicated to peaceful change turned to the use of force. The Student Nonviolent Coordinating Committee chose as its leaders young men who urged blacks to use arms against whites, while in San Francisco's Haight-Ashbury, once the haunt of the flower children, love posters were taken down and violent crime increased sharply.

When on 6 August 1965 President Johnson signed the Voting Rights Act of 1965, he stated it would 'strike away the last major shackle' of the Negro's 'ancient bonds.' There appeared to be every expectation that the civil rights struggle had been taken out of the streets, and the rioting that had disturbed several Northern cities in the summer of 1964 would not be repeated. But just five days later the worst race riot in the nation's history erupted in the Watts community of Los Angeles; six turbulent days left 34 dead, 856 injured. In 1966 riots broke out in the Negro districts of Cleveland, Chicago, and other cities, and racial insurrections in 1967 took 25 lives in Newark and 43 in Detroit, where black militants set fires and sniped at police. Northern Negroes, who had long exercised such rights as the suffrage, complained that civil rights statutes did almost nothing to alleviate the hardships of the urban ghetto: unemployment, inferior education, slum housing, and hostile police.

In 1966 Negro rioters chanted a new slogan: 'black power,' which could mean anything from a new-found sense of pride ('black is beautiful') to a determination to play the same kind of ethnic politics that groups like the Irish had found profitable to hatred of whites, reliance on violent confrontations, and a rejection of integration in favor of separate black institutions. Black nationalism had long been espoused by the Black Muslim movement born in Detroit in the Great Depression and led by Elijah Poole, who assumed the name of Elijah Muhammed. In 1964 the eloquent Malcolm X defected from the organization, only to be murdered by three Black Muslims the next year. Many of his ideas, however, were taken up by the new leaders of SNCC, Stokely Carmichael and his even more militant successor, H. Rap Brown, and by such guerilla groups as the Black Panthers. Martin Luther King commented on this movement: 'In advocating violence it is imitating the worst, the most brutal, and the most uncivilized value of American life.'

President Johnson's National Advisory Commission on Civil Disorders, headed by Governor Otto Kerner of Illinois, put the main blame for the riots on 'white racism.' It stated: 'What white Americans have never fully understood — but what the Negro can never forget — is that white society is deeply implicated in the ghetto.' It pointed out that more than 40 per cent of the country's non-whites lived below the 'poverty level,' as defined by the Social Security Administration, and deplored the fact that in many cities the principal response to the riots had been to 'train and equip the police with more sophisticated weapons.' The Commission issued a grim warning: 'Our nation is moving toward two societies, one black, one white — separate and unequal.'

The Rev. Dr. Martin Luther King, Jr. still hoped to bridge the gulf between the two societies. As the leading apostle of non-violence, he had been honored in Sweden with the award of the Nobel Peace Prize, but in the United States he had made little headway in his recent efforts on behalf of the poor of all races. He met rebuff both in Chicago, where techniques of resistance met obdurate hostility, and in Memphis, where he came to the aid of striking garbage collectors. In the early evening of 4 April 1968, as he stood on the balcony of a Memphis motel, Dr. King was shot and killed. James Earl Ray, a white man who was an escaped convict, was indicted for the crime.

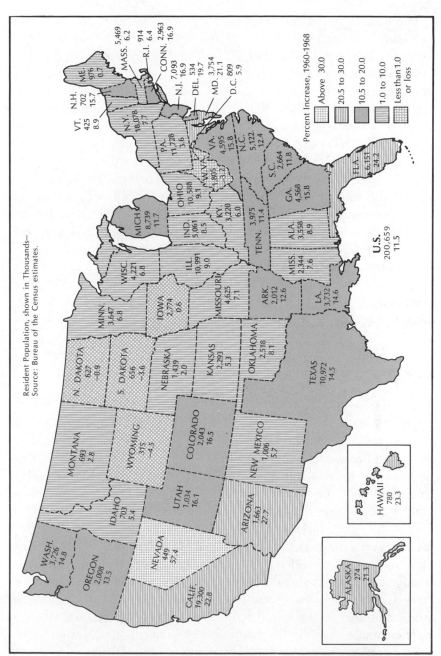

Resident Population, shown in Thousands—
Source: Bureau of the Census estimates.

Percent Increase, 1960-1968

Above 30.0
20.5 to 30.0
10.5 to 20.0
1.0 to 10.0
Less than 1.0 or loss

MASS. 5,469 6.2
R.I. 914 6.4
CONN. 2,963 16.9
N.H. 702 15.7
ME. 976 0.7
N.J. 7,093 16.9
DEL. 534 19.7
MD. 3,754 21.1
D.C. 809 5.9
VT. 425 8.9
N.Y. 18,078 7.7
PA. 11,728 3.6
VA. 4,595 15.8
W.VA. 1,805 —
N.C. 5,122 12.4
S.C. 2,664 11.8
GA. 4,560 15.8
FLA. 6,151 24.2
OHIO 10,588 9.1
KY. 3,220 6.0
TENN. 3,975 11.4
ALA. 3,558 8.9
MISS. 2,344 7.6
MICH. 8,739 11.7
IND. 5,061 8.5
ILL. 10,991 9.0
WISC. 4,221 6.8
MINN. 3,647 6.8
IOWA 2,774 0.6
MISSOURI 4,625 7.1
ARK. 2,012 12.6
LA. 3,732 14.6
N. DAKOTA 627 -0.9
S. DAKOTA 656 -3.6
NEBRASKA 1,439 2.0
KANSAS 2,293 5.3
OKLAHOMA 2,518 8.1
TEXAS 10,972 14.5
MONTANA 693 2.8
WYOMING 315 -4.5
COLORADO 2,043 16.5
NEW MEXICO 1,006 5.7
IDAHO 703 5.4
UTAH 1,034 16.1
ARIZONA 1,663 27.7
WASH. 3,726 14.8
OREGON 2,008 13.5
NEVADA 449 57.4
CALIF. 19,300 22.8

U.S. 200,659 11.5

HAWAII 780 23.3
ALASKA 274 21.3

POPULATION OF THE UNITED STATES, 1968

787

The nation grieved for the slain leader who in his thirty-nine years had contributed so much, but it reacted to his death in the same ambiguous way it had responded to his life. The death of a man who had so often cautioned against violence triggered race riots in a hundred cities, at the cost of thirty-nine lives. In Washington, D.C., smoke from burning buildings in the black slums billowed over the White House and through the cherry blossoms; on the Capitol steps, machine gunners stood guard. The rioting resulted in the biggest military build-up to deal with a civil disorder in the history of the country. On 10 April 1968, a day after Dr. King was buried in Atlanta, the House of Representatives passed and sent to the President a 'fair housing' bill designed to ban racial discrimination in 80 per cent of housing in the United States. Yet even King's death failed to move 171 Congressmen who voted in opposition. The act also set penalties for activities in interstate commerce aimed at encouraging riots. Rev. Ralph D. Abernathy carried on Dr. King's Poor People's Campaign by putting together a shanty town, 'Resurrection City, U.S.A.' in Washington, but in June the residents of Resurrection City were routed with tear gas, and the camp was demolished.

With King gone many looked toward Robert Kennedy as the one national leader who had the confidence of the poor of both races. A Kennedy campaign aide, Charles Evers, brother of the murdered Medgar Evers, later called him 'the only white man in this country I really trusted.' Kennedy had interrupted his campaign in Indiana to break the news of King's death to a Negro crowd; he explained that he could share their grief because he had lost a brother to the hand of an assassin. Kennedy won in Indiana, but when McCarthy upset him in Oregon, he had to capture the California primary of 5 June 1968 if he was to stay in the race. A little after midnight it became clear that Kennedy had won California and South Dakota on the same day. As he walked through a kitchen passageway at the Ambassador Hotel in Los Angeles, he was shot and fatally wounded. The police seized a 24-year-old Jordanian immigrant, Sirhan Bishara Sirhan, who resented Kennedy's support of Israel. At the age of forty-two, Robert Francis Kennedy was buried beside his brother in the hillside plot at Arlington National Cemetery.

The anguish over the deaths of Robert Kennedy and Martin Luther King raised probing questions about the nature of American society. Their deaths recalled other recent political murders: John Kennedy,

Medgar Evers, Rev. James Reeb, Malcolm X, the four Negro girls killed by a bomb in a Birmingham church, the three young men — James Chaney, Andrew Goodman, and Michael Schwerner — brutally murdered by enemies of civil rights in Mississippi, and too many more. The rising crime rate, the casual merchandising of slaughter on television, the resort to coercion by students at Columbia and other universities, and the lobbying by the National Rifle Association against effective gun control legislation caused many to ask whether violence was not the American way of life. Such assessments were often ill-balanced, for the United States had achieved notable success in developing peaceful solutions to social crises; yet the events of the spring of 1968, in the context of the continuing warfare in Vietnam, could not help but be disturbing. Arthur Schlesinger, Jr. told a commencement audience: 'The ghastly things we do to our own people, the ghastly things we do to other people — these must at last compel us to look searchingly at ourselves and our society before hatred and violence rush us on to more evil and finally tear our nation apart.'

The winds of violence whistled through the chinks in the American political structure in the 1968 campaign, but the party system withstood the buffeting. To the Democratic convention city of Chicago that summer came the youthful idealists of Senator McCarthy's 'Children's Crusade.' Their success in forcing a President out of office for the first time in American history had demonstrated that the political process was remarkably responsive to the popular will. But many of McCarthy's followers were frustrated by the lack of progress in the Paris negotiations between the United States and North Vietnam and were certain that only the victory of their hero would vindicate the American political system. To Chicago too came itinerant revolutionists bent on provoking a violent confrontation. In most respects the convention was exceptionally democratic; it suspended the unit rule, seated black delegates from states like Georgia and Mississippi, and provided for full debate on the Vietnam question. But the McCarthy enthusiasts, and those of Senator McGovern, who entered the race at the last minute as the heir of Robert Kennedy's following, believed the will of the people had been flouted when the presidential nomination went to Vice-President Hubert Humphrey, whose delegates had been chosen at party meetings rather than in primaries. Bitter exchanges marred the convention proceedings while in the streets anti-war demonstrators, a number of whom were deliberately provocative, clashed with Mayor Richard J. Daley's police, some of whom got altogether out of control and wielded their clubs indiscriminately. Televised accounts of the party warfare and the mayhem in the streets placed an enormous handicap on Humphrey's campaign.

Millions of Americans felt that in being asked to choose between Humphrey and the Republican nominee Richard Nixon they were offered no real choice, since both men had been identified with a 'hard' line in Vietnam and with the politics of the older generation. Humphrey countered by pointing to his outstanding record as the leader of the Senate liberals and a spokesman for civil rights. Moreover he had made a fortunate move when he picked Senator Edmund S. Muskie of Maine to be his running mate; little known before the campaign, Muskie proved to be the most popular of all the candidates. On the other hand, Nixon, as a concession to Southerners like Strom Thurmond, had selected for his vice-presidential candidate Governor Spiro T. Agnew of Maryland. By a series of racial slurs and by remarks which recalled the unhappy era of Joe McCarthy, Agnew raised doubts about Nixon's judgment of men and tempted Democratic dissidents to return to the fold.

Still other Americans expressed a different kind of dissatisfaction with the presidential choices in 1968 by building the most formidable third party in a generation. Governor George Wallace's American Independent Party appealed chiefly to those who resented gains for the Negro, especially in the South but also among some workingmen in the Northern cities. Wallace's plea for 'law and order,' although largely a euphemism for racial discrimination, also struck a chord among those who blamed the upsurge of crime and the violence of college students and anti-war demonstrators on men in authority, especially permissive Supreme Court justices. To exploit the sentiment of those who criticized Johnson for not prosecuting the war more unrestrainedly, Wallace chose as his running mate General Curtis Le May, former Air Force Chief of Staff who was known for his strident advocacy of bombing North Vietnam back to the Stone Age. But Le May's complaint about the country's 'phobia' concerning the use of nuclear weapons drove still more Democratic defectors back into the arms of their party.

Humphrey, who started out far behind, almost pulled even in the final five days of the campaign after Johnson announced he was halting the bombing of North Vietnam, but Nixon scored a narrow victory. With

31.8 million votes (43.4 per cent) Nixon gained a 301-191 margin in the Electoral College as he swept most of the West and ran well in the upper South. Humphrey, with 31.3 million votes (42.7 per cent), continued to draw most of his support from the 'Roosevelt coalition' of lower income voters, trade unionists, and minority groups in the big cities, including 85 per cent of the non-white vote. But his share of the ballots of manual workers fell off sharply, and the once-Solid South was so shattered that Humphrey captured only one Southern state, Texas. Wallace, with 9.9 million votes (13.5 per cent) and 46 electoral votes, captured four Deep South states Goldwater had carried as well as Arkansas,[1] but in the North he ran far behind the figures he had polled in the 1964 primaries as the 'white backlash' candidate. The Democrats showed they were still the majority party when they held their margin in both houses of Congress, only the third occasion that this had been achieved when the opposition party was winning the presidency. But the Vietnam war had cost the Democrats dearly. In four years a plurality of 16 million votes on the presidential line had evaporated, and for the first time a party that won a landslide victory lost control of the White House at the subsequent election.

As the grim year of 1968 drew to an end the country found excitement in a majestic voyage that suggested the potentialities of American society. In Christmas week Col. Frank Borman, Capt. James A. Lovell, Jr., and Col. William A. Anders of Apollo 8 became the first mortals to see the dark side of the moon. Many wondered why the United States, capable of so spectacular an achievement in outer space, could not approach its problems on earth with the same dedication and resourcefulness. As President Johnson prepared to turn over the reins of office to a successor known neither for his imagination nor his commitment to the redistribution of power, few could be sanguine about the prospects.

4. FROM NIXON TO CARTER

The outcome of the 1968 election set the ill-fated course of the Nixon presidency. Despite all that had befallen the Democratic administration, Nixon had won only a narrow triumph, with the smallest percentage of the popular vote of any victor since 1912. Long thought of as a

---

1. A Nixon elector in North Carolina also defected to Wallace. Goldwater, however, had also won South Carolina and Arizona.

'born loser,' he was determined to win re-election in 1972 — and by a landslide. To do so he adopted a number of strategies: moderation to appeal to the Center, divisiveness to attract the followers of George Wallace, and exploitation of the issues of cultural politics that were troubling 'Middle America.' In the end, the Nixon 'team,' not content with these expedients, did not scruple at adopting methods and policies that would reduce the presidency morally to its lowest point in the nation's history and bring about a crisis of confidence in the democratic process.

When analysts sifted through the 1968 returns, they found that voters were more concerned about 'law and order' than any other problem, even the Vietnam war, and Nixon made the most of this. The country had been shaken by five consecutive summers of rioting in the black ghettos; by campus violence; and by a sharp rise in crime, including assaults upon persons. In his inaugural address, the President declared:

> America has suffered from a fever of words; from inflated rhet-
> oric that promises more than it can deliver; from angry rhetoric that
> fans discontents into hatreds; from bombastic rhetoric that postures
> instead of persuading.
> We cannot learn from one another until we stop shouting at one
> another — until we speak quietly enough so that our words can be
> heard as well as our voices.

Nixon had some initial success in portraying himself as a promoter of domestic peace. The ghetto turbulence abruptly ended, to a certain extent because Nixon, by raising few expectations, created less possibility of disappointment. The bloodletting in Vietnam continued (one-third of American deaths in the war would occur under Nixon), but in the process of taking as long to end the war as Lincoln had required to fight the Civil War, he did reduce United States troop levels, which had peaked at 543,000 in 1968, to 39,000 on 1 September 1972. Furthermore, a reform of the draft diminished anxiety for registrants with higher numbers. In part as a consequence of these developments, the mood of protest on college campuses became muted, if only for a time.

However, Nixon's role as a builder of bridges over troubled waters proved less congenial than that of capitalizing on apprehension about social change. Millions of Americans strongly disapproved of the ideology of the 'counterculture,' which denigrated respected institutions and values, notably the work ethic. Dislike of the counterculture was especially marked among lower income voters, long the ballast of the Democratic party. In the Johnson years the 'greening of America' had taken a bewildering variety of forms, including experimentation with psychedelic drugs, uninhibited sexual behavior, and the vogue of 'acid' rock music, a volatile mixture which in Nixon's first year in office drew hundreds of thousands of young people to the Woodstock Music and Art Fair.

At the same time the counterculture was assailing American folkways, the women's liberation movement was raising challenges to traditional perceptions of sex roles and the structure of the family and even of the economy. In the 1960's two-thirds of new jobs went to women, and by 1970 43 per cent of adult women were in the labor force. Advocates of equal opportunity, who succeeded in securing legislation like the Civil Rights Act of 1964 which forbade discrimination in employment on the basis of sex, sometimes asked only that women receive equal pay for equal work. But increasingly, they advanced other demands — for child care centers, an end to restrictions on abortion, and sex quotas in hiring — that defied orthodox conceptions of woman's 'place' and the nuclear family. These innovations seemed especially unsettling in a period when the stability of the family was shaken by an 80 per cent rise in the number of divorces between 1960 and 1972.

Into this highly controverted arena of cultural politics barged the Nixon administration, led by the lubberly Spiro Agnew who took to the stump to deplore the erosion of time-honored American values. 'We have gone through a debilitating, enervating age of indulgence,' the Vice-President said. Agnew barnstormed less on the old issues of economic policy than on the latest disputes about life style, although he linked the two when he blamed changing attitudes on 'a political hedonism that permeates the philosophy of the radical liberals' and when he excoriated Dr. Benjamin Spock, author of an immensely popular manual on child-rearing and an outspoken foe of the Vietnam war. Nixon, too, berated the 'Spock-marked generation,' attacked 'abortion on demand,' and denounced the latitudinarian conclusions of the Federal Commission on Obscenity and Pornography without even reading the report he had commissioned.

Many of the new manifestations converged on the Supreme Court. In invalidating the censorship of *Lady Chatterley's Lover* in 1959, the Court stated that the First Amendment 'protects advocacy of opinion that adultery may sometimes be proper, no less than advocacy of socialism or the single tax,' and in defense of *Fanny Hill* in 1966, the justices ruled that a book could not be proscribed unless it was found 'to be utterly without redeeming social value.' During the same years when it was ending virtually all restrictions on pornography, the Warren Court stirred up an even sharper controversy by outlawing Bible-reading and prayer in public schools as a violation of the First Amendment. 'They've put the Negroes in the schools,' expostulated an Alabama Congressman, 'and now they've driven God out.' Many of the very people who were exercised about these decisions deplored the rulings of the Court in cases such as *Escobedo v. Illinois* (1964), which required that a suspect be informed of his right to remain silent and to have counsel present when he was interrogated. Though civil libertarians applauded decisions like *Gideon v. Wainwright* (1963), which stipulated that the state must provide a pauper charged with a felony with an attorney at public expense, others, frequently unreasonably, blamed the Warren Court for the dramatic rise of crime in the cities. In the climactic *Miranda* case of 1966, which broadened the 'due process' requirement of the Fourteenth Amendment, the four dissenting justices warned against returning 'a killer, a rapist or other criminal to the streets . . . to repeat his crime whenever it pleases him!'

When Nixon took office, he set out to reverse this 'permissive' jurisprudence by appointing law-and-order judges who would be 'strict constructionists,' and he was soon given the opportunity to fill several vacancies. When in 1969, the bold and innovative Chief Justice Warren retired, the President chose a conservative federal judge, Warren Burger, to replace him. That selection occasioned little comment, but when he and his maladroit Attorney-General, John Mitchell, attempted to elevate judges from Southern circuits to the High Court they were twice rebuffed by the Senate, a humiliation that had not been visited on an American President in this century. Nixon and Mitchell then came up with two more names that were so unacceptable that they did not submit them. All of this greatly distressed a Republican Senator from Nebraska who said of one of Nixon's nominees: 'There are lots of mediocre judges and people and lawyers. They are entitled to a little representation aren't they? . . . We can't have all Brandeises and Frankfurters and Cardozos and stuff like that there.'

In the end Nixon, by more respectable though still conservative appointments, did succeed in modifying the stance of the Court but not nearly to the extent he desired. In a number of decisions the 'Burger Court' softened the position of the Warren Court. Nonetheless, it also broadened the orbit of cultural politics and extended the safeguards of civil liberties and civil rights. The Court elaborated the right of a woman to an abortion during the first three months of pregnancy, curbed the imposition of the death penalty, repudiated the Attorney-General's arrogant claim that he could utilize wiretaps on domestic dissenters without a court order, and held that the government could not restrain publication of the 'Pentagon Papers,' a detailed examination of Vietnam policy which a Pentagon expert, Daniel Ellsberg, leaked to the press. In a unanimous opinion of April 1971, the Court, in a Charlotte, North Carolina, case, sustained the busing of pupils out of their neighborhoods in order to foster racial integration.

The Nixon administration found this last decision especially galling, for it had been pursuing a 'Southern strategy' to wean George Wallace's followers away from him. The aborted attempt to name a South Carolina judge to the Supreme Court had been aimed at pleasing that state's arch-conservative senator, Strom Thurmond, who regarded Agnew as the greatest Vice-President America had ever had, save only for Calhoun. Toward blacks the administration pursued a policy of 'benign neglect,' in the words of Nixon's adviser Daniel Patrick Moynihan. Sometimes 'benign neglect' implied continuing to foster racial gains but doing it surreptitiously so as not to antagonize the Wallaceites. At other times it meant outright hostility to programs of the Kennedy-Johnson era, as when Mitchell's Department of Justice opposed extension of the Voting Rights Act of 1965. When the administration asked a federal court to delay the desegregation of Mississippi schools, the NAACP asked to have the United States named a defendant, for 'it no longer seeks to represent the rights of Negro children.'

The accent on 'benign neglect' came in an era when other groups besides blacks were insisting on their rights. So substantial was the migration from the Caribbean islands in the quarter-century after World War II that there were more Puerto Ricans in New York than in San Juan, and by 1970, nearly one-quarter of a million Cubans in Florida's Dade County; both groups wanted greater recognition. Over one-fourth of the several million Mexican-Americans lived below the poverty line. Cultural nationalists furthered the cause of these 'Chicanos,' and Cesar Chavez led strikes of migrant workers in the vineyards and lettuce fields of California that evoked sympathy among liberal Democrats. However, the Nixon administration showed no understanding of the aspirations of Spanish-American groups or of the afflictions of American Indians who, with a rapidly growing population, had a life expectancy of only 46 years, compared with the national average of 69, and the country's highest rate of infant mortality. The increasing militance of Indian groups, beginning with an occupation of Alcatraz Island in San Francisco Bay and running through the ransacking of the Bureau of Indian Affairs headquarters in Washington, reached a climax in the Nixon period in a bloody confrontation on the Sioux reservation at Wounded Knee.

The hard-shelled indifference of the Nixon administration reflected the composition of its leadership. 'Richard Nixon's White House is a controlled, antiseptic place, not unlike the upper tier of a giant corporation,' observed an American journal, while a British commentary referred to the Nixon cabinet as 'a steering committee of the conformist middle class triumphant.' Dominating the White House staff were two former 'advance men,' Harry R. Haldeman and John Ehrlichman who, with their Prussian haircuts and no-nonsense comportment, seemed so much alike that they were called the 'Rosencrantz and Guildenstern' of the administration. The President for his part frequently isolated himself behind the 'Berlin Wall' erected by his two main advisers on domestic policy.

In foreign affairs, too, despite all of the buncombe about bringing the nation together, Nixon launched periodic forays that provoked paroxysms of rage. Although Nixon had claimed during the 1968 campaign that he had a plan to move the Vietnam conflict to a speedy end, the war went on, year in, year out. In 1969 massive antiwar demonstrations shook Washington, but to no avail. The President detonated an even greater explosion in 1970 when, acting secretly and without Congressional authorization, he sent American troops and bombers into Cambodia and sought to justify the invasion by saying, 'We will not be humiliated. We will not be defeated. . . . If when the chips are down, the world's most powerful nation . . . acts like a pitiful, helpless giant, the forces of totalitarianism and anarchy will threaten free nations and free institutions throughout the world.' Nixon's expansion of the fighting ignited campuses from coast to coast. Martial law was proclaimed in a number of states, including Ohio, where Kent State demonstrators firebombed the ROTC building. The situation became more inflamed when on 4

May National Guardsmen shot to death four students at Kent State University and, in an unrelated incident on 15 May, Mississippi troopers killed two students at Jackson State College. In protest, indignant students, faculty and administrators shut down scores of colleges, some for the rest of the semester.

The unmistakable evidence that he had miscalculated caused Nixon to back-track momentarily by pulling out of Cambodia, but he soon resumed a more bellicose line, in part in order to appeal to those who favored a hawkish foreign policy. When New York's mayor, John Lindsay, ordered the flag at City Hall lowered to half-staff in respect for the Kent State victims, hard-hatted construction workers rampaged through the financial district bludgeoning long-haired students and ran the flag up again. Nixon deliberately cultivated both these 'hard hats' and the disciples of George Wallace by intervening for leniency in the case of Lt. William L. Calley, Jr., convicted of slaughtering several hundred defenseless civilians at the South Vietnamese hamlet of Mylai. In 1971 the President incited new outbursts by invading Laos, and in 1972 he risked a confrontation with Russia by saturation bombing of North Vietnam and by mining harbors used by Soviet vessels there.

Yet though Nixon embarked on inflammatory adventures in foreign policy, he also undertook initiatives which lent credence to his claim to be a sponsor of *détente*. In 1969 he announced a 'Nixon Doctrine,' which implied willingness to forego any more interventions like Vietnam. He appointed as his National Security Adviser a Harvard professor, Henry Kissinger, who was regarded as a 'realist' in foreign affairs, and in 1972 the President flew to Moscow to negotiate a treaty limiting strategic missiles. He also ended the production of biological weapons. But Nixon created the greatest sensation by flying to Peking in February 1972 to confer with Premier Chou En-lai. A man who had built a career on relentless animosity to the Communist world had become the first President to contrive an opening to the People's Republic of China.

Nixon also gained stature from an extraordinary event toward which he had made no contribution — man's first voyage to the moon. On 20 July 1969, four days after they blasted off from earth, two members of the crew of Apollo 11 — Neil A. Armstrong and Col. Edwin E. Aldrin, Jr. — became the first men ever to walk on the moon. While Lt. Col. Michael Collins maneuvered their spaceship, Armstrong and Aldrin placed on the surface of the moon a plaque signed by the crew and

President Nixon that read: 'Here men from the planet earth first set foot upon the moon July 1969, A.D. We came in peace for all mankind.' Some complained that the country's resources would be better spent in coping with terrestrial problems, but more were impressed by the achievement, and Nixon, sharing the television screen with the astronauts, profited from the approbation for the journey to the Sea of Tranquility.

The President's domestic policies, too, sometimes departed from the conservatism of Attorney-General Mitchell's 'Southern strategy.' The proportion of pupils in all-black schools fell precipitously from 68 per cent in 1968 to 18 per cent in 1970, in large part because of longtime trends, some of which Nixon resisted, but also because of positive steps as when the administration sued the entire state of Georgia to end dual educational systems. A series of statutes starting with the National Environmental Policy Act of 1969 improved the quality of air and water, and the Environmental Protection Agency, created in 1970, enforced higher standards on the automobile industry and on municipalities and corporations. Frequently initiatives came not from the White House but from the Democratic Congress, as when plans to construct supersonic transport aircraft were frustrated. Still, either because of or despite the attitude of the White House, social advances continued in the Nixon years. Social security benefits increased more than 50 per cent from 1969 to 1972, and federal expenditures for education and health soared. Though these developments were offset by other moves in a reactionary direction, liberals found them a welcome surprise. 'Everybody is saying that Mr. Nixon is doing better than they expected,' noted James Reston, 'which proves the success of past failures.'

Nixon also showed more flexibility than anticipated in coping with the main domestic issue he confronted — the ailing economy. From Lyndon Johnson he had inherited an economy overstimulated by vastly increased spending on the Vietnam war. Soon he had to deal with an unpropitious combination that liberal economists had not envisaged: skyrocketing prices accompanied by rapidly mounting unemployment. The President started out by prescribing conventional nostrums, but when these failed, he turned to deficit spending. 'I am now a Keynesian,' he said; as one commentator remarked, that was 'a little like a Christian crusader saying, "All things considered, I think Mohammed was right." ' But Nixon continued to resist more direct intervention. 'Controls, Oh my God, no!' he expostulated in 1969. However, when in 1971 prices rose relentlessly, and the nation experienced its first trade deficit since 1893, he ordered a temporary freeze on wages, prices, and rents and devalued the dollar. Nixon's new policies enjoyed only moderate success. Nonetheless, he was able to make his bid for reelection at a time when many Americans were enjoying the benefits of the world's first trillion-dollar economy.

In the 1972 campaign Nixon had the decisive advantage of prevailing over both the Right and the Center sectors of the electorate. His main worry from the Right ended on 15 May 1972 when George Wallace, who showed conspicuous strength among blue-collar workers in Democratic primaries, was shot and so badly wounded that he had to withdraw from the presidential race. Nixon appropriated the Center when the Democrats chose as their Presidential nominee a factionalist, Senator George McGovern. An antiwar liberal who had made an admirable record, McGovern won the nomination as the result of changes in party procedure that alienated union chieftains and big city organizations and left the erroneous impression that he was the candidate of the counterculture. He had the further misfortune of picking as his running mate Senator Thomas Eagleton of Missouri and, after it came out that Eagleton had been treated for mental illness, dropping him from the ticket. Nixon overwhelmed McGovern with 47.2 million votes (60.7 per cent) to 29.2 million and a 520 to 17 triumph in the Electoral College; McGovern carried only Massachusetts and the predominantly black District of Columbia. Especially disappointing to McGovern was the performance of young people; an act of Congress and the Twenty-sixth Amendment, ratified in 1971, had given eighteen-year-olds the right to vote, but the majority of them did not trouble to go to the polls.

On the eve of the election Henry Kissinger had marshaled votes for Nixon by stating, 'Peace is at hand.' This welcome announcement proved premature, for in the month after his re-election the President celebrated the Christmas season by approving a merciless bombing of North Vietnam, especially of heavily populated Hanoi, that dismayed and disgusted large numbers of Americans and brought worldwide censure. However, Nixon did finally achieve a cease-fire in Vietnam in January 1973 and by the end of March the last United States troops had been withdrawn from the stricken country. In addition, the government proclaimed the end of the draft. Nixon boasted that he had achieved 'peace with honor.' In fact, the agreement acknowledged an unmitigated defeat and the term 'honor' was totally irrelevant. The war had cost 57,000 American lives, and more than 300,000 wounded; had inflicted over one million casualties on Asians; had absorbed billions of dollars in resources; and had done incalculable damage to American society and morality, and to the effectiveness of the United States in world affairs.

Returned to office by one of the most convincing margins in history, Nixon gave up all pretense of being a man of the Center and immediately veered sharply to the Right. He had hardly begun his second administration when he precipitated a serious constitutional crisis. He flouted the authority of Congress by dismantling the Office of Economic Opportunity that administered the War on Poverty, impounded funds Congress had appropriated for social purposes, and defied requests from Capitol Hill for information on the behavior of civil servants. Increasingly Nixon's aides, who supervised a White House staff over two-and-one-half times larger than that with which Roosevelt had run World War II, behaved less like servants of the people in a democratic republic and more like a Praetorian Guard. Nixon, wrote a British journalist, was asserting 'Robespierre's claim to personify the general will,' while other critics likened him to de Gaulle, a refractory ruler convinced that history was on his side, contemptuous of the legislature, and isolated from those he governed. The analogy was not wholly irrelevant, but unfortunately Nixon lacked de Gaulle's genius, his vision, and his high moral standards.

Concern about abuse of power became the leitmotif of the second Nixon administration. In the spring of 1973 the United States Attorney for Maryland launched a criminal investigation into allegations that Spiro Agnew, while county executive of Baltimore and governor of Maryland, had accepted bribes. On 10 October the Vice-President, faced with a possible prison term, pleaded *nolo contendere* (no contest) to a charge of filing a 'false and fraudulent' tax return, and resigned. A federal court fined Agnew $10,000 and sentenced him to probation for three years. Though the Department of Justice halted prosecution, it released an extensive account of Agnew's malefactions which, it stated, continued during the period when he was 'only a heartbeat away' from becoming President of the United States. Never before had so high an office in the republic been so disgraced. Under the terms of the Twenty-fifth Amendment, ratified in 1967, Nixon named as Agnew's successor the Republican Minority Leader, Representative Gerald R. Ford of

Michigan, a conservative who had never been suspected of originality. But neither had he aroused suspicions of dishonesty, and so far had the reputation of the American government sunk that this qualification, which should have been taken for granted, was regarded as an exceptional mark of distinction.

Agnew's resignation occurred in a season of mounting public indignation over a matter of far graver purport: 'the Watergate affair.' On 17 June 1972 a security guard had chanced upon intruders in the Democratic National Committee headquarters in Washington's Watergate complex. Though the culprits, who were quickly tried and convicted, were employees of the Committee to Re-elect the President (CREEP), Nixon dismissed the burglary as a 'bizarre incident,' and for a time it seemed that no more would come of the episode. But neither Judge John J. Sirica of the U.S. District Court nor reporters for the *Washington Post* were content with this explanation, and by the spring of 1973 the Nixon administration had become enmeshed in a web of duplicity and deceit.

Investigation disclosed that wrongdoing had not been limited to the Watergate break-in. Campaign officials had engaged in political sabotage and other 'dirty tricks' in New Hampshire and Florida, and the White House had connived in burgling the office of Daniel Ellsberg's psychiatrist in an attempt to find evidence that might either convict him of a crime or prove him insane; not content with this, it had even tried to tamper with the judge presiding over the trial. Both businessmen and politicians had violated the laws governing campaign contributions, and corporations were accused of subverting the election process not only in America but in Chile and other countries. Most damaging of all was the report that some of the President's closest advisers had been involved in suborning perjury and paying 'hush money' to cover up the Watergate scandal.

A Senate investigation headed by Sam Ervin, Jr., of North Carolina, shook the Nixon administration to its foundations. When, to forestall interrogation by the Senate inquiry, Nixon sought to cloak his assistants with a mantle of Executive prerogative, Ervin responded that 'divine right went out with the American Revolution and doesn't belong to White House aides.' Under pressure from the Ervin committee, John W. Dean, III, counsel to the President, confessed to having taken part in an elaborate conspiracy to conceal the Watergate transgressions, and he implicated others. L. Patrick Gray, III, acting director of the FBI, admitted that he had deliberately destroyed documents. He resigned under fire, as on 30 April 1973 did Dean, Haldeman, Ehrlichman, and Attorney-General Richard Kleindienst. Former Attorney-General Mitchell, the champion of law and order, conceded that he had attended three meetings at which bugging the Democratic headquarters was discussed. But the most startling disclosure of the Ervin committee hearings came when it developed that Nixon had been surreptitiously tape recording discussions and telephone conversations of his own Cabinet and advisers.

The tapes spelled Nixon's doom. Until this revelation, no one had demonstrated that the President himself was culpable, though such pointed questions had been asked about his tax returns and government expenditures on his lavish residences in Florida and California that he felt compelled to say, 'I am not a crook.' (In the end, he had to pay the government nearly one-half million dollars in back taxes and interest.) If he had nothing to hide about his role in the Watergate imbroglio, the tapes should clear him. But Nixon refused to turn over the tapes, even to a special prosecutor, Archibald Cox of Harvard Law School, to whom he had pledged full cooperation. When Cox went to court to obtain the tapes, Nixon ordered Attorney-General Elliot Richardson to fire him, but, to their credit, both Richardson and his assistant, William Ruckelshaus, resigned instead on 20 October 1973. The solicitor general then obliged the President by discharging Cox.

This 'Saturday night massacre,' as Washington called it, led to widespread demands for Nixon's impeachment. When the President, at bay, agreed to surrender tapes to Judge Sirica, it turned out that critical conversations were missing and that a crucial portion of one tape had been 'accidentally' erased. On 30 April 1974, to still the outcry against him, Nixon made available edited, and inaccurate, transcripts of some of the tapes, but this self-serving move backfired. The transcripts shocked the country by exposing the President's naked insensitivity to the national interest and his crude language; overnight 'expletive deleted' became a catchphrase. Cox's successor, unpersuaded by White House subterfuges about the separation of powers, subpoenaed tapes and documents of 64 additional conversations, and on 24 July, in *U.S. v. Richard M. Nixon,* the Supreme Court, while accepting the President's contention that he might invoke a claim of Executive privilege in the national security sphere, ruled unanimously that in this instance he must comply 'forthwith.'

One week later, after nationally televised deliberations, the House Judiciary Committee voted three articles of impeachment. The President was charged with betraying his oath of office by lying, obstructing justice, and manipulating the Internal Revenue Service and other agencies to breach the Constitutional rights of citizens. In desperation, Nixon played his final card. He released the transcripts of three conversations with Haldeman and, in essence, threw himself on the mercy of the Senate. But since the transcripts further incriminated him, he lost the last remnants of his support among right-wing Republicans. With no other recourse left, Richard Nixon, on 8 August 1974, brought the sordid affair to a climax by writing, 'I hereby resign the Office of President of the United States.' 'For 25 years,' wrote Bill Moyers, 'the man had massaged the baser instincts of politics.' Now he was gone, and with him went fifty-six men convicted of Watergate-related offenses, including twenty former members of the cabinet, the White House staff, and CREEP.

On the day after Nixon submitted his resignation, Gerald Ford succeeded to the presidency, the first man ever to become Chief Executive by the appointment route. Ford began with a large reservoir of good will which he quickly dissipated. On 8 September 1974 he stunned the nation by announcing that he was pardoning Nixon for all federal crimes he 'committed or may have committed or taken part in' while President. White House Press Secretary J. F. ter Horst resigned immediately as a matter of 'conscience,' and amidst a clamor of disapproval of Ford's action, which smacked of the exercise of the royal prerogative, public support for the new President dropped precipitately.

In most respects Ford's administration differed little from Nixon's. To be sure there appeared to be much less of the knavery of the Watergate era. But when Senate investigators revealed that the FBI had been involved for over one-quarter of a century in more than two hundred 'black bag jobs' against 'domestic security targets' and that the CIA had not only contravened its charter by spying on American citizens but had recruited the Mafia to assassinate Fidel Castro, Ford responded not with moral outrage but by endeavoring to suppress the evidence and punish those who wished to bring it to light. He continued to rely on Kissinger in foreign affairs and, despite the lesson of Vietnam, to contemplate intervention in the civil war in Angola. In domestic matters, Ford was more reactionary and less imaginative than Nixon. At a time of tenacious unemployment and 'double-digit' inflation, he persisted in shopworn economic policies, and repeatedly vetoed legislation for public housing, federal aid to education, health care, and other social purposes. He asked regulatory agencies to give 'maximum freedom to private enterprise' and told industrialists that he wanted Washington 'out of your business, out of your lives, out of your pockets and out of your hair.' Early in 1976 a poll found that overwhelmingly the American people thought he was 'a nice guy,' but by a big margin, too, they had concluded that 'he does not seem to be very smart about the issues the country is facing.' No one summed up his performance better than the President himself when he said, disarmingly but truthfully, 'I am a Ford, not a Lincoln.'

Ford's tribulations gave the Democrats a golden opportunity to return to power in the 1976 election, but they almost lost it. When the former governor of Georgia, James Earl Carter, Jr., emerged from the Democratic convention with his party's nomination, he held a 33-point advantage over Ford in the polls. By November, that big lead had evaporated because of a series of mishaps, such as his indiscretion in giving a frank interview to the sexually oriented magazine *Playboy*. However, in a campaign not distinguished by its concentration on serious issues, Ford made blunders of his own, especially when, in a televised debate with Carter, the President made the astounding assertion that 'there is no Soviet domination of Eastern Europe,' a remark that seemed particularly odd coming from a man who had spent much of his public life warning of the Russian menace. In the end, Jimmy Carter won, but only narrowly, polling 40.8 million votes (50.1 per cent) and 297 electoral votes to Ford's 39.1 million votes (48 per cent) and 240 electoral votes, the smallest electoral margin since 1916.

As President, Carter altered the policies of his predecessors only moderately. To be sure, he did address the energy crisis that had first disturbed the country during the Arab oil embargo of 1973, and under his aegis Congress created a Department of Energy and a series of procedures aimed at lessening American dependence on foreign oil. Carter also carried out his campaign pledge to pardon Vietnam-era draft evaders, showed courage in vetoing 'pork barrel' public works legislation, put through the first significant revision of the federal civil service laws in a century, and not only appointed two women to Cabinet posts but shepherded through Congress a 39-month extension of the deadline for ratification of the Equal Rights Amendment. However, Carter had little more success than his predecessors in coping with the dismal combination of persistent inflation, high-level unemployment, and a sagging dollar. On those occasions when the President did contemplate bolder initiatives, he had to reckon with a national mood of disapproval of government spending symbolized by California's 'Proposition 13,' which slashed property taxes without regard to the impact on social services, and with the willingness of Congress to defer to special interests. The federal tax law of 1978, said Senator Edward Kennedy, was 'the worst tax legislation approved by Congress since the days of Calvin Coolidge and Andrew Mellon.' In sum, Carter differed from Ford and Nixon less in substance than in style. His low-keyed manner deflated the pretensions of the imperial presidency, and, as a 'born-again' Christian, he brought to the White House a moral earnestness that had been largely absent at the start of the decade.

On racial matters, both the President and the Supreme Court took a middle path. Carter diverged from Ford and Nixon on civil rights primarily in his record on appointments, for he named blacks to such important posts as Secretary of Housing and Urban Development, Secretary of the Army, Solicitor General, and ambassador to the United Nations. On the other hand, he did nothing effective to lessen the scandalously high rate of unemployment among black youth or to cope with the decay of black neighborhoods. Despite the promises of his campaign, he indicated that though he was willing to do all he could to uphold rights already established, he would not move appreciably further. Similarly, the Supreme Court, when called upon to rule on the delicate issue of 'reverse discrimination,' walked a tightrope. In a landmark 5 to 4 decision in the *Bakke* case, Justice Lewis Powell joined four other judges to rule that it was permissible to consider race in determining admission to universities, but he then joined with four different judges in holding that the medical school of the University of California at Davis violated the law in setting a quota of places for blacks. The full implications of the decision remained to be seen, but the Court's action was widely interpreted as placing a limit on 'affirmative action' for blacks, other minorities, and women.

In foreign affairs, too, Carter pursued a centrist course, but in this realm his performance earned him higher grades. By presenting himself as the defender of human rights throughout the world, he restored some of the moral prestige of the presidency. Furthermore, Carter demonstrated that he was not beguiled by the globalist ambitions that had led earlier Presidents astray when he committed himself to a very gradual withdrawal of American ground troops from Korea, and even more when, in a strong show of executive leadership, he won Senate approval for treaties that would establish Panamanian control over the Panama Canal and the Canal Zone by the year 2000. If, with the encouragement of his national security adviser, Zbigniew Brzezinski, he frequently took a hard line toward the Soviet Union, he also sought assiduously to work out arms control accords with the Russians.

The President showed his willingness to move in new directions when, in December 1978, he. caught the country by surprise by announcing a dramatic change in American policy in the Orient. On January 1, 1979, he revealed, the United States would end three decades of refusal to accept the legitimacy of a Communist regime in Peking by establishing full diplomatic relations with the People's Republic of China. This meant that America was withdrawing recognition from Taiwan as the rightful government of China and abrogating its defense treaty with that island republic, though it maintained the right to sell arms to Taiwan and extracted a vague promise from Peking not to invade the country. Carter's action infuriated conservative senators, despite the fact that it had been Richard Nixon who had paved the way for recognition of Mainland China, but others agreed with the White House press officer who said, 'The idea of our not having relations with nearly a billion people is just ridiculous.' Inadvertently, the President left no doubt about what he thought the popular response would be. Unaware that a microphone had not been turned off, Carter, after presenting the news to the country, was heard to murmur: 'Massive applause throughout the nation!'

Carter's greatest success, however fragile, came in the Middle East where he took the bold risk of inviting Prime Minister Menachem Begin of Israel and President Anwar el-Sadat of Egypt to meet with him in America in September 1978. It seemed highly likely that the gathering at Camp David, the presidential retreat in the Maryland hills, would end in failure, and when instead the three men emerged with the glad tidings that they had agreed in principle, Carter scored his most impressive personal triumph since entering the White House. The euphoria, though, proved to be short-lived. A revolution in Iran ended that country's status as a Western outpost in the Middle East; the American ambassador to Afghanistan was murdered; and, in March 1979, Carter found it necessary to fly to Egypt and to Israel in quest of a peace settlement. By then it had become painfully clear that in foreign affairs as in domestic policy, Carter had many hard miles to travel.

America in the Carter years no longer seemed confident that, in Lord Bryce's words, it 'sailed a summer sea.' Carter had been elected in the year that the United States celebrated its 200th birthday, but the bicentennial had been less an occasion for self-congratulation than for sober introspection. Pundits raised searching questions about whether the values that had served the republic well in the beginning were any longer appropriate. For much of their history Americans had been buoyed by the conviction that they dwelt in a Zion settled by Chosen People, that they were citizens of, in Jefferson's words, 'the only monument of human rights and the sole depository of the sacred fire of freedom and self-government,' from which was 'to be lighted up . . . other regions of the earth.' But critics now asked whether the myth of America's uniqueness had not led to an arrogance toward the rest of the world that culminated in imperial misadventures like Vietnam. They inquired, too, whether America's faith in perpetual progress was salutary in an era when dwindling resources and the aspirations of the Third World made it imperative to nurture the environment, discipline technology, and curb population growth, and whether the United States should not accept a sense of limits. 'For the first time in the nearly four centuries of the American experiment, America as a nation is encountering failure, the final frontier of every civilization,' commented a European observer. 'It has reached the termination of boundless potentiality.'

Yet America has repeatedly shown its capacity for self-renewal. It created a nation; peopled deserts and built great cities; cut the bonds of the black slave and made its industrial system more humane; resolved the baffling problem of federalism; devised political forms to permit majority rule but protect the rights of dissenters; and fostered an economic order which, for all its failings, provided more abundance than any other in history. As the United States moved toward the year 2000, it still had the resources of character and spirit to make an important contribution to the problems confronting the world.

Perhaps no one stated the realities that loomed in the last third of this century so well as had John Kennedy. In his moving talk to the Irish parliament, he said: 'Across the gulfs and barriers that now divide us, we must remember that there are no permanent enemies. Hostility today is a fact, but it is not a ruling law. The supreme reality of our time is our indivisibility as children of God and our common vulnerability on this planet.' Yet no one knew better than Kennedy how difficult was the road to peace, at home as well as abroad. In the last speech he ever gave, at Fort Worth on 21 November 1963, he warned: 'This is a dangerous and uncertain world. . . . No one expects our lives to be easy — not in this decade, not in this century.'

Bibliography

GENERAL WORKS

1. DICTIONARIES, ENCYCLOPEDIAS, AND REFERENCE BOOKS

The American Historical Review (1895–   ) reviews all new historical literature and includes important articles and documents. The annual *Reports* of the American Historical Association (1889–   , overlapped by 5 vols. of *Papers*, 1886–91, General Index, 1884–1914) include many other articles, monographs, and source materials.

The Mississippi Valley Historical Review (1915–   ), now *The Journal of American History*, also contains many general articles and documents.

U.S. Bureau of the Census, *Historical Statistics of the United States; Colonial Times to 1957*, and *Statistical Abstract of the United States* (89 annual editions through 1968).

J. R. Commons (ed.), *The Documentary History of American Industrial Society* (10 vols.).

Oscar Handlin *et al.*, *Harvard Guide to American History*. Part i, Status, Methods and Presentation; Part ii, Materials and Tools; Parts iii–vi, classified bibliographies on successive periods.

James L. Harrison, Paul C. Beach, *et al.* (eds.), *Biographical Directory of the American Congress, 1774–1949*.

Allen Johnson & Dumas Malone (eds.), *The Dictionary of American Biography* (22 vols.), and supplementary volumes.

Richard B. Morris, *Encyclopedia of American History*.

2. HISTORIES OF THE UNITED STATES

Daniel Boorstin (ed.), *The Chicago History of American Civilization*.

H. S. Commager & R. B. Morris (eds.), *The New American Nation Series.*

E. M. Coulter and Wendell Stephenson (eds.), *A History of the South* (10 vols.), Henry David *et al.* (eds.), *Economic History of the United States* (9 vols.).

Arthur M. Schlesinger and Dixon R. Fox (eds.), *History of American Life* (13 vols.). Social development is stressed.

3. ECONOMIC AND SOCIAL HISTORY

GENERAL. Stanley Coben and Forest G. Hill, *American Economic History;* H. U. Faulkner, *American Economic History;* E. C. Kirkland, *A History of American Economic Life;* F. J. Turner, *The Frontier in American History;* Joseph Dorfman, *The Economic Mind in American Civilization* (5 vols.); Ross Robertson, *History of the American Economy.*

LABOR. J. R. Commons *et al., History of Labor in the United States* (4 vols.); H. Harris, *American Labor;* Henry Pelling, *American Labor;* S. Perlman, *History of Trade Unionism in the United States.*

IMMIGRATION. Louis Adamic (ed.), *The Peoples of America* (9 vols.); Maurice Davie, *World Immigration;* Oscar Handlin, *The Uprooted;* Marcus L. Hansen, *The Immigrant in American History* and *The Atlantic Migration 1607–1860;* Maldwyn A. Jones, *American Immigration;* Carl Wittke, *We Who Built America; the Saga of the Immigrant.*

OTHER PHASES. Roy M. Robbins, *Our Landed Heritage: The Public Domain, 1776–1936.* Tariff: F. W. Taussig, *Tariff History of the U.S.,* and Edward Stanwood, *American Tariff Controversies in the 19th Century* (2 vols.). Banking and Finance: D. R. Dewey, *Financial History of the U.S.;* W. J. Schultz & M. B. Caine, *Financial Development of the United States;* and Milton Friedman and Anna Jacobson Schwartz, *A Monetary History of the United States.*

4. FOREIGN RELATIONS

S. F. Bemis, *The Diplomatic History of the United States* and (ed.) *The American Secretaries of State and Their Diplomacy* (10 vols.); T. A. Bailey, *A Diplomatic History of the American People;* Council on Foreign Relations, *Documents on American Foreign Relations* (since 1952) and *The United States in World Affairs* (since 1931). Department of State, *Papers relating to the Foreign Relations of the U.S.* (one or more annual vols.); W. M. Malloy (ed.), *Treaties . . . between the U.S. and Other Powers, 1778–1909* (2 vols.), with supplements; D. C. McKay (ed.), *The American Foreign Policy Library* (15 vols., 1948–58) is a series of popular monographs by specialists.

5. TRAVEL

H. S. Commager, *America in Perspective;* Oscar Handlin, *This Was America;* Frank Monaghan, *French Travelers in the U.S., 1765–1932;* H. T. Tuckerman, *America and Her Commentators.*

6. GOVERNMENT AND CONSTITUTIONAL HISTORY

W. P. Binkley, *American Political Parties;* Louis Boudin, *Government by Judiciary* (2 vols.); James Bryce, *American Commonwealth* (1888); A. H. Kelly & W. A. Harbison, *The American Constitution, Its Origins and Development;* A. C. McLaughlin, *Constitutional History of the United States;* C. B. Swisher, *American Constitutional Development;* A. de Tocqueville, *Democracy in America* (translated by H. S. Commager); Charles Warren, *The Supreme Court in United States History* (2 vols.); Woodrow Wilson, *Constitutional Government in the United States.*

7. COLLECTIONS OF DOCUMENTS AND OTHER SOURCES

H. S. Commager, *Documents of American History* runs parallel to this work; Aïda di Pace Donald (ed.), *American Profiles;* R. Leopold, A. Link, and S. Coben (eds.), *Problems in American History;* Marvin Meyers *et al., Sources of the American Republic* (2 vols.); Richard B. Morris (ed.), *Documentary History of the United States;* E. E. Saveth, *Understanding the American Past* (extracts from historians' writings).

8. GEOGRAPHY

J. T. Adams, *Atlas of American History;* Isaiah Bowman, *Forest Physiography;* Ralph H. Brown, *Historical Geography of the U.S.;* Ralph H. Brown, *Historical Geography of the United States;* V. J. Esposito, *West Point Atlas of American Wars;* Harper's *Atlas of American History;* A. B. Hulbert (ed.), *Historic Highways of America* (16 vols.); C. E. Lord & E. H. Lord, *Historical Atlas of the United States;* C. O. Paullin, *Atlas of Historical Geography of the U.S.*

9. LITERATURE, PHILOSOPHY, AND RELIGION

LITERATURE. W. R. Benét & N. H. Pearson, *Oxford Anthology of American Literature;* Van Wyck Brooks, *Makers and Finders: A History of the Writer in America* (5 vols.); Harry H. Clark (ed.), *The American Writers Series* (*c.* 30 vols.); James D. Hart (ed.), *Oxford Companion to American Literature;* Jay Hubbell, *The South in Literature, 1607–1900;* Frank Luther Mott, *History of American Magazines* (4 vols.); V. L. Parrington, *Main Currents of American Thought* (3 vols.); Henry Pochmann, *German Culture in America;* R. E. Spiller, *et al.* (eds.), *Literary History of the United States*

(3 vols.); W. P. Trent (ed.), *Cambridge History of American Literature* (4 vols.).

PHILOSOPHY. Joseph Blau (ed.), *American Philosophical Addresses* and *Men and Movements in American Philosophy;* Merle Curti, *Growth of American Thought;* Herbert Schneider, *History of American Philosophy;* Stow Persons, *American Minds.*

RELIGION. Nelson Burr, *Critical Bibliography of Religion in America* (2 vols.); James W. Smith, *et al.* (eds.), *Religion in American Life* (3 vols.); Anson P. Stokes, *Church and State in the United States* (3 vols.).

10. THE FINE ARTS AND MUSIC

Wayne Andrews, *Architecture in America;* C. W. Condit, *American Building Art: The Nineteenth Century;* Royal Cortissoz, *History of American Painting;* L. H. Dodd, *The Golden Age of American Sculpture;* L. C. Elson, *The History of American Music;* J. T. Howard, *Our American Music;* O. W. Larkin, *Art and Life in America;* Lewis Mumford, *The Culture of the Cities, The City in History, Sticks and Stones,* and *Technics and Civilization;* E. P. Richardson, *Painting in America, the Story of 450 Years;* Jacques Schnier, *Sculpture in Modern America.*

11. MILITARY AND NAVAL HISTORY

Robert Heinl, *A History of the U.S. Marine Corps;* Dudley W. Knox, *A History of the U.S. Navy;* Walter Millis, *Arms and Men;* E. B. Potter (ed.), *Sea Power;* Colonel O. H. Spaulding, *The U.S. Army in War and Peace.*

12. THE HISTORY OF HISTORY

Herman Ausubel, *Historians and Their Craft;* H. Hale Bellot, *American History and Historians;* William T. Hutchinson (ed.), *The Marcus Jernegan Essays in American Historiography;* Michael Kraus, *A History of American History;* Allan Nevins, *The Gateway to History;* David Van Tassel, *Recording America's Past;* Harvey Wish, *The American Historian.*

CHAPTER I

1. GENERAL. Robert G. Athearn, *High Country Empire;* Ray Billington, *Westward Expansion;* Harold E. Briggs, *Frontiers of the Northwest;* Everett Dick, *The Sod House Frontier, 1854–1890;* Gilbert W. Fite, *The Farmer's Frontier;* Eugene W. Hollon, *The Southwest;* Paul Horgan, *Great River;* James C. Malin, *The Grassland of North America;* Earl Pomeroy, *The Pacific Slope;* Robert E. Riegel and Robert G. Athearn, *America Moves West;* Fred A. Shannon, *The Farmer's Last Frontier;* Walter P. Webb, *The Great Plains* and *The Great Frontier.*

2. THE INDIAN BARRIER. *American Heritage Book of Indians;* E. D. Branch, *The Hunting of the Buffalo;* John Collier, *Indians of the Americas;* James H. Cook, *Fifty Years on the Old Frontier;* George Crook, *General George Crook: His Autobiography;* Chester A. Fee, *Chief Joseph;* Grant Foreman, *The Five Civilized Tribes;* G. B. Grinnell, *The Story of the Indian* and *The Cheyenne Indians* (2 vols.); W. T. Hagan, *American Indians;* Helen Hunt Jackson, *A Century of Dishonor;* J. P. Kinney, *A Continent Lost, a Civilization Won;* E. P. Priest, *Uncle Sam's Stepchildren 1865–1887;* Paul Radin, *The Story of the American Indian;* B. N. Richardson, *The Comanche Barrier to the South Plains Settlement;* Flora W. Seymour, *Indian Agents of the Old Frontier;* Philip Sheridan, *Personal Memoirs* (2 vols.); Walter P. Webb, *The Texas Rangers.*

3. THE MINING FRONTIER. Hubert H. Bancroft, *Popular Tribunals* (2 vols.); Dan De Quille, *The Big Bonanza;* Russell R. Elliott, *Nevada's Twentieth Century Mining Boom;* C. W. Glassock, *Gold in Them Hills, The War of the Copper Kings,* and *The Big Bonanza;* W. Turrentine Jackson, *Treasure Hill;* Nathaniel P. Langford, *Vigilante Days and Ways;* Oscar Lewis, *Silver Kings;* George D. Lyman, *Saga of the Comstock Lode;* Effie M. Mack, *Nevada, a History of the State;* W. P. Morrell, *The Gold Rushes;* Rodman Paul, *California Gold* and *Mining Frontiers of the Far West;* Paul C. Phillips (ed.), *Forty Years on the Frontier: Journals and Reminiscences of Granville Stuart* (2 vols.); T. A. Rickard, *The History of American Mining;* Clark C. Spence, *British Investments and the American Mining Frontier, 1860–1901;* C. H. Shinn, *Mining Camps: A Study in American Frontier Government;* W. J. Trimble, *The Mining Advance into the Inland Empire;* Mark Twain, *Roughing It.*

4. CATTLE KINGDOM. Andy Adams, *The Log of a Cowboy;* Lewis Atherton, *The Cattle Kings;* E. D. Branch, *The Cowboy and His Interpreters;* Merrill Burlingame, *The Montana Frontier;* Robert Cleland, *Cattle on a Thousand Hills;* Edward E. Dale, *Cow Country* and *The Cattle Range Industry;* J. Frank Dobie, *A Vaquero of the Brush Country;* Joe B. Frantz & Julian Choate, *The American Cowboy: The Myth and the Reality;* G. R. Hebard & E. A. Brininstool, *The Bozeman Trail* (2 vols.); Stuart Henry, *Conquering Our Great American Plains;* Emerson Hough, *The Story of the Cowboy;* Winifred Kupper, *The Golden Hoof: The Story of the Sheep of the Southwest;* John Lomax, *Cowboy Songs* and *Songs of the Cattle Trail and Cow Camp;* Ernest S. Osgood, *The Day of the Cattlemen;* O. B. Peake, *The Colorado Cattle Range Industry;* Louis Pelzer, *The Cattleman's Frontier, 1850–1890;* Samuel P. Ridings, *The Chisholm Trail;* P. A. Rollins, *The Cowboy;* John T. Schlebecker, *Cattle Raising on the Plains, 1900–61;* Fred Shannon, *The Farmer's*

Last Frontier; Charles W. Towne & Edward N. Wentworth, *Shepherd's Empire;* Walter Webb, *The Great Plains;* Paul I. Wellman, *The Trampling Herd;* Edward Wentworth, *America's Sheep Trails.*

5. PASSING OF THE FRONTIER AND ORGANIZATION OF THE WEST. Leonard J. Arrington, *Great Basin Kingdom;* R. G. Athearn, *William Tecumseh Sherman and the Settlement of the West;* Mary Austin, *The Land of Little Rain;* Harold E. Briggs, *Frontiers of the Northwest;* Willa Cather, *O Pioneers, My Ántonia,* and *A Lost Lady;* Robert Cleland, *California* (2 vols.); Everett Dick, *Vanguards of the Frontier;* Edna Ferber, *Cimarron;* Dixon Ryan Fox (ed.), *Sources of Culture in the Middle West: Backgrounds versus Frontier;* Hamlin Garland, *A Son of the Middle Border* and *Boy Life on the Prairie;* Paul W. Gates, *Frontier Landlords and Pioneer Tenants;* Alfred B. Guthrie, *The Big Sky* and *The Way West;* John D. Hicks, *The Constitutions of the Northwest States;* John Ise, *Sod and Stubble: The Story of a Kansas Homestead;* Marquis James, *Cherokee Strip;* Richard Lillard, *Desert Challenge: An Interpretation of Nevada;* James C. Malin, *Winter Wheat in the Golden Belt of Kansas;* J. C. Parish, *The Persistence of the Westward Movement;* R. N. Richardson, *Texas, the Lone Star State;* Roy Robbins, *Our Landed Heritage;* Ole Rölvaag, *Giants in the Earth;* Robert Taft, *Artists and Illustrators of the Old West, 1850–1900;* Frederick J. Turner, *Significance of the Frontier in American History.*

6. DOCUMENTS. H. S. Commager, *Documents,* nos. 302, 304, 315; Robert W. Richmond and Robert W. Mardock, *A Nation Moving West;* Clark C. Spence, *The American West;* Robert V. Hine and Edwin R. Bingham, *The Frontier Experience;* Stanley Vestal, *New Sources of Indian History.*

For further references, *Harvard Guide,* ¶¶ 196, 198, 199, 208.

CHAPTER II

1. GENERAL. G. D. Bradley, *Story of the Santa Fe;* Stuart Daggett, *Chapters on the History of the Southern Pacific;* J. P. Davis, *The Union Pacific Railroad;* Carl Russell Fish, *Restoration of the Southern Railroads;* Paul Gates, *The Illinois Central Railroad and Its Colonization Work;* Julius Grodinsky, *Jay Gould* and *Transcontinental Railway Strategy;* Edward Hungerford, *The Story of the Baltimore and Ohio Railroad* (2 vols.); George Kennan, *Life of E. H. Harriman* (2 vols.); Edward C. Kirkland, *Men, Cities and Transportation, 1820–1900* (2 vols.); Wheaton Lane, *Commodore Vanderbilt;* Oscar Lewis, *The Big Four;* John Moody, *The Railroad Builders;* E. H. Mott, *Between the Ocean and the Lakes: The Story of Erie;* J. G. Pyle, *James J. Hill*

(2 vols.); William Z. Ripley, *Railroads: Rates and Regulations* (2 vols.) and *Railroads, Finance and Organization;* E. L. Sabin, *Building the Pacific Railway;* Eugene Smalley, *History of the Northern Pacific Railroad;* J. F. Stover, *American Railroads;* G. R. Taylor & I. D. Neu, *The American Railroad Network;* Nelson Trottman, *History of the Union Pacific.*

2. RAILROADS AND THE WEST. Thomas Cochran, *Railroad Leaders, 1845–1890;* Thomas Donaldson, *The Public Domain;* Robert W. Fogel, *Railroads and American Economic Growth* and *The Union Pacific Railroad;* L. H. Haney, *Congressional History of Railways, 1850–1887;* J. B. Hedges, *Henry Villard and the Railways of the Northwest;* R. C. Overton, *Burlington West: A Colonization History of the Burlington Railroad;* J. R. Perkins, *Trails, Rails and War: The Life of Grenville Dodge;* Glenn C. Quiett, *They Built the West;* Robert E. Riegel, *The Story of the Western Railroads;* Robert L. Thompson, *Wiring a Continent.*

3. REGULATION. Charles F. Adams, *Railroads;* Solon J. Buck, *The Granger Movement;* E. G. Campbell, *The Reorganization of the American Railroad System 1893–1900;* F. A. Cleveland & F. W. Powell, *Railway Promotion and Capitalization;* J. B. Crawford, *The Credit Mobilier of America;* Felix Frankfurter, *The Commerce Clause under Marshall, Taney and Waite;* Matthew Josephson, *The Robber Barons* and *The Politicos;* William Larrabee, *The Railroad Question;* Frederick Merk, *Economic History of Wisconsin;* W. Z. Ripley, *Rates and Regulations;* Fred Shannon, *The Farmer's Last Frontier;* I. L. Sharfman, *The Interstate Commerce Commission* (5 vols.).

4. THE DECLINE OF STEAMBOATING. Norman Beasley, *Freighters of Fortune;* G. A. Cuthbertson, *Freshwater: A Narrative of the Great Lakes;* G. E. Eskew, *Pageant of the Packets;* Walter Havighurst, *The Long Ships Passing;* W. J. Peterson, *Steamboating on the Upper Mississippi;* Herbert Quick, *Mississippi Steamboating;* Mark Twain, *Life on the Mississippi.*

5. DOCUMENTS. H. S. Commager, *Documents,* nos. 215, 294, 314, 318, 319; A. R. Ellingwood and W. Coombs (eds.), *The Government and Railroad Transportation;* W. Z. Ripley, *Railway Problems.*

For further references, *Harvard Guide,* ¶¶ 197, 200.

CHAPTER III

1. GENERAL. Ralph Andreano (ed.), *New Views on American Economic Development;* Alfred D. Chandler, Jr., *Giant Enterprise* and *Strategy and*

Structure; Victor S. Clark, *History of Manufactures in the United States 1860–1914;* Stanley Coben & Forest G. Hill (eds.), *American Economic History;* Thomas Cochran & William Miller, *The Age of Enterprise;* Rendigs Fels, *American Business Cycles, 1865–1897;* Milton Friedman and A. J. Schwartz, *A Monetary History of the United States;* Samuel P. Hays, *The Response to Industrialism;* Edward C. Kirkland, *A History of American Economic Life* and *Industry Comes of Age: Business, Labor and Public Policy, 1860–1897;* Simon Kuznets, *National Income;* Lewis Mumford, *Technics and Civilization;* William N. Parker, (ed.), *Trends in the American Economy in the Nineteenth Century;* Sidney Ratner, *American Taxation as a Social Force;* Ross Robertson, *History of the American Economy;* Fred A. Shannon, *America's Economic Growth;* Ida Tarbell, *The Nationalization of Business.*

2. SPECIAL INDUSTRIES AND INDUSTRIAL LEADERS. Frederick L. Allen, *The Great Pierpont Morgan;* Stanley Buder, *Pullman;* R. A. Clemen, *American Live Stock and Meat Industry;* A. H. Cole, *The American Wool Manufacture* (2 vols.); Lewis Corey, *The House of Morgan;* Richard Current, *The Typewriter and the Men Who Made It;* Paul de Kruif, *Seven Iron Men;* Paul Giddens, *The Birth of the Oil Industry* and *The Standard Oil Company of Indiana;* Burton J. Hendrick, *Andrew Carnegie* (2 vols.); Ralph and Muriel Hidy, *Pioneering in Big Business: The Standard Oil Company of New Jersey;* William T. Hutchinson, *Cyrus McCormick* (2 vols.); Meyer Jacobstein, *The Tobacco Industry;* Marquis James, *Alfred I. DuPont;* Henrietta Larson, *Jay Cooke: Private Banker;* John Moody, *Masters of Capital;* S. E. Morison, *The Ropemakers of Plymouth;* Allan Nevins, *John D. Rockefeller* (2 vols.) and *Abram Hewitt: With Some Account of Peter Cooper;* Allan Nevins & F. E. Hill, *Henry Ford* (3 vols.); H. C. Passer, *The Electric Manufacturers;* C. C. Rister, *Oil: Titan of the Southwest;* Peter Temin, *Iron and Steel in Nineteenth Century America;* H. F. Williamson and A. H. Daum, *The American Petroleum Industry;* F. P. Wirth, *Discovery and Exploitation of the Minnesota Iron Lands.*

3. TRUSTS AND TRUST REGULATION. A. A. Berle and G. S. Means, *Modern Corporation and Private Property;* J. D. Clark, *Federal Trust Policy;* John R. Commons, *Legal Foundations of Capitalism;* Eliot Jones, *The Trust Problem in the United States;* Dexter Keezer & Stacy May, *Public Control of Business;* O. W. Knauth, *The Policy of the United States Towards Industrial Monopoly;* Harry W. Laidler, *Concentration of Control in American Industry;* Henry D. Lloyd, *Wealth Against Commonwealth;* John Moody, *The Truth About the Trusts;* G. W. Nutter, *Extent of Enterprise Monopoly;* W. Z. Ripley, *Trusts, Pools, and Corporations;* H. R. Seager & G. A. Gulick, *Trust and Cor-*

poration Problems; Hans B. Thorelli, *Federal Anti-Trust Policy;* Albert Walker, *History of the Sherman Law.*

4. INVENTIONS. Roger Burlingame, *Engines of Democracy;* T. K. Derry and Trevor Williams, *A Short History of Technology to A.D. 1900;* Siegfried Giedion, *Mechanization Takes Command;* Harry Jerome, *Mechanization in Industry;* Matthew Josephson, *Edison;* Waldemar Kaempffert, *Popular History of American Inventions* (2 vols.); J. W. Oliver, *History of American Technology;* Michael Pupin, *From Immigrant to Inventor;* Holland Thompson, *The Age of Invention.*

5. BIG BUSINESS AND ITS PHILOSOPHY. Charles Barker, *Henry George;* F. B. Copley, *Frederick Taylor: Father of Scientific Management;* Sigmund Diamond, *The Reputation of the American Businessman;* Joseph Dorfman, *Economic Thought in American Civilization,* vol. 3; Sidney Fine, *Lassez Faire and the General Welfare State;* Richard Hofstadter, *Social Darwinism in the United States;* Edward C. Kirkland, *Business in the Gilded Age;* Robert G. McCloskey, *American Conservatism in the Age of Enterprise;* J. D. Rockefeller, *Random Reminiscences of Men and Events;* William G. Sumner, *The Forgotten Man and Other Essays;* Thorstein Veblen, *Theory of Business Enterprise;* Lester Ward, *Psychic Factors in Civilization;* Irvin Wyllie, *The Self-Made Man in America.*

6. DOCUMENTS. H. S. Commager, *Documents,* nos. 215, 231, 320, 339; H. U. Faulkner & F. Flugel, *Readings in the Economic History of the United States.*

For further references, *Harvard Guide,* ¶¶ 202, 206, 210.

CHAPTER IV

1. GENERAL. David Brody, *Butcher Workmen* and *Steelworkers in America;* Robert Christie, *Empire in Wood;* John R. Commons, *et al., History of Labor in the United States,* vols. 3 and 4; Gerald Grob, *Workers and Utopia;* A. L. Harris, *The Black Worker;* Herbert Harris, *American Labor;* Edward C. Kirkland, *Industry Comes of Age: Business, Labor and Public Policy, 1860–1897;* L. L. Lorwin, *The American Federation of Labor;* H. Wayne Morgan (ed.), *The Gilded Age;* Henry Pelling, *American Labor;* Mark Perlman, *The Machinists;* Selig Perlman, *History of Trade Unionism in the United States* and *A Theory of the Labor Movement;* Philip Taft, *The A. F. of L. in the Time of Gompers;* Frank Tannenbaum, *A Philosophy of Labor;* Lloyd Ulman, *The*

Rise of the National Trade Union; Norman J. Ware, *Labor Movement in the United States 1860–1895;* Charles H. Wesley, *Negro Labor in the United States 1850–1925;* Leo Wolman, *Growth of American Trade Unions 1880–1923.*

2. LABOR LEADERS AND LEADERSHIP. Charles Barker, *Henry George;* Harry Barnard, *Eagle Forgotten* (John P. Altgeld); C. R. Geiger, *The Philosophy of Henry George;* Ray Ginger, *The Bending Cross* (Eugene V. Debs); Elsie Glück, *John Mitchell;* Samuel Gompers, *Seventy Years of Life and Labor* (2 vols.); Jonathan Grossman, *William E. Sylvis;* R. E. Harvey, *Samuel Gompers;* Bernard Mandel, *Samuel Gompers;* A. E. Morgan, *Edward Bellamy;* Terence Powderly, *The Path I Trod;* Louis Reed, *Philosophy of Gompers;* Lincoln Steffens, *Autobiography* (2 vols.); Graham Taylor, *Pioneering on Social Frontiers.*

3. LABOR CONFLICTS AND INDUSTRIAL VIOLENCE. Louis Adamic, *Dynamite;* Paul W. Brissenden, *The I.W.W.;* W. G. Broehl, Jr., *The Molly Maguires;* J. R. Brooks, *American Syndicalism;* Robert Bruce, *1877: Year of Violence;* J. W. Coleman, *The Molly Maguire Riots;* J. R. Commons, et al., *History of Labor in the United States,* vol. 4; Henry David, *History of the Haymarket Affair;* Carter Goodrich, *The Miner's Freedom;* Harry W. Laidler, *Boycott and Labor Struggles;* Almont Lindsey, *The Pullman Strike;* B. S. Mitchell, *Textile Unionism in the South;* C. H. Parker, *The Casual Laborer and Other Essays;* Benjamin Rastall, *Labor History of the Cripple Creek District;* Tom Tippett, *When Southern Labor Stirs;* Leon Wolff, *Lookout:* Samuel Yellen, *American Labor Struggles.*

4. NOVELS PORTRAYING LABOR. Sherwood Anderson, *Marching Men;* Frank Harris, *The Bomb;* John Hay, *The Breadwinners;* Robert Herrick, *Memoirs of an American Citizen;* William D. Howells, *A Hazard of New Fortunes;* Jack London, *The Iron Heel;* Ernest Poole, *The Harbour;* Upton Sinclair, *The Jungle.*

5. LABOR LEGISLATION AND THE COURTS. Edith Abbott, *Women in Industry;* Edward Berman, *Labor and the Sherman Act;* M. C. Cahill, *Shorter Hours;* John R. Commons & J. B. Andrews, *Principles of Labor Legislation;* John R. Commons (ed.), *History of Labor in the United States,* vol. 3; Paul Douglas, *Social Security in the United States;* E. H. Downey, *Workmen's Compensation;* Felix Frankfurter & N. V. Greene, *The Labor Injunction;* Ernst Freund, *The Police Power;* R. Fuller, *Child Labor and the Constitution;* G. G. Groat, *Attitude of American Courts on Labor Cases;* Clyde E. Jacobs,

Law Writers and the Courts; Marc Karson, *American Labor Unions and Politics;* John Lombardi, *Labor's Voice in the Cabinet;* A. T. Mason, *Organized Labor and the Law;* I. M. Rubinow, *Social Insurance;* John Spargo, *Bitter Cry of the Children;* H. L. Sumner and E. A. Merritt, *Child Labor Legislation in the United States;* Edward E. Witte, *The Government in Labor Disputes;* Irwin Yellowitz, *Labor and the Progressive Movement in New York.*

6. DOCUMENTS. Edith Abbott (ed.), *Immigration: Select Documents and Case Records;* H. S. Commager, *Documents,* nos. 233, 295, 301, 326, 334–6, 364–6, 368; John R. Commons (ed.), *Documentary History of American Industrial Society,* vols. 4–6; A. R. Ellingswood & W. Coombs, *The Government and Labor;* James M. Landis, *Cases on Labor Law;* Carl Rauschenbush & Emmanuel Stein, *Labor Cases and Materials.*

For further references, *Harvard Guide,* ¶¶ 205, 210.

CHAPTER V

1. GENERAL. H. S. Commager (ed.), *Immigration and American History;* John R. Commons, *Races and Immigrants in America;* Oscar Handlin, *Boston's Immigrants, The Uprooted,* and *Immigration as a Factor in American History;* Marcus Hansen, *The Atlantic Migration* and *The Immigrant in American History;* M. A. Jones, *American Immigration;* Moses Rischin, *Promised City;* Carl Wittke, *We Who Built America.*

2. SPECIAL GROUPS. K. C. Babcock, *Scandinavian Element in the United States;* Emily G. Balch, *Our Slavic Fellow Citizens;* Gunter Barth, *Bitter Strength;* Rowland Berthoff, *British Immigration to Industrial America 1790–1850;* Kenneth O. Bjork, *West of the Great Divide: Norwegian Migration to the Pacific Coast;* Theodore C. Blegen, *Norwegian Migration to America* (2 vols.); Thomas Capek, *The Czechs in America;* Jerome Davis, *The Russian Immigrant;* A. B. Faust, *German Element in the United States* (2 vols.); Robert Foerster, *The Italian Emigration of Our Times;* Manuel Gamio, *Mexican Immigration to the United States;* Eric F. Hirshler (ed.), *Jews from Germany in the United States;* Florence E. Janson, *The Background of Swedish Immigration 1846–1930;* Henry S. Lucas, *Netherlanders in America 1789–1950;* William Mulder, *Homeward to Zion: Mormon Migration from Scandinavia;* Henry Pochmann, *German Culture in America;* C. C. Qualey, *Norwegian Settlement in the United States;* Theodore Saloutos, *The Greeks in the United States* and *They Remember America;* Arnold Schrier, *Ireland and the American Emigration 1850–1900;* Betty Lee Sung, *Mountain of Gold: The*

Story of the Chinese in America; William I. Thomas and Florian Znaniecki, *The Polish Peasant in Europe and America;* Carl Wittke, *The Irish in America.*

3. IMMIGRATION RESTRICTION. Marion T. Bennett, *American Immigration Policies;* William Bernard (ed.), *American Immigration Policy — A Reappraisal;* Jane P. Clark, *Deportation of Aliens from the United States to Europe;* R. L. Garis, *Immigration Restriction;* John Higham, *Strangers in the Land;* I. S. Hourwich, *Immigration and Labor;* Rodman Paul, *The Abrogation of the Gentlemen's Agreement;* Barbara Solomon, *Ancestors and Immigrants.*

4. IMMIGRANT AUTOBIOGRAPHIES, LETTERS, AND NOVELS. Louis Adamic, *Native's Return;* Mary Antin, *The Promised Land;* Theodore C. Blegen, *Land of their Choice: The Immigrants Write Home;* Abraham Cahan, *The Rise of David Levinsky;* Willa Cather, *My Antonia;* Alan Conway, *The Welsh in America: Letters from Immigrants;* Henry S. Lucas, *Dutch Immigrant Memoirs and Related Writings* (2 vols.); Jerre Mangone, *Mount Allegro;* Michael Pupin, *From Immigrant to Inventor;* Jacob Riis, *How the Other Half Lives* and *The Making of an American;* Ole Rölvaag, *Giants in the Earth* and *Peder Victorious;* Theodore Saloutos, *They Remember America.*

5. DOCUMENTS. Edith Abbott (ed.), *Historical Aspects of Immigration Problems* and *Immigration: Select Documents and Case Records;* H. S. Commager, *Documents,* nos. 233, 257, 306–7, 404, 422, 453.

For further references, *Harvard Guide,* ¶¶ 211, 226.

CHAPTER VI

1. GENERAL. L. H. Bailey, *Cyclopedia of American Agriculture* (4 vols.); O. E. Baker (ed.), *Atlas of American Agriculture;* Murray Benedict, *Farm Policies of the United States 1790–1950;* Ernest L. Bogart, *Economic History of American Agriculture;* Allan Bogue, *From Prairie to Corn Belt* and *Money at Interest;* Benjamin H. Hibbard, *A History of Public Land Policies;* Merrill Jarchow, *The Earth Brought Forth: Minnesota Agriculture to 1885;* Howard Odum, *Southern Regions of the United States;* E. L. Peffer, *The Closing of the Public Domain;* Willard Range, *A Century of Georgia Agriculture;* Roy Robbins, *Our Landed Heritage;* Aaron Sakolski, *The Great American Land Bubble;* Joseph Schafer, *Social History of American Agriculture* and *History of Agriculture in Wisconsin;* Fred A. Shannon, *The Farmer's Last Frontier;* C. C. Taylor, *The Farmers' Movement, 1620–1920;* Hamlin Garland, *Main-Travelled Roads;* U.S. Dept. of Agriculture, *Yearbook, 1889: Progress of*

Agriculture in the United States and *Yearbook, 1940: American Agriculture, the First Three Hundred Years;* Rupert Vance, *Human Geography of the South;* Walter Webb, *The Great Plains;* Harold Wilson, *The Hill Country of Northern New England;* C. Vann Woodward, *Origins of the New South.*

2. FARM PROBLEM AND AGRARIAN REVOLT. A. M. Arnett, *Populist Movement in Georgia;* Lee Benson, *Merchants, Farmers, and the Railroads;* R. P. Brooks, *The Agrarian Revolution in Georgia;* Solon J. Buck, *The Granger Movement* and *The Agrarian Crusade;* J. B. Clark, *Populism in Alabama;* Everett Dick, *The Sod House Frontier;* Elmer Ellis, *Henry Moore Teller;* Nathan Fine, *Labor and Farmer Parties in the U.S.;* P. R. Fossum, *The Agrarian Movement in North Dakota;* Paul Gates, *Fifty Million Acres: Conflicts over Kansas Land Policy;* Marion Harrington, *Populist Movement in Georgia;* F. E. Haynes, *James Baird Weaver* and *Third Party Movements Since the Civil War;* John D. Hicks, *The Populist Revolt;* O. M. Kile, *Farm Bureau Movement;* Stuart Noblin, *L. L. Polk;* Charles Otken, *The Ills of the South;* Martin Ridge, *Ignatius Donnelly;* Theodore Saloutos, *Farmer Movements in the South, 1865–1933;* Theodore Saloutos & J. D. Hicks, *Agrarian Discontent in the Middle West;* Roger Shugg, *Origins of the Class Struggle in Louisiana;* F. P. Simkins, *The Tillman Movement in South Carolina;* William Allen White, *Autobiography;* C. Vann Woodward, *Tom Watson.*

3. MACHINERY, SCIENCE, AND THE GOVERNMENT. R. L. Ardrey, *American Agricultural Implements;* Joseph Bailey, *Seaman A. Knapp;* H. N. Casson, *The Romance of the Reaper;* Paul de Kruif, *Hunger Fighters;* Philip Dorf, *Liberty H. Bailey;* L. W. Ellis & E. A. Rumely, *Power and the Plow;* Rackham Holt, *George Washington Carver;* L. D. Howard, *Fighting the Insects;* William T. Hutchinson, *Cyrus Hall McCormick* (2 vols.); D. S. Jordan & V. Kellogg, *The Scientific Aspects of Luther Burbank's Work;* Waldemar Kaempffert, *Popular History of American Inventions,* vol. 2; Leo Rogin, *Introduction of Farm Machinery in Its Relations . . . to Labor;* E. D. Ross, *Democracy's College: The Land Grant Movement in the Formative Stage;* W. H. Shepardson, *Agricultural Education in the United States;* William E. Smythe, *Conquest of Arid America;* Ray P. Teile, *Economics of Land Reclamation in the United States;* George Thomas, *Development of Institutions under Irrigation;* A. C. True & V. A. Clark, *Agricultural Experiment Stations in the United States;* W. L. Wanlass, *The United States Department of Agriculture.*

4. NOVELS. Louis Bromfield, *The Farm;* Gladys Hasty Carroll, *As the Earth Turns;* Willa Cather, *My Ántonia, O Pioneers!* and *A Lost Lady;* Doro-

thy Dondore, *The Prairie and the Making of Middle America;* Edna Ferber, *American Beauty;* Hamlin Garland, *Boy Life on the Prairie, Son of the Middle Border,* and *A Spoil of Office;* Ellen Glasgow, *Barren Ground;* Lucy Hazard, *The Frontier in American Literature;* Ed Howe, *The Story of a Country Town;* Frank Norris, *The Octopus;* Herbert Quick, *Vandemark's Folly* and *The Hawkeye;* Ole Rölvaag, *Giants in the Earth;* Thomas Stribling, *The Forge* and *The Store;* Ruth Suckow, *Folks* and *Iowa Interiors;* William Allen White, *The Heart of a Fool;* Margaret Wilson, *The Able McLaughlins.*

5. DOCUMENTS. H. S. Commager, *Documents,* nos. 214, 216, 316, 323–5; L. B. Schmidt & E. B. Ross, *Readings in the Economic History of American Agriculture.*

For further references, see *Harvard Guide,* ¶¶ 199, 209.

CHAPTER VII

1. GENERAL. Herbert Agar, *The Price of Union;* James Bryce, *The American Commonwealth* (2 vols.); Harold U. Faulkner, *Politics, Reform and Expansion 1890–1900;* Sidney Fine, *Laissez Faire and the General Welfare State;* Eric Goldman, *Rendezvous with Destiny;* Stanley Hirshson, *Farewell to the Bloody Shirt;* Richard Hofstadter, *American Political Tradition;* J. R. Hollingsworth, *The Whirligig of Politics;* Matthew Josephson, *The Politicos;* Horace Merrill, *Bourbon Democracy in the Middle West 1865–1896;* Russel B. Nye, *Midwestern Progressive Politics 1870–1950;* Ellis P. Oberholtzer, *History of the United States since the Civil War,* vol. 4; James Ford Rhodes, *History of the United States from Hayes to McKinley;* David Rothman, *Politics and Power;* Edward Stanwood, *American Tariff Controversies;* H. C. Thomas, *Return of the Democratic Party to Power;* Charles Warren, *History of the Supreme Court,* vol. 2; Leonard D. White, *The Republican Era 1865–1900;* William A. White, *Masks in a Pageant* and *Autobiography.*

2. REFORM. Geoffrey Blodgett, *The Gentle Reformers;* Carl Russell Fish, *The Civil Service and the Patronage;* E. L. Godkin, *Problems of Modern Democracy;* H. F. Gosnell, *Boss Platt and the New York Machine;* Ari Hoogenboom, *Fighting the Spoilsmen;* Carl Schurz, *Reminiscences* (one-vol. ed. by Wayne Andrews); P. P. Van Riper, *History of the United States Civil Service.*

3. BIOGRAPHIES. Harry Barnard, *Eagle Forgotten: Life of John P. Altgeld;* James J. Barnes, *John G. Carlisle;* Herbert Bass, *"I Am a Democrat";* Herbert

Croly, *Mark Hanna;* Claude Fuess, *Carl Schurz;* Mark A. Hirsch, *William C. Whitney;* George Hoar, *Autobiography of Seventy Years;* G. F. Howe, *Chester A. Arthur;* Walter Johnson, *William Allen White's America;* Margaret Leech, *In the Days of McKinley;* David S. Muzzey, *James G. Blaine;* Allan Nevins, *Grover Cleveland;* William A. Robinson, *Thomas B. Reed;* H. J. Sievers, *Benjamin Harrison;* T. C. Smith, *Life and Letters of James A. Garfield* (2 vols.); Festus Summers, *William L. Wilson and Tariff Reform;* Nathaniel W. Stephenson, *Nelson Aldrich;* J. F. Wall, *Henry Watterson;* Charles R. Williams, *Life of Rutherford B. Hayes* (2 vols.).

4. DOCUMENTS. H. S. Commager, *Documents,* nos. 297, 299, 300, 303, 308, 312, 317.

For further references, see *Harvard Guide,* ¶¶ 193, 203, 204.

CHAPTER VIII

1. GENERAL. Joseph Dorfman, *Economic Mind in American Civilization,* vol. 3; Harold U. Faulkner, *Politics, Reform and Expansion, 1890–1900* and *The Decline of Laissez Faire;* Sidney Fine, *Laissez Faire and the General Welfare State;* Eric Goldman, *Rendezvous with Destiny;* Richard Hofstadter, *The Age of Reform;* Matthew Josephson, *The Politicos* and *The President Makers;* Edward C. Kirkland, *Industry Comes of Age;* H. S. Merrill, *Bourbon Democracy in the Middle West;* Allan Nevins, *Grover Cleveland;* Arthur Schlesinger, *The Rise of the City;* William Allen White, *Masks in a Pageant.*

2. THE MONEY QUESTION AND THE PANIC OF 1893. James A. Barnes, *John C. Carlisle;* David R. Dewey, *Financial History of the United States;* Matilda Gresham, *Life of Walter Q. Gresham* (2 vols.); Mark D. Hirsch, *William C. Whitney;* W. J. Lauck, *Causes of the Panic of 1893;* J. Lawrence Laughlin, *History of Bimetallism in the United States;* D. L. McMurray, *Coxey's Army;* Wesley C. Mitchell, *A History of Greenbacks;* Alexander D. Noyes, *Forty Years of American Finance, 1865–1907;* Sidney Ratner, *American Taxation;* Irwin Unger, *The Greenback Era;* Charles Warren, *The Supreme Court,* vol. 2; F. P. Weberg, *Background of the Panic of 1893;* M. S. Wildman, *Money Inflation in the United States.*

3. THE POPULIST REVOLT. Alex M. Arnett, *The Populist Movement in Georgia;* Harry Barnard, *Eagle Forgotten: John Peter Altgeld;* John B. Clark, *Populism in Alabama;* John D. Hicks, *The Populist Revolt;* A. D. Kirwan, *Revolt of the Rednecks;* W. T. K. Nugent, *The Tolerant Populists;* Russel B. Nye,

Midwestern Progressive Politics; Norman Pollack, *The Populist Response to Industrial America;* Fred A. Shannon, *The Farmer's Last Frontier;* William D. Sheldon, *Populism in the Old Dominion;* Francis Simkins, *The Tillman Movement in South Carolina;* C. Vann Woodward, *Tom Watson: Agrarian Rebel.*

4. BRYAN AND THE ELECTION OF 1896. William J. Bryan, *Memoirs* and *The First Battle;* Paolo E. Coletta, *William Jennings Bryan I. Political Evangelist 1860–1908;* Herbert Croly, *Marcus Alonzo Hanna;* Robert F. Durden, *The Climax of Populism;* Elmer Ellis, *Henry Teller;* Paul W. Glad, *The Trumpet Soundeth: William Jennings Bryan 1896–1912* and *McKinley, Bryan and the People;* Paxton Hibben, *W. J. Bryan: The Peerless Leader;* Stanley Jones, *The Presidential Election of 1896;* H. W. Morgan, *McKinley and His America;* M. R. Werner, *Bryan;* Wayne Williams, *William Jennings Bryan.*

5. DOCUMENTS. H. S. Commager, *Documents,* nos. 280, 289, 299, 300, 311, 321–5, 327, 328, 332, 333, 337, 338, 341–3, 353.

For further references, *Harvard Guide,* ¶¶ 201, 209, 210.

CHAPTER IX

1. PHILOSOPHY AND RELIGION. A. I. Abell, *American Catholicism and Social Action* and *The Urban Impact on American Protestantism;* Mary Ellen Chase, *A Goodly Heritage;* Stewart Cole, *A History of Fundamentalism;* H. S. Commager, *The American Mind;* Merle Curti, *The Growth of American Thought;* John Dewey, *Influence of Darwin on Philosophy;* J. T. Ellis, *American Catholicism;* Washington Gladden, *Recollections;* C. H. Hopkins, *The Rise of the Social Gospel, 1865–1915;* William James, *Pragmatism, A Pluralistic Universe,* and *The Will to Believe;* Henry F. May, *The End of Innocence* and *The Protestant Churches and Industrial America;* Theodore Maynard, *The Story of American Catholicism;* Ralph Barton Perry, *The Thought and Character of William James* (2 vols.); Stow Persons (ed.), *Evolutionary Thought in America* and *American Minds;* George Santayana, *Character and Opinion in the United States* and *Winds of Doctrine;* Herbert Schneider, *A History of American Philosophy* and *Religion in Twentieth Century America;* Anson P. Stokes, *Church and State in the United States* (3 vols.); Harvey Townsend, *Philosophical Ideas in the United States;* William J. Tucker, *My Generation;* Morton G. White, *Social Thought in America;* Philip Weiner, *Evolution and the Founding of Pragmatism.*

2. SOCIAL AND LEGAL THOUGHT. Samuel Chuggerman, *Lester Ward;* John R. Commons, *Legal Foundation of Capitalism;* Bernard Crick, *The*

American Science of Politics; Merle Curti, *Growth of American Thought;*
Chester M. Destler, *American Radicalism 1865–1901;* Joseph Dorfman, *Thorstein Veblen and His America;* Felix Frankfurter, *Mr. Justice Holmes and the Supreme Court;* Edward C. Hayes (ed.), *Recent Developments in the Social Sciences;* Richard Hofstadter, *Social Darwinism in America;* Oliver W. Holmes, *Collected Legal Papers;* M. DeW. Howe, *Justice Oliver Wendell Holmes: The Proving Years;* William Jordy, *Henry Adams: Scientific Historian;* Max Lerner (ed.), *The Mind and Faith of Justice Holmes;* Howard Odum (ed.), *American Masters of Social Science;* Ernest Samuels, *Henry Adams: The Middle Years;* Harris E. Starr, *William Graham Sumner;* William G. Sumner, *The Forgotten Man and Other Essays;* Benjamin Twiss, *Lawyers and the Constitution;* Thorstein Veblen, *The Theory of the Leisure Class;* Lester Ward, *Psychic Factors in Civilization;* Charles Warren, *History of the American Bar.*

3. LITERATURE. Henry Adams, *The Education of Henry Adams;* G. N. Bennett, *William Dean Howells;* Van Wyck Brooks, *New England: Indian Summer; Howells: His Life and World; The Ordeal of Mark Twain;* and *The Confident Years;* Edwin H. Cady, *William Dean Howells;* Oscar Cargill, *Intellectual America* and *The Novels of Henry James;* Everett Carter, *Howells and the Age of Realism;* Harry H. Clark (ed.), *Transitions in American Literary History;* Malcolm Cowley, *After the Genteel Tradition;* Bernard DeVoto, *Mark Twain's America;* Dorothy Dudley, *Forgotten Frontiers: Theodore Dreiser and the Land of the Free;* Leon Edel, *Henry James;* Maxwell Geismar, *Ancestors and Rebels;* William Dean Howells, *My Mark Twain;* Alfred Kazin, *On Native Grounds;* Francis O. Matthiessen, *The James Family* and *Henry James: The Major Phase;* Emery Neff, *Edwin A. Robinson;* Vernon L. Parrington, *Beginnings of Critical Realism in America;* Henry Nash Smith & William Gibson (eds.), *Mark Twain–Howells Letters* (2 vols.); Robert E. Spiller, *et al., Literary History of the United States,* vol. 2; Walter Taylor, *The Economic Novel in America;* Edmund Wilson, *Axel's Castle;* Yvor Winters, *E. A. Robinson.*

4. JOURNALISM. Thomas Beer, *The Mauve Decade;* W. G. Bleyer, *Main Currents in the History of American Journalism;* George Britt, *Forty Years, Forty Millions: A Biography of Frank Munsey;* Oliver Carlson, *Hearst: Lord of San Simeon;* Elmer Davis, *The New York Times;* Gerald Johnson, *An Honorable Titan: Adolph Ochs;* J. M. Lee, *History of American Journalism;* Frank Luther Mott, *American Journalism* and *History of American Magazines,* vol. 3; Don Seitz, *Joseph Pulitzer: His Life and Letters;* W. A. Swanberg, *Citizen Hearst;* John Tebbel, *George Horace Lorimer and the Saturday Evening Post;* Oswald G. Villard, *Some Newspapers and Newspapermen;* B. A.

Weisberger, *The American Newspaperman;* William Allen White, *Autobiography.*

5. EDUCATION. John L. Childs, *American Pragmatism and Education;* Lawrence Cremin, *The Transformation of the School;* E. P. Cubberley, *Public Education in the United States;* Merle Curti, *Social Ideas of American Educators;* Charles W. Dabney, *Universal Education in the South* (2 vols.); John Dewey, *The School and Society* and *Democracy and Education;* Hugh Hawkins, *Pioneer: A History of the Johns Hopkins University;* Richard Hofstadter & Walter Metzger, *Academic Freedom in the United States;* Henry James, *Charles W. Eliot* (2 vols.); Edward Krug, *Charles W. Eliot and Popular Education;* Thomas LeDuc, *Piety and Intellect at Amherst College;* Robert D. Leigh, *The Public Library in the United States;* Paul Monroe (ed.), *Cyclopedia of Education* (5 vols.); S. E. Morison, *Development of Harvard University 1869–1929;* Allan Nevins, *The Land Grant Colleges;* George Pierson, *Yale College, 1871–1921;* E. D. Ross, *Democracy's College;* Richard J. Storr, *Harper's University;* Thorstein Veblen, *The Higher Learning in America;* Lawrence Veysey, *The Emergence of the American University.*

6. ART AND ARCHITECTURE. Wayne Andrews, *Architecture in America* and *Architecture, Ambition, and Americans;* Virgil Barker, *American Painting;* Cecilia Beaux, *Background with Figures;* John Burchard & Albert Bush-Brown, *The Architecture of America;* Alan Burroughs, *Limners and Likenesses;* H. S. Commager, *The American Mind;* Royal Cortissoz, *Augustus St. Gaudens* and *John La Farge;* W. H. Downes, *John Singer Sargent;* James Marston Fitch, *American Building;* Siegfried Giedion, *Space, Time and Architecture;* Ira Glackens, *William Glackens and the Ash-Can Group;* Lloyd Goodrich, *Albert Ryder; Winslow Homer;* and *Thomas Eakins;* Talbot Hamlin, *The American Spirit in Architecture;* John Kouwenhoven, *Made in America;* Oliver Larkin, *Art and Life in America;* Russell Lynes, *The Tastemakers;* Roland McKinney, *Thomas Eakins;* C. H. Moore, *Daniel H. Burnham, Architect and Planner of Cities;* Lewis Mumford, *Roots of Contemporary Architecture, The Brown Decades, Sticks and Stones,* and *The South in Architecture;* Jerome Myers, *Artist in New York;* E. P. Richardson, *Painting in America;* Marjorie Ryerson (ed.), *The Art Spirit: Robert Henri;* Augustus St. Gaudens, *Reminiscences;* Homer St. Gaudens, *The American Artist and His Times;* Montgomery Schuyler, *American Architecture* (2 vols.); Frederick Sherman, *Albert Pinkham Ryder;* Lorado Taft, *History of American Sculpture;* William Walton, *Art and Architecture at the World's Columbian Exposition* (3 vols.); Frank Lloyd Wright, *Autobiography, Modern Architecture,* and *Writings and Buildings.*

CHAPTER X

1. GENERAL. J. Bartlett Brebner, *The North Atlantic Triangle: The Interplay of Canada, the United States and Great Britain;* Foster R. Dulles, *The Imperial Years,* and *America in the Pacific;* Lionel Gelber, *The Rise of Anglo-American Friendship 1898–1906;* A. W. Griswold, *The Far Eastern Policy of the United States;* G. F. Kennan, *American Diplomacy;* William L. Langer, *The Diplomacy of Imperialism,* vol. 2; Walter LeFeber, *The New Empire;* H. Wayne Morgan, *William McKinley and His America,* and *America's Road to Empire;* Robert E. Osgood, *Ideals and Self-Interest in America's Foreign Policy;* Dexter Perkins, *Hands Off! A History of the Monroe Doctrine;* D. W. Pletcher, *The Awkward Years: American Foreign Relations Under Garfield and Arthur;* A. K. Weinberg, *Manifest Destiny;* Arthur Whitaker, *The Western Hemisphere Idea: Its Rise and Decline;* B. M. Williams, *Economic Foreign Policy of the United States;* William A. Williams, *The Tragedy of American Diplomacy.*

2. RISE OF IMPERIALISM AND MANIFEST DESTINY IN THE 'NINETIES. Harry C. Allen, *Great Britain and the United States;* Howard K. Beale, *Theodore Roosevelt and the Rise of America to World Power;* E. J. Carpenter, *America in Hawaii;* P. E. Corbett, *The Settlement of Canadian-American Disputes;* Tyler Dennett, *Americans in Eastern Asia;* William Livezey, *Mahan on Sea Power;* A. T. Mahan, *From Sail to Steam;* Ernest May, *Imperial Democracy;* Frederick Merk, *Manifest Destiny and Mission in American History;* Allan Nevins, *Henry White;* Gordon O'Gara, *Theodore Roosevelt and the Rise of the Modern Navy;* Earl S. Pomeroy, *Pacific Outpost: American Strategy in Guam;* W. D. Puleston, *Admiral Mahan;* G. H. Ryden, *The Foreign Policy of the United States in Relation to Samoa;* Harold and Margaret Sprout, *The Rise of American Naval Power;* S. K. Stevens, *American Expansion in Hawaii 1842–1898;* Richard West, *Admirals of American Empire.*

3. THE SPANISH WAR. E. J. Benton, *International Law and Diplomacy of the Spanish-American War;* W. R. Braisted, *The United States Navy in the Pacific;* F. R. Chadwick, *Relations of the United States and Spain: The War* (2 vols.); George Dewey, *Autobiography;* Orestes Ferrara, *The Last Spanish War;* H. E. Flack, *Spanish-American Diplomatic Relations Preceding the War of 1898;* Frank Freidel, *The Splendid Little War;* Frederick Funston, *Memories of Two Wars;* A. T. Mahan, *Lessons of the War with Spain;* Walter Millis, *The Martial Spirit;* B. A. Reuter, *Anglo-American Relations During the Spanish American War;* Theodore Roosevelt, *The Rough Riders;* H. S. Sar-

gent, *The Campaign of Santiago de Cuba* (3 vols.); W. S. Schley, *Forty-five Years under the Flag;* J. R. Spears, *Our Navy in the War with Spain;* Joseph Wheeler, *The Santiago Campaign;* Joseph Wisan, *The Cuban Crisis as Reflected in the New York Press.*

4. IMPERIALISM AND ANTI-IMPERIALISM. Robert Beisner, *Twelve Against Empire;* Andrew Carnegie, *Autobiography;* Royal Cortissoz, *Life of Whitelaw Reid* (2 vols.); Merle Curti, *Bryan and World Peace;* Tyler Dennett, *John Hay;* Elmer Ellis, *Henry Teller;* Margaret Leech, *In the Days of McKinley;* William V. Moody, *Poems,* ed. by Robert M. Lovett; Ernest R. May, *Imperial Democracy* and *American Imperialism;* Arthur S. Pier, *American Apostles to the Philippines;* Julius Pratt, *Expansionists of 1898;* Moorfield Storey & M. P. Lichanco, *The Conquest of the Philippines by the United States.*

5. THE OPEN DOOR. M. J. Bau, *Open Door Doctrine in Relation to China;* J. M. Callahan, *American Relations in the Pacific and in the Far East;* Charles Campbell, Jr., *Special Business Interests and the Open Door Policy;* H. Chung, *The Oriental Policy of the United States;* P. H. Clements, *The Boxer Rebellion;* Tyler Dennett, *Americans in Eastern Asia* and *John Hay;* Alfred L. P. Dennis, *Adventures in American Diplomacy;* C. O. Paullin, *Diplomatic Negotiations by American Naval Officers;* Earl S. Pomeroy, *Pacific Outpost;* Julius W. Pratt, *America's Colonial Experiment;* Paul S. Reinsch, *An American Diplomat in China;* Alfred Vagts, *Deutschland und die Vereinigten Staaten in der Weltpolitik* (2 vols.); Paul A. Varg, *Open Door Diplomat — The Life of William W. Rockhill* and *Missionaries, Chinese, and Diplomats;* W. W. Willoughby, *Foreign Rights and Interests in China.*

6. IMPERIALISM AND THE CONSTITUTION. Charles B. Elliott, *The Philippines, to the End of the Military Regime;* C. E. Magoon, *Legal Status of the Territory Acquired by the U.S. during the War with Spain;* C. F. Randolph, *Law and Policy of Annexation;* Charles Warren, *The Supreme Court in U.S. History,* vol. 2; W. F. Willoughby, *Territories and Dependencies of the U.S.*

7. DOCUMENTS. R. J. Bartlett (ed.), *The Record of American Diplomacy;* H. S. Commager, *Documents,* nos. 268, 281, 305, 329–31, 340, 345–52; Insular Cases, House Documents, 56 Cong. 2nd Sess. no. 509.

For further references, *Harvard Guide,* ¶¶ 220–25.

CHAPTER XI

1. GENERAL. Daniel Aaron, *Men of Good Hope;* J. R. Chamberlain, *Farewell to Reform;* Lawrence A. Cremin, *The Transformation of the School;* Herbert Croly, *Progressive Democracy* and *The Promise of American Life;* Roger Daniels, *The Politics of Prejudice;* Chester M. Destler, *American Radicalism 1865–1901;* Joseph Dorfman, *Economic Mind in American Civilization,* vol. 3, and *Thorstein Veblen and His America;* Ray Ginger, *Age of Excess;* Samuel Haber, *Efficiency and Uplift;* Samuel Hays, *The Response to Industrialism 1885–1914;* Richard Hofstadter, *The Age of Reform;* Matthew Josephson, *The President Makers;* Gabriel Kolko, *The Triumph of Conservatism,* and *Railroads and Regulation, 1877–1916;* Christopher Lasch, *The New Radicalism in America;* Blake McKelvey, *The Urbanization of America (1860–1915);* Arthur Mann, *Yankee Reformers in the Urban Age;* Elting E. Morison, *Turmoil and Tradition: A Study of the Life and Times of Henry L. Stimson;* David W. Noble, *The Paradox of Progressive Thought;* Russel B. Nye, *Midwestern Progressive Politics;* V. L. Parrington, *The Beginnings of Critical Realism in America;* Arthur M. Schlesinger, *The Rise of the City;* Robert Wiebe, *Businessmen and Reform;* C. Vann Woodward, *Origins of the New South, 1877–1913.*

2. POLITICAL REFORM AND ERA OF THE MUCKRAKERS. R. M. Abrams, *Conservatism in a Progressive Era;* Ray Stannard Baker, *An American Chronicle;* Charles Barker, *Henry George;* W. E. Bean, *Boss Ruef's San Francisco;* Henry F. Bedford, *Socialism and the Workers in Massachusetts;* Claude Bowers, *Beveridge and the Progressive Era;* James Bryce, *The American Commonwealth,* part V; D. M. Chalmers, *The Social and Political Ideas of the Muckrakers;* D. D. Egbert & Stow Persons (eds.), *Socialism and American Life* (2 vols.); Elmer Ellis, *Mr. Dooley's America: Life of Finley Peter Dunne;* Louis Filler, *Crusaders for American Liberalism;* Edward A. Fitzpatrick, *McCarthy of Wisconsin;* Robert M. Fogelson, *The Fragmented Metropolis;* Dewey Grantham, *Hoke Smith and the Politics of the New South;* Fred E. Haynes, *Third Party Movements in the United States;* Frederic C. Howe, *Confessions of a Reformer, Wisconsin: An Experiment in Democracy,* and *The City, the Hope of Democracy;* Tom Johnson, *My Story;* Ira Kipnis, *The American Socialist Movement 1897–1912;* A. D. Kirwan, *The Revolt of the Rednecks: Mississippi Politics 1876–1925;* Aileen S. Kraditor, *The Ideas of the Woman Suffrage Movement, 1890–1920;* B. C. and L. La Follette, *Robert M. La Follette* (2 vols.); Edwin R. Lewinson, *John Purroy Mitchel;* Peter Lyon, *Success Story: The Life and Times of S. S. McClure;* C. C. McCarthy,

The Wisconsin Idea; R. S. Maxwell, *La Follette and the Rise of Progressives in Wisconsin;* G. E. Mowry, *The California Progressives* and *The Era of Theodore Roosevelt;* R. E. Noble, *New Jersey Progressivism before Wilson;* Fremont Older, *My Story;* C. W. Patton, *The Fight for Municipal Reform;* Howard Quint, *The Forging of American Socialism;* C. C. Regier, *The Era of the Muckrakers;* D. A. Shannon, *The Socialist Party of America;* Lincoln Steffens, *The Shame of the Cities* and *Autobiography;* H. L. Warner, *Progressivism in Ohio;* Arthur and Lila Weinberg (eds.), *The Muckrakers: An Anthology;* William Allen White, *Autobiography;* Brand Whitlock, *Forty Years of It.*

3. HUMANITARIAN REFORM. Edith Abbott, *The Tenements of Chicago 1908–1935;* Graham Adams, Jr., *Age of Industrial Violence;* Jane Addams, *Forty Years at Hull House,* and *My Friend, Julia Lathrop;* Oscar Ameringer, *If You Don't Weaken;* W. D. P. Bliss (ed.), *New Encyclopedia of Social Reform;* Robert H. Bremner, *From the Depths: The Discovery of Poverty in the United States;* John R. Commons, *Myself;* Merle Curti, *The Peace Crusade;* Allen F. Davis, *Spearheads for Reform;* John C. Farrell, *Beloved Lady: A History of Jane Addams' Ideas on Reform and Peace;* George P. Geiger, *Philosophy of Henry George;* Joseph R. Gusfield, *Symbolic Crusade: Status Politics and the American Temperance Movement;* R. M. Lubove, *The Progressives and the Slums;* Arthur E. Morgan, *Edward Bellamy;* William L. O'Neill, *Divorce in the Progressive Era;* Jacob Riis, *The Battle with the Slum* and *How the Other Half Lives;* Mary Heaton Vorse, *A Footnote to Folly;* Louise Wade, *Graham Taylor;* Lillian Wald, *The House on Henry Street* and *Windows on Henry Street;* Stephen B. Wood, *Constitutional Politics in the Progressive Era.*

4. THE STRUGGLE FOR NEGRO RIGHTS. George W. Cable, *The Silent South* and *The Negro Question;* W. J. Cash, *The Mind of the South;* W. E. B. DuBois, *Dusk of Dawn, The Philadelphia Negro, Color and Democracy,* and *The Souls of Black Folk;* John Hope Franklin, *From Slavery to Freedom;* Thomas F. Gossett, *Race: The History of an Idea in America;* Alain Locke, *The New Negro: An Interpretation;* August Meier, *Negro Thought in America;* August Meier and Elliott M. Rudwick, *From Plantation to Ghetto;* Saunders Redding, *The Lonesome Road;* Seth M. Scheiner, *Negro Mecca: A History of the Negro in New York City, 1865–1920;* Allan H. Spear, *Black Chicago: The Making of a Negro Ghetto, 1890–1920;* Samuel R. Spencer, Jr., *Booker T. Washington;* Booker T. Washington, *Up From Slavery* and *The Story of the Negro;* Walter White, *How Far the Promised Land?;* C. Vann Woodward, *Strange Career of Jim Crow.*

5. IMAGINATIVE LITERATURE. Henry Adams, *Democracy;* Winston Churchill, *Coniston* and *Mr. Crewe's Career;* Jon W. DeForest, *Honest John Vane;* Theodore Dreiser, *The Titan* and *The Financier;* Paul L. Ford, *The Honorable Peter Stirling;* Edgar Lee Masters, *A Spoon River Anthology;* David G. Phillips, *The Plum Tree;* Booth Tarkington, *In the Arena;* Mark Twain, *The Gilded Age;* W. A. White, *A Certain Rich Man;* Brand Whitlock, *The Thirteenth District* and *The Turn of the Balance.*

6. SOURCES AND DOCUMENTS. C. A. Beard & B. E. Shultz, *Documents on Initiative, Referendum and Recall;* H. S. Commager, *Documents,* nos. 301, 313, 371, 376, 384, 406, 407, 432, 433; R. W. Logan (ed.), *The Negro in the United States.*

For further references, *Harvard Guide,* ¶¶ 212–15.

CHAPTERS XII AND XIII

1. GENERAL. John Blum, *The Republican Roosevelt;* Claude Bowers, *Beveridge and the Progressive Movement;* Nicholas Murray Butler, *Across the Busy Years* (2 vols.); Lewis Einstein, *Roosevelt: His Mind in Action;* Harold U. Faulkner, *The Decline of Laissez Faire;* J. S. Garraty, *Henry Cabot Lodge* and *Right-Hand Man: The Life of George W. Perkins;* Eric Goldman, *Rendezvous with Destiny;* W. H. Harbaugh, *Power and Responsibility: The Life and Times of Theodore Roosevelt;* Philip Jessup, *Elihu Root* (2 vols.); Walter Johnson, *William Allen White's America;* Matthew Josephson, *The President Makers;* R. M. Lowitt, *George Norris;* M. N. McGeary, *Gifford Pinchot;* E. E. Morison & J. M. Blum (eds.), *The Letters of Theodore Roosevelt* (8 vols.); George E. Mowry, *The Era of Theodore Roosevelt;* Henry F. Pringle, *Theodore Roosevelt* and *Life and Times of William Howard Taft* (2 vols.); Nathaniel W. Stephenson, *Nelson W. Aldrich;* Henry Stimson, *On Active Service in Peace and War.*

2. THE EXTENSIONS OF GOVERNMENT REGULATION. Frederick L. Allen, *The Great Pierpont Morgan;* F. B. Clark, *Constitutional Doctrines of Justice Harlan;* John D. Clark, *The Federal Trust Policy;* Sidney Fine, *Laissez Faire and the General-Welfare State;* Samuel P. Hays, *Conservation and the Gospel of Efficiency 1890–1920;* A. T. Mason, *Bureaucracy Convicts Itself: The Ballinger-Pinchot Controversy;* James Penick, Jr., *Progressive Politics and Conservation;* Gifford Pinchot, *Breaking New Ground,* and *The Fight for Conservation;* E. R. Richardson, *The Politics of Conservation;* Hans B. Tho-

relli, *The Federal Anti-Trust Policy;* C. R. Van Hise, *Conservation of Natural Resources;* H. W. Wiley, *An Autobiography.*

3. FOREIGN AFFAIRS: GENERAL. Eugene N. Anderson, *The First Moroccan Crisis;* Howard K. Beale, *Theodore Roosevelt and the Rise of America to World Power;* Charles S. Campbell, *Anglo-American Understanding 1898–1903;* Herbert Croly, *Willard Straight;* Tyler Dennett, *John Hay;* L. E. Ellis, *Reciprocity, 1911;* Lionel M. Gelber, *The Rise of Anglo-American Friendship;* W. H. Haas, *The American Empire;* Philip Jessup, *Elihu Root* (2 vols.); J. L. Keenleyside & G. S. Brown, *Canada and the United States;* Allan Nevins, *Henry White;* G. C. O'Gara, *Theodore Roosevelt and the Rise of the Modern Navy;* Alfred Vagts, *Deutschland und die Vereinigten Staaten in der Weltpolitik* (2 vols.).

4. FOREIGN AFFAIRS: LATIN AMERICA. J. B. and F. Bishop, *Goethals;* W. H. Callcott, *The Caribbean Policy of the United States;* H. P. Davis, *Black Democracy;* Miles Du Val, *Cadiz to Cathay;* Russell J. Fitzgibbon, *Cuba and the United States 1900–1935;* M. C. Gorgas & B. J. Hendrick, *W. C. Gorgas;* Henry C. Hill, *Roosevelt and the Caribbean;* W. D. McCain, *The United States and the Republic of Panama;* Dwight Miner, *The Fight for the Panama Route;* Dana Munro, *Intervention and Dollar Diplomacy in the Caribbean, 1900–1921;* J. Fred Rippy, *The United States and Mexico* and *The Capitalists and Colombia;* G. H. Stuart, *Cuba and Its International Relations;* Frank Tannenbaum, *The Mexican Agrarian Revolution;* Sumner Welles, *Naboth's Vineyard* (2 vols.); Arthur P. Whitaker, *The United States and South America: The Northern Republics.*

5. FOREIGN AFFAIRS: THE PACIFIC AND THE FAR EAST. Thomas A. Bailey, *Theodore Roosevelt and the Japanese-American Crisis;* P. H. Clemens, *The Boxer Rebellion;* Tyler Dennett, *Roosevelt and the Russo-Japanese War* and *Americans in Eastern Asia;* Raymond A. Esthus, *Theodore Roosevelt and Japan;* A. Whitney Griswold, *The Far Eastern Policy of the United States;* Hermann Hagedorn, *Leonard Wood* (2 vols.); Grayson Kirk, *Philippine Independence;* J. G. Reid, *The Manchu Abdication and the Powers 1908–1912;* C. F. Remer, *Foreign Investments in China;* J. S. Reyes, *Legislative History of America's Economic Policy Towards the Philippines;* S. K. Stevens, *American Expansion in Hawaii;* Charles Vevier, *The United States and China 1906–1913;* Dean C. Worcester, *The Philippines, Past and Present;* Edward H. Zabriskie, *American-Russian Rivalry in the Far East.*

6. THE ELECTION OF 1912. William J. Bryan, *Tale of Two Conventions;* Josephus Daniels, *The Wilson Era: Years of Peace, 1910–1917;* Arthur Link,

Woodrow Wilson and the Progressive Era and *Woodrow Wilson: The Road to the White House;* George Mowry, *Theodore Roosevelt and the Progressive Movement;* Victor Rosewater, *Backstage in 1912.*

7. DOCUMENTS. R. J. Bartlett (ed.), *The Record of American Diplomacy;* P. H. Clyde (ed.), *United States Policy Towards China;* H. S. Commager, *Documents,* nos. 345–52, 355, 356, 360–63, 367, 369–87, 412, 446; J. W. Gantenbein, *Evolution of Latin American Policy, passim.*

For further references, *Harvard Guide,* ¶¶ 220–25, 236–39.

CHAPTER XIV

1. WOODROW WILSON. Ray S. Baker, *Woodrow. Wilson: Life and Letters* (8 vols.), vols. 1–4; Herbert C. Bell, *Woodrow Wilson and the People;* John M. Blum, *Woodrow Wilson and the Politics of Morality* and *Joe Tumulty and the Wilson Era;* Josephus Daniels, *The Wilson Era; Years of Peace, 1910–1917;* Charles Forcey, *The Crossroads of Liberalism: Weyl, Croly and Lippmann and the Progressive Era;* J. A. Garraty, *Woodrow Wilson;* Burton J. Hendrick, *Life and Letters of Walter Hines Page* (3 vols.); David F. Houston, *Eight Years with Wilson's Cabinet;* James Kerney, *The Political Education of Woodrow Wilson;* Robert La Follette, *Autobiography;* Arthur Link, *Woodrow Wilson* (5 vols.); Walter Lippmann, *Drift and Mastery;* William G. McAdoo, *Crowded Years;* A. T. Mason, *Brandeis;* M. J. Pusey, *Charles Evans Hughes;* Frederick Palmer, *Newton D. Baker* (2 vols.); Frederick L. Paxson, *The Pre-War Years;* Charles Seymour (ed.), *The Intimate Papers of Colonel House* (4 vols.); Oswald G. Villard, *Fighting Years;* Arthur Walworth, *Woodrow Wilson* (2 vols.); Walter Weyl, *The New Democracy;* Woodrow Wilson, *The New Freedom.*

2. DOMESTIC POLICIES. Louis D. Brandeis, *Other People's Money;* John D. Clark, *The Federal Trust Policy;* William Diamond, *Economic Thought of Woodrow Wilson;* Carter Glass, *An Adventure in Constructive Finance;* W. S. Holt, *The Federal Farm Loan Bureau;* E. W. Kemmerer, *The A. B. C. of the Federal Reserve System;* J. Laurence Laughlin, *The Federal Reserve Act;* Frank W. Taussig, *The Tariff History of the United States;* A. L. Todd, *Justice on Trial: The Case of Louis D. Brandeis;* Paul M. Warburg, *The Federal Reserve System* (2 vols.).

3. FOREIGN AFFAIRS. Edward Buehrig, *Woodrow Wilson and the Balance of Power;* Howard F. Cline, *The United States and Mexico;* R. W. Curry,

Woodrow Wilson's Far Eastern Policy; Merle Curti, *Bryan and World Peace;* T. Iyenage & K. Sato, *Japan and the California Problem;* Harley Notter, *Origins of the Foreign Policy of Woodrow Wilson;* Robert Quirk, *An Affair of Honor;* Paul S. Reinsch, *An American Diplomat in China;* J. Fred Rippy, *The United States and Mexico;* George Stephenson, *John Lind of Minnesota;* Frank Tannenbaum, *The Mexican Agrarian Revolution;* Charles C. Tansill, *The Purchase of the Danish West Indies.*

4. DOCUMENTS. H. S. Commager, *Documents,* nos. 389–98, 402, 404, 410–12; Report of the Industrial Commission of 1915, 64 Cong. 1st Sess. Sen. Doc. no. 415; Report of the Pujo Committee, 62 Cong. 3d Sess. House Rep. no. 1593.

For further references, *Harvard Guide,* ¶¶ 235, 237, 238.

CHAPTER XV

1. GENERAL. Alex Arnett, *Claude Kitchin and the Wilson War Policies;* Ray Stannard Baker, *Woodrow Wilson: Life and Letters,* vols. 5 and 6; R. S. Baker & W. E. Dodd (eds.), *The Public Papers of Woodrow Wilson* (6 vols.); E. H. Buehrig, *Woodrow Wilson and the Balance of Power;* C. H. Cramer, *Newton D. Baker;* Burton J. Hendrick, *Life and Letters of Walter Hines Page* (3 vols.); A. S. Link, *Wilson the Diplomatist; and Wilson* (5 vols); V. S. Mamatey, *The United States and East Central Europe, 1914–1918;* E. R. May, *The World War and American Isolation, 1914–1917;* A. J. Mayer, *Political Origins of the New Diplomacy, 1917–1918;* Allan Nevins (ed.), *The Letters and Journals of Brand Whitlock* (2 vols.); Harley Notter, *Origins of the Foreign Policy of Woodrow Wilson;* R. E. Osgood, *Ideals and Self-Interest in America's Foreign Relations;* Frederick L. Paxson, *American Democracy and the World War,* vol. 1; Charles Seymour, *American Neutrality, 1914–1917* and *American Diplomacy During the World War;* Charles Seymour (ed.), *The Intimate Papers of Colonel House* (4 vols.).

2. STRUGGLE FOR NEUTRAL RIGHTS. Thomas A. Bailey, *The Policy of the United States Towards Neutrals;* Newton D. Baker, *Why We Went to War;* K. E. Birnbaum, *Peace Moves and U-Boat Warfare;* Edwin M. Borchard & W. P. Lage, *Neutrality for the United States;* Merle Curti, *Bryan and World Peace;* Sidney B. Fay, *Origins of the World War* (2 vols.); James W. Gerard, *My Four Years in Germany;* Hugh Gibson, *Journal from Our Legation in Belgium;* C. Hartley Grattan, *Why We Fought;* Walter Millis, *The Road to War;* Bernadotte E. Schmidt, *The Coming of the War* (2 vols.); Charles Sey-

mour, *American Neutrality 1914–1917;* D. M. Smith, *Robert Lansing and American Neutrality;* and *The Great Departure;* Arno Spindler, *La Guerre Sous-Marine* (3 vols.); Charles Tansill, *America Goes to War;* Barbara Tuchman, *The Zimmermann Telegram.*

3. PROPAGANDA. Thomas A. Bailey, *The Man in the Street: Impact of American Public Opinion on American Foreign Policy;* C. J. Child, *The German-American in Politics 1914–1917;* L. Gelber, *Rise of Anglo-American Friendship;* Harold D. Lasswell, *Propaganda Technique in the World War;* H. C. Peterson, *Propaganda for War;* Arthur Ponsonby, *Falsehood in War Time;* Armin Rappaport, *British Press and Wilsonian Neutrality;* C. E. Scheiber, *Transformation of American Sentiment Toward Germany 1898– 1914;* J. D. Squires, *British Propaganda at Home and in the United States 1914–1917;* George Sylvester Viereck, *Spreading Germs of Hate;* Johann von Bernstorff, *My Three Years in America;* Franz Rintelen von Kleist, *The Dark Invader.*

4. DOCUMENTS. H. S. Commager, *Documents,* nos. 400, 405, 408, 409, 416–18; *Official German Documents Relating to the War* (2 vols.); *Papers Relating to the Foreign Relations of the United States, 1914–1917* (6 vols.); *The Lansing Papers* (2 vols.); Carleton Savage (ed.), *Policy of the United States Toward Maritime Commerce in War* (2 vols.).

For further references, *Harvard Guide,* ¶¶ 240, 241.

CHAPTER XVI

1. MOBILIZATION. Bernard Baruch, *American Industry in War;* Daniel R. Beaver, *Newton D. Baker and the American War Effort;* J. M. Clark, *Costs of the World War to the American People;* G. B. Clarkson, *Industrial America at War;* John R. Commons, *et al., History of Labor,* vol. 4; Benedict Crowell & Robert F. Wilson, *How America Went to War* (6 vols.); Seward W. Livermore, *Politics Is Adjourned;* William G. McAdoo, *Crowded Years;* A. D. Noyes, *The War Period of American Finance;* Frederick Palmer, *Newton D. Baker: America at War* (2 vols.); F. L. Paxson, *American Democracy and the World War,* vols. 1 and 2; P. W. Slosson, *The Great Crusade and After;* Herbert Stein, *Government Price Policy During the World War;* G. S. Watkins, *Labor Problems and Labor Administration During World War* (2 vols.); W. F. Willoughby, *Government Organization in War Times and After.*

2. PUBLIC OPINION AND CIVIL LIBERTIES. Zechariah Chafee, *Free Speech in the United States;* George Creel, *How We Advertised America;*

Donald Johnson, *The Challenge to American Freedoms;* Max Lerner (ed.), *The Mind and Faith of Justice Holmes;* J. R. Mock & Cedric Larson, *Words that Won the War;* H. C. Peterson and G. C. Fite, *Opponents of War, 1917–1918;* Harry Scheiber, *The Wilson Administration and Civil Liberties;* Norman Thomas, *Conscientious Objectors in America.*

3. MILITARY AND NAVAL HISTORY. Leonard Ayres, *The War with Germany: A Statistical Summary;* Thomas G. Frothingham, *Naval History of the World War* (3 vols.) and *American Re-enforcement in the World War;* R. H. Gibson & M. Prendergast, *German Submarine War 1914–1918;* Louis Guichard, *The Naval Blockade 1914–1918;* J. G. Harbord, *The American Army in France;* John Bach McMaster, *The United States in the World War* (2 vols.); Elting Morison, *Admiral Sims and the Modern American Navy;* Frederick Palmer, *America in France: Our Greatest Battle* (the Meuse-Argonne) and *Bliss: Peacemaker;* John J. Pershing, *My Experiences in the World War* (2 vols.); Edouard Requin, *America's Race to Victory;* W. S. Sims & B. J. Hendrick, *The Victory at Sea;* David Trask, *The United States in the Supreme War Council;* George S. Viereck (ed.), *As They Saw Us.*

4. INTERVENTION IN RUSSIA. Thomas A. Bailey, *America Faces Russia;* William S. Graves, *America's Siberian Adventure 1918–1920;* George Kennan, *Russia Leaves the War* and *The Decision to Intervene;* Christopher Lasch, *The American Liberals and the Russian Revolution;* Betty M. Unterberger, *America's Siberian Expedition 1918–1920;* W. A. Williams, *American-Russian Relations 1781–1947.*

5. THE TREATY, THE LEAGUE, AND THE PEACE. Selig Adler, *The Isolationist Impulse;* Thomas Bailey, *Woodrow Wilson and the Lost Peace* and *Woodrow Wilson and the Great Betrayal;* R. S. Baker, *Woodrow Wilson and World Settlement* (3 vols.) and *What Wilson Did at Paris;* Paul Birdsall, *Versailles Twenty Years After;* Allan Cranston, *The Killing of the Peace;* Donald F. Fleming, *The United States and the League of Nations* and *The United States and the World Court;* John Garraty, *Henry Cabot Lodge;* Lawrence E. Gelfand, *The Inquiry;* W. S. Holt, *Treaties Defeated by the Senate;* E. M. House and Charles Seymour (eds.), *What Really Happened at Paris;* J. M. Keynes, *Economic Consequences of the Peace;* Robert Lansing, *The Peace Negotiations;* Étienne Mantoux, *The Carthaginian Peace;* David Hunter Miller, *The Drafting of the Covenant* (2 vols.); Harold Nicolson, *Peace Making, 1919;* K. F. Nowak, *Versailles;* Frederick Palmer, *Bliss: Peacemaker;* H. R. Rudin, *Armistice, 1918;* Gene Smith, *When the Cheering Stopped;* Harold W. V. Temperley, *et al., History of the Peace Conference*

(6 vols.); Seth P. Tillman, *Anglo-American Relations at the Paris Peace Conference of 1919.*

6. DOCUMENTS. R. J. Bartlett, *Record of American Diplomacy;* H. S. Commager, *Documents,* nos. 418, 423–9, 435, 436, 442.

For further references, *Harvard Guide,* ¶¶ 242–3.

CHAPTERS XVII AND XVIII

1. GENERAL. Frederick Lewis Allen, *Only Yesterday* and *The Big Change;* Paul Carter, *The Twenties in America;* H. U. Faulkner, *From Versailles to New Deal;* John D. Hicks, *The Republican Ascendancy;* G. H. Knoles, *The Jazz Age Revisited;* Isabel Leighton (ed.), *The Aspirin Age;* William E. Leuchtenburg, *The Perils of Prosperity, 1914–32;* George Mowry, *The Urban Nation;* James Prothro, *Dollar Decade;* Karl Schriftgiesser, *This Was Normalcy;* Preston Slosson, *The Great Crusade and After, 1914–1928;* George Tindall, *The Emergence of the New South, 1913–1945.*

2. POLITICS. S. H. Adams, *Incredible Era;* Wesley Bagby, *The Road to Normalcy;* J. Leonard Bates, *The Origins of Teapot Dome;* David Burner, *The Politics of Provincialism;* Clarke Chambers, *Seedtime of Reform;* Cedric B. Cowing, *Populists, Plungers, and Progressives;* Claude Fuess, *Calvin Coolidge;* Oscar Handlin, *Al Smith and His America;* Arthur Holcombe, *The New Party Politics;* Herbert Hoover, *American Individualism;* J. Joseph Huthmacher, *Massachusetts People and Politics, 1919–1933;* Morton Keller, *In Defense of Yesterday;* B. C. and Fola La Follette, *Robert M. La Follette,* 2 vols.; Lawrence Levine, *Defender of the Faith, William Jennings Bryan: The Last Decade, 1915–1925;* Kenneth MacKay, *The Progressive Movement;* Donald R. McCoy, *Calvin Coolidge;* Alpheus T. Mason, *William Howard Taft: Chief Justice; The Supreme Court from Taft to Warren,* and *Harlan Fiske Stone;* Edmund Moore, *A Catholic Runs for President;* Burl Noggle, *Teapot Dome;* Howard Quint and Robert Ferrell, *The Talkative President;* E. E. Schattschneider, *Politics, Pressures and the Tariff;* Andrew Sinclair, *The Available Man;* William A. White, *Masks in a Pageant* and *Puritan in Babylon;* Howard Zinn, *La Guardia in Congress.*

3. INTOLERANCE AND CIVIL LIBERTIES. John W. Caughey, *In Clear and Present Danger;* Zechariah Chafee, *Free Speech in the United States;* Stanley Coben, *A. Mitchell Palmer;* H. S. Commager, *Freedom, Loyalty, and Dissent;* Robert Cushman, *Civil Liberties in the United States;* Theodore

Draper, *The Roots of American Communism;* Robert L. Friedheim, *The Seattle General Strike;* Frederic Howe, *Confessions of a Reformer;* E. M. Morgan and G. L. Joughin, *The Legacy of Sacco and Vanzetti;* Robert Murray, *Red Scare;* John P. Roche, *Courts and Rights: The American Judiciary in Action;* Elliott M. Rudwick, *Race Riot at East St. Louis;* Francis Russell, *Tragedy in Dedham;* David Shannon, *The Socialist Party of America.*

4. POLITICAL FUNDAMENTALISM. Charles C. Alexander, *The Ku Klux Klan in the Southwest;* Herbert Asbury, *The Great Illusion;* David M. Chalmers, *Hooded Americanism;* Virginius Dabney, *Dry Messiah: The Life of Bishop Cannon;* Norman Furniss, *The Fundamentalist Controversy, 1918–1931;* Willard B. Gatewood, Jr., *Preachers, Pedagogues, & Politicians;* Ray Ginger, *Six Days or Forever?;* Kenneth T. Jackson, *The Ku Klux Klan in the City;* J. M. Mecklin, *The Ku Klux Klan;* Charles Merz, *The Dry Decade;* Peter Odegard, *Pressure Politics;* A. S. Rice, *The Ku Klux Klan in American Politics;* Andrew Sinclair, *Prohibition: The Era of Excess;* Lincoln Steffens, *Autobiography* (2 vols.); Frank Tannenbaum, *Darker Phases of the South;* James Weinstein, *The Decline of Socialism in America, 1912–1925.*

5. FOREIGN AFFAIRS. Samuel F. Bemis, *The Latin American Policy of the United States;* Dorothy Borg, *American Policy and the Chinese Revolution 1925–1928;* Raymond L. Buell, *The Washington Conference;* Howard Cline, *The United States and Mexico;* Richard Current, *Secretary Stimson;* Alexander De Conde, *Herbert Hoover's Latin American Policy;* Herbert Feis, *Diplomacy of the Dollar 1919–1932;* John K. Fairbank, *The United States and China;* R. H. Ferrell, *Peace in Their Time;* D. F. Fleming, *United States and World Organization 1920–1933;* Betty Glad, *Charles Evans Hughes and the Illusions of Innocence;* A. Whitney Griswold, *The Far Eastern Policy of the United States;* H. G. Moulton & Leo Pasvolsky, *World War Debt Settlements;* Harold Nicolson, *Dwight Morrow;* R. W. Paul, *The Abrogation of the Gentlemen's Agreement;* Dexter Perkins, *The United States and the Caribbean* and *Hands Off! A History of the Monroe Doctrine;* Merlo Pusey, *Charles Evans Hughes* (2 vols.); E. O. Reischauer, *The United States and Japan;* Frank Simonds, *American Foreign Policy in the Post-War Years;* Sara Smith, *The Manchurian Crisis 1931–32;* Henry L. Stimson & McGeorge Bundy, *On Active Service in Peace and War;* J. C. Vinson, *The Parchment Peace;* B. H. Williams, *Economic Foreign Policies of the United States.*

6. THE ECONOMY. A. A. Berle & G. C. Means, *Modern Corporation and Private Property;* A. R. Burns, *The Decline of Competition;* Charles Chapman, *Development of American Business and Banking Thought;* John K. Galbraith,

American Capitalism, and The Great Crash; Siegfried Giedon, Mechanization Takes Command; Harry Jerome, Mechanization in Industry; Simon Kuznets, The National Income and Its Composition 1919–1938; H. W. Laidler, Concentration of Control in American Industry; W. W. Leontief, The Structure of American Economy 1919–1929; Allan Nevins & Frank E. Hill, Ford: Expansion and Challenge 1915–1933; G. W. Nutter, Extent of Enterprise Monopoly 1899–1931; Otis Pease, The Responsibilities of American Advertising; The President's Committee, Recent Economic Changes in the United States (2 vols.); W. Z. Ripley, Main Street and Wall Street; Robert Sobel, The Big Board, and The Great Bull Market; George Soule, Prosperity Decade; Elmus R. Wicker, Federal Reserve Monetary Policy, 1917–1933; Thomas Wilson, Fluctuations in Income and Employment.

7. LABOR AND AGRICULTURE. Dean Albertson, Roosevelt's Farmer; Harold Barger & Hans Landsberg, American Agriculture 1899–1939; M. R. Benedict, Farm Policies of the United States 1790–1950; J. D. Black, Agricultural Reform in the United States; David Brody, Labor in Crisis: The Steel Strike of 1919; John R. Commons, et al., History of Labor, vol. 4; J. D. Durand, The Labor Force, 1890–1960; Nathan Fine, Labor and Farmer Parties in the United States; Gilbert Fite, George Peek and the Fight for Farm Parity; C. O. Gregory, Labor and the Law; Matthew Josephson, Sidney Hillman; Russell Lord, The Wallaces of Iowa; K. D. Lumpkin & D. S. Douglas, Child Workers in America; Liston Pope, Millhands and Preachers: Gastonia; Theodore Saloutos & John D. Hicks, Agricultural Discontent in the Middle West; Philip Taft, The A.F. of L. in the Time of Gompers; Mary H. Vorse, Passaic Textile Strike, 1926–27; J. A. Wechsler, Labor Baron: John L. Lewis; E. E. Witte, Government in Labor Disputes; Leo Wolman, Ebb and Flow in Trade Unionism.

8. SOCIAL AND INTELLECTUAL DEVELOPMENTS. Joseph Wood Krutch, The Modern Temper; Robert and Helen Lynd, Middletown; W. F. Ogburn (ed.), Recent Social Changes in the United States; Gilbert Osofsky, Harlem; Bernard Rosenberg & David White, Mass Culture: The Popular Arts in America; Leo Rosten, Hollywood; Gilbert Seldes, The Seven Lively Arts; Harold Stearns (ed.), Civilization in the United States; Dixon Wecter, When Johnny Comes Marching Home.

9. LITERATURE. Carlos Baker, Hemingway; Van Wyck Brooks, The Confident Years; H. M. Campbell & R. E. Foster, William Faulkner; Oscar Cargill, Intellectual America; Richard Chase, The American Novel and Its Tradition; Malcolm Cowley, After the Genteel Tradition, and Exile's Return; Bernard

Duffey, *Chicago Renaissance in American Letters;* C. A. Fenton, *The Apprenticeship of Ernest Hemingway;* Leslie Fiedler, *Life and Death in the American Novel;* Maxwell Geismar, *Rebels and Ancestors, The Last of the Provincials,* and *Writers in Crisis;* Rudolf Gilbert, *Shine, Perishing Republic: Robinson Jeffers;* Donald Heiney, *Recent American Literature;* Frederick J. Hoffman, *Freudianism and the Literary Mind* and *The Twenties;* Irving Howe, *William Faulkner;* Randall Jarrell, *Poetry and the Age;* Matthew Josephson, *Portrait of the Artist as an American;* Alfred Kazin, *On Native Grounds;* Amy Lowell, *Tendencies in Modern American Poetry;* William Manchester, *Disturber of the Peace: H. L. Mencken;* E. L. Masters, *Vachel Lindsay;* F. O. Matthiessen, *The Achievement of T. S. Eliot;* Henry F. May, *The End of American Innocence;* Arthur Mizener, *The Far Side of Paradise: Biography of F. Scott Fitzgerald;* Harriet Monroe, *A Poet's Life;* Herbert J. Muller, *Thomas Wolfe;* Emery Neff, *Edwin Arlington Robinson;* William V. O'Connor, *The Tangled Fire of William Faulkner;* Albert Parry, *Garrets and Pretenders: A History of Bohemianism in America;* Stow Persons, *American Minds;* Houston Peterson, *The Melody of Chaos;* Lawrence C. Powell, *Robinson Jeffers;* Arthur H. Quinn, *History of the American Drama from the Civil War to the Present;* Mark Schorer, *Sinclair Lewis;* Robert Sklar, *F. Scott Fitzgerald;* Robert E. Spiller, *et al., Literary History of the United States,* vol. 2; Allen Tate, *Collected Essays, 1928–1955;* Edmund Wilson, *The Shores of Light: A Literary Chronicle of the Twenties and Thirties.*

10. ART, PAINTING, AND MUSIC. John Baur, *Revolution and Tradition in American Art;* Milton Brown, *American Paintings from the Armory Show to the Depression;* Elizabeth Cary, *George Luks;* Martha Cheney, *Modern Art in America;* E. O. Christensen, *Index of American Design;* Aaron Copeland, *Our New Music;* Waldo Frank, *et al., America and Alfred Stieglitz;* Ira Glackens, *William Glackens and The Ashcan School;* Robert Henri, *The Art Spirit;* John R. Howard, *Our Contemporary Composers;* Sam Hunter, *Modern American Painting and Sculpture;* Sidney Janis, *Abstract and Surrealist Art in America;* Samuel Kootz, *Modern American Painters;* Walt Kuhn, *The Story of the Armory Show;* Oliver Larkin, *Art and Life in America;* Grace Overmyer, *Government and the Arts;* Constance Rourke, *Charles Sheeler;* James T. Soby, *Contemporary Painters.*

11. SCIENCE. L. Barrett, *The Universe and Dr. Einstein;* Helen Clapesattle, *The Doctors Mayo;* S. R. and F. T. Flexner, *William Henry Welch and the Heroic Age of American Medicine;* George Gray, *Advancing Front of Science;* Bernard Jaffe, *Men of Science in America.*

12. DOCUMENTS. H. S. Commager, *Documents*, nos. 424, 430–34, 438–41, 447–62, 465–72; George Mowry, *The Twenties*.

For further references, *Harvard Guide*, ¶¶ 245–51, 253.

CHAPTERS XIX AND XX

1. GENERAL. Charles and Mary Beard, *America in Midpassage;* John Braeman, *et al.* (eds.), *Change and Continuity in Twentieth-Century America;* Denis Brogan, *The Era of Franklin D. Roosevelt;* Paul Conkin, *The New Deal;* Mario Einaudi, *The Roosevelt Revolution;* Morton J. Frisch and Martin Diamond (eds.), *The Thirties;* Otis L. Graham, Jr., *An Encore for Reform;* Edgar Kemler, *The Deflation of American Ideals;* William E. Leuchtenburg, *The Perils of Prosperity, 1914–32* and *Franklin D. Roosevelt and the New Deal, 1932–1940;* Broadus Mitchell, *Depression Decade, 1929–1941;* Raymond Moley, *After Seven Years;* Dexter Perkins, *The New Age of Franklin D. Roosevelt;* Basil Rauch, *The History of the New Deal;* Arthur M. Schlesinger, Jr., *The Age of Roosevelt:* vol. 1, *The Crisis of the Old Order,* vol. 2, *The Coming of the New Deal,* and vol. 3, *The Politics of Upheaval;* Lester G. Seligman and Elmer E. Cornwell, Jr., *New Deal Mosaic;* Rita James Simon (ed.), *As We Saw the Thirties;* George Tindall, *The Emergence of the New South, 1913–1945;* Dixon Wecter, *The Age of the Great Depression, 1929–1941.*

2. THE DEPRESSION. Irving Bernstein, *The Lean Years: A History of the American Worker 1920–1933;* C. J. Enzler, *Some Social Aspects of the Depression;* John K. Galbraith, *The Great Crash;* Lionel Robbins, *The Great Depression;* J. A. Schumpeter, *Business Cycles.*

3. THE HOOVER ADMINISTRATION. Herbert Hoover, *Memoirs* (3 vols.); W. S. Myers & W. H. Newton, *The Hoover Administration;* Albert U. Romasco, *The Poverty of Abundance;* Gilbert Seldes, *The Years of the Locust (America, 1929–1932);* Rexford Tugwell, *Mr. Hoover's Economic Policies;* H. C. Warren, *Herbert Hoover and the Great Depression;* R. L. Wilbur & A. M. Hyde, *The Hoover Policies.*

4. ROOSEVELT AND HIS CIRCLE. Bernard Bellush, *Franklin D. Roosevelt as Governor of New York;* John M. Blum, *From the Morgenthau Diaries: Years of Crisis, 1928–1938;* James McG. Burns, *Roosevelt: The Lion and the Fox;* S. F. Charles, *Minister of Relief: Harry Hopkins and the Depression;*

Marriner Eccles, *Beckoning Frontiers;* Frank Freidel, *Franklin D. Roosevelt*
(3 vols.) and *F.D.R. and the South;* Daniel R. Fusfeld, *The Economic
Thought of Franklin D. Roosevelt and the Origins of the New Deal;* Thomas
Greer, *What Roosevelt Thought;* John Gunther, *Roosevelt in Retrospect;*
Tamara K. Hareven, *Eleanor Roosevelt;* Cordell Hull, *Memoirs* (2 vols.);
Harold Ickes, *The Autobiography of a Curmudgeon, The New Democracy,*
and *The Secret Diary of Harold L. Ickes* (3 vols.); Frances Perkins, *The
Roosevelt I Knew;* Alfred Rollins, Jr., *Roosevelt and Howe;* Eleanor Roose-
velt, *This Is My Story* and *This I Remember;* Samuel Rosenman, *Working
with Roosevelt;* Robert Sherwood, *Roosevelt and Hopkins;* Rexford Tugwell,
The Democratic Roosevelt and *The Battle for Democracy;* Henry Wallace,
New Frontiers.

5. POLITICS AND ELECTIONS. Edward C. Blackorby, *Prairie Rebel: The
Public Life of William Lemke;* Francis Broderick, *Right Reverend New
Dealer: John A. Ryan;* Robert Burke, *Olson's New Deal for California;* James
F. Byrnes, *Speaking Frankly;* James Farley, *Jim Farley's Story* and *Behind the
Ballots;* E. J. Flynn, *You're the Boss;* George Q. Flynn, *American Catholics
and the Roosevelt Presidency;* Fred Israel, *Nevada's Key Pittman;* Donald
Bruce Johnson, *The Republican Party and Wendell Willkie;* Barry Karl, *Exec-
utive Reorganization & Reform in the New Deal;* Murray Kempton, *Part of
Our Time;* Samuel Lubell, *The Future of American Politics;* D. R. McCoy,
Angry Voices: Left-of-Center Politics in the New Deal, and *Landon of Kansas;*
George Mayer, *The Political Career of Floyd B. Olson;* Charles Michelsen,
The Ghost Talks; Rev. August Ogden, *The Dies Committee;* James T. Patter-
son, *Congressional Conservatism and the New Deal;* Roy V. Peel & T. C.
Donnelly, *The 1932 Election;* Richard Polenberg, *Reorganizing Roosevelt's
Government;* E. E. Robinson, *They Voted for Roosevelt;* Allan Sindler, *Huey
Long's Louisiana;* Charles J. Tull, *Father Coughlin and the New Deal;* Frank
A. Warren, *Liberals and Communism;* George Wolfskill, *Revolt of the Con-
servatives.*

6. INDUSTRY AND FINANCE. A. A. Berle, Jr. and G. C. Means, *The
Modern Corporation and Private Property;* A. R. Burns, *The Decline of
Competition;* A. W. Crawford, *Monetary Management under the New Deal;*
Ralph de Bedts, *The New Deal's SEC;* W. O. Douglas, *Democracy and Fi-
nance;* M. S. Eccles, *Economic Balance and a Balanced Budget;* J. K. Gal-
braith and G. C. Johnson, *Economic Effects of Federal Works Expenditures,
1933–1938;* A. H. Hansen, *Full Recovery or Stagnation;* E. W. Hawley, *The
New Deal and the Problem of Monopoly;* G. G. Johnson, *The Treasury and
Monetary Policy 1933–1938;* Hugh Johnson, *Blue Eagle, from Egg to Earth;*

David Lynch, *The Concentration of Economic Power;* L. S. Lyon, *et al., The National Recovery Administration;* Ferdinand Pecora, *Wall Street Under Oath;* J. R. Reeve, *Monetary Reform Movements;* K. D. Roose, *Economics of Recession and Revival.*

7. AGRICULTURE. M. R. Benedict, *Farm Policies of the United States;* Stuart Chase, *Rich Land, Poor Land;* Gilbert Fite, *George N. Peek and the Fight for Farm Parity;* Richard S. Kirkendall, *Social Scientists and Farm Politics in the Age of Roosevelt;* Russell Lord, *The Wallaces of Iowa;* Carey McWilliams, *Factories in the Field* and *Ill Fares the Land;* E. G. Nourse, *et al., Three Years of the AAA;* A. F. Raper, *Preface to Peasantry;* John Shover, *Cornbelt Rebellion;* John Steinbeck, *The Grapes of Wrath;* Henry Wallace, *New Frontiers* and *America Must Choose.*

8. RELIEF, SOCIAL SECURITY AND LABOR. Edith Abbott, *Public Assistance;* Grace Adams, *Workers on Relief;* Arthur J. Altmeyer, *The Formative Years of Social Security;* Jerold Auerbach, *Labor and Liberty;* Irving Bernstein, *The New Deal Collective Bargaining Policy;* Josephine C. Brown, *Public Relief;* Horace R. Cayton, *Black Workers and the New Unions;* Paul Conkin, *Tomorrow a New World;* David Eugene Conrad, *The Forgotten Farmers;* Milton Derber and Edwin Young (eds.), *Labor and the New Deal;* Carroll Dougherty, *Labor under the NRA;* Paul Douglas, *Social Security in the United States;* Sidney Fine, *The Automobile Under the Blue Eagle;* Walter Galenson, *The C.I.O. Challenge to the A.F. of L.* and *Rival Unionism;* Herbert Harris, *American Labor;* Seymour E. Harris, *The Economics of Social Security;* Abraham Holtzman, *The Townsend Movement;* Donald S. Howard, *The WPA and Federal Relief Policy;* Harold L. Ickes, *Back to Work;* Edward Levinson, *Labor on the March;* Betty and E. K. Lindley, *A New Deal for Youth;* Roy Lubove, *The Struggle for Social Security;* Robert and Helen Lynd, *Middletown in Transition;* Jane de Hart Mathews, *The Federal Theatre, 1935–1939;* Lewis Meriam, *Relief and Social Security;* Grace Overmyer, *Government and the Arts;* Selig Perlman, *Labor in the New Deal Decade;* John A. Salmond, *The Civilian Conservation Corps;* Philip Taft, *The A.F. of L. from the Death of Gompers;* Mary H. Vorse, *Labor's New Millions;* Willson Whitman, *Bread and Circuses;* J. K. Williams, *Grants in Aid under Public Works Administration;* E. E. Witte, *The Development of the Social Security Act.*

9. THE TVA AND CONSERVATION. Gordon R. Clapp, *The T.V.A.;* Wilmon H. Droze, *High Dams and Slack Waters;* C. L. Hodge, *The Tennessee Valley Authority;* William E. Leuchtenburg, *Flood Control Politics;* David E.

Lilienthal, *The TVA: Democracy on the March* and *Journals: The TVA Years;* Richard L. Neuberger, *Our Promised Land;* C. H. Pritchett, *The Tennessee Valley Authority;* Paul B. Sears, *Deserts on the March;* Philip Selznick, *TVA and the Grass Roots;* Willson Whitman, *God's Valley* and *David Lilienthal.*

10. SUPREME COURT. Leonard Baker, *Back to Back;* Irving Brant, *Storm over the Constitution;* Robert K. Carr, *The Supreme Court and Judicial Review;* H. S. Commager, *Majority Rule and Minority Rights;* Richard Cortner, *The Wagner Act Cases;* E. S. Corwin, *The Twilight of the Supreme Court, Court Over Constitution, The Commerce Power vs. State Rights,* and *Constitutional Revolution, Ltd.;* Charles P. Curtis, *Lions under the Throne;* J. P. Frank, *Mr. Justice Black;* Eugene C. Gerhart, *America's Advocate: Robert H. Jackson;* Samuel Hendel, *Charles Evans Hughes and the Supreme Court;* Robert Jackson, *Struggle for Judicial Supremacy;* Samuel Konefsky, *The Legacy of Holmes and Brandeis, Justice Stone and the Supreme Court,* and *The Constitutional World of Mr. Justice Frankfurter;* Alpheus T. Mason, *Harlan Fiske Stone;* Alpheus T. Mason & William M. Beaney, *The Supreme Court in a Free Society;* Joel Paschal, *Mr. Justice Sutherland;* C. Herman Pritchett, *The Roosevelt Court;* Merlo J. Pusey, *Charles Evans Hughes* (2 vols.) and *The Supreme Court Crisis;* Bernard Schwartz, *The Supreme Court: Constitutional Revolution in Retrospect.*

11. DOCUMENTS. H. S. Commager, *Documents,* nos. 475–87, 493–520, 529, 542, 543, 549, 555; Don Congdon (ed.), *The '30s;* Louis Filler (ed.), *The Anxious Years;* Morton Keller (ed.), *The New Deal;* William E. Leuchtenburg (ed.), *The New Deal* and *Franklin D. Roosevelt;* Edgar Nixon (ed.), *Franklin D. Roosevelt and Conservation,* 2 vols.; F. D. Roosevelt and Samuel Rosenman (eds.), *The Public Papers and Addresses of Franklin D. Roosevelt* (13 vols.); Jack Salzman and Barry Wallenstein (eds.), *Years of Protest;* David Shannon (ed.), *The Great Depression;* Bernard Sternsher (ed.), *The New Deal;* Harvey Swados (ed.), *The American Writer and the Great Depression.*

For further references, *Harvard Guide* ¶¶ 256–64.

CHAPTERS XXI–XXIV

1. ROOSEVELT'S FOREIGN POLICY AND THE COMING OF THE WAR. C. A. Beard, *American Foreign Policy in the Making, 1932–1940,* and *President Roosevelt and the Coming of the War, 1941;* R. P. Browder, *The*

Origins of Soviet-American Diplomacy; A. L. C. Bullock, *Hitler;* Floyd A. Cave, *et al., Origins and Consequences of World War II;* Mark Chadwin, *The Hawks of World War II;* Winston S. Churchill, *The Gathering Storm* and *Their Finest Hour* (The Second World War, vols. 1, 2); Warren I. Cohen, *The American Revisionists;* Wayne S. Cole, *America First* and *Senator Gerald P. Nye and American Foreign Relations;* Gordon Craig and Felix Gilbert (eds.), *The Diplomats, 1919–1939;* D. E. Cronon, *Josephus Daniels in Mexico;* R. N. Current, *Secretary Stimson;* Robert Dallek, *Democrat & Diplomat: The Life of William E. Dodd;* R. A. Divine, *The Illusion of Neutrality;* Donald Drummond, *The Passing of American Neutrality;* T. R. Fehrenbach, *F.D.R.'s Undeclared War;* Herbert Feis, *Seen from E.A.* and *The Road to Pearl Harbor;* Robert Ferrell, *The Diplomacy of the Great Depression;* Lloyd Gardner, *Economic Aspects of New Deal Diplomacy;* Joseph C. Grew, *Turbulent Era* and *Ten Years in Japan;* E. D. Guerrant, *Roosevelt's Good Neighbor Policy;* Waldo H. Heinrichs, Jr., *American Ambassador: Joseph C. Grew and the Development of the United States Diplomatic Tradition;* Cordell Hull, *Memoirs,* 2 vols.; Manfred Jonas, *Isolationism in America, 1935–1941;* Toshikazu Kase, *Journey to the Missouri;* George F. Kennan, *Russia and the West under Lenin and Stalin;* William L. Langer & S. Everett Gleason, *The Challenge to Isolation 1937–1940* and *The Undeclared War 1940–1941;* Elting E. Morison, *Turmoil and Tradition: The Life and Times of Henry L. Stimson;* Arthur D. Morse, *While Six Million Died;* W. S. Myers, *The Foreign Policies of Herbert Hoover 1929–1933;* J. W. Pratt, *Cordell Hull* (2 vols.); Basil Rauch, *Roosevelt from Munich to Pearl Harbor;* E. O. Reischauer, *The United States and Japan;* Paul W. Schroeder, *The Axis Alliance and Japanese-American Relations;* Robert E. Sherwood, *Roosevelt and Hopkins: An Intimate History;* William L. Shirer, *The Rise and Fall of the Third Reich;* Henry L. Stimson & McGeorge Bundy, *On Active Service in Peace and War* (2 vols.); C. C. Tansill, *Back Door To War;* F. Jay Taylor, *The United States and the Spanish Civil War;* H. L. Trefousse, *Germany and American Neutrality;* M. S. Watson, *Chief-of-Staff: Prewar Plans and Preparations;* John E. Wiltz, *In Search of Peace* and *From Isolation to War, 1931–1941;* Roberta Wohlstetter, *Pearl Harbor: Warning and Decision;* Bryce Wood, *The Making of the Good Neighbor Policy.*

2. SHORT HISTORIES OF THE WAR. A. R. Buchanan, *The United States in World War II,* 2 vols.; V. J. Esposito (ed.), *A Concise History of World War II;* Maj. Gen. J. F. C. Fuller, *The Second World War, 1939–45;* Hans-Adolf Jacobsen, Jürgen Rohwer, *et al., Entscheidungsschlachten des zweiten Weltkrieges;* Walter Millis (ed.), *The War Reports of General George C. Marshall, General H. H. Arnold, and Admiral E. J. King.*

3. SHORT NAVAL HISTORIES. Rear Adm. Paul Auphan & Jacques Mordal, *The French Navy in World War II;* Cdr. M. A. Bragadin, *The Italian Navy in World War II;* Lt. Cdr. P. K. Kemp, RN, *Key to Victory: The Triumph of British Sea Power in World War II;* S. E. Morison, *The Two Ocean War;* Capt. S. W. Roskill, RN, *White Ensign: The British Navy at War;* Friedrich Ruge, *Der Seekrieg: The German Navy's Story, 1939–45;* U.S. Strategic Bombing Survey, Naval Analysis Div., *The Campaigns of the Pacific War* (ed. by Rear Adm. R. M. Ofstie).

4. SHORT HISTORIES OF OTHER ARMS AND ASPECTS. J. Phinney Baxter 3rd, *Scientists Against Time;* Bureau of the Budget, *The U.S. at War: Development and Administration of the War Program; Building the Navy's Bases in World War II* (History of the Bureau of Yards & Docks, vol. I); Rear Adm. Henry E. Eccles, *Logistics in the National Defense;* K. R. Greenfield, *World War II Strategy Reconsidered* and (ed.), *Command Decisions;* Richard Hewlett and Oscar Anderson, *The New World;* F. H. Hinsley, *Hitler's Strategy;* Jeter A. Isely & Philip A. Crowl, *The U.S. Marines and Amphibious War;* George H. Johnston, *The Toughest Fighting in the World* (New Guinea); Lamont Lansing, *Day of the Trinity;* Anthony Martienssen, *Hitler and His Admirals;* S. E. Morison, *Strategy and Compromise;* Theodore Roscoe, *U.S. Submarine Operations, World War II.*

5. BIOGRAPHIES AND MEMOIRS. General H. H. Arnold, *Global Mission;* General Omar Bradley, *A Soldier's Story;* Arthur Bryant, *The Turn of the Tide* and *Triumph in the West* (2 vols.), based on diaries of Field Marshal Viscount Alanbrooke; Winston S. Churchill, *The Grand Alliance, The Hinge of Fate, Closing the Ring,* and *Triumph and Tragedy* (The Second World War, vols. 3–6); Charles R. Codman, *Drive* (with Patton); Admiral of the Fleet Viscount Cunningham of Hyndhope, *A Sailor's Odyssey;* Grand Admiral Doenitz, *Memoirs: Ten Years and Twenty Days;* Anthony Eden, *Full Circle;* General Robert L. Eichelberger, *Our Jungle Road to Tokyo;* General Dwight D. Eisenhower, *Crusade in Europe;* Walter Millis (ed.), *The Forrestal Diaries;* Sir Francis de Guingand, *Operation Victory;* Fleet Admiral William F. Halsey & Lt. Cdr. J. Bryan 3rd, *Admiral Halsey's Story;* Captain B. H. Liddell Hart, *The Other Side of the Hill: The German Generals Talk* and (ed.), *The Rommel Papers;* E. J. King & Walter Whitehill, *Fleet Admiral King: A Naval Record;* S. L. A. Marshall, *Blitzkrieg, Bastogne, Island Victory,* and *Night Drop* (Normandy); Viscount Montgomery of Alamein, *The Memoirs;* Lt. Gen. Sir Frederick Morgan, *Overture to Overlord;* Robert Payne, *The Marshall Story;* Forrest Pogue, *George C. Marshall;* Ernie Pyle, *Brave Men;* Grand Admiral Erich Raeder, *My Life;* Marshal of the R. A. F.

Sir John Slessor, *The Central Blue;* H. R. Trevor-Roper, *The Last Days of Hitler;* General Albert C. Wedemeyer, *Wedemeyer Reports;* Theodore White (ed.), *The Stilwell Papers.*

6. COMPREHENSIVE OFFICIAL AND SEMI-OFFICIAL HISTORIES. AUSTRALIA. *Australia in the War of 1939–1945.* Series 1 (Army), 7 vols.; Series 2 (Navy), 2 vols.; Series 3 (Air), 4 vols.; Series 4 (Civil), 5 vols.; Series 5 (Medical), 4 vols. CANADA. Col. C. P. Stacey, *The Canadian Army 1939–1945, An Official Historical Summary,* and *History of the Canadian Army* (3 vols.); Gilbert N. Tucker, *The Naval Service of Canada* (2 vols.). GREAT BRITAIN. J. R. M. Butler (ed.), *History of the Second World War, U. K. Military Series,* includes 6 vols. on *Grand Strategy* by Butler & John Ehrman, 4 vols. on *The War at Sea* by S. W. Roskill, and the sensational *Strategic Air Offensive against Germany* (4 vols.) by Sir Charles Webster & Noble Frankland. JAPAN. Col. Takushiro Hattori, *Dai Toa Sanso Zenshi* (Complete History of the Greater East Asia War, 8 vols.), Tokyo. U.S. ARMY. Kent R. Greenfield, *et al.* (eds.), *The U.S. Army in World War II,* 65 vols. published or in preparation on individual campaigns, and vols. on Military Administration, Engineers and other Corps, the Supreme Command, etc. (*Master Index, Reader's Guide II,* published in 1960, gives an analysis of each vol.); *The American Forces in Action* (14 paper-bound vols.); Wesley F. Craven & J. L. Cate (eds.), *The Army Air Forces in World War II* (7 vols.). U.S. MARINE CORPS. *History of U.S. Marine Corps Operations in World War II,* 5 vols. published or in preparation; *Marine Corps Monographs,* 14 vols. on campaigns in the Pacific. U.S. NAVY AND COAST GUARD. Rear Adm. Julius A. Furer, *Administration of the Navy Dept. in World War II;* S. E. Morison, *History of United States Naval Operations in World War II* (15 vols.); M. F. Willoughby, *The United States Coast Guard in World War II.*

7. WARTIME DIPLOMACY. John M. Blum (ed.), *From the Morgenthau Diaries: Years of War, 1941–1945;* Robert Butow, *Japan's Decision To Surrender;* R. A. Divine, *The Reluctant Belligerent;* Herbert Feis, *The China Tangle, Churchill-Roosevelt-Stalin, The Potsdam Conference,* and *Japan Subdued;* Trumbull Higgins, *Winston Churchill and the Second Front;* W. L. Langer, *Our Vichy Gamble;* Robert Murphy, *Diplomat Among Warriors;* William L. Neumann, *Making the Peace, 1941–1945;* C. F. Romanus and Riley Sunderland, *Stilwell's Mission to China;* Gaddis Smith, *American Diplomacy during the Second World War;* J. L. Snell, *Illusion and Necessity: Wartime Origins of the East-West Dilemma over Germany,* and (ed.), *The Meaning of Yalta;* Edward Stettinius, *Roosevelt and the Russians;* Sumner Welles,

A Time for Decision; T. H. White and Annalee Jacoby, *Thunder Out of China.*

8. MOBILIZATION AND AMERICAN SOCIETY IN WARTIME. Albert A. Blum, *Drafted or Deferred;* James F. Byrnes, *Speaking Frankly;* Bruce Catton, *War Lords of Washington;* L. V. Chandler, *Inflation in the United States, 1940–1948;* Marshall Clinard, *The Black Market;* R. H. Connery, *Navy and Industrial Mobilization in World War II;* Edwin S. Corwin, *Total War and the Constitution;* Jonathan Daniels, *Frontier on the Potomac;* John Dos Passos, *State of the Union;* Herbert Garfinkel, *When Negroes March;* Jack Goodman (ed.), *While You Were Gone;* Morton Grodzins, *Americans Betrayed;* William Hassett, *Off the Record with FDR 1942–1945;* P. E. Jacobs and M. Q. Sibley, *Conscription of Conscience;* Eliot Janeway, *The Struggle for Survival;* Frederic C. Lane, *Ships for Victory;* Ulysses Lee, *The Employment of Negro Troops;* Francis Merrill (ed.), *Social Problems on the Home Front;* Gunnar Myrdal, *An American Dilemma* (2 vols.); Donald M. Nelson, *Arsenal of Democracy;* David Novik, *et al., Wartime Production Control;* H. D. Hall, *North American Supply;* W. F. Ogburn (ed.), *American Society in Wartime;* Donald H. Riddle, *The Truman Committee;* Joel Seidman, *American Labor from Defense to Reconversion;* H. M. Somers, *Presidential Agency: OWMR;* Jacobus ten Broek, *et al., Salvage: Japanese American Evacuation and Resettlement;* George Tindall, *The Emergence of the New South, 1913–1945;* War Production Board, *Industrial Mobilization for War,* vol. 1; Roland Young, *Congressional Politics in the Second World War.*

9. DOCUMENTS. Desmond Flower & James Reeves (eds.), *The Taste of Courage, The War, 1939–45;* Richard Polenberg (ed.), *America at War.*

CHAPTERS XXV AND XXVII

1. GENERAL. James M. Burns, *The Deadlock of Democracy;* Congressional Quarterly, *Congress and Nation;* Elmer Cornwell, *Presidential Leadership of Public Opinion;* Eric Goldman, *The Crucial Decade;* Erwin C. Hargrove, *Presidential Leadership;* Walter Johnson, *1600 Pennsylvania Avenue;* Richard Neustadt, *Presidential Power.*

2. POLITICS. Clifton Brock, *Americans for Democratic Action;* Stuart G. Brown, *Conscience in Politics: Adlai Stevenson;* Angus Campbell *et al., The American Voter;* Paul David *et al., Presidential Nominating Politics in 1952;* Kenneth S. Davis, *A Prophet in His Own Country;* Heinz Eulau, *Class and Party in the Eisenhower Years;* Louis Gerson, *The Hyphenate in Recent Amer-*

ican Politics and Diplomacy; L. Harris, *Is There a Republican Majority?;* Walter Johnson, *How We Drafted Adlai Stevenson;* V. O. Key, *Southern Politics in State and Nation;* Samuel Lubell, *The Revolt of the Moderates;* Herbert J. Muller, *Adlai Stevenson;* Arthur M. Schlesinger, Jr., *The Vital Center;* Charles A. H. Thomson & Frances M. Shattuck, *The 1956 Presidential Campaign;* David B. Truman, *The Congressional Party.*

3. TRUMAN AND THE FAIR DEAL. Stephen K. Bailey, *Congress Makes a Law;* E. R. Bartley, *The Tidelands Oil Controversy;* P. A. Brinker, *The Taft-Hartley Act After Ten Years;* James G. Burrow, *AMA: Voice of American Medicine;* Jonathan Daniels, *The Man of Independence;* Richard Davies, *Housing Reform During the Truman Administration;* Richard S. Kirkendall (ed.), *The Truman Period As A Research Field;* L. W. Koenig (ed.), *The Truman Administration;* R. Alton Lee, *Truman and Taft-Hartley;* Allen J. Matusow, *Farm Policies and Politics in the Truman Years;* H. A. Millis & E. C. Brown, *From the Wagner Act to Taft-Hartley;* Cabell Phillips, *The Truman Presidency;* Harry S. Truman, *Memoirs* (2 vols.).

4. CIVIL LIBERTIES. Jack Anderson and Ronald May, *McCarthy;* Alan Barth, *The Loyalty of Free Men;* Daniel Bell (ed.), *The New American Right;* Eleanor Bontecou, *The Federal Loyalty-Security Program;* Ralph Brown, *Loyalty and Security;* Robert K. Carr, *Federal Protection of Civil Rights, The House Committee on Un-American Activities,* and *To Secure These Rights;* John W. Caughey, *In Clear and Present Danger;* Whittaker Chambers, *Witness;* Harold W. Chase, *Security and Liberty;* Henry S. Commager, *Freedom, Loyalty, Dissent;* Alastair Cooke, *A Generation on Trial;* Charles Curtis, *The Oppenheimer Case;* Theodore Draper, *The Roots of American Communism;* Osmond D. Fraenkel, *Supreme Court and Civil Liberties;* Walter Gellhorn, *Security, Loyalty, and Science, The States and Subversion* and *American Rights;* Morton Grodzins, *The Loyal and the Disloyal;* Learned Hand, *The Spirit of Liberty;* Alger Hiss, *In the Court of Public Opinion;* Sidney Hook, *Heresy, Yes — Conspiracy, No;* Donald J. Kemper, *The Decade of Fear: Senator Hennings and Civil Liberties;* Milton Konvitz, *The Constitution and Civil Rights;* Earl Latham, *The Communist Controversy in Washington;* Owen Lattimore, *Ordeal by Slander;* Richard P. Longacker, *The Presidency and Civil Liberties;* Robert MacIver, *Academic Freedom in Our Time;* C. H. Pritchett, *Civil Liberties and the Vinson Court;* Michael Paul Rogin, *The Intellectuals and McCarthy;* Richard Rovere, *Senator Joe McCarthy;* David Shannon, *The Decline of American Communism;* Edward A. Shils, *The Torment of Secrecy;* S. A. Stouffer, *Communism, Conformity and Civil Liberties;* Michael Straight, *Trial by Television;* Telford Taylor, *Grand Inquest;* J. A. Wechsler, *The Age of Suspicion.*

5. THE EISENHOWER GOVERNMENT. Sherman Adams, *First-Hand Report;* Dean Albertson (ed.), *Eisenhower as President;* Marquis Childs, *Eisenhower: Captive Hero;* E. L. Dale, *Conservatives in Power: A Study in Frustration;* Robert J. Donovan, *Eisenhower: The Inside Story;* E. J. Hughes, *The Ordeal of Power;* Alan McAdams, *Power and Politics in Labor Legislation;* Martin Merson, *The Private Diary of a Public Servant;* Richard M. Nixon, *Six Crises;* Merlo J. Pusey, *Eisenhower the President;* Richard Rovere, *The Eisenhower Years: Affairs of State;* Aaron Wildavsky, *Dixon-Yates.*

6. CIVIL RIGHTS. Harry Ashmore, *The Negro and the Schools;* Monroe Berger, *Equality by Statute;* Bradford Daniel (ed.), *Black, White and Gray;* Walter Gellhorn, *American Rights;* Robert Harris, *The Quest for Equality;* Anthony Lewis, *et al.*, *Portrait of a Decade;* Donald R. Matthews & James W. Prothro, *Negroes and the New Southern Politics;* Walter F. Murphy, *Congress and the Court;* Benjamin Muse, *Ten Years of Prelude;* A. M. Rose, *The Negro in Postwar America;* Don Shoemaker (ed.), *With All Deliberate Speed: Segregation-Desegregation;* James W. Silver, *Mississippi: The Closed Society;* Frank E. Smith, *Congressman from Mississippi;* B. M. Ziegler, *Desegregation and the Supreme Court;* Howard Zinn, *SNCC: The New Abolitionists.*

7. THE WARFARE STATE. Morton Berkowitz and P. G. Bock, *American National Security;* Demetrios Caraley, *The Politics of Military Unification;* Paul Hammond, *Organizing for Defense;* Samuel Huntington, *The Common Defense* and *The Soldier and the State;* Edward A. Kolodziej, *The Uncommon Defense and Congress, 1945–1963;* William R. Kintner, *et al.*, *Forging a New Sword: A Study of the Department of Defense;* Ernest R. May (ed.), *The Ultimate Decision;* Walter Millis, *Arms and the State;* Clinton Rossiter, *The Supreme Court and the Commander-in-Chief;* John M. Swomley, *The Military Establishment.*

8. DOCUMENTS. H. S. Commager, *Documents,* nos. 567–73, 576, 578–85, 588, 592, 594–5, 597–633; *Public Papers of the Presidents: Dwight D. Eisenhower* (8 vols.); *Public Papers of the Presidents: Harry S. Truman* (8 vols.).

For further references, *Harvard Guide* ¶¶ 274–6.

CHAPTERS XXVI AND XXVIII

1. GENERAL. Dean Acheson, *Power and Diplomacy;* Herbert Agar, *The Price of Power;* Raymond Aron, *The Century of Total War;* James F. Byrnes, *Speaking Frankly;* William G. Carleton, *Revolution in American Foreign*

Policy; Jules Davids, *America and the World in Our Time;* D. D. Eisenhower, *Mandate for Change;* Louis J. Halle, *The Cold War as History;* George F. Kennan, *The Realities of American Foreign Policy;* John Lukacs, *A History of the Cold War;* Hans Morgenthau, *Dilemmas of Politics* and *Politics Among the Nations;* Robert Osgood, *Limited War;* William Reitzel *et al., United States Foreign Policy, 1945–1955;* Walt W. Rostow, *The United States in the World Arena;* J. W. Spanier, *American Foreign Policy Since World War II;* Richard P. Stebbins, *The United States in World Affairs* (annual volumes); Harry S. Truman, *Memoirs,* vol. 2; H. B. Westerfield, *Foreign Policy and Party Politics: Pearl Harbor to Korea.*

2. LIQUIDATING THE WAR. Ruth Benedict, *The Chrysanthemum and the Sword;* V. H. Bernstein, *Final Judgment: The Story of Nuremberg;* Lucius Clay, *Decision in Germany;* W. Friedman, *Allied Military Government of Germany;* Sheldon Glueck, *The Nuremberg Trials and Aggressive War;* Robert Jackson, *The Case Against the Nazi War Criminals;* E. H. Litchfield (ed.), *Governing Postwar Germany;* A. Frank Reel, *The Case of General Yamashita;* Edwin Reischauer, *The United States and Japan;* Theodore White, *Fire in the Ashes;* Robert Woetzel, *Nuremberg Trials in International Law;* Harold Zink, *American Military Government in Germany.*

3. ORGANIZATION FOR PEACE AND THE CONTROL OF ATOMIC WEAPONS. Gar Alperovitz, *Atomic Diplomacy;* Robert Batchelder, *The Irreversible Decision 1939–1950;* P. M. Blackett, *Fear, War and the Bomb;* David Bradley, *No Place to Hide;* Bernard Brodie, *The Absolute Weapon;* Harrison Brown, *The Challenge of Man's Future;* Norman Cousins, *Modern Man Is Obsolete;* R. A. Dahl & R. S. Brown, *The Domestic Control of Atomic Energy;* Pierre Gallois, *The Balance of Terror;* George Gamow, *Atomic Energy in Cosmic and Human Life;* James M. Gavin, *War and Peace in the Space Age;* Robert Gilpin, *American Scientists and Nuclear Weapons Policy;* R. G. Hewlett and O. E. Anderson, Jr., *The New World;* Herman Kahn, *On Thermonuclear War;* George Kennan, *Russia, the Atom and the West;* Henry Kissinger, *Nuclear Weapons and Foreign Policy;* Ralph Lapp, *Atoms and Peace;* P. McGuire, *Experiment in World Order;* Jeannette Muther, *History of the United Nations Charter;* James Warburg, *Disarmament: The Challenge of the 1960's;* Arthur Waskow, *The Limits of Defense.*

4. RELIEF AND RECOVERY. David A. Baldwin, *Economic Development and American Foreign Policy;* W. A. Brown, *American Foreign Assistance;* Merle Curti & Kendall Birr, *Prelude to Point Four: American Missions Overseas;* Seymour Harris, *European Recovery Program* and *Foreign Economic*

Policy for the United States; J. M. Jones, *The Fifteen Weeks;* Eugene Kulischer, *Europe on the Move;* Barbara Ward, *The Rich Nations and the Poor Nations;* George Woodbridge (ed.), *UNRRA* (2 vols.).

5. THE COLD WAR. E. H. Carr, *Soviet Impact on the Western World;* W. Phillips Davison, *The Berlin Blockade;* Roscoe Drummond and Gastro Coblenz, *Duel at the Brink;* J. F. Dulles, *War or Peace;* Herbert Feis, *Between War and Peace; Contest over Japan;* and *Potsdam;* Herman Finer, *Dulles Over Suez;* D. L. Fleming, *The Cold War* (2 vols.); Norman Graebner, *The New Isolationism;* Martin F. Herz, *Beginnings of the Cold War;* B. H. Ivanyi & A. Bell, *The Road to Potsdam;* Walter Lippmann, *The Cold War;* W. H. McNeill, *America, Britain, and Russia;* Drew Middleton, *The Defense of Western Europe;* R. E. Osgood, *NATO: The Entangling Alliance;* Henry L. Roberts, *Russia and America;* Arnold A. Rogow, *James Forrestal;* Walter B. Smith, *My Three Years in Moscow;* Edmund Stillman & William Pfaff, *The New Politics;* M. D. Taylor, *Uncertain Trumpet.*

6. THE KOREAN WAR. Carl Berger, *The Korea Knot;* Mark Clark, *From the Danube to the Yalu;* Herbert Feis, *The China Tangle;* Leland M. Goodrich, *Korea: A Study in U.S. Policy;* Trumbull Higgins, *Korea and the Fall of MacArthur;* R. T. Oliver, *Why War Came to Korea;* David Rees, *Korea: The Limited War;* Richard Rovere & A. M. Schlesinger, Jr., *The General and the President;* John Spanier, *The Truman-MacArthur Controversy;* Allen Whiting, *China Crosses the Yalu;* Courtney Whitney, *MacArthur;* C. A. Willoughby & J. Chamberlain, *MacArthur, 1944–1951.*

7. LATIN AMERICA. Robert Alexander, *Communism in Latin America;* Donald M. Dozer, *Are We Good Neighbors?;* Ronald Schneider, *Communism in Guatemala;* Arthur P. Whitaker, *Argentine Upheaval* and *The United States and Latin America: The Northern Republics.*

8. DOCUMENTS. Ruhl Bartlett (ed.), *Record of American Diplomacy;* H. S. Commager, *Documents,* nos. 557–58, 562–66, 571–75, 577, 583, 586–93, 596, 599–602; Council on Foreign Relations, *Documents on American Foreign Relations* (annual vols.).

For further references, *Harvard Guide,* ¶¶ 272–73.

CHAPTER XXIX

1. GROWTH AND THE ECONOMY. Walter Adams and H. M. Gray, *Monopoly in America;* F. M. Bator, *The Question of Government Spending;*

A. A. Berle, *The Twentieth Century Revolution;* Peter Drucker, *America's Next Twenty Years* and *The New Society;* Edward S. Flash, Jr., *Economic Advice and Presidential Leadership;* Editors of Fortune, *America in the Sixties: The Economy and the Society;* Kenneth Galbraith, *The Affluent Society* and *American Capitalism;* Walton Hamilton, *Politics and Industry;* Dale Hathaway, *Government and Agriculture;* A. E. Holmans, *United States Fiscal Policy, 1945–1959;* Robert Lekachman, *Age of Keynes;* Max Lerner, *America as a Civilization;* David E. Lilienthal, *Big Business;* Vance Packard, *The Hidden Persuaders;* Andrew Shonfield, *Modern Capitalism;* Lauren Soth, *Farm Trouble in an Age of Plenty;* Philip Taft, *Structure and Government of Labor Unions;* C. E. Warne & K. W. Lumpkin, *et al., Labor in Post War America.*

2. THE CITY. Luther Gulick, *The Metropolitan Problem;* Jane Jacobs, *The Death and Life of Great American Cities;* Lewis Mumford, *The City in History* and *The Culture of Cities;* A. C. Spectorsky, *The Exurbanites;* Christopher Tunnard & Henry H. Reed, *American Skyline;* Robert Wood, *Suburbia.*

3. SOCIETY AND THE CLASS STRUCTURE. Frederick L. Allen, *The Big Change;* Bernard Barber, *Social Stratification;* Reinhard Bendix & Seymour Lipset (ed.), *Class, Status and Power;* Alfred C. Kinsey, *et al., Sexual Behavior in the Human Male;* C. Wright Mills, *The Power Elite* and *White Collar;* Vance Packard, *The Status Seekers;* David Riesman, *et al., The Lonely Crowd* and *Faces in the Crowd;* W. Lloyd Warner, *American Life: Dream and Reality* and *Social Class in America;* William H. Whyte, *The Organization Man.*

4. EDUCATION. Jacques Barzun, *The House of Intellect* and *Teacher in America;* Arthur Bestor, *Educational Wastelands* and *The Restoration of American Learning;* James Conant, *The American High School Today* and *Slums and Suburbs;* Cyril Scott Fletcher (ed.), *Education for Public Responsibility;* Robert Hutchins, *Conflict of Education in a Democratic Society;* David Riesman, *Constraint and Variety in American Education;* Mark Van Doren, *Liberal Education.*

5. ARTS AND LETTERS. John Aldridge, *After the Lost Generation;* I. H. Baur, *Revolution and Tradition in Modern American Art;* Leo Gurko, *Heroes, Highbrows and the Popular Mind;* Talbot Hamlin, *Forms and Functions of Twentieth Century Architecture;* Randall Jarrell, *Poetry and the Age;* Archibald MacLeish, *Poetry and Experience;* Andrew C. Ritchie, *Abstract Painting and Sculpture in America;* Bernard Rosenberg & David M. White (eds.), *Mass Culture: Popular Arts in America;* Gilbert Seldes, *The Public Arts;* Lionel Trilling, *The Liberal Imagination.*

6. SCIENCE. Siegfried Giedion, *Mechanization Takes Command;* Bernard Jaffe, *Men of Science in America* and *The New World of Chemistry;* Robert

Millikan, *Autobiography;* Ruth Ellen Moore, *The Coil of Life: Great Discoveries in the Life Sciences; Scientific American Reader:* see, too, files of *The Scientific American,* especially September 1950; Mitchell Wilson, *American Science and Invention.*

CHAPTERS XXX AND XXXI

1. JFK AND LBJ. James McG. Burns, *John F. Kennedy;* Michael Davie, *LBJ;* Aida DiPace Donald (ed.), *John F. Kennedy and the New Frontier;* Helen Fuller, *Year of Trial;* Harry Golden, *Mr. Kennedy and the Negroes;* Don F. Hadwiger and Ross B. Talbot, *Pressures and Protests;* Pierre Salinger, *With Kennedy;* A. M. Schlesinger, Jr., *A Thousand Days;* Hugh Sidey, *John F. Kennedy: President;* Theodore Sorenson, *Kennedy;* Tom Wicker, *JFK and LBJ;* W. S. White, *The Professional: Lyndon B. Johnson* and *The Taft Story;* B. H. Wilkins & C. B. Friday, *The Economists of the New Frontier.*

2. POLITICS. Bernard Cosman & Robert J. Huckshorn (eds.), *Republican Politics;* Milton C. Cummings, Jr. (ed.), *The National Election of 1964;* George F. Gilder and Bruce K. Chapman, *The Party That Lost Its Head;* Seymour E. Harris, *Economics of the Kennedy Years;* Earl Mazo, *Richard Nixon;* Robert D. Novak, *The Agony of the G.O.P. 1964;* Richard H. Rovere, *The Goldwater Caper;* Eric Sevareid (ed.), *Candidates 1960;* Theodore White, *The Making of the President, 1960* and *The Making of the President, 1964.*

3. FOREIGN AFFAIRS. John R. Boettiger (ed.), *Vietnam and American Foreign Policy;* Joseph Buttinger, *Vietnam: A Dragon Embattled;* Bernard Fall, *The Two Vietnams* and *Viet-Nam Witness, 1953–66;* J. W. Fulbright, *The Arrogance of Power;* Philip L. Geyelin, *Lyndon B. Johnson and the World;* Richard N. Goodwin, *Triumph or Tragedy;* Roger Hilsman, *To Move a Nation;* Karl Meyer & Ted Szulc, *The Cuban Invasion;* Marcus G. Raskin and Bernard B. Fall (eds.), *The Viet-Nam Reader;* Arthur M. Schlesinger, Jr., *The Bitter Heritage;* Robert Shaplen, *The Lost Revolution;* Richard Stebbins, *The United States in World Affairs* (for appropriate years).

4. FROM NIXON TO CARTER. Carl Bernstein and Robert Woodward, *All the President's Men;* Henry Brandon, *The Retreat of American Power;* Rowland Evans and Robert Novak, *Nixon in the White House;* Stephen Graubard, *Kissinger;* Frank Mankiewicz, *Perfectly Clear;* R. Reeves, *A Ford not a Lincoln;* Martin Schram, *Running for President 1976;* Kandy Stroud, *How Jimmy Won;* Theodore White, *Breach of Faith;* Garry Wills, *Nixon Agonistes;* Jules Witcover, *Marathon;* James Wooten, *Dasher.*

Statistical Tables

ADMISSION OF STATES TO THE UNION

STATE	ENTERED UNION	STATE	ENTERED UNION
Alabama	1819	Montana	1889
Alaska	1959	Nebraska	1867
Arizona	1912	Nevada	1864
Arkansas	1836	New Hampshire	1788
California	1850	New Jersey	1787
Colorado	1876	New Mexico	1912
Connecticut	1788	New York	1788
Delaware	1787	North Carolina	1789
Florida	1845	North Dakota	1889
Georgia	1788	Ohio	1803
Hawaii	1959	Oklahoma	1907
Idaho	1890	Oregon	1859
Illinois	1818	Pennsylvania	1787
Indiana	1816	Rhode Island	1790
Iowa	1846	South Carolina	1788
Kansas	1861	South Dakota	1889
Kentucky	1792	Tennessee	1796
Louisiana	1812	Texas	1845
Maine	1820	Utah	1896
Maryland	1788	Vermont	1791
Massachusetts	1788	Virginia	1788
Michigan	1837	Washington	1889
Minnesota	1858	West Virginia	1863
Mississippi	1817	Wisconsin	1848
Missouri	1821	Wyoming	1890

IMMIGRANTS BY COUNTRY OF LAST PERMANENT RESIDENCE, 1820–1976

COUNTRIES	1820–1975, TOTAL	1951–1960, TOTAL	1961–1970, TOTAL	1972	1973	1974	1975	1976[1]	PER CENT 1820–1975	PER CENT 1961–1970	PER CENT 1971–1976[1]
All countries	47,099	2,515.5	3,321.7	384.7	400.1	394.9	386.2	502.3	100.0	100.0	100.0
Europe	35,961	1,325.6	1,123.4	86.3	91.2	80.4	72.8	91.6	76.4	33.8	21.1
Austria[2]	4,312	67.1	20.6	2.3	1.6	.7	.5	.6	9.2	.6	.3
Hungary		36.6	5.4	.5	1.0	.9	.6	.7		.2	.2
Belgium	201	18.6	9.2	.5	.4	.4	.4	.7	.4	.3	.1
Czechoslovakia	136	.9	3.3	1.2	.9	.4	.3	.4	.3	.1	.2
Denmark	363	11.0	9.2	.5	.4	.5	.3	.5	.8	.3	.1
Finland	33	4.9	4.2	.3	.3	.2	.2	.2	.1	.1	.1
France	742	51.1	45.2	2.9	2.6	2.2	1.8	2.6	1.6	1.4	.6
Germany[2]	6,954	477.8	190.8	7.8	7.6	7.2	5.9	8.6	14.8	5.7	1.9
Great Britain[3]	4,852	195.5	210.0	11.5	11.9	11.7	12.2	16.0	10.3	6.3	3.1
Greece	629	47.6	86.0	10.5	10.3	10.6	9.8	10.8	1.3	2.6	2.7
Ireland[4]	4,720	57.3	37.5	1.4	1.6	1.3	1.1	1.3	10.0	1.1	.3
Italy	5,270	185.5	214.1	22.4	22.3	15.0	11.0	10.0	11.2	6.4	4.2
Netherlands	356	52.3	30.6	1.0	1.0	1.0	.8	1.2	.8	.9	.3
Norway	855	22.9	15.5	.4	.4	.4	.4	.4	1.8	.5	.1
Poland[2]	503	10.0	53.5	3.8	4.1	3.5	3.5	4.0	1.1	1.6	.9
Portugal	411	19.6	76.1	9.5	10.0	10.7	11.3	13.7	.9	2.3	2.7
Spain	246	7.9	44.7	4.3	5.5	4.7	2.6	3.4	.5	1.3	1.0
Sweden	1,270	21.7	17.1	.7	.6	.6	.5	.8	2.7	.5	.2
Switzerland	346	17.7	18.5	1.0	.7	.7	.7	1.0	.7	.6	.2
U.S.S.R.[2][5]	3,354	.6	2.3	.4	.9	.9	4.7	9.2	7.1	.1	.7
Yugoslavia	106	8.2	20.4	2.8	5.2	5.0	2.9	2.9	.2	.6	.9
Other Europe	300	10.8	9.2	.9	1.9	1.9	1.4	2.8	.6	.3	.4
Asia	2,275	153.3	427.8	116.0	120.0	127.0	129.2	184.4	4.8	12.9	31.7
China[6]	488	9.7	34.8	8.5	9.2	10.0	9.2	12.9	1.0	1.0	2.4
Hong Kong	[7]143	15.5	75.0	10.9	10.3	10.7	12.5	16.9	.3	2.3	2.8
India	107	2.0	27.2	15.6	12.0	11.7	14.3	20.2	.2	.8	3.7
Iran	[7]26	3.4	10.3	2.9	2.9	2.5	2.2	3.7	.1	.3	.7
Israel	[7]70	25.5	29.6	3.0	2.9	2.9	3.5	6.4	.1	.9	.9

Japan	391	46.3	40.0	5.0	6.1	5.4	4.8	6.0	.8	1.2	1.3
Jordan	[7]29	5.8	11.7	2.4	2.1	2.5	2.3	3.1	.1	.3	.6
Korea	[7]150	6.2	34.5	18.1	22.3	27.5	28.1	37.5	.3	1.0	6.0
Lebanon	[7]35	4.5	15.2	3.0	2.6	3.0	4.0	6.8	.1	.5	.9
Philippines	[8]268	19.3	98.4	28.7	30.2	32.5	31.3	46.4	.6	3.0	8.1
Turkey	382	3.5	10.1	1.5	1.4	1.4	1.1	1.3	.8	.3	.3
Other Asia	184	11.7	40.9	16.3	18.0	16.9	15.8	23.3	.4	1.2	4.0
America	8,348	996.9	1,716.4	173.2	179.6	178.8	174.7	213.5	17.7	51.7	44.7
Argentina	[9]83	19.5	49.7	2.5	2.9	2.9	2.8	3.3	.2	1.5	.7
Brazil	[9]52	13.8	29.3	1.8	1.8	1.6	1.4	1.7	.1	.9	.4
Canada	4,048	378.0	413.3	18.6	14.8	12.3	11.2	14.9	8.6	12.4	3.9
Colombia	[9]119	18.0	72.0	5.2	5.3	5.9	6.4	7.1	.3	2.2	1.5
Cuba	[10]395	78.9	208.5	19.9	22.5	17.4	25.6	35.0	.8	6.3	5.8
Dominican Rep.	[9]170	9.9	93.3	10.8	14.0	15.7	14.1	15.0	.4	2.8	3.4
Ecuador	[9]70	9.8	36.8	4.4	4.2	4.8	4.7	5.6	.1	1.1	1.2
El Salvador	[9]31	5.9	15.0	2.0	2.0	2.3	2.4	3.1	.1	.4	.5
Guatemala	[9]30	4.7	15.9	1.7	1.8	1.6	1.9	2.6	.1	.5	.5
Haiti	[10]65	4.4	34.5	5.5	4.6	3.8	5.0	6.5	.1	1.0	1.3
Honduras	[9]28	6.0	15.7	1.0	1.4	1.4	1.4	1.6	.1	.5	.3
Mexico	1,912	299.8	453.9	64.2	70.4	71.9	62.6	74.5	4.1	13.7	16.2
Panama	[9]39	11.7	19.4	1.6	1.7	1.7	1.7	2.3	.1	.6	.4
Peru	[9]35	7.4	19.1	1.5	1.8	2.0	2.3	3.3	.1	.6	.5
West Indies	637	29.8	133.9	24.2	21.6	24.4	22.3	24.6	1.4	4.0	5.8
Other America	633	99.2	106.2	8.3	8.7	9.3	9.0	12.4	1.3	3.2	2.3
Africa	104	14.1	29.0	5.5	5.5	5.2	5.9	7.7	.2	.9	1.5
Australia and New Zealand	111	11.5	19.6	2.6	2.5	2.0	1.8	2.7	.2	.6	.6
All other countries	300	14.0	5.7	1.2	1.3	1.4	1.8	2.4	.6	.2	.4

[1] For 1976, 15 months ending Sept. 30. [2] 1938–1945, Austria included with Germany; 1899–1919, Poland included with Austria-Hungary, Germany, and U.S.S.R. [3] Beginning 1952, includes data for United Kingdom not specified, formerly included with 'Other Europe.' [4] Comprises Eire and Northern Ireland. [5] Europe and Asia. [6] Beginning 1957, includes Taiwan. [7] Prior to 1951, included with 'Other Asia.' [8] Prior to 1951, Philippines included with 'All other countries.' [9] Prior to 1951, included with 'Other America.'

Source: *Statistical Abstract*

POPULATION OF THE UNITED STATES, 1870–1974

(in Thousands)

STATE	1870	1880	1890	1900	1910	1920	1930	1940	1950	1960	1970	(estimate) 1974
New England												
Maine	627	649	661	694	742	768	797	847	914	969	992	1,047
New Hampshire	318	347	377	412	431	443	465	492	533	607	738	808
Vermont	331	332	332	344	356	352	360	359	378	390	444	470
Massachusetts	1,457	1,783	2,239	2,805	3,336	3,852	4,250	4,317	4,691	5,149	5,689	5,800
Rhode Island	217	277	346	429	543	604	688	713	792	859	947	937
Connecticut	537	623	746	908	1,115	1,381	1,607	1,709	2,007	2,535	3,032	3,088
Middle Atlantic												
New York	4,383	5,083	6,003	7,269	9,114	10,385	12,588	13,479	14,830	16,782	18,237	18,111
New Jersey	906	1,131	1,445	1,884	2,537	3,156	4,041	4,160	4,835	6,067	7,168	7,330
Pennsylvania	3,522	4,283	5,258	6,302	7,665	8,720	9,631	9,900	10,498	11,319	11,794	11,835
South Atlantic												
Delaware	125	147	168	185	202	223	238	267	318	446	548	573
Maryland	781	935	1,042	1,188	1,295	1,450	1,632	1,821	2,343	3,101	3,922	4,094
Dist of Columbia	132	178	230	279	331	438	487	663	802	764	757	723
Virginia	1,225	1,513	1,656	1,854	2,062	2,309	2,422	2,678	3,319	3,967	4,648	4,908
West Virginia	442	618	763	959	1,221	1,464	1,729	1,902	2,006	1,860	1,744	1,791
North Carolina	1,071	1,340	1,618	1,894	2,206	2,559	3,170	3,572	4,062	4,556	5,082	5,363
South Carolina	706	996	1,151	1,340	1,515	1,684	1,739	1,900	2,117	2,383	2,591	2,784
Georgia	1,184	1,542	1,837	2,216	2,609	2,896	2,909	3,124	3,445	3,943	4,590	4,882
Florida	188	269	391	529	753	968	1,468	1,897	2,771	4,952	6,789	8,090
South Central												
Kentucky	1,321	1,649	1,859	2,147	2,290	2,417	2,615	2,846	2,945	3,038	3,219	3,357
Tennessee	1,259	1,542	1,768	2,021	2,185	2,338	2,617	2,916	3,292	3,567	3,924	4,129
Alabama	997	1,262	1,513	1,829	2,138	2,348	2,646	2,833	3,062	3,267	3,444	3,577
Mississippi	828	1,132	1,290	1,551	1,797	1,791	2,010	2,184	2,179	2,178	2,217	2,324
Arkansas	484	803	1,128	1,312	1,574	1,752	1,854	1,949	1,910	1,786	1,923	2,062
Louisiana	727	940	1,119	1,382	1,656	1,799	2,102	2,364	2,684	3,257	3,641	3,764
Oklahoma			259	790	1,657	2,028	2,396	2,226	2,233	2,328	2,559	2,709
Texas	819	1,592	2,236	3,049	3,897	4,663	5,825	6,415	7,711	9,580	11,197	12,050

North Central												
Ohio	2,665	3,198	3,672	4,158	4,767	5,759	6,647	6,908	7,947	9,706	10,652	10,737
Indiana	1,681	1,978	2,192	2,516	2,701	2,930	3,239	3,428	3,934	4,662	5,194	5,330
Illinois	2,540	3,078	3,826	4,822	5,639	6,485	7,631	7,897	8,712	10,081	11,114	11,131
Michigan	1,184	1,637	2,094	2,421	2,810	3,668	4,842	5,256	6,372	7,823	8,875	9,098
Wisconsin	1,055	1,315	1,693	2,069	2,334	2,632	2,939	3,138	3,435	3,951	4,418	4,566
Minnesota	4	781	1,310	1,751	2,076	2,387	2,564	2,792	2,982	3,414	3,805	3,917
Iowa	1,194	1,625	1,912	2,232	2,225	2,404	2,471	2,538	2,621	2,758	2,824	2,855
Missouri	1,721	2,168	2,679	3,107	3,293	3,404	3,629	3,785	3,955	4,320	4,677	4,777
North Dakota	14	135	191	319	577	647	681	642	620	632	618	637
South Dakota			349	402	584	637	693	643	653	681	666	682
Nebraska	123	452	1,063	1,066	1,192	1,296	1,378	1,316	1,326	1,411	1,483	1,543
Kansas	364	996	1,428	1,470	1,691	1,769	1,881	1,801	1,905	2,179	2,247	2,270
Mountain												
Montana	21	39	143	243	376	549	538	559	591	675	694	735
Idaho	15	33	89	162	326	432	445	525	589	668	713	799
Wyoming	9	21	63	93	146	194	226	251	291	330	332	359
Colorado	40	194	413	540	799	940	1,036	1,123	1,325	1,755	2,207	2,496
New Mexico	92	120	160	195	327	360	423	532	681	951	1,016	1,122
Arizona	10	40	88	123	204	334	436	499	750	1,302	1,771	2,153
Utah	87	144	211	277	373	449	508	550	689	891	1,059	1,173
Nevada	42	62	47	42	82	77	91	110	160	285	489	573
Pacific												
Washington	24	75	357	518	1,142	1,357	1,563	1,902	2,379	2,853	3,409	3,476
Oregon	91	175	318	414	673	783	954	1,090	1,521	1,769	2,091	2,266
California	560	865	1,213	1,485	2,378	3,427	5,677	6,907	10,586	15,717	19,953	20,907
Alaska					64	64	55	59	73	226	300	337
Hawaii					154	192	256	368	423	633	769	847
Puerto Rico						1,300	1,544	1,869	2,211	2,350	2,712	
Total	38,558	50,156	62,948	75,995	92,228	107,322	124,747	132,154	151,319	179,311	203,212	211,390

Source: U.S. Bureau of the Census

URBAN AND RURAL POPULATION, 1870–1970

Census Year	URBAN * Number (in Thousands)	Per Cent of Total	RURAL Number (in Thousands)	Per Cent of Total
1870	9,902	25.7	28,656	74.3
1880	14,129	28.2	36,026	71.8
1890	22,106	35.1	40,841	64.9
1900	30,159	39.7	45,834	60.3
1910	41,998	45.7	49,973	54.3
1920	54,157	51.2	51,552	48.8
1930	68,954	56.2	53,820	43.8
1940	74,423	56.5	57,245	43.5
1950	96,847	59.0	54,479	41.0
1960	125,269	69.9	54,054	30.1
1970	149,235	73.5	53,887	26.5

* Urban: Includes all persons living in places of 2,500 or more and in densely settled urban fringe areas.

Source: U.S. Census of Population, 1970

YEAR	CANDIDATE	PARTY	POPULAR VOTE	PER CENT	ELECTORAL VOTE
1876	Tilden	Democratic	4,284,885	50.94	184
	Hayes	Republican	4,033,950	47.95	185
	Cooper	Greenback	81,740	.97	...
	Smith	Prohibition	9,522	.11	...
	Walker	American	2,636	.03	...
1880	Garfield	Republican	4,449,053	48.31	214
	Hancock	Democratic	4,442,035	48.23	155
	Weaver	Greenback	307,306	3.34	...
	Dow	Prohibition	10,487	.11	...
	Phelps	American	707	.01	...
1884	Cleveland	Democratic	4,911,017	48.89	219
	Blaine	Republican	4,848,334	48.27	182
	St. John	Prohibition	151,809	1.51	...
	Butler	Greenback	133,825	1.33	...
1888	Cleveland	Democratic	5,540,050	48.66	168
	Harrison	Republican	5,444,337	47.82	233
	Fisk	Prohibition	250,125	2.20	...
	Streeter	Union Labor	146,897	1.29	...
	Cowdrey	United Labor	2,808	.03	...
1892	Cleveland	Democratic	5,554,414	46.04	277
	Harrison	Republican	5,190,802	43.02	145
	Weaver	People's	1,027,329	8.51	22
	Bidwell	Prohibition	271,058	2.24	...
	Wing	Socialist	21,164	.19	...
1896	McKinley	Republican	7,035,638	50.88	271
	Bryan	Democratic	6,467,946	46.77	176
	Levering	Prohibition	141,676	1.03	...
	Palmer	Nat. Democratic	131,529	.95	...
	Matchett	Socialist-Labor	36,454	.27	...
	Bentley	National	13,969	.10	...
1900	McKinley	Republican	7,219,530	51.69	292
	Bryan	Democratic	6,358,071	45.51	155
	Woolley	Prohibition	209,166	1.49	...
	Debs	Socialist Democrat	94,768	.67	...
	Barker	People's	50,232	.37	...
	Malloney	Socialist-Labor	32,751	.23	...
	Ellis	Union Reform	5,098	.04	...
	Leonard	United Christian	518	.00	...
1904	Roosevelt	Republican	7,628,834	56.41	336
	Parker	Democratic	5,084,401	37.60	140
	Debs	Socialist	402,460	2.98	...
	Swallow	Prohibition	259,257	1.91	...
	Watson	People's	114,753	.85	...
	Corregan	Socialist-Labor	33,724	.25	...
	Holcomb	Continental	830	.00	...
1908	Taft	Republican	7,679,006	51.58	321
	Bryan	Democratic	6,409,106	43.05	162
	Debs	Socialist	420,820	2.83	...
	Chafin	Prohibition	252,683	1.69	...
	Hisgen	Independence	83,562	.56	...
	Watson	People's	28,131	.19	...
	Gillhaus	Socialist-Labor	13,825	.10	...
	Turney	United Christian	461	.00	...
1912	Wilson	Democratic	6,286,214	41.82	435
	Roosevelt	Progressive	4,126,020	27.45	88
	Taft	Republican	3,483,922	23.17	8
	Debs	Socialist	897,011	5.97	...
	Chafin	Prohibition	208,923	1.39	...
	Reimer	Socialist-Labor	29,079	.20	...
1916	Wilson	Democratic	9,129,606	49.28	277
	Hughes	Republican	8,538,221	46.07	254
	Benson	Socialist	585,113	3.16	...

YEAR	CANDIDATE	PARTY	POPULAR VOTE	PER CENT	ELECTORAL VOTE
1916	Hanly	Prohibition	220,506	1.19	...
	Reimer	Socialist-Labor	13,403	.07	...
	Misc.		41,894	.23	...
1920	**Harding**	**Republican**	16,152,200	61.02	404
	Cox	Democratic	9,147,353	34.55	127
	Debs	Socialist	919,799	3.47	...
	Watkins	Prohibition	189,408	.72	...
	Cox	Socialist-Labor	31,175	.12	...
	Christensen	Farmer Labor	26,541	.10	...
	Macauley	Single Tax	5,837	.02	...
1924	**Coolidge**	**Republican**	15,725,016	54.10	382
	Davis	Democratic	8,385,586	28.80	136
	La Follette	Independent, Progressive, and Socialist	4,822,856	16.60	13
	Faris	Prohibition	57,551⎫		...
	Johns	Socialist-Labor	38,958⎪		...
	Foster	Workers'	33,361⎬ .50		...
	Nations	American	23,867⎪		...
	Wallace	Com. Land	2,778⎭		...
1928	**Hoover**	**Republican**	21,392,190	58.20	444
	Smith	Democratic	15,016,443	40.80	87
	Thomas	Socialist	267,420⎫		...
	Foster	Workers'	48,770⎪		...
	Reynolds	Socialist-Labor	21,603⎬ 1.00		...
	Varney	Prohibition	20,106⎪		...
	Webb	Farm-Labor	6,390⎭		...
1932	**Roosevelt**	**Democratic**	22,821,857	57.30	472
	Hoover	Republican	15,761,841	39.60	59
	Thomas	Socialist	884,781⎫		...
	Foster	Communist	102,991⎪		...
	Upshaw	Prohibition	81,869⎬ 3.10		...
	Harvey	Liberty	53,425⎪		...
	Reynolds	Socialist-Labor	33,276⎭		...
	Coxey	Farm-Labor	7,309		...
1936	**Roosevelt**	**Democratic**	27,751,612	60.70	523
	Landon	Republican	16,681,913	36.40	8
	Lemke	Union	891,858⎫		...
	Thomas	Socialist	187,342⎪		...
	Browder	Communist	80,181⎬ 2.90		...
	Colvin	Prohibition	37,609⎪		...
	Aiken	Socialist-Labor	12,729⎭		...
1940	**Roosevelt**	**Democratic**	27,243,466	54.70	449
	Willkie	Republican	22,304,755	44.80	82
	Thomas	Socialist	99,557⎫		...
	Babson	Prohibition	57,812⎪		...
	Browder	Communist	46,251⎬ .50		...
	Aiken	Socialist-Labor	14,861⎭		...
1944	**Roosevelt**	**Democratic**	25,602,505	52.80	432
	Dewey	Republican	22,006,278	44.50	99
	Thomas	Socialist	80,518⎫		...
	Watson	Prohibition	74,758⎪		...
	Teichert	Socialist-Labor	45,336⎬ 2.70		...
	Misc. Independent		216,289⎭		...
1948	**Truman**	**Democratic**	24,179,345	49.60	303
	Dewey	Republican	21,991,291	45.10	189
	Thurmond	States Rights	1,176,125⎫		39
	Wallace	Progressive	1,157,326⎪		...
	Thomas	Socialist	139,572⎬ 5.30		...
	Watson	Prohibition	103,900⎪		...
	Misc. Independent		46,267⎭		...
1952	**Eisenhower**	**Republican**	33,936,234	55.20	442
	Stevenson	Democratic	27,314,992	44.50	89

YEAR	CANDIDATE	PARTY	POPULAR VOTE	PER CENT	ELECTORAL VOTE
1952	Hallinan	Progressive	140,023		...
	Hamblen	Prohibition	72,949		...
	Haas	Socialist-Labor	30,267		...
	Hoopes	Socialist	20,203	.30	...
	MacArthur	Constitution	17,205		...
	Dobbs	Socialist Workers	10,312		...
1956	Eisenhower	Republican	35,590,472	57.40	457
	Stevenson	Democratic	26,022,752	42.00	73 *
	Andrews	States Rights	111,178		...
	Haas	Socialist-Labor	44,450		...
	Holtwick	Prohibition	41,937	.60	...
	Misc. Independent		216,119		...
1960	Kennedy	Democratic	34,226,731	49.70	303
	Nixon	Republican	34,108,157	49.50	219
	Byrd				15 †
	Faubus	National States Rights	44,977		
	Haas	Socialist-Labor	47,522		
	Decker	Prohibition	46,203	.80	
	Dobbs	Socialist Workers	40,165		...
	Misc. Independent		324,464		...
1964	Johnson	Democratic	43,129,484	61.10	486
	Goldwater	Republican	27,178,188	38.50	52
	Haas	Socialist-Labor	45,219		...
	DeBerry	Socialist Workers	32,720		...
	Munn	Prohibition	23,267	.40	...
	Misc. Independent		235,632		...
1968	Nixon	Republican	31,770,237	43.40	301
	Humphrey	Democratic	31,270,533	42.70	191
	Wallace	American Independent	9,906,141	13.50	46
	Blomen	Socialist-Labor	52,588		...
	Gregory	New	47,097		...
	Halstead	Socialist Workers	41,300		...
	Cleaver	Peace & Freedom	36,385	.40	...
	McCarthy	New	25,858		...
	Misc. Independent		36,680		...
1972	Nixon	Republican	47,169,911	60.7	520
	McGovern	Democratic	29,170,383	37.5	17
	Schmitz	American	1,099,482		
	Spock	Peoples	78,756		
	Jenness	Socialist Workers	66,677		
	Fisher	Socialist-Labor	53,814	1.8	
	Hall	Communist	25,595		
	Munn	Prohibition	13,505		
	Hospers	Libertarian	3,673		1
	Mis. Independent		36,758		
1976	Carter	Democratic	39,147,793	50.1	297
	Ford	Republican	40,830,763	48.0	240
	McCarthy	Independent	756,691		
	MacBride	Libertarian	173,011		
	Maddox	American Independent	170,531		
	Anderson	American	160,773		
	Camejo	Socialist Workers	91,314	1.9	1 *
	Hall	Communist	58,992		
	Wright	People's	49,024		
	LaRouche	United States Labor	40,043		
	Bubar	Prohibition	15,934		
	Levin	Socialist-Labor	9,616		
	Zeidler	Socialist	6,038		
	Misc. Independent		45,366		

* In 1956 in Alabama one Democratic elector refused to vote for Stevenson and cast his ballot for Walter B. Jones.
† Six unpledged electors from Alabama, eight from Mississippi and one Oklahoma Republican who refused to vote for Nixon.
* One Republican elector from Washington voted for Ronald Reagan.

Source: *America Votes* and *Statistical Abstract of the United States*

| NAME | SERVICE | | NAME | SERVICE | |
Chief Justices in Italics	Term	Yrs.	Chief Justices in Italics	Term	Yrs.
Lucius Q. C. Lamar, Miss.	1889–1910	Yrs.	William B. Woods, Ga.	1880–1887	7
John Jay, N.Y.	1789–1795	6	Stanley Matthews, Ohio	1881–1889	8
John Rutledge, S.C.	1789–1791	2	Horace Gray, Mass.	1881–1902	21
William Cushing, Mass.	1789–1810	21	Samuel Blatchford, N.Y.	1882–1893	11
James Wilson, Pa.	1789–1798	9	Lucius Q. C. Lamar, Miss.	1888–1893	5
John Blair, Va.	1789–1796	7	Melville W. Fuller, Ill.	1888–1910	22
Robert H. Harison, Md.	1789–1790	1	David J. Brewer, Kan.	1889–1910	21
James Iredell, N.C.	1790–1799	9	William J. Brennan, Jr., N.J.	1893–1890	Yrs.
Thomas Johnson, Md.	1791–1793	2	Henry B. Brown, Mich.	1890–1906	16
William Paterson, N.J.	1793–1806	13	George Shiras, Jr., Pa.	1892–1903	11
John Rutledge, S.C.	1795–1795		Howell E. Jackson, Tenn.	1893–1895	2
Samuel Chase, Md.	1796–1811	15	Edward D. White, La.	1894–1910	16
Oliver Ellsworth, Conn.	1796–1799	4	Rufus W. Peckham, N.Y.	1895–1910	14
Bushrod Washington, Va.	1798–1829	31	Joseph McKenna, Cal.	1898–1925	27
Alfred Moore, N.C.	1799–1804	5	Oliver W. Holmes, Mass.	1902–1932	29
John Marshall, Va.	1801–1835	34	William R. Day, Ohio	1903–1922	19
William Johnson, S.C.	1804–1834	30	William H. Moody, Mass.	1906–1910	4
Brock Livingston, N.Y.	1806–1823	17	Horace H. Lurton, Tenn.	1910–1914	5
Thomas Todd, Ky.	1807–1826	19	Charles E. Hughes, N.Y.	1910–1916	6
Joseph Story, Mass.	1811–1845	34	Willis Van Devanter, Wyo.	1910–1937	27
Gabriel Duval, Md.	1811–1836	25	Edward D. White, La.	1910–1921	11
Smith Thompson, N.Y.	1823–1843	20	Joseph R. Lamar, Ga.	1911–1916	6
Robert Trimble, Ky.	1826–1828	2	Mahlon Pitney, N.J.	1912–1922	10
John McLean, Ohio	1829–1861	32	Jas. C. McReynolds, Tenn.	1914–1941	27
Henry Baldwin, Pa.	1830–1844	14	Louis D. Brandeis, Mass.	1916–1939	23
James M. Wayne, Ga.	1835–1867	32	John H. Clarke, Ohio	1916–1922	6
Roger B. Taney, Md.	1836–1864	28	William H. Taft, Conn.	1921–1930	9
Philip P. Barbour, Va.	1836–1841	5	George Sutherland, Utah	1922–1938	16
John Catron, Tenn.	1837–1865	28	Pierce Butler, Minn.	1922–1939	17
John McKinley, Ala.	1837–1852	15	Edward T. Sanford, Tenn.	1923–1930	7
Peter V. Daniel, Va.	1841–1860	19	Harlan F. Stone, N.Y.	1925–1941	16
Samuel Nelson, N.Y.	1845–1872	27	Charles E. Hughes, N.Y.	1930–1941	11
Levi Woodbury, N.H.	1845–1851	6	Owen J. Roberts, Pa.	1930–1945	15
Robert C. Grier, Pa.	1846–1870	24	Benjamin N. Cardozo, N.Y.	1932–1938	6
Benj. R. Curtis, Mass.	1851–1857	6	Hugo L. Black, Ala.	1937–1971	34
John A. Campbell, Ala.	1853–1861	8	Stanley F. Reed, Ky.	1938–1957	19
Nathan Clifford, Me.	1858–1881	23	Felix Frankfurter, Mass.	1939–1962	23
Noah H. Swayne, Ohio	1862–1881	20	William O. Douglas, Conn.	1939–1975	36
Samuel F. Miller, Iowa	1862–1890	28	Frank Murphy, Mich.	1940–1949	9
David Davis, Ill.	1862–1877	15	Harlan F. Stone, N.Y.	1941–1946	5
Stephen J. Field, Cal.	1863–1897	34	James F. Byrnes, S.C.	1941–1942	1
Salmon P. Chase, Ohio	1864–1873	9	Robert H. Jackson, N.Y.	1941–1954	13
William Strong, Pa.	1870–1880	10	Wiley B. Rutledge, Iowa	1943–1949	6
Joseph P. Bradley, N.J.	1870–1892	22	Harold H. Burton, Ohio	1945–1958	13
Ward Hunt, N.Y.	1872–1882	10	Fred M. Vinson, Ky.	1946–1953	7
Morrison R. Waite, Ohio	1874–1888	14	Tom C. Clark, Tex.	1949–1967	18
John M. Harlan, Ky.	1877–1911	34	Sherman Minton, Ind.	1949–1956	7

NAME	SERVICE		NAME	SERVICE	
Chief Justices in Italics	Term	Yrs.	*Chief Justices in Italics*	Term	Yrs.
Earl Warren, Cal.	1953–1969	16	Abe Fortas, Tenn.	1965–1969	4
John M. Harlan, N.Y.	1955–1971	16	Thurgood Marshall, N.Y.	1967–	
William J. Brennan, Jr., N.J.	1956–		*Warren E. Burger*, Minn.	1969–	
Charles E. Whittaker, Mo.	1957–1962	5	Harry A. Blackmun, Minn.	1970–	
Potter Stewart, Ohio	1959–		William H. Rehnquist, Ariz.	1972–	
Byron R. White, Colo.	1962–		Lewis F. Powell, Jr., Va.	1972–	
Arthur J. Goldberg, Ill.	1962–1965	3	John Paul Stevens, Ill.	1975–	

DISTRIBUTION OF INCOME, 1950–1974

YEAR AND COLOR	INCOME LEVEL (PER CENT DISTRIBUTION)											MEDIAN	
	Under $1,000	$1,000 to $1,999	$2,000 to $2,999	$3,000 to $3,999	$4,000 to $4,999	$5,000 to $5,999	$6,000 to $6,999	$7,000 to $9,999	$10,000 to $14,999	$15,000 to $24,999	$25,000 and over	Income	Index (1950=100)
All Families													
1950	11.5	13.2	17.8	20.7	13.6	9.0	5.2	5.8		3.3		3,319	100
1955	7.7	9.9	11.0	14.6	15.4	12.7	9.5	12.9	4.8	1.4		4,421	133
1960	5.0	8.0	8.7	9.8	10.5	12.9	10.8	20.0	10.6	3.7		5,620	169
1965	2.9	6.0	7.2	7.7	7.9	9.3	9.5	24.2	17.7	7.6		6,957	210
1970	1.6	3.0	4.3	5.1	5.3	5.8	6.0	19.9	26.8	22.3		9,867	297
1974	1.3	1.3	2.7	3.6	4.1	4.4	4.4	13.8	24.3	28.3	11.5	12,836	387
White Families													
1950	10.0	12.2	17.3	21.3	14.4	9.6	5.5	6.1		3.5		3,445	100
1955	6.6	8.7	10.4	14.3	16.0	13.4	9.9	13.9	5.3	1.5		4,605	134
1960	4.1	6.9	8.1	9.4	10.5	13.3	11.2	21.3	11.2	4.1		5,835	169
1965	2.5	5.2	6.3	6.9	7.6	9.3	9.8	25.5	18.8	8.3		7,251	210
1970	1.4	2.4	3.7	4.6	4.9	5.5	5.8	20.1	27.9	23.7		10,236	297
1974	1.1	1.0	2.2	3.1	3.7	4.2	4.2	13.5	25.1	29.7	12.4	13,356	388
Non-white Families													
1950	28.1	25.3	23.5	13.5	4.3	1.9	1.5	1.7		0.3		1,869	100
1955	19.0	20.7	17.6	17.2	11.1	5.8	4.8	3.1	0.6	(Z)		2,549	136
1960	13.4	18.3	14.8	14.0	10.4	8.7	6.7	8.7	4.3	0.6		3,233	173
1965	7.1	13.6	14.6	14.8	10.8	9.5	6.8	13.7	7.6	1.4		3,994	214
1970	3.4	7.7	9.0	8.8	8.2	9.0	7.4	18.2	17.3	10.9		6,516	349
1974	2.2	4.4	7.0	8.2	7.8	6.3	6.7	16.2	19.0	17.9	4.5	8,265	422

Z: Less than 0.05 per cent.
Source: Dept. of Commerce, Bureau of the Census, *Current Population Reports*

The Constitution of
The United States of America

We the People of the United States, in order to form a more perfect union, establish Justice, insure domestic tranquility, provide for the common defence, promote the general Welfare, and secure the Blessings of Liberty to ourselves and our Posterity, do ordain and establish this Constitution for the United States of America.

ARTICLE I

SECTION 1. All legislative Powers herein granted shall be vested in a Congress of the United States, which shall consist of a Senate and a House of Representatives.

SECTION 2. The House of Representatives shall be composed of Members chosen every second Year by the People of the several States, and the Electors in each State shall have the Qualifications requisite for Electors of the most numerous Branch of the State Legislature.
No Person shall be a Representative who shall not have attained to the Age of twenty-five Years, and been seven Years a Citizen of the United States, and who shall not, when elected, be an Inhabitant of that State in which he shall be chosen.
Representatives and direct Taxes shall be apportioned among the several States which may be included within this Union, according to

their respective Numbers, which shall be determined by adding to the whole Number of free Persons, including those bound to Service for a Term of Years, and excluding Indians not taxed, three fifths of all other Persons. The actual Enumeration shall be made within three Years after the first Meeting of the Congress of the United States, and within every subsequent Term of ten Years, in such Manner as they shall by Law direct. The Number of Representatives shall not exceed one for every thirty Thousand, but each State shall have at Least one Representative; and until such enumeration shall be made, the State of New Hampshire shall be entitled to chuse three, Massachusetts eight, Rhode-Island and Providence Plantations one, Connecticut five, New-York six, New Jersey four, Pennsylvania eight, Delaware one, Maryland six, Virginia ten, North Carolina five, South Carolina five, and Georgia three.

When vacancies happen in the Representation from any State, the Executive Authority thereof shall issue Writs of Election to fill such Vacancies.

The House of Representatives shall chuse their Speaker and other Officers; and shall have the sole Power of Impeachment.

SECTION 3. The Senate of the United States shall be composed of two Senators from each State, chosen by the Legislature thereof, for six Years; and each Senator shall have one Vote.

Immediately after they shall be assembled in Consequence of the first Election, they shall be divided as equally as may be into three Classes. The Seats of the Senators of the first Class shall be vacated at the Expiration of the second Year, of the second Class at the Expiration of the fourth Year, and of the third Class at the Expiration of the sixth Year, so that one-third may be chosen every second Year; and if Vacancies happen by Resignation, or otherwise, during the Recess of the Legislature of any State, the Executive thereof may make temporary Appointments until the next Meeting of the Legislature, which shall then fill such Vacancies.

No Person shall be a Senator who shall not have attained to the Age of thirty Years, and been nine Years a Citizen of the United States, and who shall not, when elected, be an Inhabitant of that State for which he shall be chosen.

The Vice President of the United States shall be President of the Senate, but shall have no Vote, unless they be equally divided.

The Senate shall chuse their other Officers, and also a President pro tempore, in the Absence of the Vice President, or when he shall exercise the Office of President of the United States.

The Senate shall have the sole Power to try all Impeachments. When sitting for that Purpose, they shall be on Oath or Affirmation. When the President of the United States is tried, the Chief Justice shall preside: And no Person shall be convicted without the Concurrence of two thirds of the Members present.

Judgment in Cases of Impeachment shall not extend further than to removal from Office, and disqualification to hold and enjoy any Office of honor, Trust or Profit under the United States: but the Party convicted shall nevertheless be liable and subject to Indictment, Trial, Judgment and Punishment, according to Law.

SECTION 4. The Times, Places and Manner of holding Elections for Senators and Representatives, shall be prescribed in each State by the Legislature thereof; but the Congress may at any time by Law make or alter such Regulations, except as to the Places of chusing Senators.

The Congress shall assemble at least once in every Year, and such Meeting shall be on the first Monday in December, unless they shall by Law appoint a different Day.

SECTION 5. Each House shall be the Judge of the Elections, Returns and Qualifications of its own Members, and a Majority of each shall constitute a Quorum to do Business; but a smaller Number may adjourn from day to day, and may be authorized to compel the Attendance of absent Members, in such Manner, and under such Penalties as each House may provide.

Each House may determine the Rules of its Proceedings, punish its Members for disorderly Behavior, and, with the Concurrence of two thirds, expel a Member.

Each House shall keep a Journal of its Proceedings, and from time to time publish the same, excepting such Parts as may in their Judgment require Secrecy; and the Yeas and Nays of the Members of either House on any question shall, at the Desire of one fifth of those present, be entered on the Journal.

Neither House, during the Session of Congress, shall, without the Consent of the other, adjourn for more than three days, nor to any other Place than that in which the two Houses shall be sitting.

SECTION 6. The Senators and Representatives shall receive a Compensation for their Services, to be ascertained by Law, and paid out of the Treasury of the United States. They shall in all Cases, except Treason, Felony and Breach of the Peace, be privileged from Arrest during their Attendance at the Session of their respective Houses, and in going to and returning from the same; and for any Speech or Debate in either House, they shall not be questioned in any other Place.

No Senator or Representative shall, during the Time for which he was elected, be appointed to any civil Office under the Authority of the United States, which shall have been created, or the Emoluments whereof shall have been encreased during such time; and no Person holding any Office under the United States, shall be a Member of either House during his Continuance in Office.

SECTION 7. All Bills for raising Revenue shall originate in the House of Representatives; but the Senate may propose or concur with Amendments as on other Bills.

Every Bill which shall have passed the House of Representatives and the Senate, shall, before it becomes a Law, be presented to the President of the United States; If he approves he shall sign it, but if not he shall return it, with his Objections to that House in which it shall have originated, who shall enter the Objections at large on their Journal, and proceed to reconsider it. If after such Reconsideration two thirds of that House shall agree to pass the Bill, it shall be sent, together with the Objections, to the other House, by which it shall likewise be reconsidered, and if approved by two thirds of that House, it shall become a Law. But in all such Cases the Votes of both Houses shall be determined by Yeas and Nays, and the Names of the Persons voting for and against the Bill shall be entered on the Journal of each House respectively. If any Bill shall not be returned by the President within ten Days (Sundays excepted) after it shall have been presented to him, the Same shall be a Law, in like Manner as if he had signed it, unless the Congress by their Adjournment prevent its Return, in which Case it shall not be a Law.

Every Order, Resolution, or Vote to which the Concurrence of the Senate and House of Representatives may be necessary (except on a question of Adjournment) shall be presented to the President of the United States; and before the Same shall take Effect, shall be approved by him, or being disapproved by him, shall be repassed by two thirds of the Senate and House of Representatives, according to the Rules and Limitations prescribed in the Case of a Bill.

SECTION 8. The Congress shall have Power To lay and collect Taxes, Duties, Imposts and Excises, to pay the Debts and provide for the common Defence and general Welfare of the United States; but all Duties, Imposts and Excises shall be uniform throughout the United States;

To borow Money on the credit of the United States;

To regulate Commerce with foreign Nations, and among the several States, and with the Indian Tribes;

To establish an uniform Rule of Naturalization, and uniform Laws on the subject of Bankruptcies throughout the United States;

To coin Money, regulate the Value thereof, and of foreign Coin, and fix the Standard of Weights and Measures;

To provide for the Punishment of counterfeiting the Securities and current Coin of the United States;

To establish Post Offices and post Roads;

To promote the Progress of Science and useful Arts, by securing for limited Times to Authors and Inventors the exclusive Right to their respective Writings and Discoveries;

To constitute Tribunals inferior to the supreme Court;

To define and punish Piracies and Felonies committed on the high Seas, and Offences against the Law of Nations;

To declare War, grant Letters of Marque and Reprisal, and make Rules concerning Captures on Land and Water;

To raise and support Armies, but no Appropriation of Money to that Use shall be for a longer Term than two Years;

To provide and maintain a Navy;

To make Rules for the Government and Regulation of the land and naval Forces;

To provide for calling forth the Militia to execute the Laws of the Union, suppress Insurrections and repel Invasions;

To provide for organizing, arming, and disciplining the Militia, and for governing such Part of them as may be employed in the Service of the United States, reserving to the States respectively, the Appointment of the Officers, and the Authority of training the Militia according to the discipline prescribed by Congress;

To exercise exclusive Legislation in all Cases whatsoever, over such District (not exceeding ten Miles square) as may, by Cession of particular States, and the Acceptance of Congress, become the Seat of the Government of the United States, and to exercise like Authority over all Places purchased by the Consent of the Legislature of the State in which the Same shall be, for the Erection of Forts, Magazines, Arsenals, dock-Yards, and other needful Buildings; — And

To make all Laws which shall be necessary and proper for carrying into Execution the foregoing Powers, and all other Powers vested by this Constitution in the Government of the United States, or in any Department or Officer thereof.

SECTION 9. The Migration or Importation of such Persons as any of the States now existing shall think proper to admit, shall not be prohibited by the Congress prior to the Year one thousand eight hundred and eight, but a Tax or duty may be imposed on such Importation, not exceeding ten dollars for each Person.

The Privilege of the Writ of Habeas Corpus shall not be suspended, unless when in Cases of Rebellion or Invasion the public Safety may require it.

No Bill of Attainder or ex post facto Law shall be passed.

No Capitation, or other direct, tax shall be laid, unless in Proportion to the Census or Enumeration herein before directed to be taken.

No Tax or Duty shall be laid on Articles exported from any State.

No Preference shall be given by any Regulation of Commerce or Revenue to the Ports of one State over those of another: nor shall Vessels bound to, or from, one State, be obliged to enter, clear, or pay Duties in another.

No Money shall be drawn from the Treasury, but in Consequence of

Appropriations made by Law; and a regular Statement and Account of the Receipts and Expenditures of all public Money shall be published from time to time.

No Title of Nobility shall be granted by the United States: And no Person holding any Office of Profit or Trust under them, shall, without the Consent of the Congress, accept of any present, Emolument, Office, or Title, of any kind whatever, from any King, Prince, or foreign State.

SECTION 10. No State shall enter into any Treaty, Alliance, or Confederation; grant Letters of Marque and Reprisal; coin Money; emit Bills of Credit; make any Thing but gold and silver Coin a Tender in Payment of Debts; pass any Bill of Attainder, ex post facto Law, or Law impairing the Obligation of Contracts, or grant any Title of Nobility.

No State shall, without the Consent of the Congress, lay any Imposts or Duties on Imports or Exports, except what may be absolutely necessary for executing its inspection Laws: and the net Produce of all Duties and Imposts, laid by any State on Imports or Exports, shall be for the Use of the Treasury of the United States; and all such Laws shall be subject to the Revision and Controul of the Congress.

No State shall, without the Consent of Congress, lay any Duty of Tonnage, keep Troops, or Ships of War in time of Peace, enter into any Agreement or Compact with another State, or with a foreign Power, or engage in War, unless actually invaded, or in such imminent Danger as will not admit of delay.

ARTICLE II

SECTION 1. The Executive Power shall be vested in a President of the United States of America. He shall hold his Office during the Term of four Years, and, together with the Vice President, chosen for the same Term, be elected, as follows

Each State shall appoint, in such Manner as the Legislature thereof may direct, a Number of Electors, equal to the whole Number of Senators and Representatives to which the State may be entitled in the Congress: but no Senator or Representative, or Person holding an Office of Trust or Profit under the United States, shall be appointed an Elector.

The electors shall meet in their respective States, and vote by ballot for two Persons, of whom one at least shall not be an Inhabitant of the same State with themselves. And they shall make a List of all the Persons voted for, and of the Number of Votes for each; which List they shall sign and certify, and transmit sealed to the Seat of the Government of the United States, directed to the President of the Senate. The President of the Senate shall, in the Presence of the Senate and House of Representatives, open all the Certificates, and the Votes shall then be counted. The Person having the greatest Number of Votes shall be the President, if such Number be a Majority of the whole Number of Electors appointed; and if there be more than one who have such Majority, and have an equal Number of Votes, then the House of Representatives shall immediately chuse by Ballot one of them for President; and if no Person have a Majority, then from the five highest on the List the said House shall in like Manner chuse the President. But in chusing the President, the Votes shall be taken by States, the Representation from each State having one Vote; A quorum for this Purpose shall consist of a Member or Members from two thirds of the States, and a Majority of all the States shall be necessary to a Choice. In every Case, after the Choice of the President, the Person having the greatest Number of Votes of the Electors shall be the Vice President. But if there should remain two or more who have equal Votes, the Senate shall chuse from them by Ballot the Vice President.

The Congress may determine the Time of chusing the Electors, and the Day on which they shall give their Votes; which Day shall be the same throughout the United States.

No Person except a natural born Citizen, or a Citizen of the United States, at the time of the Adoption of this Constitution, shall be eligible to the Office of President; neither shall any Person be eligible to that Office who shall not have attained to the Age of thirty five Years, and been fourteen Years a Resident within the United States.

In Case of the Removal of the President from Office, or of his Death, Resignation or Inability to discharge the Powers and Duties of the said Office, the same shall devolve on the Vice President, and the Congress may by Law provide for the Case of Removal, Death,

Resignation or Inability, both of the President and Vice President, declaring what Officer shall then act as President, and such Officer shall act accordingly, until the Disability be removed, or a President shall be elected.

The President shall, at stated Times, receive for his Services, a Compensation, which shall neither be encreased nor diminished during the Period for which he shall have been elected, and he shall not receive within that Period any other Emolument from the United States, or any of them.

Before he enter on the Execution of his Office, he shall take the following Oath or Affirmation: — "I do solemnly swear (or affirm) that I will faithfully execute the Office of President of the United States, and will to the best of my Ability, preserve, protect and defend the Constitution of the United States."

SECTION 2. The President shall be Commander in Chief of the Army and Navy of the United States, and of the Militia of the several States, when called into the actual Service of the United States; he may require the Opinion, in writing, of the principal Officer in each of the executive Departments, upon any Subject relating to the Duties of their respective Offices, and he shall have Power to grant Reprieves and Pardons for Offences against the United States, except in Cases of Impeachment.

He shall have Power, by and with the Advice and Consent of the Senate to make Treaties, provided two thirds of the Senators present concur and he shall nominate, and by and with the Advice and Consent of the Senate, shall appoint Ambassadors, other public Ministers and Consuls, Judges of the supreme Court, and all other Officers of the United States, whose Appointments are not herein otherwise provided for, and which shall be established by Law: but the Congress may by Law vest the Appointment of such inferior Officers, as they think proper, in the President alone, in the Courts of Law, or in the Heads of Departments.

The President shall have Power to fill up all Vacancies that may happen during the Recess of the Senate, by granting Commissions which shall expire at the End of their next Session.

SECTION 3. He shall from time to time give to the Congress Information of the State of the Union, and recommend to their Consideration such Measures as he shall judge necessary and expedient; he may, on extraordinary Occasions, convene both Houses, or either of them, and, in Case of Disagreement between them, with Respect to the Time of Adjournment, he may adjourn them to such Time as he shall think proper; he shall receive Ambassadors and other public Ministers; he shall take Care that the Laws be faithfully executed, and shall Commission all the Officers of the United States.

SECTION 4. The President, Vice President and all civil Officers of the United States, shall be removed from Office on Impeachment for, and Conviction of, Treason, Bribery, or other high Crimes and Misdemeanors.

ARTICLE III

SECTION 1. The judicial Power of the United States, shall be vested in one supreme Court, and in such inferior Courts as the Congress may from time to time ordain and establish. The Judges, both of the supreme and inferior Courts, shall hold their Offices during good Behaviour, and shall, at stated Times, receive for their Services, a Compensation, which shall not be diminished during their Continuance in Office.

SECTION 2. The judicial Power shall extend to all Cases, in Law and Equity, arising under this Constitution, the Laws of the United States, and Treaties made, or which shall be made, under their Authority; — to all Cases affecting Ambassadors, other public Ministers and Consuls; — to all Cases of admiralty and maritime Jurisdiction; — to Controversies to which the United States shall be a Party; — to Controversies between two or more States; — between a State and Citizens of another State; — between Citizens of different States, — between Citizens of the same State claiming Lands under Grants of different States, and between a State, or the Citizens thereof, and foreign States, Citizens or Subjects.

In all Cases affecting Ambassadors, other public Ministers and Consuls, and those in which a State shall be Party, the supreme Court shall have original Jurisdiction. In all other Cases before mentioned, the supreme Court shall have appellate Jurisdiction, both as to Law and

Fact, with such Exceptions, and under such Regulations as the Congress shall make.

The Trial of all Crimes, except in Cases of Impeachment, shall be by Jury; and such Trial shall be held in the State where the said Crimes shall have been committed; but when not committed within any State, the Trial shall be at such Place or Places as the Congress may by Law have directed.

SECTION 3. Treason against the United States, shall consist only in levying War against them, or in adhering to their Enemies, giving them Aid and Comfort. No Person shall be convicted of Treason unless on the Testimony of two Witnesses to the same overt Act, or on Confession in open Court.

The Congress shall have Power to declare the Punishment of Treason, but no Attainder of Treason shall work Corruption of Blood, or Forfeiture except during the Life of the Person attainted.

ARTICLE IV

SECTION 1. Full Faith and Credit shall be given in each State to the public Acts, Records, and judicial Proceedings of every other State. And the Congress may by general Laws prescribe the Manner in which such Acts, Records and Proceedings shall be proved, and the Effect thereof.

SECTION 2. The Citizens of each State shall be entitled to all Privileges and Immunities of Citizens in the several States.

A person charged in any State with Treason, Felony, or other Crime, who shall flee from Justice, and be found in another State, shall on Demand of the executive Authority of the State from which he fled, be delivered up, to be removed to the State having Jurisdiction of the Crime.

No Person held to Service or Labour in one State, under the Laws thereof, escaping into another, shall, in Consequence of any Law or Regulation therein, be discharged from such Service or Labour, but shall be delivered up on Claim of the Party to whom such Service or Labour may be due.

SECTION 3. New States may be admitted by the Congress into this Union; but no new State shall be formed or erected within the Jurisdiction of any other State; nor any State be formed by the Junction of two or more States, or Parts of States, without the Consent of the Legislatures of the States concerned as well as of the Congress.

The Congress shall have Power to dispose of and make all needful Rules and Regulations respecting the Territory or other Property belonging to the United States; and nothing in this Constitution shall be so construed as to Prejudice any Claims of the United States, or of any particular State.

SECTION 4. The United States shall guarantee to every State in this Union a Republican Form of Government, and shall protect each of them against Invasion; and on Application of the Legislature, or of the Executive (when the Legislature cannot be convened) against domestic Violence.

ARTICLE V

The Congress, whenever two thirds of both houses shall deem it necessary, shall propose Amendments to this Constitution, or, on the Application of the Legislatures of two thirds of the several States, shall call a Convention for proposing Amendments, which, in either Case, shall be valid to all Intents and Purposes, as Part of this Constitution, when ratified by the Legislatures of three fourths of the several States, or by Conventions in three fourths thereof, as the one or the other Mode of Ratification may be proposed by the Congress; Provided that no Amendment which may be made prior to the Year One thousand eight hundred and eight shall in any Manner affect the first and fourth Clauses in the Ninth Section of the first Article; and that no State, without its Consent, shall be deprived of its equal Suffrage in the Senate.

ARTICLE VI

All Debts contracted and Engagements entered into, before the Adoption of this Constitution, shall be as valid against the United States under this Constitution, as under the Confederation.

This Constitution, and the Laws of the United States which shall be made in Pursuance thereof; and all Treaties made, or which shall be made, under the Authority of the United States, shall be the supreme Law of the Land; and the Judges in every State shall be bound thereby, any Thing in the Constitution or Laws of any State to the Contrary notwithstanding.

The Senators and Representatives before mentioned, and the Members of the several State Legislatures, and all executive and judicial Officers, both of the United States and of the several States, shall be bound by Oath or Affirmation, to support this Constitution; but no religious Test shall ever be required as a Qualification to any Office or public Trust under the United States.

ARTICLE VII

The Ratification of the Conventions of nine States, shall be sufficient for the Establishment of this Constitution between the States so ratifying the Same.

DONE in Convention by the Unanimous Consent of the States present the Seventeenth Day of September in the Year of our Lord one thousand seven hundred and Eighty seven and of the Independence of the United States of America the Twelfth. IN WITNESS whereof We have hereunto subscribed our Names.

G° WASHINGTON
Presid^t and deputy from Virginia

AMENDMENTS
ARTICLE I

[THE FIRST TEN ARTICLES PROPOSED 25 SEPTEMBER 1789; DECLARED IN FORCE 15 DECEMBER 1791]

Congress shall make no law respecting an establishment of religion, or prohibiting the free exercise thereof; or abridging the freedom of speech, or of the press; or the right of the people peaceably to assemble, and to petition the Government for a redress of grievances.

ARTICLE II

A well regulated Militia, being necessary to the security of a free State, the right of the people to keep and bear Arms, shall not be infringed.

ARTICLE III

No Soldier shall, in time of peace, be quartered in any house, without the consent of the Owner, nor in time of war, but in a manner to be prescribed by law.

ARTICLE IV

The right of the people to be secure in their persons, houses, papers, and effects, against unreasonable searches and seizures, shall not be violated, and no Warrants shall issue, but upon probable cause, supported by Oath or affirmation, and particularly describing the place to be searched, and the persons or things to be seized.

ARTICLE V

No person shall be held to answer for a capital, or otherwise infamous crime, unless on a presentment or indictment of a Grand Jury, except in cases arising in the land or naval forces, or in the Militia, when in actual service in time of War or public danger; nor shall any person be subject for the same offence to be twice put in jeopardy of life or limb; nor shall be compelled in any Criminal Case to be a witness against himself, nor be deprived of life, liberty, or property, without due process of law; nor shall private property be taken for public use, without just compensation.

ARTICLE VI

In all criminal prosecutions, the accused shall enjoy the right to a speedy and public trial, by an impartial jury of the State and district wherein the crime shall have been committed, which district shall have been previously ascertained by law, and to be informed of the nature and cause of the accusation; to be confronted with the witnesses against him; to have compulsory process for obtaining Witnesses in his favor, and to have the Assistance of Counsel for his defence.

ARTICLE VII

In suits at common law, where the value in controversy shall exceed twenty dollars, the right of trial by jury shall be preserved, and no fact tried by a jury shall be otherwise re-examined in any Court of the United States, than according to the rules of the common law.

ARTICLE VIII

Excessive bail shall not be required, nor excessive fines imposed, nor cruel and unusual punishments inflicted.

ARTICLE IX

The enumeration in the Constitution, of certain rights, shall not be construed to deny or disparage others retained by the people.

ARTICLE X

The powers not delegated to the United States by the Constitution, nor prohibited by it to the States, are reserved to the States respectively, or to the people.

ARTICLE XI

[PROPOSED 4 MARCH 1794; DECLARED RATIFIED 8 JANUARY 1798]

The Judicial power of the United States shall not be construed to extend to any suit in law or equity, commenced or prosecuted against one of the United States by Citizens of another State, or by Citizens or Subjects of any Foreign State.

ARTICLE XII

[PROPOSED 9 DECEMBER 1803; DECLARED RATIFIED 25 SEPTEMBER 1804]

The Electors shall meet in their respective states, and vote by ballot for President and Vice-President, one of whom, at least, shall not be an inhabitant of the same state with themselves; they shall name in their ballots the person voted for as President, and in distinct ballots the person voted for as Vice-President, and they shall make distinct lists of all persons voted for as President, and of all persons voted for as Vice-President, and of the number of votes for each, which lists they shall sign and certify, and transmit sealed to the seat of the Government of the United States, directed to the President of the Senate; — The President of the Senate shall, in the presence of the Senate and House of Representatives, open all the certificates and the votes shall then be counted; — The person having the greatest number of votes for President, shall be the President, if such number be a majority of the whole number of Electors appointed; and if no person have such majority, then from the persons having the highest numbers not exceeding three on the list of those voted for as President, the House of Representatives shall choose immediately, by ballot, the President. But in choosing the President, the votes shall be taken by states, the representation from each state having one vote; a quorum for this purpose shall consist of a member or members from two-thirds of the states, and a majority of all the states shall be necessary to a choice. And if the House of Representatives shall not choose a President whenever the right of choice shall devolve upon them, before the fourth day of March next following, then the Vice-President shall act as President, as in the case of the death or other constitutional disability of the President. The person having the greatest number of votes as Vice-President, shall be the Vice-President, if such number be a majority of the whole number of Electors appointed, and if no person have a majority, then from the two highest numbers on the list, the Senate shall choose the Vice-President; a quorum for the purpose shall consist of two-thirds of the whole number of Senators, and a majority of the whole number shall be necessary to a choice. But no person constitutionally ineligible to the office of President shall be eligible to that of Vice-President of the United States.

ARTICLE XIII

[PROPOSED 31 JANUARY 1865; DECLARED RATIFIED 18 DECEMBER 1865]

SECTION 1. Neither slavery nor involuntary servitude, except as a punishment for crime whereof the party shall have been duly convicted, shall exist within the United States, or any place subject to their jurisdiction.

SECTION 2. Congress shall have power to enforce this article by appropriate legislation.

ARTICLE XIV

[PROPOSED 13 JUNE 1866; DECLARED RATIFIED 28 JULY 1868]

SECTION 1. All persons born or naturalized in the United States, and subject to the jurisdiction thereof, are citizens of the United States and of the State wherein they reside. No State shall make or enforce any law which shall abridge the privileges or immunities of citizens of the United States; nor shall any State deprive any person of life, liberty, or property, without due process of law; nor deny to any person within its jurisdiction the equal protection of the laws.

SECTION 2. Representatives shall be apportioned among the several States according to their respective numbers, counting the whole number of persons in each State, excluding Indians not taxed. But when the right to vote at any election for the choice of electors for President and Vice President of the United States, Representatives in Congress, the Executive and Judicial officers of a State, or the members of the Legislature thereof, is denied to any of the male inhabitants of such State, being twenty-one years of age, and citizens of the United States, or in any way abridged, except for participation in rebellion, or other crime, the basis of representation therein shall be reduced in the proportion which the number of such male citizens shall bear to the whole number of male citizens twenty-one years of age in such State.

SECTION 3. No person shall be a Senator or Representative in Congress, or elector of President and Vice President, or hold any office, civil, or military, under the United States, or under any State, who, having previously taken an oath, as a member of Congress, or as an officer of the United States, or as a member of any State legislature, or as an executive or judicial officer of any State, to support the Constitution of the United States, shall have engaged in insurrection or rebellion against the same, or given aid or comfort to the enemies thereof. But Congress may by a vote of two-thirds of each House, remove such disability.

SECTION 4. The validity of the public debt of the United States, authorized by law, including debts incurred for payment of pensions and bounties for services in suppressing insurrection or rebellion, shall not be questioned. But neither the United States nor any State shall assume or pay any debt or obligation incurred in aid of insurrection or rebellion against the United States, or any claim for the loss or emancipation of any slave; but all such debts, obligations and claims shall be held illegal and void.

SECTION 5. The Congress shall have power to enforce, by appropriate legislation, the provisions of this article.

ARTICLE XV
[PROPOSED 26 FEBRUARY 1869; DECLARED RATIFIED 30 MARCH 1870]

SECTION 1. The right of citizens of the United States to vote shall not be denied or abridged by the United States or by any State on account of race, color, or previous condition of servitude.

SECTION 2. The Congress shall have power to enforce this article by appropriate legislation.

ARTICLE XVI
[PROPOSED 12 JULY 1909; DECLARED RATIFIED 25 FEBRUARY 1913]

The Congress shall have power to lay and collect taxes on incomes, from whatever source derived, without apportionment among the several States, and without regard to any census or enumeration.

ARTICLE XVII
[PROPOSED 13 MAY 1912; DECLARED RATIFIED 31 MAY 1913]

The Senate of the United States shall be composed of two senators from each State, elected by the people thereof, for six years; and each Senator shall have one vote. The electors in each State shall have the qualifications requisite for electors of the most numerous branch of the State legislature.

When vacancies happen in the representation of any State in the Senate, the executive authority of such State shall issue writs of election to fill such vacancies: PROVIDED, That the legislature of any State may empower the executive thereof to make temporary appointments until the people fill the vacancies by election as the legislature may direct.

This amendment shall not be so construed as to affect the election or term of any senator chosen before it becomes valid as part of the Constitution.

ARTICLE XVIII

[PROPOSED 18 DECEMBER 1917; DECLARED RATIFIED 29 JANUARY 1919]

After one year from the ratification of this article, the manufacture, sale, or transportation of intoxicating liquors within, the importation thereof into, or the exportation thereof from the United States and all territory subject to the jurisdiction thereof for beverage purposes is hereby prohibited.

The Congress and the several States shall have concurrent power to enforce this article by appropriate legislation.

This article shall be inoperative unless it shall have been ratified as an amendment to the Constitution by the legislatures of the several States, as provided in the Constitution, within seven years from the date of the submission hereof to the States by the Congress.

ARTICLE XIX

[PROPOSED 4 JUNE 1919; DECLARED RATIFIED 26 AUGUST 1920]

The right of citizens of the United States to vote shall not be denied or abridged by the United States or by any States on account of sex.

The Congress shall have power, by appropriate legislation, to enforce the provisions of this article.

ARTICLE XX

[PROPOSED 2 MARCH 1932; DECLARED RATIFIED 6 FEBRUARY 1933]

SECTION 1. The terms of the President and Vice-President shall end at noon on the twentieth day of January, and the terms of Senators and Representatives at noon on the third day of January, of the years in which such terms would have ended if this article had not been ratified; and the terms of their successors shall then begin.

SECTION 2. The Congress shall assemble at least once in every year, and such meeting shall begin at noon on the third day of January, unless they shall by law appoint a different day.

SECTION 3. If, at the time fixed for the beginning of the term of the President, the President-elect shall have died, the Vice-President-elect shall become President. If a President shall not have been chosen before the time fixed for the beginning of his term, or if the President-elect shall have failed to qualify, then the Vice-President-elect shall act as President until a President shall have qualified; and the Congress may by law provide for the case wherein neither a President-elect nor a Vice-President-elect shall have qualified, declaring who shall then act as President, or the manner in which one who is to act shall be selected, and such person shall act accordingly until a President or Vice-President shall have qualified.

SECTION 4. The Congress may by law provide for the case of the death of any of the persons from whom the House of Representatives may choose a President whenever the right of choice shall have devolved upon them, and for the case of the death of any of the persons from whom the Senate may choose a Vice-President whenever the right of choice shall have devolved upon them.

SECTION 5. Sections 1 and 2 shall take effect on the 15th day of October following the ratification of this article.

SECTION 6. This article shall be inoperative unless it shall have been ratified as an amendment to the Constitution by the legislatures of three-fourths of the several States within seven years from the date of its submission.

ARTICLE XXI

[PROPOSED 20 FEBRUARY 1933; DECLARED RATIFIED 5 DECEMBER 1933]

SECTION 1. The eighteenth article of amendment to the Constitution of the United States is hereby repealed.

SECTION 2. The transportation or importation into any State, Territory or possession of the United States for delivery or use therein of intoxicating liquors, in violation of the laws thereof, is hereby prohibited.

SECTION 3. This article shall be inoperative unless it shall have been ratified as an amendment to the Constitution by convention in the several States, as provided in the Constitution, within seven years from the date of the submission hereof to the States by the Congress.

ARTICLE XXII

[PROPOSED 21 MARCH 1947; DECLARED RATIFIED 3 MARCH 1951]

SECTION 1. No person shall be elected to the office of the President more than twice, and no person who has held the office of President, or acted as President, for more than two years of a term to which some other person was elected President shall be elected to the office of the President more than once. But this Article shall not apply to any person holding the office of President when this Article was proposed by the Congress, and shall not prevent any person who may be holding the office of President, or acting as President, during the term within which this Article becomes operative from holding the office of President or acting as President during the remainder of such term.

ARTICLE XXIII

[PROPOSED 17 JUNE 1960; DECLARED RATIFIED 3 APRIL 1961]

SECTION 1. The District constituting the seat of Government of the United States shall appoint in such manner as the Congress may direct:

A number of electors of President and Vice President equal to the whole number of Senators and Representatives in Congress to which the District would be entitled if it were a State, but in no event more than the least populous State; they shall be in addition to those appointed by the States, but they shall be considered, for the purposes of the election of President and Vice President, to be electors appointed by a State; and they shall meet in the District and perform such duties as provided by the twelfth article of amendment.

SECTION 2. The Congress shall have power to enforce this article by appropriate legislation.

ARTICLE XXIV

[PROPOSED 27 AUGUST 1962; DECLARED RATIFIED 4 FEBRUARY 1964]

SECTION 1. The right of citizens of the United States to vote in any primary or other election for President or Vice President, for electors for President or Vice President, or for Senator or Representative in Congress, shall not be denied or abridged by the United States or any State by reason of failure to pay any poll tax or other tax.

SECTION 2. The Congress shall have power to enforce this article by appropriate legislation.

ARTICLE XXV

[PROPOSED 6 JULY 1965; DECLARED RATIFIED 23 FEBRUARY 1967]

SECTION 1. In case of the removal of the President from office or of his death or resignation, the Vice President shall become President.

SECTION 2. Whenever there is a vacancy in the office of the Vice President, the President shall nominate a Vice President who shall take office upon confirmation by a majority vote of both Houses of Congress.

SECTION 3. Whenever the President transmits to the President pro tempore of the Senate and the Speaker of the House of Representatives his written declaration that he is unable to discharge the powers and duties of his office, and until he transmits to them a written declaration to the contrary, such powers and duties shall be discharged by the Vice President as Acting President.

SECTION 4. Whenever the Vice President and a majority of either the principal officers of the executive department or of such other body as Congress may by law provide, transmit to the President pro tempore of the Senate and the Speaker of the House of Representatives their written declaration that the President is unable to discharge the powers and duties of his office, the Vice President shall immediately assume the powers and duties of the office as Acting President.

Thereafter, when the President transmits to the President pro tempore of the Senate and the Speaker of the House of Representatives his written declaration that no inability exists, he shall resume the powers and duties of his office unless the Vice President and a majority of either the principal officers of the executive department or of such other body as Congress may by law provide, transmit within four days to the President pro tempore of the Senate and the Speaker of the House of Representatives their written declaration that the President is unable to discharge the powers and duties of his office. Thereupon Congress shall decide the issue, assembling within forty-eight hours for that purpose if not in session. If the Congress, within twenty-one days after receipt of the latter written declaration, or, if Congress is not in session, within twenty-one days after Congress is required to assemble, determines by two-thirds vote of both Houses that the President is unable to discharge the powers and duties of his office, the Vice President shall continue to discharge the same as Acting President; otherwise, the President shall resume the powers and duties of his office.

ARTICLE XXVI

[PROPOSED 23 MARCH 1971; DECLARED RATIFIED 30 JUNE 1971]

SECTION 1. The right of citizens of the United States, who are 18 years of age or older, to vote shall not be denied or abridged by the United States or any state on account of age.

SECTION 2. The Congress shall have the power to enforce this article by appropriate legislation.

Index